GAY & LESBIAN LITERATURE

GAY & LESBIAN LITERATURE

INTRODUCTION TO GAY MALE LITERATURE

WAYNE R. DYNES

INTRODUCTION TO LESBIAN LITERATURE

BARBARA G. GRIER

EDITOR

SHARON MALINOWSKI

St J

St James Press

Detroit and London

STAFF

Sharon Malinowski, *Editor*

Sonia Benson, Joanna Brod, Elizabeth A. Des Chenes, Bruce Ching, Kathleen J. Edgar, Marie Ellavich,
David M. Galens, Jeff Hill, Denise E. Kasinec, Jane K. Kosek, Thomas F. McMahon
Mark F. Mikula, Susan Reicha, Terrie M. Rooney, Mary K. Ruby, Pamela L. Shelton,
Kenneth R. Shepherd, Deborah A. Stanley, and Thomas Wiloch, *Associate Editors*

Mary L. Onorato, Scot Peacock, Anders Ramsey,
and Roger M. Valade III, *Assistant Editors*

James G. Lesniak, *Senior Editor*

Victoria B. Cariappa, *Research Manager*

Mary Rose Bonk, *Research Supervisor*

Reginald A. Carlton, Andrew Guy Malonis,
and Norma Sawaya, *Editorial Associates*

Laurel Sprague Bowden, Rachel A. Dixon, Eva Marie Felts, Shirley Gates, Doris Lewandowski,
Sharon McGilvray, Dana R. Schleiffers, and Amy B. Wieczorek, *Editorial Assistants*

Cynthia Baldwin, *Art Director*
Mary Krzewinski, *Graphic Designer*

∞ ™ This book is printed on acid-free paper that meets the minimum requirements
of American National Standard for Information Sciences-
Permanence Paper for Printed Library Materials, ANSI Z39.48-1984.

ISBN 1-55862-174-1

St. James Press is an imprint of Gale Research Inc.
Printed in the United States of America.
Published simultaneously in the United Kingdom
by Gale Research International Limited
(An affiliated company of Gale Research Inc.)

I(T)P™

The trademark **ITP** is used under license.
10 9 8 7 6 5 4 3 2 1

Contents

Preface

The diverse and dynamic field of gay and lesbian literature is enjoying a period of vigorous growth. Once relegated to the literary fringe, it has survived through the efforts of small presses and specialized bookstores and now establishes its connection to the larger literary society and its expanding readership. Established presses are increasing their publications in this field; book clubs are issuing libraries of gay and lesbian literary masterpieces; scholarship is revisiting literature from a gay and lesbian perspective and dissertations are abounding; and libraries and schools are beginning to assess the importance of this literature for children and young adults.

Based upon a need for reference sources in the area of homosexuality in both academic and public libraries, and based upon an important endorsement from the Gay and Lesbian Task Force of the American Library Association's Social Responsibilities Round Table, St. James Press proudly introduces this extensive compilation of biographical, bibliographical, and critical information on more than two hundred authors who have figured prominently in gay and lesbian literature and culture since 1900.

Scope

International in scope, *Gay & Lesbian Literature* includes novelists, poets, short story writers, dramatists, journalists, editors, and writers of nonfiction, including scholars whose work has contributed significantly to the field, in addition to authors known predominantly for their work in social and political arenas. Inclusion is based upon the gay and lesbian thematic content of a writer's work and not upon sexual identity. Although the emphasis of this collection focuses upon the most eminent and frequently studied authors of gay and lesbian literature writing today, significant deceased authors from the earlier portion of the century who have exerted a major influence on contemporary gay and lesbian literature are also included, as are writers whose work promises to generate a lasting contribution to the field.

Preparation

Before preparing this edition of *Gay & Lesbian Literature,* a telephone survey of librarians was conducted and an advisory board, several members of whom are or have been active in the Gay and Lesbian Task Force of the American Library Association, was assembled to assist in the compilation of a list of featured authors and to assure that the concerns of the gay and lesbian community would be sensitively addressed. More than one thousand names were considered for possible inclusion in this volume; lists were compiled for review by the Advisory Board, whose recommendations were then incorporated. This list was then reviewed by scholars to gauge academic interest and international representation. Mailings were made to all living authors so that information might be as complete and accurate as possible.

Entry Format

Entries in *Gay & Lesbian Literature* provide in-depth biographical, bibliographical, and critical information that is unavailable in any other single reference source. The format of each entry is designed for ease of use--by students, teachers, scholars, librarians, and the general public. Entries in *Gay & Lesbian Literature* are arranged as follows:

Biographical Information

▽ Author is featured under name by which he/she is best known--if a pseudonym or variation, the author's given name follows. Any pseudonyms or name variations used for writing are also listed and cross-references appear throughout the text.

▽ Personal information about the author, including date and place of birth, country of residence or citizenship, and educational background, plus marriage and/or companion information.

▽ Summary of author's career, including employers, positions, and dates held for each career post, vocational achievements, and military service.

▽ Summary of professional, civic, and other affiliations, plus any official posts held.

▽ Recipient: List of major prizes and nominations, fellowships, and grants, honoring the author and his/her work.

▽ Agent/Addresses: Address at which author or his/her agent may be contacted.

▽ If author is deceased, the place, cause, and date of his/her death.

Writings by the Author

▽ A comprehensive list of titles, publishers, dates of original publication and revised editions, and production information for plays, televised scripts, and screenplays by the featured author are typically arranged by genre and include uncollected short fiction and nonfiction, where available. Also included is a list of recorded versions made by the author of his/her work.

Writings about the Author

▽ Adaptations: Films, plays, and other media adaptations based upon the author's work, includes stage plays, musicals, operas, teleplays.

▽ Manuscript Collections: A listing of the institutions which house significant collections of manuscripts relating to the featured author.

▽ Biography: Biographical sources on the featured author in both books and articles.

▽ Interviews: Major interviews with the featured author.

▽ Bibliography: A listing of bibliographies that have been compiled on the featured author.

▽ Critical Sources: A selected list of sources that combines the major scholarship existing on the featured author, with an emphasis on the gay and lesbian scholarship extant, plus a list of sources used in preparing the critical essay, including citations culled from scholarly, mainstream, and alternative press indexes.

▽ Author Comment: A statement made by the featured author concerning his/her own work.

Critical Essay

▽ Signed critical essays commissioned from a diverse group of scholars, librarians, and free-lance writers in the area of gay and lesbian literature, discuss the gay and lesbian content of the work of the featured authors. The approach taken with each essay varies, but the emphasis is on that which makes the author's work important to his/her own literary canon specifically and to the gay and lesbian literary or historical world generally.

Indexes

This edition of *Gay & Lesbian Literature* provides the following indexing to the featured entries:

▽   General Index: Alphabetically lists the names, name variations, and pseudonyms of featured authors.

▽   Nationality Index: Alphabetically lists featured authors according to country of origin, lengthy residence, and/or country of citizenship.

▽   Gender Index: Alphabetically lists featured authors according to gender.

▽   General Subject and Genre Index: Alphabetically lists featured authors according to genres in which their work appears, and refers readers to subjects relevant to the study of gay and lesbian literature.

▽   Awards Index: Lists recipients of gay and lesbian literary awards.

Highlights

In an effort to make this volume as useful as possible, and with the assistance of the Advisory Board, the editor has provided the following lists or appendices which may assist readers in securing additional information and may serve as an acquisitions tool for libraries seeking to augment their collections in this burgeoning field.

▽   Suggested Additional Authors of Gay and Lesbian Literature: Lists the authors whose work represents the field of gay and lesbian literature and culture, but who are not featured with an entry in *Gay & Lesbian Literature*.

▽   Important Anthologies: A selective list of important anthologies of fiction, nonfiction, poetry, drama, interviews.

Acknowledgments

The editor gratefully acknowledges the members of the advisory board for their generous expertise, valuable suggestions and assistance, and general collaboration; Claude J. Summers, Margaret Cruikshank, Alan Hollinghurst, Ron Eddy, Tracy Chevalier, and Warren Johannson for additional review of the author lists; Pamela L. Shelton for her editorial support; Kenneth R. Shepherd for his technical assistance; Michael LaBlanc, Emily McMurray, James F. Kamp, Laura Standley Berger, and Shelly Andrews for their typesetting assistance; Peter Gareffa, senior editor of biographical directories, and Donna Olendorf and Susan Trosky, for their cooperation and assistance, and for that of their staffs.

Suggestions Are Welcome

The editor hopes that you find *Gay & Lesbian Literature* a useful reference tool and welcomes comments and suggestions on any aspects of this work. Please send comments to: The Editor, *Gay & Lesbian Literature*, St. James Press, 835 Penobscot Building, Detroit, MI 48226-4094; or call toll-free at 800-347-GALE; or fax to 313-961-6599.

Introduction to Gay Male Literature

by Wayne R. Dynes

During the twentieth century, gay male writing has displayed a rich and varied profile, with fiction and poetry most prominent, while drama, biography, autobiography, literary criticism, and expository prose are also significant. Basking in today's literary freedom, it is easy to disregard the constraints that limited the scope of activity in previous decades. Outright censorship prevented "explicit" works from being published, or if they did appear they could only be distributed through clandestine channels. Some books, as the early novels of William Burroughs, had to be published abroad. Not a few authors, sensing family and peer pressures as well as external constraints, resigned themselves to producing work for the drawer. Fortunately some of these texts have survived, and have been published in our own time. A more subtle problem had to do with what the late Roger Austen termed "playing the game." Mainstream publishers would allow gay-themed novels to appear, but only with certain stipulations, as the convention of requiring the hero to die at the end. To avoid this fate, some resorted to "vanity" presses or self-publishing.

Fortunately, many gay authors were aware of the models of homoerotic-theme writing, beginning with such classical writers as Theognis, Pindar, and Catullus. Modern French literature, with such giants as Verlaine and Rimbaud, Proust and Gide, also offered encouragement. *Leaves of Grass* by Walt Whitman, especially its Calamus section, was a beacon of light. Whitman's English disciple Edward Carpenter, who lived an openly gay life, wrote prose works that conveyed accurate nonjudgmental information about the history of same-sex behavior. Another Englishman, the heterosexual sex researcher H. Havelock Ellis, also presented much useful data, but his most relevant work could not be published in the United Kingdom during his lifetime. In France the great novelist André Gide risked his reputation to publish *Corydon,* a 1924 essay defending homosexuality. More cautiously, his younger contemporary Jean Cocteau presented his insights in a metaphorical, poetic form.

On the whole novels rank as the most widely practiced and most widely read genre of creative writing relating to the gay male experience. In the United States in 1899, Alfred J. Cohen's *A Marriage Below Zero* directly focused on homosexuality, negatively; he established the long-lasting tradition of ending the tale with the suicide of the homosexual character. Nine years later Edward I. Prime-Stevenson achieved the first positive look at explicit homosexuality in an American novel in his *Imre: a Memorandum*; significantly, this book was published in Naples. In the 1920s in Paris, the American Robert McAlmon did great service as both a writer and a publisher.

In the changed climate in the United States after World War II, a number of publicly known gay novelists were able to break into the first rank of famous authors: Gore Vidal, Truman Capote, John Horne Burns, James Baldwin, Christopher Isherwood, Paul Bowles, and William Burroughs. In addition to the mainstream writers, who aimed their books at a wide general audience, another group of novelists have written works specifically for gay and lesbian readers. This fiction has ranged from high-quality literature through many gradations to semi-pornographic erotica; since the 1970s it has found a home with gay-oriented publishers such as Alyson, Gay Sunshine Press, and Knights Press in the United States, Gay Men's Press (GMP) in England, Persona in France, and Rosa Winkel Verlag in Germany. Such novels are reviewed in gay periodicals and marketed in gay bookstores, reflecting in literature the ghettoization that has increasingly characterized the gay experience in North America and northern Europe. Critics have attacked this segregation in literature, yet it has provided an outlet for creative writing by gays and lesbians uninhibited by the disparagement or squeamishness of heterosexual readers.

In the United States, the first widely successful gay-directed novel was James Barr's *Quatrefoil,* a 1950 work portraying a love affair between two Navy officers. A long hiatus followed before the Mexican American John Rechy had a major impact with his 1963 *City of Night,* a gritty semi-autobiographical depiction of the world of male prostitution. In the 1960s and 1970s gay liberation ideas slowly made their way into gay and lesbian novels. Eventually the distinction between mainstream and specialized novels faded, with many works that once would have been attributed to the latter class even achieving notice in the very respectable *New York Times Book Review*.

Recent American gay novelists of note include Christopher Bram, Donald Curzon, Robert Ferro, Harlan Greene, Allan Gurganus, David Leavitt, Armistead Maupin, Ethan Mordden, Felice Picano, James Purdy, and Edmund White. In England Neil Bartlett, Allan Hollinghurst, Adam Mars-Jones, and David Watmough have written inventive and sensitive fiction. The California writer Joseph Hansen pioneered in the field of gay detective fiction, while Samuel R. Delany addressed erotic themes in science fiction. A special genre of novels concerns AIDS: here outstanding work has been contributed by Hervé Guibert and Paul Monette. Latin American literature has produced three gay writers of distinction: the Proustian resident of Havana José Lezama Lima, the Cuban exile Reinaldo Arenas, and the Argentine chronicler of modern life Manuel Puig, author of the 1976 *Kiss of the Spider Woman*. The pederastic short novels of the Italian Pier Paolo Pasolini, best known for his films, appeared only after his death in 1975. Since that time Aldo Busi has acquired an international reputation for his fiction, informed by a saucy, "in-your-face" tone reflecting militant gay liberation. The prolific and multitalented Yukio Mishima wrote novels offering unique insights into the Japanese gay scene. The complex Australian Patrick White won the Nobel prize in literature in 1973.

As a tradition, homoerotic writing has sunk deep roots in the realm of poetry, perhaps because of its long association with love and romance, its inherent ambiguity (which makes veiled references easier than in prose), and its anchoring in a body of ancient Greek verse. In fact, modern scholarship has ascertained that even before the Greeks the Sumerian *Epic of Gilgamesh*, versions of which go back to the third millennium B.C., ranks as the first surviving homoerotic poem, treating the love between the semi-divine hero Gilgamesh and his "wild man" companion Enkidu. Cross-cultural influences of this kind, including those from Islam, China, and Japan, have played a fostering role. Helping to make these achievements better known, some gay male poets have been active as translators.

The first British golden age of homoerotic poetry came in the latter half of the nineteenth and the early twentieth centuries, witnessing an outpouring of love poems directed mostly at boys. Best known as a prose writer, Baron Corvo (Frederick Rolfe) belonged to this group. Widely read, A. E. Housman and Wilfred Owen remained in the closet. Beginning in the 1930s this traditional verse gave way to modernist poetry by Wystan Hugh Auden, Stephen Spender, Thom Gunn, and others. Auden achieved an international reputation as a man of letters, while open about his sexual orientation. In the United States the modernist Hart Crane, like so many others a disciple of Whitman, contributed *The Bridge* to American literature. His contemporary Marsden Hartley practiced poetry as a second vocation, after his modernist paintings. The California poet Robert Duncan showed a rare courage in avowing his homosexuality. After World War II Allen Ginsberg, author of *Howl*, achieved worldwide fame with intense, frankly homoerotic verse, which was a major element in the Beat literary movement, which he pioneered together with Jack Kerouac and William Burroughs. The New York writer Frank O'Hara, also active as an art critic, wrote poems based on seemingly slight incidents of daily life. His close friend John Ashbery, who lived for a long time in Paris, produced more intricate, learned work. James Broughton, Dennis Cooper, Paul Goodman, James Merrill, Jack Spicer, and many other American poets have published since censorship declined in the 1960s.

The Alexandrian poet Constantine Cavafy became a luminary of modern Greek literature through the concise lyrics he wrote in the early part of this century, many of them reflecting the world of the urban gay male. Family pressures prevented most of the openly gay work of the great Spanish poet Federico García Lorca from appearing in his own lifetime; some of it was published in the 1980s. His colleague Luis Cernuda was more fortunate in that his frank oeuvre was published during his years in exile in Mexico.

Many of the novelists who treated homoeroticism in their fiction also wrote poetry, but in recent times poetry has left the cultural mainstream and become uneconomic. In the process, it has been claimed as an art form by the underground artist and the street poet. Contemporary gay and lesbian poetry tends to be published by gay and lesbian small magazines for gay and lesbian audiences; it is uncensored but largely unread outside of a small literate gay or lesbian ghetto.

Until recently censorship restricted the treatment of homosexuality on the stage. Even celebrated playwrights like

Oscar Wilde, Noel Coward, Terence Rattigan, Tennessee Williams, and Edward Albee had to refrain from representing the theme frankly. In the 1960s the staging of the frank and sardonic works of Joe Orton in London and elsewhere represented a major breakthrough. In Canada Michel Tremblay combined an piquant awareness of French-Canadian national consciousness with gay identity. Since 1969 many little theaters in North America and England have facilitated the emergence of gay playwrights, including Robert Chesley, Harvey Fierstein, William Hoffman, Martin Sherman, Robert Patrick, Doric Wilson, and Lanford Wilson. Recently, some of this work, particularly plays dealing with the impact of AIDS on the lives of individuals, has entered the mainstream. The activist Larry Kramer has passionately indicted indifference to the AIDS crisis in plays, prose writings, and journalism. And Tony Kushner's Pulitzer-winning *Gay Fantasia* plays on Broadway.

The fields of autobiography and biography have also been important. Some autobiographies, like that of John Addington Symonds, could only be published long after the writer's lifetime. A most unusual autobiographer was the satanist Aleister Crowley. Collections of letters, such as those of Oscar Wilde and J. R. Ackerley, are also a form of autobiography, though one usually compiled by others. In fact Ackerley is best known for his *My Father and Myself*, which is both a biographical record of his bisexual father and an autobiographical account of his own gradual discovery of the fact. Diaries, of which those of Gide are the most famous and those of the composer Ned Rorem a more modest example, are sometimes deliberately published by their authors as a candid form of autobiography.

With the growth of the gay and lesbian movement, biographers began to look back at such figures as the leading lights of the Bloomsbury circle, including Lytton Strachey and John Maynard Keynes, with a new candor, and biographies dealing with homosexuality multiplied. Problems of concealment are critical in the biographies and autobiographies of homosexually involved people, though more and more mainstream biographers are at least alluding to the sexual life of their subjects, if not exploring the effects of this aspect on their work.

Literature is not only written, but studied. Literary studies proceed along a number of lines. First is what might be called the bedrock: identification of authors involved with homosexuality or lesbianism, whether positively or negatively, biographically and through analysis of their works in an effort to expose the often hidden influences of their sexuality on their creative product. Then some literary critics focus on themes, such as coming out, the growth of consciousness, friendship, interaction of characters with the mainstream society, conflict between homosexual and heterosexual desires, and "arcadia" (the attempt to find special places of refuge where gay and lesbian persons can flourish undisturbed). Another approach is literature as social reflector, an endeavor that extends to authors without known personal involvement, but who have treated (or deliberately ignored) homoeroticism in the course of their works. Then some literary works invite consideration as factors in the growth of political consciousness, in the wake of the gay-liberation movement. This realm also includes fiction, poetry, and plays concerning AIDS. In a more general way, literary study may involve interaction with emerging modes of study, including ethnic literature (for gay and lesbian fiction presents significant similarities—as well as differences—with black and other minority literatures), deconstruction, and cultural criticism, which deliberately blurs the lines between high and low culture and between literature and the other arts.

Finally, there is the field of scholarly and scientific writing. For long these fields preserved a type of objectivity that required homosexuality to be discussed only in terms of "them," others who were different from the writer. At the turn of the century pioneer studies from a sympathetic, yet objective point of view were made by German scholars, with the indefatigable Magnus Hirschfeld at their head. In the United States Parker Tyler and Vito Russo achieved wide recognition for their film studies. Recently, Yale professor John Boswell's revisionist and pro-gay studies of the European Middle Ages have had a surprising impact with the public at large. Anthropologists such as Gilbert Herdt, and scientists such as Simon LeVay have begun to include their own experiences in the presentation of their findings.

The present volume, *Gay and Lesbian Literature*, is the first of its kind. It comes at a time of tremendous surge in gay and lesbian writing of all sorts. In this context of ferment it is more important than ever to study and evaluate the distinguished record of past and present achievements.

Introduction to Lesbian Literature

by Barbara G. Grier

What a splendid gathering we have here. *Gay & Lesbian Literature* presents nothing less than information for some two hundred authors whose work has added substantially to gay and lesbian literature in the twentieth century. No work of the past has ever attempted to bring together in one source the homoerotic work that makes up so large a part of the major literature of our time. With the format and inclusiveness of *Gay & Lesbian Literature* allowing it to be used as a browsing tool as well as for research, this edition will find its way into many private libraries in addition to the institutional and public libraries of the world.

This ranging through almost one hundred years of literature allows the luxury of including authors born before 1900, and in keeping with the sexual mores and the conventions of literature in the past, the relevant homosexual literature includes many male authors born before the middle of the 1800s, but only two women born before the later 1800s. Listings of women authors highlight older notables such as Natalie Clifford Barney, Romaine Brooks, Colette, Radclyffe Hall, Vernon Lee, Gertrude Stein, Renée Vivien, and Virginia Woolf. Writers from the rich middle period include Elizabeth Bowen, Jane Bowles, Bryher, Rosamund Lehmann, Carson McCullers, Edna St. Vincent Millay, Mary Renault, and Sara Teasdale. The more contemporary group of authors, those still actively adding to the literature, include Dorothy Allison, Blanche McCrary Boyd, Margaret Cruikshank, Lillian Faderman, Katherine V. Forrest, Jewelle Gomez, Joan Nestle, Adrienne Rich, Sarah Schulman, Jeanette Winterson, and Bonnie Zimmerman.

In the late 1950s, interest in lesbian literature as a specific genre began to be documented in various small lesbian and gay periodicals. As groups of women collected, analyzed and discussed this literature, many of the writers of the period acquired mythic status, a lionization not necessarily accorded in relationship to the merit of the work as literature, thus allowing such works as those of Ann Bannon and Valerie Taylor from the "pulp" arena to be mixed with the works of Patricia Highsmith (writing as Claire Morgan) and later Jane Rule, authors of established critical reputation.

The lesbian paperback originals, a post World War II phenomenon, lasted from roughly the mid-1950s to the mid-1960s, and left at least two permanent legacies to literature: a general freeing of the sexual mores allowing much more sexually explicit material to find its way into respectable print, and burgeoning academic criticism that began to make a clear distinction between that literature written by women for women and that literature written by men, about women, for other men. The politicizing nature of the literature, albeit exclusively fiction, can be convincingly cited as one of the catalytic agents for the women's movement.

After 1969--usually cited as the birth of the modern day gay and lesbian struggle for civil rights and the birth period of the current phase of the women's movement--lesbian and gay literature began the growth phenomenon that allows us the privilege of this volume.

Jeannette Howard Foster (1889-1981), lesbian literature researcher and writer, author of *Sex Variant Women in Literature* in 1956, often predicted that we would see a day when it would not be possible to begin to cover the subject of lesbian literature in a single volume. Indeed, Foster could not today duplicate her pioneering work, which cites and briefly analyzes all known works of the literature through copyright year 1954. The intervening forty years may easily have quadrupled the available material and ironically made painfully difficult the process of distilling today's source material to bring itemization within the bounds of publication.

Knowing that *Gay & Lesbian Literature* will feed thousands of dissertations is gratifying indeed, but equally reassuring is the knowledge that it will spawn future volumes. *Gay & Lesbian Literature* is not an end summation, not a coda, but a beginning. It is a vital introduction to a rich and varied field of amazing literature.

Featured Authors

ACKERLEY, J. R. British poet and playwright whose writings are frequently rooted in autobiography, offer a vivid picture of gay life.

ALBEE, Edward. American award-winning playwright whose work often explores dysfunctional relationships and issues of truth versus illusion.

ALLEN, Paula Gunn. American educator and writer who draws upon her multicultural heritage to explicate what makes us individual and what brings us together.

ALLISON, Dorothy. American fiction writer and winner of National Book Award for *Bastard Out of Carolina* who explores the nature of domestic, personal, psychic, and sexual violence, especially from a lesbian-feminist point of view.

ALTMAN, Dennis. Australian educator and activist who uses Marxian analysis in discussions about sexual politics.

ANZALDÚA, Gloria. American poet and essayist whose work explores lesbianism within a multicultural background.

ARNOLD, June. American experimental novelist, identified as one of few lesbians who wrote political fiction, envisioned a world where it was possible for women to exert control over their own destinies.

ASHBERY, John. American poet and recipient of the Pulitzer and National Book Award whose work disavows individual consciousness and explores love in terms of generosity.

AUDEN, W. H. British and American poet, honored by numerous awards, including the Pulitzer and National Book Award, and considered to be one of the greatest poets of the twentieth century, insisted on the independence of poetry from the poet's life and disguised gender in his poems with homosexual themes.

BALDWIN, James. American novelist and essayist who examined the individual in terms of racial and sexual separatism in society, and who projected his own sexuality into his art.

BANNON, Ann. American novelist whose work reveals gay life in Greenwich Village in the 1950s and 1960s.

BARNES, Djuna. American journalist and free lance illustrator who celebrated lesbianism in her landmark novel *Nightwood,* which was informed by her experiences in Greenwich Village and, after 1920, among the expatriate artists in Paris.

BARNEY, Natalie. French writer whose own writing celebrated homosexuality without apology or remorse, established a famous Paris salon which attracted many artists and promoted their work.

BARTLETT, Neil. British playwright and novelist whose *Ready to Catch Him Should He Fall* shows a profound understanding of traditional gay male themes, attempts an honest depiction of what it means to be gay by creating characters with universal qualities and situations with universal implications.

BÉRUBÉ, Allan. American historian whose study of gay men and women in the military has influenced subsequent scholarship.

BIRTHA, Becky. African American poet and short story writer who explores racial and sexual relationships.

BLAIS, Marie-Claire. French Canadian award-winning novelist, poet, and playwright, whose work depicts characters who hold a marginal place in society.

BOSWELL, John. American award-winning historian whose work on the Middle Ages has altered contemporary perceptions about homosexuality and intolerance.

BOWEN, Elizabeth. Irish and British writer whose life and work expressed ambivalence about her personal and cultural identity, explored marginal relationships and thresholds between childhood and adulthood, innocence and experience, masculinity and femininity, tradition and modernity.

BOWLES, Jane. American fiction writer and playwright who explored the efforts of women to escape from conventional sexual roles, frequently wrote about emotional distance and a search for balance.

BOWLES, Paul. American fiction writer, poet, and composer, examines a world in which all human behavior is aberrant and dangerous.

BOYD, Blanche McCrary. American novelist who writes from the perspective of a white Southern lesbian who understands the complexity of her position and whose writing tries to mediate and understand power, autonomy, and sense of self.

BOYD, Malcolm. American theologian and writer whose celebration of homosexuality as a spiritual gift has contributed much to the growth of a separate gay and lesbian approach to religious matters and to the evolution of a more accepting theology.

BRADLEY, Marion Zimmer. American novelist, best known for her science fiction novels about the world of "Darkover," explores the universe of gender roles and human relationships, and creates characters that progress from feeling alien and outcast to forming a bond with others.

BRAM, Christopher. American writer who has expanded the traditional themes of gay male fiction by creating a more complex and sophisticated fictional narrative that is influenced by feminism and progressive domestic and international politics as well as gay liberation.

BROOKS, Romaine. American expatriate artist and memoirist, primarily known for her portraits of the Paris artistic community, consciously borrowed styles from earlier movements and used them to build a visual image of the new public lesbian of the 1920s and 1930s.

BROUGHTON, James. American poet, playwright, and filmmaker, whose work celebrates life's sensual and visionary pleasures, is a leader in the field of experimental cinema.

BROWN, Rita Mae. American activist, novelist and poet, who writes about the lives of working-class women with humor and a keen sense of storytelling.

BRYHER. British poet, novelist, and memoirist, whose interest in remodeling oneself, renaming oneself, or in veiling one's lesbianism beneath a male mask or an imagined maleness revealed itself in many of her historical novels.

BURROUGHS, William S. American novelist, poet, and canonical figure in the Beat Movement, whose work has resisted incorporation into the canon of gay literature largely because his vision of sexuality is too dark and politically incorrect.

BUSI, Aldo. Italian novelist whose work presents homosexuality not as an alternative lifestyle, nor an exotic, erotic choice, but as an integral and basic component of being.

CALIFIA, Pat. American novelist, journalist, and sex educator, whose contribution to lesbian culture has been to return sex to the dialogue on homosexuality.

CAPOTE, Truman. American writer whose work often presents homosexuality circuitously, but shows great insight into the problems of boys struggling with their sexuality.

CARPENTER, Edward. British poet and social theorist, who opened the field of sexuality to include the history of male-male love and argued for the creative role of "intermediate types" in the progress of civilization.

CATHER, Willa. American writer who wrote about lesbians and gay males metaphorically by writing about people on the margins of the dominant culture, outsiders whom she believed were the best of society.

CAVAFY, C. P. Greek poet whose erotic poems have particularly influenced a number of gay, lesbian, and bisexual artists, believed that erotic memory is more real than the actuality of love.

CERNUDA, Luis. Spanish poet who worshipped light, air, and water as they illuminated a man's body, wrote homosexual love poems and homoerotic poems that show love as a break with the social order and a joining with the natural world.

CHAMBERS, Jane. American playwright who frankly explored various aspects of lesbian relationships and is regarded as a pioneer in the field of lesbian theatre.

CHESLEY, Robert. American playwright whose *Night Sweat* initiated the AIDS-related themes in the gay theatre, wrote honestly about the joys and sorrows of being gay.

COCTEAU, Jean. French writer who wrote obliquely about homosexual relationships but infused his work with a tension caused by the contradictory desire to express and expose and an ambiguity that within his world, things are not quite what they seem.

COLETTE. French writer whose work shows strong, independent women counterpoised against weak and dependent men and restored love for one's own sex to world literature.

COMPTON-BURNETT, I. British novelist whose work is often concerned with the minute workings of power and loyalty within familial relationships challenged the primacy of the conventional values of a patriarchal and heterosexist society.

COOPER, Dennis. American poet, novelist, and playwright who writes about empty lives and sexual despair and focuses on the difficulties in being in a homophobic world that ignores and disregards the pleasures of the flesh and the world of the gay imagination.

CORINNE, Tee. American artist and fiction writer whose pioneering work in the field of lesbian erotica and celebrates the sexuality of all women.

CRANE, Hart. American poet who refined the sexual mystique of the 1920s and in whose art homosexuality hinges on its grasp of the cold facts of American cities as a source of passionate images in its celebration of male myths and engineering wonders.

CRISP, Quentin. British humorist and social critic, whose work traces four decades of attitudes and fashions of speech and behavior among homosexuals, as well as the changing attitudes toward and social acceptance of homosexuality.

CROWLEY, Aleister. British occultist and author of treatises on magic who negated Judeo-Christian traditions by inverting its tenets occupies a unique place in the history of homoerotic literature.

CROWLEY, Mart. American playwright whose *The Boys in the Band* explores the inherent emotional problems that accompany the inability to accept one's own sexuality.

CRUIKSHANK, Margaret. American educator whose scholarship in the area of homosexuality, sexism, homophobia, and ageism, has brought together several anthologies important to the study of lesbianism.

CURZON, Daniel. American novelist whose work focuses on the homosexual male experience and the relationship between gays and non-gays reveals a grim world of harsh realism that denies the simplistic and sentimental happy solution.

DALY, Mary. American teacher of theology and philosophy whose work repudiates patriarchy, especially in religion, and explores the depths of language and meaning.

D'EMILIO, John. American historian whose work in the field of gay and lesbian history provides a framework for all subsequent work in the field.

DIXON, Melvin. American novelist and poet who work attempts to push the boundaries of what is permissible in the traditions of African American and gay male fiction.

DOOLITTLE, Hilda. American award-winning poet whose work addresses lesbian sexuality indirectly but reveals an underlying homoerotic passion.

DUBERMAN, Martin Bauml. American historian whose work in homosexuality spans several genres has contributed significantly to an increased understanding of gay and lesbian history and culture.

DUFFY, Maureen. British poet and novelist whose personal history and political commitments are explicit in all her work explores the diversity and unpredictability of human sexuality and what it means to be overtly sexual in an erotophobic and homophobic world.

DUNCAN, Robert. American award-winning Beat poet and playwright who also wrote one of the first pieces to portray homosexuals as a minority group oppressed by a hostile society.

DURANG, Christopher. American playwright whose work has expanded the boundaries of satire explores the inability to make sense of human and emotional tragedy and critiques traditional gender and sexual roles.

DWORKIN, Andrea. American feminist and novelist who examines the interaction of the gay and lesbian liberation movements with themes of importance to the women's movement.

DYNES, Wayne R. American educator whose work in gay studies has earned him a lasting place in academic history as one of the authentic founders of the "gay science."

ELLIS, Havelock. British physician who was the first major writer on homosexuality in English and one of the great scientific authorities on human sexuality in the first half of the twentieth century.

FADERMAN, Lillian. American educator whose studies of lesbianism in this century have contributed significantly to the field.

FASSBINDER, Rainer Werner. German playwright and filmmaker, considered one of the foremost international figures in cinema, studied the dynamics of power in the material and personal worlds.

FEINBERG, David B. American novelist whose work captures the social and psychological hysteria surrounding AIDS.

FERRO, Robert. American novelist whose work examines the position of the gay man in relation to the nuclear family and their relationship with the gay world.

FIERSTEIN, Harvey. American playwright, whose *Torch Song Trilogy* concerns search for lasting love, advocates commitment and responsibility in relationships.

FLANNER, Janet. American novelist and journalist whose attitude toward her lesbianism was ahead of her time and atypical among the expatriate circle in which she lived.

FORD, Charles Henri. American poet and novelist whose *The Young and Evil* with Parker Tyler has become a cult classic, worked in many forms throughout his career.

FORREST, Katherine V. Canadian novelist known for her series of police procedurals featuring lesbian sleuth Kate Delafield has also written thematically complex novels concerning love, exploration, discovery and intense passion involving two women.

FORSTER, E. M. British novelist whose central theme was the conflict between social mores and personal freedom also explored the relationship between colonial exploitation and homosexual repression.

FOSTER, Jeannette Howard. American librarian whose pioneering work *Sex Variant Women in Literature* represents a monumental contribution to the development of a lesbian culture.

FOUCAULT, Michel. French philosopher and social historian whose work traces the history of discourse about sexuality and has influenced numerous students of homosexuality.

GARCÍA LORCA, Federico. Spanish poet whose view of human life was marked by existential pessimism espoused a paneroticism inspired by the eternal cycles of nature.

GENET, Jean. French novelist and playwright whose work often reveals an autobiographical element examined the sexual act as intrinsically violent and unequal and liberated some of the constraints in literature and conflicted with apologist homosexual movements of the 1940s and 1950s.

GIDE, André. French novelist and playwright, winner of the Nobel Prize, and one of the most important writers of the first half of the twentieth century, made a case for innate homosexuality in *Corydon* in 1920, and frequently explored themes of Greek love.

GIDLOW, Elsa. Canadian poet and philosopher and one of the first poets in the twentieth century to write almost exclusively and explicitly from an openly lesbian viewpoint.

GINSBERG, Allen. American poet and important figure in the Beat Movement attacked the power elite in *Howl,* and celebrates sexual freedom and its ideological corollaries in his work.

GOMEZ, Jewelle. American novelist whose work is a hybrid of politics and imagination celebrates lesbian life and sexuality and analyzes how lesbian and gay male culture can articulate and understand erotic and political difference.

GRAHN, Judy. American poet, playwright, and novelist who redefines gay and lesbian existence in positive and powerful terms by drawing on myth, tribal cultures, history and personal experience to create a new mythology of gayness as a way of being.

GREENE, Harlan. American novelist whose work looks at the difficulties in finding acceptance from society as well as the gay community itself.

GRIER, Barbara G. American journalist, editor, publisher who has helped create vast, diverse, readable, and positive lesbian literature.

GRUMBACH, Doris. American novelist whose genius resides in recreating the romantic sensibility of the past and making it understandable in terms of twentieth-century lives and sexuality.

GUNN, Thom. American poet whose work explores the boundaries between love and sexuality and between public and private acknowledgements of feeling.

GURGANUS, Allan. American fiction writer whose fictional characters are frequently marked by ambivalence about their homosexuality.

HALL, Radclyffe. English novelist and poet whose *The Well of Loneliness* has become a literary classic, wrote explicitly of same sex love.

HALL, Richard W. American fiction writer and playwright who depicts the coalescing gay world of the 1970s and 1980s.

HANSEN, Joseph. American fiction writer whose mystery novels about masculine homosexual insurance adjuster David Brandstetter are popular with gay and non-gay readers alike.

HEMPHILL, Essex. American poet and a key figure in the emergence of a distinctive African American perspective in the overall field of gay literature.

HIGHSMITH, Patricia. American novelist whose reputation as a crime novelist belies the perspective in her work on what it means to be human--and guilty--in the twentieth century.

HIRSCHFELD, Magnus. German physician and writer who became an international authority on homosexuality in his lifetime.

HOCQUENGHEM, Guy. French writer and one of the central figures in the post-Stonewall gay and lesbian movement.

HOLLERAN, Andrew. American novelist whose *Dancer from the Dance* was one of the first works to receive acclaim from outside the gay press, shows the dark side of the gay world in his work but discusses issues most pressing to the gay male community.

HOLLINGHURST, Alan. British poet and novelist who has gained significant critical attention with *The Swimming-Pool Library* focuses upon male-male relationships in his work.

HOUSMAN, A. E. British poet whose work reveals little explicit homosexual content wrote with veiled illusions to homosexuality.

HUGHES, Langston. American poet and fiction writer whose work expresses a gay spirit or chord rather than explicit gay themes.

ISHERWOOD, Christopher. British-born American novelist and playwright who wrote of alienation, isolation, sexuality, and spirituality crafted what may be the definitive portrait of pre-Hitler Germany in *The Berlin Stories*.

JAY, Karla. American educator whose work embodies the belief that it is essential for gays, and particularly lesbians, to have an appreciation of their past in order to move forward with a sense of dignity and purpose.

JOHNSTON, Jill. American journalist whose politics have forged and illumined lesbian and gay theory and have imbued it with a past.

KATZ, Jonathan. American playwright, nonfiction writer, and activist who believes that people are a product of both their natures and social conditioning and thinks that the process of historicizing sexuality and homosexuality is leading to important surprises.

KENAN, Randall. American fiction writer whose work is noted for stylistic virtuosity and thematic richness writes about complex individuals within racial and sexual types.

KEROUAC, Jack. American novelist and poet in the Beat Movement whose work often embodies an autobiographical element.

KRAMER, Larry. American playwright and activist who has ranged a war within and against a community built on sexual freedom calls for a more responsible gay male community.

KUSHNER, Tony. American playwright whose Pulitzer-winning *Gay Fantasia* goes farther than any other contemporary gay literary work in its use of gay characters and traditionally gay themes to examine a complex political, cultural, and historical reality that transcends gay ghettos and embraces all of American society.

KUZMIN, Mikhail. Russian poet and popular pre-revolutionary literary figure who wrote frankly of sexual themes.

LAWRENCE, D. H. British writer who attempted to resolve the relationships between the sexes in work that interweaves authoritarianism, sexuality, and mysticism.

LAWRENCE, T. E. British soldier known as Lawrence of Arabia whose *Seven Pillars of Wisdom* candidly comments upon freedom and lack of sexual restraint.

LEAVITT, David. American novelist and author of short fiction whose work exhibits an instinct for the ordinariness of life examines what people hold in common and what divide them.

LEDUC, Violette. French novelist whose work reveals an autobiographical element focused upon the experiences of love, sexuality, and the disappointment of female protagonists.

LEE, Vernon. This British essayist and fiction writer embodied the "new woman" who emerged at the end of the nineteenth century who found it possible to live without a male companion and to share her emotional life with women.

Le GUIN, Ursula K. American novelist whose work has become increasingly woman-centered explores the absence of gender dominance and is well known for her *Earthsea* fantasy.

LEHMANN, Rosamond. British novelist who portrayed characters loving without labels during a time when there was a dearth of good lesbian material.

LEZAMA LIMA, José. Cuban novelist and poet who displayed a biting and personal way of exploring the complexities of the origin of human sexuality.

LORDE, Audre. American essayist and short fiction writer who focused a sharp eye of language on life, love, and relationships.

LOWELL, Amy. American Imagist poet and leader in the growth of American literature whose love poems reveal fulfillment and calls for a new sexual ethic in poetry.

LYON, Phyllis Ann. American gay activist and educator whose *Lesbian/Woman* and *Lesbian Love and Liberation* with Del Martin serve as pioneering works in the field of lesbian culture.

MANN, Thomas. German novelist and short story writer who exposed and critically depicted the narcissism of Western society also wrote about the inner conflicts of individuals whose erotic propensities deviate from societal norms.

MANSFIELD, Katherine. New Zealand poet and author of short stories who employs a feminist approach to life and literature.

MARS-JONES, Adam. British short story writer who is considered one of the best writers on the subject of AIDS.

MARTIN, Del. American gay activist and writer of nonfiction whose *Lesbian/Woman* and *Lesbian Love and Liberation* with Phyllis Ann Lyon serve as pioneering works in the field of lesbian culture.

MARTINAC, Paula. American novelist and short story writer who highlights the experiences of women and targets the many common denominators between women of differing sexual orientations.

MAUGHAM, Robin. British writer who produced several works that explore homosexuality and class structure.

MAUPIN, Armistead. American novelist whose "Tales of the City" novels of gay life appeal to a wide audience.

McALMON, Robert. American publisher and author whose stories reveal autobiographical elements may be best remembered in the field of gay studies by his *Distinguished Air* in which he questions the attitude to take toward the confused lives of some gays who nevertheless generate admiration through their courage, openness, survival and sense of humor.

McCULLERS, Carson. American novelist and playwright whose work explores the variety and complexity of human isolation and expose the destructive repercussions of that alienation, especially when the separation of the individual from society is occasioned by racial and gender bigotry.

McNALLY, Terrence. American playwright of wit and intelligence whose satiric use of homosexual themes and characters has resulted in what critics refer to as the consummate gay farce, *The Ritz*.

MERRILL, James Ingram. American poet and recipient of the Pulitzer Prize and National Book Award who brings together the fine, the exotic, and the mythic, with the commonplace.

MEW, Charlotte. British poet and important turn-of-the-century lesbian writer who wrote of female sexuality, including the autoerotic and lesbian.

MILLAY, Edna St. Vincent. American poet and dramatist whose work reveals little about her private life but shows a love of freedom and risk.

MILLER, Neil. American journalist whose glimpses into the day-to-day life of gays in various communities throughout the world spotlight the vast cultural differences that impinge upon the concept of homosexuality.

MILLETT, Kate. American feminist whose work is firmly rooted in the belief that the personal is the political.

MISHIMA, Yukio. Japanese writer who wrote one of the first important books to deal with the topic of homosexuality in Japan.

MONETTE, Paul. American poet and novelist and winner of the National Book Award for *Becoming a Man* believes that telling one person's truth leaves no one out.

MORAGA, Cherríe. American educator and writer whose work examines lesbianism in terms of multicultural heritage.

MORDDEN, Ethan. American writer whose tales of gay Manhattan in the *Christopher Street* in the early 1980s reveal the era of gay self-discovery, self-expression, and self-abandon between the Stonewall revolt and the dawn of the AIDS epidemic.

NESTLE, Joan. American historian interested in changing the definition of history explores how the human soul resists social and cultural tyrannies.

NEWMAN, Lesléa. American writer whose books for children have stirred controversy in schools and libraries, explores issues of lesbian and Jewish identity as well as the political relationships between women and food.

O'HARA, Frank. American poet and dramatist who celebrated the uncertainties of his time and ridiculed the fraud of traditional poetry, families and values.

ORTON, Joe. British playwright who satirized heterosexual characters rather than promote homosexual ones.

OWEN, Wilfred. British poet who depicted the shame and horror of World War I rather than its glory and honor also revealed in his verse homosexual tendencies and leitmotifs.

PARKER, Pat. American poet who was distinctive for her willingness to engage problematic topics in her verse presented sex between women frankly and honestly.

PARNOK, Sophia. Russian poet known for the boldness of her subject matter and language.

PASOLINI, Pier Paolo. Italian writer, film critic, and theorist who viewed his subject matter from nonconforming, contrary, yet innovative perspectives.

PATRICK, Robert. American playwright whose work provides numerous images of gay male possibilities and frequently treats serious themes in comic terms.

PENNA, Sandro. Italian poet whose work displays emotions ranging from exhilaration to melancholy as it reflects upon boy love.

PICANO, Felice. American writer and a leader in the modern gay literary movement whose own work expresses a sense of coming to terms with human nature and contemporary urban living.

PRATT, Minnie Bruce. American poet and essayist who has cultivated the concepts of community and personal exchange writes of urbanism, art, love, racism, identity, family, and sex.

PRESTON, John. American writer whose prolific output spans many genres writes frankly about gay and lesbian self-esteem, sexuality, AIDS, and homophobia.

PROUST, Marcel. French novelist recognized as a twentieth-century literary giant, searches for meaning in the past in his *A la recherche du temps perdu* and believed that his theory of love was applicable to everyone.

PUIG, Manuel. Argentinean novelist and playwright, whose *Kiss of the Spider Woman* has been variously adapted, combined an interest in popular culture with techniques of experimental fiction and turned a critical eye and ear on modern society and culture.

PURDY, James. American novelist whose work sometimes displays internalized homophobia also explores possibilities when gay desire is not hidden or silent.

RAPHAEL, Lev. American short story writer who explores the place of sexual orientation within the larger context of an ethnic culture and religious tradition.

RATTIGAN, Terence Mervyn. British playwright and screen-writer and author of the well-made, genteel domestic drama of the 1950s, exposed social and sexual hypocrisy and revealed an unending sympathy for characters whose emotional lives have been hurt by a repressive culture.

RECHY, John. American writer whose semi-autobiographical *City of the Night* depicts the encounters of a male-hustler, portrays the gay male experience, AIDS, the ghettoization of gay art, with structural and stylistic diversity in numerous other fictional works.

REES, David (Bartlett). British novelist and young adult writer whose work explores social issues in general and homosexuality in particular communicated the experience which at midlife turned his own life around.

RENAULT, Mary. British-born South African novelist and historian whose *The Persian Boy* defied her own society's taboos about homosexuality.

RICH, Adrienne. American poet and prose writer whose developing feminist consciousness led to an increased awareness of her own lesbianism works to create connections and to foster community among women in her poetry and prose.

ROLFE, Frederick. British novelist whose work is primarily autobiographical and imbued with recurring homosexual themes.

ROREM, Ned. American composer and essayist who chronicled his own life in his diaries frankly described homosexual love affairs at a time when such subjects were considered unmentionable.

ROUTSONG, Alma. American novelist whose *Patience and Sarah* stands as one of the first contemporary lesbian historical novels.

RULE, Jane. Canadian novelist and author of short fiction whose critical study *Lesbian Images* represents an important contribution to lesbian literature.

RUSS, Joanna. American novelist and radical feminist who argues for a world and culture in which women's ideas and opinions are able to be heard and implemented.

RUSSO, Vito. American activist and film historian who explored and evaluated the types and ranges of imagery through which homosexuals and the idea of homosexuality were presented to the general public in cinema.

SACKVILLE-WEST, V. British poet, garden designer, and biographer whose verse reveals lesbian passion is important for living her life on her own terms, which has earned her a place as a figurehead in the assimilationist "les-bi-gay" movement of the early 1990s.

SAGARIN, Edward. American sociologist author of nonfiction who was a pioneering thinker of the American homophile movement.

SARTON, May. American poet and novelist who wrote one of the first mainstream novels to deal with an openly lesbian without apology or psychoanalytic explanation.

SCHULMAN, Sarah. American novelist who explores the interaction between the nature of art and the reality of politics.

SCOPPETTONE, Sandra. American novelist who writes powerfully and honestly about sexuality for adults and young adults alike has also created the character of Lauren Laurano for the first mainstream lesbian detective book to be published, *Everything You Have Is Mine.*

SHERMAN, Martin. American playwright whose *Bent* was the first play to publicly depict the incarceration of gays in concentration camps during World War II.

SHILTS, Randy. American journalist whose investigation into the AIDS epidemic resulted in *And the Band Played On,* studies the history of gays and lesbians in the military in *Conduct Unbecoming.*

SHOCKLEY, Ann Allen. American novelist who put the black lesbian character into twentieth-century American literature.

SMITH, Barbara. American editor and essayist who writes about homosexual black feminism was the first to characterize as lesbian the relationships between black women in classic black novels.

SPENDER, Stephen. British poet who offers a clear explication of opinions about same-gender relations and the validity of various explanations for it in *World within World.*

SPICER, Jack. American serialist poet known for some of the most moving love poetry of the century.

STEIN, Gertrude. American expatriate writer whose writing is both revelatory and secretive masked lesbian subject matter in her work.

STEWARD, Samuel M. American poet, novelist, and author of erotica, whose nonfiction describes sexual trends and how they have been expressed in literature has had a significant influence on many gay male erotic writers.

SWINBURNE, A. C. British poet who made himself a provocative public presence by deliberately transgressing the conventions by which sexuality was represented in respectable mid-Victorian literature.

TEASDALE, Sara. American poet who wrote primarily from the heart about things of the heart.

TOKLAS, Alice B. American expatriate journalist and author of cookbooks whose memoir *Staying on Alone* presents a picture of Gertrude Stein at work.

TOURNIER, Michel. French novelist whose work evinces an enormous interest in sexuality through depictions of possible forms of sexual expression that are not focused uniquely on the genitals.

TREMBLAY, Michel. French Canadian writer who creates a world in which the autobiographical element unfolds progressively as his universe expands, and the homosexual element appears objectively.

TYLER, Parker. American poet and nonfiction writer whose *The Young and Evil* with Charles Henri Ford has become a cult classic, explored issues of eroticism in film and attempted to elucidate the power of onscreen sexual archetypes upon audience's lives and sexual fantasies and emotions.

VIDAL, Gore. American writer who has gained a level of renown for his depiction of homosexual characters and themes has turned popular and psychoanalytic ideas about gender identity inside out.

VIVIEN, Renée. British-born French poet and short fiction writer whose work was influenced by Classical Greek philosophy, French symbolism, and American feminism, frequently drew from decadent and symbolist traditions giving them a unique lesbian interpretation.

WARNER, Sylvia Townsend. British poet, novelist, and short story writer whose work examines liberation from ideological constraints and awareness of alternative realities.

WARREN, Patricia Nell. American novelist whose work concerns homophobia, violence against gays and lesbians, and sadomasochism, and questions the role of sexuality and the social limitations placed on it.

WATMOUGH, David. British-born Canadian novelist and short story writer who has created a fictional alter ego in Davey Bryant epitomizes the life of the gay male in the twentieth century as he travels in search of adventure.

WAUGH, Evelyn. British novelist and satirist whose treatment of homosexuality fluctuated depending on his characters' motives and on the circumstances in which they were involved.

WEEKS, Jeffrey. British social scientist who approaches sexuality as a highly political field of study that has social and cultural as well as individual importance.

WELCH, Denton. British novelist and author of short fiction whose work exhibits relentless honesty, a vigorously pared autobiographical theme, and a flair for detail.

WHITE, Edmund. American novelist who writes novels that turn in upon their own technique and are concerned with questions of knowability and of uncertainty.

WHITE, Patrick. Australian novelist and Nobel Prize winner whose primary concern as a novelist is the exploration of the inner lives of his characters.

WILDE, Oscar. Universally acknowledged as the wittiest poet, literary critic, novelist, short story writer, and playwright of the late nineteenth century, he achieved much fame but suffered subsequent disgrace and imprisonment for homosexual offenses in the most sensational trials of the century.

WILLIAMS, Tennessee. American playwright who treated homosexuality obliquely, portrayed powerful and poetic women characters as well as many sexually magnetic males, exhibited gay vision in his work without mention of homosexuality.

WILSON, Barbara. American novelist and short story writer who provides insight into the political, social, and emotional ramifications of the struggle to redefine culture's view of women by liberating it from male expectations; using politics, humor and lyricism, she treats issues of desire, language and gender.

WILSON, Doric. American playwright who views the need to establish a distinctive gay cultural identity as the primary motivation fueling efforts for change.

WILSON, Lanford. American dramatist who explores a wide range of human emotions and situations through an often bewildering variety of characters.

WINSLOE, Christa. German sculptress, novelist and playwright whose *The Child Manuela* is considered one of the last examples of lesbian fiction to be issued before the Nazi regime obliterated homosexual literature.

WINTERSON, Jeanette. British novelist whose work reveals ungendered eroticism, homophilic references, and feminist or lesbian sensibility while not focusing solely on questions of lesbian identity and experience.

WITTIG, Monique. French novelist and feminist theorist who has devised a theory of lesbianism as the route to social revolution that has largely shaped the thinking of French and American radical lesbian feminists.

WOOLF, Virginia. British novelist, essayist, diarist, and publisher whose work exhibits homoerotic desire and expresses in repeated lesbian plots and subplots her own personal struggle to express the experiences of her own life in her texts.

YOURCENAR, Marguerite. Belgian-born American novelist who wrote about different kinds of love and the forms to express its variety.

ZIMMERMAN, Bonnie. American educator and pioneer in lesbian studies and literary criticism.

A

ABHAVANANDA. *See* CROWLEY, Aleister.

————

ACKERLEY, J(oe) R(andolph). British poet, playwright, and biographer. Born in Herne Hill, Kent, 4 November 1896. Educated at Magdalene College, Cambridge, graduated, 1921. Served in the Royal Army, 1914–18; became prisoner of war. Private secretary to ruler of state in India; assistant producer in talks department, British Broadcasting Corp. (BBC), London, 1928–35; literary editor of *Listener*, 1935–59. **Recipient:** W. H. Smith Literary Award for *We Think the World of You*, 1962. *Died 4 June 1967.*

WRITINGS

Memoirs

Hindoo Holiday: An Indian Journal. London, Chatto & Windus, and New York, Viking, 1932; published with additional material, 1952; new and expanded edition, New York, Poseidon Press, 1990.

My Dog Tulip. London, Secker & Warburg, 1956; revised, New York, Fleet Publishing, 1965.

My Father and Myself. London, Bodley Head, 1968; New York, Coward, 1969.

My Sister and Myself: The Diaries of J. R. Ackerley, edited and introduced by Francis King. London, Hutchinson, 1982.

Poetry

"The Everlasting Terror (To Bobby)," in *English Review* (London), November 1916.

"Daedalus" and "9.9.19," in *Cambridge Modern Poets, 1914–1920,* edited by Edward Lewis Davison. London, W. Heffer and Son, 1920.

With A. Y. Campbell, Edward Davison, and Frank Kendon, *Poems by Four Authors* (includes "Ghosts," "On a Photograph of Myself as a Boy," "The Portrait of a Mother," "The Conjuror on Hammersmith Bridge," and five sonnets). Cambridge, England, Bowes, 1923.

"Ditty," in *Listener* (London), 17 December 1959.

Micheldever, and Other Poems (includes "Micheldever," "The Conjuror on Hammersmith Bridge," "Ghosts," "After the Blitz,

1941," and "Missing [To F. H.]"). London, McKelvie, 1972.

"The Jacket" in *Ackerley: A Life of J. R. Ackerley* by Peter Parker. New York, Farrar, Straus, 1989.

Other

The Prisoners of War (play; produced London, 1925; broadcast by BBC Third Programme, 1953). London, Chatto & Windus, 1925; corrected edition, 1927.

Compiler and author of preface, *Escapers All* (anthology), 1932.

We Think the World of You (novel). London, Bodley Head, 1960; new and expanded edition, New York, Poseidon Press, 1989.

"Kobo Daishi," in *Listener* (London), 31 August 1961.

"I Am a Beast," in *Orient/West* (Tokyo), March–April 1964.

Contributor, *Authors Take Sides on Vietnam,* edited by Cecil Woolf and John Bagguley. London, Peter Owen, 1967.

"A Summer's Evening," in *London Magazine,* October 1969.

E. M. Forster: A Portrait (biography). London, McKelvie, 1970.

The Ackerley Letters. New York, Harcourt, 1975; as *The Letters of J. R. Ackerley,* edited by Neville Braybrooke, London, Duckworth, 1975.

*

Manuscript Collections: A collection of his manuscripts is held by Ackerley's literary executor, Francis King; a collection of letters from E. M. Forster to Ackerley is held by the Harry Ransom Humanities Research Center, University of Texas at Austin.

Biography: *The Secret Orchard of Roger Ackerley* by Diane Petre, London, Hamish Hamilton, 1975; *E. M. Forster: A Life* by P. N. Furbank (two volumes), London, Secker & Warburg, 1977–78; *A Small Cloud* by Harry Daley, London, Weidenfeld & Nicolson, 1987; *William Plomer: A Biography* by Peter F. Alexander, Oxford, Oxford University Press, 1989; *Ackerley: A Life of J. R. Ackerley* by Peter Parker, New York, Farrar, Straus, 1989.

Critical Sources: "Papa Was a Wise Old Sly Boots" by W. H. Auden, in *New York Review of Books,* 27 March 1969, reprinted in his *Forewords and Afterwords,* New York, Random House, 1973, 450–58; *Times Literary Supplement,* 31 January 1975; *New York Times Book Review,* 25 May 1975; "Love with the Perfect Dog" by A. Lurie, in *New York Times Book Review,* 12 November 1989, 12; "Dog Days" by R. Jenkyns, in *New Republic,* 18 December 1989, 31–34; "Attitudes to Ackerley" by J. G. Links, in *Encounter* (London), April 1990, 55–57; "Heavy Petting: J. R. Ackerley Goes to the Dogs" by Walter Kendrick, in *Village Voice Literary Supplement,* October 1990, 14–15; discussion of *Prisoners of War,* in *Not* *in Front of the Audience: Homosexuality on Stage* by Nicholas De Jongh, London, Routledge, 1992, 22–30.

* * *

J. R. Ackerley's writings are almost always rooted in autobiography, and because of their sexual frankness they offer a more vivid picture of the life of a gay man than do the memoirs of many of his gay contemporaries. Indeed, gay male friends of his sometimes found both his life and writings shocking. Ackerley produced only four volumes during his lifetime: the play *Prisoners of War*, the memoirs *Hindoo Holiday* and *My Dog Tulip*, and the autobiographical novel *We Think the World of You*. His most important and disturbing memoir, *My Father and Myself*, was published the year after his death. It was followed by an edition of his letters and a selection of diaries, *My Sister and Myself*.

Ackerley began his literary life writing poems, including hundreds of unpublished ones. His juvenilia reflected the homoerotic milieu of his "public" school. His experiences in World War I led him to produce poems, such as "The Everlasting Terror" and "Ghosts," whose elegiac tones indicate his love for dead comrades. In the late 1920s he composed "The Jacket," a simple but poignant reflection on the end of his love affair with a young man. "After the Blitz, 1941" and "Missing (To F. H.)," written as a civilian in the first years of World War II, reflect his love for a soldier missing at war. Other poems do not have overtly gay themes but are intimately tied to Ackerley's hatred at the exploitation of the working class, as we see in "Micheldever" or sympathy for outcasts driven to suicide, as in "The Conjuror on Hammersmith Bridge." "Ditty" is a lament on a dog's old age.

Prisoners of War and *Hindoo Holiday* indicate Ackerley's willingness to push homosexual themes as far as the times would allow. The play *Prisoners of War* takes place at a prisoner–of–war camp in Switzerland where in 1918 British soldiers live on their hope of repatriation. It may well be the first twentieth–century play produced on London or Broadway to animate its plot with homosexual desire. The protagonist, Captain Conrad, suffers from unrequited love for a shallow soldier named Grayle, and he eventually has a nervous breakdown, transferring his affection to a potted azalea. In a 1955 letter to Stephen Spender, Ackerley denies that the affection between two supporting characters is homosexual, but this view is open to debate. *Hindoo Holiday* is based on Ackerley's six months in India in 1923 and 1924 as personal secretary and companion to the Maharajah of Chhokrapur. We can tell that the elderly ruler in the play is gay through his desire to bring teenage boys to court as his "young gods" and in his amusing plans to turn his realm into a successor of the classical Greek states.

More than 20 years went by before the appearance of the famous and unusual dog story, *My Dog Tulip*, a tribute to the female Alsatian, Queenie, to which Ackerley was devoted from 1946 to her death in 1961. Because Queenie was as difficult as she was beautiful, and because Ackerley spent less energy on his cruising, desire for human love, and his regular friendships for her sake, his attitude toward her has generated much controversy. The novel *We Think the World of You* is closely based on his acquisition of this dog as a mistreated puppy from the family of a petty thief with whom

Ackerley was infatuated. The scene in which the dog responds to the two men making love after their long separation, omitted from early editions, is particularly memorable.

My Father and Myself juxtaposes the author's secret sexual and romantic life with that of his father—a man who did not marry Ackerley's mother until the children were grown, who had a second family on the side, and who might have been the kept man of a homosexual Count in his early career. Told in the disturbing impressionistic style of Ford Madox Ford's *The Good Soldier*, it reaches insight through unusual juxtapositions. Very frank for its time in its depiction of his sexual life, it recounts Ackerley's quest for the "Ideal Friend" among the lower classes and his reflections on his unrealistic romantic expectations, compulsive cruising, premature ejaculations, and fear of halitosis.

In addition to his signed book reviews in the *Listener*, Ackerley published a few short but worthwhile essays. The most famous of these is his 1967 glowing tribute to E. M. Forster with whom he had been close friends since 1922. Earlier he had written the preface to *Escapers All*, a volume of narratives by men who had escaped from prisoner–of–war camps. "A Summer's Evening" compares his affection for his dog and his Aunt Bunny. "Kobo Daishi" draws together his love of young men and dogs in the setting of a Buddhist cemetery in Japan. "I Am a Beast" concerns animal rights.

The posthumous volumes are important in understanding Ackerley's life. For example, the unflattering treatment of his sister Nancy in *My Father and Myself* should be supplemented by the diaries of 1948 to 1949 in *My Sister and Myself* which reveal Nancy's attempt at suicide, partially from emotional blackmail. Other entries offer his vivid observations of Siegfried Sassoon's disastrous attempt at married life as a road fortunately not taken. Neville Braybrooke's edition of 336 letters concentrates on the last 20 years of Ackerley's life. The section "A Visit to Japan" from late 1960 offers an interesting account of cruising young men there. Braybrooke's volume offers important information on problems of censorship in getting Ackerley's writings published.

Peter Parker's biography of Ackerley, which concentrates on the author's life more than his work, describes in detail Ackerley's loves and pick–ups, and he explains the gay milieu in which Ackerley lived. Parker also connects his subject's emotional life to his opposition to censorship of sexual matters at the BBC. Parker finds among Ackerley's closest friends and associates E. M. Forster, William Plomer, Sebastian Sprott, Stephen Spender, Francis King, James Kirkup, and Donald Windham.

Two points remain fixed in discussions of Ackerley. First, he was a truly outstanding literary editor of the *Listener*, getting the best reviewers and poets. Second, his prose style is often superb. However, some see his work as exhibitionistic, self–blinded, or gross. They show dislike for the life by criticizing the work, deploring Ackerley's disturbing family situation, love for the possessive Queenie, promiscuity and attraction to rough trade, and indulgence in alcohol. They accuse him of misanthropy, misogyny, and squandering of his talent. His fans are favorably impressed with his psychological insight into character, refusal to apologize for being gay and lustful, defiance of censorship, and ability to get past platitudes and ponder the nature of love. *We Think the World of You* (popularized by the film adaptation with Alan Bates in the Ackerley role) and *My Father and Myself* ensure his literary reputation.

—*Peter G. Christensen*

ADDISON, Jan. *See* FOSTER, Jeannette Howard.

————

ALBEE, Edward (Franklin III). American playwright, producer, and director of plays. Born in Washington, D.C., 12 March 1928. Attended Trinity College, Hartford, Connecticut, 1946–47. Has held a variety of jobs, including continuity writer for WNYC–radio, office boy, record salesperson, and counterboy; messenger for Western Union, 1955–58; producer for New Playwrights Unit Workshop, 1963—; director of own plays, including *The Zoo Story, The Sandbox,* and *Listening,* 1978—; codirector of Vivian Beaumont Theatre at Lincoln Center for the Performing Arts, New York City, 1979—. Founder of William Flanagan Center for Creative Persons, Montauk, New York, 1971. Lecturer at college campuses. U.S. State Department cultural exchange visitor to United Soviet Socialist Republic (now the Commonwealth of Independent States) and Latin American countries. Member of National Endowment grant–giving council; member of governing commission of New York State Council for the Arts. **Recipient:** Berlin Festival Award, 1959 and 1961; Rice Memorial Award, 1960; Obie Award, 1960; Argentine Critics Circle Award, 1961; best plays of the 1960–61 season honors from Foreign Press Association, 1961; Lola D'Annunzio Award, 1961; selected as most promising playwright of 1962–63 season by the New York Drama Critics, 1963; New York Drama Critics Circle Award, 1963; Foreign Press Association Award, 1963; Tony Award, 1963; Outer Circle Award, 1963; *Saturday Review* Drama Critics Award, 1963; *Variety* Drama Critics' Poll Award, 1963; *Evening Standard* Award, 1964; Margo Jones Award, with Richard Barr and Clinton Wilder, 1965; Pulitzer Prize, 1967 and 1975; American Academy and Institute of Arts and Letters Gold Medal, 1980. D. Litt. from Emerson College, 1967, and Trinity College, 1974.

WRITINGS

Plays

The Zoo Story (produced Berlin, 1959; New York and London, 1960). Included in *The Zoo Story, The Death of Bessie Smith, The Sandbox: Three Plays,* 1960.

The Death of Bessie Smith (produced Berlin, 1960; New York and London, 1961). Included in *The Zoo Story, The Death of Bessie Smith, The Sandbox: Three Plays,* 1960.

The Sandbox (produced New York, 1960). Included in *The Zoo Story, The Death of Bessie Smith, The Sandbox: Three Plays,* 1960.

The Zoo Story, The Death of Bessie Smith, The Sandbox: Three Plays. New York, Coward–McCann, 1960; as *The Zoo Story, and Other Plays* (includes *The American Dream*), London, Cape, 1962.

Fam and Yam (produced Westport, Connecticut, 1960). New York, Dramatists Play Service, 1961.

The American Dream (produced New York, 1961), introduction by Albee. New York, Coward–McCann, 1961; London, French, 1962.

Who's Afraid of Virginia Woolf? (produced on Broadway, 1962). New York, Atheneum, 1962; London, Cape, 1964.

The American Dream, The Death of Bessie Smith, Fam and Yam. New York, Dramatists Play Service, 1962.

The American Dream and The Zoo Story: Two Plays. New York, New American Library, 1963.

The Ballad of the Sad Cafe (adaptation of the novella by Carson McCullers; produced New York, 1963). Published as *The Ballad of the Sad Cafe, Carson McCullers's Novella Adapted to the Stage,* Boston, Houghton, 1963; London, Cape, 1965.

Tiny Alice (produced New York, 1964). New York, Atheneum, 1965; London, Cape, 1966.

Malcolm (adaptation of the novel by James Purdy; produced New York, 1966). Published as *Malcolm, Adapted by Edward Albee from the Novel by James Purdy,* New York, Atheneum, 1966; London, Cape/Secker & Warburg, 1967.

A Delicate Balance (produced New York, 1966). New York, Atheneum, 1966; London, Cape, 1968.

Breakfast at Tiffany's (musical; adaptation of a story by Truman Capote; music by Bob Merrill; produced Philadelphia and New York, 1966).

Everything in the Garden (adaptation of play by Giles Cooper; produced New York, 1967). New York, Atheneum, 1968.

Box [and] *Quotations from Chairman Mao Tse–Tung* (produced Buffalo, New York, and New York City, 1968). Published as *Box and Quotations from Chairman Mao Tse–Tung: Two Inter–Related Plays,* New York, Atheneum, 1969; London, Cape, 1970.

All Over (produced New York, 1971). New York, Atheneum, 1971; London, Cape, 1972.

Seascape (produced New York, 1975). New York, Atheneum, 1975; London, Cape, 1976.

Counting the Ways (produced London, 1976; Hartford, Connecticut, 1977). Included in *Counting the Ways and Listening: Two Plays,* 1977.

Listening: A Chamber Play (radio play; broadcast by BBC, 1976; produced Hartford, Connecticut, 1977). Included in *Counting the Ways and Listening: Two Plays,* 1977.

Counting the Ways and Listening: Two Plays. New York, Atheneum, 1977.

The Lady from Dubuque (produced New York, 1980). New York, Atheneum, 1980.

The Plays, Volume 1: *The Zoo Story, The Death of Bessie Smith, The Sandbox,* [and] *The American Dream,* New York, Coward–McCann, 1981; Volume 2: *Tiny Alice, A Delicate Balance, Box,* [and] *Quotations from Chairman Mao Tse–Tung,* New York, Atheneum, 1981; Volume 3: *All Over, Seascape, Counting the Ways,* [and] *Listening,* New York, Atheneum, 1982; Volume 4: *Everything in the Garden, Malcolm,* [and] *The Ballad of the Sad Cafe,* New York, Atheneum, 1983.

Lolita (adaptation of the novel by Vladimir Nabokov; produced Boston and New York, 1981). New York, Dramatists Play Service, 1984.

The Man Who Had Three Arms (produced Miami and Chicago, 1982). New York, Atheneum, 1987.

The Marriage Play (produced Vienna, 1987; San Diego, 1989).

The Sandbox and The Death of Bessie Smith, with Fam and Yam. New York, New American Library, 1988.

Finding the Sun (produced Greeley, Colorado).

Author of Introductions

Three Plays by Noel Coward: Blithe Spirit, Hay Fever, and Private Lives by Noel Coward. New York, Delta, 1965.
National Playwrights Directory, second edition, edited by Phyllis Johnson Kaye. Waterford, Connecticut, Eugene O'Neill Theater Center, 1981.
With Sabina Lietzmann, *New York.* New York, Vendome Press, 1981.
Louise Nevelson: Atmospheres and Environments. Clarkson N. Potter, Inc., 1981.
Entrances: An American Director's Journey by Alan Schneider. New York, Viking, 1986.

Other

With James Hinton, Jr., *Bartleby* (opera; adaptation of a story by Herman Melville; produced New York, 1961).

*

Adaptations: *Who's Afraid of Virginia Woolf?* (motion picture), Warner Brothers, 1966.

Biography: *Edward Albee: Tradition and Renewal* by Gilbert Debusscher, Brussels, Belgium, American Studies Center, 1967; *Edward Albee: Playwright in Protest* by Michael E. Rutenberg, New York, Avon, 1969; *Edward Albee* by Ruby Cohn, Minneapolis, University of Minnesota Press, 1969; *Edward Albee* by Richard E. Amacher, New York, Twayne Publishers, 1969, revised edition, 1982; *Albee* by C. W. E. Bigsby, Edinburgh, Scotland, Oliver & Boyd, 1969; *Edward Albee*, edited by Harold Bloom, New York, Chelsea House, 1987; *Edward Albee* by Gerry McCarthy, New York, St. Martin's Press, 1987.

Interviews: *Conversations with Edward Albee* edited by Philip C. Kolin, Jackson, University Press of Mississippi, 1988.

Bibliography: *From Tension to Tonic: The Plays of Edward Albee* by Anne Paolucci, Carbondale, Southern Illinois University Press, 1972; *Edward Albee at Home and Abroad* by Richard E. Amacher and Margaret Rule, New York, AMS Press, 1973; *Edward Albee: An Annotated Bibliography 1968-1977* by Charles Lee Green, New York, AMS Press, 1980; *Edward Albee: A Reference Guide* by Scott Giantvalley, Hall, 1987; *Contemporary Authors Bibliographic Series*, Volume 3: *American Dramatists*, Detroit, Michigan, Gale, 1989.

Critical Sources: "Not What It Seems: Homosexual Motif Gets Heterosexual Guise" by Howard Taubman, in *New York Times*, 1961; "The Play that Dare Not Speak Its Name" by Philip Roth, in *New York Review of Books*, 25 February 1965, 4; *Seasons of Discontent* by Robert Brustein, New York, Simon & Schuster, 1965; "Who's Afraid of Little Annie Fanny?," in *Ramparts*, 1967; *The Season: A Candid Look at Broadway* by William Goldman, New York, Harcourt, 1969; *Edward Albee: A Collection of Critical Essays*, edited by C. W. E. Bigsby, Englewood Cliffs, New Jersey, Prentice-Hall, 1975; *Who's Afraid of Edward Albee?* by Foster Hirsch, Berkeley, California, Creative Arts, 1978; *Edward Albee:*

The Poet of Loss by Anita Maria Stenz, The Hague and New York, Mouton, 1978; *Culture Clash: The Making of Gay Sensibility* by Michael Bronski, Boston, South End Press, 1984; *Critical Essays on Edward Albee*, edited by Philip C. Kolin and J. Madison Davis, Hall, 1986; *We Can Always Call Them Bulgarians: The Emergence of Lesbians and Gay Men on the American Stage* by Kaier Curtin, Boston, Alyson Publications, 1987; *Understanding Edward Albee* by Matthew C. Roudane, Columbia, University of South Carolina Press, 1987.

*   *   *

Edward Albee caught the attention of the public with the United States premiere of his first play, *The Zoo Story*. He followed this success with the Tony Award–winning *Who's Afraid of Virginia Woolf?* and the Pulitzer Prize–winning plays *A Delicate Balance* and *Seascape*. He has maintained his position as one of the most important playwrights of the contemporary theater, having written eight full–length original plays, nine one–acts, and five adaptations of novels by other writers. The critical praise for Albee's work has always been mixed with doubt and criticism. His earliest work positioned him, in the eyes of some critics, as a savior of the Broadway theater, but it quickly became fashionable to dismiss much of Albee's work for a variety of reasons. Some critics claimed that Albee was merely repeating himself in his middle and later work; others were more outspoken and claimed (either overtly or in more encoded language) that Albee's writing suffered because of his homosexuality. Perhaps more than any other United States playwright, Albee's career has been persistently dogged by homophobic criticism.

Albee was born in 1928. His biological parents gave him up for adoption to Reed and Frances Albee, who resided in Larchmont, New York. Albee was raised with all of the niceties of an upper–middle–class life: servants, chauffeur–driven limousines, and private tutors. Albee attended several private schools and dropped out of Trinity College after three semesters. He moved to Greenwich Village and took on a variety of jobs, including record salesperson and Western Union telegraph deliverer. Just before his thirtieth birthday, Albee decided to pursue the writing career he had been avoiding and wrote *The Zoo Story* in three weeks. After being rejected by several New York producers, the play premiered in the Schilder Theater Werkstatt in Berlin, Germany, in 1959. *The Zoo Story* was a hit; four months later, it opened in New York on a double bill with Irish author Samuel Beckett's *Krapp's Last Tape*, earning Albee national attention. His next three plays—*The Sandbox*, *The American Dream*, and *The Death of Bessie Smith*—secured him a place as a promising new playwright.

In 1962, *Who's Afraid of Virginia Woolf?* premiered on Broadway and was an instant popular and critical success. The play's strong language, harsh view of social and marital relationships, and blatant sexual subtext shocked some—the Pulitzer Prize committee decided not to award that year's prize to it, in response to which John Mason Brown and John Gassner resigned from the committee—but it was proclaimed by many to be a breakthrough in contemporary theater. Albee followed *Virginia Woolf* with an adaptation of American novelist Carson McCullers' novella *The Ballad of the Sad Cafe*, which did not fare well at the box office despite some good reviews. Albee's next work was *Tiny Alice*, an original play that consciously toys with ideas of symbolism, religious salvation, and metaphysics. The play's scheme—an ingenious puzzle motif that deals with truth and illusion (a theme that also surfaces in *Virginia Woolf,* as well as later work)—confounded most critics and audiences at the time but seems relatively obvious in retrospect. Albee then adapted American author James Purdy's darkly comic novel *Malcolm,* which received poor reviews, many critics voicing disdain of the play's overtly sexual images and situations.

Popular culture was going through many changes during this time and homosexuality, both as a theme and a social reality, was more discussable than ever before. Although Albee, following the lead of American playwright Tennessee Williams, did not announce his sexual orientation, he did little to hide it. Some critics, uneasy with the new freedom of expression manifesting itself in the arts, began to write about how homosexuals were shaping popular culture to reflect their own view of reality. In 1961, Howard Taubman wrote an article printed in the *New York Times,* "Not What It Seems: Homosexual Motif Gets Heterosexual Guise," about three unnamed playwrights who attacked marriage and women but were really writing about dysfunctional gay relationships. Taubman also argued that the homosexual influence was too strong on Broadway. The unnamed playwrights were William Inge, Tennessee Williams, and Albee. This same theme was brought up several years later by Stanley Kauffman, who also wrote in the *New York Times;* Kauffman noted that homosexuals could not write about their own lives because of anti–gay prejudice, but he still thought that their influence was far too great on popular culture. Even the relatively liberal *Ramparts* ran an article entitled "Who's Afraid of Little Annie Fanny?" which claimed: "The point is that homosexual playwrights and homosexual directors and homosexual producers have been having more and more to say about what can and can't be done in the American Theater." Philip Roth, in a *New York Review of Books* review of *Tiny Alice,* accused Albee of writing "pansy prose."

Such cultural criticism was directed at Albee, Williams, and Inge, not only because they were speaking uncomfortable truths about American culture but because they had broken the unwritten rule of refusing to directly deny their homosexuality. This criticism made a lasting impact on popular culture. It laid the foundation for the devaluation of all three men's work and, because it essentially accused homosexual artists of being anti–American cultural saboteurs, it created an atmosphere of suspicion and unease about all of their work.

Despite this atmosphere, Albee's 1967 play *A Delicate Balance*—about middle–class couples facing an existentialist, although physically palpable, void in their lives—won the Pulitzer Prize, although there was much critical grumbling about dysfunctional marriages and overwrought (meaning unmanly) writing. Albee's work *Everything in the Garden,* an adaptation of a play by English playwright Giles Cooper, was an attack on suburban materialism and loveless marriages and received stringent criticism about its view of the family and the American home.

Albee abandoned traditional narrative in *Box* and *Quotations from Chairman Mao,* two experimental plays that relied on impressionistic, pared–down dialogue to produce elusive, evocative meanings. Albee's stagecraft was changing. It was more abstractly musical and less open to overtly anti–gay criticism. *All Over* charts the final hours of a dying man and resembled a contemporary medieval morality play in which characters are delineated by the roles—Wife, Man, Doctor—and the narration is essentially a meditation on the meaning of death. Albee's dialogue is sparse and terse, indicating a

further development away from the ironic realism of his earlier plays and towards a theater of sound language rather than incident. Critical reception was mixed. No one complained about the play's attack on the emptiness of middle–class life but rather called the play cold and cerebral, the implication being that homosexuals could not write *real* heterosexual characters with or without passion.

Seascape surprised critics and audiences because, although Albee repeated his *Virginia Woolf* framework (two arguing couples confront one another and themselves), one of the couples was a pair of giant lizards. The play won a Pulitzer Prize and Albee proved himself as capable of the gentle joke as he was the bitter barb more than a decade earlier. The language of *Seascape* is more lyrical than terse, but the atmosphere is sad. If the characters in *Who's Afraid of Virginia Woolf?* discuss the inevitability of evolution, the characters in *Seascape* live it. Although critical reception to *Seascape* was generally positive, reviewers had stopped seeing Albee as either a savior of the theater or a major threat. The play was viewed with respect but not treated as though it had any resonance.

Counting the Ways and *Listening* are small chamber dramas that glisten with wit and precise language. They explore human cruelty, the impossibility of true knowledge, and death. These themes are also manifest in *The Lady From Dubuque,* in which a dying woman is visited by a mysterious older woman who claims to be her mother. More even than *A Delicate Balance* and *All Over,* the tone of *The Lady From Dubuque* is an unsettling mixture of ritual and mystery, theatrical calculation and unabashed emotion. Albee's delineation of extreme human emotion in the face of death did not please the critics and the show closed in under two weeks. *The Lady from Dubuque,* with both its negative portrayal of a marriage and its intellectualized message, seemed to fulfill the worst expectations of critics with an anti–Albee bias.

Lolita, an adaptation of American novelist and poet Vladimir Nabokov's novel, annoyed most critics. Many of them brought out the old criticisms of Albee's anti–family, anti–woman attitudes; no one seemed to understand that Albee's criticism was directed at the culture that warped institutions and people. Since Albee himself had been recently more open about his sexuality, some critics openly blamed his gayness for what they disapproved of in the play. As a somewhat closeted writer, Albee was attacked for artistic inauthenticity; as an openly gay writer he was attacked for his sexuality.

Albee's next two plays, *The Man Who Had Three Arms* and *Finding the Sun,* found small audiences. *The Man Who Had Three Arms* premiered in a regional theater and had a brief Broadway run. An attack on materialism in life and the theater—its main character, who gives a lecture throughout the play, is named Himself—the play was seen as simply autobiographical and thus a self–indulgent burst of anger. *Finding the Sun* is a complicated domestic drama of three couples that was produced at the Frazier Theater in Greeley, Colorado.

While Albee's career and reputation has declined since the mid–1970s, it is impossible to view this without considering the homophobic nature of much of the critical reception of his work. Is it possible for a playwright of his generation *not* to have his sexuality used against him in evaluating his work? If not, then what is the effect of that homophobia over Albee's whole career? These are questions that affect not only the career of Albee but of all openly gay artists.

—*Michael Bronski*

ALDON, Howard. *See* **WILSON, Doric.**

————

ALLEN, Paula Gunn. American educator, novelist, poet, editor, and essayist. Born in Cubero, New Mexico, in 1939. Holder of B.A., M.F.A., degrees; University of New Mexico, Ph.D. American studies. Lecturer, San Francisco State University, University of New Mexico, Albuquerque, and Fort Lewis College, Durango, California; professor of ethnic and Native American studies, then professor of English, University of California, Berkeley. **Recipient:** National Endowment for the Arts award; Ford Foundation grant; American Book Award, 1990, for *Spider Woman's Granddaughters.* Address: c/o Beacon Press, 25 Beacon Street, Boston, Massachusetts 02108, U.S.A.

WRITINGS

Novels

The Woman Who Owned the Shadows. San Francisco, Spinsters/ Aunt Lute Books, 1983.

Poetry

The Blind Lion. Berkeley, California, Thorp Springs Press, 1974.
Coyote's Daylight Trip. Albuquerque, New Mexico, La Confluencia, 1978.
A Cannon Between My Knees. New York, Strawberry Hill Press, 1981.
Star Child. Marvin, South Dakota, Blue Cloud Quarterly, 1981.
Shadow Country. Los Angeles, University of California Indian Studies Center, 1982.
Skins and Bones. Albuquerque, New Mexico, West End, 1988.

Editor

From the Center: A Folio: Native American Art and Poetry. New York, Strawberry Hill Press, 1981.
Studies in American Indian Literature: Critical Essays and Course Design. New York, Modern Language Association, 1983.
Spider Woman's Granddaughters: Traditional Tales and Contemporary Writing By Native American Women. New York, Fawcett, 1990.

Other

Sipapu: A Cultural Perspective. Albuquerque, New Mexico, University of New Mexico Press, 1975.
"*Hwame, Koshkalak,* and the Rest: Lesbians in American Indian Cultures," in *Conditions,* Volume 7, 1981; published in *The Sacred Hoop,* 1986.

The Sacred Hoop: Recovering the Feminine in American Indian Traditions (includes "*Hwame, Koshkalak,* and the Rest: Lesbians in American Indian Cultures" and "How the West Was Really Won"). Boston, Beacon Press, 1986; selection published as "Lesbians in American Indian Cultures," in *Hidden from History: Reclaiming the Gay and Lesbian Past,* edited by Martin Bauml Duberman, Martha Vicinus, and George Chauncey, Jr., New York, New American Library, 1989.
Grandmothers of the Light: A Medicine Woman's Sourcebook. Boston, Beacon Press, 1991.
Indian Perspectives. Southwest Parks and Monuments Association, 1992.

*

Biography: *Paula Gunn Allen* by Elizabeth I. Hanson, Boise, Idaho, Boise State University, 1990.

Interviews: *Winged Words: American Indian Writers Speak* by Laura Coltelli, Lincoln, University of Nebraska Press, 1990; with Patricia Holt, *San Francisco Chronicle,* 1990.

Critical Sources: "Native American Literature" by Patricia Holt, in *San Francisco Chronicle,* 2 July 1989; "Despite Successes, Scholars Express Ambivalence about Place of Minority Literature in Academe" by Ellen K. Coughlin, in *Chronicle of Higher Education,* 10 January 1990; review of *Spider Woman's Granddaughters* by Quannah Karvar, *Los Angeles Times Book Review,* 3 June 1990, 14; review of *Grandmothers of the Light,* in *Kirkus Reviews,* 1 August 1991, 976.

*   *   *

Poet, novelist, educator, and essayist Paula Gunn Allen is an American Indian of mixed Laguna Pueblo and Sioux descent. She is a mother, a grandmother, and a lesbian—and, as Patricia Holt noted in an interview with Allen in the *San Francisco Chronicle,* "one of the few Native American women with nationwide recognition."

Allen is the daughter of an Indian Scottish mother and a Lebanese American father. She grew up in a small New Mexican village bounded by two Native American reservations and attended a convent school during her youth. Other religious influences included a Presbyterian grandmother and a Jewish grandfather, but she was most strongly affected by her mother's stories about Native American goddesses and traditions.

Allen received her Ph.D. from the University of New Mexico in American studies. "I wanted to fit into English," she explained in an interview with Laura Coltelli in *Winged Words: American Indian Writers Speak,* "and I told the graduate dean that I wanted to focus on Native American literature. And he told me there was no such thing, which is why I have my degree in American studies." The influences on Allen's writing are as diverse as W. C. Williams and the Black Mountain School of poetry, Gertrude Stein, the romantic poets Keats and Shelley, Mozart, and cowboy music and literature.

Allen's published works include several books of poetry, a novel, a book of essays called *The Sacred Hoop: Recovering the Feminine in American Indian Traditions,* and a collection of goddess stories from Native American Civilizations, *Grandmothers of the Light: A Medicine Woman's Sourcebook.* She is the editor of several collections, including *Spider Woman's Granddaughters: Traditional Tales and Contemporary Writing by Native American Women,* which won an American Book Award in 1990, and *Studies in American Indian Literature; Critical Essays and Course Design,* which has become the standard introduction to the field.

In her introduction to *The Sacred Hoop,* Allen highlights the "major themes or issues that pertain to American Indians and that characterize the essays." One of these is that "traditional tribal lifestyles are more often gynocratic than not, and they are never patriarchal." She goes on to explain that "some distinguishing features of a woman–centered social system include free and easy sexuality and wide latitude in personal style. This latitude means that a diversity of people, including gay males and lesbians, are not denied and are in fact likely to be accorded honor."

It is this focus in Allen's work, most extensively worked in her essays "How the West Was Really Won" and "*Hwame, Koshkalak, and the Rest: Lesbians in American Indian Cultures,*" both in *The Sacred Hoop,* that makes her so important to lesbian and gay writing, thought, and history. Allen is something of an archaeologist, unearthing hidden facts about thriving ancient cultures that were both woman–centered and what we would today call "gay positive." She writes in "*Hwame, Koshkalak,* and the Rest" that "it is my contention that gayness, whether female or male, traditionally functions positively within tribal groups."

The cultures that Allen describes in *The Sacred Hoop,* unlike traditional Western modes of social organization, "focused on social responsibility rather than on privilege, and on the realities of the human constitution rather than on denial–based social fictions to which human beings are compelled to conform by powerful individuals within the society." She notes that "the colonizers saw (and rightly) that as long as women held unquestioned power of such magnitude, attempts at total conquest of the continents were bound to fail."

Because so little has been written about the gay and lesbian presence in tribal societies and what little there is often reinforces western homophobic preconceptions, much of Allen's "discussion of lesbians is necessarily conjectural, based on secure knowledge of American Indian social systems and customs that I have gathered from formal study, personal experience, and personally communicated information from other Indians." As Allen herself notes, her creative process "is somewhat western and somewhat Indian." She writes, "My Inner self, the self who knows what is true of American Indians because it *is* one, always warns me when something deceptive is going on. And with that warning, I am moved to do a great deal of reflecting, some more reading, and a lot of questioning and observing of real live human beings who are Indian in order to discover the source of my unease."

One of the finest qualities of Allen's writing is its balance, warmth, and underlying inclusiveness. "Far from a one–sided feminist view," a reviewer writes of *Grandmothers of the Light* in *Kirkus Reviews,* "the emphasis is on balance, ... seeking completion rather than adversariness and opposition." Quannah Karvar writes about *Spider Woman's Granddaughters* in the *Los Angeles Times Book Review:* "For those of us who inhabit that perilous ground where two worlds collide, Allen is a pathfinder. She is only one of many who, like Spider Woman, offer their 'light of intelligence and experience'."

Perhaps because Allen herself is the product of such varied cultural, religious, social, and literary influences, she is so well–equipped to find and explicate the things that make us individual as well as those that join us together. Allen closes one of her essays in *The Sacred Hoop* with the invocation: "Let us adjust our perspective to match that of our foresisters. Then, when we search the memories and lore of tribal peoples, we might be able to see what eons and all kinds of institutions have conspired to hide from our eyes."

—*Ira N. Brodsky*

———

ALLISON, Dorothy (E.) American novelist, poet, and author of short stories. Born in Greenville, South Carolina, 11 April 1949. Educated at Florida Presbyterian College, St. Petersburg, B.A. 1971; received master's degree in anthropology from New School for Social Research, New York. Companion of Alix Layman; one child. **Recipient:** Lambda Literary awards for *Trash,* 1988; National Book Award and Bay Area Book Reviewers Association prize for fiction for *Bastard Out of Carolina,* 1992. Agent: Frances Goldin, 305 East 11th Street, New York, New York 10003, U.S.A. Address: P.O. Box 14474, San Francisco, California 94114, U.S.A.

WRITINGS

Novels

Bastard Out of Carolina. New York, Dutton, 1992.
Cavedweller. New York, Dutton, in press.

Short Stories

Trash. Ithaca, New York, Firebrand Books, 1988.
"A Lesbian Appetite," in *Women On Women,* edited by Joan Nestle and Naomi Holoch. New York, Dutton, 1990.
"Private Rituals," in *High Risk,* edited by Amy Shoulder and Ira Silverberg. New York, Dutton, 1991.
"Her Body, Mine, and His," in *Leatherfolk: Radical Sex, People, Politics, and Practice,* edited by Mark Thompson. Boston, Alyson Publications, 1991.

Poetry

The Women Who Hate Me. Brooklyn, New York, Long Haul Press, 1983; as *The Women Who Hate Me: Poetry, 1980–1990,* Ithaca, Firebrand Books, 1991.

Other

"I Am Working on My Charm," in *Conditions: Six,* 1980.
"The Billie Jean King Thing," in *New York Native,* 18–31 May 1981.

"Confrontation: Black/White," in *Building Feminist Theory: Essays from "Quest,"* edited by Charlotte Bunch and others. New York, Longman, 1981.
Skin (essays). Ithaca, Firebrand Books, 1993.

Recordings: Keynote address for OutWrite '92: Lesbian and Gay Writers Conference, Boston, 20 March 1992, Berkeley, California, Conference Recording Service.

*

Adaptations: *Bastard Out of Carolina* (audiocassette), New York, Penguin/HighBridge, 1993; *Bastard Out of Carolina* has been optioned for film.

Interviews: "A Storyteller Out of Hell" by Bo Huston, in *Advocate,* 7 April 1992, 70–72; "Truth Is Meaner than Fiction" by Lynn Karpen, in *New York Times Book Review,* 5 July 1992, 3.

Critical Sources: Review by George Garrett of *Bastard Out of Carolina,* in *New York Times Book Review,* 5 July 1992, 3.

*   *   *

With the publication of her first novel, *Bastard Out of Carolina* in 1992, Dorothy Allison moved from relative small press obscurity to near national acclaim as a writer. Although she has written for feminist, lesbian, and gay newspapers, periodicals, and presses for almost two decades, Allison—like many other gay and lesbian writers—never received much attention from the mainstream media. What was surprising about the mainstream acceptance of *Bastard Out of Carolina* was that while the book does not deal specifically with lesbianism (a topic that is present in almost all of Allison's other writings), it explores in detail domestic, personal, psychic, and sexual violence from a specifically lesbian–feminist, and to some degree, sadomasochistic point of view. It is Allison's depictions of interpersonal violence—and especially her frank and troubling analysis of how it is intrinsic to family life and personal identity—that many readers have found disturbing in her work.

Born in 1949 to a poor white family in Greenville, South Carolina, Allison grew up in an abusive but loving family. It is from this experience that she has drawn most of the material for her fiction. During and after her college years she was active in a variety of feminist projects involving battered women, child care, and women's health. It was during this time—and with these political roots—that she began writing poems and short stories. Much of Allison's writing is an attempt to understand her own abusive upbringing and the effect it had upon her life. At the same time she is completely honest about her own sexual desires and how crucial her sexuality is for her emotional and psychic survival.

In 1983 Allison published a book of poetry, *The Women Who Hate Me.* (This was updated and re–released in 1991 under the title *The Women Who Hate Me: Poetry 1980–1990.*) It was here that Allison began to detail her love and sexual desire for women, but also how this placed her at odds with some segments of the feminist movement. While some more mainstream feminists spoke against promiscuous sexuality, sadomasochism, and butch/femme role play-

ing, Allison explored these very ideas in her life and her work. In an interview with *Advocate,* she spoke about those years: "I felt like a spy. During the daytime I was a nice, lean lesbian–feminist living in a collective; at night I was a subterranean slut." In the book's title poem, Allison writes, "The women who hate me cut me / as men can't. Men don't count. / I can handle men. Never expected better / of any man anyway."

This tension between a responsible feminist analysis of sexual freedom and an anti–sexual prejudice within a segment of the mainstream feminist movement has always fueled Allison's commitment to her writing and her politics. In 1982, speaking at a symposium on sexuality at Barnard College, Allison was picketed by feminist anti–pornography advocates. "The worst accusation though," she claims in the *Advocate* interview, "was that I was guilty of child sexual abuse because of the writing I was doing." At the time, Allison was beginning to publish the stories that would eventually appear in her 1988 collection *Trash.* These harsh, funny, emotional stories about growing up poor, socially despised, and abused also include some graphic depictions of sexuality and numerous indications that Allison was, as she put it, "addicted to violence."

The themes of personal and sexual violence in *Trash* reappear in *Bastard Out of Carolina.* Allison's fiction, like that of lesbian writers Blanche McCrary Boyd and Rita Mae Brown, is closely tied to her Southern roots. But unlike Boyd, who writes from an upper–middle–class perspective, or Brown, who usually presents a somewhat sentimental view of Southern life, Allison illuminates the hard, uncertain lives of the urban and rural poor. Allison's characters are, in common parlance, trash. *Bastard Out of Carolina* tells the story of Bone, a young girl who deeply loves and is loved by her mother and who is physically and sexually abused by her step–father. The emotional tension of the book arises from the fact that Bone's mother knows about this abuse but does nothing about it, thus on some level condoning the violence.

Allison understands the potential problems with this sort of material and has explicitly communicated the way in which she approached the novel. She told *Advocate,* "I wanted to write a book about a girl in a working class environment who loves her family and is smart and powerful. I hate victim portraits. And I hate the pornography of victimization. Half of the incest books or family violence books sell on sexual voyeurism.... It's very hard not to titillate when you're working with this kind of material, because American culture is consumed with it." What makes *Bastard Out of Carolina* so powerful is that Allison does not attempt to present her material through any lens other than simple emotional realism. She avoids sentimentality and exploitation—the narrative's emotional quality is more than enough to grip and move us—and she feels that to do otherwise would be to betray not only her fiction but her life as well.

In her story, "Her Body, Mine, and His," published in Mark Thompson's *Leatherfolk: Radical Sex, People, Politics, and Practice* in 1991, Allison describes in graphic detail a physically exhausting, tremendously powerful sexual encounter. She then writes: "I have been told that lesbians don't do this. Perhaps we are not lesbians? She is a woman. I am a woman. But maybe we are aliens? Is what we do together a lesbian act?" Much of Allison's work attempts to define an honest lesbian sexuality that takes into consideration desire, lust, past history, violence, need, class, politics, and love. Allison's prose and poetry—even when it talks about past or current violence—is an attempt to understand and redefine a whole host of physical experiences in light of the transformative power of sexuality. Later in "Her Body, Mine, and His," she writes, "The holy act of sex, my sex, done in your name, done for the only, the best reason. Because we want it." Sexuality in *Trash* and *Bastard Out of Carolina* is an instrument of self–love and salvation, a way to overcome past terrors and hurts, a way to see the present and the future. As Allison explains in the preface to *Trash:* "I write stories. I write fiction. I put on the page a third look at what I've seen in life—the condensed and reinvented experience of a cross–eyed working class lesbian, addicted to violence, language and hope, who has made the decision to live, is determined to live, on the page and on the street, for me and mine."

—*Michael Bronski*

————

ALTMAN, Dennis. Australian educator, activist, and author of nonfiction. Born in Sydney, 16 August 1943. Educated at the University of Tasmania, B.A. (with honors) 1964; Cornell University, M.A. 1966. Lecturer in politics, Monash University, Melbourne, Victoria, Australia, 1966–68; lecturer, 1969–75, then senior lecturer in American politics, 1975–80, University of Sydney, Sydney, New South Wales, Australia; regent's lecturer at University of California, Santa Cruz, 1983; visiting fellow at University of California, Institute for Health Policy Studies, San Francisco, 1984; senior lecturer, 1986–88, then reader, beginning 1989, La Trobe University, Bundoora, Victoria, Australia. Member, Global AIDS Policy Coalition, and executive board, AIDS Society for Asia and the Pacific, and International Council of AIDS Service Organizations. Contributor to periodicals, including *Politics, Nation,* and *Australian Society.* Address: La Trobe University, Bundoora, Victoria, Australia 3083.

WRITINGS

Nonfiction

Homosexual: Oppression and Liberation. New York, Outerbridge & Dienstfrey, 1971; revised, London, Allan Lane, 1974; revised, New York, New York University Press, 1993.
Coming Out in the Seventies. Sydney, Wild & Wooley, 1979.
Rehearsals for Change: Politics and Culture in Australia. Sydney, Fontana, 1980.
The Homosexualization of America, the Americanization of the Homosexual. New York, St. Martin's Press, 1982.
AIDS and the New Puritanism. London, Pluto Press, 1986; as *AIDS in the Mind of America: The Social, Political, and Psychological Impact of a New Epidemic,* Garden City, New York, Doubleday, 1986.
"AIDS and the Reconfiguration of Homosexuality," in *Homosexuality, Which Homosexuality?: Essays from the International Scientific Conference on Lesbian and Gay Studies.* London, GMP Publishers, 1989.
Paper Ambassadors: The Politics of Stamps. Australia, Angus & Robertson, 1991.

The Comfort of Men. Melbourne, Heinemann, 1993.

*

Manuscript Collections: National Library of Australia, Caberra.

*   *   *

Activism has long been the key to Dennis Altman's life and work, a fact reiterated in the essay "AIDS and the Reconceptualization of Homosexuality," where the author defines himself as an international activist–academic. The "false distinction" between these modes—that of the activist versus the role of the academic—appears to Altman to inhibit many of his fellow academics from serious political analysis of homosexuality. A self–professed "Libertarian Socialist," Altman uses Marxian analysis in his approach to discussions about sexual politics. His internationalism is well represented by his many visiting appointments at American universities, and his wide travels in America and Europe.

Altman's books explore the both image and identity of the homosexual and the effect of the AIDS crisis. In a sense, these works provide a history of modern gay culture from the heady days of gay liberation, through the confrontations and agonies of the early onset of AIDS, to a new acceptance of difference. In many of his writings, Altman discusses the possibility of a return to the nurturing structures and ideals of early gay liberation. Through this reappearance, he suggests a positive role for AIDS (though he also sees a problem in the re–emergence of establishment–oriented figures among the leadership of the gay community). Governments get short shrift from Altman, although he does praise the Australian government for its early willingness to accept guidance from gay movements.

Altman is a constructionist rather than an essentialist—that is, he believes that social and political forces play a major role in defining homosexuality. This attitude has separated him somewhat from those who seek genetic causes. He claims that the latter attitude tends to reduce one's own sense of responsibility, substituting "fitting in" with society for remaking that society. Given this belief, it is appropriate that one aspect of Altman's novel *The Comfort of Men* explores male bonding.

The distinctive flavor of Altman's work may well derive from his Australian background. In Australia, the strong tradition of mateship goes back to the country's earliest days and persists in a clear distinction between the worlds of the two sexes. Although mateship cannot simply be equated with homosexuality it certainly has strong emotional, even homoerotic, overtones. Here can be seen the interaction of politics and culture that lies behind Altman's analysis of homosexual and gay cultures in America and elsewhere. Similar in some ways to Susan Sontag's approach, his view is that straight and gay cultures interact and affect each other. *The Homosexualization of America* is an extensive treatment of this theme, interlaced with the author's Marxian analysis of the effects of capitalist commercialism.

The rapid and widespread changes brought about by AIDS tend to make writing from the 1970s and early 1980s seem dated. Many of Altman's books suffer when looked at with this kind of hindsight, but they are also linked by his tenacious claim that gay people can and should take an active role in constructing their world. The very word "liberation" is derived from anti–colonial, anti–imperial movements and he is undoubtedly influenced by his Australian background. Readers will find close parallels between Altman's explorations of the homosexual world and the Australian search for a political and literary identity.

—*Murray S. Martin*

————

ANDROS, Phil. *See* **STEWARD, Samuel M(orris).**

————

ANZALDÚA, Gloria (Evanjelina). American poet, essayist, and editor. Born in Jesus Maria of the Valley in South Texas, 26 September 1942. Educated at Pan–American University, Edinburg, Texas, B.A. 1969; University of Texas at Austin, M.A. 1973; University of California at Santa Cruz. Has taught high school English and in migrant, adult, and bilingual programs in Texas. Has taught creative writing, women's studies, Chicano studies at University of Texas at Austin, Vermont College of Norwich University, San Francisco State University, and University of California at Santa Cruz. Writer–in–residence at the Loft in Minneapolis, Minnesota; artist–in–residence at Pomona College, California. Contributing editor of *Sinister Wisdom.* Has given lectures, panels, and workshops throughout the United States, Canada, and Mexico. **Recipient:** MacDowell Artist Colony fellowship, 1982; National Endowment of the Arts award for fiction, 1991; Astraea National Lesbian Action Foundation Lesbian Writers Fund Sappho Award of Distinction, 1992. Address: c/o Literature Board, University of California, Santa Cruz, California 95064, U.S.A.

WRITINGS

Poetry

"Reincarnation (for Julie)," "Birth," "Abstractions (for H. Michaux)," "Now Let Us Go (Tinuique)," "The Visitor," and "El pecado," in *Tejidos* (Austin, Texas), fall 1976, 6–8.
"Woman," "Temple," "Guitarrera," "Helpless," and "Pesadilla," in *Tejidos* (Austin, Texas), spring 1977, 15–17.
"Holy Relics," in *Conditions: Six* (Lincoln, Nebraska), summer 1980, 144–150.
"Tres Mujeres en el Gabinete/Three Women in the Closet," in *Lesbian Poetry Anthology,* edited by Elly Bulkin and Joan Larkin. Watertown, Persephone Press, 1981.
"A Woman Lies Buried Under Me," in *Sinister Wisdom* (Lincoln, Nebraska), spring 1982, 2.
"Shadow," "Tres pajaros perdidos," and "Never, Momma," in *Third Woman* (Bloomington, Indiana), 2:1, 1984, 5–9.

"In the Name of All the Mothers Who Have Lost Children in the War/En el Nombre de Todas las Madres que Han Perdido Hijos en la Guerra," in *Ikon: Creativity and Change,* second series (New York), winter/summer 1985, 134–137.
"De las Otras," in *Companera: Latina Lesbians: An Anthology,* edited by Juanita Ramos. New York, Latina Lesbian History Project, 1987.
Borderlands—La Frontera: The New Mestiza (prose and poetry; English and Spanish). San Francisco, Spinsters Book Company, 1987.
"Nightvoice" and "Old Loyalties," in *Chicana Lesbians: The Girls Our Mothers Warned Us About.* Berkeley, California, Third Woman Press, 1991.

Short Stories

"El Paisano Is a Bird of Good Omen," in *Cuentos: Stories by Latinas,* edited by Alma Gomez, Cherríe Moraga, and Mariana Romo–Carmona. New York, Kitchen Table Women of Color Press, 1983.
"Life Line," in *Lesbian Love Stories,* edited by Irene Zahava. Freedom, California, Crossing Press, 1989.
"Ms. Right, My Soul Mate," in *Lesbian Love Stories,* Volume 2, edited by Irene Zahava. Freedom, California, Crossing Press, 1991.
"A Tale," in *Word of Mouth: Short–Short Stories by Women Writers,* edited by Irene Zahava. Freedom, California, Crossing Press, 1991.

Essays

"Speaking in Tongues: A Letter to Third World Women Writers" and "La Prieta," in *This Bridge Called My Back: Writings by Radical Women of Color* edited by Anzaldúa and Cherríe Moraga, foreword by Toni Cade Bambara. Watertown, Massachusetts, Persephone Press, 1981.
"The Homeland, Aztlan/El Otro Mexico," in *Aztlan: Essays on the Chicano Homeland,* edited by Rudolfo A. Anaya and Francisco A. Lomeli. Albuquerque, New Mexico, Academia/El Norte, 1989.
"En Rapport, In Opposition: Cobrando Cuentas a las Nuestras" and "La Conciencia de la Mestiza: Towards a New Consciousness," in *Making Face, Making Soul Hacienda Caras: Creative and Critical Perspectives by Feminists of Color,* edited by Anzaldúa. San Francisco, Aunt Lute Books, 1990.
"Bridge, Drawbridge, Sandbar or Island: Lesbians–of–Color Hacienda Alianzas," in *Bridges of Power: Women's Multicultural Alliances,* edited by Lisa Albrecht and Rose M. Brewer. Philadelphia, New Society Publishers, 1990.
"Metaphors in the Tradition of the Shaman," in *Conversant Essays: Contemporary Poets on Poetry,* edited by James McCorkle. Detroit, Wayne State University Press, 1990.

Other

Author of afterword, *This Way Daybreak Comes* by Annie Cheatham and Mary Clare Powell. Philadelphia, New Society Publishers, 1986.
"La Historia de una Marimacho," in *Third Woman* (Bloomington, Indiana), Number 4, 1989, 64–68.
"Border Crossings," in *Trivia: A Journal of Ideas* (North Amherst, Massachusetts), spring 1989, 46–51.

"People Should Not Die in June in South Texas," in *Daughters and Fathers,* edited by Irene Zahava. Freedom, California, Crossing Press, 1990.

Prietita Has a Friend—Prietita Tiene un Amigo (children's book; English and Spanish). San Francisco, Childrens Book Press, 1991.

"To(o) Queer the Writer—Loca, Escritora y Chicana," in *InVersions: Writing by Dykes, Queers, and Lesbians,* edited by Betsy Warland. Vancouver, Press Gang Publishers, 1991.

Lloronas, Women Who Howl: Autohistorias–Teorias and the Production of Writing, Knowledge and Identity. San Francisco, Aunt Lute Books, forthcoming.

Recordings: *This Bridge Called My Back: Writings by Women of Color,* Los Angeles, Pacifica Tape Library, 1983.

*

Biography: "Gloria Anzaldúa" by Hector A. Torres, in *Dictionary of Literary Biography,* Volume 122: *Chicano Writers, Second Series,* Detroit, Gale Research, 1992; *American Women Writers,* Volume 5: *From Colonial Times to the Present; A Critical Reference Guide,* edited by Carol H. Green and Mary G. Mason, New York, Continuum, 1993.

Interviews: With Eleanor J. Bader, in *Matrix* (Santa Cruz, California), May 1988, 3, 13; "Borderlands: Transformation at the Crossroads" by Maya Valverde, in *Woman of Power* (Cambridge, Massachusetts), summer 1988, 30–33; "Conversations at the Book Fair" by Suzanne de Lotbiniere–Harwood, in *Trivia: A Journal of Ideas* (North Amherst, Massachusetts), spring 1989, 37–45; "On the Borderlands with Gloria Anzaldúa," in *Off Our Backs* (New York), July 1991, 1–4.

Critical Sources: Review by Jennifer Pierce of *This Bridge Called My Back,* in *Berkeley Journal of Sociology* (Berkeley, California), Number 7, 1982, 178–180; "A Personal Reading of *This Bridge Called My Back*" by Pamela Culbreth, in *Sinister Wisdom* (Lincoln, Nebraska), Number 21, 1982, 15–28; "Una conciencia de mujer" by Margaret Randall, in *Women's Review of Books* (Wellesley, Massachusetts), December 1987, 8–9; "Dare to Write: Virginia Woolf, Tillie Olsen, Gloria Anzaldúa" by Carolyn Woodward, in *Changing Our Power: An Introduction to Womens Studies,* edited by Jo Whitehorse Cochran and others, Dubuque, Iowa, Kendall/Hunt Publishing, 1988, 336–349; "Reading Along the Dyke" by Valerie Miner, in *Out/Look* (San Francisco), spring 1988, 94–98; "Algo Secretamente Amado" by Cherríe Moraga, in *Third Woman* (Bloomington, Indiana), Number 4, 1989, 151–156; "After Reading: Borderlands/La Frontera" by Linda Nelson, in *Trivia: A Journal of Ideas* (North Amherst, Massachusetts), spring 1989, 90–101; "Living on the Borderland: The Poetic Prose of Gloria Anzaldúa and Susan Griffin" by Diane P. Freedman, in *Women and Language* (Urbana, Illinois), spring 1989, 1–4; "Borderlands La Frontera—The New Mestiza" by Vera Norwood, in *Journal of the Southwest* (Tucson, Arizona), spring 1989, 112–116; review by Arthur Ramirez of *Borderlands/La Frontera: The New Mestiza,* in *Americas Review* (Houston, Texas), fall–winter 1989, 185–187; "The Borderlands of Culture: Writing by W.E.B. Du Bois, James Agee, Tillie Olsen, and Gloria Anzaldúa" by Shelley Fisher Fishkin, in *Literary Journalism in the Twentieth Century,* edited by Norman Sims, New York,

Oxford University Press, 1990, 133–182; "The Limits of Cultural Studies" by Jose David Saldivar, in *American Literary History* (New York), summer, 1990, 251–266; "Politics, Representation and the Emergence of a Chicana Aesthetic" by Alvina E. Quintana, in *Cultural Studies* (London), October 1990, 257–263; "The Construction of Self in U.S. Latina Autobiographies" by Lourdes Torres, in *Third World Women and the Politics of Feminism,* edited by Chandra Talpade Mohanty, Ann Russo, and Lourdes Torres, Bloomington, Indiana University Press, 1991, 271–287; *Criticism in the Borderlands: Studies in Chicano Literature, Culture, and Ideology,* edited by Hector Calderon and Jose David Saldivar, Durham, North Carolina, Duke University Press, 1991; "Masquerades: Viewing the New Chicana Lesbian Anthologies" by Deena J. Gonzalez, in *Out/Look* (San Francisco), winter 1992, 80–83; "On Borderlands/La Frontera: An Interpretive Essay" by Maria Lugones, in *Hypatia* (North Amherst, Massachusetts), fall 1992, 31–38; "Making Face, Making Soul–Haciendo–Caras" by Denise A. Segura and Beatriz M. Pesquera, in *Gender & Society* (Newbury Park, California), September 1992, 519–522.

*   *   *

"Yo soy Patlache" is how Gloria Anzaldúa introduced herself at a reading in Santa Cruz, California, in April of 1993. Patlache is a Nahuatl (American Indian) word for, as Anzaldúa said, "people like her"—lesbian—but it also connotes her identity as a mestiza, a mixture of Indian, Spanish, and Mexican. Anzaldúa usually describes herself as a Chicana–Tejana, a Mexican living in Texas. These multi–identities permeate her writings of prose and poetry.

In her essay, "La Prieta," Anzaldúa writes of her early life in Hargill, a Mexican community on the Rio Grande in South Texas. She was 15 years old when her father died and the family was reduced to poverty, wearing flour sack clothing and working in the fields. Despite or perhaps because of her hard life, Anzaldúa, after learning English at nine, filled her life with stories. At night under the bed covers she read books voraciously and, because this was forbidden, told endless stories to her sister to keep her quiet. Consequently, Anzaldúa does her best writing at night.

Painting was also a part of Anzaldúa's life, and in her twenties she studied at the Pan–American University in Texas where she received her Bachelor of Arts in English, art, and education and then her Master of Arts in literature and education at the University of Texas in Austin. She moved from Texas (the first of her family in six generations to do so) and taught and wrote in Vermont and San Francisco. The move to San Francisco in the 1970s was pivotal for Anzaldúa. She encountered other female writers of color, such as Cherríe Moraga, another Chicana who was looking at issues of identity in her writings. Feeling excluded by the white feminist writers movement, they spoke together of the need for an expansion of the concept of feminism to encompass all women. In this vein they collected and coedited writings by women of color, which they published in an anthology titled *This Bridge Called My Back: Writings by Radical Women of Color* published in 1981. It was first published by the women's press, Persephone Press, and reprinted by Kitchen Table Women of Color Press. *This Bridge Called My Back,* which included poetry, essays, and stories, has been immensely important to the feminists and women of color communities. It has sold widely, been translated into Spanish, won the 1986 Before Columbus Foundation American Book Award and is used in many university classrooms around the world. An important section in *This Bridge Called My Back* titled "Between the Lines, On Culture, Class and Homophobia," contains prose and poetry written by lesbians of color whose voices had not been articulated to the reading public.

As Anzaldúa continued to write and teach creative writing, feminist studies, and Chicano studies, she searched for writings that would be a continuation of the ideas set out in *This Bridge Called My Back*. These writings would specifically, as she stated in her second anthology *Making Face, Making Soul—Hacienda Caras: Creative and Critical Perspectives by Feminists of Color*, "confront the racism in the White Women's movement in a more thorough, personal, direct, empirical and theoretical way." Before teaching a class at the University of California, Santa Cruz, Anzaldúa compiled recent material addressing these issues written by women of color. These pieces eventually made up the author's 1990 *Making Face, Making Soul—Hacienda Caras*. This anthology gave voice to many unheard writers by the dominant white community. However, the focus was more on ethnic and cultural identity than sexual identity though many writings were by lesbians of color.

Between *This Bridge Called My Back* and *Making Face, Making Soul—Hacienda Caras*, in 1987, Anzaldúa published her own book, *Borderlands—La Frontera: The New Mestiza* which brought together many of her writings for the first time. By including essays on the nature of the mestiza, histories of Mexicans living on the United States border, stories and poems of her childhood, her family and her lesbianism, and ancient myths and songs, *Borderlands—La Frontera* reaches out to encompass all who live on the borders of race, class, sexuality, and culture. The physical layout of the book echoes these concepts by playing with the idea of borders as Anzaldúa skillfully interweaves styles, (essays, stories, poems) and languages (Spanish and English). She embraces the dualities of her culture by interspersing English and Spanish in the same sentence, a writing down of her oral tradition in Chicano Spanish.

In *Borderlands—La Frontera* Anzaldúa spoke of living on the edge but in that space she was able to choose a path, that of lesbianism. "It's an interesting path, one that continually slips in and out of the white, the Catholic, the Mexican, the indigenous, the instincts. In and out of my head." She added that "it is a path of knowledge ... a way of balancing, of mitigating duality ... the coming together of opposite qualities within." According to Sonia Saldivar-Hull, Anzaldúa's poem, "To Live in the Borderlands Means You," reflects her belief that "the new mestiza ... who 'carries five races' on her back ... is also a 'new gender,' 'both woman and man,' ... she becomes a survivor because of her ability to 'live sin fronteras (without borders) / be a crossroads.'"

As Valerie Miner stated in *Out/Look*, Anzaldúa used "sexual marginality as a lens through which to consider other marginalities—national, racial, linguistic, economic." She created new images in her writings by her narrative poems, her retelling of Aztec myths, her analysis of language and folklore, her theories of race and sexuality, and her autobiographical journey from Texas to California, from farmworker to academic, writer, and theorist.

In an essay written for *Bridges of Power: Women's Multicultural Alliances*, Anzaldúa spoke more on creating a lesbian culture that "must be a mestiza lesbian culture, one that partakes of all cultures, one that is not just white in style, theory, or direction, that is not just Chicana, not just Black." She also concludes, "The danger is that white lesbians will 'claim' us and our culture as their own in the creation of 'our' new space." A further discourse on this idea is found in Anzaldúa's essay, "To(o) Queer the Writer—Loca,

Escritora y Chicana" in which she states her disbelief in the concept of lesbian writer, as lesbian is a European term that allows the white middle class gay and lesbian theorists to push queer Mestizas (her term) into a mold that does not fit.

Anzaldúa resides in Santa Cruz, California, where she studies literature at the University of California, teaches and writes essays, stories, and poems that continue to show careful attention to the complexities and excitements of writing from a lesbian mestiza point of view.

—*Jacquelyn Marie*

ARNOLD, June (Davis). American novelist. Also wrote as Carpenter. Born in Greenville, South Carolina, 27 October 1926. Raised in Houston, Texas. Educated at Vassar College, 1943–44; Rice University, B.A. 1948, M.A. 1958. Married (and divorced), four children; companion of Parke Bowman. *Died 11 March 1982.*

WRITINGS

Novels

Applesauce. New York, McGraw, 1967.
The Cook and the Carpenter (as Carpenter). Plainfield, Vermont, Daughters, Inc., 1973.
Sister Gin (one chapter originally published in *Amazon Quarterly* [Somerville, Massachusetts], 3:2, 1975). Plainfield, Vermont, Daughters, Inc., 1975; with afterword by Jane Marcus, New York, Feminist Press at the City University of New York, 1989.
Baby Houston, introduction by Beverly Lowry. Austin, Texas Monthly Press, 1987.

Other

"Feminist Presses and Feminist Politics," in *Quest: A Feminist Quarterly* (Washington, D.C.), summer 1976, 18–26.

*

Interviews: Unpublished and untranscribed conversations with June Arnold by Marie J. Kuda, 1976.

Critical Sources: Review of *The Cook and the Carpenter*, in *Village Voice*, 4 April 1974, 33; review of *The Cook and the Carpenter*, in *Ms.*, June 1974, 35; "Creating a Women's World" by Lois Gould, in *New York Times Magazine*, 2 January 1977, 10–11, 34, 36–38; unpublished and untranscribed conversation with Parke Bowman, 1978; review of *Applesauce*, in *Washington Post Book World*, 8 January 1978, E4; review of *Applesauce*, in *New York Times Book Review*, 15 January 1978, 27; review of *Sister Gin*, in *Spectator*, 3 March 1979, 23; review by Taffy Cannon of *Baby Houston*, in *Los*

Angeles Times Book Review, 19 July 1987; review by Eve Ottenberg Stone of *Baby Houston,* in *New York Times Book Review,* 26 July 1987, 10; "Bringing Up Baby" (review of *Baby Houston*) by Jane Marcus, in *Women's Review of Books,* October 1987, 4; review of *Baby Houston,* in *New Directions for Women,* November 1987, 22; review by Joyce Maynard of *Baby Houston,* in *Mademoiselle,* December 1987, 70; *The Safe Sea of Women: Lesbian Fiction 1969–1989* by Bonnie Zimmerman, Boston, Beacon Press, 1990; review of *Sister Gin,* in *Belles Lettres,* spring 1990, 22; unpublished and untranscribed conversation with Beth Dingman, 7 August 1993.

*   *   *

June Arnold had a unique vision of a world where it was possible for women to exert control over their own destinies. Her work as a novelist, feminist, and publisher contributed to the dissemination of that ideal. The women in her novels come together, draw support from one another, and gird their loins to do battle with the controlling order that oppresses them. As a cofounder of Daughters, Inc., in 1973, Arnold and her partner and attorney Parke Bowman put their theories of empowerment into practice. Together with Bertha Harris—novelist and coauthor of *The Joy of Lesbian Sex*—and feminist political guru Charlotte Bunch, Arnold and Bowman set out to take on the establishment presses that gave little attention to women's work.

Arnold's success in writing and publishing came after some 40 years of varied life experiences. She lived most of her childhood in Houston, Texas, and after a period at Vassar from 1943 to 1944, she took two literature degrees from Rice University. After being married and divorced, Arnold and her four children moved to Greenwich Village, where she wrote her first novel, *Applesauce,* published by McGraw–Hill in 1967. The author's political concerns became evident as she undertook her writing career; in response to a query from *Contemporary Authors* in the 1970s, she listed her politics as "Feminist" and her religion as "Women." With her lover Bowman she moved to Plainfield, Vermont, where they started their feminist publishing venture in the early 1970s. Daughters, Inc. published five titles annually from 1973 through 1978, including three by Arnold: *The Cook and the Carpenter,* under Arnold's pseudonym, Carpenter, *Sister Gin,* and a reprint of *Applesauce.* She also contributed to a number of periodicals including the *Village Voice, Quest, Amazon Quarterly,* the *Houston Post, Plexus,* and *Sister Courage.* Since her death in 1982, excerpts of her work have appeared in several anthologies, and the novel *Baby Houston* was published in 1987.

Generally held to be her most popular work, *Sister Gin* was an immediate success, due in no little part to an excerpt that appeared in a special "Sexuality" issue of *Amazon Quarterly.* The chapter in which the aging, slightly deaf Mamie Carter and the menopausal Su engage in sensuous sex was hailed as a *tour de force* by lesbians, feminists, and octogenarians. In *Sister Gin* Arnold dealt with the then–timely feminist issues of alcoholism, race, and obesity, treating them with insight and humor.

Arnold's fiction has generally been labeled "experimental" and "lesbian." *Applesauce* features an androgynous character that experiences life from both male and female perspectives, and has been compared more than once to Virginia Woolf's *Orlando.* The book was largely ignored by lesbians, however, until its later reprint from Daughters, Inc. *The Cook and the Carpenter,* on the other hand, made an immediate impact on the lesbian–feminist community. The book featured a commune of people with neutral names, and the author's creation of the neutral pronouns "na" and "nam" allowed free exploration and testing of preconceptions about roles and class in society. Copies of the book were passed around discussion groups, and Arnold's name became rapidly known in the lesbian subculture of the early 1970s.

Included in the first offering of titles from Daughters, Inc. was Rita Mae Brown's *Rubyfruit Jungle* as well as *The Cook and the Carpenter,* and both quickly established the reputation of the press. *Rubyfruit Jungle* eclipsed the popularity of almost every lesbian novel that had ever been published; the book sold 90,000 copies in 11 printings. With this kind of success, it was inevitable that the mainstream entertainment industry would attempt to capitalize on the book's appeal. By 1976 Daughters, Inc. was besieged by the establishment with offers for paperback and movie rights for the book. As reported by Lois Gould in the *New York Times Magazine,* Brown was in favor of the sale while others at Daughters, Inc. were uncertain about the feminist ramifications of the movie deal. The eventual sale of the film rights at a seven–figure price was perceived by some in the feminist community as a compromise of the small press' principles.

In spite of the income and attention created by *Rubyfruit Jungle,* Arnold believed in the necessity of a strong, independent women's communications network. She had envisioned presses, publishers, booksellers, magazines, writers, and women consumers linked by a media under their own control. In an article she wrote for *Quest,* Arnold noted that the "words of earlier feminists were lost because they were the property of male publishers who easily avoided reprinting them." She outlined the reasons writers should publish with feminist presses, stressing, "It is vital that we spend the energy of our imaginations and criticisms building feminist institutions that women will gain from both in money and skills." She foresaw that the establishment presses "will publish some of us—the least threatening, the most saleable, the most easily controlled or a few who cannot be ignored."

Arnold and Daughters, Inc. initiated a conference of women that she hoped would be instrumental in advancing such a women's network. In late summer of 1976 about 130 women representing over 80 presses, publishers, journals and bookstores met for seven days in a dry, hot Nebraska Campfire Girls campground. The majority of those attending the conference were lesbian, and most took to heart the various lessons learned in workshops and by networking with one another at the event. In the years since that first Women in Print conference, economics and politics have taken their toll among the participants, but the survivors are journals and presses that have allowed lesbian–feminist publishing to reach a readership that numbers in the millions. Despite this success, it is more than an exercise in fantasy to speculate on the quality and direction lesbian–feminist book publishing would have taken had not Arnold been forced to withdraw and do battle with cancer.

She and Bowman returned to Texas, where Arnold worked on a novel about her mother. *Baby Houston* was published posthumously to positive reviews. Philip Lopate, author of *The Rug Merchant,* declared in a dust jacket blurb that the book was "simply the best novel ever written about Houston." Jane Marcus in the *Women's Review of Books* called it "the novel of the year," and added that "the portrait it paints of a mother and two daughters in Houston between 1939 and 1964 is as bitter and as sweet as a good margarita."

The underground demand for *Sister Gin,* widely circulated in xeroxed fragments among women's studies classes and readers of lesbian erotica, resulted in a 1989 reprint of the work now dubbed a feminist classic. Bonnie Zimmerman in *Safe Sea of Women* (a title drawn from *Sister Gin)* praises Arnold as an experimental writer and cites her as one of few lesbians writing political fiction in the 1970s. She also notes Arnold's impact as a publisher and calls attention to the fact that of this small group of politically–aware writers of lesbian material, all, including Arnold, Elana Nachman, Monique Wittig, and Rita Mae Brown, were published by Daughters, Inc.

—*Marie J. Kuda*

————

ASHBERY, John (Lawrence). American poet, novelist, translator, playwright, and author of short stories. Also writes as Jonas Berry. Born in Rochester, New York, 28 July 1927. Educated at Deerfield Academy, 1945; Harvard University, B.A. in English literature 1949; Columbia University, M.A. in English literature 1951; New York University, graduate study in French literature 1957–58. Reference librarian, Brooklyn Public Library, Brooklyn, New York; copywriter, Oxford University Press, New York City, 1951–54, and McGraw–Hill Book Co., New York City, 1954–55; instructor in elementary French, New York University, New York City, 1957–58; art critic, European Edition of *New York Herald,* Paris, 1960–65; Paris correspondent, then executive editor, *Art News,* New York City, 1964–72; professor of English and codirector of M.F.A. Program in Creative Writing, Brooklyn College of the City University of New York, 1974–90 (distinguished professor 1980–90); Charles Eliot Norton Professor of Poetry, Harvard University, Cambridge, Massachusetts, 1989–90; Charles P. Stevenson, Jr., Professor of Languages and Literature, Bard College, Annandale–on–Hudson, New York, 1990—. Editor of *Locus Solus,* 1960–62, and of *Art and Literature,* 1963–66; poetry editor, *Partisan Review,* 1976–80; art critic, *Art International,* 1961–64, *New York,* 1978–80, and *Newsweek,* 1980–85. Chancellor, Academy of American Poets, beginning 1988. Recipient: Young Men's Hebrew Association Discovery Prize (with others), 1952; Fulbright scholarship to France, 1955–57; Yale Series of Younger Poets Prize, 1956; Poet's Foundation grants, 1962 and 1972; *Poetry*'s Harriet Monroe Poetry Award, 1963; *Poetry*'s Union League Civic and Arts Foundation Prize, 1966; Guggenheim fellowships, 1967 and 1973; National Endowment for the Arts grants, 1968 and 1969; National Institute of Arts and Letters Award, 1969; Poetry Society of America's Shelley Memorial Award, 1973; *Poetry*'s Frank O'Hara Prize, 1974; University of Chicago's Harriet Monroe Poetry Award, 1975; Pulitzer Prize, 1976; National Book Award, 1976; National Book Critics Circle Award, 1976; *Poetry*'s Levinson Prize, 1977; Rockefeller Foundation grant in playwriting, 1978; D.Litt. from Southampton College of Long Island University, 1979; named Phi Beta Kappa Poet at Harvard University, 1979; English–Speaking Union Poetry Award, 1979; Academy of American Poets fellowship, 1982; New York City Mayor's Award of Honor for Arts and Culture, 1983; Bard College's Charles Flint Kellogg Award in Arts and Letters, 1983; Bollingen prize (with others), 1985; MacArthur Foundation fellowship, 1985–90; Modern Language Association Common

Wealth Award, 1985; *Nation*'s Lenore Marshall Award, 1986; Brandeis University Creative Arts Award in Poetry, 1989. Agent: Georges Borchardt, Inc., 136 East 57th Street, New York, New York 10022, U.S.A.

WRITINGS

Poetry

Turandot, and Other Poems. New York, Tibor de Nagy Gallery, 1953.
Some Trees, introduction by W. H. Auden. New Haven, Connecticut, Yale University Press, and London, Cumberlege/Oxford University Press, 1956.
The Poems. New York, Tiber Press, 1960.
The Tennis Court Oath. Middletown, Connecticut, Wesleyan University Press, 1962.
Rivers and Mountains. New York, Holt, 1966.
Selected Poems. London, J. Cape, 1967.
Sunrise in Suburbia. New York, Phoenix Book Shop, 1968.
Three Madrigals. New York, Poet's Press, 1968.
Fragment, illustrations by Alex Katz. Los Angeles, Black Sparrow Press, 1969; included in *The Double Dream of Spring,* 1970.
Evening in the Country. St. Thomas, Virgin Islands, Spanish Main Press, 1970.
The Double Dream of Spring (includes poem "Fragment"). New York, Dutton, 1970.
The New Spirit. New York, Adventures in Poetry, 1970; included in *Three Poems,* 1972.
Three Poems. New York, Viking, 1972.
Self–Portrait in a Convex Mirror. New York, Viking, 1975; Manchester, England, Carcanet, 1977.
The Serious Doll. Privately printed, 1975.
With Joe Brainard, *The Vermont Notebook.* Los Angeles, Black Sparrow Press, 1975.
Houseboat Days. New York, Viking, and London, Penguin, 1977.
ZZZZZ, edited by Kenward Elmslie, illustrations by Karl Torok. Calais, Vermont, Z Press, 1977.
As We Know. New York, Viking, 1979.
Shadow Train. New York, Viking, and Harmondsworth, England, Penguin, 1981.
A Wave. New York, Viking, and Manchester, England, Carcanet, 1984.
Selected Poems. New York, Viking, 1985.
The Ice Storm. New York, Hanuman Books, 1987; included in *April Galleons,* 1987.
April Galleons. New York, Viking, 1987.
Flow Chart. New York, Knopf, 1991.
Hotel Lautreamont. New York, Knopf, 1992.

Novels

With James Schuyler, *A Nest of Ninnies.* New York, Dutton, 1969.

Plays

The Heroes (produced New York, 1952; London, 1982). Published in *Artists' Theatre,* edited by Herbert Machiz, New York, Grove, 1969; included in *Three Plays,* 1978.

The Compromise (produced Cambridge, Massachusetts, 1956). Published in *The Hasty Papers,* Alfred Leslie, 1960; included in *Three Plays,* 1978.

The Philosopher. Published in *Art and Literature,* Number 2, 1964; included in *Three Plays,* 1978.

Three Plays (includes *The Heroes, The Compromise,* and *The Philosopher*). Calais, Vermont, Z Press, 1978.

Art Studies and Criticism

With others, *R. B. Kitaj: Paintings, Drawings, Pastels.* Washington, D.C., Smithsonian Institution, 1981; London, Thames & Hudson, 1986.

Fairfield Porter: Realist Painter in an Age of Abstraction. Boston, New York Graphic Society, 1983.

Reported Sightings: Art Chronicles, 1957–1987, edited by David Bergman. New York, Knopf, 1989.

Editor

With others, *The American Literary Anthology/1.* New York, Farrar, Straus, 1968.

With Thomas B. Hess, *Light.* New York, Macmillan, 1969.

With Thomas B. Hess, *Art of the Grand Eccentrics.* New York, Macmillan, 1971.

With Thomas B. Hess, *Avant–garde Art.* New York, Macmillan, 1971.

With Thomas B. Hess, *Painterly Painting.* New York, Newsweek, 1971.

Penguin Modern Poets 24: Kenward Elmslie, Kenneth Hoch, James Schuyler. Harmondsworth, England, Penguin, 1974.

The Funny Place, by Richard F. Snow. Chicago, O'Hara, 1975.

Muck Arbour, by Bruce Marcus, Chicago, O'Hara, 1975.

With David Lehman, *The Best American Poetry, 1988.* New York, Scribner, 1989.

From Altar to Chimney–Piece: Selected Stories of Mary Butts by Mary Butts. Kingston, New York, McPherson, 1992.

Contributor

With Lawrence G. Blochman, *Murder in Montmarte* by Noel Vexin (as Jonas Berry). New York, Dell, 1960.

With Lawrence G. Blochman, *The Deadlier Sex* by Genevieve Manceron (as Jonas Berry). New York, Dell, 1961.

Alberto Giacometti by Jacques Dupin. Paris, Maeght Editeur, 1962.

The Dice Cup: Selected Prose Poems by Max Jacob, edited by Michael Brownstein. New York, SUN, 1979.

Every Question but One by Pierre Martory. New York, Groundwater Press, 1990.

With Mary A. Caws, *Selected Poems* by Pierre Reverdy. Winston–Salem, North Carolina, Wake Forest University Press, 1991.

With others, *Things to Translate: Selected Poems* by Piotr Sommer. Chester Springs, Pennsylvania, Dufour Editions, 1991.

And author of introduction, *Hebdomeros, and Other Writings* by Giorgio De Chirico. Exact Change, 1992.

Other

With Frank O'Hara, *Poets of the New York School.* New York, Gotham Book Mart, 1969.

Author of introduction, *The Collected Poems* by Frank O'Hara. New York, Knopf, 1971.

Author of introduction, *What a Life!* by E. V. Lucas and George Morrow. New York, Dover, 1975.

Author of foreword, *Along the Dark Shore* by Edward Byrne. Brockport, New York, BOA Editions, 1977.

Author of introduction, *The Ultimate Cigar* by Stuart Kaufman. Westtown, New York, First East Coast Theatre and Publishing Company, 1985.

Author of introduction, *The Third Rose: Gertrude Stein and Her World* by John M. Brinnin. Don Mills, Ontario, Addison–Wesley, 1987.

Author of introduction, *The Mirrored Clubs of Hell* by Gerrit Henry. New York, Arcade, 1991.

Recordings: *Treasury of 100 Modern American Poets Reading Their Poems,* Volume 17, Spoken Arts; *Poetry of John Ashbery,* Jeffrey Norton.

*

Interviews: *The Craft of Poetry: Interviews from The New York Quarterly,* edited by William Packard, Garden City, New York, Doubleday, 1964, 111–32; "The Craft of John Ashbery" by Louis A. Osti, in *Confrontation,* fall 1974, 84–96; with Raymond Gardner in *Guardian* (London), 19 April 1975, 8.

Bibliography: *John Ashbery: A Comprehensive Bibliography* by David K. Kermani, New York, Garland Publishing, 1976.

Critical Sources: *John Ashbery,* edited by David Lehman, Ithaca, New York, Cornell University Press, 1979; *Beyond Amazement: New Essays on John Ashbery,* edited by David Lehman, Ithaca, New York, Cornell University Press, 1980; *John Ashbery,* edited by Harold Bloom, New York, Chelsea House, 1985.

*   *   *

"Recondite" might be the one best word to describe John Ashbery's life and poetry. In "Fragment," he writes, "Of older / Permissiveness which dies in the / Falling back toward recondite ends." Author of a multitude of publications, Ashbery has not been speechless, but he has been reticent. In "The New Spirit" he writes, "I thought that if I could put it all down, that would be one way. And next the thought came to me that to leave all out would be another, and truer, way."

Ashbery reveals little about personal relationships—a central topic in "confessional" verse. Even when perhaps talking about himself, the poet would dissolve identities, as in *A Wave:* "Being tall and shy, you can still stand up more clearly / To the definition of what you are. You are not a sadist / But must only trust in the dismantling of that definition / Someday when names are being removed from things, when all attributes / Are sinking in the maelstrom of de–definition like spars."

Gravitating early to the arts, Ashbery came of age at the beginning of the Cold War. At Harvard he wrote his senior thesis in 1949 on W. H. Auden; at Columbia his master's thesis in 1951 on novelist Henry Green and he began a dissertation on Raymond Roussel. While still a student, Ashbery presented and performed in plays in Cambridge and Manhattan. Leaving New York in 1955, Ashbery lived in Paris until 1965. As have generations of Americans, he searched for sexual and literary freedom in France. In "The Tomb of Stuart Merrill" Ashbery celebrates one of the American exiles who met Walt Whitman before spending his life in Paris. Ashbery absorbed the work of Gertrude Stein, Guillaume Apollinaire, Marcel Proust, Arthur Rimbaud, Arthur Craven, Marcelin Pleynet, Oscar Wilde, Raymond Roussel, Max Jacob, Pierre Reverdy and many others. Ashbery found affinities with bisexual, lesbian and homosexual authors while shying away from the more openly homosexual advocates like Jean Cocteau or André Gide as well as heterosexual propagandists like André Breton.

Ashbery himself took up painting for a time and worked as an art reviewer for the *Paris Herald Tribune, Art News,* and *Newsweek.* The collected *Reported Sightings: Art Chronicles 1957–1987* in 1989 offers some autobiographical information. While in Paris, Ashbery published some of his most brilliant poetry. Auden chose the 1956 *Some Trees* for the Yale Younger Poets prize and in his introduction noticed the influence of Rimbaud. *The Tennis Court Oath* in 1962, and *Rivers and Mountains* in 1966, infused with expatriate freedom, infuriated some readers and inspired others. In later works, Ashbery has absorbed the landscapes of Long Island, Vermont, and upstate New York. In 1986, he wrote in *Sightings* that "my own progress as a writer began with my half–consciously imitating the work that struck me when I was young and new"; then came a later "doubting phase in which I was examining things and taking them apart without being able to put them back together to my liking. I am still trying to do that."

A watershed publication of reconstruction, the 1975 *Self–Portrait in a Convex Mirror* won the Harriet Monroe Poetry, Pulitzer, National Book Award, and National Book Critics Circle prizes. Ashbery has not mellowed with age, and has found new readers. His 1992 *The Hotel Lautreamont* does not abandon youthful experimentation. Lautreamont the gay poet used a pseudonym that echoes the French word for "otherness." "The governing principle seems to be not so much automatism," Ashbery writes in *Sightings,* "but that of self–abnegation, one which will reflect the realities both of the spirit (rather than the individual consciousness) and of the world perceived by it: the state in which *'Je est un autre,'* in Rimbaud's famous phrase."

Since Ashbery abjures "individual consciousness," gay themes in his work are not necessarily autobiographical. For instance, in *Self Portrait:* "Once I let a guy blow me. / I kind of backed away from the experience. / Now years later, I think of it / Without emotion." A passage in "The New Spirit" (title of Apollinaire's proclamation) could be autobiographically describing love's stages: "The animalistic one, the aristocratic one in which sex and knowledge fitted together to screen out the intriguing darkness, or the others in which idealism—child–love or sibling–love—gradually twisted the earth's barrenness into a sense from which both libertinage and liberty in its highest, most intellectual sense were subtly excluded, culminating in the (for him) highest form of love, which recognizes only its own generosity."

This "highest form of love" figures occasionally in several poems. Thus a narrator in "Litany" asks why have someone "to take care of me" and answers: "I can do it better than anyone, and have

/ All my life, and now I am tired / And a little bored with taking care of myself / And would like to see how somebody else might / Do it, even if that person falls on their face / Trying to, in the attempt."

Flow Chart: A Poem might or might not be read as a love poem. At the beginning the poem says, "I would like your / attention, not just your eyes and face. I would like to tell you / how much I love you." And the poem ends with the inevitable joys and decays of love: "Then in the car he proposed to me. In the back seat. We drank sacrificial wine. / It was so *good.*" The sequel has a familiar ring: "Then we went out and a cloud like a magician's cape / covered the sun. I'll never forget that. And we walked on awhile and I was trying to explain my embarrassing / tendency not to be able to distinguish things that happened to me years ago / from recent dreams. He was cool for a while after that. Men / never seem to know how much to erase, and afterward it's bedlam, greed and self–interest take over."

Flow Chart could be read as Ashbery's relationship to his public and to fame. Yale critic Harold Bloom claims that Ashbery has in *Hotel Lautreamont* achieved "fresh greatness as a poet" and more than ever "seems to be to the second half of our century what Stevens and Yeats were to the first." Ashbery's attitude toward fame resembles his attitude toward love. In discussing artists Thomas Hart Benton and Jackson Pollock, public shifts do not change a work, he reported in *Sightings,* "but it does illustrate that Benton's is the kind of art that cannot go on living without acceptance, while Pollock's is the kind which cannot be destroyed by acceptance since it is basically unacceptable."

Ashbery's experimentation, sexuality, and reserve have become acceptable. What remains unacceptable may be his playful gayness. His reservations reside in an understanding of the assaults on our playfulness, our joy in dreams and the movement of sound through our bodies. His view of a gay liberation would not be a meeting (or even sex) with the President. In *Hotel Lautreamont,* his poem "Oeuvres Completes" asks why we are here, and answers: "It's so the little naked man can run out into the grass / that towers over him, sprayed with dewdrops, to massacre the cold / and master the changed legions / whose breath never hurt / anything, but you are loved and it's your responsibility."

—*Charles Shively*

AUDEN, W(ystan) H(ugh). British and American poet and playwright. Born in York, 21 February 1907; came to the United States in 1939; became citizen, 1946. Educated at St. Edmund's School, Hindhead, Surrey, 1915–20; Gresham's School, Holt, Norfolk, 1920–25; and Christ Church College, Oxford, 1925–28, B.A. 1928. Served as stretcher–bearer for Loyalists during Spanish Civil War, 1937; as uniformed civilian at rank of Major, served as research chief of Morale Division, U.S. Strategic Bombing Survey in Germany, 1945. Married writer Erika Mann (daughter of German writer Thomas Mann), 15 June 1935 (divorced); companion of Chester Kallman, 1939–73. Teacher, Larchfield Academy, Helensburgh, Scotland, 1930–32; The Downs School, Colwall, 1932–35. Founded the Group Theatre, with Rupert Doone, Robert Medley, and others, 1932;

film writer for General Post Office film unit, 1935; collaborated on scripts with Benjamin Britten. Travelled extensively during the 1930s, to Iceland (for travel book with Louis MacNeice), 1936, to Spain, briefly broadcasting for Republican government in Spanish Civil War, 1937; and to China with Christopher Isherwood, 1938. Taught at St. Mark's School, Southborough, Massachusetts, and American Writers League School, 1939; New School for Social Research, New York, 1940–41, 1946–47, and 1948; Olivet College, Michigan, and University of Michigan, 1941–42; Swarthmore College, Pennsylvania, and Bryn Mawr College, Pennsylvania, 1943–45; Bennington College, Vermont, 1946; Barnard College, New York, 1947; Page–Barbour Lecturer, University of Virginia, 1949; Mount Holyoke College, Massachusetts, 1950; W. A. Neilson Research Professor, Smith College, Northampton, Massachusetts, 1953; professor of poetry, Oxford University, 1956–61. Opera librettist for music by Benjamin Britten and, with Chester Kallman, for works by Igor Stravinsky, Hans Werner Henze, and Nicolas Nabokov. Edited Yale Series of Younger Poets, 1947–57. Founder and editor, with Jacques Barzun and Lionel Trilling, of the Reader's Subscription Book Club, 1951–58, and wrote occasionally for its periodical, *Griffin;* established the Mid–Century Book Society with Jacques Barzun and Lionel Trilling, 1959–63, and wrote occasionally for its periodical, the *Mid–Century*. **Recipient:** King's Gold Medal for poetry, 1937; Guggenheim fellowship, 1942; membership in the American Academy of Arts and Letters, 1942, and their Award of Merit Medal, 1945; Pulitzer Prize in poetry, 1948; Bollingen Prize in poetry, 1954; National Book Award, 1956; Feltrinelli Prize (Rome), 1957; Alexander Droutzkoy Award, 1959; Guinness Poetry Award (Ireland), shared with Robert Lowell and Edith Sitwell, 1959; special recognition on Chicago Poetry Day, 1960; Honorary Student (fellow), Christ College, Oxford University, 1962–73; Austrian State Prize for European Literature, 1966; National Medal for Literature of National Book Committee, 1967; Gold Medal of National Institute of Arts and Letters, 1968. D. Litt., Swarthmore College, 1965; D.Litt., Oxford, 1971; D.Litt., London, 1972. *Died in his sleep in Vienna, Austria, 28 September 1973; death officially recorded as morning of 29 September 1973.*

WRITINGS

Poetry

Poems (hand–printed by Stephen Spender). [Oxford], 1928.
Poems. London, Faber, 1930; revised, 1933, 1960; New York, Random House, 1934; revised with new foreword by Stephen Spender, Elliston Poetry Foundation of the University of Cincinnati, 1965.
The Orators: An English Study (includes prose). London, Faber, 1932; revised, 1934, 1966; revised with new foreword, New York, Random House, 1967.
Poem. Bryn Mawr, Pennsylvania, Frederic Prokosch, 1933.
Two Poems. Bryn Mawr, Pennsylvania, Frederic Prokosch, 1934.
Poems (includes *The Orators* and *The Dance of Death*). New York, Random House, 1934.
Sonnet. London, Frederic Prokosch, 1935.
Look, Stranger! London, Faber, 1936; as *On This Island,* New York, Random House, 1937.
With Louis MacNeice, *Letters from Iceland.* London, Faber, and New York, Random House, 1937.
Spain. London, Faber, 1937.
Selected Poems. London, Faber, 1938.
With Christopher Isherwood, *Journey to a War.* London, Faber, and New York, Random House, 1939; revised, Faber, 1973.
Epithalamion Commemorating the Marriage of Guiseppe Antonio Borghese and Elisabeth Mann. New York, privately printed, 1939.
Another Time: Poems (includes *Spain*). New York, Random House, and London, Faber, 1940.
Some Poems. London, Faber, and New York, Random House, 1940.
Three Songs for St. Cecilia's Day. New York, privately printed, 1941.
The Double Man. New York, Random House, 1941; as *New Year Letter,* London, Faber, 1941.
The Collected Poetry of W. H. Auden. New York, Random House, 1945.
Litany and Anthem for St. Matthew's Day. Northampton, St. Matthew's, 1946.
The Age of Anxiety: A Baroque Eclogue (produced Off–Broadway, 1954). New York, Random House, 1947; London, Faber, 1948.
Collected Shorter Poems, 1930–1944. London, Faber, 1950; New York, Random House, 1951.
Nones. New York, Random House, 1951; London, Faber, 1952.
Mountains. London, Faber, 1954.
The Shield of Achilles. New York, Random House, and London, Faber, 1955.
The Old Man's Road. New York, Voyages Press, 1956.
A Gobble Poem ("snatched from the notebooks of W. H. Auden and now believed to be in the Morgan Library"). [London], 1957.
Reflections on a Forest. Greencastle, Indiana, De Pauw University, 1957.
Goodbye to the Mezzogiorno (bilingual edition). Milan, All'Insegno del Pesce d'Oro, 1958.
W. H. Auden: A Selection by the Author. Hammersmith, Penguin, 1958; as *Selected Poetry of W. H. Auden.* New York, Modern Library, 1959.
Homage to Clio. New York, Random House, and London, Faber, 1960.
W. H. Auden: A Selection, edited by Richard Hoggart. London, Hutchinson, 1961.
The Common Life, translation from the German by Dieter Leisegang. Darmstadt, Bläschke, 1964.
The Cave of the Making, translation from the German by Dieter Leisegang. Darmstadt, Bläschke, 1965.
Half–Way (limited edition). Cambridge, Massachusetts, Lowell–Adams House Printers, 1965.
About the House. New York, Random House, 1965; London, Faber, 1966.
The Platonic Blow. [New York], 1965.
The Twelve, music by William Walton. London, Oxford University Press, 1966.
Collected Shorter Poems, 1927–1957. London, Faber, 1966; New York, Random House, 1967.
Portraits. Apiary Press, 1966.
Marginalia. Cambridge, Massachusetts, Ibex Press, 1966.
River Profile. Cambridge, Massachusetts, Laurence Scott, 1967.
A Selection by the Author. London, Faber, 1967.
Selected Poems. London, Faber, 1968; revised, New York, Random House, 1979.
Two Songs. New York, Phoenix Book Shop, 1968.

Collected Longer Poems. London, Faber, 1968; New York, Random House, 1969.

A New Year Greeting, with *The Dance of the Solids* by John Updike. New York, *Scientific American*, 1969.

City without Walls, and Other Poems. London, Faber, 1969; New York, Random House, 1970.

Natural Linguistics. London, Poem–of–the–Month Club, 1970.

Academic Graffiti. London, Faber, 1971; New York, Random House, 1972.

With Leif Sjöberg, *Selected Poems*. New York, Pantheon, 1972.

Epistle to a Godson, and Other Poems. New York, Random House, and London, Faber, 1972.

Auden/Moore: Poems and Lithographs, edited by John Russell. London, British Museum, 1974.

Poems, lithographs by Henry Moore, edited by Vera Lindsay. London, Petersburg Press, 1974.

Thank You, Fog: Last Poems. London, Faber, and New York, Random House, 1974.

Collected Poems, edited by Edward Mendelson. London, Faber, and New York, Random House, 1976.

Sue. Sycamore Press, 1977.

Selected Poems, edited by Edward Mendelson. New York, Vintage, and London, Faber, 1979.

Plays

With Christopher Isherwood, *The Ascent of F6* (produced London, 1931; New York, 1939). London, Faber, 1936; revised, New York, Random House, and London, Faber, 1937.

The Dance of Death (produced London, 1934; New York, 1935; as *Come Out into the Sun*, Poughkeepsie, New York, 1935; as *The Dance of Death*, New York, 1936). London, Faber, 1933; in *Poems*, 1934.

With Christopher Isherwood, *The Dog beneath the Skin; or, Where Is Francis?* (produced London, 1936; revised version, New York, 1947). London, Faber, and New York, Random House, 1935.

With Edward Crankshaw, *No More Peace! A Thoughtful Comedy* (adaptation of play by Ernst Toller; produced London, 1936; New York, 1937). New York, Farrar and Rinehart, and London, Lane, 1937.

With Christopher Isherwood, *On the Frontier: A Melodrama in Three Acts* (produced Cambridge, 1938; London, 1939). London, Faber, 1938; New York, Random House, 1939.

The Dark Valley (radio play; broadcast, 1940). Published in *Best Broadcasts of 1939–1940*, edited by Max Wylie, New York, Whittlesey House, and London, McGraw Hill, 1940.

With Christopher Isherwood, *Two Great Plays* (contains *The Dog beneath the Skin* and *The Ascent of F6*). New York, Random House, 1959.

The Knights of the Round Table (radio adaptation of play by Jean Cocteau; broadcast, 1951; produced Salisbury, Wiltshire, 1954; New York, 1979). Published in *The Infernal Machine, and Other Plays* by Jean Cocteau, New York, New Directions, 1963.

With Christopher Isherwood, *Plays, and Other Dramatic Writings: W. H. Auden and Christopher Isherwood, 1928–1938*, edited by Edward Mendelson. Princeton, Princeton University Press, 1988.

Documentary Screenplays in Verse

Night Mail, 1936.
Coal–Face, 1936.
The Londoners, 1938.

Radio Plays

Hadrian's Wall, 1937.

With James Stern, *The Rocking–Horse Winner* (adaptation of short story by D. H. Lawrence), 1941.

Criticism and Essays

With T. C. Worley, *Education Today and Tomorrow*. London, Hogarth Press, 1939.

"Criticism in a Mass Society," in *The Intent of the Critic*, edited by Donald A. Stauffer. Princeton, New Jersey, Princeton University Press, 1941.

Address on Henry James (booklet). [New York], 1947.

"Squares and Oblongs," in *Poets at Work: Essays Based on the Modern Poetry Collections at the Lockwood Memorial Library, University of Buffalo*, edited by Charles D. Abbott. New York, Harcourt, 1948; reprinted in part in *The Dyer's Hand, and Other Essays*, 1963.

"The Ironic Hero," in *Horizon* (London), 1949.

"Yeats as an Example," in *The Permanence of Yeats*, edited by James Hall and Martin Steinmann, New York, Macmillan, 1950.

The Enchafèd Flood: The Romantic Iconography of the Sea. New York, Random House, 1950; London, Faber, 1951.

"Presenting Kierkegaard," in *The Living Thoughts of Kierkegaard*, edited by Alfred O. Mendel. New York, McKay, 1952; as *Kierkegaard*, London, Cassell, 1955.

Making, Knowing, and Judging. Oxford, Clarendon Press, 1956.

The Dyer's Hand, and Other Essays. New York, Random House, 1962; London, Faber, 1963; as *Selected Essays*, London, Faber, 1964.

Louis MacNeice: A Memorial Lecture. London, Faber, 1963.

Shakespeare, Fünf Aufsätze. [Frankfurt am Main], 1964.

Worte und Noten: Rede zur Eröffnung der Salzburger Festspiele 1968. Salzburg, Festungsverlag, 1968.

Secondary Worlds (T. S. Eliot Memorial Lectures at University of Kent, 1967). London, Faber, and New York, Random House, 1969.

A Certain World: A Commonplace Book (annotated personal anthology). New York, Random House, 1970; London, Faber, 1971.

Forewords and Afterwords, edited by Edward Mendelson. New York, Random House, and London, Faber, 1973.

Libretti, Lyrics, and Narratives

Our Hunting Fathers, music by Benjamin Britten. London and New York, Boosey & Hawkes, 1936.

Fish in the Unruffled Lakes, music by Benjamin Britten. London and New York, Boosey & Hawkes, 1937.

On This Island, music by Benjamin Britten. London and New York, Boosey & Hawkes, 1937.

Two Ballads. London and New York, Boosey & Hawkes, 1937.

Now through the Night's Caressing Grip, music by Benjamin Britten. London and New York, Boosey & Hawkes, 1938.

Ballad of Heroes, music by Benjamin Britten. London and New York, Boosey & Hawkes, 1939.

Hymn to St. Cecilia for S.S.A.T.B., music by Benjamin Britten. London and New York, Boosey & Hawkes, 1942.

For the Time Being: A Christmas Oratorio, music by Marvin David Levy (produced New York, 1959). [New York], 1944.

The Duchess of Malfi, music by Benjamin Britten (adaptation of the play by John Webster; produced New York, 1946).

With Chester Kallman, *The Rake's Progress,* music by Igor Stravinsky (produced Venice, 1951; New York, 1953; London, 1962). London and New York, Boosey & Hawkes, 1951.

With Chester Kallman, *Delia; or, A Masque of Night* (libretto). Published in *Botteghe Oscure XII* (Rome), 1953.

The Punch Review (lyrics; produced London, 1955).

With Chester Kallman, *The Magic Flute,* music by Wolfgang Amadeus Mozart (adaptation of libretto by Schikaneder and Giesecke; telecast, 1956). New York, Random House, 1956; London, Faber, 1957.

With Noah Greenberg, *The Play of Daniel: A Thirteenth Century Musical Drama* (narrative; produced New York, 1958; London, 1960). New York and London, Oxford University Press, 1959.

With Chester Kallman, *The Seven Deadly Sins of the Lower Middle Class,* music by Kurt Weill (adaptation of work by Bertholt Brecht; produced New York, 1959; Edinburgh and London, 1961). Published in *Tulane Drama Review* (New Orleans), September 1961.

Five Poems, music by Lennox Berkeley (produced New York, 1959). J. and W. Chester, 1960.

With others, *Time Cycle, for Soprano and Orchestra* (performed by New York Philharmonic under direction of Leonard Bernstein at Carnegie Hall, 1960).

With Chester Kallman, *Don Giovanni,* music by Wolfgang Amadeus Mozart (adaptation of libretto by Lorenzo da Ponte; telecast, 1960). New York and London, Schirmer, 1961.

With Chester Kallman, *Elegy for Young Lovers,* music by Hans Werner Henze (produced Stuttgart and Glyndebourne, Sussex, 1961). Mainz, Schott, 1961.

Elegy for J.F.K., music by Igor Stravinsky. London and New York, Boosey & Hawkes, 1964.

With Chester Kallman, *Arcifanfarlo, King of Fools; or, It's Always Too Late to Learn,* music by Dittersdorf (adaptation of libretto by Goldoni; produced New York, 1965).

The Twelve: Anthem for the Feast Day of Any Apostle, music by William Walton. Oxford, Oxford University Press, 1966.

With Chester Kallman, *The Bassarids,* music by Hans Werner Henze (based on *The Bacchae* by Euripides; produced as *Die Bassariden* at Salzburg Festival, Austria, 1966; in English, Santa Fe, New Mexico, 1966). Mainz, B. Schotts Söhne, 1966.

Moralities: Three Scenic Plays from Fables by Aesop, music by Hans Werner Henze. Mainz, B. Schotts Söhne, 1969.

The Ballad of Barnaby, music by students of Wykeham Rise School under the direction of Charles Turner (narrative adaptation of Anatole France's version of *Our Lady's Juggler;* performed Washington, Connecticut, 1969; New York, 1970).

With Chester Kallman, *Love's Labour's Lost,* music by Nicholas Nabokov (adaptation of play by William Shakespeare; produced at 25th Edinburgh International Festival, Scotland, 1971). Berlin, Boat & Bock, 1972.

With Chester Kallman, *The Entertainment of the Senses,* music by John Gardner (produced London, 1974). Included in *Thank You, Fog,* 1974.

Paul Bunyan, music by Benjamin Britten (produced New York, 1941; Aldeburgh, Suffolk, 1976). London, Faber, 1976.

With Chester Kallman, *The Rise and Fall of the City of Mahagonny* (adaptation of opera by Bertholt Brecht). Boston, Godine, 1976.

Contributor

I Believe, edited by Clifton Fadiman. Simon & Schuster, 1939; revised, G. Allen, 1941.

Modern Canterbury Pilgrims and Why They Chose the Episcopal Church, edited by James A. Pike. New York, Morehouse–Goreham, 1956.

Religious Drama, Volume 1, edited by Marvin Halvorsen. Peter Smith, 1957.

Memories and Commentaries by Igor Stravinsky (letters). London, Faber, 1960.

The Seven Deadly Sins, compiled by Raymond Mortimer. Sunday Times Publications, 1962.

English and Medieval Studies, edited by Norman Davis and C. C. Wrenn (tribute to J. R. R. Tolkien). Allen & Unwin, 1962.

The Contemporary Poet as Artist and Critic, edited by A. Ostroff. Boston, Little, Brown, 1964.

Poems by W. H. Auden and Others, edited by Eric W. White. Poetry Book Society, 1966.

Word in the Desert, edited by C. B. Cox and A. E. Dyson. Oxford, Oxford University Press, 1968.

Democracy and the Student Left, edited by G. F. Kennan. Boston, Little, Brown, 1968.

Editor

With Charles Plumb, *Oxford Poetry 1926.* Oxford, Blackwell, 1926.

With C. Day Lewis, *Oxford Poetry 1927.* Oxford, Blackwell, 1927.

With John Garrett, *The Poet's Tongue: An Anthology* (two volumes). London, G. Bell, 1935.

With Arthur Elton, *Mechanics.* Longmans, Green, 1936.

The Oxford Book of Light Verse. Oxford, Clarendon Press, 1938.

A Selection from the Poems of Alfred, Lord Tennyson. Garden City, New York, Doubleday, 1944; as *Tennyson: An Introduction and a Selection,* London, Phoenix House, 1946.

The American Scene, Together with Three Essays from "Portraits of Places" by Henry James. New York, Scribner, 1946.

Slick but Not Streamlined: Poems and Short Pieces by John Betjeman. Garden City, New York, Doubleday, 1947.

Intimate Journals by Charles Baudelaire, translation by Christopher Isherwood. Hollywood, Marcel Rodd, 1947.

The Portable Greek Reader. New York, Viking, 1948.

Selected Prose and Poetry of E. A. Poe. New York, Rinehart, 1950.

With Norman Holmes Pearson, *Poets of the English Language,* Volume 1: *Medieval and Renaissance Poets: Langland to Spenser;* Volume 2: *Elizabethan and Jacobean Poets: Marlowe to Marvell;* Volume 3: *Restoration and Augustan Poets: Milton to Goldsmith;* Volume 4: *Romantic Poets: Blake to Poe;* Volume 5: *Victorian and Edwardian Poets: Tennyson to Yeats.* New York, Viking, 1950, London, Eyre & Spottiswoode, 1952.

With Marianne Moore and Karl Shapiro, *Riverside Poetry 1953: Poems by Students in Colleges and Universities in New York City.* New York, Association Press, 1953.

With Chester Kallman and Noah Greenberg, *An Elizabethan Song Book: Lute Songs, Madrigals, and Rounds.* Garden City, New York, Doubleday, 1955; London, Faber, 1957; as *An Anthology of Elizabethan Lute Songs, Madrigals, and Rounds,* New York, Norton, 1970.

Selected Writings of Sydney Smith. New York, Farrar, Straus, 1956; London, Faber, 1957.

The Criterion Book of Modern American Verse. New York, Criterion, 1956; as *The Faber Book of Modern American Verse,* London, Faber, 1956.

Van Gogh: A Self Portrait (selected letters), Greenwich, Connecticut, New York Graphic Society, and London, Thames & Hudson, 1961.

The Pied Piper, and Other Fairy Tales by Joseph Jacobs. New York, Macmillan, 1963.

With Louis Kronenberger, *The Viking Book of Aphorisms: A Personal Selection.* New York, Viking, 1963; as *The Faber Book of Aphorisms,* London, Faber, 1964.

A Choice of de la Mare's Verse by Walter de la Mare. London, Faber, 1963.

Selected Poems by Louis MacNeice. London, Faber, 1964.

Nineteenth Century British Minor Poets. New York, Delacorte, 1966; as *Nineteenth Century Minor Poets,* London, Faber, 1967.

With John Lawlor, *To Nevill Coghill from Friends.* London, Faber, 1966.

Selected Poetry and Prose of Byron. New York, New American Library, 1966; London, New English Library, 1967.

Persons from Porlock, and Other Plays for Radio by Louis MacNeice. BBC Productions, 1969.

G. K. Chesterton: A Selection from His Non–Fiction Prose. London, Faber, 1970.

A Choice of Dryden's Verse. London, Faber, 1973.

George Herbert. London, Penguin, 1973.

Selected Songs of Thomas Campion. London, Bodley Head, 1974.

Editor ("Yale Younger Poets" Series)

Poems by Joan Murray. New Haven, Yale University Press, 1947.

A Beginning by Robert Horan. New Haven, Yale University Press, 1948.

The Grasshopper's Man by Rosalie Moore. New Haven, Yale University Press, 1949.

A Change of World by Adrienne Rich. New Haven, Yale University Press, 1951.

A Mask for Janus by W. S. Merwin. New Haven, Yale University Press, 1952.

Various Jangling Keys by Edgar Bogardus. New Haven, Yale University Press, 1953.

An Armada of Thirty Whales by Daniel G. Hoffmann. New Haven, Yale University Press, 1954.

Some Trees by John Ashbery. New Haven, Yale University Press, 1956.

The Green Wall by James Wright. New Haven, Yale University Press, 1957.

A Crackling of Thorns by John Hollander. New Haven, Yale University Press, 1958.

Of the Festivity by William Dickey. New Haven, Yale University Press, 1959.

Translator

With others, *Adam Mickiewicz, 1798–1855: Selected Poems.* Noonday Press, 1956.

With James and Tania Stern, *The Caucasian Chalk Circle* by Bertholt Brecht. Published in *Bertholt Brecht Plays,* Volume 1, London, Methuen, 1960.

"On Poetry," in *Two Addresses* by St. John Perse (pseudonym of Alexis Saint–Leger Leger). New York, Viking Press, 1961.

With others, *The Great Operas of Mozart.* Grossett, 1962.

With Elizabeth Mayer, *Italian Journey 1786–1788* by Johann Wolfgang von Goethe. London, Collins, and New York, Pantheon, 1962.

With Leif Sjöberg, *Markings* by Dag Hammarskjöld. New York, Knopf, and London, Faber, 1964.

With others, *Antiworlds* by Andrei Voznesenski. New York, Basic Books, 1966; bilingual edition with additional works by Voznesenski as *Antiworlds, and the Fifth Ace,* New York, Basic Books, 1967.

With Paul B. Taylor, *Völuspá: The Song of the Sybil,* with an Icelandic text edited by Peter H. Salus and Paul B. Taylor. Iowa City, Windhover Press, 1968.

With Paul B. Taylor, *The Elder Edda: A Selection* by Edda Saemundar. London, Faber, and New York, Random House, 1969.

Collected Poems by St. John Perse (pseudonym of Alexis Saint–Leger Leger). Princeton, New Jersey, Princeton University Press, 1971.

With Leif Sjöberg, *Selected Poems* by Gunnar Ekelöf. New York, Pantheon, 1972.

With Elizabeth Mayer and Louise Bogan, *The Sorrows of Young Werther, and Novella* by Johann Wolfgang von Goethe. New York, Random House, 1973.

With Leif Sjöberg, *Evening Land/Aftonland* by Pär Lagerkvist. Detroit, Michigan, Wayne State University Press, 1975.

With Paul B. Taylor, *Norse Poems.* London, Athlone Press, 1981.

Other

The English Auden: Poems, Essays, and Dramatic Writings, 1927– 1939, edited by Edward Mendelson. London, Faber, 1977; New York, Random House, 1978.

Complete Works of W. H. Auden. Princeton, New Jersey, Princeton University Press, 1989.

"The Map of All My Youth": Early Works, Friends, and Influences, edited by Katherine Bucknell and Nicholas Jenkins. New York, Oxford University Press, 1991.

Recordings: *Reading His Own Poems,* Harvard Vocarium, 1941; *Reading from His Works,* Caedmon, 1954; *Auden,* Argo, 1960; *Selected Poems,* Spoken Arts, 1968.

*

Manuscript Collections: Berg Collection at the New York Public Library; Humanities Research Center at the University of Texas, Austin; Bodleian Library, Oxford University; British Museum, London; Butler Library, Columbia University; Lockwood Memorial Library, State University of New York at Buffalo; and Swarthmore College Library.

Biography: *W. H. Auden: The Life of a Poet* by Charles Osborne, New York, Harcourt, 1979, London, Eyre Methuen, 1980; *W. H. Auden: A Biography* by Humphrey W. Carpenter, London, Allen & Unwin, and Boston, Houghton, 1981; *Conversations with Auden* by Howard Griffin, edited by Donald Allen, San Francisco, Grey Fox Press, 1981; *Britten and Auden in the Thirties* by Donald Mitchell, Seattle, University of Washington Press, 1984; *The Poet*

Auden: A Personal Memoir by A. L. Rowse, New York, Weidenfeld & Nicolson, 1987.

Bibliography: *W. H. Auden: A Bibliography, 1924–1969* by B. C. Bloomfield and Edward Mendelson, Charlottesville, University Press of Virginia, 1972; *W. H. Auden: A Reference Guide* by Martin E. Gingerich, Boston, G. K. Hall, 1977.

Critical Sources: "The Airman, Politics and Psychoanalysis" by Stephen Spender, in his *The Destructive Element,* London, Cape, 1935, 251–277; *New Verse,* November 1937 (special Auden issue); *Lions and Shadows* by Christopher Isherwood, London, Hogarth, 1938; *Modern Poetry and the Tradition* by Cleanth Brooks, Chapel Hill, University of North Carolina Press, 1939, 125–135; "Virtue and Virtuosity: Notes on W. H. Auden" by Malcolm Cowley, in *Poetry,* January 1945, 202–209; *New Bearings in English Poetry* by F. R. Leavis, London, Chatto & Windus, 1950, 226–229; *World within World* by Stephen Spender, London, Hamilton, 1951; "The Theme of Political Orthodoxy in the Thirties" by Stephen Spender, in his *The Creative Element,* London, Hamilton, 1953, 140–158; *Predilections* by Marianne Moore, New York, Viking, 1955, 84–102; *The Thirties* by Julian Symons, London, Cresset, 1960; "Operas, Criticism, and Rites of Homage" by Monroe K. Spears, in his *The Poetry of W. H. Auden: The Disenchanted Island,* New York, Oxford University Press, 1963; *Shenandoah,* winter 1967 (special Auden issue); "Gazebos and Gashouses" by Richard Ellmann, in his *Eminent Domain,* New York, Oxford University Press, 1967, 97–126; "Auden and Isherwood" by Raymond Williams, in his *Drama from Ibsen to Brecht,* revised edition, London, Chatto & Windus, 1968, 199–206; "But He's a Homosexual ..." by Benjamin DeMott, in his *Supergrow: Essays and Reports on Imagination in America,* New York, 1969; *A Reader's Guide to W. H. Auden* by John Fuller, New York, Noonday, 1970; "Auden as a Literary Critic" by Cleanth Brooks, in his *A Shaping Joy: Studies in the Writer's Craft,* New York, Harcourt Brace, and London, Methuen, 1971; *W. H. Auden: A Tribute,* edited by Stephen Spender, New York, Macmillan, 1975; *The Auden Generation* by Samuel Hynes, New York, Viking, 1977; *Early Auden* by Edward Mendelson, New York, Viking, 1981; *Auden in Love* by Dorothy J. Farnan, New York, 1984; *W. H. Auden,* edited by Harold Bloom, New York, Chelsea House, 1986; *The Hidden Law: The Poetry of W. H. Auden* by Anthony Hecht, Cambridge, Massachusetts, 1993; "Rule Britten" (review of *Benjamin Britten* by Humphrey Carpenter) by George Steiner, in *New Yorker,* 5 July 1993, 86–89.

*   *   *

Most of the critical writing on the work of W. H. Auden—one of the greatest poets of the twentieth century—makes little or nothing of his homosexuality. In his writings Auden himself urged that his poetry be read without reference to his life, instructing his executors to call on holders of letters from him to destroy them. He did not pretend to be heterosexual; but in his insistence on the independence of poetry from the poet's life, which accorded with the generally accepted critical assumptions of his time, and in the general obliqueness or absence of personal references, he discouraged readers of his poems from making specific biographical identifications. Since his death in 1973, biographical material has made clear the importance of his sexuality and of his relationship with Chester

Kallman, matters that criticism still generally ignores.

Auden was born in York, England; his father was a doctor, his mother a nurse. He grew up in the industrial city of Birmingham, and was educated at Oxford University. His work was published and applauded when he was in his early twenties, and continually so for the next 40 years. In the 1930s the messages in his works seemed revolutionary, suggesting that a political revolution would also be a social, psychological, and sexual one. In 1939 Auden immigrated to New York, which henceforth became his primary residence. This move was soon followed by his reaffirmation of the Christian faith in which he was raised, a move thought by many admirers to be an apostasy, considering the radical and irreverent Marxist, Freudian, and Darwinian echoes of his brilliant early poetry. When Auden edited, retitled, omitted, and scrambled the order of his poems for his *Collected Poetry* of 1945, some critics saw an attempt at revising his radicalism out of, and his rediscovered Christianity into, his early work.

Since adolescence Auden had known he was homosexual; he had long led an active sexual life. Shortly after arriving in New York he fell in love with Chester Kallman, an aspiring poet who was then a student at Brooklyn College. Legally, Auden was married to Erika Mann, daughter of Thomas Mann, a formality arranged to provide her with a passport out of Nazi Germany, but he considered himself married to Kallman. Shortly after their "marriage," however, Kallman had an affair with another man. Auden felt profoundly betrayed, and indeed in the grasp of demonic forces both within himself and in the world, confirming the sense of evil forces being played out on the stage of history. This sense of the existence of psychological as well as historical evil played an important role in Auden's return to religion.

Despite the differences in the kind of commitment they made to each other, Auden and Kallman were closely associated for the rest of their lives (Kallman dying shortly after Auden). They lived together and collaborated on some projects (notably the libretto for Igor Stravinsky's opera, *The Rake's Progress*). Both, evidently, had active independent sexual lives, with Auden continuing to feel a particular emotional dedication to Kallman.

Themes and subjects directly related to homosexuality are not as such central to Auden's poetry. When homosexuality or Auden's love for a particular man is behind a given poem, either the gender is disguised or it is revealed indirectly—or the poem is left unpublished. Six very early poems have recently been published in *"The Map of All My Youth";* one of them, "Chorale," is quite explicit sexually. One is struck by a sense of loneliness in the poems, which are addressed to young men whom the speaker has paid for sex. They express a resigned realism, or in the case of "Chorale," a bouncy but less than totally convincing cheerfulness about sex. Auden presents homosexual subjects more explicitly than is the rule, but all are written in German (Auden was in Germany in 1928 and 1929), and they were left unpublished.

Most of Auden's love poems are androgynous in that the gender of neither lover nor beloved is revealed. In "'The Truest Poetry is the Most Feigning'" (its title comes from Shakespeare's *As You Like It*), Auden gives mock advice to a poet writing a love poem when a coup d'état occurs: keep writing, but identify it now as an ode to "the new pot–bellied Generalissimo." "Re–sex the pronouns," he wittily advises—and this is the advice he himself often followed.

The most famous of Auden's love poems was first published without a title (Auden's habit in the 1930s), and later as "Lullaby." It begins: "Lay your sleeping head, my love, / Human on my faithless arm." It was written to a man, but as the poet Anthony Hecht remarks in *The Hidden Law: the Poetry of W. H. Auden,* the poem is "decently screened as to gender." The most acute comment on the poem (and virtually the only interpretation of Auden's work that deals directly with his homosexuality) comes in an essay by Benjamin DeMott entitled "But He's a Homosexual...." DeMott argues that "the kind of knowledge this poem gives is more vivid in homosexual art than elsewhere" because the intelligent homosexual artist must constantly question things others can take for granted. According to DeMott, Auden was aware of deep truths about all love that were brought home with inescapable particularity to the homosexual artist.

An anecdote about another work underscores the ways in which a nongendered poem springing from a homosexual situation expresses vividly aspects of heterosexual love. In 1941, Auden published a volume including the long poem, "New Year Letter"; in America the volume was entitled *The Double Man,* after a sentence from Montaigne ("We are, I know not how, double in ourselves, so that what we believe we disbelieve, and cannot rid ourselves of what we condemn.") As Humphrey Carpenter notes in *W. H. Auden: A Biography,* Auden wrote in the copy he gave Kallman: "To Chester who knows both halves." The poem is concerned with many kinds of doubleness: the private and the public spheres of life, war and peace, faith and doubt, body and soul, Eros and Agape (i.e., physical and spiritual love), and so on. But the inscription can also mean that Kallman knows the full story of Auden's sexuality, and suggests that it made Auden particularly aware of doubleness in other spheres of life.

Auden wrote poems, some unpublished, that celebrate his love for Kallman, most notably "In Sickness and in Health," with its title from the Anglican marriage ceremony, and "Epithalamion," ostensibly written to celebrate the marriage of Erika Mann's sister. Once again, indirection governs. Androgynous or heterosexual language and form express an unrevealed homosexual commitment. Guardedness and disguise are the rule. Not long after Auden discovered Kallman's infidelity to him, he was at work on what became a part of his most overtly religious work, *For the Time Being: A Christmas Oratorio.* As Carpenter describes it, "The speaker in the poem is Saint Joseph, confronted by Mary's apparent sexual infidelity when she has conceived Jesus; but Auden privately admitted that the poem was also about his own betrayal by Chester. "Joseph," he told a friend, "is me." Words that could be applied to Joseph could be equally applied to—in fact originate in—the feelings of a betrayed gay lover. Auden's deep if improbable religious faith was theologically, fundamentally incarnational: connections between the divine and the human, the bodily and the spiritual, in Auden's view, lie at the heart of Christianity.

Auden published one piece of erotica—"The Platonic Blow"— during his lifetime in unauthorized editions, including *FagRag,* using his own name. Also published posthumously was a poem called "Glad," dated 1965 and addressed to a Viennese call–boy named Hugerl, which presents a list of reasons for gladness about their friendly, contractual relationship. Although acknowledging that "you were in need of money / And I wanted sex," the speaker is "glad that I know we enjoy / Mutual pleasure." Beneath the knowing tone is a sadness, one that appears as early as the previously mentioned poems written in German.

Auden was proud occasionally to have sneaked homosexual slang into his poems, and some poems, for example, "In Praise of Limestone," which Auden and others have considered one of his finest poems, have an aura of what Freud called the "polymorphous–perverse sexuality of childhood." What the limestone landscape

represents that it ostensibly celebrates is not made at all clear. Like other Auden poems, even when it seems explicit, it is full of riddles. Anthony Hecht states that "'Limestone' is undeniably a personal and in some ways an intimate poem, overtly bearing upon a private relationship [that] ... was not, for the most part, a happy one." Usually Auden is among the clearest and most articulate of poets. But as he approaches private relationships he often becomes playful, tantalizing, ambiguous—and here it seems to add to the poem.

Besides "In Sickness and In Health," Carpenter mentions "The Prophets" and "Not as That Dream Napoleon" as having been written to Kallman. Unpublished is a verse–letter to Kallman, dated Christmas Day 1941; it appears in Dorothy J. Farnan's *Auden in Love.* In a long prose–poem on the difficulty of writing love poetry, "*Dichtung und Wahrheit* (An Unwritten Poem)," Kallman, Hugerl, and one other lover can at times be identified, according to Carpenter (*Dichtung und Wahrheit* is also the title of Goethe's autobiography, and can be translated "poetry and truth"). It concludes: "This poem I wished to write was to have expressed exactly what I mean when I think the words *I love You,* but I cannot know exactly what I mean; it was to have been self–evidently true, but words cannot verify themselves." The distancing is playful and instructive, but also has the effect of disguising the relationships behind the poems.

Awareness of Auden's homosexuality and of the story of his love for Kallman sharpens our sensitivity to the hidden depths of Auden's self. Nothing like a full analysis of Auden—one that includes awareness of his homosexuality and puts it in proper relation to his poetry—has yet been done. To understand Auden more fully we will need to understand his homosexuality not only as an abstract quality and not only as a set of biographical facts but also in terms of a particular moment in history. In a 1993 review in the *New Yorker,* the critic George Steiner notes that "men like Auden ... came of sexual age at a time when homosexual practices were fraught with opprobrium and legal peril. Discretion, evasion, public mendacity were unavoidable.... Immediately below the level of seemingly 'normal' existence, particularly for public figures, bubble the grimy, dangerous, blackmail–ridden underworld of homosexual bars, steam baths, one–night hotels, and louche resorts. [The composer Benjamin] Britten and [his beloved, the tenor Peter] Pears, whose temperaments were less robust, less mockingly exhibitionist than Auden's persisted with almost unfailing control and courage in living, and in gradually making visible, their chosen lives." Auden's homosexuality is manifested in his sensitivity to certain aspects of love, in some of the games, riddles, indirections, "re–sexing" of pronouns, deflections, omissions, and rearrangements of his work. It is far more present implicitly than by direct reference, and it is only beginning to be understood. As Steiner's comment indicates, there are pains and oppressions connected with Auden's homosexuality that belong to a particular time and place, as well as degrees of "control and courage" that will take equally long to be recognized.

—*Richard Johnson*

B

BALDWIN, James (Arthur). American civil rights activist, novelist, short story writer, playwright, poet and essayist. Born 2 August 1924, in New York City. Educated at De Witt Clinton High School, New York City, 1942. Youth minister at Fireside Pentecostal Assembly, New York City, 1938–42; variously employed as a handyman, dishwasher, and waiter in New York City, and in defense work in Belle Meade, New Jersey, 1942–46. Lecturer on racial issues at universities in the United States and Europe, 1957–87. Director of play, *Fortune and Men's Eyes,* in Istanbul, Turkey, 1970, and film, *The Inheritance,* 1973. Contributor of book reviews and essays to periodicals, including *Harper's, Nation, Esquire, Playboy, Partisan Review, Mademoiselle,* and *New Yorker.* Member of Congress on Racial Equality national advisory board, American Academy and Institute of Arts and Letters, Authors League, International PEN, Dramatists Guild, Actors' Studio, National Committee for a Sane Nuclear Policy. **Recipient:** Eugene F. Saxton fellowship, 1945; Rosenwald fellowship, 1948; Guggenheim fellowship, 1954; National Institute of Arts and Letters grant for literature, 1956; Ford Foundation grant, 1959; National Conference of Christians and Jews Brotherhood Award, 1962, for *Nobody Knows My Name: More Notes of a Native Son;* George Polk Memorial Award, 1963, for magazine articles; Foreign Drama Critics Award, 1964, for *Blues for Mister Charlie;* D.Litt. from the University of British Columbia, Vancouver, 1964; National Association of Independent Schools Award, 1964, for *The Fire Next Time;* American Book Award nomination, 1980, for *Just above My Head;* named Commander of the Legion of Honor (France), 1986. *Died in St. Paul de Vence, France, of stomach cancer, 1 December 1987.*

WRITINGS

Novels

Go Tell It on the Mountain. New York, Knopf, 1953; London, Joseph, 1954.
Giovanni's Room. New York, Dial, 1956; London, Joseph, 1957.
Another Country. New York, Dial, 1962.
Tell Me How Long the Train's Been Gone. New York, Dial, and London, Joseph, 1968.
If Beale Street Could Talk. New York, Dial, and London, Joseph, 1974.
Just above My Head. New York, Dial, and London, Joseph, 1979.
Harlem Quartet, 1987.

Short Stories

Going to Meet the Man. New York, Dial, and London, Joseph, 1965.

Contributor, *American Negro Short Stories.* New York, Hill & Wang, 1966.
"Just Above My Head," in *The Faber Book of Gay Short Fiction,* edited by Edmund White. London and New York, Faber & Faber, 1991.

Plays

The Amen Corner (produced Washington, D.C., 1955; on Broadway, 1965). New York, Dial, 1968; London, Joseph, 1969.
Giovanni's Room (based on Baldwin's novel; produced New York, 1957).
Blues for Mister Charlie (produced on Broadway, 1964). New York, Dial, 1964; London, Joseph, 1965.
One Day, When I Was Lost: A Scenario (screenplay; based on *The Autobiography of Malcolm X* by Alex Haley). London, Joseph, 1972; New York, Dial, 1973.
A Deed for the King of Spain (produced New York, 1974).
The Welcome Table, 1987.

Nonfiction

Autobiographical Notes. New York, Knopf, 1953.
Notes of a Native Son. Boston, Beacon Press, 1955; London, Mayflower, 1958.
Nobody Knows My Name: More Notes of a Native Son. New York, Dial, 1961; London, Joseph, 1964.
The Fire Next Time. New York, Dial, and London, Joseph, 1963.
Nothing Personal, photographs by Richard Avedon. New York, Atheneum, and Harmondsworth, Penguin, 1964.
With others, *Black Anti–Semitism and Jewish Racism.* R. W. Baron, 1969.
With Kenneth Kaunda, *Menschenwuerde und Gerechtigkeit* (essays delivered at the fourth assembly of the World Council of Churches), edited by Carl Ordung. Union–Verlag, 1969.
With Margaret Mead, *A Rap on Race* (transcribed conversation). New York, Lippincott, and London, Joseph, 1971.
No Name in the Street (essays). New York, Dial, and London, Joseph, 1972.
With Françoise Giroud, *Cesar: Compressions d'or.* Hachette, 1973.
With Nikki Giovanni, *A Dialogue* (transcribed conversation). New York, Lippincott, 1973; London, Joseph, 1975.
The Devil Finds Work. New York, Dial, and London, Joseph, 1976.
With others, *Harlem, U.S.A.: The Story of a City within a City,* edited by John Henrik Clarke. Berlin, Seven Seas, 1976.
The Evidence of Things Not Seen. New York, Holt, 1985.
The Price of the Ticket: Collected Nonfiction, 1948–1985. New York, St. Martin's Press, 1985.
With others, *Perspectives: Angles on African Art,* edited by Michael J. Weber. Center for African Art, 1987.

Other

"Mass Culture and the Creative Artist: Some Personal Notes," in *Culture for the Millions,* Princeton, New Jersey, Van Nostrand, 1959.

Author of introduction, *To Be Young, Gifted, and Black* by Lorraine Hansberry. New York, NAL/Dutton, 1970.

With Yoran Cazac, *Little Man, Little Man: A Story of Childhood* (children's book). New York, Dial, and London, Joseph, 1976.

"In Search of a Basis for Mutual Understanding and Racial Harmony," in *The Nature of a Humane Society,* edited by H. Ober Hess. Philadelphia, Fortress, 1976–77.

Jimmy's Blues: Selected Poems. London, M. Joseph, 1983; New York, St. Martin's Press, 1985.

Author of introduction, *The Chasm: The Life and Death of a Great Experiment in Ghetto Education* by Robert Campbell. Westport, Connecticut, Greenwood Press, 1986.

Author of introduction, *Duties, Pleasures, and Conflicts: Essays in Struggle* by Michael Thelwell. Amherst, University of Massachusetts Press, 1987.

Conversations with James Baldwin, edited by Fred L. Standley and Louis H. Pratt. Jackson, University Press of Mississippi, 1989.

*

Adaptations: *The Amen Corner* was adapted as a musical stage play by Garry Sherman, Peter Udell and Philip Rose, and produced on Broadway, 1983; *Go Tell It on the Mountain* was dramatized on "American Playhouse," Public Broadcasting System, 1985.

Interviews: "The Negro in American Culture," in *Cross Currents,* summer 1961, 205–224; "Disturber of the Peace" by E. Auchincloss and N. Lynch, in *Mademoiselle,* May 1963, 174–175, 199–207; "At a Crucial Time a Negro Talks Tough: 'There's a Bill Due That Has to be Paid,'" in *Life,* 24 May 1963, 81–86A; "A Conversation with James Baldwin" by Kenneth B. Clark, in *Freedomways,* summer 1963, 361–368; "The American Dream and the American Negro" by William F. Buckley, Jr., in *New York Times Magazine,* 7 March 1965, 32–33, 87–89; "James Baldwin Breaks His Silence," in *Atlas,* March 1967, 47–49, "James Baldwin ... in Conversation" by Dan Georgakas, in *Black Voices: An Anthology of Afro–American Literature,* edited by Abraham Chapman, New York, New American Library, 1968, 660–668; "How Can We Get the Black People to Cool It?," in *Esquire,* July 1968, 49–53, 116; "It's Hard to Be James Baldwin" by Herbert R. Lottman, in *Intellectual Digest,* July 1972, 67–68; "Why I Left America" with Ida Lewis, in *New Black Voices,* edited by Abraham Chapman, New York, New American Library, 1972, 409–419; *Black Scholar,* December 1973–January 1974, 33–42; "James Baldwin Comes Home" by Jewell Hardy Gresham, in *Essence,* June 1976, 54–55, 80, 82, 85; "James Baldwin Writing and Talking" by Mel Watkins, in *New York Times Book Review,* 23 September 1979, 35–36; "James Baldwin: Looking towards the Eighties" by Kalamu ya Salaam, in *Black Collegian,* December/January 1980, 105–110; *Baldwin: Three Interviews* by Malcolm King, Wesleyan University Press, 1985; "Interview with James Baldwin" by David C. Estes, in *New Orleans Review,* fall 1986, 59–64.

Bibliography: *Black American Writers: Bibliographical Essays,*

Volume 2: *Richard Wright, Ralph Ellison, James Baldwin, and Amiri Baraka,* edited by M. Thomas Inge and others, New York, St. Martin's Press, 1978; *James Baldwin: A Reference Guide,* edited by Fred L. and Nancy V. Standley, Boston, G. K. Hall, 1981; *Contemporary Authors Bibliographical Series,* Volume 1: *American Novelists,* Detroit, Gale, 1986.

Critical Sources: *Saturday Review,* 1 December 1956; *Saturday Review,* 1 July 1961; *Saturday Review,* 7 July 1962; *The Creative Present: Notes on Contemporary Fiction,* edited by Nona Balakian and Charles Simmons, Garden City, New York, Doubleday, 1963; *A World More Attractive: A View of Modern Literature and Politics* by Irving Howe, Horizon Press, 1963; *Saturday Review,* 2 February 1963; *Encounter,* August 1963; *Partisan Review,* summer 1963; *After Alienation: American Novels in Mid–Century* by Marcus Klein, World Publishing, 1964; *Contemporary American Novelists,* edited by Harry T. Moore, Southern Illinois University Press, 1964; *Doings and Undoings* by Norman Podhoretz, New York, Farrar, Straus, 1964; *Saturday Review,* 2 May 1964; *The Negro Novel in America* by Robert Bone, New Haven, Yale University Press, 1965; *Seasons of Discontent: Dramatic Opinions, 1959–1965* by Robert Brustein, New York, Simon & Schuster, 1965; *Encounter,* July 1965; *Saturday Review,* 6 November 1965; *New York Times Book Review,* 12 December 1965; *The Furious Passage of James Baldwin* by Fern Marja Eckman, New York, Evans, 1966; *Black on White: A Critical Survey of Writing by American Negroes* by David Littlejohn, New York, Viking, 1966; *Black Voices: An Anthology of Afro–American Literature,* edited by Abraham Chapman, New York, New American Library, 1968; *Soul on Ice* by Eldridge Cleaver, New York, McGraw–Hill, 1968; *Saturday Review,* 1 June 1968; *New York Times Book Review,* 2 June 1968; *Afro–American Writers* by Darwin T. Turner, Appleton, 1970; *The Americans* by David Frost, Stein & Day, 1970; *Modern Black Novelists: A Collection of Critical Essays,* edited by M. G. Cook, Englewood Cliffs, New Jersey, Prentice–Hall, 1971; *The Morning After* by Wilfrid Sheed, Farrar, Straus, 1971; *The Politics of Twentieth–Century Novelists* by George A. Panichas, Hawthorn, 1971; *James Baldwin: A Critical Study* by Stanley Macebuh, New York, Third Press, 1973; *James Baldwin: A Collection of Critical Essays,* edited by Kenneth Kinnamon, Englewood Cliffs, New Jersey, Prentice–Hall, 1974; *Black Fiction* by Roger Rosenblatt, Boston, Harvard University Press, 1974; *The Dark and Feeling: Black American Writers and Their Work* by Clarence Major, Joseph Okpaku, 1974; *The Theme of Identity in the Essays of James Baldwin* by Karin Moeller, Acta Universitatis Gotoburgensis, 1975; *The Nature of a Humane Society,* edited by H. Ober Hesse, Fortress, 1976; *New York Times Book Review,* 2 May 1976; *James Baldwin: A Critical Evaluation,* edited by Therman B. O'Daniel, Washington, Howard University Press, 1977; *Squaring Off: Mailer vs. Baldwin* by W. J. Weatherby, New York, Mason/Charter, 1977; *Washington Post,* 23 September 1979; *Washington Post,* 15 October 1979; *James Baldwin* by Carolyn Wedin Sylvander, New York, Ungar, 1980; *Saturday Review,* 5 January 1980; *Critical Essays on James Baldwin,* edited by Fred L. Standley and Nancy V. Burt, Boston, G. K. Hall, 1981; *Washington Post,* 9 September 1983; *Washington Post,* 25 September 1983; *Concise Dictionary of American Literary Biography: The New Consciousness, 1941–1968,* Detroit, Gale, 1987; *Dictionary of Literary Biography Yearbook: 1987,* Detroit, Gale, 1988; "On James Baldwin (1924–1987)" by Darryl Pinckney, in *New York Review of Books,* 21 January 1988, 8, 10; "A Memory of James Baldwin" by Mary McCarthy, in *New York Review of Books,* 27 April 1989, 48–49;

Washington Post, 14 August 1989; "Critical Deviance: Homophobia and the Reception of James Baldwin's Fiction" by Emmanuel Nelson, in *Journal of American Culture,* fall 1991, 91; *The Gay Novel in America,* by James Levin, New York, Garland, 1991, 143–45, 302; "James Baldwin" by Emmanuel S. Nelson, in *Contemporary Gay American Novelists,* Westport, Connecticut, Greenwood Press, 1993, 6–24.

*   *   *

Renowned novelist and essayist James Baldwin bore articulate witness to the unhappy consequences of American racial strife. His writing career began in the last years of legislated segregation; his fame as a social observer grew in tandem with the civil rights movement as he mirrored the aspirations, disappointments, and coping strategies of blacks in a hostile society. In the novels, plays, and essays he wrote during the turbulent decades of the 1950s and 1960s, Baldwin explored the psychological implications of racism for both the oppressed and the oppressor. Works such as *Notes of a Native Son* and *Nobody Knows My Name* acquainted wide audiences with his highly personal observations and his sense of urgency in the face of rising black unrest.

Baldwin's own story is as compelling as that of the characters he created within his novels. The oldest of nine children, he was raised in Harlem by his stepfather, an evangelical preacher who struggled to support a large family from whom he demanded excessively rigorous religious behavior. As a youth, Baldwin found time away from caring for his younger siblings to read and write; he was an excellent student who sought escape from the increased abusiveness of his stepfather through literature, movies, and the theatre. At the age of 14, he underwent a dramatic religious conversion. Partly in response to his nascent sexuality and partly as a further buffer against the ever–present temptations of drugs and crime, Baldwin began a junior ministry at the Fireside Pentecostal Assembly. After three years, however he lost the desire to preach as he began to question blacks' acceptance of the Christian tenets that had, in his estimation, been used to enslave them.

After graduating from high school in 1942, Baldwin took a job at a railroad site in nearby New Jersey in order to help support his family; mental instability had incapacitated his stepfather. There he was confronted daily with racism, discrimination, and the debilitating regulations of segregation—following his stepfather's death in 1946, Baldwin determined to make writing his sole profession. Tired of grappling with the overt racism then prevalent in New York City, as well as with the growing awareness of his own homosexuality, he began to find the social tenor of the United States increasingly stifling. Despite the fact that such prestigious periodicals as the *Nation, New Leader,* and *Commentary* had begun to accept his essays and short stories for publication, in 1948, at the age of 24, Baldwin moved to Paris. He would live in France, on and off, for the remainder of his life.

"Once I found myself on the other side of the ocean," Baldwin told the *New York Times,* "I could see where I came from very clearly, and I could see that I carried myself, which is my home, with me. You can never escape that. I am the grandson of a slave, and I am a writer. I must deal with both." Through some difficult financial and emotional periods, Baldwin undertook a process of self–realization that included both an acceptance of his heritage and an admittance of his bisexuality. Europe gave the young author many things: a broader perspective from which to view his own identity, the love affair with Lucien Happersberger that would dominate his later fiction, and a burst of creative energy. A wealth of essays were written, beginning with 1953's *Autobiographical Notes.* Concurrently published were novels such as *Go Tell It on the Mountain* and the play *The Amen Corner,* the first of Baldwin's works to freely explore both race and sexuality.

Many critics view Baldwin's nonfiction as his most significant contribution to American literature. His essays probed beyond problems of white versus black, uncovering the essential issues of personal identity and self–determination. But racial unrest was not the only topic of controversy that Baldwin addressed through his writing. In fictional works such as *Go Tell It on the Mountain* and 1956's *Giovanni's Room,* his bold introduction of homosexual themes provided Baldwin with another vehicle for the exploration of prejudice. "By insisting on honest explorations of gay and bisexual themes in his novels," notes Emmanuel S. Nelson in *Contemporary Gay American Novelists,* "Baldwin made a sharp break from the African–American literary conventions; through a radical departure from tradition, he helped create the space for a generation of young African–American gay writers who succeeded him. Long before the Stonewall Riots of 1969 helped liberate the gay literary imagination in the United States, Baldwin boldly made his sexuality a vital part of the vision he projected in his art. He was, in the finest sense of the work, a revolutionary."

Because Baldwin's fiction contains interracial love affairs—both homosexual and heterosexual—he came under attack from the writers of the Black Arts Movement who called for a literature exclusively by and for blacks. Eldridge Cleaver, in his book *Soul on Ice,* accused Baldwin of a hatred of blacks and "a shameful, fanatical fawning" love of whites. Baldwin refused to be pigeonholed by reverse racism—he referred to himself as an "American writer" as opposed to a "black writer" and continued to confront the issues facing a multi–racial society. What Cleaver and others saw as complicity with whites, Baldwin defended as his personal attempt to alter the violent and oppressive environment faced by minorities. The masked homophobia of the Black Arts Movement found its reflection in the mainstream media's critical response to much of Baldwin's fiction: sometimes a reviewer's response was a violent denunciation of a work's homosexual theme, but more often such themes were discreetly overlooked and responded to with silence. As Nelson asserts: "[The critics'] silence is not merely a result of blindness but a carefully defined political posture. It is a strategy of enforcing invisibility; it is a way of denying the significance of Baldwin's sexual identity and the gay content of his work."

It was Baldwin's stature as a champion of the black cause that enabled him to weather such cool and evasive critical reception. As James Levin notes in *The Gay Novel in America,* "Baldwin could write about homosexuality because his literary reputation had been confirmed and because those who wished to support him as a black writer refrained from attacking him on what seemed to be an extraneous or possibly detrimental issue." His fiction continued to explore the "full weight and complexity" of the individual in a society prone to callousness and categorization; love, both sexual and spiritual, continued to be the essential component of Baldwin's characters' quests for self–realization. John W. Aldridge observes in the *Saturday Review* that sexual love "emerges in his novels as a kind of universal anodyne for the disease of racial separatism, as a means not only of achieving personal identity but also of transcending false categories of color and gender." Homosexual encounters were, for Baldwin, a principal means to achieve important revelations.

Typically, some reviewers chose to see Baldwin's use of gay protagonists in this manner as merely a literary device: a human being whose acceptance of his own deviant nature made him uniquely capable of giving love unconditionally.

Baldwin died in 1987, a victim of cancer. The publication of his collected essays, *The Price of the Ticket: Collected Nonfiction, 1948–1985,* and his subsequent death sparked reassessments of his career and comments on the quality of his lasting legacy. In a posthumous profile for the *Washington Post,* Juan Williams wrote: "The success of Baldwin's effort as the witness is evidenced time and again by the people, black and white, gay and straight, famous and anonymous, whose humanity he unveiled in his writings. America and the literary world are far richer for his witness. The proof of a shared humanity across the divides of race, class and more is the testament that the preacher's son, James Arthur Baldwin, has left us."

—*Pamela S. Shelton*

————

BANNON, Ann. American novelist. Born Ann Weldy in Joliet, Illinois, 15 September 1932; took stepfather's name, Thayer. Educated at Hinsdale High School, Hinsdale, Illinois; University of Illinois, Champaign–Urbana (Phi Beta Kappa), B.A. 1954; California State University, Sacramento, M.A. 1969; Stanford University, Palo Alto, California, Ph.D. 1975. Has lived in California since 1957; currently lives in Sacramento. Professor of Linguistics, Department of English, Associate Dean, School of Arts and Sciences, California State University. Address: c/o Naiad Press, P.O. Box 10543, Tallahassee, Florida 32302, U.S.A.

WRITINGS

Novels

Odd Girl Out. Greenwich, Connecticut, Fawcett, 1957; reissued, Tallahassee, Naiad Press, 1983.
I Am a Woman. Greenwich, Connecticut, Fawcett, 1959; reissued, Tallahassee, Naiad Press, 1983.
Women in the Shadows. Greenwich, Connecticut, Fawcett, 1959; reissued, Tallahassee, Naiad Press, 1983.
Journey to a Woman. Greenwich, Connecticut, Fawcett, 1960; reissued, Tallahassee, Naiad Press, 1983.
Beebo Brinker. Greenwich, Connecticut, Fawcett, 1962; reissued, Tallahassee, Naiad Press, 1983.

*

Critical Sources: "When Jack Blinks: Si(gh)ting Gay Desire in Beebo Brinker" by Ma Barale, in *Feminist Studies,* fall 1992.

Ann Bannon comments: "It is a wonderful thing to want to tell stories and discover that others want to hear them; that a whole universe of interested, eager, and wholly neglected readers is waiting to hear from you. I have had that experience—when my tales of women in love with each other were first published in the late 1950s and early 1960s—and it changed my life. I doubt that I knew much more about lesbian history and culture when I began writing than did my ingenuous readers; to think that as I learned and grew, in a small way I may have helped shape their lives and perceptions of themselves, touches me deeply. I, like many readers, fell in love with one of my characters, and because of her, the books became known as the 'Beebo Brinker' series.

"After the first years of intense interest in the original Gold Medal editions, and the international translations that followed, the books seemed to fade from the consciousness of a new generation of lesbians. They were caught up with the great battles of the civil rights era and the rise of the women's movement and were looking to the future. It took the farsightedness, the drive to save the wisdom and love of the past that characterize the publishers of Naiad Press, to rescue the books from neglect. I became one of the authors whose early works they have sought out and reissued. I will always be grateful to Barbara Grier and Donna McBride, founders of Naiad, for the care they lavished on the new editions of the 1980s. Their effort gave voice to the women of an earlier era and recaptured a part of our shared history. I am proud to have been a part of it."

*   *   *

Ann Bannon is one of only a very few women who have written about being lesbian during the 1950s and 1960s in the United States. Her novels, all issued originally as paperbacks (or "pulps") with ongoing characters, reflect the repressiveness of those decades and reveal how much still needs to change. Bannon presents all the constraints, both overt (i.e. anti–gay laws) and covert, that gays endured in the 1950s: the fear of sharing one's personal life with one's coworkers, friends, or even family because it could mean losing everything; and if the police were called, there was always the risk of being thrown in jail. But Bannon also shows the gay community, with its bars, businesses, and neighborhoods, especially the bohemian Greenwich Village.

Bannon's characters reveal the duality that was, of necessity, part of gay life; many are filled with self–loathing and speak of not being "normal" and of being unable to have a long–term loving relationships. Two of Bannon's ongoing characters, Laura Landon and Jack Mann, marry—not for love or sex, but for security. Mann is a 40–something gay male who is no longer attractive to the young men he desires; and Landon finds herself in and out of love with a variety of women—including straight women and a lesbian of color—or in an oppressive relationship with Beebo Brinker (who is, perhaps, Bannon's most memorable character). Mann and Landon run away from the gay community and, more importantly, from themselves in an effort to become "happy and normal" as a straight couple in suburbia.

—*Pamela Bigelow*

BARNES, Djuna. American journalist and free lance illustrator. Also wrote as Lydia Steptoe. Born in Cornwall–on–Hudson, New York, 12 January 1892. Educated at Pratt Institute and Art Students' League. Married Courtenay Lemon in 1917 (divorced 1919). Trustee, Dag Hammarsköld Foundation, beginning 1961. Contributor to numerous journals, sometimes under pseudonym Lydia Steptoe, including *Vanity Fair, Town and Country,* and *New Yorker.* **Recipient:** National Endowment for the Arts senior fellowship, 1981; membership in the National Institute of Arts and Letters. *Died in New York City, 19 June 1982.*

WRITINGS

Novels

Ryder. London, Boni & Liveright, 1928.
Nightwood. London, Faber, 1936; New York, Harcourt, 1937.

Short Stories

Vagaries Malicieux: Two Stories. Frank Hallman, 1974.
Smoke, and Other Early Stories. Los Angeles, Sun and Moon Press, 1983.

Plays

Three from the Earth (produced New York, 1919). Included in *A Book,* 1928.
Kurzy of the Sea (produced New York, 1919). Included in *A Book,* 1928.
An Irish Triangle (produced New York, 1919). Included in *A Book,* 1928.
The Dove (produced Northhampton, New York, 1926). Included in *A Book,* 1928.
A Book. London, Boni and Liveright, 1928; as *A Night among Horses,* Boni and Liveright, 1929; as *Spillway,* London, Faber, 1962.
The Antiphon (produced Stockholm, 1961). New York, Farrar, Straus, 1958. Included in *Selected Works: Spillway, The Antiphon, Nightwood,* 1962.

Poetry

Creatures in an Alphabet. New York, Dial, 1983.

Essays

Greenwich Village as It Is, edited by Robert A. Wilson. Phoenix Book Shop, 1978.
New York, edited by Alyce Barry. Los Angeles, Sun and Moon Press, 1989.

Other

The Book of Repulsive Women: 8 Rhythms and 5 Drawings. Bruno Chap Books, 1915.
Ladies Almanack: Showing Their Signs and Their Tides; Their Moons and Their Changes; the Seasons, as It Is with Them; Their Eclipses and Equinoxes; as Well as a Full Record of Diurnal and Nocturnal Distempers. Privately printed, 1928.

Selected Works: Spillway, The Antiphon, Nightwood. New York, Farrar, Straus, 1962; as *Selected Works of Djuna Barnes: Spillway, The Antiphon, Nightwood,* New York, Farrar, Straus, 1980.
Interviews, edited by Alyce Barry. Los Angeles, Sun & Moon Press, 1985.
I Could Never Be Lonely without a Husband, edited by Alyce Barry. London, Virago, 1987.

*

Biography: *Djuna: The Life of Djuna Barnes* by A. Field, New York, Putnam, 1983; *Djuna Barnes, 1978–1981: An Informal Memoir* by Hank O' Neal, Santa Rosa, California, Paragon Press, 1990.

Critical Sources: "Introduction," *Nightwood* by T. S. Eliot, New York, New Directions, 1937; *The Widening Gyre: Crisis and Mastery in Modern Literature* by Joseph Frank, Bloomington, Indiana University Press, 1963; *Djuna: The Formidable Miss Barnes* by Andrew Field, Austin, University of Texas Press, 1985; *Women of the Left Bank: Paris, 1900–1940* by Shari Benstock, Austin, University of Texas Press, 1986; "The Outsider among the Expatriates: Djuna Barnes' Satire on the Ladies of the *Almanack*" by Karla Jay, in *Silence and Power: A Reevaluation of Djuna Barnes,* edited by Mary Lynn Broe, Carbondale, Southern Illinois University Press, 1991.

*   *   *

After nearly two decades of publishing poetry, fiction, and drawings, Djuna Barnes published her landmark novel in 1936. Both the form and the content of *Nightwood* were informed by her years, first among the bohemian writers in Greenwich Village and, after 1920, among the expatriate artists living in Paris. Barnes and many of her peers, including James Joyce, Gertrude Stein, and Ezra Pound, have made the period famous for their radical experimentation with language and literary convention. The expatriate community also offered an open–mindedness about sexuality unavailable in the United States; a large number of the women publicly identified as lesbian or bisexual, and many of the men were gay.

Nightwood, The Book of Repulsive Women, and *The Ladies Almanack* all deal more or less directly with lesbianism. *The Book of Repulsive Women,* published in a small edition in the Village in 1915, consisted of a series of poems and drawings about the female body and female sexuality; in his biography of Barnes, Andrew Field claims that "*The Book of Repulsive Women,* a full decade before Radclyffe Hall's *The Well of Loneliness,* was the first modern literary work in English to bring the theme of woman's 'bitter secret' ... to the misty fore." Field suggests that the chapbook was ignored by censors, at a time when much more discreet texts were being cut, because of "images so bold for their time that they could not even be recognized for the purposes of suppression." *The Ladies Almanack,* another small edition published 13 years later in Paris, followed the bawdy lead of *Repulsive Women.* An experimental text that falls somewhere between a long poem and a parody of an Elizabethan almanac of the seasons, it has generally been read as a playful commemoration of the women who regularly attended Natalie Barney's Paris salon. Each of the women were artists and intellectuals, most were lesbian or bisexual, and the Almanack makes no effort to hide this.

Previous to the publication of *Nightwood,* Barnes had one other major critical success with *Ryder,* published in 1928, which briefly enjoyed best–seller status in the United States. Barnes wrote the text, a series of highly experimental vignettes chronicling the history of the Ryder family, in a mock Elizabethan prose not unlike the style of the Almanack. Field has documented the extent to which Barnes' fiction follows her own family's history, and he claims that, in general, family history constitutes the main ingredient of Barnes' work. He also presents considerable evidence that *Nightwood* is based on Barnes' long and tormented relationship with Thelma Wood, an American sculptor; he consequently reads the novel as an attempt to describe and exorcise that experience; his assertion brings into focus the three main currents of Barnes' criticism and their conflicts with one another. While many critics have looked closely at Barnes' work against the backdrop of her life, the major trend has followed the lead of T.S. Eliot and Joseph Frank— a purely stylistic analysis of her experiments with language that dismisses both personal experience and social content.

In *Women of the Left Bank: Paris, 1900–1940,* Shari Benstock notes that "Barnes was considered to be the most important woman writer of the Paris community, her work generally thought to be second only to that of Joyce, with whom she shared certain literary methods." T.S. Eliot, the American poet renowned for *The Waste Land,* gave *Nightwood* his influential blessing in the form of a highly complimentary introduction. Joseph Frank sanctioned the novel's academic reputation in the 1960s when he praised "the maturity of achievement so conspicuous in every line of this work" in *The Widening Gyre;* in this landmark study of modernist form, Frank placed Barnes' work among the highly regarded texts of Marcel Proust, Joyce, and Flaubert. His attention contributed to the general interest in modernism that blossomed in the 1960s and 1970s.

It is possible, however, that important critics of style like Eliot and Frank proclaimed the value of Barnes' work at the expense of valuing the presence of challenging social critiques in her fiction. Frank manages to discuss *Nightwood* at length without naming Barnes' lesbianism or the lesbian relationship of her characters even once. Although the central narrator, Dr. Matthew O'Connor, is quite explicitly a gay male transvestite, Frank succeeds in only briefly mentioning the doctor's "homosexual inclinations." Consequently, despite a steady history of serious interest among scholars, only the recent emergence of feminist theory and gay and lesbian studies has made it possible to discuss the significance of sexuality in Barnes' work.

Benstock has contributed considerably to both the critique of previous criticism and the recuperation of Barnes' social insights. She argues that "until recently, [Barnes'] work has been placed against the Modernist tradition, where it has suffered a neglectful misreading.... [A] focus on the 'style' rather than 'substance' of these works allowed critics to mask their own ideological and political biases." In place of this formalist approach, she offers the feminist argument that "all of Djuna Barnes' writing can be read as a critique of woman's place in Western Society." As Field claims, *Ryder* is motivated by Barnes' own unusual family history, but this history is largely about women who have to negotiate their economic and sexual circumstances in relation to one man's over-

abundance of power. Even where gay subject matter does not appear in a text, Barnes always examines the social position of women in a masculine and heterosexual world.

—*Ondine E. Le Blanc*

———

BARNEY, Natalie (Clifford). French translator, poet, novelist, playwright, essayist, memoirist, and patron of the arts. Also wrote as Tryphé. Born in Dayton, Ohio, 31 October 1876. Educated at a boarding school in Fontainebleau, and at Miss Ely's School for Girls, New York. Independently wealthy after her father's death in 1902; from 1910 hosted an international literary *salon* in Paris that included Ezra Pound, Anatole France, Rémy de Gourmont, Marcel Proust, and Ranier Maria Rilke. *Died in Paris, 2 February 1972.*

WRITINGS

Memoirs

Aventures de l'esprit. Paris, Emile Paul, 1929; excerpts included in *Un panier de Framboises,* 1979; translated and annotated by John Spaulding Gatton as *Adventures of the Mind,* introduction by Karla Jay, New York, New York University Press, 1992.
Nouvelles Pensées de l'Amazone. Paris, Mercure de France, 1939.
Souvenirs indiscrets. Paris, Flammarion, 1960.
Traits et portraits. Paris, Mercure de France, 1963; New York, Arno Press, 1975.

Letters

With Pierre Louys and Renée Vivien, *Correspondances croisées: Suivies de deux lettres inedites de Renée Vivien à Natalie Barney et de divers documents* (letters and poems), edited and annotated by Jean–Paul Goujon. Muizon, Editions à L'Écart, 1983.
With Renée Vivien and Eva Palmer, *Album secret,* edited and annotated by Jean–Paul Goujon. Muizon, Editions à L'Écart, 1984.

Other

Quelques Portraits—Sonnets de Femmes, illustrations by Alice Pike Barney. Paris, Société d'Editions littéraires, 1900.
Cinq petits Dialogues grecs (as Tryphé). Paris, La Plume, 1902.
Actes et entr'actes. Paris, Sansot, 1910.
Pensées d'une Amazone (epigrams). Paris, Emile Paul, 1920; excerpts included in *Un panier de Framboises,* 1979.
The One Who Is Legion; or, A.D.'s After–Life, illustrations by Romaine Brooks. London, Partridge, 1930.
Selected Writings, edited and with an introduction by Miron Grindea. London, Adam, 1963.
Un panier de Framboises (excerpts). Paris, Mercure de France, 1979.

A Perilous Advantage: The Best of Natalie Clifford Barney, edited and translated by Anna Livia, introduction by Karla Jay. Norwich, Vermont, New Victoria, 1992.

*

Manuscript Collections: Fonds Litteraire Jacques Doucet, Paris; Beinecke Rare Book and Manuscript Library, Yale University, New Haven, Connecticut.

Biography: *Lettres à l'Amazone* by Rémy de Gourmont, Paris, 1914; revised, Paris, Mercure, 1988; *The Amazon of Letters: The Life and Loves of Natalie Barney* by George Wickes, New York, Putnam, 1976; *Portrait d'une Séductrice* by Jean Chalon, Paris, Stock, 1976, translated by Carol Barko as *Portrait of a Seductress: The World of Natalie Barney,* Crown, 1979; *The Amazon and the Page: Natalie Clifford Barney and Renée Vivien* by Karla Jay, Bloomington, Indiana University Press, 1988.

Critical Sources: *Renée Vivien* by André Germain, Paris, Cres, 1917; *Renée Vivien: Femme damnée, Femme sauvée* by Yves–Gérard Le Dantec, Aix–en–Provence, Editions du Feu, 1930; "The More Profound Nationality of Their Lesbianism: Lesbian Society in Paris in the 1920s" by Bertha Harris, in *Amazon Expedition: A Lesbianfeminist Anthology,* edited by Phyllis Birkby and others, New York, Times Change Press, 1973; "The Amazon Was a Pacifist" by Karla Jay, in *Reweaving the Web of Life: Feminist and Nonviolence,* edited by Pam McAllister, Philadelphia, New Society, 1982; "The Outsider among the Expatriates: Djuna Barnes's Satire on the Ladies of the *Almanack*" by Karla Jay, in *Lesbian Texts and Contexts: Radical Revisions,* edited by Karla Jay and Joanne Glasgow, New York, New York University Press, 1990, 204–216; "The Trouble with Heroines" by Anna Livia, in *A Perilous Advantage: The Best of Natalie Clifford Barney,* Norwich, Vermont, New Victoria, 1992, 181–193; "Adventures of the Mind: Natalie Barney Plundered Hearts, Minds, Private Parts" by Victoria Brownsworth, in *Lambda Book Report,* September–October 1992, 22–23.

*   *   *

Once as a small child, Natalie Barney was rescued from some rambunctious children by Oscar Wilde. As she recounted in *Adventures of the Mind,* she sat with him "on a raised throne" while he told her stories. Whether or not this reminiscence is apocrypha, Barney clearly saw herself as the true heir of Oscar Wilde. She had been bequeathed his witty flair for epigrams, his love for sexual adventure, and most of all, his notoriety as a sexual outlaw.

Barney wore Wilde's mantle with pride, and like him wrote plays laced with epigrams, a few of which appear in *Actes et entr'actes.* Unlike Wilde, she lacked the gift for creating a tightly knit, fast–paced plot, nor did she have any interest in reaching out to the masses with a universal story that would make her plays profitable on Broadway or London's West End. As a result, most of her plays remained unpublished and without a professional production, but Barney seemed satisfied with amateur renditions starring Colette, Mata Hari, the English poet Renée Vivien, or other friends in her

backyard in Neuilly and later, after Vivien's death in 1909, at the Temple of Friendship behind 20, rue Jacob.

Though she penned more than twenty works, Barney considered herself a lazy writer and rarely polished her epigrams, plays, or the many portraits she wrote of her friends in *Aventures de l'esprit, Traits et portraits,* and *Souvenirs indiscrets.* Having inherited enormous sums from Alfred Barney, her industrialist father, and Alice Pike Barney, her artistically talented and philanthropically inclined mother, Barney occupied herself by pursuing flesh–and–blood women, rather than elusive muses. Starting with Liane de Pougy, the famous courtesan of the Belle Epoque, Barney had affairs with the brilliant and the powerful, including Colette, Lucie Delarue–Mardrus, Djuna Barnes, Dolly Wilde (Oscar's niece), Olive Custance, Nadine Wong, and the Duchess de Clermont–Tonnerre (who wrote as Elisabeth de Gramont). She had a long, tempestuous affair with Renée Vivien (Pauline Mary Tarn), spent a half century with American artist Romaine Brooks, and began a new affair in her eighties with Janine Lahovary. In *Souvenirs indiscrets,* Barney asked, "If love needs constance and desire needs change, how can we reconcile the two?" The problem was that while Barney needed change, her lovers needed constance. Despite her call for a lesbian life that was free of patriarchal bonds, she tended to fall in love with women who may have been lesbians but who were conventional in other regards.

Her former lovers became her friends and confidantes and formed the inner circle at 20, rue Jacob, where Barney moved in 1909 and set up a salon in 1910, which met every Friday (except during wars) for over sixty years. There they were joined by writers including Gertrude Stein, Ezra Pound, Paul Valéry, Rainer Maria Rilke, William Carlos Williams, Gabriele d'Annunzio, Rabindranath Tagore, Oscar Milosz, Max Jacob, Rachilde, and Mina Loy. The Fridays included good food and witty conversation, and in 1927, Barney initiated the Académie des Femmes, her counterpart to the all–male Académie Française. Writers like Djuna Barnes read from unpublished manuscripts, and Barney raised money to help Barnes, Pound and other writers. She sold subscriptions to have Barnes' *Ladies Almanack* privately printed in 1928.

Although Barney seemed to promote others' writing instead of her own, her work was brought to the attention of the French public when Rémy de Gourmont, a recluse and one of the most brilliant Frenchmen of the early part of the twentieth century, celebrated her beauty and wit in his column in the *Mercure de France,* which was later published in book form as *Lettres à l'Amazone.* Answering the curiosity of an eager public, in 1920 Barney published a collection of epigrams entitled *Pensées d'une Amazone* and additional witticisms and thoughts in *Nouvelles Pensées de l'Amazone* in 1939. These, like most of her works, were written in French, the language of her adopted country. Her work remained almost completely unavailable in English until the early 1990s.

Barney's only attempt at sustained writing in English was a self–published novel, *The One Who Is Legion; or, A.D.'s After–Life* in 1930, which was illustrated by Romaine Brooks. The novel is the tale of the return from the grave of a gynandrous suicide, who very much resembles Renée Vivien. This Symbolist novel–manqué was only one of several literary attempts, including the pamphlet, "The Woman Who Lives with Me," in which Barney returned obsessively to her unsuccessful relationship with Vivien.

Barney's contribution to lesbian literature lies not in her loose imitations of Symbolism, her careless prose, or her halting French verse, but in the content of her oeuvre, which celebrated homosexuality without apology or remorse. In "Predestined for Free Choice," she wrote, "I have always done as I pleased." She went on to mock "right–thinking people" who made "light of our precious relationships." She saw herself as part of a lesbian literary heritage dating back to Sappho, whose reputation she and Vivien attempted to revive as they recast her as a lesbian goddess and muse.

For many lesbians, Barney's life was unparalleled in her celebration of what would later be labeled "gay pride." Though as a teenager and young adult she flirted with the idea of a "Boston marriage," by 1900, she had embraced an openly lesbian existence and used her own name to pen sonnets to other women in *Quelques Portraits—Sonnets de Femmes,* which was illustrated by Alice Pike Barney. With the exception of *Cinq petits Dialogues grecs,* which she published in 1902 under the male pseudonym of Tryphé, she refused to pretend that her effusive writings about women were by a man. In 1904, she and Vivien traveled to Lesbos, where they hoped to set up an artists' colony for lesbians. Though the project was ill–conceived and ultimately aborted when Vivien left Barney for her other lover, the Baroness de Zuylen de Nyevelt, it may have been the first lesbian attempt to reclaim historically important space for homosexual women.

Early scholarship about Vivien by Yves–Gérard Le Dantec and André Germain blamed Barney for Vivien's decline and death. André Rouveyre attacked Barney for making Rémy de Gourmont blind with infatuation. By the 1970s, presentations of Barney by Gayle Rubin and Bertha Harris tended towards adulation. Biographies by George Wickes and Jean Chalon portrayed Barney as a female Don Juan. In the late 1980s and early 1990s, Barney's reputation and work were subjected to some scrutiny. In "The Amazon Was a Pacifist," I traced her passage from pacifist to fascist, and in *The Amazon and the Page: Natalie Clifford Barney and Renée Vivien,* I questioned her relationship to feminism. In "The Trouble with Heroines," Anna Livia explored in detail Barney's anti–Semitism, a position complicated by Barney's lineage, which was one quarter Jewish. As Livia stated, "The trouble with heroines is that as soon as we discover their feet of clay, they become the scapegoat of our common failings as surely as, in their pre–lapsarian state, they embodied our common ideals." Perhaps Barney, like her idol Wilde who went from being the toast of London to a prison inmate, will profit from a sense of balance about her accomplishments and failings. As Victoria Brownsworth wrote in *Lambda Book Report,* "Barney may not be every lesbian's cup of tea, but her work is a slice of lesbian history that forms a vital link to a group of women who have functioned as role models for several generations of 20th century lesbians."

—*Karla Jay*

———

BARROW, Marilyn. *See* **GRIER, Barbara G(ene Damon).**

———

BARTLETT, Neil. British playwright, novelist, short story writer, translator, and actor. Born in Hitchin, Hertfordshire, in 1958. Edu-

cated at Magdalen College, Oxford, B.A. in English literature 1981. Founder and member of 1982 Theatre Company, London, 1982–84; staff member of Consenting Adults in Public, London, 1983, September in the Pink (London Lesbian and Gay Arts Festival), London, 1983, and International AIDS Day, London, 1986; master of ceremonies for National Review of Live Art, London, Nottingham, and Glasgow, Scotland, 1985–90; actor in plays, including *Pornography* in London, 1984, *A Vision of Love Revealed in Sleep, 1* in London, 1988, and *Lady Audley's Secret* in London, 1988; director of plays, including *More Bigger Snacks Now* in London, 1985, *The Avenging Woman* in Latvia and Canada, 1991, and *Twelfth Night* in Chicago, 1992; founder, member, director, writer, and performer, Gloria, London, 1988—. **Recipient:** Perrier Award, 1985; *Time Out/Dance Umbrella* award, 1989; Writers Guild of Great Britain award, 1991; *Time Out* award, 1992. Agent: Gloria, 16 Chenies Street, London WC1E 7EX, England, U.K.

WRITINGS

Plays

Dressing Up (produced London, 1983; directed by Bartlett).
Pornography (produced London, 1984; directed by Bartlett).
The Magic Flute (adaptation of opera by Wolfgang Amadeus Mozart; produced London, 1985; directed by Bartlett).
A Vision of Love Revealed in Sleep, 1 (produced London, 1986; directed by Bartlett).
Lady Audley's Secret (adaptation of novel by Mary E. Braddon; produced London, 1988; directed by Bartlett).
Le Misanthrope (translation of play by Molière; produced Edinburgh, 1988; London, 1989; Chicago, 1989). Bath, Absolute Classics, 1990.
A Vision of Love Revealed in Sleep, 2 (produced London, 1989; directed by Bartlett).
A Vision of Love Revealed in Sleep, 3 (produced London, 1990; directed by Bartlett). Published in *Gay Plays 3,* edited by Michael Wilcox, London, Methuen, 1990.
The School for Wives (translation of play by Molière; produced Derby, 1990; Washington, D.C., 1992; directed by Bartlett). Bath, Absolute Classics, 1990.
Bérénice (translation of play by Jean Racine; produced London, 1990). Bath, Absolute Classics, 1990.
Sarrasine (adaptation of story by Honoré de Balzac; produced Edinburgh, 1990; London, 1990; New York, 1991; directed by Bartlett).
Let Them Call It Jazz (adaptation of story by Jean Rhys; produced London, 1991; directed by Bartlett).
A Judgement in Stone, music by Nicholas Bloomfield (adaptation of novel by Ruth Rendell; produced London, 1992; directed by Bartlett).
The Game of Love and Chance (translation; produced London, 1992; directed by Bartlett).
Night After Night (produced London, 1993; directed by Bartlett, music by Bloomfield). London, Metheun, 1993.

Television Plays

That's What Friends Are For, 1988.
That's How Strong My Love Is, 1989.

Fiction

Ready to Catch Him Should He Fall (novel). London, Serpent's Tail, 1990; New York City, Dutton, 1991.
"Three Wedding Ceremonies," in *The Faber Book of Gay Short Fiction*, edited by Edmund White. London and New York, Faber & Faber, 1991.
The Ten Commandments (short stories). London, Serpent's Tail, 1992.

Other

Who Was That Man? A Present for Mr. Oscar Wilde. London, Serpent's Tail, 1988.
Where Is Love (video), 1988.
With Stuart Marshall, *Pedagogue* (video), 1988.
Now That It's Morning (screenplay), 1992.

*

Critical Sources: "Ritual and Gay Nature" by Marvin Shaw, in *Lambda Book Report,* November/December 1991; "A Reinvented Man" by Gerald Raymond, in *Advocate,* 28 January 1992, p. 69.

*   *   *

The 1988 publication of Neil Bartlett's *Who Was That Man?*, a critical, historical study of Oscar Wilde and his times, was a breakthrough for gay male writing and scholarship. Bartlett, who had made a name for himself first as a student at Oxford and later as an innovative playwright and director, attempted to view Wilde through the eyes of a late–twentieth–century gay liberationist and to unearth the gay milieu inhabited by Wilde in the latter part of the nineteenth century. Most contemporary studies of Wilde acknowledge his homosexual activity but do not position him firmly in the Victorian gay subculture. On the other hand, Bartlett's study, which was researched through newspapers, journals, police reports, crime magazines, and the literature of the period, is the first book to locate Wilde's life and ideas in a historical gay setting.

The scholarship of *Who Was That Man?* is, however, its least arresting factor. Bartlett positions himself, as the author, in a dialogue with the dead Wilde and continually probes the similarities and differences between late–Victorian and late–twentieth–century gay male culture. As a result *Who Was That Man?* becomes a reflective, meditative work about not only Oscar Wilde but the politics of sexuality, culture and history. Bartlett is particularly perceptive in untangling the contemporary argument that much of what might seem sexualized to the modern reader in Wilde's writings was in fact nothing more than a particularly flowery language of male friendship. He uses this linguistic analysis to discover how homosexuality manifested itself in mainstream culture—and especially in Wilde's writing as well the letters and journals of others—and to clarify what this may mean to society today. Bartlett's interest in

Who Was That Man? is in uncovering a gay male history and sensibility that is continuous over several historical periods and to find, by the psychological and political standards of today, a way to understand and critique that history.

These concerns are also apparent in Bartlett's stage work, particularly *A Vision of Love Revealed in Sleep* (based upon the life and writings of Victorian writer Simeone Solomon), *Lady Audley Secret* (a post–modern reinterpretation of Mary E. Baddon's popular Victorian thriller), and *Sarrasine* (adapted from a text by Honoré de Balzac). They are especially prominent in his 1991 novel *Ready to Catch Him Should He Fall,* a startling psycho–historical analysis of the gay male psyche told in mythic language and indebted heavily to the techniques of magic realism.

Although British and American gay male writing has matured a great deal in both style and theme since the Stonewall Riots in 1969, traditional forms and narratives—most strikingly the "coming out" story and the "redemption through love and/or sex" plot—have dominated most of the work produced. Bartlett's *Ready to Catch Him Should He Fall* is a radical departure from these narratives that shows a profound understanding of traditional gay male narrative themes as well as the necessity to break from them.

In attempting to understand some "truth" about gay male lives, emotions and psychology, Bartlett has created a trans–historical mythic world in which characters possess universal qualities and situations have universal implications. On the surface, *Ready to Catch Him Should He Fall* has an odd, archly written, pseudo–literary style that distances the reader as much as it draws attention to itself: "This is a picture which I took of him myself. He was so beautiful in those days—listen to me, *those days,* talking like it was ancient history. It's just that at the time it all seemed so beautiful and important, it was like some kind of historical event. *History on legs,* we used to say; a significant pair of legs, an important stomach, legendary ... *a classic of the genre. Historic.* Well it was true, all of it."

The style fits Bartlett's characterizations: there is Boy (who seems to stand for all gay youth), The Older Man, or O, (who is, apparently, all experienced gay men) and Mother, or Madam, who runs The Bar (or in this mythic world, all gay bars). The plot is simple. Boy comes to town in search of himself and meets O, who takes him in and instructs him in the ways of gay love. Madam takes the lovers under her wing to protect them from the homophobic world. When the sickly Father appears, problems ensue between Mother and him, and both Boy and O have to mediate the situation.

Bartlett's tone is derived from Jean Genet's works of magical realism, in which the most mundane aspect of gay life is celebrated and transfigured. Throughout *Ready to Catch Him Should He Fall,* Bartlett uses religious language and scatters references to other great gay works, from Wilde's *Picture of Dorian Gray* to lyrics from Stephen Sondheim's *Follies,* all of which add to the historical weight of the novel: it is clear that Bartlett really *is* talking about all of gay male life and culture. Eventually Bartlett's prose takes on a Jungian flavor, and it becomes apparent that he is using the form of a semi–traditional prose narrative in an attempt to examine all of the psychological, emotional, and psychic changes that the British gay male community has gone through in the past four decades. The growing sense of worth and independence that Boy experiences in the world of O and The Bar is equivalent to the growing gay community that has sprung up during that time. Bartlett is not interested in simple metaphors, however, and takes his story one step further by insisting that we view Madam, O, Boy and Father as representative of the nuclear family and that their journey parallels the decline of that traditional family unit as well as the need for gay men to break from it.

Bartlett's writing is direct and honest. In both *Ready to Catch Him Should He Fall* and *Who Was That Man?* he finds a way to get beneath all of the social and psychological jargon that attempts to explain gay lives and produces an honest depiction—in historical, psychological, symbolic and contemporary terms—of what it *means* to be gay.

—*Michael Bronski*

————

BEAUCHAMP, Kathleen Mansfield. *See* **MANSFIELD, Katherine.**

————

BERRY, Jonas. *See* **ASHBERY, John (Lawrence).**

————

BÉRUBÉ, Allan. American historian, educator, and author of non–fiction. Educated at University of Chicago and City College of San Francisco. Companion of Brian Keith, 1983–87 (died of complications from AIDS). Has taught gay history at University of California, Santa Cruz, and Stanford University since 1991; former editor of *Out/Look.* Contributor of articles to numerous journals and periodicals, including *Out/Look, Advocate, Mother Jones, Gay Community News, Washington Blade,* and *Body Politic.* **Recipient:** Lambda Literary Award for the best non–fiction of 1991, for *Coming Out under Fire: The History of Gay Men and Women in World War II;* National Endowment for the Arts grant, with Arthur Dong, 1992, for documentary film; awards from Alice B. Toklas Lesbian/Gay Democratic Club, *Advocate,* Gay Press Association, San Francisco Board of Supervisors, Association of Lesbian and Gay Psychologists, National Park Service, and Bay Area Physicians for Human Rights.

WRITINGS

Nonfiction

"Marching to a Different Drummer: Lesbian and Gay GIs in World War II," in *Hidden from History: Reclaiming the Gay and Lesbian Past,* edited by Martin B. Duberman, Martha Vicinus, and George Chauncey, Jr. New York, New American Library, 1989.

Coming Out under Fire: The History of Gay Men and Women in World War II. New York, Free Press, 1990.

*

Critical Sources: "Author, Filmmaker Documenting History of Military Ban on Gays" by Lynn Elber, in *Detroit Free Press,* 17 February 1993, 5C.

*   *   *

With his *Coming Out Under Fire: The History of Gay Men and Women in World War II,* Allan Bérubé won instant recognition as an accomplished historian. Written with wit, charm, and power, it was acclaimed in mainstream publications from the *New York Times Book Review* and the *Journal of American History* as well as the *Advocate* and the *Lesbian News.* As with his lectures and slide presentations, which reached large audiences well before the book appeared, the book is moving and effective in strengthening the position of gay men and women in the military. Calling *Coming Out Under Fire* the "definitive account of gays in World War II," Randy Shilts acknowledges his own indebtedness to Bérubé in the writing of *Conduct Unbecoming: Lesbians and Gays in the U.S. Military Vietnam to the Persian Gulf.*

Having studied English literature at the University of Chicago and multi–image production at the City College of San Francisco, Bérubé is a master of many media. Using visual, spoken, and written formats, he appeals effectively to popular audiences. He has produced three slide presentations on lesbian and gay history and has spoken at more than one hundred college and community forums.

Bérubé is the recipient of numerous awards and has served on the Lesbian/Gay Advisory Committee to the San Francisco Human Rights Commission. Currently living in Los Angeles, he is producing a television documentary with Arthur Dong based on his book. It is funded in part by the National Endowment for the Arts; and when completed, the documentary will bring together the results of ten years of research by Bérubé, including gay soldiers' letters, rare film footage, and government documents. Bérubé indicated to Lynn Elber in the *Detroit Free Press* that "gay and lesbian purges were conducted but the demand for troops saw the military keep homosexuals in by trying to reform them, segregating them in certain jobs or just turning a blind eye." The film will present the history of the military's ban without the sensationalism focused upon by the news media and will chart the military's campaign against homosexuals and study it from the perspective of both its victims and perpetrators.

—*William A. Percy III*

————

BIRTHA, Becky. American poet and short story writer. Born in 1948. Address: 5116 Cedar Avenue, Philadelphia, Pennsylvania 19143–1510, U.S.A.

WRITINGS

Compiler, *Literature by Black Women: A List of Books.* Privately printed, 1983.

For Nights Like This One: Stories of Loving Women. San Francisco, Frog in the Well, 1983.

Lovers' Choice (stories; includes "Johnieruth," "Babytown," "Past Halfway," "The Deep Heart's Core," "Ice Castle," "Her Ex–Lover," "Both Ways," "Route 23: 10th and Bigler to Bethlehem Pike," "The Saints and Sinners Run," and "In the Life"). Seattle, Seal Press, 1987.

Contributor, *Intricate Passions.* Banned Books, 1989.

The Forbidden Poems. Seattle, Seal Press, 1991.

*

Critical Sources: *Times Literary Supplement,* 3–9 June 1988, 623; *Belles Lettres,* July–August 1988, 15; *Village Voice,* 16 April 1991, 70; *Choice,* October 1991, 276.

*   *   *

Becky Birtha is author of *Lovers' Choice,* a volume of short stories, and *The Forbidden Poems,* her first collection of poetry. *Lovers' Choice,* published in 1987, contains many stories offering insight into the lives of lesbians. Each of the leading characters arrives at a crossroad where her choice of direction holds the potential for momentous change. Patricia Roth Schwartz commented in *Belles Lettres* that "as a Black lesbian/feminist writer, Birtha deserves praise for her courage in writing about interracial relationships, about white women from a Black woman's perspective and about Black lesbians." These elements are prevalent in "Ice Castle" and "Her Ex–Lover," each concerned with a black woman's process of coming to grips with a seemingly irrational attraction to a white woman. The adolescent Maurie's attraction to Gail in "Ice Castle" becomes for her a stepping–stone toward an awareness of her sexual orientation as well as of what it means to be black. In "Her Ex–Lover," Ernestine is eventually able to leave behind her obsession with her former lover, Lisa, allowing her to become wholeheartedly involved with her current black lover. Not all stories in *Lovers' Choice* deal with lesbian relationships. "Route 23: 10th and Bigler to Bethlehem Pike" tells of Leona May Moses, a single mother who must wrap her children in blankets and take them riding on an all–night city bus when her landlord refuses to provide heat for her apartment. "These tender, strong, enduring women," concluded Schwartz, "let us know that, as Leona May Moses insists as she takes her kids on their all–night ride, 'We ain't getting off. This trip ain't over yet.'"

Birtha followed *Lovers' Choice* with *The Forbidden Poems,* a collection in which several poems are concerned with the loss of loved ones, while others praise the strength stemming from communities of women. The poems are told from the perspective of a black woman who has recently ended a long–term relationship with her white lover. Robyn Selman noted in the *Village Voice* that "*The Forbidden Poems* is honest, open, and loaded with details of les-

bian life," and explained that "addressing her self is the speaker's main concern—as a woman, a black woman, and as a lesbian." *Choice* contributor L. J. Parascandola found that "despite a few overly sentimental lines," the poems possess "biting humor" and "a stark, direct quality."

—*Anders Ramsay*

————

BISHOP, Donald. *See* **STEWARD, Samuel M(orris).**

————

BISHOP, George Archibald. *See* **CROWLEY, Aleister.**

————

BLAIS, Marie–Claire. French Canadian novelist, poet, and playwright. Born in Québec City, Québec, 5 October 1939. Educated at Couvent Saint–Roch, Québec; Laval University (literature and philosophy), Québec. Lived in the United States, 1963–74; now lives in Québec. Clerical worker, 1956–57. **Recipient:** L'Academie Francaise Prix de la Langue Francaise, 1961; Guggenheim fellowships, 1963, 1964; Le Prix France–Québec, 1966; Prix Medicis (Paris), 1966; Prix du Gouverneur General du Canada, 1969, 1979; York University (Toronto) honorary doctorate, 1975; Ordre du Canada, 1975; Prix Belgique, 1976; Calgary University honorary professor, 1978; Prix Athanase David, 1982; Prix de l'Academie Francaise, 1983; Nessim Habif prize (Belgium), 1991; honorary doctorate, Victoria University. Agent: John C. Goodwin and Associates, 839 Sherbrooke Est, Suite 2, Montréal, Québec, Canada H2L 1K6. Address: 448 Chemin Sims, Kingsbury, Québec, Canada J0B 1X0.

WRITINGS

Fiction

La Belle Bête. Québec, Institut Littéraire du Québec, 1959; translated by Merloyd Lawrence as *Mad Shadows,* Toronto, McClelland & Stewart, London, Cape, and Boston, Little Brown, 1960.

Tête blanche. Québec, Institut Littéraire du Québec, 1960; translated by Charles Fullman, Toronto, McClelland & Stewart, and Boston, Little Brown, 1961; London, J. Cape, 1962.

Le Jour est noir. Montréal, Éditions du Jour, 1962; translated by Derek Coltman as *The Day Is Dark*, in *The Day Is Dark* [and] *Three Travelers*, 1967.

Une Saison dans la vie d'Emmanuel. Montréal, Éditions du Jour, 1965; translated by Derek Coltman as *A Season in the Life of Emmanuel*, introduction by Edmund Wilson, New York, Farrar Straus, 1966; London, J. Cape, 1967.

Les Voyageurs sacrés. Montréal, HMH, 1966; translated by Derek Coltman as *Three Travelers*, in *The Day Is Dark* [and] *Three Travelers*, 1967.

L'Insoumise. Montréal, Éditions du Jour, 1966; translated by David Lobdell as *The Fugitive*, Ottawa, Oberon Press, 1978.

The Day Is Dark [and] *Three Travelers: Two Novellas*, translated by Michael Harris. New York, Farrar Straus, 1967; Markham, Ontario, and London, Penguin, 1985.

David Sterne. Montréal, Éditions du Jour, 1967; translated by David Lobdell, Toronto, McClelland & Stewart, 1973.

Manuscrits de Pauline Archange (first book in series). Montréal, Éditions du Jour, 1968; with *Vivre! Vivre!: La Suite des manuscrits de Pauline Archange*, translated by Derek Coltman as *The Manuscripts of Pauline Archange*, New York, Farrar Straus, 1970; Toronto, McClelland & Stewart, 1982.

Vivre! Vivre!: La Suite des manuscrits de Pauline Archange (second book in series). Montréal, Éditions du Jour, 1969; with *Manuscrits de Pauline Archange*, translated by Derek Coltman as *The Manuscripts of Pauline Archage*, New York, Farrar Straus, 1970; Toronto, McClelland & Stewart, 1982.

Les Apparences (third book in series). Montréal, Éditions du Jour, 1970; translated by David Lobdell as *Dürer's Angel*, Toronto, McClelland & Stewart, 1974.

Le Loup. Montréal, Éditions du Jour, 1972; translated by Sheila Fischman as *The Wolf*, Toronto, McClelland & Stewart, 1974.

Un Joualonais, sa joualonie. Montréal, Éditions du Jour, 1973; as *A coeur joual*, Paris, Laffont, 1974; translated by Ralph Manheim as *St. Lawrence Blues*, New York, Farrar Straus, 1974; London, Harrap, 1975.

Une Liaison parisienne. Montréal, Stanké/Quinze, 1975; translated by Sheila Fischman as *A Literary Affair*, Toronto, McClelland & Stewart, 1979.

Les Nuits de l'underground. Montréal, Stanké, 1978; translated by Ray Ellenwood as *Nights in the Underground: An Exploration of Love*, Toronto, General Publishing, 1979; New York, Beaufort Books, 1983.

Le Sourd dans la ville. Montréal, Stanké, 1979; translated by Carol Dunlop as *Deaf to the City*, Toronto, Lester Orpen Dennys, 1980; Woodstock, New York, Overlook, 1987.

Visions d'Anna, ou le vertige. Montréal, Stanké, 1982; translated by Sheila Fischman as *Anna's World*, Toronto, Lester Orpen Dennys, 1985.

Pierre, la guerre du printemps 81. Montréal, Primeur, 1984; as *Pierre*, Paris, Acropole, 1986; Montréal, Boréal, 1991.

L'Ange de la solitude. Montréal, VLB Editeur, 1989.

Poetry

Pays voilés. Québec, Garneau, 1963; as *Veiled Countries*, in *Veiled Countries* [and] *Lives*, 1984.

Existences. Québec, Garneau, 1964; as *Lives*, in *Veiled Countries* [and] *Lives*, 1984.

Veiled Countries [and] *Lives*, translation by Michael Harris. Montréal, Signal, 1984.

Plays

La Roulotte aux poupées (produced Montréal, 1962); translated as *The Puppet Caravan* (televised, 1967).

Eléonor (produced Québec, 1962).

L'Exécution (produced Montréal, 1967). Montréal, Éditions du Jour, 1968; translated by David Lobdell as *The Execution*, Vancouver, Talon, 1976.

Fièvre, et autres textes dramatiques: Théâtre radiophonique (includes *L'Envahisseur*; *Le Disparu*; *Deux Destins*; *Un Couple*). Montréal, Éditions du Jour, 1974.

With Nicole Brossard, Marthe Blackburn, Luce Guilbeault, France Théoret, Odette Gagnon, and Pol Pelletier, *La Nef des sorcières (Marcelle)* (produced Montréal, 1976). Montréal, Quinze, 1976; translated by Linda Gaboriau as *A Clash of Symbols*, Toronto, Coach House Press, 1979.

L'Océan; Murmures (broadcast, 1976). Montréal, Quinze, 1977; translation by Ray Chamberlain of *L'Ocean* published as *The Ocean*, Toronto, Exile, 1977; translation by Margaret Rose of *Murmures* published in *Canadian Drama/L'Art Dramatique Canadien* (Guelph, Ontario), fall 1979.

Sommeil d'Hiver. Montréal, Éditions de la Pleine Lune, 1984.

Fière, 1985.

L'île (produced Montréal, 1991). Montréal, VLB Editeur, 1988; translated by David Lobdell as *The Island*, Ottawa, Oberon, 1991.

Un Jardin dans la tempête (broadcast, 1990); translated by David Lobdell as *A Garden in the Storm*.

Television Plays

L'Océan, Radio–Canada, 1976.

Journal en images froides, *Scénario*, Radio–Canada, 1978.

L'Exil, L'Escale, Radio–Canada, 1979.

Radio Plays

Le Disparu, *Premières*, Radio–Canada, 1971.

L'Envahisseur, *Feuillaison*, Radio–Canada, 1972.

Deux Destins, *Premières*, Radio–Canada, 1973.

Fièvre, *Premières*, Radio–Canada, 1973.

Une Autre Vie, *Premières*, Radio–Canada, 1974.

Un Couple, *Premières*, Radio–Canada, 1975.

Une Femme et les autres, *Premières*, Radio–Canada, 1976.

Murmures, *Premières*, Radio–Canada, 1976.

L'Enfant–vidéo, *Scénario*, Radio–Canada, 1977.

Le Fantôme d'une voix, *Premieres*, Radio–Canada, 1980.

Other

Author of introduction, *The Oxford Book of French–Canadian Short Stories*, edited by Richard Teleky. New York, Oxford University Press, 1980.

"L'Exil," in *Liberté*, January–February 1981.

Contributor, *Contemporary Authors Autobiography Series*, Volume 4. Detroit, Gale, 1986.

Voies de pères, voix de filles. Saint–Laurent, Québec, Lacombe, 1988.

*

Manuscript Collections: National Library of Canada, Ottawa.

Biography: *Lily Briscoe: A Self–Portrait* by Mary Meigs, Vancouver, Talonbooks, 1981; *Contemporary Authors Autobiography Series,* Volume 4. Detroit, Gale, 1986.

Interviews: "L'Insoumise des lettres canadiennes: une entrevue" by Helene Pilotte, in *Chatelaine,* August 1966, 21–23, 51–54; "Marie–Claire Blais" by Denise Bourdet, in *La Revue de Paris,* February 1967, 129–136; "Nightmare's Child" by George Russell, in *Weekend Magazine,* 23 October 1976, 11; "I Am, Simply, a Writer" by John Hofsess, in *Books in Canada,* February 1979, 8–10; "Les Vingt Années d'écriture de Marie–Claire Blais" by Donald Smith, in *Lettres Québécoises,* winter 1979–80, 51–58; "Marie–Claire Blais: 'Je veux aller le plus loin possible': une entrevue avec Marie–Claire Blais" by Gilles Marcotte, in *Voix et images* (Montréal), winter 1983, 192–209.

Bibliography: "Bibliographie de Marie–Claire Blais" by Aurélien Boivin, Lucie Robert, and Ruth Major–LaPierre, in *Voix et Images,* winter 1983, 248–95.

Critical Sources: "Marie–Claire Blais" by Edmund Wilson, in his *O Canada: An American's Notes on Canadian Culture,* New York, Farrar Strauss, 1965, 147–57; "La Thématique de l'aliénation chez Marie–Claire Blais" by Jacques–A. Lamarche, in *Cité Libre* (Montréal), July–August 1966, 27–32; "L'Espace politique et social dans le roman québécois" by George–André Vachon, in *Recherches Sociographiques,* September–December 1966, 259–279; "Prix littéraires, *Une Saison dans la vie d'Emmanuel*" by Louis Barjon, in *Etudes,* February 1967, 217–222; "Marie–Claire Blais et la révolte du roman canadien" by Roger Gillard, in *La Dryade,* summer 1967, 63–80; "Le Monde étrange de Marie–Claire Blais ou la cage aux fauves" by Gérard–Marie Boivin, in *Culture,* March 1968, 3–17; "Introduction à l'univers de Marie–Claire Blais" by Michel Brûlé, in *Revue de l'Institut de Sociologie,* 42:3, 1969, 503–513; "Note sur deux romans de Marie–Claire Blais" by Lucien Goldmann, in *Revue de l''Institut de Sociologie,* 42:3, 1969, republished in Goldmann's *Structures mentales et création culturelle,* Paris, Editions Anthropos, 1970, 401–414; *Marie–Claire Blais* by Philip Stratford, Toronto, Forum House, 1971; "Fiction as Autobiography in Québec: Notes on Pierre Valliéres and Marie–Claire Blais" by James Kraft, in *Novel* (Providence, Rhode Island), autumn 1972, 73–78; *Le Monde perturbé des jeunes dans l'oeuvre romanesque de Marie–Claire Blais: sa vie, son oeuvre, la critique,* Montréal, Editions Agence d'Arc, 1973; "*Mad Shadows* as Psychological Fiction" by Joan Caldwell, and "The Shattered Glass: Mirror and Illusion in *Mad Shadows*" by Douglas H. Parker, both in *Journal of Canadian Fiction* (Montréal), 2:4, 1973; "Marie–Claire Blais, French Canadian Naturalist" by L. Clark Keating, in *Romance Notes* (Chapel Hill, North Carolina), Number 15, 1973; *Le Monde perturbé des jeunes dans l'oeuvre romanesque de Marie–Claire Blais* by Thérèse Fabi, Montréal, Editions Agence d'Arc, 1973; *Marie–Claire Blais: le noir et le tendre* by Vincent Nadeau,

Montréal, Presses de l'Université de Montréal, 1974; "La Technique de l'inversion dans les romans de Marie–Claire Blais" by Maroussia Ahmed in *Canadia Modern Language Review* (Toronto), May 1975, 380–86; "Les Enfants de Grand–mère Antoinette" by Gilles Marcotte, in his *Notre roman à l'imparfait,* Montréal, La Presse, 1976, 93–137; "The Church in Marie–Claire Blais's *A Season in the Life of Emmanuel*" by Margaret Anderson, in *Sphinx* (Regina, Saskatchewan), Number 7, 1977; "Saphisme, Mystique et Littérature" by Gabrielle Poulin, in *Lettres Québécoises* (Montréal), 12 November 1978, 6–8; "Beauty and Madness in Marie–Claire Blais' *La Belle Bête*" by Jennifer Waelti–Walters, in *Journal of Canadian Fiction,* Numbers 25/26, 1979, 186–198; "Jean Basile, Louky Bersianik, Marie–Claire Blais, Paul Chamberland, Yves Navarre participent pour *le Berdache* à une table ronde: 'Y a–t–il une écriture homosexuelle?'" in *Le Berdache,* November 1979, 25–39; "La Révolte contre le patriarcat dans l'oeuvre de Marie–Claire Blais" (M.A. thesis) by Victor Tremblay, University of British Columbia, 1980; "Sur–vivre et sous–vivre: la sexualité dans *Une Saison dans la vie d'Emmanuel*" by Françoise Maccabée–Iqbal, in *Coincidences* (Ottawa), May–December 1980, 85–108; *Lily Briscoe: A Self–Portrait* by Mary Meigs, Vancouver, Talon, 1981; "Marie–Claire Blais' *Une Liaison parisienne:* An Ambiguous Discovery" by Camille R. La Bossière, in *Selecta* (Corvallis, Oregon), Number 2, 1981; "The Censored Word and the Body Politic: Reconsidering the Fiction of Marie–Claire Blais" by Karen Gould, in *Journal of Popular Culture* (Bowling Green, Ohio), winter 1981, 14–27; "Textes lesbiens: Language et vision utopique des nouvelles écrivaines du Québec" by Marthe Rosenfeld, in *Le Berdache,* April 1981, 40–44; *The Medusa Head* by Mary Meigs, Vancouver, Talon, 1983; "Un rituel de l'avidité" by Elène Cliché, in *Voix et images* (Montréal), winter 1983, 229–248; "From Shattered Reflections to Female Bonding: Mirroring in Marie–Claire Blais's *Visions d'Anna*" by Paula Gilbert Lewis, in *Québec Studies,* Number 2, 1984; "Redefining the Maternal: Women's Relationships in the Fiction of Marie–Claire Blais" by Mary Jean Green, in *Traditionalism, Nationalism and Feminism: Women Writers of Québec,* edited by Paul Gilbert Lewis, Westport, Connecticut, Greenwood, 1985; *L'Oeuvre romanesque de Marie–Claire Blais* by Françoise Laurent, Montréal, Fides, 1986; "Marie–Claire Blais" by Eva–Marie Kröller, in *Dictionary of Literary Biography,* Volume 53: *Canadian Writers since 1960,* Detroit, Gale, 1986; "L'Art de la fugue dans *Le Loup* de Marie–Claire Blais" by Victor Tremblay, in *French Review* (Champaign, Illinois), May 1986, 911–921; "Atomized Lives in Limbo: An Analysis of *Mad Shadows* by Marie–Claire Blais" by Coomie S. Vevaina, in *Literary Criterion* (Mysore, India), 22:1, 1987; "Marie Claire Blais" by Rosemary Lloyd, in *Beyond the Nouveau Roman,* edited by Michael Tilby, New York, Berg, 1990, 123–150; "The Question of Lesbian Identity in Marie–Claire Blais's Work" by Janine Ricouart, in *Redefining Autobiography in Twenti-eth–Century Women's Fiction,* edited by Janice Morgan and Colette T. Hall, New York, Garland, 1991, 169–190.

*   *   *

One of the most prominent and internationally recognized writers of Québec's "Quiet Revolution," Marie–Claire Blais has consistently depicted characters who hold a marginal place in society; the poor and the dispossessed, children, the physically and mentally ill, criminals, gays, lesbians and artists are rebels who transgress and thus permit a questioning of the rules of conventional society. They live in a world that is dark and alienating; pain, anguish and despair are commonplace. For Blais, the task of a writer in this world is to bear witness to the suffering of humanity. Art in any form is a means of salvation, of healing the wounds inflicted by an oppressive society. And the most consistent wound experienced by her characters, especially those who are gay and lesbian, is a split between mind and body. Blais writes the body: its pain and its pleasure. Her sensual imagery is embedded in the long, flowing sentences that have become her trademark. Her writing oscillates between the "not quite realism" of many women writers and the lyrical, existential and surreal.

Blais' first novel, *La Belle bête* (*Mad Shadows*), received mixed reviews; lauded by liberal critics, it was strongly criticized by more conservative elements of the literary institution. In an effort to escape artistic and social repression, she left Québec and lived for over 15 years in Paris and the United States, where she was "discovered" by well-known literary critic Edmund Wilson. Wilson also introduced her to painter Mary Meigs and a relationship ensued that, according to Meigs' autobiography, *Lily Briscoe: A Self-Portrait*, was to undergo almost as many variations as those depicted in Blais' novels.

The appearance of *Une Saison dans la vie d'Emmanuel* (*A Season in the life of Emmanuel*) in 1965 established Blais as a literary "genius." An attack on the hypocrisy and oppressive nature of the institutions of the traditional family and the Catholic church, this novel focusses primarily on children as society's outcasts. The sexual explorations of these children, as yet uninhibited by heterosexual convention, permit Blais' first explicit literary treatment of homosexuality, albeit in the form of fantasy, metaphor and symbol. This novel also establishes a link, which becomes a major theme in her subsequent work, between homosexuality and art, as the protagonist is censored both for his sexual and his literary activities.

Many of Blais' subsequent works include homosexual characters: *L'Insoumise* (*The Fugitive*) depicts a father who must deal with the (mistaken) suspicion that his son is gay, as well as the unrequited love of the son's male friend; *Les Manuscrits de Pauline Archange* (*The Manuscripts of Pauline Archange*) is similar to *Une Saison dans la vie d'Emmanuel* in its focus on a child protagonist's precocity both literary and (bi)sexual. In 1976 Blais collaborated with a group of Québec feminists to produce *La Nef des sorcières* (*A Clash of Symbols*), in which she portrayed a lesbian. *Visions d'Anna* (*Anna's World*) includes a lesbian character who is depicted as an independent and nurturing young woman despite her family's lack of understanding and acceptance.

Blais has written three novels that focus almost exclusively on gay and lesbian characters, and each can be seen as a further development of both her artistic vision and her political stance. *Le Loup* (*The Wolf*) is a confessional novel in which a young gay pianist, Sébastien, recounts his sexual experiences. A study of desire, seduction and sensuality, the novel explores how each new lover attempts to possess Sébastien in order to fill his own emptiness. Sébastien in turn sees himself as a Christ figure; he chooses partners who are incapable of returning his love, in an attempt to redeem them. In a violent inversion of Christian imagery, he depicts his exploits as acts of charity and redemption, but physical rather than spiritual: "carnal pity" and "sensual commiseration." Despite jealousies and emotional abuse, Sébastien continues his search for beauty in love—for it is only beauty, that of love and of art, that offers even the smallest hope for salvation, even if that salvation is only a momentary easing of the pain of existence.

The most fascinating aspect of this novel is its structure: a musical arrangement as a fugue in four parts, each focussing more or less on one lover, with memories of and dialogues with the others returning in counterpoint and harmony. Sébastien's description of his most recent lover also pertains to the novel as a whole: "a fugue woven of conflicts, torments and perpetual change." And as Victor Tremblay has pointed out in his study of this work, the musical and sexual imagery combine with that of food to produce perhaps the most sensual of all of Blais' novels.

Le Loup concludes with an idyllic dream of self-acceptance, acceptance by family and a revision of the traditional family by offering alternatives within the gay community. Attempts are made at homosexual "open marriages" and long-term "ménages à trois." Although jealousy hinders these attempts, the novel is open-ended; like a fugue, it is open to further variations.

The publication of *Les Nuits de L'Underground* (*Nights of the Underground*) coincided with Blais' return to Québec with Mary Meigs to live. Centred on a lesbian club in Montréal, the Underground, this novel is basically an extremely lyrical and complex "coming out" story. Geneviève Aurès, a Québécoise sculptor living with a man in Paris despite her attraction to women, returns to Québec for an exhibition and falls in love with Lali Dorman, a woman who stands out from the others in the club in her acceptance of her sexuality and her refusal to try to "pass" for straight. The two become lovers for a short time. Upon her return to Paris, Geneviève is finally able to leave her male partner. As expected, Lali soon moves on to other lovers and Geneviève meets Françoise, an older woman who has led a closeted double life and who is now very ill. Through Geneviève's new-found self-acceptance, Françoise also finds a new joy in life and recovers, both sexually and physically.

Throughout much of the novel, Québec's freezing winter is contrasted with scenes in the warm and steamy bar, which offer elegant and humorous vignettes of solidarity: a mixture of races, classes and what the narrator describes as a "tangled underbrush of ... various languages" and dialects. The novel concludes in spring, as the bar patrons come out into the sunshine to mix with artists, both gay and straight, in a new restaurant, and to begin a housing project that promises to integrate them into the larger community.

As in *Le Loup*, it is art that gives meaning to suffering in this subterranean world of society's outcasts. Geneviève's obsession for Lali "began as for a work of art," and as she finds herself unable to possess Lali, nor to liberate her from the pain of her past, she finally creates a bust of Lali. This act, which universalizes the beauty of a woman and the artist's love for that woman, frees Geneviève from her obsession.

Blais' latest novel, *L'Ange de la solitude*, begins in a lesbian community, depicting a group of young artists who live together in a commune. Structured around a rudimentary plot involving the disappearance and eventual death of one of the women, the narrative follows each of these women as she drifts through her own alienated psychological, artistic and romantic travels, until the tragedy brings them together to form a family.

These three novels have in common a mixture of lyricism and didacticism as they explore the difficulties involved in being gay or lesbian in a homophobic society. From *Le Loup* to *L'Ange de la solitude* there is a decreasing interest in structural experimentation and plot and the development of a more and more explicit political program. Christian imagery is gradually replaced by a more open and accepting spirituality. The diversity and complexity of gay and lesbian relationships is explored in increasing detail, as are alternatives to the traditional heterosexual family. Finally, in all three of these novels, Blais examines and rejects rigid gender roles: gay men in *Le Loup* and lesbian women in *Les Nuits de l'Underground* are described as both warrior–like and maternal in their love–making. The two lesbian novels depict characters who take on masculine names, refer to each other as "brothers" and are both sons and daughters to their parents. Sexual ambiguity is repeatedly depicted as beautiful: Geneviève describes Françoise as "at once masculinely handsome and seductively feminine." This gender–bending is one instance of the profound humanism of all of Marie–Claire Blais' work, as she attempts to reach through the suffering in order to create a world in which the individual is free, both corporally and spiritually.

—*Dawn Thompson*

BOSWELL, John (Eastburn). American historian and author of nonfiction. Born in Boston, 20 March 1947. Educated at College of William and Mary, Williamsburg, Virginia, A.B. 1969; Harvard University, Cambridge, Massachusetts, M.A. 1971, Ph.D. 1975. Assistant professor of history, Yale University, New Haven, Connecticut, 1975–81, associate professor, 1981–82, professor of history, 1982—, director of graduate studies in history, 1984–86. **Recipient:** Woodrow Wilson fellowship; Morse fellowship; Unitarian Universalist Association Frederic C. Melcher Award in recognition of an outstanding literary work contributing to religious liberalism, American Library Association's Gay/Lesbian Book Award, and American Book Award for History, for *Christianity, Social Tolerance, and Homosexuality,* 1981; Yale University's William Clyde deVane Medal for teaching and scholarship, 1982; honorary master of arts degree, Yale University, 1982. Agent: Georges Borchardt, Inc., 136 East 57th Street, New York 10022, U.S.A. Address: Department of History, Yale University, 216 HGS, New Haven, Connecticut 06520, U.S.A.

WRITINGS

Nonfiction

The Royal Treasure: Muslim Communities under the Crown of Aragon in the Fourteenth Century. New Haven, Connecticut, Yale University, 1977.
Christianity, Social Tolerance, and Homosexuality: Gay People in Western Europe from the Beginning of the Christian Era to the Fourteenth Century. Chicago, University of Chicago Press, 1980.
The Kindness of Strangers: The Abandonment of Children in Western Europe from Late Antiquity to the Renaissance. New York, Pantheon Books, 1988.

Other

"Revolutions, Universals, and Sexual Categories," in *Hidden from History: Reclaiming the Gay and Lesbian Past,* edited by Martin Bauml Duberman, Martha Vicinus, and George Chauncey, Jr. New York, New American Library, 1989.

With others, *Homosexuality in the Priesthood and Religious Life,* edited by Jeannine Gramick. New York, Crossroad Publishing, 1989.

*

Interviews: In *Newsweek,* 29 September 1980.

*   *   *

John Boswell's award–winning study *Christianity, Social Tolerance, and Homosexuality* proposes a sweeping new evaluation of how homosexuality was viewed and treated by the Church over a 1500–year period. According to Boswell's interpretation, the early Church said nothing explicitly against homosexuality until the late Middle Ages. Before that time, Boswell asserts, Church pronouncements which are now perceived to have been anti–homosexual have in fact been mistranslated or misunderstood. St. Paul's censure of homosexuality in Romans, for example, does not condemn homosexual behavior, Boswell believes, but only homosexual acts committed by normally heterosexual persons. Similar biblical censures Boswell finds are equally invalid.

Boswell sees the Church as having been tolerant toward homosexuals for many centuries, even going so far as to identify some leading clerics of the early church as homosexuals. The bans on gay marriages and on homosexual behavior in general throughout much of Europe during the fourth century Boswell attributes to a return to a rural society with the collapse of the Roman empire. Rural societies traditionally favor procreative sex over homosexuality. By the early Middle Ages and the growth of urban centers, however, homosexuality was again tolerated. Boswell speculates that there was even a flourishing homosexual culture in the early Medieval cities.

The legislation that began to condemn and outlaw homosexual behavior was first adopted in the twelfth through fourteenth centuries. At this time such Church leaders as St. Aquinas argued that homosexuality was unnatural, a view that continued to be the dominant belief among orthodox Christians for centuries. But Boswell sees the Medieval intolerance of homosexuality as having its roots in the sagging fortunes of the Crusades and a resultant hostility to those of differing beliefs and cultures, including Jews, Muslims, and homosexuals. Religious intolerance to homosexuality, according to Boswell, is less a matter of biblical injunctions than a reaction to particular historical circumstances of the late Middle Ages. Although some critics disagreed with certain of Boswell's interpretations of history and biblical meaning, many cited *Christianity, Social Tolerance, and Homosexuality* as a landmark work in its field and an important contribution to an understanding of the relationship between the Christian Church and homosexuality.

In the essay "Revolutions, Universals, and Sexual Categories" published in *Hidden from History: Reclaiming the Gay and Lesbian Past,* Boswell confronts some of the concerns critics had about *Christianity, Social Tolerance, and Homosexuality.* Specifically, Boswell addresses the question of whether there is a consistent gay community throughout history or whether what historians call "gay" has been a series of changing sexual categories created by a society undergoing constant evolution. In his essay for *Homosexuality in the Priesthood and the Religious Life,* Boswell speaks of his own research into homosexuality in Roman Catholic Church history. He emphasizes that homosexuality has long been common to the Catholic religious tradition and cites monastic sources which suggest strong emotional ties between some Medieval monks. Directing his comments to homosexual priests and nuns of today who may feel isolated and alone, Boswell asserts the long–standing role of homosexual culture in Church history and the enduring contributions of individual homosexuals to the Church.

—*Thomas Wiloch*

BOWEN, Elizabeth (Dorothea Cole). Irish and British novelist and author of short stories, memoirs, and nonfiction. Born in Dublin, 7 June 1899. Educated at Downe House, Downe, Kent; London County Council School of Art, 1918–19. Married Alan Charles Cameron in 1923 (died 1952). Associate editor, *London Magazine,* in the 1950s. Worked in a shell–shock hospital near Dublin in World War I; worked for Ministry of Information and as an air–raid warden in London during World War II. **Recipient:** Named to Irish Academy of Letters, 1937; Commander, Order of the British Empire, 1948; named a Royal Society of Literature Companion of Literature, 1965; James Tait Black Memorial Prize, 1970. D.Litt.: Trinity College, 1949, and Oxford University, 1956. *Died in London, 22 February 1973.*

WRITINGS

Novels

The Hotel. London, Constable, 1927; New York, Dial, 1928.
The Last September. London, Constable, and New York, Dial, 1929; with preface by Bowen, New York, Knopf, 1952.
Friends and Relations. London, Constable, and New York, Dial, 1931.
To the North. London, Gollancz, 1932; New York, Knopf, 1933.
The House in Paris. London, Gollancz, 1935; New York, Knopf, 1936.
The Death of the Heart. London, Gollancz, 1938; New York, Knopf, 1939.
The Heat of the Day. London, J. Cape, and New York, Knopf, 1949.
A World of Love. London, J. Cape, and New York, Knopf, 1955.
The Little Girls. London, J. Cape, and New York, Knopf, 1964.
Eva Trout; or, Changing Scenes. New York, Knopf, 1968; London, J. Cape, 1969.

Short Stories

Encounters. New York, Boni & Liveright, and London, Sidgwick & Jackson, 1923.
Ann Lee's, and Other Stories. New York, Boni & Liveright, and London, Sidgwick & Jackson, 1926.

Joining Charles, and Other Stories. New York, Dial, and London, Constable, 1929.
The Cat Jumps, and Other Stories. London, Gollancz, 1934.
Look at All Those Roses. New York, Knopf, and London, Gollancz, 1941.
The Demon Lover, and Other Stories. London, J. Cape, 1945; as *Ivy Gripped the Steps, and Other Stories,* New York, Knopf, 1946.
Selected Stories. M. Fridberg, 1946.
Early Stories (includes *Encounters* and *Ann Lee's, and Other Stories*). New York, Knopf, 1951.
Stories. New York, Knopf, 1959.
A Day in the Dark, and Other Stories. London, J. Cape, 1965.
Irish Stories. Chester Springs, Pennsylvania, Dufour, 1978; as *Elizabeth Bowen's Irish Stories,* Dublin, Poolbeg Press, 1978.
The Collected Stories of Elizabeth Bowen, introduction by Angus Wilson. New York, Knopf, 1981.

Memoirs

Seven Winters. Dublin, Cuala Press, 1942; as *Seven Winters: Memories of a Dublin Childhood,* London, Longmans, Green, 1943; as *Bowen's Court and Seven Winters,* London, Virago, 1984.
Bowen's Court, London, Longmans, Green; New York, Knopf, 1942, second edition, 1964; as *Bowen's Court and Seven Winters,* London, Virago, 1984.
Pictures and Conversations, foreword by Spencer Curtis Brown. New York, Knopf, 1975.
Bowen's Court [and] *Seven Winters: Memories of a Dublin Childhood,* introduction by Hermione Lee. London, Virago Press, 1984.

Other

Editor, *The Faber Book of Modern Stories.* Faber, 1937.
English Novelists. London, Collins, and New York, Hastings House, 1942.
Anthony Trollope: A New Judgement. London, Oxford University Press, 1946.
Why Do I Write?: An Exchange of Views between Elizabeth Bowen, Graham Greene, and V. S. Pritchett. London, Marshall, 1948; Folcroft, Pennsylvania, Folcroft, 1969.
Collected Impressions (nonfiction). London, Longmans, Green, and New York, Knopf, 1950.
The Shelbourne Hotel. New York, Knopf, 1951; as *The Shelbourne: A Centre of Dublin Life for More than a Century,* London, Harrap, 1951.
Editor, *Stories* by Katherine Mansfield. Vintage, 1956; as *Thirty–four Short Stories,* London, Collins, 1957.
A Time in Rome (nonfiction). London, Longmans, Green, and New York, Knopf, 1960.
Seven Winters: Memories of a Dublin Childhood and Afterthought: Pieces about Writing. New York, Knopf, 1962.
Afterthought: Pieces about Writing (essays). London, Longmans, Green, and New York, Knopf, 1964.
The Good Tiger (children's fiction). New York, Knopf, 1965.
Editor and author of introduction, *Doctor Thorne* by Anthony Trollope. New York, Modern Library, 1985.
The Mulberry Tree: Writings of Elizabeth Bowen, edited by Hermione Lee. New York, Harcourt, 1987.
Author of introduction, *The Stories of William Sansom* by William Sansom. Salem, New Hampshire, Ayer Company Publishers.

Adaptations: *The Heat of the Day* (stage play), by Harold Pinter, London, Faber, 1989.

Manuscript Collections: Berg Collection, New York Public Library; Ransom Humanities Research Center, University of Texas at Austin; Houghton Library, Harvard University.

Biography: *Elizabeth Bowen: Portrait of a Writer* by Victoria Glendinning, London, Weidenfeld & Nicolson, 1977, New York, Avon, 1978; "Elizabeth Bowen" by Janet E. Dunleavy, in *Dictionary of Literary Biography,* Volume 15: *British Novelists, 1930–1959,* Detroit, Michigan, Gale, 1983; *Elizabeth Bowen* by Patricia Craig, New York, Viking, 1986; *Elizabeth Bowen* by Phyllis Lassner, Savage, Maryland, Barnes & Noble, 1989.

Bibliography: *Elizabeth Bowen: A Descriptive Bibliography* by J'nan M. Sellery, Austin, Texas University Press, 1977.

Critical Sources: *Elizabeth Bowen* by Jocelyn Brooke, London, Longmans, Green, 1952; "Elizabeth Bowen: Romance Does Not Pay," in *The Vanishing Hero: Studies in Novelists of the Twenties,* London, Eyre & Spottiswoode, 1956; *Elizabeth Bowen: An Introduction to Her Novels* by William Heath, Madison, University of Wisconsin Press, 1961; "The World of Elizabeth Bowen," in *The Contemporary English Novel* by Frederick Karl, New York, Farrar, Straus, 1962; "The Giant Located: Elizabeth Bowen," in *The Lunatic Giant in the Drawing Room: The British and American Novel Since 1930* by James Hall, Bloomington, Indiana University Press, 1968; *Elizabeth Bowen* by Allan E. Austin, Boston, Twayne Publishers, 1971; *Patterns of Reality: Elizabeth Bowen's Novels* by Harriet Blodgett, The Hague, Mouton, 1975; *Elizabeth Bowen* by Edwin J. Kenny, Lewisburg, Pennsylvania, Bucknell University Press, 1975; "Elizabeth Bowen" in *Lesbian Images* by Jane Rule, Garden City, New York, Doubleday, 1975; *Elizabeth Bowen: An Estimation* by Hermione Lee, London, Vision Press, 1981; *Elizabeth Bowen,* edited by Harold Bloom, New York, Chelsea House, 1987; *How Will the Heart Endure: Elizabeth Bowen and the Landscape of War* by Heather Bryant Jordan, Ann Arbor, University of Michigan Press, 1992.

*   *   *

Like Radclyffe Hall's Stephen Gordon, Elizabeth Bowen was endowed with a masculine name before birth and was expected to be a boy. And even though "no one, from the moment the sex was announced, said a word against Elizabeth for not being Robert," she wholeheartedly took on the role of "son and heir" to the family estate, Bowen's Court. Bowen is vague in her autobiographical works about the effect this may have had on her childhood, or on her personal and artistic development, but it is clear to readers of her fiction that she remained, all through her career, preoccupied with gender and gender roles.

Throughout her life and works, Bowen was to express a marked ambivalence about her personal and cultural identity. As a member of the dying Anglo–Irish ascendancy class, she felt caught between the world of romantic Ireland and of an increasingly cosmopolitan English literary scene. The perception of the Anglo–Irish as "English in Ireland, Irish in England" contributed to a kind of alienation from both and, Bowen claims, developed in her the habit of de-tached observation necessary to her development as a novelist. Neither did the particular social dynamics of Irish colonialism escape Bowen's acute awareness, especially in its sexual manifestation; the discourse of English political domination was shot through with references to Ireland as feminine/feminized and the Irish landscape as a female body. Bowen's second novel, *The Last September,* set in County Cork during the Anglo–Irish War, explores this complex blend of power, sexuality, identity, gender and violence.

The main characters—usually female—in Bowen's novels tend to occupy liminal states—thresholds between childhood and adulthood, innocence and experience, masculinity and femininity, tradition and modernity. Lois, the protagonist of *The Last September,* teeters at age 20 on the brink of womanhood, but without a viable model of femininity to grasp. The novel is peopled with ineffectual, emasculated men and silly or domineering women—all living under the compulsion of tradition, trying to fit into stiflingly conventional roles of marriage and Irish society. On the margins of Danielstown, the Irish estate, circulate the socio–sexual misfits: Marda, a 29–year–old "New Woman," resisting, then finally succumbing to, the necessity of marriage; Lawrence, the Oxford–educated nephew, cynical and aesthetic and probably homosexual; and the Montmorencys, a middle–aged, childless couple who seem to have reversed their traditional husband and wife roles.

Even in Bowen's novels set in England, an interest in marginal relationships remains primary. Since the stories are more concerned with examining the emotional lives of the characters than the physical and sexual side, overtly gay or lesbian characters are rare. Extremely intense same–sex relationships, however, pervade many of Bowen's stories and novels. Her first novel, *The Hotel,* published in the United States in 1928, the same year as *The Well of Loneliness,* stands in contrast to Hall's story in its refusal to portray homosexual relationships and lesbian tendencies as tragic or abnormal. The lesbian couple with whose quarrel and reconciliation the novel opens and closes may be neurotic, but they are decidedly not tragic. The main plot, however, revolves around 22–year–old Sydney Warren's obsessive attraction to the charismatic, middle–aged widow, Mrs. Kerr, who is wintering at the same Riviera hotel. Sydney realizes that she is being used when she is dropped after the arrival of Mrs. Kerr's son Ronald, who soon has a similar revelation about his relationship with his mother. In her frustration, Sydney accepts a proposal of marriage from James Milton, an intellectual clergyman, only to change her mind a few weeks later. At the end of the novel, Sydney, like Lois at the conclusion of *The Last September,* having rejected the conventional inanities of heterosexual love and marriage, stands at the door of a new and uncertain modern world—a world that Bowen declines to sketch for her reader.

In Bowen's work, as in her life, social convention and tradition offer security, rootedness, and a kind of steady contentment; yet this convention is also a kind of fiction. Bowen's own marriage to Alan Cameron, which lasted from 1923 until his death in 1952, while the basis of emotional security and professional support, was studded with affairs, passionate and intense in a way that her marriage never could be. And just as these affairs took their course outside the realm of her conventional marriage, so most lesbian relationships in her stories occur outside of, though often alongside, the context of heterosexual love and marriage.

In a 1964 novel, *The Little Girls,* three middle–aged women, school chums in childhood, come together to dig up a treasure chest they had buried as little girls, before the Great War. The reunion revives long buried emotions as the women replay their childhood roles of subjection and domination, passion and repression. Their adult understanding of their past reveals new dimensions to their early friendship: Clare's awkward devotion to Diana is recast as lesbian desire; Diana's vague charm, as girlish coyness; and Sheila's prim superiority as repressed anger. Like other lesbian relationships and romantic friendships in Bowen's novels, the unusual and intense friendship of the three women—as children and much later in middle–age—brackets the conventional lives they have led in between, as wives, mothers and career women.

Bowen's strength as a novelist lies in the extraordinary psychological depth of her characterizations combined with remarkable economy of language. Moreover, her acute sense of observation never allows her to indulge in sentimental or dishonest representations of human relationships; it is this imperative that opens a narrative space, however marginal, for the sympathetic portrayal of lesbian psychology and relationships.

—*Allison Rolls*

———

BOWLES, Jane (Sydney Auer). American novelist, playwright, and author of short stories and nonfiction. Born in New York City, 22 February 1917. Educated at Stoneleigh in Massachusetts; privately tutored in Leysin, Switzerland, 1932–34. Married composer and author Paul Bowles in 1938. Converted to Catholicism, c. 1971. Writer in the United States during the late 1930s and early 1940s; contributor to *Vogue, Harper's Bazaar,* and *Mademoiselle;* after World War II, lived in Mexico, Panama, France, and Ceylon; lived in Tangier, Morocco, 1948–73. *Died in Málaga, Spain, 4 May 1973.*

WRITINGS

Fiction

Plain Pleasures (short story; originally published in *Harper's Bazaar* [New York], 1942). London, Peter Owen, 1966.
"Andrew," in *Antaeus* (New York), 1971.
"Emmy Moore's Journal," in *Antaeus* (New York), 1971.
Two Serious Ladies (novel). New York, Knopf, 1943; London, Peter Owen, 1965; with introduction by Francine du Pleasix Gray, London, Virago, 1979.

Plays

In the Summer House, background music by Paul Bowles (produced New York, 1953; Dublin, 1969). New York, Random House, 1954.

Other

Song of an Old Woman (song). New York, Schirmer, 1946.
Two Skies (song). New York, Schirmer, 1946.
The Collected Works of Jane Bowles (includes "Camp Cataract," originally published in *Harper's Bazaar* [New York], 1949), introduction by Truman Capote. New York, Farrar Straus, 1966; expanded as *My Sister's Hand in Mine,* New York, Ecco Press, 1977.

Feminine Wiles, introduction by Tennessee Williams. Santa Barbara, California, Black Sparrow Press, 1976.
Out in the World: Selected Letters of Jane Bowles, 1935–1970, edited by Millicent Dillon. Santa Barbara, California, Black Sparrow Press, 1985.

*

Manuscript Collections: Humanities Research Center, University of Texas, Austin.

Biography: *A Little Original Sin: The Life and Work of Jane Bowles* by Millicent Dillon, New York, Holt, Rinehart, & Winston, 1981.

Critical Sources: "The World and Art of Jane Bowles (1917–1973)" by Robert E. Lougy, in *CEA Critic* (Rochester, New York), winter 1986–summer 1987, 157–173; "Imagination, Control and Betrayal in Jane Bowles' 'A Stick of Green Candy'" by Mark T. Bassett, in *Studies in Short Fiction* (Newberry, South Carolina), winter 1987, 25–29; "Jane Bowles: Experiment as Character" by Millicent Dillon, in *Breaking the Sequence: Women's Experimental Fiction,* edited by Ellen G. Friedman and Miriam Fuchs, Princeton, New Jersey, Princeton University Press, 1989, 140–147; *The Dream at the End of the World: Paul Bowles and the Literary Renegades in Tangier* by Michelle Green, New York, HarperCollins, 1991.

*   *   *

During an Atlantic crossing by ocean liner at the age of 17, Jane Bowles was on deck reading Louis–Ferdinand Céline's novel *Voyage to the End of Night* when a stranger approached, recounts Robert E. Lougy in *CEA Critic.* "I see you're reading Céline," he remarked. "He is the greatest writer in the whole world," she replied. The man smiled. "Céline," he said, "c'est moi." After a long talk with the famous novelist, the young girl vowed to become a writer herself. Upon her return to New York, she began the novel that was eventually published as *Two Serious Ladies* in 1943. *Two Serious Ladies* earned accolades from such writers as Tennessee Williams, Truman Capote, Alan Sillitoe, and John Ashbery. The novel also established Bowles' underground reputation as a prose stylist of unique qualities who explored the efforts of women to escape from conventional sexual roles. Despite her small body of published work—a single novel, a play, seven short stories, and selected letters—Bowles holds a respected, if minor, position in contemporary literature, partly due to popular interest in her troubled life and partly to being rediscovered by lesbians and feminists who see in her a prototypical spokesperson.

In Bowles' fiction, characters are emotionally distanced from one another and yet unable to survive alone. In story after story she writes of two women, either sisters or friends, who long to break free of bourgeois morality but crave the stability it provides. Bowles' characters are on a search for balance in their personal lives, a balance between action and passivity, between independence and security. In the story "A Quarreling Pair," for example, two sisters with contrasting personalities argue over their approaches to life. The stronger sister wishes the pair to stay at home, while the other sister, adventurous but high–strung, wants to leave. Bowles' play *In the Summer House* focuses on a mother and daughter who, despite their respective marriages, want to maintain their own dangerously insulated relationship.

Two Serious Ladies is Bowles' most sustained examination of her essential fictional conflict. Christina Goering and Frieda Copperfield are friends who follow different paths to what they believe is personal fulfillment. Christina sells off her possessions and takes a string of lovers in a quest to achieve self–styled sainthood. But she ruthlessly and quite unconsciously uses people along the way. Frieda works up the nerve to leave her husband and live in a sleazy hotel with a prostitute named Pacifica, becoming an emotionally disturbed alcoholic. Christina and Freida experiment with both homosexual and heterosexual relationships as a possible means of finding happiness, but neither woman is satisfied with her relationships. When they meet again after many years, however, both friends believe they have found what they wanted. Christina sees herself as nearly a saint, while Frieda claims to possess a daring and self–confidence she never had before. The novel is comically gothic in style, recounting in deadpan prose the arbitrary and motiveless choices the women make. At story's end, the idea occurs to Christina that both women may be "piling sin upon sin," but she dismisses the possibility as being "of considerable interest but of no great importance."

Of considerable interest to many of Bowles' readers is the relationship between her own life and her fiction. A lesbian who had a string of female lovers and many affairs, Bowles was known to enter parties and announce, "I'm a lesbian and this is my lover," yet she never created a character who was that open about her sexuality. Time and again in her stories Bowles depicts lesbianism as a symptom of a disturbed personality, something engaged in by lost souls searching for emotional stability. Her failure to portray healthy lesbian characters may be due in part to her own ill health and emotional problems. She suffered from alcoholism, drug dependence, and a manic–depressive nature, which led to periodic emotional breakdowns and suicide attempts. Her health problems led to a severe stroke at the age of 40 which disabled her for the rest of her life. The true connection between Bowles' life and art remains a subject of continuing critical debate and reader interest.

Part of the Bowles' legend consists of the years she spent living in Tangier, Morocco, with her husband, novelist Paul Bowles. Tangier, because of its international zone status before Morocco achieved independence, was for many years an open port where emigrés from around the world could enter visa–free. Smugglers, gunrunners, drug dealers, and other criminals gave the city a dangerous, colorful image attractive to many literary figures. Following André Gide's example, many gay writers and artists made Tangier a stopping point during the 1950s, and no stay was complete without visiting the Bowles' household. Among their many callers were Truman Capote, Allen Ginsberg, Susan Sontag, Jack Kerouac, William Burroughs, Tennessee Williams, and Christopher Isherwood.

—*Thomas Wiloch*

———

BOWLES, Paul (Frederick). American composer, translator, poet, novelist, and author of short fiction. Born in New York City, 30 December 1910. Educated at School of Design and Liberal Arts and University of Virginia; also studied with Aaron Copland, 1930–32, and Virgil Thomson, 1933–34. Married Jane Sydney Auer in 1938 (died 1973). Music critic, New York *Herald–Tribune,* 1942–46; visiting professor, San Fernando Valley State College, San Fernando, California, 1968. Composer for plays, operas, film scores, and ballets, and of songs and chamber music. Since 1947 has lived in Tangier. **Recipient:** Guggenheim fellowship, 1941; National Institute of Arts and Letters Award in Literature, 1950; Rockefeller grant, 1959; National Endowment for the Arts creative writing fellowship, 1978, and senior fellowship, 1980; American Book Award nomination, 1980, for fiction. Agent: William Morris Agency, 1350 Avenue of the Americas, New York, New York 10019, U.S.A. Address: 2117 Tanger Socco, Tangier, Morocco.

WRITINGS

Novels

The Sheltering Sky. London, Lehmann, and New York, New Directions, 1949.
Let It Come Down. London, Lehmann, and New York, Random House, 1952.
The Spider's House. New York, Random House, 1955; London, Macdonald, 1957; revised, Santa Rosa, California, Black Sparrow Press, 1982.
Up Above the World. New York, Simon & Schuster, 1966; London, Owen, 1967.

Short Stories

"A White Goat's Shadow: A Story," in *Argo,* December 1930.
"Bluey, Pages from an Imaginary Diary (1919)," in *View,* October 1943.
"Here to Learn," in *Antaeus* (New York), summer 1979.
The Delicate Prey, and Other Stories. New York, Random House, 1950.
A Little Stone: Stories. London, Lehmann, 1950.
The Hours after Noon. London, Heinemann, 1959.
A Hundred Camels in the Courtyard. San Francisco, City Lights Books, 1962.
The Time of Friendship. New York, Holt Rinehart, 1967.
Pages from Cold Point, and Other Stories. London, Owen, 1968.
Three Tales. New York, Hallman, 1975.
Things Gone and Things Still Here. Santa Rosa, California, Black Sparrow Press, 1977.
Collected Stories of Paul Bowles, 1939–1976, introduction by Gore Vidal. Santa Rosa, California, Black Sparrow Press, 1979.
Midnight Mass, and Other Stories. Santa Rosa, California, Black Sparrow Press, 1981.
Unwelcome Words. Bolinas, California, Tombouctou Books, 1988.
Call at Corazon, and Other Stories. London, Owen, 1988.
"Pages from Cold Point," in *The Faber Book of Gay Short Fiction,* edited by Edmund White. London and New York, Faber & Faber, 1991.

Poetry

Two Poems. New York, Modern Editions Press, 1933.

Scenes. Santa Rosa, California, Black Sparrow Press, 1968.
The Thicket of Spring: Poems, 1926–1969. Santa Rosa, California, Black Sparrow Press, 1972.
Next to Nothing. Kathmandu, Starstreams, 1976.
Next to Nothing: Collected Poems, 1926–1977. Santa Rosa, California, Black Sparrow Press, 1981.

Screenplays

With Tennessee Williams, *The Wanton Countess* (originally released as *Senso* by Gore Vidal, Luchino Visconti, and Tennessee Williams, c. 1949), Domenico Forges Davanzati, 1954.
Paul Bowles in the Land of the Jumblies, Gary Conklin, 1969.

Uncollected Nonfiction

"Fez," in *Holiday* (New York), July 1950.
"The Secret Sahara," in *Holiday* (New York), January 1953.
"Paris! City of the Arts," in *Holiday* (New York), April 1953.
"Europe's Most Exotic City," in *Holiday* (New York), May 1955.
"The Incredible Arab," in *Holiday* (New York), August 1956.
"The Worlds of Tangier," in *Holiday* (New York), March 1958.
"The Moslems," in *Holiday* (New York), April 1959.
"Casablanca," in *Holiday* (New York), September 1966.
"Cafe in Morocco," in *Holiday* (New York), August 1968.
"What's So Different about Marrakesh?," in *Travel and Leisure* (New York), June–July 1971.
"Morocco Perceived," in *Esquire* (New York), March 1975.

Translator

No Exit by Jean–Paul Sartre. New York, French, 1946.
Lost Trail of the Sahara by Roger Frison–Roche. London, Hale, 1956; Englewood Cliffs, New Jersey, Prentice Hall, 1962.
A Life Full of Holes by Driss ben Hamed Charhadi. New York, Grove, 1963.
Love with a Few Hairs by Mohammed Mrabet. London, Owen, 1967.
The Lemon by Mohammed Mrabet. London, Owen, 1969.
M'Hashish by Mohammed Mrabet. San Francisco, City Lights Books, 1969.
For Bread Alone by Mohamed Choukri. London, Owen, 1973.
Jean Genet in Tangier by Mohamed Choukri. Ecco Press, 1974.
The Boy Who Set the Fire, and Other Stories by Mohammed Mrabet. Santa Rosa, California, Black Sparrow Press, 1974.
Hadidan Aharam by Mohammed Mrabet. Santa Rosa, California, Black Sparrow Press, 1975.
The Oblivion Seekers, and Other Writings by Isabelle Eberhardt. San Francisco, City Lights Books, 1975.
Harmless Poisons, Blameless Sins by Mohammed Mrabet. Santa Rosa, California, Black Sparrow Press, 1976.
Look and Move On by Mohammed Mrabet. Santa Rosa, California, Black Sparrow Press, 1976.
The Big Mirror by Mohammed Mrabet. Santa Rosa, California, Black Sparrow Press, 1977.
Five Eyes: Short Stories by Five Moroccans. Santa Rosa, California, Black Sparrow Press, 1979.
Tennessee Williams in Tangier by Mohamed Choukri. Cadmus Editions, 1979.
The Beach Cafe by Mohammed Mrabet. Santa Rosa, California, Black Sparrow Press, 1980.

The Chest by Mohammed Mrabet. Bolinas, California, Tombouctou Books, 1983.
The Beggar's Knife by Rodrigo Rey Rosa. San Francisco, City Lights Books, 1985.
Marriage with Papers by Mohammed Mrabet. Bolinas, California, Tombouctou Books, 1986.
Dust on Her Tongue by Rodrigo Rey Bosa. London, Owen, 1989.
The Pelcari Project by Rodrigo Rey Rosa. London, Owen, 1991.

Other

Yallah (travel). Zurich, Manesse, New York, McDowell Obolensky, 1957.
Their Heads Are Green and Their Hands Are Blue (travel). New York, Random House, 1963; as *Their Heads Are Green,* London, Owen, 1963.
Without Stopping: An Autobiography. London, Owen, and New York, Putnam, 1972.
In the Red Room. Los Angeles, Sylvester & Orphanos, 1981.
Points in Time. London, Owen, 1982, New York, Ecco Press, 1984.
Aperture. New York, Aperture Foundation, 1984.
Two Years Beside the Strait: Tangier Journal, 1987–1989. London, Owen, 1990; as *Days: Tangier Journal, 1987–1989,* New York, Ecco Press, 1991.
Author of preface, *View: Parade of the Avante Garde, 1940–1947,* edited by Charles Henri Ford. New York, Thunders Mouth Press, 1991.

Published Music: *Tornado Blues* (chorus); *Music for a Farce* (chamber music); *Piano Sonatina; Huapango 1 and 2; Six Preludes for Piano; El Indio; El Bejuco; Sayula; La Cuelga; Sonata for Two Pianos; Night Waltz* (two pianos); Songs: *Heavenly Grass; Sugar in the Cane; Cabin; Lonesome Man; Letter to Freddy; The Years; Of All the Things I Love; A Little Closer, Please; David; In the Woods; Song of an Old Woman; Night Without Sleep; Two Skies; Que te falta?; Ya Llego; Once a Lady Was Here; Bluebell Mountain; Three; On a Quiet Conscience; El Carbonero; Baby, Baby; Selected Songs,* Santa Fe, Soundings Press, 1984.

Operas: *Denmark Vesey,* 1937; *The Wind Remains,* 1941.

Ballets: *Yankee Clipper,* 1937; *Pastorella,* 1941; *Sentimental Colloquy,* 1944; *Blue Roses,* 1957.

Incidental Music: For plays: *Horse Eats Hat,* 1936; *Dr. Faustus,* 1937; *My Heart's in the Highlands,* 1939; *Love's Old Sweet Song,* 1940; *Twelfth Night,* 1940; *Liberty Jones,* 1941; *Watch on the Rhine,* 1941; *South Pacific,* 1943; *Jacobowsky and the Colonel,* 1944; *The Glass Menagerie,* 1945; *Twilight Bar,* 1946; *On Whitman Avenue,* 1946; *The Dancer,* 1946; *Cyrano de Bergerac,* 1946; *Land's End,* 1946; *Summer and Smoke,* 1948; *In the Summer House,* 1953; *Edwin Booth,* 1958; *Sweet Bird of Youth,* 1959; *The Milk Train Doesn't Stop Here Anymore,* 1963. For films: *Roots in the Soil,* 1940; *Congo,* 1944.

Recordings: *The Wind Remains,* M.G.M.; *Cafe Sin Nombre,* New Music; *Sonata for Two Pianos,* Concert Hall; *Night Waltz,* Columbia; *Scenes d'Anabase,* Columbia; *Music for a Farce,* Columbia; *Song for My Sister,* Disc; *They Cannot Stop Death,* Disc; *Night Without Sleep,* Disc; *Sailor's Song,* Disc; *Rain Rots the Wood,* Disc; *Sonata for Flute and Piano,* Art of This Century; *Six Preludes,*

Golden Crest; *Huapango 1 and 2*, New Music; *El Bejuco and El Indio*, Art of This Century; *Blue Mountain Ballads*, Music Library; *Concerto for Two Pianos, Winds and Percussion*, Columbia; *Once a Lady Was Here, Song of an Old Person*, New World; *A Picnic Cantata*, lyrics by James Schuyler, Columbia, 1955; *Six Latin American Pieces*, Etcetera, 1984; *Five Songs*, GSS, 1984; *Six Preludes, Eleven Songs*, 1989.

*

Manuscript Collections: Humanities Research Center, University of Texas, Austin.

Biography: "An Evening with Paul Bowles" by Richard Rumbold, in *London Magazine* (London), November 1960, 65–73; "Paul Bowles," in *Contemporary Authors Autobiography Series*, Detroit, Gale Research, 1989, 81–95.

Interviews: "Talk with Paul Bowles" by Harvey Breit, in *New York Times Book Review*, 9 March 1952, 19; "An Interview with Paul Bowles" by Oliver Evans, in *Mediterranean Review*, winter 1971, 3–15; "Conversations in Morocco" by Michael Rogers, in *Rolling Stone* (New York), 23 May 1974, 48–58.

Bibliography: *Paul Bowles: A Descriptive Bibliography* by Jeffrey Miller, Santa Rosa, California, Black Sparrow Press, 1986.

Critical Sources: "Paul Bowles and the Natural Man" by Oliver Evans, in *Recent American Fiction*, Boston, Houghton Mifflin, 1963; *Another Way of Living: A Gallery of Americans Who Choose to Live in Europe* by John Bainbridge, New York, Holt Rinehart, 1968; *Paul Bowles: The Illumination of North Africa* by Lawrence D. Stewart, Carbondale, Southern Illinois University Press, 1974; *Paul Bowles: Staticity and Terror* by Eric Mottram, London, Aloes, 1976; *The Fiction of Paul Bowles: The Soul Is the Weariest Part of the Body* by Hans Bertens, Amsterdam, Rodopi, and Atlantic Highlands, New Jersey, Humanities Press, 1979; *Review of Contemporary Fiction* (Elmwood Park, Illinois), 2:3 (Paul Bowles issue), 1982; *Paul Bowles: The Inner Geography* by Wayne Pounds, Bern, Switzerland, Lang, 1985; *Twentieth–Century Literature* (Hempstead, New York), fall–winter (Paul Bowles issue), 1986; *A World Outside: The Fiction of Paul Bowles* by Richard F. Patteson, Austin, University of Texas Press, 1987; *An Invisible Spectator: A Biography of Paul Bowles* by Christopher Sawyer–Laucanno, London, Bloomsbury, 1989, New York, Ecco Press, 1990.

*   *   *

Because Paul Bowles has chosen to live in Tangier, Morocco, for over four decades, the city and its Muslim culture figure prominently in many of his novels and short stories. In the usual Bowles' story, a Westerner arrives in the primitive, somewhat barbaric society of Morocco, is overwhelmed by the differing way of life, sheds his civilized veneer, and succumbs to mental collapse. Bowles' fictional world is one where violence lies just below the surface normality and the constraints of civilization are easily discarded. This vision is presented in a careful, detached prose which height-

ens the tension and ambiguity. In some of his stories Bowles includes homosexual characters, although they are oftentimes depicted as violent or emotionally–troubled individuals. His lesbian characters are stereotypes. In his private life Bowles has enjoyed a number of homosexual relationships, particularly with young Arabs, but his fiction tends to depict such behavior—and most human behavior, to be sure—as abnormal and dangerous.

Bowles began writing as a child, creating poems, stories and music, and even publishing work in the legendary *transition* magazine at the age of 16. During a trip to Paris in 1931 he met and befriended Gertrude Stein and her companion, Alice B. Toklas. Stein was adamant that the surrealist–inspired poetry Bowles was then writing should be abandoned, telling the young author that he was "no poet at all." The advice moved Bowles to look seriously at a music career instead. With friend Aaron Copland's encouragement, he sought work as a composer. Soon he was writing music for the New York stage and Hollywood films. It was some ten years before he began writing prose again, this time trying his hand at short fiction. Stein reacted favorably to the change in genre. "Go on with them," she advised.

When in 1942 Bowles' wife Jane began her novel *Two Serious Ladies*, Bowles himself began writing seriously again. He was soon publishing stories in *Harper's Bazaar, Mademoiselle, Partisan Review*, and other magazines, gathering many of these early works together in the collection *The Delicate Prey, and Other Stories*. The stories published here are typical of Bowles' nihilistic vision. The title story tells of a cunning criminal who lures three brothers into the mountains, murders the two older brothers, then tortures, mutilates, rapes and murders the youngest. In "A Distant Episode," a Western linguist ventures into the Moroccan wilderness to study nomadic tribesmen only to be taken prisoner by them. They cut out his tongue, dress him in a suit of flattened tin cans, and make him dance for their amusement.

Among the best of Bowles' stories are several dealing with specifically homosexual characters. "Pages from Cold Point," perhaps the best known of these stories, traces the moral disintegration of a Mr. Norton, a divorced college professor. Blinded by lust to the consequences of his actions, Norton seduces his teenaged son, Racky. The ensuing relationship turns the boy into a sexual predator who uses blackmail, violence and money to force others to his will. In "The Echo," Bowles tells of a woman who leaves her marriage to live with a lesbian lover in Columbia. When the woman's neurotic daughter visits and discovers the nature of the relationship, she assaults the lover in an act both of outrage and familial rebellion. The lover is a stereotypical lesbian, butch and blue–jeaned, playing a decidedly masculine role. (In his later novel *Let It Come Down*, Bowles again created a lesbian stereotype in Eunice Goode, who wears pants, slugs down gin and talks like a truck driver.) Although both "Pages from Cold Point" and "The Echo" depict homosexuals as violent, predatory, and troubled individuals, hedonism—and a civilization whose intellectuals have degenerated into self–absorbed, morally reckless creatures—are Bowles' real targets in "Pages from a Cold Point," while dysfunctional family relations plague the characters in "The Echo." Since Bowles' world is one in which all human behavior is aberrant, his depiction of homosexuality as something unhealthy, a problem, a symptom of emotional or moral disease, does not differ significantly from his depiction of heterosexuality.

Bowles and his late wife Jane Bowles entertained many prominent gays in literature and the arts at their residence in Tangier. For many years an international port which could be entered without a visa, Tangier attracted criminal elements from around the world. Literary people who enjoyed the dangerous ambience of the port, the easy access to drugs, and the tolerance of the residents also frequented Tangier. Bowles has said that he found it a convenient place to board ocean liners for travel to any part of the world. During the 1950s the port was particularly popular with the international gay community, and the Bowles served as frequent hosts.

—*Thomas Wiloch*

BOX, Edgar. *See* **VIDAL, Gore.**

BOYD, Blanche McCrary. American novelist and essayist. Born in Charleston, South Carolina, in 1945. Teaches writing at Connecticut College, New London, Connecticut. Address: c/o Connecticut College, Box 1421, New London, Connecticut 06320, U.S.A.

WRITINGS

Novels

Nerves. Plainfield, Vermont, Daughters, Inc., 1973.
Mourning the Death of Magic. New York, Macmillan, 1977.
The Revolution of Little Girls. New York, Knopf, 1991.

Other

The Redneck Way of Knowledge: Down–Home Tales (includes "Growing Up Racist" and "Ambush"). New York, Knopf, 1981.
"The Way It Should Be Remembered," in *New York Times Magazine,* 19 November 1989.

*

Critical Sources: "Creating a Women's World" by Lois Gould, in *New York Times Magazine,* 2 January 1977, 10–38; *The Safe Sea of Women: Lesbian Fiction, 1969–1989* by Bonnie Zimmerman, Boston, Beacon Press, 1990; "The Surprise of the New" by Sarah Schulman, in *Advocate,* 21 May 1991, 90.

*   *   *

Blanche McCrary Boyd's writing career has spanned more than 20 years, at least two genres and several artistic identifications. Her first novel *Nerves,* was published in 1973 by Daughters, Inc., a collectively run publishing house founded by writers June Arnold, Bertha Harris, Patty Bowman and Charlotte Bunch that was dedicated to bringing new feminist voices to print. (Their greatest success was Rita Mae Brown's first novel, *Rubyfruit Jungle,* also published in 1973, which has since become a lesbian classic.)

On the surface *Nerves* was domestic Southern gothic that chronicled and explored the troubled underpinning of the dysfunctional nuclear family from the point of view of the 14–year–old Diane. But the trappings of the family gothic—a genre that has appealed to other Southern women writers such as Flannery O'Connor, Carson McCullers and gay male writers like Tennessee Williams, Harlan Greene—are subverted by Boyd's conscious intervention of a feminist politic. The byzantine and often emotionally unhealthy family relationships (so often the trademark of the gothic) are viewed as the direct result of male power. The narrative tensions in *Nerves* come from the struggle of the female characters to create their own autonomy and overcome not only the power of their past family history, but the troubled history of the American South itself. This is a theme that would be repeated and elaborated upon in Boyd's next two novels *Mourning the Death of Magic* and *The Revolution of Little Girls.* The setting of each of the novels is Charleston, South Carolina, Boyd's birthplace and the city in which she grew up and returned to live several times as an adult.

Each of Blanche McCrary Boyd's novels creates an essentially female centered universe in which the younger women—Diane in *Nerves,* Galley in *Mourning the Death of Magic* and Ellen in *The Revolution of Little Girls*—constantly encounter emotional, psychic and sometimes material obstacles to their gaining some autonomy over their lives and sexuality. Each of these characters becomes, at some point in their lives, a lesbian. But Boyd's novels never reduce complex emotional and political arrangements to a simple case of gender disenfranchisement and in each of the novels it is the younger women's mothers and aunts who are coagents of their disempowerment. In the context of Boyd's female–centered universe, this creates a situation in which the generations of women characters refract and reflect one another. Halfway through *The Revolution of Little Girls* (Boyd's most successful and critically acclaimed novel) Ellen is pursued by a small troop of phantom pre–pubescent girls who are at once a materialization of past and possible selves as well as a sign that the need to break from the past is inevitable.

Many of these themes are also present in *The Redneck Way of Knowledge,* a collection of nonfiction pieces that originally appeared in the *Village Voice.* Many of the fictionalized events of the novels reappear as personal *reportage,* although Boyd's social concerns—especially about racial issues—are delved into more deeply. In "Growing Up Racist" she explores the complexities of being Southern and attempting to embrace an anti–racist politic. In "Ambush" she explores the complicated social relationships that led to a clash of violence and murder between the Klan and the Communist Worker's Party. Issues of race are also present in the novels—Lena, in *Nerves,* is described as wondering "if it was nerves making her see, for the first time, how much of her life was built on the lives of black people. [I]t was as if, when she walked on her carpets, she stepped on bodies"—and Boyd is particularly concerned with how white women, already socially constrained, deal with their own complicity in racial oppression.

Blanche McCrary Boyd writes from the perspective of a white Southern lesbian who understands the complexity of her position—as an oppressed gender and sexual minority as well as a member of a dominant racial class—and whose writing is continually attempting to mediate and understand both the imbalance of power in her life as well as to establish her own autonomy and sense of self.

—*Michael Bronski*

———————

BOYD, Malcolm. American theologian, novelist, playwright, and editor. Born in New York City, 8 June 1923. Educated at University of Arizona, Tucson, B.A. 1944; Divinity School of the Pacific, B.D. 1954; Oxford University, Oxford, England, 1954–55; studied at an ecumenical institute in Geneva, Switzerland; Union Theological Seminary, New York City, S.T.M. 1956; participated in a work–study program at Taize Community, France, 1957. Companion of Mark Thompson. Copywriter, scriptwriter, and producer of radio programs, Foote, Cone & Belding (advertising agency), Hollywood, California, 1945–46; writer and producer, Republic Pictures and Samuel Goldwyn Productions, Hollywood, 1947–49; cofounder, vice president, and general manager, Pickford, Rogers, & Boyd, New York City, 1949–51; rector, St. George's Episcopal Church, Indianapolis, Indiana, 1957–59; Episcopal chaplain, Colorado State University, Ft. Collins, 1959–61; Protestant chaplain, Wayne State University, and assistant priest, Grace Episcopal Church, Detroit, 1961–64; assistant pastor, Church of the Atonement, Washington, D.C., 1964–65; national field representative to American universities and colleges, Episcopal Society for Cultural and Racial Unity, 1965–68; writer–priest in residence, St. Augustine by–the–Sea Episcopal Church, Santa Monica, California, 1981—; director, Institute of Gay Spirituality and Theology, Los Angeles, 1987—. Lecturer, World Council of Churches, 1955 and 1964; columnist, *Pittsburgh Courier,* 1962–65; participated in voter registration drives in Alabama and Mississippi, 1963 and 1964; resident fellow of Calhoun College, Yale University, New Haven, Connecticut, 1968–71, associate fellow, 1971–75; resident guest, Mishkenot Sha'ananim, Jerusalem, Israel, 1974; host of television programs, including *Sex in the Seventies,* CBS–TV, 1975; president of Los Angeles chapter of PEN, 1984–87; chaplain, AIDS Commission of the Episcopal Diocese of Los Angeles, 1989—; contributing editor, *Renewal and Integrity Forum*; contributor of reviews and articles to newspapers and periodicals, including *Los Angeles Times Book Review, New York Times, Advocate, Ms., Modern Maturity, Episcopalian, United Church Herald,* and *Christian Century.* Member of the Film Awards Committee, National Council of Churches, 1965; Los Angeles City/County AIDS Task Force, beginning 1985. **Recipient:** Integrity International Award, 1978; Union of American Hebrew Congregations Award, 1980. Address: c/o St. Augustine–by–the–Sea Episcopal Church, 1227 Fourth Street, Santa Monica, California 90401, U.S.A.

WRITINGS

Nonfiction

Crisis in Communication. Garden City, New York, Doubleday, 1957.
Christ and Celebrity Gods. New York, Seabury, 1958.

Focus: Rethinking the Meaning of Our Evangelism. Wilton, Connecticut, Morehouse, 1960.
If I Go Down to Hell. Wilton, Connecticut, Morehouse, 1962.
The Hunger, the Thirst. Wilton, Connecticut, Morehouse, 1964.
Are You Running with Me, Jesus? New York, Holt, 1965; revised, Boston, Beacon Press, 1990.
Free to Live, Free to Die. New York, Holt, 1967; revised and abridged, 1970.
Malcolm Boyd's Book of Days. New York, Random House, 1969.
As I Live and Breathe: Stages of an Autobiography. New York, Random House, 1969.
Human Like Me, Jesus. New York, Simon & Schuster, 1971.
With Paul Conrad, *When in the Course of Human Events.* London, Sheed & Ward, 1973.
Christian: Its Meanings in the Age of Future Shock. New York, Hawthorn, 1975.
Am I Running with You, God? Garden City, New York, Doubleday, 1977.
Take Off the Masks. Garden City, New York, Doubleday, 1977; revised, Philadelphia, New Society, 1984; revised, New York, San Francisco, 1993.
Look Back in Joy: Celebration of Gay Lovers. San Francisco, Gay Sunshine, 1981; revised, with photographs by Crawford Barton, Boston, Alyson Publications, 1990.
Half Laughing/Half Crying: Songs for Myself. New York, St. Martin's Press, 1986.
Gay Priest: An Inner Journey. New York, St. Martin's Press, 1987.
Deges, Boundaries, and Connections. Seattle, Broken Moon Press, 1992.
Rich with Years: Daily Meditations on Growing Older. San Francisco, HarperCollins, in press.

Fiction

The Fantasy World of Peter Stone, and Other Fables. New York, Harper, 1969.
The Lover. Waco, Texas, Word, Inc., 1972.
The Runner. Waco, Texas, Word, Inc., 1974.
The Alleluia Affair. Waco, Texas, Word, Inc., 1975.

Plays

They Aren't Real to Me (produced New York, 1962).
The Job (produced New York, 1962).
Study in Color (produced New York, 1962).
Boy (produced New York, 1964).
The Community (produced New York, 1964).

Editor

On the Battle Lines. Wilton, Connecticut, Morehouse, 1964.
The Underground Church. London, Sheed & Ward, 1968.
With Nancy Wilson, *Amazing Grace: Stories of Lesbian and Gay Faith.* Trumansburg, New York, Crossing Press, 1991.

Contributor

Christianity and Contemporary Arts. Nashville, Tennessee, Abingdon, 1962.
Witness to a Generation, by Edward Fiske. New York, Bobbs–Merrill, 1967.

You Can't Kill the Dream. Atlanta, John Knox, 1968.
Gay Spirit: Myth and Meaning, edited by Mark Thompson. New York, St. Martin's Press, 1987.
Contemporary Authors Autobiography Series (autobiographical sketch), Volume 11. Detroit, Gale, 1990.

Other

My Fellow Americans (interviews). New York, Holt, 1970.
With Ervin Zavada, *Are You Running with Me, Jesus* (screenplay; based on author's book of the same title).

*

Adaptations: All of Boyd's plays have appeared on television; *The Job, Study in Color, Boy* (film), New York, Anti–Defamation League of B'nai B'rith.

Manuscript Collections: Malcolm Boyd Collection and Archives, Boston University Library.

Biography: *Contemporary Authors Autobiography Series,* Volume 11, Detroit, Gale, 1990, 43–60.

Interviews: "Malcolm Boyd Takes Another Step With Integrity," in *Advocate,* 8 September 1976, 15–16; *Contemporary Authors New Revision Series,* Volume 26, Detroit, Gale, 1989, 66–70.

Malcolm Boyd comments: "I salute diversity as a hallmark of creation and I believe in the integration of sexuality and spirituality as a way toward wholeness."

*   *   *

The complex variety of career paths taken by activist Malcolm Boyd are bound together by a common theme: expressing the truth of one's inner nature and spiritual needs with openness and honesty. Since his ordination as an Episcopal priest in 1955, Boyd has written on a broad field of subjects, from his 1965 collection of prayers for the contemporary world *Are You Running with Me Jesus?,* which brought him national acclaim, to the meditation texts of *The Book of Days* and articles in popular periodicals and newspapers such as *Ms., Parade,* the *New York Times* and the *Washington Post.* His contributions to the evolving body of American gay and lesbian journalism are similarly diverse, with features on such topics as the emerging gay community in the former Soviet Union and the struggle of homosexuals with organized religion for recognition and equality at the altar appearing frequently in the *Advocate.* Much of Boyd's gay–themed writing is autobiographical in nature, as he uses his own life as a forum for the explication of his views and insights on social reforms, spirituality and political change. The three works for which he is most widely known, *Take Off the Masks, Look Back in Joy: Celebration of Gay Lovers,* and *Gay Priest: An Inner Journey,* reveal the development of Boyd's private journey and growth.

At the time of its initial publication in 1978, two years after John McNeill's groundbreaking study *The Church and the Homosexual,*

Take Off the Masks was virtually unique as an autobiography of an openly gay member of the clergy, preceded only by Troy Perry's *The Lord Is My Shepherd and He Knows I'm Gay* in 1972. Despite the subsequent appearance of such works as Salmon Sherwood's *Kairos: Confessions of a Gay Priest,* Johannes DiMaria–Kuiper's *Hot under the Collar,* and the anthology *Lesbian Nuns: Breaking Silence,* Boyd's volume retains its primacy as the opening dialogue against the subordination of human spiritual needs to the bureaucracy of faith, a condition that he termed "Churchianity". The demand that individuals be seen as precious, unique and valuable, irrespective of race, beliefs or sexual orientation, is an outgrowth of Boyd's own outreach ministry at Colorado State University in 1959 as well as his involvement in the civil rights movement. Through the story of the author's life and passage into wholeness, *Take Off the Masks* inveighs against the separation of people by barriers of any kind. The idea that a prominent clergyman would not only admit to being homosexual but actually celebrate it as a spiritual gift contributed both to the growth of a separate gay and lesbian approach to religious matters and to the evolution of a more accepting theology.

The format of the brief essays that form the body of *Look Back in Joy: Celebration of Gay Lovers* recalls the pages of *Are You Running with Me, Jesus?* The collection frankly explores the gamut of emotions that comprise gay relationships of all types, from the most transient encounters to lifetime commitments. The final section presents vignettes from the construction of Boyd's own partnership. Taken as a whole, the work is a melding of the activist focus of much of the author's previous writing with the spiritual aspects emerging from the gay and lesbian movement of the 1980s. The growing spiritual aspect of the gay and lesbian movement would be more fully developed and explored in such anthologies as *Gay Spirit: Myth and Meaning* and *Amazing Grace: Stories of Lesbian and Gay Faith.*

Gay Priest: An Inner Journey is in many ways a combination of the passion, anger, and purpose of *Take Off the Masks* and the poetic style of *Look Back in Joy.* It completes the inner picture of the writer by deepening his sense of life experience, a quality that was also achieved in Boyd's *Half Laughing/Half Crying: Songs for Myself,* published in 1986. The conflict between religion and society for possession of the souls of gays and lesbians has been played out in the words of dozens of books, essays, and poems since the Stonewall Riots of 1969. The writings of Malcolm Boyd offer a consistently humane perspective on this debate as seen from the battlefield of integrity, faith and sexuality.

—*Robert B. Marks Ridinger*

BOYD, Nancy. *See* **MILLAY, Edna St. Vincent.**

BRADLEY, Marion Zimmer. American novelist, genre writer, critic and musician. Has also written as Lee Chapman, John Dexter, Miriam Gardner, Morgan Ives, and Elfrida Rivers. Born in Albany, New York, 3 June 1930. Educated at New York State College for

Teachers (now State University of New York at Albany), 1946–48; Hardin–Simmons University, Abilene, Texas, B.A. 1964; graduate study at University of California, Berkeley. Married 1) Robert A. Bradley in 1949 (divorced, 1964), one son; 2) Walter Henry Breen in 1964 (divorced); one son and one daughter. Editor of *Marion Zimmer Bradley's Fantasy Magazine*. **Recipient:** Hugo Award nomination, 1963; Nebula Award nominations, 1964 and 1978; Invisible Little Man Award, 1977; Leigh Brackett Memorial Sense of Wonder Award, 1978; Locus Award for best fantasy novel, 1984. Address: P.O. Box 72, Berkeley, California 94701, U.S.A.

WRITINGS

Novels

The Catch Trap. New York, Ballantine, 1979.

Romance Fiction

I Am a Lesbian (as Lee Chapman). Derby, Monarch, 1962.
Spare Her Heaven (as Morgan Ives). Derby, Monarch, 1963.
My Sister, My Love (as Miriam Gardner). Derby, Monarch, 1963.
Twilight Lovers (as Miriam Gardner). Derby, Monarch, 1964.
Knives of Desire (as Morgan Ives). San Diego, Corinth, 1966.
No Adam for Eve (as John Dexter). San Diego, Corinth, 1966.

Gothic Fiction

The Strange Women (as Miriam Gardner). Derby, Monarch, 1962.
Castle Terror. New York, Lancer, 1965.
Souvenir of Monique. New York, Ace, 1967.
Bluebeard's Daughter. New York, Lancer, 1968.
Dark Satanic. New York, Berkley Publishing, 1972.
Drums of Darkness: An Astrological Gothic Novel. New York, Ballantine, 1976.
The Inheritor. New York, Tor Books, 1984.
Witch Hill. New York, Tor Books, 1990.

Fantasy Fiction

The House between the Worlds. Garden City, New York, Doubleday, 1980; revised, Del Rey, 1981.
The Mists of Avalon. New York, Knopf, 1982; London, Michael Joseph, 1983.
Web of Darkness, edited by Hank Stine, illustrations by V. M. Wyman and C. Lee Healy. Virginia Beach, Donning, 1983; Sevenoaks, England, New English Library, 1985.
Web of Light, edited by Hank Stine, illustrations by C. Lee Healy. Virginia Beach, Donning, 1983.
Night's Daughter. New York, Ballantine, and London, Sphere, 1985.
With Vonda McIntyre, *Lythande* (anthology). New York, DAW Books, 1986.
The Fall of Atlantis (includes *Web of Light* and *Web of Darkness*). Riverdale, New York, Baen Books, 1987.
The Firebrand. New York, Simon & Schuster, 1987; London, M. Joseph, 1988.
With Julian May and Andre Norton, *Black Trillium.* Garden City, New York, Doubleday, 1990.

Science Fiction

The Door Through Space (bound with *Rendezvous on Lost Planet* by A. Bertram Chandler). New York, Ace Books, 1961.
Seven from the Stars (bound with *Worlds of the Imperium* by Keith Laumer). New York, Ace Books, 1962.
The Colors of Space. New York, Monarch, 1963; revised, illustrations by Barbi Johnson, Norfolk, Virginia, Donning, 1983.
Falcons of Narabedla [and] *The Dark Intruder, and Other Stories.* New York, Ace Books, 1964.
The Brass Dragon (bound with *Ipomoea* by John Rackham). New York, Ace Books, 1969; London, Methuen, 1978.
With Paul Edwin Zimmer, *Hunters of the Red Moon.* New York, DAW Books, 1973; London, Arrow, 1979.
Endless Voyage. New York, Ace Books, 1975; expanded as *Endless Universe,* 1979.
The Ruins of Isis, edited and illustrated by Polly and Kelly Freas. Donning, 1978; London, Arrow, 1985.
With Paul Edwin Zimmer, *The Survivors.* New York, DAW Books, 1979; London, Arrow, 1985.
Survey Ship, illustrations by Steve Fabian. New York, Ace Books, 1980.
Warrior Woman. New York, DAW Books, 1988; London, Arrow, 1988.
Witch Hill. Tor Books, 1990.

"Darkover" Series

The Sword of Aldones [and] *The Planet Savers.* New York, Ace Books, 1962; with introduction by Bradley, Boston, Gregg Press, 1977; London, Arrow, 1979; as *Planet Savers: The Sword of Aldones,* New York, Ace Books, 1984.
The Bloody Sun. New York, Ace Books, 1964; London, Arrow, 1978; revised, New York, Ace Books, 1979; with introduction by Bradley, Boston, Gregg Press, 1979.
Star of Danger. New York, Ace Books, 1965; London, Arrow, 1978; with introduction by Bradley, Boston, Gregg Press, 1979.
The Winds of Darkover (bound with *The Anything Tree* by John Rackham). New York, Ace Books, 1970; London, Arrow, 1978; with introduction by Bradley, Boston, Gregg Press, 1979.
The World Wreckers. New York, Ace Books, 1971; London, Arrow, 1979; with introduction by Bradley, Boston, Gregg Press, 1979.
Darkover Landfall. New York, DAW Books, 1972; London, Arrow, 1976; with introduction by Theodore Sturgeon, Boston, Gregg Press, 1978.
The Spell Sword. New York, DAW Books, 1974; London, Arrow, 1978; with introduction by Bradley, Boston, Gregg Press, 1979.
The Heritage of Hastur. New York, DAW Books, 1975; with introduction by Susan Wood, Boston, Gregg Press, 1977; London, Arrow, 1979.
The Shattered Chain. New York, DAW Books, 1976; London, Arrow, 1978; with introduction by Bradley, Boston, Gregg Press, 1979.
The Forbidden Tower. New York, DAW Books, 1977; with introduction by Bradley, Boston, Gregg Press, 1979; London, Arrow, 1980.
Stormqueen! New York, DAW Books, 1978; with introduction by Bradley, Boston, Gregg Press, 1979; London, Arrow, 1980.
The Ballad of Hastur and Cassilda (poem). Berkeley, Thendara House, 1978.

The Bloody Sun [and] *To Keep the Oath*. Boston, Gregg Press, 1979.
Contributor, *Legends of Hastur and Cassilda* (short stories), edited by Bradley. Berkeley, Thendara House, 1979.
Two to Conquer. New York, DAW Books, 1980; London, Arrow, 1982.
The Keeper's Price, and Other Stories (short stories). New York, DAW Books, 1980.
Contributor, *Tales of the Free Amazons* (short stories), edited by Bradley. Berkeley, Thendara House, 1980.
Sharra's Exile. New York, DAW Books, 1981; London, Arrow, 1983.
Children of Hastur (contains *The Heritage of Hastur* and *Sharra's Exile*). Garden City, New York, Doubleday, 1981.
Hawkmistress! New York, DAW Books, 1982; London, Arrow, 1985.
Contributor, *Sword of Chaos, and Other Stories* (short stories), edited by Bradley. New York, DAW Books, 1982.
Thendara House. New York, DAW Books, 1983; London, Arrow, 1985.
Oath of the Renunciates (contains *The Shattered Chain* and *Thendara House*). Garden City, New York, Doubleday, 1983.
City of Sorcery. New York, DAW Books, 1983; London, Arrow, 1986.
Contributor, *Free Amazons of Darkover: An Anthology* (short stories), edited by Bradley. New York, DAW Books, 1985.
With the Friends of Darkover, *Red Sun of Darkover* (short stories). New York, DAW Books, 1987.
The Other Side of the Mirror. New York, DAW Books, 1987.
Contributor, *Four Moons of Darkover* (short stories), edited by Bradley. New York, DAW Books, 1988.
The Heirs of Hammerfell. New York, DAW Books, 1989.
With the Friends of Darkover, *Domains of Darkover* (short stories). New York, DAW Books, 1990.
With the Friends of Darkover, *Leroni of Darkover* (short stories). New York, DAW Books, 1991.
With the Friends of Darkover, *Renunciates of Darkover* (short stories). New York, DAW Books, 1991.
Rediscovery: A Novel of Darkover. New York, DAW Books, 1993.
Towers of Darkover, edited by Bradley. New York, DAW Books, 1993.

Short Stories

"Centaurus Changeling," in *Magazine of Fantasy and Science Fiction*, April 1954.
The Parting of Arwen (as Elfrida Rivers). Baltimore, T–K Graphics, 1974.
The Jewel of Arwen. Baltimore, T–K Graphics, 1974.
Contributor, *Thieves' World*, edited by Robert Lynn Asprin. New York, Ace Books, 1979.
The Best of Marion Zimmer Bradley, edited by Martin H. Greenberg. Chicago, Academy Chicago, 1985; Mapes Monde Editore, 1991.
Contributor, *Spell Singers*, edited by Alan Bard Newcomer. New York, DAW Books, 1988.
Jamie, and Other Stories: The Best of Marion Zimmer Bradley, edited by Martin H. Greenberg. Chicago, Academy Chicago, 1992.

Nonfiction

With Gene Damon, *Checklist: A Complete, Cumulative Checklist of Lesbian, Variant, and Homosexual Fiction in English*. Rochester, Texas, privately printed, 1960.

Men, Halflings, and Hero Worship (criticism). Baltimore, T–K Graphics, 1973.
The Necessity for Beauty: Robert W. Chambers and the Romantic Tradition. Baltimore, T–K Graphics, 1974.
Editor, *A Gay Bibliography*. New York, Arno Press, 1975.
With Alfred Bester and Norman Spinrad, *Experiment Perilous: Three Essays in Science Fiction*. New York, Algol Press, 1976.
"One Woman's Experience in Science Fiction," in *Women of Vision*, edited by Denise DuPont. New York, St. Martin's Press, 1988.

Other

Songs from Rivendell. Privately printed, 1959.
Translator, *El Villano en su Rincon* by Lope de Vega. Privately printed, 1971.
In the Steps of the Master (teleplay novelization). New York, Tempo Books, 1973.
Can Ellen Be Saved? (teleplay novelization). New York, Tempo Books, 1975.
Contributor, *Essays Lovecraftian* edited by Darrell Schweitzer. Baltimore, T–K Graphics, 1976.
The Darkover Cookbook. Berkeley, Friends of Darkover, 1977.
The Maenads (poetry). Portland, Oregon, Garvin & Levin, 1978.
Author of introduction, *The Breaking of the Seals* by Francis Ashton, edited by Hank Stine, illustrations by Randy Bruce. Virginia Beach, Donning, 1982.
Editor, and contributor, *Greyhaven: An Anthology of Fantasy*. New York, DAW Books, 1983.
Editor, *Sword and Sorceress: An Anthology of Heroic Fantasy* (multiple volumes). New York, DAW Books, 1984—.
Contributor, *Contemporary Authors Autobiography Series* (autobiographical sketch), Volume 10. Detroit, Gale, 1989.
Editor, *Spells of Wonder*. New York, DAW Books, 1989.
Author of foreword, *Harper's Encyclopedia of Mystical and Paranormal Experiences*, edited by Rosemary E. Guiley. San Francisco, Harper, 1991.

*

Biography: *Marion Zimmer Bradley* by Rosemarie Arbur, Mercer Island, Washington, Starmont House, 1985; *Twentieth–Century Science Fiction Writers*, Chicago, St. James Press, 1986; *Contemporary Authors Autobiography Series*, Volume 10, Detroit, Gale, 1989.

Interviews: *Publishers Weekly*, 30 October 1987, 49–50.

Bibliography: *Leigh Brackett, Marion Zimmer Bradley, Anne McCaffrey: A Primary and Secondary Bibliography* by Rosemarie Arbur, Boston, G. K. Hall, 1982.

Critical Sources: "Marion Zimmer Bradley" by Laura Murphy, in *Dictionary of Literary Biography*, Volume 8: *Twentieth–Century American Science Fiction Writers*, Detroit, Gale, 1981; "Recent Feminist Utopias" by Joanna Russ, in *Future Females: A Critical Anthology*, edited by Marleen S. Barr, Bowling Green, Ohio, Bowling Green State University Popular Press, 1981; "Marion Zimmer Bradley's Ethic of Freedom" by Susan Shwartz, in *The Feminine Eye: Science Fiction and the Women Who Write It*, edited by Tom Staicar, New York, Ungar, 1982; "Marion Zimmer Bradley," in *The*

Science Fiction Source Book, edited by David Wingrove, New York, Van Nostrand Reinhold, 1984; *Women Worldwalkers: New Dimension of Science Fiction and Fantasy,* edited by Jane B. Weedman, Lubbock, Texas Tech Press, 1985; "Marion Zimmer Bradley," in *Anatomy of Wonder: A Critical Guide to Science Fiction,* edited by Neil Barron, third edition, New York, Bowker, 1987; "Marion Zimmer Bradley," in *Reader's Guide to Twentieth–Century Science Fiction,* compiled and edited by Marilyn Fletcher and James Thorson, Chicago, American Library Association, 1989; "Heterosexual Plots and Lesbian Subtexts: Toward a Theory of Lesbian Narrative Space" by Marilyn R. Farwell, in *Lesbian Texts and Contexts: Radical Revisions,* edited by Karla Jay and Joanne Glasgow, New York University Press, 1990, 92; *The Gay Novel in America* by James Levin, New York, Garland, 1991.

* * *

According to science fiction and fantasy author Marion Zimmer Bradley in *Jamie, and Other Stories: The Best of Marion Zimmer Bradley,* women's liberation, not space exploration, is the great event of the twentieth century. Influenced by C. L. Moore and Leigh Brackett—female pioneers in the male–dominated field of science fiction of the thirties and forties—Bradley is one of the first science fiction writers to feature independent female characters such as Cassiana in the 1954 "Centaurus Changeling," Taniquel in the 1964 *The Bloody Sun,* and Melitta of Storn, the hero of the 1970 *The Winds of Darkover.* She is also one of the first to continually explore the universe of gender roles and human relationships.

Bradley denies that she is a feminist, and decries the use of literature as propaganda and polemic. A storyteller above all else, she emphasizes in her essay in *Women of Vision* that "it's okay for a woman in a story to have whatever love life suits her, but the real work of the world must come first." Nevertheless, her enthusiasm for women's rights and gay rights is apparent in her works.

Lifelong science fiction and fantasy fan turned prolific author, Bradley is best known for her science fiction novels about the world of Darkover and for her best–selling mainstream Arthurian fantasy novel *The Mists of Avalon.* Her works also include many non–Darkover science fiction novels and short stories, fantasies based on myth and legend, lesbian romances written under pseudonyms, Gothics, bibliographies of gay and lesbian fiction, and a mainstream gay novel set in the circus milieu of the forties, *The Catch Trap.* As the editor of *Marion Zimmer Bradley's Fantasy Magazine* and many Darkover and non–Darkover anthologies, Bradley has served as role model and mentor for the work of her numerous fans, some of whom, such as Mercedes Lackey, Jennifer Roberson, and Diana Paxson, have built successful professional writing careers of their own.

The artistry of Bradley's writing has progressed steadily throughout her career. Having learned her craft writing potboilers, formula fiction tied to strict deadlines and genre parameters, she was finally freed of length restrictions by publisher Don Wollheim of DAW Books. The resulting work, *The Heritage of Hastur* in 1975, marks the beginning of her mature Darkover novels in which adventure is combined with in–depth exploration of psychological, sexual, spiritual, and social issues. It was at this time that Bradley made the decision to not be locked into the concepts of the earlier novels. In 1979 an extensive rewrite of *The Bloody Sun* was published, and in 1981 a completely new novel, *Sharra's Exile,* based on the events in

The Sword of Aldones, replaced that novel in the official Darkover chronology.

Liberated from being the sole financial support of her family by her second husband Walter Breen, Bradley was able at last to take the time to realize her literary potential in two carefully researched and well–written mainstream fantasies based on myth and legend, *The Mists of Avalon* in 1982, and *The Firebrand* in 1987. *The Mists of Avalon* gained international recognition for Bradley's work beyond her cult Darkover fandom.

Bradley writes with awareness and sensitivity about differences in cultures and lifestyles. Many of her characters initially hide their true identities and struggle to adapt to alien ways. Attempting to hide her Terran background from her Darkovan Renunciate sisters, Magda Lorne remarks literally and figuratively in the novel *Thendara House,* "I never realized how Terran I was until I *had* to be Darkovan 28 hours a day, ten days a week."

Eventually most of Bradley's characters come to terms with who they are. This can be a complex multi–level process developed through several novels. For instance, in the Darkovan trilogy *The Shattered Chain, Thendara House,* and *City of Sorcery,* Magda learns to accept the activation of her "laran" psi powers, to openly express her awakened love for her freemate Jaelle n'ha Melora and for her lover Camilla n'ha Kyria, to understand and respect the female–centered orientation of the Free Amazons/Order of Renunciates, to develop a healthy pride without guilt in her professional accomplishments, and to reconcile many social and spiritual aspects of her Terran/Darkovan cultural heritage.

Many of Bradley's characters are developed according to a similar plot formula. As they come of age sexually or psychically or both, they progress from feeling alien and outcast to forming a bond with a group, family, or individual, while retaining responsible self–determination. For example, in the Darkover novel *The Heritage of Hastur,* young Lord Regis Hastur experiences the awakening of his psychic "laran," accepts his gay identity and his love for schoolmate and paxman Danilo Syrtis, and chooses to take control of his destiny as the heir to the Comyn telepathic dynasty rather than escape to Terra. Likewise, in the mainstream gay novel *The Catch Trap,* trapeze artist Tommy Zane sorts out his sexual identity while trying to fit into the family and circus culture of the Flying Santellis. For the love of Mario Santelli, Tommy chooses to forgo a promising career as a flyer to become Mario's catcher.

However, Bradley's plots are not always developed according to a simple formula. In the science fiction novel *The Ruins of Isis,* Unity scholar Cendri Owain observes the subjugation of men by the Matriarchate of the planet Isis. While she makes friends with powerful woman leaders and participates in traditional Isis mating rituals, Cendri never completely loses her culture shock. In the end she and her husband accept each other as loving equals and work together to bring legal and educational equality to men and women on the planet. Similarly, the plots of Bradley's short stories about Lythande, the Adept of the Blue Star, depend on the premise that Lythande remain hidden and an outsider. As she travels disguised as a male minstrel (her lyrics consist of paraphrases of Sappho), her identity as a woman is divulged only at the risk of losing her magic powers. Bradley portrays Lythande as a woman cursed to conceal her true self forever.

Bradley peoples her worlds with characters representing many types of gender roles and relationships. According to researcher Marilyn Farwell, *The Mists of Avalon,* although predominantly heterosexual, contains a clear lesbian subtext. While the two loves of the priestess Morgaine's life are men, Lancelet and Accolon, the concept of sisterhood in the Goddess is pervasive throughout the novel, and is intensified in several love scenes between Morgaine and another priestess, Raven.

Native Darkovan culture exhibits a vast variety of relationships, in contrast to Terrans who are depicted mostly as conservative heterosexuals. Two forms of Darkovan marriage are recognized, the permanent *di catenas,* using bracelets representing chains, and freemate marriage, a more temporary legal bond between a man and woman or between two women. *Nedestro* children born out of wedlock are accepted casually, as are gay relationships preceding heterosexual marriage. Female lovers of women, such as Camilla n'ha Kyria, and female lovers of men, such as Rafaella n'ha Doria, serve together in the Free Amazons/Order of Renunciates.

Heterosexuals, gays, lesbians, and bisexuals on Darkover share the stage with virginal or celibate Keepers of the towers where psychic matrix technology is controlled, and with the rarely seen indigenous residents of Darkover, the androgynous *chieri,* who appear as their partners desire them to be. The Explorers in the non–Darkover novel *Endless Universe* are sterile (they steal or purchase children to replenish their numbers) and are quite lacking in sex–role differentiation. In Bradley's early short story "Centaurus Changeling," the natives of the planet Megaera practice polygamy.

Bradley also introduces characters who sexually exploit and enslave others, such as the men of the Darkovan Dry Towns who keep their women in chains, the women of Isis who put property tattoos on their men and call them "it" rather than "he," and the gay character Dyan Ardais in *The Heritage of Hastur* who uses his "laran" power to psychically and sexually humiliate and terrorize Danilo Syrtis. Ajax murders and then brutally rapes the corpse of the Amazon warrior Penthesilea in *The Firebrand,* and in *Rediscovery* Ryan Evans plots to use the Darkovan drug kireseth to increase the "useful life" of child prostitutes.

However, Bradley more than balances her portrayal of the dark side of human relationships with positive influences such as the Free Amazons/Order of Renunciates who renounce the marital enslavement of the Dry Towns and the "laran" breeding program of the Comyn telepaths. In addition, there is a men's resistance movement on Isis, with its motto "We were not born in chains." In the name of the Goddess, groups such as the Amazon tribes and Priestesses of the Serpent Mother in *The Firebrand,* the Wise Sisterhood in *City of Sorcery,* and the Priestesses of Avalon in *The Mists of Avalon* all provide similar counterweights to those who would dominate and enslave.

Inherent in Bradley's storytelling is a message of acceptance and respect for oneself and for others, an affirmation of human rights and human dignity. Her explanation of the matter in *Sword and Sorceress: An Anthology of Heroic Fantasy* is characteristically plain–spoken and modest: "There is only one purpose in fiction, and that is to entertain the reader, and to make her—or him—think."

— *Jeanette Smith*

————

BRAM, Christopher. American novelist and author of short stories and screenplays. Born in Buffalo, New York, 22 February

1952. Educated at College of William and Mary, Williamsburg, Virginia (editor, *William and Mary Review,* 1973–74), B.A. (with honors) 1974. Reporter, *Virginian–Pilot,* Norfolk, Virginia, 1971; benefit authorizer, Social Security Administration, Flushing, New York, 1978–79; clerk, Scribner Bookstore, New York City, 1979–86; typesetter, *New York Native,* New York City, 1986–87. Contributor to magazines, including *Premiere, New York Times Book Review, New York Native, Lambda Book Report, Advocate, New York Newsday, Frontiers,* and *Night and Day* (under pseudonym Thersites); contributing editor of *Christopher Street,* 1979–82. Agent: Donadio & Ashworth, Inc., 231 West 22nd Street, New York, New York 10011, U.S.A.

WRITINGS

Novels

Surprising Myself. New York, Donald I. Fine, 1987.
Hold Tight. New York, Donald I. Fine, 1988.
In Memory of Angel Clare. New York, Donald I. Fine, 1989.
Almost History. New York, Donald I. Fine, 1992.

Other

Contributor, *Aphrodisiac: Fiction from Christopher Street.* New York, Coward, 1980.
"Meeting Imelda Marcos" in *Men on Men 3,* edited by George Stambolian. New York, Dutton, 1990.
"Greenwich Village" in *Hometowns,* edited by John Preston. New York, Dutton, 1991.
With Draper Shreeve, *George and Al* (screenplay).
With Draper Shreeve, *Business–like* (screenplay).
With Draper Shreeve, *Dangerous Music* (screenplay).
The Lost Language of Cranes (unproduced feature screenplay; based on novel by David Leavitt).

*

Interviews: "The Making of *Hold Tight*" by Paul Webb, in *Lambda Book Report,* August/September 1988; "Anyplace Gay, USA" by Philip Gambone, in *Bay Windows,* 18 January 1990; "Man of the World" by Jim Marks, in *Advocate,* 5 May 1992; "Christopher Bram Makes History" by Dale Reynolds, in *Frontiers,* 5 June 1992; "Christopher Bram's Fertile Imagination" by Trey Graham, in *Washington Blade,* 4 September 1992.

Critical Sources: Review of *Surprising Myself* by Richard Hall, in *Advocate,* 18 August 1987; review of *Surprising Myself* by John Brosnahan, in *Booklist,* 15 May 1988, 1573; review of *Hold Tight* by John Preston, in *Advocate,* 17 June 1988; review of *In Memory of Angel Clare* by Michael Bronski, in *Lambda Book Report,* August/September 1989; "Shallowest Depths" by Dennis Harvey, in *Bay Area Reporter,* 17 September 1989; *The Gay Novel in America* by James Levin, New York, Garland, 1991; "A Man of the World: In His Latest Novel, *Almost History*" by Jim Marks, in *Advocate,* 5

May 1992, 83; review of *Almost History* by Michael Bronski, in *The Guide to the Northeast,* June 1992, 14; "Christopher Bram" by Mark E. Bates, in *Contemporary Gay American Novelists,* edited by Emmanuel S. Nelson, Westport, Connecticut, Greenwood Press, 1993, 29–36.

Christopher Bram comments: "It's often assumed that a gay or lesbian imagination is a narrow imagination, exclusively focused on private emotion and private parts. But being gay can also open doors into areas outside one's personal experience. What do I know about career diplomats? Very little. But because the State Department protagonist of *Almost History* was gay, I had a vested interest in his life, a foothold in his world. I knew firsthand the lies you tell yourself to deny inconvenient emotions. From that base, I could build the rest of Jim Goodall's life, his fussy masculinity, his frustrated principles, the zigzags of his thirty–some years as 'a houseguest of history.'

"Something similar has happened in most of my books. I use my sexuality to flesh out my intellectual curiosity, which is the other half of my writer's capital. My current work–in–progress follows the last days of an elderly movie director in 1957, who's gay, English and a veteran of the First World War.

"I see myself as part of a recent wave of gay and lesbian writers who use their sexuality as a vantage point from which to view the rest of the world, without denying that identity: Allan Gurganus, Tony Kushner, Dorothy Allison, Randall Kenan, Michael Nava, Jenifer Levin, Lev Raphael and Philip Gambone. I strive to write *through* my gay identity about things that should matter to everyone: family, love, race, politics, death, history, the body in the world, the kitchen and the moon."

*   *   *

Christopher Bram first came to the attention of lesbian and gay readers when his story "Aphrodisiac" was published in *Christopher Street* in 1978. It later gained a wider readership when it served as the title story for the 1980 anthology *Aphrodisiac: Fiction from Christopher Street.* His appearance in *Christopher Street*—at the time the major publishing outlet for Manhattan–based gay writers—placed him in the tradition of urban gay male writers like Robert Ferro, Felice Picano and Andrew Holleran, among others. Such writers were known for their straightforward narrative styles and subject matter centered specifically upon the immediate issues of gay male life: coming out, finding a lover, and creating, or reclaiming a safe emotional, physical and psychological gay space. In was within these conventions that Bram published his first novel, *Surprising Myself,* in 1987.

The publication of *Surprising Myself* met with a generally positive response (*Booklist* called it "the gay novel of the year,") and its "coming out" story—a perennial theme in gay male novels from the 1906 *Imer* to the more contemporary works of John Fox or Michael Chabon—made the book both accessible and comfortable for the common gay reader. But while other writers remained secure and happy in this genre, Bram seemed to chafe at its stylistic and narrative restrictions.

In 1988 he published *Hold Tight* in which an American sailor is made to work in a gay brothel during World War II to extract secrets from German spies. The novel expanded the usual "coming out" theme and placed it in a broader historical and philosophical context. On the surface *Hold Tight* (which takes its title comes from a 1940s Andrews Sisters song) is a complex hybrid of several genres: the World War II spy novel (in the style of Eric Ambler), the classic post–war gay novel (such as Fritz Peters' *Finistere*), the slightly "daring" woman's narrative in which the main character must engage in sexual activity to save her country (Hitchcock's *Notorious* comes to mind), as well as the traditional gay porn novel in which any plot is an excuse to have sex. Although *Hold Tight* has a conventional feel to it, Bram proved that he was a master at using and subverting genre while expanding the parameters of what was possible in the contemporary gay male narrative. Most importantly, *Hold Tight* presented a viable way for readers to deal with larger themes in a positive context of gay male sexuality, among them the interplay of global and personal politics and the role that alternative sexuality plays in governmental policy decisions. These same themes were to appear again, four years later, in *Almost History,* a novel that specifically deals with the interaction between the personal and the political.

Bram departed from these more abstract concerns in his 1989 novel *In Memory of Angel Clare,* in which a tightly knit group of Manhattan friends discovers after the death of their good friend Clarence Laird, (nicknamed Angel Clare after the character in *Tess of the D'Urbervilles*), that they have "inherited" his most recent lover, an immature young student named Michael. *In Memory of Angel Clare* is half comedy–of–mismanners and half philosophical exploration of what the idea of "community" really means. Bram understands that his material is sensitive, but he is never unaware of its humorous and instructional potential. *Angel Clare* is a comic novel of social criticism—much like Mary McCarthy's *The Group*—and at a time when most novels dealing with AIDS veered towards the sentimental, *Angel Clare* was a daring and notable exception.

With the publication of *Almost History* in 1992, Bram elaborated on the themes of his earlier novels. *Almost History* tells the story of Jim Goodall, a career diplomat who comes out late in life and attempts to juggle the responsibilities of job, family and new sexuality with the evolution of his own personal politics as well as that of United States foreign policy. Bram manages to create a fictional world in which gay male sexuality is a decisive force but not the only concern of the author or his characters. In *Almost History* Bram has created a new, more complex and sophisticated model for the gay male fiction narrative that is influenced by feminism and progressive domestic and international politics as well as gay liberation. In his work he has consistently pushed the boundaries of content and the narrative possibilities in gay male fiction.

—*Michael Bronski*

————

BROCK, Rose. *See* **HANSEN, Joseph.**

BROOKS, Romaine. Pseudonym for Beatrice Romaine Goddard. American expatriate artist and memoirist. Born in Rome, Italy, 1874. Educated at various schools in the United States, Italy and Switzerland; studied art at La Scuola Nazionale and Circolo Artistico in Rome, the Académie Colarossi in Paris, and with Gustave Courtois in Paris. Married John Ellingham Brooks, c. 1902 (marriage ended); companion of author Natalie Barney, beginning 1915. *Died in Nice, France, 7 December 1970.*

WRITINGS

Illustrator, *The One Who Is Legion; or, A.D.'s After–Life* by Natalie Barney. London, Partridge, 1930.
Romaine Brooks: Portraits—Tableaux—Dessins. Paris, Braun & Cie, 1952; New York, Arno Press, 1975.
Romaine Brooks, 1874–1970: Poitiers, Musée Sainte–Croix, 27 juin–30 septembre 1987. Poitiers, Le Musée, 1987.
Romaine 70 dessins. France; privately printed.
No Pleasant Memories (unpublished memoirs).
A War Interlude or On the Hills of Florence during the War (unpublished memoirs).

*

Biography: *Romaine Brooks: Thief of Souls* by Adelyn D. Breeskin, Washington, Smithsonian Institution Press, 1971, second edition, 1986; *Between Me and Life: A Biography of Romaine Brooks* by Meryle Secrest, Garden City, New York, Doubleday, 1974; *Romaine Brooks* by Francoise Werner, Paris, Plon, 1990.

Critical Sources: "American Women Artists and the Female Nude Image" (dissertation) by Florence Rebecca McEwin, University of North Texas, 1986; "The Eye of Be*Hold*Her: The Lesbian Vision of Romaine Brooks," in *Sinister Wisdom* (Rockland, Maine), spring 1981, 35–42; *Women of the Left Bank: Paris, 1900–1940* by Shari Benstock, Austin, University of Texas Press, 1986; "The Rare, Subtle Talent of Romaine Brooks" by Adelyn D. Breeskin, in *Art News,* October 1989, 156–159; "Fleurs du Mal or Second–hand Roses?: Natalie Barney, Romaine Brooks, and the 'Originality of the Avant–Garde'" by Bridget Elliott and Jo–Ann Wallace, in *Feminist Review,* spring 1992, 6–30; "Fashion, Character and Sexual Politics in Some Romaine Brooks' Lesbian Portraits" by Sandra Langer, Article 131, Lesbian–Feminist Study Clearinghouse, University of Pittsburgh, Pittsburgh, Pennsylvania.

*   *   *

Romaine Brooks, primarily known as a visual artist, contributed to gay and lesbian literature as an illustrator and a portraitist. Her talent as a painter and her 50–year association with her friend and lover Natalie Barney brought her into the heart of the Paris literary and artistic community. Born into a wealthy American family, Brooks spent an unhappy childhood both caring for her brother St. Mar, who was severely mentally ill, and attempting to appease her abusive mother. Brooks' unpublished memoirs, *No Pleasant Memo-*

ries, reflect the physical and psychological cruelty to which she was subjected. The atmosphere created by her mother's violence, neglect, and obsession with the supernatural helped influence Brooks to write, at age 85, "My dead mother gets between me and life."

In 1898, Brooks left America for Europe. A small allowance from her mother allowed her to study art at La Scuola Nazionale and at Circolo Artistico in Rome. A few years later Brooks attended Académie Colarossi, and studied in the studio of Gustave Courtois in 1905. She married John Ellingham Brooks in 1903, but dismissed him after a few months, admonishing him to "go back to his boys in Italy" according to Brooks biographer Meryle Secrest in *Between Me and Life.*

In 1915, Brooks met Natalie Barney at a tea party given by Lady Anglesey. Barney, the center of a coterie of artists and lesbians, was to become Brooks' primary partner in life and love until 1969. Neither woman hesitated to use the privileges of their class to display her lesbianism. Brooks painted many of the women who participated in Barney's salon; she also illustrated Barney's novel, *One Who Is Legion.* In this work, themes of suicide, resurrection, and androgyny are clearly reminiscent of the death of Natalie's lover Renée Vivien.

Brooks' first one–woman exhibition at Galeries Durand–Ruel in Paris in 1910 was a tremendous success. The exhibit consisted of 13 studies, all of women or young girls. At the time, Guillaume Appollinaire wrote in *L'Intransigeant* that the artist painted "with strength, but too much sadness." This overall sadness permeates much of Brooks' work. The women in her portraits often appear angry and rather grim. Frequently rendered in gray, black, and white, Brooks' subjects are sharply outlined and presented against sepulchral backgrounds. Many, including the artist in her self–portrait, are painted wearing male attire. Brooks also painted male members of the artistic community of Paris. Among her subjects were author Jean Cocteau, ballerina Ida Rubenstein, poet Gabriele d'Annunzio, pianist Renatta Borgatti, Natalie Barney, and Una, Lady Troubridge (the lover of author Radclyffe Hall).

During Brooks' 1971 retrospective at the Whitney, critic Hilton Kramer described her figure paintings as "very strong and very cold ... impressively eerie, suggesting a kind of icy eroticism." Some critics have dismissed Brooks' painting as derivative of earlier movements. It has been argued by Bridget Elliott and Jo–Ann Wallace in *Feminist Review* that Brooks consciously borrowed styles from earlier movements and used them to build a visual image of the new, public lesbian of the 1920s and 1930s.

—*Melissa J. Delbridge*

BROUGHTON, James (Richard). American poet, playwright, and filmmaker. Born in Modesto, California, 10 November 1913. Educated at Stanford University, B.A. 1936; New School for Social Research, 1943–45. Married Suzanna Hart in 1962 (divorced 1978), one son and one daughter; companion of Joel Singer since 1978. Has had a variety of jobs, including merchant marine, printer, ghostwriter, waiter, and book reviewer for the *New York Herald Tribune.* Involved with Art in Cinema (experimental film group), San Francisco Museum, late 1940s, and with the San Francisco poetry move-

ment, late 1950s and early 1960s; founded Centaur Press with
Kermit Sheets; wrote for Interplayers theater; resident playwright,
Playhouse Repertory Theatre, San Francisco, 1958–64; lecturer in
creative arts, San Francisco State University, 1964–76; instructor
in film, San Francisco Art Institute, 1968–82. Has given public
readings of his poetry nationwide. Member of board of directors,
Farallone Films, 1948—, and Anthology Film Archives, 1969—.
Recipient: Alden Award for drama, 1945; James D. Phelan Award
for drama, 1948, and for creative cinema, 1987; Edinburgh Film
Festival Award of Merit, 1953; Cannes Film Festival Prix du fantaisie
poetique, 1954; Oberhausen Film Festival Hauptpreis der
Kurzfilmtage, 1968; Avon Foundation grant–in–aid, 1968; Eugene
O'Neill Theatre Foundation playwright fellowship, 1969; Bellevue
Film Festival grand prize, 1970; Guggenheim fellowships, 1970–71
and 1973–74; *Film Culture* Twelfth Independent Film Award, 1975;
National Endowment for the Arts grants, 1976, 1982; City of San
Francisco Citation of Honor, 1983; San Francisco Art Institute
D.F.A., 1984; American Film Institute Maya Deren Award, 1989;
National Poetry Association Lifetime Achievement Award, 1992.
Address: P.O. Box 1330, Port Townsend, Washington 98368, U.S.A.

WRITINGS

Poetry

Songs for Certain Children. San Francisco, Adrian Wilson, 1947.
The Playground. San Francisco, Centaur Press, 1949.
The Ballad of Mad Jenny. San Francisco, Centaur Press, 1949.
Musical Chairs: A Songbook for Anxious Children. San Francisco,
   Centaur Press, 1950.
An Almanac for Amorists. Paris, Collection Merlin, New York,
   Grove Press, and London, Halcyon, 1955.
True and False Unicorn. New York, Grove Press, 1957.
The Water Circle: A Poem of Celebration. San Francisco, Pterodac-
   tyl Press, 1965.
Tidings. San Francisco, Pterodactyl Press, 1965.
Look In, Look Out. Eugene, Oregon, Toad Press, 1968.
High Kukus. New York, Jargon Society, 1968.
A Long Undressing: Collected Poems, 1949–1969. New York, Jar-
   gon Society, 1971.
Going through Customs. San Francisco, Arion Press, 1976.
Erogeny. San Francisco, ManRoot Press, 1976.
Odes for Odd Occasions. San Francisco, ManRoot Press, 1977.
Song of the Godbody. San Francisco, ManRoot Press, 1978.
Hymns to Hermes. San Francisco, ManRoot Press, 1979.
Shaman Psalm. Mill Valley, California, Syzygy Press, 1981.
Graffiti for the Johns of Heaven. Mill Valley, California, Syzygy
   Press, 1982.
Ecstasies. Mill Valley, California, Syzygy Press, 1983.
Atteindre l'inevitable. France, Nadir Press, 1985.
A to Z. Mill Valley, California, Syzygy Press, 1986.
Vrai et Fausse Licorne. France, Editions Aeolian, 1987.
Hooplas: A Collection of Celebratory Verse. Branford, Connecti-
   cut, Pennywhistle Press, 1988.
75 Life Lines. New York, Jargon Society, 1988.
Special Deliveries: New and Selected Poetry. Seattle, Broken Moon
   Press, 1990.

Plays

A Love for Lionel (produced New York, 1944).
Summer Fury (produced Palo Alto, California, 1945). Published in
   Best One Act Plays of 1945, edited by Margaret Mayorga, New
   York, Dodd, 1946.
The Playground (verse play; produced Oakland, California, 1948).
   San Francisco, Centaur Press, 1949.
Eggs of the Ostrich (adaptation from the French of Andre Roussin),
   1956.
Burning Questions (produced San Francisco, 1958).
The Last Word (produced San Francisco, 1958). Boston, Baker,
   1958.
Where Helen Lies (produced New York, 1959). University of Colo-
   rado at Colorado Springs, 1961.
The Rites of Women (produced San Francisco, 1959).
How Pleasant It Is to Have Money (produced San Francisco, 1964).
Bedlam (produced San Francisco, 1967).

Screenplays

With Sydney Peterson, *The Potted Psalm,* 1946.
Mother's Day, Farallone Films, 1948.
Adventures of Jimmy, Farallone Films, 1950.
Four in the Afternoon, Farallone Films, 1951.
Loony Tom and Happy Lover, Farallone Films, 1951.
The Pleasure Garden, London, Flights of Fancy Committee for
   Farallone Films, 1953.
The Bed, Farallone Films, 1968.
Nuptiae, Farallone Films, 1969.
The Golden Positions, Farallone Films, 1970.
This Is It, Farallone Films, 1971.
Dreamwood, Farallone Films, 1972.
High Kukus (includes poems from *High Kukus*), Farallone Films,
   1973.
Testament (film autobiography), Farallone Films, 1974.
The Water Circle, Farallone Films, 1975.
Erogeny, Farallone Films, 1976.
With Joel Singer, *Together,* Farallone Films, 1976.
With Joel Singer, *Windowmobile,* Farallone Films, 1977.
With Joel Singer, *Song of the Godbody* (includes the poem from
   Song of the Godbody), Farallone Films, 1977.
Hermes Bird, Farallone Films, 1979.
With Joel Singer, *The Gardener of Eden,* Farallone Films, 1981.
With Joel Singer, *Shaman Psalm* (includes the poem from *Shaman
   Psalm*), Farallone Films, 1982.
With Joel Singer, *Devotions,* Farallone Films, 1983.
With Joel Singer, *Scattered Remains,* Farallone Films, 1988.

Other

The Right Playmate. New York, Farrar, Straus, and London, Hart–
   Davis, 1952.
Something Just for You. Pisani Press, 1966.
The Androgyne Journal (autobiography). Oakland, California,
   Scrimshaw Press, 1977; revised, Seattle, Broken Moon Press,
   1991.
Seeing the Light. San Francisco, City Lights Books, 1977.
Making Light of It. San Francisco, City Lights Books, 1992.
Coming Unbuttoned, A Memoir. San Francisco, City Lights Books,
   1993.

Recordings: *San Francisco Poets,* Evergreen Records, 1958; *The Bard & the Harper,* MEA Records, 1965; *Songs from a Long Undressing* (cassette), Syzygy Press, 1987; *True & False Unicorn* (cassette), Syzygy Press, 1987; *Graffiti for the Johns of Heaven* (cassette), Syzygy Press, 1987; *Ecstasies* (cassette), Syzygy Press, 1987; *The Androgyne Journal* (cassette), Broken Moon Press, 1993.

*

Manuscript Collections: Kent State University Library, Kent, Ohio.

Interviews: With William Packard, in *New York Quarterly,* Number 42, 1990.

Critical Sources: *Experimental Cinema* by David Curtis, New York, Universe Books, 1971; *Visionary Film* by P. Adams Sitney, New York, Oxford University Press, 1974; "James Broughton" by Idris McElveen in *Dictionary of Literary Biography,* Volume 5: *American Poets since World War II,* Detroit, Gale, 1980, 107–112; *The Great American Poetry Bake–Off, Fourth Series,* by Robert Peters, Metuchen, New Jersey, Scarecrow Press, 1991.

James Broughton comments: "It can take a long time to become what you always were. Trusting your individual uniqueness challenges you to lay yourself open. Wide open. I had to make a strong identification with Whitman's defiant stance against the conservative poets of his day before I could trust my own peculiar yawp. And I earned no recognition until I did this.

"In my book, *True and False Unicorn,* I said of the unicorn, 'Despite his delicacy he is indestructible.' A unique delicacy is not a fragile thing. Consider the rose, the cloud, the rain. In the long run the dandy can outmaneuver the brute, the bird is more resourceful than the rhino.

"As a child I loved everything that went on in a theater: dance, vaudeville, drama, movies. I had a toy theater, a magic lantern, a stage in the attic. Shakespeare shaped my image of the world as a dramatic circus. The theme of my film, *The Bed,* I phrased thus, 'All the world's a bed, and men and women merely dreamers.'

"My films are extensions of my poetic view of life. I think of them as being similar to Blake's illustrated poems, since most of them employ poetry on the soundtracks. They are as personal as my writing and as handmade. Hence, like poetry, they have little commercial value. I am, in all I do, first and foremost a poet, and one who believes in living poetically."

*   *   *

In his poetry and his films, California native James Broughton has celebrated life's sensual and visionary pleasures. Broughton describes himself as a pansexual androgyne, not a bisexual nor a homosexual nor a heterosexual. From 1952 to 1978, he was married to Susanna Hart, and they had a son and a daughter. In 1978 he married Joel Singer, a photographer and filmmaker born in Montréal.

Broughton has stated that an angel appeared to him when he was three years old, told him that he would become a poet, and advised him to chart his own course in life. At age ten, his parents sent him to military school. Later Broughton attended Stanford University, and after earning a B.A., he joined the merchant marine. He eventually settled in New York, entered the theater scene, and studied at the New School for Social Research before returning to San Francisco. It was there that he learned poetry reading and was introduced to filmmaking. His first film, *The Potted Psalm,* made with Sydney Peterson, was shown as part of the Art in Cinema movement in San Francisco and established Broughton as a leader in the field of experimental cinema, and his later award–winning works, *The Pleasure Garden* and *The Bed,* added to that reputation.

Broughton's poems have been collected in two handsome volumes. In "I Am a Medium," the preface to *A Long Undressing, Collected Poems: 1949–1969,* Broughton explains his life's calling as "something larger than his personal life, his craft, his published works." His *Special Deliveries, New and Selected Poems* begins with a similar preface that echoes the earlier one and carries it forward. The poem is dated at Port Townsend, Washington, on the 170th anniversary of Walt Whitman's birth: "A poet has to allow everything to happen to him or he can make nothing happen for others.... I don't really know anything unless I can feel it.... I say only what it tells me and I try to stand by it. And I don't have to believe it if I know that I know. The message from my angel repeats over and over: Attain the Inevitable. Allness is ripe."

—*Charles Shively*

———

BROWN, Daniel Russell. *See* **CURZON, Daniel.**

———

BROWN, Rita Mae. American activist, novelist, poet, translator, essayist, and author of screenplays. Born in Hanover, Pennsylvania, 28 November 1944. Educated at Broward Junior College, A.A. 1965; University of Florida; New York University, B.A. 1968; New York School of Visual Arts, Manhattan, cinematography certificate 1968; Institute for Policy Studies, Washington, D.C., Ph.D. 1973. With others, founded Student Homophile League at New York University, and opened the first women's center in New York City. Photo editor, Sterling Publishing, New York City, 1969–70; lecturer in sociology, Federal City College, Washington, D.C., 1970–71; visiting member of faculty in feminist studies, Goddard College, Plainfield, Vermont, 1973; president, American Artists, Inc., Charlottesville, Virginia, 1980—. Former member of National Gay Task Force and National Women's Political Caucus; member of board of directors of Human Rights Campaign Fund (New York City), 1986. **Recipient:** Writers Guild of America award and Emmy award nomination for television special *I Love Liberty,* 1983; Emmy award nomination for *Long Hot Summer,* 1985; New York Public Library's Literary Lion award, 1986; named Charlottesville's favorite author, 1990. Address: c/o American Artists, Inc., P.O. Box 4671, Charlottesville, Virginia 22905, U.S.A. Agent: Julian Bach Literary Agency, Inc., 747 Third Avenue, New York, New York 10017, U.S.A.

WRITINGS

Novels

Rubyfruit Jungle. Plainfield, Vermont, Daughters, Inc., 1973.
In Her Day. Plainfield, Vermont, Daughters, Inc., 1976.
Six of One. New York, Harper, 1978.
Southern Discomfort. New York, Harper, 1982.
Sudden Death. New York, Bantam, 1983.
High Hearts. New York, Bantam, 1986.
Bingo. New York, Bantam, 1988.
Venus Envy. New York, Bantam, 1993.

Mystery Series with Sneaky Pie Brown

Wish You Were Here. New York, Bantam, 1990.
Rest in Pieces. New York, Bantam, 1992.

Poetry

The Hand that Cradles the Rock. New York University Press, 1971.
Songs to a Handsome Woman. Baltimore, Diana Press, 1973.
The Poems of Rita Mae Brown. Freedom, California, Crossing Press, 1987.

Screenplays

Slumber Party Massacre, Sante Fe Productions, 1982.
Rubyfruit Jungle (based on her novel).
Cahoots.

Television Series

I Love Liberty, ABC–TV, 1982.
Long Hot Summer (remake of 1958 film based on *The Hamlet* by William Faulkner), NBC–TV, 1985.
My Two Loves, ABC–TV, 1986.
The Alice Marble Story, Gross–Weston Productions, 1986.
Southern Exposure, NBC–TV, 1990.

Television Films

The Girls of Summer, 1989.
Selma, Lord, Selma, 1989.
Rich Men, Single Women, 1989.
Sweet Surrender, 1989.
The Thirty–nine Year Itch, CBS–TV, 1990.
Home, Sweet, Home (cable), FKA, 1990.
The Mists of Table Dancing, Universal, 1987.

Essays

"Take a Lesbian to Lunch" and "Hanoi to Hoboken, a Round Trip Ticket," in *Out of the Closets: Voices of Gay Liberation,* edited by Karla Jay and Allen Young. New York, Douglas, 1972.
"The Last Straw," in *Class and Feminism: A Collection of Essays from the Furies,* edited by Charlotte Bunch and Nancy Myron. Baltimore, Diana Press, 1974.
"Living with Other Women" and "The Shape of Things To Come," in *Lesbianism and the Women's Movement,* edited by Nancy Myron and Charlotte Bunch. Baltimore, Diana Press 1975.
A Plan Brown Wrapper. Baltimore, Diana Press, 1976.
"Queen For a Day: A Stranger in Paradise," in *Lavender Culture,* edited by Karla Jay and Allen Young. New York, Jove/HBJ, 1978.

Other

Translator, *Hrotsvitra: Six Medieval Latin Plays.* New York University Press, 1971.
Starting from Scratch: A Different Kind of Writer's Manual. New York, Bantam, 1988.

*

Interviews: With Carole Horn, in *Washington Post,* 24 October 1977, 1; with Patricia Holt, in *Publishers Weekly,* 2 October 1978, 16–17; with Armistead Maupin, in *Interview,* February 1982, 50; "The Unthinkable Rita Mae Brown Spreads Around a Little 'Southern Discomfort'" by Karen G. Jackovich, in *People,* 26 April 1982, 75–77; *Contemporary Authors, New Revision Series,* Volume 11, Detroit, Gale, 1984; "Life Without Martina" by Mark Uehling and Nikki Finke Greenberg, in *Newsweek,* 19 August 1985, 9–10; "Unsinkable Rita Mae Brown" by Jean Carr–Crane, in *Lambda Book Report,* December 1988–January 1989, 4.

Critical Sources: "Poetry Power" by F. Chapman in *Off Our Backs,* April 1972, 27; "Utopian Vision of the Lesbian Muse" by P. Bennett, in *Gay News,* 24 June 1978, 8; "Southern Belles Lettres" by A. Denham, in *Nation,* 19 June 1982, 759; "Rita Mae Brown: Feminist Theorist and Southern Novelist" by Martha Chew, in *Southern Quarterly* (Hattiesburg, Mississippi), fall 1983, 61–80; reprinted in *Women Writers of the Contemporary South,* edited by Peggy Whitman Prenshaw, Jackson, University Press of Mississippi, 1984; "*Rubyfruit Jungle:* Lesbianism, Feminism, and Narcissism" by Leslie Fishbein, in *International Journal of Women's Studies* (Montréal, Québec), March–April 1984, 155–159; "Questions of Genre and Gender: Contemporary American Versions of the Feminine Picaresque" by James Mandrell, in *Novel,* winter 1987, 149–170; "Uses of Classical Mythology in Rita Mae Brown's *Southern Discomfort*" by Daniel B. Levine, in *Classical and Modern Literature* (Terre Haute, Indiana), fall 1989, 63–70; *The Safe Sea of Women: Lesbian Fiction, 1969–1989* by Bonnie Zimmerman, Boston, Beacon Press, 1990; review by Marilyn Stasio of *Wish You Were Here,* in *New York Times Book Review,* 16 December 1990, 33; review by Marilyn Stasio of *Rest in Pieces,* in *New York Times Book Review,* 6 September 1992, 17.

Rita Mae Brown is perhaps the widest read openly lesbian author publishing in the 1980s and 1990s. Like many other feminist and lesbian writers—Jewelle Gomez, Dorothy Allison, Robin Morgan, Sarah Schulman and Barbara Smith—she got her start and found her inspiration in the energy of the early women's liberation movement. Although Brown is now read for her well–received and well–publicized mainstream novels (including a mystery series allegedly cowritten with her cat, Sneaky Pie Brown) many of her current readers know nothing of her more political past.

Born to an unwed couple ("Let's say I had illegitimate parents," she always quips), Brown was adopted by a working–class family while still a young child. She grew up in Florida and attended Howard Junior College as well as the University of Florida (from which she was expelled in 1963 for being a lesbian). After moving to Manhattan, Brown received her bachelor's degree from New York University and went on to the New York School of Visual Arts; she later received her doctorate from the Institute of Policy Studies in Washington, D.C. During this time, Brown became a very visible member of the newly emerging women's liberation movement and later the radical lesbians. She was also a member of the RAT collective, an underground newspaper that laid the groundwork for much early women's liberation theory. Later, Brown was a member of the "Furies" collective, which produced some of the movement's finest theoretical and positional works.

It was in this political environment that Brown began writing. Many of her early political essays are examples of precise, impassioned and hard thinking. It was her political commitments that led Brown to write her first novel, *Rubyfruit Jungle,* published by the feminist, collectively run publisher Daughters Press. *Rubyfruit Jungle* (the title refers to female genitalia) was a runaway best seller, selling more than 35,000 copies in its first years. A cross between *The Adventures of Huckleberry Finn* (its heroine's name is Molly Bolt) and a lesbian *Tropic of Cancer* (Brown consciously served up her pungent social critiques with bawdy humor) *Rubyfruit Jungle*—even with its graphic lesbian sex and its heart–on–its–sleeve progressive politic—managed to find a crossover audience.

Brown's identification with an overtly feminist press made the gender, sexual and class politics in both *Rubyfruit Jungle* and the author's next novel, *In Her Day,* clearly apparent. *Six of One* drew upon these same themes but was positioned as more of a mainstream work, detailing the lives of the lovable eccentrics in Runnymead, a small town on the Pennsylvania–Maryland border (a setting to which Brown would later return in *Bingo*). Brown's concerns about the lives of working–class people, the social and psychological experiences of women, the reality of racism and the oppression of lesbians are still present in this work but less explicitly articulated, woven into the subtext of the narrative.

In much of Brown's newer, mainstream work, there is a mixture of traditional plotting, raucous—sometimes bawdy—humor, and a keen sense of storytelling. *Southern Comfort* is a multi–generational family saga set in Montogmery, Alabama, that uses the same tone and character types as *Six of One* and *Bingo*. In *Sudden Death,* a "roman a clef" based on Brown's well–publicized affair with tennis champion Martina Navratilova, the author returns to some of the themes of her earlier feminist essays, examining the responsibilities and respect that women owe one another. In *High Hearts,* Brown again returns to the Southern regionalism of her earlier novels, only this time with a Civil War setting and a heterosexual heroine who turns to transvestism in order to fight. When not writing fiction, Brown has also been very successful in writing for television, completing more then a dozen major projects and at least one produced screenplay.

—*Michael Bronski*

—————

BRYHER. British poet, novelist, memoirist, and author of nonfiction. Born Annie Winifred Ellerman in Margate, Kent, 2 September 1894; name legally changed c. 1918. Educated in Eastbourne, Sussex, and by private tutor. Married 1) the writer and publisher Robert Menzies McAlmon in 1921 (divorced 1927); 2) the writer and editor Kenneth Macpherson in 1927 (divorced 1947); companion of Imagist poet Hilda Doolittle (H.D.); adopted Doolittle's daughter Perdita with Macpherson c. 1930. Associated with Doolittle's Paris literary circle, including Ezra Pound, James Joyce, John Gould Fletcher, and others. Regular contributor to *Saturday Review* and *Sphere,* 1917–18; cofounder and editor, with Macpherson, of the cinema magazine *Close–Up* in Territet, Switzerland, and London, 1927–33; formed the literary magazine *Life and Letters Today,* 1935. Member of Interplanetary Association. *Died in Switzerland, 28 January 1983.*

WRITINGS

Poetry

Region of Lutany, and Other Poems (as Annie Winifred Ellerman). London, Chapman & Hall, 1914.
With others, *Arrow Music.* J. & E. Bumpus, 1922.

Nonfiction

Amy Lowell: A Critical Appreciation. Andover, Hampshire, Eyre & Spottiswoode, 1918.
A Picture Geography for Little Children, Part 1: *Asia.* London, J. Cape, 1925.
West (travel). London, J. Cape, 1925.
Film Problems of Soviet Russia. London, Pool, 1929.
With Robert Herring and Dallas Bower, *Cinema Survey.* Brendin, 1937.

Novels

Development, preface by Amy Lowell. London, Macmillan, 1920.
Two Selves. Contact Press, 1923; Chaucer Head, c. 1927.
Civilians. Territet, Switzerland, Pool, 1927.
With Trude Weiss, *Lighthearted Student.* London, Pool, 1930.
The Fourteenth of October. New York, Pantheon, 1952.
The Player's Boy. New York, Pantheon, 1953.
The Roman Wall. New York, Pantheon, 1954.

Beowulf: Roman d'une maison de thé dans Londres bombarde. Paris, Mercure de France, 1948; translated as *Beowulf,* New York, Pantheon, 1956.
Gate to the Sea. New York, Pantheon, 1958.
Ruan. New York, Pantheon, 1960.
The Coin of Carthage. London, Harcourt, 1963.
Visa for Avalon. London, Harcourt, 1965.
This January Tale. London, Harcourt, 1966.
The Colors of Vand. London, Harcourt, 1969.

Memoirs

The Heart to Artemis: A Writer's Memoirs. London, Harcourt, 1962.
The Days of Mars: A Memoir, 1940–1946. London, Harcourt, 1972.

Other

Translator, *The Lament for Adonis* by Bion of Smyrna. A. L. Humphreys, 1918.
Paris 1900, translation by Sylvia Beach and Adrienne Monnier. La Maison des Amis Livres, 1938.
Editor, with Kenneth Macpherson, *Close–Up: A Magazine Devoted to the Art of Films* (ten volumes). New York, Arno, 1970.

*

Manuscript Collections: Magdalene College, Cambridge University, England.

Critical Sources: Review by Marianne Moore of *Beowulf,* in *Saturday Review,* Number 39, 1956; "Celtic Saga" (review of *Ruan*) by Sylvia Beach, in *Saturday Review,* Number 43, 1960; *Herself Defined: The Poet H.D. and Her World* by Barbara Guest, Garden City, New York, Doubleday, 1984; *Penelope's Web: Gender, Modernity, H.D.'s Fiction* by Susan Stanford Friedman, Cambridge, Cambridge University Press, 1990; "Multiplying the Past: Gender and Narrative in Bryher's Gate to the Sea" by Ruth Hoberman, in *Contemporary Literature,* 31:3, 1990.

*   *   *

In her World War II memoir, *The Days of Mars,* Bryher renames her longtime lover, the poet H.D., as "cousin": "I begged my cousin Hilda (H.D.), who was an American by birth, to rejoin her relatives there." Naming and renaming persons and roles proved a significant issue in Bryher's life and in her literature; she particularly enjoyed exploring "male" dress and "male" literary covers. This interest in remodeling oneself, renaming oneself, or in veiling one's lesbianism beneath a male mask or in an imagined maleness revealed itself in many of her historical novels.

Bryher produced a prolific amount of writing in a wide variety of genres, yet she never overtly addressed her own lesbianism or any other lesbianism. Her novels lack the keystones of historical fiction—namely, detailed research and verisimilitude of setting—precisely because the author used historical settings to both distance herself from, and to signal her relationship to, lesbianism. For ex-

ample, in *The Fourteenth of October,* Bryher sets her main character, Wulf, in the landscape of the Battle of Hastings. In the first few pages of the novel, young Wulf and his mentor Leofwen discuss the former's disinterest in war and the machineries of battle. In Bryher's texts, the recurring type of male figures, exemplified by characters like Wulf, disdain or inept at the roles required of males during war. By placing these characters in historical settings, Bryher could both "participate" in war as well as redefine the nature of the warring participants.

In designing such men as primary characters, Bryher shifted the predominant masculine code to read more ambiguously; in this way, her male and female characters feel more alike than dissimilar. In terms of a lesbian literary masking technique, Bryher's male personae afforded her not only an opportunity to assume male roles, but also to bring maleness and femaleness to a point of proximity. This proximity is well exemplified in *The Fourteenth of October,* when Wulf likens his lady love, Laurel, to himself. It is apparent in the work that Wulf loves Laurel for her likeness to him rather than for any heterosexual attractive force of difference. And, even though Bryher depicts this couple as physically heterosexual, the attributes expressed by Wulf that ultimately make Laurel desirous to him prove to be homoerotic.

An autobiographical impulse prevalent in Bryher's historical novels concerns a triangulated love affair. In their own life together, Bryher and H.D. involved themselves in several "menages a trois." Bryher married Kenneth MacPherson as a cover for a relationship that he and H.D. had consummated, while the three of them lived, loved, wrote and traveled together for a time. Barbara Guest in *Herself Defined: The Poet H.D. and Her World* refers to this group as "the newest menagerie of three," alluding to the repeated attraction that a threesome provided the two women. In *The Fourteenth of October,* such a threesome comes alive. Laurel, Rafe, and Wulf remain an inseparable group until Rafe and Laurel decide to marry. Wulf, hearing about this decision from a third party, refuses to believe it. Although Bryher depicts this triangle as ultimately sundered by an "ordinary" two–party, heterosexual love, she asserts her own stance through that of her primary male persona who cannot abide the suggestion of an "ordinary" relationship.

In *The Player's Boy,* Bryher designed yet another type of warring world, that involving rivalries among actors in a seventeenth–century European traveling theater troupe. In this novel, the author depicts her primary male character, Sands, as inept in his male role by situating him in more explicitly homoerotic relationships than she does characters such as Wulf. Sands must ultimately decide whether he wants to spend his life with his good friend Martin as a sailor or remain on the stage as a mediocre player; in the end, his fear of the relationship renders him unable to accompany the sailor. Over the remainder of the plot, Sands becomes involved with another man who betrays him and participates in an ill–fated love triangle. It is only when he finally prepares to die that Sands realizes he should have gone to sea with Martin.

Bryher took greater risks in works like *The Player's Boy* by bringing a homosexual relationship to the page, although she still masked her own lesbianism beneath a subtly gay male plot. Never a flamboyant or direct writer of lesbian literature, Bryher sacrificed intention to form, and clarity of intent and effectiveness of style for depiction of encoded artifacts regarding homosexual relationships. These artifacts reveal the fears through which she struggled to write the verisimilitude that represented her life.

—*Renée R. Curry*

BURROUGHS, William S(eward). American novelist, poet, and author of short stories. Also writes under pseudonyms William Lee and Willy Lee. Born in St. Louis, Missouri, 5 February 1914. Educated at Harvard University, A.B. 1936, graduate study, 1938; University of Vienna, 1937; Mexico City College, 1949–50. Served in the United States Army, 1942. Married 1) Ilse Herzfeld Klapper, 1937 (divorced 1946); 2) Joan Vollmer, 1946 (died 1951, of an accidental gunshot wound); one son, the writer William S. Burroughs, Jr. (died, 1981). Advertising copywriter in New York City in early 1940s; has also worked as bartender, exterminator, and private detective. Actor in motion picture *Drugstore Cowboy,* 1989. **Recipient:** National Institute of Arts and Letters award in literature, 1975, named member of American Academy and Institute of Arts and Letters, 1983. The Nova Convention, a four–day arts festival held in New York in 1978, and the Final Academy, held in London in 1982, were organized as tributes to Burroughs. Address: c/o William S. Burroughs Communications, P.O. Box 147, Lawrence, Kansas 66044, U.S.A.

WRITINGS

Novels

Junkie: Confessions of an Unredeemed Drug Addict (as William Lee; bound with *Narcotic Agent* by Maurice Helbrant). New York, Ace Books, 1953; London, Digit, 1957; published separately under name William S. Burroughs, New York, Ace Books, 1964; unexpurgated edition published as *Junky,* New York, Penguin, 1977.
The Naked Lunch. Paris, Olympia Press, 1959; as *Naked Lunch,* New York, Grove, 1962; London, Calder, 1964.
The Soft Machine. Paris, Olympia Press, 1961; enlarged, New York, Grove, 1966; enlarged, London, Calder & Boyars, 1968.
The Ticket That Exploded. Paris, Olympia Press, 1962; revised, New York, Grove, 1967; London, Calder & Boyars, 1968.
Dead Fingers Talk (contains excerpts from *Naked Lunch, The Soft Machine,* and *The Ticket That Exploded*). London, Calder, 1963.
Nova Express. New York, Grove, 1964; London, Cape, 1966.
The Wild Boys: A Book of the Dead. New York, Grove, 1971; London, Calder & Boyars, 1972; revised, London, Calder, 1979.
Short Novels. London, Calder, 1978.
Port of Saints. Berkeley, California, Blue Wind Press, 1979; London, Calder, 1983.
The Soft Machine, Nova Express, The Wild Boys. New York, Grove, 1980.
Cities of the Red Night: A Boy's Book. London, Calder, and New York, Holt, 1981.
The Place of Dead Roads. New York, Holt, 1983; London, Calder, 1984.
Queer. New York, Viking, 1985; London, Pan Books, 1986.
The Western Lands. New York, Viking, 1987.
Routine. Plashet, 1987.
Tornado Alley. Cherry Valley, New York, Cherry Valley Editions, 1989.

Short Stories

Exterminator! New York, Viking/Seaver, 1973; London, Calder & Boyars, 1975.

Early Routines. Santa Barbara, California, Cadmus Editions, 1981.
The Streets of Chance. New York, Red Ozier Press, 1981.
"The Wild Boys," in *The Faber Book of Gay Short Fiction,* edited by Edmund White. London and New York, Faber & Faber, 1991.

Contributor

A Casebook on the Beat, edited by Thomas Parkinson. New York, Crowell, 1961.
The Final Academy: Statements of a Kind, edited by Roger Ely. Final Academy, 1982.

Films

With Brion Gysin, *Towers Open Fire,* 1963.
With Antony Balch, *Bill and Tony,* 1966.
Blade Runner: A Movie. Berkeley, California, Blue Wind Press, 1979.
The Cut–Ups.

Composer

Old Lady Sloan, recorded by Mortal Micronotz, 1982.

Other

With Brion Gysin, *The Exterminator.* San Francisco, Auerhaun Press, 1960.
With Brion Gysin, Sinclair Beiles, and Gregory Corso, *Minutes to Go* (poems). Paris, Two Cities Editions 1960; San Francisco, Beach Books, 1968.
With Allen Ginsberg, *The Yage Letters.* San Francisco, City Lights Books, 1963.
Takis (exhibition catalog). [New York], 1963.
Roosevelt after Inauguration (as Willy Lee). New York, Fuck You Press, 1964; as *Roosevelt after Inauguration, and Other Atrocities,* San Francisco, City Lights Books, 1979.
Valentine's Day Reading. New York, American Theatre for Poets, 1965.
The White Subway, edited by James Pennington. London, Aloes Books, 1965.
Health Bulletin: APO:33: A Metabolic Regulator. New York, Fuck You Press, 1965; revised as *APO:33: A Report on the Synthesis of the Apomorphine Formula,* San Francisco, Beach Books, 1966.
With Lee Harwood, *Darayt.* Lovebooks, 1965.
With Claude Pelieu and Carl Weissner, *So Who Owns Death TV?* San Francisco, Beach Books, 1967.
They Do Not Always Remember. New York, Delacorte, 1968.
Ali's Smile. Brighton, Unicorn Books, 1969.
The Dead Star. San Francisco, Nova Broadcast Press, 1969.
With Daniel Odier, *Entretiens avec William Burroughs.* Paris, Editions Pierre Belfond, 1969; revised, enlarged, and translated as *The Job: Interviews with William S. Burroughs* (includes *Electronic Revolution*), New York, Grove, and London, Cape, 1970; with additional material as *The Job: Topical Writings and Interviews,* London, Calder, 1984.
The Last Words of Dutch Schultz: A Fiction in the Form of a Film Script. London, Cape Goliard Press, 1970; New York, Viking/Seaver, 1975.
With Carl Weissner, *The Braille Film.* San Francisco, Nova Broadcast Press, 1970.

With Claude Pelieu, *Jack Kerouac* (in French). Paris, L'Herne, 1971.

Electronic Revolution. Blackmoor Head Press, 1971.

With Brion Gysin and Ian Somerville, *Brion Gysin Let the Mice In,* edited by Jan Herman. West Glover, Vermont, Something Else Press, 1973.

Mayfair Academy Series More or Less. Brighton, Urgency Press Rip–Off, 1973.

The Book of Breeething. Ingatestone, OU Press, 1974; Berkeley, California, Blue Wind Press, 1975.

With Eric Mottram, *Snack: Two Tape Transcripts.* London, Aloes Books, 1975.

With Charles Gatewood, *Sidetripping.* New York, Strawberry Hill, 1975.

Cobble Stone Gardens. Cherry Valley, New York, Cherry Valley Editions, 1976.

The Retreat Diaries (bound with *The Dream of Tibet* by Allen Ginsberg). New York, City Moon, 1976.

Naked Scientology. Bonn, Expanded Media Editions, 1978.

With Brion Gysin, *The Third Mind.* New York, Viking, 1978; London, Calder, 1979.

Doctor Benway: A Variant Passage from "The Naked Lunch." Bradford Morrow, 1979.

Ah Pook Is Here, and Other Texts (includes *The Book of Breeething, Electronic Revolution*). London, Calder, 1979; New York, Riverrun, 1982.

Letters to Allen Ginsberg, 1953–1957. New York, Full Court Press, 1981.

A William Burroughs Reader, edited by John Calder. London, Pan Books, 1982.

The Burroughs File (includes *The White Subway, Cobble Stone Gardens,* and *The Retreat Diaries*). San Francisco, City Lights Books, 1984.

The Four Horsemen of the Apocalypse. Left Bank Books, 1984.

The Adding Machine: Collected Essays. London, Calder, 1985; New York, Seaven, 1986.

Interzone. New York, Viking, 1989.

Uncommon Quotes (poetry). Caravan of Dreams Productions, 1989.

Recordings: *Call Me Burroughs,* 1965; *William S. Burroughs/John Giorno,* 1975; *You're the Man I Want to Share My Money With,* 1981; *Nothing Here Now but the Recordings,* 1981; *Revolutions per Minute (The Art Record),* 1982.

*

Manuscript Collections: Burroughs Archives in Lawrence, Kansas, and the Robert H. Jackson Collection, Cleveland, Ohio.

Biography: *With William Burroughs: A Report from the Bunker* by Victor Bockris, New York, Seaver, 1981; *Literary Outlaw: The Life and Times of William S. Burroughs* by Ted Morgan, New York, Holt, 1988; *The Dream at the End of the World: Paul Bowles and the Literary Renegades in Tangier* by Michelle Green, New York, HarperCollins, 1991; *William Burroughs: El Hombre Invisible* by Barry Miles, Winnipeg, Manitoba, Hyperion, 1993.

Interviews: *The Job: Interviews with William S. Burroughs,* edited by Daniel Odier, New York, Grove, and London, Cape, 1970.

Bibliography: *William S. Burroughs: An Annotated Bibliography of His Works and Criticism* by Michael Barry Goodman, New York, Garland, 1975; *William S. Burroughs: A Bibliography 1953–1973* by Joe Maynard and Barry Miles, Charlottesville, University Press of Virginia, 1978; *William S. Burroughs: A Reference Guide* by Michael B. Goodman and Lemuel B. Coley, New York, Garland, 1990.

Critical Sources: *William Burroughs: The Algebra of Need* by Eric Mottram, Buffalo, New York, Intrepid Press, 1971, second edition, Marion Boyers, London, 1977; *Naked Angels: The Lives and Literature of the Beat Generation* by John Tytell, New York, McGraw–Hill, 1976; *Contemporary Literary Censorship: The Case History of Burroughs' Naked Lunch* by Michael B. Goodman, Metuchen, New Jersey, Scarecrow Press, 1981; *With William Burroughs: A Report from the Bunker,* edited by Victor Bokris, New York, Seaver, 1981; *William Burroughs* by Jennie Skerl, Boston, Twayne Publishers, 1985; *Contemporary Gay American Novelists,* edited by Emmanuel S. Nelson, Westport, Connecticut, Greenwood Press, 1993.

*   *   *

Along with Allen Ginsberg and Jack Kerouac, William S. Burroughs ranks as one of the three canonical figures of the Beat trend in American writing. Notable for their gripping, often phantasmagoric imagery and nonlinear structure, Burroughs' mature prose writings utilize and carry forward techniques pioneered by such avant–garde European writers as James Joyce, Louis–Ferdinand Celine, and Jean Genet. More broadly, his works continue the European tradition of the carnivalesque, a non–realistic mode of fiction and art that is seen in the work of François Rabelais, Hieronymus Bosch, and Pieter Bruegel the Elder.

Since the accidental death of his wife Jane Vollmer in Mexico City in 1951, Burroughs has lived an exclusively homosexual life. He portrays gay experience through the prisms of street life and expanded consciousness, the latter stemming in part from his experience as a drug user. Burroughs has also embraced a theme of general relevance: he warns against encroaching social control through the tentacular extension of bureaucracy and the techniques of mind manipulation that it characteristically employs. His break with accepted fictional devices of narrative continuity meshes with his non–authoritarian social philosophy. Burroughs' libertarian approach has gained him many adherents among young people, straight and gay alike, who seek to rebel against constraint. His books have been compared to science–fiction, but it seems more accurate to say that he influenced this field rather than its influencing him. Despite the acknowledged beauty of much of his writing, Burroughs has never quite achieved recognition in academia—a rejection that many of his admirers would regard as an advantage. He has influenced the pop culture of music: the rock bands Steely Dan, Soft Machine, and Naked Lunch purloined their names from his work, while the generic term "heavy metal" derives from his novel *The Soft Machine.*

The grandson of the inventor of the adding machine, Burroughs was born in the Midwest. Recognizing early on that their son was timid and reclusive, his parents took corrective action by sending him for a stay on a ranch in New Mexico. The intended cure failed, and Burroughs came to realize that not only was he attracted to members of his own sex, but that he was different in other ways.

His feelings of alienation grew when he attended Harvard University and encountered large groups of "careerist" fellow students.

The years from 1936 to 1944 were passed in seemingly aimless drifting. Burroughs worked as an advertising copywriter, exterminator, bartender, and private detective, also serving a brief stint in the United States army—experiences that later provided essential material for his books. In New York City in the late forties, he became friendly with Allen Ginsberg and Jack Kerouac, for whom he served as mentor. Burroughs also became fascinated by the world of petty criminality and drug addiction that he encountered in the city. Influenced by his hustler friend Herbert Huncke, Burroughs started taking drugs in 1944 and did not stop until 1957.

After his marriage, Burroughs moved first to Texas and Louisiana, then on to Mexico City in 1949. His novel *Queer,* about a doomed affair with a heterosexual man, documented the author's Mexican period. About the same time, he wrote *Junkie: Confessions of an Unredeemed Drug Addict,* which Ginsberg managed to place with Ace Books, a pulp publisher. Both works were straightforward narratives recounting details of the writer's own life.

In 1954 Burroughs moved to Tangier, Morocco. When he settled there, the city was an international zone, governed by the consuls of eight European nations. A place where almost anything went—including smuggling and dubious financial transactions—Tangier hosted merchants who sold hard drugs over the counter. Local boys fought to make themselves available for sexual purposes. Drugs and sex were powerful attractions for many expatriates. Like Burroughs, many of the European residents lived on a small annuity, supplied in some cases by relatives who preferred that the "black sheep" lived abroad. Struggling with, and succumbing to, his drug addiction, Burroughs nonetheless managed to accumulate a stock of over one–thousand typed pages that formed the basic material for his quartet of novels, *Naked Lunch, The Soft Machine, The Ticket That Exploded,* and *Nova Express.*

Naked Lunch first appeared under the Paris imprint of Olympia Press, a common venue for works deemed too explicit to pass muster under America's then strict censorship laws. However these laws were soon to crumble, and the legal struggles over the American publication by Grove Press contributed to the dismantling of literary censorship in the United States. In his preface to *Naked Lunch,* Burroughs explained the title as "the frozen moment when everyone sees what is on the end of every fork." The book's lack of conventional narrative structure has sometimes been explained as the result of careless stacking of pages on the writer's desk, yet the abrupt transitions seem more a deliberate effort to derail expectations of realism and linear storytelling. The atmosphere is that of a special zone (a hyperreal projection of Tangier) in which it appears that "anything goes," but which in reality is the battle ground of sinister forces. The book portrays a society menaced by fanatical efforts on the part of the authorities to control the population by many forms of addiction, not just that of drugs. Other groups seek their own transformation, such as the Liquefactionists, who aim at the merger of all sentient beings into one vast blob, and the homosexual Divisionists, who grow clones of themselves for sexual purposes. In the view of many critics, the nightmare Burroughs depicts stems ultimately from the collision between the instrumental reason of the Enlightenment, with its vision of control through social engineering, and the anarchic human forces that resist this domination. The book contains graphic scenes of gay sex, generally sadomasochistic, showing Burroughs' fascination with hanging at the time. The crude narrative and repetitiveness of these episodes reflects the author's familiarity with the "blue movies," porno-graphic short films shown clandestinely in Western countries.

At some point, Burroughs seems to have recognized that the experimental techniques of disrupting consciousness he had practiced in the tetralogy had reached their term. In any event, *The Wild Boys: A Book of the Dead* adopts a more conventional narrative with new material. The theme is one near the author's heart. The "Wild Boys" of the title are a tribal group of hashish–smoking homosexual outlaws who began in Morocco and spread throughout the world. Reflecting the misogyny of Burroughs' later years, the boys have learned to clone themselves so that women are completely excluded from their society which, in Burroughs' eyes at least, is a kind of utopia. Their wily rebelliousness lets them escape the otherwise pervasive social control. Although the style had changed, Burroughs is still concerned with the problem and social control and how to escape it. The characters in this book reappear in the sequel, *Port of Saints,* which is made up of a series of "out-takes," material drafted for—but not used—in *The Wild Boys.* Another book along these lines is *Cities of the Red Night,* which features a libertarian colony of gay pirates in eighteenth–century Madagascar. Offering a change of scene, *The Place of Dead Roads* is a Western set in the 1890s.

The body of Burroughs' writing has resisted incorporation into the canon of "gay literature," largely because his vision of sexuality is too dark and too lacking in "political correctness." Instead, Burroughs has found much more acceptance among young, often heterosexual readers who have punk and anarchist allegiances. Rejecting all party lines, including that of the political wing of gay liberation, the work of Burroughs stands on its own. Although Burroughs is committed to personal liberation, some of his attitudes and concerns—sadomasochism, violence for personal kicks, and misogyny—are perceived as outside the mainstream. Yet it is precisely the fact that Burroughs is not assimilable to the norms of middle–class respectability that has assured him a continuing audience among young people.

—*Wayne R. Dynes*

———

BUSI, Aldo. Italian novelist. Born in Montichiari (Brescia), 1948. Left school at an early age to work at odd jobs in Milan. Traveled and lived in various European capitals and in the United States where he worked at a variety of jobs, such as sanitation worker, real estate agent, and waiter. Fluent in German, English, and French. Literary translator of Goethe, John Ashbery, Heimitovon Doderer, Meg Wolitzer, Christina Stead, Lewis Carroll, and Paul Bailey. Contributor to the Italian magazine, *Epoca.* Address: c/o Antiche Olura, 8, 25018 Montichiari Brescia, Milan, Italy.

WRITINGS

Novels

Seminario sulla gioventù. Milan, Adelphi, 1984; translated by Stuart Hood as *Seminar on Youth,* New York, Farrar Straus Giroux, 1989.

La Vita standard di un venditore provvisorio do collant. Milan, Mondadori, 1985; translated by Raymond Rosenthal as *The Standard Life of a Temporary Pantyhose Salesman,* New York, Farrar Straus Giroux, 1988.

La Delfina Bizantina. Milan, Mondadori, 1986.

Una Pioggia angelica (novella from manuscript of *Sodomie in Corpo 11*). Brescia, L'Obliquo, 1987.

Sodomie in Corpo 11. Milan, Mondadori, 1988; translated by Stuart Hood as *Sodomies in Elevenpoint,* London, Faber and Faber, 1992.

Altri abusi ["Other Abuses"]. Milan, Leonardo, 1989.

L'Amore è una budella gentile. Milan, Leonardo, 1991.

Sentire le donne. Milan, Bompiani, 1991.

Le persone normali. Milan, Mondadori, 1992.

Manuale del perfetto Gentilomo ["Handbook for the Perfect Gentlehomo"]. Milan, Sperling Kupfer, 1992.

Vendita Galline Km 2 ["Free Range Chickens 2 Miles"]. Milan, Mondadori, 1993.

Manuale della perfetta Gentildonna ["Handbook for the Perfect Gentlewoman"]. Milan, Sperling Kupfer, forthcoming.

Manuale del perfetto Gentiluomo ["Handbook for the Perfect Gentleman"]. Milan, Sperling Kupfer, forthcoming.

Other

Pâté d'homme (three act play in comic book format), illustrations by Dario Cioli, adaptation by Carmen Covito. Milan, Mondadori, 1989.

Alice nel Paese delle Meraviglie (translation of Lewis Carroll's *Alice in Wonderland*). Milan, Mondadori, 1989.

With Denis Gaita and Davide Tortorella, *Pazza* (musical lyrics and short stories; text accompanied by cassette, performance by Aldo Busi). Milan, Bompiani, 1990.

Decamerone: da un italiano all'altro (modernized edition of *Decameron* by Giovanni Boccaccio). Milano, Rizzoli, 1990–91.

*

Critical Sources: "Neo–barocchismo in 'Somodie in Corpo 11' di Aldo Busi" by Livio Borriello, in *Paragone,* Number 39, 1988, 95–98; "Busi: l'iperralismo della rappresentazione e la negazione della verosimiglianza" by Angela Ferraro, in *Da Verga a Eco: Strutture e tecniche del romanzo italiano,* edited by Gabriele Catalano, Naples, Tullio Pironti, 1989, 527–541; "Du dessin et de la couleur dans le roman italien" by Patrizia Lombardo, in *Critique,* 46:514, 1990, 162–178; "Aldo Busi" by Maria Pia Ammirati, in *Il Vizio di scrivere: Letture su Busi, De Carlo, Del Giudice, Pazzi, Tabucchi e Tondelli,* Soveria Mannelli, Italy, Rubbettino, 1991, 25–50.

Aldo Busi comments: "I am not a gay writer because if I had been straight I wouldn't have been a heterosexual writer: I would have been exactly the writer I am now, let's say, a writer. I don't see any specific link between one's own sexuality and the laws of true, not targeted literature."

*   *   *

Aldo Busi's first two novels, *Seminario sulla gioventù* (*Seminar on youth*) and *La Vita standard di un venditore provvisorio di*

collant (*The Standard Life of a Temporary Pantyhose Salesman*), combine to produce a macabre sort of bildungsroman. The former is concerned with the limited wanderings and ruminations of a small town boy, Barbino, as he drifts through Milan and Paris, as a waiter, toy boy, and finally is kept by a hoping older woman, Arlette. The latter is the sometimes hilarious, sometimes grotesque, account of the external and internal travels of a doctoral candidate, Angelo Basarovi, as he serves as a translator, on a temporary basis—which stretches over years—for Celestino Lometto, the delightfully repugnant head of a small pantyhose firm.

Seminario begins by depicting the odd and harsh life in a rural village of Barbino's early years; his hatred for his mother, his absent father, and his introduction to male sex by rough adult hands in wooded places. As a waiter in Milan, Barbino serves up more than dinner to the rich clientele. In Paris, he fares no better, trysting with a bizarre bevy of characters, attempting to score big amid old letches with peculiar sexual tastes, sinking deeper and deeper into indigence. Finally he is taken in by Arlette, but her insistent attempts at forced domesticity eventually oblige Barbino to leave. Busi ends with Barbino's escape to England—a closure which suggests a new beginning, a new novel.

Angelo, in *La Vita standard,* seems a matured Barbino. Relatively content with his lot, living with his mother, sunning himself on the gay beaches at Lake Garda and leisurely pursuing an advanced degree, Angelo accepts a temporary, part–time position as a translator for Lometto, the director of a local pantyhose firm. The tumultuous and hilarious relationship of the gay translator and his straight boss follows. Their riotous excursions north produce constant bickering over money and morals; each continuously conniving to bamboozle the other as they create complicated intrigues with the strangest clients over the affairs of nylon tights. Gradually, Angelo becomes more and more involved with the bizarre financial and personal undertakings of the entire pantyhose dynasty.

In both of these novels, Busi entwines autobiographical elements around his fiction. In two later works, *Sodomie in Corpo 11* (*Sodomy in Elevenpoint*) and *Altri abusi* ("Other Abuses"), the author discards the artificiality of fictive protagonists and takes center stage himself, as if the "I" protagonist had emerged, fully formed, from his earlier, pupal characters. The Milan–Paris–London excursions of Barbino and the Austria–Germany junkets of Angelo, have evolved into a full–time occupation. The new Busi author/character is a traveling writer/journalist, purged of all excess baggage; no home, no family, no lover, in order to immerse himself totally in the act of writing. His travels take him everywhere and anywhere, from Finland to Colombia, Portugal to Tunisia, Iceland to Japan, Sanremo to Korea. He discards objective journalism and writes about what he sees, combining memory, sensation, social comment and literary criticism in a vocabularic sea of stream of consciousness and picaresque imagery. Nothing is sacred from the author's sharp pen. He decries the fallout of totalitarian South American governments and the poverty it engenders, describes the boredom of Finnish life, punctuates the prejudice of Italians, paries with a priest in a Vatican confessional, mocks the insistence of sports spectators at the Games and disparages the inanity of contemporary music.

Homosexuality is ever present in these novels. Busi and his protagonists are constantly on the prowl, throughout the world, searching for sex on planes and in trains, and in more exotic places, like truck stops, turkish baths, rest rooms, barrooms, and abandoned buildings. While Busi's language is noted for its "linguistic accumulation," descriptions of sexual encounters seem intentionally spartan. In Busi's writings, homosexuality is not considered an alternative lifestyle, nor is it viewed as an exotic, erotic choice. Busi is neither an activist nor apologist. Homosexuality is fundamental to this writer; and, as such, is an integral and basic component of his very being. On the last page of *Altri abusi,* Busi clarifies his position. "One is born homosexual and becomes heterosexual, and the force one uses to become heterosexual is not less than that needed to remain homosexual. For this reason, I have never succeeded in being able to consider heterosexuals as different. Different from whom? From each other? Maybe, but nothing more."

Artistically, this translates into a pervasive theme, directly and simply described. These natural acts, no matter how abstruse they might seem to some readers, are rarely elaborated linguistically or rhetorically amplified. Livio Borriello, in his article in *Paragone,* observes that the "obsessive repetitiveness of erotic situations tends to discarnate and abstract them into a dimension which is purely rhetorical." Sexual need is not a moral question in Busi, but more of a biological appetite which requires periodic satiety in order to maintain a healthy body and soul, and thus, optimal conditions for literary creativity.

Maria Pia Ammirati, in her Busi chapter in *Il Vizio di scrivere,* observes that each of Busi's protagonists has "difficulty in his relationships with other homosexuals." A closer examination of Busi's writings; however, reveals that it is not homosexuals but relationships that are perceived as difficulties in Busi's works. From *Seminario* to *Altri abusi* there is a continuous, intentional movement away from social constraints. Busi, the writer, strives for independence in order to better observe his surroundings, so as to comment, without conventional social bias, on the state and ramifications of what he sees. Thus there is little to do with close friends, lovers, and domestic issues in Busi's novels. Busi needs to be alone, to be free from as many distractions as possible, so as to concentrate body and soul on his writing. One of the last lines of *Altri abusi* encapsulates the author's definition of a writer. "A writer can not limit himself to live like anyone else: he must decide once and for all to exist, and that's it—like the sea. And the sea does not know what a sea is, nor does it even care."

—*Joseph P. Consoli*

C

CALIFIA, Pat. American novelist, journalist, and sex educator. Born in Texas, 8 March 1954. Educated at San Francisco State University, San Francisco, California, B.A. 1977. Columnist, *Advocate,* San Francisco, beginning 1981; editor, *Advocate Men,* 1990–91. Former member of board of directors, National Leather Society. Address: 2215R Market Street, Box 261, San Francisco, California 94114, U.S.A.

WRITINGS

Nonfiction

Contributor, *Caught Looking: Feminism, Pornography and Censorship,* by Hannah Alderfer. Caught Looking, Inc., 1987.
Sapphistry: The Book of Lesbian Sexuality, introduction by Phyllis Lyon, illustrations by Tee Corinne. Tallahassee, Naiad Press, 1980; revised, 1988.
"A Personal View of the History of the Lesbian S/M Community and Movement in San Francisco," in *Coming to Power: Writings and Graphics on Lesbian S/M.* Boston, Alyson Publications, 1982; revision edited by Samois.
Editor, *The Lesbian S/M Safety Manual.* Boston, Alyson Publications, 1988.
Editor, *The Advocate Adviser.* Boston, Alyson Publications, 1990.
Contributor, *The Persistent Desire: A Femme–Butch Reader,* edited by Joan Nestle, Boston, Alyson Publications, 1992.
Editor, *The Sexpert.* New York, Badboy, 1992.
Contributor, *Madonnarama: Essays on Sex and Popular Culture,* edited by Lisa Frank and Paul Smith. San Francisco, Cleis Press, 1993.
Sensual Magic. New York, Masquerade, 1993.

Fiction

"Jessie," in *Coming to Power.* Boston, Alyson Publications, 1982.
Macho Sluts: Erotic Fiction. Boston, Alyson Publications, 1988.
Doc and Fluff: The Distopian Tale of a Girl and Her Biker. Boston, Alyson Publications, 1990.
"The Vampire," in *Daughters of Darkness: Lesbian Vampire Stories,* edited by Pam Keesey. San Francisco, Cleis Press, 1993.
Melting Point. Boston, Alyson Publications, 1993.

*

Interviews: "Sadomasochism: Fears, Facts, Fantasies" by Nancy Wechsler, *Gay Community News* (Boston), 15 August 1981, 6–8.

Critical Sources: *Contemporary Feminist Thought* by Hester Eisenstein, Boston, G. K. Hall, 1983, 116–124; "Surveying Contemporary Lesbian Erotica" by Susie Bright, in *Lambda Rising Book Report* (Washington, D.C.), 1:4, 1988, 4; *Safe Sea of Women: Lesbian Fiction, 1969–1989* by Bonnie Zimmerman, Boston, Beacon Press, 1990; "Lesbian Sex Wars in the 1980s" by Lillian Faderman, in her *Odd Girls and Twilight Lovers: A History of Lesbian Life in Twentieth–Century America,* New York, Columbia University Press, 1991, 246–270; "Lesbian Erotica: Flogging the Velvet Dream" by Marie J. Kuda, in *Gay Chicago,* 5 December 1991, 21–25.

Pat Califia comments: "While I agree that racism and violence against women are serious issues, I do not believe we can combat these social ills by stigmatizing, censoring, or persecuting sexual minorities within the gay and lesbian community. The position that S/M and pornography have occupied in the debates about eliminating misogyny, rape, and battery of women has largely been a symbolic one. It is much easier to mobilize public sentiment against 'perverts' and effect a purge in the women's movement than it is to attack the real sources of woman–hating. In my work, I have tried to make all people more aware of their sexual options, encourage women especially to minimize danger when they take sexual risks, support the formation of self–aware deviant communities, increase lesbian visibility by creating more provocative images of dyke passion, and *make people keep thinking*—even while they are jacking off!"

*   *   *

Pat Califia would not wince at being called a sexual radical, but there was a time when any woman who accepted for herself the label "lesbian" was deemed such. The public examination of women's sexual appetites and adventures that rode in on the tail of the women's movement of the 1960s and 1970s had its counterpart in the lesbian community as well. Arbiters of a new orthodoxy among the lesbian–feminist communities, attempting to redefine "lesbian" as a political entity with an option to practice sexual expression or not, came flat up against a new wave of lesbians who were reclaiming and testing the boundaries of lesbian sexuality. While heterosexual women followed the lead of supermarket press and women's magazines in the quest for orgasm, the lesbian community broke out into a series of "sex wars" in which the opposing camps were basically cultural feminists versus sexual radicals. Califia caused the polarization of the erotica–pornography debates between so–called radicals and those she labeled the "puritan" element, taking the position that consensual S/M as practiced by lesbians was not inconsistent with feminism.

Califia (she renamed herself after an Amazon queen) was raised in a Mormon family and came out as a lesbian in Salt Lake City, Utah.

After moving to San Francisco in 1973, she encountered a community of women sex researchers, historians, and photographers—women like Tee Corinne, Marsha Seeley, Amber Hollibaugh, and Honey Lee Cottrell—who were exploring and documenting lesbian sexual gratification and erotica. Califia was one of the women who founded Samois, a support group for lesbian leatherwomen involved in S/M. Together with feminist theorist Gayle Rubin and others, she contributed to the anthology *Coming to Power,* first published by Samois in 1982. *Coming to Power* was a collection of fiction, graphics, position papers, philosophy, and other nonfiction intended as both outreach and as an aggressive response to the perceived attack from lesbian anti–porn factions. Califia's personal view of the background of the confrontation takes up the better part of her chapter on the history of San Francisco's S/M movement.

Coming to Power caused an immediate furor, not only because of its content, but also because that content made the book's distribution a politically charged issue. Lesbian, gay, and feminist bookstores were in a quandary; some sold it only under the counter, some would not carry it at all. As copies began to circulate, both the volume's underground reputation and the demand for it grew. The popularity of *Coming to Power* was in no little part due to another of Califia's contributions: an erotic short story entitled "Jessie."

Califia's nonjudgmental primer on the varied forms of lesbian sexual activity, *Sapphistry: The Book of Lesbian Sexuality* had been issued two years before *Coming to Power,* to much the same reception among booksellers. Before *Sapphistry* there had been two earlier attempts at lesbian sex manuals: one a slick, heavily–illustrated volume from an establishment press, and the other a slim, reticent, beautifully–illustrated book from a lesbian press that strove hard to be politically correct. Califia's work was all–encompassing, with an introduction by pioneer activist Phyllis Lyon, and illustrations by Tee Corinne, and it garnered both critical and political approval. Within a year of its 1980 publication, the demand for *Sapphistry* was so great that it finally secured a place on bookstore shelves. The issues generated by the publication of both *Coming to Power* and *Sapphistry* fueled lesbian discussion groups and conference workshops for a decade.

Califia's interest in sexual health and safety prompted subsequent editions of *Sapphistry,* revised to include information on AIDS awareness and prevention—many women, especially lesbians in monogamous relationships, were unaware of their vulnerability to the disease. Her *Lesbian S/M Safety Manual,* published in 1988, was the first book devoted specifically to women's perspectives on sexually transmitted diseases, emotional safety, prophylactics, and the importance of communication and sexual contracts in S/M. Califia went on to write a sex advice column for the *Advocate,* a national gay newspaper with a principally male readership. *The Sexpert* and *The Advocate Adviser* are collections of her witty and thoughtful responses to reader queries as originally published in her columns.

In addition to her works of nonfiction, Califia has written on sexual subjects for a number of mainstream journals. Her fiction continues to attract readers despite the ambivalence of some reviewers. Susie Bright, maven of the sexually experimental and former editor of *On Our Backs,* wrote in *Lambda Rising Book Report* that the stories in *Macho Sluts* did not measure up to the promise of "Jessie." However, Califia's novel *Doc and Fluff: The Distopian Tale of a Girl and Her Biker* received a review from *Lambda Book Report* advising readers to wear "asbestos gloves" as this was her "hot, wet, trashy best."

Several anthologies of vampire stories and lesbian erotica include examples of Califia's short fiction; editor Joan Nestle's *The Persistent Desire* included three of her butch–femme poems. And in her contribution to 1993's *Madonnarama: Essays on Sex and Popular Culture,* Califia takes on the entertainment icons who dabble in the counter–culture to turn a profit without a personal investment and at a price for those they deem disposable.

Califia's contribution to lesbian culture has been to return "sex" to the dialogue on homosexuality. She has prodded an intellectual faction bent on creating an image of lesbianism grounded in celibacy and support networks, and has poked at those fighting sexual violence by aligning themselves with some pretty scary right–wing bedfellows. Most significantly, through her writings, Califia has persisted, sometimes on shaky ground and often with a sense of humor, in calling for sexual tolerance and equality.

—*Marie J. Kuda*

* * *

CAPOTE, Truman. American novelist, playwright, and author of short stories. Born Truman Streckfus Persons in New Orleans, Louisiana, 30 September 1924; name legally changed. Educated at Trinity School and St. John's Academy, both in New York City, and in public schools in Greenwich, Connecticut. Newspaper clipper and cartoon cataloger, *New Yorker,* New York City, c. 1943–44; worked as a filmscript reader and free–lance writer of anecdotes for a digest magazine. Appeared in motion picture *Murder by Death,* Columbia, 1976. **Recipient:** O. Henry Award, 1946, 1948, and 1951; National Institute of Arts and Letters creative writing award, 1959; Mystery Writers of America Edgar Award, 1966; Emmy Award, 1967. *Died in Los Angeles, of liver disease complicated by phlebitis and multiple drug intoxication, 25 August 1984.*

WRITINGS

Novels

Other Voices, Other Rooms. New York, Random House, and London, Heinemann, 1948; with introduction by the author, New York, Random House, 1968.
The Grass Harp. New York, Random House, 1951; with *A Tree of Night, and Other Stories,* New York, New American Library, 1956.
Breakfast at Tiffany's: A Short Novel and Three Stories. New York, Random House, 1958; as *Breakfast at Tiffany's,* London, Hamilton, 1959.
In Cold Blood: A True Account of a Multiple Murder and Its Consequences (nonfiction novel; first serialized in *New Yorker*). New York, Random House, 1965; London, Hamilton, 1966.

Short Stories

A Tree of Night, and Other Stories. New York, Random House, 1949; London, Heinemann, 1950; with *The Grass Harp,* New York, New American Library, 1956.

A Christmas Memory (first published in *Mademoiselle*), illustrations by Etienne Delessert. New York, Random House, 1966.

The Thanksgiving Visitor (first published in *McCall's*). New York, Random House, 1968.

Music for Chameleons: New Writing (includes "Nocturnal Turnings or How Siamese Twins Have Sex"). New York, Random House, 1980; London, Hamilton, 1981.

Miriam: A Classic Story of Loneliness (first published in *Mademoiselle*). Mankato, Minnesota, Creative Education, 1982.

One Christmas (first published in *Ladies Home Journal*). New York, Random House, 1983.

Jug of Silver (children's book), illustrations by James Hoys. Mankato, Minnesota, Creative Education, 1986.

Nonfiction

Local Color (sketches). New York, Random House, 1950.

The Muses Are Heard: An Account (first published in *New Yorker*). New York, Random House, 1956; as *The Muses Are Heard: An Account of the Porgie and Bess Visit to Leningrad*, London, Heinemann, 1957.

The Dogs Bark: Public People and Private Places. New York, Random House, 1973; London, Weidenfeld & Nicolson, 1974.

Then It All Came Down: Criminal Justice Today Discussed by Police, Criminals, and Corrections Officers, 1976.

Plays

The Grass Harp: A Play (adaptation of the novel by Capote; produced on Broadway, 1952; produced as a musical on Broadway, 1971). New York, Random House, 1952.

With Harold Arlen, *The House of Flowers* (libretto; based on a story by Capote; produced on Broadway, 1954; revised and produced Off–Broadway, 1968). New York, Random House, 1968.

Screenplays

With John Huston, *Beat the Devil,* United Artists, 1954.

With William Archibald and John Mortimer, *The Innocents* (based on the novel by Henry James), Twentieth Century–Fox, 1961.

With Eleanor Perry, *Trilogy* (based on the stories "Miriam," "Among the Paths to Eden," and "A Christmas Memory" by Capote), Allied Artists, 1969.

Television Plays

A Christmas Memory (based on the story by Capote), ABC–TV, 1966.

Among the Paths to Eden (based on the story by Capote), 1967.

The Thanksgiving Visitor (based on the story by Capote), ABC–TV, 1968.

Laura, 1968.

Behind Prison Walls, 1972.

With Tracy Keenan Wynn and Wyatt Cooper, *The Glass House,* 1972.

Crimewatch, 1973.

Other

Observations, photographs by Richard Avedon. New York, Simon & Schuster, and London, Weidenfeld & Nicolson, 1959.

Selected Writings, introduction by Mark Schorer. New York, Random House, and London, Hamilton, 1963.

Author of introduction, *The Collected Works of Jane Bowles.* New York, Farrar, Strauss, 1966.

The Thanksgiving Visitor (first published in *McCall's*). New York, Random House, 1968; London, Hamilton, 1969.

With Eleanor and Frank Perry, *Trilogy: An Experiment in Multimedia.* New York, Macmillan, 1969.

Three by Truman Capote. New York, Random House, 1985.

Answered Prayers: The Partial Manuscript (first serialized in *Esquire*), edited by Joseph Fox. New York, Random House, 1986; as *Answered Prayers: The Unfinished Novel,* 1987.

A Capote Reader. New York, Random House, 1987.

Recordings: *Children on Their Birthdays,* Columbia, c. 1950.

*

Adaptations: *Breakfast at Tiffany's* (film), Paramount, 1961; *Breakfast at Tiffany's* (a musical adaptation) by Edward Albee and Bob Merrill, produced Philadelphia and New York, 1966; *In Cold Blood* (film), Columbia, 1967.

Biography: "The Private World of Truman Capote" by Anne Taylor Fleming, in *New York Times Magazine,* 9 July 1978, 22–25, and 16 July 1978, 12–13, 15, 44; *Truman Capote: The Story of His Bizarre and Exotic Boyhood by an Aunt Who Helped Raise Him* by Marie Rudisill and James C. Simmons, New York, Morrow, 1983; *Capote: A Biography* by Gerald Clarke, New York, Simon & Schuster, 1986; *Truman Capote: Dear Heart, Old Buddy* by John Malcolm Brinnin, New York, Delacorte, 1986; *Dear Genius; A Memoir of My Life with Truman Capote* by Jack Dunphy, New York, McGraw, 1987; *Lost Friendships: A Memoir of Truman Capote, Tennessee Williams, and Others* by Donald Windham, New York, Morrow, 1987; *A Bridge of Childhood: Truman Capote's Southern Years* by Marianne Moates, New York, Holt, 1989.

Interviews: With Eric Norden, in *Playboy,* March 1968, 51–62, 160–170; *Conversations with Capote* by Lawrence Grobel, New York, New American Library, 1985; *Truman Capote: Conversations,* edited by M. Thomas Inge, Jackson, University of Mississippi Press, 1987.

Bibliography: "Truman Capote: A Bibliography" by Jackson R. Bryer, in *Truman Capote's "In Cold Blood": A Critical Handbook,* edited by Irving Malin, Belmont, California, Wadsworth, 1968, 239–69; *Truman Capote: A Checklist* by Kenneth Starosciak, New Brighton, Minnesota, Kenneth Starosciak, 1974; *Truman Capote: A Primary and Secondary Bibliography* by Robert J. Stanton, Boston, G. K. Hall, 1980; "Truman Capote: A Bibliographical Checklist" by Robert A. Wilson, in *American Book Collector,* July/August 1980, 8–15.

Critical Sources: *Truman Capote's "In Cold Blood": A Critical Handbook,* edited by Irving Malin, Belmont, California, Wadsworth, 1968; *The Worlds of Truman Capote* by William L. Nance, New York, Stein & Day, 1970; *Playing the Game: The Homosexual Novel in America* by Roger Austen, Indianapolis, Bobbs–Merrill, 1977;

Like a Brother, Like a Lover: Male Homosexuality in the American Novel and Theater from Herman Melville to James Baldwin by Georges–Michel Sarotte, translation by Richard Miller, Garden City, New York, Doubleday, 1978; *Truman Capote* by Helen S. Garson, New York, 1980; *The Homosexual As Hero in Contemporary Fiction* by Stephen Adams, New York, Barnes & Noble, 1980; "Truman Capote" by Craig Goad, in *Dictionary of Literary Biography,* Volume 2: *American Novelists since World War II,* Detroit, Gale, 1980, updated for *Concise Dictionary of American Literary Biography: The New Consciousness, 1941–1968,* Detroit, Gale, 1987; *Truman Capote* by Kenneth T. Reed, Boston, Twayne Publishers, 1981; *Gay Fictions, Wilde to Stonewall: Studies in a Male Homosexual Literary Tradition* by Claude J. Summers, New York, Continuum, 1990; "El Chiasme en Proust y Capote: Arte y suicidio" by Hugo Beccacece, in *La Nació—Suplemento Literario,* 5 August 1990, 1–2; *The Gay Novel in America* by James Levin, New York, Garland, 1991; *Truman Capote: A Study of His Short Fiction* by Helen S. Garson, New York, Twayne Publishers, 1992; "Truman Capote" by Peter G. Christensen, in *Contemporary Gay American Novelists,* edited by Emmanuel S. Nelson, Westport, Connecticut, Greenwood Press, 1993.

*   *   *

Truman Capote achieved meteoric fame between 1945 and 1958 for two memorable novels, *Other Voices, Other Rooms* and *The Grass Harp,* and two volumes of stories, *A Tree of Night, and Other Stories* and *Breakfast at Tiffany's,* all much stronger on atmosphere and characterization than on plot. Some works stressed a dark vision of life; others were more sentimental, including what is perhaps his best story, "A Christmas Memory." Capote's fame enabled him to travel with the artistic, famous, and wealthy, and led him to write inconsequential pieces of journalism. After a comeback with the true crime novel *In Cold Blood: A True Account of a Multiple Murder and Its Consequences,* he lost the good will of friends and critics with a series of four scandal–mongering stories, which were supposed to be parts of his magnum opus, *Answered Prayers,* which was apparently never finished. Years of writer's block, drug–addiction problems, and humiliating incidents lost Capote critical support and led to a major devaluation of his work that has continued to the present.

The bulk of Capote's fiction does not feature gay themes; when it does, healthy mutual relationships between men do not appear. In "Shut a Final Door" from *A Tree of Night, and Other Stories,* a young man named Walter, who is starting to disintegrate emotionally, flees from New York to New Orleans without confronting all his inner demons, one of which may well be homosexuality. "A Diamond Guitar," from *Breakfast at Tiffany's,* takes place in a southern prison where a middle–aged convict, Schaeffer, falls in love with a young Cuban, Tico Feo, who has just been incarcerated. The sensitive Schaeffer is betrayed by the streetwise Tico Feo during a prison break. "Unspoiled Monsters," the first of the stories in the unfinished *Answered Prayers,* is full of gay name–dropping and bits of gossip.

The one "gay book" for which Capote will be remembered is his first novel, *Other Voices, Other Rooms.* It centers on the emotional dislocation of 13–year–old Joel Harrison Knox, who, in the deep American South of the 1930s, goes off to live with his cousin Randolph, a stranger. In the eighth chapter of the novel, Randolph tells Joel the story of the great love of his life; this passage is one of the few in which Capote does not approach homosexuality circuitously. *Other Voices, Other Rooms* has received attention in surveys of American gay fiction. To some the novel is a sympathetic study of a lonely boy who will surely turn out to be gay in his later teens. Others find that the Southern Gothic trappings only enforce stereotypes of gay male grotesqueness, effeminacy, and escapism. The novel succeeds as art because of this complexity.

Homosexuality emerges as a difficult–to–assess subtext in *In Cold Blood.* This famous nonfiction documentary novel, based on the 1959 murder of the Clutter family in Holcomb, Kansas, reveals much about the two murderers, Perry Smith and Eugene ("Dick") Hickock, yet it has also been accused of distorting their personalities. In a 1966 interview later collected in M. Thomas Inge's *Truman Capote: Conversations,* George Plimpton asked Capote if there was any sexual attraction between Perry and Dick, and Capote said there was not. This may be true; however, the handful of brief references to homosexuality in the novel makes one wonder if the issue is more complicated. It may be that Capote was guided by the understandable desire not to turn public attention to homosexual attraction with respect to such brutal murderers.

The nonfiction collection *The Dogs Bark: Public People and Private Places* contains several journalistic pieces that feature gay and lesbian bisexual personalities that are not presented as such. In "The White Rose," Capote writes about going to visit French writer Sidonie–Gabrielle Colette in Paris in 1947 and receiving an expensive paper weight from her as a present. His attempts to validate great writers outside of the sexual mainstream, unfortunately, seem to deteriorate to name–dropping, since he never offers any sharp characterization of their work or their social defiance. Capote wanted to be seen in the tradition of gay French writing, often comparing himself to French novelist Marcel Proust.

Other short pieces tell about visits to vacation spots recognizable as haunts of the gay jet set—Ischia, Tangier, and Taormina. Some brief celebrity sketches are devoted to American novelist and playwright Jane Bowles, British photographer Cecil Beaton, French author and artist Jean Cocteau, and French writer André Gide. The essay on the last encounter of Cocteau and Gide, in Sicily in 1950, according to Donald Windham's memoir, is a fantasy that could not have taken place. Two essays on living in Brooklyn, New York, give little sense of the vital gay scene there in the 1940s. Although weak, these pieces are more important in understanding Capote than is generally recognized. Capote's failure—perhaps cowardice—in confronting the gay potential of this material constitutes the opposite pole of his later obsession with writing tell–all stories of what really happened in the world of the jet set.

In the collection of essays and stories, *Music for Chameleons: New Writings,* one of the most interesting pieces is the last one in the volume, "Nocturnal Turnings or How Siamese Twins Have Sex." Rambling but moving, it includes his perhaps most famous statement: "But I'm not a saint yet. I'm an alcoholic. I'm a drug addict. I'm homosexual. I'm a genius. Of course, I could be all four of these dubious things and still be a saint. But I shonuf ain't no saint yet, nawsuh." The romantic French tradition of locating homosexuality between addiction and genius contrasts strongly with the view of homosexuality in *Answered Prayers,* where it is much closer to everyday vulgarity and social climbing.

What remains effective in Capote's work is his insight into the problems of boys struggling with their sexuality, as in *Other Voices, Other Rooms,* and the disturbing view of male bonding in a repressive society, as in *In Cold Blood.*

—*Peter G. Christensen*

———

CARPENTER. *See* **ARNOLD, June (Davis).**

———

CARPENTER, Edward. British poet, editor, social theorist, craftsman, and curate. Born in Brighton, East Sussex, 29 August 1844. Educated at Brighton College, 1854–63; Heidelberg University; and Trinity Hall, Cambridge (fellow, 1869), 1864–69. Companion of George Merrill, beginning c. 1898. In holy orders, beginning 1869; curate of St. Edward's, Cambridge, 1870; travelled to Rome, Naples and Florence, Italy, c. 1873; relinquished orders and fellowship, 1874; staff lecturer on astronomy, University Extension movement in the North of England. Travelled to the United States, 1877 and 1884. Worked as a sandalmaker and market gardener, Derbyshire, beginning 1883. Founder of socialist society, Sheffield, 1885. *Died in Guildford, 28 June 1929.*

WRITINGS

Poetry

Narcissus, and Other Poems. London, H. S. King, 1873.
Moses: A Drama in Five Acts (verse play). London, E. Moxon & Son, 1875; revised as *The Promised Land,* London, Swan, 1911.
Towards Democracy. Manchester, England, 1883.
Chants of Labour, 1888.
The Story of Eros and Psyche from Apuleius, and The First Book of the Iliad of Homer, Done into English. London, Swan, 1900.
Who Shall Command the Heart? (sequel to *Towards Democracy*). London, Swan, 1902.

Nonfiction

The Religious Influence of Art. London, Bell & Daldy, 1870.
Cooperative Production, with Reference to the Experiment of Leclaire: A Lecture. Manchester, England, John Heywood, 1883.
Desirable Mansions: A Tract (first published in *Progress*). Manchester, England, John Heywood, 1883.
Modern Money–Lending and the Meaning of Dividends: A Tract. Manchester, England, John Heywood, 1883.
Modern Science: A Criticism. Manchester, England, John Heywood, 1885.

England's Ideal: A Tract Re–Printed from "To–Day," May, 1884. Manchester, England, John Heywood, 1885.
England's Ideal, and Other Papers on Social Subjects. London, Swan, 1887.
Civilization: Its Cause and Cure, and Other Essays. London, Swan, 1889; enlarged, London, Allen & Unwin, 1921.
With Edward Maitland, *Vivisection* (two essays). London, Humanitarian League, 1893.
Marriage in Free Society. Manchester, England, Labour Press Society, 1894.
Woman, and Her Place in a Free Society. Manchester, England, Labour Press Society, 1894.
Homogenic Love, and Its Place in a Free Society. Manchester, England, Labour Press Society, 1894.
Sex–Love, and Its Place in a Free Society. Manchester, England, Labour Press Society, 1894.
Love's Coming–of–Age: A Series of Papers on the Relations of the Sexes. Manchester, England, Labour Press Society, 1896.
The Need of a Rational and Humane Science. London, G. Bell & Sons, 1897.
An Unknown People (first published in *Reformer*). London, A & H. B. Bonner, 1897.
The Village and the Landlord. [London], 1907.
Angels' Wings: A Series of Essays on Art and Its Relation to Life. London, Swan, 1898.
Empire, in India and Elsewhere (first published in *Human Review*). [London], 1900.
The Art of Creation: Essays on the Self and Its Powers. London, George Allen, 1904.
Vivisection: An Address Given before the Humanitarian League. London, Humanitarian League, 1904.
Prisons, Police and Punishment: An Inquiry into the Causes and Treatment of Crime and Criminals. London, Fifield, 1905; excerpts published as *Non–Governmental Society,* 1911.
The Simplification of Life, from the Writings of Edward Carpenter, edited by Harry Roberts. London, A. Treherne, 1905.
Days with Walt Whitman, with Some Notes on His Life and Work. London, George Allen, 1906.
The Intermediate Sex: A Study of Some Transitional Types of Men and Women. London, Swan, 1908.
British Aristocracy and the House of Lords (first published in *Albany Review*). London, Fifield, 1908.
With T. S. Dymond, D. C. Pedder, and the Fabian Society, *Socialism and Agriculture.* London, Fifield, 1908.
The Inner Self: Delivered in the King's Weigh House Church. London, Christian Commonwealth, 1912.
The Drama of Love and Death: A Study of Human Evolution and Transfiguration. London, George Allen, 1912.
Intermediate Types among Primitive Folk: A Study in Social Evolution. London, George Allen, 1914.
The Healing of Nations and the Hidden Sources of Their Strife. London, Allen & Unwin, 1915.
The Story of My Books (originally published in *English Review*). London, Allen & Unwin, 1916.
Towards Industrial Freedom. London, Allen & Unwin, 1917.
Pagan and Christian Creeds: Their Origin and Meaning. London, Allen & Unwin, 1920.
The Teachings of the Upanishads: Two Lectures to Popular Audiences. London, Allen & Unwin, 1920.
Some Friends of Walt Whitman. London, British Society for the Study of Sex Psychology, 1924.

With George Barnefield, *The Psychology of the Poet Shelley*. London, Allen & Unwin, 1925.

Editor

Forecasts of the Coming Century, by a Decade of Writers. Manchester, England, Labour Press, 1897.
Ioläus: An Anthology of Friendship. London, Swan, and Boston, C. E. Goodspell, 1902.
Light from the East: Being Letters on Gñanam, the Divine Knowledge, by Sir Ponnambalam Arunachalam. London, Allen & Unwin, 1927.

Travel Sketches

From Adam's Peak to Elephanta: Sketches in Ceylon and India. London and New York, Macmillan, 1892; excerpts published as *A Visit to a Gñáni or Wise Man of India*, London, George Allen, 1911.
Sketches from Life in Town and Country, with Some Verses. London, George Allen, 1908.

Other

My Days and Dreams (memoir). London, Allen & Unwin, 1916.
Selected Writings, Volume 1: *Sex*. InBook Distribution Co., 1984.

*

Biography: "Edward Carpenter and the Double Structure of Maurice" by Robert K. Martin, in *Literary Visions of Homosexuality*, edited by Stuart Kellogg. New York, Haworth, 1983; "Alternative Service: Families in Recent American Gay Fiction" by David Bergman, in *Kenyon Review*, winter 1986, 72–90; "Commanding the Heart: Edward Carpenter and Friends" by S. Rowbotham, in *History Today*, September 1987.

Bibliography: "Figuring in History: The Reputation of Edward Carpenter, 1883–1987: Annotated Secondary Bibliography" by Tony Brown, in *English Literature in Review, 1880–1920*, Part 1, 32:1, 35–64; Part 2, 32:2, 170–210; *A Bibliography of Edward Carpenter*, Gordon Press Publishers.

Critical Sources: *Edward Carpenter, an Exposition and an Appreciation*, by E. Lewis, 1915; *Edward Carpenter, in Appreciation*, edited by G. Beith, 1931; *Coming Out: Homosexual Politics in Britain from the Nineteenth Century to the Present* by Jeffrey Weeks, London, Quartet, 1977.

*   *   *

Edward Carpenter describes his middle-class beginnings in his memoir, *My Days and Dreams*. His mother had been subjected to "a baneful parental influence—Scottish pride and puritanism." His father came from a naval family and served as a magistrate in Brighton, England, where Edward was born, one of ten children. While his brothers entered the army, navy, and civil service, his sisters, Lady Hyatt and Lady Daubeney, encouraged his interests in nature, flowers, music and literature. Carpenter entered Trinity Hall in Cambridge, was ordained in 1870, and was interviewed by the Prince of Wales as a tutor for the future George V. As vicar under social reformer E. D. Maurice, Carpenter turned to social service among the working classes and relinquished holy orders in 1874.

Though primarily a writer of nonfiction, Carpenter published several books of poetry; his work in this genre was greatly influenced by Walt Whitman. In 1868, a friend presented Carpenter with the first English edition of Whitman's *Leaves of Grass*, and after corresponding with the poet, Carpenter visited Whitman in Camden, New Jersey, in 1877. In 1883, Carpenter published *Towards Democracy*, a poem of nearly five hundred pages. In a "Note" to the 1922 edition, Carpenter compared Whitman's "full-blooded, copious, rank, masculine style" to his own "milder radiance, as of the moon compared with the sun."

Carpenter's prose works fall into three interrelated parts: political, religious and sexual. In politics, Carpenter was essentially an anarchist and utopian socialist. In 1883, an inheritance enabled him to purchase a farm near Sheffield, where he assembled a cooperative group that did market gardening and made sandals. He championed women's rights, vegetarianism, simple living and environmental concerns. Some have seen him as a model for George Bernard Shaw's Morrell, the clergyman in *Candida*.

Carpenter's works on spirituality attempted to bring all the areas of his life together, as well as all the peoples and faiths of the world. While he left the Church of England, he never relinquished what he saw as a universal and divine love inherent in each person. *The Drama of Love and Death: A Study of Human Evolution and Transfiguration* searched for a faith that would not be hobbled by one particular class or nation. One of his last books, *Light from the East: Being Letters on Gñanam, The Divine Knowledge*, like his lectures on the Upanishads, searched for a new faith for the industrial age.

His writings on politics and religion might seem dated, but Carpenter's writings on sexuality, particularly those on homosexuality, have continued to attract followers. Carpenter opened the field of homosexual studies in several directions. His anthology of male friendship, *Ioläus: An Anthology of Friendship*, provided a history of male-male love, and *Intermediate Types among Primitive Folk: A Study in Social Evolution* provided an anthropology of homosexuality. In *Love's Coming-of-Age*, Carpenter challenged "the arbitrary notion that the function of love is limited to child-bearing, and that any love not concerned with the propagation of the race must necessarily be of a dubious character." But he went further than defending his own sexuality; he provided a subtle argument for the creative role of what he called "intermediate types" in the progress of civilization. In *Coming Out*, Jeffrey Weeks argues that Carpenter "reverses the usual picture of evolution by arguing that it was the existence of a variety of sexual types which led to important differentiations in social life and activities."

Carpenter was truly international. He traveled extensively, journeying to Japan, India, the United States, Africa, Greece, and Italy. Many of his ideas came from the German liberation movements; he adopted the notion of a third sex, the Uranian, an inborn Platonic seed. The idea of inheriting one's sexual orientation remains a controversial issue; Carpenter certainly believed he was born a homosexual. His epic *Towards Democracy* concludes: "Lo what a world I create for my own, my lovers, / ... Thus, dear ones, building up these spheres of ourselves continually for the joyance of each other, it shall come about that at length / We shall need no other world, no other worlds."

—*Charles Shively*

_____

CARR, H. D. *See* **CROWLEY, Aleister.**

_____

CASEY, Gladys. *See* **GRIER, Barbara G(ene Damon).**

_____

CATHER, Willa (Sibert). American editor, educator, novelist, poet, journalist, and author of short stories. Born in Back Creek Valley, Virginia, 7 December 1873. Educated at the University of Nebraska, A.B. 1895. Lived with her secretary, Edith Lewis. Newspaper correspondent in Nebraska, c. 1890–95; telegraph editor and drama critic, *Daily Leader,* Pittsburgh, Pennsylvania, 1897–1901; teacher of English and Latin and head of English department, Allegheny High School, Pittsburgh, 1902–05; managing editor, 1906–11, full–time writer, 1911–47, *McClure's,* New York City. **Recipient:** Pulitzer Prize for fiction, 1922; Howells Medal for fiction, 1930; Prix Femina Américaine for distinguished literary accomplishment, 1932; National Institute of Arts and Letters Gold Medal, 1944; honorary degrees: University of Nebraska, University of Michigan, University of California, Columbia University, Yale University, Princeton University, Creighton University, and Smith College. *Died in New York City of a cerebral hemorrhage, 24 April 1947.*

WRITINGS

Novels

Alexander's Bridge. Boston, Houghton, 1912; as *Alexander's Bridges,* London, Heinemann, 1912; revised, Boston, Houghton, 1922; with introduction by Sharon O'Brien, New York, New American Library, 1988.
O Pioneers! Boston, Houghton, 1913.

The Song of the Lark. Boston, Houghton, 1915; with new preface by the author, London, J. Cape, 1936; revised, with introduction by A. S. Byatt, New York, Virago, 1982; reprinted, with foreword by Doris Grumbach, Boston, Houghton, 1988.
My Ántonia, illustrations by W. T. Bends. Boston, Houghton, 1918; reprinted, with introduction by Walter Havighurst, 1949.
One of Ours. New York, Knopf, 1922; reprinted, with introduction by Stanley T. Williams, 1926.
A Lost Lady. New York, Knopf, 1923.
The Professor's House. New York, Knopf, 1925; reprinted, with introduction by A. S. Byatt, New York, Virago, 1981.
My Mortal Enemy. New York, Knopf, 1926; reprinted, with introduction by A. S. Byatt, New York, Virago, 1982.
Death Comes for the Archbishop. New York, Knopf, 1927; reprinted, with introduction by A. S. Byatt, New York, Virago, 1981.
Shadows on the Rock. New York, Knopf, 1931; reprinted, with introduction by A. S. Byatt, New York, Virago, 1984.
Lucy Gayheart. New York, Knopf, 1935.
Sapphira and the Slave Girl. New York, Knopf, 1940.

Short Stories

The Troll Garden. New York, McClure, Phillips, 1905; reprinted, with afterword, by Katherine Anne Porter, New York, New American Library, 1961; edited with introduction and notes by James Woodress, Lincoln, University of Nebraska Press, 1983.
Youth and the Bright Medusa. New York, Knopf, 1920.
Obscure Destinies. New York, Knopf, 1932.
The Old Beauty, and Others. New York, Knopf, 1948.
Five Stories (includes article by George N. Kates). St. Paul, Minnesota, Vintage Book, 1956.
Early Stories of Willa Cather, edited by Mildred R. Bennett. New York, Dodd, 1957.
Willa Cather's Collected Short Fiction, 1892–1912, edited by Virginia Faulkner. Lincoln, University of Nebraska Press, 1965; revised, 1970.
Uncle Valentine, and Other Stories, edited by Bernice Slote. Lincoln, University of Nebraska Press, 1973.
Willa Cather: Twenty–four Stories, selected with introduction by Sharon O'Brien. New York, New American Library, 1987.
The Short Stories of Willa Cather, edited by Hermione Lee. New York, Virago, 1989.

Poetry

April Twilights. San Francisco, Badger, 1903; edited by Bernice Slote, Lincoln, University of Nebraska Press, 1968.
April Twilights, and Other Poems. New York, Knopf, 1923; enlarged, 1933; edited by Bernice Slote, Lincoln, University of Nebraska Press, 1962.

Nonfiction

Willa Cather on Writing. New York, Knopf, 1949; with foreword by Stephen Tennant, Lincoln, University of Nebraska Press, 1988.
Willa Cather in Europe: Her Own Story of the First Journey, edited with introduction and incidental notes by George N. Kates, New York, Knopf, 1956.

The Kingdom of Art: Willa Cather's First Principles and Critical Statements, 1893–1896, edited by Bernice Slote. Lincoln, University of Nebraska Press, 1966.

The World and the Parish: Willa Cather's Articles and Reviews, 1893–1902 (two volumes), edited by William M. Curtin. Lincoln, University of Nebraska Press, 1970.

Willa Cather in Person: Interviews, Speeches, and Letters, selected and edited by L. Brent Bohlke. Lincoln, University of Nebraska Press, 1986.

Other

Editor and ghostwriter, *The Life of Mary Baker G. Eddy, and the History of Christian Science,* by Georgine Milmine. Garden City, New York, Doubleday, 1909.

Ghostwriter, *My Autobiography,* by S. S. McClure. New York, Stokes, 1914.

Editor and author of introduction, *The Best Stories of Sarah Orne Jewett* (two volumes). Boston, Houghton, 1925.

Not under Forty (essays). New York, Knopf, 1936.

The Novels and Stories of Willa Cather (13 volumes). Boston, Houghton, 1937–41.

Writings from Willa Cather's Campus Years, edited by James R. Shively. Lincoln, University of Nebraska Press, 1950.

*

Adaptations: *O Pioneers!* (drama; adaptation by Darrah Cloud; produced Boston, 1990.)

Biography: *Willa Cather: A Critical Biography* by E. K. Brown, New York, Knopf, 1953; *Willa Cather: A Memoir* by Elizabeth Shepley Sergeant, Philadelphia, Lippincott, 1953; *Willa Cather Living* by Edith Lewis, New York, Knopf, 1953; *Willa Cather: The Emerging Voice* by Sharon O'Brien, New York, Oxford University Press, 1987; *Willa Cather: A Literary Life* by James Woodress, Lincoln, University of Nebraska Press, 1988.

Critical Sources: *Willa Cather: A Critical Introduction* by David Daiches, Ithaca, New York, Cornell University Press, 1951; *The Landscape and the Looking Glass: Willa Cather's Search for Value* by John H. Randall III, Boston, Houghton, 1960; *Willa Cather's Imagination* by David Stouck, Lincoln, University of Nebraska Press, 1975; "Cather and Her Friends" by James Woodress, in *Critical Essays on Willa Cather,* Boston, G. K. Hall, 1983; "The Thing Not Named: Willa Cather as a Lesbian Writer" by Sharon O'Brien, in *Signs,* Number 9, 1984, 576–599; *Perilous: Willa Cather's Romanticism* by Susan Rosowski, Lincoln, University of Nebraska Press, 1986; "Displacing Homosexuality: The Use of Ethnicity in Willa Cather's *My Ántonia*" by Katrina Irving, in *Modern Fiction Studies,* Number 36, 1990, 91–119.

*   *   *

On the question of Willa Cather's lesbianism, James Woodress writes in *Critical Essays on Willa Cather,* "Documentary evidence does not exist to dispose of the question in one way or another."

Certainly Cather herself always remained silent on her sexuality, partly because of the era in which she lived, partly because of her own sense of privacy. For this reason there is no first–hand evidence of Cather's lesbianism; there is, however, an abundance of circumstantial evidence. While still in high school Cather began referring to herself as William Cather, Jr., and shocked some people in her hometown of Red Cloud, Nebraska, with her announced intention of studying medicine, a profession that was almost exclusively male at that time. Cather began her studies at the University of Nebraska in 1890, and during her early college days in Omaha she caused a stir by dressing in men's clothing and wearing her hair cropped short. A college English class soon convinced Cather to concentrate on literary studies rather than medicine, and she proved herself to be such a brilliant writer and thinker that she began working as a professional critic of theater, art, music, and literature while still an undergraduate. A few years after earning her degree Cather met, and almost certainly fell in love with, Isabelle McClung, the daughter of a wealthy, conservative Pittsburgh judge. From 1901 until 1906 Cather and Isabelle McClung shared a bedroom in the McClung family mansion, and their friendship continued for some 30 years despite McClung's 1916 marriage to musician Jan Hambourg. Important clues to the exact nature of Cather's relationship with McClung were lost when, late in life, the intensely private Cather destroyed all the correspondence that had passed between them. In 1908 Cather and Edith Lewis, then a proofreader, entered into what was known as a Boston marriage—a living arrangement between two single women that provided companionship, economic support, and, possibly, love. Cather and Lewis would continue to live and travel together until Cather's death in 1947. Besides McClung and Lewis, Cather had close relationships with a number of other women, including the writers Elizabeth Shepley Sargeant, Dorothy Canfield Fisher, Zoë Akins, and Sarah Orne Jewett, who was Cather's literary mentor.

As with her life, Cather's writing gives only indirect evidence of her sexual orientation. None of Cather's female characters is overtly lesbian, though many of them might be. In particular there are Cather's strong female characters who reject nineteenth–century standards of female behavior and thus remove themselves from the socially approved triad of birth–marriage–death. Thea Kronberg of *The Song of the Lark* not only achieves a successful professional singing career without a man, but achieves it in part due to the death of a man who would have married her and bound her to a conventional family life. Alexandra Bergson of *O Pioneers!* works tirelessly, manages her farm more efficiently than her brothers manage theirs, and puts off marriage until she is past childbearing age. As for male characters, Cather created a number who might be gay, though as with her female characters, their homosexuality is never made explicit. Almost certainly gay are the characters Harvey Merrick of "The Sculptor's Funeral" and Paul of "Paul's Case." Merrick is an artist with a "ladylike voice" who is mocked by the citizens of his hometown because he appreciates beauty and doesn't share the local obsession with turning a profit. Paul is a tragic, sensitive teenager who escapes from his dull hometown to the artistic vitality of New York and there spends a night carousing with "a wild San Francisco boy, a freshman at Yale."

From the novel *My Ántonia* there are the probably homosexual characters of Peter and Pavel, a pair of Russian immigrants who share a farm, a bed, and a terrible secret: back in Russia, they threw a bride and groom off a wedding–party sled in order to escape ravenous wolves. Katrina Irving, writing in *Modern Fiction Studies,* calls Peter and Pavel's action "a clear allegory for the adoption of homosexuality." Besides Cather's treatment of character, other evidence of her lesbianism is found in her adoption of male personae to describe female beauty. This is seen most clearly in her short story "Coming, Aphrodite!," in which the male protagonist, artist Don Hedger, spies on his beautiful neighbor as she exercises in the nude.

Whether hinted at or simply ignored, neither heterosexuality nor homosexuality in themselves are major themes in Cather's work. Instead, her writing focuses on two themes that seem far removed from the author's sexuality. One of these themes is the American West, and the other is art. The West—particularly Nebraska—is central to some of Cather's best short fiction, including the three stories that comprise *Obscure Destinies:* "Neighbor Rosicky," which tells the story of a Bohemian immigrant–farmer; "Old Mrs. Harris," which describes a family similar to Cather's own; and "Two Friends," a child's remembrance of friendship and conflict between two small–town businessmen. The West also figures prominently in some of Cather's most celebrated novels. *O Pioneers!* and *My Ántonia* take place in Nebraska, while *Death Comes for the Archbishop* is set in the Southwest (a place that Cather first saw, and fell in love with, in 1912). Although Cather's western childhood and date of birth might have aligned her with such western Naturalist writers as Frank Norris and Hamlin Garland, her writing bears little resemblance to the work of the Naturalists. While Cather does manage to write of the West as a place of economic and social conflict (a subject that was Garland's obsession), she also writes lovingly and somewhat nostalgically of the land and its immigrant pioneers. Unlike some of the more socially conscious, politically active writers of her time, Cather possessed the breadth of view, artistic sensibility, and streak of conservatism needed to see life in America as encompassing more than just political struggle.

Cather's obsession with all forms of art (and what it means to be an artist) runs throughout her work. In her fiction her ideas on art and the artistic life are most clearly stated in the short stories from the collection *Youth and the Bright Medusa.* Besides "Paul's Case" and "The Sculptor's Funeral," both of which deal with the artistic mind in conflict with the small–minded materialism of mid–America, *Youth and the Bright Medusa* includes such stories as "Coming, Aphrodite!," which examines the problem of love as a hindrance to an artistic career, and "The Diamond Mine," which considers what is left for the artist once success and fame have been won. Even Cather's war novel, *One of Ours,* features a sensitive, artistic protagonist (partly based on her cousin, Lt. G. P. Cather) who falls in love with a French culture that appreciates beauty and art in a way that the practical, money–grubbing culture of America cannot. Cather's writing about art and artists is most heavily influenced by the work of Henry James, whom she greatly admired. Her first novel, *Alexander's Bridge,* is widely considered to be an imitation of Henry James' style.

Cather's interests in the West and art are not kept separate in her writing. For example *The Song of the Lark,* a novel which is in many ways Cather's artistic autobiography, brings together the West and art as it tells the story of Thea Kronberg, a minister's daughter born in the tiny Colorado railroad town of Moonstone. Though Thea rankles at the repression of small–town life, she is nurtured by both the stark western beauty that surrounds Moonstone and the few local residents who recognize her innate potential as a musician and an artist. Eventually Thea must go east to develop her talents, and her artistic quest includes stops in Chicago, New York, and Europe. The East gives Thea culture and initiates her into the "religion" of art, but a communion with a western setting—the ancient, mystical Indian ruins of the Southwest—is necessary to complete the maturation of Thea's artistic soul. Like so many Cather characters, and like Cather herself, Thea combines the raw natural beauty and energy of the West with the refined artistic and cultural traditions of the East to produce a new and powerful art.

Cather's interests in art and the West are not as contradictory as they might at first seem. Her artists are always unconventional types, independent Bohemian dreamers and strivers who reject the social roles that society would prescribe for them. Similarly, her westerners are independent spirits who, because of their closeness to the land and their immigrant status, are set apart from the run of middle–America. It is no accident that the nationality of so many of Cather's immigrant westerners is Bohemian, for they share with her Bohemian artists the status of cultural outsiders. If, as Sharon O'Brien writes in *Signs,* Cather is a "lesbian writer forced to disguise or to conceal the emotional sources of her fiction, reassuring herself that the reader fills the absence in the text by intuiting the subterranean, unwritten subtext," then the author's cultural outsiders—whether they are opera stars or immigrant sod–busters—are part of that subtext. Though Cather could not, or would not, write directly about lesbians or gays, she writes of them metaphorically by writing about people on the margins of the dominant culture. Moreover, Cather frequently portrays outsiders not only as persons of worth to society, but as the best of society. For Cather, cultural outsiders, the people on the borders and frontiers, are society's dreamers and thinkers, pioneers and artists. This vision is her great contribution to gay and lesbian literature.

—Donald A. Barclay

———

CATTY, Charles. *See* **MEW, Charlotte (Mary).**

———

CAVAFY, C(onstantine) P(eter). Greek poet. Name transliterated as Constantin, Konstantinos; also Patrou, Petrou; also Kavafis, Kavifis, Kabaphe, Kabaphes. Born in Alexandria, Egypt, 17 April 1863; spent part of childhood in England and Constantinople. Civil servant, Egyptian Ministry of Public Works, Alexandria, 1885–1933. *Died in Alexandria, Egypt, 29 April 1933.*

WRITINGS

Greek Texts

Piimata ["Poems"] (two volumes), edited by George P. Savidis. Athens, Ikaros, 1963.

Peza ["Prose Texts"], edited by G. Papoutsakis. Athens, Fexis, 1963.

Anekdota Pexa ["Unpublished Prose Texts"], edited by M. Peridis. Athens, Fenix, 1963.

Anekdota Piimata ["Unpublished Poems"], edited by George P. Safidis. Athens, Ikaros, 1968.

Epistoles ston Mario Vaïno ["Letters to Mario Vaïno"], edited by E. Moshos. Athens, Estia, 1979.

Anekdota Simiomata Piitikes ke Ithikis ["Unpublished Notes on Poetics and Ethics"], edited by George P. Savidis. Athens, Ermis, 1983.

To Apokirigmena ["The Rejected Poems"], edited by George P. Savidis. Athens, Ikaros, 1983.

Poetry

Poiemata. Athens, Eridanos, 1935.

The Complete Poems of Cavafy (includes all canonical poems plus 33 early poems), translation by Rae Dalven, introduction by W. H. Auden. London, Chatto & Windus, and New York, Harcourt, 1961; expanded edition adds 63 of 75 unpublished poems, New York, Harcourt, 1976.

The Poems, translation by John Mavrogordato, introduction by Rex Warner. London, Hogarth Press, 1951; second edition (includes translation of all 154 canonical poems), 1962.

Hapanta, 1963.

Poiemata 1896–1933, 1966.

Fourteen Poems by C. P. Cavafy: Chosen and Illustrated with Twelve Etchings by David Hockney, translation by Nikos Stangos and Stephen Spender. London, Editions Alecto, 1966.

Autgrapha poiemata (1896–1910), 1968.

K. P. Kabaphe anekdota poiemata 1882–1923, 1968.

Passions and Ancient Days, translation and introduction by Edmund Keeley and George Savidis. New York, Dial Press, 1971.

Selected Poems, 1972.

Kavaphika, 1974.

Collected Poems (bilingual edition includes all canonical poems plus 21 unpublished poems), translation by Edmund Keeley and Philip Sherrard, edited by George Savidis. New Jersey, Princeton University Press, and London, Hogarth Press, 1975.

Three Poems of Passion, translation by Edmund Keeley and George Savidis. Verona, Italy, Plain Wrapper Press, 1975.

Homage to Cavafy (collection of translations of ten of the erotic poems and Duane Michals' photographs of male nudes). Danbury, New Hampshire, Addison House, 1978.

Poems of Constantine Cavafy, translation by George Khairallah. Beirut, Heidelberg, 1979.

Cavafy as I Knew Him; with Twelve Annotated Translations of His Poems and a Translation of the "Golden Verses of Pythagoras" by Memas Kolaitis. Santa Barbara, California, Kolaitis Dictionaries, 1980.

Three Poems of Cavafy, translation by Lawrence Durrell. Edinburgh, Tragara Press, 1980.

Contributor, *Voices of Modern Greece: Selected Poems,* translated and edited by Edmund Keeley and Philip Sherrard. New Jersey, Princeton University Press, 1981.

Contributor, *The Dark Crystal: An Anthology of Modern Greek Poetry,* selected and translated by Edmund Keeley and Philip Sherrard. Athens, D. Harvey, 1981.

Erotika poiemata. Athens, Erato, 1984.

The Greek Poems of C. P. Cavafy, Volume 1: *The Canonical Poems,* Volume 2: *The Non–Canonical Poems,* translation by Memas Kolaitis. New Rochelle, New York, A. D. Caratzas, 1988–89.

Uncollected Verse

"The Gods Abandon Antony," "Alexandrian Kings," "In the Month of Athyr," "Morning Sea," and "Darius," in *Pharos and Pharillon* by E. M. Forster, translation by George Valassopoulo. London, 1923; reprinted, Berkeley, Creative Arts, 1980, 55, 95–96.

"Darius," translation by George Valassopoulo, in *Nation and the Athenaeum,* 6 October 1923, 14.

"The City," translation by George Valassopoulo, in *Nation and the Athenaeum,* 5 April 1924, 16.

"Theodotus," translation by George Valassopoulo, in *Nation and the Athenaeum,* 21 July 1924, 380.

"Ithaca," translation by George Valassopoulo, *Criterion,* 2:8, 1924, 431–32.

"Ionicon," "The Ides of March," "Manuel Comnenus," and "Come Back," translation by George Valassopoulo, in *Oxford Outlook* 6:26, 1924, 94–95.

"For Ammones Who Died at the Age of 29 in the Year 610" and "If He Did Die," translation by George Valassopoulo, in *Criterion,* 8:30, 1928, 33–34.

"Of Coloured Glass," "The Trojans," and "The Afternoon Sun," translation by Robert Liddell, in *Personal Landscape: An Anthology of Exile,* edited by Robin Fedden. London, Editions Poetry London, 1945, 108–10 (with accompanying essay, 101–07).

"Waiting for the Barbarians," translation by Richard Lattimore, in *Kenyon Review,* spring 1955, 291–92.

"King Demetrius," "Nero's Term," "Orophernes," and "The Retinue of Dionysus," translation by Rob Swigart, in *Antaeus,* autumn 1972, 144–47.

"Fifteen Poems," translation by Cavafy's brother, John Cavafy, in *St. Andrews Review,* autumn–winter 1974, 37.

"Candles" and "In the Cafe," in *American Poetry Review,* September–October 1975, 40.

"Ithaca," translation by Edouard Roditi, in *Chicago Review,* winter 1975–1976, 33.

"The Unpublished Drafts of Five Poems on Julian the Apostate by C. P. Cavafy," edited by R. Lavagnini, in *Byzantine and Modern Greek Studies,* Number 7, 1981, 55–88 (includes accompanying essay "The Julian Poems of C. P. Cavafy" by G. W. Bowerstock, 89–104).

"Three Cavafy Poems" (contains "The Afternoon Sun," "On an Italian Shore," and "Days of 1908"), translation by James Merrill, in *Grand Street,* winter 1987, 124–26.

Prose

Peri ekklesias kai theatrou, 1963.

"Ars Poetica," in *Charioteer,* 10, 1968.

Peza ["Prose Texts"] (includes "Give Back the Elgin Marbles," "Persian Manners," "Misplaced Tenderness," "Romaïc Folklore of Enchanted Animals," "Masks," and diary extracts from Cavafy's trip to Greece). Athens, Ekdoseis P. Phykire, 1982.

"Cavafy's Reading Notes on Gibbon's 'Decline and Fall,'" edited by Diane Haas, in *Folia Heohellenica,* Number 4, 1982, 25–96.

"In Broad Daylight," translation by James Merrill of "Is to Fos tis Imeras," in *Grand Street,* spring 1983, 99–107.

Manuscript Collections: Cavafy Archive, Benaki Museum, Athens; E. M. Forster Archive, Cambridge University (which includes unpublished Cavafy translations by George Valassopoulo).

Critical Sources: "The Poetry of C. P. Cavafy" by E. M. Forster, in his *Pharos and Pharillon,* Richmond, Surrey, Hogarth Press, 1923, 110–17; "Constantine Cavafy and the Greek Past" by C. M. Bowra, in his *The Creative Experiment,* London, Macmillan, 1949, 29–60; "The Complete Poems of C. P. Cavafy" by E. M. Forster, in his *Two Cheers for Democracy,* London, Edward Arnold, 1951, 247–50; "Cavafis and the Permanence of Greek History" by Edward Roditi, in *Poetry,* March 1953, 389–92; "Constantin Cavafis" by Philip Sherard, in *The Marble Threshing Floor: Studies in Modern Greek Poetry,* 1956; *Présentation Critique de Constantin Cavafy, 1863–1933* (includes the canonical poems and a lengthy critical introduction), translation by Marguerite Yourcenar and Constantin Dimaras, Paris, Gallimard, 1958; "Introduction" by W. H. Auden, in *The Complete Poems of Cavafy* by Constantine Cavafy, translation by Rae Dalven, New York, Harcourt, 1961, vii–xv; *Constantine Cavafy* by Peter Bien (Columbia Essays on Modern Writers Pamphlet 5), New York, Columbia University Press, 1964; "The Poetics of Cavafy" by A. Decavalles, in *Charioteer,* Number 10, 1968, 69–71; "Cavafy: The Historic and Erotic" by Stephen Spender, in *New York Review of Books,* 15 June 1972, 12–13; "The 'New' Poems of Cavafy" by Edmund Keeley, in *Modern Greek Writers,* edited by Edmund Keeley and Peter Bien, Princeton University Press, 1972, 123–43; *Cavafy: A Critical Biography* by Robert Lidell, London, Duckworth, 1974; "Marvelous Poet" by James Merrill, in *New York Review of Books,* 17 July 1975, 12–17; *Cavafy's Alexandria: Study of a Myth in Progress* by Edmund Keeley, Cambridge, Harvard University Press, 1976; *Alexandria Still: Forster, Durrell, and Cavafy* by Jane Lagoudis Pinchin, Princeton, Princeton University Press, 1977; "C. P. Cavafy" by William Plomer, in *Electric Delights,* Boston, David Godine, 1978, 1251–1254; "Cavafis and His Translators into English" by Kimon Kriar, in *Journal of the Hellenic Diaspora,* spring 1978, 17–40; *Kavafy: The One String-Lyre Player* by Stavros Mellisinos, Athens, Melissinos, 1979; *Love and the Symbolic Journey in the Poetry of Cavafy, Eliot, and Seferis: An Interpretation with Detailed Poem–by–Poem Analysis* by K. Kapre–Karka, New York, Pella, 1982; *Mind and Art of C. P. Cavafy: Essays on His Life and Work* by Denise Harvey, 1983; *Journal of the Hellenic Diaspora,* spring–summer 1983 (special Cavafy issue); "Eroticism and Poetry" by Margaret Alexiou, in *Journal of the Hellenic Diaspora,* spring–summer 1983, 45–65; *The Dark Brain of Piranesi,* translation by Richard Howard, New York, Farrar, Straus, Giroux, 1984, 154–98; *The Poetics of Cavafy: Textuality, Eroticism, History* by Gregory Jusdanis, Princeton University Press, 1987. *C. P. Cavafy* by Christopher Robinson, Bristol Classical Press, 1988; "Cavafy's Homosexuality and His Reputation Outside Greece" by Peter Bien, in *Journal of Modern Greek Studies,* October 1990, 197–211; "An Unsought–for–Calling (My Life as a Translator from the Modern Greek)" by Rae Dalven, in *Journal of Modern Greek Studies,* Number 8, 1990, 307–316.

*   *   *

C. P. Cavafy has gained worldwide fame for the canon of his 153 short poems published posthumously in Alexandria in 1935. A son of Greek parents living in Alexandria, he wrote his poems in mod-

ern Greek, drawing on both the demotic and purist traditions. He was also fluent in English and French, languages whose literature he knew well. He divided his poems into three categories, historical, philosophical, and erotic. Cavafy wrote uninspired traditional love poems during his twenties and thirties. Beginning in 1904, he became more accepting of his gay orientation and consequently produced erotic poems of a much higher quality. Margaret Alexiou suggests that 47 of the 153 canonical poems are in the erotic group, and that 16 of the 75 poems first published only in 1968 also fit into this category. The erotic poems, unusual for their time, have generally not been considered as outstanding as the poems in the historical and philosophical categories, on which Cavafy's fame principally rests. However, the erotic poems have been particularly influential on a number of gay, lesbian, and bisexual artists.

Cavafy had far less interest in Classical Greece, which has often been of appeal to gay men, than in the Hellenistic world and the Byzantine Empire. He was particularly inspired by the last days of the Ptolemies, Cleopatra, and her lover Mark Antony. Cavafy was influenced by the dramatic monologues of Tennyson and Browning, and many of his best poems are either monologues by or addresses to figures in historical or mythic/historical settings. The most admired poems include "Expecting the Barbarians," "The City," "Trojans," "The God Forsakes Antony," and "Ithaca." The resignation and detachment toward ideologies, great historical events, and patriotic fanfares reinforce the value given to the private world, even that of brief encounters, in the erotic poetry. Not surprisingly for such a private poet, Cavafy's outward life was uneventful. Although he was born into a family of wealthy Greek merchants in Alexandria, family fortunes plummeted upon Cavafy's father's death. Cavafy went to Liverpool (where the family business had a branch) to live from the ages of nine to 16. Except for a period in Constantinople from 1882 to 1885, the rest of his life was led in Alexandria, except for a few trips to Athens. He led the life of a bachelor clerk in the Irrigation Service.

It has been very hard to piece together the story of Cavafy's romantic life. The emotional tone of his poetry about contemporary Alexandria was set by the casual nocturnal sexual encounters in the Quartier Attarine in which he also took part. In later years Cavafy enjoyed the admiring company of young men, who would come to discuss life and art in his apartment in the Rue Lepsius, located in a rather seedy part of the city. Cavafy published in periodicals and circulated his poems in broadsheets and little booklets. Although he had a specific plan for the arrangement of his work, the body of personally selected poems on which he wanted his fame to rest was not published until two years after his death. Cavafy was recognized as a literary figure within his lifetime, and Cavafy's brother John made the first translations of the poems into English. However, his posthumous fame is much greater.

Cavafy's first major champion in the English–speaking world was E. M. Forster, who met him during his World War I stay in Alexandria. Forster promoted his friend's work in England without calling attention to Cavafy's homosexuality, and he encouraged their mutual friend George Vlassopoulo to translate the corpus of poems. Only a little over a dozen were published, so the project was taken up by John Mavrogordato, professor of Greek and Byzantine Studies at Oxford, who completed a translation of 154 poems by 1937. It was not, however, in print until 1951, by which time a few translations with accompanying appreciations had also been published by Robert Liddell, Cavafy's future biographer. An essay by C. W. Bowra on Cavafy in 1949 and Rex Warner's preface to the Mavrogordato translation assured his fame in English.

Lawrence Durrell in the *Alexandria Quartet* (1957–1960) often referred to Cavafy as the presiding poet of the city he called the "great wine–press of love" and peopled with characters such as the gay transvestite Scobie. W. H. Auden's preface to Rae Dalven's translation of the poems in 1961 brought further attention to the place of homosexuality in Cavafy's poetry. Auden was only one of many homosexual and bisexual poet/translators to respond to Cavafy. He was followed by Stephen Spender (in a volume with illustrations by David Hockney), Edouard Roditi, and James Merrill. In France, Marguerite Yourcenar had already translated Cavafy in the 1950s. Later, Richard Howard translated her long essay on Cavafy, including its many French translations of Cavafy, into English. Duane Michals has issued a small volume of ten Cavafy poems interspersed with his own photographs of male nudes.

The complete translations of the canonical poems by Mavrogordato and Dalven were followed by those of Edmund Keeley/Philip Sherrard in 1975, George Khairallah in 1979, and Memas Kolaitis in 1988, as well as a set of 41 poems by Kimon Friar in 1973. Although Keeley/Sherrard are the most famous of the translators of the complete sets, and Keeley has written more on Cavafy than any other English–language critic, all have had their champions. Peter Bien in a valuable 1990 article discusses the various translations in terms of their possible appeal to gay audiences. He notes that Khairallah, the least known, is the most sexually up–front and colloquial in his versions. Cavafy offers many challenges to translators, as he uses a unique mixture of old and new word forms, avoids metaphor, and refers to obscure historical events and situations.

The erotic poems have provoked debate in two areas: their emotional quality and their position in Cavafy's complete works. Even non–heterosexual writers have found some of the sexuality troubling. Auden calls attention to the poet's transmutation of unhappy sexual encounters into the stuff of poetry, while wondering what becomes of the poet's partner, who most likely will not recast trivial or harmful sexual experiences. Yourcenar finds some of the erotic poetry marred by an unhealthy sentimentality. Spender implies that Cavafy's poetry is set up within the limiting view that erotic memory is more real than the actuality of love. On an affirmative note, Liddell in 1948 remarked to Cavafy's credit that he never resorted to Proust's disguise of homosexuality and his association of it with sickness and perversion.

Many of the major critics have stressed that homosexuality and eroticism are very important in Cavafy's work and that they resonate in various ways. Pinchin remarks on the number of times the old poet remembers himself as young and beautiful, thus using the literary motif of the double to good effect. Sherrard and Merrill each relate Cavafy's cult of the beauty of the male body to the Greek legacy. Kapre–Karka finds the erotic poetry capable of suggesting a drama of spiritual search. Keeley in *Cavafy's Alexandria* discusses Cavafy's decision to reveal his erotic preferences over the years "with increasing—if never total candor," so that the eroticism could be merged into the myth of Alexandria and transcend the limitations of confessional poetry. For Peter Bien Cavafy sets up the sexual decadence in his poetry in relation to the decline of his family, the Greek community of his city, and of Alexandria itself. Other critics, such as Seferis and Patoukolos, have claimed that criticism has overstressed the sexuality.

Many of the erotic poems make no direct mention of the gender of either partner. The relatively low use of personal pronouns in Greek and Cavafy's strategy of direct address also contribute to indirection. "Gray," "Far Off," "The Afternoon Sun," "On the Ship," and "At the Next Table" are all poems in which an older man reflects on someone he had loved briefly or whose beauty he had worshipped. The third–person poems often include character sketches or anecdotes. In "He Asked about the Quality," a man in a shop to buy a handkerchief makes an assignation with the salesman. The most shocking of the erotic poems is the non–canonical "The Bandaged Shoulder," in which the speaker takes the beloved's bloody rag to his mouth to taste. Cavafy also wrote poems overlapping the three categories he created. Some erotic poems are set in the historical past. "Understanding" is a philosophical poem which explains the poet's belief that only through his youthful pursuits could he create himself as an artist.

Margaret Alexiou believes that in the poem "Hidden Things" Cavafy makes it clear that who he was cannot be deduced from what he said. For Alexiou, Cavafy used masks, and the eroticism in his poetry is not autobiographical nor even subjective in the usual sense. Instead, eroticism is an aspect of the recollection and fantasy which permeate his attitude to myth and history. Although some readers may find the poems more subjective than Alexiou does, we do well to keep in mind that if we choose to read Cavafy as an erotic poet on an intense, emotional level we are appropriating a more distanced, mediated body of work to our own needs.

—*Peter Christensen*

CAVE, Thomas. *See* **STEWARD, Samuel M(orris).**

CAYER, D. M. *See* **DUFFY, Maureen (Patricia).**

CERNUDA, Luis (Luis Cernuda y Bidon). Spanish poet, educator, and critic. Born in Seville, 21 September 1902. Educated at University of Seville, 1919–25; University of Madrid, doctorate in law. Lecturer in Spanish language and literature, University of Toulouse, France, 1929–30; worked in a bookstore, Madrid; served in diplomatic and other posts for the Spanish Republican government in Madrid, Paris, London, and Valencia, Spain, c.1936–38; teacher of Spanish language and literature at Glasgow University, Scotland; Cambridge University, England; and the Instituto Espagnol, London; professor of Spanish, Mount Holyoke College, South Hadley, Massachusetts, 1947–52. *Died in Mexico City, Mexico, of a heart attack, 5 November 1963.*

WRITINGS

Poetry

Perfil del aire. [Spain], 1927; expanded as *Perfil del aire, con otras obras olvidadas e ineditas documentos y epistolario,* edited by Derek Harris, Suffolk, England, Boydell & Brewer, 1971.

Egloga, elegia, oda. [Spain], 1928; with lithographs by Gregorio Prieto, Madrid, Ediciones de Arte y Bibliofilia, 1970.

Un rio, un amor. [Spain], 1929.

Los placeres prohibidos. [Spain], 1931.

La invitacion a la poesia. Spain, M. Altoguirre, 1933; with introduction by Carlos–Peregrin Otero, Barcelona, Barral, 1975.

Donde habite el olvido. [Spain], 1934.

Invocaciones. [Spain], 1934–35.

La realidad y el deseo ["Reality and Desire"]. Madrid, Ediciones del Arbol, 1936; second edition (includes *Las Nubes*), Mexico City, Editorial Seneca, 1940; third edition (augmented), [Mexico], 1958; as *La realidad y el deseo, 1924–1962* (includes *Desolation of the Chimera*), Mexico City, Fondo de Cultura Economica, 1964.

Las nubes. [Spain], 1940; revised, Madrid, Catedra, 1984.

Ocnos. London, Dolphin, 1942; revised, Madrid, Insula, 1949; with introduction by Cesare Acutis, Torino, Italy, 1966; with introduction and notes by D. Musacchio, Barcellona, Barral, 1977.

Como quien espera el alba [and] *La realidad y el deseo.* Buenos Aires, Argentina, Losada, 1947.

Vivir sin estar viviendo. [Mexico City], 1949.

Variaciones sobre tema mexicano. Mexico City, Porrua y Obregon, 1952.

Con las horas contadas. [Mexico City], 1956.

Desolacion de la quimera. Mexico City, J. Mortiz, 1962.

Antologia poetica, selection and introduction by Rafael Santos Toroella. Barcelona, Plaza & Janes, 1970; second edition, selection by Philip Silver, Madrid, Alianza, 1975; English/Spanish version edited and translated by Reginald Gibbons as *The Poetry of Luis Cernuda,* Berkeley, University of California Press, 1977.

Poesia completa. Barcelona, Barral, 1974.

With Vicente Aleixandre, *Selected Poems.* Providence, Rhode Island, Copper Beech, 1974.

Ocnos seguido de variaciones sobre tema mexicano, prologue by Jaime Gil de Biedma. Madrid, Taurus, 1977.

Antologia. Madrid, Catedra, 1981.

Sonetos clasicos sevillanos. Madrid, El Observatorio, 1986.

The Young Sailor, and Other Poems, translation and introduction by Rick Lipinski, illustrations by Alex Kouval. San Francisco, Gay Sunshine, 1987.

Criticism

Estudios sobre poesia espagnola contemporanea. Madrid, Guadarrama, 1957.

Pensamiento poetico en la lirica inglesa: Siglo XIX. Mexico City, Imprenta Universitaria, 1958.

Poesia y literatura. Barcelona, Barral, 1960.

Poesia y literatura II. Barcelona, Barral, 1964.

Critica, ensayos y evocaciones, edited by Luis Maristany. Barcelona, Barral, 1970.

Other

Tres narraciones (stories). Buenos Aires, Ediciones Iman, 1948.

Translator, *Poemas de Friedrich Hoelderlin.* Madrid, Visor, 1974.

Prosa completa, edited by Derek Harris and Luis Maristany. Barcelona, Barral, 1975.

Epistolario inedito (letters). Seville, Servicio de Publicaciones del Ayuntamiento, 1981.

La familia interrupida ["The Interrupted Family"]. Barcelona, Sirmio, 1988.

Recordings: *Antologia poetica: voz del autor.* Mexico City, Universidad Nacional Autonoma de Mexico, 1975.

*

Biography: *Cuatro poetas espanoles contemporaneos* by Pablo Luis Avila, Milano, Italy, La Goliardica, 1968; *Luis Cernuda* by Salvador Jimenez–Fajardo, Boston, Twayne Publishers, 1978.

Bibliography: *Poesia y reflexion: la palabra en el tiempo* by Manuel Ballestero, Madrid, Taurus, 1980; *Luis Cernuda y la "Generacion del 27"* by Cesar Real Ramos, Salamanca, Mexico, Ediciones Universidad de Salamanca, 1983.

Critical Sources: *"Et in Arcadio Ego": A Study of the Poetry of Luis Cernuda* by Philip Silver, London, Tamesis, 1965; *Other Voices: A Study of the Late Poetry of Luis Cernuda* by Alexander Coleman, Chapel Hill, University of North Carolina Press, 1969; *Luis Cernuda: A Study of the Poetry* by Derek Harris, London, Tamesis, 1973.

*   *   *

Born in Spain, and one of that country's great poets, Luis Cernuda spent most of his life in exile. As a student, he had studied André Gide, taught in Toulouse, and closely studied such French surrealists as René Crevel and Pierre Reverdy. In Gerado Diego's *Anthology of Contemporary Spanish Poetry,* Cernuda claimed no Castilian ancestry but a mix of "Galician and French blood," and a friend (Nobel laureate Vicente Aleixandre) described him "de un negro definitivo."

He supported the Spanish Republic even more actively than his intimate friend (and perhaps lover) Federico García Lorca who was killed by the Falangists in August, 1936. In April, Lorca had saluted Cernuda as "divine, and to whom must be extended again water, reed, and penumbra for his incredible renovated swan." In May, Lorca had read his homosexual love poems, *Dark Sonnets* (not published until 1983), to Cernuda and other friends. Cernuda in turn wrote "To A Dead Poet (F. G. L.)," an elegy for his murdered amigo: "They killed you, because you were / Green in our arid land." *La realidad y el deseo* incorporated Cernuda's first six books of poetry; the second edition in 1940 added *Las nubes;* the third edition in 1958 added four more works; and the final edition in 1964 added *Desolation of the Chimera.* Cernuda's additions and corrections resemble Walt Whitman's continuous reworking of *Leaves of Grass.*

Cernuda found his love of poetry and of males very early. After his military father died in 1920, he read the romantic poet Gustavo Adolfo Bécquer (1836–1870), and at 14 began writing his own poems, often for men he loved. He lived with his mother and two sisters, but not long after his first book was published in 1927, his mother died. He never again returned to Seville.

At no time in his life did Cernuda question his being a poet or his being a homosexual. He never expressed any desire to be straight; indeed, he demonstrated contempt for the family, the state and religion—all of which he identified as persecutors of his love. His play La familia interrupida ("The Interrupted Family'), not published until 1988 emphasized disruption. His World War II poem "La Familia" asks, "Isn't your praised conjugal action / Fruit only of studied insensibility?" He conceived his love not only as contrary but even revolutionary: "A spark of those pleasures," he sang, "Shines at the hour of revenge. / Its brightness could destroy your world."

Cernuda's transforming love had to be created from scratch. In his prose–poem Ocnos, he concluded that "you can think, feel or believe only what enters you first through sex, our only gate into the heart and the mind." For him sexual passion was illumination: "I adored you as if you were the sum of all beautiful bodies, / Without veils that alter love's hidden image." The most homoerotic moments in Cernuda's works have been beautifully translated by Pick Lipinski and published by Gay Sunshine Press under the title The Young Sailor, and Other Poems. Significantly gay poems come in every part of Cernuda's work. In his first book, he claimed, "I exist, I know it well, / Because the world lets its / Amorous presence shine through / To my senses." And 30 years later, in a poem also published in The Young Sailor, he can find the same illumination on a California beach: "Málibu, / Fairy name. / Enchanted power."

Noble laureate Octavio Paz, to whom Cernuda wrote an eloquent poem, explains that "for Cernuda love is a break with the social order and a joining with the natural world. And it is a break not only because his love differs from that of most but because all love shatters human laws." Thus the sea, sailors, lilacs, muscles, the sun, birds, and all the parts of our bodies provide entrances like lighthouses or swimming suits into another world, another side.

While travelling along paths untrodden, Cernuda claimed a special history. He wrote a memorial poem after André Gide's death, a poem celebrating the love of Rimbaud and Verlaine, a poem for Michelangelo's "David" and "Dostoyevsky and Physical Beauty." And "Ludwig of Bavaria Listens to Lohengrin" from his last book celebrates Ludwig's surrendering, "No longer king but slave to manly beauty."

Cernuda's search through history led him away from Christianity to the Greeks, Arabs, Aztecs, and Gnostics. He translated into Spanish Holderlin's poems, which celebrated the Greeks. Cernuda worshiped light, air, and water as they illuminated a man's body. These forces were his ancestors. He addressed the Aztec god of air, Quetzalcoatl, the plumed serpent: "Who makes me a feather between your wings."

Exiled from Spain in 1938, Cernuda was blown like a feather around the world. He taught Spanish in Surrey, Glasgow, Cambridge, and London (1944–46). He then went to Mt. Holyoke College but found New England too grey for his taste; he fled to Mexico but held temporary appointments at UCLA and San Francisco State.

Cernuda deeply loved Mexico, which he first visited in 1949, thrilled to be again among Spanish speakers after a decade among Anglophones. He was further rejuvenated by a passionate love affair with his "Salvador," for whom he wrote a stunning series of "Poems for the Body." His epilogue concluded: "(If a man can foretell / Sum it all up) / Your image at my side / Perhaps will smile at me as it smiled at me today, / Illuminating this dark and remote existence / With love, the only light of the world." Certainly Cernuda foretold his own death, since he had prepared all his papers and left his teaching position before he was found dead in a friend's bathroom, 5 November 1963, in Mexico City.

—Charles Shively

CERNUDA y BIDON, Luis. *See* **CERNUDA, Luis.**

CHALLENS, Mary. *See* **RENAULT, Mary.**

CHAMBERS, (Carolyn) Jane. American playwright, novelist, and author of screenplays. Born in Columbia, South Carolina, 27 March 1937. Educated at Rollins College, 1953–54; Pasadena Playhouse, 1955–56; Goddard College, B.A. 1971. Companion of Beth Allen. Stage actor, 1956–61; free–lance journalist, 1962–64; writer and broadcaster for WMTW–TV in Poland Spring, Maine, 1964–66; director of avocation at Poland Spring Job Corps Center, 1967–69, and at Jersey City Job Corps Center in New Jersey, 1969–71; television writer and playwright, 1971–77; teacher of creative writing at Goddard College, beginning in c. 1971; full–time writer, 1977–83; playwright in residence for The Glines (theatre company that presents works with gay themes), New York City, beginning in 1980. Writer for *Search for Tomorrow* (television serial), CBS–TV, 1973–74. Contributor of feature articles to *New York Times* and *Harper's*. Founder of the New Jersey Women's Political Caucus, 1971; board member of Off–Off–Broadway Alliance; women's program planning committee member of American Theatre Association. **Recipient:** Religious Arts Guild Rosenthal Award for poem "Ejected," 1971; Connecticut Educational Television Award for best religious drama, *Christ in a Treehouse*, 1971; Eugene O'Neill fellowship for *Tales of the Revolution, and Other American Fables*, 1972; Writers Guild of America award for *Search for Tomorrow*, 1973; Office of Advanced Drama Research award for *The Common Garden Variety*, 1976; Creative Artists Public Service Program grant, 1977; DramaLogue Critics Circle Award and Villager Downtown Theatre Award for *Last Summer at Bluefish Cove*, 1982; Fund for Human Dignity award, 1982. *Died in Greenport, New York, of a brain tumor, 15 February 1983.*

WRITINGS

Plays

The Marvelous Metropolis (produced New York, c. 1962).
Tales of the Revolution, and Other American Fables (produced Waterford, Connecticut, 1972).
Random Violence (produced New York, 1973).
Mine! (produced New York, 1974).
The Wife (produced New York, 1974).
Jamboree (produced New York, 1974).
A Late Snow (produced New York, 1974). Published in *Gay Plays: The First Collection,* New York, Avon, 1979; New York, JH Press, 1989.
The Common Garden Variety (produced Los Angeles, 1976).
My Blue Heaven (produced Off–Broadway, 1981). New York, JH Press, 1981.
Last Summer in Bluefish Cove (produced New York, 1980, Los Angeles, 1985). New York, JH Press, 1982.
Kudzu (produced New York, 1981).
The Quintessential Image (produced Minneapolis, Minnesota, 1983; New York, 1989).
Eye of the Gull.
Deadly Nightshade.
One Day Short at the Jamboree.
Bluff.

Television Plays

Christ in a Treehouse, Connecticut Educational Television, 1971.
Curfew!, WNYC–TV, 1972.

Screenplays

Here Comes the Iceman, 1972.
Grass Roots, 1973.
Gotcha, 1975.

Novels

Burning. Jove Press, 1978.
Chasin' Jason. New York, JH Press, 1987.

Other

Contributor, *Along with All the Once Beloved Things* (poetry anthology), edited by Jeanne Foster Hill. Worship Arts Clearing House, Unitarian Universalist Association, 1972.
Warrior at Rest: A Collection of Poetry. New York, JH Press, 1984.

*

Adaptations: *In Her Own Words (A Portrait of Jane),* a biographical portrait of Chambers interwoven with excerpts of her own writings compiled by John Glines, was performed in New York City, 1989.

Biography: "Jane Chambers" by Penny M. Landau, in *Notable*

Women in American Theatre: A Biographical Dictionary, edited by Alice M. Robinson, Vera Mowry Roberts, and Milly S. Barranger, Westport, Connecticut, Greenwood Press, 1989; "Jane Chambers: In Memoriam" by Penny M. Landau, in *Women and Performance: A Journal of Feminist Theory* (New York), winter 1984, 55–57.

Critical Sources: *Contemporary Authors,* Volume 85–88, Detroit, Gale, 1980; "New York, New York" by Tish Dace, in *Other Stages,* 25 June 1980; review by Frank Rich of *Last Summer at Bluefish Cove,* in *New York Times,* 27 December 1980, 13; "That 'Girls in the Sand' Family Is Making Waves" by Janice Arkatov, in *Los Angeles Times,* 17 August 1983; "Gay Plays, Gay Theatre, Gay Performance" by Terry Helbing, in *Drama Review,* March 1981; "Notes on Lesbian Theatre" by Emily Sisley, in *Drama Review,* March 1981; review by Lawrence Christon of *Last Summer at Bluefish Cove,* in *Los Angeles Times,* 24 January 1983; review by Dick Lochte of *Last Summer at Bluefish Cove,* in *Los Angeles Magazine,* December 1985, 46; review by John Simon of *The Quintessential Image,* in *New York,* 14 August 1989, 77; "Comedy of Self–Acceptance and a Portrait of the Writer" by Stephen Holden, in *New York Times,* 17 August 1989.

*   *   *

In stage plays such as *A Late Snow* and *Last Summer in Bluefish Cove,* Jane Chambers frankly explored various aspects of lesbian relationships—from the emotional and physical love between two women, to the curious and skeptical attitudes of family members and friends, to the protagonists' hopes and struggles for acceptance. Regarded as a pioneer in the field of lesbian theatre, Chambers received several prestigious awards for her writings and was active in a number of theatre and gay rights organizations.

Born in 1937 in Columbia, South Carolina, Chambers grew up in Orlando, Florida. She developed an early interest in writing and, as a teenager, she created scripts for her high school's radio station and local public radio. During the early 1950s she furthered her pursuits at Rollins College, dabbling into the art of writing plays. Chambers also gained experience in television, penning scripts for a show in which she frequently performed and served as producer, *Youth Pops a Question.* Later, she worked at a television station in Maine where she created a children's show.

Enamored with acting, Chambers ventured to the Pasadena Playhouse in California in the mid–1950s to begin a serious study of the craft. After seeking roles in Off–Broadway productions and coffee–house theatre in New York City, she became a free–lance journalist in 1962, and saw production of her first play, *The Marvelous Metropolis.* After four years as the director of avocation at the Job Corps Center, first in Maine and then in New Jersey, Chambers earned a bachelor's degree from Goddard, where she also held a position as creative writing instructor.

Her own work soon began to draw attention. She penned the award–winning *Christ in a Treehouse* for Connecticut Educational Television and won the Religious Arts Guild Rosenthal Award for her poem "Ejected." Her work on the daytime serial *Search for Tomorrow* earned her additional writing kudos, while her stage play, 1972's *Tales of the Revolution, and Other American Fables,* was honored with the Eugene O'Neill Prize. About the same time, Chambers tried her hand at writing screenplays such as *Here Comes the Iceman, Grass Roots,* and *Gotcha.* Her engaging play *Late Snow,* which featured lesbians who are snowbound in a cabin, was produced in 1974.

Her first novel, entitled *Burning,* was published in 1978. Partially set in the modern day, the book was billed as a gothic suspense thriller as its characters are possessed by spirits from the late seventeenth century. The story's two protagonists had been lesbians in their earlier lives, but their relationship ended in sorrow— one woman was burned by citizens who believed she was a witch and the other was forced into marriage. Their tortured souls are finally quieted as the twentieth–century women continue their age– old love affair.

It was also during the 1970s that Chambers met Beth Allen, who would become her business manager and companion. A founder of the New Jersey Women's Political Caucus and the Interart Theatre in New York City, Chambers worked in various organizations to bring gay rights issues to light. In the early 1980s, Chambers described her motivations for writing to *Contemporary Authors.* "I write from my experience and interests," she explained. "I have always felt a strong identification with the underdog and much of my work is set in minority or ethnic subcultures. I am not writing about social injustice—I am writing about specific people who happen to be victims of that injustice. I do not consciously create my characters—I just look up one day and notice that they are standing in front of my typewriter. They are a determined lot who will not budge until I write a story or a play for them to live in." Continuing to pursue that impetus, Chambers wrote more plays that focused on the gay experience, some of which were produced by the Glines theatre company in New York City.

Last Summer at Bluefish Cove, considered one of her best plays, was written for the First Gay American Arts Festival, and was produced in 1980. In it, Cambers delves into the life of a naively straight woman who has been diagnosed with cancer and has come to Bluefish Cove to vacation. She meets another woman on the beach, a lesbian who invites her to a party where it soon becomes apparent that identities have been misjudged. Central to the play are the other female protagonists—the lesbians who are also vacationing at the resort town. The play also examines the hardships associated with terminal disease, yet maintains an element of humor in the various situations that the women encounter. The play was acknowledged with a Dramalogue Critics Circle Award and the Villager Downtown Theatre Award.

Shortly after the production of *Last Summer at Bluefish Cove,* Chambers herself was diagnosed with terminal cancer. She continued to pen plays such as *The Quintessential Image* and *My Blue Heaven,* a comedy focusing a lesbian couple who becomes overwhelmed with expressions of concern and curiosity from those outside the gay community. Such works contributed to her being named the recipient of the fifth annual Fund for Human Dignity award in 1982. Other factors included her dedication to and involvement in organizations attempting to increase public awareness of gay rights issues. She lost her battle to cancer on 15 February 1983. *Warrior at Rest: A Collection of Poetry* and the novel *Chasin' Jason* were published posthumously.

—*Kathleen J. Edgar*

———

CHAMBERS, Jessie. *See* **LAWRENCE, D(avid) H(erbert Richards).**

CHAPMAN, Lee. *See* **BRADLEY, Marion Zimmer.**

———

CHESLEY, Robert. American playwright. Born in Jersey City, New Jersey, c. 1943. Lived in San Francisco, beginning in the early 1980s; companion of Gene Weber. Contributed to periodicals, including the *Advocate. Died in San Francisco, of AIDS–related complications, 5 December 1990.*

WRITINGS

Plays

Hell, I Love You (produced San Francisco, c. 1981).
City Pieces (three one–act plays; produced New York, 1981).
Stray Dog Story (produced San Francisco, 1982), illustrations by Kimble Mead, introduction by Nicholas Deutsch. New York, JH Press, 1984.
Jerker; or, The Helping Hand: A Pornographic Elegy with Redeeming Social Value and a Hymn to the Queer Men of San Francisco in Twenty Phone Calls, Many of Them Dirty (produced New York, 1987).
Hard Plays—Stiff Parts: The Homoerotic Plays of Robert Chesley, illustrations by Art Jagonasi, introduction by Bert Herrman. San Francisco, Alamo Square Press, 1990.
Night Sweat (produced New York, 1985).

*

Interviews: "Playwright Robert Chesley: Waking up to the Dark Side of Romance in Night Sweat" by David Lamble, in *Advocate,* 29 May 1984, 48–49.

Critical Sources: Obituary, *New York Times,* 8 December 1990.

*   *   *

The career of playwright Robert Chesley spanned the 1980s, the decade of AIDS, and was finally claimed by it; and he believed in addressing the sorrows and joys of being gay openly and frankly. Prior to his relocation from the New York City area to San Francisco and the appearance of the first of his more than 20 one–act and seven full–length plays in 1981, his writings and interviews with such prominent figures of the then–contemporary gay subculture as Doric Wilson and Ensign Vernon Berg appeared in the *Advocate.* Of particular interest are the numerous reviews of theatrical productions and various acts that he covered, ranging from Eric Bentley's *Are You Now or Have You Ever Been* and Lanford Wilson's *The Fifth of July* to Gretchen Cryer's *I'm Getting My Act Together and Taking It on the Road* and the *Pink Satin Bombers.* He represents a pattern common to many gay writers in the first generation after the Stonewall Riots in his exploration of subtle emotional dynamics within gay relationships, a shedding of the skin of stereotype to confront sometimes uncomfortable realities and present them to the audience. His exposure to a wide range of performance, style, and technique in his capacity of reviewer provided a useful period of apprenticeship in which his own ideas could crystallize.

His debut with the Theatre Rhinoceros' 1981 production of *Hell, I Love You* in San Francisco bears similarities to other works of the period in that it is structured around a dialogue between two gay men. In this instance, the two protagonists are almost quintessentially mismated, one desiring a varied and active social life while his partner is contented with a good book and a quiet evening at home. The pairing of opposites to form a matrix of creative tension recalls Martin Sherman's 1975 work *Passing By.* Their discussions are used by Chesley to analyze possible coping strategies for interpersonal questions being evolved within the gay community, a theme that would recur in his better-known later works *Night Sweat* and *Jerker.* Critical reception found fault with Chesley's depiction of maintaining the balance between libido and basic affection and his illustration of certain elements of the gay life then in full bloom in San Francisco. The Theatre Rhinoceros production was shortly followed by the New York City premiere, sponsored by the Chelsea Gay Association Theater Project, of a group of one-act plays collectively entitled *City Pieces.*

Chesley's next contribution to New York's gay theater companies came with the 1982 production of *Stray Dog Story,* a modern satiric fable whose central topic is the sense of alienation from self and shared community experience frequently endured during adaptation to a gay lifestyle. Taking a basic plot motif from the popular folk tale of Cinderella, it tells the story of Buddy, a dog who is transformed into a gay man through the good offices of his "Fairy Dog Mother" and eventually becomes homeless. His total lack of knowledge of how to be human and function among people mirrors the questioning, learning, and reintegration so much a part of the coming out process of acceptance of a gay identity.

The challenges of expression presented to the theater by the impact on society of the AIDS pandemic called for the creation of a new genre of plays, to channel the intense emotional experiences associated with the disease and give them comprehensible form. This tradition, later to include such works as Larry Kramer's powerful 1985 production *The Normal Heart* and William Hoffman's *As Is,* was initiated by Chesley with *Night Sweat.* The play was described by the *New York Times* as "the first full-length drama dealing with the AIDS crisis to be produced in New York." It tells the story of Richard, who has just been diagnosed with the disease and has decided to avail himself of the services of a new club called the Coup de Grace, where, for a fee of ten thousand dollars, individual suicides can be staged complete with props and costumes. Scenarios available depict many of the behaviors popular in the gay community of the time, such as disco dancing and an obsession with matters of style. Its mood of black comedy recalls the medieval morality plays and the artistic depiction of the "Dance of Death," a phrase borrowed by one character who wishes to die while partying. In the end, having summoned up the apocalyptic mood of the times, Chesley rejects despair as the only response, choosing to say to the audience, "You can wake up from this night-

mare." Written in the fourth year of the AIDS pandemic, it bears a further similarity to medieval plague literature in that the disease is never explicitly named, being present as a looming shadow of fear and grief. This refusal to surrender courage and to dare to love despite a reality turned potentially fatal is a theme also expressed in much of his later work.

On 31 August 1986, station KPFK–FM in Los Angeles broadcast, as part of its weekly gay program *IMRU (I Am, Are You?),* excerpts from Chesley's play *Jerker,* in which the plot unfolds the story of two gay men who become acquainted purely telephonically and develop a relationship. The play consists of 20 lengthy conversations, some of which use sexually explicit language, in keeping with the plot and subject matter. On 16 April 1987, the radio station was cited by the Federal Communications Commission as being in violation of the law under regulations prohibiting the description or depiction of sexual activities in an offensive manner, the first such investigation done by the agency since 1975. It was recommended by the Commission that the Justice Department prosecute the Pacifica Foundation, operators of the station, on the grounds of broadcasting obscenity. Upon review, the Department declined further action, stating that KPFK had been within the legal guidelines promulgated by the FCC at air time, although the regulations in question were quickly modified.

Jerker opens with a divided stage representing two bedrooms in different neighborhoods of San Francisco, gateways into the worlds of the two main characters, who over the course of the hour-long play gradually move in voice from the emotionally intense but empty connection of phone sex to an intimate linkage of mutual support and caring. Never meeting, the gradual withdrawal of one partner, his replacement of direct access with an answering machine and final disconnection due to death from AIDS make the play one of the most powerful of all the AIDS dramas. Chesley's willingness to place gay realities, from slang and attitudes up to and including shifts in lifestyle occasioned by AIDS, frankly before the audience, is starkly visible in the full title of the play: *Jerker, or the Helping Hand: A Pornographic Elegy with Redeeming Social Value and a Hymn to the Queer Men of San Francisco in Twenty Phone Calls, Many of Them Dirty.* Here, the creator of the genre of AIDS theater has moved beyond the externals of the disease to its underlying matrix of pain and raw feeling, continuing to portray the essential humanity of gay people forced to confront the ultimate questions of death, identity, and sexuality. The final scene closes with the surviving member of the conversation alone and silent, a foreshadowing of the writer's own demise on 5 December 1990 from AIDS-related complications.

—*Robert B. Marks Ridinger*

———

COCTEAU, Jean (Maurice Eugene Clement). French poet, playwright, novelist, painter, musician, screenwriter, and filmmaker. Born in Maisons Laffitte, Seine–et–Oise, 5 July 1889. Studied at Lycee Condorcet, Paris; privately educated. Served as a civilian ambulance driver in Rheims during World War I, later went to Belgium and served with marine–rifleman group; served in auxiliary corps in Paris. Companion of writer Raymond Radiguet, 1920–23. Founded the review *Scheherazade* with Maurice Rostand and others; founded Editions de la Sirene with Blaise Cendrars, 1918; contributor to *Paris–Midi,* 1919; author of series for *Ce Soir,* 1937–38; produced cartoon for a tapestry commissioned by the Gobelins, 1948. Member of Academie Francaise, Academie Royale de Belgique, Academie Mallarme, American Academy, German Academy, Academie du Disque, and Association France–Hongrie; president of Academie de Jazz; honorary member, National Institute of Arts and Letters. **Recipient:** Prix Louions–Delluc, 1946; Grand Prix de la Critique Internationale, 1950; Grand Prix du Film Avante–garde, for film, 1950; honorary doctorate from Oxford University, 1956; Commandeur de la Legion d'Honneur, 1961. *Died in Milly, France, of a heart attack, 11 October 1963.*

WRITINGS

Poetry

La Lampe d'Aladin. Paris, Societe d'Editions, 1909.
Le Prince frivole. Paris, Mercure de France, 1910.
La Danse de Sophocle. Paris, Mercure de France, 1912.
Le Cap de Bonne–Esperance. Paris, Editions de la Sirene, 1919.
L'Ode a Picasso. Paris, Francois Bernouard, 1919.
With Andre Lhote, *Escales.* Paris, Editions de la Sirene, 1920.
Poesies: 1917–1920. Paris, Editions de la Sirene, 1920.
Vocabulaire. Paris, Editions de la Sirene, 1922.
Plain–Chant. Paris, Stock, 1923.
Poesie, 1916–1923. Paris, Gallimard, 1924.
La Rose de Francois. Paris, Francois Bernouard, 1924.
Cri ecrit. Montpellier, France, Imprimerie de Montane, 1925.
Pierre Mutilee. Paris, Editions des Cahiers Libres, 1925.
L'Ange heurtebise. Paris, Stock, 1925.
Opera: Oeuvres poetiques 1925–1927. Paris, Stock, 1927; revised as *Oeuvres poetiques: 1925–1927,* Paris, Dutilleul, 1959.
Morceaux choisis. Paris, Gallimard, 1932; as *Poemes,* Lausanne, Switzerland, H. Kaeser, 1945.
Mytholgie, lithographs by Giorgio di Chirico. Paris, Editions de Quatre–Chemins, 1934.
Allegories. Paris, Gallimard, 1941.
Leone. Paris, Nouvelle Revue Francaise, 1945; in *Poemes,* 1948; translated by Alan Neame as *Leoun,* London, England, 1960.
La Crucifixion. Paris, P. Morihien, 1946; in *Poemes,* 1948.
Poemes (includes *Leone, Allegories, La Crucifixion,* and "Neige"). Paris, Gallimard, 1948.
Anthologie poetique de Jean Cocteau. Paris, Le Club Francais du Livre, 1951.
Le Chiffre sept. Paris, Seghers, 1952.
Appogiatures, with a portrait of the author by Modigliani. Monaco, Editions du Rocher, 1953.
Dentelle d'eternite. Paris, Seghers, 1953.
Clair–Obscur. Monaco, Editions du Rocher, 1954.
Poemes: 1916–1955. Paris, Gallimard, 1956.
Contributor, *Corps memorabiles* by Paul Eluard. Paris, Seghers, 1958.
De la Brouille. Liege, Belgium, Editions Dynamo, 1960.
Ceremonial espagnol du Phoenix [with] *La Partie d'echecs.* Paris, Gallimard, 1961.
Le Requiem. Paris, Gallimard, 1962.

Faire–Part, foreword by Jean Marais and Claude–Michel Cluny. Paris, Librairie Saint–Germain des Pres, 1968.

Nonfiction

Le Coq et l'arlequin, with a portrait of the author by Picasso. Paris, Editions de la Sirene, 1918; translated by Rollo H. Myers as *Cock and Harlequin: Notes Concerning Music,* London, Egotist Press, 1921; in *A Call to Order,* 1923.
Dans le ciel de la patrie. Paris, Societe Spad, 1918.
Le Secret professionnel (autobiography). Paris, Stock, 1922; in *A Call to Order,* 1923; translated by Richard Howard as *Professional Secrets: The Autobiography of Jean Cocteau,* edited by Robert Phelps, New York, Farrar, Straus, 1970.
Dessins. Paris, Stock, 1923; translated as *Drawings,* New York, Dover, 1972.
Picasso. Paris, Stock, 1923.
La Rappel a l'ordre. Paris, Stock, 1926; with *Le Coq et l'arlequin* and *Le Secret professionnel* translated by Rollo H. Myers as *A Call to Order,* New York, Holt, 1923; London, Faber & Gwyer, 1926.
Romeo et Juliette: Pretext a mise en scene d'apres le drame de William Shakespeare. Paris, Se Vend au Sans Pariel, 1926.
Le Mystere laic. Paris, Editions de Quatre Chemins, 1928; as *Essai de critique indirecte: Le mystere laic–Des beaux arts consideres comme un assassinat,* introduction by Bernard Grasset, Paris, Grasset, 1932.
Opium: Journal d'une desintoxication, illustrations by Cocteau. Paris, Stock, 1930; translated by Ernest Boyd as *Opium: The Diary of an Addict,* London, and New York, Longmans Green, 1932; translated by Margaret Crosland and Sinclair Road as *Opium: The Diary of a Cure,* London, P. Owen, 1957, revised, 1968.
Le Livre blanc. Paris, Editions du Signe, 1930; as *The White Paper,* Olympia Press, 1957; with *The Naked Beast at Heaven's Gate* by P. Angelique, Greenleaf Classics, 1968; as translated by Margaret Crosland *Le Livre blanc,* London, P. Owen, 1969.
Portraits–Souvenir, 1900–1914, illustrations by Cocteau. Paris, Grasset, 1935; translated by Margaret Crosland as *Paris Album, 1900–1914,* London, W. H. Allen, 1956.
Contributor, *La Vie de Darius Milhaud* by Gea Augsbourg. Paris, Correa, 1935.
60 dessins pour Les Enfants terribles. Paris, Grasset, 1935.
Mon premier voyage: Tour du monde en 80 jours. Paris, Gallimard, 1936; translated by Stuart Gilbert as *Round the World Again in Eighty Days,* London, G. Routledge, 1937; translated by W. J. Strachan as *My Journey Round the World,* London, P. Owen, 1958.
Dessins en marge du texte des Chevaliers de la table ronde. Paris, Gallimard, 1941.
Le Greco. Paris, Le Divan, 1943.
Portrait de Mounet–Sully, illustrations by Cocteau. Paris, F. Bernouard, 1945.
La Belle et la bete: Journal d'un film. Paris, Janin, 1946; translated by Ronald Duncan as *Diary of a Film,* New York, Roy, 1950; as *Beauty and the Beast: Diary of a Film,* New York, Dover, 1972.
Poesie critique, edited by Henri Parisot. Paris, Editions des Quatres Vents, 1946; in two volumes, Paris, Gallimard, 1959.
With Paul Claudel, Paul Eluard, and Stephane Mallarme, *De la musique encore et toujours!,* preface by Paul Valery. Paris, Editions du Tambourinaire, 1946.

La Difficulte d'etre. Paris, P. Morihien, 1947; translated by Elizabeth Sprigge as *The Difficulty of Being,* introduction by Ned Rorem, London, P. Owen, 1966; New York, Coward, 1967.

Le Foyer des artistes. Paris, Plon, 1947.

L'Eternel retour. Paris, Nouvelles Editions Francaises, 1947.

Drol de menage, illustrations by Cocteau. Paris, P. Morihien, 1948.

Editor, *Almanach du theatre et du cinema.* Paris, Editions de Flore, 1949.

Maalesh: Journal d'une tournee de theatre. Paris, Gallimard, 1949; translated by Mary C. Hoeck as *Maalesh: Theatrical Tour in the Middle East,* London, P. Owen, 1956.

Dufy. Paris, Flammarion, 1950.

With Andre Bazin, *Orson Welles.* Paris, Chavane, 1950.

Modigliani. Paris, F. Hazin, 1950.

With others, *Portrait de famille.* Paris, Fini, 1950.

Jean Marais. Paris, Calmann–Levy, 1951.

Entretiens autour de cinematographe, recuellis par Andre Fraigneau. Paris, A. Bonne, 1951; translated by Vera Traill as *Cocteau on Film: A Conversation Recorded by Andre Fraigneau,* England, Roy, 1954; New York, Dover, 1972.

Journal d'un inconnu. Paris, Grasset, 1952; translated by Alec Brown as *The Hand of a Stranger,* London, Elek Books, 1956; New York, Horizon, 1959.

Reines de la France. Paris, Grasset, 1952.

With Julien Green, *Gide vivant.* Paris, Amiot–Dumont, 1952.

Venise images par Ferruccio Leiss [and] *L'Autre face de Venise par Jean Cocteau.* Milan, Italy, D. Guarnati, 1953.

Carte blanche, illustrations by Cocteau. Lausanne, Switzerland, Mermod, 1953.

With others, *Prestige de la danse.* Paris, Clamart, 1953.

Discours de reception de M. Jean Cocteau a l'Academie francaise et reponse de M. Andre Maurois. Paris, Gallimard, 1955.

Look to the Glory of Your Firm and the Excellence of Your Merchandise, for If You Deem These Good, Your Welfare Becomes the Welfare of All, translation by Lewis Galantiere. Montrouge, France, Draeger, c. 1955.

Aux confins de la Chine. Paris, Edition Caracteres, 1955.

Colette: Discours de reception a l'Academie Royale de Belgique. Paris, Grasset, 1955; excerpts edited and translated by Margaret Crosland as *My Contemporaries,* London, P. Owen, 1967, Philadelphia, Chilton, 1968.

Le Dragon des mers. Paris, Georges Guillot, 1955.

Contributor, *Marbe et decoration.* Federation Marbriere de France, c. 1955.

Journals, edited and translated by Wallace Fowlie, illustrations by Cocteau. New York, Criterion Books, 1956.

Adieu a Mistinguett. Liege, Belgium, Editions Dynamo, 1956.

Art et sport. Limoges, France, Savonnet, 1956.

Impression: Arts de la rue. Liege, Belgium, Editions Dynamo, 1956.

Temoignage, illustrations by Picasso. Paris, P. Bertrand, 1956.

Le Discours de Strasbourg. Metz, France, Societe Messine d'Editions et d'Impression, 1956.

Le Discours d'Oxford. Paris, Gallimard, 1956; translated by Jean Stewart as "Poetry and Invisibility," in *London Magazine,* January 1957.

With Louis Aragon, *Entretiens sur le Musee de Dresde.* Paris, Cercle d'Art, 1957; translated as *Conversations on the Dresden Gallery,* New York, Holmes, 1983.

Erik Satie. Liege, Belgium, Editions Dynamo, 1957.

La Chapelle Saint Pierre, Villefranche sur Mer. Paris, Editions du Rocher, 1957.

La Corrida du premier mai. Paris, Grasset, 1957.

Impression, Arts de la rue [and] *Eloge de l'imprimerie.* Liege, Belgium, Editions Dynamo, 1957.

Comme un miel noir (in French and English). Paris, L'Ecole Estienne, 1958.

With Roloff Beny and others, *Merveilles de la Mediterranee.* Paris, Arthaud, 1958.

Paraprosodies precedees de 7 dialogues. Monaco, Editions du Rocher, 1958.

Contributor, *De bas en haut* by G. Coanet. Metz, France, La Societe Messine d'Editions et d'Impressions, 1958.

La Salle des mariages, Hotel de ville de Menton. Monaco, Editions du Rocher, 1958.

La Canne blanche. Paris, Editions Estienne, 1959.

Gondole de morts. Milan, Italy, All'Insegne del Pesce d'Oro, 1959.

Guide a l'usage des visiteurs de la Chapelle Saint Blaise des Simples. Monaco, Editions du Rocher, 1960.

De la brouille. Liege, Belgium, Editions Dynamo, 1960.

Notes sur Le Testament d'Orphee. Liege, Belgium, Editions Dynamo, 1960.

Decentralisation. [Paris], 1961.

Du Serieux. Paris, [1961].

With others, *Insania pingens.* Basel, Switzerland, Ciba, 1961; as *Petits maitres de la folies,* Lausanne, Switzerland, Clairfontaines, 1961.

Le Cordon ombilical. Paris, Plon, 1962.

Picasso: 1916–1961, original lithographs by Picasso. Monaco, Editions du Rocher, 1962.

Discours a l'Academie royale de langue et de litterature francaises. Liege, Belgium, Editions Dynamo, 1962.

Hommage. Liege, Belgium, Editions Dynamo, 1962.

Interview par Jean Breton (contains "Malediction au laurier" and "Hommage a Igor Stravinsky"). [Paris], 1963.

Adieu d'Antonio Ordonez. Paris, Editions Forces Vives, 1963.

Contributor, *La Comtesse de Noailles.* Paris, Librairie Academique Perrin, 1963.

Contributor, *Expositions les peintres temoins de leur temps* (catalog). Luneville, France, Le Musee, 1964.

Entretien avec Andre Fraigneau (interview), preface by Pierre de Boisdeffre. Paris, Union Generale d'Editions, 1965.

Pegase. Paris, Nouveau Cercle Parisien du Livre, 1965.

Entre Radiguet et Picasso. Paris, Editions Hermann, 1967.

With Raymond Radiguet, *Paul et Virginnie.* Paris, Edition Speciale, 1973.

Novels

Le Potomak. Paris, Societe Litteraire de France, 1919; definitive edition, Stock, 1924.

Le Grand Ecart, illustrations by Cocteau. Paris, Stock, 1923; translated by Lewis Galantiere as *The Grand Ecart,* New York, Putnam, 1925; with *La Voix humaine,* Paris, Club des Editeurs, 1957; translated by Dorothy Williams as *The Miscreant,* London, P. Owen, 1958.

Thomas l'imposteur. Paris, Nouvelle Revue Francaise, 1923; revision edited by Bernard Garniez, New York, Macmillan, 1964; translated by Lewis Galantiere as *Thomas the Imposter,* Englewood Cliffs, New Jersey, Appleton, 1925; translated by Dorothy Williams as *The Imposter,* New York, Noonday Press, 1957.

Les Enfants terribles. Paris, Grasset, 1929; revision edited by Jacques Harde, Blaisdell, 1969; translated by Samuel Putnam as

Enfants Terribles, New York, Harcourt, 1930; translated by Rosamund Lehmann as *The Children of the Game,* England, Harvill, 1955; as *The Holy Terrors,* Norfolk, Connecticut, New Directions, 1957.

La Fin du Potomak. Paris, Gallimard, 1940.

Deux travestis, illustrations by Cocteau. Paris, Fournier, 1947.

Plays

Le Boeuf sur le toit. [Paris], 1920.

Les Maries de la tour Eiffel. Paris, Nouvelle Revue Francaise, 1924; translated by Dudley Fitts as *The Eiffel Tower Wedding Party,* in *The Infernal Machine, and Other Plays,* Norfolk, Connecticut, New Directions, 1963; as *The Wedding on the Eiffel Tower,* in *Modern French Plays,* New York, Faber, 1964.

Orphee. Paris, Stock, 1927; as *Orphee: A Tragedy in One Act* (produced New York, 1954), translated by Carl Wildman, New York, Oxford University Press, 1933; in *Five Plays,* 1961; translated by John Savacool as *Orphee,* Norfolk, Connecticut, New Directions, 1963.

Translator, *Oedipe Roi* [and] *Romeo et Julliette.* Paris, Plon, 1928.

Antigone. Paris, Nouvelle Revue Francaise, 1928; translated by Carl Wildman, in *Four Plays,* 1961.

La Voix humaine (produced France, 1930). Published with *Le Grand ecart,* Paris, Club des Editeurs, 1957; translated by Carl Wildman as *The Human Voice* (produced New York, 1980), London, Vision Press, 1951.

La Machine infernale. Paris, Grasset, 1934; with introduction and notes by W. M. Landers, London, Harrap, 1957; translated by Carl Wildman as *The Infernal Machine,* New York, Oxford University Press, 1936; translated by Albert Bermel as *The Infernal Machine,* Norfolk, Connecticut, New Directions, 1963.

Les Chevaliers de la table ronde. Paris, Gallimard, 1937; translated by W. H. Auden as *The Knights of the Round Table,* Norfolk, Connecticut, New Directions, 1963.

Les Parents terribles. Paris, Gallimard, 1938; revised, edited by R. K. Totton, New York, Methuen, 1972; translated by Charles Frank as *Intimate Relations,* in *Four Plays,* 1962.

Les Monstres sacres. Paris, Gallimard, 1940; translated by Edward O. Marsh as *The Holy Terrors,* in *Four Plays,* 1962.

La Machine a ecrire. Paris, Gallimard, 1941; translated by Ronald Duncan as *The Typewriter,* Durham, England, Dobson, 1957.

Renaud et Armide. Paris, Gallimard, 1943.

L'Aigle a deux tetes. Paris, Gallimard, 1946; translated by Ronald Duncan as *The Eagle Has Two Heads,* New York, Funk, 1948; translated by Carl Wildman as *The Eagle with Two Heads,* in *Four Plays,* 1962.

Theatre (two volumes). Paris, Gallimard, 1948; augmented edition (two volumes), Paris, Grasset, 1957.

Un Tramway nomme desir (adaptation of *A Streetcar Named Desire* by Tennessee Williams; produced Paris, 1949). Paris, Bordas, 1949.

Bacchus. Paris, Gallimard, 1952; translated by Mary C. Hoeck as *Bacchus: A Play,* Norfolk, Connecticut, New Directions, 1963.

Cher menteur (adaptation of play by Jerome Kilty; produced Paris, 1960). Paris–Theatre, 1960.

Five Plays (includes *Orphee*). New York, Hill & Wang, 1961.

Four Plays (contains *Antigone, Intimate Relations, The Holy Terrors,* and *The Eagle with Two Heads*). London, MacGibbon & Kee, 1962.

L'Impromptu du Palais–Royal. Paris, Gallimard, 1962.

Screenplays

And director, *Le Sang d'un poete* (produced, 1930). Paris, Editions du Rocher, 1948, revised, 1957; translated by Lily Pons as *Blood of a Poet,* London, Bodley Press, 1949; in *Two Screenplays,* 1968.

La Comedie du bonheur (produced, 1940).

And performer, *Le Baron fantome* (produced, 1942).

And director with Jean Delannoy, *L'Eternal retour* (produced, 1943). Paris, Nouvelles Editions Francaises, 1948.

Les Dames du Bois du Boulogne (produced, 1944).

And director, *La Belle et la bete* (adaptation from the fairy tale by Mme. Leprince de Beaumont; produced, 1945). Paris, Editions du Rocher, 1958; in *Screenplays, and Other Writings on the Cinema,* 1968; bilingual edition, New York, New York University Press, 1970.

Ruy Blas (adaptation from the play by Victor Hugo; produced, 1947). Paris, Editions du Rocher, 1947.

La Voix humaine (adaptation of his own play; produced, 1947).

And director, *L'Aigle a deux tetes* (adaptation of his own play; produced, 1947).

Noces de sable (produced, 1948).

And director, *Les Parents terribles* (adaptation of his own play; produced, 1948). Paris, Le Monde Illustre, 1949; translated and adapted by Charles Frank as *Intimate Relations* (also known as *Disobedient*), 1952; published with *Les Enfants terribles,* Paris, Club des Librairies de France, 1962.

Les Enfants terribles (adaptation of his own novel; produced, 1948); with *Les Parents terribles,* Paris, Club des Librairies de France, 1962.

And director, *Orphee* (adaptation of his own play; produced, 1949). Paris, Andre Bonne, 1951.

And director, *Santo Sospiro* (short; produced, 1951).

Ce Seicle a cinquante ans (short; produced, 1952).

La Coronna nagra (produced, 1952).

And director, *Le Rouge est mis* (short; produced, 1952).

And director, *Le Testament d'Orphee* (produced, 1959). Paris, Editions du Rocher, 1959; translated by Carol Martin–Sperry as *The Testament of Orpheus,* in *Two Screenplays,* 1968.

Two Screenplays, translation by Carol Martin–Sperry. Columbus, Ohio, Orion Press, 1968; in *Screenplays, and Other Writing on the Cinema,* 1968.

Screenplays, and Other Writings on the Cinema. Columbus, Ohio, Orion Press, 1968.

Opera

Oedipus rex: Opera–oratorio en deux actes d'apres Sophocle. France, Boosey & Hawkes, 1949; with *Orpheus* [and] *The Infernal Machine,* translation by Carl Wildman, New York, Oxford University Press, 1962.

Ballet Scenarios

Le Dieu bleu. [France], 1912.

Parade. [France], 1917.

Letters

Lettre a Jacques Maritain. Paris, Stock, 1926; excerpts translated as *Journals,* 1956; as *Lettre a Maritain: Response a Jean Cocteau,*

Paris, Stock, 1964.
Art and Faith: Letters between Jacques Maritain and Jean Cocteau.
    New York, Philosophical Library, 1948.
Lettre aux Americains. Paris, Grasset, 1949.
Editor, *Choix de lettres de Max Jacob a Jean Cocteau: 1919–1944.*
    Paris, P. Morihien, 1949.
Lettre sur la poesie. Paris, Dutilleul, 1955.
Lettres a André Gide avec quelques reponses d'André Gide. Paris,
    La Table Ronde, 1970.
*Mon Premier voyage, Des beaux–arts consideres comme un
    assasinat, Lettre a Maritain.* Paris, Vialetay, 1973.
Lettres a Milorad. Paris, Editions Saint–Germain–des–Pres, 1975.

Other

Oeuvres completes (ten volumes). Paris, Marguerat, 1947–50.
Theatre de Poche. Paris, P. Morihien, 1949; as *Nouveau theatre de
    poche,* Paris, Editions du Rocher, 1960.
Author of notes and introduction, *Jean Cocteau chez les sirens:
    Une experience de linguistic sur le discours de reception a
    l'Academie francaise de M. Jean Cocteau,* compiled by Jean
    Dauven, illustrations by Picasso. Monaco, Editions du Rocher,
    1956.
Cocteau par lui–meme, edited by Andre Fraigneau. Paris, Editions
    du Seuil, 1957.
Editor, *Amedo Modigliani: Quinze dessins.* Paris, Leda, 1960.
Ceremonial espagnal du phenix [and] *La Partie d'eches.* Paris,
    Gallimard, 1961.
Opera [and] *Le Discours du grand sommeil,* preface by Jacques
    Brosse. Paris, Gallimard, 1967.
Opera [and] *Plain–Chant.* Paris, Livre de Poche, 1967.
Le Cap de Bonne Esperance [and] *Discours du grand sommeil.*
    Paris, Gallimard, 1967.
Pages choisies, edited by Robert Prat. Paris, Hachette, 1967.
Opera [and] *Des mots, De mon style.* Paris, Tchou, 1967.
Cocteau's World (anthology), edited and translated by Margaret
    Crosland. London, P. Owen, 1971; New York, Dodd, 1973.
Du cinematographie (collected works), edited by André Bernard
    and Claude Gauteur. Paris, P. Belfond, 1973.
Entretiens sur le cinematographie, edited by André Bernard and
    Claude Gauteur. Paris, P. Belfond, 1973.
*Orphee: Extraits de la tragedie d'Orphee ainsi que des films Orphee
    et Le Testament d'Orphee.* Paris, Bordas, 1973.
Poesie de journalism, 1935–1938. Paris, P. Belmond, 1973.

*

Biography: *Jean Cocteau* (contains a study of Roger Lannes, poems, and a bibliography), Paris, Segher, 1945, revised, 1969; *Cocteau
on the Film: A Conversation Recorded by Andre Fraigneau,* New
York, Dobson, 1954; *The Journals of Jean Cocteau,* edited and
translated by Wallace Fowlie, New York, Criterion Books, 1956;
Jean Cocteau by Margaret Crosland, New York, Knopf, 1956;
Cocteau by Andre Fraigneau, New York, Grove, 1961; *Jean Cocteau:
The History of a Poet's Age* by Wallace Fowlie, Bloomington, Indiana University Press, 1966; *Jean Cocteau: The Man and the Mirror*
by Elizabeth Sprigge and Jean–Jacques Kihm, London, Gollancz,
1968; *An Impersonation of Angels: A Biography of Jean Cocteau* by
Frederick Brown, New York, Viking, 1968; *Jean Cocteau* by Rene

Gilson, New York, Crown, 1969; *Cocteau: A Biography* by Francis
Steegmullen, Boston, Little, Brown, 1970; *Jean Cocteau* by Bettina
L. Knapp, Boston, Twayne Publishers, 1970.

Critical Sources: *Le Diable au corps* by Raymond Radiguet,
Paris, Grasset, 1923, translated by Kay Boyle as *Devil in the Flesh,*
Paris, Black Sun Press, 1932; *Le Bal du comte d'Orgel* by Raymond
Radiguet, Paris, Grasset, 1924, translated by Violet Schiff as *Count
d'Orgel,* New York, Grove, 1970; *Album masques: Jean Cocteau*
by Milorad and Jean–Pierre Joecker, Paris, Persona, 1983; *Raymond
Radiguet* by James P. McNab, Boston, Twayne Publishers, 1984.

*   *   *

Although Jean Cocteau's homosexuality undergirds most of what
he wrote, relatively few of his works address gay issues in explicit
terms. Exceptions are his novella *Le Livre blanc,* many erotic drawings and lithographs, and a number of short texts—both prose and
poetry—that were published posthumously.

It is as a poet that Cocteau wished to be remembered. He gave the
name *poesie* (poetry) to all of his creations from novels such as *Les
Enfants terribles* to critical essays such as *Le Secret professionnel,*
or even to films, such as *Orphee.* It was not enough to write poetry.
Cocteau made the poet—and Orpheus in particular—his ideal, and
then tried to identify, body and soul, with that figure. In interviews
and in his personal journals, such as *La Difficulte d'etre* or *Journal
d'un inconnu,* Cocteau repeatedly described a life–feeling of inad-
equacy, anxiety, and incompleteness. Through a fusion or identification with the idealized poet, Cocteau attempted to give to his life
direction and unity, and to rationalize a deep sense of estrangement.
If identification with Orpheus represents one strata for coping with
alienation—a strategy that some critics found to be no more than
role–playing, a theatrical gesture, a pose—identification with a stronger, male lover was for Cocteau another. Each of his lovers, such as
the writer Raymond Radiguet, or Jean Bourgoint, the inspiration
for Paul of *Les Enfants terribles,* or Jean Brais the actor, became not
just companions but a source of artistic inspiration and even "a
better half," the stronger complement of a self viewed as fragmentary.

The prototype of this stronger "other," an object of endless
fascination throughout Cocteau's life, was one Pierre Dargelos, a
school classmate at the petit lycee Condorcet in Paris, who was
incorporated into Cocteau's poetic universe to become a stellar
presence in a personal mythology. From work to work, in his principal manifestations, including, for example, *Le Livre blanc, Les
Enfants terribles,* and the film *Le Sang d'un poete,* Dargelos is a big,
strong, handsome, aggressive boy, the complete opposite of the
puny, self–deprecating youth who not only loves him, but wishes
to become him.

Dargelos makes his first major appearance in *Le Livre blanc.* Like
so many of Cocteau's texts, this novella was written in the company of a lover who served as a source of inspiration. Cocteau
wrote it in 1927, in the company of Jean Desbordes, a young writer
who would later die at the hands of Gestapo torturers. Just three
years earlier, André Gide, who had little esteem for Cocteau, had
written *Corydon,* his eulogy on homosexuality, and Cocteau may
have wanted to outdo him. But, unlike Gide, Cocteau was unwilling
to be recognized as the author of a gay text. The first edition of 21
copies of *Le Livre blanc* bore no signature. A larger run in 1930 had

erotic drawings that were clearly Cocteau's but were signed "M. B. Arrington"; here too, Cocteau denied, at least in public, that the novella was his.

The title *Le Livre blanc* gives the impression of being an official document, a research paper of sorts. In a sense, it is. It is the fast-paced chronicle of the narrator's life, centered entirely upon his (homo)sexual desires and experiences, from his first sexual awakening as a young boy to his infatuation with the school bully Dargelos. It also involves the narrator's realization that, whereas his school companions become heterosexual, he remains gay. Many of the episodes, including the encounter with a sailor nicknamed Pas de Chance ("No Luck") in Toulon, a naval base in the south of France, are clearly autobiographical.

Le Livre blanc, with its light touch, constant changes of scene, and determined salacity, is reminiscent of eighteenth-century tales. Like eighteenth-century heroes before him, the twentieth-century protagonist of *Le Livre blanc* finally decides that he must leave France, where his sexuality is barely tolerated. But the novella is also "pure" Cocteau. Many of the images that are more fully developed by Cocteau in later works are found here, from gypsies to mirrors, sailors to centaurs; all are explicitly sexual, undisguised, unsublimated. It becomes clear that sexuality—more precisely homosexuality—is at the heart of all of Cocteau's work, though it is often masked.

Dargelos makes his most remarkable appearance in *Les Enfants terribles,* Cocteau's finest novel. The setting, as in *Le Livre blanc,* is the petit lycee Condorcet. But *Les Enfants terribles* offers a fascinating study in the transformation of the raw material of "naked" desire into the refined material of gilded myth. The encounter between Paul, the puny, retiring protagonist, and his idol Dargelos is described in the first pages of the novel.

Dargelos is a preternatural, aggressive, "phallic" demigod who is strong, tall, and insolent. He hurls a snowball that penetrates Paul's open mouth, and another that strikes him full in the chest. This is described as a dreadful blow, a blow from a marble fist. Paul's last view of Dargelos is of an erect figure standing bemused, with his hands at his sides, in a supernatural light. In *Les Enfants terribles,* the revelation of Dargelos' supernatural beauty is a mythical beginning for Paul: his death to the world, since he is forced by his wound to leave school and stay at home, and his rebirth to a new life. He and his sister make of their room a sacred space and refuse all contact with the debased reality of the outside world. Their rather puzzling service is to childhood, to poetry perhaps, to the "inside." Dargelos is never far from Paul's thoughts and actually becomes the instrument of his death.

Paul's closeted or cloistered life in *Les Enfants terribles* makes little sense in objective terms; the ostensible ideal served, that of childhood or poetry, is elusive, and even unconvincing for some. But, as the mythical account of a homoerotic infatuation, cutting the protagonist off from the world, throwing him back into a more private world, it can be more readily understood.

If Cocteau felt compelled to mask, redefine, or otherwise disguise what was at base a homosexual impulse he could, in other cases, simply change the gender of the love object. He did so, for example, in the long poem *Plain-Chant,* written in the summer of 1922 while staying at the village of Pramousquier in the south of France. He had fled Paris in the company of his young lover Raymond Radiguet, who would die of typhoid late the following year. While Radiguet corrected the proofs of his first novel, *Le Diable au corps,* and wrote the major part of his second one, *Le Bal du comte d'Orgel,* Cocteau was also creating a number of works.

He drew beautiful sketches of his sleeping companion, composed *Plain-Chant,* as well as an adaptation of Sophocles' play *Antigone,* and two novels of his own, *Le Grand Ecart* and *Thomas l'Imposteur.*

It is hard to imagine a more creative period than that shared by Cocteau and Radiguet in the summer of 1922. In terms of the quality and volume of the work produced by both artists, it is without equal. But Cocteau, as ever, was reluctant to reveal his homosexuality forthrightly. *Plain-Chant* is a 40-page love-poem, among Cocteau's finest poetry, inspired by Radiguet. In classical meter and rhyming verse, which reflects Radiguet's reaction against the Surrealists' advocacy of modernism at all costs, Cocteau explores the most basic of themes; poetry, love, and death. Unrequited love forms the background to most of *Plain-Chant.* In the second section—there are three in all—Cocteau explores the theme of the loved one, identified as a woman, but obviously based on Radiguet, who escapes from the lover's embrace into sleep, which is represented as a realm close to that of death. While the verse is beautiful, it does not describe love returned. The poet tries to become one with his lover, but the sense of complete fusion is of short duration. Even when he holds his lover in his arms, he is reminded of his separateness. In sleeping, the other passes into a realm which denies him entry. His "mistress" is part of his dreams, but he cannot enter "hers." The other escapes his embrace. The demon of jealousy awakens in his heart, to make their separation still more complete.

Just as Cocteau's homosexuality informs *Plain-Chant,* so it is at the heart, in varying degrees of exposure or concealment, of just about everything that he wrote. His perceived need to disguise, conceal, or sublimate this sexuality, accompanied by the strong, contradictory desire to express and to expose, creates a constant ambiguity, a sense that within his world, things are not quite what they seem to be. It is perhaps this—conscious or subliminal—awareness of ever-present tension and paradox at the core of Cocteau's work that has divided his readers so sharply into opposing camps. Certainly few French writers of this century have attracted so much adulation, or so much opprobrium.

—*James P. McNab*

COLETTE, (Sidonie-Gabrielle). French journalist, novelist, and author of short stories. Also wrote as Willy; Colette Willy. Born in Saint-Sauveru-en-Puisaye, Burgundy, 28 January 1873. Married 1) Henry Gauthier-Villars in 1893 (divorced 1910); 2) Baron Henri de Jouvenel des Ursins in 1912 (divorced 1925), one daughter; 3) Maurice Goudeket in 1935. Music hall dancer and mime, 1906–11; began as columnist, became dramatic critic and story editor, 1911–19, *Le Matin,* Paris; contributor to the review *Le Film.* Elected to Académie Royale de Langue et de Littérature Françaises, Anna de Noailles chair, c. 1936; elected to Académie Goncourt (first female member), 1945, elected president, 1949. **Recipient:** Légion d'Honneur chevalier, 1920, officer, 1928, commandeur, 1936, grand officer, 1953; Médaille d'Or de la Ville de Paris, 1953; received state funeral, France's highest posthumous honor. *Died in Paris, 3 August 1954.*

WRITINGS

Novels

Claudine à l'école (as Willy). Paris, Ollendorff, 1900; translated by Janet Flanner as *Claudine at School,* London, Gollancz, 1930; translated by H. Mirande, New York, A. & C. Boni, 1930.

Claudine à Paris (as Willy). Paris, Ollendorff, 1901; translated as *Claudine in Paris,* London, Gollancz, 1931; translated by James Whitall as *Young Lady of Paris,* New York, A. & C. Boni, 1931.

Claudine en ménage (as Willy). Paris, Mercure de France, 1902; as *Claudine amoureuse,* Paris, Ollendorff, 1902; translated by Frederick A. Blossom as *The Indulgent Husband,* New York, Farrar & Rinehart, 1935.

Claudine s'en va: Journal d'Annie (as Willy). Paris, Ollendorff, 1903; translated by Frederick A. Blossom as *The Innocent Wife,* New York, Farrar & Rinehart, 1935; translated by Antonia White as *Claudine and Annie,* London, Secker & Warburg, 1962.

Minne (as Willy). Paris, Ollendorff, 1904; included in *L'Ingénue libertine,* 1909.

Dialogues de bêtes (as Colette Willy). Paris, Mercure de France, 1904; enlarged as *Douze Dialogues de bêtes,* 1930; in *Creatures Great and Small,* 1957.

Les Egarements de Minne (as Willy). Paris, Ollendorff, 1905; revised version included in *L'Ingénue libertine,* 1909.

Le Retraite sentimentale (as Colette Willy). Paris, Mercure de France, 1907; translated by Margaret Crosland as *Retreat from Love,* London, Owen, and Bloomington, Indiana University Press, 1974.

Les Vrilles de la vigne (as Colette Willy). Paris, Editions de la Vie Parisienne, 1908.

L'Ingénue libertine (as Colette Willy; contains *Minne* and *Les Egarements de Minne*). Paris, Ollendorff, 1909; translated by Rosemary Carr Benét as *The Gentle Libertine,* New York, Farrar & Rinehart, and London, Gollancz, 1931.

La Vagabonde (as Colette Willy). Paris, Ollendorff, 1910; translated by Charlotte Remfry–Kidd as *Renée la vagabonde,* Garden City, New York, Doubleday, 1931; translated by Enid McLeod as *The Vagabond,* London, Secker & Warburg, 1954.

Prrou, Poucette et quelques autres (as Colette Willy). Paris, Librairie des Lettres, 1913.

L'Entrave. Paris, Librairie des Lettres, 1913; translated by Viola Gerard Garvin as *Recaptured,* London, Gollancz, 1931; Garden City, New York, Doubleday, Doran, 1932; translated by Antonia White as *The Shackle,* London, Secker & Warburg, 1964; as *The Captive,* New York, Penguin, 1970.

La Paix chez les bêtes. Paris, Georges Crès, 1916; in *Creatures Great and Small,* 1957.

Les Enfants dans les ruines. Paris, Editions de la Maison du Livre, 1917.

Dans la foule. Paris, Georges Crès, 1918.

La Chambre éclairée. Paris, Edouard Joseph, 1920.

Chéri. Paris, Fayard, 1920; translated by Janet Flanner, New York, A. & C. Boni, 1929; London, Gollancz, 1930.

Le Voyage égoïste. Paris, Editions d'Art Edouard Pelletan, 1922.

Le Blé en herbe. Paris, Flammarion, 1923; translated by Ida Zeitlin as *The Ripening,* New York, Farrar & Rinehart, 1932; translated by Roger Senhouse as *Ripening Seed,* London, Secker & Warburg, 1955; New York, Farrar, Straus & Cudahy, 1956.

Rêverie du nouvel an. Paris, Stock, 1923.

La Femme cachée. Paris, Flammarion, 1924; translated by Margaret Crosland as *The Other Woman,* London, Owen, 1971.

Aventures quotidiennes. Paris, Flammarion, 1924.

Quatre Saisons. Paris, Philippe Ortiz, 1925.

L'Enfant et les sortilèges. Paris, Durand, 1925.

La Fin de Chéri. Paris, Flammarion, 1926; translated as *The Last of Chéri,* New York, Putnam, 1932; translated by Roger Senhouse, London, Secker & Warburg, 1951.

La Naissance du jour. Paris, Flammarion, 1928; translated by Rosemary Carr Benét as *A Lesson in Love,* New York, Farrar & Rinehart, and as *Morning Glory,* London, Gollancz, 1932; translated by Enid McLeod as *Break of Day,* New York, Farrar, 1961.

La Seconde. Paris, Ferenczi, 1929; translated by Viola Gerard Garvin as *The Other One,* New York, Cosmopolitan Book, and as *Fanny and Jane,* London, Gollancz, 1931.

Prisons et paradis. Paris, Ferenczi, 1932, revised, 1935.

La Chatte. Paris, Grasset, 1933; translated by Morris Bentinck as *Saha the Cat,* New York and London, Farrar & Rinehart/T. W. Laurie, 1936; with *Gigi,* London, Secker & Warburg, 1953.

Duo. Paris, Ferenczi, 1934; translated by Frederick A. Blossom, New York, Farrar & Rinehart, 1935.

Bella–Vista. Paris, Ferenczi, 1937.

Le Toutounier. Paris, Ferenczi, 1939.

Julie de Carneilhan. Paris, Fayard, 1941; with *Chambre d'hôtel,* translated by Patrick Leight Fermor, London, Secker & Warburg, and, with *Chambre d'hôtel* and *Gigi,* New York, Farrar, Straus & Young, 1952.

Short Stories

L'Envers du music–hall. Paris, Flammarion, 1913; translated by Anne–Marie Callimachi as *Music–hall Sidelights,* with *Mes Apprentissages,* London, Secker & Warburg, 1957, and with *Mitsou,* New York, Farrar, Straus & Cudahy, 1958.

Mitsou; ou, Comment l'esprit vient aux filles (includes *En camarades, pièce en deux actes*). Paris, Fayard, 1919; translated by Jane Terry as *Mitsou; or, How Girls Grow Wise,* New York, A. & C. Boni, 1930; translated by Raymond Postgate as *Mitsou,* with *L'Envers du music–hall,* New York, Farrar, Straus & Cudahy, 1958.

Chambre d'hôtel. Paris, Fayard, 1940; translated by Patrick Leigh Fermor as *Chance Acquaintances,* with *Julie de Carneilhan,* London, Secker & Warburg, and with *Gigi* and *Julie de Carneilhan,* New York, Farrar, Straus & Young, 1952.

Le Képi. Paris, Fayard, 1943.

Trois ... six ... neuf. Paris, Corrêa, 1944.

Gigi et autres nouvelles. Lausanne, La Guilde du Livre, 1944; translated by Patrick Leigh Fermor as *Gigi,* with *Julie de Carneilhan* and *Chambre d'hôtel,* New York, Farrar, Straus & Young, 1952; with *La Chatte,* London, Secker & Warburg, 1953.

The Stories of Colette, translation by Antonia White. London, Secker & Warburg, 1958; as *The Tender Shoot, and Other Stories,* New York, Farrar, Straus & Cudahy, 1959.

Plays

With Léopold Marchand, *Chéri, comédie en quatre actes* (based on her own novel). Paris, Librairie Théâtrale, 1922.

La Vagabonde (based on her own novel; produced in Paris). Paris, Impr. de l'Illustration, 1923.

With Anita Loos, *Gigi* (based on her own novel). Paris, France–Illustration, 1954.

Memoirs

La Maison de Claudine. Paris, Ferenczi, 1922; revised, 1930; translated by Enid McLeod and Una Vicenzo Troubridge as *My Mother's House,* with *Sido,* London, Secker & Warburg, and New York, Farrar, Straus & Young, 1953.

Sido; ou, Les Points cardinaux. Paris, Editions Kra, 1929; revised, Paris, Ferenczi, 1930; translated by Enid McLeod as *Sido,* with *La Maison de Claudine,* London, Secker & Warburg, and New York, Farrar, Straus & Young, 1953.

Ces Plaisirs. Paris, Ferenczi, 1932; as *Le Pur et l'impur,* Paris, Armes de France, 1941; translated by Edith Dally as *The Pure and the Impure,* New York, Farrar & Rinehart, 1933; translated as *These Pleasures,* London, White Owl, 1934.

Mes Apprentissages: Ce que Claudine n'a pas dit. Paris, Ferenczi, 1936; translated by Helen Beauclerk as *My Apprenticeships,* with *L'Envers du music–hall,* London, Secker & Warburg, 1957.

Journal à rebours. Paris, Fayard, 1941; translation by David Le Vay, in *Looking Backwards,* 1975.

De ma fenêtre. Paris, Armes de France, 1942; enlarged as *Paris de ma fenêtre,* Geneva, Milieu du Monde, 1944; translation by David Le Vay, in *Looking Backwards,* 1975.

L'Etoile vesper. Geneva, Milieu du Monde, 1946; translated by David Le Vay as *The Evening Star,* London, Owen, 1973; Indianapolis, Indiana, Bobbs–Merrill, 1974.

Journal intermittent. Paris, Fleuron, 1949; translation by David Le Vay, in *Places,* 1970.

Le Fanal bleu. Paris, Ferenczi, 1949; translated by Roger Senhouse as *The Blue Lantern,* London, Secker & Warburg, and New York, Farrar, Straus, 1963.

Earthly Paradise: An Autobiography Drawn from Her Lifelong Writings, translation by Helen Beauclerk and others, edited by Robert Phelps. London, Secker & Warburg, and New York, Farrar, Straus, 1966.

Looking Backwards (includes *De ma fenêtre* and *Journal à rebours*). Bloomington, Indiana University Press, 1975.

Letters

Une Amitié inattendue: Correspondance de Colette and Francis Jammes, edited by Robert Mallet. Paris, Emile–Paul, 1945.

Lettres à Hélène Picard, edited by Claude Pichois. Paris, Flammarion, 1958; excerpts included in *Letters from Colette,* 1980.

Lettres à Marguerite Moréno, edited by Claude Pichois. Paris, Flammarion, 1959; excerpts included in *Letters from Colette,* 1980.

Lettres de la vagabonde, edited by Claude Pichois and Roberte Forbin. Paris, Flammarion, 1961; excerpts included in *Letters from Colette,* 1980.

Lettres au petit corsaire, edited by Claude Pichois and Roberte Forbin. Paris, Flammarion, 1963; excerpts included in *Letters from Colette,* 1980.

Lettres à ses pairs, edited by Claude Pichois and Roberte Forbin. Paris, Flammarion, 1973; excerpts included in *Letters from Colette,* 1980.

Letters from Colette, translation by Robert Phelps. New York, Farrar, 1980.

Collected Works

Oeuvres complètes (15 volumes), compiled and with an introduction by Colette and Maurice Goudeket. Paris, Flammarion, 1949–50; enlarged as *Oeuvres complètes de Colette* (16 volumes), Paris, Club de l'Honnête Homme, 1973–76.

Colette: Oeuvres, edited by Claude Pichois. Paris, Gallimard, 1984–86.

Other

Les Heures longues, 1914–1917 (journalism). Paris, Fayard, 1917.

Histoires pour Bel–Gazou. Paris, Stock, 1930.

Renée Vivien. Abbeville, France, Edouard Champion, 1928.

La Jumelle noire (four volumes). Paris, Ferenczi, 1934–38.

Discours de réception à l'Académie Royale de Langue et de Littérature Françaises de Belgique. Paris, Grasset, 1936.

Mes Cahiers. Paris, Armes de France, 1941.

De la patte à l'aile. Paris, Corrêa, 1943.

Flore et Pomone. Paris, Galerie Charpentier, 1943.

Nudité. Paris, Mappemonde, 1943.

Broderie ancienne. Monaco, Editions du Rocher, 1944.

Belles Saisons. Paris, Galerie Charpentier, 1945.

Pour un herbier. Lausanne, Mermod, 1948; translated by Roger Senhouse as *For a Flower Album,* New York, McKay, 1959.

Trait pour trait. Paris, Fleuron, 1949.

La Fleur de l'âge. Paris, Fleuron, 1949.

En Pays connu. Paris, Manuel Bruker, 1949.

Chats de Colette. Paris, A. Michel, 1950.

Creatures Great and Small: Creature Conversations; Other Creatures; Creature Comforts (includes *Dialogues de bêtes* and *La Paix chez les bêtes*), translation by Enid McLeod. New York, Farrar, Straus & Cudahy, 1957.

Paysages et portraits. Paris, Flammarion, 1958.

Notes Marocaines. Lausanne, Mermod, 1958.

Découvertes. Lausanne, Mermod, 1961.

Contes des mille et un matins. Paris, Flammarion, 1970; translated by Margaret Crosland and David Le Vay as *The Thousand and One Mornings,* London, Owen, and New York, Bobbs–Merrill, 1973.

Places (includes *Journal intermittent*), translation by David Le Vay. London, Owen, 1970; Indianapolis, Indiana, Bobbs–Merrill, 1971.

Journey for Myself: Selfish Memories, translation by David Le Vay. London, Owen, 1971.

*

Adaptations: *La Seconde* and *Claudine at School* (drama); *Gigi* (film), Metro–Goldwyn–Mayer, 1958.

Manuscript Collections: Bibliothèque Nationale, Paris.

Biography: *Près de Colette* by Maurice Goudeket, Paris, Flammarion, 1956, translated by Enid McLeod as *Near Colette,* New York, Farrar, Straus & Cudahy, 1957; *Colette: The Difficulty of Loving* by Margaret Crosland, Indianapolis, Bobbs–Merrill, 1973; *Colette libre et entravée* by Michèle Sarde, Paris, Stock, 1978, translated by Richard Miller as *Colette, Free and Fettered,* New York, Morrow, 1980; *Colette* by Joanna Richardson, London, Methuen, 1983.

Critical Sources: *Colette* by Elaine Marks, New Brunswick, Maine, Rutgers University Press, 1960; *Colette* by Margaret Davies, London, Oliver & Boyd, 1961; *Colette: The Woman, The Writer*, University Park & London, University of Pennsylvania Press, 1981; *Europe*, November/December 1981 (special Colette issue).

*   *   *

Sidonie Gabrielle Colette, the descendent of a long line of journalists and writers, was born on 28 January 1873 in Saint–Sauveur–en–Puisaye in the department of Yonne. At 18 she fell passionately in love with the 35–year–old Henry Gauthier–Villars, better known as Willy, a music critic and journalist who published work written by others under his own name. Although he was a notorious philanderer, Colette was drawn by his worldliness and married him in 1893. For the next 13 years she lived with him in Paris.

Willy inspired her to write her first novel, *Claudine à l'école*. The heroine, Claudine, is a headstrong, sensual and outspoken girl of 15 who becomes intensely infatuated with one of the younger teachers, Aimée, who tutors her in English at home. Their affair is interrupted by the domineering headmistress, who is also in love with the assistant. Claudine manages to eavesdrop one day on an intimate moment enjoyed by the two women in their quarters. Later the headmistress intimates to Claudine that she might have replaced the younger teacher as her favorite.

The next volume in the series, *Claudine à Paris,* moves the 17–year–old Claudine to the capital. A long illness requires her hair to be cropped and her social contacts are restricted to her father's older sister and the latter's grandson, Marcel, an effeminate boy who is having an affair of his own with a male schoolmate. The liaison has already created problems for them at the lycée and provoked the scornful ire of Marcel's father. The plot turns on Claudine's infatuation and eventual marriage to the good–looking Renaud. In the third novel, *Claudine en ménage,* Renaud—modeled on one facet of Willy—is a superfluous figure, and the plot turns on Claudine's involvement with another woman, Rézi, which is central to the story and portrayed with great subtlety and effect. Sensually aroused, Claudine feels drawn to the ultra–feminine, charmingly built Rézi. Instead of objecting, the husband encourages their liaison, which is conducted behind the closed curtains of a Parisian rendez–vous. The work is not pornographic, there are no explicit details, but the style perfectly conveys the abandonment to pleasure. It also effectively portrays an escape from bondage into wild, uninhibited freedom when it dawns on Claudine that Renaud is sharing Rézi with her in a *ménage à trois.* In this novel Colette's lyrical prose matured and gained the contour that enabled her to counterpose the two poles of her existence—the realm of sexuality, love, and jealousy; and the yearning for the freedom of the outside world.

This work was followed by *Claudine s'en va: Journal d'Annie,* which introduces a new character, Annie, a friend of Claudine's, who spends a great deal of her time traveling. She attends the Wagner Festival in Bayreuth, which was historically reputed as a homosexual gathering place as early as 1895. Annie flees loneliness but only in the hope of finding the right man at the next turn of the road.

Since the royalties from her novels all went to Willy, Colette was financially dependent upon him, and as she prepared for a break with him, she trained herself for a stage career as a dancer and a mime. In the meantime, in the company of such lesbian figures of the literary world as Renée Vivien, Natalie Barney, Lucie Delarue–Mardrus, and Valtesse de la Bigne, she met a woman whose maiden name was Mathilde de Morny, the youngest daughter of the Duc de Morny and the former wife of the Marquis de Belbeuf. De Morny had married when she was 18 but divorced in 1903 without ever really having lived as the Marquis' wife. Nicknamed "Missy" and renowned for her lesbian affairs, she was decidedly masculine, with short hair and a plain face and figure. And she always dressed like a man. She fell in love with Colette just as the latter's marriage was ending. In November of 1906 she left Willy's domicile, and on 13 February 1907 a separation of property was granted.

However, even earlier on 3 January 1907, a true scandal broke. Missy had outlined a mime–play titled *Rêve d'Égypte,* in which an old scholar fascinated by the occult lore of ancient Egypt falls in love with a mummy. The mummy stands up, unwinds her bandages, and dances seductively in front of him. Missy played the male role, Colette the female. When the performance began at the Moulin Rouge, a riot began, orchestrated by the de Morny clan and the members of the Jockey Club, to which the Marquis de Belbeuf belonged. The music was drowned out by noise; the stage was pelted with projectiles of every kind. The climax of the disturbance came when Colette and Missy exchanged a long kiss and obscene insults began to fill the hall.

The next day the Paris newspapers reported the scandal in a vein highly critical of both the actresses and Willy. But what followed this episode was so outrageous that it has been blacked out even in the most explicit biographies. Freed by the separation from Willy, Colette and the Marquise de Morny presented themselves at the registry office in Paris applying to have their marriage recorded. The nonplussed registrar, however, allegedly rejected the marriage although he observed that he "found no text that prohibits such a marriage." This daring act qualifies Colette as the patroness of lesbian marriage—one of the most controversial demands of the contemporary homosexual movement.

Despite the break with Willy, Colette went on writing, and now the inspiration came from Missy, whose house in Paris and villa at Le Crotoy on the Baie de Somme were always open to her. The prose "Nuit Blanche" in the collection of essays *Les Vrilles de la vigne* shed light on their friendship, which overflowed into love and brought emotional and physical gratification. Only the last essay reveals the bed partners to be both women: "You will give me pleasure, leaning over me, your eyes filled with maternal anxiety, you who seek, through your passionate *amie,* the child you did not have."

The music hall years of Colette's life added immensely to her legend—legend more than fact, because while she was copiously photographed, she had no talent as actress or dancer. Her mimicry and actions were in silhouette, but she lacked a gift for either facial expression or choreography. However, this phase brought her into contact with another profession in which homosexuality has traditionally been tolerated if not encouraged. Colette herself gravitated more toward lesbian intellectuals and writers, but could also move in a milieu where female homosexuality, if not too provocative, was accepted. The years from 1906 to 1911 were the high point of Colette's engagement with Lesbos. She formed a friendship with Renée Vivien, whose house on the Avenue du Bois was close to hers on Rue de Villejust. In *Le pur et l'impur,* Colette evokes this early twentieth–century lesbian microsociety together with a literary portrait of Vivien, whose real name was Pauline Tarn, and who wrote French poetry of Sapphic inspiration. She severely criticized Marcel Proust's depiction of Gomorrah, dismissing it as a male fantasy because it replicated the quite alien world of the male homosexual. The bisexual woman is more easily accepted by the male, who sees in her passion for her own sex only a charming caprice, not a threat to his masculinity. Colette's Lesbos has more in common with a gynaeceum or an eighteenth–century convent than with a depraved counterpart of Sodom. It is a refuge not just from male domination, but from a hierarchy of dominance and submission. It is more than a difference of sexual orientation, it is a difference of status. Colette assigns to female homosexuality a specific character by referring it to femininity and detaching it from the male counterpart. In other women she could find the emotional satisfaction, the fidelity, the harmony in love that she sought in vain from the opposite sex.

At the same time she experienced at first hand, and with no ideological prejudice, the world of the music hall. She could later write of it as an insider, one who shared the problems, the anxieties, the conflicts and affinities of its denizens, but at the same time as one who had lived in other strata of French society and knew intimately milieux that were closed to them, so that she could muster the detachment needed for psychological insight and grasp the truth. The collection of short stories, *L'Envers du music–hall,* reflects this period of her life.

The other side of her androgynous nature recalled her to the world of male affection. In December 1910 she met Henri de Jouvenel, one of the subdirectors of the daily paper *Le Matin,* and became his mistress in September of 1911. In December of 1912, when she was already two months pregnant, they were married. As La Baronne de Jouvenel she entered upon a very different life, playing hostess for her husband, who had been elected to the Chamber of Deputies from Corrèze, where his family had a château. But her career had not lost its importance; no longer mime, but journalist, when the First World War broke out she traveled widely, to Venice in particular, and accompanied her husband to Rome in 1917 when he was French delegate to the commission for the *petite entente.* Her articles were collected in *Les Heures longues, 1914–1917.*

After the war ended, she returned to fiction with *Mitsou; ou, Comment l'esprit vient aux filles,* a work that filled Marcel Proust with admiration. He wrote to Colette that the book had moved him to tears and that one scene in particular, in a restaurant, had so outclassed his own handling of similar episode as to make his literary effort pathetic. In the following year she produced the work deemed her masterpiece, *Chéri.* It relates the love of a hero barely out of adolescence with Léa, a woman of 49 who has not "abandoned her search for happiness." It attained a success that was merited particularly by its beauty and economy of form and by the masterful, true–to–life depiction of the magnificent heroine. The counterpart in real life commenced the following year when Colette began to educate her stepson Bertrand de Jouvenel in the ways of love, an affair that became public knowledge to the accompaniment of disapproval and scandal. It led to divorce from her second husband in 1923.

The remaining years of her career saw her, a recognized and successful writer, living after 1926 at her villa at Saint–Tropez and composing one novel after another in which strong, independent women are counterposed to weak and dependent men, like the one who ends his literary existence by committing suicide in *La Fin de Chéri.* Her lesbian affairs involved her with two *amantes,* the film star Marguerite Moréno, and an anonymous foreign noblewoman, both of whom she skillfully but discretely characterized in *Ces Plaisirs.*

In 1935 she married Maurice Goudeket and settled permanently at the Palais–Royal in Paris. Increasingly crippled as the result of an injury and of arthritis, she was ultimately confined to a wheelchair and then to bed, but basked in the homage accorded a national heroine. In 1945 she became the first woman ever elected to the Académie Goncourt, and in 1949 was chosen to be its president. Shortly before her death she received the Médaille d'Or de la Ville de Paris and was promoted to Grand Officier de la Légion d'Honneur. The Fourth Republic honored her with a national funeral, although she was denied the last rites of the Catholic Church, on 7 August 1954.

In the emergence of homosexuality from post–medieval invisibility, different roles fell to different nations. If Germany took the lead on the scientific and political fronts, France made the crucial breakthrough in the cultural sphere. What Proust and Gide did for male homosexuality, Colette did for lesbianism: they restored love for one's own sex to world literature. By attempting to register her liaison with the Marquise de Morny, Colette even became the patroness of lesbian marriage. Her writings are a legacy to the lesbian and feminist movements of today, a record of the evolving consciousness of a modern woman living, loving and struggling to be free.

—*Warren Johansson*

———

COLTON, James. *See* **HANSEN, Joseph.**

———

COMMONS, Giselle. *See* **CORINNE, Tee (A.)**

———

COMPTON–BURNETT, I(vy). British novelist. Born in Pinner, Middlesex, c. 5 June 1884. Educated at Royal Holloway College, University of London (Founders Scholar, 1906), B.A. (classics) 1907. Companion of writer Margaret Jourdain, beginning 1919. **Recipient:** Commander of the Order of the British Empire, 1951; James Tait Black Memorial Prize, 1956; D.Litt., University of Leeds, 1960; Dame Commander of the Order of the British Empire, 1967. *Died in London, 29 August 1969.*

WRITINGS

Novels

Dolores. Edinburgh, Scotland, Blackwood, 1911.
Pastors and Masters. London, Heath Cranton, 1925.
Brothers and Sisters. London, Heath Cranton, and New York, Harcourt, 1929.
Men and Wives. London, Heinemann, and New York, Harcourt, 1931.

More Women Than Men. London, Heinemann, 1933.
A House and Its Head. London, Heinemann, 1935.
Daughters and Sons. London, Gollancz, 1937; New York, Norton, 1938.
A Family and a Fortune. London, Gollancz, 1939.
Parents and Children. London, Gollancz, 1941.
Elders and Betters. London, Gollancz, 1944.
Manservant and Maidservant. London, Gollancz, 1947; as *Bullivant and the Lambs,* New York, Knopf, 1948.
Two Worlds and Their Ways. London, Gollancz, and New York, Knopf, 1949.
Darkness and Day. London Gollancz, and New York, Knopf, 1951.
The Present and the Past. London, Gollancz, 1953; New York, Messner, 1954.
Mother and Son. London, Gollancz, and New York, Messner, 1955.
A Father and His Fate. London, Gollancz, 1957; New York, Messner, 1958.
A Heritage and Its History. London, Gollancz, 1959; New York, Simon & Schuster, 1960.
The Mighty and Their Fall. London, Gollancz, 1961; New York, Simon & Schuster, 1962.
A God and His Gifts. London, Gollancz, 1963; New York, Simon & Schuster, 1964.
The Last and the First. London, Gollancz, and New York, Knopf, 1971.
Collected Works (19 volumes). London, Gollancz, 1972.

*

Manuscript Collections: Humanities Research Center, University of Texas, Austin.

Biography: *The Life of Ivy Compton–Burnett* by Elizabeth Sprigge, New York, Brazillier, 1973; *Ivy When Young: The Early Life of I. Compton–Burnett* by Hilary Spurling, London, Gollancz, 1974.

Critical Sources: *I. Compton–Burnett* by Pamela Hansford Johnson, London, Longmans, Green, 1951; *The Novels of I. Compton–Burnett* by Robert Liddell, London, Gollancz, 1955; *Ivy Compton–Burnett* by Frank Baldanza, New York, Twayne Publishers, 1964; *Ivy and Stevie: Ivy Compton–Burnett and Stevie Smith: Conversations and Reflections* by Kay Dick, London, Duckworth, 1971; *The Art of I. Compton–Burnett* by Charles Burkhart, London, Gollancz, 1972; *A Compton–Burnett Compendium* by Violet Powell, London, Heinemann, 1973; *Lesbian Images* by Jane Rule, Garden City, New York, Doubleday, 1975; *Herman and Nancy and Ivy: Three Lives in Art* by Charles Burkhart, London, Gollancz, 1977, 74–108.

*   *   *

Often considered a challenging and eccentric novelist, Ivy Compton–Burnett worked outside the mainstream of literary Modernist experimentalism from the 1930s through the 1950s. Adhering to the stricture of an indistinct narrative voice, Compton–Burnett's novels rely primarily on dialogue for their exposition. For this reason, and because of her educational background in clas-

sical Greek drama, Compton–Burnett is often regarded as a "dramatic" novelist. Yet her fiction is far less concerned with the large cosmic questions that haunt Greek tragedy than it is with the more commonplace limitations of human nature and society. This concern is most often manifested in her fascination with relationships—especially familial—and the minute workings of power and loyalty within these intrapersonal bonds.

Compton–Burnett's critics often attribute this preoccupation with family dynamics to her own upbringing. She was the eldest daughter of the seven children of James Compton–Burnett, a doctor who apparently studied under noted psychoanalyst Sigmund Freud in Vienna, and his second wife, Katherine Rees. Five children from James' first marriage also lived in the household. Within this large family, clear groupings occurred: Ivy and her two brothers formed a close bond based on education and literary tastes; Katherine's youngest four daughters, all interested in music, formed the next group (Ivy claimed to despise music and thus remained distant from this group); because Katherine favored her own children, the five children of the first marriage formed their own group; while the parents—never particularly nurturing or emotionally involved with the children—made up the top rung of the family hierarchy. While in early adulthood, Compton–Burnett experienced the disintegration of this family structure with the deaths of her parents and two brothers and the double suicide of two younger sisters. After a period of extended mourning and healing, Compton–Burnett began writing novels, most set in pre–World War I England, centered around the theme of familial relationships.

The advantages of a classical education, uncommon for young women in the early twentieth century, prepared Compton–Burnett for a career as a writer, though she was vague about any early literary aspirations she may have had. Similarly, she acknowledged few literary influences—though she admitted a literary kinship with Jane Austen. Like Austen, she writes in a detached and ironic voice about marriage, courtship, and family life, dissecting with precision the dynamics of power and authority among the English gentry. Moreover, she shares with Austen that fascination with the economic side of social relations; marriage is, for most of Compton–Burnett's female characters, a means of financial, rather than emotional, security—few of them marry for love. These themes, with few variations, dominate the bulk of her oeuvre.

While relatively open about her early family life and influences, Compton–Burnett remained reticent about her personal life. She refused to consider writing an autobiography, claiming, in an interview with Kay Dick in Dick's book *Ivy and Stevie,* that "there'd be so much I wouldn't want to reveal. I don't mean important things, but all sorts of hundreds of little things that everybody keeps to himself." She never married, though she makes reference in a later interview to an early attachment to a young man killed in the war. The great relationship of her life was with Margaret Jourdain, an authority on English furniture and country houses, with whom Compton–Burnett lived for 35 years. While the relationship clearly provided her with emotional support and companionship, both partners claimed that they were a "neuter" couple. As in her novels, sexual behavior seems an irrelevant detail in Compton–Burnett's life, and there seems to be no evidence that she ever had a sexual relationship with anyone, male or female. She stood, as Jane Rule asserts in her study, *Lesbian Images* at the "asexual extreme of lesbian sensibility."

While, in some ways, extremely conservative and conventional, Compton–Burnett exercised a tremendous tolerance that extended to the characters in her fiction. Though she has been called "amoral" for her portrayal of a world in which wrong is not always punished and for her refusal to pass judgment on her characters' failings, her novels register an extreme sensitivity to those limitations and temptations that exist for real human beings in difficult situations. The rejection of this literary convention parallels the rejection of the Victorian social and domestic values in her novels. Rarely does the reader find a traditional heterosexual relationship or family unit: An uncle marries his nephew's fiancee; a husband raises his children by his wife's sister and his son's wife; a woman begins an affair with the mother of her brother's son—family structures are as fluid as individual sexuality.

Compton–Burnett's fifth book, *More Women Than Men,* most explicitly explores the nature of emotional and sexual attachment in the context of a complicated network of familial relations. The story takes place in a girl's school, of which Josephine Napier is the headmistress. She acts as a benevolent dictator over her female staff, as well as over her husband and adopted child, Gabriel, the son of her brother Jonathan who maintains a long–term homosexual relationship (the happiest and most compelling in the book) with Felix Bacon, son of a local aristocrat. When Josephine's husband dies and Gabriel marries, Josephine transfers her affection to Felix, who has come to work as drawing master at the school. The death of Felix's father catalyzes him into conventionality wherein he leaves Jonathan to marry Helen Keats, one of the school teachers. Assuming his familial mantel, he takes up residence in his ancestral home. Josephine eventually attaches herself to another of her teachers, Maria Rosetti, who is Gabriel's actual mother and is privy to Josephine's terrible secret—her partial responsibility for the death of Gabriel's young wife. In the end, a kind of emotional and economic equilibrium is established—characters are neatly paired off, with a clean distribution of fortunes among them—though without the parallel moral equilibrium.

The story is conveyed almost entirely through dialogue, with minimal authorial comment or intrusion. And because the author makes no attempt to differentiate characters by speech mannerisms or diction, the characters all remain on the same moral plane and readers are left to draw their own conclusions. Josephine's murderous act is reported in exactly the same matter–of–fact tone as the school recital or Felix and Jonathan's embraces. While this aspect of Compton–Burnett's novels is clearly what leads many critics to dismiss her as willfully difficult, more recent feminist scholars consider it a deliberate attempt to subvert traditional patriarchal modes of narrative and replace them with a wider vision of social and emotional relations, including the normalization of gay and lesbian relationships.

Ivy Compton–Burnett left no criticism of her own with which to illuminate her narrative practices, while the few interviews she granted furnish her readers with a morass of contradictory facts and memories. What is clear is her challenge to the primacy of the conventional values of patriarchal and heterosexist society, as well as to traditional literary and narrative imperatives, however successful that challenge may have been.

—*Allison Rolls*

———

COOPER, Dennis. American poet, novelist, playwright, and author of short stories. Born in Pasadena, California, 10 January 1953. Educated at Pasadena City College and Pitzer College. Founder

of *Little Caesar* magazine, 1976, and Little Caesar Press, 1978. Program director for Beyond Baroque Foundation, Venice, California, beginning in 1979. Art critic for *Art Forum* and *Art Scribe,* beginning 1987. **Recipient:** Ferro–Grumley Foundation Award, 1990. Agent: Ira Silverberg Communications, 61 Fourth Avenue, Third Floor, New York, New York 10003, U.S.A.

WRITINGS

Poetry

The Terror of Earrings (chapbook), 1973.
Tiger Beat (chapbook), 1978.
Antoine Monnier (chapbook), 1978.
Idols. New York, Sea Horse Press, 1979.

Fiction

Closer (novel). New York, Grove, 1989.
Frisk (novel). New York, Grove Weidenfeld, 1991.
Wrong (short stories). New York, Grove Weidenfeld, 1992.

Plays

The Undead (produced Los Angeles, 1989).
Knife/Tape/Rope (produced New York, 1989).

Other

The Tenderness of Wolves. Freedom, California, Crossing Press, 1981.
Safe. New York, Sea Horse, 1984.
He Cried: Poems and Stories. New York, Black Star, 1984.
"The Outsiders" in *Men on Men,* edited by George Stambolian. New York, Plume, 1986.
Editor, with Richard Hawkins, *Against Nature: A Group Show of Work by Homosexual Men.* Los Angeles, Los Angeles Contemporary Exhibition, 1989.
With Lucinda Barnes, *Charles Ray* (interviews). Newport Beach, California, Newport Harbor Art Museum, c. 1990.
Contributor, *Discontents: An Anthology of New Queer Writers.* New York, Amethyst, 1991.
"Wrong" in *High Risk,* edited by Amy Schoulder and Ira Silverberg. New York, Dutton, 1991.
Jerk. Artspace Books, 1992.
"My Mark," in *The Faber Book of Gay Short Fiction,* edited by Edmund White. London and New York, Faber & Faber, 1991.

*

Biography: "Dennis Cooper" by Earl Jackson, Jr., in *Contemporary Gay American Novelists,* edited by Emmanuel S. Nelson, Westport, Connecticut, Greenwood Press, 1992, 77–82.

Interviews: With Richard Myer, in *Cuz,* New York, The Poetry Project, 1988, 52–69.

Critical Sources: "The Lost Boys" by Edmund White, in *Times Literary Supplement* (London) 5 April 1989, 92; "Naked Lunchroom: Dennis Cooper's Teenage Wasteland" by Vince Aletti, in *Village Voice Literary Supplement*, May 1989, 28; "Running on Emptiness" by Robert Gluck, in *San Francisco Chronicle*, 4 June 1989, 9; "The Brink of Darkness" by Bo Huston, in *Advocate*, 1 October 1989, 57; "Dennis Cooper Hits Home" by Eric Latsky, in *L.A. Weekly.* 13–19 June 1990, 20–27.

*   *   *

While much gay male writing since the Stonewall incident of 1969 has followed the lead of Walt Whitman in celebrating the expansive joys of the gay body electric, poet and novelist Dennis Cooper has embarked on the opposite course: pinpointing the precise physical boundaries of the human body and examining that object in surgical detail. While he is most famous (perhaps even notorious) for writing about the disembowelment and dismemberment of teenage boy characters in his novels *Closer* and *Frisk*, Cooper has always been as interested in charting the limits of the emotional and psychological in the everyday lives of his characters.

Born in Pasadena, California, in 1953, Cooper attended Pasadena City College, as well as Pitzer College, and later traveled to Britain. When he returned to the West Coast in 1976, he founded *Little Caesar Magazine*, which featured contemporary poetry and interviews with artists and musicians. Two years later he founded Little Caesar Press. A year after that he became the program director of Beyond Baroque Foundation, an avant garde organization that teaches, among other subjects, writing and performance. During this time, Cooper began writing poetry and short prose pieces and published three chapbooks, *The Terror of Earrings, Tiger Beat*, and *Antoine Monnier*, before publishing his first full book of poems, *Idols*, in 1979.

From his earliest pieces, Cooper has detailed the empty lives and sexual despair of middle–class Southern California teenagers. He often uses an almost documentary technique to look at their lives. The poem "Ed Hong" (from *Idols*) is an example of this: "When they snapped his picture/ he was on LSD/ and flunking everything. / You would have said: / 'beautiful loser. / good for a rape and an O.D.'"

As Cooper progressed, he became much more concerned with documenting and examining the physical violence that his characters endure as well as perpetrate on themselves and others. In a long prose piece, "The Hurd," which appears in *The Tenderness of Wolves*, Cooper details the life of a killer of teenaged boys. The prose is straightforward and non–sensational, as emotionally blank and as metaphysically frightening as the lives of his characters. But even through the gruesome killings, Cooper's murderer is in search of some definition of human knowledge. After murdering one boy the killer fantasizes: "He'd face the girls who had slept with the boy, toss them a few easy questions like 'What does he do when you blow him?' and 'How much hair in his ass?' They'd pipe up the answers and think the man jealous. Then he'd narrow his eyes and ask, 'When you hack off his balls with a knife, and slap his face to keep him aware, does he scream for God or for his mother?'"

This passage prefigures the themes of Cooper's two most popular and critically acclaimed books, *Closer* and *Frisk*. The first book examines the quest for ultimate knowledge of another person: knowing what someone screams at his death is a form of power—a form of personal and social control in a world that is so out of control only the personal experience of violence will satisfy the desire for knowledge. In *Frisk* the narrator, Julian, hires a hustler, named Pierre. After he touches, smells, licks, and tastes every inch of the prostitute, Julian asks Pierre to expel bodily waste: "'I'm not being abject,' I say. 'It's not, Ooh, shit, piss, how wicked,' or anything. It's, like I said, information.' Pierre nods. 'Then what are you going to do with it?' he asks. 'I don't mean with my shit, I mean with the information?' My face scrunches up. 'Uh, create a mental world ... uh, wait. Or a situation where I could kill you and understand ... shit, I sound ridiculous.'" Later in the novel Julian's boyhood friend regales him with detailed descriptions of murdering, disemboweling, and dismembering a young boy: "Then we cut him apart for a few hours and studied everything inside the body...." He then ,makes a plea to the narrator to join him in this pursuit: "We'll do it ourselves. It's totally easy. Nothing's happened to me. I feel strong, powerful, clear all of the time. Nothing bothers me anymore. I'm telling you, Julian, this is some kind of ultimate truth."

The second theme present in Cooper's books is the inability of his characters (and by extension his readers) to "feel" anything in a material culture that continually deadens or negates them. When George, a young man in *Closer* meets up with Tom—a man intent on disemboweling him—George is drawn and yet oblivious to the idea. "'It just some Novocain,' Tom muttered, 'so I can take you apart, sans your pointless emotions.'" Tom proceeds to carve up George's body and when the boy makes a joke everything changes. "When Tom didn't laugh George bit his lip. That's all it took. He burst into tears. He felt a couple of slashes across his back. 'I said no fucking emotions!' Tom yelled. 'Do you want me to kill you or not?' 'No,' George sobbed. "Well, then what are you doing here?' 'I don't know,' George blubbered, 'I don't know.'"

Cooper's characters live in a world so emotionally suffocating that commonplace intimacy is never enough to surmount the overwhelming isolation and boredom of everyday life. Violence, death, and dismemberment—finding out what is *really* inside someone—is one of the few opportunities these characters have to connect to another human being. Disembowelment is the only way some of these people can come close to a real emotion. While other gay male writers have dwelt on the endless opportunities open to their characters, Cooper focuses on how difficult it still is to live in a homophobic world that ignores and disregards the pleasures of the flesh and the world of the gay imagination. It is a world that has presumed that AIDS signifies punishment and that sexual pleasure is innately suspect. Cooper's characters are not instruments of evil but rather men who are trying to find human connection in a mad world.

—*Michael Bronski*

———————

CORINNE, Tee (A.) American artist, novelist, and author of short stories. Has also written as Giselle Commons. Born 3 November 1943, in St. Petersburg, Florida. Educated at University of South Florida, B.A.; and Pratt Institute, M.F.A., 1968. Writer, editor, artist, and art books columnist for *Feminist Bookstore News*,

1987—; founding coeditor of *Blatant Image: A Magazine of Feminist Photography;* cofounder and past cochair of Gay and Lesbian Caucus of the College Art Association. **Recipient:** Lambda Literary Award, 1989. Address: P.O.B. 278, Wolf Creek, Oregon 97497, U.S.A.

WRITINGS

Novels

The Sparkling Lavender Dust of Lust. Austin, Texas, Banned Books, 1991.

Short Stories

Dreams of the Woman Who Loved Sex. Austin, Texas, Banned Books, 1987.
Lovers: Love and Sex Stories. Austin, Texas, Banned Books, 1989.

Art Books

Cunt Coloring Book. San Francisco, Pearlchild, 1975; as *Labiaflowers.* Tallahassee, Naiad Press, 1981.
The So; or, Women Writers' Group Picture Book. Grants Pass, Oregon, Pearlchild, 1982.
Yantras of Womanlove: Diagrams of Energy. Tallahassee, Naiad Press, 1982.
The Southern Oregon Women Writers Group Gourmet Eating Society and Chorus Picture Book. Sunny Valley, Oregon, Pearlchild, 1982.
Drawings '83. Grants Pass, Oregon, Pearlchild, 1984.
Women Who Loved Women. Grants Pass, Oregon, Pearlchild, 1984.
Lesbian Muse: The Women Behind the Words. Portland, Oregon, Chance Publications, 1989.
Family: About Growing Up in an Alcoholic Family. North Vancouver, British Columbia, Gallerie, 1990.

Editor

Intricate Passions: A Collection of Erotic Short Fiction. Austin, Texas, Banned Books, 1989.
Riding Desire: An Anthology of Erotic Writing. Austin, Texas, Banned Books, 1991.
The Poetry of Sex: Lesbians Write the Erotic. Austin, Texas, Banned Books, 1992.
With others, *All of Our Secrets Exposed.* Days Creek, Oregon, Niaodagain, 1993.

Illustrator

The Marquise and the Novice by Victoria Ramstetter. Tallahassee, Naiad Press, 1981.
The Outlander by Jane Rule. Tallahassee, Naiad Press, 1981.
Sapphistry: The Book of Lesbian Sexuality by Pat Califia. Tallahassee, Naiad Press, 1988.

Other

"Clementina Hawarden, Photographer" (as Giselle Commons), in

Sinister Wisdom: A Journal of Words and Pictures for the Lesbian Imagination (Rockland, Maine), winter 1978.
"The Drainage Ditch," in *Pleasures: Women Write Erotica,* edited by Lonnie Barbach. Garden City, New York, Doubleday, 1984.
"Notes on Writing Sex," in *An Intimate Wilderness,* edited by Judith Barrington. Portland, Oregon, Eighth Mountain Press, 1991.
Contributor, *I Am My Lover* by Honey Lee Cottrell.

*

Interviews: With Joanne Stato, in *Off Our Backs,* July 1991.

Critical Sources: *Sinister Wisdom: A Journal of Words and Pictures for the Lesbian Imagination* (Charlotte, North Carolina), 1:3, 1977; *Blatant Image: A Magazine of Feminist Photography* (Sunny Valley, Oregon), 1:1, 1981, 21, 48–49; *Sapphistry: The Book of Lesbian Sexuality* by Pat Califia, second edition, Tallahassee, Naiad, 1983; "Encouraging Flirtatious Belligerence" by Lee Lynch, in *Bay Windows,* 22 January 1987; "Surveying Contemporary Lesbian Erotica" by Susie Bright, in *Lambda Rising Book Report: A Contemporary Review of Gay and Lesbian Literature* (Washington, D.C.), 1:4, 1988, 4; "Words to Lust By" by Jan Zita Grover, in *Women's Review of Books,* November 1990; *Stolen Glances: Lesbians Take Photographs,* edited by Tessa Boffin and Jean Fraser, London, Pandora Press, 1991, 223–228; "Southerners and Social Issues" by Paula Martinac, in *Lamba Book Report* (Washington, D.C.), November/December 1991, 30; "The Sparkling Lavender Glow of Success" by Victoria A. Brownworth, in *Windy City Times,* 6 February 1992; "Placing Eroticism in the Context of Lesbian Life" by Victoria A. Brownworth, in *Philadelphia Gay News,* 12–18 June 1992.

Tee Corinne comments: "In my work I have sought to bring generosity, beauty, and grace to the understanding of women's and lesbian sexuality and history, and to lesbian literary personalities. I'm interested in establishing ways to communicate across barriers of taboo, negative stereotyping, and benign ignorance."

*   *   *

Tee Corinne, an artist, researcher, and educator, is a pioneer in the field of lesbian erotica. While her enduring reputation may be for her work as a photographer, graphic artist, and illustrator, her impact on the creation of contemporary lesbian culture as a sex educator and writer are no less important, though more difficult to measure. Her images and words have appeared in almost every lesbian–read periodical of substance since the mid–1970s. In addition, Corinne was one of the early, undocumented lesbian cultural ambassadors, spreading the results of her research and creativity by giving slideshows and lectures at women's bookstores, universities, lesbian centers, women's festivals, and bars anywhere and everywhere in the United States.

Concurrent with the re–examination of sexuality engendered by women's liberation groups, Corinne was part of a movement to explore and redefine lesbian sexuality and eroticism. In the mid–1970s, she became involved with the San Francisco Sex Information Switchboard. During this period she created a number of lesbian related sex education materials—including a sexually explicit film intended to respond in a non–pornographic manner, to the often–raised question of what lesbians do in bed—that were distributed to women's sexuality and therapy groups. Her slide show, in which she used two anatomically correct rag dolls, less threateningly answered the same query for a wider audience. It was distributed nationally through Multi–Media Resource Center and was included as a short subject when Corinne toured with her other slide lectures. Multi–Media also distributed her set of 36 color slides of female genitalia (with diagram and teaching guide) for use by women's studies and consciousness–raising groups. These images, and the drawings in *Cunt Coloring Book* (later briefly renamed *Labiaflowers*), were intended to reclaim the word and the images from prior negative history. Corinne contributed 16 color plates of female genitalia to complement Honey Lee Cottrell's black and white photography in *I Am My Lover,* a book on women's masturbation.

Corinne survived on a small inheritance from her mother, an artist. She published several of her works under her own imprint, Pearlchild, and learned first hand the vagaries and prejudices of printers and the publishing establishment when dealing with explicitly lesbian materials. She was among 130 publishers and media women gathered in Nebraska for the 1976 Women in Print conference. Here she renewed old acquaintances and made new ones that would contribute to the wider dissemination of her work. She met Catherine Nicholson and Harried Desmoines, who were premiering a new lesbian magazine, *Sinister Wisdom: A Journal of Words and Pictures for the Lesbian Imagination.* Corinne's solarized cover photo of lesbian lovers sold out the periodical's third issue. When the photo was offered as a fund–raising poster, it became the first nationally–recognized image of lesbians by a lesbian artist. Other connections enabled her to offer her slide lectures in cities like Chicago, where hundreds of women gathered for the fourth national Lesbian Writers' Conference in 1977; Corinne's program "Lesbian Sexual Imagery in the Fine Arts" placed lesbian images, often created by men, in a feminist historical context.

Over the years Corinne has offered many programs and exhibits, either of her own work or the results of her research, often in tandem with women with whom she had an intimate and creative relationship. She was one of the artists invited to exhibit in GALAS—The Great American Lesbian Artists Show. An exhibit of her solarized photos, "Dyke Cream," was followed by a joint venture with Cottrell, "Cool Verbages and Hot Images." A slide lecture, "Styles of Being Lesbian in Paris, 1890–1945: An Herstorical ReVision," was presented in conjunction with historian Frances Doughty. Several series of greeting and post cards offered images of Caroline Overman as characters out of classic lesbian fiction, while others had portraits of movement figures like entertainer Pat Bond, *Feminist Bookstore News* publisher Carol Seajay, or Cottrell. Cottrell images were especially popular in Corinne's "politically incorrect" series, a response to the doyennes of a new lesbian feminist orthodoxy.

Corinne's first full–length photographic exploration of sexual imagery was *Yantras of Womanlove: Diagrams of Energy.* Art critic Jan Zita Grover, whose comments accompany excerpts from *Yantras* in *Stolen Glances: Lesbians Take Photographs,* notes that Corinne's technical choices, "solarization, flipped negatives, [and] negative images function not only as protection of the individual model's identity, but also as a correlative for the status of the public lesbian: present yet invisible," which results "in a body of work on sexuality that cannot be understood in terms familiar to art/academic analysis." While completing *Yantras,* Corinne and a core group

founded the Feminist Photography Ovulars, which offered workshops in advanced and experimental photography and also resulted in the creation of *Blatant Image: A Magazine of Feminist Photography.* The Oregon community inspired Corinne's book of drawings *The Southern Oregon Women Writer's Group Gourmet Eating Society and Chorus Picture Book.*

At about this time Corinne's published emphasis would shift from visual to verbal sexual imagery. Her story "The Drainage Ditch" appeared in *Pleasures: Women Write Erotica* under the pseudonym Giselle Commons. Another book of images, *Women Who Loved Women,* which features 103 pictures of lesbian foremothers, with commentary, preceded two popular volumes of her erotic prose, *Lovers* and *Dreams of the Woman Who Loved Sex.* In 1989, she collected stories from 24 of her favorite lesbian authors, photographed each woman, and published the resulting anthology as *Intricate Passions: A Collection of Erotic Short Fiction.*

Corinne's erotic photographs and stories celebrate the sensuality of women of all sizes, colors, and degrees of ability, expressing their sexual joy in myriad ways. Her work continues to be anthologized; her portrait photography, historical research, and commentary appear regularly in the gay and lesbian press; and her analysis, like "Notes on Writing Sex," surfaces in works of cultural criticism for academia and women at large.

—*Marie J. Kuda*

———

CORVO, Baron. *See* **ROLFE, Frederick (William Serafino Austin Lewis Mary).**

———

CORVO, Frederick Baron. *See* **ROLFE, Frederick (William Serafino Austin Lewis Mary).**

———

CORY, Donald Webster. *See* **SAGARIN, Edward.**

———

CRANE, (Harold) Hart. American poet. Born in Garrettsville, Ohio, 21 July 1899. Educated at public schools in Cleveland, Ohio. Mechanic bench hand and shipyard laborer in Ohio during the 1910s; reporter for the *Plain Dealer,* Cleveland, 1919; advertising manager for the *Little Review,* New York City, 1919; shipping clerk for Rheinthal & Newman, New York City, 1919; advertising copywriter in Cleveland and New York City c. 1920s; worked in sales,

New York City, in the 1920s. Frequent contributor to periodicals, including *Modern School* and *Pagan*. **Recipient:** Helen Waire Levinson Prize, 1930; Guggenheim fellowship, for the study of European culture pertaining to American poetry, 1931–32. *Committed suicide by drowning in the Gulf of Mexico, 27 April 1932.*

WRITINGS

Poetry

White Buildings, foreword by Allen Tate. New York, Boni & Liveright, 1926.
The Bridge. Paris, Black Sun Press, 1930; New York, Horace Liveright, 1930.

Collected Verse

The Collected Poems of Hart Crane, edited by Waldo Frank. New York, Liveright, 1933.
Voyages: Six Poems from White Buildings, illustrations by Leonard Baskin. New York, Museum of Modern Art, 1957.
The Complete Poems and Selected Letters and Prose of Hart Crane, edited by Brom Weber. Garden City, New York, Doubleday, 1966.
Seven Lyrics. Cambridge, Massachusetts, Ibex Press, 1966.
Ten Unpublished Poems. New York, Gotham Book Mart, 1972.
The Poems of Hart Crane, edited by Marc Simon. New York, Liveright, 1986.

Letters

Twenty–one Letters from Hart Crane to George Bryan, edited by Joseph Katz, Hugh C. Atkinson, and Richard A. Ploch. Columbus, Ohio State University Press, 1969.
Robber Rocks: Letters and Memories of Hart Crane, 1923–1932, edited by Susan Jenkins Brown. Middletown, Connecticut, Wesleyan University Press, 1969.
With others, *The Letters of Hart Crane and His Family,* edited by Thomas S. W. Lewis. New York, Columbia University Press, 1974.
With Yvor Winters, *Hart Crane and Yvor Winters: Their Literary Correspondence,* edited by Thomas Parkinson. Los Angeles, University of California Press, 1978.

*

Manuscript Collections: Columbia University Library, New York City.

Biography: *Hart Crane: The Life of an American Poet* by Philip Horton, New York, Norton, 1937; *Hart Crane: A Biographical and Critical Study* by Brom Weber, London, Bodley Press, 1948; *Hart Crane* by Vincent G. Quinn, Boston, Twayne Publishers, 1963; *Hart Crane* by Monroe K. Spears, Minneapolis, Minnesota, University of Minneapolis Press, 1965; *Voyager: A Life of Hart Crane* by John Unterecker, New York, Farrar, Strauss, 1969.

Bibliography: *Hart Crane: A Descriptive Bibliography* by Joseph Schwartz and Robert C. Schweik, Pittsburgh, Pennsylvania, University of Pittsburgh Press, 1972; *Hart Crane: A Reference Guide* by Joseph Schwartz, Boston, G. K. Hall, 1983.

Critical Sources: *Hart Crane's Sanskrit Charge: A Study of The Bridge* by L. S. Dembo, Ithaca, New York, Cornell University Press, 1960; *Hart Crane: An Introduction and Interpretation* by Samuel Hazo, New York, Barnes & Noble, 1963; *The Poetry of Hart Crane: A Critical Study* by R. W. B. Lewis, Princeton, New Jersey, Princeton University Press, 1967; *Hart Crane: An Introduction to the Poetry* by Herbert A. Leibowitz, New York, Columbia University Press, 1968; *The Broken Arch: A Study of Hart Crane* by R. W. Butterfield, Edinburgh, 1969; *The Merrill Studies in "The Bridge,"* edited by David R. Clark, Columbus, Ohio, Merrill, 1970; *Hart's "Bridge"* by Sherman Paul, Champaign, Illinois, University of Illinois Press, 1972; *Hart Crane: The Patterns of His Poetry* by M. D. Uroff, Champaign, Illinois, University of Illinois Press, 1974; *Hart Crane's "The Bridge": A Description of Its Life* by Richard P. Sugg, Tuscaloosa, University of Alabama Press, 1976; *Vision of the Voyage: Hart Crane and the Psychology of Romanticism* by Robert Combs, Memphis, Tennessee, Memphis State University Press, 1978; *Hart Crane's Divided Vision: An Analysis of The Bridge* by Helge Normann Nilsen, Oslo, Norway, Universitetssforlaget, 1980; *Hart Crane's Holy Vision: "White Buildings"* by Alfred Hanley, Atlantic Highlands, New Jersey, Duquesne University Press, 1981; *Critical Essays on Hart Crane,* edited by David R. Clark, Boston, G. K. Hall, 1982; *Hart Crane: A Collection of Critical Essays,* edited by Alan Trachtenberg, Englewood Cliffs, New Jersey, Prentice–Hall, 1982; *Splendid Failure: Hart Crane and the Making of "The Bridge"* by Edward Brunner, Urbana and Chicago, University of Illinois Press, 1983; "The Bridge" in *On the Modernist Long Poem* by Margaret Dickie, Iowa City, University of Iowa Press, 1986; *Hart Crane: The Contexts of "The Bridge"* by Paul Giles, New York, Cambridge University Press, 1986; *Hart Crane's Harp of Evil: A Study of Orphism in "The Bridge"* by Jack C. Wolf, Troy, New York, Whitson, 1986; *Transmemberment of Song: Hart Crane's Anatomies of Rhetoric and Desire* by Lee Edelman, Stanford, California, Stanford University Press, 1987.

*   *   *

"When the Pulitzers showered on some dope / ... few people would consider why I took / to stalking sailors," wrote Robert Lowell as Crane in the sonnet, "Words for Hart Crane." The poem continues, "I / Catullus redivivus, once the rage / of the Village and Paris, used to play my role / of homosexual, wolfing the stray lambs / who hungered by the Place de la Concorde."

Such frank admissions of homosexuality are not to be found in Crane's own poetry; he gave the reader few glimpses into his private life, but directed his erotic passion to language itself, which he fashioned into one of the purest lyrical styles in American literature. But Lowell, writing in 1959, 27 years after Crane's suicide, has him confess to dark psychological secrets as the base of his art. For Lowell and others writing in the 1950s, the homosexual was a tragic figure, and a homosexual artist's main subject was the suffering and exile borne of his deviant existence.

But Crane's homosexuality lies in his art, in its grasp of the cold facts of American cities as a source of passionate images, and in its celebration of male myths like the Conquest of the New World, the Machine Age, and such engineering wonders as the Brooklyn Bridge. In forming large areas of experience into personal vision, he followed Walt Whitman, who had turned the whole of American experience into one of universal love, the coming together of races and of the world's strangers into spiritual and sexual union. Crane was less sanguine about such prospects, but he did believe that a new poetry of the machine and the facts of labor and urban life would revive an old art and stake out America's voice in world literature.

But to do so meant going against the grain of American literary tastes and attitudes, which favored plain speech and moral arguments. Instead, Crane schooled himself on "absolutist" poetry, as he called it, in the work of Donne, Blake, Baudelaire, Rimbaud, and others. "Absolutist" poetry, in contrast to "impressionist" poetry, as he wrote in his little essay, "General Aims and Theories," treats experience as fundamentals of spiritual life: "The impressionist is interesting as far as he goes—but his goal has been reached when he has succeeded in projecting certain selected factual details into his reader's consciousness. He is really not interested in the causes (metaphysical) of his materials, their emotional derivations or their utmost spiritual consequences."

Crane's view of poetry is that it must engage the terms of one's cultural era and find in them the immortal gods and powers underlying art in all ages. Daily life is a debris of shifting particles in which only the most creative intellect can discern the archetypes of imagination. To get at them requires a "'logic of metaphor' which antedates our so–called pure logic, and which is the genetic basis of all speech, hence consciousness and thought–extension," he wrote in "General Aims and Theories." Crane identified impressionism with materialistic values and the rejection of myths and archetypes in the American mind. His absolutism gave Romantic poetry a new agenda: to interpret the modern city through Greek myths.

White Buildings, his first book, is a clear application of the principles set forth in "General Aims." The title refers to the sunny villages of the Caribbean, which he first visited in 1916 when he followed his mother to the Isle of Pines, south of Cuba, following her separation from his father. Crane's grandfather owned a fruit ranch there, and at 17, we learn from hints in the poems, Crane had his first sexual experiences. He associated the sunny beaches and bright buildings with sensuality and Greek passion.

Crane's poems corroborate Wallace Stevens' view of Caribbean islands as a realm of imagination, a poetic coast rich in the metaphors of edenic nature, palms, fern gardens, bougainvillea, a native life given to leisure, carnivals, and easy love. Here was an offshoot of Mediterranean culture rich in memories of the love goddess Aphrodite and her male counterpart, Dionysus. Crane's poems refer often to both gods; "For the Marriage of Faustus and Helen" celebrates the continuing sway of pagan love in the modern age.

But Crane's women are a bit too abstract, mythical figures whom he academically sketches into existence. They are not the palpable creatures of French poetry, in red shoes and swirling skirt, but conscious symbols of the sensuality missing in America. Crane's Caribbean is ancient Arcadia revamped for the Jazz Age, replete with white villas, crystal beaches, and sultry young natives. Crane's world coincides with the wild, frenzied demi–monde that whirled around the pillars of Jay Gatsby's mansion in F. Scott Fitzgerald's *The Great Gatsby,* published in 1925, a year prior to *White Buildings.* Crane went far in defining the sexual mystique of the 1920s, and in celebrating the role of black culture in its formation. Little wonder Tennessee Williams found Crane a kindred spirit a decade later; Williams culled a title for his play on sexual immolation,

"Summer and Smoke," from a line in Crane's poem "Emblems of Conduct." Crane's poetry proved a rich lode for titling other works, including the song "Riders on the Storm" by the rock band The Doors, which was taken from "Praise for an Urn," and Clayton Eshleman's essay book, *Antiphonal Swing,* from the closing line of *The Bridge.*

White Buildings is an unabashed revel in sexuality; nearly every poem describes a scene of seduction and outright surrender to the lures of Circe, Aphrodite, or to Dionysian impulses. Verbal play on the word "garden" abounds, as in "Garden Abstract," where Eve's attraction to forbidden fruit is hailed as the doorway to sexual freedom. Noon, sun–bleached walls, the white light of the moon, and cups of wine furnish the erotic tokens of the book, whose subtext of encounter, submission, and sexual elation is laced with Greek myth. Crane was in open revolt from his Christian upbringing, and his book was greeted by the bohemian fringe of New York as the articulation of their own sexual attitudes.

Warming the American landscape with erotic scenes from Caribbean life had its psychological motives as well. No doubt the harsher facts of American enterprise composed part of Crane's impression of his father, the difficult, loveless manufacturer of candy in Cleveland, who saw Crane's literary pursuits as foolish and wasteful. Paganizing the rough, impersonal life he knew in Ohio via an imagery he found on the Isle of Pines was one solution to dealing with his father; another was his homosexuality, which distanced him from his father and gave him a more neutral stance to social convention.

The men Crane admired were models of affection and sensitivity; the poets he revered include Whitman, Baudelaire, Rimbaud, men of great passion and inventiveness, the opposites of his stern parent. In "Episode of Hands," he celebrates the kindness of a laborer who attended him after he injured his hand working in his father's factory where, "The unexpected interest made him flush. / Suddenly he seemed to forget the pain." Masculinity redeemed itself in such moments and filled the gap left by his own father: "And factory sounds and factory thoughts / Were banished from him by that larger, quieter hand / That lay in his with the sun upon it. / And as the bandage knot was tightened / The two men smiled into each other's eyes." Homosexuality remolded the image of the male for Crane; he could celebrate the achievements of male society based on bonds of loyalty and love and thus avoid the problematic role of his own father.

The poems of *White Buildings,* etched in brilliant lyric phrases, are a psycho–sexual code in which a young man escapes from paternal tyranny and discovers freedom through erotic encounters. Because such events are bound up with psychological pain, Crane does not confess them to the reader but raises their condition to mythical generalities as if addressed directly to his father. The characters and situations of his poems argue the same end, the rightness of affection, understanding, and sexual license as counterpoints to an unstated life of cold, deliberate striving.

Something of the same situation governs the writing of *The Bridge,* where he champions the selfless work of Washington Roebling in building the Brooklyn Bridge. Here is another positive image of the male as loving contributor to mankind, using his genius to unify life. The bridge is viewed as joining sky and earth, eternity and the drift of daily life, the very things "absolutist" poetry must seek to do. The whole poem is a hymn to the male spirit—as explorer, builder, founder of a nation, inventor of ships, trains, river boats, automobiles, and airplanes, as the creator of the wonders of transportation and the city.

But in "Three Songs" we confront the tawdrier aspects of modern America and its victimization of women and minorities. In "Quaker Hill" Crane traces the degradation of Christianity to honky–tonk parlors and the "pain that Emily [Dickinson] and Isadora [Duncan] knew!" Crane was many decades ahead of his time transforming his father's monocultural world with the healing powers of pagan gods, the "daemons" that are no more. Edgar Allan Poe, another pagan disciple of love, is also invoked as he identifies the narrator of "The Tunnel" as his alter ego. The poem closes with "Atlantis," where the bridge is a great wind harp vibrating to the winds of universal love.

Crane wrote love poems using the harsh materials of the modern landscape. He peopled his Caribbean beaches with Aphrodite, Circe, Dionysus, and Helen, and with the frail, broken figure of Christ (in "Lachrymae Christi"), who he utilized as the symbol of his own woes. He offered an idyllic world of love and passion to balance the stark realities of the modern age. For Crane the vast steel metropolises belonged to the cold logic of his father, and the warm, sunny world of Cuba was the garden world of his mother and of the female spirit. In *The Bridge* he set out to forge a redeeming metaphor of the city that would countervail the pessimism of T. S. Eliot's "The Waste Land," and reveal masculinity's own deep wells of passion and love.

Crane's homosexuality resides in the erotic power of his images, where he takes the female's role as the struck, pierced, or wounded lover, as in "To the Cloud Juggler": "Wrap us and lift us; drop us then, returned / Like water, undestroyed,—like mist, unburned ... / But do not claim a friend like him again, / Whose arrow must have pierced you beyond pain." And in "Old Song," where "the thorn in sharpened shade / Weathers all loneliness." And again in "Reply," where "words / Shall come to you through wounds prescribed by swords." The fringe world of male encounter is captured in "The hot fickle wind, the breath of males," and elsewhere as "blood, suet and sweat,—the rigmarole / of wine and mandolins. Midnight; and maybe love."

Subtle, indirect, symbolic language expressed Crane's most passionate feelings for other men. What he said about Greek goddesses he meant for the men he was drawn to. The dense configurations of his lyricism were partly the exuberance of a deep poetic talent, and partly a protective code of writing in an intolerant age. Crane's lush poetry influenced the styles of subsequent writers from Tennessee Williams to Robert Lowell and Frank O'Hara.

Crane's sunny beaches and languorous days of love have become the stereotype of gay resorts. Key West and Fire Island are stock images of gay cruising grounds, but Crane was the first to transpose Greek eros onto the sandy edges of the New World. When he took his life in the Caribbean coming home to New York, he chose the waters near Cuba for his resting place.

—*Paul Christensen*

———

CRISP, Quentin. British actor, humorist, social critic, commercial artist, and memoirist. Born Dennis Pratt in Sutton, Surrey, 25 December 1908; immigrated to the United States in 1977. Actor in films, including *The Bride,* Columbia, 1985, and in stage produc-

tions, including *The Naked Civil Servant* and *The Importance of Being Earnest.* Contributor to *New York* magazine and the *New York Times.* **Recipient:** Special Drama Desk Award for unique theatrical experience, 1979. Address: 46 East Third Street, New York, New York 10003, U.S.A.

WRITINGS

Autobiographies

The Naked Civil Servant. London, J. Cape, 1968; revised, with a new forward by Michael Holroyd, New York, New American Library, 1983.
How to Become A Virgin (sequel to *The Naked Civil Servant*). London, Duckworth, and New York, St. Martin's Press, 1981.

Other

Color in Display. London, Blandford Press, 1938.
How to Have a Lifestyle (social history). London, Cecil Woolf, 1975.
With A. F. Stuart, *Lettering for Brush and Pen.* London, F. Warne, 1976.
Love Made Easy. London, Duckworth, 1977.
An Evening with Quentin Crisp (one–man show; produced New York, 1978).
Chog: A Gothic Tale, illustrations by Gahan Wilson. New York, Methuen, 1979.
With Donald Carroll, *Doing It with Style.* New York, F. Watts, 1981.
With John Hofsess, *Manners from Heaven: A Divine Guide to Good Behavior.* New York, Harper, 1984.
The Wit and Wisdom of Quentin Crisp, edited by Guy Kettelhack. New York, Harper, 1984.
How to Go to the Movies (film criticism). New York, St. Martin's Press, 1988; London, Hamilton, 1990.
Quentin Crisp's Book of Quotations: 1000 Observations on Life and Love by, for, and about Gay Men and Women, edited by Amy Appleby. New York, Macmillan, 1989.

Recordings: *An Evening with Quentin Crisp,* DRG, 1979.

*

Adaptations: *The Naked Civil Servant* was adapted as a television play, 1975.

Interviews: "Crisply Quentin: The Naked Civil Servant Turns Survivor–Circuit Celebrity" by Jim Bigwood, in *Advocate,* 8 March 1979, 33–35; "Crisp Thoughts on the Perils of Gay Celebrity," in *Advocate,* 1 October 1985, 8–9.

*   *   *

The phenomenon known as Quentin Crisp was born Dennis Pratt in Sutton, Surrey in 1908. Following a fairly conventional childhood for the time and education at a public school, he embarked upon a life of being, as he frankly states in the opening pages of *The Naked Civil Servant,* "not merely a self–confessed homosexual but a self–evident one." This entailed a move to London in the late 1920s and a highly varied series of occupations ranging from commercial artist to modelling and writing. Beginning with the 1938 work *Color in Display,* his literary creation has ranged from articles for the travel section of the *New York Times* to film commentary for *Christopher Street* and observations on society and manners for the *Advocate.* The three works for which he is best known as a gay writer are his two volumes of autobiography, *The Naked Civil Servant* and *How To Become a Virgin,* published in 1968 and 1981 respectively, and the 1989 compilation *Quentin Crisp's Book of Quotations.*

The Naked Civil Servant was, at the time of its initial publication in London, virtually the only such work by a homosexual who was open about his sexual identity. Covering his (often violent) experiences with the working class population of London from 1926 until the late 1960s, it presents a virtually unparalleled account of the social atmosphere of Depression–era England, the Blitz and World War II years, and post–war recovery, from the perspective of a deliberately marginalized individual. Of particular interest to the student of gay and lesbian history are the descriptions of attitudes and fashions of speech and behavior among some homosexuals over the four decades. The title of *The Naked Civil Servant* is a reference to Crisp's periodic work as an artist's model. The work established the author's reputation as a wit and humorist with a clear sense of the absurd and a sharp eye for manners and aesthetics, and was adapted as a play for television in December of 1975. The book's 1981 sequel, *How to Become A Virgin,* covers the period in the author's life when his pen name was legally adopted and he immigrated to the United States. Crisp was, however, severely criticized by the London homosexual newspaper *Gay News* for representing an extremely effeminate and stereotyped image of gay men.

Following his relocation to New York City in 1977, Crisp developed his one–man show from the London pub theaters into the performance piece, *An Evening with Quentin Crisp,* which opened at Players Theatre in 1978. While the piece is reminiscent of *Tru,* a work on the life of author Truman Capote, and the dramatization of Mark Twain's writings by actor Hal Holbrook, in this case the author himself is on stage to play out the aesthetic quality initiated in *The Naked Civil Servant* and to answer questions.

Quentin Crisp's Book of Quotations: 1000 Observations on Life and Love by, for, and about Gay Men and Women) presents selections from an assemblage of publications ranging from the homoerotic poetry of the ancient world to the more recent poems of Walt Whitman and Allen Ginsberg to the California Penal Code. Its intent is to trace the changing attitudes toward and social acceptance of homosexuality—among both heterosexuals and homosexuals—as reflected in print over the centuries. Offering his own view of the gay community's current relationship with mainstream society, Crisp notes in the preface, "If the gay community ever wished to enter the real world, it no longer does."

—*Robert B. Marks Ridinger*

————

CROWE, F. J. *See* **JOHNSTON, Jill.**

CROWLEY, Aleister (Edward Alexander Crowley). British occultist, poet, and novelist. Also wrote as Frater Perdurabo; Count Vladimir Svareff; George Archibald Bishop; St. E. A. of M. and S.; A Gentleman of the University of Cambridge; Abhavananda; H. D. Carr; Master Therion; Rev. C. Verey. Born in Leamington, Warwickshire, 12 October 1875. Educated at Malvern and Tonbridge schools; Trinity College, Cambridge. Reported to have been a German agent in the United States during World War I. Married Rose Kelly in 1903; companion of poet Victor Neuburg. Founder and chief administrator, Argentinum Astrum (also known as the Silver Star or A.A.), 1908–47; founder and chief administrator, Abbey of Thelema, Cefalu, Sicily, 1920–29. Affiliated with Hermetic Order of the Golden Dawn (member of inner circle of the Red Rose and Golden Cross until 1900), Ordo Templi Orientis (head of the British branch). *Died in Hastings, Sussex, 1 December 1947.*

WRITINGS

Poetry

Aceldama, a Place to Bury Strangers In, 1898.
Jephthah, 1898.
Jezebel (as Count Vladimir Svareff), 1898.
The Mother's Tragedy, 1898.
Songs of the Spirits, 1898.
The Tale of Archais, 1898.
White Stains. Privately printed, 1898.
The Soul of Osiris, 1901.
Alice: An Adultery, 1903.
The Argonauts, 1904.
Snowdrops from a Curate's Garden, 1881 A.D. Privately printed, 1904.
The Sword of Song, 1904.
Rosa Mundi, 1905.
Gargoyles, 1906.
Clouds without Water. London, privately printed, 1909.
Bagh–i Mu'attar (also known as *The Scented Garden of Abdullah the Satirist of Shiraz*). London, privately printed, 1910.

Prose

Knox Om Pax (essays). Limited edition, 1907; as *Knox Om Pax: Essays in Light,* introduction by Martin P. Starr, Chicago, Teitan Press, 1990.
The World's Greatest Tragedy. [Paris], 1910.

Occult Treatises

The Book of Lies (as Frater Perdurabo). [London], 1913.
Magick in Theory and Practice, 1929.
The Book of the Law, 1938.
The City of God: A Rhapsody. London, Ordo Templi Orientis, 1943.
The Book of Thoth (as Master Therion), 1944.
Magick without Tears, edited by Israel Regardie. St. Paul, Minnesota, Llewellyn, 1973; with Marcelo Motta as *Magick without Tears: Unexpurgated, Commented (Being the Oriflamme, Volume VI, Numbers 3–4),* Nashville, Tennessee, Society Ordo Templi Orientis International, c. 1983.
Magical and Philosophical Commentaries of The Book of the Law,

edited and annotated by John Symonds and Kenneth Grant. Montréal, 93 Publishing, 1974.

The Law Is for All: An Extended Commentary on The Book of the Law, edited and introduced by Israel Regardie. St. Paul, Minnesota, Llewellyn, 1975; second edition, Phoenix, Arizona, Falcon Press, 1983.

Magick and Mysticism: Being Book Four Commented, Part II (Being the Oriflamme, Volume VI, Number 2). Nashville, Tennessee, Society Ordo Templi Orientis International, c. 1982.

Translator

And editor, *The Book of the Goetia of Solomon the King: Translated into the English Tongue by a Dead Hand and Adorned with Divers Other Matters Germane Delightful to the Wise.* Inverness, Scotland, Society for the Propagation of Religious Truth, 1904.

The Key of the Mysteries. London, Rider, 1969.

Collections

The Works of Aleister Crowley (three volumes). Foyers, Scotland, Society for the Propagation of Religious Truth, 1905–07.

The Vision and the Voice, introduction and footnotes by Israel Regardie. Dallas, Texas, Sangreal Foundation, 1952.

The Gospel According to St. Bernard Shaw. Limited edition, 1953; as *Crowley on Christ,* edited and introduced by Francis King, London, Daniel, 1974.

The Confessions of Aleister Crowley: An Autohagiography, edited by John Symonds and Kenneth Grant. New York, Hill & Wang, c. 1969; London, Routledge & Kegan Paul, 1979.

The Magical Record of the Beast 666: The Diaries of Aleister Crowley, 1914–1920, edited by John Symonds and Kenneth Grant. London, Duckworth, 1972.

Gems from the Equinox: Instructions by Aleister Crowley for His Own Magical Order, edited by Israel Regardie. St. Paul, Minnesota, Llewellyn, 1974.

The Complete Astrological Writings, edited with annotations by John Symonds and Kenneth Grant. London, Duckworth, 1974.

Aleister Crowley's Astrology: With a Study of Neptune and Uranus: Liber DXXXVI, edited and introduced by Stephen Skinner. New Jersey, Spearman, 1974.

The Qabalah of Aleister Crowley. New York, Samuel Weiser, 1974; as *777, and Other Qabalistic Writings of Aleister Crowley: Including Gematria & Sepher Sephiroth,* edited and introduced by Israel Regardie. York Beach, Maine, Samuel Weiser, 1982.

The Holy Books of Thelema. York Beach, Maine, Samuel Weiser, 1983.

Eight Lectures on Yoga, introduction by Israel Regardie. Phoenix, Arizona, Falcon Press, 1985.

Aleister Crowley: Selected Poems, selected and introduced by Martin Booth. London, Crucible, 1986.

Golden Twigs, edited and introduced by Martin P. Starr. Chicago, Teitan Press, 1988.

Portable Darkness: An Aleister Crowley Reader, edited with commentary by Scott Michaelsen. New York, Harmony Books, c. 1989.

Amrita: Essays in Magical Rejuvenation, edited by Martin P. Starr. Kings Beach, California, Thelema Publications, 1990.

Other

The Rites of Eleusis (drama), 1910.

The Diary of a Drug Fiend (fictional biography). London, 1922; New York, Dutton, 1923.

Moonchild (novel), 1929.

The Stratagem, and Other Stories (short stories), 1929.

*

Biography: *The Great Beast: The Life and Magick of Aleister Crowley* by John Symonds, London, Rider, 1915; *The Eye in the Triangle: An Interpretation of Aleister Crowley* by Israel Regardie, St. Paul, Minnesota, Llewellyn, 1970; *The Legend of Aleister Crowley: Being a Study of the Documentary Evidence Relating to a Campaign of Personal Vilification Unparalleled in Literary History* by Percy Reginald Stephensen and Israel Regardie, Phoenix, Arizona, Falcon Press, third edition, 1983; *Aleister Crowley: A Memoir of 666* by Alan Burnett–Rae, edited by Victor Hall, London, Vision Press, 1971; *The Heart of the Master* by Khaled Khan, Montréal, 93 Publishing, 1973; *Aleister Crowley and the Hidden God* by Kenneth Grant, London, Muller, 1973; *The Magical World of Aleister Crowley* by Francis King, New York, Coward, 1978; *The Magician of the Golden Dawn: The Story of Aleister Crowley* by Susan Roberts, Chicago, Contemporary Books, c. 1978; *Aleister Crowley: The Nature of the Beast* by Colin Wilson, San Bernardino, California, Borgo Press, c. 1987; *The Aleister Crowley Scrapbook* by Sandy Robertson, York Beach, Maine, Samuel Weiser, 1988; *The Legacy of the Beast: The Life, Work, and Influence of Aleister Crowley* by Gerald Suster, York Beach, Maine, Samuel Weiser, 1989.

Bibliography: *A Crowley Cross–Index* by Will Parfitt and A. Drylie, Bath, Somersetshire, ZRO, 1976.

Critical Sources: *The Star in the West: A Critical Essay Upon the Works of Aleister Crowley* by John Frederick Charles Fuller, London and New York, Walter Scott, 1907; *Roll Away the Stone: An Introduction to Aleister Crowley's Essays on the Psychology of Hashish* by Israel Regardie, St. Paul, Minnesota, Llewellyn, 1968; "Carta de Raul Leal a João Gaspar Simões a propósito de *Vida e Obra de Fernando Pessoa* e de Aleister Crowley," in *Persona: Publicação do centro de estudos pessoanos,* August 1982, 54–57; "Aleister Crowley et l'androgyne: Imaginaire décadent et magia sexualis" by Frédéric Monneyron, in *Cahiers victoriens & édouardiens,* April 1991, 63–71.

*   *   *

Beneath the rational surface of modern society there flourishes a subterranean world of occult belief and practice: astrology, clairvoyance, divination, thaumaturgy, black magic and similar doings rejected by the scientific mind which denies their efficacity. Androgyny has been, if not a prerequisite, at least a positive attribute in that milieu, in a straight line that runs from the shaman of primitive cultures to the trance medium of today. Aleister Crowley plunged headlong into that world, acquired international notoriety for the diabolic wickedness that he openly advertised, and has retained a reputation as a foremost practitioner of sexual heterodoxy.

Crowley's initiation into homosexuality came in adolescence from a clergyman. During his last year at Trinity College, Cambridge, he met Herbert Pollitt, who called himself Diane de Rougy after the celebrated courtesan and actress of that day, Liane de Pougy, and performed as a female impersonator on the stage. Crowley admitted that "the relation between us was that ideal intimacy which the Greeks considered the greatest glory of manhood and the most precious prize of life." Pollitt was undoubtedly the source of some of the homoerotic poems in *The Scented Garden of Abdullah the Satirist of Shiraz*, also entitled *Bagh–i–Mu'attar*, published privately in 1910.

Crowley's interest in the occult waxed enormously through his participation from 1898 to 1900 in the Order of the Golden Dawn, an offshoot of Theosophy. The specific role of homosexuality in his life can be appreciated only if one grasps the relationship of sexuality to magic. Some occultists adhere to the belief that the deployment of sexual energy can be used for the enhancement and evolution of consciousness. The occult tradition in this domain appeals to sundry pagan cults, to the Knights Templar, the Rosicrucians, the Illuminati, the Freemasons and others. Underlying the sexual magic is the assumption that at the moment of climax, duality or objectivity ceases, the opposition of male and female is abolished, and the vacuum thus formed in the magician's consciousness magnetically attracts the desired object of the performance. Crowley was instructed in this lore in 1912 by a German, Theodor Reuss, an adept of the world of fringe Masonry and an agent of the German secret service, who enlightened him as to the vital importance of sexual magic and initiated him into the highest degrees of the Ordo Templi Orientis (Order of the Templars of the East) and made him "Supreme and Holy King" of the English–speaking section he was supposed to found.

Crowley called each sexual act "a magical affirmation," a means of expressing his hidden nature, of discovering his true will, and of influencing the course of events in the outside world—an act of goetic magic, which is to say magic performed by invoking and employing a spirit. He performed such rites with both sexes, but the homosexual mode is best recorded in a typescript entitled *The Paris Working*, compiled in the French capital during the first six weeks of 1914. It records a series of invocations of Mercury (more often called by his Greek name Hermes in the text) and of Jupiter for the usual purpose of obtaining wisdom from the one god and priestly power from the other; the sexual rite performed by the two magicians was expected to be far more powerful, and the results far more practical: gold and creative inspiration. The practices were ascribed to the Oriental Templars, who in Crowley's belief had indeed committed the sacrilege for which they had been tortured and executed in the fourteenth century. He scorned and satirized in a book of verse, *White Stains*, the naïveté of a Krafft–Ebing who could find in such actions only the expression of a psychopathic personality tainted with hereditary degeneracy.

Crowley's contribution to the science and art of sexual magic lay in dedicated and persistent experimentation, both heterosexual and homosexual, on the basis of which he wrote manuals of technique for expanding and refining human intelligence and consciousness. In his time he revealed these techniques only to high grade initiates, but in due course they were written down and published in such works as *De Arte Magica*, a commentary on his *Liber Agape*, and a major appendix to *Secret Rituals of the OTO*. However, in all of his extensive corpus of esoteric writing there is little that does not possess a sexual allusion or overtone.

As poet and author of treatises on magic, Crowley occupies a unique place in the history of homoerotic literature in the twentieth century. He negated the Judeo–Christian tradition by inverting its tenets: reviving sodomy with members of the same sex as an instrument of pagan sexual magic, the very reason for which it was condemned and forbidden by both religions. His public defiance of convention earned him, at the height of his fame, the title of "the wickedest man in the world," although by the 1970s it would have been devaluated to just another flamboyant "gay lifestyle." In sharp contrast, the scientific view of the world that rejects the magical and supernatural has stripped the acts themselves of their demonic aura and the taboo of its validity; it has consigned such beliefs to a long superseded, archaic stage of human consciousness.

—*Warren Johansson*

CROWLEY, Edward Alexander. *See* **CROWLEY, Aleister.**

CROWLEY, Mart. American playwright and author of screenplays. Born in Vicksburg, Mississippi, 21 August 1935. Educated at University of California, Los Angeles; Catholic University of America, Washington, D.C., B.A. 1957. Production assistant on various movies filmed in New York City, 1957–59; assistant to Elia Kazan, Newtown Productions, New York City, 1959–60; secretary to actress Natalie Wood, 1961–62; producer of film adaptation of *The Boys in The Band*, 1970; producer of television series *Hart to Hart*, Los Angeles, 1979–83; writer of television movies.

WRITINGS

Plays

The Boys in the Band (produced Off–Broadway, 1968; London, 1969). New York, Farrar, Straus, 1968; London, Weidenfeld and Sons, 1969.
Remote Asylum (produced Los Angeles, 1970).
A Breeze from the Gulf (produced Off–Broadway, 1973; London, 1992). New York, Farrar, Straus, 1974.
The Spirit of It All (produced Williamstown, Massachusetts, 1984).
For Reason That Remain Unclear (produced Washington, D.C., 1993).

Screenplays

Cassandra at the Wedding (adaptation; unproduced), Twentieth Century–Fox, 1963.

And producer, *The Boys in the Band,* National General, 1970.
Jane (adaptation; unproduced), Columbia Pictures, 1975.
Tough Customers (unproduced), Warner Brothers, 1977.
Seasons Greetings (unproduced), Twentieth Century–Fox, 1978.
Dance A Little Closer (adaptation of *The Spirit of It All;* unproduced), Warner Brothers, 1990.

Television Plays

There Must Be A Pony (movie; adaptation of a novel by James Kirkwood), Columbia Pictures Television, 1986.
Bluegrass (miniseries; adaptation of a novel), ABC–TV, 1988.
People Like Us (miniseries; adaptation of a novel), NBC–TV, 1989.
Remember (miniseries; adaptation of a novel), CBS–TV, 1993.

*

Adaptations: *The Boys in the Band* (sound recording), A & M, 1969.

Critical Sources: Review by Clive Barnes, in *New York Times,* 15 April 1968, 36; "Theater" by Martin Duberman, in *Partisan Review,* summer 1968, 418; "How Anguished Are Homosexuals" by Donn Teal, in *New York Times,* 1 June 1969, 23; *The Season: A Candid Look at Broadway* by James Goldman, New York, Harcourt, 1969; "Mart Crowley" by Stuart W. Little and Arthur Cantor, in *The Playmakers,* New York, Dutton, 1971, 287; *Like a Brother, Like a Lover: Male Homosexuality in the American Novel and Theater from Melville to James Baldwin* by Georges–Michel Sarotte, translated by Richard Miller, Garden City, New York, Doubleday, 1978; *5001 Nights at the Movies* by Pauline Kael, New York, Holt, 1982; *Culture Clash: The Making of Gay Sensibility* by Michael Bronski, Boston, South End Press, 1984; *We Can Always Call Them Bulgarians* by Kaier Curtin, Boston, Alyson Publications, 1987; *The Celluloid Closet* by Vito Russo, revised edition, New York, Harper, 1987; "The Boys in the Band Come Back: Self–Hatred or Proud History?" by Wendell Rickets, in *Outlook,* summer 1990, 62–67; *Not in Front of the Audience: Homosexuality on Stage* by Nicholas de Jongh, New York, Routledge, 1992; *Acting Gay: Male Homosexuality in Modern Drama* by John M. Clum, New York, Columbia University Press, 1992; "What's So Bad about *The Boys in The Band?*" by William Spencer, in *Guys,* August 1993, 92–100.

*   *   *

Mart Crowley was born in Vicksburg, Mississippi in 1935. He was educated at Catholic University in Washington, D.C., where he received a B.A. in 1957. Crowley then worked on films in New York City and became a production assistant for Elia Kazan in 1959. Relocating to California, he worked as Natalie Wood's secretary for two years beginning in 1961. He later sold a screenplay to Twentieth Century–Fox and worked in various capacities in the television production industry. *The Boys in the Band,* his first play, was produced Off–Broadway by Theater Four in 1968, and it was an instant critical and popular hit.

The Boys in the Band shook up the theater world. Not only did Crowley's play exhibit wit, energy, and verve, but it was one of the early stage productions to authentically present the everyday lives of gay men. These were people who clearly had relationships, sexual and otherwise, with one another; they were gay men who were being defined within and by their own world rather than as intruders in the world of heterosexuality.

Structurally, *The Boys in The Band* is a conventional, well–constructed drama in which a number of characters inhabit a single set talking with one another. The occasion is a birthday party given by Michael at his Upper East Side apartment for his friend Harold. Various guests show up—announced and unannounced—and after drinking and party games (similar to those in Edward Albee's *Whose Afraid of Virginia Woolf?*), psychological and emotional truths are exposed.

In *5001 Nights at the Movies* Pauline Kael compared Crowley's play to the "gathering of bitchy ladies in *The Women* [a play by Clare Booth], but with a '40s–movie bomber–crew cast: A Catholic, a Jew, a Negro, a hustler, one who is butch, one who is nelly, and so on." But for all of its conventionality, *The Boys In The Band* is a solid, effective piece of writing. Crowley took a handful of gay stereotypes, turned them into human beings and supplemented them with an array of non–stereotyped gay characters. He created a world in which an obvious gay presence was visible but clearly intended it to be viewed in a broader context. The play was a hit—it ran for over a thousand performances—but it prompted differing reactions from the mainstream media than it did from gay reviewers.

Many of New York's major critics liked the show because they felt it told the truth about gay male life: all homosexuals were unhappy, self–hating, and self–destructive. Clive Barns peppered his *New York Times* review with words like "fairy–queens," "queers," and "screamingly fag," and dwelt upon how unhappy all of the characters were. He also proclaimed that Crowley's play "is the frankest treatment of homosexuality I have ever seen on the stage." He added that "the special self–dramatization and frightening self–pity—true I suppose of all minorities, but I think especially true of homosexuals—is all the same laid on too thick sometimes." Gay critics (especially after the Stonewall Riots in June of 1969, which occurred while the play was still running) hated the play because they felt that it perpetuated stereotypes regarding male homosexuals, suggesting that they were maladjusted and dissatisfied with their sexual identity. Gay theater historian Kaier Curtin wrote in *We Can Always Call them Bulgarians* that "even by many who initially found it amusing and entertaining, Crowley's dramatic guilt–trip was eventually damned as another negative, stereotypical portrait of the gay community."

Both of these views—the positive notices from the mainstream media and the negative response from gay critics—misinterpret the play. Of the eight characters in *The Boys in the Band,* only two are really unhappy—Michael and Harold, the host of the party and its guest of honor. The rest of the characters have fairly routine human and relationship problems, but are by no means drastically unhappy, nor do they find being gay problematic. At the end of the play, Harold—noted for his truthful if hurtful *bon mots*—tells Michael, "You are a sad and pathetic man. You're a homosexual and you don't want to be. But there is nothing you can do to change it." Crowley's point is that it is not homosexuality itself that causes emotional problems, but rather the inability to accept one's sexuality.

After the success of *The Boys in the Band,* Crowley wrote *Remote Asylum,* a play that again featured the character Michael from

The Boys in the Band. The play did poorly at its 1970 opening in Los Angeles. In 1973 *A Breeze From the Gulf*—again featuring Michael—was moderately well–received Off–Broadway but went unproduced for a number of years before being staged in London in 1992. Crowley has continued to work in television, including a four–season stint as producer of *Hart to Hart.* He has also written two other stage plays, *The Spirit of It All* and *For Reasons That Remain Unclear.*

—*Michael Bronski*

———

CRUIKSHANK, Margaret. American educator, editor, and author of nonfiction. Born in Duluth, Minnesota, 1940. Educated at Benedictine schools; San Francisco State University, M.A.; Loyola University, New Orleans, Louisiana, Ph.D. Affiliate scholar, Center for Research on Women, Stanford University, Palo Alto, California, 1981–88; faculty member, City College of San Francisco, 1981—. Address: City College of San Francisco, Ocean and Phelan Avenues, San Francisco, California 94112, U.S.A.

WRITINGS

Nonfiction

The Gay and Lesbian Liberation Movement. New York, Routledge, 1992.

Editor

The Lesbian Path. Originally published, 1980; revised and enlarged, San Francisco, Grey Fox Press, 1985.
Lesbian Studies: Present and Future. Old Westbury, New York, Feminist Press, 1982.
New Lesbian Writing: An Anthology (poetry and prose). San Francisco, Grey Fox Press, 1984.
Fierce with Reality.

Other

Thomas Babington Macaulay (biography/literary criticism). Boston, Twayne Publishers, 1978.
"Lesbians in the Academic World," in *Our Right to Love: A Lesbian Resource Book,* edited by Ginny Vida. Englewood Cliffs, New Jersey, Prentice–Hall, 1978.
"Cuban Lesbians Arrive in Seattle," in *Out and About,* January 1981.
"Lesbian Studies: Some Preliminary Notes," in *Radical Teacher,* spring 1981.
"Notes on Recent Lesbian Autobiographical Writing," in *Journal of Homosexuality,* fall 1982.

Margaret Cruikshank comments: "I want my books to change lives. They could not have been conceived or produced without two developments in the 1970s: the coming out of many thousands of gay people and the great impact of women's liberation. While attacking the intertwined social evils of sexism, homophobia, and ageism, I stand apart from ideologies and political agendas. I identify both with the lesbians and gay men who thrive as outsiders/outcasts and with those who work within mainstream institutions."

*   *   *

Margaret Cruikshank is the author and editor of a number of publications that both identify issues surrounding the study of homosexuality in the academic/classroom setting and define the lesbian as a visible and unique presence within the women's movement. Among her edited works are three well–received anthologies: *The Lesbian Path,* an early collection of autobiographical profiles of 38 lesbians and their experiences being lesbian, *Lesbian Studies: Present & Future,* a resource guide for educators, and *New Lesbian Writing: An Anthology,* a work consisting of poems and short fiction by lesbian authors.

In *The Lesbian Path,* both well known and emerging lesbian writers discuss their early struggles, conflicts and discoveries. The collection covers many topics, including the experiences of young lesbians, "coming out" stories, the particular problems and conflicts of religion and lesbianism, growing up, careers, and coming out and raising children. *The Lesbian Path* was revised in 1985, with the new revision containing both original essays from the earlier edition plus new selections from well–known authors such as Jane Rule, Judy Grahn and May Sarton.

Lesbian Studies: Present & Future is designed for researchers and educators who wish to incorporate the study of the lesbian in their research and/or classroom. The collection contains information about how lesbians perceive themselves in the academic world, the teaching of lesbian fiction and poetry, classroom psychology, and topics for further research, including lesbian biography, lesbian history, older lesbians, women in prison and lesbians in textbooks. The work also contains several syllabi for teaching a course on lesbianism as well as a lengthy bibliography.

Writers such as Marilyn Hacker, Jane Rule and Elsa Gidlow are included in *New Lesbian Writing: An Anthology,* a collection of fiction and nonfiction. This is a mature collection of lesbian writings that profiles the work of writers not yet previously published or well known to American audiences. The entries are international in scope and the collection goes far in promoting the diversity of spirit in the lesbian nation.

In her latest work, *The Gay and Lesbian Liberation Movement,* Cruikshank traces the political and social history of the emerging gay and lesbian identity in society. Although it covers a broad spectrum of ideas, the text is largely intended to clarify past and present issues surrounding the quest for equality and freedom of choice. Cruikshank sees women as central to the feminist movement, the precursor to the gay liberation movement. Chapters in *The Gay and Lesbian Liberation Movement* include "Gay and Lesbian Liberation as a Sexual Freedom Movement," "Gay and Lesbian Liberation as a Political Movement," "Gay Culture and Community," and "Lesbian Feminism."

—*Jane Jurgens*

CURZON, Daniel. American educator, novelist, and short story writer. Born Daniel Russell Brown in Litchfield, Illinois, 19 March 1938. Educated at University of Detroit, Ph.B. 1960; Kent State University, Kent, Ohio, M.A. 1961; Wayne State University, Detroit, Ph.D. 1969. Companion of John Gettys. One son, Zachary. Instructor in English, University of Detroit, 1962–65; instructor in English, Wayne State University, 1965–69; lecturer in English, University of Maryland, London division, 1970–72, Far East Division, 1972–74; lecturer in English, California State University, Fresno, 1974–76; instructor, City College San Francisco, 1980—. Author of scholarly articles as Daniel Brown; contributor of short stories to magazines. **Recipient:** Bay Area Theater Critics Circle nomination for best script for *Sex Show,* 1977; University of Calgary Best of Series Award for *Last Call,* 1982. Agent: Jeffrey Simmons, 10 Lowndes Square, London SW1 X9HA, England, U.K. Address: 416 Dorado Terrace, San Francisco, California 94112, U.S.A.

WRITINGS

Novels

Something You Do in the Dark. New York, Putnam, 1971; revised, Port Washington, New York, Ashley Books, 1979.
The Misadventures of Tim McPick. Los Angeles, John Parke Custis Press, 1975.
Among the Carnivores. Port Washington, New York, Ashley Books, 1978.
From Violent Men. San Francisco, IGNA Books, 1983.
The World Can Break Your Heart. Stamford, Connecticut, Knights Press, 1984.
Curzon in Love. Stamford, Connecticut, Knights Press, 1988.
Superfag (unpublished).
I, the Bard (unpublished).
Only the Good Parts (unpublished).
Not Sold in Stores; or, Skulduggery (unpublished).

Short Stories

The Revolt of the Perverts. San Francisco, Leland Mellott Books, 1978.
"Two Bartenders, a Butcher, and Me," in *Aphrodisiac: Fiction from Christopher Street.* New York, Coward–McCann, 1980; Chatto & Windus, 1984.
"Virility," in *On the Line: New Gay Fiction,* edited by Ian Young. Trumansburg, New York, Crossing Press, 1981.
Human Warmth, and Other Stories. San Francisco, Grey Fox Press, 1981.
"Victor" and "Two Bartenders, a Butcher, and Me," in *Mae West Is Dead: Recent Lesbian and Gay Fiction,* edited by Adam Mars–Jones. London, Faber, 1983.
Sacred Cows (unpublished).

Plays

Sex Show: Comedy Madness (15 satirical skits; produced San Francisco, 1977).
Desert Isle. Published in *GPU News,* August 1977.
Sex Education (skit from *Sex Show*), published in *Arts and Letters,* December 1977.

Your Town (one–act satire; produced San Francisco, 1978).
Beneath the Surface (satire; produced San Francisco, 1979).
Comeback (musical drama; staged reading, Berkeley, California, 1980), music by Dan Turner.
Last Call (produced San Francisco, 1980; Calgary, 1982). Published in *Alternate,* July 1981.
Beer and Rhubarb Pie (one–act version produced San Francisco, 1981; staged reading of three–act version, New York, 1990). Published in *Alternate,* February 1981.
Don't Rub Me the Wrong Way (comedy; staged reading, New York, 1981).
The Birthday Girl (produced San Francisco, 1982).
Margaret and Ernie vs. the World (produced San Francisco, 1982).
Demons (staged reading, San Francisco, 1983).
Rev. What's His Name (skit in *The AIDS Show;* produced San Francisco, 1984). Published in *West Coast Plays,* fall 1985.
Cinderella II: Happily Ever After (musical comedy; produced San Francisco, 1984), music by Dan Turner.
The Murder of Gonzago (comedy; produced San Francisco, 1986).
No Mince Pies (musical comedy; staged reading San Francisco, 1987), music by Dan Turner.
My Unknown Son (produced New York, 1987; Off–Broadway, 1988).
Animal Farm (one–act satire based on novel by George Orwell; produced San Francisco, 1983).
One Man's Opinion (one–act; produced Seattle, 1984).
Immortality (one–act; produced San Francisco, 1986).
Contributor of two short plays, *Homosexual Acts* (produced Off–Broadway, 1991).
The New Zoo Story (one–act; produced San Francisco, 1993).
The Third Part of Henry IV (sequel to William Shakespeare's *Henry IV*).
The Blasphemer: The Ayatollah's Edict (docu–drama based on Salman Rushdie affair).
When Bertha Was a Pretty Name (comedy).
Stuck (comedy).
Pixies in Peril (parody of J. R. R. Tolkien's *The Hobbit*).
Avatars (comedy).
The Birthday Boy (gay version of *The Birthday Girl*).
Half to Death (comic thriller).
Sour Grapes (one–act companion piece to *The Murder of Gonzago*).

Other

"The Problems of Writing Serious Gay Literature," in *Margins,* spring, 1975.
"Do We Need a Wholesome Gay Literature?," in *Blueboy,* January 1978.
The Joyful Blue Book of Gracious Gay Etiquette (satire). San Francisco, IGNA Books, 1982.
"Gay Literature after 'City of Night'" (interview), in *Los Angeles Times Book Review,* 2 October 1988.
Dropping Names: The Delicious, Dishy Memoirs of Daniel Curzon. Published in *James White Review,* 1993.

*

Manuscript Collections: Gay and Lesbian Archives of San Francisco Public Library.

Biography: "Daniel Curzon" by John Gettys, in *Contemporary Gay American Novelists,* edited by Emmanuel S. Nelson, Westport, Connecticut, Greenwood Press, 1992.

Interviews: "From Violent Men: An Interview with Novelist Daniel Curzon" by David John Lamble, in *California Voice* (San Francisco), 3 June 1983, 2–3, 13; "Gay Literature After 'City of Night'" by Daniel Curzon, in *Los Angeles Times* (Los Angeles), 2 October 1988, 15; unpublished interview with Daniel Curzon by Tom W. Kelly, May 1993.

Critical Sources: *Like a Brother, Like a Lover: Male Homosexuality in the American Novel and Theatre from Herman Melville to James Baldwin* by Georges–Michel Sarotte, Garden City, New York, Anchor Press/Doubleday, 1978; *The Gay Novel in America* by James Levin, New York, Garland, 1991.

Daniel Curzon comments: "My epitaph, I hope, will read: 'He told the truth and trusted people enough to take it. He also wrote lots of comedy. This gets ignored.'"

*   *   *

As a San Francisco resident who arrived in 1976, during the heyday of gay liberation, Daniel Curzon has published novels focussing on the homosexual male experience and the relationship between gays and non–gays. His trademark is a grim world view that denies the simplicity and dishonesty of romantic, sentimental, and happy plots and resolutions. Rather, he opts for harsh realism, taking an intensely honest, critical look at gays, non–gays, homophobia, and oppressive social structures. Curzon's published work primarily focuses on gay male characters fighting for acceptance, pride, and respect in a hateful world incapable of understanding them. His books also reflect the powerful need for gay men to have loving relationships as well as the difficulty of achieving this goal. Since 1980 the author and John Gettys have been lovers, and in 1983 Curzon coparented a child with a lesbian couple.

Having written plays since his early childhood in Detroit, Curzon acted and directed with the Players, a theatre group at the University of Detroit, where he received a degree in English in 1960. Since completing his doctoral degree at Wayne State University in 1969, he has supported himself almost exclusively by teaching English. Desperate to escape a mind–numbingly narrow life in Detroit, he accepted a position with the University of Maryland in 1969 and for over three years taught at various U.S. military bases in England, Thailand, Vietnam, Okinawa, and Japan. During this time, his first book, *Something You Do in the Dark,* was published and, to maintain employment, he adopted the pseudonym Daniel Curzon, his actual surname being Brown. In 1974 he accepted an appointment at California State University, Fresno, where he taught, among other courses, a class in gay literature. At this time Curzon founded and published six issues of *Gay Literature,* a magazine devoted to serious writing. In 1976 he settled in San Francisco and taught part–time while running the International Gay News Agency. He currently teaches at City College of San Francisco, where he gained full–time status and tenure in 1988. Despite the demands of teaching and the wildly conflicting critical responses to his work, Curzon continues to write plays and novels about the gay community.

Past and current geographic locations and social circumstances comprise the essential warring elements in his work: harsh plot elements that reflect the harsh, unequivocal demands he makes on all of society, including the gay community itself. His collective work calls for an end to homophobia and total acceptance of homosexual men and women as full–class citizens.

Constantly approaching literature through different modes of storytelling, Curzon has worked to re–design literary genres around gay themes. Genres used in his published novels include the angry–young–man drama, surreal comedy, and satire. Ironically, despite the pervasively dark outlook of his novels, one of his best–selling works to date is *The Joyful Blue Book of Gracious Gay Etiquette,* a satire on Victorian books of good manners, which informs about bathhouse manners and pre–AIDS health concerns, among other issues, and makes tongue–planted–angrily–in–cheek references to police and military discrimination against gays. Even in his manically surreal comedy *The Misadventures of Tim McPick,* which features an Everygay's journey through an insane world, Curzon depicts life as a pointless succession of inanities amid singularly–focused manic oddballs and mindless herd beasts. *Curzon in Love,* a novel in three sections, unfolds utilizing naturalism, Cowardesque comedy, and an *Arabian Nights* style of storytelling, respectively.

From Violent Men epitomizes the anger and unrelenting narrative that has garnered Curzon fame and respect while also creating elements of controversy. His storytelling creates an interweaving of plots and plottings as various characters pursue their poorly–planned goals, all with ultimately disastrous results.

Curzon's writing rejects what he considers "glib, socio–babble, C–minus–mind demands that women and certain pre–selected 'minorities' and, increasingly, gays be portrayed as though they have some kind of collective virtue and are excused from the same scrutiny and criticism given to other groups." Nor do these groups have a monopoly on pain suffering, and he feels that "writing that is 'minority–mongering,' 'I'm–more–oppressed–than–thou pamphleteering,' is self–serving and self–defeating." The philosophy underlying his work is that "while one must certainly have the courage to try to change what makes life harder than it needs to be, people in our time ascribe far too many of their sorrows simply to the conveniently provided 'isms'—chiefly racism and sexism, which have gone from being accurate observations to analysis-stopping, new orthodoxies now descending into parodies of themselves as much as Catholicism and Marxism did before them, with only knee-jerk 'liberal' or knee-jerk 'conservative' interpretations expressed." As homosexuals begin to take their place in the social spotlight after the long struggle, Curzon sees the same rigidity, the same parody forming, to be followed by the same loss of faith. All this makes him sigh, for he feels that "human beings should have the insight to realize and the courage to admit that life itself, the human condition itself, for most people most of the time has only small victories and is more commonly a kind of mutating virus which keeps inventing new disappointments and discontents for everyone."

—*Tom W. Kelly*

D

DALY, Mary. American teacher of theology and philosophy, feminist, and essayist. Born in Schenectady, New York, 16 October 1928. Educated at College of St. Rose, B.A. 1950; Catholic University of America, M.A. 1952; St. Mary's College, Notre Dame, Indiana, Ph.D. 1954; University of Fribourg, Switzerland, S.T.D. 1963, Ph.D. 1965. Teacher of philosophy and theology, Cardinal Cushing College, Brookline, Massachusetts, 1954–59; assistant professor, 1966–69, and then associate professor of theology, 1969—, Boston College, Chestnut Hill, Massachusetts. Teacher of theology and philosophy, U.S. Junior Year Abroad programs, University of Fribourg, Switzerland, 1959–66. Member of American Catholic Philosophical Association, American Academy of Religion, American Academy of Political and Social Science, American Association of University Professors, National Organization for Women, Society for the Scientific Study of Religion. Agent: Charlotte Raymond, 23 Waldron Court, Marblehead, Massachusetts 01945, U.S.A. Address: Department of Theology, Carney Hall, Boston College, Chestnut Hill, Massachusetts 02167, U.S.A.

WRITINGS

Nonfiction

Natural Knowledge of God in the Philosophy of Jacques Maritrain. Rome, Catholic Book Agency, 1966.

The Church and the Second Sex. New York, Harper, 1968; revised with new "feminist postchristian" introduction by author, Boston, Beacon Press, 1984; revised with new "archaic afterwords" by author, 1985.

Beyond God the Father: Toward a Philosophy of Women's Liberation. Boston, Beacon Press, 1973; revised, 1985.

Gyn/Ecology: The Metaethics of Radical Feminism. Boston, Beacon Press, 1978.

Pure Lust: Elemental Feminist Philosophy. Boston, Beacon Press, 1984.

Websters' First New Intergalactic Wickedary of the English Language, edited by Jane Caputi. Boston, Beacon Press, 1987.

Women and Poverty. State Mutual Book and Periodical Service, 1989.

Industrial Development and Irish National Identity, 1922–1939. Syracuse, New York, Syracuse University Press, 1992.

Contributor

The New Catholic Day: Catholic Theologians of the Renewal, edited by William Jerry Boney and Lawrence E. Molumby. Atlanta, John Knox, 1968.

Demands for Christian Renewal, edited by William J. Wilson. Maryknoll Publications, 1968.

Sisterhood Is Powerful, edited by Robin Morgan. New York, Random House, 1970.

Voices of the New Feminism, edited by Mary Lou Thompson. Boston, Beacon Press, 1970.

*

Interviews: "Five Boston–Area Feminists Interviewed," in *Boston Globe,* 13 January 1985, BGM 12.

Critical Sources: "That Women Be Themselves" by Adrienne Rich, in *New York Times Book Review,* 11 February 1979, 10; "The Croning of a Woman" by Rita Mae Brown, in *Washington Post Book World,* 11 February 1979, F3; "Taking Off on a Daly Journey" by Erica Smith, in *Herizons,* June 1984, 23–24; review of *Pure Lust* by Demaris Wehr, in *New York Times Book Review,* 22 July 1984, 14; "Famous Lust Words" by Marilyn Frye, in *Women's Review of Books,* August 1984, 3; "Mary Daly's *Pure Lust*" by Eileen Manion, in *Canadian Journal,* fall 1985, 134–137; "Embracing Motherhood: New Feminist Theory" by Heather Jon Maroney, in *Canadian Journal,* winter 1985, 40–64; "On Political Courage, Witches, and History" (excerpt of keynote address to National Women's Political Caucus in Portland, Oregon) by Vermont Governor Madeleine M. Kunin, in *Ms.,* November 1987, 84; "Erratic, Ecstatic, Eccentric" by Julia Penelope, in *Women's Review of Books,* December 1987, 5; "Chasing through the Wickedary" by Debra Ratterman, in *Off Our Backs,* January 1988, 17; "What Snools These Mortals Be" by Coral Lansbury, in *New York Times,* 17 January 1988, Section 7, 9; "BC's Treatment of Feminist–Thinker Daly Protested" by James L. Franklin, in *Boston Globe,* 23 March 1989, 31; "Snools Deny Daly Tenure: Hags Revolt," in *Off Our Backs,* May 1989, 11; "Teacher Fights School Over Feminism and Beliefs" by Peter Steinfels, in *New York Times,* 10 May 1989, A31.

*　*　*

Mary Daly's first book, *The Church and the Second Sex,* published in 1968, placed her among the radical feminist theologians and resulted in her prompt dismissal from a teaching job at Boston College. Student demonstrations for "academic" freedom led to Daly's reinstatement, but the book, which discussed in bitter terms the submissive role of women in the Catholic Church, established Daly once and for all as an enemy of "the prevailing religion of the entire planet": patriarchy. Five years later, in *Beyond God the Father, Toward a Philosophy of Women's Liberation* she leapt into what Erica Smith called in *Herizons* "the post–Christian era" in which Daly "began to understand more clearly the nature of the beast and the name of the demon: patriarchy, the interconnections among the structures of oppression in a patriarchal society and the destructive dynamics which these structures generate in their victims became more and more visible."

In 1978's *Gyn/Ecology: The Metaethics of Radical Feminism,* Daly is concerned not only with those malfunctioning (she uses the term "male–functioning") mythologies of the Christian Church clearly hostile to women, but also with creating (discovering) the female cosmos, a space of self–representation and assertion where words lose their negative connotations. Hags, Crones, Harpies, Furies, and Spinsters are the true women who represent life. On the other side of the barricade, Daly places men, i.e., the enemy. But as Rita Mae Brown notices in her discussion of the book in *Washington Post Book World,* "Daly, in her righteous anger at the total rape of womankind, still does not address the question of why so many women comply in their own 'living–death'." However, *Gyn/Ecology* proposes solutions that will lead to the final triumph of women—and one of the main demands is the recognition of the power of language.

1984's *Pure Lust: Elemental Feminist Philosophy* is an exploration of the depths of language and meaning. Considered by its author "a sisterwork to *Beyond God the Father* and *Gyn/Ecology,*" *Pure Lust* moves through three realms: Archespheres (Discerning our origins), pyrospheres (remaining and reclaiming our passions and virtues), and Metomorphospheres (deep changes that occur when we break through the mazes and mazes of phallocratic double–think.)" *Pure Lust* is an existential journey, something that Daly names "the break through the foreground." It also plays on the double meaning of words and their interchangeability. Thus gynecide (the killing of women) is accompanied by the killing of words. Naturally, the author's task is to find the "right" words for the newly–discovered female cosmos. *Webster's First Intergalactic Wickedary of the English Language,* "conjured by Mary Daly...in Cahoots with Jane Caputi," in 1987, is considered by Julia Penelope in *Women's Review of Books* to be an "erratic, ecstatic, eccentric" piece of writing that deconstructs and reconstructs language in feminist terms. In a world where male language has "messed" with female minds, the acquisition of a new language is mandatory. Daly refuses again to be "at a loss for words"; if such a language does not exist, it is because the hidden layers of English have not been developed. The *Wickedary* offers women a language that can serve them. As Penelope puts it, "the Wickedary is a Sin–thesis." It is, in other words, Daly's theory of the original sin of language revisited.

—*Dayana Stetco*

DAMON, Gene. *See* **GRIER, Barbara G(ene Damon).**

DAVISON, Lawrence H. *See* **LAWRENCE, D(avid) H(erbert Richards).**

D'EMILIO, John. American historian and writer of nonfiction. Born in New York City, 21 September 1948. Educated at Columbia University, B.A. 1970, Ph.D. 1982. Companion of college administrator Jim Oleson since 1983. Associate professor of U.S. history and gay history, University of North Carolina at Greensboro, 1983—. Cochair of board of directors of National Gay and Lesbian Task Force, 1989–91; fellow of Center for Advanced Studies in the Behavioral Sciences, 1990–91. **Recipient:** American Library Association's Gay/Lesbian Book Award, 1984. Address: Department of History, University of North Carolina at Greensboro, Greensboro, North Carolina 27412, U.S.A.

WRITINGS

The Civil Rights Struggle: Leaders in Profile. New York, Facts on File, 1979.
Sexual Politics, Sexual Communities: The Making of a Homosexual Minority in the United States, 1940–1970. Chicago, University of Chicago Press, 1983.
With Estelle Freedman, *Intimate Matters: A History of Sexuality in America.* New York, Harper, 1988.
"Gay Politics and Community in San Francisco Since World War II," in *Hidden from History: Reclaiming the Gay and Lesbian Past,* edited by Martin Bauml Duberman, Martha Vicinus, and George Chauncey, Jr. New York, New American Library, 1989.
Making Trouble: Essays on Gay History, Politics, and the University. London, Routledge, 1992.

*   *   *

Minority communities often define their relationship to the dominant society through cultural components that provide identity and continuity. Memories of the past are especially important, as mainstream histories and media often exclude or trivialize significant people and events out of ignorance or deliberate prejudice. In few cases has this exclusion been as thorough and complete as for gays and lesbians prior to the Stonewall Riots of 1969. One of the themes that quickly emerged in the gay liberation movement discussion groups after the uprising was a need to learn about the past of the American homosexual community. In his various researches and writings, John D'Emilio has contributed to the reclaiming of this hidden history for more than a decade.

Born in New York City, D'Emilio received his undergraduate and graduate education at Columbia University, completing his Ph.D. in 1982. While his formal involvement in analyzing gay and lesbian history began with his doctoral thesis (subsequently published as *Sexual Politics, Sexual Communities: The Making of A Homosexual Minority in the United States, 1940–1970*), his role as a founding member of the Gay Academic Union in 1973 had already brought him to consider questions regarding the viability of writing the histories of sexuality. During the time when D'Emilio was pursuing his research, the first significant compilation of original source documents on the history of homosexuals in the United States was published. Jonathan Katz's *Gay American History: Lesbians and Gay Men in the U.S.A.* established beyond question that a valid historical study of a community whose own members were accustomed to regarding themselves as marginal was indeed possible. It is against this framework of changing social and subcultural perceptions that D'Emilio's work may most profitably be considered.

The study, which became *Sexual Politics, Sexual Communities,* was the first attempt to clearly delineate the social, historical and political antecedents to the gay liberation movement of the early 1970s. Opening with a consideration of the place of homosexuality in American culture and its metamorphosis from solely an expression of sexuality to a fuller indication of individual identity, successive chapters examine the two decades prior to the Stonewall Riots of 1969, the gradual evolution of urban homosexual communities in the aftermath of World War II, attitudes toward homosexuality in the 1950s and the famous purges of suspected gays and lesbians from all branches of the military as well as the State Department. The book also covers the founding, activities and philosophy of the Mattachine Society and the Daughters of Bilitis, and the impact of the social ferment of the 1960s on what had become known as the "homophile" movement, with particular attention given to the revolution in attitudes toward sexuality of any sort. The militant activism of the early 1960s in the eastern United States is examined through a review of the work of the Mattachine Society of Washington, D.C., and New York City and its debt to the civil rights movement. The experience of the San Francisco gay and lesbian community is also posited as a model of the types of changes that were to occur in many American cities. A final section brings the analysis up to the beginnings of the gay liberation movement. The comprehensive treatment and documentation of *Sexual Politics, Sexual Communities* provided the historical framework for all subsequent work in the field of gay history such as Allan Bérubé's *Coming Out Under Fire* and Randy Shilts' *The Mayor of Castro Street.*

Following his appointment to the faculty of history at the University of North Carolina at Greensboro, with a specialization in gay history, D'Emilio continued to expand his interest in sexuality as an element of social development. A collaboration with Estelle Friedman resulted in *Intimate Matters: A History of Sexuality in America* in 1988.

In the 1992 anthology *Making Trouble,* D'Emilio's widely distributed writings on historiography as it relates to the gay community may be assessed as a whole. Topics addressed range from a consideration of the origin and demise of the first attempt at founding a gay liberation movement in the United States in 1924, through the politics of sexuality during the Cold War and the formation of San Francisco's homosexual communities, to the coming of the AIDS pandemic and the creation of the NAMES Project Quilt. Of particular interest are the articles discussing the foundation of gay history as a genuine field of investigation (and its varied receptions by the academic community) and sexual identity as an issue on campus.

—*Robert B. Marks Ridinger*

* * *

DEXTER, John. *See* **BRADLEY, Marion Zimmer.**

DIXON, Melvin. American novelist, poet, translator, and educator. Born in Stamford, Connecticut, 29 May 1950. Educated at Wesleyan University, Middletown, Connecticut, B.A. 1971; Brown University, Providence, Rhode Island, M.A. 1973, Ph.D. 1975. Companion of Richard Horovitz (died). Assistant professor of English, Williams College, Williamstown, Massachusetts, 1976–80; member of the English department of Queens College of the City University of New York, Flushing, 1980–92. Contributing editor to *Callaloo.* **Recipient:** National Endowment for the Arts poetry fellowship, 1984; New York Arts Foundation artist fellowship in fiction, 1988; Nilon Award, 1989. *Died of complications from AIDS, 26 October 1992.*

WRITINGS

Novels

Trouble the Water. New York, Fiction Collective Two/University of Colorado Press, 1989.
Vanishing Rooms. New York, Dutton, 1991.

Poetry

Climbing Montmartre. Broadside Press, 1974.
Change of Territory. Charlottesville, University Press of Virginia, 1983.
The Collected Poetry. Charlottesville, University Press of Virginia, 1991.

Translations

Drumbeats, Masks, and Metaphor: Contemporary Afro–American Theatre. Cambridge, Massachusetts, Harvard University Press, 1983.
The Collected Poems of Léopold Sédar Senghor. Charlottesville, University Press of Virginia, 1991.

Other

Ride Out the Wilderness: Geography and Identity in Afro–American Literature, (criticism). Champaign, University of Illinois Press, 1987.
"Red Leaves," in *Men on Men 2,* edited by George Stambolian. New York, New American Library, 1988.
Contributor, *Brother to Brother,* edited by Essex Hemphill. Alyson Publications, 1991.
"I'll be Somewhere Listening for My Name," in *Sojourner: Black Gay Voices in the Age of AIDS,* edited by B. Michael Hunter. New York, Other Countries Press, 1993.

*

Interviews: With Darryl Grant, in *Washington Blade,* 26 April 1991, 43, 52; with Clarence Bard Cole, in *Christopher Street,* 14:1, 1991, 24–27.

Critical Sources: "Melvin Dixon: Wrestling with Baldwin" by V.

R. Peterson, in *Essence,* August, 1991, 42; *Contemporary Gay American Novelists,* edited by Emmanuel S. Nelson, Westport, Connecticut, Greenwood Press, 1993.

* * *

At the time of his death due to complications from AIDS in 1992, Melvin Dixon was considered one of the most noted gay African American writers in the United States. In less than ten years he had produced two novels, a book of poems, two volumes of translation and a work of literary and cultural criticism. All of the books met with positive critical press and his literary scholarship was highly praised. While his scholarly work is respected—in particular his translations of Léopold Sédar Senghor's poetry and his critical volume *Ride Out the Wilderness: Geography and Identity in Afro–American Literature*—it is his fiction writing that is most innovative.

Most gay male literature since Stonewall has received scant attention from mainstream critics; gay writing by African American men has had to function under the double burden of being ignored by both the mainstream and a wide white gay readership. Although Dixon's *Vanishing Rooms* managed to gain some crossover critical reception and audience with white gay reviewers and readers, it did not receive the attention that other books of its stature have. This is due to Dixon's insistence on focusing on the primacy of African American themes and continually posing difficult questions about race, violence and homophobia.

In *Trouble the Water*, Dixon takes two traditional genres: the return of a Northern African American to the South (a traditional Black narrative theme that Dixon explored in depth in *Ride Out of the Wilderness*) as well as the more extravagant Southern gothic. *Trouble the Water* tells the story of Jordan Henry, who was raised as a young boy by his strong willed grandmother Mother Harriet in Pee Dee, North Carolina. Later in life, Jordan, now a Harvard graduate and professor, returns home with his wife only to be embroiled in a destructive struggle—orchestrated by his grandmother on her deathbed—that is centered around family history.

Trouble the Water draws on several African–American literary traditions—the use of biblical imagery, the idea of home as being a haven of security, and the notion that education represents a form of economic and psychological progress—and then reverses them. The climb to the mountaintop, on which Pee Dee is situated, might have conjured up images of Moses, Noah and the Transfiguration, but in Dixon's world there is no such enlightenment. Although Jordan returns to find his "roots" in Pee Dee, he discovers little emotional or historical comfort there, but rather a past that refuses to let go and move forward. While his advanced "Northern" education has situated him better in the world, it has not, as Booker T. Washington might imply in his writings, proved to be any emotional or physic panacea. History, Dixon seems to be saying, is always a trap unless we face it with unsentimental hearts and minds.

The Southern Gothic themes—most notably used by such white authors as Faulkner, Flannery O'Connor, Lillian Hellman and Tennessee Williams—are used by Dixon in a more straightforward manner. Family secrets, festering hates and deathbed manipulations are all consciously used by the author to explore the capability of the human heart for destruction. Mired in history and tradition, the residents of Pee Dee are trapped because they can see no other alternatives.

The characters in *Vanishing Rooms* are also trapped by history. The novel begin with Metro, the white lover of the African American Jesse, queer–bashed and murdered by a gang of white youths. From this beginning, Dixon has fashioned a series of three overlapping narratives: by Jesse, Ruella, an African American woman who befriends him, and Lonny, the troubled white boy who is part of the murderous gang. These interlocking chapters explicate the murder, detail Metro and Jesse's relationship and describe Jesse's dealing with his grief at his lover's death.

If the plot structure of *Vanishing Rooms* turns on three narratives, its thematic structure revolves around three political ideas: the nature of homophobic violence, the social construct and parameters of male homosexuality, and the eroticization of race. Dixon approaches each of these contested topics and attempts to discover a "hidden" side to them that fuels his character's actions and ideas.

We see in the "Lonny" sections of *Vanishing Rooms* how the young man is both attracted to homosexuality and repulsed by his own feelings. When Metro is attacked and killed by the gang, Lonny undergoes a breakdown as well as a catharsis. Dixon seems to imply that the two prevailing thoughts about homophobia and homophobic violence—the first that it is simply a hatred of "difference," the second that it is a recognition and then an attraction—are both inadequate to describe the phenomenon. Lonny is neither *simply* a "homophobe" or *simply* a "closet case." Dixon's vision is too complex to allow either simplistic analysis to stand.

After Metro is murdered, Jesse finds comfort, as well as a sexual relationship, with Ruella. There is no doubt that Jesse remains homosexually identified throughout the novel and such interludes of heterosexual activity are quite rare in contemporary gay male fiction, even though it may occur in everyday life. Since the theoretical underpinnings of much gay fiction is to establish, in the face of overwhelming homophobia, the validity of homosexuality, non–homosexual behavior—and especially nurturing heterosexual behavior—is quite deviant. *Vanishing Rooms* attempts to broaden the boundaries of gay male fiction by insisting that we acknowledge, in our writings, the possibilities and realities of the actual world.

The relationship of Metro and Jesse forms the center of *Vanishing Rooms* and although both of them attempt to be cognizant of what it means in a racist culture to be involved in an interracial homosexual relationship, at times they are unable to establish themselves as completely separate from their environment. The climax of the interpersonal problems comes when—in an attempt to be aggressively sexy and "low"—Metro calls Jesse a "nigger" during their lovemaking. Jesse is enraged and repeatedly hits Metro who responds by masturbating until he reaches orgasm. The interplay of racism and racist language, the pushing of the boundaries of eroticism, and the violence that ensues from reflexive, non–thinking action permeates the book. Although Dixon is clear about what constitutes racism he is also insistent on examining the ways in which both Metro and Jesse contribute to their interpersonal violence.

In his fiction, Melvin Dixon attempted to push the boundaries of what is permissible in the traditions of African American and gay male fiction. By insisting that race and sexuality be dealt with in each genre, he enlarged the possibilities for all writers and readers.

—*Michael Bronski*

DOMINI, Rey. *See* **LORDE, Audre (Geraldine).**

————

DOOLITTLE, Hilda. American poet, playwright, novelist, and translator. Also wrote as H. D. Born in Bethlehem, Pennsylvania, 19 September 1886. Educated at Bryn Mawr College, 1900–06. Married Richard Aldington in 1913; one daughter. Literary editor of the *Egoist,* 1916–17; contributing editor of the cinema journal *Close–Up,* 1927–31. **Recipient:** *Poetry* Guarantors Prize, 1915; Levinson Prize, 1938, and Harriet Monroe Memorial Prize, 1958, both for work published in *Poetry;* Brandeis University Creative Arts Medal for lifetime of distinguished achievement, 1959; National Institute and American Academy of Arts and Letters Award of Merit Medal for poetry, 1960. *Died in Zurich, Switzerland, of a heart attack, 27 September 1961.*

WRITINGS

Novels as H. D.

Palimpsest. Paris, Contact Editions, and Boston, Houghton, 1926; revised, Carbondale, Southern Illinois University Press, 1968.
Hedylus. Boston, Houghton, and Oxford, Blackwell, 1928; revised, Redding Ridge, Connecticut, Black Swan Books, 1980.
Kora and Ka. Dijon, France, Darantiere, 1934; Berkeley, Bios, 1978.
Bid Me to Live: A Madrigal. New York, Grove, 1960; enlarged, Redding Ridge, Connecticut, Black Swan Books, 1983.

Poetry as H. D.

Sea Garden. London, Constable, Boston and New York, Houghton, 1916.
The Tribute and Circe: Two Poems. Cleveland, Clerk's Private Press, 1917.
Hymen. London, Egoist Press, and New York, Holt, 1921.
Heliodora, and Other Poems. Boston, Houghton, and London, Cape, 1924.
Red Roses for Bronze. London, Chatto & Windus, Boston and New York, Houghton, 1931.
The Usual Star. Dijon, France, Darantiere, 1934.
What Do I Love? London, Brendin, 1944.
The Walls Do Not Fall. London and New York, Oxford University Press, 1944; included in *Trilogy,* 1973.
Tribute to the Angels. London and New York, Oxford University Press, 1945; included in *Trilogy,* 1973.
The Flowering of the Rod. London and New York, Oxford University Press, 1946; included in *Trilogy,* 1973.
Helen in Egypt. New York, Grove, 1961.
Two Poems (originally published in *Life and Letters Today,* 1937). Berkeley, California, ARIF, 1971.
Priest and A Dead Priestess Speaks. Port Townsend, Washington, Copper Canyon Press, 1983.

Translator

Choruses from the Iphigenia in Aulis by Euripides. Cleveland, Ohio, Clerk's Private Press, 1916.
Ion by Euripedes. Boston, Houghton, 1937.

Collected Works

Collected Poems of H. D. New York, Boni & Liveright, 1925.
H. D., edited by Hugh Mearns. New York, Simon & Schuster, 1926.
Selected Poems of H. D. New York, Grove, 1957.
Trilogy: The Walls Do Not Fall, Tribute to the Angels, The Flowering of the Rod. New York, New Directions, and Cheadle, England, Carcanet, 1973.
Collected Poems 1912–1944, edited by Louis L. Martz. New York, New Directions, 1983.
Selected Poems, edited by Louis L. Martz. Cheadle, England, Carcanet Press, 1989.

Other

Hippolytus Temporizes: A Play in Three Acts. Boston, Houghton, 1927; revised, Redding Ridge, Connecticut, Black Swan Books, 1985.
Borderline—A Pool Film with Paul Robeson. London, Mercury, 1930.
The Hedgehog (children's fiction). London, Brendin, 1936.
By Avon River (poetry and prose). New York, London and Toronto, Macmillan, 1949, revised, Redding Ridge, Connecticut, Black Swan Books, 1986.
Tribute to Freud, with Unpublished Letters to Freud by the Author. New York, Pantheon, 1956; enlarged, Boston, Godine, 1974; second edition published as *Tribute to Freud: Writing on the Wall,* New York, New Directions, 1984.
Temple of the Sun. Berkeley, California, ARIF, 1972.
Hermetic Definition. New York, New Directions, and Oxford, Carcanet, 1972.
The Poet and the Dancer (originally published in *Life and Letters Today,* December, 1935). San Francisco, Five Trees Press, 1975.
Contributor, *Images of H. D.,* by Eric Walter White. London, Enitharmon, 1976.
End to Torment: A Memoir of Ezra Pound, edited by Norman Holmes Pearson and Michael King. New York, New Directions, 1979.
HERmione. New York, New Directions, 1981; published as *Her,* London, Virago, 1984.
The Gift (memoir). New York, New Directions, 1982.
Notes on Thought and Vision and The Wise Sappho. San Francisco, City Lights Books, 1983.

*

Manuscript Collections: Beinecke Library, Yale University, New Haven, Connecticut.

Biography: *H. D.: The Life and Work of an American Poet* by Janice S. Robinson, Boston, Houghton, 1982; *Herself Defined: The Poet H. D. and Her World* by Barbara Guest, Garden City, New York, Doubleday, 1984.

Bibliography: Jackson R. Bryer and Pamela Roblyer, "H. D." A Preliminary Checklist," in *Contemporary Literature,* Number 10, 1969, 632–675.

Critical Sources: *Images of H. D.* by Eric Walter Shite, London, Enitharmon, 1976; *Women of the Left Bank, Paris, 1900–1940* by Shari Benstock, Austin, University of Texas Press, 1986; *H.D.: The Career of That Struggle* by Rachel Blau DuPlessis, Brighton, England, Harvester Press, 1986; "Lesbian Romanticism: H.D.'s Fictional Representations of Frances Gregg and Bryher" by Cassandra Laity, in *Paint It Today* by H.D., New York University Press, 1992; "Introduction" by Robert Spoo, in *Asphodel* by H.D., Durham, North Carolina, and London, Duke University Press, 1992.

*   *   *

Literature critics writing about Hilda Doolittle have tended to focus their discussion on one among a series of possible splittings they find in her work: the word from the object, language from experience, public from private, or even a splitting of the self into two different selves. Those critics who have recuperated H. D. into the fields of feminist criticism and gay and lesbian studies generally stress the closeting of H.D.'s work. The work published during her lifetime—mostly poetry—addresses lesbian sexuality only very indirectly. The largely autobiographical prose manuscripts unearthed after her death take her lesbian relationships as their main subject.

H. D. is generally known as a Modernist poet, and her career as such was sanctioned quite early by Ezra Pound, the self–proclaimed "high priest of Modernism." H. D. visited Pound in London in 1911, before she thought of herself as a poet. Pound introduced her to a large literary circle that included William Butler Yeats, May Sinclair, and H. D.'s future husband, Richard Aldington. By 1912, intense discussions among Doolittle, Pound, and Aldington instigated the formulation of Imagism. As an aesthetic doctrine, Imagism sought to bridge the gap between word and object by concentrating poetic language—unemotional, uncluttered, unembellished—so intensely on its subject that it would become an object in its own right. Imagism also rejected the values of the immediately previous generations in favor of something "new." "Nermes of the Ways," published in *Poetry* magazine in 1913 with the signature of "H. D., Imagiste," is often referred to as the first Imagist poem.

H. D.'s career blossomed from there. She produced her first volume of poetry, *Sea Garden,* in 1916 and a second, *Hymen,* in 1921. Only four years later, H.D.'s work was gathered in *Collected Poems.* Successful in the sphere that would later be labeled high modernism—which rejected any sentimentality equated with the "weaknesses" of femininity—H. D. was in a position to be admired as few other women poets were. She earned the sanction of Pound, a demanding critic, and continued to derive her poetic authority from highly partriarchal fields. Much of H. D.'s early poetic work grew out of translation exercises; she would translate, alter, and borrow the forms and imagery of classical Greek poetry into her own creations. In *H. D.: The Career of That Struggle,* feminist critic Rachel Blau DuPlessis explains that "to enter the classics is

to confront the issue of cultural authority, for knowledge of Greek and Latin, formerly barred to women and certain males, was the sigil of knowledge and authority." H. D.'s poetry, based so obviously in a rare knowledge of this rigorous discipline, could not be dismissed as feminine drivel, either by her peers or by later critics. Feminist criticism, however, began in the 1980s to point out that H. D. subtly manipulates that classicism to serve her specifically as a female poet. She did so, DuPlessis claims, by "insistently making the matriarchal female power of the mother–goddess figures dominant."

A similar reworking of classical sources characterizes the novels that H.D. published during her lifetime, most notably *Palimpsest.* This experimental text presents three separate stories which nonetheless overlay and illuminate one another, each story foregrounding the extent to which the female protagonist's intimacy with another woman allows her to become more fully creative. Although this fiction and her poetry clearly valued women's relationships with one another, any lesbianism was very buried; all of the work that explicitly addresses lesbian desire was suppressed by both H. D. during her lifetime and by the critical establishment for many years after her death in 1961.

The one surviving manuscript of *Asphodel,* composed in 1921–22, has "destroy" written across the title page. It followed the composition of *Paint It Today* in 1921 and preceded *HERmione* in 1926–27, both of which closely relate events from H. D.'s own life. The autobiographical *Bid Me Live,* composed in 1939, was published as early as 1960, but this work emphasizes the protagonist's relationships with men and downplays homoeroticism. The earlier three pieces focus quite heavily on relationships modeled after H. D.'s involvements with two significant female lovers, Frances Gregg and Winifred Ellerman, commonly known as Bryher. Naturally, H. D.'s centrality to gay and lesbian studies has depended on the availability for study and publication of these manuscripts.

Frances Gregg, with whom H. D. became involved when she was a teenager, has been identified as the paramount passion of the poet's life. Gregg was traveling with H. D. during the London visit in 1911, but abruptly left to marry a man back in the United States; several critics have conjectured that H. D.'s own marriage was impelled by her grief over this loss. *Asphodel,* which begins where *HERmione* ends, moves its protagonist, Hermione Gart, away from that dangerously consuming passion for her female companion, described in *HERmione,* toward a healthier, more supportive relationship with a different lover. Critics generally agree that this is largely a paean to Bryher, with whom H. D. lived from 1919 to 1946.

In her introduction to *Paint it Today*—a novel that briefly covers the same material—Cassandra Laity refers to Gregg as the "love of [H.D.'s] life" and as her "muse." The latter is probably the more significant, since it pulls together the explicit lesbianism of these texts with the creative concerns of the work that was never closeted. In *Women of the Left Bank, Paris, 1900–1940,* Shari Benstock describes H. D.'s creative work as requiring a sense of self that was gendered and sexualized; consequently, according to Benstock, H.D.'s bisexuality confronted her with "the writing moment [that] always brought with it this crisis of sexual identity." Laity develops this idea further when she asserts that in all of H. D.'s work "homoerotic passion often appears to underlie all poetic expression."

—*Ondine E. Le Blanc*

DUBERMAN, Martin Bauml. American historian, playwright, biographer, and educator. Born in New York, New York, 6 August 1930. Educated at Yale University, New Haven, Connecticut, B.A. 1952 (Phi Beta Kappa); Harvard University, Cambridge, Massachusetts, M.A. 1953, Ph.D. 1957. Instructor and assistant professor, Yale University, 1957–62; assistant professor, 1962–65, associate professor, 1965–67, and professor of history, 1967–71, Princeton University, Princeton, New Jersey; distinguished professor, beginning 1971, Herbert H. Lehman College, City University of New York; founder and head of the Center for Lesbian and Gay Studies, beginning 1991. Historical advisor, *Utopian Communities in America* film project, *Sesame Street* series on late nineteenth-century New York, and labor history series for the National Endowment for the Arts; drama critic, *Show* and *Partisan Review;* member of editorial board, *Signs;* member of the board of directors, National Gay Task Force, Lion Theatre Group, and Glines Theatre. **Recipient:** Morse fellow, Yale University, 1961–62; Bancroft Prize for history, 1962; American Council of Learned Societies grant, 1963; Princeton University McCosh faculty fellowship, 1963–64; Vernon Rice Drama Desk Award, 1963–64; National Book Award nomination, 1966; Rockefeller Foundation grant, 1967–68, fellow, 1976; American Academy Award, 1971; National Academy of Arts and Letters award for contributions to literature, 1971. Address: History Department, Herbert H. Lehman College, New York, New York 10468, U.S.A.

WRITINGS

Biographies

Charles Francis Adams 1807–1887. Boston, Houghton, 1961.
James Russell Lowell. Boston, Houghton, 1966.
Paul Robeson. New York, Knopf, 1989.

Plays

In White America (produced New York, 1963; London, 1964). Boston, Houghton, 1964; London, Faber, 1965.
Metaphors. In *Collision Course* (produced New York, 1968). New York, Random House, 1968.
Groups (produced New York, 1968).
The Colonial Dudes (produced New York, 1969). Included in *Male Armor*, 1975.
The Electric Map (produced New York, 1970). Included in *The Memory Bank*, 1970; included in *Male Armor*, 1975.
The Memory Bank (includes *The Recorder* and *The Electric Map*). New York, Dial, 1970.
Payments (produced New York, 1971). Included in *Male Armor*, 1975.
Soon (adaptation of a story by Joseph Martinez Kookoolis, Scott Fagan, and Robert Greenwald; produced New York, 1971), music by Joseph Martinez Kookoolis and Scott Fagan.
Dudes (produced New York, 1972).
The Recorder (produced London, 1974). Included in *The Memory Bank*, 1970; included in *Male Armor*, 1975.
Elagabalus (produced New York, 1973). Included in *Male Armor*, 1975.
Male Armor: Selected Plays 1968–1974 (includes *Metaphors; The Colonial Dudes; The Recorder; The Guttman Ordinary Scale;*

Payments; The Electric Map; and *Elagabalus*). New York, Dutton, 1975.
Visions of Kerouac (produced New York, 1976). Boston, Little Brown, 1977.
Mother Earth: An Epic Drama of Emma Goldman's Life. New York, St. Martin's Press, 1991.

Television Plays

The Deed, 1969.
Mother Earth: The Life of Emma Goldman, 1971.

Historical Studies

Editor and contributor, *The Antislavery Vanguard: New Essays on the Abolitionists.* Princeton, New Jersey, Princeton University Press, 1965.
Black Mountain: An Exploration in Community. New York, Dutton, 1972; London, Wildwood House, 1974.
About Time: Exploring the Gay Past. New York, Sea Horse, 1986; revised, New York, Meridian Books, 1991.
Editor, with Martha Vicinus and George Chauncey, Jr., and contributor, *Hidden from History: Reclaiming the Gay and Lesbian Past.* New York, New American Library, 1989.
Stonewall. New York, Dutton, 1993.

Contributor

Democracy and the Student Left. Boston, Little, Brown, 1968.
A Radical Reader. New York, Harper, 1970.
The Best Short Plays of 1970. Radnor, Pennsylvania, Chilton, 1970.
The Best Short Plays of 1972. Radnor, Pennsylvania, Chilton, 1972.
Readings in Human Sexuality. New York, Harper, 1976.

Other

The Uncompleted Past: Collected Essays, 1961–1969. New York, Random House, 1969.
Cures: A Gay Man's Odyssey (autobiography). New York, Dutton, 1991.

*

Adaptations: *In White America* was filmed for television in 1970; the BBC has purchased *Stonewall* for a television film.

Interviews: *Gay Sunshine Interviews,* Volume 2, edited by Winston Leyland, Gay Sunshine Press, 1982, 55–74; "From the Abolitionists to Gay History: An Interview with Martin Bauml Duberman," in *Radical History Review,* September 1988; "PW Interviews: Martin Bauml Duberman," in *Publishers Weekly,* 13 January 1989, 72.

*   *   *

Martin Bauml Duberman is unique among gay writers in having achieved distinction as a scholar, biographer, historian, founder of the largest center for lesbian and gay studies in America, playwright, and leader in the fight for equality and diversity. From the very beginning of his career, Duberman has been recognized as an authority on important figures from New England history and letters. Educated at Yale and Harvard, he won the Bancroft Prize in 1962 for his biography of Charles Francis Adams. Four years later he produced a life of James Russell Lowell.

Although a full professor at Princeton, he subsequently left that university in 1971 to become distinguished professor at Herbert H. Lehman College of the City University of New York, where he could be closer to the cultural, social, and political issues of concern to him. Already in 1963 he had written and had produced on Broadway *In White America,* an evening of theater that documents two hundred years of African American history and suffering. The play brought Duberman immediate international acclaim, and he has subsequently had numerous other plays produced. Many of the author's dramatic works were collected in *Male Armor: Selected Plays, 1968–1974,* including *Metaphors, The Colonial Dudes, The Recorder, The Guttman Ordinary Scale, Payments, The Electric Man,* and *Elagabalus.* In all of these Duberman attempts to raise social consciousness, continuing the effort he began with *In White America.*

His many other projects include *The Antislavery Vanguard: New Essays on the Abolitionists,* which Duberman edited. His outstanding reputation in African American studies led Paul Robeson's family to choose him in 1988 to write the official biography of that beloved actor, singer, and activist.

By the 1970s Duberman had elected to speak out for yet another of America's minorities: homosexuals. The 1972 book *Black Mountain: An Exploration in Community* studies the nature and evolution of the influential Black Mountain artists' colony and experimental educational institution in North Carolina. In describing how one of its members is driven out because of his homosexuality, Duberman disclosed his own sexual orientation. He has produced a prodigious amount of writing on gay subjects, in particular the 1986 study *About Time: Exploring the Gay Past* and 1989's *Hidden from History: Reclaiming the Gay and Lesbian Past.* In 1991, Duberman founded The Center for Lesbian and Gay Studies, which he still heads. The same year he published *Cures,* an autobiography detailing, with wit and verve, his psychological odyssey and his public coming out. It enjoyed instant success. Like the lessons of his plays, the portrait Duberman traces of his treatment by doctors to "cure" him of his homosexuality and of the help he provided in 1975 to Howard Brown, Mayor Lindsay's Commissioner of Public Health, the highest public official to come out at that time, has set the issue of gay rights squarely before the public. The book has also inspired and given courage to gay men and lesbians faced with similar challenges in their own lives.

Duberman's 1993 work *Stonewall* provides the first book–length study of the events generated by the Stonewall Rebellion of 28 June 1969. It includes sketches of the lives of six gay and lesbian activists from that exciting era in the history of the American movement. This book, like the many that came before it, demonstrates Duberman's ability to produce valuable works related to the issue of homosexuality, and to do so in many different genres. These writings represent a significant contribution to the better understanding of gay and lesbian history and culture.

—*William A. Percy III*

DUFFY, Maureen (Patricia). British poet and novelist. Has also written as D. M. Cayer. Born in Worthing, Sussex, October 1933. Educated at Trowbridge High School for Girls, Wiltshire; Sarah Bonnell High School for Girls; King's College, London, 1953–56, B.A. (with honours) in English 1956. Taught school for five years. Cofounder, Writers Action Group, 1972; Writers Guild of Great Britain, joint chair, 1977–78, and president, 1985–89; Greater London Arts Literature Panel, chair, 1979–81; vice–chair, 1981–86, chair, 1989—; British Copyright Council; Authors Lending and Copyright Society, chair, 1982—; vice president, Beauty without Cruelty; fiction editor, *Critical Quarterly,* Manchester, 1987. Member of Gay and Lesbian Humanist Association; vice president of European Writers Congress. **Recipient:** City of London Festival Playwright's prize, 1962; Arts Council bursary, 1963, 1966, 1975; Society of Authors travelling scholarship, 1976. Royal Society of Literature, fellow, 1985. Agent: Jonathan Clowes Ltd., Ironbridge House, Bridge Approach, London NW1 8BD, England, U.K.

WRITINGS

Poetry

Lyrics for the Dog Hour. London, Hutchinson, 1968.
The Venus Touch. London, Weidenfeld & Nicolson, 1971.
Actaeon. Rushden, Northamptonshire, Sceptre Press, 1973.
Evesong. London, Sappho, 1975.
Memorials of the Quick and the Dead. London, Hamish Hamilton, 1979.
Collected Poems 1949–1984. London, Hamish Hamilton, 1985.

Plays

The Lay–Off (produced London, 1962).
The Silk Room (produced Watford, Hertfordshire, 1966).
Rites (produced London, 1969). Published in *New Short Plays 2,* London, Methuen, 1969.
Solo, Olde Tyme (produced Cambridge, England, 1970).
A Nightingale in Bloomsbury Square (produced London, 1973). Published in *Factions,* edited by Giles Gordon and Alex Hamilton, London, Joseph, 1974.

Television and Radio Plays

Josie (television play), 1961.
Only Goodnight (radio play), 1981.

Novels

That's How It Was. London, Hutchinson, 1962; New York, Dial, 1984.
The Single Eye. London, Hutchinson, 1964.
The Microcosm. London, Hutchinson, and New York, Simon & Schuster, 1966.
The Paradox Players. London, Hutchinson, 1967; New York, Simon & Schuster, 1968.
Wounds. London, Hutchinson, and New York, Knopf, 1969.
Love Child. London, Weidenfeld & Nicolson, and New York, Knopf, 1971.

I Want to Go to Moscow: A Lay. London, Hodder & Stoughton, 1973; as *All Heaven in a Rage,* New York, Knopf, 1973.
Capital. London, Cape, 1975; New York, Braziller, 1976.
Housespy. London, Hamish Hamilton, 1978.
Gor Saga. London, Eyre Methuen, 1981; New York, Viking, 1982.
Scarborough Fear (as D. M. Cayer). London, Macdonald, 1982.
Londoners: An Elegy. London, Methuen, 1983.
Change. London, Methuen, 1987.
Illuminations. London, Sinclair–Stevenson, 1991.
Occam's Razor. London, Sinclair–Stevenson, 1993.

Nonfiction

The Erotic World of Faery. London, Hodder & Stoughton, 1972.
The Passionate Shepherdess: Aphra Behn 1640–1689. London, Cape, 1977; New York, Avon, 1979.
Inherit the Earth: A Social History. London, Hamish Hamilton, 1980.
Men and Beasts: An Animal Rights Handbook. London, Paladin, 1984.
A Thousand Capricious Chances: A History of the Methuen List 1889–1989. London, Methuen, 1989.

Editor

With Alan Brownjohn, *New Poetry 3.* London, Arts Council, 1977.
Oroonoko, and Other Stories by Aphra Behn. London, Methuen, 1986.
Love Letters between a Nobleman and His Sister by Aphra Behn. London, Virago, 1987.
Five Plays by Aphra Behn. London, Heinemann Educational, 1990.

Other

Translator, *A Blush of Shame* by Domenico Rea. London, Barrie & Rockliff, 1968.

*

Manuscript Collections: King's College, University of London.

Critical Sources: *Transatlantic Review 45,* London, spring 1973; *Guide to Modern World Literature* by Martin Seymour–Smith, London, Wolfe, 1973, as *Funk & Wagnalls Guide to Modern World Literature,* New York, Funk & Wagnalls, 1973; *An Encyclopedia of British Women Writers,* edited by Paul Schlueter and June Schlueter, London, Garland, 1988, 145; *British Women Writers: A Critical Reference Guide,* edited by Janet Todd, New York, Continuum, 1989, 196–97.

Maureen Duffy comments: "I am presently at work on a biography of Henry Purcell."

*   *   *

Maureen Duffy stands out among contemporary British novelists as a writer and thinker whose personal history and political commitments are explicit in all of her work. Born in 1933 to working–class parents in Worthing, Sussex, Duffy has always turned to her class roots in her novels. Before and after graduating from King's College in 1956, she taught school for five years. Duffy began her writing career in 1961 with the premiere of *Josie,* a television play. This was quickly followed by *The Layoff,* a stage play produced in London in 1962 and the publication of her first novel, *That's How It Was,* the same year. *That's How It Was* met with sound critical and popular reception. Hailed as a fine, honest depiction of working–class British life, critics noted that Duffy avoided both sentimentalization and cliche. Even the birth of Paddy, the book's heroine, is shockingly honest: "Lucky for me I was born at all really, I mean she could have decided not to bother. Like she told me she was tempted, head in the gas oven, in front of a bus, oh a thousand ways."

What most critics did not comment upon in their reviews of *That's How It Was* was the strong feminist undertones of Duffy's contextualization of Paddy's relationship with her mother. Although the novel portrays the sexuality of its characters honestly, it also sets the tone for much of Duffy's more openly lesbian, feminist, and political work. In this work, the diversity and unpredictability of human sexuality is handled with a keen eye for erotic truth as well as an understanding of what it means to be overtly sexual in an erotophobic and homophobic world. In the 1964 *The Single Eye* Duffy examines the intricate homosexual and heterosexual relationships among a group of London artists and also explores how the creation of art functions as an erotic activity. It was during this time that Duffy's lesbianism became known, a fact she never denied. In *The Single Eye,* a character discussing the huge range of possible sexual and emotional human responses declares, "I've got too many sins of the flesh on my own to come down heavily on other people's."

This attitude infuses Duffy's 1966 *The Microcosm,* a look at the lives of three women in a London lesbian bar called The House of Shades. If Duffy's earlier work was more naturalistic, it was in *The Microcosm* that she began experimenting with new form. The book contains stream–of–consciousness passages reminiscent of author James Joyce's work, first– and second–person narration, as well as pastiches from earlier works of literature (particularly Daniel Defoe's *Moll Flanders*). This narrative method is intrinsic to Duffy's material as she attempts to find new ways to approach and describe the lives of ordinary people—many of whom are social outcasts—without falling into the traps set by traditional narrative. By focusing almost entirely on an all–female world in *The Microcosm,* Duffy was beginning to explore not only lesbianism but the specific relationship of women to the material world.

This theme also surfaced, harshly, in her 1969 one–act play *Rites,* based, in part, on *The Bacchae* by the Greek playwright, Euripides. Set in a woman's washroom, the play focuses on a group of working–class women who kill another woman whom they mistake for a man. At the climax of the play, one of the characters comments in self defense, "She couldn't have been happy," and another responds fiercely "Why not, she was alive?" Although Duffy understands that women occupy a specific place in the world in terms of class, gender, race and economic opportunity, she is unwilling to posit a feminism that excuses women of responsibility to a larger and greater good. In her 1971 novel *The Love Child,* Duffy explores the psyche of a manipulative young girl who attempts (and to some degree succeeds) in destroying the lives of her family. The book ends with the suicide of her mother's lover and the young woman stating, "She will have no more lovers except me.... I am my mother's lover now. But I didn't know, I didn't know," indicating that Duffy has a complicated and sophisticated psychological view of relationships between women.

The response "Why not, she was alive?" that resonates at the end of *Rites* articulates another theme in Duffy's writing and situates her in a world that understands a wide range of political options and work, especially her concern with the animal rights movement. Both the 1973 *All Heaven in a Rage* and the 1981 *Gor Saga* examine the relationship between humans and the rest of the living world. This relationship takes on an even more metaphysical aspect in the 1972 nonfiction work *The Erotic World of Faery*. On one level this is a psychoanalytic look at myth, fairy tales and folk legends, but on a more profound level Duffy examines the complex relationship between human consciousness and the material world, between a politic of responsibility and a politic of consciousness. The use of the word "erotic" in the title underlies Duffy's persistent interest in how human eroticism, sexuality, and sensuality profoundly shape our understanding and actions in the world. It is this world–view that has permitted Duffy to write so easily of sexuality and sexual difference and to integrate these ideas into a broader politic.

Duffy's interest in the unconscious and the effect of the erotic on our everyday lives is complimented by her firm understanding of economics and the workings of the material world, particularly in how it relates to class and economics. In her introduction to *That's How It Was* Duffy writes, "It is a political book in the sense that national and international politics govern the physical condition of Paddy's and her mother's life, and in this sense politics have remained a major element in all my later writing." This has also fueled Duffy's interest in the writings of Aphra Behn (the first woman in Britain to make a living from writing). Besides *The Passionate Shepherdess: Aphra Behn 1640–1689*, a biography, she has also edited three volumes of Behn's work. Duffy's interest in the economics of writing has also led her to work with, and often take a leadership position in, the Writers Guild of Great Britain, the Author's Lending and Copyright Society, and the British Copyright Council.

—*Michael Bronski*

———

DUNCAN, Robert. American poet and playwright. Also wrote as Robert Edward Symmes until 1942. Born Edward Howard Duncan in Oakland, California, 7 January 1919; adopted in 1920 and given name Robert Edward Symmes; took original surname, 1941. Educated at University of California, Berkeley, 1936–38 and 1948–50. Served in the United States Army, 1941. Companion of Jess Collins. Editor, *Experimental Review*, 1938–40, *Phoenix*, and *Berkeley Miscellany*, 1948–49, Berkeley, California; teacher at Black Mountain College, Black Mountain, North Carolina, 1956; assistant director of Poetry Center, 1956–57, and lecturer in poetry workshop, 1965, San Francisco State College, California; lecturer in creative writing workshop, University of British Columbia, Vancouver, 1963; organizer of and participant in poetry readings and workshops, San Francisco. **Recipient:** Ford grant, 1956–57; *Poetry* Union League Civic and Arts Foundation Prize, 1957; *Poetry* Harriet Monroe

Prize, 1961; Guggenheim fellowship, 1963–64; *Poetry* Levinson Prize, 1964; Miles Poetry Prize, 1964; National Endowment for the Arts grants, 1965 and 1966–67; *Poetry* Eunice Tietjens Memorial Prize, 1967; National Book Critics Circle Award nomination, 1984; Shelley Memorial Award, 1984; National Poetry Award, 1985; Before Columbus Foundation American Book Award, 1986; Bay Area Book Reviewers Association Fred Cody Award for Lifetime Literary Excellence, 1986. *Died in San Francisco, of a heart attack, 7 January 1988.*

WRITINGS

Poetry

Heavenly City, Earthly City. Berkeley, California, Bern Porter, 1947.
Poems 1948–49. Berkeley, California, Berkeley Miscellany Editions, 1949.
Medieval Scenes. San Francisco, Centaur Press, 1950; with preface by the author, Kent, Ohio, Kent State University Libraries, 1978.
The Song of the Border–Guard, 1952.
Fragments of a Disordered Devotion. San Francisco, privately printed, 1952.
Caesar's Gate: Poems 1949–1950 with Collages by Jess Collins. Palma de Mallorca, Divers Press, 1955; as *Caesar's Gate: Poems 1949–1950 with Paste–Ups by Jess*, with preface by the author, Berkeley, California, Sand Dollar, 1972.
Contributor, *Faber Book of Modern American Verse*, edited by W. H. Auden. New York, Faber, 1956.
Letters: Poems MCMLIII–MCMLVI, illustrations by Duncan. Highlands, North Carolina, Jargon, 1958.
Selected Poems. San Francisco, City Lights Books, 1959.
The Opening of the Field. New York, Grove, 1960; London, J. Cape, 1969.
Roots and Branches. New York, Scribner, 1964; London, J. Cape, 1970.
Writing, Writing: A Composition Book of Madison 1953, Stein Imitations (poems and essays). Albuquerque, New Mexico, Sumbooks, 1964.
Wine. Berkeley, California, Oyez, 1964.
Uprising. Berkeley, California, Oyez, 1965.
A Book of Resemblances: Poems 1950–1953. New Haven, Connecticut, Henry Wenning, 1966.
Of the War: Passages 22–27. Berkeley, California, Oyez, 1966.
The Years as Catches: First Poems (1939–1946). Berkeley, California, Oyez, 1966.
Boob. Privately printed, 1966.
Epilogos. Los Angeles, Black Sparrow Press, 1967.
The Cat and the Blackbird (for children), illustrations by Jess Collins. San Francisco, White Rabbit Press, 1967.
Christmas Present, Christmas Presence! Los Angeles, Black Sparrow Press, 1967.
Bending the Bow. New York, New Directions, 1968; London, J. Cape, 1971.
My Mother Would Be a Falconess. Los Angeles, Oyez, 1968.
Names of People. Los Angeles, Black Sparrow Press, 1968.
The First Decade: Selected Poems 1940–1950. London, Fulcrum Press, 1968.
Derivations: Selected Poems 1950–1956. London, Fulcrum Press, 1968.

Play Time, Pseudo Stein [and] *1942, a Story* [and] *A Fairy Play: From the Laboratory Records Notebook of 1953, a Tribute to Mother Carey's Chickens.* New York, Poets Press, 1969; with preface by the author, San Francisco, Tenth Muse, 1969.

Achilles' Song. [Phoenix], 1969.

Poetic Disturbances. San Francisco, Maya, 1970.

Bring It Up from the Dark. Cody's Books, 1970.

Tribunals: Passages 31–35. Los Angeles, Black Sparrow Press, 1970.

Structure of Rime XXVIII: In Memoriam Wallace Stevens. Storrs, University of Connecticut, 1972.

Poems from the Margins of Thom Gunn's Moly. San Francisco, privately printed, 1972.

A Seventeenth Century Suite in Homage to the Metaphysical Genius in English Poetry (1590–1690): Being Imitations, Derivations, and Variations upon Certain Conceits and Findings Made among Strong Lines, c. November 5, 1971–December 16, 1971. San Francisco, privately printed, 1973.

Contributor, *The Male Muse: Gay Poetry Anthology,* edited by Ian Young. Trumansburg, New York, Crossing Press, 1973.

With Jack Spicer, *An Ode and Arcadia.* Berkeley, California, Ark Press, 1974.

Dante. Canton, New York, Institute of Further Studies, 1974.

The Venice Poem. Burlington, Vermont, Poet's Mimeo, 1978.

Veil, Turbine, Cord, and Bird. Brooklyn, New York, Jordan Davies, 1979.

The Five Songs. La Jolla, Friends of the University of California—San Diego Library, 1981.

Ground Work: Before the War. New York, New Directions, 1984.

The Regulators. Barrytown, New York, Station Hill Press, 1985.

Ground Work II: In the Dark. New York, New Directions, 1987.

Selected Poems, edited by Robert J. Bertholf. New York, New Directions, 1993.

Plays

Faust Foutu (produced San Francisco, 1955). Published as *Faust Foutu: Act One of Four Acts: A Comic Mask, 1952–1954,* decorations by the author, San Francisco, White Rabbit Press, 1958; published as *Faust Foutu: An Entertainment in Four Parts,* Stinson Beach, California, Enkido Surrogate, 1959.

Medea at Kolchis: The Maiden Head (produced Black Mountain, North Carolina, 1956). Berkeley, California, Oyez, 1965.

Essays

"The Homosexual in Society," in *Politics,* August 1944.

"Notes on Poetics Regarding Olson's 'Maximus,'" in *Black Mountain Review* (Black Mountain, North Carolina), spring 1956; revised, in *Review,* January 1964.

"Pages from a Notebook" and autobiographical statement, in *The New American Poetry,* edited by Donald M. Allen. New York, Grove, 1960.

As Testimony: The Poem and the Scene. San Francisco, White Rabbit Press, 1964.

The Truth and Life of Myth: An Essay in Essential Autobiography. New York, House of Books, 1968.

Contributor, *The Artistic Legacy of Walt Whitman: A Tribute to Gay Wilson Allen,* edited by Edwin Haviland Miller. New York, New York University Press, 1970.

Fictive Certainties: Five Essays in Essential Autobiography. New York, New Directions, 1979.

Contributor, *Convivio: A Journal of Poetics from New College of California,* edited by John Thorpe. Bolinas, California, Tombouctou Books, 1983.

Contributor, *Hill Field: Poems and Memoirs for John Montague* by William Kennedy. Coffee House Press, 1989.

Contributor

Author of preface, *O!* by Jess Collins. New York, Hawk's Well Press, 1960.

Author of preface, *Elegies and Celebrations* by Jonathan Williams. Jargon, 1962.

Author of introduction, *Translation* by Jess Collins. Los Angeles, Black Sparrow Press, 1971.

Author of introduction, *Dodeka* by John Taggart. Milwaukee, Wisconsin, Membrane Press, 1979.

Other

The Artist's View. [San Francisco], 1952.

The Sweetness and Greatness of Dante's "Divine Comedy" (lecture presented at Dominican College of San Raphael, 1965). San Francisco, Open Space, 1965.

Six Prose Pieces. Rochester, Michigan, Perishable Press, 1966.

Adam's Way: A Play on Theosophical Themes. San Francisco, 1966.

Audit/Robert Duncan (originally appeared in special issue of *Audit/Poetry*). Audit/Poetry, 1967.

A Selection of Sixty-five Drawings from One Drawing Book, 1952–1956. Los Angeles, Black Sparrow Press, 1970.

Notes on Grossinger's "Solar Journal: Oecological Sections." Los Angeles, Black Sparrow Press, 1970.

A Prospectus for the Prepublication of Ground Work to Certain Friends of the Poet. Privately printed, 1971.

An Epithalamium, 1980.

Quand le Grand Foyer, 1981.

In Blood's Domain, 1982.

Towards an Open Universe. Published in *Poets on Poetry,* edited by Howard Nemerov, New York, Basic Books, 1966; Aquila Publishing, 1982.

In Passage, 1983.

*

Manuscript Collections: Bancroft Library, University of California, Berkeley; Kent State University Library, Kent, Ohio; Lockwood Memorial Library, State University of New York at Buffalo; Archive for New Poetry, University of California, San Diego; Washington University Library, Saint Louis; Wilbur Cross Library, University of Connecticut, Storrs.

Biography: "'The Barbaric Friendship with Robert': A Biographical Palimpsest" by Ekbert Faas, in *Mosaic,* winter 1978; *Young Robert Duncan: Portrait of the Poet as Homosexual in Society* by Ekbert Faas, Los Angeles, Black Sparrow Press, 1983; *Robert Duncan: A Descriptive Biography* by Robert J. Bertholf, preface by Robert Creeley, Los Angeles, Black Sparrow Press, 1986; *Robert Duncan* by Mark Andrew Johnson, Boston, Twayne Publishers, 1988.

Bibliography: *A Bibliography of the White Rabbit Press* by Johnston Alastair, Berkeley, California, Poltroon Press, 1985; *Robert Creeley, Edward Dorn, and Robert Duncan: A Reference Guide* by Willard Fox, Boston, G. K. Hall, 1989.

Critical Sources: *Origin,* June 1963 (special Duncan issue); *Audit,* Number 4, 1967 (special Duncan issue); "'Towards a Possible Music': The Poetry of Robert Duncan" by Ian Reid, in *New Poetry,* April 1973; *Maps,* Number 6, 1974 (special Duncan issue); *Godawful Streets of Man* by Warren Tallman, Coach House Press, 1976; "Robert Duncan in Canada" by George Bowering, in *Essays on Canadian Writing,* Number 4, 1976; *Robert Duncan: Scales of the Marvelous,* edited by Robert J. Bertholf and Ian Reid, New York, New Directions, 1979; *The Lost America of Love: Rereading Robert Creeley, Edward Dorn, and Robert Duncan* by Sherman Paul, 1981.

*   *   *

Born Edward Howard Duncan, 7 January 1919, in Oakland, California, Duncan lost his mother shortly after his birth and was adopted by a well–off couple. His adoptive parents, Edwin and Minnehaha Symmes, were members of the Hermetic Brotherhood, an offshoot of Helena Blavatsky's Theosophical Society. The Hermetic Brotherhood received from sources unknown a prediction that Duncan would come to epitomize the decadence and termination of civilization in his lifetime. Duncan used the name Symmes until he reverted to his birth name in 1942.

Duncan studied at the University of California at Berkeley from 1936 to 1938, where he took part in radical politics and published his first poems. In 1940, Duncan moved on to New York, where he traveled in gay circles—meeting Parker Tyler, Sanders Russell, the artist Tchelitchew, the music theorist Lou Harrison, the novelists Charles Henri Ford and James Baldwin, utopian Paul Goodman, and numerous poets, including W. H. Auden.

In 1944, Duncan published his now–famous essay, "The Homosexual in Society," appearing in the August issue of *Politics* that year; his commentary was one of the first written pieces to portray homosexuals as a minority group, a minority severely oppressed by a hostile society. Duncan's observations, since legitimized, distressed many in the gay community. Auden, for example, attempted to block publication of the essay, noting that he earned a good part of his livelihood by teaching "and in that profession one is particularly vulnerable" to that hostile society Duncan wished to confront.

Duncan returned to California in 1945 and in 1946, at the urging of Werner Vortriede, he began studying with Ernst Kantorowicz, the eminent German–Jewish medievalist in exile who had been a disciple of Stefan George and an important member of his *Georgekreis.*

Themes dealing with the resolution of political and sexual dichotomy and with the relationship between earthly reality and heavenly vision, which Duncan had first put forward in *Politics* in 1944, he pursued in *Heavenly City, Earthly City, Caesar's Gate: Poems, 1949–1950,* and *Medieval Scenes,* with some success. In these verses, and often elsewhere, medieval heretics represent the gay glitterati of his own circles. Such practices show that throughout his career Duncan was a *romantic.*

In 1946, Duncan met and became the fractious friend of serialist poet Jack Spicer. Together, they became activists in the San Francisco Renaissance. Despite Duncan's full–fledged involvement in radical politics, he never did forsake establishmentarian appearances like so many of his cohorts. Yet from first to last Duncan was *out* in the most modern sense of the word: "I am not afraid to be a queen," he noted brazenly. Nonetheless, Duncan received nearly all the standard awards of an established poet of his day: a Ford grant in 1956, a Guggenheim fellowship in 1963, a Miles Poetry Prize (1964), National Endowment for the Arts grants in the 1960s, and the National Poetry Award in 1985. Additionally, Duncan was respected by the *Poetry* establishment in Chicago (winning the Harriet Monroe Prize in 1961 and thus establishing his name as an up–and–coming American poet). He was an editor of *Experimental Review, Phoenix,* and the *Berkeley Miscellany* in the 1940s and served as a reader, workshop director, and lecturer for several decades. In the mid–1950s, Duncan taught at the now–famous Black Mountain College in North Carolina which—following the Iowa Poetry Workshop—became the Mecca of American poetry for a brief time (until 1956). Here, he had an opportunity to widen the discourse of the confessional and post–confessional poets. Duncan was also given the chance to reject the by–then antiseptic New Criticism with such contemporaries as Charles Olson, the "Dogtown" poet of Gloucester and author of the "open–field" *Maximus* poems, and the gay poets Robert Creeley and Garret Lansing. During his time at Black Mountain College, Duncan also showed interested in the work of lesbian poets, particularly the writings of Gertrude Stein and the bisexual Hilda Doolittle.

As he captured the prestigious *Poetry* prizes in 1961, 1964, and 1967, Duncan's reputation as an American poet came to equal even that of Creeley, a fellow–traveler; and, although he never reached the popular rank of several of the largely gay "San Francisco School" such as Allen Ginsberg (perhaps the most widely read) or Lawrence Ferlinghetti (owner of City Lights Book Store and perhaps the most musical of the San Francisco romantics), he won earlier and greater acceptance in the academic and nearby intellectual worlds. Duncan was not the *essential* anarchist but recognized in the poets of his day an anarchy he could not work without. Despite his reputation as a "Beat" poet, Duncan was less a "people's poet" than a "poet's poet"—serious, calculating, traditionalist in an Emersonian or Whitman tradition with a firm foundation in Milton and Blake. Musically, he was more akin to the sophisticated rhythms of Stravinsky rather than to those of the Beatles. Straight poets had little effect on him, though Ezra Pound, Dylan Thomas, and William Carlos Williams were outstanding exceptions in this regard. Duncan was more of a wrestling theorist than a dancing lyricist, a professional poet with far less patience for amateurism than he generally let on. Today, a small Duncan academic industry has sprung up to interpret his main–line vision of American society. His most popular work has proven to be *Bending the Bow,* which enjoyed some popularity when it was published at the height of the romantic revolution of the 1960s.

—*William A. Percy III*

DUNCAN, Edward Howard. *See* DUNCAN, Robert.

DURANG, Christopher (Ferdinand). American playwright and actor. Born in Montclair, New Jersey, 2 January 1949. Educated at Harvard University, B.A. 1971; Yale University, M.F.A. 1974. Actor with Yale Repertory Theatre, New Haven, Connecticut, 1974, appearing in such plays as *The Idiots Karamazov* and *Das Lusitania Songspiel;* drama teacher at Southern Connecticut College, New Haven, Connecticut, 1975; playwriting teacher at Yale University, New Haven, Connecticut, 1975–76. **Recipient:** Columbia Broadcasting System (CBS) fellowship, 1975–76; Rockefeller Foundation grant, 1976–77; Guggenheim fellowship, 1978–79; Tony Award, 1978; Off–Broadway Award, 1980; Lecomte du Nuoy Foundation grant, 1980–81. Agent: Helen Merrill, 337 West 22nd Street, New York, New York 10011, U.S.A.

WRITINGS

Plays

The Life Story of Mitzi Gaynor, or Gyp (produced New Haven, Connecticut, 1973).
Better Dead Than Sorry (produced 1973).
With Albert Innaurato, *I Don't Generally Like Poetry but Have You Read "Trees?"* (cabaret; produced New York, 1973).
With Albert Innaurato, *The Idiots Karamazov* (produced New Haven, Connecticut, 1974). New York, Dramatists Play Service, 1980.
With Wendy Wasserstein, *When Dinah Shore Ruled the Earth* (produced New Haven, Connecticut, 1975).
Death Comes to Us All, Mary Agnes (produced New Haven, Connecticut, 1975). Included in *The Nature and Purpose of the Universe, Death Comes to Us All, Mary Agnes, and 'Dentity Crisis: Three Short Plays,* 1979.
The Vietnamization of New Jersey (produced New Haven, Connecticut, 1976). New York, Dramatists Play Service, 1978.
A History of the American Film (produced Waterford, Connecticut, 1976; New York, 1978). New York, Dramatists Play Service, 1978.
With Sigourney Weaver, *Das Lusitania Songspiel* (produced with *Titanic,* New York, 1976; revised version produced New York, 1979).
With Sigourney Weaver, *Titanic* (produced with *Das Lusitania Songspiel,* New York, 1976). New York, Dramatists Play Service, 1983; included in *Christopher Durang Explains It All for You: Six Plays,* 1990.
The Marriage of Bette and Boo (produced 1976). New York, Dramatists Play Service, 1985.
'Dentity Crisis (produced New Haven, Connecticut, 1978). Included in *The Nature and Purpose of the Universe, Death Comes to Us All, Mary Agnes, and 'Dentity Crisis: Three Short Plays,* 1979; and in *Christopher Durang Explains It All for You: Six Plays,* 1990.
The Nature and Purpose of the Universe (produced New York, 1979). Included in *The Nature and Purpose of the Universe, Death Comes to Us All, Mary Agnes, and 'Dentity Crisis: Three Short Plays,* 1979; and in *Christopher Durang Explains It All for You: Six Plays,* 1990.
Sister Mary Ignatius Explains It All for You (produced New York, 1979). New York, Dramatists Play Service, 1980; included in *Sister Mary Ignatius Explains It All for You, and The Actor's*

Nightmare: Two Plays, 1982; and in *Christopher Durang Explains It All for You: Six Plays,* 1990.
Beyond Therapy (produced New York, 1981). Garden City, New York, Doubleday, 1981; included in *Christopher Durang Explains It All for You: Six Plays,* 1990.
The Actor's Nightmare (produced New York, 1981). Included in *Sister Mary Ignatius Explains It All for You, and The Actor's Nightmare: Two Plays,* 1982; and in *Christopher Durang Explains It All for You: Six Plays,* 1990.
Baby with the Bathwater. New York, Dramatists Play Service, 1984.
With Robert Altman, *Beyond Therapy* (screenplay; based on a play by Durang), Sandcastle, 1987.
Media Amok (produced Cambridge, Massachusetts, 1992).

Collected Plays

The Nature and Purpose of the Universe, Death Comes to Us All, Mary Agnes, and 'Dentity Crisis: Three Short Plays. New York, Dramatists Play Service, 1979.
Sister Mary Ignatius Explains It All for You, and The Actor's Nightmare: Two Plays. New York, Dramatists Play Service, 1982.
Baby with the Bathwater and Laughing Wild: Two Plays. New York, Grove, 1988.
Christopher Durang Explains It All for You: Six Plays (contains *The Nature and Purpose of the Universe, 'Dentity Crisis, Titanic, The Actor's Nightmare, Sister Mary Ignatius Explains It All for You,* and *Beyond Therapy*). New York, Grove, 1990.

*

Critical Sources: *The American Theater* by Ethan Mordden, New York, Oxford, 1981; *Kicking the Habit: A City Confronts Religious Prejudice* (pamphlet), Milwaukee, A Catholic League Publication, 1983.

*   *   *

Christopher Durang came to prominence as a playwright in the early 1970s while the American Theater was going through a radical renaissance. The theater of the 1950s was defined by the social realism of Arthur Miller and the lyrical drama of Tennessee Williams, and the plays of 1960s owed much of their tone to the emergence of writers such as Edward Albee, Terrence McNally and Lanford Wilson, all of whom began their careers off–Broadway and were noted for their rebellion against the political and social status-quo, as well as a departure from conventional forms. By the 1970s, the political and thematic rebellion of the decade before came to seem mild–mannered. The new wave of playwrights—David Rabe, Albert Innaurato, Thomas Babe, David Mamet, and Christopher Durang—were angrier, more blatantly anti–social, more scathing in their satire and social vision. Of these five, it was Durang who chose to manifest his social critique in the form of satire. His work has, to a large degree, expanded the boundaries of socially acceptable (and sometimes unacceptable) satiric comedy.

Durang was born and raised an observant Catholic in a New Jersey suburb. He attended Catholic grammar and high schools. His parents divorced, after a difficult marriage, in his early teenage years. He wrote several plays during this time and after graduating Harvard University in 1971 attended Yale Drama School. His mother died in 1979 after years of struggling with cancer. Since 1975 he has lived and worked in Manhattan.

Although Durang has written more than a dozen produced plays, he has gained notable success with half that many. Such early plays as *The Nature and Purpose of the Universe,* from 1971, *The Marriage of Bette and Boo,* 1973, and *Titanic,* 1974, with their savage portraits of the nuclear family at war with itself, show Durang's preoccupation with the inability to make sense of human and emotional tragedy. The plays also provide critiques of traditional gender and sexual roles. These themes appear again in *A History of the American Film,* published in 1978. Although this play was viewed by many critics as a simple fantasia on the history of Hollywood movies, it is instead a sharp–witted look at how many people are literally trapped in a life–scenario proscribed by Hollywood fantasies, as well as by history itself. Much of Durang's work up to this point was predicated on the philosophical premise that human suffering was surely inevitable, probably meaningless, and impossible to alleviate.

The appearance of *Sister Mary Ignatius Explains It All For You*—on a 1979 bill of one–acts by various playwrights, including Tennessee Williams and David Mamet—manifested a shift in Durang's vision. Here the idea of inevitable human suffering was given a face in Sister Mary Ignatius, a Roman Catholic nun. Ignatius, by her interpretations of church dogma—some crazily idiosyncratic, others theologically sound—demanded that her students (in essence, the audience) accept the hardships that life has handed out to them. The crisis of the play is precipitated by four ex–students who have come to make her pay for the fact that as children she had promised them a world, based upon Catholic theology, that made sense. Although the students do not dislodge Sister Mary Ignatius—she in fact kills two of them—they do attempt to stage some sort of metaphysical revolt. The play ends, however, with the appropriate catechism question: "'What are some of the perfections of God?' Some of the perfections of God are: God is eternal, all–good, all–knowing, all–present, and almighty."

Sister Mary Ignatius is a moral play; it asks the eternal, if predictable question: how can God allow evil in the world? (a question Durang asks in almost all of his work, no doubt a result of his Catholic upbringing). Despite this moral foundation, the play was forcefully and rigorously attacked by its critics as being blatantly anti–Catholic. Durang's satiric wit, presented with more compassion than in any of his previous plays, managed to garner him a great deal of public and critical attention. The play was later to receive its own full evening production, along with the author's *The Actor's Nightmare,* in 1981.

Gender and sexuality have always been a target of Durang's satire. Homosexual and transvestite men appear in *The Nature and Purpose of the Universe, Titanic, Sister Mary Ignatius,* while *A History of the American Film* is preoccupied with the sexual underpinnings of the nuclear family. In *Beyond Therapy,* from 1981, Durang took on the question of romantic relationships by looking at various sexualities, the efficacy of therapy, the impossibility of Manhattan restaurants, and the seeming improbability of personal happiness. Structured as a sex farce, *Beyond Therapy* comes closer than any Durang play to implying that its characters might have a chance at escaping their misery. This theme is repeated again in *Baby and the Bathwater,* published in 1984, in which the main character is subjected to a Durangian nightmare childhood that includes a gender switch. The play is brought to a quiet resolution,

however, that suggests an ability to make peace with the past injustices of the world. This mood is also reflected in Durang's 1985 rewrite of 1973's *The Marriage of Bette and Boo.* Autobiographically inspired, *The Marriage of Bette and Boo* depicts the emotional horrors of a Catholic childhood taxed by chronic family tragedy. The harsh humor of the original version is moderated in the rewrite; Durang still allows his characters to rampage and hurt one another, but he is now willing to allow their hurt and feelings to emerge as well.

Laughing Wild, from 1987, is perhaps the clearest and most optimistic example of Durang's world view. In a long monologue, a character muses: "And think about God. You know, it was nice to believe in God, and an afterlife, and I'm sometimes envious of the people who seem comfortable because they still have this belief. But I remember when everyone won Tonys for *Dreamgirls,* and they all got up there thanking God for letting them win this award, and I was thinking to myself: God is silent on the Holocaust, but he involves himself in the Tony Awards? It doesn't seem likely."

It is in *Laughing Wild* that Durang also brings an articulation of institutionalized homophobia—especially in religion—further than he has before. During a prolonged skit in which God decides that homosexuals, Haitians, and hemophiliacs should get AIDS—"anything beginning with an h," He explains—Durang savages not so much religious belief as the devastating misuse of the political and cultural power of some organized religions.

Christopher Durang brought to his earlier work a gay male sensibility of parody and cultural criticism, especially in such works as *Titanic* and *A History of the American Film.* This playful sense later turned more overtly angry at the treatment of homosexuals (as well as others) by organized religion, the government, and the institution of the family in plays like *Sister Mary Ignatius* and *Laughing Wild.* The satiric promise of his early career has been fulfilled and augmented by a sharper, more cogent sense of political understanding.

—*Michael Bronski*

———

DWORKIN, Andrea. American feminist, novelist, and essayist. Born in Camden, New Jersey, 26 September 1946. Educated at Bennington College, B.A. 1968. Has worked as a waitress, receptionist, secretary, typist, salesperson, factory worker, paid political organizer, and teacher. Regular contributor to periodicals, including *America Report, Christopher Street, Gay Community News, Ms., Social Policy,* and *Village Voice.* Member of PEN, Women's Institute for Freedom of the Press, Authors League of America. Agent: Elaine Markson, 44 Greenwich Avenue, New York, New York 10011, U.S.A.

WRITINGS

Nonfiction

Women Hating: A Radical Look at Sexuality. New York, Dutton, 1974.

Our Blood: Prophecies and Discourses on Sexual Politics (essays and speeches; includes "Lesbian Pride"). New York, Harper, 1976.

Contributor, *Take Back the Night: Women on Pornography.* New York, Morrow, 1980.

Pornography: Men Possessing Women. New York, Putnam, 1981.

Right–Wing Women: The Politics of Domesticated Females. New York, Putnam, 1983.

Intercourse. Free Press, 1987.

With Catharine A. MacKinnon, *Pornography and Civil Rights: A New Day for Women's Equality.* Organizing Against Pornography, 1988.

Letters from a War Zone (essays). New York, Dutton, 1989.

Novels

Ice and Fire. London, Secker & Warburg, 1986.

Mercy. London, Secker & Warburg, 1990; Four Walls Eight Windows, 1991.

Ruins.

Short Stories

The New Woman's Broken Heart. Frog in the Well, 1980.

*

Interviews: With Elizabeth Wilson, in *Feminist Review,* June 1982, 23–29; *Contemporary Authors New Revision Series,* Volume 16, Detroit, Gale, 1985, 98–101.

Critical Sources: "A Grim Parable of Sexual Ideology" by Sherie Posesorski, in *Globe and Mail* (Toronto), 2 August 1986; "Men As Beasts" by Barbara Amiel, in *Times* (London) 4 June 1987; "Bitterness and Sexual Aggression" by Naomi Black, in *Globe and Mail* (Toronto) 11 July 1987; "The Bare–faced Feminist" by Catherine Bennett, in *Times* (London), 18 May 1988, 122; "Changing My Mind About Andrea Dworkin" by Erica Jong, in *Ms.,* June 1988, 60–64; "Taking the Lid Off" by Hermione Lee, in *Times Literary Supplement* (London), 3–9 June 1988, 611; "Street Fighting Feminist" by Lore Dickstein, in *New York Times Book Review,* 29 October 1989, 11; review by Brian Morton of *Mercy,* in *Bookseller,* 21 September 1990, 837; review by Sarah Kent of *Mercy,* in *Time Out,* 26 September–3 October 1990, 37; "Powerful Voice Against Violent Oppression of Women" by Brian Morton, in *Glasgow Herald,* 4 October 1990; "The Return of Carry Nation" by Camille Paglia, in *Playboy,* October 1992, 36.

*   *   *

One of the most vital and, until recently, least examined aspects of the literature of the gay and lesbian liberation movements that emerged during the 1970s is its interaction with, and treatment of, themes of importance to the women's movement. The demands of openly lesbian feminists created a crisis of conscience within the Women's Liberation movement; no less a figure than Betty Friedan referred to them as the "lavender menace." Out of the fierce debates aimed at assisting newly–awakened women with the complex task

of understanding and defining their multiple oppressions arose a stream of writing of many diverse viewpoints, whose goal was the exploration of the roots of then–current political and social limits and the ways in which these might be challenged. A particularly influential group of militant authors gradually coalesced in the San Francisco Bay Area, represented by such women as poets Pat Parker and Judy Grahn, and the philosopher Susan Griffin. While each would come to find her own voice with which to call for change, few were as insistently controversial as their counterpart in the New York City area, Andrea Dworkin.

Born in Camden, New Jersey, in 1946, and raised on the street where poet Walt Whitman's house stood, Dworkin began writing in elementary school and debated whether to pursue a career in law or become a writer. Her final decision was made in part because, as she later stated in an interview, "the change that happens from writing is very deep" and one of her goals was to alter society. Involving herself in demonstrations against the Vietnam War—and the entire counterculture movement—while a student at Bennington College, Dworkin's first direct experience of the costs of promoting alternative political positions came when she was arrested during a demonstration and held for four days in the New York City Women's House of Detention. Upon her release, she immediately went public with graphic descriptions of the ways in which she had been brutalized by both prison employees and inmates. No woman, Dworkin protested, whatever her status, should be subjected to such indignities.

The anger and outrage generated by this event fueled her initial determination to explore and challenge what she saw as a male–dominated system of power allocation in contemporary society. In 1974, following a period of travel and residence in Crete and the Netherlands, the first of her books appeared. The result of three years of thought, it bore a simple blunt title. *Woman Hating: A Radical Look at Sexuality* conveyed both Dworkin's subject and manifesto.

In the opening paragraphs of the book's introduction, Dworkin outlines her basic agenda for promoting change. "This book is an action, a political action where revolution is the goal. It has no other purpose," she writes. "The commitment to ending male dominance as the fundamental psychological, political and cultural reality of earth–lived life is the fundamental revolutionary commitment, ... a commitment to transformation of the self and transformation of ... reality on every level, ... an analysis of sexism, ... what it is, how it operates on us and in us."

Such rhetoric represents a logical extension of one of feminism's basic tenets into a complete framework for cultural dissection. But, while many feminists and lesbian separatists would have otherwise agreed with some of her premises, Dworkin's radical, vigorous attacks on any institution or practice that she viewed as oppressive to women—in any form—swiftly marked her as independent and distinctive. Between 1974 and 1976, riding the wave of publicity generated by her first work, Dworkin became a familiar figure on the lecture circuit, speaking at Smith College, at a conference held at Boston College entitled "Alternatives to the Military–Corporate System," at a host of major universities in and around New York City, as well as to the National Organization for Women. The complete texts of nine of these speeches were published in 1976 as *Our Blood.* Of particular value to the history of homosexual literature is the address she delivered on 28 June 1975, at a rally for Lesbian Pride Week held in Central Park. Published as "Lesbian Pride," it sets out clearly the author's vision of what it means to be a lesbian in all its manifestations and provides a standard for the evaluation of her subsequent writing from this perspective.

The majority of works published after *Our Blood* continued the analysis of feminist issues Dworkin began in *Woman Hating*. The issue of pornography was most notable among them. With the formation of the San Francisco–based Women Against Violence in Pornography and the Media in 1976, the topic swiftly occasioned considerable debate within all sections of the women's community. Dworkin's view of pornography as a genre that both justifies and celebrates male power over women—thus supporting the basic tenets of the American ideal of masculinity—should be seen in the context of both lesbian feminist philosophy and the women's liberation movement's anger at any reduction of woman to mere object. Realizing her early dreams of effecting change in society through legal channels, Dworkin and lawyer Catherine MacKinnon drafted an ordinance that defined pornography as a type of sex discrimination and those hurt by it as having been deprived of their rights. The ordinance was passed into law in Indianapolis, Indiana, and Minneapolis, Minnesota. It was in the process of being introduced in Los Angeles and Cambridge, Massachusetts, when it was declared unconstitutional in 1986. Some of the ordinance's most vocal opponents were feminists who believed that its passage would place limits on the rights of women to explore all types of sexuality. Dworkin published a collection of writings tracing her involvement with this subject in 1989, under the title *Letters from A War Zone*.

Most of Dworkin's literary work dates from after 1980. Highly varied in form, pieces range from contributions to *Ms.* and the *Village Voice* to works published in *Gay Community News* and *Christopher Street*. Her only collection of short stories, *The New Woman's Broken Heart*, was followed by two autobiographical novels: *Ice and Fire* and the more lengthy *Mercy*, notable for its author's simultaneous praise and condemnation of Walt Whitman for his unrealistic dreams of true democracy in America. Through her professional affiliations with the Authors League of America, the Women's Institute for Freedom of the Press, and PEN, Dworkin continues a tradition of radical lesbianism—born of Stonewall—into the future.

—*Robert B. Marks Ridinger*

DYNES, Wayne R. American educator, editor, and author of nonfiction. Born in Fort Worth, Texas, 23 August 1934. Educated at University of California at Los Angeles, B.A. 1956; New York University, Institute of Fine Arts, Ph.D. 1969 (Woodrow Wilson fellow, 1956–57; university fellow, 1957–58; Fulbright fellow, University of London, 1963–65). Lecturer, Vassar College, 1967–68; instructor, 1968–69, assistant professor, 1969–70, adjunct associate professor, 1974–75, and visiting adjunct professor, 1992, Columbia University; visiting associate professor at University of Pennsylvania, 1971; adjunct associate professor, 1972–74, associate professor, 1974–85, and professor of art history, 1986—, Hunter College of the City University of New York. Editorial representative at Istituto per la Collaborazione Culturale, Rome, 1958–60; translation editor of *Encyclopedia of World Art,* McGraw–Hill Book Co., New York, 1960–63; editor of *Gesta,* International Center of

Medieval Art, 1970–73; editor of *Cabirion and Gay Books Bulletin,* 1979–85; editor of Gai Saber Monograph Series, 1979—; editor of *Garland Gay and Lesbian Studies,* 1989—. Member of editorial board, *Journal of Homosexuality,* 1989—, and *Journal of the History of Sexuality,* 1990—. **Recipient:** Gay Academic Union Scholarship (GAU) Award, 1981; PSC–CUNY research award, 1984–85; CUNY Scholar Incentive Award, 1986, 1992. Address: 90 Morningside Drive, 2K, New York, New York 10027, U.S.A.

WRITINGS

Nonfiction

Palaces of Europe. London, Paul Hamlyn, 1969.
The Illuminations of the Stavelot Bible. New York, Garland, 1978.
With Peter Basquin, Marlies Danziger, and Gerald Pinciss, *Explorations in the Arts* (Humanities text based on an interdisciplinary course taught at Hunter College). New York, Holt, 1985.
Homolexis: A Historical and Cultural Lexicon on Homosexuality. New York, Gay Academic Union, 1985.
With Marshall Neal Myers, *Hieronymus Bosch and the Canticle of Isaiah.* New York, Cabirion Press, 1987.
Homosexuality: A Research Guide. New York, Garland, 1987.
Editor, with Warren Johansson, William A. Percy, and Stephen Donaldson, *Encyclopedia of Homosexuality* (two volumes). New York, Garland, 1990.
With Stephen Donaldson, *Major Lines of Investigation in Gay/Lesbian Studies.* New York, GAU, 1992.
Historiography of Art History, 1993.
Editor, with Stephen Donaldson, *Concise Encyclopedia of Homosexuality.* New York, Macmillan, forthcoming.

Editor, with Stephen Donaldson; *Studies in Homosexuality* Series

Asian Homosexuality. New York, Garland, 1992.
Cross–Cultural Studies of Homosexuality. New York, Garland, 1992.
History of Homosexuality in Europe and America. New York, Garland, 1992.
Homosexual Themes in Literary Studies. New York, Garland, 1992.
Homosexuality and Government, Politics and Prisons. New York, Garland, 1992.
Homosexuality and Homosexuals in the Arts. New York, Garland, 1992.
Homosexuality and Medicine, Health, and Science. New York, Garland, 1992.
Homosexuality and Psychology, Psychiatry and Counseling. New York, Garland, 1992.
Homosexuality and Religion and Philosophy. New York, Garland, 1992.
Homosexuality in the Ancient World. New York, Garland, 1992.
Homosexuality: Discrimination, Criminology, and the Law. New York, Garland, 1992.
Lesbianism. New York, Garland, 1992.
Sociology of Homosexuality. New York, Garland, 1992.

Other

"Orpheus without Eurydice," in *Gai Saber,* 1:3–4, 1978.

"Christianity and the Politics of Sex," in *Homosexuality, Intolerance and Christianity,* edited by Warren Johansson. New York, Gay Academic Union, revised, 1985.

"Portugayese," in *Male Homosexuality in Central and South America,* edited by S. O. Murray. San Francisco, Instituto Obregon, 1987.

"Wrestling with the Social Boa Constructor," in *Forms of Desire: Sexual Orientation and the Social Construction Controversy,* edited by E. Stein. New York, Garland, 1990.

"Homosexuality," in *Encyclopedia of the 1890s,* edited by G. A. Cevasco. New York, Garland, 1993.

*

Wayne R. Dynes comments: "In the present intellectual climate of relativism and nihilism, I remain a rationalist, committed to weighing and improving ideas, always comparing them with empirical data, so that human knowledge, which is a unity, may advance ever closer to truth. Only this unceasing quest for truth can establish a firm foundation for social justice."

*   *   *

In the formative period of gay studies in the United States, Wayne R. Dynes towered over his contemporaries by virtue of both his Central European education and the breadth of his intellectual horizon. Trained at the Institute of Fine Arts of New York University and the Warburg Institute of the University of London, he brought to the emerging field the legacy of his émigré teachers—the profound culture instilled by Erwin Panofsky, Karl Lehmann, and Richard Krautheimer in New York, and the philosophical insight of Sir Karl Popper in London. Dynes is today professor of art History at Hunter College of the City University of New York.

As far back as the 1950s Dynes had made contact with the leaders of ONE in Los Angeles. In 1971 he became an early member of the Gay Task Force of the American Library Association led by Barbara Gittings. Two years later he was a founder of the Gay Academic Union, which held its first conference at John Jay College in New York City in November 1973. In the winter of 1973 and 1974 he organized the Scholarship Committee of the New York Chapter of GAU, which has been his focus of activity ever since.

Along with hosting monthly meetings of the Scholarship Committee in his New York apartment, he edited *Gay Books Bulletin,* later the *Cabirion,* hailed as the premier journal of gay scholarship. Assembling a group of devoted collaborators, he gathered the results of their discussions first in the 1985 *Homolexis: A Historical and Cultural Lexicon of Homosexuality.* In 1987 he issued *Homosexuality: A Research Guide,* which instantly earned the status of the standard bibliography of the field.

His crowning achievement was as editor–in–chief of the 1990 *Encyclopedia of Homosexuality,* with 770 articles in two volumes——the largest work ever published on the subject in any language. The transcendent objectivity of the book, its joining of the legacy of the pre–1933 German movement with a critical approach to the thinking of earlier generations and with methodological advances of recent decades, and the international scope of its entries have made it incomparable and irreplaceable. It ranks with the *Encyclopédie* of Diderot and D'Alembert and the *Larousse du XIXe* siècle as one of the great reference works that projected a new image of the world. At the same time it scorned the intellectual fashions of the hour to lay a solid and enduring foundation for insightful research in the future. A *Concise Encyclopedia of Homosexuality* is being edited to celebrate the 25th anniversary of the Stonewall Uprising in 1994.

Most recently, Dynes has edited the *Garland Gay and Lesbian Studies* and a set of volumes of reprints of major articles under the series title of *Studies in Homosexuality.* His rigorous intellectual training, his command of many languages and disciplines, and the depth and breadth of his investigations find no parallel in the contemporary United States, where beside him most self–styled gay scholars are little more than propagandists or dilettantes. He has earned a lasting place in academic history as one of the authentic founders of the "gay science."

—*Warren Johansson*

E-F

EARLY, Jack. *See* **SCOPPETTONE, Sandra.**

———

ELLERMAN, Annie Winifred. *See* **BRYHER.**

———

ELLIS, (Henry) Havelock. British physician, anthropologist, and essayist. Born in Croydon, Surrey, 2 February 1859. Educated at St. Thomas Hospital, London, 1880–c. 1887; received licentiate in Medicine, Surgery, and Midwifery from Society of Apothecaries, 1889. Married Edith Lees in 1891. Taught school in Australia, c. 1870s; editor, "Mermaid Series: The Best Plays of the Old Dramatists," 1887–1896. Member of the Fellowship of the New Life. *Died in Hintlesham, 8 July 1939.*

WRITINGS

Nonfiction

The Criminal. London, W. Scott, 1890.
Man and Woman: A Study of Human Secondary Sexual Characters. London, W. Scott, 1894.
Studies in the Psychology of Sex: Volume 1: *Sexual Inversion,* as *Das kontraere Geschlechtsgefuehl,* Germany, 1896; with John Addington Symonds, London, Wilson & Macmillan, 1897; revised without coauthor as Volume 2, 1901; Volume 2: *The Evolution of Modesty, the Phenomena of Sexual Periodicity, Auto–Eroticism,* 1899, revised as Volume 1, 1900; Volume 3: *The Analysis of the Sexual Impulse, Love and Pain, the Sexual Impulse in Women,* 1903; Volume 4: *Sexual Selection in Man: Touch, Smell, Hearing, Vision.* 1905; Volume 5: *Erotic Symbolism, the Mechanism of Detumescence, the Psychic State in Pregnancy,* 1906; Volume 6: *Sex in Relation to Society,* 1910; Volume 7: *Eonism, and Other Supplementary Studies,* 1928.
A Study of British Genius. London, Hurst & Blackett, 1904.
The Problem of Race Regeneration, 1911.
The Task of Social Hygiene. London, Constable, 1912.

The Play–Function of Sex. London, British Society for the Study of Sex Psychology, 1921.
Psychology of Sex: A Manual for Students. London, Heinemann, 1933.
Sex and Marriage: Eros in Contemporary Life, edited by John Gawsworth. London, Williams & Norgate, 1951.

Literary Criticism

The New Spirit. London, G. Bell, 1890; with new preface, London, W. Scott, 1892.
Affirmations. London, W. Scott, 1898; new edition, London, Constable, 1915.
Views and Reviews: A Selection of Uncollected Articles, 1884–1932. London, Desmond Harmsworth, 1932.
From Rousseau to Proust. London, Constable, 1934.
From Marlowe to Shaw: The Studies, 1876–1936, in English Literature, edited by John Gawsworth. London, Williams & Norgate, 1950.

Essays

The Nationalization of Health. London, T. Fischer Unwin, 1892.
Mescal: A New Artificial Paradise, 1897.
A Note on the Bedborough Trial. London, University Press, 1898.
The Nineteenth Century: A Dialogue in Utopia. London, Grant Richards, 1900.
The Soul of Spain. London, Constable, 1908.
The World of Dreams. London, Constable, 1911.
Essays in War–Time. London, Constable, 1916.
Women, and The Objects of Marriage: Two Essays. London, British Society for the Study of Sex Psychology, 1918.
The Philosophy of Conflict, and Other Essays in War–Time. London, Constable, 1919.
Little Essays of Love and Virtue. London, A. & C. Black, 1922; in *On Life and Sex,* 1948.
The Dance of Life. London, Constable, 1923.
The Colour–Sense in Literature (originally appeared in *Contemporary Review,* May 1896). London, Ulysses Book Shop, 1931.
Concerning Jude the Obscure (first published in *Savoy,* October 1896). London, Ulysses Book Shop, 1931.
More Essays in Love and Virtue. London, Constable, 1931; in *On Life and Sex,* 1948.
My Confessional: Questions of Our Day. London, John Lane, 1934.
Selected Essays. London, J. M. Dent, 1936.
Morals, Manners, and Men. London, Watts, 1939.
On Life and Sex (includes *Little Essays of Love and Virtue* and *More Essays of Love and Virtue*). London, Heinemann, 1948.

Memoirs

Impressions and Comments: First Series, London, Constable, 1921; *Second Series,* London, Constable, 1921; *Third series,* London, Constable, 1924.
Fountain of Life: Being the Impressions and Comments of Havelock Ellis. 1930.
My Life. London, Heinemann, 1940; revised, bibliography by Alan Hull Walton, London, Spearman, 1967.

Editor

The Pillars of Society, and Other Plays, by Heinrich Ibsen, 1888.
The Pentameron, and Other Imaginary Conversations, by Walter S. Landor, 1889.
Life in Nature by James Surgeon Hinton, 1932.
The Dramatist by Christopher Marlowe, 1951.

Translator

Germinal, by Emile Zola, 1894.
Sonnets, with Folk Songs from the Spanish. Golden Cockerel Press, 1925.

Other

Women and Marriage; or, Evolution in Sex (originally appeared in *Westminster Review*). London, W. Reeves, 1888.
Kanga Creek: An Australian Idyll (novel). Golden Cockerel Press, 1922.
The Art of Life: Gleanings from the Works of Havelock Ellis (essays, criticism, and nonfiction). London, Constable, 1929.
Chapman. London, Nonesuch Press, 1934.
Poems, selected by John Gawsworth. London, Richards, 1937.
The Genius of Europe. London, Williams & Norgate, 1950.
The Unpublished Letters of Havelock Ellis to Joseph Ishill. Berkeley Heights, New Jersey, privately printed, 1954.

*

Biography: *The Sage of Sex: A Life of Havelock Ellis* by Arthur Calder–Marshall, New York, Putnam, 1959; *Havelock Ellis, Philosopher of Sex* by Vincent Brome, Routledge & Kegan Paul, 1979; *Havelock Ellis: A Biography* by Phyllis Grosskurth, New York, Knopf, 1980.

Interviews: With Herman Bernstein, in *Celebrities of Our Time,* New York, Joseph Lauren, 1924, 136–142.

Critical Sources: *Havelock Ellis, Artist of Life: A Study of His Life and Work* by John Stewart Collis, William Sloane Associates, 1959; "The First of the Yea–Sayers: Henry Havelock Ellis" by Edward M. Brecher, in *The Sex Researchers,* Boston, Little, Brown, 1969, 3–49; "Havelock Ellis" by Paul Robinson, in *The Modernization of Sex: Havelock Ellis, Alfred Kinsey, William Masters, and Virginia Johnson,* New York, Harper, 1976, 1–41.

Henry Havelock Ellis was the first major writer on homosexuality in English, and one of the great scientific authorities on human sexuality in the first half of the twentieth century. Educated as a physician, from his first articles published in medical journals and monographs in the early 1890s to his death in 1939, he waged a campaign to inform and enlighten a public still in the grip of Victorian ignorance and prudery, and to create a viable science of sexual attraction and behavior. At the outset he collaborated with John Addington Symonds, who had privately published two essays, *A Problem in Greek Ethics* in 1883, and *A Problem in Modern Ethics* in 1891, and both names figured on *Das konträre Geschlechtsgefühl* in 1896, the German translation of *Sexual Inversion,* but Symonds' family pressured Ellis to remove the name of the deceased from the English version of the following year.

Sexual Inversion was the second volume of *Studies in the Psychology of Sex,* published in six volumes between 1897 and 1910. Like all writing on homosexuality in English at that time, it was a derivative work, heavily dependent upon the publications on the subject in Germany and Austria, and especially the books and articles of Magnus Hirschfeld and his collaborators on the Wissenschaftlich–humanitäre Komitee, which it conveniently summarized for the English reader. But the *Studies* as a whole had a comprehensive character embracing all facets of sexuality, normal and abnormal, in a way that no German work except perhaps Iwan Bloch's *The Sexual Life of Our Time in Its Relations to Modern Civilization* in 1907 had done. They introduced a new way of thinking about sexuality that stripped it of the aura of the magical and demonic in which the Judeo–Christian tradition had invested it, and placed it instead in a framework of empirical biology and sociology. They are purely descriptive, as Ellis resisted the analytic approach of modern depth psychology to the very end, but as such a landmark and an imperishable classic.

In all three editions of *Sexual Inversion,* the last published in 1915, Ellis upheld the neo–Aristotelian view that true, primary homosexuality is inborn, constitutionally determined, spontaneous, and unmodifiable by any accident of psychological development or chance vicissitude in the life of the individual. To the end of his life he rejected the neo–Thomistic conception of homosexuality as secondary and acquired by fixation at an immature stage of psychosexual development, seduction in adolescence, or vicious habit in adulthood, even though its psychoanalytic formulation was gaining ground as a rationalization of theological homophobia. Ellis thus faithfully continued the tradition begun by Karl Heinrich Ulrichs and ratified by Westphal and Krafft–Ebing, but gave it his own interpretation. By citing case histories collected mainly by correspondence with miscellaneous writers, though not by statistical surveys of the kind initiated by Hirschfeld and amplified by Kinsey, he sought to refute the notion that homosexuality could be a form of "masturbatory insanity," or that the homosexual was a satyr, a debauchee who turned to unnatural vice because he had ceased to derive any thrill from normal sexuality. Ellis argued that homosexuality paralleled color blindness, a phenomenon discovered by Dalton in 1794, as a condition that fundamentally altered the subject's perception of the surrounding world, but was outwardly visible to no one.

Ellis could thus argue for the legal tolerance and social acceptance of the invert, and his book was the first major plea in the English–speaking world for reform of the penal statutes—made even harsher by the Criminal Law Amendment Act of 1885 that added "gross indecency" to the list of crimes. It meant that any sexual activity between males that disgusted or outraged a nominally heterosexual judge or jury could earn a sentence of two years' imprisonment—with or without hard labor. Received in many American jurisdictions, it made the plight of the homosexual even more precarious. And the "infamy of fact" inherited from the Middle Ages was perpetuated and reinforced by the moral purity campaigns of the Victorian age.

Like his German contemporaries, Ellis invoked the data of animal behavior and of comparative anthropology to prove that homosexuality was not "unnatural," that it was not the result of "cultural decadence," but occurred in many species of animal and among human beings at all stages of civilization, from the most primitive to the most cultured. He assembled case histories to show that sexual inversion could run in families, and that the subjects experienced their fondness for their own sex at an early age, before they had been "corrupted" by anyone or even suspected how Western society stigmatized the overt behavior. The book was not just a detached collection of empirical findings, it was an apologia for those whom Victorian morality branded criminals and outcasts addicted to the filthiest of all vices. Ellis argued that this attitude had not always prevailed, certainly not in the Greek civilization that was one of the wellsprings of modern Western culture, and that homoerotic bonding could even possess a utility for the social order.

The work of Havelock Ellis had little measurable impact in his lifetime. He held no university chair, headed no institute, and founded no school. At his death in 1939 the criminal laws in England and the United States were still unchanged. But 18 years later, his legacy bore fruit: when in September 1957 the Wolfenden Committee delivered its report recommending repeal of the laws against buggery and gross indecency, it was solidly endorsed by the liberal wing of the establishment, and the Homosexual Law Reform Society put through the changes in a single decade. Although by the middle of the century *Studies in the Psychology of Sex* belonged to the history of the subject, it posed many questions that remain for researchers of the future to answer. Most important of all, in place of the irrational hatred and loathing inculcated by the Judeo–Christian tradition, Ellis bequeathed to the modern world an enlightened and rational attitude toward not just love for one's own sex, but all the manifold phenomena of human sexuality.

—*Warren Johansson*

FADERMAN, Lillian. American educator, editor, and author of nonfiction. Born in the Bronx, New York, 18 July 1940. Educated at University of California, Berkeley, A.B. 1962; University of California, Los Angeles, M.A. 1964, Ph.D. 1967. Affiliated with California State University, Fresno, beginning in 1967, associate professor, 1971–72, professor of English, 1973—, chair of department, 1971–72, dean of School of Humanities, 1972–73, assistant vice–president of academic affairs, 1973–76; visiting professor, University of California, Los Angeles, 1989–91. Contributor to *Massachusetts Review, New England Quarterly, Journal of Popular Culture, Conditions, Signs, Journal of Homosexuality,* and *Journal of the History of Sexuality.* Member of Modern Language Association of America. Address: Department of English, California State University, Fresno, California 93740, U.S.A.

WRITINGS

With Barbara Bradshaw, *Speaking for Ourselves: American Ethnic Writing.* Glenview, Illinois, Scott, Foresman, 1969.

Editor, with Luis Omar Salinas, *From the Barrio: A Chicano Anthology.* Canfield Press, 1973.

"Warding Off the Watch and Ward Society: Amy Lowell's Treatment of the Lesbian Theme," in *Gay Books Bulletin* (New York), summer 1979.

With Brigitte Eriksson, *Lesbian–Feminism in Turn–of–the–Century Germany.* Tallahassee, Naiad Press, 1980; as *Lesbians in Germany: 1890s to 1920s,* Tallahassee, Naiad Press, 1990.

Surpassing the Love of Men: Romantic Friendship and Love between Women from the Renaissance to the Present. New York, Morrow, 1981.

Scotch Verdict. New York, Morrow, 1983.

Odd Girls and Twilight Lovers: A History of Lesbian Life in Twentieth Century America. New York, Columbia University Press, 1991.

"Harlem Nights: Savvy Women of the '20s Knew Where to Find New York's Lesbian Life," in *Advocate,* 26 March 1991, 54.

*

Critical Sources: "Women Who Love Women" by Carolyn G. Heilbrun in *New York Times Book Review,* 5 April 1981, 12; "The Invention of the Lesbian" by Joanna Russ in *Washington Post Book World,* 3 May 1981, 6; "Sapphic Bliss" by Keith Walker in *Times Literary Supplement,* 4 September 1981, 1014; "Rogues, Misers and Madmen" by Allan Massie in *Spectator,* 16 March 1985, 28–29; "Women in Love" by Susan Brownmiller in *Washington Post Book World,* 23 June 1991, 1, 10; review by Patricia Sarles of *Odd Girls and Twilight Lovers,* in *Library Journal,* August 1991, 128; "Out of the Closet and into History" by Jeffrey Escoffier in *New York Times Book Review,* 28 June 1992, 1, 24; "Talking Heads" by Jane Mills in *New Statesman and Society,* 17 July 1992, 48.

*   *   *

Lillian Faderman, a professor of English at California State University in Fresno, documents the history of lesbianism in two volumes: *Surpassing the Love of Men: Romantic Friendship and Love between Women from the Renaissance to the Present* and *Odd Girls and Twilight Lovers: A History of Lesbian Life in Twentieth Century America.* In the first work, Faderman examines the shifts in societal views toward lesbianism that have taken place from the sixteenth century to the twentieth century. In her second title, *Odd Girls and Twilight Lovers,* she concentrates on the changes in social attitudes toward lesbianism that have transpired from the beginnings of the twentieth century through to the present.

Faderman was inspired to research and write *Surpassing the Love of Men* after discovering romantic letters that poet Emily Dickinson penned around the mid–1800s to Sue Gilbert, who later became Dickinson's sister–in–law. When the letters were edited for publication in the 1920s, they were purged of all references to romantic love. In *Surpassing the Love of Men,* Faderman suggests that the passionate sections were deleted to avoid any connection to lesbianism, a sexual orientation that Austrian psychoanalyst Sigmund Freud declared around the turn of the century was "morbid." Faderman believes that Freud's statement, combined with the negative views of other sexologists of the time, led to lesbianism becoming socially unacceptable.

In *Surpassing the Love of Men,* Faderman provides evidence that, from the 1500s through to the twentieth century, "romantic friendships" between women were not only fairly common, but public as well. Passion was frequently expressed through letters, poems, and diary entries, and the relationships were generally considered benign and virtuous. Such relationships were viewed with suspicion only when a lesbian attempted to usurp a male's power or if she sought to attain the status of a male. And if a woman chose to marry another woman, both involved were prosecuted.

Faderman reports that because of the opinions of authority figures like Freud, attitudes toward lesbians began to change near the beginning of the twentieth century. Society, in general, began to view lesbians as "diseased" and such women were told to hate themselves. They were forced into secrecy and faced censure if their sexual orientations were revealed. The author concludes that the condemnation of lesbians has been one way in which males have attempted to dominate women. By dictating the social acceptability of various sexual orientations, she states, men have been able to control who women love, how women live, and how—by making them dependent on the financial security of a traditional marriage—women survive economically.

In *Odd Girls and Twilight Lovers,* Faderman focuses on the shifts in public reaction to lesbianism that have occurred during the twentieth century. Faderman bases her work on personal letters, unpublished manuscripts, diaries, songs, and nearly two hundred interviews. She reports that as women became increasingly educated and as they entered the workforce in larger numbers in the twentieth century, they no longer needed to rely on men for financial security. Consequently, love between women came to be viewed not with sentimentality—as it had previously—but with condemnation. Moreover, Faderman contends that since Freud emphasized the sexual nature of the relationships, lesbians could no longer live together without raising suspicions that they were sexually involved.

In addition, Faderman reveals that in certain decades in particular—namely the 1910s, 1930s, and 1950s—lesbians faced repression in the form of federal employers who terminated suspected homosexuals for alleged security reasons, and in the form of anxious heterosexuals who encouraged raids on gay bars. Faderman points out, though, that even during periods of severe social strictures, the lesbian culture continued to grow. According to Jane Mills in *New Statesman and Society,* one of the particular merits of *Odd Girls and Twilight Lovers* is that Faderman moves "from turn-of-the-century sexologists who introduced a poisonously reductive definition of lesbianism as genital contact to present-day lesbians and gays, who have gained ... power to define themselves."

—Denise Kasinec

————

FARR, Hilary. *See* **FOSTER, Jeannette Howard.**

FASSBINDER, Rainer Werner. German playwright, author of screenplays, director, and producer of plays and films. Born in Bad Woerishofen, Bavaria, 31 May 1946. Educated at public schools in Germany, and at Fridi–Leophard Studio, Munich, c. 1966. Married actress Ingrid Caven in 1970 (divorced). Actor in Munich Action Theatre, 1967–68, and in motion pictures, including *Tonys Freunde,* 1967; *Baal,* 1969; *Katzelmacher,* 1969; *Warnung vor einer heiligen Nutte,* 1971; and *Faustrecht der Freiheit,* 1975. Director of plays, including *Iphigenie auf Taurus, Pioniere in Ingolstadt, Ajax, Anarchie in Bayern,* and *Das bisschen Realitaet, das ich brauche.* Director of films, including *The Merchant of Four Seasons, Satan's Brew, The Marriage of Maria Braun,* and *Lola.* Founder of Munich Antiteatre, 1968, and cofounder of Film–Verlag der Autoren, 1970. **Recipient:** West German Film Critics Prize, 1969; Federal Film Prize, 1969 and 1970; Cannes Film Festival critic's award, 1974; Berlin Film Festival first prize, 1979; Berlin Film Festival Golden Bear Prize, 1982; German Academy of Producing Arts television award; Gerhard Hauptmann prize; and other film awards. *Died in Munich, West Germany (now Germany), of an overdose of cocaine and sleeping pills, 10 June 1982.*

WRITINGS

Plays

Adapter, Johann Wolfgang Goethe, *Iphigenie auf Taurus* (produced Munich, 1968).

Pioniere in Ingolstadt (adaptation of play by Marie–Louise Fleisser; produced Munich, 1968).

Ajax (adaptation of the writings of Sophocles; produced Munich, 1968).

Orgie Ubu (adaptation of the play *Ubu Roi* by Alfred Jarry; produced Munich, 1968).

Anarchie in Bayern (produced Munich, 1969).

Werwolf (produced Munich, 1969).

Katzelmacher (produced Munich). Frankfurt, Verlag der Autoren, 1969.

With John Gay, *Die Bettleroper* (produced Munich). Frankfurt, Verlag der Autoren, 1970.

Das brennende Dorf (adaptation of the writings of Lope de Vega; produced Munich). Frankfurt, Verlag der Autoren, 1970.

Blut am Hals der Katze (produced Munich). Frankfurt, Verlag der Autoren, 1970.

Bremer Freiheit [and] *Ein buergerliches Trauerspiel* (produced Munich). Frankfurt, Verlag der Autoren, 1971.

Die bitteren Traenen der Petra von Kant (produced Munich). Frankfurt, Verlag der Autoren, 1973.

With Hans Guenther Pflaum, *Das bisschen Realitaet, das ich brauche* (produced Munich). Munich, Hanser, 1976.

Antiteater (plays; contains *Katzelmacher, Preparadise Sorry Now,* and *Die Bettleroper*). Frankfurt, Suhrkamp, 1970.

Antiteater Two (plays; contains *Das Kaffehaus,* adaptation of the play by Carlo Goldoni, *Bremer Freiheit,* and *Blut am Hals der Katze*). Frankfurt, Suhrkamp, 1972.

Stuecke Three (plays; contains *Die bitteren Traenen der Petra von Kant, Das brennede Dorf,* and *Der Muell, die Stadt und der Tod*). Frankfurt, Suhrkamp, 1976.

Screenplays

Der Stadtstreicher (short film), Roser–Film, 1965; English version released as *The City Bums.*

Das kleine Chaos (short film), Roser–Film, 1966; English version released as *The Small Chaos.*

Liebe ist kaelter als Tod, Antiteater–X–Film, 1969; English version released as *Love Is Colder than Death.*

Katzelmacher, Antiteater–X–Film, 1969.

Goetter der Pest, Antiteater–X–Film, 1969; English version released as *Gods of the Plague.*

With Michael Fengler, *Warum laeuft Herr R. amok?,* Antiteater/Mara–Film, 1969; English version released as *Why Does Herr R. Run Amok?*

Der amerikanische Soldat, Antiteater, 1970; English version released as *The American Soldier.*

With Michael Fengler, *Die niklashauser Fahrt,* Janus Film, 1970; English version released as *The Niklashauser Drive.*

Rio das Mortes, Janus Film/Antiteater–X–Film, 1970.

Whity, Atlantis Film/Antiteater–X–Film, 1970.

Warung vor einer heiligen Nutte, Antiteater–X–Film/Nova International, 1970; English version released as *Beware of a Holy Whore.*

Haendler der vier Jahreszeiten, Tango Film, 1971; English version released as *The Merchant of Four Seasons.*

Die bitteren Traenen der Petra von Kant, Tango Film, 1972.

Effi Briest (adaptation of the novel by Theodore Fontane), Tango Film, 1974.

With Christian Hohoff, *Faustrecht der Freiheit,* Tango Film, 1975; English version released as *Fox and His Friends; Survival of the Fittest* and *Fist–Right of Freedom.*

With Kurt Raab, *Mutter Kuesters faehrt zum Himmel,* Tango Film, 1975; English version released as *Mother Kuesters Goes to Heaven.*

Satansbraten. Albatros Productions, 1976; English version released as *Satan's Brew.*

Chinesisches Roulette, Albatros–Film/Les Films du Losange, 1977; English version released as *Chinese Roulette.*

Die dritte Generation, Tango Film/Project Filmproduktion im Filmverlag der Autoren, 1978; English version released as *The Third Generation.*

Die Ehe der Maria Braun, Albatros Film, 1978; English version released as *The Marriage of Maria Braun.*

In einem Jahr mit 13 Monden, [West Germany], 1978; English version released as *In a Year with 13 Moons.*

With Peter Marthesheimer and Pea Frohlich, *Lola,* United Artists Classics, 1982.

With Daniel Schmid, *Schatten der Engel* (adaptation of *Der Muell, die Stadt und der Tod*), [Germany], 1976.

Television Plays

Pioniere in Ingolstadt (adaptation of the play by Marie–Louise Fleisser), Janus Film/Antiteater, 1971; released in United States as *Recruits in Ingolstadt.*

Acht Stunden sind kein Tag (contains "Jochen und Marion," "Oma und Gregor," "Franz und Ernst," "Harald und Monika," and "Irmgard und Rolf"), WDR–TV, 1972–73; English version released as *Eight Hours Don't Make a Day.*

Wildwechsel (adaptation of the play by Franz Xaver Kroetz), Intertel, 1973; English version released as *Game Pass.*

With Fritz Mueller–Scherz, *Welt am Draht* (adaptation of the novel by Daniel F. Galouye), WDR–TV, 1973; English version released as *World on a Wire.*

Angst isst die Seele auf, Tango Film, 1974; English version released as *Ali: Fear Eats the Soul.*

Martha, WDR–TV, 1974.

Ich will doch nur, dass ihr Mich liebt, [West Germany], 1976; English version released as *I Only Want You to Love Me.*

Berlin Alexanderplatz (based on the novel by Alfred Doeblin), Teleculture Films, 1980.

Querelle (based on the novel *Querelle de Brest* by Jean Genet). [West Germany], 1982; Triumph Films, 1983.

Bolwieser (adaptation of the book by Oskar Maria Graf), Bavaria Atelier, 1983; English version released as *The Stationmaster's Wife.*

Other

Frauen in New York.

*

Critical Sources: *Fassbinder,* edited by Tony Rayns, British Film Institute, 1976.

*   *   *

At the time of his death at the age of 36, Rainer Werner Fassbinder was considered to be one of the foremost film directors in the world. Not only had his films met with critical and popular success, but his output was prodigious: from 1965 until his death 17 years later he wrote and directed 41 full–length feature films as well as a dozen shorts. He was also a driving force in the West German theater scene, where he wrote and directed more than a dozen stage works. Along with directors Wim Wenders and Werner Herzog, Fassbinder was one of the pioneers of German New Wave cinema. But his position as an out gay artist also placed him in the vanguard of exploring the potentials and parameters of a contemporary gay aesthetic in film.

Fassbinder was born in Bad Worishofen, Bavaria, West Germany. He was the only child of a middle–class family; his father was a physician and his mother a noted translator who had rendered Truman Capote, among others, into German. Fassbinder grew up watching Hollywood films, and this perhaps more than anything else was the main influence on his sensibility and directorial vision. He particularly respected the work of German emigree filmmaker Douglas Sirk, who specialized in women's films and who was one of Hollywood's major artists in the 1940s and 1950s. Fassbinder left home at the age of 16 and began working in the theater in Berlin, Frankfurt, and Nurenberg. He joined the Munich Action Theater in 1967 but quickly broke from it and started his own Antiteater, a communal acting endeavor that performed in bars, empty theaters, and unused movie houses. From this group he eventually put together a repertory company of performers who were to appear in his films over the next 15 years.

Although he continued to write and direct for the stage until

1976, Fassbinder's main artistic outlet was film. He directed his first short film, *Der Stadtstreicher* (released in the United States as *The City Bums*) in 1965 and by 1969 was making his first full–length feature, *Liebe ist Kaelter ais Tod* (*Love is Colder than Death*). Many of his early films were stark portrayals of German working–class life that focused on the post–war economic problems of German workers and their families. Even in these early works, Fassbinder was particularly interested in the lives of his women characters and wrote many of the roles for the dynamic women actors in his company: Ingrid Craven, Irm Harmann, Hanna Schygulla, Eva Mattes and Margarit Carstensen, among others. His use of female performers and characters to convey the emotional essence of his work clearly placed Fassbinder in a tradition of gay male sensibility.

With the release of the 1972 *Die bitteren Traenen der Petra von Kant* ("The Bitter Tears of Petra von Kant"), Fassbinder began to establish an artistic vision and pattern that would continue for the next decade. Based on his own stage play, *Petra von Kant* ostensibly tells the story of several dysfunctional lesbian relationships, but beneath this is an examination of power dynamics. While earlier Fassbinder films looked at clearly defined power struggles in the material world, *Petra von Kant* moved this theme into the realm of the personal. Borrowing technique from Douglas Sirk, the film is shot in lurid colors (reminiscent of the unworldly Technicolor of the 1950s) and framed in odd, dislocating camera angles. The script itself is a mixture of realistic dialogue and dreamy, sometimes surreal, images. This Brechtian juxtaposition allowed Fassbinder to place his political ideas in a broader—more psychological and cultural—context. The extreme emotions, the elaborate art direction, and the use of melodrama in conjunction with the clear delineation of social power located Fassbinder's work somewhere between serious, high camp, and traditional Marxist art. This same technique in style and ideology is also clearly present in his 1975 *Faustrecht der Freiheit* (*Fox and His Friends*), in which a working–class gay man is preyed upon by wealthier gay men after he wins the lottery. Both films were picketed by gay activist groups when they were released in the United States for what was seen to be homophobic representations of gay people. They have since become staples in lesbian and gay film festivals.

Like many gay artists from Oscar Wilde, in his verse drama *Salome,* to Charles Ludlum, in his mock–tragedy *Camille,* Fassbinder's work is fueled to a large degree by reinterpreting older cultural artifacts. In 1974 he wrote and directed a version of Fontane's *Effie Briest* and would later reinterpret such works as Douglas Sirk's *All That Heaven Allows* (*Ali: Fear Eats the Soul,* 1974); Clare Booth Luce's *The Women* (*Frauen in New York,* 1977); von Sternberg's *The Blue Angel* (*Lola,* 1981); and Jean Genet's *Querelle de Brest* (*Querelle,* 1982). In addition to this, Fassbinder also continually used artifacts from popular culture—from The Platters singing "The Great Pretender" at the end of *The Bitter Tears of Petra von Kant* to Oscar Wilde's "The Ballad of Reading Gaol" in *Querelle*—to locate and reinforce his ideas in the realm of a politicized popular culture.

Fassbinder scored his biggest hit in 1978 with *Die Ehe der Maria Braun* (*The Marriage of Maria Braun*). In this film he retold post–war German economic history using the Hollywood genre of the woman's film. Using the frame of such films as *Mildred Pierce* and *Imitation of Life,* Fassbinder traces the career and love life of Maria Braun, who begins as a homeless bar girl and becomes a prominent business woman. Fassbinder charts not only the rise of the German economy but the ensuant political changes—including radical ter-

rorism—as well. Although he was using an established form; Fassbinder placed his own political spin upon it. Whereas in the traditional women's film the protagonist is saved from a loveless life of success by love, Maria Braun's downfall comes from her romantic sentimentality. *The Marriage of Maria Braun* became the first of a trilogy, and a similar idea is present in the second installment, *Lola.* In this film, as a feminist twist on the misogynistic *The Blue Angel,* the heroine has more integrity as a prostitute than as the wife of an important businessman. The third segment of the trilogy *Veronika Voss* in 1981, was a cynical retelling of Billy Wilder's 1950 film *Sunset Boulevard,* mixed with Fassbinder's own thoughts on the evils of the popular press as well as doctors. All three of these films show the influence of Hollywood culture, as well as feminism, on Fassbinder's work.

Fassbinder's last film, *Querelle*—taken from the novel by Jean Genet—was a highly stylized meditation on male eroticism and aesthetics. In this film Fassbinder created of a gay–male–centered universe: all of the characters are constructed from stereotypes that appear in gay pornography, the set itself is a series of subtle, and not–so–subtle phallic images, and the lurid colors and lighting resemble not only cheap Hollywood thrillers, but also the covers of 1950s American gay pulp paperback novels. Fassbinder's eye for sexual fetish juxtaposed with his grand scale direction made *Querelle* look as though it was Uniform Night at a leather bar as directed by Busby Berkeley. His gay male aesthetic sensibility found its full fruition in *Querelle,* and the open homoeroticism of the film—much of which, unlike *Fox and His Friends,* is presented in a positive light—stands in sharp contrast to his more ironic portrayals of female sexuality in his earlier work. *Querelle* was Fassbinder's last work before he died in Munich on 10 June 1982.

—*Michael Bronski*

FEINBERG, David B. American novelist and essayist. Born in Lynn, Massachusetts, 25 November 1956. Educated at Massachusetts Institute of Technology, S.B. 1977, New York University, M.A. 1981. Manager of MLACC for Modern Language Association of America since 1981. Active member of AIDS Coalition to Unleash Power (ACT UP). Regular contributor of stories and reviews to *Tribe, Outweek, Advocate, Gay Community News, Mandate, James White Review,* and *QW.* **Recipient:** Lambda Literary Award for Gay Men's Fiction; American Library Association Gay/Lesbian Book Award for Fiction; New York Public Library Books to Remember Committee. Address: c/o Modern Language Association of America, 10 Astor Place, New York, New York 10003, U.S.A.

WRITINGS

Novels

Eighty–Sixed. New York, Viking, 1989.
Spontaneous Combustion. New York, Viking, 1991.

Short Stories

"The Age of Anxiety," in *Men on Men 2,* edited by George Stambolian. New York, New American Library, 1988.
"If A Man Answers," in *Men on Men 4,* edited by George Stambolian. New York, New American Library, 1992.

Essays

"Queer and Loathing at the FDA: Revolt of the Perverts," in *Tribe,* (Baltimore), winter 1989.
"Notes From the Front Line," in *NYQ* (New York), 8 December 1992.
"Memorial Services From Hell," in *Gay Community News* (New York), April 1993 (special March on Washington promotional issue).

*

Biography: "David B. Feinberg" by Jane S. Carducci, in *Contemporary Gay Male Novelists,* edited by Emmanuel S. Nelson, Westport, Connecticut, Greenwood Press, 1992, 122–127.

Interviews: "The Guilt Behind the Book" by Nina Reyes, in *Next* (Boston), 8 March 1989, 36; "Epidemic of Laughter" by Joel Weinberg, in *Advocate* (Los Angeles), 14 March 1989, 46–47; "The Inspiration of David Feinberg" by Owen Keenhan, in *Outlines* (Chicago), December 1991, 29; "Interview" by Jim Provenzano, in *NYQ* (New York), 8 December 1991, 36.

Critical Sources: "When Sex Was All That Mattered" by Catherine Texier, in *New York Times Book Review,* 26 February 1989, 9; "AIDS—This Side of the Abyss" by Bob Summer, in *Lambda Rising Book Report,* February/March 1989, 10; "Bounced From the Bar of Life" by Daniel Curzon, in *Los Angeles Times,* 5 March 1989, C21; "AIDS and the American Novel" by Emmanuel Nelson, in *Journal of American Culture* (Bowling Green, Ohio), spring 1990, 47–53; "The Further Adventures of B. J. Rosenthal" by Robert Friedman, in *Sentinel,* 21 November 1991, 37; "Young, Single, and HIV–Positive" by Scott Bradfield, in *New York Times,* 17 November 1991, 11; "Between the Lines" by Michael Bronski, in *Guide* (Boston), December 1991, 19; *The Gay Novel in America* by James Levin, Boston, Garland, 1991.

*   *   *

The advent of AIDS, first reported in the *New York Times* in July of 1981, completely changed the tone and terrain of gay male fiction writing. While most post–Stonewall gay male fiction dealt with either coming out as a gay man, coming to terms with being a gay man, or discovering a place in the gay community, the reality of AIDS essentially fractured the limited scope of such inquiries. To a large degree, pre–AIDS gay male literature was a literature of discovery; post–AIDS, it is now a literature of immediate crisis. The tensions and quandaries of individuals, as well as a community, living with the continual onslaught of serious illness were bound to affect both the style and the narrative content of gay male writing in the 1980s and 1990s. The novels of David Feinberg are good examples of one kind of fiction narrative strategy for dealing with the AIDS crisis. Immediate in tone and subject, Feinberg captures the social and psychological hysteria surrounding AIDS, containing it in a loosely knit, highly effective genre of first–person, confessional narrative.

David Feinberg was born in 1956 in Lynn, Massachusetts. He attended the Massachusetts Institute of Technology and later received an M.A. from New York University. While living for a time in Los Angeles, he came out in 1977 after attending the Gay Pride March. Feinberg began writing fiction in Los Angeles, and his first novel, *Calculus,* remains unpublished. After moving to New York City, he joined a gay male writing group and finally found a narrative voice with which he was comfortable. This voice—decidedly Jewish, definitely New York, and emotionally volatile—became the inspiration for B. J. Rosenthal, the narrator of his two novels *Eighty–Sixed* and *Spontaneous Combustion.* During this time the gay community began to organize against the AIDS epidemic and Feinberg joined AIDS Coalition to Unleash Power (ACT UP), an AIDS activist group that focused upon direct–action politics. Feinberg's involvement with ACT UP focused his political energy and greatly influenced both the tone and the content of his two novels.

In its first half, entitled "1980: Ancient History," *Eighty–Sixed* is a cross between the non–linear structure of a Jack Kerouac novel and the intense self–revelation/self–analysis of the work of Philip Roth. B. J. Rosenthal's voice is so strong and consistent that it allows Feinberg to deliver a tirade of description, opinion, and digression. He spins a circuitous plot involving his character's experiences with work, the search for sex, and the attempts to enjoy the delights of Manhattan while overcoming a sense of guilt whenever he has fun. In the book's second half, "1986: Learning How to Cry," AIDS begins to infiltrate Rosenthal's world when many of his friends and sex partners begin getting sick. It is then that Feinberg's (and Rosenthal's) compulsive narration begins to build to a strong emotional climax. And although there are no enormous plot developments—issues of work, sex, and guilt are joined by the need to take care of a sick friend—Feinberg effectively describes the enclosing terror and fear of living in a world dominated by AIDS.

Spontaneous Combustion takes up where *Eight–Sixed* leaves off. B. J. Rosenthal discovers that he is HIV–positive, falls in love with his (heterosexual) doctor, looks for a lover, and joins ACT UP before ultimately getting used to the fact that he may, at some point in the future, become symptomatic with AIDS. Like *Eighty–Sixed,* the structure of *Spontaneous Combustion* is essentially a long jazz riff on the nature of life, sex, and death. Feinberg's most salient narrative coup is his ability to capture the frenetic quality of New York gay life without sacrificing either the mordant wit that acts as a defense against AIDS or the ever–present emotional terror of the disease.

As a stylist, Feinberg uses prose that recalls, curiously, the "then I did this, and then I did that" conversational poetry of gay poet Frank O'Hara. Neither *Eighty–Sixed* nor *Spontaneous Combustion* has a traditional narrative structure but move along, incident by incident, in an artful approximation of everyday life. The use of such a style attempts to convey the more open structure of urban gay life. Feinberg's use of camp, trenchant wit, and epigrammatic speech recalls the writings of Oscar Wilde as well as such gay stylists as Alfred Chester and Neil Bartlett.

In his tone, Feinberg clearly recalls the novels of Philip Roth by incorporating the compulsive self–analysis and the heightened awareness of being an "outsider." Roth's identity is that of a Jew who feels he lives outside the Jewish community. Likewise, Feinberg's is that of a gay Jew whose sexuality places him outside the Jewish community. Moreover, Feinberg's Jewishness marks him as an outsider to the gay community, and his health status as HIV–positive places him (irrevocably) outside the realm of the healthy. This sense of being the "outsider" allows Feinberg to establish his credentials as a social critic who is passionately concerned with questions of personal and social morality. For Feinberg, the moral questions of how casual sexual partners treat one another is as important as how ACT UP is attempting to force the United States government to act honorably and ethically about AIDS.

—*Michael Bronski*

FERRO, Robert (Michael). American novelist and educator. Born in Cranford, New Jersey, 21 October 1941. Educated at Rutgers University, B.A. 1963; University of Iowa, M.F.A. and M.A. 1967. Companion of Michael Grumley. Teacher, Adelphi University, Garden City, New York. *Died in Hohokus, New Jersey, of complications from acquired immunodeficiency syndrome (AIDS), 11 July 1988.*

WRITINGS

Novels

The Others. New York, Scribner, 1977.
The Family of Max Desir. New York, Dutton, 1983.
The Blue Star. New York, Dutton, 1985.
Second Son. New York, Crown, 1988.

Short Stories

"The Aviary," in *A True Likeness: Lesbian and Gay Writing Today,* edited by Felice Picano. New York, The Sea Horse Press, 1980.
"Frank's Party," in *First Love/Last Love: New Fiction from Christopher Street,* edited by Michael Denneny, Charles Ortleb, and Thomas Steele. New York, Putnam, 1985.
"Second Son," in *Men on Men,* edited by George Stambolian. New York, New American Library, 1986.

Other

With Michael Grumley, *Atlantis: The Autobiography of a Search.* Garden City, New York, Doubleday, 1970.

*

Biography: "Forward" by Edmund White, in *Life Drawing* by Michael Grumley, New York, Grove, 1991.

Critical Sources: *The Gay Novel* by James Levin, New York, Irvington, 1983; "Introduction" by George Stambolian, in *Men on Men,* edited by Stambolian, New York, New American Library, 1986; "Introduction" by George Stambolian, in *Men on Men 3,* edited by Stambolian, New York, Dutton, 1990; *Gaiety Transfigured Gay Self–Representation in American Literature* by David Bergman, Madison, University of Wisconsin Press, 1991; "Introduction" by Felice Picano, in *Men on Men 4,* edited by George Stambolian, New York, Dutton, 1992.

*   *   *

The novels of Robert Ferro are unique because, while much of the gay male writing that appeared in the 1970s deals with the world of the gay ghetto and the evolution of a distinctive, urban gay male identity, Ferro's novels are firmly rooted in the biological family. Ferro was concerned with exploring the position of the gay man in relation to his nuclear family and, by extension, their relationship with the gay world. But Ferro's fiction is not simply concerned with the material world of family ties and gay relationships; running through all of his work is a strong sense of the fantastic and the extraordinary. Human connections occur on physical, metaphysical, or spiritual planes, and this strong sense of mysticism and otherworldliness separates Ferro's writing from much other gay fiction.

Born in New Jersey in 1941, Ferro attended Rutgers University and the University of Iowa, where he received an M.F.A. in writing in 1967. It was there that he met Michael Grumley, who was to be his lover for 21 years until their deaths in 1988. Ferro and Grumley moved to New York and collaborated on *Atlantis: The Autobiography of a Search,* an account of a summer–long boat trip taken in order to discover the lost continent. Ferro worked at a variety of jobs during the 1970s and continued writing. The immediate result was *The Others,* an intricate novel about a collection of ghost–like characters travelling together on a boat, all of them searching for some greater sense of reality. The novel was both clever and effective, a contemporary retelling of Sutton Vane's classic play *Outward Bound* with a modern sensibility. After the publication of *The Other,* Ferro worked to support Grumley's writing, which was considerably successful. Their situations then reversed and Ferro began to write full–time with the help of Grumley.

Ferro's first work produced during this period was *The Family of Max Desir.* The narrative of the novel is two layered and emblematic of Ferro's future work. Max, a gay man in his thirties, wants his close–knit upper–middle–class Italian family to accept his relationship with his lover, Nick. Most of his family members are willing, but Max's father, John, steadfastly refuses. When Max's mother becomes ill and dies, the family is thrown into a crisis that eventually culminates in John accepting Max's lover into the family and his own decision to become a lay–monk in a religious order. Interwoven with the domestic narrative, Ferro fashioned another story of urban spiritualism and the supernatural in which Max partakes in Haitian voodoo ceremonies and hears a mysterious voice commanding him to write about the Queen of Iala and distant mysterious planets. These two disparate narratives are actually bound together by the idea of the mysterious in everyday life and the commonplaceness of the other world. In his afterward to Grumley's novel *Life Drawing,* George Stambolian wrote that Ferro thought gay men, and "especially gay artists," had "a kind of shamanistic access to alternative existences and a special knowledge of death."

This theme is clearly present in Ferro's next work, *The Blue Star*. Here Ferro charts the lives of two men over 20 years and interweaves the emotional reality of the relationship with a narrative full of fanciful Italianate romance and a subplot about the secret building of a Masonic Temple beneath New York City's Central Park in the late 1800s. Again Ferro merges the mundane with the fabulous, the everyday with the extraordinary, in an attempt to convey the inner psychic lives of his gay characters. The presence of the ornate, mysterious, and completely submerged Masonic Temple in the center of Manhattan stands not so much as a symbol of a hidden gay existence in a thriving metropolis as it does a latent mystical ability that is possessed by gay men in the contemporary world.

Second Son is Ferro's last work and a finer tuning of his earlier themes. Here two gay men with an unnamed, fatal disease affecting homosexuals (AIDS is never mentioned by name) meet and fall in love. Half of the book is an examination of how their respective families handle their relationship and their health, while the other half of the novel is an exploration of their plans to go to the planet Splendora, where their health will be restored. Much of the domestic material is very close to *The Family of Max Desir*—the old family house in New Jersey, the response of varying family members—but the supernatural aspects of the novel are an advance over Ferro's earlier work. If the Masonic Temple in *The Blue Star* was a symbol of inner life, the trip to Splendora has more emotional resonance. One of the themes in western gay male sensibility and writing has always postulated a safe place; the planet Splendora is the newest addition to this tradition. Ferro's impulse to find a safe place for gay men to think and live—an imaginary romantic Italy, an accepting biological family, a disembodied voice with news from the Queen of Iala, a hidden Masonic Temple with a secret brotherhood, or the Planet Splendora— signifies an attempt to reconcile the difficulty of living in a homophobic, material world with the power of the gay imagination.

Both Ferro and Grumley lived and wrote with AIDS since the early 1980s. Grumley finished writing his novel *Life Drawing* in 1987. (It was published posthumously in 1991.) After a trip to Italy late that year, both men were forced to return to New York because of a decline in Grumley's health. Ferro nursed Grumley for the last weeks of his life; he died on 28 March 1988. Ferro died ten weeks later.

—*Michael Bronski*

———————

FIERSTEIN, Harvey. American playwright. Born in Brooklyn, New York, 6 June 1954. Educated at Pratt Institute, B.F.A. 1973. Founding actor in Gallery Players Community Theater, Brooklyn, New York, 1965; female impersonator in New York City, beginning 1971; actor in plays, including Andy Warhol's *Pork*, 1971, *Xircus: The Private Life of Jesus Christ*, *The Trojan Women*, *Vinyl Visits an FM Station*, *The Haunted House*, 1991, and *Pouf Positive*, 1991; actor in his own plays, *International Stud*, 1976–79, *Fugue in a*

Nursery, 1979–80, *Widows and Children First!*, 1979–81, *Torch Song Trilogy*, 1981–83, and *Safe Sex*, 1987; actor in the film *Garbo Talks*, 1984, in the film adaptation of *Torch Song Trilogy*, 1988, in the television adaptation *Tidy Endings*, 1988, in the television play *In the Shadow of Love: A Teen AIDS Story*, 1991, and in the films *The Harvest*, 1992, *Mrs. Doubtfire*, 1993, and *White Lies*, 1994. Guest appearances on the television series *Miami Vice, Cheers*, and *Murder She Wrote;* narrator of film *The Times of Harvey Milk*. **Recipient:** Four Villager Awards, 1980; Obie Award, 1982; Tony Award, 1983, 1984; Oppenheimer Award, 1983; Drama Desk Award, 1983; Dramatists Guild's Hull–Warriner Award, 1983; Theater World Award, 1983; Fund for Human Dignity Award, 1983; Los Angeles Drama Critics Circle Award, 1984; two Academy of Cable Excellence Awards for best dramatic special and writing, 1988; grants from Rockefeller Foundation, Ford Foundation, Creative Artists Public Services, and Public Broadcasting System. Address: c/o Green, Siegal, and Associates, 8730 Sunset Boulevard, Suite 470, Los Angeles, California 90069, U.S.A.

WRITINGS

Plays

In Search of the Cobra Jewels (produced New York, 1972).
Freaky Pussy (produced New York, 1973).
Flatbush Tosca (produced New York, 1975).
The International Stud (produced New York, 1978; included in *Torch Song Trilogy* and produced New York, 1981; London, 1985). Included in *Torch Song Trilogy*, 1981.
Fugue in a Nursery (produced New York, 1979; included in *Torch Song Trilogy* and produced New York, 1981; London, 1985). Included in *Torch Song Trilogy*, 1981.
Widows and Children First! (produced New York, 1979; included in *Torch Song Trilogy* and produced New York, 1981; London, 1985). Included in *Torch Song Trilogy*, 1981.
Torch Song Trilogy (includes *The International Stud, Fugue in a Nursery*, and *Widows and Children First!;* produced New York, 1981; London, 1985). New York, Gay Presses of New York, 1981; London, Methuen, 1984.
Spookhouse (produced New York, 1982; London, 1987). Published in *Plays International* (London), July 1987.
La Cage aux Folles, music and lyrics by Jerry Herman (adaptation of the play by Jean Poiret; produced Boston and New York, 1983; London, 1986).
Safe Sex (includes *Manny and Jake, Safe Sex*, and *On Tidy Endings*; produced New York, 1987). New York, Atheneum, 1987.
Forget Him (produced New York, 1988).
With Charles Suppon, *Legs Diamond* (produced New York, 1988).

*

Adaptations: *Torch Song Trilogy* was filmed by New Line Cinema, 1988; *On Tidy Endings* was adapted for television as *Tidy Endings* and broadcast on Home Box Office, 1988.

Interviews: In *Playboy* (Chicago), August 1988, 43; in *Video Review* (New York), July 1989, 60.

Critical Sources: "Daring Climb from Obscurity" by Michiko Kakutani, in *New York Times,* 14 July 1982, 17; "Fragments of a Trilogy: Harvey Fierstein's 'Torch Song'" by Kim Powers, in *Theater* (New York), spring 1983, 63–67; "His Heart Is Young and Gay" by Jack Kroll, in *Newsweek,* 20 June 1983, 71; "Dignity in Drag: Torch Song's Great Balls of Fierstein" by Jay Scott, in *Film Comment* (New York), January/February 1989, 9.

*   *   *

Harvey Fierstein's play *Torch Song Trilogy* concerns a gay Jewish man, not unlike Fierstein himself, who is searching for a lasting love. His ordinary domestic desire and the normalcy with which he is presented make the play one of the few times in stage history when homosexuals have been presented as healthy people. No suicidal tendencies, no drug or alcohol problems, Fierstein's gay characters are overwhelmingly down–to–earth and accessible to both gay and straight audiences. *Torch Song Trilogy* began life in a small Off–Off–Broadway theater, moved to a larger theater when audience interest demanded it, and won Fierstein a host of awards.

The trilogy begins with Arnold Beckoff, a drag queen, falling in love with the bisexual Ed, but neither man can commit himself to a stable relationship; Ed is involved with a woman named Laurel, while Arnold has sexual relations in the back room of a local gay bar. When Ed leaves him for Laurel, Arnold must begin his quest for love anew. The second play, *Fugue in a Nursery,* begins a year later with Arnold and his new lover Alan being invited to Ed and Laurel's country house for a weekend. Through a series of interweaving conversations that take place on a large bed, the two couples discuss the difficulties of love. In the last play, *Widows and Children First!,* Alan has been murdered and Ed has left Laurel to live with Arnold again.

Some critics found the trilogy to be overly concerned with monogamy and family matters. Fierstein's emphasis on commitment and responsibility were counter to the values of many gay liberationists. But speaking to Jack Kroll in *Newsweek,* Fierstein argued that "gay liberation should not be a license to be a perpetual adolescent. If you deny yourself commitment then what can you do with your life?" Speaking to Michiko Kakutani in the *New York Times,* Fierstein explained that *Torch Song Trilogy*'s Arnold shared the same aspirations all people have: "Everyone wants what Arnold wants—an apartment they can afford, a job they don't hate too much, a chance to go to the store once in a while and someone to share it all with."

Fierstein used this same approach in his adaptation of *La Cage aux folles* as a musical for the stage. Written by the French playwright Jean Poiret as a farcical comedy, and already twice filmed, the play was rendered in Fierstein's version as a study of family relationships. The story centers on a middle–aged homosexual couple: Albin, a transvestite, and Georges, a nightclub owner. Georges must come to terms with his son, the result of a youthful heterosexual fling, when the son becomes engaged to the daughter of a local politician. Hoping to make a good impression, Georges asks Albin to leave when the future in–laws are due to visit, resulting in anger and hurt feelings. The couple's problems are complicated due to the fact that they both consider Georges' son as their own. In this manner, the situation is presented as a family relationship like any other, despite the fact that both mother and father are men. Some critics found the musical to be far too melodramatic and

mainstream, despite the openly gay characters featured. But audiences responded positively, and *La Cage aux folles* was a popular success as well as a winner of six Tony awards.

Fierstein's next trilogy of plays, *Safe Sex,* explores the problems of loving and relationships in the time of AIDS. In the first of the three one–act plays, *Manny and Jake,* two gay men discuss the future of their relationship when one of them suspects he has contracted the HIV virus. The second play, *Safe Sex,* shows another gay couple using the fear of AIDS to avoid intimacy. The last play, *On Tidy Endings,* tells of a bisexual man who has died of AIDS, leaving his wife and gay lover behind. The cable television adaptation of *On Tidy Endings,* broadcast on Home Box Office as *Tidy Endings,* starred Fierstein and won four awards for cable excellence, including one for best dramatic special and one for Fierstein's writing.

—*Thomas Wiloch*

FISKE, Irene. *See* **GRIER, Barbara G(ene Damon).**

FLANNER, Janet. American novelist and journalist. Also wrote as Genêt. Born in Indianapolis, Indiana, 13 March 1892. Educated at University of Chicago, c. 1912–1913. Married William Lane Rehm in 1920 (divorced 1922). Cinema critic, *Indianapolis Star,* Indianapolis, Indiana, 1916–17; worker at a reform school in Philadelphia, Pennsylvania; foreign correspondent and columnist, under the name Genêt, *New Yorker,* New York City, 1925–75; wartime broadcaster and free–lance writer. Cofounder of Lucy Stone League, 1921. **Recipient:** French Legion of Honor, 1947; Smith College honorary degree, 1958; National Book Award, 1966. *Died in New York City, 7 November 1978.*

WRITINGS

Novels

The Cubical City. New York, Putnam, 1926; with afterword by the author, Carbondale, Southern Illinois University Press, 1974.

Nonfiction

An American in Paris: Profile of an Interlude between Two Wars. New York, Simon & Schuster, and London, Hamilton, 1940.
Contributor, *The New Yorker Book of War Pieces.* New York, Reynal & Hitchcock, 1947.

Men and Monuments. New York, Harper, and London, Hamilton, 1957; with introduction by Rosamond Bernier, New York, Da Capo Press, 1990.

Biography

Petain: The Old Man of France. New York, Simon & Schuster, 1944.

Letters

Paris Journal, edited by William Shawn, Volume 1: *1944–1965,* New York, Atheneum, 1965; London, Gollancz, 1966; Volume 2: *1965–1971,* New York, Atheneum, 1971.
Paris Was Yesterday: 1925–1939, edited by Irving Drutman. New York, Viking, 1972; London, Angus & Robertson, 1973.
London Was Yesterday: 1934–1939, edited by Irving Drutman. New York, Viking, and London, M. Joseph, 1975.
Darlinghissima: Letters to a Friend, edited by Natalia Danesi Murray. New York, Random House, 1985.

Translations

Cheri, by Colette. New York, A. & C. Boni, 1929; London, Gollancz, 1930; with introduction by Wallace Fowlie, San Francisco, George F. Ritchie, 1983.
Claudine at School, by Colette. New York, A. & C. Boni, 1930; London, Gollancz, 1930.
Souvenirs: My Life with Maeterlinck, by Georgette Le Blanc. New York, Dutton, 1932; as *Maeterlinck and I,* London, Methuen, 1932.

Other

With Marcel Vertès, *The Stronger Sex.* New York, Hyperion Press, 1941.
Master, 1956.
Author of commentary, *Conversation Pieces* by Constantin Alajalov. New York and London, Studio Publications, 1942.
The Surprise of the Century, 1957.
Author of foreword, *Two: Gertrude Stein and Her Brother, and Other Early Portraits* by Gertrude Stein. New Haven, Connecticut, Yale University Press, and London, Geoffrey Cumberlege/ Oxford University Press, 1951.
Author of introduction, *The Pure and the Impure* by Colette. New York, Farrar, Straus, 1967.
Author of introduction, *Ross, The New Yorker, and Me* by Jane Grant. New York, Reynal/Morrow, 1968.
Author of introduction, *Colette: The Difficulty of Loving* by Margaret Crosland. New York, Bobbs–Merrill, 1973.
Author of foreword, *Published in Paris: American and British Writers, Printers, and Publishers in Paris, 1920–1939* by Hugh Ford. New York, Macmillan, 1975.
Janet Flanner's World: Uncollected Writings, 1932–1975, edited by William Shawn. New York, Harcourt, 1979.

*

Adaptations: *Letters from Paris* (a vocal score comprising nine prose extracts from Flanner's *Paris Journal*) was set to music, New York, Boosey & Hawkes, c. 1969.

Manuscript Collections: Library of Congress, Washington, D.C.

Biography: *Genêt: A Biography of Janet Flanner* by Brenda Wineapple, New York, Ticknor & Fields, 1989.

Interviews: "Genêt" by Roy Newquist, in *Counterpoint,* Chicago, Rand McNally and Company, 1964; "Conversation Piece" by Mary McCarthy, *in New York Times Book Review,* 21 November 1965, 5, 88–91; "Janet Flanner" by Michael Mok, in *Publisher's Weekly,* 12 June 1972, 16–7.

Critical Sources: *Women of the Left Bank: Paris, 1900–1940* by Shari Benstock, Austin, University of Texas Press, 1986; "On Her Mouth You Kiss Your Own: Lesbian Conversations in Exile, 1924–1936" (dissertation) by Luita Deane Spangler, University of New Hampshire, 1992.

*   *   *

Journalist, novelist, and translator Janet Flanner spent over 50 years of her life in Paris as the *New Yorker's* American correspondent. Although never secretive about her lesbianism, she made a clear distinction between her private and public life, which enabled her to both move in the avant–garde literary and artistic circles of Paris and succeed as a journalist in the more repressive America.

Daughter of a prosperous businessman and a Quaker mother, Flanner was born and educated in Indianapolis. At 17, after traveling in Germany with her family, Janet became acutely aware of the insularity and limitations of her midwestern home. Shortly after her father's suicide in 1912, Janet attended the University of Chicago for a year. Her college career was unsuccessful, and after brief periods of employment in a Quaker girls' reformatory and writing art and drama criticism for the *Indianapolis Star,* in 1918 Janet married William Lane Rehm, a friend from the University of Chicago. The couple moved to New York, and took an apartment in Greenwich Village.

It was there that Flanner met her first great love, Solita Solano, drama editor of the *New York Tribune.* In 1921, the two women left what they saw as the restrictive environment of America for Europe. Flanner and Rehm obtained an amicable divorce. In 1922, after touring Greece, Constantinople, and Austria, the women settled in Paris. There, Flanner became friends with Ernest Hemingway, Kay Boyle, Gertrude Stein, Djuna Barnes (in whose *Ladies' Almanack* she and Solano appear as the journalists Nip and Tuck), and other leading writers and artists. Flanner found herself surrounded by others who had come to Paris to escape the artistic and sexual restrictions of the United States. She did not identify exclusively with any of the prominent salons of the period, although she spent time among the coteries of Gertrude Stein and Alice Toklas, Natalie Barney, and Sylvia Beach.

In her autobiographical novel, *The Cubical City,* Flanner criticized the repressive sexual mores forced upon American women. The protagonist, Delia Poole, a designer of stage scenery in New York, refuses a proposal of marriage and pursues the enjoyment of physical love. As a woman, she is unable to do this without recriminations. The novel is sharply critical of the cultural requirement that women conform to sexual standards inimical to their female nature. In contrast to the submission required of women in heterosexual marriage, Flanner emphasizes the sustenance and nurturing inherent in woman–identified love and friendship.

Flanner considered herself primarily a journalist, and it is through her twice–monthly "Letter from Paris" in the *New Yorker* that she is chiefly known. Using the pen–name "Genêt," Flanner kept the American public abreast of life in the French capitol. For over 50 years she wrote witty and informative columns concerning cultural events, sports, and political developments. These were later published as *Paris Journal* and *Paris Was Yesterday: 1925–1939.* Women figured prominently in her "Letters." She reviewed exhibits of their art; wrote on female fashion from an aesthetic and economic point of view; commented on their accomplishments in sports; and expressed concern for their working conditions.

In 1967, Flanner translated Colette's *Le pur et l'impur,* a collection of sketches of lesbian life. Flanner's introduction to the translation is almost documentary in style, revealing more about her respect for the author than her reaction to the work itself. Flanner's attitude toward her lesbianism was for the most part ahead of her time and atypical among the expatriate circle in which she lived. She was a happy woman remarkably free of internalized homophobia and committed to feminism. Her relationships with women were not based on heterosexual models. Her long relationship with Solano was loving, trusting, and apparently non–monogamous. Memoirs and letters of both lesbian and heterosexual women demonstrate the respect and acceptance with which they viewed Flanner.

—*Melissa J. Delbridge*

———————

FORD, Charles Henri. American poet, novelist, editor, and screenwriter. Born in Brookhaven, Mississippi, 10 February 1913. Companion of artist Pavel Tchelitchew. Editor, *Blues: A Magazine of New Rhythms,* Columbus, Missouri, 1929–30; founder and editor of *View* magazine and View Editions, New York City, 1940–47; artist with exhibitions at Institute of Contemporary Arts, London, 1955; Galerie Marforen, Paris, 1956; Galerie du Dragon, Paris, 1957 and 1958; Cordier and Ekstrom Gallery, New York City, 1965; New York Cultural Center, 1975; Carleton Gallery, 1975; Iolas Gallery, 1976; Robert Samuel Gallery, 1980; Akehurst Gallery, London, Vintage Gallery, Amsterdam, and Guillaune Giallozzie Gallery, 1993. **Recipient:** Fourth Annual Avant–Garde Film Festival Award, 1966. Agent: Oscar Collier, 280 Madison Avenue, New York, New York 10016, U.S.A.

WRITINGS

With Parker Tyler, *The Young and Evil* (novel). Paris, Obelisk Press, 1933; New York, Olympia Press, 1960; with introduction by Stephen Watson and illustrations by Pavel Tchelitchew, New York, Seahorse Press, 1988; London, Gay Men's Press, 1989.

Poetry

A Pamphlet of Sonnets. Majorca, Caravel Press, 1936.

The Garden of Disorder, and Other Poems. London, Europa Press, and New York, New Directions, 1938.
ABC's. Prairie City, Illinois, James A. Decker, 1940.
The Overturned Lake. Cincinnati, Little Man Press, 1941.
Poems for Painters. New York, View Editions/Vanguard, 1945.
The Half–thoughts, the Distances of Pain. New York, Prospero Pamphlets, 1947.
Sleep in a Nest of Flames. New York, New Directions, 1949.
Spare Parts. New York, New View, 1966.
Silver Flower Coo. New York, Kulchur, 1968.
Flag of Ecstasy: Selected Poems, edited by Edward B. Germain. Los Angeles, Black Sparrow Press, 1972.
7 Poems. Kathmandu, Bardo Matrix, 1974.
Om Krishna: Special Effects. Cherry Valley, New York, Cherry Valley Editions, 1979.
Om Krishna II. Cherry Valley, New York, Cherry Valley Editions, 1981.
Secret Haiku: Om Krishna III. New York, Red Ozier Press, 1982.
Haiku and Imprints I [and] *II* (two volumes). Kathmandu, Operation Minotaur, 1984–85.
Handshakes from Heaven. Paris, Handshake, 1985.
Handshakes from Heaven II. Paris, Handshake, 1986.
Emblems of Arachne. New York, Catchword Papers, 1986.
Out of the Labyrinth: Selected Poems. San Francisco, City Lights Books, 1990.

Screenplays

Poem Posters, 1966.
Johnny Minotaur, 1971.

Other

Contributor, *Readies for Bob Brown's Machine,* edited by Bob Brown. Cagnes–sur–Mer, Roving Eye Press, 1931.
Contributor, *Americans Abroad: An Anthology,* edited by Peter Neagoe. The Hague, Servire, 1932.
Contributor, *365 Days,* edited by Kay Boyle, Laurence Vail, and Nina Conarain. London, Cape, 1936; New York, Harcourt, 1936.
Contributor, *New Directions in Prose and Poetry,* Volumes 3–6 and 13–15, edited by James Laughlin and others. New York, New Directions, 1938.
Translator, editor, and contributor, *The Mirror of Baudelaire* by Charles Baudelaire. New York, New Directions, 1942.
Editor, *A Night with Jupiter, and Other Fantastic Stories.* New York, View Press, 1945; London, Dobson, 1947.
The American Genius: An Anthology of Poetry with Some Prose, edited by Edith Sitwell. London, Lehmann, 1951.
Editor, *View: Parade of the Avante Garde, 1940–1947,* foreword by Paul Bowles. New York, Thunders Mouth Press, 1991.
Contributor, *Cold–Drill 1991,* edited by Bob Moore. Idaho, Boise State University, 1991.

*

Manuscript Collections: Humanities Research Center, University of Texas, Austin; Yale University, New Haven, Connecticut; J. Paul Getty Library, Malibu, California.

Interviews: Unpublished interview with Steven Watson, 27 July 1986; "An Interview with Charles Henri Ford" by Jerry Rosco, in *Playguy* (New York), September 1991, 62–67; "Charles Henri Ford" by Paul Cummings, in *Pavel Tchelitchew: Nature Transformed* (New York, Michael Rosenfeld Gallery), April 1993, 3–6.

Critical Sources: "Introduction" by William Carlos Williams to *The Garden of Disorder, and Other Poems,* New York, New Directions, 1938; "Introduction" by Edith Sitwell to *Sleep in a Nest of Flames,* New York, New Directions, 1949; *The Divine Comedy of Pavel Tchelitchew* by Parker Tyler, New York, Fleet, 1967; *Published in Paris: American and British Writers, Printers, and Publishers in Paris, 1920–1939* by Hugh Ford, New York, Macmillan, 1975; *Tracking the Marvelous: A Life in the New York Art World* by John Bernard Myers, New York, Random House, 1983; "Introduction" by Stephen Watson to *The Young and Evil,* London, Gay Men's Press, 1989; "Foreword" by Paul Bowles, in *View: Parade of the Avante Garde, 1940–1947,* New York, Thunders Mouth Press, 1991; "A Legend in His Rhyme" by Jerry Rosco, in *New York Native,* 22 July 1991, 25.

*   *   *

On the dust jacket of the 1933 novel Charles Henri Ford authored with Parker Tyler, American writer Gertrude Stein commented, "*The Young and Evil* creates this generation as *This Side of Paradise* by Fitzgerald created his generation." Unlike the novels of F. Scott Fitzgerald or Ernest Hemingway, however, *The Young and Evil* features protagonists who are unapologetic Greenwich Village homosexuals. Published in Paris by Obelisk Press, the book was banned in the United States and England. With the original edition numbering 2,500, British Customs seized and burned 500 copies. But the early homophobic reaction only contributed to the novel's legendary status within twentieth-century, pre–Stonewall gay literature.

Somewhat like the French writer, artist, and filmmaker Jean Cocteau, Ford worked in many forms throughout his long and colorful career. He published his first poem in the *New Yorker* at 14, and began publishing and editing *Blues: A Magazine of New Rhythms* at the age of 16 in 1929. The precocious Southerner produced nine issues of *Blues* and received contributions from some celebrated American expatriates. Stein wrote in her *Autobiography of Alice B. Toklas,* "Of all the little magazines which as Gertrude Stein loves to quote, have died to make verse free, perhaps the youngest and freshest was the *Blues*. Its editor Charles Henri Ford has come to Paris and he is as young and fresh as his *Blues* and also honest which also is a pleasure."

Before Ford's 1931 arrival in Paris with writer friend Djuana Barnes, he spent much of 1930 in Greenwich Village with another young poet, Parker Tyler. Through shared experience and their correspondence, they assembled the material that Ford fictionalized as *The Young and Evil*. Steven Watson's in–depth introduction to the 1988 edition of the novel somewhat clarified the extent of coauthorship. Ford claimed primary writing credit while acknowledging the major influence of Tyler's letters and that Tyler wrote a few chapters. When Ford returned to Columbia, Mississippi, from New York, in summer 1930, he began to shape the manuscript, giving it the working title "Love and Jump Back." He took the first draft with him to Paris the following spring.

Ford flourished among the expatriates and in 1932 he met his lover of the next 23 years, the Russian Neo–Romantic artist Pavel Tchelitchew. That Tchelitchew was living with a lover, musician Allen Tanner, and a sister, Choura, was only one problem with the relationship. Another was that Tchelitchew and his work had fallen out of favor with the ever–fickle Stein. Worse, poet Edith Sitwell loved Tchelitchew beyond reason and for years she blamed Ford for weakening the friendship. Nevertheless, the histrionic Russian often said he saw in Charles a blue–eyed Huckleberry Finn, and when they lived together Ford discovered an artistic genius who strongly influenced his own near–surrealist artwork and poetry. On the occasion of a spring 1993 exhibit of Tchelitchew art in New York, Ford told interviewer Paul Cummings: "Pavlik could influence my taste and I could blossom from having wonderful paintings by him in front of my eyes. That became the kind of standard that made me see other things with renewed eyesight."

After several quick rejections by New York and London houses, *The Young and Evil* was published by Jack Kahane's Obelisk Press in August 1933. Karel and Julian are the novel's Tyler and Ford characters, respectively. Julian's friend Theodosia is drawn from Ford's friend Kathleen Tankersley Young. The last of the story's five main characters are Louis and Gabriel, a pair of dark, vagabond poets. Also modeled from real–life friends, Louis, bisexual, and Gabriel, heterosexual but modern, personify the allure and the distress of the bohemian Greenwich Village landscape, with its dubious clubs and cafes on MacDougal Street, its student intellectuals, and tenement apartments. Karel is drawn to Louis and Louis is drawn to Gabriel. That the attraction is not merely sexual or romantic is basic to the theme. The narrative is as untraditional as the prose of Stein or James Joyce, with occasional waves of surrealism. Quote marks are dispensed with and there's scarcely a comma on the horizon, but the writing is compelling and clear: "All writers have at least one fugitive piece Julian said. He looked at Gabriel's meeting in the center eyebrows and the eyes beneath were as beautiful as before. A man cannot love a woman and a woman cannot love a man he thought not really. He thought so looking at Gabriel." Small editions of *The Young and Evil* appeared in 1960 and 1975. With the help of writer and publisher Felice Picano, a Seahorse Press edition was printed in New York in 1988, including the Steven Watson introduction and reproductions of the watercolors Tchelitchew had painted into Ford's personal copy. In 1989, Gay Men's Press in London released another edition.

Ford's broader reputation is as an avante–garde artist and art publisher. From 1940 to 1947 his *View* magazine featured the American and European vanguard in art as well as poetry and prose. "The aim of *View* was not to shock, but to surprise," Paul Bowles wrote in his foreword to the 1991 Thunder's Mouth Press anthology, *View: Parade of the Avante–Garde, 1940–1947.* Ford's 1966 volume of visually stunning collage and color, *Spare Parts,* is also a book of poetry. Galleries have exhibited his art and photography for five decades. His 1965 documentary film *Poem Posters* features many of his fellow artists, including Andy Warhol, to whom Ford introduced performance artist Gerard Malanga. His full–length *Johnny Minotaur,* filmed in Crete in 1971, is a homoerotic cult classic.

Ford's 19 books of poetry, ranging from lyrical surrealist to haiku, contain gay poems but in the main are universal. *Out of the Labyrinth* contains an elegy to a Warhol star, "Candy Darling," and includes these lines: "To small heartless caterpillars you are the sorcerer saint dissolving in star–showers / Exquisite aberration, the garment of decay was not for you / Like an upside–down butterfly or a man without eyebrows in all that rushing annihilation yours was the historic aura of a peacock's grace."

Pavel Tchelitchew died in Rome in 1957 but Ford's prolific and varied work continued. For decades he maintained homes in New York, Paris, Crete, and Katmandu, Nepal. His constant companion since the early seventies is photographer and artist Indra Tamang. His sister is Broadway actress Ruth Ford, who was married to Hollywood actor Zachary Scott. Ford's works contracted to Southern Illinois University Press include *I Will Be What I Am: Letters from Paris, 1931–34,* and the autobiography, *Water from A Bucket.* When interviewed for *Playguy* magazine, Ford was asked if he were concerned about the explicit nature of his and other gay autobiographies. "Not only should we not worry," he said, "but we should push it forward.... We've got to fight the Puritanism that we've been saddled with since the days of *The Young and Evil.*"

—*Jerry Rosco*

FORREST, Katherine V(irginia). Canadian novelist and author of short fiction. Born in Windsor, Ontario, 20 April 1939. Educated at Wayne State University, Detroit, Michigan, and University of California, Los Angeles. Fiction editor, Naiad Press, Tallahassee, Florida. Member of International PEN. **Recipient:** *Lambda* Literary Award, for *The Beverly Malibu* and *Murder By Tradition.* Address: P.O. Box 31613, San Francisco, California 94131, U.S.A.

WRITINGS

Novels

Curious Wine. Tallahassee, Naiad Press, 1983.
Daughters of a Coral Dawn. Tallahassee, Naiad Press, 1984.
An Emergence of Green. Tallahassee, Naiad Press, 1986.

Novels ("Kate Delafield" Series)

Amateur City. Tallahassee, Naiad Press, 1984.
Murder at the Nightwood Bar. Tallahassee, Naiad Press, 1987.
The Beverly Malibu. Tallahassee, Naiad Press, 1991.
Murder By Tradition. Tallahassee, Naiad Press, 1991.

Short Stories

Dreams and Swords. Tallahassee, Naiad Press, 1987.

Editor

With Barbara Grier, *The Erotic Naiad.* Tallahassee, Naiad Press, 1992.

With Barbara Grier, *The Romantic Naiad.* Tallahassee, Naiad Press, 1993.

*

Critical Sources: "Utopia and Ideology in Daughters of a Coral Dawn and Contemporary Feminist Utopias" by Holda M. Zaki, in *Women's Studies: An Interdisciplinary Journal,* 14:2.

Katherine V. Forrest comments: "From the beginning, lesbian and gay lives were my writing focus because of my own membership in a community starved for accurate images of itself in print. My work is intended as a reflection of our lives, and of a cultural identity that incorporates all races, all colors, all creeds. Gay and lesbian literature, in my opinion, has become the most dynamic literature in America because of the sheer diversity of lesbian and gay lives. As a people, we have literally had to invent our lives, and, as lesbian editor Carol DeSanti of Dutton has remarked, ours remain 'the only untold stories'."

* * *

Although she has written a number of novels featuring complex themes and plots, Katherine Virginia Forrest is perhaps best known for her series of police procedurals featuring lesbian detective Kate Delafield. The popularity of the Delafield books is due in large part to both their tight construction and empathetic heroine. "My objective in the series is to present entertaining fiction and also lesbian life in process," the author once noted, "a woman in a high visibility job who must deal with her sexual identity in a totally homophobic atmosphere."

Forrest introduced readers to her fictional sleuth in *Amateur City.* In this work—as well as the other books in Forrest's mystery series—Delafield is presented as strong, self assured, and independent, but not above engaging in a romantic interlude while investigating a case. Delafield is, however, a "closeted" figure who goes to great lengths to separate her personal and professional life. On the job, she is diligent, correct, and patient, with meticulous eye for detail. Mindful of the human element in her work, she has compassion for both the victim and the victim's family.

In *The Beverly Malibu,* Delafield, together with her partner Ed Taylor, investigates the especially gruesome murder of Owen Sinclair, a Hollywood director living in a Los Angeles apartment complex called the Beverly Malibu. During the course of the investigation, Forrest introduces a cast of bizarre characters and individual side plots that keep the reader guessing at the outcome. To further complicate matters, Delafield becomes involved emotionally and sexually with two of the prime suspects.

The LAPD detective is pressured to take on a case involving the murder of Teddie Crawford, a young gay man, in *Murder By Tradition.* As her investigation proceeds, Delafield is drawn so deeply into the case that it imperils both her career and her personal life. For the first time, Delafield's careful attempts to kept her sexual orientation separate from her professional life are jeopardized and, ultimately, threatened with exposure.

Apart from her "Delafield" work, Forrest has also written a number of thematically complex novels. Her first work, *Curious*

Wine, is a sustained romantic fantasy about love, exploration, discovery and intense passion involving two women, Diana Holland and Lane Christianson. In *Daughters of a Coral Dawn,* the author introduces readers to Megan, Laurel, and the other women of Cybele who have fled their homeland—Earth—in search of a world of their own without men. *An Emergence of Green* explores themes of jealousy, indecision, loyalty and doubt, as well as the emergence of lesbian identity in all its complexity. Forrest has also collaborated with Barbara Grier in a compilation of lesbian erotica entitled *The Erotic Naiad: Love Stories by Naiad Press Authors.*

—*Jane Jurgens*

FORSTER, E(dward) M(organ). British novelist, playwright, essayist, biographer, and nonfiction writer. Born in London, 1 January 1879. Educated at King's College, Cambridge, B.A. (second–class honors in classics) 1900, B.A. (second–class honors in history) 1901, M.A. 1910. Lived in Greece and Italy after leaving Cambridge in 1901, remaining abroad until 1907, except for a brief visit to England in 1902; helped found, and contributed to, the *Independent Review.* Lectured at Working Men's College, London, for a period beginning in 1907; made first trip to India in 1912; Red Cross volunteer in Alexandria, 1915–19. Returned to England after the war where he was literary editor of the Labor Party's *Daily Herald* for a time, and contributed reviews to journals including *Nation* and *New Statesman;* served as private secretary to the Maharajah of Dewas State Senior, 1921; lived in England, writing and lecturing, 1921–70. Clark Lecturer at Cambridge University, 1927, Rede Lecturer at Senate House, Cambridge, 1941, W. P. Ker Lecturer at University of Glasgow, 1944; made lecture tour of United States in 1947. Member of the general advisory council of the British Broadcasting Corp., and writer of numerous broadcasts; was a vice–president of the London Library; honorary corresponding member of American Academy of Arts and Letters and the Bavarian Academy of Fine Arts; was president of Cambridge Humanists, and member of Reform Club. **Recipient:** Dewas State Senior Tukojirao Gold Medal (India), 1921; James Tait Black Memorial Prize, and Prix Femina/Vie Heureuse, both 1925; King's College, Cambridge, fellow, 1927–30, honorary fellow, 1946–70; Royal Society of Literature Benson Medal, 1937; Companion of Honour, 1953; Companion of Royal Society of Literature; Order of Merit, 1969. Recipient of honorary doctorates from University of Aberdeen, 1931, University of Liverpool, 1947, Hamilton College, 1949, Cambridge University, 1950, University of Nottingham, 1951, University of Manchester, 1954, Leiden University, 1954, and University of Leicester, 1958. *Died in Coventry, 7 June 1970.*

WRITINGS

Novels

Where Angels Fear to Tread. Edinburgh and London, Blackwood, 1905; New York, Knopf, 1920.

The Longest Journey. Edinburgh and London, Blackwood, 1907; New York, Knopf, 1922.
A Room With a View. London, Arnold, 1908; New York, Putnam, 1911.
Howards End. London, Arnold, and New York, Putnam, 1910.
A Passage to India. London, Arnold, and New York, Harcourt, 1924.
Maurice. London, Arnold, and New York, Norton, 1971.
The Lucy Novels: Early Sketches for "A Room with a View," edited by Oliver Stallybrass. London, Arnold, and New York, Holmes & Meier, 1973.
The Manuscripts of "Howards End," edited by Oliver Stallybrass. London, Arnold, and New York, Holmes & Meier, 1973.
The Manuscripts of "A Passage to India," edited by Oliver Stallybrass. London, Arnold, and New York, Holmes & Meier, 1978.

Short Stories

The Celestial Omnibus, and Other Stories. London, Sidgwick & Jackson, 1911; New York, Knopf, 1923.
The Story of the Siren. Richmond, Leonard and Virginia Woolf at the Hogarth Press, 1920.
The Eternal Moment, and Other Stories. London, Sidgwick & Jackson, and New York, Harcourt, 1928.
The Collected Tales of E. M. Forster (previously published as *The Celestial Omnibus* and *The Eternal Moment*). New York, Knopf, 1947; as *Collected Short Stories of E. M. Forster,* London, Sidgwick & Jackson, 1948.
The Life to Come, and Other Stories. London, Arnold, 1972; as *The Life to Come, and Other Short Stories,* New York, Norton, 1973.
Arctic Summer, and Other Fiction, edited by Elizabeth Heine and Oliver Stallybrass. London, Arnold, and New York, Holmes & Meier, 1980.
The New Collected Short Stories by E. M. Forster. London, Sidgwick & Jackson, 1987.
"Dr. Woolacott," in *The Faber Book of Gay Short Fiction,* edited by Edmund White. London and New York, Faber & Faber, 1991.

Plays

The Heart of Bosnia (produced, 1911).
Pageant of Abinger, music by Ralph Vaughan Williams (produced, 1934).
England's Pleasant Land, a Pageant Play. London, Hogarth Press, 1940.

History

The Government of Egypt, Recommendations by a Committee of the International Section of the Labour Research Department, with Notes on Egypt by E. M. Forster. London, Labour Research Department, 1921.
Alexandria: A History and a Guide. Alexandria, W. Morris, 1922; Garden City, New York, Doubleday, 1961; London, Michael Haag, 1982.
Pharos and Pharillon. Richmond, Hogarth Press, and New York, Knopf, 1923.
Anonymity: An Enquiry, Richmond, Hogarth Press, 1925.

Literary Criticism

Aspects of the Novel (Clark lecture, 1927). London, Arnold, and New York, Harcourt, 1927.
Sinclair Lewis Interprets America. Cambridge, Massachusetts, Harvard Press, 1932.
Virginia Woolf: The Rede Lecture. Cambridge, Cambridge University Press, 1942; New York, Harcourt, 1942.
The Development of English Prose Between 1918 and 1939 (W. P. Ker Lecture, 1944). Glasgow, Jackson, 1945.
Aspects of the Novel, and Related Writings, edited by Oliver Stallybrass. London, Edward Arnold, 1974; New York, Holmes & Meier, 1974.

Essays

Abinger Harvest. London, Arnold, and New York, Harcourt, 1936.
Two Cheers for Democracy. London, Arnold, 1951.

Contributor

T. E. Lawrence by His Friends, edited by Arnold W. Lawrence. London, J. Cape, 1937.
Writers in Freedom, edited by Hermon Ould. London, Hutchinson, 1942.
Talking to India, edited by George Orwell. London, Allen & Unwin, 1943.
Peter Grimes: Essays. London, John Lane for the Governors of Sadler's Wells Foundation, 1945.
Freedom of Expression: A Symposium, edited by Herman Ould. London, Hutchinson, 1945.
Mahatma Gandhi: Essays and Reflections on His Life and Work by S. Radhakrishnan (second edition). London, Allen & Unwin, 1949.
Hermon Ould: A Tribute. [London], 1952.
The Fearful Choice: A Debate on Nuclear Policy, conducted by Philip Toynbee, Detroit, Wayne State University Press, 1959.

Letters

Selected Letters of E. M. Forster, edited by Mary Lago and P. N. Furbank: Volume 1, *1879–1920,* Cambridge, Massachusetts, Harvard University Press, 1983; Volume 2, *1921–1970,* Cambridge, Massachsetts, Harvard University Press, 1984.
Original Letters from India. London, Hogarth Press, 1986.

Other

A Letter to Madan Blanchard (belles lettres). Hogarth Press, 1931; New York, Harcourt, 1932.
Goldsworthy Lowes Dickinson (biography). London, Edward Arnold, 1934; New York, Harcourt, 1934.
What I Believe. London, Hogarth Press, 1939.
Nordic Twilight (political pamphlet). London, Macmillan, 1940.
A Diary for Timothy (screenplay), 1945.
With Eric Crozier, *Billy Budd: An Opera in Four Acts* (libretto; adaptation of the novel by Herman Melville), music by Benjamin Britten. London and New York, Boosey & Hawkes, 1951.
Desmond MacCarthy. Mill House Press, 1952.
The Hill of Devi. London, Edward Arnold, and New York, Harcourt, 1953.

Battersea Rise (first chapter of *Marianne Thornton*). New York, Harcourt, 1955.
Marianne Thornton (1797–1887): A Domestic Biography. London, Arnold, and New York, Harcourt, 1956.
E. M. Forster: Selected Writings, edited by G. B. Parker. London, Heinemann Educational, 1968.
"Albergo Empedocle," and Other Writings by E. M. Forester (previously unpublished material written 1900–15), edited by George H. Thomson. New York, Liveright, 1971.
Goldsworthy Lowes Dickinson, and Related Writings, edited by Oliver Stallybrass. London, Edward Arnold, and New York, Holmes & Meier, 1973.
Commonplace Book (facsimile edition). London, Scolar Press, 1978; revised edition edited by Philip Gardner, London, Scolar Press, and Stanford, Stanford University Press, 1985.
The Hill of Devi, and Other Indian Writings, edited by Oliver Stallybrass. London, Edward Arnold, and New York, Holmes & Meier, 1983.
The Abinger Edition of E. M. Forster (14 volumes), edited by Oliver Stallybrass and Elizabeth Heine. London, Arnold, and New York, Holmes & Meier, 1972–84.

*

Adaptations: *A Room with a View* (play adaptation by Stephen Tait and Kenneth Allott; produced in Cambridge, 1950), London, Edward Arnold, 1951; *A Passage to India* (play adaptation by Santha Rama Rau; produced London, 1960, and on Broadway, 1962), London, Edward Arnold, 1960; *Where Angels Fear to Tread* (play adaptation by Elizabeth Hart), S. French, 1963; *Howards End* (play adaptation by Lance Sieveking and Richard Cottrell; produced London, 1967); *A Passage to India* (television adaptation by John Maynard; produced by the BBC, and broadcast by NET in 1968); *Howards End* (television adaptation by Pauline Macaulay; produced by the BBC, and broadcast in 1970; *A Passage to E. M. Forster* (play compiled by William Roerick and Thomas Coley; based on Forster's works; produced at Theatre de Lys in New York, 1970); *A Passage to India* (film adaptation directed by David Lean), Columbia Pictures, 1984; *A Room with a View* (film adaptation by Merchant–Ivory Productions), Cinecom, 1986; *Maurice* (film adaptation by Merchant–Ivory Productions), Cinecom, 1987.

Manuscript Collections: E. M. Forster Archive at King's College Library, King's College, Cambridge; Humanities Research Center, University of Texas, Austin.

Biography: *E. M. Forster: A Life* (two volumes), London, Secker & Warburg, Volume 1: *The Growth of a Novelist (1870–1914),* 1977, Volume 2: *Polycrates' Ring (1914–1970),* 1978, one–volume edition published as *E. M. Forster: A Life,* New York, Harcourt, 1978; *E. M. Forster and His World* by Francis King, London, Thames & Hudson, and New York, Scribner, 1978.

Bibliography: *A Bibliography of E. M. Forster* by B. J. Kirkpatrick, London, Hart–Davis, 1965, revised, Oxford, Clarendon Press, 1968; *E. M. Forster: An Annotated Bibliography of Writings about Him,* edited by Frederick P. W. McDowell, DeKalb, Northern Illinois University Press, 1977.

Critical Sources: "The Novels of E. M. Forster" by Virginia Woolf, in *Atlantic Monthly,* November 1927, 642–648, republished in her *The Death of the Moth,* New York, Harcourt, 1942, 104–112; *The Achievement of E. M. Forster* by J. B. Beer, London, Chatto & Windus, and New York, Barnes & Noble, 1962; *Forster: A Collection of Critical Essays,* edited by Malcolm Bradbury, Englewood Cliffs, New Jersey, Prentice–Hall, 1966; *E. M. Forster* by Frederick P. W. McDowell, New York, Twayne Publishers, 1969; "Introduction" by Oliver Stallybrass, *The Life to Come, and Other Short Stories,* New York, Avon, 1972, vii–xxvii; *E. M. Forster: The Personal Voice* by John Colmer, London, Routledge & Kegan Paul, 1975; "Children of the Sun: A Narrative of "Decadence" by Martin Green, in *England After 1918,* New York, Basic Books, 1976; "The Homosexual Vision of E. M. Forster" by Dennis Altman, in *Cahiers D'Etudes Victoriennes* (Montpellier), Numbers 4–5 (special E. M. Forster issues), 1977, 85–96; "The Evolution of E. M. Forster's *Maurice*" by Philip Gardner, "*Maurice* as Fantasy" by Kathleen Grant, "'Fresh Woods and Pastures New': Forster Criticism and Scholarship since 1975" by Frederick P. W. McDowell, and "Moments in the Greenwood: *Maurice* in Context" by Ira Bruce Nadel, in *E.M. Forster: Centenary Revaluations,* edited by Judith Scherer Herz and Robert K. Martin, Toronto, University of Toronto Press, 1982, 177–190, 191–203, 204–223, 311–329; *E. M. Forster: A Guide to Research,* by Claude J. Summers, New York, Ungar, 1983; *The Short Narratives of E. M. Forster* by Judith Scherer Herz, New York, St. Martin's Press, 1988; "The Under–Plot in E. M. Forster's *The Longest Journey*" by Tariq Rahman, in *Durham University Journal,* Number 83, 1991, 59–67.

*   *   *

Perhaps the first book that comes to mind when thinking of E. M. Forster is *A Passage to India.* As a late Victorian, Forster inherited the precepts of "Empire" that emerge most clearly in Kipling, but he brought to them an inquiring mind that was dissatisfied with the twilight shallowness of Edwardian days. For Forster, the conflict between social mores and personal freedom was central; all his works deal in some way with this theme. A common second theme—the relationship between colonial exploitation and homosexual repression—has not been as widely studied (yet it seems likely that Forster made the connection). The short story, "The Boat," about a cross–cultural homosexual encounter, neatly links both ideas, illustrating the kind of novel Forster might have written if he had allowed himself to write openly about what was closest to his heart.

From a gay perspective, interest in Forster's work is often centered on the author's posthumous publications such as the novel *Maurice* and short story collections like *The Life to Come.* To these may be added *The Longest Journey,* with its homosexual sub–theme and concern with the joys and problems of friendship. Many early Forster critics were nonplussed by the author's decision to refrain from creative writing, to which he once responded: "I should have been a more famous writer if I had written or rather published more, but sex has prevented the latter." Forster's posthumous publications have had the task of remedying this omission (largely because,

in his lifetime, the author destroyed most of his "sexy" writings).

It is important to remember that *Maurice* was actually written in 1913. At that time, homosexuality was a taboo topic, and admitting to it could lead to social disaster. The Austro–Hungarian empire had just been rocked by a homosexual scandal (the Redl affair, in which a high–ranking officer had been blackmailed because of his homosexuality), and a similar scandal had taken place in the court of Wilhelm II in Germany. In England, the trials of Oscar Wilde were still fresh in the public's mind, while the Wolfenden recommendations for the relaxation of laws against homosexuals were before parliament. At the time of *Maurice*'s composition, blackmail and suicide were natural components of life for middle– and upper–class homosexuals. In his personal life, Forster was fortunate enough to be associated with groups that were quite open about homosexuality, such as the Cambridge Apostles from King's College, and later, the Bloomsbury Group. Interestingly, Forster's 1960 postscript to *Maurice* proposes a reintegration of homosexuals into society, a proposal tempered by the author's understanding that most people were uncomfortable with the idea.

In a sense, Forster's writings were precursors of the later "decadence" so well described by Martin Green in *Children of the Sun*—a revolt against the patriarchal rules of an earlier Britain. Forster's female characters are both strong and sensitive, and his most admired male characters exhibit the same quality. Forster's writings also explore a peculiarly British gay trait: the glorification of relationships with men from the lower classes. In *Maurice,* for example, the title character is a gamekeeper, a pairing repeated in "Arthur Snatchfold," and "The Obelisk," in which sailors follow the usual ways of seamen in port—taking sex where they can find it.

This division in thinking was also evident among literary critics, some of whom used the author's posthumous output as a way of downgrading all Forster's works; others saw in them a key for unlocking further meanings. Revaluation is the fate of many writers, and in Forster's case all new estimations inevitably involved his personal life. In *Cahiers D'Etudes Victoriennes,* Dennis Altman noted that Forster was led by his homosexuality to resist middle–class conventions, while at the same time understanding that these same conventions prevented him from being open. In many ways, Forster saw his homosexuality as a kind of escape–valve, the greenwood which represented both a refuge and place of exile. *Maurice* has been viewed by some critics as an ironic pastoral fantasy as well as a commentary on social injustice particular to its times; taken in this sense, the novel has a certain nostalgic charm somewhat removed from society's reality. Nevertheless, *Maurice* still reflects Forster's favorite advice—"only connect."

In his many critical writings, Forster insisted on the need for craftsmanship and careful attention to style. Many critics feel that the author succeeded at craftsmanship more than he cared to admit (even though some of his work should be taken as "jeux d'esprit" rather than finished "art"). The question that must be asked—and which must remain unanswered—concerns the types of novels Forster *might* have written. An intriguing part of the answer lies in the concepts behind such stories as "The Boat," and "Arthur Snatchfold," where the themes so evident in Forster's earlier writing are gradually transformed into another way of looking at the world. The same sense persists of the importance of friendship across classes and cultures, a sense of total sharing which Forster called "the eternal moment."

—*Murray S. Martin*

FOSTER, Jeannette Howard. American librarian, author of fiction and nonfiction, poet, and translator. Also wrote under the pseudonyms of Hilary Farr, Jan Addison, and Abigail Sanford. Born in Oak Park, Illinois, 3 November 1895. Educated at University of Chicago, 1912–14, A.A. 1914; Rockford College, Rockford, Illinois, A.B. in chemistry and engineering 1918; University of Chicago, M.A. in English and American literature 1922; Emory University, Atlanta, Georgia, B.S. in library science 1932; University of Chicago, Ph.D, 1935. Associate professor of English, Hamline University, St. Paul, Minnesota, 1922–31; science librarian, Antioch College, Yellow Springs, Ohio, 1932–33; librarian, Hollins College, Virginia, 1935–37; professor of library science, Drexel Institute, 1937–48; librarian, Kinsey Institute for Sex Research, Bloomington, Indiana, 1948–52; reference librarian, University of Kansas, Kansas City, Missouri 1952–60; assistant librarian, Lindenwood College, St. Charles, Missouri, beginning 1963. Contributor to *Library Quarterly,* and contributor of reviews, fiction, poetry, and criticism, sometimes under pseudonyms of Hilary Farr, Jan Addison, and Abigail Sanford, to the *Ladder.* **Recipient:** Third annual Gay Book Award, Task Force on Gay Liberation of the American Library Association for *Sex Variant Women in Literature,* 1974. *Died in a nursing home in Pocahantas, Arkansas, 26 July 1981.*

WRITINGS

Nonfiction

An Approach to Fiction through Characteristics of Its Readers, 1936.
Sex Variant Women in Literature: A Historical and Quantitative Survey. New York, Vantage Press, 1956; London, Frederick Muller, 1958; Baltimore, Diana Press, 1975; Tallahassee, Naiad Press, 1985.

Poetry

With Valerie Taylor, *Two Women: The Poetry of Jeanette Foster and Valerie Taylor.* Chicago, Womanpress, 1976.
Two Women Revisited: The Poetry of Jeanette Foster and Valerie Taylor. Austin, Texas, Banned Books, 1991.

Other

Translator, *A Woman Appeared to Me* by Renée Vivien, introduction by Gayle Rubin. Weatherby Lake, Missouri, Naiad Press, 1976.

*

Bibliography: *Women and Sexuality in America: A Bibliography* by Nancy Ann Sahli, Boston, G. K. Hall, 1984, 14.

Critical Sources: *The Lesbian in Literature* by Barbara Grier (as Gene Damon), San Francisco, Daughters of Bilitis, 1967, second edition, Reno, Nevada, The Ladder, 1975; third edition, Tallahassee, Naiad Press, 1981; *Homosexuality: Lesbians and Gay Men in Society, History, and Literature,* edited by Jonathan Katz, New York, Arno Press, 1974; unpublished correspondence with Jeannette Howard Foster, 1974–79; *Gay American History: Lesbians and Gay Men in the U.S.A.—A Documentary* by Jonathan Katz, New York, Crowell, 1976; "The X–Rated Bibliographer: A Spy in the House of Sex" by Karla Jay, in *Lavender Culture,* New York, Jove/Harcourt, 1978, 259; *Women's Studies* by Esther Stineman, Colorado, Libraries Unlimited, 1979, 470, 473; *Surpassing the Love of Men* by Lillian Faderman, New York, Morrow, 1981; untranscribed conversations with Joe Gregg, 1981–85; *Wolf Girls at Vassar: Lesbian and Gay Experiences 1930–1990* by Anne MacKay, New York, St. Martin's Press, 1993, 52.

*   *   *

It is difficult to fully assess Jeannette Howard Foster's contribution to the development of a lesbian culture. Her "opus" as she called it, *Sex Variant Women in Literature: A Historical and Quantitative Survey,* was truly a pioneer effort. Prior to her book, no work had attempted an examination of the lesbian in literature. In addition, Foster was a librarian, teacher, translator, fiction writer, poet, and reviewer. The ripples of her influence are being extended daily by the current generation of academics, writers, librarians and educators.

Foster was born in Oak Park, Illinois, on 3 November 1885 and died in a nursing home in Pocahantas, Arkansas, on 26 July 1981. She earned undergraduate degrees in chemistry and American and English literature from Rockford College, received an M.A. in literature from the University of Chicago, a B.S. in library science from Emory University in Atlanta, and took her Ph. D. in library science from the University of Chicago, where her thesis was on the reading habits of the modern American woman.

During Foster's long career she taught creative writing, literature, and college English; was a professor of library science at Drexel, Columbia, and Emory; worked as librarian at Hollins College, Antioch College, Lindenwood, Hamline University, the University of Missouri in Kansas City, and the special library of the Institute for Sex Research at Indiana University.

Foster formed friendships with Janet Flanner while at the University of Chicago and May Sarton while the latter was poet in residence at Lindenwood. She was one of Kinsey's first librarians and served as librarian to the President's Advisory Committee on Education in Washington, D.C.

In 1974 Foster was recipient of the Third Annual Gay Book Award from the then Task Force on Gay Liberation of the American Library Association for *Sex Variant Women in Literature,* originally self–published through a "vanity" press. Foster's study is a scholarly work, chronologically organized, which examines the "variant ... emotional reaction(s) among women as these appear in literature." In her introduction, she detailed the "difficulty in gaining access" to much of the material she wished to consider. Her original intention to "include only works seen at first hand" was taxed by cataloging obscurities, inaccessible or lost material, and closed collections. "No class of printed matter except outright pornography has suffered more critical neglect, exclusion from libraries, or omission from collected works than variant belle–lettres," she wrote. Undaunted, she spent more than 30 years pursuing rare works. She revealed many devious plans to get at lost classics, including one case in which she was locked in a room by a friendly librarian in a distant city and given one day to read a rare French manuscript in the original. Karla Jay in an interview with Foster recounts the same story and adds: "I believe that her dedication was so great that had the only sexual library been the Pope's ... she would have become a nun to gain access to it."

Foster's book critically examines 324 examples of "variant woman" literature in such languages as French, German, and English and from the ancient writers and the Bible through to the mid–twentieth century. The assumptions Foster made in evaluating "variant" literature presaged later feminist criticism and remains unchallenged. Her pioneer work has been recognized as a cornerstone title for a variety of gay men and lesbians active in the counter–culture as well as those interested in scholarly research, including Barbara Grier who praised it as "essential to any collection of lesbian literature" in her bibliographies and has often cited Foster's influence on her own research.

Jonathan Katz used Foster as a frequent reference source and, in fact, dedicates his trail breaking *Gay American History* to her. Lillian Faderman acknowledges Foster's "indispensable" contribution and cites her throughout *Surpassing the Love of Men* in a manner which reflects upon the value of her scholarship. Loeb and Stineman included it in their recommended core bibliography, *Women's Studies*, as did Sahli in her *Women and Sexuality in America,* calling it a "pioneering work with significant influence on more recent studies ... [which] should remain a standard for many years to come." In the early 1970s while Arno Press was developing its series of reprints, *Homosexuality: Lesbians and Gay Men in Society, History and Literature,* Foster's book was the source authority for the inclusion of most of the lesbian titles. Gail Ellen Dunlap, one of the *Wolf Girls At Vassar* in the 1950s, notes that she "didn't like the popular dyke literature" but did include Foster's book in her reading. Chicago's Gerber–Hart Library and Midwest Gay and Lesbian Resource Center (under the leadership of librarian Joe Gregg, one of Foster's students) used *Sex Variant Women in Literature* as a guide to collection development, eventually succeeding in obtaining a grant to purchase a significant body of lesbian titles drawn from her "opus." Catalogs of rare booksellers from New York to Berkeley have listed her work at premium prices, annotating their entries with comments like: "Her discussions and insights [are] ... impressive for the quality of her scholarship and intelligent understanding. But when one considers that hers was a voyage without maps, the number of titles and authors she discovered for the world of letters is nothing short of staggering." It is difficult to find a work on lesbian literature or history that does not make some reference to Foster or her work.

After being contacted in the 1960s by Barbara Grier, then editor of the *Ladder,* Foster contributed reviews, fiction, poetry, and criticism to the journal under a variety of names including her own. Hilary Farr, Jan Addison and Abigail Sanford are a few of the pseudonyms she used—the latter two drawn from the surnames of her grandfathers.

In correspondence with the writer, Foster indicated that in the early 1970s she was being asked to grant reprint rights to her "opus" by two different factions: one urged reprint with a trade publisher or university press for the widest exposure, the other appealed to her to let the work be done by a lesbian–feminist press for political reasons. Foster yielded to the latter, and Diana Press brought out a paperback edition of *Sex Variant Women in Literature* in 1975. Foster was generally pleased but had reservations about the book—as a librarian she noted the margins were insufficient to permit hardcover rebinding, a necessity for inclusion in library collections. When Diana Press failed, a third edition was brought out, also in

paper, by Naiad Press. These editions have made her work more readily available to a new generation of scholars.

In 1976, Foster published a collection of her poetry written between 1916 and 1938. This work, *Two Women* (reprinted 15 years later as *Two Women Revisited*), as well as a translation from the French of Renée Vivien's *A Woman Appeared to Me* were both issued by lesbian presses. Foster wrote of her joy at living long enough to see three of her works in print. She was especially pleased with *A Woman Appeared to Me*—the first translation into a prose work based on Vivien's affair with Violet Shilleto and her relationship with Natalie Clifford Barney. With the exception of a few individual poems translated and published in little magazines, this was the first major Vivien work to be published.

During the late 1970s many well known activists made pilgrimages to see Foster. She was praised and lionized. When her expenses began to exceed her resources, nascent gay and lesbian newspapers rallied to an appeal from novelist Valerie Taylor and photographer Tee Corinne for donations to ease the plight of the then nursing–home–bound pioneer. Benefits and fund–raisers were held around the country, further extolling her work and enhancing her reputation. A movement was begun to create nursing/retirement homes for lesbians.

In addition to the above, Foster contributed articles to *Library Quarterly* and other professional journals, had a story published in the late 1920s in *Harper's,* and at the time of her death left at least one unpublished novel, *Home is the Hunter,* and dozens of unpublished poems. During the latter part of her life, Dr. Foster had cataloged her personal library of over two thousand volumes.

—*Marie J. Kuda*

FOUCAULT, Michel. French philosopher, social historian, and translator. Born in Poitiers, 15 October 1926. Educated at École Normale Supérieure; Sorbonne, University of Paris, licence in philosophy 1948, licence in psychology 1950, diploma in psycho–pathology 1952, Ph.D. 1960. Teacher of philosophy and French literature, University of Lille, University of Uppsala, University of Warsaw, University of Hamburg, University of Clermont–Ferrand, University of Sao Paulo, and University of Tunis, 1960–68; professor, University of Paris, Vincennes, France, 1968–70; chairman of history of systems of thought, College de France, 1970–84. Director, *Zone des tempetes,* 1973–84; contributor to periodicals, including *Critique.* **Recipient:** Center of Scientific Research (France) Medal, 1961, for philosophical work. *Died in Paris, of complications resulting from AIDS, 25 June 1984.*

WRITINGS

Nonfiction

Maladie mentale et personnalité. Paris, Presses Universitaires de France, 1954; revised as *Maladie mentale et psychologié,* 1962; translated by Alan Sheridan as *Mental Illness and Psychology,* New York, Harper, 1976.

Folie et déraison: Histoire de la folie à l'âge classique. Paris, Plon, 1961; abridged edition, Paris, Union Generale, 1964; translated by Richard Howard as *Madness and Civilization: A History of Insanity in the Age of Reason,* New York, Pantheon, 1965, London, Tavistock, 1967.

Naissance de la clinique: Une Archéologie du regard medical. Paris, Universitaires de France, 1963; translated by A. M. Sheridan Smith as *The Birth of the Clinic: An Archaeology of Medical Perception,* New York, Pantheon, and London, Tavistock, 1973.

Raymond Roussel. Paris, Gallimard, 1963; translated as *Death and the Labyrinth: The World of Raymond Roussel,* Garden City, New York, Doubleday, 1986.

Les Mots et les choses: Une Archeologie des sciences humanes. Paris, Gallimard, 1966; translated as *The Order of Things: An Archaeology of the Human Sciences,* New York, Pantheon, 1971.

L'Archeologie du savoir. Paris, Gallimard, 1969; translated by A. M. Sheridan Smith as *The Archaeology of Knowledge* (includes "The Discourse on Language"), New York, Pantheon, 1972.

L'Ordre du discours. Paris, Gallimard, 1971; translated as "The Discourse on Language," in *The Archaeology of Knowledge,* 1972.

(Editor) *Moi, Pierre Rivière, ayant égorgé ma mère, ma soeur et mon frère ... Un Cas de parricide au XIXe siècle.* France, 1973; translated by Frank Jellinek as *I, Pierre Riviere, Having Slaughtered My Mother, My Sister, and My Brother ... A Case of Parricide in the 19th Century,* New York, Pantheon, 1975, London, Peregrine, 1978.

Ceci n'est pas une pipe: Deux Lettres et quatre dessins de Rene Magritte. Montpellier, France, Fata Morgana, 1973; translated by James Harkness as *This Is Not a Pipe: Illustrations and Letters by Rene Magritte,* Berkeley, University of California Press, 1983.

Surveiller et punir: Naissance de la prison. Paris, Gallimard, 1975; translated by Allan Sheridan as *Discipline and Punish: The Birth of the Prison,* New York, Pantheon, 1977.

Les Machines à guérir (aux origines de l'hôpital moderne). Paris, Institute de l'Environnement, 1976.

Histoire de la sexualité, translated by Robert Hurley as *The History of Sexuality,* Volume 1: *La Volonté de savoir,* Paris, Gallimard, 1976, as *Discipline and Punishment: The Birth of the Prison,* New York, Pantheon, 1978; Volume 2: *L'Usage des Plaisirs,* Paris, Gallimard, 1984, as *The Use of Pleasure,* New York, Pantheon, 1985; Volume 3: *Souci de Soi,* Paris, Gallimard, 1984, as *The Care of the Self,* New York, Pantheon, 1987.

Language, Counter–Memory, Practice: Selected Essays and Interviews, edited and translated by Donald F. Bouchard, additional translation by Sherry Simon. Ithaca, New York, Cornell University Press, 1977.

Author of introduction, *Herculine Barbin: Being the Recently Discovered Memoirs of a Nineteenth–Century French Hermaphrodite,* translation by Richard McDougall. New York, Pantheon, 1980.

Power/Knowledge: Selected Interviews, and Other Writings, 1972–1977. New York, Pantheon, 1981.

The Foucault Reader, edited by Paul Rabinow. New York, Pantheon, 1984.

With Maurice Blanchot, *Foucault–Blanchot,* translation by Jeffrey Mehlman and Brian Massumi. Zone Books, 1987.

Politics, Philosophy, Culture: Interviews, and Other Writings, 1977–1984, edited by Lawrence D. Kritzman, introduction by Alan Sheridan. London, Routledge, 1988.

Translator

Le Rêve et l'existence by Ludwig Binswanger. Paris, Desclée de Brouwer, 1954; translated by Forrest Williams and Jacob Needleman as *Dream and Existence,* edited by Keith Hoeller, Revision Exist. Psychology, 1986.

With others, *Études de style* by Leo Spitzer. Paris, Gallimard, 1962.

Anthropologie du point de vue pragmatique by Immanuel Kant. Paris, Vrin, 1964.

*

Bibliography: *Michel Foucault: An Annotated Bibliography: Tool Kit for a New Age* by Michael Clark, New York, Garland, 1983.

Critical Sources: *Foucault* by Annie Guédez, Paris, Editions Universitaires, 1972; *Foucault* by Angèle Kremer–Marietti, Paris, Seghers, 1974; *Michel Foucault: The Will to Truth* by Alan Sheridan, London, Tavistock, 1980; *Michel Foucault: An Introduction to the Study of His Thought* by Barry Cooper, New York and Toronto, Edwin Mellen, 1981; *Michel Foucault: Beyond Structuralism and Hermeneutics* by Hubert L. Dreyfus and Paul Rabinow, afterword by Michel Foucault, Chicago, University of Chicago Press, 1982, second edition, 1983; *Michel Foucault: Social Theory and Transgression* by Charles E. Lemert and Garth Gillan, New York, Columbia University Press, 1982; *Psycho Politics: Laing, Foucault, Goffman, Szasz, and the Future of Mass Psychiatry* by Peter Sedgwick, London, Pluto, and New York, Harper, 1982; *Michel Foucault and the Subversion of Intellect* by Karlis Racevskis, Ithaca, New York, Cornell University Press, 1983; *Foucault, Marxism and Critique* by Barry Smart, London, Routledge, 1983; *Michel Foucault* by Mark Cousins and Athar Hussain, New York, St. Martin's Press, and London, Macmillan, 1984; *Foucault, Marxism, and History: Mode of Production Versus Mode of Information* by Mark Poster, Cambridge, England, Polity Press, and New York, Blackwell, 1984; *Cultural Analysis: The Work of Peter L. Berger, Mary Douglas, Michel Foucault, and Jürgen Habermas* by Rovert Wuthnow and others, London, Routledge, 1984; *Prophets of Extremism: Nietzsche, Heidegger, Foucault, Derrida* by Allan Megill, Berkeley, University of California Press, 1985; *Michel Foucault: The Freedom of Philosophy* by John Rajchman, New York, Columbia University Press, 1985; *Foucault: A Critical Reader* by David Couzens Hoy, Oxford, Blackwell, 1986; *Michel Foucault* by Didier Eribon, translated by Betsy Wing, Cambridge, Harvard University Press, 1992; *The Passion of Michel Foucault* by James Miller, New York, Simon & Schuster, 1993; "Subject and Abject: The Examined Life of Michel Foucault" by Alexander Nehamas, in *New Republic,* 15 February 1993, 27–36.

*   *   *

Michel Foucault has been called one of the most influential modern philosophers to have emerged since the 1960s. A contemporary of Jean Paul Sartre, Foucault's work has influenced a generation of scholars in a variety of disciplines.

Foucault was born on 15 October 1926, in Poitiers, France. He was educated at the Ecole Normale Superieure, and the Sorbonne at the University of Paris where he received his diploma in 1952. Between 1952 and 1960, he taught at the University of Lille, the University of Uppsala, the University of Warsaw and the University of Hamburg. He returned to Paris in 1960 and received his doctorate for his thesis *Folie et deraison: Historie de la folie a l'age classique* (*Madness and Civilization: A History of Insanity in the Age of Reason*). In this major work, published the following year, Foucault traced the influences that philosophical, religious and scientific writings have had upon modern treatises of psychiatry. Between 1966 and 1970, he taught at the University of Clermont–Ferrand, the University of Tunis, and the University of Paris in Vincennes, France. He became famous in 1966 with the publication of *Les mots et les choses: Une archeologie des sciences humanes* (*The Order of Things: An Archaeology of the Human Sciences*). In 1970 he was appointed Chair of history and systems of thought and was elected to the College de France, a prestigious French educational institution.

In the early– to mid–seventies, Foucault made several trips to the United States and taught at the University of California, Berkeley. At this time he began to speak openly of his homosexuality and began producing one of his most influential works, *Histoire de la sexualité* (*The History of Sexuality*). A student of Nietzsche and of Marxist philosopher Louis Althausser, Foucault studied a wide variety of social institutions, including prisons, mental institutions, medical clinics and universities. He came to believe that those in power manipulate prevailing attitudes to suit their ends and redefine the ideas of insanity, illness, sexuality and criminality in order to identify and oppress undesirables and sexual "deviants." These social attitudes in turn become "principles of exclusion" through which society defines itself. Throughout history, individuals and groups are merely elements in a network of control and manipulation over which they are powerless.

In his three–volume work, *The History of Sexuality,* Foucault defines the history of sex and sexuality as a history of repression by those in power. Such power has manifested itself in terms of censorship, prohibition or non–recognition. Such power relations can be complex and subtle as well as overt. In the first volume,

Discipline and Punishment, Foucault discovers that the prevailing negatives attitudes toward sex and sexuality between the sixteenth and nineteenth centuries did little to repress but much to encourage a deluge of written discourse about the topic. People could not stop thinking and writing about "it." The result of this "explosion" of knowledge was to redefine and rediscover different forms of sexuality. In the next two volumes, Foucault traces the history of discourse about sexuality back to the beginnings of Western Civilization. In the second volume, *The Use of Pleasure,* Foucault demonstrates that the Greeks revealed through their writings the proper codes of behavior regarding sexual behavior. Sex was not the romantic end of one's being but a regulated social institution with strict codes necessary for maintaining social cohesion and control. In the third volume, *The Care of the Self,* the author continues his analyses of the ancient world to the Romans and their strict sexual codes of moderation and restraint.

Foucault impresses readers by his broad, tolerant and mature definitions of the nature of sex and sexuality. His theories and personality have had a profound impact on studies of sexuality, especially upon studies of homosexuality as well as upon the homosexual community itself. In his work, Foucault attacks rigid stereotypes and oppressive models. Believing we are all creatures of history, he maintains that societies in different times and in different places in history have had their own unique habits, customs and manners which set them apart from other societies. The terms that one society uses to define itself as a "society" in a particular time and place may have little or no meaning in another time and place. His strength as a social historian lies in his ability to see "contingency" where other historians only see "necessity." He refused to define the homosexual as "transhistorical," i.e., a given and a constant in all periods of history. The concept of "homosexuality" was not at all times in history recognized and was not defined by the same standards. Foucault saw the need to define the behavior of individuals according to the standards of their own time and culture.

—Jane Jurgens

G

GARCÍA LORCA, Federico. Spanish poet, dramatist, lecturer, illustrator, and musician. Born in Fuentevaqueros, Granada, 5 June 1898. Educated at University of Granada, 1914–19; University of Madrid, degree in law, 1923; Columbia University, 1929. Organizer, Cante Jondo Festival, Madrid, 1922; coeditor, *Gallo* (literary magazine), Granada, 1928; artistic director, director, and producer, La Barraca (traveling university theater group), 1932–35; director of plays, including *Blood Wedding*, 1933. *Executed by a firing squad in Viznar, Granada, Spain, 19 August 1936.*

WRITINGS

Poetry

Libro de poemas. Madrid, Maroto, 1921.

Canciones (includes "Canción del mariquita" ["Song of the Pansy"]; "Narciso," "(Narciso)" ["Narcissus"]; and "Soneto" ["Sonnet"]). Málaga, Spain, Litoral/Imprenta Sur, 1927; translated by Federico García Lorca and Philip Cummings as *Songs,* edited by Daniel Eisenberg, Pittsburgh, Pennsylvania, Duquesne University Press, 1976.

Primer romancero gitano. Madrid, Revista de Occidente, 1928; as *Romancera gitano,* 1929; translated by Langston Hughes as *Gypsy Ballads,* Beloit, Wisconsin, Beloit College, 1951; translated by Carl W. Cobb as *Lorca's Romancero gitano: A Ballad Translation and Critical Study,* Jackson, University Press of Mississippi, c. 1983.

Poema del cante jondo. Madrid, Ulises/Iberoamericana, 1931; partially translated by Keith Waldrop as *Poem of the Gypsy Seguidilla,* Providence, Rhode Island, Burning Deck, 1967; translated by Carlos Bauer as *Poem of the Deep Song,* San Francisco, City Lights Books, 1987.

Oda a Walt Whitman. Mexico City, Alcancía, 1933; as *Ode to Walt Whitman,* in *Ode to Walt Whitman, and Other Poems,* San Francisco, City Lights Books, 1988.

Llanto por Ignacio Sanchez Mejias. Madrid, Cruz & Raya/Arbol, 1935; translated by A. L. Lloyd as *Lament for the Death of a Bullfighter, and Other Poems,* London, Heinemann, and New York, Oxford University Press, 1937.

Seis poemas gallegos. Santiaga de Compostela, Spain, Nós, 1935; as *Six Galician Poems,* in *Ode to Walt Whitman, and Other Poems,* 1988.

Primeras canciones. Madrid, Héroe, 1936; as *First Songs* in *Ode to Walt Whitman, and Other Poems,* San Francisco, City Lights Books, 1988.

Poems, translation by Stephen Spender and J. L. Gili. New York, Oxford University Press, 1937; Oxford, England, Dolphin, 1939.

Poeta en Nueva York (includes "Tu infancia en Mentón" ["Your Childhood in Menton"] and "Oda a Walt Whitman"). Mexico City, Séneca, 1940; translated by Rolfe Humphries as *The Poet in New York, and Other Poems of Federico García Lorca,* introduction by J. Bergamin, New York, Norton, 1940; translated by Ben Belitt as *Poet in New York,* introduction by Angel de Rio, New York, Grove Press, 1955.

The Selected Poems of Federico García Lorca, translation by Stephen Spender and J. L. Gili. London, Hogarth Press, 1943; New York, Transatlantic Arts, 1947.

Poemas pósthumos. Mexico City, Mexicanas, 1945.

Diván del Tamarit. Barcelona, A.D.L., 1948; translated by Edwin Honig as *Divan* in *Divan, and Other Writings,* Providence, Rhode Island, Bonewhistle Press, 1974; in *Four Puppet Plays; The Divan Poems,* 1990.

Siete poemas y dos dibujos inéditos, edited by Luis Rosales. Madrid, Cultura Hispánica, 1949.

The Selected Poems of Federico García Lorca (bilingual edition), edited with an introduction by Francisco García Lorca and Donald M. Allen, translation by Roy Campbell, and others. New York, New Directions, 1955.

Lorca, translation by J. L. Gili. London, Penguin, 1960–65.

With Juan Ramon Jimenez, *Lorca and Jimenez: Selected Poems,* translation by Robert Bly. Sixties Press, 1967.

The Lieutenant Colonel and the Gypsy, translation and illustrations by Marc Simont. Garden City, New York, Doubleday, 1971.

Lorca/Blackburn, Poems by Federico García Lorca: Translations by Paul Blackburn. Northampton, Massachusetts, Mulch Press, 1976; as *Lorca/Blackburn: Poems,* San Francisco, Momo's Press, 1979.

The Cricket Sings: Poems and Songs for Children (bilingual edition), translation by Will Kirkland. New York, New Directions, 1980.

Suites (includes "En el bosque de las toronjas de luna" ["In the Forest of the Moon Grapefruits"]), edited by André Belamich. Barcelona, Ariel, 1983.

Inéditos de Federico García Lorca: Sonetos del amor oscuro, 1935–1936, compiled by Marta Teresa Casteros. Buenos Aires, Instituto de Estudios de Literatura Latinoamericana, 1984.

Antología comentada/Federico García Lorca: selección, introduction and notes by Eutimio Martín, illustrations by author. Madrid, Ediciones de la Torre, 1988–89.

Sonnets of Love Forbidden, translation by David K. Loughran. Missoula, Montana, Windsong, 1989.

Collected Poems, edited by Christopher Maurer. New York, Farrar, Straus, 1991.

Plays

El maficio de la mariposa (produced Madrid, 1920). Included in

Obras Completas, Madrid, Aguilar, 1954; as *The Butterfly's Evil Spell*, in *Comedies*, 1954.

Mariana Pineda: Romance popular en tres estampas (produced Barcelona, 1927). Madrid, Farsa, 1928; as *Romance de las muerte de Torrijos*, in *El Dia Grafico*, 1927; translated by James Graham–Luján as *Mariana Pineda: A Popular Ballad in Three Prints*, in *Tulane Drama Review* (New Orleans, Louisiana), winter 1962; translated by Robert G. Harvard as *Mariana Pineda: A Popular Ballad in Three Engravings*, Warminster, England, Aris & Phillips, 1987.

La zapatera prodigiosa: Farsa violenta (produced Madrid, 1930). Losada, 1944; as *The Shoemaker's Prodigious Wife*, in *From Lorca's Theater*, 1941; in *Comedies*, 1954; as *The Prodigious Cobbler's Wife*, in *Two Plays of Misalliance*, 1989.

Bodas de sangre (produced Madrid, 1933; translated by Jose A. Weissberger as *Bitter Oleander*, produced New York, 1935). Cruz & Raya/Arbol, 1936; translated by Gilbert Neiman as *Blood Wedding*, Norfolk, Connecticut, New Directions, 1939; as *Blood Wedding*, in *Three Tragedies of Federico García Lorca*, 1947, London, Falcon, 1948; in *Three Tragedies*, 1977.

Amor de Don Perlimplín con Belisa en su jardín (produced Madrid, 1933). Included in *Obras completas*, 1938; as *The Love of Don Perlimplín with Belisa, in His Garden*, in *Comedies*, 1954; in *Two Plays of Misalliance*, 1989.

Yerma: Poema tragico (produced Madrid, 1934). Buenos Aires, Anaconda, 1937; as *Yerma*, in *From Lorca's Theater*, 1941; in *Three Tragedies*, 1977; translated by Ian Macpherson and Jaqueline Minett as *Yerma: A Tragic Poem* (bilingual edition), introduction by John Lyon, Warminster, England, Aris & Phillips, 1987.

Retabillo de Don Cristóbal (puppet play; produced Buenos Aires, 1934). Valencia, Subcomisariado de Propaganda del Comisariado General de Guerra, 1938; translated by Edwin Honig as "In the Frame of Don Cristóbal," in *Some Little Known Writings of Federico García Lorca*, New York, New Directions, 1944.

Doña Rosita la soltera; o, El lenguaje de las flores: Poema granadino del novecientos (produced Barcelona, 1935). Included in *Obras Completas*, 1938; as *Doña Rosita the Spinster*, in *Comedies*, 1954.

Los titeres de Cachiporra: Tragecomedia de Don Cristóbal y la sena Rosita: Farsa (puppet play; produced Madrid, 1937). Losange, 1953; translation by William I. Oliver, in *New World Writing*, New York, New American Library of World Literature, 1955.

La casa de Bernarda Alba: Drama de mujeres en los pueblos de Espana (produced Buenos Aires, 1945). Losada, 1944; in *Three Tragedies*, 1977.

El público: Amor, teatro, y caballos en la obre de Federico García Lorca (contains *El público*, produced San Juan, Puerto Rico, 1978, and *Comedia sin titulo*, produced Madrid, 1989), edited by Rafael Martínez Nadal. Oxford, England, Dolphin, 1970; revised as *El público: Amor y muerte en la obra de Federico García Lorca*, Mexico, J. Mortiz, 1974; revised as *El público y comedia sin titulo: Dos obras postumas*, Oxford, England, Dolphin, 1978; translated by Carlos Bauer as *The Public, and Play Without a Title*, New York, New Directions, 1983.

Así que pasen cinco años (produced Madrid, 1978). Included in *Obras completas*, 1938; translated by William B. Logan and Angel G. Orrios as *Once Five Years Pass*, in *Once Five Years Pass, and Other Dramatic Works*, Barrytown, New York, Station Hill, 1989.

Comedies (contains *The Butterfly's Evil Spell*, *The Shoemaker's Prodigious Wife*, *The Love of Don Perlimplín with Belisa, in His Garden*, and *Doña Rosita the Spinster*), translation by Robert L. O'Connell and James Graham–Luján, introduction by Francisco García Lorca. New York, New Directions, 1954; enlarged as *Five Plays: Comedies and Tragicomedies*, 1963.

Three Tragedies (contains *Blood Wedding*, *Yerma*, and *The House of Bernarda Alba*), translation by Sue Bradbury. London, Folio Society, 1977.

Two Plays of Misalliance: The Love of Don Perlimplín [and] *The Prodigious Cobbler's Wife*. Warminster, England, Aris & Phillips, 1989.

Four Puppet Plays; The Divan Poems. Riverdale–on–Hudson, New York, Sheep Meadow, 1990.

Letters

Federico García Lorca: Cartas a sus amigos, edited by Sebastián Gasch. Barcelona, Cobalto, 1950.

García Lorca: Cartas, postales, poemas, y dibujos (includes letters and poems), edited by Antonio Gallego Morell). Madrid, Monedo y Crédito, 1968.

Epistolario, edited by Christopher Maurer. Madrid, Alianza, 1983; translated in part and edited by David Gershator as *Selected Letters*, New York, New Directions, 1983.

"Federico García Lorca escribe a su familia desde Nueva York y La Habana (1929–1930)," in *Poesía*, 1985.

Collections

Obras completas, edited by Guillermo de Torre. Losada, 1938–46.

From Lorca's Theater: Five Plays of Federico García Lorca (contains *The Shoemaker's Prodigious Wife*), translation by Richard O'Connell and James Graham–Luján, introduction by Stark Young. New York, Scribner, 1941.

Obras completas, edited with commentary by Arturo de Hoyo, introductions by Jorge Guillen and Vicente Aleixandre. Aguilar, 1954.

Obras, edited with commentary by Mario Hernández. Madrid, Alianza, 1981; revised, 1983.

Ode to Walt Whitman, and Other Poems (contains *Oda a Walt Whitman*, *Seis poemas gallegos*, and *Primeras canciones*), translation by Carlos Bauer. San Francisco, City Lights Books, 1988.

Plays Two: Lorca (part of "World Dramatists" series). London, Heinemann Educational, 1990.

Barbarous Nights: Legends and Plays, translation by Christopher Sawyer–Laucanno. San Francisco, City Lights Books, 1991.

Illustrator

Federico García Lorca: Dibujos. Granada, Spain, Ministerio de Cultura, 1986; translated by Christopher Maurer as *Line of Light and Shadow: The Drawings of Federico García Lorca*, edited with an introduction by Marion Hernández, Durham, North Carolina, Duke University Museum of Art, 1991.

Lorca—The Drawings: Their Relation to the Poet's Life and Work by Helen Oppenheimer. London, F. Watts, 1987.

Other

Impresiones y paisajes (travelogue). Granada, P. V. Traveset, 1918; translated by Lawrence H. Klibbe as *Impressions and Landscapes,* Lanham, Maryland, University Press of America, 1987.

Cinco forsas breves; seguidas de Así que pasen cinco años. Losange, 1953.

Conferencias y charlas. Havana, Consejo Nacional de Cultura, 1961.

Casidas. Madrid, Arte ye Bibliofilia, 1969.

Prosa. Madrid, Alianza, 1969.

Granada, paraíso cerrado y otras páginas granadinas. Granada, Sanchez, 1971.

A Concordance to the Plays and Poems of Federico García Lorca, edited by Alice M. Pollin and Philip H. Smith. Ithaca, New York, Cornell University Press, 1975.

Autógrafos, edited by Rafael Martínez Nadal. Oxford, England, Dolphin, 1975.

Viaje a la luna (filmscript), edited by Laffranque. Loubressac, France, Braad, 1980; translated by Richard Diers as *Trip to the Moon,* in "A Filmscript by Lorca," in *Windmill Magazine,* spring 1963.

From the Havana Lectures, 1928: "Theory and Play of the Duende" and "Imagination, Inspiration, Evasion" (bilingual edition), translation by Stella Rodriguez, preface by Randolph Severson, introduction by Rafael Lopez Pedraza. Dallas, Texas, Kanathos, 1981.

Lola, la comedianta, edited by Piero Menarini. Madrid, Alianza, 1981.

Conferencias, edited by Christopher Maurer. Madrid, Alianza, 1984; partially translated by Christopher Maurer as *Deep Song, and Other Prose,* New Directions, and London, Boyars, 1980.

How a City Sings from November to November (lecture; bilingual edition), translation by Christopher Maurer. Tiburon–Belvedere, California, Cadmus Editions, 1984.

La niña que riega la albahaca y el príncipe preguntón, in *Anales de la literatura española contemporañea,* 1984.

Tres diálogos. Granada, Universidad de Granada/Junta de Andalucía, 1985.

Alocuciones argentinas, edited by Marion Hernández. Madrid, Fundación Federico García Lorca/Crotalón, 1985.

Oda y burla de Sesostris y Sardanápalo/Federico García Lorca: edición de Miguel García–Posada. El Ferrol de Caudillo, Spain, Sociedad de Cultura Valle–Inclán, 1985.

Alocución al pueblo de Fuentevaqueros. Granada, Comisión del Cincuentenario, 1986.

Teatro inconcluso, edited by Laffranque. Granada, Universidad de Granada, 1986.

Four Suites, translation by Jerome Rothenberg. College Park, Maryland, Sun and Moon Press, 1989.

*

Adaptations: *Yerma, The Love of Don Perlimplín with Belisa, in His Garden* (operas and ballets); *Blood Wedding* (opera; film; ballet, 1981); poetry and the first act of *Doña Rosita la soltera* (musical recording), New World Records, Bronx Arts Ensemble, 1985, 1987, and 1988.

Manuscript Collections: Fundación García Lorca, Consejo Superior de Investigaciones Científicas, Madrid.

Biography: *Federico García Lorca* by John A. Crow, Los Angeles, University of California Press, 1945; *Federico García Lorca* by Reed Anderson, New York, Grove Press, 1984; *Federico García Lorca* by Ian Gibson, Volume 1: *De Fuente Vaqueros a Nueva York (1898–1929),* Barcelona, Grijalbo, 1985, Volume 2: *De Nueva York a Fuente Grande (1929–1936),* Barcelona, Grijalbo, 1987, translated as *Federico García Lorca: A Life,* New York, Pantheon, 1989; *In the Green Morning: Memories of Federico* by Francisco García Lorca, translation by Christopher Maurer, New York, New Directions, 1986.

Bibliography: *Lorca: A Collection of Critical Essays* by Manuel Duran, Englewood Cliffs, New Jersey, Prentice–Hall, 1962; *Federico García Lorca y su mundo: Ensayo de una bibliografía general,* edited by Joseph L. Laurenti and Joseph Siracusa, Metuchen, New Jersey, Scarecrow Press, 1974; *García Lorca: A Selectively Annotated Bibliography of Criticism,* edited by Francesca Colecchia, New York, Garland, 1979; *García Lorca: An Annotated Primary Bibliography* by Francesca Colecchia, New York, Garland, 1982; "Bibliografía lorquiana reciente," regular listing in *Boletín de la Funación Federico García Lorca,* 1987—.

Critical Sources: *Lorca: A Collection of Critical Essays,* edited by Manuel Duran, Englewood Cliffs, New Jersey, Prentice–Hall, 1962; *A la recherche de Lorca* by Jean–Louis Schonberg, Neuchâtel, Editions de la Baconnière, 1966; *Lorca: poeta maldito* by Francisco Umbral, Madrid, Biblioteca Nueva, 1968; *Lorca's "The Public": A Study of an Unfinished Play and of Love and Death in Lorca's Work,* New York, Schocken, 1974; "La Barraca" by Luis Sáenz de la Calzada, in *Teatro universitario,* Madrid, Revista de Occidente, 1976; "Homosexualidad en la Generacion del 27. Una conversacion con Jaime Gil de Biedma" by Bruce Swansey and José Ramón Enríquez, in *El homosexual ante La sociedad enferma,* edited by José Ramón Enríquez, Barcelona, Tusquets, 1978, 193–216; *Lorca's "Romancero gitano": A Ballad Translation and Critical Study* by Carl Cobb, Jackson, University Press of Mississippi, c. 1983; *La miel es mas dulce que la sangre. Las Epocas lorquiana y freudiana de Salvadord Dalí* by Rafael Santos Torroella, Barcelona, Seix Barral, 1984; *Lorca: The Gay Imagination* by Paul Binding, London, GMP, 1985; *El rio: Novelas de caballeria* by Luis Cardoza y Aragon, Mexico City, Fondo de Cultura Economica, 1986; *Federico García Lorca, heterodoxo y mártir. Análisis y provección de La obra juvenil inédita* by Eutimio Martin, Madrid, Siglo 21, 1986; *Federico García Lorca v la cultura de la homosexualidad: Lorca, Dalí, Cernúda, Gil–Albert; Prados v la voz silenciada del amor homosexual* by Angel Sahuquillo, University of Stockholm, 1986, second edition, Alicante, Instituto de Cultura "Juan Gil–Albert"—Diputacion de Alicante, 1991; "La sensibilidad homoerotica en el Romancero gitano" by Luis Antonio de Villena, in *Campus (Revista de la Universidad de Granada),* December 1986, 27–30; "El publico" by Rafael Martinez Nadal, in *Amor v muerte en la obra de Federico García Lorca,* third edition, Madrid, Hiperión, 1988; "The Social and Sexual Geography of *Poeta en Nueva York*" by John K. Walsh, in *"Cuando yo me muera ... ": Essays in Memory of Federico García Lorca,* edited by C. Brian Morris, Lanham, Maryland, University Press of America, 1988, 105–127; "Reaction to the Publication of the 'Sonetos del amor oscuro'" by Daniel Eisenberg, in *Bulletin of Hispanic Studies,* Number 65, 1988, 261–271; "'Las cintas del vals':

Three Dance–Poems from Lorca's *Poeta en Nueva York*" by John K. Walsh, in *Romanic Review,* Number 79, 1988, 502–516; "City of Night: García Lorca's Old–Fashioned Modernism" by John Ash, in *Village Voice* (New York), 26 July 1988, 52–53; *Lorca's Late Poetry: A Critical Study* by Andrew A. Anderson, Liverpool, England, Francis Cairns, 1990; "Lorca and Censorship: the Gay Artist Made Heterosexual" by Daniel Eisenberg, in *Angelica: Revista de Literatura,* Number 2, 1991, 121–145; *El drama oculto: Buñuel, Dalí, Falla, García Lorca y Sánchez Mejías* by Emilio Valdivielso Miquel, Madrid, Ediciones de la Torre, 1992.

*   *   *

Federico García Lorca is probably Spain's most famous twentieth–century author, and may be counted, alongside such figures as the novelist Miguel de Cervantes, the poet and dramatist Lope de Vega, the poet Serafin Estébanez Calderón, and the novelist and playwright Benito Pérez Galdós, among the most outstanding Spanish writers of all time. Born in a small farming community outside Granada in 1898, Lorca grew up the first son in a comfortable landowning family that was orthodox Catholic but fairly liberal politically. In 1909 the family moved into the city of Granada, and there Lorca received his secondary education. Subsequently, he started courses at the local university. In 1919 he transferred to the University of Madrid and, more importantly, to a student residence, known simply as the Residencia de Estudiantes, which was based on the examples of Oxford and Cambridge colleges. Early letters, dating from even before the move to Madrid, suggest that Lorca was at least in the process of becoming aware of his own sexual nature, a process that was doubtlessly accelerated by the atmosphere of the all–male Residencia and the new friendships he made there.

From what remains of his library and from references in his writings, we know that throughout this period he was reading very widely, and among the authors identified are the Greek philosopher Plato, the French poet Paul Verlaine, the Irish poet and dramatist Oscar Wilde, the French novelist Marcel Proust, and the French poet and novelist Jean Cocteau (American poet Walt Whitman came rather later). Details of Lorca's personal life through the 1920s are still rather sketchy, but from 1923 on we do know that he became involved in an increasingly intense friendship with the painter Salvador Dalí. Dalí's sensationalistic memoirs are entirely unreliable, especially with regard to their personal dealings; on the other hand, there is ample textual documentation of their joint elaboration of a complex aesthetic theory and a series of cliquish private references centered on the figure of Saint Sebastian. The relationship came to an end in 1928, due in part to Dalí's growing interest in French Surrealism, which Lorca rejected, and also in part to Dalí's transfer of loyalties to the Spanish film director Luis Buñuel; together Buñuel and Dalí went on to make the first Surrealist film, 1929's *Le Chien andalou*, which has been interpreted by some as a veiled commentary on Lorca's sexuality.

In the later 1920s Lorca was also involved in an affair with a young sculptor, Emilio Aladrén, the break–up of which was one of the factors that contributed to a depression that, in turn, led to his being sent by his family on a trip to America in the summer of 1929—the first time he had set foot outside Spain. In New York at the end of the "roaring twenties," Lorca was able to observe a very different attitude to morals and sexuality than he had known in

Granada or Madrid; there also he discovered Whitman's volume of poetry *Leaves of Grass* and met the American poet Hart Crane. Back in Spain in the 1930s, and coinciding with the years of the Second Republic, he adopted a more open or even defiant attitude to his personal sexuality, as did another contemporary Spanish poet and intimate of Lorca, Luis Cernuda. During the 1930s, among many other activities, Lorca served as director of a Madrid student theater troupe, La Barraca, and his last important relationship was with Rafael Rodríguez Rapún, an engineering student who was a leading member of the group.

In much of the as yet unpublished juvenilia from 1916 to 1920 (prose, poetry and drama), Lorca, in the grip of a powerful late–Romantic malaise, identifies with several roles, among them the suffering Christ–figure and the sad clown of Pierrot, a traditional comic character. In the contemporary travelogue *Impresiones y paisajes* (*Impressions and Landscapes*), he condemns what he perceives as the unhealthy lives of cloistered monks.

Chronologically, Lorca's first explicit treatment of a homosexual motif is found in the poem "Canción del mariquita" ("Song of the Pansy") from *Canciones,* an ironic description of the primping of an effeminate Andalusian while the rest of the townsfolk sneak glances and gossip. Of interest also are three other poems all from the same collection that focus on the Narcissus motif: "Narciso," "(Narciso)," and "Soneto."

An uncollected pair of poems entitled "Normas" treats, in fairly difficult and opaque imagery, the twin "norms" of homosexual and heterosexual love. The speaker wishes that he were sexually aroused by a woman's naked body (associated with daytime and the sun); rather he is attracted to a male adolescent (associated with nighttime and the moon), whom he nevertheless resists or rejects. These same two "norms" are contrasted in a sonnet, "Adán" ("Adam"). Using the biblical couple Adam and Eve as archetypes, the procreative—but also the bloody, potentially violent and cyclical—aspects of heterosexuality, symbolized by dawn, are set against what is seen as the more neutral and static barrenness of homosexuality, again identified with the moon.

From this same period there is a third, unfinished, and, until recently, unpublished poem, entitled "Oda y burla de Sesostris y Sardanápalos ("Ode and Mockery of Sesostris and Sardanapalus"). Although still somewhat ironic in tone, the centrality of the theme of homosexual eroticism is now much plainer. Following tradition, Sardanapalus, the Assyrian king, is depicted as the very incarnation of effeminacy and lasciviousness; the reasons for the presence of Sesostris (Rameses II, "the Great") and for his equation with Sardanapalus are less clear, but both figures are roundly condemned for their self–serving lust and abandon, against which is contrasted the purity and restraint of the ancient Greeks.

Lorca's famous collection *Poeta en Nueva York* (*Poet in New York*) contains at least two poems that address homosexuality directly. "Tu infancia en Mentón" ("Your Childhood in Menton") reflects on a relationship gone sour, the speaker reproaching the beloved, again in fairly dense metaphorical language, for his distance and lack of commitment. "Oda a Walt Whitman" ("Ode to Walt Whitman"), written under the direct impact of the American poet (read in Spanish translation), is much different. The poem presents Lorca taking stock and constructing something approaching a manifesto (the poem was first published in a slim, private, limited edition in Mexico City in 1933). As in "Normas," the poet is at pains to stress the equal legitimacy of all kinds of authentic love. Whitman is held up as a model of virility fully in harmony with nature, while invective is heaped upon the "maricas de las ciudades" ("city queers") who, in Lorca's eyes, pervert and degrade sex and love through their insincerity, effeminacy and affectation. Although extremely explicit judged within the context of Lorca's previous works and by the standards of the period and the culture, the harshness of this diatribe seems to modern eyes misplaced at best, prejudiced and verging on the homophobic at worst.

Lorca worked on the "Ode" in New York and Cuba; his play *El público* ("The Audience") was started in Cuba and finished back in Spain. Here one of the principal themes is homosexuality, but again understood as a part of the all–embracing phenomenon of love and sex in the world. Among the main characters we find the bisexual Director, the Walt–Whitmanesque Man 1, the effeminate Man 2, and the sadomasochistic Man 3 (but also Shakespeare's Juliet and Helen of Troy). Not surprisingly, Man 1 often seems to function as a mouthpiece and a model for the attitudes and point of view that Lorca endorses. However, the message is to an extent simultaneously undermined: Man 1 dies at the end of the play, all human relationships are shown to be difficult to sustain and inherently problematical, and the notions of identity and authenticity espoused by Man 1 are subtly called into question.

The "Oda a Walt Whitman" is as close as Lorca ever came to a programmatic statement on the subject of homosexuality, but it is possible, on the basis of a number of texts (both those mentioned here and others), to abstract a set of evolving ideas that equally concern his sexuality and writerly preoccupations. Taking his cue from the German philosopher Friedrich Nietzsche, Lorca seems to have associated the clear, cool, firm control of the Apollonian principle both with certain manifestations of homosexuality and with the writer's craft. The latter involves the need to transmute lived experience into art, to make something marble–like and enduring out of the ephemeral and the turbid, which in turn are associated with the irrational abandon of the Dionysian principle. Allied with these ideas, friends have reported that in later years Lorca would explain to them a half–joking, half–serious theory involving what he identified as the three basic types of human beings. These were the "ente" (literally "the entity"), the everyday heterosexual; the "subente" ("sub–entity"), the effeminate and affected homosexual who sometimes masqueraded as a heterosexual; and finally the "epente" (which plays on the linguistic term "epenthesis"), whom Lorca defined as the being who creates, but does not procreate—the model of the writer/homosexual.

After *Poeta en Nueva York*, a later collection, *Diván del Tamarit* ("Divan"), presents a whole series of poems about a love affair, mostly viewed from after its ending. The identity of the beloved is kept deliberately vague, and the speaker's observations and feelings (sadness, nostalgia, self–reproach, remorse, recrimination, and so on) could apply equally well to a heterosexual or homosexual relationship gone wrong. However, some of the imagery seems to gain in focus and coherence if the person addressed is conceived of as male.

Later still is the unfinished cycle of "Sonetos del amor oscuro" ("Sonnets of Dark Love"), which is known to have had an autobiographical inspiration in the relationship with Rodriguez Rapun. The appellation "dark love" suggests that the love is essentially unhappy and emotionally disturbing, as well as clandestine. In the titles and texts the speaker typically refers to his "love" or "beloved," and in the 11 sonnets only one adjectival ending identifies the "other" as specifically male. As before, although the element of homosexuality may add further complications, it is clear that the emotions felt and lessons to be learnt are intended to be universal in nature.

Toward the end of his life, Lorca also outlined a number of unrealized dramatic projects, among them *La bola negra* ("The Black Ball") and *La destruccion de Sodoma* ("The Destruction of Sodom"). In the former, a young man was to be denied membership in the local gentlemen's club (hence the title) because of his homosexuality; the latter was planned to retell fairly closely the biblical story, stressing the "corruption" of the inhabitants of the town, the attractiveness of the angels, and Lot's incest.

Aside from his poetry and theatre—and, to a lesser extent, his prose—there is also a substantial corpus of drawings left by Lorca. Subjects worthy of mention here are a whole series of sad clowns, Pierrots and Harlequins; two nude Venuses with graphically, and rather violently, treated genitalia; two Saint Sebastians; a young sailor seated on the lap of a bearded man; a group of three sailors and a cabin boy; and several other versions of sailors, often standing outside taverns.

The number of Lorca's works that deal more or less explicitly with homosexual themes is not high when measured against his total output. On the other hand, in general, heterosexual relationships are not depicted either in a more positive or negative light than homosexual ones in Lorca's writings, and human relationships are typically seen as problematical, one–sided, unhappy and often short–lived. Beyond this, a number of critics have sought to apply theories of homosexual inspiration or aesthetics that would "explain" many, if not all, of Lorca's compositions, regardless of their explicit sexual content. Similarly, psychological approaches tend to suggest that any of his works dealing with frustration, secrecy, unhappiness or sterility (and there are many) could be the result of Lorca's own situation, and that they could thus be read obliquely as referring to the homosexual dilemma. While this remains a matter of interpretation, what is undeniably true is that there are a number of compositions that lament the absence of children or the inability to procreate; examples of this include the set of poems "En el bosque de las toronjas de luna" ("In the Forest of the Moon Grapefruits") from the collection *Suites,* and the tragedy of maternal frustration, *Yerma.*

Lorca's view of human life was strongly marked by existential pessimism, and yet at the same time he espoused a kind of paneroticism inspired by the eternal cycles of nature. Although in strictly chronological terms he was not the first twentieth–century Spanish poet to treat homosexual themes (that distinction likely belongs to Luis Cernúda), because of the brilliance of his work and the circumstances of his death, Lorca has become something of a cause celebre. Transformed first into a political martyr figure, all mention of his homosexuality was carefully avoided for many years. More recently, in an attempt to remedy this very deliberate omission, it has probably been over–emphasized and pressed into the service of various modern causes. We still await a well documented, properly balanced, and adequately sophisticated full–length study of the subject as it affected his life, his work, and the complex interrelationship between them.

—*Andrew A. Anderson*

GARDNER, Miriam. *See* **BRADLEY, Marion Zimmer.**

GENÊT. *See* **FLANNER, Janet.**

———

GENET, Jean. French playwright, poet, and novelist. Born in Paris, 19 December 1910. Abandoned by his mother shortly after birth; raised by a peasant couple. Convicted of theft at age 16 and sentenced to reform school; escaped to join French Foreign Legion; deserted after a few days; survived by begging, theft, dealing in narcotics, and prostitution; received presidential pardon from life sentence, 1948. **Recipient:** *Village Voice* Off–Broadway Award (Obie), 1960, 1961; French Literary Grand Prix, 1983. *Died in Paris, of throat cancer, 15 April 1986.*

WRITINGS

Novels

Notre–Dame des Fleurs. Monte Carlo, Aux dépens d'un amateur, 1944; translated by Bernard Frechtman as *Our Lady of the Flowers,* Paris, Morihien, 1949; New York, Grove Press, 1963.

Miracle de la rose. Lyons, L'Arbalète, 1946; translated by Bernard Frechtman as *Miracle of the Rose,* London, Blond, 1965; New York, Grove Press, 1966.

Pompes funèbres. Privately printed, 1947; revised edition, 1948; translated by Bernard Frechtman as *Funeral Rites,* New York, Grove Press, and London, Blond, 1969.

Querelle de Brest. Privately printed, 1947; translated by Gregory Streatham as *Querelle of Brest,* London, Blond, 1966; translated by Hollo Anselm as *Querelle,* New York, Grove Press, 1974.

Journal du voleur. Paris, Gallimard, 1949; translated by Bernard Frechtman as *The Thief's Journal,* Paris, Olympia Press, 1954; New York, Grove Press, 1964.

Plays

Haute Surveillance (produced Theatre des Mathurins, 1949). Paris, Gallimard, 1949; translated by Bernard Frechtman as *Death-watch* (produced New York, 1958), with *The Maids,* in *Two Plays,* 1954; published as *Deathwatch: A Play,* Faber, 1961.

Les Bonnes, pièce en un acte; Les Deux Versions précédées d'une lettre de l'auteur (produced Paris, 1947). Sceaux, France, J. J. Pauvert, 1954; translated by Bernard Frechtman as *The Maids* (produced New York, 1955), with *Deathwatch,* in *Two Plays,* 1954; as *Les Bonnes et comment jouer Les Bonnes,* Décines, L'Arbalète, 1963.

Two Plays (contains *The Maids* and *Deathwatch*), translation by Bernard Frechtman. New York, Grove Press, 1954.

Le Balcon (produced London, 1957). Décines, L'Arbalète, 1956; revised by the author and translated by Bernard Frechtman as *The Balcony* (produced London, 1957), London, Faber, 1957; New York, Grove Press, 1958; revised, Décines, L'Arbalète, and New York, Grove Press, 1960.

Les Nègres: Clownerie (produced Paris, 1959; translated as *The Blacks,* produced New York, 1961). Décines, L'Arbalète, 1958; translated by Bernard Frechtman as *The Blacks: A Clown Show,* London, Faber, and New York, Grove Press, 1960.

Les Paravents (produced Berlin, 1961). Décines, L'Arbalète, 1961; translated by Bernard Frechtman as *The Screens* (produced New York, 1971), New York, Grove Press, 1962; London, Faber, 1963.

Poetry

Chants secrets. Lyons, 1944; Décines, L'Arbalète, 1945.

Poèmes. Lyons, L'Arbalète, 1948; translated by Steven Finch as *Treasures of the Night: Collected Poems,* San Francisco, Gay Sunshine Press, 1981.

The Complete Poems of Jean Genet. San Francisco, Man–Root, 1981.

Screenplays

Un Chant d'amour. 1950.

Mademoiselle, 1965.

Genet, 1981.

Other

Le Condamné à mort. Fresnes, 1942; translated by Diane de Prima as *The Man Sentenced to Death,* 1950; translated by Steven Finch as *The Man Sentenced to Death,* San Francisco, Gay Sunshine Press, 1981.

La Galère. Paris, Y. Loyau, 1947.

L'Enfant criminel et 'Adame Miroir. Paris, Morihien, 1949.

Lettre à Leonor Fini. Paris, Y. Loyau, 1950.

Les Beaux Gars. [Paris], 1951.

Oeuvres complètes (five volumes). Paris, Gallimard, 1951–79.

L'Atelier d'Alberto Giacometti, Les Bonnes, suivi d'une lettre, L'Enfant criminel, [and] *Le Funambule.* Décines, L'Arbalète, 1958.

Lettres à Roger Blin. Paris, Gallimard, 1966; translated by Richard Seaver as *Letters to Roger Blin: Reflections on the Theater,* New York, Grove Press, 1969; as *Reflections on the Theatre, and Other Writings,* London, Faber, 1972.

May Day Speech, description by Allen Ginsberg. San Francisco, City Lights Books, 1970.

Un Captif amoureux. Paris, Gallimard, 1986; translated by Barbara Bray as *Prisoner of Love,* New York, HarperCollins, 1989.

What Remains of a Rembrandt Torn into Four Equal Parts and Flushed Down the Toilet. Hanuman Books, 1988.

Lettres à Olga et Marc Barbezat. Décines, L'Arbalète, 1988.

*

Adaptations: *The Balcony* (film), Continental, 1963; *The Maids* (filmed stage performance), 1975; *Querelle of Brest* (film); *Deathwatch* (film); *Poison* (film; based on the novels *Our Lady of the Flowers, Miracle of the Roses,* and *The Thief's Journal*), Zeitgeist, 1991. Selections from Genet's works have been recorded on Caedmon Records, including a reading by Genet, in French, from *Journal du voleur.*

Biography: *Aveux spontanés, conversations avec ...* by Robert Poulet, Paris, Plon, 1963, 109–114; *Jean Genet: A Biography of Deceit, 1910–1951* by Harry E. Stewart and Rob Roy McGregor, New York, Peter Lang, 1989.

Interviews: In *Playboy*, April 1964, 45–55; "Conversation with Jean Genet" by Pierre Démeron in *Oui*, November 1972, 62–102; "Jean Genet Talks to Hubert Fichte: Translation from the French by Patrick McCarthy" by Hubert Fichte in *New Review*, April 1977, 9–21, republished in *Gay Sunshine Interviews*, edited by Winston Leyland, San Francisco, Gay Sunshine Press, 1978.

Bibliography: *Jean Genet and His Critics: An Annotated Bibliography, 1943–1980* by Richard C. Webb, New Jersey and London, Scarecrow Press, 1982.

Critical Sources: *Saint Genet, comedien et martyr* by Jean–Paul Sartre, Paris, Gallimard, 1952, translated by Bernard Frechtman as *Saint Genet: Actor and Martyr*, New York, Braziller, 1963; *The Imagination of Jean Genet* by J. H. McMahon, New Haven, Connecticut, Yale University Press, 1964; *Jean Genet* by Tom F. Driver, New York, Columbia University Press, 1966; *Jean Genet* by Bettina Knapp, Boston, Twayne Publishers, 1968; *Jean Genet: A Critical Appraisal* by Philip Thody, New York, Stein & Day, 1968; *The Vision of Jean Genet* by Richard N. Coe, New York, Grove Press, 1968; *The Theatre of Jean Genet: A Casebook* edited by Coe, New York, Grove Press, 1970; *A Genetic Approach to Structures in the Work of Jean Genet* by Camille Nash, Cambridge, Massachusetts, Harvard University Press, 1978; *The Pathological Vision. Jean Genet, Louis–Ferdinand Céline and Tennessee Williams* by Robert Hauptmann, New York, Peter Lang, 1983, 1–50.

*   *   *

The biography of Jean Genet is simultaneously well–known and obscure. Though Genet's own accounts of his early life varied and readers often confuse his actual life with his novelistic semi–autobiographical accounts, some of the basic facts have been verified. Genet was born in 1910 (though even the year is not entirely certain) to an unwed mother, Gabrielle Genet, in Paris. Genet's mother left him in the care of a state orphanage while he was still an infant. Genet makes clear in his work the profound effect on him of this abandonment. The misogynistic sentiments found in Genet's work are thought to have resulted in part from his mother's actions; he at times castigates all women for what he perceived as an original betrayal. Especially in his early work, Genet simply ignored women, as he wrote almost exclusively about male relationships.

At the age of nine, Genet was adopted, or "loaned out" as Jean–Paul Sartre calls it in his work, *Saint Genet: comédien et martyr* (*Saint Genet: Comedian and Martyr*), to a peasant couple in the Morvan region of central France. After several years of good study habits and conduct, Genet became a thief. Sartre described Genet's own statement in *Journal d'un Voleur* (*The Thief's Journal*), "I have decided to be what crime made of me," as a deeply existential moment. Whether or not Genet as a boy understood the profundity of his choice to steal, Genet, as author, insisted that to become a thief, or to become a homosexual, involved a conscious adoption of the role. He wrote in *The Thief's Journal*: "I recognized myself as

being the coward, the traitor, the thief, the homo that they saw in me.... With a little patience and reflection, I discovered within myself sufficient reason for being called by those names." Genet was not a victim of his abandonment and adoption, or later of poverty and prostitution, rather he turned these circumstances into possibilities in which to explore the furthest reaches of these states of degradation. Through the profound isolation of his moral and aesthetic choices, he approached "saintliness."

Around the age of 15, Genet entered a reformatory, Mettray, where the intensity of his identification as an outlaw grew. Though Genet felt that his homosexuality preceded his thievery, he did not act on his same sex desires until others had caught and punished him for stealing. Mettray figures nostalgically, even lovingly, in Genet's second novel, *Le miracle de la rose* (*The Miracle of the Rose*). Though the other "colonists" (juvenile inmates) at Mettray seemed to despise Genet's marked acceptance of his homosexual desire and even spat on him, it is in Mettray that Genet transcended this scorn to embrace what he described as the feminine, secondary role of lover and adorer, unable to attain the "masculine" position of the admired, the adored, the beloved. All the same structures carry over from Mettray to the adult prison portrayed in *The Miracle of the Rose,* including adolescent male bullying and allegiances based on threats and betrayals, as well as those based admiration and longing.

The circumstances of Genet's "graduation" from Mettray are inexact. Genet's clearest account states that upon leaving Mettray, between the ages of 18 and 20, he joined the French Foreign Legion, was stationed in Syria, met a young Syrian lover there, deserted his post, then began wandering all over Europe as a beggar and a thief. Though readers today may be shocked at Genet's extreme poverty, thievery, and prostitution as he depicts it in *The Thief's Journal*, one must recall that Genet began his wanderings around the time of the Great Depression, when many people shared similar destitution. The semi–autobiographical *The Thief's Journal* follows Genet from city to city and prison to prison across Europe as he steals or prostitutes himself, often to support an either brutish or ridiculous small–time gangster. The details of Genet's abject travels are reasonably accurate in the book, though Genet fails to mention any of the legitimate work he performed, such as tutoring French while in Czechoslovakia. Nowhere in these early fictions does Genet describe his literary influences, his reading, nor tentative attempts at writing. Yet, it is unlikely that Genet achieved such beauty of style without widely studying other authors.

Genet's primary source of income well into his thirties was theft. He was arrested and deported repeatedly from various countries and finally landed in Fresnes Prison in France. It was in prison, apparently as a challenge to another prisoner whose poetry Genet despised, when Genet finally reflected upon the meaning of his experiences, and began to write. His first poem, "Le condamné à mort," though appreciated by Cocteau at the time, does not hold up well. This poem as well as his first novel–length work, the complexly narrated reverie *Notre–Dame des fleurs* (*Our Lady of Flowers*), were smuggled out of prison and published in small press runs. A small group of astute readers (in addition to Cocteau, there were Sartre and Simone de Beauvoir, for example) exalted Genet's work and successfully petitioned the president of the Republic of France to free Genet from the threat of lifetime imprisonment. Other well–known authors, such as François Mauriac, denounced Genet's work as morally degrading, perverse, and pornographic.

Reading Genet's works as gay literature may inspire in the individual reader the profound contradictory impulses of his early critics. Genet is certainly among the most explicit of critically accepted gay male writers when he describes not only the emotional and psychological details of gay male relations, but sometimes in great detail the physical acts as well. Many of the descriptions of physical sexuality between men contain tender moments, caresses, gentleness, and grace. Far from romanticized, however, these sexual encounters take place between career criminals, whom Genet depicts as petty braggarts and fakes. Genet often counterpoints the tenderest gestures of intimacy with vivid, sometimes brutal descriptions of the power relationships of the sexual actors. The gay male reader searching for some acknowledgment of his own sexuality may be horrified or delighted by Genet's insistence on the sexual act as intrinsically violent and unequal, requiring dominance and submission. *Querelle de Brest* (translated into English as *Querelle* and filmed in 1983 under the same title by Rainer Werner Fassbinder) reaches an apex of sex mixed with violence. Only after both Querelle and another character, Gil, have murdered do they seek gratification from a previously undiscovered homosexual desire.

After reading Sartre's *Saint Genet: comédien et martyr,* published in 1952, Genet seems to have felt so thoroughly exposed and evaluated that he underwent an authorial crisis and stopped writing for several years. Perhaps this block in writing had as much to do with the changes in Genet's circumstances as it did with his reading of Sartre's analysis. Genet's earlier works were primarily autobiographical or depicted only the criminal element of his experience. When Genet removed himself from the society of criminals, while in no sense joining a literary establishment or a bourgeois milieu, he lost contact with the thief's argot and the thief's philosophy on which he based his novelistic work. Though Genet maintained an outlaw perspective, he altered the voice of his work from fictional autobiography to the shifting narrative voice of the drama. Before *Saint Genet,* Genet had written, in addition to his fictional works, two plays, *Haute surveillance* (*Deathwatch*) and *Les Bonnes* (*The Maids*), which had been produced for the stage. After his break in writing, Genet wrote only plays and none with the criminal, prison, or homosexual milieu of his earlier works. Most recent appreciation and analysis of Genet focuses on his dramatic work, which continues to be staged, and which many critics have called among the most important theater of the twentieth century.

Despite the obvious breaks in time, subject, and genre, Genet's themes of play–acting, power, submission and policing, evident from his first major work, *Our Lady of Flowers,* provide continuity to his artistic production. In the plays, the characters overtly assume roles, even if they are not always those of the thief or the homosexual. In *Les Bonnes* (*The Maids*) two sisters take on the role of their mistress, "Madame," and her maid in a complex tale in which their play–acting has consequences in the real world; the maids blackmail Madame's lover, and one sister, playing out her role to the end, insists on drinking poisoned tea intended for Madame. Genet had wanted to add a further layer of complexity by having men act the part of the maids, but the original director of the play rejected the idea. In *Le balcon* (*The Balcony),* once again the role–playing which seems to be strictly defined and contained, both in space and in time, crosses all boundaries of the fabulous bordello in which the male customers act out powerful roles as bishops, judges, executioners. What appears to be an actual revolution in the city surrounding the brothel may be only an elaborate component of the entertainment. Irma, the "Madame" of this play, turns to the audience at the end of the play, instructing them: "You must now go home, where everything—you can be quite sure—will be falser than here." As in his novels, Genet asserts that the task of the

individual is both to recognize that all action is ritualized within preconceived roles and that the individual must choose the role and its consequent rituals.

Genet's last two plays, *Les nègres* (*The Blacks*) and *Les paravents* (*The Screens*), reflect his concerns as they evolve from questions of the bourgeois norm and sexual behavior, to criticism of Western colonialism and oppression of Third World peoples. In his mid–50s Genet again abandoned writing, this time for political activism in support of the oppressed blacks and Arabs he had depicted in his last two plays. Despite Genet's involvement in the Black Panther Party in the United States, then in the Palestinian Liberation Front, he never supported the gay liberation movement or gay activism. The movement for homosexual rights might have provided a modicum of acceptability for Genet, but he preferred to retain his outlaw status. Genet's final work, published at the time of his death in 1986, *Un captif amoureux* (*Prisoner of Love*), details his long experience living with Palestinians in their exile and resistance. Where he had earlier idealized the brutal, criminal European thug, in this, his last literary work, Genet instead idealizes the young Arab revolutionary.

Although Genet's early works liberated some of the constraints which had limited frank discussion of homosexuality in literature, their necessary link between homosexuality and criminality strongly conflicted with the polite, often apologist homosexual movements of their time, the late 1940s and the 1950s. American writers, such as Gore Vidal in *The City and the Pillar* and James Baldwin in *Giovanni's Room,* who strove during the same period to emphasize how completely normal, if not bland, was the average homosexual male, fit much better into the post–war American movement of gay identity and liberation politics. However, Genet's reputation and influence as a radical, outlaw queer is bound to increase in the United States as queer activism displaces in part the liberation movement. Todd Haynes' 1991 film, *Poison,* which adapts fragments of Genet's imagery and narrative, illustrates that the stylized eroticism, decentered narrator, and besieged outsiders of Genet's texts continue to be timely and will likely engender a renaissance of Genet studies in the current queer theory and post–modern critical schools.

—*Terry L. Allison*

GENTLEMAN of the UNIVERSITY of CAMBRIDGE, A. *See* **CROWLEY, Aleister.**

GIDE, André (Paul Guillaume). French novelist and playwright. Born in Paris, 22 November 1869. Educated at private and public schools in Paris. Worked with the Red Cross and in a convalescent home for soldiers during World War I; became director of Foyer Franco–Belge. Married Madeleine Rondeaux in 1895 (died 1938);

one daughter, with Elisabeth van Rysselberghe. Cofounder, *La Nouvelle Revue française*, 1909, and *L'Arche* (North African literary magazine); literary critic, *La Revue blanche*. Mayor of La Roque, Normandy, France, 1896; juror, Rouen, France, 1912; special envoy, Colonial Ministry in Africa, 1925–26. **Recipient:** Royal Society of London honorary fellowship, 1924; Goethe Medal, 1932; Nobel Prize in literature, 1947; honorary doctorate in letters, University of Oxford, 1947; Frankfort am Main (Germany) Goethe Plaque, 1949; American Academy of Arts and Letters honorary corresponding member, 1950. *Died in Paris, of pneumonia, 19 February 1951.*

WRITINGS

Novels

Le Voyage d'Urien. Paris, Librairie de l'Art Independant, 1893; second edition, 1894; translated with introduction and notes by Wade Baskin as *Urien's Voyage,* New York, Philosophical Library, 1964.

Paludes. Paris, Librairie de l'Art Independant, 1895.

Le Promethee mal enchaine. Paris, Mercure, 1899; translated by Lilian Rothermere as *Prometheus Illbound,* London, Chatto & Windus, 1919; revised, Paris, Gallimard, 1925.

L'Immoraliste. Paris, Mercure, 1902; translated by Dorothy Bussy as *The Immoralist,* New York, Knopf, 1930; translated by Richard Howard as *The Immoralist,* New York, Knopf, 1970.

La Porte etroite. Paris, Mercure, 1909; revised, 1959; translated by Dorothy Bussy as *Strait Is the Gate,* New York, Knopf, 1924.

Isabelle. Paris, Gallimard, 1911; translated by Dorothy Bussy as *Isabelle,* in *Two Symphonies,* 1931.

Les Caves du Vatican: Sotie. Paris, Gallimard, 1914; New York, Macmillan, 1956; translated by Dorothy Bussy as *The Vatican Swindle,* New York, Knopf, 1925; as *Lafcadio's Adventures,* New York, Knopf, 1928; as *The Vatican Cellars,* London, Cassell, 1952.

La Symphonie pastorale. Paris, Editions de la Nouvelle Revue Francaise, 1919; translated by Dorothy Bussy as *The Pastoral Symphony,* in *Two Symphonies,* 1931.

Les Faux–Monnayeurs. Paris, Gallimard, 1926; translated by Dorothy Bussy as *The Counterfeiters,* New York, Knopf, 1927; as *The Coiners,* London, Cassell, 1950.

L'Ecole des femmes. Paris, Gallimard, 1929; translated by Dorothy Bussy as *The School for Wives,* New York, Knopf, 1929; with *Robert: Supplement a "L'Ecole des femmes"* [and] *Genevieve,* 1950.

Robert: Supplement a "L'Ecole des femmes." Paris, Gallimard, 1929; translated by Dorothy Bussy, with *Genevieve; or, The Unfinished Confidence* [and] *The School for Wives,* New York, Knopf, 1950.

Two Symphonies: "Isabelle" and "The Pastoral Symphony," translation by Dorothy Bussy. New York, Knopf, 1931; as *La Symphonie pastorale* [and] *Isabelle,* London, Penguin Books, 1963.

Genevieve; ou, La Confidence inachevee. Paris, Gallimard, 1936; translated by Dorothy Bussy as *Genevieve; or, The Unfinished Confidence* with *The School for Wives* [and] *Robert Supplement a "L'Ecole des femmes."* New York, Knopf, 1950.

L'Ecole des femmes [with] *Robert: Supplement a "L'Ecole des femmes"* [and] *Genevieve; ou, La Confidence inachevee.* Paris, Gallimard, 1944; translated by Dorothy Bussy as *The School for Wives* with *Robert: Supplement a "L'Ecole des femmes,"* [and] *Genevieve; or, The Unfinished Confidence,* New York, Knopf, 1950.

Thesee. New York, Pantheon, 1946; translated by John Russell as *Theseus,* New York, New Directions Publishing, 1949.

"Marshlands" and "Prometheus Misbound": Two Satires, translation by George D. Painter. New York, New Directions Publishing, 1953; McGraw, 1965.

Plays

Saul: Drame en cinq actes (produced Paris, 1922). Paris, Mercure, 1900; enlarged edition, 1904.

Le Roi Candaule (produced Paris, 1901). Paris, Editions de la Revue Blanche, 1901.

Le Retour de l'enfant prodigue (produced Monte Carlo, Monaco, 1928). Paris, Bibliotheque de l'Occident, 1909; translated by Aldyth Thain as *The Return of the Prodigal Son,* Salt Lake City, Utah State University Press, 1960.

Bethsabe. Paris, Bibliotheque de l'Occident, 1912.

Philoctete (produced, 1919).

Oedipe: Drame en trois actes (produced Antwerp, 1931). Paris, Gallimard, 1931.

Les Caves du Vatican: Farce en trois actes et dix–neuf tableaux (produced Montreux, 1933). Paris, Ides et Calendes, 1948; revised (produced Paris, 1950), Paris, Gallimard, 1950.

Persephone (produced Paris, 1934). Paris, Gallimard, 1934; translated by Samuel Putnam as *Persephone,* New York, Gotham Book Mart, 1949.

Le Treizieme Arbre (produced Marseilles, 1935).

Le Retour. Paris, Ides et Calendes, 1946.

Robert; ou, L'Interet general (produced Tunis, 1946). Paris, Ides et Calendes, 1949.

With Jean–Louis Barrault, *Le Proces: Piece tiree du roman de Kafka* (produced 1947). Paris, Gallimard, 1947; translated and adapted by Jacqueline and Frank Sundstrom as *The Trial,* London, Secker & Warburg, 1950; translated by Leon and Joseph Katz as *The Trial: A Dramatization Based on Franz Kafka's Novel,* New York, Schocken, 1964.

Persephone: Melodrame en trois tableaux d'André Gide, music by Igor Fedorovich Stravinski. Paris, Boosey & Hawkes, 1950.

Letters

Lettres. Liege, France, A la Lampe d'Aladdin, 1930.

Correspondance, 1899–1926, Paul Claudel–André Gide. Paris, Gallimard, 1945; translated by John Russell as *The Correspondence, 1899–1926, between Paul Claudel and André Gide,* New York, Pantheon, 1952.

Correspondance Francis Jammes–André Gide. Paris, Gallimard, 1948.

Correspondance, 1909–1926, Rainer Maria Rilke–André Gide, edited by Renée Lang. Paris, Correa, 1952.

Correspondence Paul Valery–André Gide, 1890–1942, edited by Robert Mallet. Paris, Gallimard, 1955; translated by June Guicharnaud as *Self–Portraits: The Gide–Valery Letters, 1890–1942,* Chicago, University of Chicago Press, 1966.

Correspondance André Gide–Charles Peguy, 1905–1912, edited by Alfred Saffrey. Persan, Imprimerie de Persan–Beaumont, 1958.

The Correspondance of André Gide and Edmund Gosse, 1904–1928, edited by Linette F. Brugmans. New York, New York University Press, 1959; London, P. Owen, 1960.

Correspondance André Gide–Arnold Bennett, 1911–1931: Vingt ans d'amitie litteraire, edited by Linette F. Brugmans. Geneva and Paris, Droz & Minard, 1964.

Correspondance André Gide–Roger Martin du Gard, 1913–1951 (two volumes), edited by Jean Delay. Paris, Gallimard, 1968.

Correspondance, André Gide–François Mauriac, 1912–1950, edited by Jacqueline Morton. Paris, Gallimard, 1971.

Correspondance d'André Gide et Georges Simenon, edited by Francis Lacassin and Gilbert Sigaux. Paris, Plon, 1973.

With Charles Brunard, *Correspondance avec André Gide et souvenirs.* Paris, La Pensee Universelle, 1974.

With Albert Mockel, *Correspondance (1891–1938),* edited by Gustave Vanwelkenhuyzen. Geneva, Droz, 1975.

With Henri Gheon, *Correspondance* (two volumes), edited by Jean Tipi and Anne–Marie Moulenes. Paris, Gallimard, 1976.

Correspondance André Gide–Jules Romains, edited by Claude Martin. Paris, Flammarion, 1976.

With Jacques–Emile Blanche, *Correspondance: 1892–1939,* edited by Georges–Paul Collet. Paris, Gallimard, 1979.

André Gide–Justin O'Brien, Correspondance, 1937–1951, edited by Jacqueline Morton. Lyons, France, Centre d'Etudes Gidiennes, 1979.

Correspondance André Gide–Dorothy Bussy, 1918–1951 (three volumes), edited by Jean Lambert. Paris, Gallimard, 1979–82; translated by Richard Tedeschi as *Selected Letters of André Gide and Dorothy Bussy,* London, Oxford University Press, 1983.

With François–Paul Alibert, *Correspondance: 1907–1950,* edited by Claude Martin. Lyons, France, Presses Universitaires de Lyon, 1982.

André Gide–Jean Giono, Correspondance, 1929–1940, edited by Roland Bourneuf and Jacques Cotnam. Lyons, France, Centre d'Etudes Gidiennes, Universite Lyon II, 1984.

D'un monde a l'autre: La Correspondance André Gide–Harry Kessler (1903–1933), edited by Claude Foucart. Lyons, France, Centre d'Etudes Gidiennes, Universite Lyon II, 1985.

Correspondance avec Jef Last (1934–1950), edited by C. J. Greshoff. Lyons, France, Presses Universitaires de Lyon, 1985.

With Anna de Noailles, *Correspondance (1902–1928),* edited by Claude Mignot–Ogliastri. Lyons, France, Centre d'Etudes Gidiennes, Universite Lyon II, 1986.

With Thea Sternheim, *Correspondance (1927–1950),* edited by Claude Focart. Lyons, France, Centre d'Etudes Gidiennes, Universite Lyon II, 1986.

Correspondance avec Francis Viele–Griffin (1891–1931), edited by Henry de Paysac. Lyons, France, Presses Universitaires de Lyon, 1986.

With Jacques Copeau, *Correspondance* (two volumes), edited by Jean Claude. Paris, Gallimard, 1987.

Correspondance avec André Ruyters (1895–1950), edited by Claude Martin and Victor Martin–Schmets. Lyons, France, Presses Universitaires de Lyon, 1987.

Collected Works

Philoctete; Le Traite du Narcisse; La Tentative amoureuse; El Hadj. Paris, Mercure, 1899.

Morceaux choisis. Paris, Editions de la Nouvelle Revue Francaise, 1921.

Pages choisise. Paris, Georges Cres, 1921.

Divers: Caracteres; Un Esprit non prevenu; Dictees; Lettres. Paris, Gallimard, 1931.

Oeuvres completes (15 volumes), edited by Louis Martin Chauffier. Paris, Gallimard/Editions de la Nouvelle Revue Francaise, 1932–39.

Le Retour de l'enfant prodigue, precede de cinq autres traites: Le Traite du Narcisse, La Tentative amoureuse, El Hadj, Philoctete, Bethsabe. Paris, Gallimard, 1932; translated by Dorothy Bussy as *The Return of the Prodigal, Preceded by Five Other Treatises; With "Saul," a Drama in Five Acts,* London, Secker & Warburg, 1953.

Theatre. Paris, Gallimard, 1942.

Theatre complet (eight volumes). Paris, Ides et Calendes, 1947–49.

My Theater: Five Plays and an Essay, translated by Jackson Mathews. New York, Knopf, 1952.

Poesie; Journal; Souvenirs. Paris, Gallimard, 1952.

Ne jugez pas; Souvenirs de la cour d'assises; L'Affaire Redureau; La Sequestree de Poitiers. Paris, Gallimard, 1957.

Romans, recits, et soties: Oeuvres lyriques, edited with notes and bibliography by Yvonne Davet and Jean–Jacques Thierry. Paris, La Pleiade/Gallimard, 1958.

Oeuvres. Paris, Gallimard, 1960.

Translator

Typhon by Joseph Conrad. Paris, Nouvelle Revue Francaise, 1918.

With others, *Oeuvres choisies* by Walt Whitman. Paris, Nouvelle Revue Francaise, 1918.

Antoine et Cleopatre by William Shakespeare. Paris, Lucien Vogel, 1921.

Le Mariage du Ciel et de l'Enfer by William Blake. Paris, Claude Aveline, 1923.

Hamlet by William Shakespeare (bilingual edition). New York, Schiffrin, 1944; Paris, Gallimard, 1946.

Other

Les Cahiers d'André Walter. Paris, Librairie de l'Art Independant, 1891; first half translated with introduction by Wade Baskin as *The White Notebook,* New York, Philosophical Library, 1964; as *The Notebooks of André Walter,* New York, Philosophical Library, 1968.

Le Traite du Narcisse: Theorie du symbole. Paris, Librairie de l'Art Independant, 1891.

Les Poesies d'André Walter. Paris, Librairie de l'Art Independant, 1892.

La Tentative Amoureuse; ou, Le Traite du vain desir. Paris, Librairie de l'Art Independant, 1893.

Les Nourritures terrestres. Paris, Mercure, 1897.

Si le grain ne meurt (autobiography). Bruges, Belgium, Imprimerie Ste. Catherine, c. 1920; Paris, Gallimard, 1926; translated by Dorothy Bussy as *If It Die: An Autobiography,* New York, Random House, 1935; as *If It Die,* London, Secker & Warburg, 1950.

Les Nouvelles Nourritures. Paris, Gallimard, 1935.

The Journals of André Gide (four volumes), edited and translated by Justin O'Brien. New York, Knopf, 1947–51; as *Journals,* London, Secker & Warburg, 1948–55; as *Journals, 1889–1949,* London, Penguin Books, 1967; as *The Journals of André Gide,*

1889–1949, New York, Vintage, 1956; abridged edition as *The Journals of André Gide* (two volumes), Evanston, Illinois, Northwestern University Press, 1987.
Les Nourritures terrestres. Translated by Dorothy Bussy as *The Fruits of the Earth*, New York, Knopf, 1949; with *Les Nouvelles Nourritures*, Paris, Club des Libraires de France, 1956; as *Fruits of the Earth*, London, Secker & Warburg, 1962; with *Later Fruits of the Earth*, 1970.
Les Nouvelles Nourritures [and] *Les Nourritures terrestres.* Paris, Club des Libraires de France, 1956; as *Later Fruits of the Earth*, London, Penguin/Secker & Warburg, 1970.
Notes on Chopin. Westport, Connecticut, Greenwood Press, 1978.
Dostoevsky. Westport, Connecticut, Greenwood Press, 1979.
Amyntas: North African Journals. New York, Ecco Press, 1988.

*

Adaptations: *La Symphonie pastorale* (film) by Pierre Bost and Jean Aurenche, preface by J. Delannoy, Nouvelle Edition, 1948; *La Symphonie pastorale* (three–act play), F. De Wolfe & Robert Stone, 1954; *L'Immoraliste* (play *André Gide's "The Immoralist"*) by Ruth and Augustus Goetz, Dramatists Play Service, 1962.

Manuscript Collections: Bibliotheque Litteraire Jacques Doucet, Paris.

Biography: *Le Dialogue avec André Gide* by Charles Du Bos, Correa, 1947; *The Journals of André Gide* (four volumes) edited and translated with introduction and annotations by Justin O'Brien, New York, Knopf, 1947–51; *Recollections of André Gide* by Roger Martin du Gard, translation by John Russell, New York, Viking, 1953; *Portrait of André Gide* by Justin O'Brien, New York, Knopf, 1953; *Madeleine et André Gide* by Jean Schlumberger, Paris, Gallimard, 1956, translated by Richard H. Akeroyd as *Madeleine and André Gide*, Tuscaloosa, Alabama, Portals Press, 1980; *La Jeunesse d'André Gide* by Jean Delay (two volumes), Paris, Gallimard, 1956, translated by June Guicharnaud as *The Youth of André Gide*, Chicago, University of Chicago Press, 1963; *André Gide par lui-meme* by Claude Martin, Paris, Seuil, 1964; *André Gide: His Life and Art* by Wallace Fowlie, New York, Macmillan, 1965; *Conversations with André Gide* by Claude Mauriac, translation by Michael Lebeck, New York, Braziller, 1965; *André Gide: A Critical Biography* by George D. Painter, New York, Atheneum, 1968; *Vie d'André Gide, 1869–1951: Essai de biographie critique* by Pierre de Boisdeffre, Paris, Hachette, 1970; *Les Cahiers de la petite dame: Notes pour l'histoire authentique d'André Gide* by Maria van Rysselberghe (four volumes), Paris, Gallimard, 1973–77; *La Maturite d'André Gide: De "Paludes" a "l'Immoraliste," 1895–1902* by Claude Martin, Paris, Klincksieck, 1977; *André Gide, qui etes–vous?* by Eric Marty, Paris, La Manufacture, 1987.

Bibliography: *Bibliographie des ecrits d'André Gide, 1891–1952* by Arnold Naville, Paris, Guy le Prat, 1949; *Index detaille des quinze volumes de l'Edition Gallimard des "Oeuvres completes" d'André Gide* by Justin O'Brien, Paris, Pretexte, 1954; *Bibliographie chronologique de l'oeuvre d'André Gide* by Jacques Cotnam, Boston, G. K. Hall, 1974; *Inventaire bibliographique et index analytique de la correspondance d'André Gide, publiee de 1897 a 1971* by Jacques Cotnam, Boston, G. K. Hall, 1975; "Inventaire des traductions des oeuvres d'André Gide," in *Bulletin des Amis d'André Gide*, Numbers 28–58, 1975–83; *La Correspondance generale d'André Gide* by Claude Martin and others, Lyons, Centre d'Etudes Gidiennes, Universite Lyon II, 1985; *An Annotated Bibliography of Criticism on André Gide, 1973–1988* by Catharine Savage Brosman, New York, Garland, 1990.

Critical Sources: *Histoire du roman français depuis 1918* by Claude–Edmonde Magny, Paris, Seuil, 1950; *André Gide: L'Insaisissable protee* by Germaine Bree, Paris, Belles Lettres, 1953, translated as *André Gide*, New Brunswick, New Jersey, Rutgers University Press, 1963; *Les Precieux* by Bernard Fay, Paris, Perrin, 1966; *Entretiens sur André Gide*, edited by Marcel Arland and Jean Mouton, Netherlands, Mouton, 1967; *André Gide* by Albert J. Guerard, Cambridge, Massachusetts, Harvard University Press, 1969; *André Gide* by Thomas Cordle, Boston, Twayne Publishers, 1969; *Gide: A Study of His Creative Writings* by G. W. Ireland, New York, Oxford University Press, 1970; *Gide: A Collection of Critical Essays*, edited by David Littlejohn, Englewood Cliffs, New Jersey, Prentice–Hall, 1970; "Profil d'une oeuvre 5" by Geneviève Idt, in *André Gide/Les Faux–Monnayeurs*, Paris, Hatier, 1970; *Les Critiques de notre temps et Gide*, edited by Michel Raimond, Paris, Garnier, 1971; *Les Caves du Vatican d'André Gide* by Alain Goulet, Paris, Larousse, 1972; "Gide and Sexual Liberation" by John Weightman, in *The Concept of the Avant–Garde*, LaSalle, Illinois, Library Press, 1973; "Corydon and Ménalque" by Richard Ellmann, in *Golden Codgers*, New York and London, Oxford University Press, 1973; *Gide's Art of the Fugue: A Thematic Study of "Les Faux–Monnayeurs"* by Karen Nordenhaug Ciholas, Chapel Hill, University of North Carolina Department of Romance Languages, 1974; "Gide and the Confidence Game of Fiction" by Robert Alter, in *Partial Magic: The Novel as Self–Conscious Genre*, Berkeley, University of California Press, 1975, 159–179; "Gide et l'espace autobiographique" by Philippe Lejeune, in *Le Pacte autobiographique*, Paris, Seuil, 1975; *André Gide and the Art of Autobiography: A Study of "Si le grain ne meurt"* by C. D. E. Tolton, Toronto, Macmillan, 1975; *André Gide ou l'ironie de l'écriture* by Martine Maisani–Léonard, Montréal, Presses de l'Université de Montréal, 1976; *Gide: A Study* by Christopher Bettison, Totowa, New Jersey, Rowman and Littlefield, and London, Heinemann, 1977, also published as *A Student's Guide to Gide*, Heinemann, 1979; *Portraits of Artists: Reflexivity in Gidean Fiction, 1902–1946* by Arthur E. Babcock, New York, French Literature Publications, 1982; *Fiction et vie sociale dans l'oeuvre d'André Gide* by Alain Goulet, Paris, Minard, 1986; *André Gide and the Codes of Homotextuality* by Emily S. Apter, Stanford French and Italian Studies, Saratoga, California, ANMA Libri, 1987; "André Gide" by Elaine D. Cancalon, in *Dictionary of Literary Biography*, Volume 65: *French Novelists, 1900–1930*, Detroit, Gale, 1988; "C.R.D.N. Seventy Years After" by Claude Courove, in *Gay Books Bulletin*, Number 5, 23–25.

* * *

André Gide was one of the most important writers of the first half of the twentieth century. He was also an avowed homosexual—a pederast who primarily directed his desire toward young boys. It would of course be possible to study his life and works from the narrow point of view of the development of homosexual theories, but it is certainly more interesting to analyze the relationship between Gide's homosexuality and the more encompassing theme of total liberation from constraints, which is the key to a profound understanding of his work.

For Gide, becoming aware of his sexual orientation led to various kinds of social rebellion. Gide's defense of individual liberties began before World War I when bourgeois values and conservative politics were very much in force. His thinking was in advance of many of the "acceptable" authors of the times. Only after the influence of the postwar surrealist movement did other figures catch up with Gide who had already questioned the importance of one's "roots" and the validity of family, religion, and ideologies. Gide had also begun an attempt at self–analysis which he tried to keep objective by avoiding hypocrisy and self–delusion. The gradual evolution of his stance on the liberation of the individual within society goes hand in hand with his practice and defense of pederasty.

Although Gide would later make a case for innate homosexuality in *Corydon* in 1920, it would seem that his early childhood upbringing as described in his memoirs *If It Die* played an important role. At the age of nine, Gide was suspended from school for masturbation and threatened with castration by a doctor. Gide's father died when he was 11 and he was brought up by a strictly religious mother who regulated every aspect of his behavior. Her Calvinist ethic equated any outward manifestation of sexuality with sin. Gide became aware of homosexual desires during two trips to North Africa (in 1893 and 1895). Encounters with Arab boys whose beauty he admired, as well as conversations with Oscar Wilde, made him aware for the first time of the joy and liberation experienced through sexual satisfaction. These first physical contacts occurred in the beauty of a natural setting (for example on the desert sand) and were henceforth linked in Gide's mind to an intense communion with nature ("fervor") and to the principles of "déracinement" (uprooting), "dénuement" (denuding or the peeling away of all socially learned behavior), and "disponibilité" (readiness to benefit completely from each new experience).

Despite this new state of mind, the young Gide was emotionally in love with his cousin Madeleine. He decided to consult a doctor who advised him to marry so that his "true nature" would take over. André and Madeleine were wed in October, 1895, but the doctor's prediction did not come true. Paradoxically Gide's inability to have physical relations with his wife resulted from the intensity of his love for her. He idealized her and in his mind, spiritual and physical love were distinctly separate. Madeleine's resignation and suffering were not truly known until Gide's publication in 1947, nine years after her death, of *Et nunc manet in te,* a self–accusatory account of their marriage. Spiritual and physical love coincided very rarely for Gide. His portrayal of women as saints or seductresses was attenuated only in his later works when he began to realize that women too can become liberated. His long–standing friendship with Maria Van Rysselberghe and her daughter Elizabeth (for whom Gide fathered a daughter, Catherine) helped him to pass one final hurdle in the fight against social constraints and to make of him, near the end of his life, one of the first feminists.

Not all of Gide's novels deal with pederasty. The ones that do, follow a very gradual evolution. In the early books, there is a suggestion of latent homosexuality, a search for purity and the failure of heterosexual couples. With the publication of the theoretical work *Corydon,* in 1920 and 1924, Gide outwardly defends homosexuality, but novels published before that time are still more suggestive than explicit. Homosexual encounters in his works are usually limited to physical adventures and, with a few exceptions

where sentiment is suggested, rarely include spiritual love or moral attachment. Finally in 1925 Gide's major novel, *The Counterfeiters,* presents the possibility of love between an adult man and his adolescent charge. Not until the trilogy, written in the thirties, did Gide even conceive of the question of lesbianism.

Gide's first book, *The Notebooks of André Walter,* illustrates a desire for absolute purity and the denial of carnal pleasure. It tells the story, in diary style, of Walter's love for his cousin Emmanuèle, his renunciation of that love, and his ultimate insanity and death. The book, influenced by Johann Wolfgang von Goethe's *Die Leiden des jungen Werthers,* is written in an uncontrolled lyric style which accentuates its narcissism. *The Lovers' Attempt,* another short book written in 1893, expresses the failure of consummated physical love. Rachel and Luc satisfy their desire but their happiness soon turns to boredom.

The first work in which homosexuality plays a major role is *The Fruits of the Earth* (1897). This song to nature (divided into eight books) is an idealized description of the North African trips. Whereas encounters with young Arab boys presented here are less explicit than those described in the memoirs, they are lyricized and are very closely associated with the theme of total liberation propounded by Menalcas, whose speech fills the first part of Book IV. Menalcas, who was fashioned after Oscar Wilde, announces most of the themes that would concern Gide throughout his career: "Every day, and from hour to hour, I wanted nothing but to be more and more simply absorbed into nature.... I made myself ductile, conciliatory, at the disposal of each one of my senses.... Families, I hate you! closed circles ... doors fast shut; jealous possessions of happiness.... My claim was not to love anyone in particular—man or woman—but friendship itself, or affection, or love.... My happiness is made of fervor. Through the medium of all things without distinction, I have passionately worshipped." Gide's homosexual encounters, which broke down the puritanism of his youth, opened his mind and body to the liberation of sensuality that produced the principles expounded by Menalcas.

Both the philosophy of the work and its structure is informed by the relationship of man to boy. The book is told to a young imagined listener called Nathaniel. This foreshadows discussions of Greek love which will be described later in *Corydon.* But, at the end of the work, true to his credo of total detachment, the narrator tells Nathaniel to throw away his book: "Shake yourself free of it.... Leave me; now you are in my way.... I have exaggerated my love for you and it occupies me too much. I am tired of pretending I can educate anyone.... Throw away my book; say to yourself that it is *only one* of the thousand possible postures in life. Look for your own."

Similar themes are expressed in Gide's first major novel, *The Immoralist.* The story is told in the first person by its protagonist, Michel, who, having been cured of tuberculosis during a wedding trip to North Africa, becomes aware of the limitless possibilities of man. Like the narrator of the *Fruits of the Earth,* he too undergoes a transformation that strips him of all social and moral attachments. When his wife becomes gravely ill, Michel cannot stop himself from forcing her to follow him through all the stages of their first trip until she finally dies. After her death, Michel is at loose ends and asks his friends (to whom he has narrated his tale) to give him a reason for living.

The theme of homosexual love is only implicit in *The Immoralist.* Michel's marriage (as Luc and Rachel's relationship) is a failure, and although he does make love to his wife, he seems constantly more attracted by the Arab boys with whom he spends a great deal of his time. But he is still attracted primarily by their beauty and health, and no sexual encounters occur in the novel. The tale does however include suggestive passages. At the story's end, Michel's servant is a young Arab boy, Ali. Rather than anger the boy, Michel dismisses his sister with whom he had spent several nights. The story ends with the following words: "She has not taken offence; but every time I meet her, she laughs and declares that I prefer the boy to her. She makes out that it is he who keeps me here. Perhaps she is not altogether wrong."

Lafcadio's Adventures (or *The Vatican Swindle*), is a vast satire of almost all the characters and situations that Gide had already treated to this point. The main plot turns around the attempt by a clever con man named Protos (a name that suggests changing form and therefore disguise) to extract money from the rich by convincing them to liberate the Pope who has supposedly been imprisoned. An entire family, centered around three sisters and their husbands, is involved in a series of strange events. These couples, once again, demonstrate the impossibility of fulfillment through heterosexual marriage. Julius is a hypocritical novelist whose fidelity to his wife Marguerite is a manifestation of the conventional behavior he performs to get ahead in society. Anthime, a scientist who is parodied by Gide throughout most of the work, is ever at odds with his religious wife, until she rebels against his newly found asceticism. Fleurissoire and his friend Blafaphas both love Arnica. She finally decides in favor of Fleurissoire after trying out both family names and finding his less horrid. In order to placate Blafaphas, Fleurissoire swears never to consummate his marriage. But he falls prey to an affectionate prostitute during his ill–fated crusade to deliver the Pope. Gide makes fun of all his major preoccupations: writing (through the character of Julius), religious freedom (Anthime), rebellion against society's constraints (through Protos), and marriage (through Fleurissoire). Lafcadio, a young man who at first seems to be less of a caricature than the others, turns out to be the ultimate parody of complete detachment and rebellion. The theme of pederasty itself is parodied here in Lafcadio's long and amusing account of his childhood. Various "uncles" (his mother's lovers) create for Lafcadio a childhood filled with games, esthetic pursuits, and a return to nature and nudity. The satire gave no indication that Gide would next write a serious work, *Corydon*.

Gide had thought of *Corydon* as early as 1900. Oscar Wilde's imprisonment, degradation, and death in that year had greatly affected him. But he postponed the actual writing of the book until much later out of prudence and fear of hurting his wife. In 1911, 22 copies of an anonymous work entitled *C.R.D.N.* appeared. The definitive edition was not published until 1924. Gide had finally decided that the importance of what he considered a "social mission" outweighed all other considerations. After receiving the Nobel Prize in 1947, Gide wrote a preface to the American edition of *Corydon* in which he stated that the treatise was his most important work.

The final version of *Corydon* consists of four Socratic dialogues in which a narrator (sometimes blatantly homophobic, sometimes just the devil's advocate) interviews a young man named *Corydon* (the name is taken from a shepherd in Virgil's second *Eclogue* who loved another shepherd). The young man tells the story of his "coming out" and defends pederasty with scientific and social documentation. Dialogue I states that homosexuality is natural and that homosexuals are healthy and virile, not perverse or depraved as was usually thought. In Dialogue II Corydon expounds the scientific foundation for male homosexuality. According to Alain Goulet "His central thesis rests on the affirmation that, in nature, 'sexual in-

stinct' does not exist ... and pleasure must be dissociated from procreation" (my translation). Abundant examples of homosexual behavior in the animal kingdom prove its foundation in nature.

Dialogues III and IV speak of the universality of homosexuality in man, using examples from diverse cultures, literature, history, and the fine arts. However, the most striking defense comes from the praise of the practice known as "Greek love." Having abandoned his original posture, which argued that physical pleasure was always dissociated from emotional love, Gide (through the words of Corydon) describes the moral good that comes from the love between an adolescent and an older man who is a father figure, a mentor, and a lover. Thanks to such a relationship, the young man is protected from unsafe sexual encounters (with prostitutes, etc.), grows up under the loving moral, emotional, and physical guidance of an elder, and may eventually marry if his orientation turns out to be heterosexual. In this way, Gide broadens his defense of pederasty into a theory for an ideal social structure. *Corydon* was an extremely important work since it helped to liberate many young homosexuals from feelings of guilt and abnormality. It was one of the first attempts to change the reactions of society and to permit homosexuals to live fulfilling lives. Unfortunately, Gide had not yet become aware of the same need for liberation among women.

The Counterfeiters, was one of many early twentieth–century works (like those of Virginia Woolf, Marcel Proust and James Joyce) that revolutionized the form of the novel. The story itself is extremely complex, dealing with three separate families connected in various ways. Their story is told both by an omniscient narrator— who ironically questions his own omniscience—and through Edouard's diary. Edouard, who has links to all three families and other peripheral characters, is a novelist writing a novel also entitled *The Counterfeiters,* in which another novelist is also writing a novel, and so on *ad infinitum.*

The theory of Greek love is illustrated in the novel through the relationship of Edouard and his nephew Olivier. Many misunderstandings plague their early contacts. Because of their emotions each feels intimidated. Unable to communicate, each goes his own way: Edouard hires Olivier's best friend, Bernard, as his secretary, and Olivier himself is exploited by another novelist, Passavant. Finally though, in a poignant scene, Olivier declares his love and goes to live with Edouard. Many of the novel's characters live according to some stereotyped image that comes from legend, myth, or literature and which makes of them moral "counterfeiters." Olivier is no exception. Since he assumes that he will never be able to surpass the experience of his first night of love with Edouard, he tries to commit suicide. He is saved from the consequences of what he believes is a heroic act by Edouard, who will be his mentor, lover, and father figure. Olivier, it is suggested, will thrive both emotionally and intellectually because of this relationship.

Despite its illustration of Greek love, the novel is more balanced than the theoretical work *Corydon.* Bernard, who is perhaps the strongest character and real hero of the book, is clearly heterosexual from the beginning. It is also shown how some pederasts exploit youth, as in the case of Passavant. Moreover, the theme of "counterfeiting" applies even to Edouard, whose early relationship with Laura is not quite honest and who fails to call a doctor for Olivier for fear of an inquest. As always, Gide puts into question his most cherished beliefs. How long will Edouard remain with Olivier? The question is left unanswered, but the last sentence of Edouard's diary and of this open–ended novel shows interest in another adolescent: "I am most curious to know Caloub " says Edouard.

From 1929 to 1936 Gide finally turned his fictional interests toward the plight of women in society. For the first time, in *The School for Wives,* the narrator is a woman. Eveline tells of her marriage to Robert, who covers up his hypocrisy and opportunism under the guise of religion and social conformity. Her story ends with her departure for a hospital at the front lines. She dies soon after of contagion, having sacrificed her life in order to break away from her stifling marriage. The second book of the trilogy is Robert's defense, and the third, entitled *Geneviève,* is the family story told again in first person by the daughter.

Geneviève despises her father and tries to encourage her mother's feeble attempts at independence. But the real feminist rebellion is yet to come and is only suggested here. Her friend Gisèle dreams of a career that will "allow me to help women by teaching them to know themselves, to become aware of their value." Finally in *Geneviève* the possibility of physical love among women is suggested. Geneviève experiences an almost violent attraction for her classmate, Sara. These troubling feelings are heightened when she sees a nude portrait of Sara painted by her artist father. It is the narrator later on who can explain this emotion which the adolescent girl does not yet understand: "I was racked by unfamiliar pangs, which I did not know to be desire, because I thought desire could only be felt for a person of the opposite sex." Geneviève becomes aware of women's plight mainly through literature. Her thinking develops in the direction of independence and liberation from male domination, but the only action she takes is to ask an older friend to father her baby. He refuses.

It was difficult for Gide at this point to carry the story of feminism much farther. Several attempts at continuing Geneviève's narration were never published. At this point in his career he turned to nonfiction and expressed his social concerns.

Gide was certainly one of the first liberators and many of his ideas have become accepted tenets of contemporary society. His fiction reveals an ever increasing awareness of the expression of homosexual love from the first latent suggestions to the celebration of Greek love in *Corydon* and *The Counterfeiters.* Finally, near the end of his fictional writings, he attempted to enter the ranks of the early feminist movement. Our own society owes him a great debt for his ground breaking ideas and their sincere expression.

—*Elaine D. Cancalon*

———

GIDLOW, Elsa. British, Canadian, and American poet and philosopher. Born in Hull, Yorkshire, 1898; grew up in Montréal; came to the United States in the early 1920s. Educated at McGill College (now University). Companion of 1) Violet Henry–Anderson (died); 2) Isabel Quallo. Journalist and editor of in–house industry periodicals, 1918–21; English secretary, Consulate of Serbians, Croatians and Slovenians, Montréal, 1922; poetry editor, then associate editor, *Pearson's,* New York City, 1921–26; editor, *Pacific Coast Journal of Nursing,* San Francisco, 1926–28; free–lance writer, 1940–68. Contributor to periodicals, including *Canadian Bookman, Feminist Studies, Forum, Pacific Weekly,* and *San Francisco Review.* Cofounder and owner of Druid Heights Books (publisher). Cofounder, 1962, treasurer, and member of the board, Society for Comparative

Philosophy. **Recipient:** Southern California Women for Understanding Lesbian Rights Award, 1981. *Died in Marin County, California, of a heart attack, 8 June 1986.*

WRITINGS

Poetry

On a Grey Thread. Will Ransom, 1923.
California Valley with Girls. Privately printed, 1932.
From Alba Hill. Privately printed, 1933.
Wild Swan Swinging. Privately printed, 1954.
Letters from Limbo. Privately printed, 1956.
Moods of Eros. Mill Valley, California, Druid Heights Books, 1970.
Makings for Meditation: A Collection of Parapoems, Reverent and Irreverent, illustrations by Dearie Swick. Mill Valley, California, Druid Heights Books, 1973.
Sapphic Songs: Seventeen to Seventy. Baltimore, Diana Press, 1976; revised as *Sapphic Songs: Eighteen to Eighty, the Love Poetry of Elsa Gidlow.* Tallahassee, Naiad Press, 1982.

Other

Wise Man's Gold (drama in verse), 1972.
Ask No Man Pardon: The Philosophical Significance of Being Lesbian (essay), photographs by Ruth Mountaingrove. San Francisco, Booklegger Press, 1975.
Elsa, I Come With My Songs: The Autobiography of Elsa Gidlow. San Francisco, Booklegger Press, 1986.
Contributor, *A Lesbian Love Advisor* by Celeste West, illustrations by Nicole Ferentz. Pittsburgh, Cleis Press, 1989.
Shattering the Mirror.

*

Adaptations: Selections from *Sapphic Songs* were set to music by K. Gardner as *Two Sapphic Songs,* Stonington, Maine, Sea Gnomes' Music, 1982.

Biography: *In My Own Way* by Alan Watts, New York, Random House, 1973; "Elsa Gidlow's Sapphic Songs," in *American Poetry– Review* (Philadelphia), January 1978; "Footprints on the Sands of Time," in *Frontiers,* 4:3, 1979.

*   *   *

Elsa Gidlow, a pioneer Bay Area lesbian poet, was the first American female poet of the early twentieth century to write almost exclusively and explicitly from an openly lesbian viewpoint. She was born in Yorkshire, England, in 1898, and her freethinking English parents moved when she was six to primitive quarters in the tiny schoolless French Canadian village of Tetreauville, Québec. Between early fear of her hard–drinking, ambitious father (who often declaimed popular poems), household chores, and helping her overburdened but always singing mother with younger children, Gidlow soon found her own secret place, a large rock between giant tree roots at the edge of a stream, where she developed a poetic fantasy life, an abiding dislike for snow, a longing for knowledge, and a hope for a salubrious climate.

Her "practical" father, who took correspondence courses, taught first–aid to railroad workers, and travelled comfortably on the job while keeping his wife tight–budgeted and pregnant, hoping for another son, thought Elsa's interest in poetry impractical: "You have to make something of yourself." After a year travelling across Canada on the railroad as his secretary, Gidlow moved with her family to Montréal when she was 16. There she took a typing job, joined a library, experienced her first passionate friendship (the woman she loved got married), brought together a bohemian literary group, published a "little magazine" with much gay material, and took courses at McGill College (now University). At school she and her friends discovered the works of Havelock Ellis, Edward Carpenter, Baudelaire, Rimbaud, Verlaine, and other writers who seemed liberating at the time. Finding the classic literature of India also deeply influenced her.

Gidlow was inspired during her adolescence by reading press accounts of the feminist protests of the Pankhursts and their compatriots in London. Seeing the appalling conditions of her mother and the many infant deaths in the poor village, and being accosted by men who exhibited themselves, she resolved very early that she would never marry. In "Footprints on the Sands of Time" she wrote, "When I filled out forms, I used to wonder if I really existed. For example: grammar school (none); high school (none); college (none); degrees (none); post graduate record (none); honors and awards (none); marriages (none); children (none); religious affiliation (none). I do have a birth certificate."

Gidlow called poetry "a poet's way into the world, a path to connection ... a key to unlocking her deepest self, discovering where that self joins with all that appears to be outside of it, ultimately to realize inseparability from the 'self' of every other being, human and non–human. If that suggests religion I cannot deny the resemblance ... it comes to me forcibly that I am in the realm of the sacred ... in its gut level place in human life, most particularly in the life of woman ... our awe in the face of the whole mystery of our being, of Being itself, not any institutionalized doctrine or belief."

She published her first collection of poetry, *On a Grey Thread,* a book of explicit and passionate lesbian love verse, in 1923, when she "was too ignorant and too courageous to know better." Unmolded by the literary lions of the early twentieth century, her verse always lacked the defensiveness of so many gay and lesbian writers. She trusted her love and gloried in it—no lurking in the dark, no fear of discovery, no sense of guilt, no glorying in willful degradation.

In *Ask No Man Pardon: The Philosophical Significance of Being Lesbian,* a 1975 pamphlet, she notes the continued fear and ignorance regarding Sapphic love, as opposed to the social imperatives, "Male and female created he them" and "go forth and multiply," contrasting this with Nature's apparent love of diversity and spontaneity. "It appears to be natural to delight in union," she says, regardless of whether procreation is intended. If the way of the woman who takes delight in other women "was unnatural, as claimed, why was so much pressure, so much conditioning, required to mold ... her to the socially prescribed role? ... Who instructs the dolphin, or the pine ... how to grow and function? How should they need instruction, being cells of the being of the Universal Mother, carrying within themselves her design?" She notes that

botanists regard each new variation with interest and excitement, never asking if the fritillary butterfly is abnormal for not conforming to the pattern of the monarch. While not demeaning the contribution of mothers, she discusses the signal contributions women–loving–women have made and can make to society if they are not forced into roles contrary to their own natures.

In 1981 the Southern California Women for Understanding and the International Gay and Lesbian Archives held a reception for Gidlow in the Hollywood Hills after presenting SCWU's 1981 Lesbian Rights Award to her. Her last remaining copy of *On a Grey Thread*—possibly the first book of open lesbian verse published in America—as well as a lock of the long hair she had cut in 1923 (swearing never again to wear it long), and other historically important personal mementos, were displayed under glass on the patio—and stolen. Miraculously, they were returned to the Archives weeks later by a chagrined woman who said, "My lover is a klepto," and left.

Gidlow left behind a frank, sensitive and challenging autobiography in *Elsa, I Come With My Songs,* and was a contributor to Celeste West's *A Lesbian Love Advisor.* In her graceful and moving appearance in the film *The Word Is Out,* asked when she became a lesbian, Gidlow replied, "I never know what that means! I feel I was born this way!"

—*Jim Kepner*

GINSBERG, Allen. American poet. Born in Newark, New Jersey, 3 June 1926. Educated at Columbia University, A.B. 1948. Served in the U.S. military during World War II; discharged. Worked variously as a spot welder in the Brooklyn Naval Yard, 1945, as a dishwasher, 1945, and on various cargo ships, 1945–56; worked as a literary agent, a reporter for a New Jersey union newspaper, and as a copy boy for *New York World Telegram,* all 1946; night porter for the May Co. in Denver, Colorado, 1946; book reviewer for *Newsweek* in New York City, 1950; market research consultant in New York City and San Francisco, 1951–53; instructor at the University of British Columbia, Vancouver, Canada, 1963; founder and treasurer of the Committee on Poetry Foundation, 1966—; organizer of the Gathering of the Tribes for a Human Be–In, San Francisco, 1967; cofounder, codirector, and teacher, Jack Kerouac School of Disembodied Poetics at the Naropa Institute (the first Buddhist–inspired accredited college in the western hemisphere), Boulder, Colorado, 1974—. Has given poetry readings and has exhibited his photographs around the world in such countries as Austria, England, France, Germany, India, Japan, Peru, Poland, and Russia. Participant and speaker at numerous conferences, including the Gay and Lesbian Writers Conference in San Francisco, 1990. Has appeared in numerous films, including Robert Frank's *Pull My Daisy,* 1960, *Wholly Communion,* 1965, *Don't Look Back,* 1967, and *Renaldo and Clara,* 1978. Member of the National Institute of Arts and Letters, PEN, and the New York Eternal Committee for Conservation of Freedom in the Arts. **Recipient:** Woodbury Poetry Prize; Guggenheim fellowship, 1963–64; National Endowment for the Arts grant, 1966; National Institute of Arts and Letters award, 1969; National Book Award for Poetry for *The Fall of America,*

1974; National Arts Club Medal of Honor for Literature, 1979; National Endowment for the Arts fellowship, 1986. Address: P.O. Box 582, Stuyvesant Station, New York, New York, U.S.A.

WRITINGS

Poetry

Howl, and Other Poems, introduction by William Carlos Williams. San Francisco, City Lights Books, 1956; revised, Grabhorn–Hoyem, 1971; as *Howl Annotated,* with facsimile manuscript, New York, Harper, 1986.
Siesta in Xbalba and Return to the States. Privately printed, 1956.
Kaddish, and Other Poems, 1958–1960. San Francisco, City Lights Books, 1961.
Empty Mirror: Early Poems. New York, Totem Press/Corinth Books, 1961.
The Change. Writer's Forum, 1963.
Kral Majales ["King of May"]. Kensington, California, Oyez, 1965.
Wichita Vortex Sutra. Housman's, 1966; Brunswick, Maine, Coyote Books, 1967.
TV Baby Poems. London, Cape Goliard, 1967; New York, Grossman, 1968.
Airplane Dreams: Compositions from Journals. Toronto, House of Anansi, 1968; San Francisco, City Lights Books, 1969.
With Alexandra Lawrence, *Ankor Wat.* London, Fulcrum Press, 1968.
Scrap Leaves, Tasty Scribbles. Poet's Press, 1968.
Wales—A Visitation, July 29, 1967. London, Cape Goliard, 1968.
The Heart Is a Clock. Gallery Upstairs Press, 1968.
Message II. Gallery Upstairs Press, 1968.
Planet News: 1961–1967. San Francisco, City Lights Books, 1968.
For the Soul of the Planet Is Wakening.... Desert Review Press, 1970.
The Moments Return. Grabhorn–Hoyem, 1970.
Ginsberg's Improvised Poetics, edited by Mark Robison. Buffalo, New York, Anonym Books, 1971.
New Year Blues. New York, Phoenix Book Shop, 1972.
Open Head. Melbourne, Australia, Sun Books, 1972.
Bixby Canyon Ocean Path Word Breeze. New York, Gotham Book Mart, 1972.
Iron Horse. Toronto, Coach House Press, 1972; San Francisco, City Lights Books, 1974.
The Fall of America: Poems of These States, 1965–1971. San Francisco, City Lights Books, 1972.
The Gates of Wrath: Rhymed Poems, 1948–1952. Bolinas, California, Grey Fox Press, 1972.
Sad Dust Glories: Poems during Work Summers in Woods, 1974. Berkeley, California, Workingmans Press, 1975.
First Blues: Rags, Ballads, and Harmonium Songs, 1971–1974. New York, Full Court Press, 1975.
Mind Breaths: Poems 1971–1976. San Francisco, City Lights Books, 1978.
Poems All Over the Place: Mostly Seventies. Cherry Valley, New York, Cherry Valley Editions, 1978.
Mostly Sitting Haiku. Fanwood, New Jersey, From Here Press, 1978; revised and expanded, 1979.
Careless Love: Two Rhymes. Red Ozier Press, 1978.

With Peter Orlovsky, *Straight Hearts' Delight: Love Poems and Selected Letters.* Berkeley, Gay Sunshine, 1980.
Plutonian Ode, and Other Poems, 1977–1980. San Francisco, City Lights Books, 1982.
Collected Poems, 1947–1980. New York, HarperCollins, 1984.
White Shroud Poems: 1980–1985. New York, HarperCollins, 1986.

Prose

Prose Contribution to Cuban Revolution. Artists Workshop Press, 1966.
Allen Verbatim: Lectures on Poetry, Politics, Consciousness, edited by Gordon Ball. New York, McGraw, 1975.
Your Reason and Blake's System. Hanuman Books, 1988.

Letters

With William S. Burroughs, *The Yage Letters.* San Francisco, City Lights Books, 1963.
The Visions of the Great Rememberer. Amherst, Massachusetts, Mulch Press, 1974.
To Eberhart from Ginsberg. Lincoln, Massachusetts, Penmaen Press, 1976.
With Neal Cassady, *As Ever: Collected Correspondence of Allen Ginsberg and Neal Cassady.* Berkeley, California, Creative Arts, 1977.

Journals

Indian Journals: March 1962–May 1963; Notebooks, Diary, Blank Pages, Writings. San Francisco, City Lights Books, 1970.
Notes after an Evening with William Carlos Williams. New York, Samuel Charters, 1970.
Journals: Early Fifties, Early Sixties, edited by Gordon Ball. New York, Grove, 1977.
Japan and India Journals, 1960–64, by Joanne Kyger, with photographs by Ginsberg and others. Bolinas, Tombouctou Books, 1981.

Contributor

The Marijuana Papers (essays), edited by David Solomon. New York, Bobbs–Merrill, 1966.
Background Papers in Student Drug Abuse, edited by Charles Hollander. U.S. National Student Association, 1967.
Pardon Me Sir, but Is My Eye Hurting Your Elbow? (plays), edited by Bob Booker and George Foster. Geis, 1968.
Contributor of commentary, *May Day Speech,* by Jean Genet. San Francisco, City Lights Books, 1970.
Poetics of the New American Poetry (essays), edited by Donald M. Allen and Warren Tallman. New York, Grove, 1973.
Philip Glass: The Hydrogen Jukebox. Woodstock, New York, Beekman Publications, 1992.

Photograph Books

Reality Sandwiches. San Francisco, City Lights Books, 1963; Berlin, Nishen, 1989.
Allen Ginsberg and Robert Frank. Tokyo, Galerie Watari, 1985.
Allen Ginsberg Fotografier 1947–1987. Arhus, Denmark, Forlaget Klim, 1987.

Allen Ginsberg: Photographs, introduction by Robert Frank, with photographs by Ginsberg. Pasadena, California, Twelvetrees, 1991.
Snapshot Poetics. San Francisco, Chronicle Books, 1993.

Other

Translator with others, *Poems and Antipoems* by Nicanor Parra. New York, New Directions, 1967.
Compiler, *Documents on Police Bureaucracy's Conspiracy against Human Rights of Opiate Addicts and Constitutional Rights of Medical Profession Causing Mass Breakdown of Urban Law and Order.* Privately printed, 1970.
The Fall of America Wins a Prize (speech text). New York, Gotham Book Mart, 1974.
Chicago Trial Testimony. San Francisco, City Lights Books, 1975.
With others, *Madiera and Toasts for Basil Bunting's Seventy-fifth Birthday,* edited by Jonathan Williams. East Haven, Connecticut, Jargon Society, 1977.
With Robert Creeley, *The Cantos (125-143) Ezra Pound,* edited by Michael Andre. New York, Unmuzzled Ox Press, 1986.
With others, *Nuke Chronicles.* Bowling Green, New York, Contact Two, 1980.

Recordings: *Songs of Innocence and of Experience by William Blake Tuned by Allen Ginsberg,* 1970; *Birdbrain,* 1981; *First Blues: Songs,* 1982; *The Lion for Real,* 1989.

*

Adaptations: *Kaddish* (play; produced Brooklyn Academy of Music, Brooklyn, New York, 1972).

Manuscript Collections: Papers housed in special collections in the Butler Library at Columbia University, and the Humanities Research Center at the University of Texas, Austin.

Biography: *A Casebook of the Beat,* edited by T. Parkinson, New York, Crowell, 1961; *Howl of the Censor* by J. W. Ehrlich, San Carlos, California, Nourse, 1961; *The Sullen Art* by David Ossman, New York, Corinth Books, 1963, 87–95; *Mystery of the Universe: Notes on an Interview with Allen Ginsberg* by Edward Lucie–Smith, Turret Books, 1965; *Allen Ginsberg in America* by Jane Kramer, New York, Random House, 1968, as *Pater–familias: Allen Ginsberg in America,* London, Gollancz, 1970; *Allen Ginsberg* by Thomas F. Merrill, Boston, Twayne Publishers, 1969; *Allen Ginsberg in the Sixties* by Eric Mottram, Seattle/Brighton, Unicorn Bookshop, 1972; *Ginsberg* by Barry Miles, New York, Simon & Schuster, 1989; *Dharma Lion* by Michael Schumacher, New York, St. Martin's Press, 1992.

Interviews: With Thomas Clark, in *Writers at Work: The Paris Review Interviews,* third series, New York, Viking, 1967, 279–320; with Paul Carroll, in *Playboy,* April 1969, 81; with Alison Colbert, in *Partisan Review,* 38:3, 1971, 289–309; with John Tytell, in *Partisan Review,* 41:2, 1974, 255–309; *Gay Sunshine Interview: Allen Ginsberg with Allen Young,* Bolinas, California, Grey Fox Press, 1974; with Paul Geneson, in *Chicago Review,* summer 1975, 27–35; with Paul Portugés, in *Boston University Journal,* 25:1, 1977, 47–59.

Bibliography: "Allen Ginsberg: A Bibliography and Biographical Sketch" by Edward Z. Menkin, in *Thoth,* winter 1967, 35–44; *A Bibliography of Works by Allen Ginsberg* by George Dowden, San Francisco, City Lights Books, 1971; *Allen Ginsberg: An Annotated Bibliography 1969–1977* by Michelle P. Kraus, Metuchen, New Jersey, Scarecrow Press, 1980.

Critical Sources: *Alone with America: Essays on the Art of Poetry in the United States since 1950* by Richard Howard, New York, Atheneum, 1969, 145–152; "Allen Ginsberg: Angel Headed Hipster" by George W. Lyon, Jr., in *Journal of Popular Culture,* winter 1969, 391–403; "The Prophetic Voice of Allen Ginsberg" by Stephen Hahn, in *Prospects: An Annual of American Cultural Studies,* Number 2, 1976, 527–567; "Allen Ginsberg: The Origins of 'Howl' and 'Kaddish'" by James Breslin, in *Iowa Review,* spring 1977, 82–108; *The Visionary Poetics of Allen Ginsberg* by Paul Portugés, Santa Barbara, California, Ross–Erikson, 1978; "The Survival of Allen Ginsberg" by Mark Shechner, in *Partisan Review,* 46:1, 1979, 105–112; "Moloch's Poet: A Retrospective Look at Allen Ginsberg's Poetry" by Fred Moramarco, in *American Poetry Review,* September–October 1982, 10–18; *The Post–Moderns: The New American Poetry Revised* by D. Allen and G. Butterick, New York, Grove, 1982; *On the Poetry of Allen Ginsberg,* edited by Lewis Hyde, Ann Arbor, University of Michigan Press, 1984; *Best Minds: A Tribute to Allen Ginsberg,* edited by Bill Morgan and Bob Rosenthal, New York, Lospecchio Press, 1986; *The Portable Beat Reader,* edited by Ann Charters, New York, Viking, 1992.

*   *   *

Allen Ginsberg grew up in Paterson, New Jersey, in a house of politics and poetry. His father, Louis, was a teacher and a published poet known in literary circles in New York. His mother, Naomi, plagued with bouts of paranoia and delusion over her political causes, nonetheless was active in communist groups throughout her years before incarceration in various asylums. The young Ginsberg grew up under the conventionality of his father's poetry and the duress of a sick mother whom he was often called upon to care for. He would rebel against both parents out of shame and anger and then strive to merge their different worlds into his own writing.

From early adolescence on, Ginsberg was aware of homosexual stirrings, and for the need to conceal them. After being drawn to Columbia in pursuit of a man he was attracted to in high school, Ginsberg seemingly led a double life as a student and tormented closet lover. He wrote much bad verse in those years, then, in 1945, befriended the novelist Jack Kerouac, a drop–out from Columbia several years before. Ginsberg was expelled for sheltering Kerouac in his dorm room and for having scrawled an obscenity on his dorm window. He moved into a communal apartment nearby and fell in with the demimonde society of William Burroughs and his cronies in the drug and skin trades. He flung himself into the fleshpots of 42nd Street, and took his "real" education in the underground classics of the era from Burroughs, who tutored Kerouac; Lucien Carr, a classmate; and Neal Cassady, an idol of the Beats to come.

Ginsberg drifted briefly, but his bad–boy persona was only skin deep. He returned to Columbia to study until 1948 when he became entangled in the fencing of stolen property then being stored in his apartment by Herbert Huncke. Huncke was reputedly the coiner of the word "Beat," a word that referred to the tired, down–and–out, and jazz–crazed postwar generation coming of age in America. Ginsberg copped a plea of insanity and rusticated in Columbia's own psychiatric ward, where he met Carl Solomon, a second tutor in underground culture. Ginsberg's 1955 masterpiece "Howl" is dedicated to this well–read, savvy bohemian.

After writing orderly and rhyming verses, which William Carlos Williams, a willing mentor and member of the original Modernist generation, dismissed as amateurish, Ginsberg threw up his literary ambitions and took odd jobs in New York. He was stymied by a conventional education and the misadventures of his love life.

When Neal Cassady came into New York City from Denver in 1946, leaving behind a father who was a notorious derelict of that city's Skid Row, he took command of the Burroughs group with legendary spiels on any subject. Ginsberg and Kerouac both listened, spellbound by a spontaneous street–honed eloquence not heard since pioneer days. They took notes, labored over his style, and—with the aid of mind–altering drugs—began to incorporate that lush cascade of words into their own writing. Kerouac was the more adept at it, and was soon advocating a new mode of prose that strung together vast outpourings of mind from chemically–induced states. The outcome was his ground–breaking 1957 novel, *On the Road.*

Ginsberg's progress was slower, with more to give up from his father's example. Cassady had liberated him, and Kerouac and Burroughs provided alternative art forms. Not until he left New York in December of 1953, bound for Mexico and California—where his some–time lover, Cassady, now resided—did he make the plunge to open forms and write his classic, "Siesta in Xbalba," which predates "Howl."

Ginsberg's homosexuality was a link to his mother's underground life as a communist; both went against the American grain. It was not until his romance with Cassady that he came out to friends. Now, with Burroughs' world opened to him and art as its expression, he devised a method of splicing and rapid–fire phrasing that gave him a voice. Minted with that voice was his vision of a natural world of harmonious dynamics. Ginsberg abandoned conventional philosophy (and literature) to cultivate a view of nature as the sum of erotic forces willingly merging to create life, a view he derived in part from study of the Modernist poet, Ezra Pound.

Homosexuality was at the base of his esthetic; a code of permissive sexuality eliminated the resistance and seduction of orthodox love. Cleared of these antithetical principles, Ginsberg's poetry could apply the dynamics of homosexuality to the rest of experience, and begin to merge the otherwise irresolvable and antagonistic elements of life into a cosmic hymn. Out of such musing (and close study of the elliptical joinery of the Japanese haiku) came a spontaneous poetry, made famous by his phrase "hydrogen jukebox" in "Howl," where fragments and categorical opposites form polysemous wholes. Ginsberg has said his youthful studies of Cezanne's painting, with their cubist angles joined together to form human figures and landscapes, was another breakthrough to his method.

Ginsberg's language took a path around the more aggressive forms of conventional grammar, where a subject is made to strike or transform an object through the verb. In Ginsberg's poetry, images cohere loosely through enjambments and strings of hyphenated clauses, fusing together the desiderata of daily life into "reality sandwiches," as he later called them. His world is slightly skewed through drugs or an aroused surrealistic humor. A parade of low–lifers, tramps, ragamuffins and drag queens, addicts, criminals—the marginal life

Whitman had blessed in his 1855 "Song of Myself"—convenes in the poetry of *Howl, and Other Poems, Kaddish* in 1961, and *Reality Sandwiches* in 1963.

"Howl" champions the downtrodden while castigating the "system" in America. The nemesis of the young and free–spirited is a puritanical government living by the old oppositional philosophy. Ginsberg deconstructs some of that authority in "Howl" and in his 1958 "Kaddish," an elegy to his dead mother in which he employs elements of repressive Christianity, militarism, and corporate oligarchy in defining a version of "Moloch," the god who devours children. Early on, Ginsberg was against war; he had declared himself a homosexual in World War II and received a psychological discharge. Thereafter he opposed war as commercial venturing that squandered innocent life. He was active against the Vietnam War as well.

"Howl" attacked the power elite, but a poetry of encompassing reality in all its forms was the weapon he aimed at smug propriety and repression. Where others hid their sexual preferences under masks of convention, Ginsberg drew his sexual life directly into poetry, graphically describing his amours and orgasms in vivid, sometimes lurid detail. "Sweet Boy, Gimme Yr Ass" and "Come All Ye Brave Boys" from *Mind Breaths* in 1978 are representative of the genre: dense, erotic, and funny, motivated partly by a desire to shock the heterosexual reader.

Even with sex on dining tables and floors, in backseats and bedrooms, there is no power play by the lover; in many of these erotic episodes Ginsberg plays the submissive partner, the clown, the meek hedonist taking pleasure from willing participants. He says in "Love Returned" of a young lover, "I don't have to beg ... he's willing & trembles."

Ginsberg met his life–long companion Peter Orlovsky at a Christmas party in San Francisco in 1954; Ginsberg has celebrated this relationship as the mainspring of harmony in his life. The troubled affair with Cassady, who had married in his absence, and misadventures with females before and after, added a plaintive note to his earlier, self–absorbed lyrics; with Orlovsky the poems shift to boisterous eroticism and excess. Against such freedom lay the establishment with its war economy and waste, its repression and relentless exploitation of "consumers." Here was the only enemy to pagan joy, and like his mother Naomi before him, he railed against these powers at poetry readings, sit–ins, and meditations with peaceniks and anti–nuke groups.

Ginsberg's writing is a coherent celebration of sexual freedom and its ideological corollaries, civil rights, ecology, and pacifism. He drew ideas from a wide variety of sources to write his poetry and was attracted to Hinduism and Buddhism because of their theology of harmonious relations between spirit and flesh, gods and mortals, death and life. These too play a prominent role in his poems as forms of human integration.

Like Robert Duncan, his counterpart on the West Coast, Ginsberg believed in a mode of spontaneous composition in which to capture the mind at play. Man corrupts only when he imposes a stifling logic to his thoughts; the raw energies of nature are inherently virtuous and coherent, but human eyes are often blind to the original beauty of creation. The sexual urge in all its forms is part of that original energy; like Whitman, Ginsberg celebrates love between men as another of its forms and a binding power of otherwise formless masses of humanity.

—*Paul Christensen*

GODDARD, Beatrice Romaine. *See* **BROOKS, Romaine.**

––––––

GOMEZ, Jewelle. American novelist, social activist, and teacher of creative writing. Born in Boston, Massachusetts, 11 September 1948. Educated at Northeastern University, B.A. 1971; Columbia University School of Journalism, M.S. 1973. Companion of Diane Sabin, beginning 1992. Worked in production, WGBH–TV, Boston, for *Say Brother,* 1968–71; WNET–NY, New York City, 1971–73; and for the Children's Television Workshop, New York City, 1970s; worked in various capacities, including stage manager, at Off–Broadway theatres, 1975–80; lecturer in women's studies and English, Hunter College, 1989–90; director of Literature Program, New York State Council on the Arts, 1989–93. Founding board member, Gay and Lesbian Alliance Against Defamation (GLAAD); member of Feminist Anti–Censorship Taskforce (FACT); member of board of advisors, Cornell University Human Sexuality Archives, National Center for Lesbian Rights, and *Multi–Cultural Review* magazine. **Recipient:** Ford Foundation fellowship, 1973; Beards Fund award for fiction, 1985; Barbara Deming/Money for Women Award for fiction, 1990; Lambda Literary awards for fiction and science fiction for *The Gilda Stories,* 1991. Agent: Frances Goldin, 305 East 11th Street, New York, New York 10003, U.S.A.

WRITINGS

The Lipstick Papers (poetry). Jersey City, New Jersey, Grace Publications, 1980.
Flamingoes and Bears (poetry). Jersey City, New Jersey, Grace Publications, 1986.
The Gilda Stories: A Novel. Ithaca, New York, Firebrand Books, 1991.
"A Celebration of Butch–Femme Identities in the Lesbian Community," in *The Persistent Desire: A Butch–Femme Reader,* edited by Joan Nestle. Boston, Alyson Publications, 1992.
Forty–three Septembers (essays). Ithaca, New York, Firebrand Books, 1993.

*

Interviews: *Out/Look,* spring 1992, 63–72.

Critical Sources: Keynote address presented at Creating Change Conference in Arlington, Virginia, by Jewelle Gomez, 1991; "Bold Types" by Barbara Findlen, in *Ms.,* July/August 1991, 87; "No Either/Or" by Victoria Brownworth, in *Outweek,* 22 May 1991, 54–55; "Jewelle Gomez and Minnie Bruce Pratt" by Jane Troxell, in *Washington Blade,* 8 November 1991, 42–43; review by Robert Morrish of *The Gilda Stories,* in *Multi–Cultural Review,* 1:1, 1992, 549–550; "A Novelist's Sense of Family" by Esther Ivrem, in *New York Newsday,* 28 July 1992.

Jewelle Gomez comments: "The strategic efforts of the dominant culture to make invisible or belittle the contributions and influence of people of color, women and lesbians in the United States make my writing a survival technique for myself and the millions of others like me. I write out of a deep sense of history that was instilled by living with my great–grandmother until I was 22 years old. She looked at history with an unflinching eye, but still felt hopeful about the world. That is the perspective I try to take in my fiction and essays. I want to write about larger–than–life characters who still reflect the struggles that each of us must face every day. That is why writing fantasy fiction appeals to me. I enjoy creating in a form that is considered light weight because so many 'heavy' ideas can be slipped in. The principals of feminism and all the social changes they imply cam be made to represent the value system of benign vampires without feeling didactic.

"Another important element which I became aware of because of my great–grandmother, and which I bring to my work, is the importance of acknowledging and using our full selves as we go about our work. My great–grandmother was African American, but she was also Native American. She was born on a reservation in Iowa and lived to see the first man walk on the moon. She carried with her many contradictions, as we all do. In order to be fully myself, and to write as fully as I want, I keep all the elements of my life under consideration: Black, lesbian, feminist, former Catholic, part of the Black Nationalist movement of the 1960s and the anti–war movement of the 1970s. All these elements of who I am are important and none should be sacrificed. I think I write for all of the people who were important to me in each of the phases of my life, whether it's my best friend from high school, my regular customers when I used to wait tables in a bar, the women who worked with me at Gimbels department store or the students who take my courses, or other writers I admire, living or dead."

*   *   *

The fiction and poetry of Jewelle Gomez is a hybrid of politics and imagination. Although Gomez is a noted writer with a novel, two books of poetry and a collection of essays to her name, she is also known as an astute political organizer and activist.

Born in Boston in 1948, Gomez graduated from Northeastern University in 1971 and Columbia School of Journalism in 1973. Her earliest work was in public television and between 1968 and 1971 she worked on the Boston–based series *Say Brother,* one of the first weekly Black television programs. In the mid–1970s she helped produce the Children's Television Workshop in New York. After years of teaching creative writing and Women's Studies she became the director of the Literature Program of the New York State Council on the Arts between 1989 and 1993.

During this time Gomez was also involved as a social activist with a special interest in issues of lesbian and gay representation. She was a founding board member of Gay and Lesbian Alliance Against Defamation (GLAAD), an organization that agitated against homophobic depictions in the print and electronic media, as well as a member of the Feminist Anti–Censorship Taskforce, a group founded to supply a feminist, sex–positive analysis of anti–pornography campaigns.

While much of Gomez's two books of poetry—*The Lipstick Papers* in 1980, and *Flamingoes and Bears* in 1986—is a celebration of lesbian life and sexuality, much of her other writing consists of more detailed analyses of how lesbian and gay male culture can articulate and understand erotic and political difference. In a keynote address presented at the 1991 Creating Change Conference in Arlington, Virginia, Gomez spoke about the need for the lesbian and gay community to analyze how it uses and misuses power: "We have power. White men have power they use over each other and over women. They use it to the benefit of each other and the few lesbians they find acceptable. Lesbians use their power of acceptance in their various social circles for each other and against others they don't think are cool enough or well–dressed enough ... [b]lack gays use our power to 'dis' to keep ourselves isolated from the movement ... [s]ome lesbians curse the power of sexual imagery without ever examining what that power means to lesbians."

Part of Gomez's analysis of power is manifest in how the lesbian and gay community, as well as the mainstream media, construct images of homosexuals. On a 1990 panel celebrating butch/femme identity, held at the Gay and Lesbian Community Center in Manhattan, Gomez noted: "As a writer who's also black, who's also a lesbian, a good part of my early life was spent examining mythology and stereotypes that were damaging to me. In order for me to write characters and create situations that I thought were true to the spirit of people I wanted to represent, I had to confront many stereotypes." Gomez's warning against stereotypes is moderated, however, by an injunction against looking for easy acceptability. At the Creating Change Conference she noted that "desire for acceptance is the antithesis to the desire for change. I fight every day not to return to that desire to be accepted into the familiar order of things."

Gomez's novel, *The Gilda Stories* is an eloquent explication of her political theories. Spanning 200 years—from 1850 to 2050—*The Gilda Stories* tells the story of an African American lesbian vampire making her way through history and across cultures in a continual attempt to make sense of her life. By reclaiming several genres—the horror story, the picaresque and the social history novel—and reimagining them from a lesbian–feminist point of view, Gomez inserted her sensibility and politics and managed to interrupt and change a traditionally male narrative. The effect of *The Gilda Stories* is not only to present us with positive images of lesbians but also to allow us to see how a whole range of traditional writing, by excluding women, gay people or people of color, is limited by its own exclusive point of view. As such it is as much a work of literary criticism as it is a novel in its own right.

—*Michael Bronski*

———

GRAHN, Judith Rae. *See* **Grahn, Judy.**

———

GRAHN, Judy. American poet, playwright, novelist, and writer of nonfiction. Has also written as Carol Silver. Born Judith Rae Grahn in Chicago, Illinois, 28 July 1940. Educated at San Francisco State University, B.A. 1984; and at various other institutions. Served in the U.S. armed forces; discharged in 1961. Has held a variety of jobs, including waitress, short–order cook, clerk, barmaid, artist's model, typesetter, photographer's assistant, and nurse's aide, all prior to 1969; cofounder, publisher, editor, and printer, Women's Press Collective, Oakland, California, 1969–78; instructor of literature and lesbian cultural classes at New College of California, San Francisco, beginning in 1984; instructor of a course on Gertrude Stein at Stanford University, 1988; teacher in women's writing programs in Cazenovia, New York, Ithaca, New York, Berkeley, California, and San Francisco; gives lectures and poetry readings; conducts workshops. **Recipient:** American Poetry Review Poem of the Year Award, 1979; National Endowment for the Arts grant, 1980; Before Columbus Foundation American Book Award, 1983; American Library Association Gay Book of the Year Award, 1985; with Alice Walker, Tillie Olsen, Janice Mirikitani, and Alice Adams, Women's Foundation (San Francisco) Women of Words Award, 1985; Lambda Book Award for Nonfiction, 1988; Outlook Foundation Pioneer Gay Writer Award, 1989.

WRITINGS

Poetry

The Common Woman Poems. San Francisco, self–published, 1969.
Edward the Dyke, and Other Poems. Oakland, California, Women's Press Collective, 1971.
Elephant Poem Coloring Book. Oakland, California, Women's Press Collective, 1972.
Contributor, *No More Masks!: An Anthology of Poems by Women.* Garden City, New York, Anchor/Doubleday, 1973; revised, New York, HarperCollins, 1993.
A Woman Is Talking to Death. Oakland, California, Women's Press Collective, 1974.
She Who: A Graphic Book of Poems with Fifty–four Images of Women. Oakland, California, Women's Press Collective, 1978.
The Work of a Common Woman: The Collected Poetry of Judy Grahn, 1964–1977 (contains *Edward the Dyke, and Other Poems, The Common Woman, She Who, A Woman Is Talking to Death,* and "Confrontations with the Devil in the Form of Love"), introduction by Adrienne Rich. Oakland, California, Diana Press, 1978.
The Queen of Wands. Freedom, California, Crossing Press, 1982.
Spider Webster's Declaration: He Is Singing the End of the World Again. San Francisco, Interval Press, 1983.
Contributor, *The Penguin Book of Homosexual Verse,* edited by Stephen Coote. New York, Penguin, 1983.
Descent to the Roses of the Family (chapbook). Iowa Women's Press, 1986.
The Queen of Swords. Boston, Beacon Press, 1987.
Contributor, *Gay and Lesbian Poetry in Our Time,* edited by Carl Morse and Joan Larkin. New York, St. Martin's Press, 1988.
Contributor, *The American Reader,* edited by Diane Perita. New York, HarperCollins, 1991.
Contributor, *Before Columbus Foundation Poetry Anthology.* New York, Norton, 1991.
Contributor, *An Intimate Wilderness,* edited by Judith Barrington. Portland, Oregon, Eighth Mountain Press, 1991.

Contributor, *Lesbian Culture,* edited by Julia Penelope and Susan Wolfe. Freedom, California, Crossing Press, 1993.

Plays

The Cell (produced Yellow Springs, Ohio, 1968).
She Who (produced San Francisco, 1973).
The Queen of Wands (produced Ithaca, New York, 1985; London and other European cities, 1986).
The Queen of Swords (produced Oakland, California, 1989).

Novels

Mundane's World. Freedom, California, Crossing Press, 1988.

Nonfiction

"Menstruation: From the Sacred to the Curse and Beyond," in *The Politics of Women's Spirituality,* edited by Charlene Spretnak. Garden City, New York, Doubleday, 1982, 265–279.
Another Mother Tongue: Gay Words, Gay Worlds. Boston, Beacon Press, 1984; updated and expanded, Boston, Beacon Press, 1990.
"Flaming without Burning: The Role of Gay People in Society," in *Advocate,* March 1985.
The Highest Apple: Sappho and the Lesbian Poetic Tradition. San Francisco, Spinsters Ink, 1985.
"Vessels of Life and Death: Gay Spirituality in 1986," in *Advocate,* December 1986.
Really Reading Gertrude Stein: A Selected Anthology. Freedom, California, Crossing Press, 1989.
Contributor, *Classical and Medieval Literature Criticism.* Detroit, Gale Research, 1989.
"Drawing in Nets," in *Conversant Essays: Contemporary Poets on Poetry,* edited by James McCorkle. Detroit, Wayne State University Press, 1990.
"The Common Woman, A Map of Seven Poems," in *Inversions: Writing by Dykes, Queers, and Lesbians,* edited by Betsy Warland. Vancouver, Press Gang Publishers, 1991.
"Healing from Incest through Art," in *She Who was Lost is Remembered,* edited by Louise Wisechild. Seattle, Seal Press, 1991.
Blood, Bread and Roses: How Menstruation Created the World. Boston, Beacon Press, 1993.

Editor

Lesbians Speak Out. Trumansburg, New York, Diana Press, 1974.
And author of introduction, *True to Life Adventure Stories,* Volume 1. Trumansburg, New York, Diana Press, 1978.
And author of introduction, *True to Life Adventure Stories,* Volume 2. Freedom, California, Crossing Press, 1989.

Other

Author of article, in *Sexology* (as Carol Silver), c. 1964.
Movement in Black, foreword by Audre Lorde. Trumansburg, New York, Diana Press, 1978.
Author of introduction, *The Shameless Hussy: Selected Poetry and Prose.* Freedom, California, Crossing Press, 1980.
"Boys at the Rodeo" (short story), in *True to Life Adventure Stories,* Volume 2, edited by Grahn. Freedom, California, Crossing Press, 1989.

Recordings: *Where Would I Be without You: The Poetry of Pat Parker and Judy Grahn,* Olivia Records, 1975; *Lesbian Concentrate,* Olivia Records, 1978; *March to Mother Sea: Healing Poems for Baby Girls Raped at Home,* LavenderRose Productions, 1990; *A Woman is Talking to Death,* Watershed, 1991.

*

Adaptations: *The Common Woman Poems* (one–woman stage play; performed in Australia); *Edward the Dyke* (stage play; performed off–Broadway); *A Woman is Talking to Death* (interpretive dance; performed in Seattle); "Contemplating Chrystos" (interpretive dance; performed in San Francisco); "Funeral Plainsong" (musical presentation; performed in New York).

Interviews: With John Felstiner, in *Women Writers of the West Coast: Speaking of Their Lives and Careers,* edited by Marilyn Yalom, Santa Barbara, California, Capra, 1983; "Warrior/Dyke" by Judith Beckett, in *Women of Power,* winter/spring 1986; with Lynne Constantine and Suzanne Scott, in *Belles Lettres,* March/April 1987; "Lesbian Memory and Creation" by Dell Richards, in *Outlines* (Chicago), August 1988; *Contemporary Authors,* Volume 122, Detroit, Gale, 1988; "The Women–in–Print Movement, Some Beginnings" by Carol Seajay, in *Feminist Bookstore News,* three issues, beginning May/June 1990.

Critical Sources: "Judy Grahn" by Lisa Tipps, in *American Women Writers,* New York, Ungar, 1980; "Helen of Troy and Female Power" by Lynda Koolish, in *San Francisco Chronicle,* 20 February 1983; "The Re–Vision of the Muse: Adrienne Rich, Audre Lorde, Judy Grahn, Olga Broumas" by Mary J. Carruthers, in *Hudson Review* (New York), summer 1983, 293–322; *Women Writers of the West Coast: Speaking of Their Lives and Careers* edited by Marilyn Yalom, Santa Barbara, California, Capra, 1983; "In the House of Women" by Michele Aina Barale, in *Women's Review of Books,* October 1985; review by Myrna Hughes of *The Queen of Swords,* in *San Francisco Chronicle,* 26 February 1986; *Stealing the Language: The Emergence of Women's Poetry in America* by Alicia Suskin Ostriker, Boston, Beacon Press, 1986; "The Politics of the Refrain in Judy Grahn's *A Woman Is Talking to Death*" by Amitai F. Aviram, in *Women and Language* (Fairfax, Virginia), spring 1987, 38–43; *Feminism and Poetry: Language Experience, Identity in Women's Writing* by Jan Montefiore, London and New York, Pandora Press, 1987; "Uncommon Poetry of a Common Woman" by Margaret Spillane, in *New Haven Independent,* 23 June 1988; "Judy Grahn's Gynopoetics: *The Queen of Swords*" by Sue Ellen Case, in *Studies in the Literary Imagination* (Atlanta), fall 1988, 47–67; "*Mundane's World:* How Do We Get There from Here" by Jennie Ruby, in *Off Our Backs,* July 1989; "Up to the Earth" by Ursula K. Le Guin, in *The Women's Review of Books,* February 1989; *The Safe Sea of Women: Lesbian Fiction, 1969–1989* by Bonnie Zimmerman, Boston, Beacon Press, 1990; *The Reflowering of the Goddess* by Gloria Orenstein, Elmsford, New Jersey, Pergamon Press, 1990; review by Catharine R. Stimpson of *Really Reading Gertrude Stein,* in *Women's Review of Books,* May 1990, 6; review of *Another Mother Tongue,* in *Lambda Book Report,* January 1991, 37; review by Karla Jay of *Really Reading Gertrude Stein,* in *American Book Review,* April/May 1991, 22; "A Mundane Utopia" by Ron Erickson," in *Trumpeter,* winter 1992; She

Who is a Tree: Judy Grahn and the Work of a Common Woman" by Alicia Suskin Ostriker, in *Poetry East* (Ann Arbor, Michigan), 1993.

Judy Grahn comments: "I think it is important for people to know that an open, working–class lesbian poet who surfaced in 1970 with the word 'dyke' in the title of her first book is now considered literary canon. I've seen my work taught in conjunction with Plath, Rich, Plato, and Milton, and best of all, used by common people to transform their lives. Now I feel capable of becoming a world class philosopher, using the best gifts of my communities and my spirits to help reshape the world."

*   *   *

Since being discharged from the armed forces for lesbianism in 1961, Judy Grahn has worked consistently in her writing to redefine gay and lesbian existence in positive and powerful terms. As Grahn relates in the preface to *Another Mother Tongue: Gay Words, Gay Worlds,* the less–than–honorable discharge, rejection by several family members and friends for her sexuality, and several other incidents including being beaten in public "for looking like a dike" made her "angry and determined enough to use my life to reverse a perilous situation." Grahn further states in the preface that if she had been born into the earlier tribal culture of her European ancestors, she would have been one of the European equivalents of a shaman, such as a hag or wise–woman. Born into twentieth–century America, she says she instead became "a very purposeful Lesbian poet."

Grahn's purpose has been in public evidence since her first book of poems. She explains in *Another Mother Tongue* that she titled the first collection *Edward the Dyke* "to begin to defuse the terror people have of the word" and "to tie it to me, so I could never deny it." *Edward the Dyke* was published by the Woman's Press Collective, which Grahn, Wendy Cadden and other women began in 1970. However, even before 1970, Grahn had been active on behalf of homosexual rights. In 1963, she joined the Mattachine Society in front of the White House for an early gay–rights protest; in 1964, she wrote a pro–homosexual article for *Sexology* magazine, using the name "Carol Silver" as a pseudonym. Under her own name, she first published several poems from *Edward the Dyke* in the *Ladder,* an underground lesbian magazine.

Since 1970, Grahn has been drawn to increasingly ambitious projects. *The Common Woman Poems* is a cycle of verse that both depicts and valorizes the lives of "ordinary" women. Her long poem, "A Woman is Talking to Death," weaves together the description of a fatal motorcycle accident with a meditation on racism, lesbian existence, betrayal, and love as redemption. Mary J. Carruthers' *Hudson Review* essay, "The Re–Vision of the Muse," notes that these elements are combined to portray "the futility of trying to work within a society fascinated by destruction." With *The Queen of Wands,* Grahn has commenced a four–volume cycle of poems based on the four suits of the Tarot deck. She has moved into prose with *Another Mother Tongue,* a ten–year research and writing project that both traces and creates a history of gay culture. *The Highest Apple,* originally intended to be a chapter of *Another Mother Tongue,* links Sappho with eight other lesbian poets from the nineteenth and twentieth centuries, including Grahn herself, to create a theory of lesbian poetics. Grahn has gone on to expand her prose efforts with *Mundane's World,* her first novel, and *Really*

Reading Gertrude Stein, a series of poetic critical essays introducing selected writings by Stein.

Her writings draw generously from myth, tribal cultures, history, and personal experience to create a new mythology of gayness as a way of being. *The Queen of Swords,* a poetic play, equates a modern woman's coming out process with the story of the mythological figures of Inanna and Persephone, who journey to the underworld then return to the land of the living. In *Another Mother Tongue,* Grahn traces the roots of words, symbols, and attributes associated with gayness in order to establish the idea of a gay culture and spiritual function that transcends temporal and national boundaries. For example, she traces the word "dyke," or "dike," back to the goddess Dike, whose name means "balance" or "the path," and relates this balancing attribute to gay identity and purpose. "One of the major homosexual/shamanic functions in any society," states Grahn in *Another Mother Tongue,* "is to *cross over* between these two essentially different worlds [of male and female] and reveal them to each other."

Grahn brings this same valorization of what it means to be gay to her poetry, as is evidenced in the title poem from *She Who:* "I am the wall at the lip of the water / I am the rock that refused to be battered / I am the dike in the matter, the other / I am the wall with the womanly swagger / I am the dragon, the dangerous dagger / I am the bulldyke, the bulldagger." Continuing the work she began with her first book, Judy Grahn continues to use her office as poet and writer to transform and create positive meanings for being lesbian and gay.

—*Jayne Relaford Brown*

———

GREENE, Harlan. American novelist and author of nonfiction. Born in Charleston, South Carolina, 19 June 1953. Educated at College of Charleston, B.A. 1975. Companion of psychiatrist Olin Jolley. Archivist and assistant director of South Carolina Historical Society, Charleston, 1976–89; director of North Carolina Preservation Consortium, Durham, 1990—. Agent: Theron Raines, Raines & Raines, 71 Park Avenue, Suite 4A, New York, New York 10016, U.S.A.

WRITINGS

Novels

Why We Never Danced the Charleston. New York, St. Martin's Press, 1984.
What the Dead Remember. New York, Dutton, 1991.

Other

Editor, with Frank Q. O'Neill, *South Carolina Historical Magazine Index 71–81, 1970–1980, with Additions and Corrections 1–53, 1900–1952* (revised edition). Spartanburg, South Carolina, Reprint Co., 1981.

Charleston: City of Memory (nonfiction), photographs by N. Jane Iseley. Greensboro, North Carolina, Legacy, 1987.
"Charleston, South Carolina" in *Hometowns: Gay Men Write about Where They Belong,* edited by John Preston. New York, Dutton, 1991.
"What She Gave Me" in *A Member of the Family: Gay Men Write about Their Closest Relations,* edited by John Preston. New York, Dutton, 1992.

                                    *

Biography: "Charleston, South Carolina," in *Hometowns: Gay Men Write about Where They Belong,* edited by John Preston, New York, Dutton, 1991, 55–67; "What She Gave Me," in *A Member of the Family: Gay Men Write about Their Closest Relations,* edited by John Preston, New York, Dutton, 1992.

Critical Sources: "Hirsch Hess, Ripe for Salvation" by Edith Milton, in *New York Times Book Review,* 24 June 1984, 29; review of *What the Dead Remember,* in *Publishers Weekly,* 18 October 1991, 49; "Lost Horizons: New Gay Male Novels Display Style and Grace, but What's the Point?" by Felice Picano, in *Advocate,* 22 October 1991, 82–84; "The Rules of Sexual Attraction: Preserving an Extinct Species" by Stan Leventhal, in *Lambda Book Report,* November/December 1991, 15; *The Gay Novel in America* by James Levin, Garland, 1991, 339.

                              *   *   *

Young men struggling to accept and understand their homosexuality populate Harlan Greene's novels, *Why We Never Danced the Charleston* and *What the Dead Remember.* Recognized by some reviewers as semiautobiographical, Greene's work emphasizes the difficulties that gays experience in finding acceptance from society as well as from within the gay community itself. As the setting for the first novel and much of the second, Greene's hometown of Charleston, South Carolina, plays a pivotal role in the development of both stories.

Why We Never Danced the Charleston follows three young men—the narrator and two friends—as they attempt to cope with their emerging sexuality in the hostile environment of Charleston in the 1920s. The breakup of a relationship plunges one of them into a fatally self–destructive depression. "Many books seem thinly disguised autobiography," remarked James Levin in *The Gay Novel in America,* "but this is clearly a work of the imagination and as such it is a far finer literary achievement." The 13–year–old narrator of *What the Dead Remember,* spending a summer on an island near Charleston, also seeks to come to terms with his homosexuality. The conflicts of his relationships that summer resurface when he returns to Charleston many years later and must choose between the friendship of one man and the camaraderie of the city's closeted gays. "Greene's style is spare, evocative, precise, compelling," Stan Leventhal commented in *Lambda Book Report.* "Once again he has created a remarkable tale which takes the reader to the heart and soul of an intriguing milieu."

"I know I am not unique in thinking about my hometown the way one might feel about a first lover," Greene wrote in *Home-* *towns: Gay Men Write about Where They Belong.* "Invoking a dream of innocence, I thought the city and I would be together forever, but Charleston broke my heart and made me angry." As a boy, Greene learned to recognize the complex though subtle weighing of credentials that determined a resident's place in Charleston society. He was raised in the most exclusive part of town, a point in his favor, but his family's reputation for nonconformity excluded him from numerous guest lists. Later, his homosexuality sealed his fate among many Charlestonians, and the release of *Why We Never Danced the Charleston* further isolated him, especially from other homosexuals. Greene had believed his book would bridge the distance between him and the town's other gay men, who considered him "odd." Instead, it strengthened their rejection. Greene eventually realized the discomfort his book had caused the others. "I was a threat to them now," he wrote in *Hometowns.* "Being seen with me in public was poison. It was tantamount to advertising their own homosexuality."

Persuaded by his companion Olin Jolley, whom Greene met in Charleston, that "there is no use living in a culture that demeans you, no matter how politely," Greene eventually agreed to move away. "But I still think of Charleston; I return to her often and always will," he concluded in *Hometowns.* "I claim her now; even though I know she will never claim me."

                                                —*Deborah A. Stanley*

                              ——————

GRIER, Barbara G(ene Damon). American journalist, editor, publisher, and author of short stories. Has also written as Marilyn Barrow; Gladys Casey; Gene Damon; Irene Fiske; Vern Niven; Lennox Strang; Lennox Strong. Born in Cincinnati, Ohio, 4 November 1933. Educated in Kansas City, Kansas. Companion of publisher Donna J. McBride since 1971. Author of column "Lesbiana," 1957–72, then fiction and poetry editor, 1966–67, then editor, 1968–72, then publisher, 1970–72, *Ladder,* Reno, Nevada; author of column "Reader at Large," in *Tangents,* 1965–70; cofounder and publisher, beginning 1972, member of board of directors, beginning 1973, treasurer, beginning 1976, vice–president and general manager, 1980, and chief executive officer, beginning, 1987, Naiad Press, Tallahassee, Florida. Has contributed short stories and articles to periodicals under pseudonyms of Marilyn Barrow, Gladys Casey, Gene Damon, Irene Fiske, Vern Niven, Lennox Strang, and Lennox Strong. Address: c/o Naiad Press, P.O. Box 10543, Tallahassee, Florida 32302, U.S.A.

WRITINGS

Nonfiction

With Marion Zimmer Bradley, *Checklist: A Complete, Cumulative Checklist of Lesbian, Variant, and Homosexual Fiction in English.* Rochester, Texas, privately printed, 1960.
With Lee Stuart, *The Lesbian in Literature: A Bibliography* (as Gene Damon). San Francisco, Daughters of Bilitis, 1967; second

edition with Jan Watson and Robin Jordan, Reno, Nevada, The Ladder, 1975; third edition, as Barbara Grier, Tallahassee, Naiad Press, 1981.

"The Least of These," in *Sisterhood is Powerful.* 1970.

The Index, 1974.

Editor, with Coletta Reid, *The Lavender Herring: Lesbian Essays from the Ladder.* Baltimore, Diana Press, 1976.

Lesbiana: Book Reviews from the Ladder, 1966–1972, introduction by Ann Leeson. Reno, Nevada, Naiad Press, 1976.

Editor, with Coletta Reid, *Lesbian Lives: Biographies of Women from the Ladder.* Baltimore, Diana Press, 1976.

Editor, with Coletta Reid, *The Lesbian's Home Journal: Stories from the Ladder,* illustrations by Ellen Vogel. Baltimore, Diana Press, 1976.

Contributor, *The Lesbian Path,* edited by Peg Cruikshank. Labyris Books, 1979.

Contributor, *The Coming Out Stories,* edited by Julia P. Stanley and Susan J. Wolfe. Watertown, Massachusetts, Persephone Press, 1979.

Author of foreword, *Before Stonewall: The Making of a Gay and Lesbian Community* by Andrea Weiss. Tallahassee, Naiad Press, 1988.

Editor, with Katherine V. Forrest, *The Erotic Naiad.* Tallahassee, Naiad Press, 1992.

Editor, with Katherine V. Forrest, *The Romantic Naiad.* Tallahassee, Naiad Press, 1993.

*

Manuscript Collections: Gay and Lesbian Center, San Francisco Main Public Library.

Biography: "Clinging Vine," in *Heartwomen* by Sandy Boucher, San Francisco, Harper, 1982.

Interviews: *Christopher Street,* October 1976.

Critical Sources: Address by Barbara G. Grier to *Second Annual Lesbian Writer's Conference,* Chicago, 1978.

Barbara G. Grier comments: "Unlike many people I have had a richly blessed life—fortunate enough to have been lesbian and to have been supported and loved by my family. It has seemed only right and proper to spend my life giving back some of this fortune to my community and, through some luck and chance, everything I have been given to do has led naturally to the next step. The book collecting became the reviewing became the editing became the magazine publishing became the book publishing and so on. I have had, all of this time, a single goal. I have always believed that the best thing I might leave behind is a world in which any woman, anywhere, might say to herself 'I am a lesbian' and be able to go to a nearby store or library and find a book that will say to her, 'Yes, you are a lesbian, and you are wonderful.'"

*   *   *

Barbara G. Grier has devoted much of her career to writing,

editing, and publishing articles and books pertaining to lesbians and lesbianism. Writing under her own name as well as various pseudonyms, she contributed a wealth of material to the pioneer lesbian periodical the *Ladder,* also serving as the publication's editor from 1968 until 1972. Later, she and her companion, Donna McBride, cofounded the Naiad Press, which has grown to become the world's largest lesbian book publisher.

Born November 4, 1933, in Cincinnati, Ohio, Grier became aware of her homosexuality in her youth. Beginning at the age of eight, she fell in love repeatedly with slightly older girls as her family moved to various locations throughout the country. When she was 12 and her family was living in Detroit, Michigan, she told her mother of her sexual orientation. Her sympathetic mother explained the term "lesbian" and later joked that she had read Radclyffe Hall's *The Well of Loneliness* while she was pregnant with Grier and that she had marked her daughter.

During her childhood Grier became an avid reader. When she asked a librarian for books about people who love others of the same sex, she was dismayed to learn that she could not check out such works. She found ways to gain access to the adult section, however. Grier did not become seriously interested in lesbian fiction until age 16 when she found *The Well* in the library. Grier told this writer that she believes literature is the most important part of coming out—in helping to find an identity and a sense of connectedness to the lesbian past. Asked in an October 1976 *Christopher Street* interview if she had been frightened off by the negative descriptions of homosexuality that she read in early books, she replied "No," adding "I've always felt very good about myself."

Receiving much of her education in Kansas City, Kansas, Grier graduated from high school in 1951. For a time she helped support her divorced mother and two younger sisters. When she was 18, she became the companion of an older, married librarian. They ran off to Denver for two years before spending some 20 relatively isolated years in or near Kansas City, Kansas, where they both worked for the public library. Grier also began a more than 15–year association with the *Ladder,* the pioneering lesbian periodical which started in San Francisco in 1956 as a 12–page mimeographed newsletter. While Grier worked for the *Ladder,* the periodical expanded before its demise in 1972 to a 56–page magazine with some 3,800 subscribers.

Grier's work with the *Ladder* commenced several months after the periodical's debut as she began submitting book reviews. From 1957 until 1972 she wrote a column called "Lesbiana," a breezy and to–the–point summary of current lesbian literature. She also created a series called "Living Propaganda" and she wrote an entire issue alone. In addition she contributed to other periodicals, including *ONE Magazine* and the *Mattachine Review.* From October, 1965, until March, 1970, *Tangents* carried her "Reader at Large" column, which summarized the gay literature of the day. When preparing this work, later reprinted by Tangents in the form of two pamphlets, Grier attempted to feature titles that appealed to a variety of tastes. She culled reviews in various publications, looking for telltale signs of often obscure books that might be of interest, and hunted down those that were, informing her readers without pedantry or condescension how the subject was treated. From 1966 to 1967 she became fiction and poetry editor for the *Ladder,* before assuming editorship from 1968 until 1972. From 1970 until 1972, she was the magazine's publisher.

In the meantime, Grier began making a living at free–lance writing. She received no monetary compensation for her work on various gay publications as such periodicals could not afford to pay writers or staffers at that time. In February, 1966, while living in Kansas City, she was instrumental in finding a place for the initial meeting of the National Conference of Homophile Organizations—event planners wanted to meet equidistant between the coasts and hoped the conferences could set policy for the growing movement.

In time Donna McBride came to work on the *Ladder* and a love blossomed between her and Grier. Ending her longtime relationship with the librarian, Grier eventually moved with McBride to the rural town of Bates City, Missouri. Following the relocation, their lives became more social, with more travel and speaking engagements. After years of city living, Grier and McBride lived on a five–acre farm (called 20 rue Jacob in honor of American author Natalie Barney's Paris address). Together they raised trees, learned the joys of gardening, and continued the search for lesbian literature.

Grier and McBride's work for the *Ladder* ended in 1972, when the magazine folded. The periodical's long–anonymous financial supporter withdrew her funding after the magazine's focus switched from lesbian to lesbian–feminist issues. In 1973 Grier and McBride started Naiad Press with the assistance of two older women, just retired, who supplied the start–up funds for the lesbian/feminist publishing house. Naiad's first book was 1974's *Latecomer* by Sarah Aldridge. For nine years Grier and McBride did all work for Naiad Press while holding down regular jobs. The publishing house has since grown into a considerable business, with successful books like Jane Rule's *Outlander* and *Desert of the Heart*, Sheila Ortiz Taylor's *Faultline*, and Katherine V. Forrest's *Curious Wine*.

Naiad Press became a major force in developing new genres in lesbian literature, including mysteries, westerns, science fiction, and erotic fiction (as opposed to erotic stories about lesbians written by and for heteromales). The publisher also helped create today's market in which lesbians are among the nation's top book purchasers. When Naiad Press issued Rosemary Curb and Nancy Manahan's controversial book *Lesbian Nuns: Breaking Silence*, the publicity helped the publisher gain a larger customer base, with most new patrons also ordering heavily from the house's substantial back–list. Naiad Press attempts to keep virtually all back titles in print—an unusual practice but one driven by the memory of days when positive literature about lesbians was almost non–existent. Grier is resolved that every young lesbian coming out should have ready access to a wide variety of books which support their sexual orientation.

In addition to her duties with Naiad Press, Grier has also seen the publication of a number of her own titles. These include *The Lesbian in Literature: A Bibliography* with Lee Stuart; *Lesbiana: Book Reviews from the Ladder, 1966–1972*; and *The Lavender Herring: Lesbian Essays from the Ladder, Lesbian Lives: Biographies of Women from the Ladder*, and *The Lesbian's Home Journal: Stories from the Ladder*, all edited with Coletta Reid. In 1980 McBride and Grier moved Naiad Press to Tallahassee, Florida. Between their publishing activities, they joined in the massive 1987 and 1993 gay rights marches on Washington, D.C., Naiad Press began receiving hundreds of visitors each year—to many lesbians the publishing complex is like a shrine, a mecca. In addition, a number of Naiad Press books were optioned for film. Two have reached the screen—*Desert of the Heart* (as *Desert Hearts*) and *Claire of the Moon* from the novel of the same name.

Starting her career in lesbian literature at a time when such material was thought to be very scarce, hard to find, often illegal, usually buried in symbolism or euphemism, and most often extremely negative, Grier has made a substantial contribution to the field. Through her work as reviewer and anthologist, and finally and importantly as a publisher, she has helped create vast, diverse, readable, and positive lesbian literature. Her research, started back in those dark days, produced massive card files "overflowing with unworked information—probably three thousands cards," she related at the Second Annual Lesbian Writer's Conference in Chicago in 1978. Describing "notes on women I've personally not had time to research fully, or even at all," she explained that all her subjects "need to be talked about because all the women out there are really waiting to hear.... There are many women to find, many lesbians to write about and for.... We have to go out on the hills and listen for the fine wild sweet singing of our past and record it for our future."

Grier decided to donate these files and other private papers, along with the records of Naiad Press and her collection of well more than 15,000 books (including many books about gay males which she collected until 1968), to the new Gay and Lesbian Center at the San Francisco Main Public Library. She had been contacted by several primarily male gay archives and had investigated some one hundred institutional library archives interested in receiving the collection before making her decision. An 18–wheeler semi–trailer was used to send the first batch, appraised at $400,000. Funds have been raised from the Xerox Corporation and the National Endowment for the Humanities for de–acidification and to guarantee its preservation in perpetuity. Much of her periodical collection had already been shipped to the June Mazer Lesbian Collection in West Hollywood.

Grier and McBride plan to retire from Naiad Press on 3 January 2000, when the former will be 67 years old. Both believe that the publishing house will continue to thrive long after their departure.

—*Jim Kepner*

GRUMBACH, Doris (Isaac). American novelist, essayist, and educator. Born in New York City, 12 July 1918. Educated at Washington Square College, A.B. 1939; Cornell University, M.A. 1940. Served in the U.S. Navy WAVES. Married Leonard Grumbach, 1941 (divorced 1972); four children. Companion of Sybil Pike. Title writer for Metro–Goldwyn–Mayer, New York City, 1940–41; proofreader and copyeditor, Time, Inc., 1941–42; associate editor of *Architectural Forum*, 1942–43; English teacher at Albany Academy for Girls, Rochester, New York, 1952–55; variety of positions from instructor to professor of English at College of St. Rose, Albany, New York, 1952–73; literary editor for *The New Republic*, 1973–75; professor of American literature, American University, Washington, D.C., 1975–85. Columnist for *Critic*, 1960–64; *National Catholic Reporter*, 1968–76; *New York Times Books Review*, 1976–83; *Saturday Review*, 1977–78; and *Chronicle of Higher Education*, 1979–84. Contributor of reviews and criticism to *New York Times Books Review, Chicago Tribune, Commonweal, Los Angeles Times, Nation, Washington Post, New Republic*, National Public Radio, and the *MacNeil–Lehrer Newshour*. Member of American Association of University Professors, PEN, Phi Beta Kappa. Agent: Maxine Groffsky, 2 Fifth Avenue, New York, New York 10011, U.S.A.

WRITINGS

Novels

The Spoils of Flowers. Garden City, New York, Doubleday, 1962.
The Short Throat, the Tender Mouth. Garden City, New York, Doubleday, 1964.
Chamber Music. New York, Dutton, 1979.
The Missing Person. New York, Putnam, 1981.
The Ladies. New York, Dutton, 1984.
The Magician's Girl. New York, MacMillan, 1987.

Other

The Company She Kept (biography). New York, Coward, 1967.
Contributor, *The Postconcilor Parish,* edited by James O'Gara. New York, Kennedy, 1967.
Contributor, *Book Reviewing,* edited by Silvia E. Kameran. New York, Writer Inc., 1978.
Coming into the End Zone (autobiography). New York, Norton, 1991.

Recordings: *The Craft of My Fiction,* Archive of Recorded Poetry and Literature, 1985.

*

Interviews: With Wendy Smith, in *Publishers Weekly,* 6 September 1991, 84–85; "Idol Time" by Jane Troxell, in *Lambda Book Report,* January/February 1992, 11–13.

Critical Sources: Review by Paula Deitz of *The Magician's Girl,* in *New York Times Book Review,* 1 February 1987, 22; review by Noel Perrin of *Coming into the End Zone,* in *New York Times Book Review,* 22 September 1991, 12.

*   *   *

Doris Grumbach's writing career has flourished for more then three decades. Born Doris Issac in 1918 in Manhattan to a middle–class family, she attended Washington Square College and later received an M.A. from Cornell in 1940. She held a variety of writing and editorial jobs, from title writer for the Metro–Goldwyn–Mayer offices in New York to copy editor at *Mademoiselle* to associate editor at *Architectural Forum,* before she married Leonard Grumbach, a professor of physiology, in 1941. After raising four daughters, Grumbach began teaching as an instructor at the College of Saint Rose in Albany, New York, in 1955. She retired in 1973, a full professor. It was during her tenure at the College of Saint Rose that Grumbach began writing fiction. Her first novel, *The Spoils of the Flowers,* was published in 1962 and was followed two years later by *The Short Throat, the Tender Mouth.* Both works were noted for their elegance and compact structure as well as their ability to delineate character. It was this characteristic that was to surface as Grumbach's forte in her later works.

It was perhaps because *The Short Throat, the Tender Mouth* dealt with the varied and mostly unhappy lives of a group of undergradu-

ates that Grumbach was asked to write a critical biography of Mary McCarthy, whose 1964 novel *The Group* also dealt with a group of college friends. The result was *The Company She Kept.* Grumbach approached the material by interpreting all of McCarthy's fiction as strictly autobiographical and drawing direct parallels between the author's life and her novels. Grumbach had extensively interviewed McCarthy for the book and while her subject seemed willing to divulge personal material in the beginning, she objected strenuously to the completed manuscript. Although McCarthy did not dispute any of the facts Grumbach had included in the book, McCarthy claimed that she had not given Grumbach permission to use certain intimate details of the interview. The disagreement was reported in the press and the manuscript was amended to meet McCarthy's demands. In an article in the *New York Times Book Review,* Grumbach wrote, "The value of the whole experience lies, for me, in the recognition of how difficult, even well–neigh impossible, it is to write a book that deals with a living person."

Grumbach took her own advice and her next four novels all dealt with actual people, all of whom were dead. In *Chamber Music,* Grumbach drew a fictional portrait of the American composer Edward McDowell and his wife Marian. Written as the memoirs of the 90–year–old Caroline MacLaren, *Chamber Music* told the story of her loveless marriage to Robert MacLaren, his homoerotic attachment to men, his death from tertiary syphilis, and her joyful, life–fulfilling affair with Anna Baehr, the woman who had nursed Robert through the last stages of his illness. While much of the story is based upon fact—Edward McDowell did die of syphilis and Marian did found an artists colony in his name—Grumbach has stated that their lives were an inspiration rather than a diagram for *Chamber Music.*

This was the first time that Grumbach dealt with a major homosexual theme in her work, though there were gay and lesbian characters in both of her early novels, and the gay content of *Chamber Music* caused some critical comment, since the notion of "outing" even the dead was considered daring. The book was well–received, however, and her next novel *The Missing Person* was based upon the life of Marilyn Monroe. Grumbach transposed Monroe's life back to the 1930s, and the book is a critical look at how the film industry, as well as popular culture, can destroy a life. In a introductory note to the novel, Grumbach noted that "this novel is a portrait, not of a single life but of many lives melded into one, typical of the women America often glorifies and elevates, and then leaves suspended in their lonely and destructive fame." Much of the critical opinion of *The Missing Person* was not positive, perhaps because, despite Grumbach's denial, the title character was so clearly based on Monroe and it was difficult for reviewers to create any distance between reality and fiction.

Grumbach's next novel, *The Ladies,* was set in the past and in it she recreated the eighteenth–century lives of Lady Eleanor Butler and Sarah Ponsonby, two aristocratic Irish women who fled their repressive families, moved to Wales and lived openly as a couple. In their own time, Butler and Ponsonby gained a substantial reputation—they were known as The Ladies of Llangollen—for their intelligence and wit as well as their relationship. Grumbach sticks close to the facts of Butler and Ponsonby's lives, and the power of the novel comes from her detailed account of how the two women created their own world—a world of gardens, gazebos, and animals—as a refuge from, and a talisman against, the hostile outside world. Grumbach's genius was to recreate the romantic sensibility of the times and make it understandable in terms of twentieth–century lives and sexuality.

In *The Magician's Girl,* Grumbach used details from the lives of several personalities, including Sylvia Plath, Anne Sexton, Zelda Fitzgerald, Diane Arbus, Ezra Pound, and James Laughlin, to tell the story of three American women from the 1920s to the 1970s. The critical reception to the book was mixed and many critics complained, as they had with *The Missing Person,* that the well-known facts of the lives of actual people confused the reading of this fictional account. Grumbach introduces gay material here as well (one of the women is a lesbian), and, taken as a group, her last four novels attempt to recreate in fiction the real lives, both open and hidden, that women have led.

Grumbach's next book, *Coming into the End Zone,* written when she was 70, is an autobiography. A meditation on her later years, she was moved to write it partially as a response to the death of so many gay male friends who have died of AIDS, including her editor Bill Whitehead and the author Robert Ferro. While much of the book is filled with the details of a writer's life, it is also a coming-out story as Grumbach tells of her relationship with Sybil Pike and their move from Washington, D.C., to Sargentville, Maine. Grumbach never explicitly mentions her lesbianism in *Coming into the End Zone* but her relationship with Pike is central to the book. In an interview in *Lambda Book Report,* Grumbach stated of her life and her relationship with Pike, "I don't mind saying I'm gay, I just don't think the details should be public. We share a bedroom; if that offends people, they can leave. We live openly but privately."

—*Michael Bronski*

———

GUNN, Thom(son William). British and American poet, essayist, and educator. Born in Gravesend, Kent, England, 29 August 1929; came to the United States in the middle 1950s. Educated at University College School, Hampstead; Trinity College, Cambridge, B.A. in English 1953, M.A. 1958; Stanford University, Stanford, California, 1954–55 and 1956–58. Served in the British Army National Service, 1948–50. Poetry reviewer, *Yale Review,* New Haven, Connecticut, 1958–64. From 1958, lecturer, then associate professor of English until 1966, visiting lecturer, 1973–90, senior lecturer from 1990, University of California, Berkeley. Since 1966 freelance writer. Reviewer for *Poetry, Threepenny Review,* and *Times Literary Supplement.* **Recipient:** Levinson Prize, 1955; Somerset Maugham Award, 1959; American Institute of Arts and Letters grant, 1964; National Institute Award in literature, 1964; American Academy Award in literature, 1964; Rockefeller Award, 1966; Guggenheim fellowship, 1971; W. H. Smith Award, 1980; PEN/Los Angeles Prize, for poetry, 1983; Robert Kirsch Award, for body of work, 1988; Lila Wallace/Reader's Digest fellowship, 1991; Forward Prize, 1992; MacArthur fellowship, 1993; Lenore Marshall Prize, 1993. Address: 1216 Cole Street, San Francisco, California 94117, U.S.A.

WRITINGS

Poetry

Thom Gunn. Oxford, Fantasy Press, 1953.

Fighting Terms: A Selection. Oxford, Fantasy Press, 1954; revised, New York, Hawk's Well Press, 1958; revised, London, Faber, 1962.
The Sense of Movement. London, Faber, 1957; Chicago, University of Chicago Press, 1959.
With Ted Hughes, *Selected Poems.* London, Faber, 1957.
My Sad Captains, and Other Poems. London, Faber, and Chicago, University of Chicago Press, 1961.
A Geography. Washington, D.C., Stone Wall Press, 1966.
Positives: Verses by Thom Gunn, photographs by Ander Gunn. London, Faber, 1966; Chicago, University of Chicago Press, 1967.
Touch. London, Faber, 1967; Chicago, University of Chicago Press, 1968.
The Garden of the Gods. Roslindale, Massachusetts, Pym–Randall, 1968.
Poems, 1950–1966: A Selection. London, Faber, 1969.
The Explorers: Poems. R. Gilbertson, 1969.
The Fair in the Woods. Oxford, Sycamore Press, 1969.
Sunlight. New York, Albondocani Press, 1969.
Moly, London, Faber, 1971.
Moly [and] *My Sad Captains.* New York, Farrar, Straus, 1973.
Mandrakes. London, Rainbow Press, 1973.
Songbook. New York, Albondocani Press, 1973.
To the Air. Boston, David Godine, 1974.
Jack Straw's Castle. New York, F. Hallman, 1975.
Jack Straw's Castle, and Other Poems. London, Faber, and New York, Farrar, Straus, 1976.
The Missed Beat. Newark, Vermont, Janus Press, 1976.
Selected Poems 1950–1975. London, Faber, and New York, Farrar, Straus, 1979.
Games of Chance. Omaha, Nebraska, Abattoir Editions, 1979.
Talbot Road. New York, Helikon Press, 1981.
The Passages of Joy. London, Faber, 1982; New York, Farrar, Straus, 1982.
Lament. Champaign, Illinois, Doe Press, 1985.
Sidewalks. New York, Albondocani Press, 1985.
The Hurtless Trees. New York, Jordan Davies, 1986.
Night Sweats. Florence, Kentucky, R. L. Barth, 1987.
Undesirables. Durham, England, Pig Press, 1988.
The Man with Night Sweats. London, Faber, and New York, Farrar, Straus, 1992.
Collected Poems. London, Faber, 1993; New York, Farrar, Straus, 1994.

Essays

The Occasions of Poetry: Essays in Criticism and Autobiography, edited with introduction by Clive Wilmer. London, Faber, and New York, Farrar, Straus, 1982; expanded, San Francisco, North Point Press, 1985.
Shelf Life. Ann Arbor, University of Michigan Press, 1993; London, Faber, 1994.

Editor

Poetry from Cambridge 1951–52: A Selection of Verse by Members of the University. London, Fortune Press, 1952.
With Ted Hughes, *Five American Poets.* London, Faber, 1962.
And author of introduction, *Selected Poems of Fulke Granville.* London, Faber, and Chicago, University of Chicago Press, 1968.
Ben Jonson: Poems. Harmondsworth, Middlesex, Penguin, 1974.

Recordings: *Faber Poetry Cassette,* with Thom Gunn and Craig Raine reading from their works, London, Faber, 1982.

                                    *

Manuscript Collections: University of Maryland.

Bibliography: *Thom Gunn: A Bibliography, 1940–1978* by George Bixby and Jack W. C. Hagstrom, London, B. Rota, 1979.

Critical Sources: *Thom Gunn and Ted Hughes* by Alan Bold, Edinburgh, Oliver & Boyd, 1976; *The Homosexual Tradition in American Poetry* by Robert K. Martin, Austin, University of Texas Press, 1979; *Dictionary of Literary Biography,* Volume 27: *Poets of Great Britain and Ireland, 1945–1960,* Detroit, Gale, 1984; *Three Contemporary Poets: Thom Gunn, Ted Hughes, and R. S. Thomas* edited by A. E. Dyson, London, Macmillan, 1990.

Thom Gunn comments: "I think of myself as an Anglo–American poet. My poetry is an attempt to *grasp,* with grasp meaning both to *take hold of* in a first bid at possession, and also to *understand.*"

                        *   *   *

As a British born and raised expatriate who has lived in San Francisco for 40 years, Thom Gunn occupies a unique place in both American and English poetry today. Born in Kent in 1929 to a middle–class English family—both of his parents were journalists—he followed the usual course for a boy of his class. He attended University College School and after a two year stint in the British Army National Service beginning in 1948 (all British young men of the time were required to serve) he went up to read English at Trinity College, Cambridge and received his B.A. in 1953. He had begun writing during this period and his first book was 1954's *Fighting Terms.* The book was well–received, although even the most favorable reviews admitted that it was the work on an undergraduate. These early poems—an exploration of the boundaries between love and sexuality, between public and private acknowledgements of feeling—indicate where Gunn's later work would go. This new fame placed Gunn in the middle of an emerging group of British poets—including Philip Larkin, Kingsley Amis, John Wain and Donald Davie—who were to be labeled by the critical press as The Movement. While these other poets eventually became mainstays of the British literary scene, Gunn moved to California soon after the publication of *Fighting Terms* to maintain his relationship with Mike Kitay, an American he had met and fallen in love with at Cambridge. Gunn's move to the States was a permanent one and was to influence all of his future work.

It is impossible to underestimate the effect that coming out had on Gunn's poetry and life. In a short autobiographical essay "My Life Up Until Now," he notes that Kitay "became the leading influence on my life, and thus on my poetry.... [I]t is not easy to speak of a relationship so long–lasting: so deep, and so complex, nor of the changes it has gone through, let alone of the effect it has had upon my writing." If the beginnings of Gunn's poetry can be traced to his coming out, the evolution of his poetry can also be seen as a

response to a series of comings out. Much of Gunn's writing can be traced to his own erotic education: his first entry into a gay bar ("a straight couple took me there.... It excited me so much that the next night I returned there on my own."), his exploration of his attraction to leather ("I was much taken by the American myth of the motorcyclist ... part free spirit and part hoodlum."), and his use of LSD ("We tripped also at home, on rooftops, at beaches and ranches some went to the opera loaded on acid.").

The influence of American culture on the content of Gunn's work is incalculable but his technique has remained as tight and precise as other British poets of his generation. *Moly* and *My Sad Captains* showed the prevalence of Gunn's homoeroticism in juxtaposition with his formal style. In "Three" he watches a father, mother, and young boy at a nude beach: "Only their son / Is brown all over. Rapt in endless play / In which all games make one, / His three year old nakedness is everyday." In *Jack Straw's Castle,* Gunn is even more open about his sexual inner life. From the opening poem, "The Bed": "We lie soft–caught, still now it's done, / Loose–twined across the bed / Like wrestling statues; but it still goes on / Inside my head." What might have been a traditional heterosexual narrative is completely transformed by the classical, homoerotic image of "wrestling statues."

In *Passages of Joy,* the homoeroticism is open and unabashed. In "Sweet Things" he writes: "How handsome he is in / his lust and energy, in his / fine display of impulse. Boldly 'How about now?' I say / knowing the answer. My boy I could eat you whole." But *Passages of Joy* also has a melancholy side. "The Victim" is a formal, rhymed account of the life of Nancy Spingarn, the women who lived with and was allegedly murdered by punk rocker Sid Vicious; "New York" details the poet's bedding a speed freak whose body is beginning to manifest signs of the drug use. The sadness evident in some of Gunn's earlier poems—the poet's response to the human condition—has evolved to reflect an acceptance of life's difficulties—tragedy touches the lives, albeit in small ways, of almost everyone.

It was a decade until Gunn published another collection and in that period the AIDS epidemic occurred. *The Man with Night Sweats* was published in 1992 and is suffused with a sadness only hinted at the in the earlier work. Even the occasional, usually celebratory, poem is somber. "Lines for My 55th Birthday": "The love of old men is not worth a lot. / Desperate and dry even when it is hot. / You cannot tell what is enthusiasm / And what is involuntary clawing spasm." The poems that appear earlier are overshadowed by the those inspired by AIDS that appear at the end of the volume. Gunn has not lost his ability to draw sustenance from sexuality and at times creates shocking juxtapositions as with "In Time of Plague": "My thoughts are crowded with death / and it draws so oddly on the sexual / that I am confused / confused to be attracted / by, in effect, my own annihilation." There are laments to specific friends here as well as meditation on the number of personal losses the poet has suffered.

Throughout all of the verse, Gunn still adheres to the strictly honed form he has worked with since the mid–1950s and it is this tight technique that makes the work even more moving. In "A Blank," the final poem in the collection, Gunn remembers the grief of the past decade as he sees a friend who has just adopted a child: "The year of griefs being through, they had to merge / In one last grief, with one last property: / To view itself like loosened cloud lose edge, / And pull apart, and leave a voided sky." The poem ends with a degree of hope—a human connection amid so much death. The image of the child in the poem—a "fair–topped organism dense with charm"—is reminiscent of that small boy on the nude beach in "Three": a simple possibility in a confusing and dangerous world.

—*Michael Bronski*

———————

GURGANUS, Allan. American novelist and short story writer. Born in Rocky Mount, North Carolina, 11 June 1947. Educated at Monterey Language School, 1966; Radioman and Cryptography School, 1966; University of Pennsylvania, 1966–67; Pennsylvania Academy of Fine Arts, 1966–67; Harvard University, 1969–70; Sarah Lawrence College, B.A. 1972; University of Iowa Writers' Workshop, M.F.A. 1974 (Danforth fellow, 1972–75); Stanford University, 1974–76 (Wallace Stegner fellow, 1975). Served in the United States Navy, 1966–70; served in Southeast Asia as message decoder on aircraft carrier U.S.S. *Yorktown;* received citation. Has held a variety of jobs including desk clerk and salesperson of art reproductions, Cambridge, Massachusetts, 1969–70; night security guard in vitamin factory, Bronxville, New York, 1970–72; instructor of fiction writing at Stanford University, Stanford, California, 1974–76, Duke University, Durham, North Carolina, 1976–78, Sarah Lawrence College, Bronxville, New York, 1978–86, and University of Iowa Writers' Workshop. Member of the Board of Directors, Yaddo artists retreat; cofounder, Writers for Harvey Gantt, a series of nationwide readings; artist, with paintings represented in many private and public collections, including one–man show at Phillipe Daverio Gallery, Milan, 1991. **Recipient:** PEN Syndicated Fiction prizes; National Endowment for the Arts fellowship, 1976 and 1987; Ingram Merrill Award, 1986; American Academy of Arts and Letters Sue Kaufman Prize for first fiction, 1990; English–Speaking Union of the United States Books across the Sea Ambassador Book Award for fiction, 1990; North Carolina Literary and Historical Association Sir Walter Raleigh Cup for fiction, 1990; *Los Angeles Times* Book Prize for the best work of American fiction, 1991; nomination for PEN–Faulkner Prize, 1991; Southern Book Award, 1991; Episcopal Caring Response to AIDS award for fund–raising work; numerous museum purchase prizes for artwork. Agent: Amanda Urban, International Creative Management, 40 West 57th Street, New York, New York 10019, U.S.A.

WRITINGS

Breathing Lessons (limited edition chapbook). North Carolina Wesleyan College Press, 1981.
Good Help (limited edition chapbook). North Carolina Wesleyan College Press, 1988.
"Adult Art," in *Men on Men 2: Best New Gay Fiction,* edited by George Stambolian. New York, New American Library, 1988.
Oldest Living Confederate Widow Tells All (novel). New York, Knopf, 1989.
Blessed Assurance: A Moral Tale (limited edition chapbook). North Carolina Wesleyan College Press, 1990.
White People (short stories and novellas). New York, Knopf, 1991.

"Forced Use," in *The Faber Book of Short Gay Fiction,* edited by Edmund White. London and New York, Faber & Faber, 1991.

Uncollected Short Stories

"America Competes," in *Harper's,* July 1988.
"Reassurance," in *Harper's,* 1989.
"Under This Very Mall," in *Harper's,* April 1989.
"Nativity, Caucasian," in *Harper's,* November 1990.
"Ode to Boy," in *Yale Review,* October 1992.
"The Practical Heart," in *Harper's,* July 1993.

Essays

"The Civil War in Us: Why Shiloh's Ghosts Are Restless Now," in *New York Times,* 8 October 1990, A17.
"The Sense of Life," in *Arts Magazine,* April 1991.
"What's Wrong with This Picture?," in *New York Times Book Review,* 1 December 1991.
"I, Gurganus," in *Interview,* January 1991.
"Relax, It's Almost Over," in *New York Times,* 31 December 1991, A21.
"Where Babies Come From," in *Interview,* June 1992.
"To Boy," in *Harper's,* March 1993, 31.
"Why We March," in *New York Times,* 25 April 1993, E17.

Recordings: *White People* (includes "America Competes" and "Nativity, Caucasian"), New York, Random House, 1991.

*

Adaptations: *Oldest Living Confederate Widow Tells All* (sound recording), Random House Audiobooks, 1989; *Oldest Living Confederate Widow Tells All* (teleplay), NBC–TV, 1992; *Reassurance: An Evening with Allan Gurganus* (drama; performed New York).

Biography: "Allan Gurganus" by Sam Staggs, in *Publishers Weekly,* 11 August 1989, 438–439; "Mouth of the South" by Tom Prince, in *New York,* 21 August 1989, 110–123; "He's 42. She's 99—Together They Make the South Rise Again" by Susan Reed, in *People Weekly,* 18 September 1989, 68–70.

Interviews: "If Grandma Had Been Homer" by Barth Healey, in *New York Times Book Review,* 13 August 1989, 20; "An Author Finds a Voice to Recall the South" by Mervyn Rothstein, in *New York Times,* 14 August 1989, B1, C11; with D. C. Denison, in *Writer,* October 1991, 19; with Ed Sikov, in *Gay Community News* (Boston), 22 March 1992, 10, 20.

***

Allan Gurganus says that he began reading seriously while he was laid up in a navy hospital for seven weeks with double pneumonia; he continued to read during his tour of duty on the USS Yorktown, which had a well–stocked library. Gurganus began keeping a journal and writing imitations of the authors he read. After leaving the Navy, he enrolled at Sarah Lawrence College where he was awarded two years' academic credit for the 1200 or so books he had read in the Navy. At Sarah Lawrence, he studied writing under Grace Paley; after graduating he attended the Iowa Writers' Workshop where his teachers included John Irving, Stanley Elkin, and John Cheever. Cheever soon became a close friend and valued mentor: he directed Gurganus to his first literary agent and sent his first completed short story, "Minor Heroism," to New Yorker fiction editor William Maxwell, who published the story in November 1974. Gurganus' "Minor Heroism," which deals with the awkward and sometimes painful relationship between a World War II veteran and his gay son, became the first short story about an explicitly gay character to appear in such a venerable arbiter of American literary standards as the New Yorker.

While Gurganus is, as he told Gay Community News, "completely and utterly committed to being gay" himself, many of his fictional characters are markedly ambivalent about their homosexuality. Only Bryan, the semi-autobiographical protagonist and narrator of "Minor Heroism," is portrayed as an openly gay man fully integrated into the gay community. But when he reappears in the subsequent works "Breathing Room" and "A Hog Loves its Life," Bryan's allusions to his own sexuality have grown more ambiguous with the passage of time; he reveals that after the loss of an "actor friend," he has been twice married and twice divorced. "Bryan is inevitably still trying to please his parents in some way," Gurganus explained in Gay Community News. "This, in part, accounts for his bad attempts at marriage and his ambivalence about his own sexuality."

A number of Gurganus' stories feature protagonists who lead double lives—husbands and fathers who engage in clandestine homosexual affairs or encounters. In "Art History," a school teacher is dismissed and ultimately arrested for sexual misconduct with his young male students. In "Adult Art," a school superintendent consummates a clandestine affair with a young nerd while they watch heterosexual pornographic films together. "I've got this added tenderness," Gurganus' narrator says by way of explaining his sporadic homosexual liaisons. "I never talk about it. It only sneaks up on me every two or three years. It sounds strange but feels so natural. I know it'll get me into big trouble." In "Forced Use," a scholar driving home from an academic conference has an anonymous—albeit brutally passionate—sexual encounter with a young man at a state park.

Gurganus was at Yaddo, the artists' retreat in Saratoga Springs, New York, in 1981 when he read an article in the New York Times about a woman who, by virtue of having become the child bride of an aged Civil War veteran in the 1880s, was now "the oldest living Confederate widow." The 30 pages he typed entirely in the voice of the nonagenarian woman ultimately became the opening section of Gurganus' critically acclaimed and commercially successful first novel, Oldest Living Confederate Widow Tells All, published in 1989. While it features no overtly gay or lesbian characters, Gurganus' novel is rich with homoerotic subtexts that are central to the work, including that of the relationship between Will Marsden, the protagonist whose elderly widow, Lucy, is the novel's narrator, and Ned Smythe, his best friend, with whom he joined the Confederate army when both were only 13 years of age. While Ned is killed by Yankee gunfire within the first 12 pages of the novel, Will's love for the young martyr and his inconsolable grief at his loss are fundamental to all that follows. "The fact that it was in some ways the overriding emotional connection of Willie Marsden's life is irrefutable," Gurganus told Gay Community News. "Questions of gender and questions of tenderness between people of the same sex come up in other contexts as well," the author continued. "In some ways, Lucy's great love relationships in the book are with other women. Shirley, her childhood friend who dies young, and Castalia, who's her kind of erotic emanation, give her, in some ways, more comfort than any man manages to do."

Gurganus currently makes his home in both New York and Chapel Hill, and has remained active in both writing and public speaking—he was asked to be the keynote speaker at OutWrite '92, held by Gay and Lesbian Writers in Boston. Among his more recent published works are "Where Babies Come From," a recollection of how nine-year-old renegade Spanky once taught seven-year-old Gurganus and his younger brother the rudiments of sex (through oral lecture and visual aids, not hands-on practicum), and "Ode to Boy," a lyrical meditation on the nature and culture of adolescent boys.

—Michael Broder

H

H. D. *See* DOOLITTLE, Hilda.

———————

HALL, (Marguerite) Radclyffe. English novelist, poet, and author of short stories. Born in Bournemouth, Hampshire, c. 1886. Educated in Germany and at King's College, London. Companion of Ladye Mabel Batten, 1908–16; companion of Lady Una Troubridge. **Recipient:** James Tait Black Memorial Book Prize, c. 1926; Femina–Vie Heureuse Prize, c. 1926; Eichelbergher Humane Award gold medal, c. 1926. *Died in London, 7 October 1943.*

WRITINGS

Poetry

'Twixt Earth and Stars: Poems. London, John and Edward Bumpus, 1906.
A Sheaf of Verses: Poems. London, John and Edward Bumpus, 1908.
Poems of the Past and Present. London, Chapman & Hall, 1910.
Songs of Three Counties, and Other Poems. London, Chapman & Hall, 1913.
The Forgotten Island. London, Chapman & Hall, 1915.

Novels

The Forge. London, Arrowsmith, 1924.
The Unlit Lamp. London, Cassell, 1924.
A Saturday Life. London, Arrowsmith, 1925.
Adam's Breed. London, Cassell, 1926.
The Well of Loneliness. London, J. Cape, 1928.
The Master of the House. London, J. Cape, 1932.
The Sixth Beatitude. London, Heinemann, 1936.

Other

Miss Ogilvy Finds Herself (short stories). London, Heinemann, 1934.

*

Biography: *The Life of Radclyffe Hall* by Lady Una Troubridge, New York, Citadel, 1973; *Radclyffe Hall at the Well of Loneliness: A Sapphic Chronicle* by Lovat Dickson, New York, Scribner, 1975; *The Life and Death of Radclyffe Hall* by Lady Una Troubridge, London, Jonathan Cape, 1984; *Our Three Selves: A Life of Radclyffe Hall* by Michael Baker, London, Hamish Hamilton, 1985.

Critical Sources: "The Personality of Radclyffe Hall" by Clifford Allen, in *Homosexuality and Creative Genius,* edited by Hendrik M. Ruitenbeek, New York, Astor–Honor, 1967, 183–188; "Radclyffe Hall" in *Lesbian Images* by Jane Rule, Garden City, New York, Doubleday, 1975, 50–61; *Beyond the Well of Loneliness* by Claudia Stillman Franks, Avebury, 1982; "The Myth of the Mannish Lesbian: Radclyffe Hall and the New Woman" by Esther Newton, in *Hidden From History: Reclaiming the Gay and Lesbian Past,* edited by Martin B. Duberman, Martha Vicinus, and George Chauncey, Jr., New York, New American Library, 1989, 281–293; *Reflecting on the Well of Loneliness* by Rebecca O'Rourke, London, Routledge, 1989.

*   *   *

Radclyffe Hall, the famous English author of *The Well of Loneliness,* was born near Surrey Lawn, West Cliff, near the town of Bournemouth. As the child of a wealthy and privileged, albeit troubled, family, she received a university education at King's College in London with a brief post–college year in Dresden, Germany. Although she was given the name of Marguerite Radclyffe–Hall, she was raised as a boy and wrote under the name of Radclyffe Hall. To her friends and acquaintances she was known as John.

Between 1906 and 1915, Hall composed five volumes of poetry; in all but four of these, she is explicit in her expression of same sex love. *A Sheaf of Verses* and *Poems of the Past and Present,* written soon after she had met Mabel Veronica Ballen ("Ladye"), her literary patron and her first long–standing friend and lover, are filled with passionate declarations expressing confidence and power. In *Songs of Three Counties, and Other Poems* and *The Forgotten Island,* Hall continues her lyrical declarations of earthly love to a woman but introduces a religious note in an expression of love and devotion to God.

Between 1924 and 1936, Hall published seven novels and a collection of short stories. Only two of Hall's novels deal directly with lesbian themes: *The Unlit Lamp* and *The Well of Loneliness.* In both of these works, Hall pleads for the individual's freedom to pursue happiness and fulfillment and for public sympathy and compassion for the homosexual. *The Unlit Lamp,* a precursor to *The Well,* explores the role of parental manipulation and control in a growing lesbian relationship. In this story about the Ogden family, Hall focuses on the relationship between Mrs. Odgen and her daughter Julia, and Julia's relationship with Elizabeth Rodney. Julia is torn between her growing love and devotion toward Elizabeth and her mother's jealousy and disapproval.

The Well of Loneliness undoubtedly represents Hall's bravest and best–known work. Published in England in 1928, the book was initially well–received by critics. Famous English critics of the Bloomsbury Circle, such as Desmond MacCarthy and Rebecca West, praised the novel more for its positive social statement on lesbianism, less for its artistic skill. Despite the added support of the general public, the novel was banned in England in the year of its publication under the Obscene Libel Act. In the book, Stephen Gordon, the female protagonist, is a lesbian in search of an identity. Isolated from herself in body and mind, Stephen is the "sexual invert," the outcast of society who must yield to the power that drives her. She often envies women who are able to accept their own bodies and their femininity.

Both *The Unlit Lamp* and *The Well* seem to support the theory that homosexuality is biologically determined, inherited from the parents, and is, therefore, unavoidable and irreversible; however, Hall does not rule out the possibility that upbringing and general environment are factors in the development of the homosexual identity. Despite *The Well*'s somber mood, moralistic tone, and dated content—at least by contemporary standards—the novel has endured and has enjoyed immense popularity.

Lady Una Troubridge, Hall's companion and lover for almost 30 years, recorded their life together in a work entitled *The Life and Death of Radclyffe Hall*. Published soon after Hall's death in 1943, Troubridge's book provides many insights into their long life together which was, by and large, happy and fulfilling but not without conflicts. If Troubridge's account can be taken as true, it suggests that Hall's portrayals of lesbians, especially that of Stephen Gordon in *The Well*, were not autobiographical, though many readers have interpreted them in this manner. Hall, according to Troubridge, seems to have fully and enthusiastically accepted herself as a lesbian and a woman and, because of this, enjoyed a more serene existence than her lesbian characters did. Despite this variance between her real and literary worlds, Hall's fiction and poetry represent a prominent and pioneering effort in support of lesbianism.

—*Jane Jurgens*

––––––––

HALL, Richard W(alter). American novelist, playwright, and author of short stories. Born Richard Hirshfeld in New York, New York, 26 November 1926; name legally changed in 1938. Educated at Harvard University; New York University, M.A. c. 1972. Served in the United States Army during World War II; became sergeant. Companion of 1) Dan Allen, 1960–65; 2) Arthur Marceau (died, 1989). Junior copywriter, J. Walter Thompson, New York City, 1949–52; founder and manager of Alumni Publications, New York City, 1952–64; worked in public relations for corporations including Western Electric and Celanese, 1964–69. Taught at Inter–American University, San Juan, Puerto Rico, and served as acting director of its university press, 1971–75. Contributing editor, *Advocate*, 1976–82; book reviewer for *San Francisco Chronicle*; contributor to *New Republic*, *Opera News*, and *Village Voice*. Elected to Na-

tional Book Critics Circle, 1978. *Died in Manhattan, New York, of AIDS–related complications, 29 October 1992.*

WRITINGS

Novels

The Butterscotch Prince. New York, Pyramid Books, 1975; revised, Boston, Alyson Publications, 1983.
Family Fictions: A Novel (semi–autobiography). New York, Viking, 1991.

Short Stories

Couplings: A Book of Stories (contains "The Prisoner of Love," "The Taste of Spring," "Colors," "Death in San Juan," "The Servant Problem," "The Household God," "The Judgment of Midas," "The Koan," "The Bad Penny," "A Touch of Fat," and "The Boy Who Would Be Real"). San Francisco, Grey Fox Press, 1981.
Letter from a Great–Uncle, and Other Stories (contains "Letter from a Great–Uncle," "The Purple Prince," "The Night Visitors," "The Piano," "Backwards," "The Lost Chord," "A Rose in Murcia," and "The Lesson of the Master"). San Francisco, Grey Fox Press, 1985.
Fidelities: A Book of Stories. New York, Viking, 1992.

Plays

Love Match (produced New York, 1977). Included in *Three Plays for a Gay Theater, and Three Essays*, 1983.
The Prisoner of Love (produced New York, 1979). Included in *Three Plays for a Gay Theater, and Three Essays*, 1983.
Happy Birthday, Daddy (produced New York, 1982.) Included in *Three Plays for a Gay Theater, and Three Essays*, 1983.

Other

Editor, with Dan Allen, *New Lives in the New World* (textbook). New York, Collier Macmillan, 1974.
"Henry James: Interpreting an Obsessive Memory," in *Literary Visions of Homosexuality*, edited by Stuart Kellogg. New York, Haworth Press, 1983.
Three Plays for a Gay Theater, and Three Essays (contains *Love Match*, *The Prisoner of Love*, and *Happy Birthday, Daddy*, plus "The Elements of Gay Theater," "Gay Theatre: Notes from a Diary," and "The Transparent Closet: Gay Theater for Straight Audiences"). San Francisco, Grey Fox Press, 1983.

*

Interviews: "The Dilemmas of Richard Hall" by Jim Marks, in *Lambda Book Report*, September–October 1992, 25.

Critical Sources: "Reflections at Middle Age" by Michael Lynch, in *Body Politic*, August 1985, 36; *Liberation and Disillusionment: The Development of Gay Male Criticism and Popular Fiction* by

Michael J. Clark, Los Colinas, Texas, Liberal Press, 1987, 69–74; *The Gay Novel in America* by James Levin, New York, Garland Publishing, 1991, 275; "Why the Schanbergs Became the Shays" by Matthew Stadler, in *New York Times Book Review,* 28 July 1991, 6; "A Family Denies Itself" by Michael Upchurch, in *San Francisco Chronicle Book Review,* 7 July 1991, 8; "Richard Hall" by Claude J. Summers, in *Contemporary Gay American Novelists,* edited by Emmanuel S. Nelson, Westport, Connecticut, Greenwood Press, 1993.

                      *   *   *

One of the greatest problems of researching and following the development of gay and lesbian literature in the United States lies in the virtual invisibility of many of its writers from the perspective of mainstream critical awareness. This is particularly true of those writers whose work is centered in formats difficult to locate, such as poetry or short stories. The case of Richard W. Hall is a particularly clear illustration of this phenomenon.

Born Richard Hirshfeld in New York City on 24 November 1926, Hall's name was altered by his mother following an anti–Semitic incident involving his sister in 1938. Upon graduating from high school in 1943, he attended Harvard under the accelerated wartime regimen, completing a major in English literature cum laude in 1948. Following four years of working as a copywriter, in 1952 he founded his own publishing firm specializing in materials for corporate distribution to employees, which he directed until 1964. The early 1960s were also noteworthy for his abandonment of attempts to alter his sexual orientation through psychoanalysis and the establishment of his first same sex relationship. A period of six years in the public relations field for various corporations was followed by his return to academic life, the attainment of an M.A. in English education from New York University in 1970, and his appointment to the faculty of Inter–American University at San Juan, Puerto Rico. It was at this time he began work on the manuscript which would appear in 1975 as his first novel, *The Butterscotch Prince,* and contributed both fiction and nonfiction pieces to the pages of lesbian and gay publications as well as more standard media such as the *Village Voice.*

In 1976, Hall accepted the job of contributing editor for books for the national gay newsmagazine the *Advocate,* a position he would occupy until 1982. During his tenure, he interviewed many contemporary writers whose works touched on the theme of homosexuality in some fashion, among them Eric Bentley, Marguerite Yourcenar, and John Boswell, and was elected to the National Book Critics Circle in 1978, becoming its first openly gay member. His literary output shifted from the novel to an emphasis on short stories and plays during the early years of the 1980s, a time that saw the productions of *Love Match, The Prisoner of Love,* and *Happy Birthday, Daddy,* all of which were published in 1983 under the collective title *Three Plays for a Gay Theater.* Service as a board member of The Glines, the principal company for gay theater in New York City, also enabled him to have a clear picture of the wide range of materials being produced as the response of the gay theater community to the challenges posed by the birth of a rapidly transforming gay and lesbian subculture and the increasing horrors of the AIDS epidemic.

The Butterscotch Prince falls into the class of mystery fiction begun by Joseph Hansen in 1970 with the first of what would become the dozen books featuring openly gay insurance claims investigator David Brandstetter, *Fadeout.* Originally intended as a pornographic piece, *The Butterscotch Prince* follows the efforts by a black gay man to unravel the murder of his lover, discussing along the way the issues of combining love and sex successfully and internalized homophobia, two subjects widely debated in the gay community in that decade. The question of claiming one's identity recurs in Hall's only other novel, *Family Fictions,* issued in 1991.

The literary form for which Hall is best known, his short stories, have appeared in three major collections: *Couplings: A Book of Stories, Letter from a Great Uncle, and Other Stories* and *Fidelities: A Book of Stories.* While most of the critical attention given to Hall's writings assess the accuracy of his depictions of the coalescing gay world of the 1970s and 1980s, his own philosophy of the function of homosexual literature has received less attention. In several articles on the development and future of gay and lesbian books and small press which appeared in the *Advocate* in 1983, Hall outlined the problems facing the genre. The greatest obstacle (as revealed by a survey of a dozen bookshops specializing in these materials) was one of awareness on the part of the potential audience for lesbian and gay writing of its wide variety and richness. The AIDS epidemic was seen as having changed the course of gay fiction away from a realistic depiction of the urban homosexual lifestyle (defined in such works as Andrew Holleran's *Dancer from the Dance*) toward a paradigm where "a whole orthodoxy based on the pleasure principle is no longer available.... [A] new world is waiting to be born." Following his own diagnosis, Hall contributed to the emergence of this new frame of writing until his death on 29 October 1992, in Manhattan, leaving a legacy of uniquely gay critical perspectives.

—*Robert B. Marks Ridinger*

————

HANSEN, Joseph. American novelist, short story writer, poet, and educator. Also writes as Rose Brock; James Colton. Born in Aberdeen, South Dakota, 19 July 1923. Educated at public schools in Aberdeen, South Dakota; Minneapolis, Minnesota; and Pasadena, California, 1929–42. Married Jane Bancroft in 1943; one daughter. Member of editorial staff of *One,* beginning 1962; cofounder and staff member, *Tangents,* 1965–70. Producer of radio show *Homosexuality Today,* KPFK–FM, Los Angeles, 1969. Creative writing teacher, Beyond Baroque Foundation, Venice, California, 1975–76; University of California, Los Angeles, beginning 1977. Contributor of verse to periodicals, including *Atlantic, Harper's, New Yorker,* and *Saturday Review;* contributor of short fiction to *Bachy, South Dakota Review, Tangents,* and *Transatlantic Review;* contributor of articles to *Armchair Detective, New Review,* and *Writer.* **Recipient:** National Endowment for the Arts grant, 1974; British Arts Council lecture tour grant, 1975. Agent: Stuart Krichevsky, Sterling Lord Literistic Inc., 1 Madison Avenue, New York, New York 10010, U.S.A.

WRITINGS

Novels

Fadeout. New York, Harper, 1970; London, Harrap, 1972.
Death Claims. New York, Harper, and London, Harrap, 1973.
Troublemaker. New York, Harper, and London, Harrap, 1975.
The Man Everybody Was Afraid Of. New York, Holt, and London, Faber, 1978.
Skinflick. New York, Holt, 1979; London, Faber, 1980.
A Smile in His Lifetime. New York, Holt, 1981; London, P. Owen, 1982.
Gravedigger. New York, Holt, and London, P. Owen, 1982.
Backtrack. Woodstock, Vermont, Countryman Press, 1982; London, Gay Men's Press, 1987.
Job's Year. New York, Holt, 1983; London, Arlington, 1988.
Nightwork. New York, Holt, and London, P. Owen, 1984.
Steps Going Down. Woodstock, Vermont, Countryman Press, 1984; London, Arlington, 1986.
The Little Dog Laughed. New York, Holt, 1986.
Early Graves. New York, Mysterious Press, 1987.
Obedience. New York, Mysterious Press, 1988.
The Boy Who Was Buried This Morning. New York, Viking, 1990.
A Country of Old Men: The Last Dave Brandstetter Mystery. New York, Viking, 1991.
Living Upstairs. New York, Dutton, 1993.

Short Stories

"Murder on the Surf," in *Mystery Monthly* (New York), December 1976.
The Dog, and Other Stories. Los Angeles, Momentum Press, 1979.
Brandstetter and Others: Five Fictions. Woodstock, Vermont, Countryman Press, 1984.
"The Olcott Nostrum," in *Alfred Hitchcock's Mystery Magazine* (New York), December 1987.
"The Owl in the Oak," in *Alfred Hitchcock's Mystery Magazine* (New York), March 1988.
Bohannon's Book: Five Mysteries. Woodstock, Vermont, Countryman Press, 1988.
"Molly's Aim," in *Ellery Queen's Mystery Magazine* (New York), June 1989.
Bohannon's Country. New York, Viking, 1993.

Novels as Rose Brock

Tarn House. New York, Avon, 1971; London, Harrap, 1975.
Longleaf. New York, Harper, and London, Harrap, 1974.

Novels and Short Stories as James Colton

Lost on Twilight Road. Fresno, California, National Library, 1964.
Strange Marriage. Los Angeles, Argyle Books, 1965.
The Corrupter, and Other Stories (short stories). San Diego, Greenleaf, 1968.
Known Homosexual. Los Angeles, Brandon House, 1968; revised edition published under name Joseph Hansen as *Stranger to Himself,* Hollywood, Major, 1977; as *Pretty Boy Dead,* San Francisco, Gay Sunshine Press, 1984.
Gard. New York, Award, 1969.

Cocksure. San Diego, California, Greenleaf Classics, 1969.
Hang–Up. Los Angeles, Brandon House, 1969.
The Outward Side. New York, Olympia, 1971.
Todd. New York, Olympia, 1971.

Contributor

The New Yorker Book of Poems. New York, Viking, 1974.
Killers of the Mind. New York, Random House, 1974.
Different. New York, Bantam, 1974.
Literature of South Dakota. University of South Dakota Press, 1976.
Years Best Mystery and Suspense Stories, 1984. Walker, 1985.
Murder, California Style. New York, St. Martin's Press, 1987.
Mammoth Book of Private Eye Stories. Carroll & Graf, 1988.
City Sleuths and Tough Guys. New York, Houghton, 1989.
Under the Gun. New York, Plume, 1990.

Other

One Foot in the Boat (poetry). Los Angeles, Momentum Press, 1977.
Contributor, *Colloquium on Crime: Eleven Renowned Mystery Writers Discuss Their Work,* edited by Robin W. Winks. New York, Scribner, 1986.
Rotten Rejections: A Literary Companion. Pushcart, 1990.

*

Adaptations: Four of Hansen's poems have been adapted into lyrics by composer Richard Rodney Bennett as *Vocalese,* produced London in 1983, and later broadcast by the British Broadcasting Corporation (BBC).

Critical Sources: *Poetry News, Calendar & Reviews of Southern California Readings and Publications,* November, 1981: "Joseph Hansen's Anti–Pastoral Crime Fiction," in *Clues: A Journal of Detection* (Bowling Green, Ohio), spring/summer, 1986; *The Gay Novel in America* by James Levin, New York, Garland, 1991.

*   *   *

Joseph Hansen—a novelist, artist, and poet who also writes under the pseudonyms James Colton and Rose Brock—was born on 19 July 1923, in the railroad town of Aberdeen, South Dakota. Taught to read with "progressive" flash cards and forced by a strep throat infection at age seven into an eight–month isolation, Hansen developed his imagination through reading such works as Carl Sandburg's *Abraham Lincoln—The Prairie Years* at an early age. When he returned to school, he proved himself a bright student, and he made friends easily. In 1933, as the Great Depression ravaged much of America, Hansen's father lost his shoe store and the family moved to Minneapolis, Minnesota. It was there that Hansen learned to ice skate, read books such as Jack London's *White Fang* and Mark Twain's *Huck Finn,* and wrote "Philosophy from a Boy to Older Folks," a treatise on solving national problems.

A few years later, the family joined the migration to California, driving an old Marmon with cartons and suitcases tied on, and sharing cramped quarters with in–laws on ten Altadena acres of citrus and beehives. Hansen began writing sonnets and putting the psalms of David into contemporary English, being guided briefly by Episcopal choirmaster–organist Raymond Hill through art books and classical recordings. As his love of music and literature grew, he tried writing a comic opera, edited the John Marshall Junior High School paper, acted in school plays, and immersed himself in evangelical church activities. For a time he entertained the notion of becoming a minister. It was his love of the written word, however, that eventually drew him in the direction of his life's work in writing.

Despite Hansen's respect for a religious and pure way of life, he admits to one theft: stealing, from the school library in 1938, William Rose Benet's *Fifty Poets,* an anthology in which each poet is represented by their best poem. The book was, and remains, precious to him, demonstrating that he was not alone in his hunger to write verse. "My family then were not my father, mother, sister, brother," Hansen stated in *Poetry News, Calendar & Reviews of Southern California Readings and Publications.* "My family were these: Edgar Lee Masters, Edward Arlington Robinson, Anna Hampstead Branch, Robinson Jeffers ... and so many others. And once I had found them, I tried my faltering best to be worthy of them. I hope that somewhere, in some school library, at this moment, some 15–year–old misfit like my long–lost self has chanced to come upon a book of poems that will mean as much to him as that one meant to me."

Entering Pasadena City College in 1939, Hansen eased up on religion and found exciting new friends and activities. He worked as a page at the public library and discovered, in writers such as Walt Whitman, Henry David Thoreau, and Ralph Waldo Emerson, help for his self–doubts. His lover, Bobker Ben Ali of the Pasadena Playhouse, helped even more, introducing Hansen to the works of Homer, Socrates, Charles–Pierre Baudelaire, James Joyce, Jean Cocteau, Arthur Rimbaud, and composers Erik Satie and Igor Stravinsky—as well as a rich diet of theatre. He spent many hours, still underage, at Hollywood's intimate jazz clubs, hearing great jazz for the price of a beer. In August, 1943, he married an aircraft plant worker named Jane Bancroft, who had come into his place of work. They have one daughter, Barbara, and a West Los Angeles houseful of other kids, dogs, cats, and more exotic pets (Hansen's books *Strange Marriage* and *A Smile in His Lifetime* partly address their life together).

As Hansen finished school and began married life, he turned to his writing skills to earn a living. From 1962 to 1965, he was an editor of *One* magazine (the first openly sold "avowed" American publication for homosexuals). After an angry schism, he helped launch an aesthetically superior periodical, also titled *One.* He was later forced, for legal reasons, to rename the magazine *Tangents.* His work on *Tangents* included writing editorials, stories, reviews, and a news column. Jane contributed artwork, layouts, reviews, and an advice column. Aside from work with *Tangents* (also known as the Homosexual Information Center), Hansen and his wife participated in inter–group homophile movement activities during the late 1960s. *Todd,* a novel he would later write under the pseudonym James Colton, was inspired by Los Angeles' Gay Liberation Front, organized at *Tangents'* garage–office. The magazine folded in 1970, at a time when Hansen's fiction work was just becoming widely known. He felt that the periodical had said what it had to say to the homosexual audience. At this stage in his career, Hansen felt that he could reach a wider audience, one that included heterosexual readers, with novels.

It took years for Hansen to get published and, until 1970, his writing on homosexual themes appeared under the Colton pseudonym (*One* magazine editor Don Slater insisted he use a pen name). Starting with *Lost on Twilight Road* and concluding with *Todd* in 1971, the novels serve as some of the better gay erotica available, even if some were written speedily.

It is his fine mystery novels about masculine homosexual insurance adjuster David Brandstetter, however, that have solidified Hansen's popularity with readers both gay and non–gay. From *Fadeout* in 1970 (the first novel he sold to a major publisher), the series (he had not intended it to be ongoing) has been well received by both readers and critics, although his American reception was perfunctory until after he had received high praise and popularity in England—the *London Times* called him the best writer of his kind since Dashiell Hammett (*The Maltese Falcon, The Thin Man*). Popularity for novels such as *Skinflick* and *Nightwork* followed in France, Holland, and Japan. 1987's *Early Graves* was Hansen's first novel to deal with the issue of AIDS—a subject he took up with trepidation but handled masterfully. In the novel, Brandstetter investigates the murders of young men infected with the HIV virus. *Obedience,* written in 1988, explores the Vietnamese community in Southern California.

Because protagonists of his favorite mystery writer, Ross MacDonald, did not age or develop, Hansen decided to trace real growth and change in his own lead character, as well as the changes in the Southern California landscape that Brandstetter inhabited. The investigator and his male lovers aged through the series and gay life underwent many transformations—though Hansen spurns the term gay and any concept of gay community or uniqueness.

Aside from his work as Colton and the popular Brandstetter novels, Hansen kept busy with other writings. *Backtrack,* published in 1982, covers a non–exploitive man–boy relationship and attacks a common stereotype of homosexual relationships. While gay characters predominate, the writing is non–exploitive—a change from the Colton novels, whose publishers wanted detailed and steady sex scenes. Hansen also wrote the non–mysteries *A Smile in His Lifetime,* dedicated to his wife, and *Job's Year.* In the 1950s, he worked on scripts for the TV series *Lassie;* in 1969 and 1974, he published the gothic novels *Tarn House* and *Longleaf* under the pseudonym Rose Brock (his mother's maiden name was Rosebrock); he also published a booklet of exquisite verse, *One Foot in the Boat,* in 1977, and produced many fine short stories.

Hansen insists he is a homosexual—not a gay—writer, as if that would make him a lesser writer. Still, his early Brandstetter novels have an elegance and an eye for interior decoration that set off his otherwise spare, "hardboiled" style descended from authors like Hammett and Raymond Chandler. He created Brandstetter to confound the stereotypes with which homosexuals were too often portrayed, to illustrate that there are just as many "macho" homosexuals as there are effeminate ones—that homosexuals come in the same variety of personalities as heterosexuals. Asked if he is the model for Brandstetter, Hansen admitted some resemblance but, unlike his fictional creation, he admits to being a sensitive and emotional person. Asked if he saw a Brandstetter film in the future, he said in 1981 that offers had come and gone, but most studios were fearful of presenting a real gay character, one that strayed from the popular Hollywood image of a gallivanting, flamboyant queen. Perhaps today, Hansen's concept of homosexuals on film is more likely.

Not all gay critics approve of Hansen's work. James Levin argues in *The Gay Novel in America* that while the author's 1975 novel *Troublemaker* provides a full portrayal of the gay subculture rather than simply individual homosexual characters, Hansen begins to show contempt for gay liberation. Levin points in particular to the novel's expectation that gay relationships should abandon gender roles, and he also argues that Hansen's antagonism toward gay activism and goals increases in each successive novel. This argument is a bit one–sided; some of the gay activists that Hansen presents as caricatures are, in fact, caricatures in real life. Hansen's talent is his eye for what is contemptible, silly, and admirable in gay life.

Hansen also involved himself in activities outside of writing. When police beat his daughter at a Century City, California, anti–war protest, his poster of police beating a demonstrator became a hit among many counter culture groups. At the urging of a local businessperson, Hansen also started a series of poetry workshops. This eventually led to teaching creative writing at Beyond Baroque, at the University of California, Irvine, and at University of California, Los Angeles Extension. A leading member of the Venice Poet's Circle, his verse has appeared in the *Atlantic, Harper's, New Yorker,* and *Saturday Review.*

—*Jim Kepner*

———

HEMPHILL, Essex. American editor, poet, and essayist. Born in the United States, c. 1956. Raised in Washington, D.C. Affiliated with the film productions *Looking for Langston,* by Isaac Julien, and *Tongues Untied,* by Marlon Riggs.

WRITINGS

Earth Life (poetry chapbook), privately printed, 1985.
Conditions (poetry chapbook), privately printed, 1985.
Editor, *Brother to Brother* (anthology). Boston, Alyson Publications, 1991.
Ceremonies: Prose and Poetry. New York, New American Library, 1992.

*

Critical Sources: *Los Angeles Times Book Review,* 8 September 1991, 18; review by Donald Suggs of *Brother to Brother,* in *Village Voice,* 1 October 1991, 74; review by David Trinidad of *Brother to Brother,* in *Village Voice Literary Supplement,* June 1992, 7–8; *Advocate,* 2 June 1992, 38; review by Thomas Tavis of *Brother to Brother,* in *Library Journal,* 1 October 1992, 88.

*   *   *

Since the beginning of the modern gay liberation movement in the 1970s, a steadily growing body of literature by gay and lesbian writers has explored issues of gay identity, the gay community, and the place of gay men and lesbians in mainstream society. As the movement gained an even greater momentum in the 1980s, the contributions of black gay and lesbian writers assumed increasing importance. As an editor, poet, and essayist, Essex Hemphill has been a key figure in the emergence of a distinctive African American perspective in the overall field of gay literature.

Although Hemphill grew up in a comfortable working–class neighborhood in Washington, D.C., he still had to contend with the racism that he observed around him. And as he entered adolescence and became increasingly aware of his own homosexuality, he had to contend with yet another kind of oppression, although he might have been a few years shy of learning that the word for that oppression was "homophobia." As Hemphill writes in his book *Ceremonies: Prose and Poetry,* "My sexual curiosity would have blossomed in any context, but in Southeast Washington, where I grew up, I had to carefully allow my petals to unfold. If I had revealed them too soon they would have been snatched away, brutalized, and scattered down alleys. I was already alert enough to know what happened to the flamboyant boys at the school who were called 'sissies' and 'faggots.' I could not have endured then the violence and indignities they often suffered."

In his twenties, Hemphill was attracted to the ideas embodied in the black nationalist movement that flourished in the 1960s and 1970s. But as he got older, he began to question the rhetoric that had previously inspired him. "I moved away from black nationalism," Hemphill relates in an *Advocate* article by Craig Allen Seymour II, noting that this doctrine proved "too narrow a politic for the interests that reside in me." He also found that a narrowly defined lesbian and gay political ideology could not adequately accommodate his personal vision, and went on to seek his own unique creative voice.

That literary voice had to accommodate the numerous conflicts and contradictions that Hemphill faced, both as an African American male in a predominantly white society afflicted by racism, and as a gay man in a predominantly heterosexual society afflicted by homophobia. And as many black gay writers, including Hemphill, have expressed repeatedly in recent years, being both black and gay carries a special burden because the homophobia that characterizes the black community in contemporary American society is qualitatively different, and in some ways more intense, than that of the predominantly white mainstream. Throughout American history, the culture of slavery and racism often encouraged white men to bolster their own sense of masculinity by asserting their dominance over black men. In response to this violent and abusive history, the black community placed a high premium on strong male images. Homosexuality, understood only through stereotypes of effeminacy and submissiveness, was particularly repugnant in this context. Thus, where many in white America were reluctant to tolerate homosexuals, many in black America were reluctant even to acknowledge that homosexuals existed in their community. Moreover, the racism that prevailed in mainstream American society could also be found in the newly emerging and predominantly white gay community, an especially frustrating and disheartening fact for the many black gay men and lesbians seeking to participate in the newfound gay liberation of the past 25 years.

Given these multiple layers of oppression and rejection, black gay and lesbian writers were truly courageous in staking out a new literary terrain for themselves. The writings of 35 such black gay men were gathered by Hemphill in *Brother to Brother,* and anthology of poetry and prose. The pieces in this collection are primarily autobiographical, lending a personal immediacy to discussions of racism, religious intolerance, homophobia, and life in the age of AIDS. Given the sensitivity of these topics, *Brother to Brother* could not help but be controversial. The book is divided into four sections, each with a distinct theme. The first section, called "When I Think of Home," focuses on varying notions of home and family, from those we grow up in to those we choose and create for ourselves as adults. The second section, called "Baby, I'm for Real," explores the false identities that black gay men create for themselves and hide behind, identities that often represent what they wish they could truly be or could truly have, including white skin or heterosexuality. The third section, called "Hold Tight, Gently," considers life in the age of AIDS, and includes personal accounts of dealing with the epidemic, or at times of choosing not to deal with it. The final section, "The Absence of Fear," contrasts the way black men are represented in mainstream culture with the way black men represent themselves. It includes discussions of homoerotic images of black men by the gay white photographer Robert Mapplethorpe, as well as recent films by and about black gay men, including Isaac Julien's *Looking for Langston* and Marlon Riggs' *Tongues Untied.* Hemphill himself contributes a selection of poetry to *Brother to Brother* that, according to Donald Suggs in his *Village Voice* review of the book, "effectively brackets and enlarges many of the conflicts in the anthology."

Ceremonies, an anthology of poetry and prose written entirely by Hemphill, spans the author's writing career, and includes pieces from his self–published 1985 chapbooks *Earth Life* and *Conditions* as well as previously unpublished work. Like the writings by Hemphill and others in *Brother to Brother,* the poems and essays in *Ceremonies* continue to explore the double burden of being a minority within a minority. "One of Hemphill's most persistent themes [is] the outsider confronting the dominant culture," wrote David Trinidad in his *Village Voice Literary Supplement* review of the book. Hemphill "has forged—with few role models to emulate, and with little or no support from the white gay literary establishment—an identity and a style characterized by anger and point–blank honesty," according to Trinidad. In addition to overtly political pieces, Hemphill includes love poems, celebrations of sexuality, and affirmations of gay identity, along with heartfelt and moving accounts of the fears and dangers of growing up black and gay. "He makes passionate common sense," wrote Thomas Tavis in his *Library Journal* review, concluding that "this is urgent, fiercely telling work." According to Seymour, writing in the *Advocate,* Hemphill "is poised to become the most widely known black gay writer since James Baldwin."

—*Michael Broder*

————

HIGHSMITH, (Mary) Patricia. American novelist. Has also written as Claire Morgan. Born Mary Patricia Plangman in Fort Worth, Texas, 19 January 1921; took stepfather's name. Educated at Barnard College in Manhattan, B.A. 1942. Has spent much of her time living in Switzerland. Member of the Detection Club. **Recipient:** Mystery Writers of American Scroll and Grand Prix de Litterature Policiere, both 1957, for *The Talented Mr. Ripley;* Crime Writers Association of England Silver Dagger Award for best for-

eign crime novel of the year, 1964, for *The Two Faces of January;* Le Prix Litteraire, 1987. Agent: Aarianne Ligginstorfer, Diogenes Verlag, Sprechstrasse 8, 8032 Zurich, Switzerland.

WRITINGS

Novels

Strangers on a Train. New York, Harper, 1950.
The Price of Salt (as Claire Morgan). New York, Coward, 1952; reprinted with new afterword by the author, Tallahassee, Naiad Press, 1984.
The Blunderer. New York, Coward, 1954; as *Lament for a Lover,* New York, Popular Library, 1956.
The Talented Mr. Ripley. New York, Coward, 1955.
Deep Water. New York, Harper, 1957.
A Game for the Living. New York, Harper, 1958.
This Sweet Sickness. New York, Harper, 1960.
The Cry of the Owl. New York, Harper, 1962
The Two Faces of January. Garden City, New York, Doubleday, 1964.
The Glass Cell. Garden City, New York, Doubleday, 1964.
The Storyteller. Garden City, New York, Doubleday, 1965; published in England as *A Suspension of Mercy.*
Those Who Walk Away. Garden City, New York, Doubleday, 1967.
Ripley Under Ground. Garden City, New York, Doubleday, 1970.
A Dog's Ransom. New York, Knopf, 1972.
Ripley's Game. New York, Knopf, 1974.
Edith's Diary. New York, Simon and Schuster, 1977.
The Boy Who Followed Ripley. New York, Crowell, 1980.
People Who Knock on the Door. New York, Mysterious Press, 1983.
The Mysterious Mr. Ripley (contains *The Talented Mr. Ripley, Ripley Under Ground,* and *Ripley's Game*). New York, Penguin, 1985.
Found in the Street. New York, Atlantic Monthly, 1987.
Ripley Under Water. New York, Knopf, 1991.

Short Stories

The Snail Watchers and other Stories. Garden City, New York, Doubleday, 1970; published in England as *Eleven.*
Little Tales of Misogyny (in German). Berlin, Diogenes Verlag, 1974; English edition, London, Heinemann, 1977; New York, Mysterious Press, 1986.
The Animal Lover's Book of Beastly Murder. London, Heinemann, 1975.
Slowly, Slowly in the Wind. London, Heinemann, 1979; New York, Mysterious Press, 1984.
The Black House. New York, David and Charles, 1979.
Mermaids on the Golf Course, and Other Stories. London, Heinemann, 1985.
Tales of Natural and Unnatural Catastrophes. London, Heinemann, and New York, Atlantic Monthly, 1987.

Other

Plotting and Writing Suspense Fiction. New York, Writer's Inc., 1966.

Adaptations: *Strangers on a Train* was adapted for a film directed by Alfred Hitchcock; *The Talented Mr. Ripley* was filmed as *Purple Noon* by Louis Malle; and *Ripley's Game* was filmed as *The American Friend* by Wim Wenders; Highsmith's work has also been used as the basis for television scripts, particularly for the "Alfred Hitchcock Presents" series in the 1960s.

Critical Sources: *Don't Never Forget: Collected Views and Reviews* by Brigid Brophy, New York, Holt, 1966; *Mortal Consequences: A History—From the Detective Story to the Crime Novel* by Julian Symons, New York, Harper, 1972; *The Gay Novel in America* by James Levin, New York, Garland, 1991.

*   *   *

In her essay "Detective Fiction: The Modern Myth of Violence?" Brigid Brophy postulates that the popularity of the detective and crime novel is predicated not upon readers receiving a vicarious thrill in partaking in imaginary crime but in their relief that a perpetrator is always uncovered (and usually punished) at the end of the book. The emotional payoff of the crime novel isn't "who done it?" but the secure knowledge that the reader is (at least metaphorically) innocent. For Brophy, guilt is so integral to the contemporary human condition that readers need constant reassurance of their own innocence. The novels and stories of Patricia Highsmith posit an idiosyncratic response to Brophy's theorem because in them guilt and innocence are inextricably intertwined; often perpetrators go unpunished, while those who are technically innocent are punished. In Highsmith's world, "guilt" and "innocence" are relative, situational terms that depend more upon psychological states of mind than actual crimes or events.

Highsmith's output over four decades has been prodigious, including 20 crime novels, six collections of short crime fiction, and a how-to-book for suspense writing as one of the earliest, positive depictions of lesbian life. It has been her crime fiction, however, which has garnered the most acclaim. Her first novel, *Strangers on a Train,* was made into a classic film by Alfred Hitchcock and several of her other novels also made the transition to the screen, most notably *The Talented Mr. Ripley,* which was made into *Purple Noon* by Louis Malle, and *Ripley's Game,* which was filmed as *The American Friend* by Wim Wenders. Highsmith's work has also been used as the basis for television scripts, particularly for the "Alfred Hitchcock Presents" series in the 1960s.

Much of Highsmith's fiction begins with ingenious, if contrived, plot devices—the traded murders of *Strangers on a Train,* the complicated foreign intrigue in *The Two Faces of January,* the elaborate forgery in *Ripley Under Ground*—but it is a finely honed psychological insight and delicate ironic sensibility that gives Highsmith's work its depth and resonance. It is the author's understanding of the intricacies of human nature that allows her to place her unpleasant characters in such unsavory situations and never let us lose sympathy for them. In Highsmith's work, the conscious act and the unconscious wish are never far apart; it is not uncommon in her books that a character wished dead by an enemy suddenly turns up dead or at least missing. Her genius is in allowing the reader to partake in crossing this thin line between desire and action, guilt and innocence.

Although most of Highsmith's male characters are ostensibly heterosexual, a strong theme of male homoeroticism runs through

her work. In *Strangers on a Train,* the psychopathic Charles Bruno is characterized by such traditional homosexual male signifiers as a doting mother and a meticulous personal appearance. In the five books that chart the criminal career of Tom Ripley, Highsmith carefully plays at a homoerotic context in all of his male relationships even though Ripley enters into a heterosexual marriage and would never consider himself a homosexual. This homoeroticism is particularly strong in *The Talented Mr. Ripley,* the first of the series, as well as in *The Boy Who Followed Ripley.* This latter novel featured scenes in several gay bars, Ripley disguising himself by showing up in full drag, and a 16–year–old patricidal boy who falls in love with the protagonist. There are also strong hints of homoeroticism in such novels as *A Game For the Living* (1958), *The Two Faces of January, A Dog's Ransom,* and *People Who Knock on the Door.*

The persistence of male homoeroticism in Highsmith's work is indicative of, and consistent with, her interest in guilt and the unconscious. While none of Highsmith's characters who exhibit homoerotic feelings are particularly positive—everyone in Highsmith's world is, to some degree, guilty—they are not judged or condemned for their sexual desires. Male homoeroticism, for Highsmith, seems to signify for the writer an almost platonic state of natural desire and social transgression, of sexual innocence and societal guilt.

Interestingly, Highsmith's one overtly lesbian novel, *The Price of Salt,* is a fairly realistic look at lesbian lives in the 1950s. Although Highsmith is fully aware of the pressures of homophobia, the book is distinguished by a happy ending. This stands in sharp contrast not only to the bulk of writings about homosexuals of the period but also to the rest of Highsmith's work which dwells, sometimes unremittingly, on the precariousness and instability of human emotions and relationships. Because *The Price of Salt* is an isolated work—there is nothing else like it in Highsmith's oeuvre—it is unclear if she intends it to be a psychological statement about lesbian sexuality. Because it was written and published at a time when most depictions of lesbianism or male homosexuality required some form of punishment it was, and remains, a political statement.

Although Highsmith has a reputation as a crime novelist, it is a category that is far too narrow to suit the breadth and range of her psychological perceptions and her talents as a writer. Patricia Highsmith's work is essentially a meditation on what it means to be human—and therefore, in her terms, guilty—in the twentieth century.

—*Michael Bronskl*

————

HILD, Jack. *See* **PRESTON, John.**

————

HIRSCHFELD, Magnus. German physician, editor, and writer on the subject of sexuality. Also wrote as Th. Ramien. Born in Kolberg, Prussia (now Kolobrzeg, Poland), 14 May 1868. Educated in Breslau, Strasbourg, Munich, and Berlin; received M.D. Practiced medicine in Magdeburg, Saxony, and Charlottenburg, Berlin. On 14 May 1897, founded the Wissenschaftlich–humanitäre

Komitee, dedicated in general to the overthrow of legal intolerance of homosexuals in Germany. Editor of *Jahrbuch für sexuelle Zwischenstufen* (23 volumes), beginning 1899. Presided over conferences of the World League for Sexual Reform on a Scientific Basis, Berlin, 1921, Copenhagen, 1928, London, 1929, and Vienna, 1930. Travelled the world on a lecture tour, beginning November 1931, collecting material for the Institute for Sexual Science in Berlin. Fled Germany after the Nazis came to power, settling in France. *Died in Nice, France, 14 May 1935.*

WRITINGS

Nonfiction

Sappho und Sokrates (as Th. Ramien). [Germany], 1896.
Der urnische Mensch. Leipzig, M. Spohr, 1903.
Die Homosexualität des Mannes und des Weibes. Berlin, L. Marcus, 1914.
Warum hassen uns die Völker? Eine Kriegspsychologische betrachtung von dr. Magnus Hirschfeld. Bonn, A. Marcus and E. Weber, 1915.
Kriegspsychologisches. Bonn, A. Marcus and E. Weber, 1916.
Verstaatlichung des gesundheitswesens. Berlin, Verlag neues vaterland, E. Berger, 1919.
With Berndt Götz, *Sexualgeschichte der menschheit.* Berlin, P. Langenscheidr Gmbh., 1929.
With Richard Linsert, *Liebesmittel: Eine darstellung der geschlechtlichen reixmittel.* Berlin, Man, 1930.
With Ewald Bohm, *Sexualerziehung: Der weg durch natürlichkeit zur neuen moral.* Berlin, Universitas, deutsche verlags-aktiengesellschaft, 1930.
Geschlechtskunde. Stuttgart, J. Püttmann, 1930.
Geschlecht und verbrechen. Leipzig, Schneider, 1930.
Editor, *Sittengeschichte der jüngsten seit: Eine darstellung der kultur, sittlichkeit und erotik des zwanzigsten jahrhunderts.* Leipsig, Schneider, 1930.
Sittengeschichte des weltkriegs. Leipzig, Schneider, 1930.
Sexual Pathology, Being a Study of the Abnormalities of the Sexual Functions: An Exhaustive Treatise on Sexual Symbolism, Hypereroticism, Impotence, etc.: Based upon Research, Observations and Recent Clinical Data Gathered at the Institute for Sexual Science in Berlin, translation by Jerome Gibbs. Newark, Julian Press, 1932; new edition translated by Jerome Gibbs as *Sexual Pathology: A Study of Derangements of the Sexual Instinct,* New York, Emerson Books, 1939.
Die weltreise eines sexualforschers, mit 47 abbildungen. Brugge, Bözberg–verlag, 1933; translated by O. P. Green as *Men and Women: The World Journey of a Sexologist,* New York, Putnam, and as *Women East and West: Impressions of a Sex Expert,* London, Heinemann, 1935.
La science et l'amour, par le dr. Magnus Hirschfeld. L'âme et l'amour, psychologie sexologique. Paris, Gallimard, 1935; translated by John Rodker as *Sex in Human Relationships,* London, John Lane, 1935.
Sexual Anomalies and Perversions, Physical and Psychological Development and Treatment: A Summary of the Works of the Late Professor Dr. Magnus Hirschfeld ... Compiled as a Humble Memorial by His Pupils: A Textbook for Students, Psychologists, Criminologists, Probation Officers, Judges, and Educationists.
London, F. Aldor, 1936.
Racism, edited and translated by Eden and Cedar Paul. London, Gollancz, 1938.
With Andreas Gaspar, *Sittengeschichte der beiden Weltkriege sowie der Zwischen– und Nachkriegszeit:* Volume 1: *Sittengeschichte der beiden Weltkriege sowie der Zwischen– und Nachkriegszeit;* Volume 2: *Sittengeschichte des Ersten Weltkrieges;* Volume 3: *Zwischen zwei Katastrophen,* Hanau, Schustek, 1966.
The Transvestites: The Erotic Urge to Cross–Dress, translation by Michael A. Lombardi–Nash. Buffalo, New York, Prometheus Books, 1991.

*

Biography: *Magnus Hirschfeld: A Portrait of a Pioneer in Sexology* by Charlotte Wolff, London, Quartet Books, 1986; *Magnus Hirschfeld: Leben und Werk eines jüdischen, schwulen und sozialistischen Sexologen* by Manfred Herzer, Frankfurt am Main and New York, Campus Verlag, 1992.

Bibliography: *The Writings of Dr. Magnus Hirschfeld: A Bibliography* by James D. Steakley, Toronto, Canadian Gay Archives, 1985.

Critical Sources: "Homosexual Emancipation in Germany before 1933: Two Traditions" by Harry Oosterhuis, in *Journal of Homosexuality,* November 1991, 1–27.

*   *   *

Born in Kolberg on the Baltic coast of Prussia (today Kolobrzeg in Poland) in 1868, Magnus Hirschfeld settled in Charlottenburg, a suburb of Berlin, where from 1896 onward he became the world's leading authority on homosexuality in his lifetime and the founder of the Wissenschaftlich–humanitäre Komitee (Scientific–Humanitarian Committee), the world's first homosexual rights organization. Throughout his life he unceasingly published books, articles, and pamphlets on homosexuality and other facets of sexual psychology, and founded and edited the first scientific journal dedicated to the subject, the *Jahrbuch für sexuelle Zwischenstufen,* which appeared in 23 volumes between 1899 and 1923. Exiled from his homeland by National Socialist persecution and deprived of German citizenship, he died in Nice in 1935.

When Magnus Hirschfeld founded the Komitee in 1897, his intellectual and political resources were ones inherited from his predecessors. First of all, he uncritically accepted the umbrella concept of homosexuality invented by Karl Heinrich Ulrichs and Károly Mária Kertbeny in the 1860s, with the neo–Aristotelian gloss that it was inborn and "natural." This concept he sought to locate in the framework of the Darwinian biology that in progressive circles had acquired the status of dogma, and he did so by devising the notion that homosexuals were an evolutionary "third sex," intermediate between the male and the female. Such an assertion he sought to validate by statistical data that projected the image of an individual with marked inversion of secondary and tertiary sexual characteristics. This theory was in keeping with the folk beliefs that had existed since antiquity, recognizing homosexuals as being visibly different from others. Hirschfeld was forced to turn a blind eye to the fact that the majority of predominantly or exclusively homosexual individuals are not of this stamp; the atypical pederast of both ancient and modern times has never existed.

What Hirschfeld and his forerunners could not revive was the pagan Greek religion, which had conferred the blessing and example of the gods on pederasty. They had, however, a vast corpus of classical texts referring to homoerotic relationships between adults and children in positive, even glowing terms——but Hirschfeld himself was no apologist for pederasty. With the heritage of classical antiquity he played a double game. On the one hand he sought to appropriate it in order to prove that homosexuality had a positive, noble, heroic side; but on the other—in his never–ending struggle for repeal of paragraph 175 of the Penal Code of the German Reich that criminalized male homosexuality—he asked that the age of consent be raised from 14 to 16. This change would effectively have excluded the modern pederast from any benefit of the law. Hirschfeld's political stance was therefore contorted if not riddled with dishonesty, and by 1910 he placed ever less emphasis on the "third sex" concept—a concession that left the collectivity of those attracted to their own sex undefined.

This was a gap his collaborator Kurt Hiller attempted to fill when in the spring of 1918, in the wake of the discussion of minority rights provoked by President Wilson's Fourteen Points, Hiller defined homosexuals as a biological minority equally deserving of tolerance and protection. But the whole weight of the Judeo–Christian tradition, which in this sphere of life had survived intact the assaults of the Enlightenment and of classical liberalism, still precluded acceptance of this principle. Furthermore, the image of a national minority was too clearly etched in the European mind, not just by theoretical analyses but by everyday experience, for lovers of their own sex to be accorded such a privileged status. So the movement led by Hirschfeld never gained the validation which it sought by "scientific" and legal arguments.

Throughout his 39–year career as a champion of homosexual rights, Hirschfeld steadfastly and uncompromisingly upheld the neo–Aristotelian view that true, primary homosexuality is inborn, constitutionally determined, spontaneous, and unmodifiable by any accident of psychological development or chance vicissitude in the life of the individual. He firmly rejected the neo–Thomistic conception of homosexuality as secondary and acquired by fixation at an immature stage of psychosexual development, seduction in adolescence, or vicious habit in adulthood. He thus faithfully continued the tradition of the movement begun by Karl Heinrich Ulrichs, but strove to give it a more scientific foundation.

Hirschfeld's magnum opus, 1914's *Die Homosexualität des Mannes und des Weibes,* remains even now the fullest and most comprehensive synthetic work ever written on the subject, and for those who are able to consult it, an inexhaustible treasury of information, including references to hundreds of now forgotten books and articles written between 1864 and 1913. Its 39 chapters and three indexes summarize virtually everything that had been learned in the Germany of the Second Reich. If the approaches of modern depth psychology, gender studies, and literary criticism were lacking, it was because they lay beyond the intellectual horizon of that day.

Hirschfeld never resolved the contradictions inherent in the theological–forensic concept of homosexuality which he had inherited from his predecessors. Although his own empirical findings showed that homosexual individuals run the entire gamut from those who exhibit the perfect normal type of their sex to those who possess little more of the sex to which society conventionally assigns them

than the genital organs, he persisted in relating homosexuality to evolutionary intersexuality. Even though he applied the logic of a separatist movement in claiming that sexual orientation was biologically determined and unalterable, as an assimilated Jew writing on the racial question, he echoed the assimilationist line of the Central Association of German Citizens of the Jewish Faith—heedless of the incompatibility between them. While always claiming the legacy of the *paiderasteia* of Greco–Roman antiquity for homosexuality, he permanently and irrevocably alienated the leaders of the pederastic wing of the German movement, who felt no identity with the effeminate homosexuals and viraginous lesbians whom he paraded as proof of his theories. Although he was a Social Democrat and a member of the Sozialistische Ärzteverein, the program of the sexual reform movement to which he belonged was in the final analysis individualistic—a tendency that led the Marxist–Leninist parties ultimately to repudiate it after 1933. Last of all, he could not give his followers a self–definition and a collective identity acceptable to German society. This failure doomed his lifelong campaign for toleration.

Reviled by the National Socialists as "one of the most repulsive monstrosities that even the Semitic race has ever produced," Hirschfeld nevertheless bequeathed a precious legacy, if not to the American gay rights movement, which scarcely knew his work and his theories, at least to future researchers, who will find in the vast corpus of material that he assembled and published both a stimulus and a challenge to refine the concepts that he formulated. It is these future researchers who will attempt to structure the ever–increasing data on love for one's own sex into a coherent multi–dimensional picture.

—*Warren Johansson*

———

HIRSHFELD, Richard. *See* HALL, Richard W(alter).

———

HOCQUENGHEM, Guy. French novelist, short story writer, and journalist. Born in the suburbs of Paris in 1946. Educated at Lycée Henri–IV, École Normale Supérieure. Radical activist in the 1968 movement in France, a leader in the Front Homosexuel d'Action Révolutionnaire (FHAR); became professor of philosophy at University of Paris, Vincennes–St. Denis; columnist for *Libération* and *Gai–Pied Hebdo. Died in Paris, of AIDS–related causes, 28 August 1988.*

WRITINGS

Nonfiction

Le désir homosexuel. Paris, Éditions universitaires, 1972.
L'Après–Mai des faunes: volutions. Paris, B. Grasset, 1974.
Co–ire: album systématique de l'enfance. Fontenay–sous–Bois, France, Revue du Cerfi, 1976.
La dérive homosexuelle. Paris, J.–P. Delarge, 1977.

With Jean Louis Bory, *Comment nous appelez–vous déjà? Ces hommes que l'on dit homosexuels.* Paris, Calmann–Levy, 1977.

La beauté du métis: reflexions d'un francophobe. Paris, Ramsay, 1979.

Le gay voyage: guide et regard homosexuels sur les grandes métropoles. Paris, Albin Michel, 1980.

With Jean Luc Hennig, *Les français de la honte: la morale des Français d'aujourd'hui racontée par eux–mêmes.* Paris, Albin Michel, 1983.

With René Scherer, *L'âme atomique: pour une esthétique d'ère nucléaire.* Paris, Albin Michel, 1986.

Lettre ouverte à ceux qui sont passés du col Mao au Rotary. Paris, Albin Michel, 1986.

With René Scherer, *Pari sur l'impossible: études fouriéristes.* Saint–Denis, Presses Universitaire de Vincennes, 1989.

Novels

L'amour en relief. Paris, Albin Michel, 1982.
Les petits garçons. Paris, Albin Michel, 1983.
La colère de l'agneau. Paris, Albin Michel, 1985.
Eve. Paris, Albin Michel, 1987.
Les voyages et aventures extraordinaires du frère Angelo. Paris, Albin Michel, 1988.

Other

Fin de Section (stories). Paris, C. Bourgois, 1975.
Race d'Ep!: un siècle d'images de l'homosexualité (screenplay and commentary). Paris, Hallier, 1979.
With Lionel Soukaz, *Race d'Ep!* (film adaptation), 1979.
Minigraphie de la presse parisienne (commentary on Honoré de Balzac's *Monographie de la presse parisienne,* published in same volume). Paris, Albin Michel/J.E. Hallier, 1981.

*

Biography: "L'écrivain Guy Hocquenghem est mort: la beauté du métis" by René de Ceccatty, in *Le Monde* (Paris), 30 August 1988, 34; "Le voyage extraordinaire de frère Guy" by Gilles Anquetil, in *Nouvel Observateur* (Paris), 2–8 September 1988, 30–31.

Interviews: "La révolution des homosexuels" by François Paul–Boncour, in *Nouvel Observateur* (Paris), 10–16 January 1972, 32–35; "The New French Culture" by Douglas Crimp, in *October* (Cambridge, Massachusetts), winter 1981, 105–117.

Critical Sources: "L'apocalypse selon saint Guy Hocquenghem" by Grégoire Mataro, in *Le Monde des Livres* (Paris), 8 November 1985, 29; "Hocquenghem vend la mêche" by Guillaume Faye, in *Eléments Pour la Civilisation Européene,* autumn 1986, 54–55; "*Eve* de Guy Hocquenghem: Enfin un roman nécessaire" by Bertrand Poirot–Delpech, in *Le Monde des Livres,* 18 September 1987, 15; "Guy Hocquenghem: *Les Voyages et aventures extraordinaire du frère Angelo*" by Vincent Landel, in *Magazine Litteraire,* October 1988, 92–93; "The Best of Times, the Worst of Times: the Emerging Literature of AIDS in France" by David Wetsel, in *AIDS: the Literary Response,* edited by Emmanuel S. Nelson, Twayne Publishers, New York, 1992, 95–113.

Among American readers of gay and lesbian literature, Guy Hocquenghem is not a well–known name, yet in the French–speaking West, he is one of the central figures in the "post–Stonewall" gay and lesbian movement. Because little of Hocquenghem's work has been translated into English, his relative obscurity is understandable; as yet, only one of his theoretical works, *Le désir homosexuel* (*Homosexual Desire*) and his first novel, *L'amour en relief* (*Love in Relief*), have been published in English translations (and the former into several other languages as well). It is likely, too, that Hocquenghem's leftist positions, his work in a collage of non–traditional and traditional literary forms, and his overlapping theoretical approaches to the better– known figures of Michel Foucault and the team of Gilles Deleuze and Félix Guattari have made him less likely to be translated.

Hocquenghem became a celebrity in January 1972, after giving an interview to *Nouvel Observateur* in which he discussed his coming of age in the gay rights and leftist movements and his desire to reconcile these radical movements in his own life. The author became an articulate spokesman for "Le Front Homosexuel d'Action Révolutionnaire" (FHAR, or the Homosexual Movement for Revolutionary Action), continuing his leadership by pamphleteering not only for gay and lesbian rights, but also against French insularity and bourgeois values. Along with his stance regarding homosexual rights, Hocquenghem's dedication to anti–racism is also evident in his polemical and fictional works, especially in those books that explore the relationship between the French and their largest immigrant group, the North Africans.

Hocquenghem's theoretical works on homosexuality mesh well with what is now called "Queer Theory." In his preface to *L'Après–Mai des faunes,* Deleuze describes one of Hocquenghem's central ideas: "L'homosexuel ne serait pas celui qui en reste au *même* sexe, mais celui qui découvre d'innombrable sexes dont nous n'avons pas l'idée?" (Wouldn't the homosexual not be one who stays with the *same* sex, but one who discovers innumerable sexes which we have not conceived?) Hocquenghem often restated Foucault's prescription that "bodies and pleasure," not sexual identities, should prevail. In his introduction to *Homosexual Desire,* Hocquenghem attributes some specificity to homosexual desire, noting that "homosexuality expresses something—some aspect of desire—which appears nowhere else, and that something is not merely the accomplishment of the sexual act with a person of the same sex." Despite his critical theoretical analysis of homosexuality as an adopted identity, Hocquenghem was not only active in gay politics and publishing; he also wrote specifically about the gay subculture in works such as the travel guide, *Le gay voyage.* Hocquenghem also broke the taboo surrounding the discussion of childhood sexuality in *Les petits garçons* and, in his novel *Eve,* continued his rejection of Freudian psychological explanations for sexuality.

The variety and quality of Hocquenghem's literary productions was considerable for his short life, yet he is likely to be remembered primarily for specific works like *Homosexual Desire, La beauté du métis,* and for his novels. Both *Eve* and *Love in Relief* are especially interesting in that they contain elements of science fiction that explore the connections between the human body and technology. Hocquenghem's theme of twin or dual existence is evident most strongly in *Eve,* in which twin characters named Adam and Eve share the exact chromosomal material. The novel's description of intrusive medical procedures makes literal Hocquenghem's historical and theoretical discussion about the invasion of bodies by modern technologies. *Love in Relief* also describes a drastic bodily invasion as government scientists secretly implant a vision prosthesis onto the head of a young, blind Tunisian man named Amar, who previously learned about bodies through touch, smell, taste, and hearing. In the novel, science's creeping technical manipulation of the body serves as counterpoint to Amar's free–floating sexual experiences, which he refuses to define using the "scientific" terms of homosexuality or bisexuality. He states: "I have no sexual tastes, in your sense of the word. The imaginary is reserved for the sighted. Thus I am not homosexual."

Hocquenghem's final two novels, *Les voyages extraordinaires du frère Angelo,* and *La colère de l'agneau,* feature early Christian figures as central characters (in the former, a Renaissance monk; in the latter, St. John, the "beloved of Christ"). Though these novels are far removed in setting from Hocquenghem's other works, they share with the author's earlier novels the theme of "bodies and pleasure." In these works, Hocquenghem rewrites the history of Christianity to unveil its earliest Gnostic elements and to disavow the present church's fascination with the suppression of the body and submission of the spirit.

Hocquenghem's early death from AIDS–related causes at age 42 ended in midstream a creative, scholarly, and activist life. Still, Hocquenghem left the reader of French—and perhaps in the future the reader of English—with an intelligent, spirited, multi–faceted legacy.

—*Terry L. Allison*

————

HOLLERAN, Andrew. Pseudonym. American novelist and non-fiction writer. Born c. 1943. Educated at Harvard University; University of Iowa. Served with U.S. Army in West Germany (now Germany).

WRITINGS

Novels

Dancer from the Dance. New York, Morrow, 1978.
Nights in Aruba. New York, Morrow, 1983.

Short Stories

"Nipples," in *Aphrodisiac: Fiction from Christopher Street.* New York, Coward, McCann & Geoghgan, 1980.
"Ties," in *First Love/Last Love: New Fiction from Christopher Street,* edited by Michael Denneny, Charles Ortleb and Thomas Steele. New York, Putnam, 1985.
"Friends at Evening," in *Men on Men,* edited by George Stambolian. New York, Plume, 1986.
"Lights in the Valley," in *Men on Men 3,* edited by George Stambolian. New York, Plume, 1990.
"Sunday Morning: Key West," in *The Faber Book of Gay Short Fiction,* edited by Edmund White. London and New York, Faber & Faber, 1991.

Essays

"Four by Andrew Holleran: Nostalgia for the Mud; Fast–Food Sex; Dark Disco; Male Nudes and Nude Males," in *The Christopher Street Reader,* edited by Michael Denneny, Chuck Ortleb and Thomas Steele. New York, Coward–McCann, 1983.
"The Fear," in *Personal Dispatches: Writers Confront AIDS,* edited by John Preston. New York, St. Martin's Press, 1988.
Ground Zero. New York, Morrow, 1988.
"An Essay," in *Tribe* (Baltimore), spring 1990.
"My Uncle Sitting Beneath the Tree," in *A Member of the Family,* edited by John Preston. New York, Dutton, 1992.

Other

Author of introduction, *The Normal Heart* by Larry Kramer. New York, New American Library, 1985.
Author of afterword, *Men on Men 4,* edited by George Stambolian. New York, Dutton, 1992.

*

Critical Sources: *The Gay Novel* by James Levine, New York, Irvington Publishers, 1983; *Gayiety Transigured: Gay Self–Representation in American Literature* by David Bergman, Madison, University of Wisconsin Press, 1991.

* * *

When Andrew Holleran's *Dancer from the Dance* was published in 1978 it was an immediate popular and critical success. This was probably the first time a post–Stonewall gay novel captured the attention of mainstream reviewers. (Although such varied books as Gore Vidal's 1948 *The City and the Pillar,* James Baldwin's 1956 *Giovanni's Room,* and John Rechy's 1963 *City of Night* had attracted critical attention from the national press, they were not identified as belonging to the distinct genre of "gay fiction.") The positive reception of *Dancer from the Dance* set a standard for acceptance that much gay male and lesbian literature has attempted to live up to ever since. And although *Dancer from the Dance* seemed to appear out of nowhere—at least for mainstream critics, who had not been paying attention to the burgeoning field of gay writing that began around 1969—the novel and its author had secure roots in a contemporary and historical gay male sensibility.

The birth of the gay liberation movement in 1969 brought about an explosion of new venues for cultural and artistic expression as well opening up new venues for gay work. Along with the founding of openly gay, and overtly political newspapers, journals and magazines such as *Come Out* (Manhattan), *Gay Sunshine* (San Francisco) and *Fag Rag* (Boston), gay men in many cities also formed writers groups in which they discussed ideas and politics, shared their work and supported one another. In Manhattan, The Violet Quill Club—with members Felice Picano, Edmund White, Michael Grumley, Robert Ferro, George Whitmore, Christopher Cox and Andrew Holleran—met irregularly to discuss the potential as well as the problems of autobiographical fiction. *Dancer from the Dance* was one of the first works of gay fiction to be published by a Violet

Quill member. (Edmund White's *Nocturnes for the King of Naples* also came out in 1970.)

Although the subject matter of *Dancer from the Dance* was drawn from the glittering disco world of Manhattan's gay male nightlife, the book's tone was meditative, almost melancholic. Its main character, a beautiful young man named Malone, transverses the gay social world looking for salvation in the form of emotional or erotic transcendence. By re-creating, in hallucinatory imagery, New York City's sexual underground and by idealizing Malone as a beautiful lost soul, Holleran managed to invent—and join together—two complimentary mythologies: the jaded, sexual, material world juxtaposed with the reactions and experience of the young, unspoiled innocent. This first world was described earlier by such writers as John Rechy (in *City of Night* and *Numbers*) and served as the background for many of the pulp novels with gay male themes that were popular in the 1950s and 1960s.

The idea of the uncorrupted, homoerotic innocent originated in the poetry of the Uranian writers of the Victorian era and has continued to appear in gay writing ever since. By updating these themes to the very contemporary worlds of disco and Fire Island, Holleran created a new version of old gay myths that resonated with contemporary, post–Stonewall readers. While much gay male literature of the period was intent on vocalizing the idea that "gay is good" as a much needed remedy to accepted social, moral and legal homophobia, Holleran's gay world had a dark side as well.

Holleran published his much awaited second novel in 1983. *Nights in Aruba* also told the story of an innocent who is torn between the personal, social and political freedom of gay life and his duties as a son to his aging parents. This theme of split desire echoed *Dancer from the Dance* and while the first book posited the dichotomy as innocence and experience, the second manifested it as the difference between a closeted, ostensibly heterosexual life and an open gay one. Although *Nights in Aruba* was well–received by gay and straight critics it did not have the huge social impact of *Dancer from the Dance.* This was possibly because AIDS was beginning to emerge as *the* most important issue in the gay male community and most other discussions about coming out, dealing with family and inventing a new social and physical world that accommodated homosexuality seemed less pressing. It was at this time that Andrew Holleran moved from New York City, where he had spend the better part of a decade, to a small town near Gainsville, Florida.

Andrew Holleran began writing essays about AIDS—mostly for *Christopher Street*—in the mid–1980s. These were collected in *Ground Zero* and in a surprising way they are a continuation and an obverse reflection of the world of *Dancer from the Dance.* The sense of doom and a tragic underside to gay sexuality that permeates Holleran's writing in *Dancer,* and to a lesser degree *Nights in Aruba,* has completely manifested itself in *Ground Zero.* But Holleran is careful never to make easy analogies that imply that AIDS is somehow a natural result of gay male sexual activity, as others have done. The sense of doom and despair in *Dancer* is a metaphysical condition of being human. In all of his essays on AIDS Holleran takes a forthrightly, materialistic position: AIDS is a physical condition that is caused by a virus, it has no other meanings.

Holleran is even suspicious about his own inclination and ability to write about AIDS. In an essay published in *Tribe,* Holleran writes: "I'm horrified to say this, but in a real sense AIDS is incredible material. It's not material in the sense that it's an aesthetic object, because it's happening and it's too real. At the time AIDS began not only did I not want to write about it, I also felt deeply

worthless writing about it. I felt that of all the things you can do about AIDS, writing about it is one of the most pointless."

Much of *Ground Zero* has to do with Holleran's attempt to find a comfortable way to write about AIDS. If art and literature is an act of transformation, how is it possible to transform this basic terrible, and terrifying, fact of the human condition? In *Ground Zero* Holleran writes about friends who have died, memories from pre–AIDS years, the limitations of art, and the inescapable state of mourning in which he and many of his friends live. In an attempt to describe AIDS—not the disease, but the state of a culture living with the disease—Holleran spends most of his time writing around it, discussing the reflections, circumstances and parameters of what he calls "the plague" rather than the illness itself. What is most evident in Holleran's writings on AIDS is how the idea of family—once posited in *Nights in Aruba* as antithetical to the social and sexual camaraderie of gay life—now takes on new meanings. While *Dancer from the Dance* offers a look at gay social relationships, they are not as resonant as the nuclear family ties of *Nights in Aruba.* Throughout *Ground Zero* Holleran describes the love and caretaking exhibited by a gay male community in the same terms he had earlier ascribed to biological families.

AIDS, in *Ground Zero,* is too huge, too indefinite, and too complex an experience to capture in the act of writing. The essays in *Ground Zero* are some of the best writing that has been done about AIDS precisely because Holleran realizes, and admits, not only the limits of art, but the limits of human understanding as well.

—*Michael Bronski*

HOLLINGHURST, Alan. British poet and novelist. Born in Stroud, Gloucestershire, 26 May 1954. Educated at Magdalen College, Oxford, B.A. 1975, M.Litt. 1979. *Times Literary Supplement,* London, assistant editor, 1982–84, deputy editor, 1985–90, poetry editor, 1991—.

WRITINGS

Contributor, *Poetry Introduction Four.* London, Faber, 1978.
Confidential Chats with Boys (verse). Oxford, Sycamore Press, 1982.
Contributor, *LRB Anthology.* Junction, 1983.
"A Thieving Boy," in *Firebird Two.* London, Penguin, 1983.
The Swimming–Pool Library (novel). London, Chatto & Windus, 1988; New York, Random House, 1989.
"The Swimming–Pool Library" (excerpt), in *The Faber Book of Gay Short Fiction,* edited by Edmund White. London and New York, Faber & Faber, 1991.

*

Critical Sources: "Last Summer" by Jon Savage, in *New Statesman,* 4 March 1988, 27; "Not Every Age Has Its Pleasures" by

Catherine R. Stimpson, in *New York Times Book Review,* 9 October 1988, 8.

*   *   *

Alan Hollinghurst is known primarily for the novel *The Swimming–Pool Library,* a story in the colonialist tradition of gay male writing. His early poetry and short stories, often concerned with gay issues, is not widely available. *Confidential Chats with Boys,* an early book of verse, consists of only five 20–line poems. The title seems to derive from a pre–World War I sexual advice book which at least in part warns boys against the approaches of homosexual men. "There are things in trousers called men," begins the first of the five witty, sad poems which describe a gay childhood. The slim pamphlet appeared in 1982, the same year in which Hollinghurst began as Assistant Editor of the *Times Literary Supplement.*

Hollinghurst's novel, *The Swimming–Pool Library,* gained significant critical attention at the time of its publication, first in London in 1988, then in New York in 1989. The enigmatic title refers to the protagonist's role of prefect at his school's swimming pool; all roles as prefect were called "librarian." This nostalgic use of an arcane term in many ways characterizes the novel, which firmly places itself in a male, British, homoerotic, but also a colonialist tradition in which men of the upper classes seek erotic adventure through contacts with exotic foreigners or the romanticized working class. This same tradition is also displayed in Hollinghurst's earlier "A Thieving Boy" in 1983, a story of betrayal which also depicts male English homosexual desire wandering abroad for satisfaction.

Set in 1983, *The Swimming–Pool Library* is the first–person narrative of an upper class, educated but unambitious William Beckwith. (Beckwith's name echoes that of earlier gay writer William Beckford, author of *Oriental Tales.*) In an interview for the *New York Times Book Review,* Hollinghurst denied any resemblance between himself and his protagonist. The novel is unabashedly male and homosexual; and when it appeared, *The Swimming–Pool Library* was celebrated as a paean to the pre–AIDS era of seemingly unfettered sexual contact. Early in the novel Beckwith reflects, "I was riding high on sex and self–esteem—it was my time, my *belle époque*—but all the while with a taint flicker of calamity, like flames around a photograph, something seen out of the corner of the eye." That something, presumably, is AIDS.

Beckwith's history intersects with that of Lord Nantwich. While cruising in a public lavatory, Nantwich collapses and Beckwith revives him. The novel's great irony is that Nantwich, 83, an old colonial hand, had suffered from the persecution of Beckwith's financial benefactor, his grandfather, who conducted a 1950s' campaign of homosexual persecution. Nantwich draws Beckwith into writing his biography. During the course of his research, Beckwith finally learns that his current wealth and leisure have in part been built upon the ruin of Nantwich's and other gay men's careers. Paralleling Beckwith's relationship with his grandfather, Hollinghurst establishes a gay male genealogy which links Beckwith to Nantwich, the post–colonial to the colonial. Beckwith's occasional readings of Nantwich's early diaries, which include a number of well–known gay male figures from the first half of the twentieth century, also assert male homosexuality as an unbroken historical tradition, a tradition into which Hollinghurst, by writing this novel, also inserts himself.

The Swimming–Pool Library depicts an almost exclusively male society. Though Beckwith's mother is mentioned and his sister once speaks on the telephone, all other characters are male. Even the opera which some characters attend is *Billy Budd,* a shipboard opera with an all–male cast by a gay male composer, Benjamin Britten. In this world absent of women, Hollinghurst revels in the naked physicality of men, but also depicts a wide range of male–male relationships: grandfather to grandson; friend to friend; brother to brother (though in–laws); uncle to nephew; patron to patronized; lover to lover.

Hollinghurst writes convincingly, sometimes beautifully, as in the oxymoron at the end of the phrase "spoken in a uniquely homosexual tone of bored outrage." Although the colonialist tradition has inspired Hollinghurst's always fluid, sometimes brilliant writing, Jon Savage, in his review for *New Statesman,* finds that "the book's apparent snobbery masks a sharp look at the English class system."

—*Terry L. Allison*

———

HOUSMAN, A(lfred) E(dward). British poet and editor. Also wrote as Tristram. Born in Fockbury, Worcestershire, 26 March 1859. Educated at St. John's College, Oxford, pass degree 1882; M.A. Civil servant with Her Majesty's Patent Office, London, 1882–92; professor of Latin, University College, London, 1892–1911; Kennedy Professor of Latin, Trinity College, Cambridge, 1911–36. Founder with A. W. Pollard of undergraduate periodical *Ye Rounde Table* and contributor (as Tristram). *Died in Cambridge, c. 30 April 1936.*

WRITINGS

Poetry

A Shropshire Lad. London, Kegan Paul, 1896; with notes and biography by Carl J. Weber, Westport, Connecticut, Greenwood Press, 1980.
Last Poems. New York, Holt, 1922.
More Poems, edited by Laurence Houseman. New York, Knopf, 1936.
The Collected Poems of A. E. Housman. London, J. Cape, 1939; New York, Holt, 1940; revised as *Collected Poems,* introduction by John Sparrow, New York, Penguin Books, 1956.
Manuscript Poems: Eight Hundred Lines of Hitherto Uncollected Verse from the Author's Notebooks, edited by Tom Burns Haber. Minneapolis, University of Minnesota Press, 1955; as *The Manuscript Poems of A. E. Housman: Eight Hundred Lines of Hitherto Uncollected Verse from the Author's Notebooks,* Oxford, Oxford University Press, 1955.
Complete Poems: Centennial Edition, introduction by Basil Davenport, commentary by Tom Burns Haber. New York, Holt, 1959.

Editor

With others, *M. Manilii Astronomica* (five volumes). Grant Richards, 1903–30; as *Astronomicon*, Georg Olms, 1972.

D. Junii Juvenalis Saturae. Grant Richards, 1905; revised, Cambridge, Cambridge University Press, 1931; as *Saturae*, London, Greenwood Press, 1969.

M. Annaei Lucani Belli civilis libri decem. Oxford, Basil Blackwell, 1926; Cambridge, Harvard University Press, 1950.

Lectures

Introductory Lecture Delivered in University College, London. Cambridge, Cambridge University Press, 1892; New York, Macmillan, 1937.

The Name and Nature of Poetry (criticism). New York, Macmillan, 1933.

The Confines of Criticism: The Cambridge Inaugural, 1911, with notes by John Carter. Cambridge, Cambridge University Press, 1969.

Letters

Thirty Housman Letters to Witter Bynner, edited by Tom Burns Haber. New York, Knopf, 1957.

A. E. Housman to Joseph Ishill: Five Unpublished Letters, edited by William White. Oriole Press, 1959.

The Letters of A. E. Housman, edited by Henry Maas. Cambridge, Harvard University Press, 1971.

Sir James G. Frazer and A. E. Housman: A Relationship in Letters. Dunham, North Carolina, Duke University Press, 1974.

Fifteen Letters to Walter Ashburner, with notes and introduction by Alan S. Bell. Tragara Press, c. 1976.

Collections

A Centennial Memento, commentary by William White. Oriole Press, 1959.

A. E. Housman: Selected Prose, edited by John Carter. Cambridge, Cambridge University Press, 1961.

Poetry and Prose: A Selection, edited by F. C. Horwood. London, Hutchinson, 1971.

The Classical Papers of A. E. Housman (three volumes), collected and edited by J. Diggle and F. R. D. Goodyear. Cambridge, Cambridge University Press, 1972.

Collected Poems and Selected Prose, edited by Christopher Ricks. Allen Lane, 1988.

*

Biography: *A. E. Housman* by Andrew S. F. Gow, New York, Macmillan, 1936; *Alfred Edward Housman: Recollections* by Katharine E. Symons and others, New York, Holt, 1937; *My Brother, A. E. Housman* by Laurence Housman, New York, Scribner, 1938; *A. E. Housman and W. B. Yeats* by Richard Aldington, New York, Peacock Press, 1955; *A. E. Housman: Man behind a Mask* by Maude M. Hawkins, Henry Regnery, 1958; *A. E. Housman: Scholar and Poet* by Norman Marlow, London, Routledge & Kegan Paul, 1958; *A. E. Housman* by Tom Burns Haber, Boston, Twayne Publishers, 1967; *A. E. Housman: The Scholar–Poet* by Richard Perceval Graves, New York, Scribner, 1979; *A. E. Housman: A Critical Biography* by Norman Page, New York, Schocken, 1983;

Bibliography: *A. E. Housman: Selected Prose,* edited by John Carter, Cambridge, Cambridge University Press, 1961; *The Making of "A Shropshire Lad": A Manuscript Variorum,* edited by Tom Burns Haber, Seattle, University of Washington Press, 1966.

Critical Sources: "Introduction" by John Sparrow, in *The Collected Poems,* New York, Penguin Books, 1956; *A. E. Housman: A Divided Life* by George L. Watson, London, Hart–Davis, 1957, Boston, Beacon Press, 1958; *Santayana: The Later Years: A Portrait with Letters* by Daniel Cory, New York, George Braziller, 1963; *Housman's Land of Lost Content: A Critical Study of "A Shropshire Lad"* by B. J. Leggett, Knoxville, University of Tennessee Press, 1970; *The Poetic Art of A. E. Housman: Theory and Practice* by B. J. Leggett, Lincoln, University of Nebraska Press, 1978; "A.E. Housman's 'The Love of Comrades'" by William Whallon, in *Housman Society Journal,* Number 14, 1988, 51–54; "Housman's 'Others, I am not the first'" by Laurence Perrine, in *Victorian Poetry,* autumn–winter 1990, 135–138; *A. E. Housman* by Keith Jebb, Seren Books, Poetry Wales Press, 1992.

*   *   *

It is only possible to refer to the poetry of A. E. Housman as "gay" in the current sexual sense of the term, because the prevailing mood of his verse is one of all–pervading gloom. Housman, as John Sparrow wrote in his introduction to the 1956 Penguin edition of the *Collected Poems,* was a "truly unhappy man." Famous for his cold, humorless, and even caustic personality, Housman seems to describe his own condition in poem XLI of *A Shropshire Lad:* "I see / In many an eye that measures me / The mortal sickness of a mind / Too unhappy to be kind." The philosophy underlying the poems is pessimistic: human existence is to be stoically endured, not actively enjoyed. Life is short, frequently painful, and ends with annihilation. Hope is a delusion, and the idea of an afterlife an empty myth; no one who dies ever lives again. Thus, the only thing "gay" about Housman's verse is the homosexual sensibility underlying it.

The philosopher George Santayana, Housman's contemporary, is reported to have said that the sentiment of Housman's poetry is unmistakably homosexual. If that is indeed the case, it must also be said that the homosexual meaning is more readily apparent in the last two collections of Housman's verses—*More Poems* and *Additional Poems*—than in the poems published during Housman's lifetime. These two final collections were assembled by Housman's brother, the novelist Laurence Housman, and issued after the poet's death. The poetry published during Housman's lifetime—*A Shropshire Lad* (his first collection of poems, published in 1896, when Housman was 37 and a professor of Latin at the University of London) and *Last Poems* (published in 1922, when he was 63 and the Kennedy Professor of Latin in Cambridge University)—contains no explicitly homosexual statements or themes.

Housman never came out of the closet during his lifetime. Publicly to declare oneself a homosexual in Victorian England was all but impossible, and Housman was careful, in his published poetry and in his life, to conceal his sexual nature. It was only after his death in 1936, with the publication of the two final collections of his verse, that Housman's sexual orientation could be seen through the frankly homosexual content of several of the posthumously published poems. Also, the homosexual character of these posthumous poems enables us to read many of the pieces included in the two collections published during Housman's lifetime in terms of the homosexual sensibility expressed in the ones published after his death. For instance, poem XXXII of *Last Poems* is about boyhood musings in the greenwood round Bromsgrove, near Birmingham, where Housman grew up. The lines of this poem could be expressive of any boy's sentiments, but the open homosexuality of some of the posthumous poems causes us to read the sentiment of this poem in a special way: "It was not foes to conquer, / Nor sweethearts to be kind, / But it was friends to die for / That I would seek and find." The poems of the two collections not published until after Housman's death were composed about the same time as the two collections published during his lifetime, so that there is no discontinuity of sentiment between them. The only difference is in the frankness with which homosexual meaning is stated in the posthumous poems.

When we read Housman's poetry in terms of the way that it expresses the homosexuality of its author, we can perceive certain attitudes and themes. One of these is resentment against "Whatever brute and blackguard made the world" (poem IX of *Last Poems*) for making Housman different from other men. Poem XII of *Additional Poems,* entitled "An Epitaph," expresses this resentment at being created awry: "I never sigh, nor flush, nor knit the brow, / Nor grieve to think how ill God made me, now. / Here, with one balm for many fevers found, / Whole of an ancient evil, I sleep sound." We also see this idea, when viewed from the perspective of the posthumously–published poems, expressed in poem XLV of *A Shropshire Lad:* "But play the man, stand up and end you, / When your sickness is your soul." This idea of homosexuality as a constitutional liability is expressed very poignantly in poem XLIV of *A Shropshire Lad.* This poem was based on a newspaper account that Housman had read of a Woolwich cadet who had shot himself. The poem begins by praising the young man for taking his life, observing that "Yours was not an ill for mending, / 'Twas best to take it to the grave," and continues: "Oh you had forethought, you could reason, / And saw your road and where it led, / And early wise and brave in season / Put the pistol to your head." The poet observes that, instead of waiting for "disgrace and scorn," "You shot dead the household traitor, / The soul that should not have been born." Suicide, therefore, is justified as a solution to the plight of being constituted differently from other men. Nevertheless, it is nobler to endure the pain and stoically make the best of the situation. In poem IX of *Last Poems* Housman says, "The troubles of our proud and angry dust / Are from eternity, and shall not fail. / Bear them we can, and if we can we must."

Housman's poems also express his bitter resentment of society for discriminating against the person constituted differently from his fellows. In Victorian England, homosexuality was not only perceived as an aberration, but homosexual acts were regarded as criminal. In 1895, Oscar Wilde, the brilliant dramatist and novelist, was tried for sodomy, convicted and imprisoned. Poem XVIII of the posthumous *Additional Poems* is believed to be a response to the Wilde scandal. In the poem, Wilde's condition is represented by the plight of a young man sent to prison for having red hair: "'Tis a shame to human nature, such a head of hair as his; / In the good old time 'twas hanging for the colour that it is; / Though hanging isn't bad enough and flaying would be fair / For the nameless and abomi-

nable colour of his hair." The poem leaves no doubt of Housman's position on the question of whether homosexuality is an inherent predisposition or a matter of personal choice: "He can curse the God that made him for the colour of his hair." In another poem (XII of *Last Poems*) of a somewhat more ambiguous nature, Housman expresses the same resentment of society's refusal to acknowledge homosexuality as a constitutional difference: "Please yourselves, say I, and they / Need only look the other way. / But no, they will not; they must still / Wrest their neighbour to their will, / And make me dance as they desire / With jail and gallows and hell–fire."

Not only were the laws of Housman's society opposed to homosexual relationships, but he also had the misfortune to fall hopelessly and permanently in love with a young man who was heterosexual and impatient of Housman's devotion. Among Housman's classmates at St. John's College, Oxford University, during the late 1870s, was a handsome, athletic, and intelligent science student, Moses Jackson. The two young men, though utterly different in physique and temperament, became good friends; but Jackson evidently rejected overtures of Housman's that implied something more than friendship, and he evidently did so with crushing finality. Housman never recovered from this rejection, and many of his poems express the bitterness of unrequited love. A splendid example of this condition is poem XIII of *A Shropshire Lad,* one of Housman's best–known lyrics: "When I was one–and–twenty / I heard a wise man say," the poem begins, and reports the wise man's advice: give your money but not your heart away. "But I was one–and–twenty, / No use to talk to me." "The heart out of the bosom," the wise man continues, "Was never given in vain; / 'Tis paid with sighs a plenty / And sold for endless rue.'" The poem concludes: "And I am two–and–twenty, / And oh, 'tis true, 'tis true."

In poem XV of *A Shropshire Lad,* we find one of many expressions of frustrated love in Housman's verse when he characterizes himself as "One the long nights through must lie / Spent in star–defeated sighs." The humiliation and pain of rejection suffered by Housman in his obsession with Jackson is expressed in one of the frankest poems published before the final posthumous collection *Additional Poems.* This poem, number XXXI of the also posthumous *More Poems,* begins "Because I liked you better / Than suits a man to say, / It irked you, and I promised / To throw the thought away." But the poem makes clear that the "thought" was never thrown away, and that it remained with the poet for good. His loneliness and frustration are expressed in poem XIX of *More Poems* which ends with the statement "I, Who only spend the night alone / And strike my fist upon the stone." For Housman, therefore, the homosexual man in Victorian England was, like the souls in Dante's *Inferno,* condemned to "sanza speme vivemo in disio": to live in desire without hope.

Though Housman's verses are filled with disappointment, frustration, and defeat, they do not indulge much in self–pity. The world is an inhospitable abode, but a man must make the best of it. And Housman's poetry has a manly, and frequently military, air. There is nothing effeminate about Housman's tone. He reiterates the theme of masculine courage, responsibility to one's comrades, honor, and stoical endurance. His ideal seems to be that of the Homeric heroes, of the loving comradeship of Achilles and Patroclus, or the tradition of homosexual love that obtained among some groups of the fierce Samurai warriors of Japan. In such traditions as these, replete with manliness, martial discipline, and courage, homoerotic love could be celebrated openly, honored, and revered. In poem XXXVII of the posthumous *More Poems,* the soldier narrator says that he lost his heart not on a rose–filled summer evening, but in the "blood and smoke and flame" of battle; and not to a woman, but to "a soldier and a foeman, / A chap that did not kill me, but he tried; / That took the sabre straight and took it striking / And laughed and kissed his hand to me and died."

Denied emotional fulfillment in his daily life, Housman apparently achieved a kind of vicarious satisfaction through his poetry. This seems to be the case particularly in those poems that celebrate imaginary adventures with a beloved male comrade. The most lyrical of these is number XLII of *A Shropshire Lad* entitled "The Merry Guide." In this poem, the narrator imagines encountering in the woods one day the handsome and athletic young god Mercury. This smiling divinity takes the narrator on an airborne journey throughout the English countryside. The two companions "fare on for ever," but the smiling god never speaks to the narrator. Mercury, in this poem, seems a complex symbol of the beauty and charm in nature and life, and perhaps also of the particular beauty and charm of the young Moses Jackson, forever attracting but never responding to Housman's appeals.

Another poem celebrating manly adventures, but this time in a bizarre way, is the strange piece entitled "Hell Gate." In this poem (number XXXI of *Last Poems*), begun in the 1890s and not completed until 1922, the setting is hell, and the action of the poem describes an insurrection there by the military figure of "Ned," whom the narrator had "known before." With a musket blast, Ned slays the ruler of the underworld, and, together with the narrator, successfully escapes. The poem celebrates a blow, even if only an imaginary one, against "tyranny and terror."

Ultimately, however, the message of Housman's verses seems to be that for gay persons like him there is no place where happiness and satisfaction can be found. In poem XLVI of the posthumous *More Poems,* titled "The Land of Biscay," the narrator sees a magnificent golden ship approaching the shore. "Oh, said I, my friend and lover, / take we now that ship and sail / Outward in the ebb of hues and / steer upon the sunset trail; / Leave the night to fall behind us / and the clouding counties leave: / Help for you and me is yonder, / in a haven west of eve." But as the golden ship nears the shore, the narrator hears the helmsman call out: "Landsman of the land of Biscay, / have you help for grief and me?" In response, the narrator can only shake his head, leaving himself upon the shore and the helmsman upon the sea, and each with only grief for companion.

—*William G. Holzberger*

————

HUGHES, (James) Langston. American poet, novelist, dramatist, lyricist, and author of children's literature. Born in Joplin, Missouri, 1 February 1902. Educated at Columbia University, New York City, 1921–22; Lincoln University, Pennsylvania, A.B. 1929. Held a variety of jobs including assistant cook, launderer, busboy, and seaman on voyages to Africa and Europe; lived at various times in Mexico, France, Italy, Spain, and the Soviet Union. Madrid correspondent for the *Baltimore Afro–American,* 1937; visiting professor in creative writing, Atlanta University, 1947; poet in residence, Laboratory School, University of Chicago, 1949; columnist for *Chicago Defender* and *New York Post.* Member of Authors Guild, Dramatists Guild, American Society of Composers, Authors, and Publishers (ASCAP), PEN, National Institute of Arts and Letters, and Omega Psi Phi. **Recipient:** *Opportunity* magazine first prize for poetry, 1925; *Crisis* Amy Spingarn Contest prizes for poetry and essays, 1925; Witter Bynner undergraduate poetry contest first prize, 1926; *Palms* Intercollegiate Poetry Award, 1927; Harmon Gold Medal for Literature, 1931; Rosenwald fellowships, 1931 and 1941; Guggenheim fellowship, for creative work, 1935; National Institute and American Academy of Arts and Letters Award in Literature, 1946; American Academy of Arts and Letters grant, 1947; Anisfeld–Wolfe Award, for best book on racial relations, 1954; National Association for the Advancement of Colored People's Spingarn Medal, 1960. Litt.D. from Lincoln University, 1943, Howard University, 1963, and Western Reserve University, 1964. *Died in New York City, of congestive heart failure, 22 May 1967.*

WRITINGS

Poetry

The Weary Blues. New York and London, Knopf, 1926.
Fine Clothes to the Jew. New York and London, Knopf, 1927.
The Negro Mother, and Other Dramatic Recitations. New York, Golden Stair Press, 1931.
Dear Lovely Death. Amenia, New York, Troutbeck Press, 1931.
The Dream Keeper, and Other Poems. New York, Knopf, 1932.
Scottsboro Limited: Four Poems and a Play in Verse. New York, Golden Stair Press, 1932.
A New Song. New York, International Workers Order, 1938.
With Robert Glenn, *Shakespeare in Harlem.* New York, Knopf, 1942.
Jim Crow's Last Stand. Atlanta, Negro Publication Society of America, 1943.
Freedom's Plow. New York, Musette Publishers, 1943.
Lament for Dark Peoples, and Other Poems. Holland, 1944.
Fields of Wonder. New York, Knopf, 1947.
One–Way Ticket. New York, Knopf, 1949.
Montage of a Dream Deferred. New York, Holt, 1951.
Ask Your Mama: 12 Moods for Jazz. New York, Knopf, 1961.
The Panther and the Lash: Poems of Our Times. New York, Knopf, 1967.

Novels

Not Without Laughter. New York, Knopf, 1930.
Tambourines to Glory. New York, John Day, 1958; London, Gollancz, 1959.

Short Stories

The Ways of White Folks. New York, Knopf, and London, Allen & Unwin, 1934.
Simple Speaks His Mind. New York, Simon & Schuster, 1950; London, Gollancz, 1951.
Laughing to Keep from Crying. New York, Holt, 1952.
Simple Takes a Wife. New York, Simon & Schuster, 1953; London, Gollancz, 1954.
Simple Stakes a Claim. New York and Toronto, Rinehart, 1957; London, Gollancz, 1958.

Something in Common, and Other Stories. New York, Hill & Wang, 1963.
Simple's Uncle Sam. New York, Hill & Wang, 1965.

Autobiographies

The Big Sea: An Autobiography. New York, Knopf, and London, Hutchinson, 1940.
I Wonder as I Wander: An Autobiographical Journey. New York and Toronto, Rinehart, 1956.

Nonfiction

A Negro Looks at Soviet Central Asia. Moscow and Leningrad, Cooperative Publishing Society of Foreign Workers in the U.S.S.R., 1934.
The Sweet Flypaper of Life, photographs by Roy De Carava. New York, Simon & Schuster, 1955.
With Milton Meltzer, *A Pictorial History of the Negro in America.* New York, Crown, 1956; fourth edition published as *A Pictorial History of Black Americans,* 1973.
Fight for Freedom: The Story of the NAACP. New York, Norton, 1962.
With Meltzer, *Black Magic: A Pictorial History of the Negro in American Entertainment.* Englewood Cliffs, New Jersey, Prentice–Hall, 1967.
Black Misery. New York, Knopf, 1969.

Children's Literature

With Arna Bontemps, *Popo and Fifina: Children of Haiti.* New York, Macmillan, 1932.
The First Book of Negroes. New York, F. Watts, 1952; London, Bailey & Swinfen, 1956.
The First Book of Rhythms. New York, F. Watts, 1954; London, Bailey & Swinfen, 1956.
Famous American Negroes. New York, Dodd, 1954.
Famous Negro Music Makers. New York, Dodd, 1955.
The First Book of Jazz. New York, F. Watts, 1955; London, Bailey & Swinfen, 1957; revised, New York, F. Watts, 1976.
The First Book of the West Indies. New York, F. Watts, and London, Bailey & Swinfen, 1956; as *The First Book of the Caribbean,* London, E. Ward, 1965.
Famous Negro Heroes of America. New York, Dodd, 1958.
The First Book of Africa. New York, F. Watts, 1960; London, Mayflower, 1961.

Omnibus Volumes

The Langston Hughes Reader. New York, Braziller, 1958.
Selected Poems of Langston Hughes. New York, Knopf, 1959.
The Best of Simple. New York, Hill & Wang, 1961.
Five Plays by Langston Hughes, edited by Webster Smalley. Bloomington, Indiana University Press, 1963.
Don't You Turn Back (poems), edited by Lee Bennett Hopkins. New York, Knopf, 1969.
Good Morning Revolution: The Uncollected Social Protest Writings of Langston Hughes, edited by Faith Berry. New York, Lawrence Hill, 1973.

Plays

Mulatto (produced New York, 1935).
Little Ham (produced Cleveland, Ohio, 1936).
Emperor of Haiti, 1936.
With Arna Bontemps, *When the Jack Hollers* (produced Cleveland, Ohio, 1936).
Joy to My Soul (produced Cleveland, Ohio, 1937).
Soul Gone Home (produced Cleveland, Ohio, 1937).
Front Porch (produced Cleveland, Ohio, 1938).
Little Eva's End, 1938.
Limitations of Life, 1938.
The Em–Fuehrer Jones, 1938.
Don't You Want to Be Free? (produced New York, 1938).
Author of libretto, *The Organizer,* music by James P. Johnson (produced New York, 1939).
The Sun Do Move (produced Chicago, 1942).
For This We Fight, 1943.
Author of lyrics, *Street Scene* by Elmer Rice, music by Kurt Weill (produced New York, 1947). New York, Chappell, 1948.
Author of libretto, *Troubled Island,* music by William Grant Still (opera; produced New York, 1949). New York, Leeds Music, 1949.
Author of libretto, *The Barrier,* music by Jan Meyerowitz (produced New York, 1950).
Author of lyrics, *Just around the Corner* by Amy Mann and Bernard Drew (produced Ogunquit, Maine, 1951).
Author of libretto, *The Glory Round His Head,* music by Jan Meyerowitz. New York, Broude Brothers, 1953.
Author of libretto, *Esther,* music by Jan Meyerowitz (produced Urbana, Illinois, 1957).
Simply Heavenly, music by David Martin (produced New York, 1957). New York, Dramatists Play Service, 1959.
Author of libretto, *The Ballad of the Brown King,* music by Margaret Bonds (produced New York, 1960). New York, Sam Fox, 1961.
Black Nativity (produced New York, 1961).
Gospel Glow (produced New York, 1962).
Tambourines to Glory (produced New York, 1963).
Author of libretto, *Let Us Remember Him,* music by David Amram (produced San Francisco, 1963).
Jericho–Jim Crow (produced New York, 1964).
The Prodigal Son (produced New York, 1965).
With Zora Neale Hurston, *Mule Bone* (produced on Broadway, 1991).
Soul Yesterday and Today.
Angelo Herndon Jones.
Mother and Child.
Trouble with the Angels.
Outshines the Sun.

Other

Editor, *Four Lincoln University Poets.* Lincoln, Pennsylvania, Lincoln University, 1930.
Translator, *San Gabriel* by Federico García Lorca, 1938.
Way Down South (screenplay), 1942.
Translator, "When the Tom–Tom Beats" and "Guinea" by Jacques Roumain and "Opinions of the New Chinese Student" by Refino Pedroso, in *Anthology of Contemporary Latin–American Poetry,*

edited by Dudley Fitts. Norfolk, Connecticut, New Directions, 1942.

Translator, with Mercer Cook, *Masters of the Dew* by Jacques Roumain. New York, Reynal & Hitchcock, 1947.

Translator, with Ben Frederic Carruthers, *Cuba Libre* by Nicolas Guillén. Los Angeles, Ward Richie, 1948.

Editor, with Arna Bontemps, and translator of "Really I Know," "Trite without Doubt," and "She Left Herself One Evening" by Leon Damas, in *The Poetry of the Negro, 1746–1949.* Garden City, New York, Doubleday, 1949; revised as *The Poetry of the Negro, 1746–1970,* 1970.

Translator, *Gypsy Ballads* by Federico García Lorca. Beloit, Wisconsin, Beloit College, 1951.

Editor, with Waring Cuney and Bruce M. Wright, *Lincoln University Poets.* New York, Fine Editions, 1954.

Translator, *Selected Poems of Gabriela Mistral.* Bloomington, Indiana University Press, 1957.

Editor, with Arna Bontemps, *The Book of Negro Folklore.* New York, Dodd, 1958.

Editor and author of introduction, *An African Treasury: Articles, Essays, Stories, Poems by Black Africans.* New York, Crown, 1960; London, Gollancz, 1961.

Editor and translator, "Flute Players" by Jean–Joseph Rabearivelo and "Those Who Lost Everything" and "Suffer, Poor Negro" by David Diop, in *Poems from Black Africa.* Bloomington, Indiana University Press, 1963.

Editor, *New Negro Poets: U.S.A.,* foreword by Gwendolyn Brooks. Bloomington, Indiana University Press, 1964.

Editor, *The Book of Negro Humor.* New York, Dodd, 1966.

Editor and author of introduction, *The Best Short Stories by Negro Writers: An Anthology from 1899 to the Present.* Boston and Toronto, Little, Brown, 1967.

With Arna Bontemps, *Arna Bontemps–Langston Hughes Letters: 1925–1967,* edited by Charles H. Nichols. New York, Dodd, 1980.

*

Manuscript Collections: James Weldon Johnson Memorial Collection, Beinecke Library, Yale University, New Haven, Connecticut; Schomburg Collection, New York Public Library; Lincoln University Library, Pennsylvania; Fisk University Library, Nashville, Tennessee.

Biography: *Langston Hughes: A Biography* by Milton Meltzer, New York, Crowell, 1968; *Langston Hughes: Poet of His People* by Elizabeth P. Myers, Easton, Maryland, Garrard, 1970; *Black Troubador: Langston Hughes* by Charlamae H. Rollins, Chicago, Rand McNally, 1970; *Langston Hughes: Before and Beyond Harlem* by Faith Berry, Westport, Connecticut, Lawrence Hill, 1983; *The Life of Langston Hughes* by Arnold Rampersad, New York, Oxford University Press, Volume 1: *1902–1941: I, Too, Sing America,* 1986, Volume 2: *1941–1967: I Dream a World,* 1988.

Bibliography: *A Bio–Bibliography of Langston Hughes, 1902–1967* by Donald C. Dickinson, Hamden, Connecticut, Shoestring Press, 1967; *Langston Hughes and Gwendolyn Brooks: A Reference Guide* by R. Baxter Miller, Boston, G. K. Hall, 1978; *The Art and Imagination of Langston Hughes* by R. Baxter Miller, Lexing-

ton, University Press of Kentucky, 1989.

Critical Sources: "The Tragic Mulatto Theme in Six Works by Langston Hughes" by Arthur P. Davis, in *Phylon,* winter 1955, 195–204; *Langston Hughes* by James Emanuel, New York, Twayne Publishers, 1967; "The Literary Experiments of Langston Hughes" by James Emanuel, in *CLA Journal,* June 1967, 335–344; "Langston Hughes: Cool Poet" by Arthur P. Davis, in *CLA Journal,* June 1968, 280–296; "Langston Hughes as Playwright" by Darwin T. Turner, in *CLA Journal,* June 1968, 297–309; "A Word about Simple" by Blyden Jackson, in *CLA Journal,* June 1968, 310–318; *Langston Hughes: Black Genius,* edited by Therman B. O'Daniel, New York, Morrow, 1971; "Langston Hughes: The Minstrel as Artificer" by Stanley Schatt, in *Journal of Modern Literature,* September 1974, 115–120; *Concordance to Langston Hughes* by Peter Mandelik and Stanley Schatt, Detroit, Gale, 1975; *Langston Hughes: The Poet and His Critics* by Richard K. Barksdale, Chicago, American Library Association, 1977; "Five Stories about a Man Named Hughes: A Critical Reflection" by George Houston Bass, in *Langston Hughes Review,* spring 1982, 1–12; "'For a Moment I Wondered': Theory and Form in the Autobiographies of Langston Hughes" by R. Baxter Miller, in *Langston Hughes Review,* fall 1984, 1–6; "Beyond the Mountain: Langston Hughes on Race/Class and Art" by Amritjit Singh, in *Langston Hughes Review,* spring 1987, 37–43; *Langston Hughes and the Blues* by Steven C. Tracy, Urbana and Chicago, University of Illinois Press, 1988.

*   *   *

"What happens to a dream deferred? / Does it dry up like a raisin in the sun? / And fester like a sore—and then run? / Does it stink like rotten meat? / Or crust and sugar over like a syupy sweet? / Maybe it just sags like a heavy load. / OR DOES IT EXPLODE?"—from *Harlem.*

The phrase "a dream deferred," applicable to the suppressed longings of both blacks and gays, recurs often in the verse of Langston Hughes. The assertion that Hughes was gay has been made in print often, so most gays have assumed the matter was beyond question. But he seems, like many gays in times past, to have taken care not to leave affidavits around, and his biographers flatly disagree. Faith Berry, in *Langston Hughes Before and Beyond Harlem,* says repeatedly that he was. Arnold Rampersad, writing in *The Life of Langston Hughes,* denies it, saying that people assumed Hughes was because he often went around with pretty, effeminate young men. Rampersad says that Countee Cullen, Noel Sullivan, Alain Locke, and others tried to seduce Hughes, but each decided he must be asexual. Friends noted that his occasional flirtations with women seemed to lack any sexual component. He remained a lifelong bachelor, though a brief stay in Reno led some to assume he was getting a divorce.

Hughes was raised in Kansas, moving briefly with his family when he was six to Mexico. An earthquake cut short their stay. His mostly Indian grandmother, last surviving widow of John Brown's raid, cared for him until her death, when he was returned to his waitress mother. He came to poetry by accident, being elected class poet of his grammar school without ever having written a verse. He soon learned that not all whites were bigoted, but was fascinated by the movements and language of his own people, richly reflected later in his writings. Over his mother's strong objections, he spent some time with his tight–fisted negro–hating father, a prosperous businessman in Mexico, and gave a vivid account of his restricted life on his father's ranch in *The Big Sea.*

Hughes resisted his father's insistence that he become a mining engineer and begged to be sent to Columbia, where he would be near the Harlem Renaissance, then being widely written about. To break from his father's rule, he began teaching English, earning enough to move to New York, where he plunged into the intellectual ferment and partying of the Harlem Renaissance. *The Big Sea* gives a heady account of that, without indicating the gayness of many of the participants who became his closest friends. Rebelling against Harlem's elegant night life, much of which was for whites only, because it was a romantic radical thing to do, he impulsively shipped out on a freighter bound for Africa—the source of his blood, a destination as magnetic for him as Harlem. He was piqued to find that because of his light skin, black Africans did not regard him as a negro.

More than one of Hughes' poems seem to cover equally well the condition of being black or being gay. Some of his strongest verse, characterized by bitter clowning, seems to strike a gay chord, as do "Port Town," "Desire," "Vagabonds," "Refugee in America," and in many verses Hughes wrote as from a woman's viewpoint, as in "Madame, To You." But his writings touched gay themes very rarely. Among his most powerful poems are: "The Negro Speaks of Rivers" (written on a train crossing the Mississippi while he was enroute to Mexico, or the second time to visit his father, it was his first poem to be published—in 1921 in *Crisis*—and the most anthologized); "I, Too, Sing America"; "Freedom Train"; "The Weary Blues"; and the long "Freedom's Plow." "Cafe: 3 a.m." from his *Selected Poems* stands out: "Detectives from the vice squad / with weary sadistic eyes / spotting fairies / Degenerates / some people say. / But God, Nature / or somebody / made them that way. / Police lady or lesbian / over there? / Where?"

The biographies of Hughes are important for gay readers interested in how to evaluate the "was he–wasn't he" question that dominates gay history, and his autobiographies, *The Big Sea* and *I Wonder as I Wander,* as well as the wonderful folk humor of *Simple Speaks His Mind,* read beautifully, making a strong analogy to the gay spirit even if homosexuality is very rarely mentioned. His life story resembles that of many isolated gays who grew up in the midwest feeling the oppression of discrimination—but Hughes never lifted the veil, if veil there was. His work seems to express gay spirit, even if non–black gay readers looking for explicitly sexy passages will find little beyond a few passages that might have double meaning.

—Jim Kepner

I-J

INCOGNITEAU, Jean–Louis. *See* **KEROUAC, Jack.**

———

ISHERWOOD, Christopher (William Bradshaw). British–born American novelist, playwright, editor, and translator. Born in High Lane, Cheshire, 26 August 1904; immigrated to the United States, 1939; naturalized citizen, 1946. Educated at Repton School, 1919–22; Corpus Christi College, Cambridge, 1924–25; medical student at King's College, London, 1928–29. Companion of artist Don Bachardy. Secretary to French violinist Andre Mangeot and his Music Society String Quartet, London, 1926–27; private tutor, London, 1926–27; English teacher, Berlin, Germany, 1930–33; film scriptwriter, Gaumont Films, England; dialogue writer, Metro–Goldwyn–Mayer, Hollywood, California, 1940; worked in hostel for Central European refugees, American Friends Service Committee, Haverford, Pennsylvania, 1941–42; coeditor, with Swami Prabhavananda, *Vedanta and the West,* Vedanta Society of Southern California, 1943–45. Guest professor, Los Angeles State College (now California State University, Los Angeles) and University of California, Santa Barbara, 1959–62; Regents Professor, University of California, Los Angeles, 1965, and University of California, Riverside, 1966. **Recipient:** Brandeis University Creative Arts Award, 1974–75; PEN award for body of work, 1983; Common Wealth Award for distinguished service in literature, 1984. *Died in Santa Monica, California, of cancer, 4 January 1986.*

WRITINGS

Novels

All the Conspirators. London, J. Cape, 1928.
The Memorial: Portrait of a Family. London, Hogarth, 1932; New York, New Directions, 1946.
The Last of Mr. Norris. New York, Morrow, 1935; as *Mr. Norris Changes Trains,* London, Hogarth, 1935; in *The Berlin Stories,* 1946.
Sally Bowles. London, Hogarth, 1937; in *The Berlin Stories,* 1946.
Goodbye to Berlin. New York, Random House, 1939; in *The Berlin Stories,* 1946.
Prater Violet. New York, Random House, 1945.
The Berlin Stories (contains *Mr. Norris Changes Trains, Sally Bowles,* and *Goodbye to Berlin*). New York, J. Laughlin, 1946; as *The Berlin of Sally Bowles,* London, Hogarth Press, 1975.

The World in Evening. New York, Random House, 1954.
Down There on a Visit. New York, Simon & Schuster, 1964.
A Single Man. New York, Simon & Schuster, 1964.
A Meeting by the River. New York, Simon & Schuster, 1967.

Plays

With W. H. Auden, *The Dog beneath the Skin; or, Where Is Francis?* (produced London, 1936; revised and produced London, 1937). New York, Random House, 1935.
With W. H. Auden, *The Ascent of F6* (produced London, 1937; New York, 1939). New York, Random House, 1937.
With W. H. Auden, *A Melodrama in Three Acts: On the Frontier* (produced Cambridge, England, 1938). London, Faber, 1938; as *On the Frontier: A Melodrama in Three Acts,* New York, Random House, 1939.
The Adventures of the Black Girl in Her Search for God (based on a novella by George Bernard Shaw; produced Los Angeles, 1969).
With Don Bachardy, *A Meeting by the River* (based on novel by Isherwood; produced Los Angeles, 1972; on Broadway, 1979).
With W. H. Auden, *Plays, and Other Dramatic Writings: W. H. Auden and Christopher Isherwood, 1928–1938,* edited by Edward Mendelson. Princeton, New Jersey, Princeton University Press, 1988.

Screenplays

With others, *Little Friend,* Gaumont, 1934.
With others, *A Woman's Face,* Metro–Goldwyn–Mayer, 1941.
With Robert Thoeren, *Rage in Heaven* (based on novel by James Hilton), Metro–Goldwyn–Mayer, 1941.
With others, *Forever and a Day,* RKO, 1943.
With Ladislas Fodor, *The Great Sinner,* Loew's, 1949.
Diane, Metro–Goldwyn–Mayer, 1955.
With Terry Southern, *The Loved One* (based on novel by Evelyn Waugh), Filmways, 1965.
With Don Magner and Tony Richardson, *The Sailor from Gibraltar* (based on novel by Marguerite Duras), Woodfall, 1967.
With Don Bachardy, *Frankenstein: The True Story* (based on novel by Mary Shelley; produced, 1972), New York, Avon, 1973.

Autobiographies

Lions and Shadows. London, Hogarth, 1938; New York, New Directions, 1947.
Kathleen and Frank. New York, Simon & Schuster, 1971.
Christopher and His Kind. New York, Farrar, Straus, 1980.
October, illustrations by Don Bachardy. Pasadena, California, Twelvetrees, 1983.

Editor

Vedanta for the Western World. Marcel Rodd, 1945; as *Vedanta and the West,* New York, Harper, 1951.
Vedanta for Modern Man. New York, Harper, 1951.
Great English Short Stories. New York, Dell, 1957.

Translator

Penny for the Poor by Bertolt Brecht. London, Hale, 1937; as *Threepenny Novel,* New York, Grove, 1956.
With Swami Prabhavananda, *Bhagavad–Gita: The Song of God.* Hollywood, Marcel Rodd, 1944; as *The Song of God: Bhagavad–Gita.* New York, Harper, 1951.
And editor, with Swami Prabhavananda, *Crest–Jewel of Discrimination* by Swami Shankara. Hollywood, Vedanta Press, 1947.
Intimate Journals by Charles Baudelaire. Hollywood, Marcel Rodd, 1947.
And editor, with Swami Prabhavananda, *How to Know God: The Yoga Aphorisms of Patanjali.* New York, Harper, 1953.

Other

With W. H. Auden, *Journey to War.* New York, Random House, 1939.
The Condor and the Cows: A South American Travel Diary. New York, Random House, 1949.
An Approach to Vedanta. Hollywood, Vedanta Press, 1963.
Ramakrishna and His Disciples (biography). New York, Simon & Schuster, 1965.
Exhumations: Stories, Articles, Verses. New York, Simon & Schuster, 1966.
The Legend of Silent Night (television special; adaptation of a story by Paul Gallico), American Broadcasting Company, 1969.
Essentials of Vedanta. Hollywood, Vedanta Press, 1969.
My Guru and His Disciple. New York, Farrar, Straus, 1980.
With Sylvain Mangeot, *People One Ought to Know* (poems). Garden City, New York, Doubleday, 1982.
The Wishing Tree: Christopher Isherwood on Mystical Religion, edited by Robert Adjemian. Hollywood, Vedanta Press, 1987.
"Mr. Lancaster," in *The Faber Book of Gay Short Fiction,* edited by Edmund White. London and New York, Faber & Faber, 1991.
"Hollywood Homophobia Doesn't Stop Everyone," in *Advocate,* 14 January 1992, 76.

*

Adaptations: *I Am a Camera* (stage adaptation by John Van Druten of *The Berlin Stories*) was produced in 1951; *Cabaret* (a stage musical adaptation by Joe Masteroff, John Kander, and Fred Ebb of *I Am a Camera* and *The Berlin Stories*) was produced on Broadway in 1966; *Cabaret* (screen adaptation by Jay Preston Allen of the stage musical) was filmed by Allied Artists, 1972.

Biography: *Christopher Isherwood* by Carolyn G. Heilbrun, New York, Columbia University Press, 1970; *Isherwood: A Biography of Christopher Isherwood* by Jonathan Fryer, London, New English Library, 1977; *Christopher Isherwood: A Critical Biography* by Brian Finney, New York, Oxford University Press, 1979; *Chris-*

topher Isherwood: A Personal Memoir by John Lehmann, New York, Holt, 1988.

Bibliography: *Christopher Isherwood: A Bibliography 1923–1967* by Selmer Westby and Clayton M. Brown, California State College at Los Angeles Foundation, 1968; "Christopher Isherwood: A Checklist, 1968–1975" by Stathis Orphanis, in *Twentieth–Century Literature,* October 1976, 354–61; *Christopher Isherwood: A Reference Guide* by Robert W. Funk, Boston, G. K. Hall, 1979; *Christopher Isherwood: A Bibliography of His Personal Papers,* edited by James White and William H. White, Montrose, Alabama, Texas Center for Writers Press, 1987; "A Bibliography of Isherwood" by Cal Gough, in *Lambda News,* August 1991, 29.

Critical Sources: *The Modern Novel in Britain and the United States* by Walter Allen, New York, Dutton, 1964; "Insights into Isherwood" by Angus Wilson, in *Observer,* 20 March 1966; *Christopher Isherwood* by Carolyn C. Heilbrun ("Columbia Essays on Modern Literature 53"), New York, Columbia University Press, 1970; "Irony and Style: The Example of Christopher Isherwood" by Alan Wilde, in *Modern Fiction Studies,* winter 1970; *Christopher Isherwood* by Alan Wilde ("Twayne's United States Authors Series 173"), New York, Twayne, 1971; "*Goodbye to Berlin*: Refocusing Isherwood's Camera" by David P. Thomas, in *Contemporary Literature,* winter 1972; "Christopher Isherwood—A Profile" by Brian Finney, *New Review,* August 1975; *The Auden Generation: Literature and Politics in England in the 1930s* by Samuel L. Hynes, London, Bodley Head, 1976; *Christopher Isherwood* by Francis King ("Writers and Their Work 240"), Harlow, Essex, Longman, 1976; "'Camp' and Politics in Isherwood's Berlin Fiction" by Peter Thomas, in *Journal of Modern Literature,* February 1976; "Sexuality in Isherwood" by Jonathan H. Fryer, in *Twentieth–Century Literature,* October 1976; "Art, Sex, and Isherwood" by Gore Vidal, in *New York Review of Books,* 9 December 1976, 10–18; "*Lions and Shadows*" by Hugh Brogan, *Twentieth–Century Literature,* October 1976; *Christopher Isherwood: Myth and Anti–Myth* by Paul Piazza, New York, Columbia University Press, 1978; "Christopher Isherwood: The Novelist as Homosexual" by D. S. Savage, in *Literature and Psychology,* 29:1–2, 1979; *Christopher Isherwood* by Claude J. Summers, New York, Ungar, 1980; "The Secret of Issyvoo" by Stephen Spender, in *Observer,* 12 January 1986; "Stranger in Paradise" by John Boorman, in *American Film,* October 1986; *Isherwood's Fiction: The Self and Technique* by Lisa M. Schwerdt, London, Macmillan, 1989; *Gay Fictions, Wilde to Stonewall: Studies in a Male Homosexual Literary Tradition* by Claude J. Summers, New York, Continuum, 1990; "Not a Single Man: Artist Don Bachardy Pays Tribute to Loves Old and New" by Charlie Scheips, in *Advocate,* 12 March 1991, 62; "Christopher Isherwood: Hero of Our Time" by Foster Corbin, in *Lambda News,* August 1991, 26–28.

*   *   *

When Christopher Isherwood died on 4 January 1986, he was widely mourned as a deeply revered icon of contemporary Anglo–American gay culture, a courageous teacher who had wrestled with themes that haunt the twentieth–century psyche—alienation and isolation, sexuality and spirituality—and who had voiced the fears and aspirations of gay men in difficult and dangerous times. His fascinating life's journey from an angry young man of the 1920s and 1930s to the ironic moralist and gay liberation activist of the 1970s and 1980s was itself the source of his art. Isherwood found in his mirror the personal reflection of universal predicaments, yet his work was never self–indulgent. Indeed, his greatest contribution to gay literature was to depict the homosexual as a faithful mirror of the human condition.

He was born Christopher William Bradshaw Isherwood on 26 August 1904 into an old and distinguished family, the principal landowners in Cheshire, England. In May of 1915, while a student at St. Edmund's preparatory school in Surrey, he learned of the death of his father in World War I, a loss that would haunt his early writings. He was educated at Repton School and Corpus Christi College, Cambridge, but was sent down from the university without a degree in 1925 for answering examination questions facetiously. Shortly thereafter he renewed his friendship with W. H. Auden, his former classmate at St. Edmund's, with whom he was to share a sporadic and unromantic sexual relationship for over ten years. Auden, who quickly emerged as his generation's greatest poet, cast Isherwood in the role of literary mentor and soon introduced him to a fellow Oxford undergraduate, Stephen Spender. The trio formed the nucleus of the "Auden Gang," the young poets and novelists who dominated the English literary scene of the 1930s.

From 1930 to 1933, Isherwood lived in Berlin, where the city's political excitement and sexual freedom became the stuff of his art. He immersed himself in the world of male prostitutes, living almost anonymously in shabbily genteel and working class areas of the city and translating his experience of the demimonde into what would eventually become the definitive portrait of pre–Hitler Germany, the "Berlin Stories." During his stay in Berlin, Isherwood fell in love with a working–class youth, Heinz, with whom he was to wander restlessly from one European country to another in search of a place where the two could settle together. The odyssey finally ended when Heinz had to return to Germany, where he was arrested, sentenced to prison for homosexual activities, and then to service in the German army. Isherwood's knowledge of Heinz's conscription in the German army contributed to his pacifism on the eve of the outbreak of World War II.

Having collaborated with Auden on three avant–garde plays and having supported various leftist causes, Isherwood gained a reputation for ideological commitment in the 1930s. But partly because of his growing self–consciousness as a homosexual, he deeply distrusted communism and became increasingly uncomfortable with the vacuity of political rhetoric of all stripes. In 1939, Isherwood and Auden emigrated to the United States, settling at first in New York City. But whereas Auden found the city exhilarating, Isherwood was soon deeply depressed. He decided to settle in Los Angeles, where he soon found a job in the motion picture industry. In 1940, under the influence of a Hindu monk and surrogate father, he converted to vedantism, a philosophy that would influence all his later work.

Isherwood was a conscientious objector during World War II and became a United States citizen in 1946. In 1953, he fell in love with an 18–year–old college student, Don Bachardy, who was to achieve independent success as a portrait artist. The relationship was to last the rest of Isherwood's life. At the conclusion of his 1980 autobiography, *Christopher and His Kind,* he described Bachardy as "the ideal companion to whom you can reveal yourself totally and yet be loved for what you are, not what you pretend to be." During the 1970s and 1980s Isherwood and Bachardy were active participants in the burgeoning American gay liberation movement,

a movement that Isherwood's work of the 1950s and 1960s had anticipated and inspired.

The impact of Isherwood's homosexuality on his writing is pervasive and incalculable, experienced both directly and indirectly. His interest in certain psychological predicaments and in recurring character types and themes, as well as his fascination with the anti–heroic hero, his rebellion against bourgeois respectability, his empathy with "The Lost" (his code name for the alienated and the excluded), and his ironic perspective, are all related to his awareness of himself as a homosexual. Even when suppressed or disguised for legal or artistic reasons, homosexuality is a felt presence in Isherwood's novels. It is a crucial component of the myth of the outsider that he developed so painstakingly, and a symbol not merely of alienation and isolation, but also of individuality and of the variousness of fully human possibilities.

In his early works, Isherwood presents homosexuality unapologetically and naturally. He domesticates aspects of gay life that lesser writers sensationalized, and he reveals considerable insight into the dynamics of gay relationships. His first novel, *All the Conspirators,* published in 1928, indicts the repression of homosexual feelings, a motif that will recur throughout his canon; while his second novel, 1932's *The Memorial,* brilliantly portrays a homosexual's grief at the loss of his best friend in World War I. *The Berlin Stories* (consisting of the novels *The Last of Mr. Norris,* 1935, *Sally Bowles,* 1937, and *Goodbye to Berlin,* 1939), which brought him international fame, depicts a wide range of homosexual characters, from Baron Kuno von Pregnitz, whose secret fantasies revolve around English schoolboy adventure stories, to Peter Wilkinson and Otto Nowak, who share a spoiled homosexual idyll on Reugen Island. In *The Berlin Stories,* the unhappiness that plagues the gay characters is attributed not to their homosexuality but to their infection with the soul sickness that denies life and distorts reality, an infection that they share with everyone else in the doomed city. In the early works, the gay characters are juxtaposed with the heterosexual ones to reveal beneath their apparent polarities a shared reality of the deadened spirit.

Isherwood's American novels, beginning with *The World in the Evening,* published in 1954, focus more directly on the social plight of the homosexual in a homophobic society. In these novels, Isherwood anticipates the concerns of the nascent gay liberation movement, as he presents homosexuals as a legitimate minority among the sea of minorities that constitute Western democracies. By conceiving of homosexuals as an aggrieved minority, Isherwood both softens the stigma linked to homosexuality and encourages solidarity among gay people, while also implying the possibility of a political redress to injustice by forming alliances with other disadvantaged minorities. The dilemma faced by the gay characters of Isherwood's later novels is crystallized in their apparently irreconcilable needs to assert their individuality and to feel a sense of community.

In Bob Wood, the Quaker artist of *The World in the Evening,* Isherwood offers one of the earliest sympathetic portraits of a gay activist in Anglo–American literature. Wood bitterly criticizes the heterosexual majority for its failure to accept the gay minority. Sick of futile discussions of the etiology of homosexuality, he would like to "march down the street with a banner saying, 'We're queer because we're queer because we're queer.'" But even this protest, wildly unlikely in the 1940s, when the action of the novel takes place, is impossible: his lover, Charles, a Jew who has changed his name, "is sick of belonging to these whining, militant minorities." After much soul searching, Wood finally enlists in the Navy, despite the ban against homosexuals in the United States military. His motives are defiant rather than patriotic: "what they're claiming is that us queers are unfit for their beautiful pure Army and Navy—when they ought to be glad to have us." Wood's militancy and his solidarity with other homosexuals are extremely rare in the literature of the 1950s.

Isherwood's sensitivity to the injustices felt by homosexuals is also apparent in 1964's *Down There on a Visit.* Ambrose, an expatriate Englishman who has created an anarchic community on a Greek island, fantasizes a homosexual kingdom in which heterosexuality is illegal: "meanwhile it'll be winked at, of course, as long as it's practiced in decent privacy. I think we shall even allow a few bars to be opened for people with those unfortunate tendencies, in certain quarters of the larger cities." This comic riff parodies the unjust reality in which homosexuals are excluded from the larger community, even as it also betrays Ambrose's secret desire for involvement in the world.

In Isherwood's 1964 masterpiece *A Single Man,* the need for community is also an issue. Focusing on George, a late–middle–aged and lonely expatriate Briton grieving at the death of his lover of many years, the novel more fully develops the context of gay oppression than do the earlier works and places it within a still larger context of spiritual transcendence. *A Single Man* regards the assertions of individual uniqueness and minority consciousness as necessary worldly and political goals, but it finally subsumes them in the vedantic idea of the universal consciousness. In making concrete this resolution, the novel presents a moving portrait of male homosexual love, and George emerges as an "Everyman" figure whose homosexuality is a simple given. Presaging the gay liberation movement, *A Single Man* presents homosexuality as a human variation that should be accorded respect and depicts homosexuals as a minority whose grievances need to be addressed.

Isherwood's final novel, *A Meeting by the River,* pivots on the unsuccessful attempt of a bisexual movie producer to dissuade his younger brother from taking final vows as a Hindu monk. The producer, Patrick, finally retreats to a cowardly conformity, but his Whitmanesque vision of a homosexual union "in which two men learn to trust each other so completely that there's no fear left and they experience and share everything together in the flesh and in the spirit" complements his brother's search for spiritual brotherhood in a monastery. This vedantic novel discovers in the concept of brotherhood a means of escaping the imprisoning ego.

Described by Gore Vidal as "the best prose writer in English," Isherwood was a masterful stylist, a subtle ironist, a witty and compassionate moralist, and an insightful observer of the human condition. He was, in fact, one of the best writers of his generation. Central to his achievement was his depiction of homosexuality in casual, occasionally elevated, and always human terms. Incorporating gay liberation perspectives into his novels, especially the need for solidarity among homosexuals and the recognition of homosexuals as a legitimate minority, Isherwood created characters whose homosexuality is an integral part of their personality and an emblem of their common humanity.

—*Claude J. Summers*

IVES, Morgan. *See* BRADLEY, Marion Zimmer.

JAY, Karla. American educator, activist, editor, translator, and author of nonfiction. Born in Brooklyn, New York, 22 February 1947. Educated at Barnard College, New York, A.B. in French 1968; New York University, M. Phil. in comparative literature 1978, Ph.D., 1984. Associate adjust professor, 1974–83, assistant professor, 1983–87, associate professor, 1987–90, professor of English and American literature, women's studies, gay studies, and English as a second language, Pace University, New York, 1990—. Adjunct instructor, Brooklyn College of the City University of New York, 1974, LaGuardia Community College, New York, 1975, and College of New Rochelle, New Rochelle, New York, 1975–77. Editor of the "The Cutting Edge: Lesbian Life and Literature" series for New York University Press, 1992—; general editor of series of books of new scholarship and biography in any field, reprints of classics, and first publication of lost or never–published works, 1992—; contributor to *Lesbian Tide, Majority Report, Ms., New York Times Book Review,* and *Village Voice.* Member of Modern Lanuage Association, delegate, 1988–90, member of executive committee of division of gay languages and literature, 1988–92, cochair of Lesbian and Gay Caucus, 1993—; member of board of directors, Center for Lesbian and Gay Studies, CUNY Graduate Center, New York, 1988–90; member of board of directors of Money for Women Fund (now the Barbara Deming/Money for Women Fund), 1979–85, president, 1979–85; member of National Women's Studies Association, 1981—. Member of Board of Scholars, *Ms.Magazine,* 1992—; associate editor, *Concerns,* 1992—. **Recipient:** American Library Association Gay Book Award finalist for best book, 1978; National Gay Press Association best interview, 1983; Stonewall Awards Foundation best journalist (woman), 1983; Getty Foundation travel grant, 1985; National Endowment for the Humanities Travel to Collection grants, 1984 and 1989; New York Council for the Humanities speaker in the humanities, 1985—; Lambda Literary Awards finalist for best nonfiction for *The Amazon and the Page,* 1989; Lamda Literary Awards finalist for best anthology for *Lesbian Texts and Contexts,* 1991; Lambda Literary Awards finalist for best small press book for *A Perilous Advantage,* 1993; several grants, including one from Gay Academic Union in support of research on Natalie Clifford Barney and Renée Vivien in Paris. Agent: Sydelle Kramer, Frances Goldin Literary Agency, 305 East 11th Street, New York, New York 10003, U.S.A.

WRITINGS

Editor

With Allen Young, *Out of the Closets: Voices of Gay Liberation.* New York, Douglas Books, 1972; second edition, Jove, 1978; 20th anniversary edition with introduction by Jay and John D'Emilio, New York, New York University Press, 1992.

With Allen Young, *Lavender Culture.* New York, Jove Publications, 1978.

With Joanne Glasgow, coauthor of introduction, and contributor of essay on Djuna Barnes, *Lesbian Texts and Contexts: Radical Revisions.* New York, New York University Press, 1990.

Nonfiction

With Allen Young, *After You're Out: Personal Experiences of Gay Men and Lesbian Women.* New York, Links Books, 1975.

With Allen Young, *The Gay Report: Lesbians and Gay Men Speak Out about Sexual Experiences and Lifestyles.* New York, Summit, 1979.

The Amazon and the Page: Natalie Clifford Barney and Renée Vivien (biography and literary study). Bloomington, Indiana University Press, 1988.

"The Future of Lesbian and Gay Literature," in *Lambda Book Report,* September/October 1991, 6–9.

Other

Translator, with Yvonne M. Klein, and author of introduction, *The Woman of the Wolf, and Other Stories* (translation of *La Dame à la Louve* and short stories and prose poems by Renée Vivien). New York, Gay Presses of New York, 1983.

"The Outsider among the Expatriates: Djuna Barnes' Satire on the Ladies of the *Almanack,*" in *Silence and Power: A Reevaluation of Djuna Barnes,* edited by Mary Lynn Broe. Carbondale, Southern Illinois University Press, 1991.

Author of introduction, *A Perilous Advantage: The Best of Natalie Clifford Barney,* translation by Anna Livia. Norwich, Vermont, New Victoria, 1992.

Author of introduction, *Adventures of the Mind* by Natalie Clifford Barney, translation by John Gatton. New York, New York University Press, 1992.

*

Critical Sources: "An Antidote to Hemlock" by Louie Crew, in *The Gay Academic,* Palm Springs, California, ETC Publications, 1978, xix; "The Future of Lesbian and Gay Literature" by Karla Jay, in *Lambda Book Report,* September/October 1991, 6–9; *Stonewall* by Martin B. Duberman, New York, Dutton, 1993.

*   *   *

Karla Jay is a political and literary activist with an amazingly diverse and impressive string of credentials. A vital and unique catalyst and contributor to gay and lesbian culture because of her dual position as both activist and academic, Jay has made her scholarship accessible to eager lesbian and gay audiences at conferences and workshops—she was among those itinerant historians who presented slide shows on aspects of gay/lesbian culture before general academic acceptance and publication made such work more easily available. Together with Allen Young, Jay has coedited three books that rank among the most important means through which gay and lesbian culture was communicated during the 1970s. At a time when anything not run off on a copying machine was slightly suspect—books with establishment imprimaturs were seen as sell-outs to the enemy—the professionally published work of Jay and Young found acceptance and even praise within the community. It was then thought that the only reason major publishing houses would produce a gay/lesbian book was to coopt the message or to make money off an issue or writer that could not be ignored; it was a tribute to Jay's standing that, within the community, her veracity or motives were never impugned.

Jay's credibility has been earned—she had paid her dues "on the streets" during both the feminist and gay/lesbian liberation move-

ments of the late 1960s and early 1970s. She participated in both Redstockings and the Gay Liberation Front, protested at the "Miss America Pageant," and was wiretapped by the FBI; she lectured, wrote, panned, and prodded the nascent homosexual community. Jay authored dozens of articles for *Lesbian Tide,* never losing sight of the position of the lesbian as a minority within a minority. *Out of the Closets,* which she and Young published in 1972, and *Lavender Culture,* published six years later, made gay/lesbian politics and aesthetics widely accessible to a people who were just gaining a sense of their own identity, as well as interested heterosexuals. To a generation of gays and lesbians coming to terms with their sexuality and questioning their identity, the books of Jay and Young offered a sense of community and continuity. Where homosexuals of a generation earlier had come up against libraries with empty shelves or religious and medical references to "sickness" in their search for a sense of self, Jay and a new breed of activist academics were circulating the source material for comprehending individual identity in a new cultural context.

Louie Crew wrote in *The Gay Academic* that before Stonewall, "it would have been virtually unthinkable for any academic on this side of retirement and on either side of tenure" to put the lie to the stereotypes that "would have us gay only when some of us commit crimes or when we are sexually aroused, saying at other times we are 'just persons'." In their books, Jay and Young collected material that retold the history of oppression and accomplishments, disseminated position papers, documented confrontations between activists and establishment professional organizations: they raised the questions and posed the answers that were essential to building a community.

Jay understood that it was essential for gays—particularly lesbians—to have an appreciation of their past if they were to move forward with a sense of dignity and purpose. If women were hidden from history, lesbians were buried deep, but in *The Gay Report* lesbians finally surfaced on equal footing with gay males. The fact that the report on which the book was based—5,000 surveys returned by gay people from all over North America—was not an establishment–funded study but a grassroots response to post–Kinsey questions like "Who *are* gays?" and "What do they want?" led to challenges to its credibility from the old guard and praise from activists and gay academics.

Jay continued to write, lecture, and review books while pursuing the research and translating necessary to complete her doctorate in comparative literature. The factors in her decision to research the writing and lives of Natalie Barney and Renée Vivien exemplify gay/lesbian culture at work. She first heard of Barney and Vivien from feminist academic Gayle Rubin, who offered a paper on them at a Gay Academic Union conference in the early 1970s. Subsequently, historian Jonathan Katz asked her to review their works and select those to be included as reprints in a series on homosexuality that he was editing for Arno Press. Later, Jeanette Howard Foster, doyenne of lesbian literature studies, bequeathed to Jay several first editions of works by Barney and Vivien in their original French. English translations of *The Woman of the Wolf,* a collection of short stories by Vivien, and *The Amazon and the Page,* on the personal literary relationship of the women and their Paris circle, are among Jay's contribution to gay/lesbian culture.

From the time it was published in 1990, *Lesbian Texts and Contexts: Radical Revisions* served as a launching pad for explosive reevaluations of lesbians in literature. No less a bombshell than Millett's *Sexual Politics* of a generation earlier, the essays included in *Lesbian Texts and Contexts* reached a segment of the popular audience as well. In general, Jay is critical of the reading patterns of the majority of the gay/lesbian community—too much fruit salad and not enough meat and potatoes. While observing in *Lambda Book Report* that gay and/or lesbian studies and related academic works continue to be published, she bemoans many readers' choice of "mainly or only romances, mysteries and erotica ... forcing publishers to produce more of them and few works of high literary quality.... We cannot create a viable and sustainable culture on pulp alone."

—*Marie J. Kuda*

JEAN–LOUIS. *See* **KEROUAC, Jack.**

JOHNSTON, Jill. British and American journalist and critic. Has also written as F. J. Crowe. Born in London, 17 May 1929. Married Richard John Lanham in 1958 (divorced 1964); one son and one daughter. Author of column, "Dance Journal," *Village Voice,* New York City, 1959–75; critic, *Art in America,* New York City, 1983–87. Contributor to *Art News,* 1959–65.

WRITINGS

Autobiographies

Autobiography of a Father: Volume 1: *Mother Bound,* New York, Knopf, 1983; Volume 2: *Paper Daughter,* New York, Knopf, 1985.

Other

Marmalade Me (selections from "Dance Journal" column). New York, Dutton, 1971.
Lesbian Nation: The Feminist Solution. New York, Simon & Schuster, 1973.
Editor, with Bertha Harris, Esther Newton, and Jane O'Wyatt, *Amazon Expedition: A Lesbian–Feminist Anthology.* San Rafael, California, Times Change Press, 1973.
Gullibles Travels. New York, Links Books, 1974.
Author of introduction, *To the Man Reporter from the Denver Post* by Chocolate Waters. Denver, Colorado, Eggplant Press, 1980.

*

Critical Sources: *New York,* 24 May 1971.

In 1969 a panel of performers, critics, collectors and artists, including Andy Warhol, met in New York City to discuss the writings of Jill Johnston. The title of the panel was "The Disintegration of a Critic," although Gregory Battcock, a panel member and prominent art theorist claims in his introduction to Johnston's collected dance criticism *Marmalade Me,* that an alternate title might have been "The Disintegration of Criticism."

Johnston began writing art and dance criticism in the mid–1950s. She contributed to *Art News,* wrote frequently for *Art in America* from 1959 to 1965, and authored the column "Dance Journal" in the *Village Voice* from 1959 to 1975. Her earliest pieces were straightforward, traditional criticism, but during the mid–1960s Johnston's writing turned more personal. Battcock writes in his introduction "[A] major discovery by Jill Johnston is simply, that criticism is a unique form that does not necessarily depend upon another specific object or phenomenon for its own existence or worth. However, that criticism does possess a unique identity has not yet been sufficiently demonstrated. Before it can be demonstrated, the *possibility* needs to be conceived and the new, potentially vital form must be envisioned." Through her dance and art criticism Jill Johnston began to construct a new *idea* of cultural criticism which placed her own life, emotions, thoughts and actions in the foreground as works of art (granted mostly in progress) with the cultural context surrounding her life as background.

By the late 1960s many of her columns were more about her life than the work she was ostensibly critiquing and by late 1969—after the Stonewall Riots—she came out. Her writing grew even more personal and her style had became strictly stream–of–consciousness: current events, foreign phrases, literary references and what she had for lunch were likely to be thread together along with thoughts on politics, feminism, identity and sex in a necklace of provocative ideas and juxtapositions. Most of these early pieces from 1967 to 1969 were later collected in *Marmalade Me.*

In 1970 Johnston's "Dance Journal" became, in essence, a weekly meditation on the emerging politic of lesbian feminism. Johnston coined the term "Lesbian Nation"—which became the title of her 1973 book, a collection of *Village Voice* essays—to describe an emotional, psychological and possibly physical space in which lesbians can find a sense of community and strength that are denied in a purely patriarchal world. Much of Johnston's writing at this point posited a clearly political viewpoint. In her "Conclusion" to *Lesbian Nation* she wrote: "Within just two years the meaning of the word lesbian has changed from private subversive activity to political revolutionary identity."

Johnston's revolutionary identity, however, was also distinctly personal as well. Johnston's odyssey was the basis for her political thinking and she understood the extent that her life and actions formed her political ideology. In *Lesbian Nation* she wrote: "I'm persona non grata with every 'group' in the country, just for openers. The woman's lib people don't like the way I swim. The Gay Liberation Front says I wouldn't get any support from *them.* Both organizations think I'm a male chauvinist pig, probably because I take more girls to bed (or want to or pretend to) than I have a right to—as though nobody was ever luring *me* to bed. A black man once told me that LeRoi Jones and the like wanted my head on a platter. The artists were never pleased that I began to find their lives more interesting than their art."

Although Johnston was a major theorist of early lesbian feminism, her life and her politics were distinctly her own. Her emphasis on sexuality—she was never hesitant to tell who she found attractive or with whom she had sex—separated her from many other contemporary feminists whose analysis centered more upon economic and gender discrimination and oppression than sexuality. In her next book, *Gullibles Travels,* a collection of *Village Voice* pieces from 1973, Johnston's style eschewed traditional capitalization, punctuation, grammar and syntax in favor of a highly idiosyncratic sense of sound and style. Johnston had created a completely new prose form to convey the complexity and inner meaning of her life and experiences.

If *Lesbian Nation* is overtly polemic—Johnston critiques Sigmund Freud, Friedrich Engles, and Hollywood from a feminist perspective—the essays in *Gullibles Travels* are intensely personal. These led the way to her next two books, *Mother Bound* and *Paper Daughter.* Although both volumes are formal autobiographies, written in traditional linear prose and narrative style, they are the logical continuation of her earlier pieces. In *Lesbian Nation* and *Gullibles Travels,* Johnston's search for her familial roots (she was raised by her mother and never knew the facts of her father's life) is the attempt to make sense of the past while living in the present. Both books again display her fascination with Freud, with popular culture, with the construction of family and community and with using language to represent herself.

If *Lesbian Nation* and *Gullibles Travels* presented readers with, in Gregory Battcock's words, "the disintegration of U criticism," *Mother Bound* and *Paper Daughter* were attempts to create a new self, or personal, criticism. There are many personal episodes alluded to in *Lesbian Nation* and *Gullibles Travels* that are delineated here: the early years in Catholic boarding school, her six year marriage to John Lanham, the intrigues of the art world, her three nervous breakdowns and her near inability to deal with the fame and notoriety that came with her public announcements about her private life. Along with everything else they contain, both *Mother Bound* and *Paper Daughter* explicate gay liberation, the second wave of feminism, and other political and cultural movements, and place them securely in the context of the social upheavals of the 1960s. In this Johnston has not only forged and illuminated lesbian and gay theory with her own life but has given it a history as well.

—*Michael Bronski*

K

K. M. *See* MANSFIELD, Katherine.

———

KATZ, Jonathan (Ned). American editor, dramatist, and nonfiction writer. Born in New York City, 2 February 1938. Educated at Antioch College, 1956–57; City College of New York (now City College of the City University of New York), 1957–60; and New School for Social Research. Free–lance textile designer at Prince Studio, New York City, 1960–65; partner and free–lance textile designer at New Group, Inc., New York City, 1965–70; textile designer at Henry Glass, Inc., New York City, 1970–72, 1976. Researcher and editor of recordings for Caedmon Recordings, including *Black Pioneers,* 1968–69, and *Red Man/White Man: Documents of Conflict.* **Recipient:** Louis M. Rabinowitz Foundation grants for researching and writing a radio play, 1967, and for continued research on the American history of homosexual oppression and resistance, 1976; American Library Association Gay Book Award, 1975. Agent: Joan Raines, Raines & Raines, 475 Fifth Avenue, New York, New York 10017, U.S.A.

WRITINGS

Radio Plays

The Dispute over the Ownership of Anthony Burns, WBAI–FM, 1967.
Inquest at Christiana, WBAI–FM, 1968.

Plays

Coming Out! A Documentary Play about Gay Life and Liberation in the U.S.A. (two–act; produced New York, 1972–73). New York, Arno, 1975.
Comrades and Lovers (a theatre piece about Whitman; readings given in New York, Boston, Chicago, Atlanta, and Lawrence Kansas).

Nonfiction

Resistance at Christiana: The Fugitive Slave Rebellion, Christiana, Pennsylvania, September 11, 1851; A Documentary Account. New York, Crowell, 1974.

Gay American History: Lesbians and Gay Men in the U.S.A; A Documentary. New York, Harper, 1976, revised, Meridian, 1992.
Gay/Lesbian Almanac: A New Documentary in Which Is Contained, in Chronological Order, Evidence of the True and Fantastical History of Those Persons Now Called Lesbians and Gay Men. New York, Harper, 1983.
The Invention of Heterosexuality, forthcoming.

Editor

Documents of the Homosexual Rights Movement in Germany, 1836–1927. New York, Ayer, 1975.
A Gay Bibliography: Eight Bibliographies on Lesbian and Male Homosexuality; An Original Anthology. New York, Ayer, 1975.
A Gay News Chronology, 1969–1975: Index and Abstracts of Articles from the New York Times. New York, Ayer, 1975.
Government versus Homosexuals: An Original Anthology. New York, Ayer, 1975.
A Homosexual Emancipation Miscellany, 1835–1952: An Original Anthology. New York, Ayer, 1975.
Homosexuality: Lesbians and Gay Men in Society, History, and Literature. New York, Ayer, 1975.
I Am a Woman by Ann Bannon. New York, Ayer, 1975.
Journey to a Woman by Ann Bannon. New York, Ayer, 1975.
Odd Girl Out by Ann Bannon. New York, Ayer, 1975.
Women in the Shadows by Ann Bannon. New York, Ayer, 1975.
Lesbianism and Feminism in Germany, 1895–1910: An Original Anthology. New York, Ayer, 1975.
Miss Marianne Woods and Miss Jane Pirie against Dame Helen Cumming Gordon. New York, Ayer, 1975.
Arts and Education Handbook: A Guide to Productive Collaborations. Washington, D.C., National Assembly of State Arts Agencies, 1988.

Other

With Bernard Katz, *Black Woman: A Fictionalized Biography of Lucy Terry Prince.* New York, Pantheon, 1970.
"Melville's Secret Sex Text," in *Village Voice Literary Supplement,* 13 April 1982.

*

Critical Sources: *American History Review,* February 1976.

*   *   *

Jonathan Katz grew up in Greenwich Village and felt insecure during his formative years. He attended many different colleges but ultimately dropped out, blaming the poor quality of his teachers for his decision. Like many gays, he entered psychoanalysis, hoping to erase his homosexuality, but was lucky to find a therapist who helped him understand and accept himself.

He worked on documentary plays in the late 1960s for New York's Pacifica radio station, WBAI–FM, leading to his research on a major fugitive slave demonstration in Pennsylvania, which informed his publication *Resistance at Christiana*. He was coauthor with his father, Bernard Katz, of *Black Woman*, a half fictional biography of Lucy Terry Prince. From about 1960 to 1972 he designed textiles.

Katz was gradually coming out until a homophobic article in *Harper's* impelled him to join the militant Gay Activist Alliance— whose members sat in at the *Harper's* office. "I think there's something healthy about Gays focusing on their particular problems and starting from their own sense of anger at their oppression," he stated of this event. "How can Gays make the world better for themselves unless they assert themselves?"

His interest in gay history surfaced in writing the docu–drama, *Coming Out!*, directed by David Roggensak, produced at the Gay Activist Alliance's Firehouse in New York City in 1972. The work was later presented at Washington Square United Methodist and at David Gaard's The Night House, with newly discovered material included. Critics called it funny, intensely moving, fast–paced, vital and inspirational.

Until rehearsals began, Katz had used the pen name John Swift, but "realized I just couldn't do a play called *Coming Out*, that advocates liberation and openness, and use a phony name." The play featured an all–gay ensemble, and although Katz had hoped that the play would not have been cast with such restrictions, he felt that the gay and lesbian actors brought something special to it, "speaking from their own experience."

He loved the detective work that went into researching his works, tracking down information on obscure gay persons. He had a difficult time finding material about women, however. Families destroyed letters, as did the subjects themselves in order to avoid being remembered as gay. Katz spent endless hours in the New York Public Library tracking down material, and sometimes cried in the library when he unearthed some sought–after fact. He discovered much evidence of oppression, but less material about resistance, such as a transvestite's 1890s diary describing New York gay bars and a group set up to resist police raids.

His ground–breaking, beautiful and inspiring volume *Gay American History: Lesbians and Gay Men in the U.S.A.* contained over 150 documents about the oppression of gays since 1566: "treatment" by doctors, women who passed as men, information about gay Native Americans, resistance, and love. It gave most gays a first hint of a rich but heretofore unknown history and inspired other research. His extensive notes covered further examples of persecution, love letters, and survival against great odds. Katz became a star on the gay lecture circuit. *Gay American History*'s weakly written sequel, *The Gay Almanac*, also included important documents, but bent to the social construction theory which stated that gay community or identity only became possible about 1880. The second book's two sections, which focused on early oppression and resistance after 1890 respectively, obscured the stages of transition to gay consciousness evident in the first volume. The *Almanac* introduction seemed to erase earlier ages from gay history since other societies presumably defined homosexual acts differently.

Katz also oversaw the 69–volume Arno reprint series *Homo-sexuality: Lesbians and Gay Men in Society, History and Literature* and edited or compiled several specific works in the series, which with his *Gay American History,* tripled access to information about a subject that had consisted of material provided by the ancient Greeks; "discrete" biographies of a few scattered kings, queens and artists; and work from 20 years of the current homophile/gay movement. In preparing *Gay American History* on a skimpy budget, Katz disdained the "Great Man" approach to history, looking for documents about all kinds of gays, especially ordinary ones. Of the work, he expressed in unpublished correspondence: "I hope to indicate some of the deeper relations between gay life, liberation and oppression, and the wider American society.... The book will be important if I can just indicate all the work there is to be done, if it helps open up the area of gay history ... and take it away from the doctors."

In a letter to Craig Hanson, who had analyzed the different poles of the gay movement, Katz said, "I tend toward the radical utopians, but have a pragmatic sense of what is possible under present social conditions." His comment referred to the reality of homophobia (a term that Hanson helped launch). In Katz's opinion, homophobia was not restricted to fear; he felt that it also incorporated feelings of "hate and even attraction."

Katz was a founder of the Gay Academic Union, whose first two conventions in New York City brought hundreds of academics out of the closet, but conflict between radicals such as Katz and the radical feminists against more conservative scholars decimated the group. Its energy was passed to large caucuses in specific disciplines, including sociology, history, psychology, and anthropology. In 1974 he urged the Gay Academic Union to consider starting a Gertrude Stein–Walt Whitman Homosexual Studies Collection at the New York University Library or elsewhere. He inspired and encouraged excellent work by John D'Emilio and later gay historians.

Since *Almanac,* Katz has earned his living by speaking, publishers' advances and very odd jobs. His theatre piece, *Comrades and Lovers,* about Whitman and his men, has had successful readings in New York, Boston, Chicago, Atlanta and Lawrence, Kansas. He calls himself a "most extreme" constructionist (based on the idea that homosexuality came into existence around 1880 when society defined gays as such, that ancient Greek male–male practices were therefore something else, and that gayness is created by how society defines homosexuals—as opposed to the "essentialist" view that gays have always been around, however gays happened to be defined locally). He is a work on a book, *The Invention of Heterosexuality,* intended for 1994 publication. He dismisses the "mushy middle" view that people are a product of both their natures and social conditioning. He says the process of historicizing sexuality and homosexuality is leading to important surprises. He marched in Washington in 1979 and 1987 and insists that even in the midst of the great tragedy of AIDS, gays need to recover their history. He still feels Marxism has great intellectual potential. Today, he says, is an exciting time, but as gays develop new clout, as the military issue advances, they must keep pushing. He denies that the term outing applies to telling the truth about people who are dead—even if families object—but insists that outing living people must be done with great care—oppressive times may come again. While historians still debate the theories, Katz's contribution to self-knowledge, history, and gay pride are incalculable.

—*Jim Kepner*

KENAN, Randall. American educator and author of fiction. Born in Brooklyn, New York, 12 March 1963. Educated at University of North Carolina B.A. 1985. Editor, Alfred A. Knopf, New York City, 1985–89; lecturer at Sarah Lawrence College, Bronxville, New York, beginning 1989, Vassar College, Poughkeepsie, New York, beginning 1989, and Columbia University, New York City, beginning 1990. **Recipient:** New York Foundation of the Arts grant, 1989; MacDowell Colony fellowship, 1990. Address: Sarah Lawrence College, Bronxville, New York 10708, U.S.A.

WRITINGS

Fiction

A Visitation of Spirits (novel). New York, Grove Press, 1989.
Let the Dead Bury Their Dead, and Other Stories. New York, Harcourt, 1992.

*

Critical Sources: "Debut of a Virtuoso" (review of *A Visitation of Spirits*) by George Garrett, in *Tribune Books* (Chicago), 13 August 1989, 6; *Lambda Book Report,* January 1991, 37; "Carolina Dreamin'" (review of *Let the Dead Bury Their Dead*) by Valerie Miner in *Nation,* 6 July 1992, 28; "Randall Kenan: To Live and Die in Dixie" (review of *Let the Dead Bury Their Dead*) by Jean Hanff Korelitz in *Washington Post Book World,* 2 August 1992, 1, 11.

*   *   *

Randall Kenan's first two fictional publications have drawn much attention for their stylistic virtuosity and thematic richness. They work together, as well as singly, to bring to life a small African American community in North Carolina called Tims Creek. Critics have been impressed by Kenan's skill in filling that community with magical as well as realistic imagery and complex individuals within racial and sexual types.

Readers were first introduced to Tims Creek in the novel *A Visitation of Spirits.* Horace Thomas Cross, a brilliant student, is led to relive much of his life, and generations of his family's history, through a long night in April 1984, which ends in tragedy. Taking him on this tour towards doom are demons which may be real or figurative—for Cross is full of confusion and guilt, and disgusted by his own homosexuality. Interspersed with this narrative is one in which Cross' older cousin, the Reverend James Malachai Green, takes his aunt and uncle to visit a dying relative in December 1985. On the way, the trio provide perspective on Cross and the town's history. Besides these time leaps, the narrative also shifts between various third and first–person narrations, including discourses on subjects from chicken plucking to contemporary music. "Truth is," George Garrett wrote in the *Tribune Books,* "Kenan tries pretty much of everything and pretty much gets away with all of it, too."

Kenan continues to explore Tims Creek, and the human condition, from an even greater variety of perspectives in *Let the Dead Bury the Dead, and Other Stories.* "Each of these stories," said

Valerie Miner in the *Nation,* "builds on and resonates with the others, giving readers a textured appreciation for Tims Creek, pious and witty, poor and affluent, black and white." In the title novella, Horace Cross' surname turns out to be that of the plantation owner whose slaves escaped and founded the town in a then–isolated swamp. A history of the founding and development of the town—from which myth and chronicle are hard to separate—is related in the novella through a variety of prisms: oral history, diary entries, and letters, all recorded by Reverend Green, whose unfinished opus is incorporated into a heavily annotated academic treatise by the narrator "RK" in the late 1990s. "The result," commented Jean Hanff Korelitz in the *Washington Post Book World,* "is a conjuring at once specific to one imaginary corner of the south and yet somehow evocative of the entire region and period." The conjuring, as well as sensuality—lost, recovered, genuine, manipulative, hetero– and homo–erotic—run throughout the remaining stories in the collection, as do humorous and enlightening (but non–didactic) encounters, such as that between Booker T. Washington and two former schoolmates in 1909.

The liveliness, variety, and dexterity of the writer has been impressive to many. Miner concluded, "Kenan explores the territories in between the living and the dead, between the fantastic and mundane in an energetic, inventive prose that never descends to contrivance or sentimentality."

————

KEROUAC, Jack (Jean–Louis Lebrid de Kerouac). American novelist and poet. Also wrote as Jean–Louis Incogniteau; Jean–Louis; John Kerouac. Born in Lowell, Massachusetts, 12 March 1922. Educated at Horace Mann School for Boys; Columbia College, 1940–42; New York School for Social Research, 1948–49. Served with U.S. Merchant Marine, 1942 and 1943, and U.S. Navy, 1943. Married 1) Frankie Edith Parker in 1944 (annulled 1945); 2) Joan Haverty in 1950 (divorced); one daughter; 3) Stella Sampas in 1966. Held a variety of jobs, including odd jobs in garages; sports reporter, *Sun,* Lowell, Massachusetts, 1942; railroad brakeman, Southern Pacific Railroad, San Francisco, 1952–53; traveled around the United States and Mexico; fire lookout, United States Agriculture Service, northwest Washington, 1956. Regular contributor of column "The Last Word" to *Escapade,* 1959–61; contributor to *Columbia Review* (as Jean–Louis Incogniteau), and *New World Writing* (as Jean–Louis). **Recipient:** American Academy of Arts and Sciences grant, 1955. *Died in St. Petersburg, Florida, of a stomach hemorrhage, 21 October 1969.*

WRITINGS

Novels

The Town and the City (as John Kerouac). New York, Harcourt, 1950; London, Eyre & Spottiswoode, 1951; under name Jack Kerouac, Grosset, 1960.
On the Road. New York, Viking, 1957; London, Deutsch, 1958; as *On the Road: Text and Criticism,* notes by Scott Donaldson, New York, Penguin, 1979.

The Dharma Bums. New York, Viking, 1958; London, Deutsch, 1959.

The Subterraneans. New York, Grove, 1958; London, Deutsch, 1960; in *The Subterraneans as Two Novels,* 1973.

Doctor Sax: Faust Part Three. New York, Grove, 1959; London, Deutsch, 1977.

Maggie Cassidy: A Love Story. New York, Avon, 1959; London, Panther, 1960.

Excerpts from Visions of Cody. New York, New Directions, 1960; enlarged as *Visions of Cody,* New York, McGraw, 1972; London, Deutsch, 1973.

Tristessa. New York, Avon, 1960; London, World, 1963; in *Visions of Gerard and Tristessa,* 1963.

Big Sur. New York, Farrar, Straus, 1962; London, Deutsch, 1963.

Visions of Gerard (as John Kerouac). New York, Farrar, Straus, 1963; in *Visions of Gerard and Tristessa,* 1963; under name Jack Kerouac, New York, McGraw, 1976.

Visions of Gerard and Tristessa. London, Deutsch, 1963.

Desolation Angels. New York, Coward–McCann, 1965; London, Deutsch, 1966.

Satori in Paris. New York, Grove, 1966; London, Deutsch, 1967; with *Pic,* New York, Grove, 1986.

Vanity of Duluoz: An Adventurous Education, 1935–46. New York, Coward–McCann, 1968; London, Deutsch, 1969.

Pic. New York, Grove, 1971; in *The Subterraneans as Two Novels,* 1973; with *Satori in Paris,* New York, Grove, 1986.

The Subterraneans as Two Novels (contains *The Subterraneans* and *Pic*). London, Deutsch, 1973.

With William S. Burroughs, *And the Hippos Were Boiled in Their Tanks.*

The Sea Is My Brother.

Buddha Tells Us.

Secret Mullings about Bill.

Poetry

Mexico City Blues: Two Hundred Forty–two Choruses. New York, Grove, 1959.

Hugo Weber. Portents, 1967.

Someday You'll Be Lying. Privately printed, 1968.

A Lost Haiku. Privately printed, 1969.

Scattered Poems. San Francisco, City Lights Books, 1971.

With Albert Saijo and Lew Welch, *Trip Trap: Haiku along the Road from San Francisco to New York, 1959.* Bolinas, California, Grey Fox Press, 1973.

Heaven and Other Poems. Bolinas, California, Grey Fox Press, 1977.

San Francisco Blues. Beat Books, 1983.

Hymn: God Pray for Me. Dover, New Hampshire, Caliban, 1985.

American Haikus. Dover, New Hampshire, Caliban, 1986.

Other

Contributor, *January 1st 1959: Fidel Castro.* New York, Totem Press, 1959.

Rimbaud. San Francisco, City Lights Books, 1959.

The Scripture of the Golden Eternity (philosophy and religion). New York, Totem Press/Corinth Books, and London, Centaur, 1960.

Nosferatu (Dracula) (pamphlet). New York, New York Film Society, 1960.

Author of introduction, *The Americans.* New York, Grove, 1960.

Lonesome Traveler (autobiography). New York, McGraw, 1960; London, Deutsch, 1962.

Book of Dreams. San Francisco, City Lights Books, 1961.

Ad lib narrator, *Pull My Daisy* (screenplay). New York, Grove, and London, Evergreen, 1961.

A Pun for Al Gelpi (broadside). New York, Cambridge, 1966.

A Memoir in Which Is Revealed Secret Lives and West Coast Whispers. Aurora, Oregon, Giligia, 1970.

Not Long Ago Joy Abounded at Christmas, 1972.

Two Early Stories. Atlanta, Aloe Editions, 1973.

Home at Christmas. Oliphant, 1973.

Old Angel Midnight. Trappe, Maryland, Unicorn Bookshop, 1976.

With Allen Ginsberg, *Take Care of My Ghost, Ghost* (letters). Ghost Press, 1977.

Une veille de Noel. Knight, 1980.

With Carolyn Cassady, *Dear Carolyn: Letters to Carolyn Cassady.* California, Pennsylvania, Unspeakable Visions, 1983.

Visions of America (limited edition). Sudbury, Massachusetts, Water Row Press, 1991.

Before the Road: Young Cody and the Birth of Hippie.

Recordings: With Steve Allen, *Poetry for the Beat Generation,* Hanover, 1959; *Blues and Haikus,* Hanover, 1959; *Readings by Jack Kerouac on the Beat Generation,* Verve, 1959; *The Jack Kerouac Collection* (includes *Poetry for the Beat Generation, Blues and Haikus,* and *Readings by Jack Kerouac on the Beat Generation*), Rhino Records, 1990.

*

Adaptations: *The Subterraneans* (film), Metro–Goldwyn–Mayer, 1960; a play based on Kerouac's life and works, New York, 1976.

Manuscript Collections: Columbia University Library, New York.

Biography: *Kerouac: A Biography* by Ann Charters, San Francisco, Straight Arrow, 1973; *Visions of Kerouac* by Charles E. Jarvis, Lowell, Massachusetts, Ithaca Press, 1973; *Heart Beat: My Life with Jack and Neal* by Carolyn Cassady, Berkeley, California, Creative Arts, 1977; *Jack's Book: An Oral Biography of Jack Kerouac* by Barry Gifford and Lawrence Lee, New York, St. Martin's Press, 1978; *Desolate Angel: Jack Kerouac, the Beat Generation, and America* by Dennis McNally, New York, McGraw, 1979; *Memory Babe: A Critical Biography of Jack Kerouac* by Gerald Nicosia, New York, Grove, 1983; *Kerouac: Visions of Rocky Mount,* edited by John J. Dorfner, Sudbury, Massachusetts, Water Row Press, 1991.

Bibliography: *A Bibliography of Works by Jack Kerouac, 1939–1975* by Ann Charters, New York, Phoenix Book Shop, 1975; *Jack Kerouac: A Bibliography of Biographical and Critical Material, 1950–1979* by T. E. Nisonger, Bull Bibliography, 1980; *Jack Kerouac: An Annotated Bibliography of Secondary Sources, 1944–1979* by Robert J. Milewski, Metuchen, New Jersey, Scarecrow Press, 1981.

Critical Sources: *A Casebook on the Beat,* edited by Thomas Parkinson, New York, Crowell, 1961; *No Pie in the Sky: The Hobo as American Culture Hero in the Works of Jack London, John Dos Passos, and Jack Kerouac* by Frederick Feied, New York, Citadel, 1964; *Nothing More to Declare* by John Clellon Holmes, New York, Dutton, 1967, 68–86; *The Beat Generation* by Bruce Cook, New York, Scribner, 1971; *Naked Angels: The Lives and Literature of the Beat Generation* by John Tytell, New York, McGraw, 1976, 52–78, 140–211; *Jack Kerouac: Prophet of the New Romanticism* by Robert A. Hipkiss, Lawrence, University of Kansas Press, 1977; *On the Road: Text and Criticism,* edited by Scott Donaldson, New York, Viking, 1979; *Kerouac's Crooked Road: Development of a Fiction* by Tim Hunt, Hamden, Connecticut, Archon, 1981; *Jack Kerouac* by Warren French, Boston, Twayne Publishers, 1986; *What Happened to Kerouac?* (documentary film) by Richard Lerner, 1986.

*   *   *

Any appraisal of Jack Kerouac's work immediately butts up against the autobiographical content of the books, allowing little separation between the author and his writing. Beginning with his debut novel, *The Town and the City,* through his more famous efforts such as *On the Road,* Kerouac's subject nearly always involve Kerouac and his companions, and in most regards, the books remain very true to the facts of his existence. In many cases, the factual basis of his work has made analysis of his impact more fruitful; critics have been better able to assess Kerouac as a voice of the Beat generation because the books explicitly outline his relationship to other figures in the group, including Neal Cassady, Allen Ginsberg, and William S. Burroughs, all of whom figure as characters in *On the Road* and other Kerouac titles.

When addressing the depiction of homosexual relationships in Kerouac's books, however, one finds that certain aspects of his life were more accessible through his fiction than others. In this area it is the absence of autobiographical material that is notable, making Kerouac a more enigmatic figure. At the same time, his treatment of same sex relationships illumines an issue that was somewhat taboo, even for an author who was thought to be a saboteur of mainstream American values in the 1950s.

Kerouac's treatment of gays becomes clear when one considers the predominance of homosexuals and bisexuals among those people who are the focus of his autobiographical accounts. First on this list is Ginsberg, who met Kerouac when both were students at Columbia University in the early 1940s. According to Gerald Nicosia's biography, *Memory Babe: A Critical Biography of Jack Kerouac,* Ginsberg summoned the courage to reveal his homosexuality and his attraction to Kerouac early in their relationship. Kerouac, according to Nicosia, initially reacted negatively, but the men remained close friends and Kerouac gradually came to accept Ginsberg's sexuality. Neal Cassady later became Ginsberg's lover, Kerouac's friend, and, eventually, the quintessential Beat hero of many of Kerouac's novels. Cassady was renown for his sexual prowess with women, but was nonetheless perfectly comfortable with homosexual encounters. Burroughs, another of Kerouac's close acquaintances and a central figure in the Beat movement, likewise engaged in homosexual relations.

Kerouac clearly had a considerable exposure to gay relationships through his friends, whom he often used as models for the literary characters in his autobiographical novels; however, their homosexuality is conspicuously absent in these works. Only rarely is there a reference to anything gay, despite the fact so many of his friends were gay or bisexual and the social and literary world in which he traveled was so imbued with homosexuality. When Kerouac does mention homosexuality in his books, it is often quite inconsequential—like meeting some fellow writers in a "Frisco" gay bar before going off to someone's house for a night of drinking in *The Subterraneans*—or sometimes a portrayal of gay characters as flawed and fatalistic. In *The Town and the City,* part four ends with the suicide of a handicapped homosexual, Waldo Meister. Meister takes his own life after being spurned by his inamorata, Kenny Wood, the person responsible for the accident that maimed Meister. Kerouac paints a ghoulish portrait of Waldo stalking Kenny. While leaving a nightclub with a group of people, Kenny takes his girlfriend by the arm to go home and is grabbed by Waldo in a supplicating way. "I said let go, you old fairy!" Kenny screams and sends Waldo sprawling across the pavement. While his friends berate him for abusing a poor cripple, Kenny advises them, "You're not acquainted with the facts." After Waldo's suicide, it is Kenny who must go to the morgue to identify the mangled corpse.

More revealing are passages from *On the Road,* a book that concentrates on Kerouac's relationships with Ginsberg, Burroughs, and especially Cassady. While the novel reflects their real life journeys and experiences, the emphasis is on heterosexuality—Burroughs and his wife (known as Bull and Jane Lee, respectively, in the book) and Cassady's romantic exploits with a variety of women. Homosexuality is noticeably omitted, and when it is mentioned, it is referred to in negative terms and derided by stereotypic portrayals—the depiction of the mincing "fairy" that sits in with a San Francisco jazz band being a prime example—or incidents have been altered in Kerouac's retelling. For example, in *On the Road* when Dean (Cassady's fictional name in the book) and Sal (Kerouac) are traveling east from San Francisco in a travel–bureau car, the driver of the car is described as a "fag" who is targeted by Dean as a source of money. In a Sacramento hotel room Dean tries to hustle the man, promising sex for money, but when the man becomes sullen and suspicious, Sal and Dean leave the room with no cash. Biographical accounts of this incident, however, claim that a sexual encounter did take place and that Kerouac was kept up all night by the bedroom athletics of Cassady and the driver. Here we see Kerouac carefully manipulating his account in regard to gay relations. In the fictional account the homosexual act is not consummated, and Kerouac's Beat hero, Dean, emerges unscathed from his same sex flirtation. In the end he appears more as a trickster figure who is scheming to separate the "fag" from his money rather than a man who would willingly engage in sex with another man.

Such incidents point to paradox regarding Kerouac's role as a social provocateur in the years following World War II. On one hand, he was viewed as a radical threat to the conservative values of the 1950s, a stance that was exemplified in his controversial writings about drugs, alcohol, and heterosexual sex. When it came to addressing the behavior of gays, however, Kerouac's writings remained much closer to the mainstream. While his personal relationships seemed to have been marked by an acceptance of others' homosexuality, his books adopt the status quo position of ignoring or attacking same sex relationships.

—*Richard Alexei*

KEROUAC, John. *See* **KEROUAC, Jack.**

———

KILINA, Patricia. *See* **WARREN, Patricia Nell.**

———

KIMITAKE, Hiraoka. *See* **MISHIMA, Yukio.**

———

KRAMER, Larry. American playwright, novelist, and activist. Born in Bridgeport, Connecticut, 25 June 1935; grew up in a suburb of Washington, D.C. Educated at Yale University, New Haven, Connecticut, B.A. 1957. Served in the U.S. Army, 1957. Messenger, William Morris Agency, New York City, 1958; telex operator, Columbia Pictures, New York City, 1958–59; assistant story editor, Columbia Pictures, New York City, 1961; production executive, Columbia Pictures, London, 1961–65; assistant to the president, United Artists, 1965; associate producer, *Here We Go Round the Mulberry Bush* (film), United Artists, 1967; producer, *Women in Love* (film), United Artists, 1969; writer and activist, New York City, 1971—. Cofounder of Gay Men's Health Crisis, New York City, 1981; founder of AIDS Coalition to Unleash Power (ACT UP), 1987; frequent contributor to periodicals, including *Advocate, New York Native, New York Times,* and *Village Voice.* **Recipient:** Academy of Motion Picture Arts and Sciences nomination, for best screenplay adaptation, and British Film Academy nomination, for best screenplay, 1970, both for *Women in Love;* Foundation of the Dramatists Guild Marton Award, 1986; City Lights Award, for best play, 1986; Sarah Siddons Award, for best play, 1986; Olivier Award nomination, for best play, 1986; Human Rights Campaign Fund's Arts and Communication Award, 1987; Obie Award, Lucille Lortel Award, and the Dramatists Guild Hull–Warriner Award, 1993, all for *Destiny of Me.* Address: c/o Arthur B. Kramer, Esquire, 919 Third Avenue, New York, New York 10022, U.S.A.

WRITINGS

Plays

Four Friends (produced New York, 1973).
Sissies' Scrapbook (produced New York, 1974).
The Normal Heart (produced New York, 1985), introduction by Andrew Holleran. New York, New American Library, 1985.

Just Say No (produced New York, 1988). New York, St. Martin's Press, 1989.
The Destiny of Me (produced New York, 1992). New York, New American Library/Plume, 1993.

Other

Women in Love (screenplay; adaptation of the novel by D. H. Lawrence), United Artists, 1969.
Faggots (novel). New York, Random House, 1978.
Reports from the holocaust: The making of an AIDS activist (nonfiction). New York, St. Martin's Press, 1989.
"129,001 and Counting" (speech), in *Village Voice,* 10 December 1991, 18.
"A Man's Life, and the Path to Acceptance" (essay), in *New York Times,* 4 October 1992, B–1.

*

Adaptations: *Indecent Materials* (theatre piece; produced New York Shakespeare Festival, 1990).

Biography: "The Cry of *The Normal Heart*" by Dinitia Smith, in *New York,* 3 June 1985, 42–46; "Larry Kramer" by Ken Gross, in *People,* 9 July 1990, 72–75; "The Spent Rage of the Playwright" by Paula Span, in *Washington Post,* 20 October 1992, E–1; "A Normal Heart" by Otis Stuart, in *Village Voice,* 27 October 1992, 110–112; "Kramer vs. Kramer" by Michael Shnayerson, in *Vanity Fair,* October 1992, 228–231.

Interviews: "Using Rage to Fight the Plague" by Janice C. Simpson, in *Time,* 5 February 1990, 7–8; "AIDS Activism" by Marcia Pally, in *Tikkun,* July 1990, 22–24; "Kramer vs. the World" by Victor Zonana, in *Advocate* (Los Angeles), 1 December 1992, 40–48, and 15 December 1992, 43–48; with David Nimmons, in *Playboy,* September 1993.

Critical Sources: Review by Paul Berman of *The Normal Heart,* in *Nation,* 11 May 1985, 569–570; "AIDS on Stage" by Gerald Weales, in *Commonweal,* 12 July 1985, 406–447; "AIDS Words" by Gregory Kolovakos (review of *Reports from the Holocaust*), in *Nation,* 1 May 1989, 598–602; "The Literature of AIDS" by Mark Caldwell (review of *The Normal Heart*), in *Dissent,* summer 1990, 342–347; "Larry Kramer and the Rhetoric of AIDS" by David Bergman, in *Gaiety Transfigured: Gay Self-Representation in American Literature,* Madison, University of Wisconsin Press, 1991, 122–138; "Reborn with Relevance" by William A. Henry III (review of *The Destiny of Me*), in *Time,* 2 November 1992, 69; "You Gotta Have Heart" by Jack Kroll (review of *The Destiny of Me*), in *Newsweek,* 2 November 1992, 104; "AIDS Drama: Displacing Camille" by John M. Clum, in *Acting Gay: Male Homosexuality in Modern Drama,* New York, Columbia University Press, 1992, 39–82; "AIDS Enters the American Theatre: *As Is* and *The Normal Heart*" by Joel Shatsky, in *AIDS: The Literary Response,* edited by Emmanuel S. Nelson, New York, Twayne Publishers, 1992, 131–139; "Rage and Remembrance: The AIDS Plays" by D. S. Lawson, in *AIDS: The Literary Response,* edited by Emmanuel S. Nelson, New York, Twayne Publishers, 1992, 140–154; "The Gay White Way" by William A. Henry III, in *Time,* 17 May 1993, 62–63.

"Kramer equals controversy," wrote Paula Span in the *Washington Post.* From the time he burst on the gay literary scene with his novel *Faggots,* Larry Kramer has waged a war within and against a community built on sexual freedom. At first and for many years a seeming lone voice in the wilderness, Kramer has slowly won gay men from many circles over to his call for a more responsible gay male community, one that would think less about sex and more about compassion. Along the way, he has openly attacked high–profile figures both inside and outside the gay community, the former breaking a tacit rule against criticizing one's own. As well, few have done more to advance the cause of people infected with HIV, from his participation in the founding of both the Gay Men's Health Crisis and the AIDS Coalition to Unleash Power (ACT UP), to his prolific writings of both fiction and nonfiction concerning the AIDS crisis.

Kramer's writing career began in 1969 after almost a decade working in London for Columbia Pictures and United Artists, with the screen adaptation of D. H. Lawrence's novel *Women in Love.* Although the film reproduces the affectionate relationship between Rupert and Gerald (as well as the homoerotic nude wrestling match) from the novel, its primary focus remains on the two heterosexual relationships. Kramer himself was still a closeted gay man during this time, taking female dates to parties and having short–term affairs with several of them. Despite an Academy Award nomination for his *Women in Love* screenplay, Kramer was fired from his next film project and, in 1971, moved to New York City where he began writing plays.

Kramer's first attempts in the theatre are all but forgotten. His first play, *Four Friends,* opened and closed on the same night in 1973. His second, *Sissies' Scrapbook,* opened a year later to mixed reviews and only a slightly longer run at Playwrights Horizons. Frustrated by his own inability to sustain a lasting personal relationship (either gay or straight), Kramer began writing a novel about one gay man's search for love in a world concerned primarily with sex. "There wasn't a relationship in the world that could sustain the promiscuity we were asking these relationships to sustain," he told Dinitia Smith in *New York.* Although his novel, *Faggots,* appeared in 1978 to caustic reviews from the gay press (e.g., the *Gay Community News* called it "appalling" and "offensive" because of its satirical critique of promiscuity, then widely regarded as a fundamental plank of the gay liberation platform), it also generated a positive response. Having sold more than 400,000 copies over the years, it is now considered a cornerstone of the gay literary canon; however, at the time, Kramer became the villain of the gay press, while authors like Ethan Mordden and Andrew Holleran, whose *Dancer from the Dance* provides an admiring and sympathetic portrait of the gay 1970s in counterpoint to Kramer's novel, became the darlings.

In 1980, the sight of a young man carrying his dying lover on New York's Fire Island awakened the true activist in Kramer. A year later, with the AIDS crisis still in its early stages and a gay community largely in denial, Kramer called 80 of his friends to his apartment, where, that evening, they founded the Gay Men's Health Crisis, an AIDS services organization. Kramer was in almost constant disagreement with the rest of the group over political strategy and safe–sex recommendations, and he was eventually ousted from the organization in 1983. Still a writer, but now an AIDS activist as well, Kramer combined his two careers in his 1985 play *The Normal Heart.* What Mark Caldwell in *Dissent* called "covert psychoautobiography," *The Normal Heart* is the angry story of Ned Weeks, a Kramer–based character who founds an AIDS organi-

zation, fights with the other members, eventually gets kicked out, and loses his lover to the disease before the final curtain. The play continues Kramer's attack on promiscuity ("All we've created is generations of guys who can't deal with each other as anything but erections."), attacks Ronald Reagan and the *New York Times,* and "outs" then–New York City mayor Ed Koch, years before Michelangelo Signorile popularized this practice in *OutWeek.* Ironically, it is Kramer himself who creates the line that best sums up all the attacks he has received within the gay community, when a character says to Ned, "After years of liberation, you have helped make sex dirty again for us—terrible and forbidden."

Kramer produced a phenomenal success with *The Normal Heart.* The play holds the record for the longest run at the New York Shakespeare Festival's Public Theatre, and has received over six hundred world–wide productions. Although many reviewers agreed with Paul Berman in the *Nation* when he called the script "amateurish," *The Normal Heart* was almost universally praised for its frank and overt handling of such an urgent social crisis. Years later, Jack Kroll in *Newsweek* called it "the breakthrough play on [AIDS]."

Kramer did not sit still. In 1987, through a rallying call–to–arms at New York's Lesbian and Gay Community Services Center, he founded the AIDS Coalition to Unleash Power (ACT UP), a direct–action group committed to ending the AIDS crisis. In 1988, Kramer himself tested positive for HIV. He wrote numerous essays and op–ed pieces in both the gay and straight press, many of which were collected and published as *Reports from the holocaust: The making of an AIDS Activist.* The book, which concludes with a lengthy essay written specifically for the collection, provides an excellent history of the AIDS movement, albeit from one point of view. In the final essay, Kramer continues his attack on serial sex: "There's no question that the promiscuity of some gay men was unwittingly responsible for AIDS killing so many of us." He also found himself, once again, under attack as well. Gregory Kolovakos in the *Nation* called Kramer a "hate–monger," his politics "meanspirited and exclusionary," and his point "the old wages–of–sin argument."

In the same year that *Reports from the holocaust* was published, New York's WPA Theatre produced Kramer's new play, *Just Say No.* A farce of sexual hypocrisy, the play was ill–received in its scheduled limited run. It would seem at this point that Kramer was becoming, as John M. Clum states in *Acting Gay,* "better known as AIDS polemicist and activist than as playwright." Kramer, however, would produce another major success in 1992 with *The Destiny of Me* which opened to favorable reviews at New York's Lucille Lortel Theatre, and played runner–up to Tony Kushner's "Gay Fantasia," *Angels in America* for the 1993 Pulitzer Prize. Continuing the story of *The Normal Heart*'s Ned Weeks, now HIV positive and undergoing experimental treatment, the play weaves in flashbacks from Ned's childhood as he struggles with his emerging homosexuality. William A. Henry III said in *Time:* "More than a play about AIDS and death, *The Destiny of Me* is a play about homosexuality and life. It is irate, not about dying but about having been unable to live and love."

Kramer is currently at work on his second novel, titled *The American People.* Though still an activist, he now commits more time to writing. As he told Victor Zonana in the *Advocate,* "I would like to say emphatically that I am not burned–out or tired. There just comes a time when you have to decide how your resources can be better spent." Always controversial, Kramer has nonetheless garnered respect from most in the gay community and press (even those he vehemently attacks), and is now a regular columnist for the

Advocate. In an essay for the *New York Times,* Kramer clarifies the importance of his homosexuality in his journey to acceptance: "This journey, from discovery through guilt to momentary joy and toward AIDS, has been my longest, most important journey, as important—no, more important—than my life with my parents, than my life as a writer, than my life as an activist. Indeed, my homosexuality, as unsatisfying as much of it was for so long, has been the single most important defining characteristic of my life."

—*Bradley Boney*

————

KRAMER, Ted. *See* **STEWARD, Samuel M(orris).**

————

KUSHNER, Tony. American playwright. Born in New York City, c. 1956; raised in Lake Charles, Louisiana; lives in Brooklyn, New York. Educated at Columbia University, 1978, and the New York University graduate theatre program. Worked as a switchboard operator at the United Nations Plaza Hotel, 1979–85; assistant director at the St. Louis Repertory Theatre, 1985–86; artistic director, New York Theatre Workshop, 1987–88. Member, AIDS Coalition to Unleash Power (ACT UP), a direct action political advocacy group. **Recipient:** National Endowment for the Arts fellowship, 1985, 1988; London *Evening Standard* Award for drama; Los Angeles Drama Critics Circle award; Pulitzer Prize in drama for *Millennium Approaches,* 1993.

WRITINGS

Plays

La Fin de la Baleine: An Opera for the Apocalypse (produced New York, 1982).
Yes Yes No No: The Solace–of–Solstice, Apogee/Perigee, Bestial/ Celestial Holiday Show (produced St. Louis, 1985; directed by Kushner).
The Heavenly Theatre (produced New York, c. 1986).
In Great Eliza's Golden Time (produced St. Louis, 1986).
The Illusion (adaptation of a play by Pierre Corneille; produced New York, 1988).
A Bright Room Called Day (produced London, and New York, 1990).
Angels in America: A Gay Fantasia on National Themes, Part 1: *Millennium Approaches* (in West End, and Los Angeles, 1992; on Broadway, 1993); Part 2: *Perestroika* (produced on Broadway, 1993).

Adaptations: Robert Altman has acquired the film rights to *Angels in America.*

Critical Sources: "An Angel Sat Down at His Table" by Susan Cheever, in *New York Times,* 13 September 1992; "A Playwright Spreads His Wings" by Hilary de Vries, in *Los Angeles Times,* 25 October 1992, 3, 74–76; "Avenging Angel" by Tad Friend, in *Vogue,* November 1992, 158–165; "A Playwright in the Power of 'Angels'" by David Patrick Stearns, in *USA Today,* 12 November 1992, D13; "Tony Kushner's Paradise Lost" by Arthur Lubow, in *New Yorker,* 30 November 1992, 59–64; "Kushner is Soaring with His 'Angels'" by Kevin Kelly, in *Boston Globe,* 14 April 1993, 65; "On Wings of 'Angels' Epic" by Steve Murray, in *Atlanta Journal and Atlanta Constitution,* 25 April 1993, M1; "A Broadway Godsend" by Jack Kroll, in *Newsweek,* 10 May 1993, 56–58; "Tony Kushner: Angels on Broadway" by Cathy Madison, in *Columbia* (New York), spring 1993, 40–41; "Kushner's *Angels* Ascends to a Pulitzer" by Thomas Vinciguerra, in *Columbia College Today* (New York), spring/ summer 1993, 50.

*   *   *

At age 36, playwright Tony Kushner did not have a long list of productions to his credit, but he did have a Pulitzer Prize for a play that *Newsweek* called "the biggest event involving the gay movement in the history of American popular culture." That play was *Angels in America,* which opened to rave reviews at the Royal National Theatre in London in 1992, and found an equally enthusiastic reception among critics and audiences alike on Broadway the following year. Subtitled "A Gay Fantasia on National Themes," *Angels in America* actually comprises two companion plays, *Millennium Approaches* and *Perestroika,* each of which runs for three– and–one–half hours. Epic in scope as well as in design, *Angels in America* goes farther than any other contemporary gay literary work in its use of gay characters and traditionally gay themes to examine a complex political, cultural, and historical reality that transcends gay ghettos and embraces all of American society.

Viewing the 1980s through the intersecting lenses of Reaganite politics, the burgeoning gay community, and the emerging AIDS epidemic, *Angels in America* explores such themes as denial, hypocrisy, repression, self–loathing, self–acceptance, and self–love. Kushner's truly inspired master stroke was the decision to include among his cast of characters an historical figure, the highly controversial attorney Roy Cohn, who gained notoriety in the 1950s as the chief counsel to Senator Joseph McCarthy. As McCarthy's trusted assistant, Cohn zealously pursued an anti–Communist crusade that destroyed the lives of countless Americans and culminated in the executions of Julius and Ethel Rosenberg for treason. What makes Cohn such a sublime focal point for Kushner's epic drama is the fact that this unscrupulous lawyer (who flouted the Constitution in his efforts to prosecute its perceived offenders) vehemently asserted his hatred of homosexuals while denying his own homosexuality. Moreover, he vigorously asserted that he was suffering from liver cancer right up to his death in 1986, when it was patently clear that he was dying of AIDS–related causes.

In addition to Roy Cohn, *Angels in America* focuses on Cohn's fictional protege Joe Pitt, a Mormon from Salt Lake City, Utah, who must confront the fact that he is a homosexual; Joe's wife, Harper, whose psychotic hallucinations contain some of the play's profoundest truths; Prior Walter, whose battle with AIDS transforms him into a prophetic recipient of angelic revelation; and Prior's lover Louis Ironson, who finds that despite his sweeping humanistic rhetoric, he does not have the courage to stand by Prior when the latter becomes ill. Joining these central figures is a wide range of peripheral characters, straight and gay, living and dead, human and divine, in a sweeping panorama that encompasses the most elemental realities of mortal life and the most sublime fantasies of divine imagination. "Part One of the play is about despair," Tony Kushner told *Vogue.* "Part Two therefore must be about hope, but ... our hope may simply be, as Prior says, an addiction to being alive."

Angels in America came to Broadway at a pivotal moment in gay America's struggle to join the mainstream, just one month after a massive march on Washington for the rights of sexual minorities that itself drew momentum from highly publicized ballot initiatives to limit gay rights in Oregon and Colorado, and an intense public debate on the armed forces' ban on military service by homosexuals. Kushner's work also followed closely on a number of other plays dealing with AIDS, the gay community, and gay–straight interaction, including Larry Kramer's *The Destiny of Me,* Paul Rudnick's *Jeffrey,* and William Finn's Broadway musical, *Falsettos.* But Kushner's play enjoyed far greater critical and popular acclaim than any previous drama about gay life in the age of AIDS, and— despite the fact that his first commercial productions went virtually unnoticed—left the author widely acknowledged as one of the best and most important young playwrights of his generation.

—*Michael Broder*

―――――

KUZMIN, Mikhail (Alexeyevich). Russian musician, poet, novelist, playwright, essayist, and author of short stories. Born in Yaroslavl, in 1872. Educated at St. Petersburg University; studied under Nikolay Rimsky–Korsakov 1891–94. Companion of poet Vsevolod Knyazev (committed suicide, 1913); companion of Yury Yurkun. *Died in Leningrad, of pneumonia, 1936.*

WRITINGS

Drama

Istorya rytsaria d'Alessio, 1905.
O Alexee, cheloveke Bozhem, 1907.
Venetsianskie bezumtsy, 1912; translated as *Venetian Madcaps,* 1973.

Poetry

Seti ["Nets"]. [Russia], 1908.
The Chimes of Love (poetry set to music). [Russia], 1910.
Osennie ozera ["Autumn Lakes"]. [Russia], 1912.
Glinyanie golubki ["Clay Doves"]. [Russia], 1914.
Dvum ["Pathfinder"]. [U.S.S.R.], 1918.
Zanaveshennye kartinki ["For the Two"]. [U.S.S.R.], 1920.

Alexandryskie pesni. [U.S.S.R.], 1921; translated as *Alexandrian Songs,* 1980.
Ekho. [U.S.S.R.], 1921; translated as *Echo,* 1921.
Nezdeshnie vechera ["Otherworldly Evenings"]. [U.S.S.R.], 1921.
Paraboly ["Parabola"]. [U.S.S.R.], 1923.
Forel razbyvaet lyod, 1929; translated as *The Trout Breaks the Ice,* 1980.

Novels

Krilya, 1906; translated by Neil Granoien and Michael Green as *Wings: Prose and Poetry,* Ann Arbor, Michigan, 1972.
Plavayushchie puteshestvuyushchie, 1914.

Collected Works

Sobranie sochineny (poetry, plays, novels, short stories, and essays; nine volumes), 1914–18.
Sobranie stikhov ["Collected Poetry"] (three volumes), edited by John E. Malmstad and Vladimir Markov. Munich, Wilhelm Fink Verlag, 1977–78.
Selected Prose and Poetry (poetry, short stories, and plays), edited and translated by Michael Green. Ann Arbor, Michigan, Ardis, 1972.
Prose (eight volumes), edited and introduced by Vladimir Markov. Berkeley, California, Berkeley Slavic Specialties, 1984–88.

Other

"O prekrasnoy yastnosti" (essay), 1910.
Contributor, *A Captive Spirit: Selected Prose,* edited by Marina Tsvetayeva. Ann Arbor, Michigan, Ardis, 1980.

*

Biography: "The Death and Resurrection of Mikhail Kuzmin" by Simon Karlinsky, in *Slavonic Review,* Number 38, 1979, 92–96; "Russia's Gay Literature and Culture: The Impact of the October Revolution," by Simon Karlinsky, in *Hidden From History: Reclaiming the Gay and Lesbian Past,* edited by Martin Bauml Duberman, Martha Vicinus, and George Chauncey, Jr., New York, New American Library, 1989; "Dear Old Worlds and the Age to Come: Toward a Portrait of Mikhail Kuzmin" by A. Lavrov and P. Timenchik, in *The Selected Works of Mikhail Kuzmin* (in Russian), Leningrad, Khudozhestvennaya Literatura, 1990; "Mikhail Kuzmin: A Chronicle of His Life and Times" by John Malmstad, in *A History of Russian Literature,* edited by Victor Terras, New Haven, Connecticut, Yale University Press, 1991.

Critical Sources: "Pre–Revolutionary Art," in *Literature and Revolution* by Leon Trotsky, translation by Rose Strunsky, New York, International Publishers, 1925, 19–55; "After the Symbolists," in *Modern Russian Literature: From Chekhov to the Present* by Marc Slonim, New York, Oxford University Press, 1953, 211–233; *Selected Prose and Poetry* by Mikhail Kuzmin, edited with introduction by Michael Green, Ann Arbor, Michigan, Ardis, 1980, ix–xxviii; "Russia's Gay Literature and History from the Eleventh to the Twentieth Centuries" by Simon Karlinsky, in *Gay Roots,* edited by Winston Leyland, San Francisco, Gay Sunshine Press, 1991, 81–104; "Introduction: Mikhail Kuzmin" by N. Bogomolov, in *Eros:Russia: The Silver Age* (in Russian), edited by Aleksandr Shuplyov, Moscow, Leptos Publishers, 1992.

* * *

Mikhail Kuzmin was one of the most popular literary figures of pre–revolutionary Russia, yet much of his work was explicitly homoerotic and thus very risque. Oddly enough it was with the publication, in 1905, of his first cycle of poetry, explicitly homosexual, called *Alexandrian Songs* that his reputation as a poet skyrocketed. This was relatively early on in world literature—as well as in Russia—for gay material to be not only published but read by a wide public. Kuzmin followed this book with Russia's first erotic gay novel, *Wings.* Both of these works were first published in *Scales,* one of the most popular literary journals of the day.

Trained as a musician—he studied under Rimsky–Korsakov in St. Petersburg—Kuzmin came to poetry later in life and did not begin to publish until the age of 30. An educated and well–travelled man, the times he spent both in Egypt and in Italy greatly influenced his writing, as well as helping him come to terms with his sexuality. When Kuzmin returned to Russia, friend and statesman Georgy Chicherin, who was also gay, introduced him to Sergey Diaghelev and the World of Art group where he found both intellectual challenge and support for his lifestyle. Kuzmin continued to meet and move in various literary circles throughout his life, although he never adhered to any particular one.

When *Wings* was published in 1906, it created a huge scandal. An autobiographical coming–of–age story about a young man who travels throughout his native Russia and Italy and discovers his homosexuality during the course of his travels, *Wings* was popular with the general public due to its sexual theme. However, besides its daring defense of homosexuality, Kuzmin's novella also includes numerous insightful commentaries on literature, art, and philosophy. The work was reprinted several times until 1921; it was not published again in Soviet Russia until its inclusion in a 1992 anthology of Russian erotica.

Kuzmin was also notorious for his performances at the renowned St. Petersburg cabaret "The Stray Dog," where he accompanied himself on the piano to the recital of his poems. His poetry lent itself to this medium because of its flippant charm and lightness of tone. Other prominent poets, actors, and dancers would frequent this lively bohemian center—poets Anna Akhmatova and Vladimir Mayakovsky, actress Olga Glebova–Sudeykina, and many more. Kuzmin wrote short dramatic pieces that were produced there and elsewhere. He appreciated the young Akhmatova so much that he wrote the introduction to her first book of poetry, *Evening.*

Many literary and artistic figures of the times both admired Kuzmin and were influenced by him. Lesbian poet Marina Tsvetaeva was a close friend of the poet—she confided in him the troubles she was having with her own love affair and attended parties in his honor while in St. Petersburg. In a prose piece about Kuzmin—named after his book of poems, *Otherworldly Evenings*—Tsvetaeva marvels at the prominence of Kuzmin's eyes, then writes: "In Moscow there were legends about Kuzmin. Legends grew up about every poet, and they are always composed out of some envy and maliciousness. The refrain to the word Kuzmin was 'affected, made-

up.'" Kuzmin lived with writer–friends Vyacheslav Ivanov and Lydia Zinovyeva–Annibal for a time, at their place called The Tower, also a literary center. Both of them were rumored to have same–sex affairs as well—Zinovyeva–Annibal authored a work of lesbian fiction titled "Thirty–three Freaks."

A prolific writer, Kuzmin produced not only poetry and fiction, but plays, essays, reviews, and music. In the year following the Russian Revolution, he wrote a cycle of poems called "Draped Pictures," which he did not originally intend for publication and which some people considered pornographic. Kuzmin was unconcerned with all the criticism surrounding the homosexual theme in his writings, and published his works in Germany when difficulties arose in the Soviet Union. He believed in the power of art: "I prefer a book over nature, an engraving to the shade of a spring grove, and in the vernal ode I hear the sound of the real spring rain." Music continued to shape his work, and he was one of the few poets in Russia who successfully wrote in free verse.

The last book published by Kuzmin was 1929's *Trout Breaks the Ice.* At the time of its publication, "Socialist Realism" was the literary fashion being dictated by Stalin. Kuzmin, considered old–fashioned and "bourgeois," was already being severely put down by some Soviet critics. *Trout Breaks the Ice* is a major work and contains what critics consider to be his finest verse. The poems symbolically refer to a real love affair he had with another poet, Vsevolod Knyazev, who left Kuzmin for a woman and then killed himself in 1913. Kuzmin was deeply hurt when their relationship fell apart and was obsessed with it throughout his life. Yury Yurkun, with whom he fell in love after Knyazev and lived with for the remainder of his life, also appears in the poetic storyline.

In the surrealistic *Trout Breaks the Ice* the dead come alive and interact with uninvited guests—the trout is in the background breaking up ice, repeatedly bringing up the image of Russia. The question of love for a woman versus the deeper love for a man is explored through various poetic forms and rhythms. It is a very complex, concise poem that alludes to Kuzmin's past bohemian lifestyle, his travels through'life, his loves. Anna Akhmatova's *Poem Without a Hero* is considered to be a polemic with Kuzmin's *Trout Breaks the Ice.* She thought he was being too flippant in his poem about his former lover's death. "We took everything seriously," writes Akhmatova, "but in Kuzmin's hands everything turned into a toy."

Although he did not publish poetry in his final years, Kuzmin continued to write and translate. He gave his last public recitation in 1928—to an unexpectedly packed hall. He read the draft version of *Trout Breaks the Ice* and it was very well–received. The organizers were not very pleased when a group of homosexuals bounded up to the stage at the end and showered their hero, Kuzmin, with a multitude of flowers. But several years later, Kuzmin would become a tragic figure in Soviet Petersburg, lost in the shuffle of Soviet culture, until his death from pneumonia in 1936. He had brought the culture of homosexual love to the fore in Russian literature but, because of political events, this development was cut short. As translator Michael Green says in his introduction to *Selected Poetry and Prose,* "self–acceptance, cheerfulness, irony were essential ingredients of Kuzmin's 'gayness.'"

—*Sonja Franeta*

L

LAWRENCE OF ARABIA. *See* LAWRENCE, T(homas) E(dward).

———

LAWRENCE, D(avid) H(erbert Richards). British novelist, poet, playwright, and essayist. Also wrote as Jessie Chambers and Lawrence H. Davison. Born in Eastwood, Nottinghamshire, 11 September 1885. Educated at Nottingham University College, teacher training certificate 1908. Married Frieda von Richthofen Weekley in 1914. Manufacturer's clerk, 1899; pupil–teacher, first at Eastwood British School, then at Ilkeston, Derbyshire, 1902–06; junior assistant master, Davidson Road School, Croydon, 1908–11; writer. **Recipient:** James Tait Black Memorial Prize, 1921. *Died in Vence, France, of tuberculosis, 2 March 1930.*

WRITINGS

Novels

The White Peacock. New York, Duffield, 1911; London, J. M. Dent, 1935.

The Trespasser. New York, M. Kennerley, 1912.

Sons and Lovers. New York, M. Kennerley, 1913.

The Rainbow. London, Methuen, 1915; expurgated edition, New York, B. W. Huebsch, 1916.

Women in Love. New York, privately printed, 1920; London, M. Secker, 1921.

The Lost Girl. London, M. Secker, 1920; New York, T. Seltzer, 1921.

Aaron's Rod. New York, T. Seltzer, 1922.

The Captain's Doll: Three Novelettes. New York, T. Seltzer, and as *The Ladybird, The Fox, The Captain's Doll,* London, M. Secker, 1923.

Kangaroo. New York, T. Seltzer, 1923; as *Kangaroo: The Corrected Edition,* foreword by Raymond Southall, Sydney, Collins, 1990.

With M. L. Skinner, *The Boy in the Bush.* New York, T. Seltzer, 1924.

St. Mawr. New York, Knopf, 1925.

St. Mawr, together with "The Princess." London, M. Secker, 1925.

The Plumed Serpent (Quetzalcoatl). New York, Knopf, 1926; with introduction by William York Tindall, 1951.

Sun (expurgated edition). E. Archer, 1926; unexpurgated edition, Paris, Black Sun Press, 1928.

Lady Chatterley's Lover. Florence, Italy, G. Orioli, 1928; expurgated edition, New York, Knopf, 1932; unexpurgated edition, London, Heinemann, 1956; with introduction by Mark Schorer, New York, Grove, and as *The Complete and Unexpurgated Edition of Lady Chatterley's Lover* (includes decision by Federal Judge Frederick vanPelt Bryan which lifted the post office ban), New York, Pyramid Books, 1959; with preface by Lawrence, "A Propos of *Lady Chatterley's Lover,*" London, Heinemann, 1982; with preface by Archibald MacLeish and introduction by Mark Schorer, New York, Modern Library, 1983.

The Escaped Cock. New York, Black Sun Press, 1929; as *The Man Who Died,* New York, Knopf, 1931.

The Virgin and the Gypsy. New York, Knopf, 1930.

The First Lady Chatterley. New York, Dial, 1944; as *The First Lady Chatterley: The First Version of Lady Chatterley's Lover,* foreword by Frieda Lawrence, London, Heinemann, 1972.

The Fox. London, Sphere, 1971.

John Thomas and Lady Jane. New York, Viking, and as *John Thomas and Lady Jane: The Second Version of Lady Chatterley's Lover,* London, Heinemann, 1972.

Mr. Noon (unfinished), edited by Lindeth Vasey. Cambridge, Cambridge University Press, 1984.

Short Stories

The Prussian Officer, and Other Stories. London, Duckworth, 1914; New York, Viking, 1984.

England, My England, and Other Stories. New York, T. Seltzer, 1922.

Glad Ghosts. London, E. Benn, 1926.

The Woman Who Rode Away, and Other Stories. New York, Knopf, 1928.

Rawdon's Roof. Norfolk, England, Elkin Mathews & Marrot, 1928.

Love among the Haystacks, and Other Pieces, with a reminiscence by David Garnett. London, Nonesuch Press, 1930; New York, Viking, 1933.

The Lovely Lady. London, M. Secker, 1932; New York, Viking, 1933.

A Modern Lover. New York, Viking, 1934.

A Prelude. Merle Press, 1949.

Complete Short Stories (three volumes). London, Heinemann, 1955; as *The Collected Short Stories of D. H. Lawrence,* 1974; New York, Viking, 1961.

The Horse Dealer's Daughter. Oxford, School of Art Press, 1963.

The Rocking–Horse Winner, edited by Dominick P. Consolo. London, C. E. Merrill, 1969.

The Princess, and Other Stories. Harmondsworth, Penguin, 1971.

The Mortal Coil, and Other Stories, edited by Keith Sagar. Harmondsworth, Penguin, 1971.

You Touched Me, illustrations by Sandra Higashi. Mankato, Minnesota, Creative Education, 1982.

Poetry

Love Poems and Others. London, Duckworth, 1913; New York, M. Kennerley, 1925.
Amores. New York, B. W. Huebsch, 1916.
Look! We Have Come Through! London, Chatto & Windus, 1917; as *Look! We Have Come Through! A Cycle of Love Poems,* England, Ark Press, 1958; Austin, University of Texas Humanities Research Center, 1971.
New Poems. London, M. Secker, 1918.
Bay. England, Beaumont, 1919.
Tortoises. New York, T. Seltzer, 1921; as *Tortoises: Six Poems,* Williamstown, Massachusetts, Cheloniidae Press, 1983.
Birds, Beasts, and Flowers. New York, T. Seltzer, 1923.
The Collected Poems of D. H. Lawrence (two volumes). London, M. Secker, 1928.
Pansies. New York, Knopf, London, M. Secker, and with 14 additional poems, privately printed, 1929.
Nettles. London, Faber, 1930.
Last Poems, edited by Richard Aldington and Giuseppe Orioli. Florence, Italy, G. Orioli, 1932; New York, Viking, 1933.
Fire, and Other Poems, foreword by Robinson Jeffers, note by Frieda Lawrence. Grabhorn Press, 1940.
The Complete Poems of D. H. Lawrence. London, Heinemann, 1964; New York, Viking, 1971.

Plays

The Widowing of Mrs. Holroyd: A Drama in Three Acts (produced London, 1926). London, M. Kennerley, 1914.
Touch and Go: A Play in Three Acts (produced Oxford, 1979). New York, T. Seltzer, 1920.
David: A Play (produced London, 1927). New York, Knopf, and London, M. Secker, 1926.
A Collier's Friday Night (produced London, 1973). Privately printed, 1940; Norwood, Pennsylvania, Norwood Editions, 1976.
Complete Plays. London, Heinemann, 1965; New York, Viking, 1966.
The Daughter–in–Law (produced London, 1967). London, Royal Court Theatre Program for Performances, 1967.
The Fight for Barbara (produced London, 1967).
Plays, introduction by Malcolm Elwin. Portland, Oregon, Heron Books, 1969.

Travel Sketches

Twilight in Italy. London, B. W. Huebsch, 1916; New York, Viking, 1958.
Sea and Sardinia. New York, T. Seltzer, 1921; New York, Viking, 1963.
Mornings in Mexico. New York, Knopf, 1927.
Etruscan Places. New York, Viking, 1932.

Nonfiction

Movements in European History (as Lawrence H. Davison). Oxford, Oxford University Press, 1921.
Psychoanalysis and the Unconscious. New York, T. Seltzer, 1921.
Fantasia of the Unconscious. New York, T. Seltzer, 1922.
Studies in Classic American Literature (essays). New York, T. Seltzer, 1923; London, Penguin, 1977.
Reflections on the Death of a Porcupine, and Other Essays. Philadelphia, Centaur Press, 1925.
Pornography and Obscenity. London, Faber, 1929; New York, Knopf, 1930; as *Pornography and Obscenity: An Essay,* Alicat Book Shop, 1948.
Assorted Articles. New York, Knopf, 1930.
Apocalypse. Florence, Italy, G. Orioli, 1931; New York, Viking, 1932.
We Need One Another, introduction by Henry Hart, drawings by John P. Heins. Oxford, Equinox, 1933.
Phoenix: The Posthumous Papers of D. H. Lawrence, edited and with introduction by Edward D. McDonald. New York, Viking, 1936.
Sex, Literature, and Censorship: Essays, edited by Harry T. Moore. London, Twayne Publishers, 1953.
The Symbolic Meaning: The Uncollected Versions of Studies in Classic American Literature, preface by Harry T. Moore. Philadelphia, Centaur Press, 1962.
Phoenix II: Uncollected, Unpublished, and Other Prose Works. New York, Viking, 1968.
Lawrence on Hardy and Painting: Study of Thomas Hardy [and] *Introduction to These Paintings.* London, Heinemann Educational, 1973.
Study of Thomas Hardy, and Other Essays. Cambridge, Cambridge University Press, 1985.

Letters

The Letters of D. H. Lawrence. New York, Viking, 1932.
D. H. Lawrence: Reminiscences and Correspondence. London, M. Secker, 1934.
D. H. Lawrence's Letter to "The Laughing Horse." Privately printed, 1936.
Letters to Bertrand Russell. New York, Gotham Book Mart, 1948.
Eight Letters to Rachel Annand Taylor. Pasadena, California, Castle Press, 1956.
Collected Letters (two volumes). New York, Viking, 1962.
Lawrence in Love: Letters to Louie Burrows. Nottinghamshire, University of Nottingham, 1968.
The Quest for Rananim: D. H. Lawrence's Letters to S. S. Koteliansky, 1914 to 1930. Montréal, McGill–Queen's University Press, 1970.
Letters from D. H. Lawrence to Martin Secker, 1911–1930. Privately printed, 1970.
The Centaur Letters. Austin, University of Texas Humanities Research Center, 1970.
Consciousness. Los Angeles, Press of the Pegacycle Lady, 1974.
Letters to Thomas and Adele Seltzer. Paris, Black Sparrow Press, 1976.
The Letters of D. H. Lawrence (three volumes). Cambridge, Cambridge University Press, 1979–84.

The Letters of D. H. Lawrence and Amy Lowell, 1914–1925. Paris, Black Sparrow Press, 1985.

Other

My Skirmish with Jolly Roger. New York, Random House, 1929; revised as *A Propos of Lady Chatterley's Lover, Being an Essay Extended from "My Skirmish with Jolly Roger,"* London, Mandrake Press, 1930; as *A Propos of Lady Chatterley's Lover,* London, M. Secker, 1931.
The Paintings of D. H. Lawrence, introduction by Lawrence. London, Mandrake Press, 1929.
The Triumph of the Machine, drawings by Althea Willoughby. London, Faber, 1930.
The Spirit of Place: An Anthology Compiled from the Prose of D. H. Lawrence, edited and with an introduction by Richard Aldington. London, Heinemann, 1935.
The Universe and Me. New York, H. Taylor, 1935.
D. H. Lawrence's Unpublished Forward to "Women in Love," 1919, preface by Nathan van Patten. Gelber, Lilienthal, Inc., 1936.
Ten Paintings. Manchester, England, Carcanet, 1982.

*

Adaptations: *The Rocking–Horse Winner* (radio play adaptation by W. H. Auden of story by Lawrence), 1941; *Sons and Lovers, Women in Love, Kangaroo, Lady Chatterley's Lover,* and *The Fox* have been adapted for film; *The Fox* was adapted as a play; *Lady Chatterley's Lover* was released as a sound recording.

Biography: *D. H. Lawrence: A Personal Record* by E. T. (pseudonym for Jessie Chambers), London, J. Cape, 1935; *Portrait of a Genius, but...* by Richard Aldington, London, Heinemann, 1950; *D. H. Lawrence: Novelist* by F. R. Leavis, London, Chatto & Windus, 1955; *D. H. Lawrence: A Composite Biography* by Edward Nehls, Madison, University of Wisconsin Press, Volume 1, 1957, Volume 2, 1958, Volume 3, 1959; *D. H. Lawrence and the New World* by David Cavitch, Oxford, Oxford University Press, 1969; *D. H. Lawrence: The Man and His Work; the Formative Years, 1885–1919* by Emile Delavenay, London, Heinemann, 1972; *D. H. Lawrence: The Man Who Lived,* edited by Robert B. Partlow, Jr. and Harry T. Moore, Carbondale, Southern Illinois University Press, 1980; *The Life of D. H. Lawrence* by Keith Sagar, London, Methuen, 1980.

Bibliography: *A Bibliography of the Writings of D. H. Lawrence* by Edward D. McDonald, Philadelphia, Centaur, 1925; *A Bibliography of D. H. Lawrence* by Warren Roberts, London, Hart–Davis, 1963; revised, 1982; *D. H. Lawrence: An Annotated Bibliography,* edited by James C. Cowan, DeKalb, Northern Illinois University Press, 1981.

Critical Sources: *D. H. Lawrence: A Collection of Critical Essays,* edited by Mark Spilka, Englewood Cliffs, New Jersey, Prentice–Hall, 1963; *Twentieth–Century Interpretations of "Women in Love":* *A Collection of Critical Essays,* edited by Stephen J. Miko, Englewood Cliffs, New Jersey, Prentice–Hall, 1969; *D. H. Lawrence: The Critical Heritage,* edited by R. P. Draper, London, Routledge & Kegan Paul, 1970; *Twentieth–Century Interpretations of "Sons and Lovers": A Collection of Critical Essays,* edited by Judith Farr, Englewood Cliffs, New Jersey, Prentice–Hall, 1970; "D. H. Lawrence and Homosexuality" by Geoffrey Meyers, in *D. H. Lawrence: Novelist, Poet, Prophet,* edited by Stephen Spender, New York, Harper, 1973, 135–158; "The Influence of Forster's *Maurice* on *Lady Chatterley's Lover*" by Dixie King, in *Contemporary Literature,* Number 23, 1982, 65–82; "D. H. Lawrence and His Men" by Joseph Patton, in *In Touch For Men,* Number 63, January 1982, 75–77; "D.H. Lawrence and Sex" by Donald Gutierrez, in *Liberal and Fine Arts Review,* Number 3, 1983, 43–56; "Getting Even with John Middleton Murry" by Donald Gutierrez, in *Interpretations,* Number 15, 1983, 31–38; "Toward a Resolution of Gender Identity Confusion: The Relationship of Henry and March in *The Fox*" by Jan Good, in *D. H. Lawrence Review,* Number 18, 1985–86, 217–227; "Kangaroo Revisited" by Murray S. Martin, in *D. H. Lawrence Review,* Number 18, 1985–86, 201–215; "'Men in Love?' D.H. Lawrence, Rupert Birkin and Gerald Crich" by George Donaldson, in *D. H. Lawrence: Centennial Essays,* edited by Mara Kalnins, Bristol, England, Bristol Classical, 1986; "La Perversion dans Women in Love" by Herve Fourtina, in *Etudes Lawrenciennes,* Number 4, 1989, 71–86; *The Challenge of D.H. Lawrence,* edited by Keith Cushman, Madison, University of Wisconsin Press, 1990; "Gerald et Birkin, du 'Prologue' a la version definitive de Women in Love" by Jacqueline Gouirand, in *Etudes Lawrenciennes,* Number 5, 1990, 29–50; *D. H. Lawrence* by John Worthen, London, Edward Arnold, 1991.

* * *

Although *Lady Chatterley's Lover* is the novel that first comes to mind when Lawrence is mentioned, it is by no means as central to his body of work as might be thought. Throughout his life and his work he had difficulty in resolving the relationships between the sexes. The interweaving of authoritarianism, sexuality, and mysticism, though enriching his writing, can be baffling to the casual reader. Although he maintained a strong belief in his need for a deep male–female relationship (in which, he, the male would always take the lead), he sought at the same time a close relationship with a man. As Donald Gutierrez has suggested in his analysis of the short story "Jimmy and the Desperate Woman," the ideal arrangement for Lawrence was a ménage à trois, with a strong homosexual element. From a different perspective, Jan Good, in her study of "The Fox," shows that Lawrence was deeply conscious of his feminine side, a personality mix–up that ran counter to all he had learned about the attributes society expected of a man. She suggests that this is more than simply homosexuality, and more than simply resistance to willful women, but rather a search for the ideal strong man, a replacement for the father against whom he had sided in defending his mother.

These concepts need to be kept in mind when reading his works. It is evident that his ideal friendships were those with men. As several critics have said, he was deeply aware of sex as a kind of touchstone of character. He wrote freely about 'manly love' a phrase used by Whitman and Carpenter, and in his letters spoke often of friendship between man and man, meaning an inviolable pledge, but characteristically claimed never to have formed such a friendship himself. Rather than speak directly of homosexuality he defined these relationships as *Blutbruderschaft,* a socially acceptable alternative. His own problematic personality, notably his need to be the leader and his fear of subjection, got in the way, as with John Middleton Murry, whose rejection of such a relationship was excoriated in several short stories.

For one who was so clearly fascinated by sexuality, Lawrence was strangely reserved in writing about sex. Even the 'infamous' sodomy of *Lady Chatterley's Lover* is described only obliquely. Dixie King has pointed out the close parallels with E. M. Forster's *Maurice,* notably the cross–class nature of the affair and the possible identification Lawrence felt with Lady Chatterley. Fascination with strong, young men reappears often in his novels, as in the nude swimming scene in *The Peacock.* As Joseph Patton has suggested, he was greatly moved by Carpenter's ideas of a new society that would allow the open expression of love between men, yet he was restrained by the mores of his times. The friendship between Rupert Birkin and Gerald Crich in *Women in Love* is clearly homoerotic if not homosexual, and this thought is reinforced by the prologue, where Birkin muses on his attachment to young, strong males. The passage, which contrasts the hot attraction he felt for men with the kinship he felt for women, might well have been about Lawrence himself. As George Donaldson has suggested in his study of the novel, it might as easily have been called "Men in Love." It is also possible that it reflects the uneasy relationship between the Lawrences and the Murrys, since Katherine Mansfield was, at least in part, the model for Gudrun. A reading with this context in mind makes clearer some of the tortuous scenes in the novel. Lawrence tended to incorporate his personal experiences into his novels and thus to reexamine his own feelings. In this connection, the otherwise extraneous lesbian affair of Ursula in *The Rainbow* becomes clearer when it is realized that it represents a fictionalized version of Katherine Mansfield's own lesbian experiences as recounted to Frieda Lawrence. The parallel in both cases is too striking to be accidental.

One of Lawrence's lesser known novels, *Mr. Noon,* is about homoerotic friendship between men. As demonstrated by Earl Ingersoll, the novel grew out of Lawrence's need for strong male friendships. On the one occasion when he had the chance to experience first–hand life in a country where such relationships were seen as basic to society Lawrence, in effect, opted out. As the contributor has pointed out in his study of *Kangaroo,* Lawrence in Australia had the opportunity to see in action the ultimate in male bonding—mateship—which carries with it unquestioning loyalty, and certainly supersedes any female friendships. In the novel it is mixed in with the semi–fascist movements that thrived in post–World War I Australia, so that it sometimes becomes difficult to separate the sexual from the political.

Both were very attractive to Lawrence, but the semi–autobiographical hero, Lovat, finally rejects mateship in favor of the mysticism which became dominant in Lawrence's later, American writing. It is, in this way, a bridge between the authoritarian novels and the mystical novels. Written at great speed and contemporaneous with the events that spurred it, *Kangaroo* is probably the novel most clearly reflective of Lawrence's own life. This has not always been appreciated by the critics, who have concentrated on the political events in its story (are they real or invented?) rather than on its reaction to mateship. The eventual rejection of mateship sprang

from Lawrence's aversion to final commitment, a reaction common in his novels.

There have been several studies of sexuality in Lawrence's novels. One of the most accessible is that by John Worthen. There are also several relevant essays in *The Challenge of D.H. Lawrence,* edited by Keith Cushman. Feminist critics have found Lawrence an attractive subject because of his ambivalent attitude towards women, and his difficulties in setting out the terms of an ideal relationship between the sexes. Their studies have made clearer the ways in which he identified with women himself. These have been seen in both Jungian and Freudian terms, the latter because of the closeness to his mother and its subsequent effects on his relationships with other women. Certainly his personality was strongly affected by the sexually divided world of the Nottinghamshire coal country. This also may have sponsored his flirtation with fascism, though it is possible here to draw a parallel to the homosexual fixations on uniforms and powerful men. Sado–masochism is undoubtedly inherent in much of his writing and the male dominance of his later works is similar to that in much gay writing. A good example is *The Prussian Officer.*

Lawrence's conflicted personality makes it difficult to be precise about his sexual attitudes. He was probably bisexual, but sought cover in a kind of mystical friendship. His interest in men as lovers and friends flickers throughout, but rarely becomes the principal theme. When it does, as in *Kangaroo* and *Mr. Noon,* he tends to draw away and distance himself from the implications. His mysticism and his later fascination with dualism reflect his (and his generation's) disenchantment with the certainties of an earlier age. His vision of the future was not always clear, but he certainly recognized that suppressing sexual feelings would not make life any more bearable. Though he may not offer any easy solutions, he certainly helped remove the blinders that had prevented people from facing squarely that sexual relationships were basic to being human.

—*Murray S. Martin*

———

LAWRENCE, T(homas) E(dward). British soldier, archeologist, arabist, and author of autobiographies. Known as Lawrence of Arabia; also wrote as T. E. Shaw. Born in Tremadoc, Caernavonshire, Wales, 15 August (some sources say 1 August or 16 August) 1888. Name legally changed to T. E. Shaw in 1927. Educated at Jesus College, Oxford, 1907–10, graduated with first–class honors, 1910; postgraduate travelling scholarship from Magdalen College, 1910. Archaeologist and traveller on expeditions to Southwest Asia and the Middle East, 1910–14; liaison officer between British and Arab forces, British Intelligence Service, 1914–18; technical advisor on Middle Eastern affairs, Versailles Peace Conference, 1918; Middle East advisor to colonial secretary Winston Churchill, until mid–1920s; served in Royal Air Force under name John Hume Ross, until 1923; served in Royal Tank Corps under name T. E. Shaw, 1923–25; re–enlisted in Royal Air Force, 1925–35. *Died from injuries sustained in a motorcycle accident, 19 May 1935.*

WRITINGS

Autobiographies

Seven Pillars of Wisdom: A Triumph. Privately printed, 1922; revised edition, 1926; abridged edition published as *Revolt in the Desert,* New York, Doran, 1927; complete edition, New York, Doran, 1935.

The Diary of T. E. Lawrence, MCMXI. London, Corvinus Press, 1937.

The Mint: Notes Made in the Royal Air Force Depot between August and December, 1922, and at the Cadet College in 1925. Garden City, New York, Doubleday, 1955.

Archaeology

With C. Leonard Woolley, *Carchemish: Report on the Excavation at Djerbis on behalf of the British Museum* (two volumes). London, British Museum, Part 1, 1914; Part 2, 1921.

With C. Leonard Woolley, *The Wilderness of Zinn,* 1915.

The Influence of the Crusades on Military Architecture—to the End of the XIIth Century (B.A. thesis, 1910), published as *Crusader Castles* (two volumes). London, Golden Cockerel Press, 1936.

Letters

Letters from T. E. Shaw to Bruce Rogers (as T. E. Shaw). New York, privately printed, 1933.

More Letters from T. E. Shaw to Bruce Rogers (as T. E. Shaw), edited by Bruce Rogers. New Fairfield, Connecticut, privately printed, 1936.

The Letters of T. E. Lawrence, edited by David Garnett. London, J. Cape, 1938.

Shaw–Ede: T. E. Lawrence's Letters to H. S. Ede, 1927–1935, foreword and running commentary by H. S. Ede. London, Golden Cockerel Press, 1942.

T. E. Lawrence to His Biographers Robert Graves and Liddell Hart. London, Cassell, 1938; Westport, Connecticut, Greenwood Press, 1976.

The Home Letters of T. E. Lawrence and His Brothers, edited by M. R. Lawrence. Oxford, Basil Blackwell, 1954.

Letters to E. T. Leeds, commentary by E. T. Leeds, edited with an introduction by J. M. Wilson, memoir of E. T. Leeds by D. B. Harden, illustrations by Richard Kennedy. Gloucestershire, England, Whittington Press, 1988.

The Selected Letters of T. E. Lawrence, edited by Malcolm Brown. London, J. M. Dent, 1988; New York, Norton, 1989.

Other

Translator, *The Odyssey of Homer,* introduction by Bernard Knox. New York, Oxford University Press, 1935.

Oriental Assembly (essays). Imperial War Museum, 1939.

Men in Print (criticism), 1940.

The Essential T. E. Lawrence: Selections from His Writings. London, J. Cape, 1951; edited by David Garnett, Viking, 1963; with a preface by David Garnett, New York, Oxford University Press, 1992.

Evolution of a Revolt: Early Postwar Writings of T. E. Lawrence (essays), edited with an introduction by Stanley and Rodelle Weintraub. University Park, Pennsylvania State University Press, 1968.

Minorities (poetry), edited by J. M. Wilson, preface by C. Day. London, J. Cape, 1971; as *Minorities: Good Poems by Small Poets and Small Poems by Good Poets,* Garden City, New York, Doubleday, 1972.

*

Adaptations: *Lawrence of Arabia* (film), Columbia, 1962.

Manuscript Collections: The bulk of Lawrence's letters, personal papers and manuscripts are located at the Bodleian Library, Oxford University.

Biography: *With Lawrence in Arabia* by Lowell Thomas, New York, Century Company, 1925; *Lawrence and the Arabs* by Robert Graves, illustrations edited by Eric Kennington, maps by Herry Perry, London, J. Cape, 1928, New York, Paragon House, 1991; *Lawrence of Arabia: The Man Behind the Legend* by Sir Basil Henry Liddell Hart, New York, De Capo Press, 1935; *Lawrence, the Story of His Life* by Edward Robinson, New York, Oxford University Press, 1935, Folcroft, Pennsylvania, Folcroft Library Editions, 1979; *T. E. Lawrence* by Charles E. Carrington, London, P. Davies, 1935, New York, Haskell House, 1977; *Lawrence of Arabia* by R. H. Kiernan, London, Harrap, 1935, Folcroft, Pennsylvania, Folcroft Library Editions, 1977; *Lawrence the Rebel* by Edward Robinson, London, Lincolns–Prager, 1946, Folcroft, Pennsylvania, Folcroft Library Editions, 1979; *Lawrence of Arabia: The Man and the Motive* by Anthony Nutting, New York, C. N. Potter, 1961; *Lawrence and His Desert Raiders* by James Barbary, illustrations by Elma Cameron, New York, Meredith Press, 1968; *Lawrence of Arabia: A Biographical Enquiry* by Richard Aldington, London, Collins, 1969; *The Secret Lives of Lawrence of Arabia* by Phillip Knightley and Colin Simpson, New York, McGraw–Hill, 1970; *Lawrence* by Douglas Orgill, New York, Ballantine Books, 1973; *T. E. Lawrence* by Peter Ludwig Brent, New York, Putnam, 1975, London, Weidenfeld & Nicolson, 1975; *A Prince of Our Disorder: The Life of T. E. Lawrence* by John E. Mack, Boston, Little, Brown, 1976; *Lawrence of Arabia and His World* by Richard Perceval Graves, New York, Scribner, 1976; *T. E. Lawrence* by Desmond Stewart, London, Hamish Hamilton, 1977; *Oxford's Legendary Son, the Young Lawrence of Arabia* by Paul J. Marriott, Oxford, 1977; *Solitary in the Ranks: Lawrence of Arabia As Airman and Private Soldier* by H. Montgomery Hyde, London, Constable, 1977; *Lawrence of Arabia* by Phillip Knightley, Nashville, Tennessee, T. Nelson, 1977; *Lawrence of Arabia* by Richard Ebert, illustrations by Roy Schofield, Milwaukee, Wisconsin, Raintree Publishers, 1979; *The Confessions of T. E. Lawrence: The Romantic Hero's Presentation of Self* by Thomas J. O'Donnell, Athens, Ohio University Press, 1979; *T. E. Lawrence: An Hitherto Unknown Biographical/Bibliographical Note* by Donald Weeks, Edinburgh, 1983; *Recollections of T. E. Lawrence* by E. Thurlow Leeds, Whittier, California, Bonibel Press, 1986; *In the Footsteps of Lawrence of Arabia* by Charles Blackmore, London, Harrap, 1986; *T. E. Lawrence: A Biography* by Michael Yardley, New York, Stein & Day, 1987; *Images of Lawrence* by Stephen Ely Tabachnick and Christopher Matheson, London, J. Cape, 1988; *A Touch of Genius: The Life of T. E. Lawrence* by Malcolm Brown, London, J. M. Dent, 1988, New York, Paragon House, 1989; *Lawrence of Arabia: The Authorized Biography of T.E. Lawrence* by Jeremy Wilson, New York, Atheneum, 1990; *Authorized Biographer: The Research and Writing of "Lawrence of Arabia"* by J. M. Wilson, Fordingbridge, Castle Hill Press, 1990; *The Golden Warrior: The Life and Legend of Lawrence of Arabia* by James Lawrence, London, Weidenfeld & Nicolson, 1990; *The Medievalism of Lawrence of Arabia* by M. D. Allen, University Park, Pennsylvania State University Press, 1991.

Bibliography: *Thomas Edward Lawrence (1888–1935): A Checklist of Lawrenciana, 1915–1965* by Guyla Bond Houston, Stillwater, Oklahoma, 1967; *T. E. Lawrence (of Arabia): A Collector's Booklist* by David George William Disbury, England, Egham, 1972; *T. E. Lawrence: A Bibliography* by Elizabeth Duval, New York, Haskell House, 1972; *T. E. Lawrence: A Reader's Guide* by Frank Clements, Hamden, Connecticut, Archon Books, 1973; *T. E. Lawrence: A Bibliography* by Jeffrey Meyers, New York, Garland, 1974; *Bibliographical Notes on T. E. Lawrence's Seven Pillars of Wisdom and Revolt in the Desert* by T. German–Reed, Norwood, Pennsylvania, Norwood Editions, 1977; *T. E. Lawrence: A Bibliography* by Philip M. O'Brien, Boston, G. K. Hall, 1988; *T.E. Lawrence: A Guide to Printed and Manuscript Materials* by Jeremy Wilson, Fordingbridge, Castle Hill Press, 1990.

Critical Sources: *Private Shaw and Public Shaw: A Dual Portrait of Lawrence of Arabia and G. B. S.* by Stanley Weintraub, New York, G. Braziller, 1963; *The Wounded Spirit: A Study of Seven Pillars of Wisdom* by Jeffrey Meyers, preface by Sir Alec Kirkbride, London, Martin, Brian, & O'Keeffe, 1973; *Lawrence of Arabia: The Literary Impulse* by Stanley and Rodelle Weintraub, Baton Rouge, Louisiana State University Press, 1975; *T. E. Lawrence: A Critical Study* by Robert Warde, New York, Garland, 1987.

*   *   *

Thomas Edward Lawrence became well known to the general public after the release of Sam Spiegel's and David Lean's epic film production *Lawrence of Arabia* in 1962. However, the tall, flamboyant figure cast by actor Peter O'Toole in the title role bore little resemblance to the real Thomas Edward Lawrence, a short man who was known for his shyness. While the Spiegel–Lean production did little to illumine the personal life of the real Lawrence, it did succeed in capturing the heroism—even the glory—surrounding the Lawrence legend, as well as some of the mystery surrounding this remarkable individual. It also reinforced the persistent hold Lawrence's mystique has always had on the popular imagination. More recently, two major biographical works on Lawrence—1990's *Lawrence of Arabia: The Authorized Biography of T.E. Lawrence* by Jeremy Wilson and *A Prince of Our Disorder: The Life of T.E. Lawrence,* published in 1976 by John E. Mack—have clarified many points about the life of Lawrence and have accounted for many discrepancies in previous biographical accounts. Using both primary and secondary sources, Wilson and Mack have each made an honest attempt to analyze both the professional and the personal aspects of Lawrence's life, as well as his place in history.

Lawrence was born on 16 August 1888, in Tremadoc, a village in North Wales, the second of five sons of Thomas Nobert Tighe Chapman and Sarah Junner. In his writings, Lawrence often refers to his illegitimacy, a fact that he viewed with great significance throughout his adult life. The elder Chapman changed the family name to Lawrence and frequently moved his wife and sons to various locations. Before he was eight years old, Lawrence had lived in Wales, Scotland, the Isle of Man, Jersey, France, and southern England before finally settling with his family in Oxfordshire, England. Lawrence, called "Ned" by family members, attended the City of Oxford High School in 1896–1907, and Jesus College, Oxford in 1907. During his school years, he excelled in history, geology, archaeology, and architecture, especially the architecture of the Middle Ages. His B.A. thesis, published as *Crusader Castles* in 1936, was a study of the castles and fortifications of twelfth–century Syria and Palestine. Between 1911–1914, Lawrence participated, sporadically, in an archaeological dig at Carchemish in Turkey under the subsequent directorships of famous Oriental scholars D. G. Hograth, R. Campbell Thompson, Flinders Petrie, and C. L. Woolley. During these years at Carchemish, Lawrence became familiar with Arab culture and language and also became acquainted with an Arab boy by the name of Dahoum. His relationship with Dahoum had a lasting effect on Lawrence and would later color his views on Arab culture. In his correspondence, Lawrence reveals the intimacy and obvious joy of their relationship. To Lawrence, the boy represented all that the West was not: innocence, purity, and goodness, without sexual inhibitions. Much later, after the death of Dahoum, Lawrence was to write a passionate dedicatory poem to Dahoum entitled "To S.A." which served as an introductory poem to his epic masterpiece *Seven Pillars of Wisdom: A Triumph.*

When Britain declared war on Turkey during World War I, Lawrence served as a British military intelligence officer in Cairo. Beginning in 1916, he played an important part in rallying Arab forces to launch guerilla attacks against the Turkish army. At the end of the war, Lawrence returned to Britain as a national hero having attained the rank of Colonel. He entered the political arena as a spokesman on behalf of Arab sovereignty. Lobbying for the Arab cause at the Paris Peace Conference in 1919, Lawrence continued his efforts towards Arab sovereignty until 1921.

To escape public scrutiny, Lawrence joined the Royal Air Force (R.A.F.) in 1922 under the assumed name of John Hume Ross. In 1923, after his identity was revealed, he enlisted in the Royal Tank Corps as T. E. Shaw. Lawrence entered the R.A.F. once again in 1925, where he remained for the next ten years. After his retirement from the British military in 1935, Lawrence rented a cottage at Clouds Hill, near the military camp in Bovington in order to study and write. He was tragically killed shortly thereafter in a motorcycle accident on 19 May 1935.

Major interest in the literary works of Lawrence continues to grow among historians. Although much of his work remains in manuscript form, it is slowly finding its way to publishers. Among Lawrence's best known works are the lengthy *Seven Pillars of Wisdom* and *The Mint,* as well as several volumes of posthumously published letters. Lawrence published a less–daunting, abridged version of his *Seven Pillars,* entitled *Revolt in the Desert,* which was also popular with the reading public.

Unquestionably Lawrence's most famous work, *Seven Pillars of Wisdom* is a semi–autobiographical account of the Arab revolt against the Turks in World War I. His romantic and idealized depiction of Arab manners and customs is unique. Within the work, the author candidly comments upon the freedom and lack of sexual restraint of Arab boys, a characteristic that was often expressed in homosexual activity. In *Seven Pillars,* Lawrence wrote a now famous account of his capture by the Turks at the garrison of Deraa, where he endured torture and rape at the hands of the Turkish soldiers. The author's somewhat confusing account of the episode is painful in its detail and has often been perceived by critics as a sexual awakening. Describing the brutality of this incident, Lawrence recounts: "I remembered smiling idly at him, for a delicious warmth, probably sexual, was swelling through me: and then that he flung up his arms and hacked with the full length of his whip into my groin." Lawrence was to relive the agony of Deraa many times in his later writings and the episode is often directly linked by his detractors to Lawrence's "flagellation disorder" in later life.

Critics and biographers of Lawrence have narrowly defined the question of Lawrence's sexuality or asexuality solely on the basis of the degree of erotic content in his relationships. They find no revealing evidence of Lawrence having a sustained relationship with another man—consequently, Lawrence was without "homosexual passion." Whether or not Lawrence ever acted upon his "passions" has never been clear in his writings but evidence that such a passion existed is present in many of those same writings. Lawrence reveals, in personal documents, that men were indeed his inspiration: "I take no pleasure in women. I have never thought twice or even once of the shape of a woman: but men's bodies, in repose or in movement—especially the former, appeal to me directly and very generally." Although Lawrence numbered many women among his friends, including the wife of George Bernard Shaw, he felt most at home in the company of men. *The Mint,* an account of his time in the R.A.F., is a testimony to the brotherhood of that group and reveals the special comfort Lawrence found when he was around military men. The discipline, the companionship, the camaraderie of like–minded men was appealing to Lawrence. During the R.A.F. years, Lawrence enjoyed a special friendship with Guy "Jock" Chambers who he referred to in his writings as "beautiful, like a Greek God," and with whom he enjoyed a relationship that was mutually agreeable.

What immediately impresses the reader of Lawrence's writings is that the author is able to discuss topics that were obviously painful to him with openness, candor, compassion, and sensitivity. If Lawrence himself felt sexually constricted, inhibited, or even ignorant of the basics of sex, he shows a remarkable tolerance and honesty when viewing the actions of others. Throughout the prodigious amount of writing that he produced during his tumultuous lifetime, Lawrence's humanitarian attitude toward sexuality extends far beyond its time.

—*Jane Jurgens*

LEAVITT, David. American novelist and author of short stories. Born in Pittsburgh, Pennsylvania, 23 June 1961; grew up in Palo Alto, California. Educated at Yale University, New Haven, Connecticut, B.A. (Phi Beta Kappa) 1983. Companion of author and teacher Gary Glickman. Reader and educational assistant, Viking–Penguin, Inc., New York City, 1983–84. Contributor of essays and stories to periodicals. Member of PEN. **Recipient:** Yale University Willets Prize for fiction, 1982; O. Henry Award, 1984; PEN/Faulkner Award nomination, and National Book Critics Circle Award nomination, both for *Family Dancing,* 1984; Guggenheim fellowship,

1989. Agent: Andrew Wylie, 48 West 75th Street, New York, New York 10023, U.S.A.

WRITINGS

Stories

Family Dancing (contains "Territory," "Counting Months," "The Lost Cottage," "Aliens," "Danny in Transit," "Family Dancing," "Radiation," "Out Here," and "Dedicated"). New York, Knopf, 1984.
A Place I've Never Been (includes "A Place I've Never Been," "Houses," "Ayor," "Chips at Home," "Gravity," "Spouse Night," "I See London, I See France," "My Marriage to Vengeance," "Roads to Rome," and "When You Grow to Adultery"). New York, Viking, 1990.
"When You Grow to Adultery," in *The Faber Book of Gay Short Fiction,* edited by Edmund White. London and New York, Faber & Faber, 1991.

Novels

The Lost Language of Cranes. New York, Knopf, 1986.
Equal Affections. New York, Weidenfeld & Nicolson, 1989.

Other

"The New Lost Generation," in *Esquire,* May 1985, 85.
"New Voices and Old Values," in *New York Times Book Review,* 12 May 1985.
Author of introduction, *These Young People Today: Writers under 35* (special issue of *Mississippi Review*), spring/summer, 1986.
"Italy's Secret Gardens," in *Vogue,* June 1988.
"The Way I Live Now," in *New York Times Magazine,* 9 July 1989, 28.
"Almodovar on the Verge," in *New York Times Magazine,* 22 April 1990.
"Mad about Milan," in *Vogue,* March 1990.

*

Adaptations: *The Lost Language of Cranes* (teleplay; British production appeared as part of "Great Performances" series), PBS, 1992.

Interviews: *Contemporary Authors,* Volume 122, Detroit, Gale, 1988; with Sam Staggs, in *Publishers Weekly,* 24 August 1990, 47.

Critical Sources: "Domestic Disclosures" (review of *Family Dancing*) by Wendy Lesser, in *New York Times Book Review,* 2 September 1984, 7–8; "Ordinary Lives Filled with Love and Loss" (review of *Equal Affections*) by Michiko Kakutani, in *New York Times,* 31 January 1985, 16; "The New Romantics" (review of *Family Dancing*) by Darryl Pinckney, in *New York Review of Books,* 29 May 1986, 30; review of *The Lost Language of Cranes,* in *Publishers Weekly,* 8 August, 1986, 55; "Sexual Politics, Family Secrets" (review of *The Lost Language of Cranes*) by Phillip Lopate, in *New*

York Times Book Review, 5 October 1986, 3; "Gays of Our Lives" (review of *The Lost Language of Cranes*) by Adam Mars–Jones, in *New Republic,* 17 November 1986, 43; "Post–Counterculture Tristesse" by Carol Iannone, in *Commentary,* February 1987, 57–61; "Papa and Son" (review of *The Lost Language of Cranes*) by Adrianne Blue, in *New Statesman,* 13 February 1987, 31; "Fiction Chronicle" (review of *The Lost Language of Cranes* by Michael Gorra, in *Hudson Review* (New York), spring 1987, 136–148; "David Leavitt" in *Reasons to Believe: New Voices in American Fiction* by Michael Schumaher, New York, St. Martin's Press, 1988, 175–190; review of *Equal Affections,* in *Publishers Weekly,* 18 November 1988, 69; "David Leavitt's Family Affairs" (review of *Equal Affections*) by Alan Hollinghurst, in *Washington Post Book World,* 22 January 1989, 4; "Everyone Is Somebody's Child" (review of *Equal Affections*) by Beverly Lowry, in *New York Times Book Review,* 12 February 1989, 7; "Terminal Addiction" (review of *Equal Affections*) by David Gates, in *Newsweek,* 13 February 1989, 78; review of *Equal Affections,* in *People,* 20 February 1989, 27; review of *A Place I've Never Been,* in *Publishers Weekly,* 13 July 1990, 40; "Everybody Loves Somebody Sometime" (review of *A Place I've Never Been*) by Wendy Martin, in *New York Times Book Review,* 26 August 1990, 11; "Family, Lovers, Loyalty, Betrayal" (review of *A Place I've Never Been*) by James N. Baker, in *Newsweek,* 3 September 1990, 66; "Aspects of Love" (review of *A Place I've Never Been*) by Jonathan Penner, in *Washington Post Book World,* 7 October 1990, 7; "Out of the Closet, Onto the Bookshelf" by Edmund White, in *New York Times Magazine,* 16 June 1991, 22; "David Leavitt" by D. S. Lawson, in *Contemporary Gay American Novelists,* edited by Emmanuel S. Nelson, Westport, Connecticut, Greenwood Press, 1993, 248–253.

*   *   *

David Leavitt's work exhibits not only "a genius for empathy," as Wendy Lesser noted, reviewing *Family Dancing* in the *New York Times Book Review,* but also a canniness, an instinct for the ordinariness of life. In his stories and novels, it is what people hold in common, including those things that divide them, that provide him with his subject. It is not surprising, then, to find that families play so prominent a part.

In his debut collection of stories, *Family Dancing,* published in 1985, Leavitt introduced elements that would carry through his next three books—homosexuality, family, illness, and the ways in which individual lives strain the bonds of affection. His characters, educated, articulate, middle–class, love one another and fail to love. Jonathan Keates, writing in the *Times Literary Supplement* (London), has said that "the kind of people David Leavitt writes about are exceedingly hard to dislike. Their waking thoughts, and occasionally their dreams as well, are furrowed with mutual solicitude, their arms sinewy from the exercise of reaching out, their consciences pitted with minor and tolerable quilts." In "Territory," a young gay man returning home to visit his mother, bringing with him the lover she has known of but never met, discovers that love is not immediately or infinitely elastic. "I'm very tolerant, very understanding," his mother tells him. "But I can only take so much." Borders are overstepped, and revealed by the transgression. Similarly, Rose, the wife and mother in Leavitt's first novel, *The Lost Language of Cranes,* pushes beyond what she is willing to accept by the admission that not only her son but her husband too is gay,

is lost or abandoned, as much by her own choice as by the choices others make.

Where in the work of many gay writers, women are omitted or somehow erased, in Leavitt's fiction women are central and essential. They appear, however, as either facilitators, bringing men together, or as aggravated and aggrieved judges. Many critics have pointed out that his female characters are commonly the most strongly–drawn in his work, yet their position is agonistic, unresolved.

Women retain the center in Leavitt's later work. His second novel, *Equal Affections,* offers another analogue of the reluctant mother. Indeed, one can see in *Equal Affections* a drawing–together of the individual notes he has sounded from the start. In his circling back to common themes and familiar characters, Leavitt appears to be tapping the sides of a very particular box, testing it, not so much finding weaknesses in it as trying, as if for the first time, to see exactly what is there. His is an art of limited but precise dimensions. "I've never thought of myself as naive," he commented in an essay he wrote for *Esquire* in 1985. "I've never imagined that I might lead a sheltered life. I am, after all, 'sophisticated,' have been to Europe, understand dirty jokes and the intricacies of sexually transmitted diseases. This is my milieu, the world I live in, and I have almost never stepped beyond its comfortable borders. A safety net surrounds my sophisticated life, and the question is, of course, how did it get there? Did I build it myself? Was it left for me?"

—*Kevin Ray*

LEDUC, Violette. French novelist and autobiographer. Born in Arras, Pas de Calais, 8 April 1907; grew up in Valenciennes. Educated at boarding schools. Married (later divorced). Worked in Paris before World War II as a switchboard operator, messenger, and as editorial secretary and publicity writer for Plon (publisher); black market trader in Normandy during World War II. *Died in Faucon, France, 28 May 1972.*

WRITINGS

Fiction

Ma mère ne m'a jamais donné la main, 1945.
L'Asphyxie. Paris, Gallimard, 1946; translated by Derek Coltman as *In the Prison of Her Skin,* London, Hart–Davis, 1970.
L'Affamée. Paris, Gallimard, 1948.
Ravages. Paris, Gallimard, 1955; translated by Derek Coltman and published with *Thérèse and Isabelle,* 1966.
La Vieille Fille et le mort [and] *Les Boutons dorés.* Paris, Gallimard, 1958; *Les Boutons dorés* translated by Dorothy Williams as *The Gold Buttons,* London, P. Owen, 1961, Transatlantic, 1962; translated by Derek Coltman as *The Old Maid and the Dead Man* and *The Gold Buttons,* in *The Woman with the Little Fox: Three Novellas,* 1966.
Trésors à prendre. Paris, Gallimard, 1960.

La femme au petit renard. Paris, Gallimard, 1964; translated by Derek Coltman as *The Lady and the Little Fox Fur,* London, P. Owen, 1967; as *The Woman and the Little Fox,* in *The Woman and the Little Fox: Three Novellas,* 1966.

The Woman and the Little Fox: Three Novellas (includes *The Old Maid and the Dead Man, The Gold Buttons,* and *The Woman and the Little Fox*), translation by Derek Coltman. New York, Farrar, Straus, 1966.

Thérèse et Isabelle. Paris, Gallimard, 1966; translated by Derek Coltman as *Thérèse and Isabelle,* with *Ravages,* London, Arthur Baker, 1966; New York, Farrar, Straus, 1967.

Le Taxi. Paris, Gallimard, 1971; translated by Helen Weaver as *The Taxi,* New York, Farrar, Strauss, 1972.

Autobiographies

La Bâtarde, foreword by Simone de Beauvoir. Paris, Gallimard, 1964; translated by Derek Coltman, New York, Farrar, Straus, 1965.

La Folie en tête. Paris, Gallimard, 1970; translated by Derek Coltman as *Mad in Pursuit,* New York, Farrar, Strauss, and London, Hart–Davis, 1971.

La Chasse à l'amour. Paris, Gallimard, 1973.

*

Adaptations: *Thérèse and Isabelle* (film), Amsterdam Film Corp./ Audubon Films, 1968.

Critical Sources: "Foreword" by Simone de Beauvoir, in *La Bâtarde,* translation by Derek Coltman, New York, Farrar, Straus & Giroux, 1965; "Lesbian Intertextuality" by Elaine Marks, in *Homosexualities and French Literature,* edited by George Stambolian and Elaine Marks, Ithaca, Cornell University Press, 1979; *Violette Leduc* by Isabelle de Courtivron, Boston, Twayne Publishers, 1985.

*   *   *

The first work of Violette Leduc's to achieve any critical recognition, *La Bâtarde,* published in 1964 with a preface by Simone de Beauvoir, assured Leduc of a *succès de scandale.* This autobiography, daring in style and subject matter, brought both notoriety and acclaim to Leduc, who had, in fact, been quietly publishing fiction for some two decades. Much of Violette Leduc's writings inhabits the shady area between fiction and autobiography. Her earliest novels, *L'Asphyxie,* in 1946, *L'Affamée,* in 1948, and *Ravages,* in 1955, can be read as fictional counterparts of *La Bâtarde,* which was her first volume of autobiography. The later volumes, *La Folie en tête,* in 1970, and *La Chasse à l'amour,* in 1973, pick up Leduc's life after she has started writing and are less tightly connected to her fiction. However, in the case of the first three novels, it is nearly impossible to separate Leduc's life from her fiction. Rare is the writer who provides us with both the fiction and the facts of her life in nearly parallel formats. Rarer still is the writer who intentionally creates an autobiographical voice that directs the reader to her fictions to fill in areas of her autobiography. Such, however, is Violette Leduc.

Leduc's works, whether fiction or autobiography, center almost exclusively on the experiences of love, sexuality, and the disappointment of their female protagonists. Leduc's own bisexuality defines nearly all the relationships in her texts. Her distrust of men and the fear of pregnancy instilled in her at an early age by her mother inform the narratives of *L'Asphyxie, L'Affamée* and *Ravages.* Leduc's sexual and emotional experiences with women and men and her prolonged relationships with homosexual writers and intellectuals such as Maurice Sachs and Jean Genêt all make their way into these novels. Finally, through it all, there is Simone de Beauvoir: Beauvoir, whom Leduc first idolized from afar; who, after meeting Leduc, became one of her staunchest supporters; who in a sense is the intended audience of all of Leduc's texts.

Leduc's relationship with Simone de Beauvoir can also serve as a typical example of the intricately overlapping nature of her fictional and autobiographical writings and of their highly complex chronology. *L'Affamée* presents a hallucinatory vision of the beginnings of that ambiguous relationship with 'Madame,' the object of the narrator's fixation. The narrator's struggle to reach Madame is told in a series of unconnected, frequently violent fantasies that usually begin in the café where Madame writes. Ultimately, the narrator comes to terms with her separation from Madame and understands that the barrier will only be eliminated through writing. Thus the novel ends with the narrator returning home to write. *La Folie en tête* involves the meeting with Beauvoir, preceded by a long period during which Leduc watched Beauvoir as she sat writing in cafés. But of course it was *L'Asphyxie,* not *L'Affamée,* that first brought Leduc to Beauvoir's attention. *L'Affamée,* then, is equally a confession of Leduc's obsession with Beauvoir and a defining of their later relationship in terms of writing, rather than sexuality. Not surprisingly, Madame reappears in Leduc's fiction, including *Trésors à prendre.*

A more obvious lesbian relationship was to be the prologue to Leduc's novel *Ravages.* That prologue, "Thérèse et Isabelle," was cut from the original Gallimard edition of the novel because it was too explicit in its description of lesbian sexual acts between the narrator, Thérèse, and another schoolgirl. Indeed, the erotic scenes of the "Isabelle" episode shocked because of their frankness. Although the passages are graphic, they are equally lyric in tone; sensual, without seeming sordid. Oddly enough, the Gallimard censorship brought about another twist in Leduc's "novel" of her life. Jacques Guérin convinced Leduc to create a fake manuscript version of the text which he published in a limited collector's edition. This same Guérin, a homosexual with whom Leduc became obsessed, is revealed as her tormentor in *La Folie en tête,* and did indeed contribute to her nervous breakdown. Eventually the reception of "Thérèse et Isabelle" elicited enough interest that Gallimard published the censored text separately.

Ravages recounts Thérèse's second relationship with a woman, a schoolteacher named Cécile whom Thérèse meets after leaving school and being parted from Isabelle. Thérèse and Cécile are a typical bourgeois couple, except of course that they are of the same sex. Cécile is the ideal provider for Thérèse, who has nothing to do other than be a housewife. The doldrums of this existence lead to Thérèse's flight to a more Bohemian lifestyle ... with a man. The complexity of gender roles, traditional and nontraditional, and the tensions they create form the backdrop of the Cécile episode. Thérèse's marriage to the man she runs off with, an abortion, and a divorce lead her to renounce all sexual relations.

Many episodes in *Ravages* parallel *La Bâtarde.* For example, a comparison of the Violette and Isabelle narrative to "Thérèse et

Isabelle" reveals a similarity of tone in the sexual passages, although the language is less metaphoric. It also reveals the strategies by which Leduc creates herself through fiction and autobiography. The two accounts share some elements, yet they also contradict each other in significant ways. The most striking perhaps is the end of the affair between the two girls. Whereas the fictional Thérèse is taken from the boarding school a month after the girls' promise never to leave one another, the real Isabelle visits Violette later during summer break. Violette and Hermine lead the same sort of unexceptional bourgeois existence as Thérèse and Cécile, though again the novelist's account differs somewhat from the autobiographer's. These differences expose the conscious self–fashioning so characteristic of Leduc's style: only by layering the factual over the fictional account does the reader begin to have a complete vision of Leduc herself. Ultimately, writing became a catharsis for Leduc, a way of reconciling the fragmented pieces of her existence and of fashioning an entire self.

—*Edith J. Benkov*

———

LEE, Vernon. Pseudonym for Violet Paget. British essayist, novelist, and author of short stories. Born in Boulogne–sur–Mer, France, 14 October 1856. *Died in San Gervasio, Italy, 13 February 1935.*

WRITINGS

Essays

Studies of the Eighteenth Century in Italy. London, Satchell, 1880; Chicago, McClurg, 1908.

Belcaro: Being Essays on Sundry Aesthetical Questions. London, Satchell, 1881.

Euphorion: Being Studies of the Antique and the Medieval in the Renaissance (two volumes). London, Unwin, and Boston, Roberts Brothers, 1884; revised as one volume, London, Unwin, 1885.

Juvenilia: Being a Second Series of Essays on Sundry Aesthetical Questions (two volumes). London, Unwin, 1887; revised as one volume, Boston, Roberts Brothers, 1887.

Renaissance Fancies and Studies: A Sequel to "Euphorion." London, Smith, Elder, 1895; New York, Putnam, 1896.

Limbo, and Other Essays. London, Richard, 1897; enlarged edition, London, Lane, Bodley Head, and New York, Lane, 1908.

Hortus Vitae: Essays on the Gardening of Life. London, Lane, Bodley Head, and New York, Lane, 1903.

The Enchanted Woods, and Other Essays on the Genius of Place. London, Lane, Bodley Head, and New York, Lane, 1905.

Vital Lies: Studies of Some Varieties of Recent Obscurantism (two volumes). London, Lane, Bodley Head, and New York, Lane, 1912.

The Tower of the Mirrors, and Other Essays on the Spirit of Places. London, Lane, Bodley Head, and New York, Lane, 1914.

The Golden Keys, and Other Essays on the Genius Loci. London, Lane, Bodley Head, and New York, Dodd, Mead, 1925.

Travel Sketches

Genius Loci: Notes on Places. London, Richard, 1899; New York, Lane, 1908.

The Spirit of Rome: Leaves from a Diary. London, Lane, Bodley Head, and New York, Lane, 1906.

The Sentimental Traveller: Notes on Places. London, Lane, Bodley Head, and New York, Lane, 1908.

Short Stories

A Phantom Lover: A Fantastic Story. Edinburgh, Blackwood, and Boston, Roberts Brothers, 1886.

Hauntings: Fantastic Stories. London, Heinemann, and New York, Lovell, 1890.

Vanitas: Polite Stories. London, Heinemann, and New York, Lovell, Coryell, 1892; enlarged, London, Lane, Bodley Head, and New York, Lane, 1911.

Penelope Brandling: A Tale of the Welsh Coast in the Eighteenth Century. London, Unwin, 1903.

Pope Jacynth, and Other Fantastic Tales. London, Richards, 1904; New York, Lane, 1907.

Sister Benvenuta and the Christ Child: An Eighteenth Century Legend. New York, Kennerley, 1905; London, Richards, 1906.

The Snake Lady, and Other Stories, 1954.

Novels

Ottilie: An Eighteenth–Century Idyl. London, Unwin, 1883; included in *The Prince of the Hundred Soups.* New York, Harper, 1886.

Miss Brown (three volumes). London, Blackwood, 1886; revised in one volume, New York, Harper, 1885.

Louis Norbert: A Two–Fold Romance. London, Lane, Bodley Head, and New York, Lane, 1914.

Plays

Satan the Waster: A Philosophic War Trilogy. London, Lane, Bodley Head, and New York, Lane, 1920.

Adriadne in Mantua: A Romance in Five Acts. Oxford, Blackwell, 1903; Portland, Maine, Mosher, 1906.

Other

The Countess of Albany (biography). London, Allen, and Boston, Roberts Brothers, 1884.

Baldwin: Being Dialogues on Views and Aspirations. London, Unwin, and Boston, Roberts Brothers, 1886.

Althea: A Second Book of Dialogues on Aspirations and Duties. London, Osgood, McIlvaine, 1894.

The Child in the Vatican. Portland, Maine, Mosher, 1900.

Chapelmaster Kriesler: A Study of Musical Romanticists. Portland, Maine, Mosher, 1901.

In Umbria. Portland, Maine, Mosher, 1901.

Gospels of Anarchy, and Other Contemporary Studies. London, Unwin, 1908; New York, Brentano's, 1909.

Laurus Nobilis: Chapters on Art and Life. London, Lane, Bodley Head, and New York, Lane, 1909.

With Clementina Anstruther–Thomson, *Beauty and Ugliness, and Other Studies in Psychological Aesthetics.* London, Lane, Bodley Head, and New York, Lane, 1912.

The Beautiful: An Introduction to Psychological Aesthetics. Cambridge, Cambridge University Press, and New York, Putnam, 1913.

The Ballet of the Nations: A Present–day Morality. London, Chatto & Windus, and New York, Putnam, 1915.

Peace with Honour: Controversial Notes on the Settlement. London, Union of Democratic Control, 1915.

The Handling of Words, and Other Studies in Literary Psychology. London, Lane, Bodley Head, and New York, Dodd, Mead, 1923.

Proteus, or the Future of Intelligence. London, Kegan Paul, Trench, Trübner, and New York, Dodd, Mead, 1925.

The Poet's Eye: Notes on Some Differences between Verse and Prose. London, Hogarth Press, 1926.

For Maurice: Five Unlikely Stories. London, Lane, Bodley Head, 1927.

Music and Its Lovers: An Empirical Study of Emotional and Imaginative Responses to Music. London, Allen & Unwin, 1932; New York, Dutton, 1933.

Vernon Lee's Letters. London, privately printed, 1937.

*

Manuscript Collections: Colby College, Waterville, Maine.

Biography: *Vernon Lee: Violet Paget, 1856–1935* by Peter Gunn, Oxford, Oxford University Press, 1964.

Bibliography: "'Vernon Lee': A Reintroduction and Primary Bibliography" by Phyllis F. Mannocchi, in *English Literature in Transition 1880–1920,* 26:4, 1983, 231–267; "'Vernon Lee': A Commentary and Annotated Bibliography of Writings about Her" by Carl Markgraf, in *English Literature in Transition 1880–1920,* 26:4, 1983, 268–312.

Critical Sources: "Vernon Lee, a Lonely Lady" by Anne Fremantle, in *Commonweal,* New York, 25 June 1954, 297–99; "Vernon Lee and Kit Anstruther–Thomson: A Study of Love and Collaboration between Romantic Friends" by Phyllis A. Mannocchi, in *Women's Studies,* 12:2, 1986, 129–148; *The Lesbian Imagination: Victorian Style; A Psychological and Critical Study of "Vernon Lee"* by Burdett Gardner, New York, Garland, 1987.

*   *   *

Violet Paget benefited from an exceptional and privileged childhood. The travels of her family exposed her to three cultures other than her own and allowed her to become fluent in French, German, and Italian. Moreover, she was encouraged at an early age by her mother to develop her talents and her knowledge and pursue a career in letters. This fortuitous conjunction of multiculturalism and a liberal upbringing explains to a great extent the seeming ease with which Violet Paget created the cosmopolitan intellectual Vernon Lee. As an adult, Lee frequented English and European literary and artistic circles, counting among her friends and acquaintances such

notables as Edith Wharton, John Singer Sargent, Walter Pater, Oscar Wide, Bernard Berenson, Henry James, and the Rossettis. Her career spanned six decades, during which she published 45 major works, ranging from essays on subjects as diverse as art history, music, courtly love, travel, and literary theory to fiction, including novels, plays, and fantastic short stories.

Like many other nineteenth–century women, Lee chose a male pseudonym when she embarked on a serious career. Her choice reflected her perception of the prevailing attitudes towards women's writing. As she noted in a letter to a friend in 1878, "No one reads a woman's writing on art or history or aesthetics with anything but unmitigated contempt." One might also venture that "Vernon Lee" suited the dictates of Victorian propriety by creating a nominal male persona in her personal life as well. She tended towards masculine dress, and, more to the point, all of Vernon Lee's significant emotional relationships were with women. Again, Victorian propriety plays a role here. Young or unmarried women needed traveling companions to assure their moral well–being. Vernon Lee's first passionate attachment, in her early 20s, was to her "companion" Mme. Annie Meyers. Next, she traveled with another companion, Mary Robinson. In her 30s, her great friend was Kit Anstruther–Thomson. Later in life, her house in Italy was visited by many notable women intellectuals, artists, and friends throughout the early twentieth century.

Yet, with the exception of her "aesthetic" collaboration with Kit Anstruther–Thomson, these "romantic friendships" seem to have had no overt influence in her theoretical writings, nor do they seem to appear in her fiction. Her letters, on the other hand, speak frankly of her attachments. That correspondence, which has only recently become available, reveals a woman who wrote freely of her feelings to those women she loved and who wrote with equal feeling about them to her other friends. It is possible, however, to see in Lee's entire corpus of work a tension between the sensual and the cerebral that goes beyond Victorian morality. While there is no explicit "lesbian" aesthetic theory expounded, nor any clearly defined lesbian relationship in her literary works, the juxtaposition of the negative images of sensual, obsessive, or self–sacrificing love relationships in her fiction with her highly refined theory of aesthetics may offer some clues to the tenuous position of the lesbian writer. Moreover, Lee did on occasion transform events and people from her personal life into elements of her fiction. Indeed, her novel *Miss Brown,* in 1884, with its unflattering portraits of a circle of "aesthetes" and their friends, effectively alienated the Rossettis and their Pre–Raphaelite group from Lee and nearly ended her friendship with Henry James. A later work, the short tale "Lady Tal," in 1892, caused a similar scandal with its thinly disguised portraits of Lee and Henry James, finally bringing that friendship to an abrupt end.

These contemporary reactions to *Miss Brown* and "Lady Tal" justify a closer reexamination of Lee's fiction for parallels between the complex relationship of the male authorial persona and the woman writing behind that voice and Lee's own sexuality. Thus, critics have suggested that her fantastic tales, with their often obsessive or destructive emotional relationships, mirror Lee's relationships with women. At the same time, stories such as "Medea da Carpi" and "Oke of Okehurst" depict powerful, albeit dangerous women, who offer a certain freedom from Victorian constraints. A more provocative case is her 1903 play, *Ariadne in Mantua,* whose cross–dressing heroine, Magdalen/Diego, is perhaps the most complicated of these layerings. In *Ariadne,* Lee creates a character who, though dressed as a man, regrets not being recognized as the woman she is by the man she loves, the Duke of Mantua. The Duke's fiancee is disturbed by the presence of Diego/Magdalen and perhaps feels some attraction toward him/her. The final act of this drama includes a play within a play—the story of Ariadne—whose lament is a song written by Lee's former lover, Mary Robinson. The ambiguous nature of the relationships among the characters and the multiple levels of relationships within and without the play, give some clue of the complexity of Lee's psyche.

The exceptional nature of the collaboration between Vernon Lee and Kit Anstruther–Thomson merits a separate discussion. Their ten–year relationship resulted in the Vernon Lee's first foray into the field of aesthetics with her 1897 essay "Beauty and Ugliness." The later collection, *Beauty and Ugliness, and Other Studies in Psychological Aesthetics,* in 1912, and *The Beautiful,* in 1913, also attest to the extent of Anstruther–Thomson's importance to Lee's aesthetic development. Lee had just learned of the impending marriage of Mary Robinson, the "first great friendship and love of [her] life" when she went to stay at the home of the Anstruther–Thomson's. A friendship developed quickly and intensely between Lee and Anstruther–Thomson, resulting in her accompanying Lee back to Italy. Lee used Anstruther–Thomson as a sort of "medium" to study empathetic responses to works of art. In 1924, three years after Anstruther–Thompson's death, Lee edited and had published a collection of her friend's essays, *Art and Man.* Lee's introduction to the volume reveals the strength, passion, and intellectual nature behind their relationship.

Vernon Lee embodies the "new woman" who emerged at the end of the nineteenth century. She was a writer, an intellectual, and an independent spirit who found it+1X equally possible to live without a male companion and to share her emotional life with women.

—*Edith J. Benkov*

———

LEE, William. *See* **BURROUGHS, William S(eward).**

———

LEE, Willy. *See* **BURROUGHS, William S(eward).**

———

Le GUIN, Ursula K(roeber). American novelist, essayist, editor, and author of short stories and children's books. Born in Berkeley, California, 21 October 1929; daughter of anthropologist Alfred L. Kroeber and author Theodora Kroeber. Educated at Radcliffe College, A.B. 1951 (Phi Beta Kappa); Columbia University, A.M. 1952 (faculty fellow, 1952; Fulbright fellow, 1953). Married historian Charles Alfred Le Guin in 1953; three children. Instructor in French, Mercer University, Macon, Georgia, 1954–55; and Univer-

sity of Idaho, Moscow, 1956. Lecturer or writer in residence in programs and workshops, including Clarion West, Portland State University, Pacific University, University of Reading, England, the First Australian Workshop in Speculative Fiction, Indiana University Writers Conference, Revelle College at University of California, San Diego, Kenyon College, Tulane University, Bennington College, Flight of the Mind. Creative consultant for Public Broadcasting Service, for television production of *The Lathe of Heaven,* 1979. Member of Authors League, Writers Guild West, PEN, Science Fiction Research Association, Science Fiction Writers Association, Amnesty International of the U.S.A., Nature Conservancy, National Organization for Women, National Abortion Rights Action League. **Recipient:** *Boston Globe–Horn Book* Award for *A Wizard of Earthsea,* 1968; Science Fiction Writers Association's Nebula Award, and International Science Fiction Association's Hugo Award for *The Left Hand of Darkness,* 1969; Newbery Silver Medal Award for *The Tombs of Atuan,* 1972; Hugo Award for *The Word for World Is Forest,* 1972; National Book Award finalist for *The Farthest Shore,* 1972; Hugo Award for *The Ones Who Walk Away from Omelas,* 1973; *Locus* Award, 1973; Hugo Award, Nebula Award, Jupiter Award, and Jules Verne Award for *The Dispossessed,* 1975; Nebula Award for "The Day before the Revolution," 1975; Gandalf Award for fantasy writing, 1979; University of Rochester Janet Heidinger Kafka Award for *Always Coming Home,* 1986; Prix Lectures–Jeunesse for *Very Far Away from Anywhere Else,* 1987; International Fantasy Award and Hugo Award for *Buffalo Gals,* 1988; Pushcart Prize for "Bill Weisler," 1991; American Academy and Institute of Arts and Letters Harold D. Vursell Award, 1991; Nebula Award for *Tehanu,* 1991. Honorary degrees from Bucknell University, Lawrence University, University of Oregon, Western Oregon State College, Lewis and Clark College, Occidental College, Emory University, Kenyon College, and Portland State University. Lives in Portland, Oregon. Literary Agent: Virginia Kidd, P.O. Box 278, Milford, Pennsylvania 18337, U.S.A. Dramatic Agent: Ilse Lahn, 5300 Fulton Avenue, Van Nuys, California 91401, U.S.A.

WRITINGS

Novels

Rocannon's World (bound with *The Kar–Chee Reign* by Avram Davidson). New York, Ace Books, 1966; London, Tandem, 1972; included in *Three Hainish Novels,* 1978.
Planet of Exile (bound with *Mankind under the Lease* by Thomas M. Disch). New York, Ace Books, 1966; London, Tandem, 1972; included in *Three Hainish Novels,* 1978.
City of Illusions. New York, Ace Books, 1967; London, Gollancz, 1971; included in *Three Hainish Novels,* 1978.
The Left Hand of Darkness. New York, Ace Books, and London, MacDonald, 1969.
The Lathe of Heaven. New York, Scribner, 1971; London, Gollancz, 1972.
The Dispossessed: An Ambiguous Utopia. New York, Harper, and London, Gollancz, 1974.
The Word for the World Is Forest (novella). New York, Putnam, and London, Gollancz, 1976.
Very Far Away from Anywhere Else. New York, Atheneum, 1976; as *A Very Long Way from Anywhere Else,* London, Gollancz, 1976.

Three Hainish Novels (contains *Rocannon's World, Planet of Exile,* and *City of Illusions*). Garden City, New York, Doubleday, 1978.

Malafrena. New York, Putnam, 1979; London, Gollancz, 1980.

The Beginning Place. New York, Harper, 1980; as *Threshold;* London, Gollancz, 1980.

The Visionary: The Life Story of Flicker of the Serpentine (novella; bound with *Wonders Hidden* by Scott R. Sanders). Santa Barbara, California, Capra, 1984.

Always Coming Home (includes tape cassette of *Music and Poetry of the Kesh*), music by Todd Barton, illustrations by Margaret Chodos, diagrams by George Hersh. New York, Harper, 1985; London, Gollancz, 1986; published without cassette, New York, Bantam, 1987.

Short Stories

The Wind's Twelve Quarters. New York, Harper, 1975; London, Gollancz, 1976.

Orsinian Tales. New York, Harper, 1975; London, Panther, 1978.

The Water Is Wide. Portland, Oregon, Pendragon Press, 1976.

Orsinian Tales. New York, Harper, 1976.

Gwilan's Harp. Northridge, California, Lord John Press, 1981.

The Compass Rose. New York, Harper, and London, Gollancz, 1982.

The Eye of the Heron, and Other Stories. New York, Harper, and London, Gollancz, 1983.

Searoad: Chronicles of Klatsland (includes "Quoits"). New York, HarperCollins, 1991.

"In the Drought," in *Xanadu,* edited by Jane Yolen.

Children's Fiction

A Wizard of Earthsea, illustrations by Ruth Robbins. Boston, Parnassus, 1968; London, Gollancz, 1971; included in *The Earthsea Trilogy,* 1977.

The Tombs of Atuan (sequel to *A Wizard of Earthsea*), illustrations by Gail Garraty. New York, Atheneum, 1970; London, Gollancz, 1972; included in *The Earthsea Trilogy,* 1977.

The Farthest Shore (sequel to *The Tombs of Atuan*), illustrations by Gail Garraty. New York, Atheneum, and London, Gollancz, 1972; included in *The Earthsea Trilogy,* 1977.

The Earthsea Trilogy (includes *The Wizard of Earthsea, The Tombs of Atuan,* and *The Farthest Shore*). London, Gollancz, 1977.

Leese Webster, illustrations by James Brunsman. New York, Atheneum, 1979.

The Adventure of Cobbler's Rune, illustrations by Austin. New Castle, Virginia, Cheap Street, 1982.

Adventures in Kroy. New Castle, Virginia, Cheap Street, 1982.

Solomon Leviathan's 931st Trip around the World, illustrations by Alicia Austin. New Castle Virginia, Cheap Street, 1984.

A Visit from Dr. Katz, illustrations by Ann Barrow. New York, Atheneum, 1988.

Catwings, illustrations by S. D. Schindler. Shapleigh, Maine Orchard Books, 1988.

Catwings Return, illustrations by Schindler. Shapleigh, Orchard Books, 1989.

Fire and Stone, illustrations by Laura Marshall. New York, Atheneum, 1989.

Tehanu: The Last Book of Earthsea (sequel to *The Farthest Shore*). New York, Atheneum, and London, Gollancz, 1990.

Fish Soup, illustrations by Patrick Wynne. New York, Atheneum, 1992.

A Ride on the Red Mare's Back, illustrations by Julie Downing. Shapleigh, Orchard Books, 1992.

Poetry

Wild Angels (collection of early works). Santa Barbara, California, Capra, 1975.

With Theodora K. Quinn, *Tillai and Tylissos.* Red Bull, 1979.

Walking in Cornwall: A Poem for the Solstice, illustrations by C. A. Le Guin. Portland, Oregon, Pendragon Press, 1979.

Torrey Pines Reserve (broadsheet). Northridge, California, Lord John Press, 1980.

Hard Words, and Other Poems. New York, Harper, 1981.

In the Red Zone, illustrations by Henk Pander. Northridge, California, Lord John Press, 1983.

Buffalo Gals, and Other Animal Presences (short stories and poetry), illustrations by Margaret Chodos. Santa Barbara, California, Capra, 1987; New York, New American Library, 1988.

Wild Oats and Fireweed. New York, Harper, 1988.

No Boats, illustrations by Le Guin. Ygor and Buntho Make Books, 1991.

Essays

Dreams Must Explain Themselves (limited edition). New York, Algol Press, 1975.

The Language of the Night: Essays on Fantasy and Science Fiction (criticism), edited by Susan Wood. New York, Putnam, 1978; revised and edited by Le Guin, Berkeley, California, Women's Press, 1990.

Dancing at the Edge of the World: Thoughts on Words, Women, Places (criticism). New York, Grove, and London, Gollancz, 1989.

Way of the Water's Going: Images of the Northern California Costal Range (essay with text from *Always Coming Home*), photographs by Ernest Waugh and Alan Nicholson. New York, Harper, 1989.

Editor

Nebula Award Stories XI. New York, Harper, and London, Gollancz, 1977.

With Virginia Kidd, *Interfaces: An Anthology of Speculative Fiction.* New York, Ace Books, 1980.

With Virginia Kidd, *Edges: Thirteen New Tales from the Borderlands of the Imagination.* New York, Pocket Books, 1980.

Other

From Elfland to Poughkeepsie (lecture). Portland, Oregon, Pendragon Press, 1973.

No Use to Talk to Me (radio play). Originally published in *The Altered Eye,* edited by Lee Harding, Melbourne, Nostrilia Press, 1976; New York, Berkley Publishing, 1980.

The Art of Bunditsu, illustrations by Le Guin. Nekobooks, 1982.

King Dog: A Screenplay (bound with *Dostoevsky: A Screenplay* by Raymond Carver and Tess Gallagher). Santa Barbara, California, Capra, 1985.

With composer Elinor Armer, *Uses of Music in Uttermost Parts* (music and text; produced San Francisco and Seattle, 1986).
With Vonda N. McIntyre, *A Winter Solstice Ritual from the Pacific Northwest,* illustrations by Le Guin. Ygor & Buntho Make Books, 1991.
With Paul Preuss, *The Left Hand of Darkness* (screenplay).

Recordings: *The Ones Who Walk Away from Omelas, and Other Stories,* Alternate World, 1976; *The Lathe of Heaven,* Alternate World, 1976; *Gwilan's Harp and Intracom,* Caedmon, 1977; with Todd Barton, *Music and Poetry of the Kesh,* Valley Productions, 1985; with David Bedford, *Rigel Nine: An Audio Opera,* Charisma, 1985; *The Left Hand of Darkness,* Warner Audio, 1985.

*

Adaptations: *The Word for World Is Forest* (sound recording), Book of the Road, 1968; *The Lathe of Heaven* (teleplay), PBS, 1979; *The Tombs of Atuan* (filmstrip with record or cassette), Newbery Award Records, 1980; *The Earthsea Trilogy* (abridged sound recording), Colophon, 1981; "The Ones Who Walk Away from Omelas" (drama with dance and music; performed Portland Civic Theatre, 1981); the screenplay *The Left Hand of Darkness* is being considered for production.

Manuscript Collections: University of Oregon Library, Eugene.

Biography: *Women Writers of the West Coast: Speaking of Their Lives and Careers,* edited by Marilyn Yalom, Santa Barbara, California, Capra, 1983; "Ursula Le Guin," in *Concise Dictionary of American Literary Biography: Broadening Views, 1968–1988,* Detroit, Gale, 1989; *Authors and Artists for Young Adults,* Volume 9, Detroit, Gale, 1992.

Interviews: "Ursula Le Guin: From a Public Dialogue between Le Guin and Anne Mellor, Professor of English, Stanford University, November 6, 1980," in *Women Writers of the West Coast Speaking of Their Lives and Careers,* edited by Marilyn Yalom, Santa Barbara, California, Capra Press, 1983.

Bibliography: *Ursula K. Le Guin: A Primary and Secondary Bibliography* by Elizabeth Cummins Cogell, Boston, Hall, 1983.

Critical Sources: "Wholeness and Balance in the Hainish Novels of Ursula Le Guin" by Douglas Barbour, *Science–Fiction Studies,* spring 1974; *Structural Fabulation: An Essay on the Future of Fiction* by Robert Scholes, University of Notre Dame Press, 1975; *Writers of the 21st Century Series: Ursula K. Le Guin,* edited by Joseph D. Olander and Martin Harry Greenberg, New York, Taplinger, 1979; *Extrapolation,* edited by Thomas D. Clareson, fall 1980 (special Ursula K. Le Guin issue); *Ursula K. Le Guin* by Barbara J. Bucknall, New York, Ungar, 1981; "*The Beginning Place:* Le Guin's Metafantasy" by Brian Attebery, in *Children's Literature,* Number 10, 1982; "Chronosophy, Aesthetics, and Ethics in Le Guin's *The Dispossessed: An Ambiguous Utopia*" by James W. Bittner, in *No Place Else: Explorations in Utopian and Dystopian Fiction,* edited by Eric S. Rabkin, Martin H. Greenberg, and Joseph D. Olander, Carbondale, Southern Illinois University Press, 1983; *Approaches to the Fiction of Ursula K. Le Guin* by James W. Bittner,

Ann Arbor, Michigan, UMI Research Press, 1984; "Ursula Le Guin: In a World of Her Own" by Nora Gallagher, in *Mother Jones,* January 1984, 23–27, 51–53; *Ursula K. Le Guin* by Charlotte Spivak, Boston, Twayne Publishers, 1984; *Erotic Universe: Sexuality and Fantastic Literature* by Donald Palumbo, New York, Greenwood Press, 1986; "Art, Myth and Ritual in Le Guin's *Left Hand of Darkness*" by Anna Valdine Clemens, in *Canadian Review of American Studies,* winter 1986; "Utopian and Dystopian Pessimism: Le Guin's *The Word for World Is Forest* and Tiptree's 'We Who Stole the Dream'" by Soren Baggesen, in *Science–Fiction Studies,* March 1987; *Le Guin and Identity in Contemporary Fiction* by Bernard Selinger, Ann Arbor, UMI Research Press, 1988; *Understanding Ursula K. Le Guin* by Elizabeth Cummins, Columbia, University of South Carolina Press, 1990; *Radical Imagination: Feminist Conceptions of the Future in Ursula Le Guin, Marge Piercy, and Sally Miller Gearhart,* New York, P. Lang, 1991; "Places Where a Woman Could Talk: Ursula K. Le Guin and the Feminist Linguistic Utopia" by Kristine J. Anderson, in *Women and Language,* spring 1992; "Beyond Words: The Impact of Rhythm as Narrative Technique in *The Left Hand of Darkness*" by Nora Barry and Mary Prescott, in *Extrapolation,* summer 1992.

Ursula K. Le Guin comments: "Since *The Left Hand of Darkness,* which was written 25 years ago, my work has become increasingly woman–centered. The first three books of my fantasy *Earthsea* take place in a traditionally male–dominated society, even though the second of them, *The Tombs of Atuan,* is set in a little world of only women and girls (and eunuchs). In the fourth Earthsea book, *Tehanu,* I turned this power structure on its head by showing it from the point of view of the truly powerless—an old woman and an abused girl—and to offer the hope of a different, better definition of power—power as enablement not as domination.

"In the 1970s I wrote an anarchist utopia, *The Dispossessed,* which though still male–centered and predominantly heterosexual at least shows a completely gender–equal society, in which bisexuality and homosexuality are taken for granted.

"In the 1980s I was at last able to write a utopia from a non–phallocentric point of view: *Always Coming Home,* which is, I think, a genuinely feminist novel. Though I wish I had shown more of the gay/lesbian side of life in my future California, the book shows a world where there is no gender dominance of any kind.

"Two recent stories with lesbian main characters are 'Quoits,' in my collection *Searoad,* and 'In the Drought,' in Jane Yolen's anthology *Xanadu.* Work in progress includes a collaboration with Judith Barrington on a kind of guide to etiquette for straight people with their gay and lesbian friends, and a series of science–fiction stories involving all sorts of variations on love, sex, and marriage—thought experiments you might call them."

*   *   *

Highly acclaimed for her contributions to numerous genres, Ursula K. Le Guin has written for children and adults alike. Although Charlotte Spivack finds Le Guin "an entertaining writer" whose work "can be read with enjoyment and adequate understanding without reference to anything else," she points out that Le Guin is "a novelist with a genuinely mythopoetic imagination." In her novels for older readers, she presents complex and detailed worlds. "The highly original cosmos that she has created through her fiction is not only rich in populated planets," remarks Spivack, "but also peopled with morally and psychologically complex characters and thronging with images, ideas, and archetypes." One of Le Guin's strengths as a novelist is that she poses questions about the way her characters interact with one another, hoping that, by raising the questions, her readers will become more aware of how things are and how things might be.

Within her novels, Le Guin is especially known for her liberal utopian societies. For instance, one such society is found in *The Left of Hand of Darkness,* for which she won both the Nebula and Hugo awards for best science fiction novel for 1969. *The Left of Hand of Darkness* is generally considered to be one of her best works. Set in the distant future on the planet Gethen, the novel examines a society, complete with accounts of legends and myths and descriptions of religious ceremonies, that is androgynous. Only during an oestrus period do the inhabitants assume one gender or the other. Once out of the oestrus period, they do not assume the traditional roles of either gender. By using this device, Le Guin is able to discuss such issues as gender identity and its role in society and issues of friendship based on that gender identity.

In an interview with Nora Gallagher in *Mother Jones,* Le Guin indicated that the novel had its origins in her increasing involvement in feminism: "I began to want to define and understand the meaning of sexuality and the meaning of gender, in my life and in our society. Much had gathered in the unconscious—both personal and collective—which must either be brought up into consciousness, or else turn destructive.... I was and am a fiction writer. The way I did my thinking was to write a novel. That novel, *The Left Hand of Darkness,* is the record of my consciousness, the process of my thinking." Spivack suggests that in her work Le Guin also incorporates Taoism, which asserts "the mutual interdependence of male and female, visually depicted in the yin–yang symbol of interlocking dark and light semicircles." Although Le Guin provides some evidence that it is possible for a society to develop without the pressures and tensions of male/female conflicts, she has been criticized for her use of the male pronoun in relation to these androgynous people throughout *The Left Hand of Darkness,* which tends to inculcate and perpetuate American gender–linked stereotypes.

However, in an interview with *Something about the Author,* Le Guin remarked on the rationale behind using "he" to refer to her characters throughout the novel: "In 1967, while I was writing *The Left Hand of Darkness,* nobody had discussed the sexist implications of the pronouns. It was before the women's movement became interested in gender bias in language—the fact that 'he' is supposedly 'universal' and therefore embraces women. It doesn't as a matter of fact." When given the opportunity to work on a screenplay version of the novel, Le Guin noted in her interview that she altered the language and "got away from the masculine tinge which colors the book."

Although Le Guin does not allow her characters to have same–sex relationships, thus perpetuating a heterosexual society with its mores instead of a truly utopian society where people are free to choose their partners because of attraction not gender, in *The Left Hand of Darkness,* she presents a hypothetical world and allows her readers to think about the possibilities open to a society in which people are androgynous. "Le Guin's fiction offers a thrilling personal vision of a universe, a whirling, expanding infinity in its complexity," observes Spivack, who concludes, "She has already created a galaxy with profoundly human relevance, and her reading public can only wait with soaring expectancy for what will follow next."

—*Pamela Bigelow*

————

LEHMANN, Rosamond (Nina). British novelist, editor, and translator. Born in Bourne End, Buckinghamshire, 3 February 1901. Educated at Girton College, Cambridge (scholar; honorary fellow, 1986), 1919–22. Married 1) Leslie Ruciman (divorced); 2) Wogan Philipps in 1928; one son and one daughter (died). Codirector of John Lehmann Ltd. (publishing company), 1946–53; president of English Centre; international vice–president of PEN; vice–president of the College of Psychic Studies; council member of Society of Authors. **Recipient:** Commandeur dans l'Ordre des Arts et Lettres, 1968; Commander of the British Empire, 1982. *Died in London, 12 March 1990.*

WRITINGS

Novels

Dusty Answer. London, Chatto & Windus, and New York, Holt, 1927.

A Note in Music. London, Chatto & Windus, and New York, Holt, 1930.

Invitation to the Waltz. London, Chatto & Windus, and New York, Holt, 1932.

The Weather in the Streets. London, Collins, and New York, Reynal, 1936.

The Ballad and the Source. London, Collins, 1944; New York, Reynal, 1945.

The Echoing Grove. London, Collins, and New York, Harcourt, 1953.

A Sea–Grape Tree. London, Collins, 1976; New York, Harcourt, 1977.

Memoirs

The Swan in the Evening: Fragments of an Inner Life. London, Collins, and New York, Harcourt, 1967.

With Cynthia Hill Sandys, *Letters from Our Daughters* (two volumes). London, College of Psychic Studies, 1972.

Other

Letter to a Sister. London, Hogarth, 1931; London, Harcourt, 1932.

No More Music (play; produced London, 1938). London, Collins, 1939; New York, Reynal, 1945.

Editor, with others, *Orion: A Miscellany 1–3* (three volumes). London, Nicholson & Watson, 1945–46.

The Gipsy's Baby, and Other Stories. London, Collins, 1946; New York, Reynal, 1947.

Translator, *Genevieve* by Jacques Lemarchand. London, Lehmann, 1947.

Translator, *The Holy Terrors* by Jean Cocteau. New York, New Directions, 1957.

With W. Tudor Pole, *A Man Seen Afar*. London, Spearman, 1965.

With W. Tudor Pole, *Zeuge im Leben Jesu*. Zurich, Origo–Verlag, 1969.

Editor, with C. H. Sandys, *The Awakening Letters*. London, Spearman, 1978.

Author of foreword, *My Dear Alexias: Letters to Rosamond Lehmann* by W. Tudor Pole, edited by Elizabeth Gaythorpe. London, Spearman, 1979.

Author of introduction, postscript, and captions, *Rosamond Lehmann's Album* (photographs). London, Chatto & Windus, 1985.

*

Adaptations: *The Weather in the Streets* was filmed in 1983.

Biography: *Virginia Woolf and Her World* by John Lehmann, New York, Harcourt, 1975; *Gay American History; Lesbians and Gay Men in the U.S.A.* by Jonathan Katz, New York, Crowell, 1976; *Elizabeth Bowen: A Biography* by Victoria Glendinning, New York, Avon Books, 1977; *Rosamond Lehmann: An Appreciation* by Gillian Tindall, London, Chatto & Windus, 1985; *Rosamond Lehmann: A Thirties Writer* by Ruth Siegel, New York, P. Lang, 1989.

Bibliography: *Women Loving Women: A Select and Annotated Bibliography of Women Loving Women in Literature* edited by Marie J. Kuda, Chicago, Womanpress, 1975.

Critical Sources: *Sex Variant Women in Literature; A Historical and Quantitative Survey* by Jeannette H. Foster, New York, Vantage, 1956; *Rosamond Lehmann* (part of Twayne's English Authors Series) by Diana E. LeStourgeon, New York, Twayne Publishers, 1965; *Subjective Vision and Human Relationships in the Novels of Rosamond Lehmann* by Wiktoria Dorosz, Uppsala, Sweden, Universitet, 1975; *Virginia Woolf and Her World* by John Lehmann, New York, Harcourt, 1975; *Gay American History: Lesbians and Gay Men in the U.S.A.* by Jonathan Katz, New York, Crowell, 1976, 422; *Elizabeth Bowen: A Biography* by Victoria Glendinning, New York, Avon, 1977, 128; *Rosamond Lehmann* by Judy Simons, New York, St. Martin's Press, 1992.

*　　*　　*

Rosamond Lehmann has been considered by critics to be a minor British writer in a Jamesian mode. The author of 13 books, a play, a handful of short stories, and a few critical essays, she was an outsider in the Bloomsbury circle—traces of her can be found in almost every biography and collection of letters that touched the famous literary group. Her brother John Lehmann managed Hogarth Press for Leonard and Virginia Woolf; her sensual, almost sexual,

word–portrait of Virginia is quoted in one of his memoirs. She had an ongoing friendship with Elizabeth Bowen, and in correspondence with Dora Carrington was privy to some of the peregrinations of the androgynous artists and intellects surrounding Woolf and Lytton Strachey.

Lehmann wrote her first novel when she was 24. *Dusty Answer*, published in 1927, has a leitmotif of homosexuality and lesbianism which, unnamed, was often missed by readers and some reviewers. The young protagonist, Judith Earle, lives next door to four boys, cousins with whom she has varying degrees of romantic attachment during her college years. At Cambridge, she forms an intense romantic friendship with Jennifer, who loves her passionately. Roddy, one of the cousins to whom Judith is most attracted, forms an overtly gay relationship with Tony. The two young men flow in and out of the book until the ending scene. After two years of unrequited love, Jennifer goes off with Geraldine—in a final letter written to Judith years later, this relationship is clearly lesbian and collapses because of Geraldine's possessive jealousy and Jennifer's wandering eye. In essence, Judith loses the two people she loves most to homosexuality. Even when she is being seduced or courted, her thoughts wander to comparisons with Jennifer—while swimming with her lover Julian, Judith thinks back to Jennifer "slipping the clothes down off white shoulder and breast, talking and laughing. A tide of memories; Jennifer's head burning in the sunlight, her body stooping towards the water.... Where had it all gone—Where was Jennifer?—Whom enchanting now?—How faintly remembering Judith? Compared with that tumultuous richness, how sickly, how wavering was this present feeling—what a sorry pretense! Would one ever be happy again?"

In the final pages of the novel, Judith and Jennifer exchange letters—both seem to be longing for the old passion of their first love. They plan a reunion at a tea shop near the college, but Jennifer does not appear. The reader is left with the final image of Judith, stoic, now free of both her old loves, as Tony and Roddy walk by the tea shop.

Lesbian readers, even today, bring their own interpretation to the ending of *Dusty Answer*. Judith has been pursuing men because of her latent lesbianism. Midway through the novel, she tells Julian, who wants her to be his mistress: "I'd go to her [Jennifer] now this minute if I knew where she was. But I don't.... Help me forget her."

To the lesbian reader, Judith's eagerness to rejoin Jennifer leaves the potential for a post–ending lesbian relationship. Novelist Valerie Taylor, in writing the bibliographic annotation for *Dusty Answer* in *Women Loving Women*, concurred with Jeannette H. Foster's opinion that the novel was autobiographical and that the lesbian content was exceptional for its day. Barbara Gittings, one of the founders of the New York Daughters of Bilitis, editor of the lesbian magazine the *Ladder* from 1963 to 1966, and head of the American Library Association Gay Lesbian Task Force for almost 20 years, has written of searching for a lesbian identity in libraries of the 1950s. "Then I began to find other books. I remember specifically ... *Dusty Answer* by Rosamond Lehmann.... [F]iction made a big difference, because here were human beings that were fleshed out in a dimension that simply wasn't available in the scientific materials, which were always examining us from a clinical point of view in which we were diseased case histories."

Foster notes that a plethora of college romances or boarding school novels, "more or less negative contributions, all by American women, probably stemmed from Miss Lehmann's *Dusty Answer*." Foster may be alluding to the quickie, for–profit paperback originals that began flooding the market in the post–war years, although she points out that Sheila Donisthrope's 1931 book *Love-liest of Friends,* a "fairly obvious rebuttal to [Radclyffe Hall's] *Well of Loneliness*" has the description of a character that is "lifted verbatim from the description of Jennifer" in *Dusty Answer.* Foster also noted that male reviewers tended to be "unsympathetic" to the works of women writers with variant, or lesbian, themes.

Lehmann "made her name" with *Dusty Answer,* and her subsequent novels were also successful—*The Ballad and the Source* went through several printings and was a Book–of–the–Month Club selection in the United States. Victoria Glendinning, in her biography of author Elizabeth Bowen, describes Lehmann thusly: "She was famous not only for her talent but for her looks. She was unequivocally beautiful—dark–haired, creamy." For the generation of pre–*Rubyfruit,* pre–Naiad Press romance lesbians in search of positive images, *Dusty Answer* hit a responsive chord. It was heavily autobiographical, written by a woman of position and beauty, with attractive characters and no labels, just rapturous love. It did not have the attendant baggage of an obscenity trial as would *The Well of Loneliness,* published just one year later, nor the prerequisite dismal ending of future lesbian fiction. For American women who were creating lesbian fantasies around the censored screen images of Greta Garbo, Marlene Dietrich, and Katherine Hepburn, the nonjudgmental presentation of the romance between Judith and Jennifer was palpable—and they could extend it with their own happy postscript.

Throughout the rest of her writings, the light touch of Lehmann's fiction assured her continued popularity. Foster notes that Lehmann's 1936 novel *Weather in the Streets* "skimmed variance fleetingly" and Taylor annotates *The Ballad and the Source:* "Romantic quasi–sexual attachment among English schoolgirls. Social pressure explicit." In those early years when there was a dearth of good lesbian material, Lehmann's portrayal of her characters loving without labels presented an oasis for the mind and heart.

—*Marie J. Kuda*

LEZAMA LIMA, José. Cuban novelist, poet, and essayist. Born José María Andrés Fernando Lezama Lima in Campamento Militar de Columbia, 19 December 1910. Educated at Colegio San Francisco de Paula, 1920–28; Universidad de La Habana, law degree. Lawyer in private practice, Cuba, 1938–40; counsellor in charge of judicial matters, Consejo Superior de Defensa Social, Castillo del Principe (prison), Havana, c. 1940; worked for various government agencies in Cuba, 1940–59; director of department of literature and publications, Consejo Nacional Cultura, Havana, 1959–76. Co-president of the Unión de Escritores y Artistas de Cuba (Cuban Writers and Artists Union), 1961; advisor, Centro Cubano de Investigaciones Literarias (Cuban Center for Literary Research), c. 1962. Founder and editor, *Verbum* (literary review), 1937; coeditor, *Espuela de Plata* (literary review), 1939–41; founder and editor, *Nadie Parecía* (literary review), 1942–44; founder and editor, *Orígenes* (literary review), 1944–56. *Died in Havana, 9 August 1976.*

WRITINGS

Novels

Muerte de Narciso. Havana, Ucar, García, 1937.
Enemigo rumor. Havana, Ucar, García, 1941.
Aventuras sigilosas. Havana, Orígenes, 1945.
La fijeza. Havana, Orígenes, 1949.
Aristedes Fernández, 1950.
Tratados en La Habana. Havana, Universidad Central de Las Villas, 1958.
Paradiso. Havana, Unión Nacional de Escritores y Artistas de Cuba, 1966; revised, Mexico City, Era, 1968; translated by Gregory Rabassa, New York, Farrar, Straus, and London, Secker & Warburg, 1974.
Esferaimagen: Sierpe de don Luis de Góngora; Las imágenes posibles. Barcelona, Tusquets, 1970.
Algunos tratados en La Habana. Editorial Anagrama, 1971.
Introducción a los vasos órficos. Barcelona, Barral, 1971.
Las eras imaginarias. Madrid, Fundamentos, 1971.
Coloquio con Juan Ramón Jiménez. Estudios Gráficos de CBA, 1973.
Cangrejos y golondrinas. Buenos Aires, Calicanto, 1977.
Fragmentos a su imán. Havana, Arte & Literatura, 1977.
Oppiano Licario. Havana, Arte & Literatura, 1977.
Imagen y posibilidad, edited by Ciro Bianchi Ross. Havana, Letras Cubanas, 1981.
El reino de la imagen. Caracas, Venezuela, Ayacucho, 1981.
Juego de las decapitaciones. Barcelona, Montesinos, 1982.
Relatos. Madrid, Alianza, 1987.
Confluencias. Havana, Letras Cubanas, 1988.

Poetry

Dador. Havana, Ucar, García, 1960.
Possible imagen de José Lezama Lima. Barcelona, Sinera, 1969.
Poesía completa. Havana, Instituto del Libro, 1970; enlarged, Havana, Letras Cubanas, 1985.

Collections

Orbita de Lezama Lima, edited by Armando Alvarez Bravo. Havana, Unión de Escritores y Artistas de Cuba, 1966.
Los grandes todos. Montevideo, Uruguay, Arca, 1968; as *Lezama Lima,* Buenos Aires, Alvarez, 1968.
Obras completas (two volumes), edited by Cintio Vitier. Mexico City, Aguilar, 1975, 1977.
The Poetic Fiction of José Lezama Lima, by Raymond D. Souza. Columbia, University of Missouri Press, 1983.
Cercanía de Lezama Lima, by Carlos Espinosa. Havana, Letras Cubanas, 1986.

Other

Analecta del reloj (essays). Havana, Orígenes, 1953.
Author of introduction, *Gradual de laudes,* by Angel Gaztelu. Havana, Orígenes, 1955.
La expresión americana (lectures). Havana, Instituto Nacional de Cultura, Ministerio de Educación, 1957; enlarged, Montevideo, Arca, 1969.

Editor, *Antología de la poesía cubana* (three volumes). Havana, Consejo Nacional de Cultura, 1965.

Selector and author of introduction, *Juan Clemente Zenea: Poesía.* Havana, Academia de Ciencias de Cuba, 1966.

La cantidad hechizada (essays). Havana, Unión Nacional de Escritores y Artistas de Cuba, 1970.

Cartas (1939–1976) (letters), edited and introduced by Eloísa Lezama Lima. Madrid, Orígenes, 1979.

Cuentos (short stories). Havana, Letras Cubanas, 1987.

Mi correspondencia con Lezama Lima (letters), by José Rodríguez Feo. Havana, Unión de Escritores y Artistas de Cuba, c. 1989.

*

Biography: *Lezama Lima: El ingenuo culpable* by Reynaldo González, Havana, Letras Cubanas, 1988.

Bibliography: *Sobre José Lezama Lima y sus lectores: Guía y compendio bibliográfico* by Justo C. Ulloa, Boulder, Colorado, Society of Spanish and Spanish–American Studies, c. 1987.

Critical Sources: "Para llegar a Lezama Lima" by Julio Cortázar, in his *La vuelta al día en ochenta mundos,* Mexico City, Siglo XXI, 1967, 135–155; "Cartas: sobre el *Paradiso* de Lezama" by Emir Rodríguez Monegal and Mario Vargas Llosa, in *Mundo Nuevo* (Paris), October 1967, 89–95; "Vidas para leerlas" by Guillermo Cabrera Infante, in *Vuelta,* April 1980, 4–16; *Sobre José Lezama Lima y sus lectores: guía y compendio bibliográfico* by Justo C. Ulloa, Boulder, Colorado, Society of Spanish and Spanish American Studies, 1987; *Lezama Lima* by Eugenio Suárez–Galbán, Madrid, Taurus, c. 1987; *José Lezama Lima's Joyful Vision: A Study of Paradiso, and Other Prose Works* by Gustavo Pellón, Austin, University of Texas Press, 1989; *José Lezama Lima: Poet of the Image* by Emilio Bejel, illustrations by Vicente Dopico, Gainesville, University of Florida, c. 1990.

*   *   *

A major Cuban novelist and poet, José Lezama Lima achieved international notoriety with the publication of *Paradiso,* one of the most original and controversial novels of the 1960s to emerge from writers in the small island–nation. In *Paradiso,* as well as in its sequel *Oppiano Licario,* Lezama developed a narrative style which, combined with his unique poetic canon as expressed in his essays, produced a different kind of autobiographical novel in Cuba. The abstruse construction of these two novels presents neither a specific ideology nor a strict psychological analysis of the characters, but it displays instead a biting and very personal way of exploring the complexities of the origin of human sexuality.

Lezama was born in the military camp Columbia, near Havana, on 19 December 1910; he was the second child of José María Lezama y Rodda, an artillery lieutenant in the Cuban army, and of the former Rosa Lima y Rosado, daughter of revolutionary exiles residing in Florida during the Cuban War of Independence from Spain. Lezama's personal memories from early childhood prominently

figure in his novels, poems, and essays, and he constantly alludes to his relationship with his family as the controlling force that molded his works.

Following the death of his father in 1919, Lezama, his two sisters, and his mother moved into their maternal grandmother's house in Havana. After the marriage of his sisters, Lezama continued to live with his mother until her death in 1964. His mother became his closest friend and critic, and she had such an overwhelming influence in his life that he even acquired her unique way of modulating speech. It was not until after her death, and only because she had requested him to do so, that he married María Luisa Bautista Treviñu, an old friend of the family. Lezama and María Luisa lived in his mother's house until Lezama's death on 9 August 1976.

Lezama's early schooling was at the Colegio San Francisco de Paula, where his father had also been educated. Because of young Lezama's constant asthma attacks, most of his childhood was spent closed up in his room. It was during this early period of his life that Lezama developed a passion for reading as a means of combating his sleepless nights. In secondary school, Lezama distinguished himself in art, philosophy, and literature courses. His high–school years are recreated in *Paradiso,* although obscure metaphorical associations and allusions to his many readings diminish the autobiographical impact. One can discern, however, his early fascination with sexuality in the numerous references that appear in the chapters dedicated to the adolescent years of José Cemí, the protagonist of *Paradiso* and Lezama's alter ego.

In 1929, Lezama enrolled at the University of Havana as a law student. Cuba was suffering under the dictatorship of Gerardo Machado, and Lezama, not unlike many other students, joined demonstrations against the regime. Because of the political turmoil of the times, Machado closed the university for four years, thus interrupting Lezama's studies. But the young Cuban welcomed this interruption, for it furnished him with the much needed time to focus and to read avidly every source of knowledge available to him. The political events he witnessed, and the intricate philosophical discussions on the origins of sexuality he engaged in with his fellow classmates at the university, provided Lezama with details for further imagery that he would later use in *Paradiso* in the chapters dealing with political unrest, phallic symbolism, and homoerotic love.

With the fall of Machado and the reopening of the university in 1934, Lezama continued his law studies, mainly to please his mother. But his copious reading and his contact with Cuban intellectuals had changed his attitude towards his professional life. He was now sure that he wanted to devote his energies to a life of culture and poetry. In 1937, he published his most consequential poem, "Muerte de Narciso" ("The Death of Narcissus"), where he plays masterfully with the image of the flower, with the mythic figure of Narcissus, with Nature, with absence and presence, and with the life cycle to convey the reader to metaphysical levels. This poem is an excellent example of the various layers of meaning that are interwoven in all of Lezama's intricate creations. Here the symbolism of the mirror as an instrument of contemplation and reflection suggests multiple connotations. It is also a strong image of love for the self or the same and its latent destructive consequences.

In 1937 Lezama also began to edit a series of literary reviews devoted to literature and art which would prepare the way for the founding of Lezama's most important literary organ, *Orígenes.* Essays constitute his greatest contribution to *Orígenes.* Those essays contain the core of his poetics, which had an immense impact on his collaborators as well as on the configuration of his own poetic and narrative production. The concepts of "vivencia oblicua" (oblique experience), "súbito" (unexpected intellectual enlightenments), and "eras imaginarias" (imaginary eras) are expounded in these essays and are crucial elements of his writings, which function mainly through poetic associations and not by causal connections. In *Orígenes,* Lezama also published several short stories and the first five chapters of *Paradiso.*

Lezama published *Paradiso* in 1966, two years after the death of his mother. In this novel, Lezama seems to exteriorize the inner tensions and doubts silently suppressed during the period he lived with his mother. The novel encompasses the familiar, mythical, intellectual, and poetic worlds experienced by the author during his formative years. The structure of *Paradiso* is the result of Lezama's own poetic canon, and it can be divided into four subtly unified conceptual units: 1) the genealogical construct built around the image of the family tree and detailed descriptions of Jose Cemí's family; 2) the sexual construct which explores multiple manifestations of man's sexual origins; 3) the application of Lezama's poetic construct in which the author experiments with the notions of time and space; and 4) the educational construct that contains Cemí's formal initiation into poetry during his encounter with his intellectual mentor, Oppiano Licario.

The first edition of *Paradiso,* published by UNEAC (Unión de Escritores y Artistas de Cuba) in 1966, caused an immediate uproar in Cuba's intellectual circles. Because of detailed descriptions of homosexual encounters, *Paradiso* was classified as pornographic by revolutionary government officials and summarily removed from circulation. However, the ban lasted only a few months, because the novel had already been recognized for its literary merits by intellectuals abroad. Nonetheless, the sexual content in the novel continued to incite controversy. In 1967, the Uruguayan critic Emir Rodríguez Monegal wrote a letter in *Mundo Nuevo* criticizing Peruvian novelist Mario Vargas Llosa's failure to see the importance of homosexuality in the novel. He pointed out that without real attention to the homosexual aspects of the novel, it is impossible to place *Paradiso* in its proper perspective. For Monegal these episodes are connected to Lezama's poetic conceptions as stated in the latter's essays. In 1968, the Argentine critic and novelist Julio Cortázar commented in his essay "Para llegar a Lezama Lima" ("How to Approach Lezama Lima"), published in *La vuelta al día en ochenta mundos* ("Around the Day in Eighty Worlds"), that in *Paradiso*'s homosexual references there are metaphorical allusions to Jules Verne's *Journey to the Center of the Earth,* in 1864. Although Cortázar perceptively uncovered hidden puns in which Icelandic orography is used to describe homoerotic incidents, he also recognized that homosexuality in *Paradiso* is an important component not because it presents a new source of "pornographic" materials for the avid reader of this kind of literature, but because it is rooted in mythological, anthropological, and poetic concepts which go beyond any superficial reading.

Finally, in a 1980 essay entitled "Vidas para leerlas" (Lives to be Read), the Cuban novelist Guilleimo Cabrera Infante offered a different reading of the theme of homosexuality in *Paradiso.* Cabrera Infante stressed aspects of Lezama's own homosexuality and linked the publication of *Paradiso* to the poet's silent protest against the persecution homosexuals were suffering in Communist Cuba.

Notwithstanding the controversial reception of *Paradiso* and the many attempts to justify its sexual content, it is apparent that the four constructs in the novel are directly linked to Lezama's preoccupation with man's sexual origins. *Paradiso* is a compendium of all of his previous works where obscure and learned refer-

ences abound in the crowded pages. It is a permutation of texts in which Lezama's postulates contained in his essays and poems are fused with remembrances, readings, and information borrowed from other texts (iconography, cultural, historical, religious or fictional). Such a permutation enriches the immense and hermetic metaphor of the *rite de passage* that José Cemí must endure before realizing his destiny of becoming a poet. It is precisely in his initiation that phallic images and homosexual scenes become dominant, with the desire to portray vividly this ritual passage, Lezama creates a variety of images based on a great number of phallic symbols. Many of these phallic symbols have as their archetypal model the most remote cultures of antiquity in which phallic emblems were the center of worship in rituals celebrating the constant regeneration of life. The loose assortment of graphic symbols drawn by the writer throughout this period of initiation are later integrated into a final image of resurrection. This is done by means of a pictorial description of vegetation festivals and by means of esoteric debates between Cemí and two of his close friends at the university, Fronesis and Foción. In their highly intellectual conversations, the perfect state of man after resurrection and multiple expressions of homosexual and sexual modes are skillfully scrutinized. Once all the different theories have been discussed, Lezama, through Jose Cemí, sums up his opinion of the dark mystery surrounding homosexuality, women, and Eros in general. His aim has been to examine the topic carefully and exhaustively. Because of his Catholic upbringing and given the difficulty of summarizing such an extensive field of knowledge, Lezama ends the discussion among the three friends by relating the position on homosexuality of well–known Catholic thinkers such as Saint Augustine and Saint Thomas Aquinas.

Concerned with disparate comments made by critics regarding the theme of homosexuality in *Paradiso,* Lezama decided to write a sequel that would add another dimension to the discussion and clarify his poetic intentions. But although *Oppiano Licario* was thus conceived it is almost as hermetic as *Paradiso.* In *Oppiano Licario,* Lezama focuses his attention on the educational, poetic, and sexual constructs present in his first novel and emphasizes the cognitive development of Jose Cemí, who is the integrative character in both novels. In *Oppiano Licario,* Cemí continues his apprenticeship, which culminates with his symbolic sexual encounter with Inaca Eco Licario, Oppiano Licario's sister. Inaca represents the missing link in his formative period, and she contributes to the poet's cognitive formation by providing him with a sense of perspective and the capability of reconstructing fragments into a unifying whole. Unfortunately, Lezama's original intention of integrating all of his poetic concepts in *Oppiano Licario* and of clarifying some of the most controversial and obscure episodes of *Paradiso* were cut short by his sudden death, brought about by pneumonia in 1976.

In *Paradiso* and *Oppiano Licario,* Cemí is the main character whose ultimate poetic fulfillment becomes the crux of the intricate metaphorical construction. The insertion of the sexual construct in both novels opens for Cemí other avenues that he must consider in his journey toward becoming a poet. This metaphorical scrutiny of sexuality is enriched through Lezama's conception of a triad in which the three friends symbolically represent key fragments of the portrait of the poet. But even though Fronesis and Foción completed the image of totality that Cemí must embody, the character of Foción is continually fraught with negative attributes. Foción symbolizes the errant element that must be suppressed. In *Paradiso,* Foción is the acknowledged homosexual member of the group. He tries in vain to justify homosexuality by suggesting among many possibilities a primordial stage of androgyny, but as in the case of other homosexual characters depicted in both novels, Foción is portrayed in unfavorable terms as an incomplete being who ends his life in a destructive state of madness. The fate of Lezama's homosexual characters seems to underscore the fact that Lezama's novels are not an apology for homosexuality as some readers have insinuated. It is apparent that in both novels, the poet pursues higher goals probably found within Cemí's own philosophical arguments with his two friends. In this context, homosexuality and its phallic correlative function as metaphors: they are the poetic signs of an undaunted intellectual search for answers to the different manifestations of sexuality at a time and in a society where homosexuality was perceived as an undesirable deviant sexual inclination.

—*Justo C. Ulloa and Leonor A. Ulloa*

LORDE, Audre (Geraldine). American librarian, educator, poet, essayist, and author of short stories. Also wrote as Rey Domini. Born in New York City, 18 February 1934. Educated at National University of Mexico, 1954; Hunter College (now Hunter College of the City University of New York), B.A. 1960; Columbia University, New York City, M.L.S. 1962. Married Edwin Ashley Rollins in 1962 (divorced 1972); one son, one daughter. Librarian, Mount Vernon Public Library, Mount Vernon, New York, 1961–63; head librarian, Town School Library, New York City, 1966–68; lecturer in creative writing, City College, New York City, 1968; lecturer in education department, Herbert H. Lehman College, Bronx, New York, 1969–70; associate professor of English, John Jay College of Criminal Justice, New York City, beginning 1970; professor of English, Hunter College, New York City, 1981–87, Thomas Hunter professor, 1987–92. Visiting professor, Tougaloo University, Tougaloo, Mississippi, and Atlanta University, Atlanta, Georgia, both 1968. Visiting lecturer throughout the United States, Europe, Africa, and Australia. Founder, Kitchen Table: Women of Color Press and Sisterhood in Support of Sisters in South Africa. Poetry editor, *Chrysalis* and *Amazon Quarterly*. Contributor of short stories to *Venture* magazine as Rey Domini. **Recipient:** National Endowment for the Arts grants, 1968, 1981; Creative Artists Public Service grant, 1972, 1976; National Book Award nominee, 1974; American Library Association Gay Caucus Book Award, 1981, for *The Cancer Journals;* Borough of Manhattan President's Award, 1987, for literary excellence; Before Columbus Foundation's American Book Award, 1989; Triangle Publications Group's Bill Whitehead Award for lifetime contribution to literature, 1990; Sappho Award for contribution to literature on multicultural lesbian identity, 1990; Fund for Free Expression Award, 1991; named New York State Poet Laureate, 1992; honorary doctorates: Oberlin College, Haverford College, State University of New York at Binghampton. *Died in St. Croix, Virgin Islands, of liver cancer, 20 November 1992.*

WRITINGS

Poetry

The First Cities. New York, Poets Press, 1968.
Cables to Rage. London, Breman Press, and Detroit, Broadside Press, 1970.
From a Land Where Other People Live. Detroit, Broadside Press, 1973.
The New York Head Shop and Museum. Detroit, Broadside Press, 1974.
Coal. New York, Norton, 1976.
Between Our Selves. Point Reyes, California, Eidolon Editions, 1976.
The Black Unicorn. New York, Norton, 1978.
Chosen Poems, Old and New. New York, Norton, 1982; revised as *Undersong: Chosen Poems Old and New,* New York, Norton, 1992.
Our Dead behind Us. New York, Norton, 1986.

Contributor

Beyond the Blues: New Poems by American Negroes, edited by Rosey Poole. Lympne, Kent, Hand & Flower Press, 1963.
Sixes and Sevens, edited by Paul Bremen. London, Breman, 1963.
New Negro Poets, U.S.A., edited by Langston Hughes. Bloomington, Indiana University Press, 1964.
The New Black Poetry, edited by Clarence Major. New York, International Press, 1969.
Natural Process: An Anthology of New Black Poetry, edited by Ted Wilentz and Tom Weatherly. New York, Hill & Wang, 1970.
Afro–American Poetry, edited by Bernard Bell. Boston, Allyn & Bacon, 1972.
Black Sister: Poetry by Black American Women, 1746–1980, edited by Erlene Stetson. Bloomington, Indiana University Press, 1981.
Confirmation: An Anthology of African–American Women, edited by Amina and Amiri Baraka. New York, Quill Press, 1983.

Essays

Sister Outsider: Essays and Speeches. Trumansburg, New York, Crossing Press, 1984.
A Burst of Light: Essays. Ithaca, New York, Firebrand Books, 1988.

Other

"Poems Are Not Luxuries," in *Chrysalis,* Number 3, 1977.
Uses of the Erotic: The Erotic as Power. Brooklyn, New York, Out and Out Books, 1978.
"Scratching the Surface: Some Notes on Barriers to Women and Loving," in *Black Scholar,* April 1978.
"Man Child: A Black Lesbian–Feminist's Response," in *Conditions: Four,* winter 1979.
"An Open Letter to Mary Daly," in *Top Ranking: A Collection of Articles on Racism and Classism in the Lesbian Community,* edited by Joan Gibbs and Sara Bennett, Brooklyn, February 3rd Press, 1980.
The Cancer Journals (personal diary). Argyle, New York, Spinsters Ink, 1980.

Zami: A New Spelling of My Name (biomythography). Trumansburg, New York, Crossings Press, 1982.

*

Interviews: With Anita Cornwell, in *Sinister Wisdom* (Rockland, Maine), fall 1977, 15–21; with Deborah Wood, in *In the Memory and Spirit of Frances, Zora, and Lorraine: Essays and Interviews on Black Women and Writing,* Washington, D.C., Institute for the Arts and the Humanities, 1979; with Karla M. Hammond, in *Denver Quarterly,* spring 1981, 10–27.

Bibliography: *Modern American Woman Poets* by Jean Gould, New York, Dodd, Mead, 1985, 288–296.

Critical Sources: "Broadsides: Good Black Poems, One by One" by Helen Vendler, in *New York Times Book Review,* September 1974, 320–321; "Nothing Safe: The Poetry of Audre Lorde" by Joan Larkin, in *Margins,* August 1975, 23–25; "On the Edge of the Estate" by Sandra M. Gilbert, in *Poetry* (Chicago), 104:24, 1977, 296–301; review by Gloria Hull of *Between Ourselves,* in *Conditions: One,* 1977, 97–100; "The Re–Vision of the Muse: Unnaming and Renaming in the Poetry of Audre Lorde, Pat Parker, Sylvia Plath, and Adrienne Rich" by Pamela Annas, in *Hudson Review* (New York), summer 1983, 293–322; "No More Buried Lives: The Theme of Lesbianism in Lorde, Naylor, Shange, Walker" by Barbara Christian, in *Feminist Issues,* spring 1985, 3–19; "Audre Lorde" by Irma McClaurin–Allen, in *Dictionary of Literary Biography,* Volume 41: *Afro–American Poets Since 1955,* Detroit, Gale, 1985; "The Black Woman as Artist and Critic: Four Versions" by Margaret B. MacDowell, in *Kentucky Review* (Lexington), spring 1987, 19–41.

*   *   *

One of the most extraordinary facets of the explosion of gay and lesbian literature since the Stonewall Riots in 1969, is the multitude of ways in which the common experiences of the community have been drawn, sung, and celebrated in poetry and prose. Of less prominence, until recently, has been that body of writing addressing the needs, dreams, and hopes of gay men and lesbians outside mainstream homosexual culture. While some of this exclusion has been the result of a conscious choice on the part of group members—such as adherents of the Radical Faerie philosophy—often this marginalization is due to the reflection, within the homosexual world, of attitudes and trends prevalent in society at large. The most powerful of these have been racism and discrimination against women—as challengers of social limits and often on the basis of their status and sexual orientation. While writings by openly gay black men have only recently become a recognized part of the literature (with such anthologies as Joseph Beam's *In the Life,* for example), black women have possessed a visible and active presence in the creation of the current homosexual world almost from its birth through both their willingness to challenge accepted liberationist philosophies and the power of their individual and collective voices. One of the first and most influential of these voices was that of Andre Lorde.

Lorde was born in New York City in 1934; she was raised to fit the mold of many young women maturing in that metropolitan area. She enrolled at the National University of Mexico in 1954 and continued her postsecondary education at Hunter College and Columbia University, where she received her bachelor's degree and her professional certification in the field of librarianship in 1961. Lorde joined the staff of the Mount Vernon Public Library, the first in a series of positions which over the next three decades would expose her to the disparate influences of Saint Clare's School of Nursing, Lehman College, City College of the City University of New York, and the John Jay College of Criminal Justice. Her marriage to Edwin A. Rollins in 1962 completed the matrix out of which her public sharing of private insights, griefs, and fierce joys would soon begin to arise in her first book of verse. The diversity of her creative gifts would prove to be well matched to the breadth of issues facing the communities of lesbians, women, and African Americans she would address in her personal essays, journals—and especially in her vital and intense poetry.

To understand a written work, the reader must have a clear picture of its author's vision—of the private road he or she has followed in developing both as an artist and a human being. Lorde presents a particularly complex picture due to the wide variety of causes and environments she has experienced. Nowhere in her work is this more openly presented than in her 1982 volume *Zami, A New Spelling of My Name: A Biomythography.* In an interview with Mari Evans for the 1984 publication *Black Women Writers: A Critical Evaluation,* she noted that she began to write because there was no visible source saying what she needed and wanted to hear to serve as a channel for the pain of her gradual comprehension of the world. *Zami* is perhaps the most coherent expression of this, telling, as it does, a dual story of her life from childhood in Harlem before World War II to her completion of higher education in 1962 and the coalescence of her identities as both lesbian and aware black woman in America. Lorde's characterization of the text as a new species of writing, a "biomythography," is in keeping with her adoption of—and seeking for—traditional ancestral beliefs and symbols from prior generations of women.

This search had a particularly personal aspect for her, a granddaughter of the Caribbean island of Grenada, as she recalled the tales her mother told her of the ways of the offshore island of Carriacou where she had been raised prior to immigrating to New York City. In some ways, the key to Lorde's entire career as a writer and activist lies in a description of her mother's island home on the opening page of *Zami.* "This is the country of my foremothers, my fore–bearing mothers, those Black island women who defined themselves by what they did." Self–definition through chosen actions and open admittance of the joys and sorrows of making those choices is a thread common to much of her work throughout her life. Even the title reflects her choice to claim her heritage: Zami is "a Carriacou name for women who work together as friends and lovers," a beautifully apt term for the fusion and fashioning of diverse cultures evident in all her works. The book is also representative of a more limited group of lesbian autobiographies, foreshadowing later works such as Holly Near's 1990 work *Fire In the Rain, Singer in the Storm* and *Long Time Passing: Lives of Older Lesbians,* a collection published in 1986.

The two volumes of essays and speeches compiled from those delivered by Lorde at various institutions of higher learning and political conferences in the gay and lesbian community during the 1980s provide the reader with both a window into the continuing growth of her consciousness as lesbian and activist and as a bridge into the deepening power of her poetic voice. The first, 1984's *Sister Outsider,* contains 15 selections written or delivered between 1976 and 1983, including an extended interview and self–analysis conducted with fellow lesbian poet Adrienne Rich. Of the essays, the text of a paper given at the Modern Language Association's December, 1977, meeting in Chicago as part of the "Lesbian and Literature" panel is particularly valuable for comprehension of Lorde's deeply personal visions. Other papers touch upon the creative uses to which anger can be put as a generator of change, explore the concept of "the personal as political" and of eroticism as a source of power for women. *Sister Outsider*'s 1988 successor, *A Burst of Light,* presents five shorter essays dealing with Lorde's first three years of living with cancer, her views on the then–ongoing discussion of sadomasochism within the lesbian community (represented by such writers as Pat Califia), frank and moving opinions on being a lesbian mother, and the comparative situation of African Americans and the blacks of South Africa under apartheid. Readers of black lesbian and gay writings of any political slant will find the third essay "I Am Your Sister: Black Women Organizing Across Sexualities" valuable for the links it establishes with other major writers such as Langston Hughes, Alice Dunbar–Nelson, and Angelina Weld Grimke, and the perspective it provides on the emergence of contemporary male poets such as Essex Hemphill and Assoto Saint.

Lorde's encounters with the pain of cancer and mastectomy may also be traced through the pages of the 1980 prose collection *The Cancer Journals,* which she termed "a piece of meaning words on cancer as it affects my life and my consciousness as a woman, a black lesbian feminist mother." Recognition of the place of such a testament in lesbian literature came with the designation of *The Cancer Journals* as the American Library Association's Gay Task Force Book of the Year for 1981.

The truest voice of Lorde will, however, be found in her poetry, for as she stated in the opening line of her 1977 essay *The Transformation of Silence Into Language and Action:* "I have come to believe over and over again that what is most important to me must be spoken, made verbal and shared, even at the risk of having it bruised or misunderstood." Beginning with her earliest book, 1968's *The First Cities*—written while she was the recipient of a grant from the National Endowment for the Arts—she focused a spare sharp eye of language on life and love, including her lesbian relationships. Three of her collections, *Cables To Rage, From A Land Where Other People Live,* and *New York Head Shop and Museum* were published in the 1970s by Detroit's Broadside Press, one of the centers of publication for new African American poets such as Nikki Giovanni. It would be these editions of Lorde's work that would begin to bring her influence to the wider audience of black lesbian writers, as exemplified by the early writings of California lesbian poet Pat Parker. The imagery in *The First Cities* and *Cables to Rage* is a blend of uniquely spicy twists of language, the topics central to life as a black person in America at that time. These works would come to be recognized as some of the most vital contributions to the Black Arts Movement. The poems of these first volumes would later be collected and published under the title *Coal* in 1976. Perhaps most significant for the history of modern black gay and lesbian poetry is "Martha," which one critic noted as "the first poetic expression of Lorde's homosexuality."

A Creative Artists Public Service grant in 1972 provided the basis for generating her third book of poetry, *From A Land Where Other People Live,* published in 1973. Its lines express a maturation of the anger over injustices which had been present in *Cables*

To Rage, as well as addressing more fully the author's identity as an African American woman and its differing dimensions as mother, sister, and teacher. A nomination for the National Book Award for poetry for the year also served to further widen public awareness of Lorde as a leading feminist voice. Her fourth book, the 1974 *New York Head Shop and Museum,* is perhaps the most overtly political, using her visions of New York City as a matrix to explore her radical political views, foretelling the depth and power of such successor volumes as 1978's *The Black Unicorn.* Through her founding of Kitchen Table: Women of Color Press and work as poetry editor of *Chrysalis* and *Amazon Quarterly,* Lorde attempted to provide the rising generations of women writers who would follow her the venue she had not been able to find for the literary reflection of her inner selves so much desired.

Indefatigable in both claiming her life and cherishing her many–faceted insights, Lorde's honors included being named poet laureate of New York State in 1991. She died at her home on St. Croix in the Virgin Islands in late November of 1992, a victim of the liver cancer she had lived with for over a decade.

—*Robert B. Marks Ridinger*

LOWELL, Amy (Lawrence). American poet. Born in Brookline, Massachusetts, 9 February 1874. Privately educated. Companion of actress Ada Russell. An early leader of the Imagist movement. **Recipient:** Pulitzer Prize for poetry for *What's O'Clock,* 1926. *Died of a cerebral hemorrhage, 12 May 1925.*

WRITINGS

Poetry

With Katherine Bigelow Lawrence Lowell and Elizabeth Lowell, *Dream Drops; or, Stories from Fairy Land, by a Dreamer.* Boston, Cupples & Hurd, 1887.
A Dome of Many–Coloured Glass. Boston and New York, Houghton, 1912.
Sword Blades and Poppy Seed. New York, Macmillan, 1914.
Men, Women and Ghosts. New York, Macmillan, 1916.
Can Grande's Castle. New York, Macmillan, 1918.
Pictures of the Floating World. New York, Macmillan, 1919.
Fir–Flower Tablets: Poems Translated from the Chinese (from translations of Florence Ayscough). Boston and New York, Houghton, 1921.
Legends. Boston and New York, Houghton, 1921.
A Critical Fable. Boston and New York, Houghton, 1922.
What's O'Clock, edited by Ada Dwyer Russell. Boston and New York, Houghton, 1925.
East Wind, edited by Ada Dwyer Russell. Boston and New York, Houghton, 1926.
Ballads for Sale, edited by Ada Dwyer Russell. Boston and New York, Houghton, 1927.

Selected Poems of Amy Lowell, edited by John Livingston Lowes. Boston and New York, Houghton, 1928.
The Complete Poetical Works of Amy Lowell. Boston, Houghton, 1955.
A Shard of Silence, Selected Poems, edited by G. R. Ruihley. New York, Twayne Publishers, 1957.

Other

Six French Poets: Studies in Contemporary Literature (criticism). New York, Macmillan, 1915.
Editor and contributor, *Some Imagist Poets: An Anthology.* Boston and New York, Houghton, 1915.
Editor and contributor, *Some Imagist Poets, 1916: An Annual Anthology.* Boston and New York, Houghton, 1916.
Editor and contributor, *Some Imagist Poets, 1917: An Annual Anthology.* Boston and New York, Houghton, 1917.
Tendencies in Modern American Poetry (criticism), 1917.
John Keats (biography). Boston and New York, Houghton, 1925.
Contributor, *Poetry and Poets: Essays,* edited by Ferris Greeslet. Boston and New York, 1930.

*

Biography: *Amy Lowell: A Chronicle* by S. Foster Damon, New York, Houghton, 1935; *Amy: The World of Amy Lowell and the Imagist Movement* by Jean Gould, New York, Dodd, Mead, 1975; *The Thorn of a Rose: Amy Lowell Reconsidered* by Glenn R. Ruihley, Hamden, Connecticut, Archon Books, 1975.

Critical Sources: Introduction to *The Imagist Poem: Modern Poetry in Miniature,* edited by William Pratt, New York, Dutton, 1963; "Some Imagist Essays: Amy Lowell" by Claire Healey, in *New England Quarterly,* March 1970, 134–138; introduction to *Imagist Poetry,* edited by Peter Jones, Middlesex, England, Penguin, 1972; "Warding Off the Watch and Ward Society: Amy Lowell's Lesbian Poetry" by Lillian Faderman, in *Gay Books Bulletin,* spring 1979, 23–27; "Amy Lowell and the Music of Her Poetry" by Jane Ambrose, in *New England Quarterly,* March 1989, 45–62; "'The Naked Majesty of God': Contemporary Lesbian Erotic Poetry" by Caroline Halliday, in *Lesbian and Gay Writing,* edited by Mark Lilly, Philadelphia, Temple University Press, 1990, 76.

*   *   *

In a passage from *A Critical Fable,* Amy Lowell describes her life in these terms: "Bronco–busting with rainbows is scarcely a game / For middle–aged persons inclined to the tame." These lines exemplify more than just Lowell's lighthearted sense of humor. The tone indicates the courage and passion with that Lowell defended both her art and her life. In addition, the lines are a fine example of Imagism, the pre–World War I European literary movement which Lowell espoused and brought to America.

Born into a high–society Boston family in 1874, Lowell published her first serious book of verse, *A Dome of Many–Coloured Glass,* when she was 38 years old in 1912. This was a phenomenal year in American literature because it also included first–time pub-

lications by poets Robert Frost and Edna St. Vincent Millay. In 1913, Lowell recognized herself as a budding poet of the *Imagiste* school, which rejected the fuzzy sentimentality of Romanticism in favor of striking, hard–edged imagery. She immediately went to London to find Ezra Pound, the dashing yet quixotic spokesperson for the movement, and returned to Boston to become the most vocal American proponent of Imagism.

T.S. Eliot termed the Imagist movement "the starting point of modern poetry" because it stimulated a new trajectory of literary development. But, besides promoting it, Lowell contributed to the American offshoot of Imagism with her experiments in "polyphonic prose," a form of free verse that incorporated a prose–like rhythm. Lowell's contributions constituted a break with the original European movement, causing Pound to ruefully scorn the American branch as "Amygisme." Nevertheless, Lowell's poems soon joined those of other Imagists in anthologies and the London periodical, *The Egoist: An Individualist Review.*

Lowell's interest in dramatic presentation was a link to the two women who inspired the public and personal spheres of her life, the actresses Eleanora Duse and Ada Russell. Duse, a famous Italian stage actress, had enchanted Lowell in 1902 with her art and her person, and engendered a devotion that lasted all of Lowell's life. In her Pulitzer Prize–winning book of verse, *What's O'Clock,* published posthumously in 1925, Lowell's six sonnets to Duse, which had earlier been deemed too controversial for readers, were finally made public, and they clearly reveal the poet's awe and adoration for Duse. From her, Lowell learned that art had the power to enter and indeed to order the flow of one's life, and that the expression of one's inner self could be lived out in a dramatic and opulent manner.

If Duse was Lowell's artistic ideal, who proved that life was at the core of all good art, then Ada Russell was the heart of Lowell's life, and it was she who inspired Lowell to believe that truth was at the core of beauty. Russell, a divorcee, was her muse and companion for 13 years, until Lowell's death in 1925. Their relationship was a bond of love, presumably platonic, which was acknowledged by their friends but not permanently recorded, since Ada's first duty as Lowell's executrix was to "cremate" all personal correspondence in Lowell's effects. Regardless of the details of their relationship, Lowell was a passionate person, and it was Ada's strength which gave her the courage to free herself from the many strictures imposed on her as a member of the Lowell family.

Of course, the wealth and prestige of her exalted social position also gave her the independence to live as she pleased and to subsidize other impassioned writers of the budding modern era, particularly D. H. Lawrence, a sensualist whose work she preferred to James Joyce's. S. Foster Damon reports Lowell's words in *Amy Lowell: A Chronicle:* "D. H. Lawrence's eroticisms never strike me as otherwise than beautiful because of his point of view in regard to them. On the other hand, James Joyce's attempts in that line are as disagreeable as putrefied meat." Lowell encouraged other contemporary poets, some of them unconventional women like herself, such as Hilda Doolittle (H. D.) and Bryher (a later companion to H. D.), and promoted the work of Emily Dickinson and the early work of Edna St. Vincent Millay. Another unconventional writer of the time was Gertrude Stein, and Lowell shared an astonishing number of similarities with her, including the same week, month and year of birth; the role of youngest child in the family; a stubborn nature and quick temper; and a tendency toward tomboyishness that matured into a liking for men's styles in clothing. In addition, both women took female companions as mates and both objected to obscene or pornographic literature. Despite all these commonalities, the women seem never to have crossed paths, although Lowell once declared that she didn't like Stein's work.

Like Stein, Lowell did not shrink from notoriety. Lowell understood that her flamboyant image, as well as her status as a Boston heiress and sister of the president of Harvard University, all combined to arouse the public's curiosity about her. Unfortunately, critics as well as the public seemed more obsessed with her eccentricities than with her art. And in the context of New England at the turn of the century, Lowell's unconventionalities seemed abnormal. She smoked small, black Manilla cigars—an "unladylike" choice but with the advantage that cigars burn more slowly than cigarettes, and so would last through long hours as she composed her verses. She was not above taking pleasure in defying the social convention which made smoking taboo for women; she once caused an unsuspecting young man to blush as she compared unwrapping her cigar to undressing a lady layer by layer, then lit up and inhaled seductively. Lowell liked to sleep until 3:00 in the afternoon, entertain until midnight, and then write until nearly dawn—the perfect time for her to contemplate the moon and revel in its inspiration. She demanded 16 pillows and a sybaritic–sized bath, but the ample proportions of her body made these necessities. She also demanded that mirrors be draped in black, another concession to her life–long obesity. Finally, she wore her hair in a severe pompadour in a vain attempt to add height to her five–foot stature.

This hairstyle was Russell's responsibility, and Lowell, carefully watching the reflection of her friend's gently moving hands in the mirror, was inspired to write: "The movement of your hands is the long, golden running of light from a rising sun." This line is found in the poem "In Excelsis" and is one of Lowell's many tributes to Ada's halcyon beauty. In the same poem she writes: "I drink your lips, / I eat the whiteness of your hands and feet. / My mouth is open ... / I cry and shout ... / My throat sings the joy of my eyes / The rushing gladness of my love." Russell was the inspiration for virtually all of the love poetry, and Lowell's spiritual devotion to her is unmistakable. Throughout the many love poems in Lowell's nine collections of verse, Ada figures as a ubiquitous presence, a woman in an aura of purple tints, pearlized by the moon's glow. In *Pictures of the Floating World,* the section entitled "Two Speak Together" is a compilation of verses celebrating passion, both physical and emotional. And in *Sword Blades and Poppy Seed,* Lowell plays with sexual symbolism in "The Basket" and "The Giver of Stars."

Although there is no explicit mention of homosexuality in Lowell's published writings or the correspondence that remained after her death, Lowell practiced tolerance and advocated respect and nurturing of the spiritual truths found in the company of women; before Ada, Lowell's life (and thus her art) was cold and incomplete, but after Ada, Lowell would extol the fulfillment and self–confidence she enjoyed among women. Ada, her daughter Lorna, and Ada's grandchildren all inspired Lowell to celebrate the beauty in the mundane—a spring day, lilacs, grackles, a gardener's basket, a morning bath, or a country sky. There is sensuous joy in this passage from "A Spring Day": "You are the colour of the sky when it is fresh–washed and fair ... / I smell the stars ... / They are like tulips and narcissus ... / I smell them in the air."

Throughout her career, Lowell wrote as an Imagist. Her last book of verse, *Ballads for Sale,* was edited by Ada and published in 1927, and after that, interest in both Lowell's life and her art waned until the 1970s, when fresh contemplations of the poet appeared in the form of critical and biographical studies. Consequently, her articulate descriptions of subtle feminine nuances can be found in

contemporary lesbian works. For example, the title for Caroline Halliday's essay, "The Naked Majesty of God," in *Lesbian and Gay Writing* is borrowed from Lowell's poem "The Sisters," a thoughtful commentary addressed to poets Sappho, Elizabeth Barrett Browning, and Emily Dickinson.

Lowell remained a leader in the growth of American literature long after her schism with Pound. In addition to love poetry, her writings include Modernist experiments in shifting points of view, shifting time, fragmentary snapshots, exotic sensuality and settings, shifting flows of poetic cadence, and self–reflexivity. She was led to the Haiku form by Oriental lacquer prints. She wrote poems about writing poems and a giddy epic fable about the young lions of modern American poetry, herself included. In *East Wind,* Lowell collected 13 folk tales and transcribed them into New England dialects and speech patterns. Lowell's final work and one of her finest accomplishments is her two–volume biography of poet John Keats.

Lowell's love poetry repeatedly shows she was fulfilled in loving women, and her psycho–sexual response provides the heat in her verses. Against the context of her time, this represents a revolutionary call for a new sexual ethic in poetry. The image of the call is made radiantly palpable in "Clear, with Light Variable Winds": "The moonlight shines on the straight column of water, / And through it he sees a woman, / Tossing the water–balls. / Her breasts point outwards, / And the nipples are like buds of peonies. / Her flanks ripple as she plays, / And the water is not more undulating / Than the lines of her body / 'Come', she sings, 'Poet!'"

—*Cecily M. Barrie*

———

LYON, Phyllis Ann. American gay activist, sex educator, and writer of nonfiction. Born in Tulsa, Oklahoma, 10 November 1924, raised primarily in the San Francisco Bay area; has lived in San Francisco since 1953. Educated at University of California, Berkeley, 1946 (wartime class of 1947; worked on *Daily Californian*); Institute for Advanced Study of Human Sexuality, Doctor of Education (originally Doctor of Arts) in Human Sexuality, 1976; diplomate, American Board of Sexology; previously board certified by American College of Sexologists. Domestic partner of gay activist and writer Del Martin, beginning 14 February 1953; one surrogate daughter. Chico Enterprise–Record, Chico, California, reporter, 1947–49; associate editor, *Architect and Engineer,* and editorial assistant, *Pacific Builder and Engineer,* Seattle, Washington, 1949–52; James S. Baker Export Company, San Francisco, traffic manager, 1954–64; Glide Urban Center, San Francisco, administrative assistant for operational education department, 1965–68; National Sex Forum, associate director, 1968–72, codirector, 1973–87; LyMar Associates (consulting firm), San Francisco, partner, 1972—; Institute for Advanced Study of Human Sexuality, San Francisco, cofounder, professor and registrar, 1976–87. Minister of Universal Life Church, Inc., 1969—. Lecturer at numerous colleges and universities, and presenter of workshops and seminars on lesbianism, homosexuality, and women's sexuality. Cofounder of Daughters of Bilitis, 1955; cofounder and board member of Citizens Alert, 1965–72; cofounder of National Sex Forum, 1968; founding member and then chairperson of Citizens Advisory Board of the Center for Special Problems of the San Francisco Public Health Department, 1973. Former board member of Genesis Church and Ecumenical Center, Friends of San Francisco Deputies and Inmates, San Francisco Women's Centers, Institute for Advanced Study of Human Sexuality, Institute's Alumni Association and Association of Sexologists; served on advisory boards of Senior Action in a Gay Environment (SAGE), New York, Human Rights Campaign Fund; currently a member of advisory board of Institute for Study of Human Resources, and Gay and Lesbian Historical Society of Northern California, 1991—; member of Gay/Lesbian Outreach to Elders Advisory Committee; member of Pat Bond Old Dyke Award Committee, 1991—. Cofounder of National Lesbian Feminist Organization, Lesbian Lobby, and Alice B. Toklas Lesbian/Gay Democratic Club, 1972. Former member of National Gay/Lesbian Task Force, Lesbian Mothers and Friends, Gay Rights National Lobby, Gay Academic Union, National Women's Political Caucus, Lesbian/Gay Advisory Committee and Women's Advisory Committee to Mayor Dianne Feinstein. Served on Mayor Feinstein's Task Force on Health Benefits, which researched the feasibility of extending health benefits to lesbian/gay domestic partners of city workers. Member of National Organization for Women (NOW), Lesbian Caucus, and Lesbian Agenda for Action. Contributor with others to periodicals, including *Spectrum* and *Engage*. **Recipient:** Award from San Francisco Chapter of Daughters of Bilitis, 1962; American Library Association Gay Book Award for *Lesbian/Woman,* 1972; Prosperos Award of Merit, 1972; Humanist Community of San Jose certificate of recognition, 1973; San Francisco Board of Supervisors certificate of merit and achievement, 1978, commendation, 1980; Southern California Women for Understanding First Lesbian Rights Award, 1979; award for work in lesbian and women's movements and for services to Alice B. Toklas Memorial Democratic Club, 1979 and 1986; David Award for outstanding contribution to gay community, 1983; Cable Car Outstanding Award of Merit, 1988; Long Beach Lambda Democrat Club's Franklin E. Cook Memorial Award for contributions to the cause of human rights, 1989; Earl Warren Civil Liberties Award from the Northern California Chapter of American Civil Liberties Union, 1990. Editor, *Ladder,* 1956–60. Address: 330 Ellis Street, Suite 406, San Francisco, California 94102, U.S.A.

WRITINGS

Nonfiction

With Del Martin, *Lesbian/Woman.* San Francisco, Glide Publications, 1972; revised, New York, Bantam, 1973; updated, San Francisco, Volcano Press, 1991.
With Del Martin, *Lesbian Love and Liberation.* San Francisco, Multi Media Resource Center, 1973.

Contributor

"Who Is a Lesbian?," in *Les Gais,* February–March 1968.
"The Reality of Lesbianism" (originally appeared in *Motive,* March–April 1969). Published as *The New Woman,* New York, Bobbs–Merrill, 1970.
"A Lesbian Approach to Theology," in *Is Gay Good? A Symposium on Homosexuality, Theology, and Ethics,* edited by W. Dwight Oberholtzer. Westminster Press, 1971.
Sexual Latitude—For and Against. New York, Hart Publishing, 1971.
"The New Sexuality and the Homosexual," in *The New Sexuality,* edited by Herbert A. Otto. Palo Alto, California, Science and Behavior Books, 1971.
"Lesbians—the Key to Women's Liberation," in *Trends,* July–August 1973.
"Lesbian Mothers," in *Ms.,* October 1973.
"Lesbian Mothers: Legal Realities," in *GPU News,* April 1975.
With Del Martin, "Reminiscences of Two Female Homophiles," in *Our Right to Love,* edited by Ginny Vida. Englewood Cliffs, New Jersey, Prentice–Hall, 1978.
With Del Martin, "The Older Lesbian," in *Positively Gay,* edited by Betty Berzon and Robert Leighton. Millbrae, California, Celestial Arts, 1979; updated and edited by Betty Berzon, 1992.
With Del Martin, "Anniversary," in *The Lesbian Path,* edited by Margaret Cruikshank. Monterey, California, Angel Press, 1980; revised and enlarged, San Francisco, Grey Fox Press, 1985.
With Del Martin, "Lesbian Women and Mental Health Policy," in *Women and Mental Health Policy,* edited by Lenore E. Walker. Beverly Hills, California, Sage Publications, 1984.
"A Historic Consultation," in *Open Hands,* winter 1990.

[Please refer to entry on Del Martin for essay.]

M

MacADAM, Preston. *See* PRESTON, John.

———

MANN, (Paul) Thomas. German novelist, short story writer, essayist, and critic. Also wrote as Paul Thomas. Born in Lübeck, Germany, 6 June 1875; voluntary exile in Switzerland, 1933; German citizenship revoked, became naturalized Czech citizen, 1936; immigrated to United States, 1938; naturalized American citizen, 1944; immigrated to Switzerland, 1952. Educated at Technische Universität, Munich, c. 1895. Served in the Royal Bavarian Infantry, 1900. Married Katja Pringsheim in 1905; three sons and three daughters. Coeditor (as Paul Thomas), *Der Frühlingssturm: Monatsschrift für Kunst, Litteratur, und Philosophie* (periodical), 1893; apprentice, South German Fire Insurance Co., Munich, Germany, 1894–95; reader and copyreader, *Simplicissimus,* Munich, 1898–1900; coeditor of "Romane der Welt" series, Knauer, beginning 1927; coeditor, *Mass und Wert: Zweimonatsschrift für freie deutsche Kultur* (periodical), beginning 1937; lecturer in humanities, Princeton University, Princeton, New Jersey, 1938–40; consultant in Germanic literature, Library of Congress, Washington, D.C., 1942–44; author and presenter of broadcasts for British Broadcasting Corporation (BBC). Member of Munich Censorship Council, 1912–13; German correspondent, *Dial,* beginning 1920; founding member of literary section, Prussian Academy of Arts, 1926; member of advisory committee for Bermann–Fischer, Allert de Lange, and Querido (publishers), *Forum Deutscher Dichter,* 1938–39; honorary chairperson, Union of German Writers; honorary member: German Academy of Arts, Schiller Society, German Academy of Language and Poetry, Gerhart Hauptmann Society, Society of Those Persecuted by the Nazi Regime. **Recipient:** Bänernfeld Prize, 1904; Nobel Prize for Literature, 1929; Herder Prize for exiled writers from Czechoslovakia, 1937; Cardinal Newman Award, 1938; Frankfurt, Germany's Goethe Prize, and East Germany Goethe Prize, 1949; American Academy of Arts and Letters medal of service, 1949; Accademia Nazionale dei Lincei's Feltrinelli Prize, 1952; Officer's Cross of the French Legion of Honor, 1952; honorary citizen of Lübeck, West Germany, 1955; Netherlands Cross of Orange–Nassau, 1955; West Germany Order of Merit in the Sciences and Arts, 1955; honorary doctorates: University of Bonn, 1919 (withdrawn 1936, restored 1947); Harvard University, 1935; Columbia University, 1938; Rutgers University, 1939; Dubuque University, 1939; University of California at Berkeley, 1941; Hebrew Union University, 1945; Lund University, 1949; Oxford University, 1949; Cambridge University, 1953; Friedrich Schiller University, 1955; Technische Hochschule, Zurich, Switzerland, 1955. *Died of phlebitis in Zurich, Switzerland, 12 August 1955.*

WRITINGS

Novels

Buddenbrooks: Verfall einer Familie (two volumes). Berlin, S. Fischer, 1901; translated by H. T. Lowe–Porter as *Buddenbrooks: The Decline of a Family* (two volumes), New York, Knopf, 1924; with "Lübeck as a Way of Life," New York, Knopf, 1964.
Königliche Hoheit. Berlin, S. Fischer, 1909; translated by A. Cecil Curtis as *Royal Highness: A Novel of German Court Life,* New York, Knopf, 1916.
Bekenntnisse des Hochstaplers Felix Krull: Buch der Kindheit. Vienna, Rikola, 1922; enlarged, Amsterdam, Querido, 1937; enlarged as *Bekenntnisse des Hochstaplers Felix Krull: Der Memoiren erster Teil,* Frankfurt, S. Fischer, 1954; translated by Denver Lindley as *Confessions of Felix Krull, Confidence Man: The Early Years,* New York, Knopf, 1955.
Der Zauberberg: Roman (two volumes). Berlin, S. Fischer, 1924; translated by H. T. Lowe–Porter as *The Magic Mountain* (two volumes), New York, Knopf, 1927.
Die Geschichten Jaakobs. Berlin, S. Fischer, 1933; translated by H. T. Lowe–Porter as *Joseph and His Brothers,* New York, Knopf, 1934; as *The Tales of Joseph,* London, M. Secker, 1934; in *Joseph and His Brothers,* 1948.
Der junge Joseph. Berlin, S. Fischer, 1934; translated by H. T. Lowe–Porter as *Young Joseph: Joseph and His Brothers II,* New York, Knopf, and London, M. Secker, 1935; in *Joseph and His Brothers,* 1948.
Joseph in Aegypten. Vienna, Bermann–Fischer, 1936; translated by H. T. Lowe–Porter as *Joseph in Egypt: Joseph and His Brothers III,* New York, Knopf, and London, Secker, 1938; in *Joseph and His Brothers,* 1948. *Lotte in Weimar.* Stockholm, Bermann–Fischer, 1939; translated by H. T. Lowe–Porter as *The Beloved Returns,* New York, Knopf, and under original title, London, M. Secker, 1940.
Die vertauschten Köpfe: Eine indische Legende. Stockholm, Bermann–Fischer, 1940; translated by H. T. Lowe–Porter as *The Transposed Heads: A Legend of India,* New York, Knopf, 1941.
Joseph der Ernährer. Stockholm, Bermann–Fischer, 1943; translated by H. T. Lowe–Porter as *Joseph the Provider: Joseph and His Brothers IV,* New York, Knopf, 1944; in *Joseph and His Brothers,* 1948.
Doktor Faustus: Das Leben des deutschen Tonsetzers Adrian Leverkühn, erzählt von einem Freunde. Stockholm, Bermann–Fischer, 1947; as *Doctor Faustus: The Life of the German Composer Adrian Leverkühn as Told by a Friend,* New York, Knopf, 1948.
Joseph and His Brothers, translated by H. T. Lowe–Porter. New York, Knopf, 1948.

Der Erwählte: Roman. Frankfurt, S. Fischer, 1951; translated by H. T. Lowe–Porter as *The Holy Sinner,* New York, Knopf, 1951.

Short Stories

Der kleine Herr Friedemann: Novellen. Berlin, S. Fischer, 1898; title story included in *Children and Fools,* 1928.
Tristan: Sechs Novellen. Berlin, S. Fischer, 1903; title story included in *Death in Venice, and Other Stories,* 1925; "Tonio Kröger" included in *The German Classics of the 19th and 20th Centuries,* 1914; as *Tonio Kröger,* edited with notes and introduction by John Alexander Kelly, London, F. S. Crofts, 1931; second edition edited by Elizabeth M. Wilkinson, London, Basil Blackwell, 1968.
Der kleine Herr Friedemann und anderer Novellen. Berlin, S. Fischer, 1909; translated as *Little Herr Friedemann, and Other Stories,* London, Penguin, 1972.
Der Tod in Venedig: Novelle. Munich, Hyperion, 1912; translated by Kenneth Burke as *Death in Venice,* in *Death in Venice, and Other Stories,* 1925; translated by David Luke, in *Death in Venice, and Other Stories,* 1988.
Das Wunderkind. Berlin, S. Fischer, 1914; title story included in *Children and Fools,* 1928.
Herr und Hund. Bound with *Gesang vom Kindchen,* Berlin, S. Fischer, 1919; translated by Herman George Scheffauer as *Bashan and I,* New York, Holt, and London, Collins, 1923; as *A Man and His Dog,* New York, Knopf, 1930.
Wälsungenblut. Munich, Phantasus, 1921; as "Blood of the Walsungs," in *Stories of Three Decades,* 1936.
Kino: Romanfragment. Gera, Germany, Blau, 1926.
Unordnung und frühes Leid. Berlin, S. Fischer, 1926; translated by Herman George Scheffauer as *Early Sorrow,* London, M. Secker, 1929, New York, Knopf, 1930; translated by H. T. Lowe–Porter as *Early Sorrow* (published with *Mario and the Magician*), London, M. Secker, 1934; as "Disorder and Early Sorrow," in *Stories of Three Decades,* 1936.
Mario und die Zauberer: Ein Tragisches Reiseerlebnis. Berlin, S. Fischer, 1930; translated by H. T. Lowe–Porter as *Mario and the Magician,* London, M. Secker, 1930, New York, Knopf, 1931; translated with *Early Sorrow,* London, M. Secker, 1934.
Das Gesetz: Ersählung. Los Angeles, Pazifische Press, and Stockholm, Bermann–Fischer, 1944; translated by H. T. Lowe–Porter as *The Tables of the Law,* New York, Knopf, 1945.
Die Betrogene: Ersählung. Olten, Switzerland, Vereinigung Oltner Bücherfreunde, 1953; translated by Willard Trask as *The Black Swan,* New York, Knopf, 1954.
Das Eisenbahnunglück: Novellen. Munich, Piper, 1955.
Ersählungen. Frankfurt, S. Fischer, 1957.

Essays

Friedrich und de grosse Koalition. Berlin, S. Fischer, 1915.
Betrachtungen eines Unpolitischen. Berlin, S. Fischer, 1918; translated by Walter D. Morris as *Reflections of a Nonpolitical Man,* New York, Ungar, 1983.
Rede und Antwort: Gesammelte Abhandlungen und kleine Aufsätze. Berlin, S. Fischer, 1922.
Goethe und Tolstoi: Vortrag. Aachen, Germany, Verlag "Die Kuppel," 1923; revised as *Goethe und Tolstoi: Zum Problem der Humanität,* Vienna, Bermann–Fischer, 1932; as "Goethe and Tolstoy," in *Three Essays,* 1929, and in *Order of the Day,* 1942.

Okkulte Erlebnisse. Berlin, Häger, 1924; as "An Experience in the Occult," in *Three Essays,* 1929.
Bemühungen: Neue Folge der gesammelten Abhandlungen und kleinen Aufsätze. Berlin, S. Fischer, 1925.
Three Essays, translation by H. T. Lowe–Porter. New York, Knopf, 1929.
Die Forderung des Tages: Reden und Aufsätze aus den Jahren 1925–1929. Berlin, S. Fischer, 1930.
Lebensabriss. Published in *Die Neue Rundschau* (Germany), 7 July 1930; translated by H. T. Lowe–Porter as *A Sketch of My Life,* Paris, Harrison, 1930, New York, Knopf, 1960.
Past Masters, and Other Essays, translation by H. T. Lowe–Porter. New York, Knopf, 1933.
Goethes Lufbahn als Schriftsteller: Vortrag. Munich, Oldenbourg, 1933.
Leiden und Grösse der Meister. Berlin, S. Fischer, 1935.
Freud und de Zukunft: Vortrag. Vienna, Bermann–Fischer, 1936; as "Freud and the Future," in *Freude, Goethe, Wagner: Three Essays,* 1937.
Freud, Goethe, Wagner: Three Essays, translation by H. T. Lowe–Porter and Rita Matthias–Reil. New York, Knopf, 1937.
Schopenhauer. Stockholm, Bermann–Fischer, 1938; in *The Living Thoughts of Schopenhauer,* 1939.
Achtung, Europa! Aufsätze zur Zeit. Stockholm, Bermann–Fischer, and London, Longmans, Green, 1938.
Deutschland und die Deutschen: Vortrag. Stockholm, Bermann–Fischer, 1947; in *Addresses Delivered at the Library of Congress, 1942–1949,* 1963.
Nietzsches Philosophie im Lichte unsere Erfahrung. Berlin, Suhrkamp, 1948; as "Nietzsche's Philosophy in Light of Recent History," in *Last Essays,* 1958.
Neue Studien. Stockholm, Bermann–Fischer, and Berlin, Suhrkamp, 1948.
Goethe/Wetzlar/Werther. Copenhagen, Rosenkilde og Bagger, 1950.
Michelangelo in seine Dichtungen. Cellerina, Quos Ego Verlag, 1950.
Der Künstler und die Besellschaft: Vortrag. Vienna, Frick, 1953.
Altes und Neues: Kleine Prosa aus Fünf Jahrzehnten. Frankfurt, S. Fischer, 1953.
Versuch über Schiller: Seinem Andenken zum 150. Frankfurt, S. Fischer, 1955; as "On Schiller," in *Last Essays,* 1958.
Leiden und Grösse der Meister. Frankfurt, S. Fischer, 1956.

Letters

Ein Briefwechsel. Zurich, Oprecht, 1937; translated by H. T. Lowe–Porter as *An Exchange of Letters,* New York, Knopf, 1936.
Leiden an Deutschland: Tagebuchblätter aus den Jahren 1933 un 1934. Los Angeles, Pazifische Presse, and New York, Rosenberg, 1946.
Briefe an Paul Amann, 1915–1952, edited by Herbert Wegener. Lübeck, Germany, Schmidt–Römhild, 1959; translated by Richard and Clara Winston as *Letters to Paul Amann,* Middletown, Connecticut, Wesleyan University Press, 1960.
Thomas Mann—Karl Kerenyi: Gesprächen in Griefen, edited by Karl Kerenyi. Zurich, Rhein, 1960; translated by Alexander Gelley as *Mythology and Humanism: The Correspondence of Thomas Mann and Karl Kereny,* Ithaca, New York, Cornell University Press, 1975.
Thomas Mann an Ernst Bertram: Briefe aus den Jahren 1910–1955, edited by Inge Jens. Pfullingen, Neske, 1960.

Briefe, 1899–1955 (three volumes), edited by Erika Mann. Frankfurt, S. Fischer, 1961–65; partially edited and translated by Richard and Clara Winston as *The Letters of Thomas Mann, 1889–1955*, Berkeley, University of California Press, 1990.

With Robert Fäsi, *Briefwechsel*, edited by Robert Fäsi. Atlantis, 1962.

Thomas Mann—Heinrich Mann: Briefwechsel, 1900–1949, edited by Ulrich Dietzel. Berlin, Aufbau, 1965; enlarged, 1975.

Thomas Mann—Heinrich Mann: Briefwechsel, 1900–1949, edited by Hans Wysling. Frankfurt, S. Fischer, 1968; enlarged, 1984.

Hermann Hesse—Thomas Mann: Briefwechsel, edited by Anni Carlsson. Frankfurt, S. Fischer, 1968; enlarged by Anni Carlsson and Volker Michels, Frankfurt, Suhrkamp, 1975; translated by Ralph Manheim as *The Hesse—Mann Letters; The Correspondence of Hermann Hesse and Thomas Mann, 1910–1955*, New York, Harper, 1975.

Thomas Mann und Hans Friedrich Blunck: Briefwechsel und Aufzeichnugen, edited by Walter Blunck. Troll–Verlag, c. 1969.

Letters of Thomas Mann, 1889–1955 (two volumes), translation by Richard and Clara Winston. New York, Knopf, 1970.

With Erich Kahler, *Briefwechsel im Exil*, edited by Hans Wysling. Germany, Thomas Mann Gesellschaft, 1970; translated by Richard and Clara Winston as *An Exceptional Friendship: The Correspondence of Thomas Mann and Erich Kahler*, Ithaca, New York, and London, Cornell University Press, 1975.

Briefwechsel mit sinem Verleger Gottfried Bermann Fischer, 1932–1955, edited by Peter de Mendelssohn. Frankfurt, S. Fischer, 1973.

Briefe an Otto Grautoff, 1894–1901, und Ida Boy–Ed, 1902–1928, edited by Peter de Mendelssohn. Frankfurt, S. Fischer, 1975.

Thomas Mann, edited by Hans Whysling. Heimeran, 1975.

Die Briefe Thomas Manns (extracts and indexes; five volumes), edited by Yvonne Schmidlin, Hans Bürgin, and Hans Otto Mayer. Frankfurt, S. Fischer, 1976–1987.

With Alfred Neumann, *Briefwechsel*, edited by Peter de Mendelssohn. Darmstadt, Germany, Schneider, 1977.

Briefwechsel mit Autoren. Berlin, S. Fischer, 1988.

Editor

Nacht und Tag: Roman by Erich von Mendelssohn. Leipzig, Verlag der weissen Bücher, 1914.

And author of introduction, *The Living Thoughts of Schopenhauer*, translation by H. T. Lowe–Porter. London, Longmans, Green, 1939.

Die Welt als Wille und Vorstllung by Arthur Schopenhauer. Zurich, Claassen, 1948.

And author of introduction, *The Permanent Goethe*. New York, Dial, 1948.

Collections

The German Classics of the 19th and 20th Centuries, Volume 19, edited by Kuno Francke and William Guild Howard. New York, German Publications Society, 1914.

Novellen (two volumes). Berlin, S. Fischer, 1922.

Gesammelte Werke in zehn Bänden. Berlin, S. Fischer, 1925; enlarged as *Gesammelte Werke in dreizehn Bänden*, Frankfurt, S. Fischer, 1960–1974.

Death in Venice, and Other Stories, translation by Kenneth Burke. New York, Knopf, 1925; translated by H. T. Lowe–Porter, New York, Knopf, 1928; as *Death in Venice, and Seven Other Stories*, New York, Vintage, 1964.

Children and Fools, translation by Herman George Scheffauer. New York, Knopf, 1928.

Stories of Three Decades, translation by H. T. Lowe–Porter. New York, Knopf, 1936.

Stockholmer Gesamtäsgabe der Werke (12 volumes). Stockholm, Bermann–Fischer, 1937.

Order of the Day: Political Essays and Speeches of Two Decades, translation by Agnes E. Meyer, Eric Sutton, and H. T. Lowe–Porter. New York, Knopf, 1942.

Adel des Geistes: Sechzehn Versuche zum Problem der Humanität. Stockholm, Bermann–Fischer, 1945; translated by H. T. Lowe–Porter as *Essays of Three Decades*, New York, Knopf, 1947; enlarged as *Adel des Geistes: Zwanzig Versuche zum Probelm der Humanität*, Berlin, Aufbau, 1955.

Mein Zeit: 1875–1950: Vortrag. Frankfurt, S. Fischer, 1950.

Nachlese: Prosa, 1951–1955. Frankfurt, S. Fischer, 1956.

Das erzählerische Werk: Taschenbuchausgabe in zwölf Bänden. Frankfurt, S. Fischer, 1957.

Sorge um Deutschland: Sechs Essays. Frankfurt, S. Fischer, 1957.

Last Essays, translation by Richard and Clara Winston, H. T. Lowe–Porter, and Tania and James Stern. New York, Knopf, 1958.

Stories of a Lifetime, translation by H. T. Lowe–Porter. London, Secker & Warburg, 1961.

Wagner und unsere Zeit: Aufsätze, Betrachtungen, Briefe, edited by Erika Mann. Frankfurt, S. Fischer, 1963; translated by Allan Blunden as *Pro and Contra Wagner*, introduction by Erich Heller, Chicago, University of Chicago Press, 1985.

Das essayistische Werk (eight volumes), edited by Hans Bürgin. Frankfurt, S. Fischer, 1968.

Notizen: Zu Felix Krull, Königliche Hoheit, Versuch über das Theater, Maja, Geist und Kultur, Ein Elender, Betrachtungen eines Unpolitischen, Doktor Faustus und anderen Werken, edited by Hans Wysling. Heidelberg, Winter, 1973.

Romane und Erzählungen (ten volumes). Berlin, Aufbau, 1974–1975.

Gesammelte Werke in Einzelbänden (14 volumes), edited by Peter de Mendelssohn. Frankfurt, S. Fischer, 1980—.

Death in Venice, and Other Stories, translation by David Luke. New York, Bantam, 1988.

Other

Bilse und ich. Munich, Bonsels, 1906.

Fiorenza (three–act play; performed Frankfurt, 1907). Berlin, S. Fischer, 1906; in *Stories of Three Decades*, 1936.

Gesang vom Kindchen (narrative poem). Bound with *Herr und Hund*, Berlin, S. Fischer, 1919.

Von deutscher Republik (speech). Berlin, S. Fischer, 1923; as "The German Republic," in *Order of the Day*, 1942.

Author of afterword, *Die Wahlverwantschaften* by Johann Wolfgang von Goethe. Leipzig, List, 1925.

Das Ehebuch, edited by Count Hermann Keyserling. Celle, Kampmann, 1925.

Pariser Rechenschaft. Berlin, S. Fischer, 1926.

Lübeck als geistige Lebensform (speech). Lübeck, Germany, Quitzow, 1926; translated by Richard and Clara Winston as "Lübeck as a Way of Life and Thought," in *Buddenbrooks,* New York, Knopf, 1964.

Ausgewählte Prosa, edited by J. van Dam. Groningen and The Hague, Netherlands, Wolters, 1927.

Die erzählenden Schriften (three volumes). Berlin, S. Fischer, 1928.

Zwei Festreden. Leipzig, Germany, Reclam, 1928.

Hundert Jahre Reclam: Festrede. Leipzig, Germany, Reclam, 1928.

Sieben Aufsätze. Berlin, S. Fischer, 1929.

Author of introduction, *Ausgewählte Werke* (six volumes), by Theodor Fontane. Leipzig, Germany, Reclam, 1929.

Deutsche Ansprache: Ein Appell an die Vernunft. Berlin, S. Fischer, 1930.

Goethe als Repräsentant des bürgerlichen Zeitalters (speech). Vienna, Bermann–Fischer, 1932; as "Goethe as Representative of the Bourgeois Age," in *Essays of Three Decades,* 1947.

Author of introduction, *Jakob Wassermann: Bild, Kampf und Werke* by M. Karlweis. Amsterdam, Querido, 1935.

Author of foreword, *Zehn Millionen Kinder: Die Erziehung der Jugend im Dritten Reich* by Erika Mann. Amsterdam, Querido, 1938.

Vom künftigen Sieg der Demokratie (speech). Zurich, Oprecht, 1938; as *The Coming Victory of Democracy,* translation by Agnes E. Meyer, New York, Knopf, and London, Secker & Warburg, 1938.

Dieser Friede. Stockholm, Bermann–Fischer, 1938; translated by H. T. Lowe–Porter as *This Peace,* New York, Knopf, 1938.

War and Democracy. Los Angeles, The Friends of the Colleges at Claremont, 1940.

Author of preface, *"God is My Führer": Being the Last 28 Sermons* by Martin Niemöller. New York, Philosophical Library, 1941.

Deutsche Hoerer! 25 Radiosendungen nach Deutschland (speeches). Stockholm, Bermann–Fischer, 1942; translated by H. T. Lowe–Porter as *Listen Germany! 25 Radio Messages to the German People over the B.B.C.,* New York, Knopf, 1943; enlarged as *Deutsche Hoerer! 55 Radiosendungen nach Deutschland,* Stockholm, Bermann–Fischer, 1945.

The War and the Future. Washington, D.C., Library of Congress, 1944.

Author of introduction, *The Short Novels of Dostoevsky,* translation by Constance Garnett. New York, Dial, 1945.

With Frank Thiess and Walter von Molo, *Ein Streitgespräch über die äussere und innere Emigration.* Dortmund, Germany, Druckschriften–Vertriebsdienst, 1946.

Author of introduction, *Gedichte: Peter Schlemihls wundersame Geschichte* by Adelbert von Chamisso. Oldenburg and Mainz, Germany, Lehrmittel–Verlag, 1947.

Author of introduction, *Jeunesse* by Frans Masereel. Zurich, Oprecht, 1948.

Die Enstehung des Doktor Faustus: Roman eines Romans, Amsterdam, Bermann–Fischer, 1949; translated by Richard and Clara Winston as *The Story of a Novel: The Genesis of Doctor Faustus,* New York, Knopf; as *The Genesis of a Novel,* London, Secker, 1961.

Goethe und die Demokratie. Zurich, Oprecht, 1949.

Author of introduction, *Suchende Jugend: Griefwechsel mit jungen Leuten* by Alfred Kantorowicz. Berlin, Kantorowicz, 1949.

Ansprache im Goethe—Jahr 1949. Frankfurt, Suhrkamp, and Weimar, Germany, Thüringer Volksverlag, 1949.

Author of foreword, *Klaus Mann zum Gedächtnis.* Amsterdam, Querido, 1950.

Lob der Vergänglichkeit. Frankfurt, S. Fischer, 1952.

Gerhart Hauptmann: Rede, gehalten am 9. November 1952 im Rahmen der Frankfurter Gerhart–Hauptmann–Woche (speech). Gütersloh, Germany, Bertelsmann, 1953.

Author of afterword, *Abrizz der Psychoanalyse; Das Unbehagen in der Kultur* by Sigmund Freud. Frankfurt and Hamburg, S. Fischer, 1953.

Author of foreword, *Gespräche mit Casals* by José María Corredor. Bern, Switzerland, Scherz, 1954.

Ansprache im Schiller–Jahr 1955. Berlin, Aufbau, 1955.

Author of foreword, *Kleine Menagerie* by Alexander Moriz Frey. Wiesbaden, Germany, Limes, 1955.

Author of foreword, *Und die Flamme soll euch night versengen: Letzte Briefe zum Told Verurteilter aus dem europäischen Widerstand,* edited by Piero Malvezzi and Giovanni Pirelli, translation by U. Muth and P. Michael. Zurich, Steinberg, 1955.

Author of introduction, *Die schösten Erzählungen der Welt: Hausbuch unvergänglicher Prosa.* Munich, Vienna, and Basel, Desch, 1955–1956.

Meerfahrt mit Don Quijote. Weisbaden, Germany, Insle, 1956.

Author of foreword, *Die Erzählungen* by Heinrich von Kleist. Frankfurt, S. Fischer, 1956.

Author of foreword, *Mein Stundenbuch.* Munich, List, 1957.

Addresses Delivered at the Library of Congress, 1942–1949. Washington, D.C., Library of Congress, 1963.

Thomas Mann: Tagebücher (six volumes), edited by Peter de Mendelssohn. Frankfurt, S. Fischer, 1977–80; selections translated by Richard, Clara, and Krishna Winston as *Thomas Mann Diaries: 1918–1939,* edited by Hermann Kesten, New York, Abrams, 1982.

Frage und Antwort: Interviews mit Thomas Mann 1909–1955, edited by Volkmar Hansen and Gert Heine. Hamburg, Knaus, 1983.

Tagebücher, 1944–1946, edited by Inge Jens. Berlin, S. Fischer, 1986.

*

Adaptations: *Buddenbrooks* (film), Germany, 1923 and 1959; "Buddenbrooks" (television series), Germany, 1982; *Tonio Kröger* (film), France/Germany, 1968; *Death in Venice* (film), Warner Brothers, 1971; *Disorder and Early Torment* (film), Jugendfilm, 1977; *The Transposed Heads* (musical drama), 1984–86; *The Confessions of Felix Krull* (film) Filmaufbau, 1957; "The Confessions of Felix Krull" (television series), Germany, 1981.

Manuscript Collections: Yale University, New Haven, Connecticut; Thomas–Mann–Archiv, Berlin; Thomas–Mann–Archiv, Lübeck, Germany; Thomas–Mann–Archiv, Zürich; Sammlung Ida Herz, Nuremberg, Germany; Sammlung Hans–Otto–Meyer, Düsseldorf.

Biography: *The Turning Point: Thirty–Five Years in This Century* by Klaus Mann, New York, Fischer, 1943; *Essays on Thomas Mann* by Georg Lukács, translation by Stanley Mitchell, London, Merlin Press, and New York, Grosset & Dunlap, 1964; *Thomas Mann: Profile and Perspectives* by André von Gronicka, New York, Random House, 1970; *Unwritten Memories* by Katja Mann, translation by Hunter and Hildegarde Hannum, New York, Knopf, 1975;

The Brothers Mann: The Lives of Heinrich and Thomas Mann, 1871–1950, 1875–1955 by Nigel Hamilton, New Haven, Yale University Press, 1979.

Bibliography: *Das Wek Thomas Manns* by Hans Bürgin, edited by Walter A. Reichart and Erich Neumann, Frankfurt, S. Fischer, 1959.

Critical Sources: "Die Ehe im Übergang," translation by Dieter W. Adolphs, in *Das Ehebuch,* edited by Count Hermann Keyserling, Celle, Kampmann, 1925; *Germanic Review,* December 1950 (special Mann issue); *The Arrow and the Lyre: A Study of the Role of Love in the Works of Thomas Mann* by Frank Donald Hirschbach, The Hague, Nijhoff, 1955; letter from Mann to Hermann Lange, translation by Dieter W. Adolphs, in *Briefe, 1899–1955* (three volumes), edited by Erika Mann, Frankfurt, S. Fischer, 1961–65, partially edited and translated by Richard and Clara Winston as *The Letters of Thomas Mann, 1889–1955,* Berkeley, University of California Press, 1990; *Die Homosexualität in der literarischen Tradition: Studien zu den Romanen von Jean Genet* by Marion Luckow, Stuttgart, Enke, 1962; *Thomas Mann: A Collection of Critical Essays,* edited by Henry Hatfield, Englewood Cliffs, New Jersey, Prentice–Hall, 1964; *Thomas Mann: A Chronicle of His Life* by Hans Bürgin and Hans–Otto Mayer, translation by Eugene Dobson, University of Alabama Press, 1965; "Thomas Mann: Eros, Narcissism, Caritas; The Role of Love in the Dialectics of his Works" (dissertation) by David A. Myers, Sidney, 1966; *Thomas Mann: The Use of Tradition* by Terence J. Reed, London, Oxford University Press, 1974; *Male and Female: An Approach to Thomas Mann's Dialectics* by Inta Miske Ezergailis, The Hague, Nijhoff, 1975; *Der Zauberer: Das Leben des deutschen Schriftstellers Thomas Mann* by Peter de Mendelssohn (2 volumes), Frankfurt, Fischer, 1975–92; *From the Magic Mountain: Mann's Later Masterpieces* by Henry Hatfield, Ithaca, New York, Cornell University Press, 1979; *Thomas Mann: The Devil's Advocate* by T. E. Apter, New York, New York University Press, 1979; *Thomas Mann: The Making of an Artist, 1875–1911* by Richard Winston, New York, Knopf, 1981; *Narzissmus und illusionäre Existenzform: Zu den Bekenntnissen des Hochstaplers Felix Krull* by Hans Wysling, Bern and Munich, Francke, 1982; *Brother Artist: A Psychological Study of Thomas Mann's Fiction* by James R. McWilliams, Lanham, Maryland, University Press of America, 1983; *Eros und Poesis: Über das Erotische im Werk Thomas Mann* by Claus Sommerhage, Bonn, Bouvier, 1983; *Erotische Phantasien bei Thomas Mann: Wälsungenblut, Bekenntnisse des Hochstaplers Felix Krull, Der Erwählte, Die vertauschten Köpfe, Joseph in Ägypten* by Mechthild Curtius, Königstein, Athenäum, 1984; *Thomas Mann–Kommentar zu sämtlichen Erzählungen* by Hans Rudolf Vaget, Munich, Winkler, 1984; *Thomas Mann: Modern Critical Views,* edited by Harold Bloom, Chelsea House, 1986; *Die Gestalt des Schönen: Untersuchung zur Homosexualität in Thomas Manns Roman "Der Zauberberg"* by Gerhard Härle, Königstein, Hain, 1986; *Die Dialektik von Logos und Eros im Werk von Thomas Mann* by Frederick Alfred Lubich, Heidelberg, Winter, 1986; *Männerweiblichkeit: Zur Homosexualität bei Klaus und Thomas Mann* by Gerhard Härle, Frankfurt, Athenäum, 1988; *Selbstvergessenheit, Drei Wege zum Werk: Thomas Mann, Franz Kafka, Bertolt Brecht* by Reinhard Baumgart, Munich and Vienna, Hanser, 1989; *"We of the Third Sex": Literary Representations of Homosexuality in Wilhelmine Germany* by James W. Jones, New York and Frankfurt, Peter Lang, 1990; "Der Narziß Thomas Mann und die Pathologisierung seiner Homosexualität: Zu einem 'neuen Konzept' der Thomas–Mann–Forschung" by Karl Werner Böhm, in *Psyche 44,* 1990, 308–332; "'Noch einmal also dies': Zur Bedeutung von Thomas Manns 'letzter Liebe' im Spätwerk" by James Northcote–Bade, in *Thomas Mann Jahrbuch 3,* 1990, 139–148; *Thomas Mann's Doctor Faustus: A Novel at the Margin of Modernism,* edited by Herbert Lehnert and Peter C. Pfeiffer, Columbia, South Carolina, Camden House, 1991; "Heimsuchung und süßes Gift": Erotik und Poetik bei Thomas Mann, edited by Gerhard Härle, Frankfurt, Fischer, 1992.

*   *   *

Thomas Mann is one of the most celebrated German novelists. Born in Lübeck, Germany, on 6 June 1875, he was the second son of the senator and affluent grain merchant Thomas Johann Heinrich Mann and his German–Creole wife Julia. At the age of 18, he followed his recently widowed mother to Munich, which became his principle residence for the next four decades. After receiving international acclaim for his novels *Buddenbrooks* and *Der Zauberg* (*The Magic Mountain*) as well as for his novellas, above all *Der Tod in Venedig* (*Death in Venice*), he was granted the Nobel Prize for Literature in 1929. As an ardent adversary of National Socialism, Mann moved to Switzerland in 1933. In 1938, he took up residence in the United States. Due to the high regard Americans had for his artistic accomplishments and for his brilliant command of public speech, he became the main spokesperson of the German exile movement. It was in the United States that he finished his "Joseph" tetralogy as well as the novel *Lotte in Weimar* (*The Beloved Returns*), and wrote the novel *Doktor Faustus* (*Doctor Faustus*). He left the United States in 1952 to return to Switzerland, where he completed the novel *Bekenntnisse des Hochstaplers Felix Krull* (*Confessions of Felix Krull, Confidence Man*). He died on 12 August 1955 in Zurich, Switzerland.

Mann's public role as representative of the German culture and his aim to express his ideas in a universally intelligible way did not allow him to openly admit his bisexuality. The only authority to which he confided his sexual orientation was his diary, and he burned most of the journals he had written before 1933. The remaining diaries were unsealed and subsequently published 20 years after his death. It was only then his readers were provided with clear evidence of the autobiographical nature of the homoerotic elements in his novels and novellas. These diaries point out that several characters in his works secretly commemorate young men to whom Mann had been attracted. However, his artistic practice to either encode such autobiographical elements into mere cryptographic references, to secretly identify with literary figures who are disguised as women, and to symbolically heighten the depiction of homoeroticism into a universally human sphere discourages readers from regarding his works as, strictly speaking, gay and lesbian literature.

Mann's first books, *Der kleine Herr Friedemann* ("Little Herr Friedemann") of 1898, is a collection of short stories portraying the conflict between characters who conform with societal norms such as marriage, career, and economic success, and protagonists who fail to become part of mainstream society. The latter figures are longing for love and happiness, yet they either come to terms with the unattainability of their goals, or they die of despair after the individuals they love—mostly women who are characterized as childless, cold, and elegant—have publicly disgraced them. The subtitle of Mann's first novel, *Buddenbrooks* of 1901, is "Decline of a Family." This preordained fate of the Buddenbrooks is fulfilled by Hanno, their last male descendent who proves unable to continue the tradition of his family and is helplessly in the power of an oppressive school system. However, what he gains in return for this social and physical demise is a higher level of spiritualization: before he dies at the age of 15, he is granted an elevated form of happiness through the appreciation of nature and Wagner's music. While the protagonists of Mann's early works do not disclose any homoerotic desire, their unsuccessful attempts to be accepted point decisively at the repressive societal undercurrents which are also directed against deviant sexual orientations.

The novella *Tonio Kröger,* of 1903, depicts a character who shares many traits with Hanno Buddenbrook, yet manages to live beyond his adolescence. As a schoolboy, he only has one friend, Hans Hansen. Hans' name, his blond hair, and his blue eyes make him a stereotypical German, while Tonio's first name and southern European appearance are indications of his "foreignness" to the dominant society. Throughout his works, Mann uses this leitmotif technique, i.e., sets of stereotypical attributes which are repeated verbatim, in order to establish symbolic unity and to relativize the plot through irony. Hans Hansen is the first fictional character who secretly commemorates a person to whom Mann had been homoerotically attracted. A few months before his death, Mann confessed in a letter to his former fellow student, Hermann Lange, that the model for Hans Hansen was their classmate Armin Martens: "[Armin] was my first love, and never again in my life was I granted an equally tender, blissful, and grievous love." While Martens did not acknowledge Mann's revelry, Hans Hansen does at least concede to a distanced friendship with Tonio. Unlike Hanno, however, Tonio does not simply compensate his unfulfilled love with the appreciation of nature and music, but he actively pursues the career of an artist. At the same time, he disapproves of the cold attitude of decadent artists who "despise of 'mankind'" and worship art for art's sake, and declares himself for a love of "bourgeois" life, even though he himself is excluded from it. The novella ends with Tonio's appeal to his friend, the "cold" artist Lisaweta, to "not chide this love...; it is good and fruitful. There is longing in it, and a gentle envy; a touch of contempt and no little innocent bliss."

In his letter to Lange, Mann also defines the artistic importance of his homoerotic experiences as the "rousing of a feeling which is destined to be transformed into a lasting work of art." What he does not disclose, though, is the fact that *Tonio Kröger* was written during the time of his intensely homoerotic bonding with the painter Paul Ehrenberg. In 1905, this intimate relationship came to an end when Mann married Katharina Pringsheim, a young and well–to–do woman of Jewish descent, who would become his life–long partner and the mother of his six children. His marriage procured an elegant lifestyle and introduced him to Germany's cultural elite. At that time, he had already become highly acclaimed as the author of *Buddenbrooks.* His new social role of a family man and cultural exponent did not only impede future erotic relationships with men, but it also determined and limited Mann's choice of literary subjects. He abandoned the plan for the novel "Maya," an artistic reflection of his friendship with Paul Ehrenberg, and began to write the novel *Königliche Hoheit* (*Royal Highness*), which tells the story of a prince and future statesman whose social and intellectual isolation is revoked when he marries a young and affluent woman of Native American ancestry.

Der Tod in Venedig (*Death in Venice*), which appeared in 1912, depicts the last few weeks of the life of the fictional character Gustav von Aschenbach, who is presented as the celebrated author of the novel *Maya.* His works have become part of the school curriculum and are presented to Germany's youth as a model of stylistic discipline and moral integrity. Despite his extraordinary success, he is yet another of Mann's protagonists who are excluded from mainstream society: he is an outsider by virtue of his role as a national idol. Being widowed and an intellectually solitary man in his fifties, he finds it increasingly difficult to live up to these public and self–imposed expectations. He frequently seeks refuge from his artistic and public duties through traveling, especially to Venice and the nearby elegant beach resort, Lido. It is during one of these vacations that he falls in love with the polish boy Tadzio. Even though Tadzio, whose family is staying in the same luxurious hotel and occupies a canopied beech–chair close to Aschenbach's, will never engage in a conversation with his worshiper, he is well aware of Aschenbach's infatuation with him, enjoys the other's adoration of his beautiful body, and engages in an exchange of secret gazes. Aschenbach's obsession is so strong that he makes light of all warnings of Venice being subjected to an outbreak of cholera; one day it is too late, and all of Venice is put in quarantine. He has lost any self–control and pursues his beloved Tadzio, helplessly roaming about the death–stricken streets and canals of the famous and once so beautiful city. He dies in complete disgrace in his canopied chair at the nearly deserted beach, not only intoxicated by cholera, but also by his obsession with Tadzio, whom he deems divine.

Tadzio is one of the young men who commemorate a person to whom the author had been homoerotically attracted: During his stay in Lido in May of 1911, Mann had glimpsed the Polish boy Wadyslaw ("Adzio"), Baron Moes. In *Death in Venice*, this homoerotic experience is symbolically heightened through the allusion to mythology: Mann's modern–day Venice is imperceptibly transformed into a classical landscape where the ancient gods Apollo and Dionysus wage a battle for Aschenbach's soul. In his essay, "Die Ehe im Übergang" ("Marriage in the State of Transition") of 1925, Mann presents his view of homoeroticism and its symbolic meaning in his own works, especially *Death in Venice*. He draws a parallel between art and Eros: Homoerotic love is like art for art's sake, self–serving, childless, and without the potential for commitment and faithfulness. In this regard, Aschenbach's demise is the price modern art must pay for its newly gained independence and loss of social responsibility. However, by largely diverting from the given subject, marriage, this essay pays homage to homoeroticism, and it also serves as an apologia of homoerotic love as the true origin of artistic creativity.

The works Mann finished after 1918 share the same basic patterns of encoding or directly portraying homoerotic experiences: Just as in *Death in Venice*, mythical forces as well as individual men wage jealous battles for the male protagonists' intellect, love, and souls, thereby artistically varying and redefining the relationship between life, the human intellect ("Geist"), and art. Mann's next and highly acclaimed work, *The Magic Mountain* of 1927, reveals the intellectual heightening of Hans Castorp, a young engineer, through the battle between the characters Settembrini and Naphta, who represent opposing intellectual stances of the early twentieth century. Eros is represented by the Russian woman Clawdia Chauchat, whose seduction of Castorp is described by using phallic symbolism, thereby only superficially disguising yet another commemoration of Mann's own homoerotic experiences.

Joseph, the biblical title figure of Mann's novel tetralogy, is destined to become a cofounder of the chosen people of Israel. In order to fulfill this destiny, he follows in the steps of his forefathers. However, Mann goes beyond this mythical symbolism by emphasizing the psychological aspects of the plot: Joseph relies on the support of a number of father figures, but he also must learn to cope with an ever–present majority of male enviers and enemies, beginning with his half–brothers who resent his naive pride in being their father's favorite son. After a long series of setbacks, he finally assumes the role of Egypt's protector. He has become a wise states-man who resembles Mann's political idol, Franklin Delano Roosevelt. Joseph's fateful tenacity is symbolized by his long-lasting chastity. However, when Mut–em–enet, the wife of his earlier Egyptian master, Potiphar, develops an irresistible passion for Joseph, she comes very close to seducing him. Mann's diaries reveal that Mut–em–enet's passion commemorates the "central love experience of [his] first twenty–five years," i.e., his relation-ship with Paul Ehrenberg.

When Mann moved to the United States in 1938, he had inter-rupted his work on the "Joseph" tetralogy to write the novel *Lotte in Weimar* (*The Beloved Returns*), which appeared in 1939. This novel is a portrait of Germany's most famous writer, Johann Wolfgang von Goethe. Mann paints the picture of an older man who, despite his great fame and many social amenities, is intellectually isolated. He has not overcome the loss of his only intellectual equal, Friedrich von Schiller, and is surrounded by a group of jealous worshipers. The central part of this work, however, departs from the description of these external circumstances and puts the reader into the protagonist's own perspective, thereby disclosing the processes of a creative mind. It is here that Mann reveals his view of bisexuality as the driving force of artistic creativity.

Before resuming his work on *Joseph*, Mann also wrote the no-vella *Die vertauschten Köpfe* (*The Transposed Heads*), of 1940. While *The Beloved Returns* limits its idolization of bisexuality to the artistic and creative realm, *The Transposed Heads* takes advan-tage of the supernatural elements of its model, an Indian legend, in order to visualize the consequences of transposing the heads of different characters onto the bodies of others whom they desire. Thus, Nanda, a beautiful and sensual herdsman, has his body ex-changed with the trunk of his sophisticated and highly intellectual bosom–friend, Schridaman. In some respect, this novella overcomes the dichotomy of life and art, as presented in *Tonio Kröger*: Both men gain from the transposition of their bodies, in that Nanda's mere physical beauty becomes spiritually refined and Schridaman's intellect is enriched with sensuality. However, both must realize that their mutual attraction was based on the fact that they pos-sessed different qualities. Consequently, they both lose their quar-rel over Schridaman's wife, Sita. Whomever she considers to be her husband can not satisfy her desires: Schridaman's new body has lost its attraction of being secretly desired, and when she is united with his former body, she misses his intellect. Finally, all three agree to commit suicide, since they realize that they have destroyed the basis for their happiness on Earth, as limited as it may have been.

Doktor Faustus (*Doctor Faustus*) of 1947, depicts the life of the German composer, Adrian Leverkühn. Through employing the "Montage" technique (i.e., the incorporation of an abundance of literary and non–literary models), Mann reinterprets the Faust leg-end in the light of German history. Thus, Leverkühn's life embodies the entire cultural development of Germany. He is the prototype of the German character who has to go his own way without concern for his own destruction or that of others. While *Doctor Faustus* is considered one of Mann's highest accomplishments, a number of critics have found fault with the fact that this novel is laden with historic symbolism. However, this symbolism only superficially

covers a highly personal, self–critical undercurrent. The picture Mann paints of Munich society during the first third of the twen-tieth century would not stand the claim of being truly representa-tive of Germany's history; instead, it is of autobiographical nature. Leverkühn is yet another of Mann's protagonists who are sur-rounded by a group of jealous worshipers, including the first–per-son narrator, Serenus Zeitblom. The only person he is close to— and addresses with the informal "du"—is Rudolf Schwerdtfeger, whose model is, once again, Paul Ehrenberg. Since Mann depicts this relationship without disguising one of the two lovers as a woman, *Doctor Faustus* can be considered his novel with the most explicit homoerotic content. However, the portrayal of Mut–em-enet's love is much more compelling, while Zeitblom's jealous, if not hateful and homophobic perspective of his rival does not grant the reader an unbiased view of Leverkühn's relationship with Schwerdtfeger. In addition, the *Joseph* tetralogy remains concilia-tory, whereas the aim of *Doctor Faustus* is tragedy. Thus, Schwerdtfeger is brutally killed by his female lover, Ines Institoris, in an act of desperation when she hears of his engagement with Marie Godeau, the woman to whom Leverkühn had wished to propose. With this double betrayal Schwerdtfeger contributes to his friend's destiny of not being granted a fulfilling love relationship for the sake of creating great art.

Mann's last novella, *Die Betrogene* (*The Black Swan*) of 1953, presents another form of betrayal by telling the story of a middle–aged woman who initially mistakes the symptoms of uterine cancer as a reawakening of her fertility. Rosalie von Tümmler is another self–representation of the author who disguises as a woman: In his diaries Mann repeatedly refers to his love of Klaus Heuser, which lasted from 1927 to 1935, as one of his happiest passions. Cer-tainly, his passion for Heuser is reflected in von Tümmler's illu-sionary rejuvenation. Like Mann's early works, *The Black Swan* reflects the influences of Nietzsche's non–ethical, but aesthetic understanding of deception as the basis for creativity, and of Schopenhauer's view of death as redemption, which is implicitly paraphrased by Rosalie who calls death "a great instrument of life." The eminent Mann scholar Hans Rudolf Vaget sees *The Black Swan* as Mann's attempt to cope aesthetically with the reawakening of a homoerotic passion that, 25 years after the termination of his friend-ship with Paul Ehrenberg, deeply disturbed him and appeared to be a betrayal by nature, i.e. the overwhelming power of a "wrong" passion for a young man. Vaget concludes his discussion of this novella in his *Thomas–Mann–Kommentar* as follows: "[Mann], the deceiving and deceived artistic master, reveals himself in this self–projection as the 'betrayer' who has ultimately been recon-ciled with nature, i.e. his own [sexual] nature."

Mann's last novel translated into English, *Confessions of Felix Krull, Confidence Man*, appeared in 1955. The conception of this work dates back to the first few years after Mann's wedding, and can be seen as a reflection of his own troubled self–understanding of that time. The title character stems from the sphere of Maya and therefore lives by the motto that the world's highest postulate is to be deceived. Without true ambition and sense of commitment, he loves to assume various roles in order to please the self–deceiving expectations of others. By impersonating his friend, the Marquis de Venosta, he assists the Marquis with acquitting himself of the expectations of his family, while he, Krull alias Venosta, can travel around the world and enjoy the privileges of an aristocrat. Scholars such as Hans Wysling have argued that this novel is a reflection of Mann's narcissistic nature. While this work undoubtedly exposes and critically depicts the narcissism of Western society, it also addresses the inner conflicts of individuals whose erotic propensities deviate from societal norms. Felix Krull's obsession with fulfilling the erotic desires of others obliterates his ability to love and reduces his eroticism to narcissism. At the same time, he overcomes the limitations of the egotistical self and learns to see the world with a notion of universal sympathy. *Confessions of Felix Krull* is the final artistic testimony of the greatest psychologist of Eros in the history of German literature.

—*Dieter W. Adolphs*

———

MANSFIELD, Katherine (Kathleen Mansfield Beauchamp). New Zealand and British poet, and author of short stories and children's verse. Also wrote as K. M. and Boris Petrovsky. Born in Wellington, 14 October 1888. Educated at Queen's College, London, 1903–06. Married 1) the musician George Bowden on 2 March 1909 (separated 2 March 1909; divorced April 1918); 2) John Middleton Murry on 3 May 1918. Worked briefly as a movie extra and in the chorus of an opera, London, 1908; coeditor of periodicals, including *Rhythm, The Blue Review,* and *Signature,* c. 1912–15; translator, with S. S. Koteliansky, of diaries and letters of Anton Chekhov; author of verse for children. Contributor to periodicals, including *New Age, English Review, Open Window,* and *Athenaeum,* sometimes under the names K. M. and Boris Petrovsky. *Died in Fontainbleau, France, of a lung hemorrhage resulting from tuberculosis, 9 January 1923.*

WRITINGS

Short Stories

In a German Pension. London, S. Swift, 1911; with introduction by John Middleton Murry, New York, Knopf, 1926.
Prelude. London, Hogarth Press, 1918; enlarged as *The Aloe,* introduction by John Middleton Murry, New York, Knopf, 1930.
Je ne parle pas francais. Heron Press, 1920; in *Bliss, and Other Stories,* 1920.
Bliss, and Other Stories (contains "Je ne parle pas francais"). London, Constable, 1920; New York, Knopf, 1921.
The Garden Party, and Other Stories. New York, Knopf, 1922.
The Doves' Nest, and Other Stories, edited by John Middleton Murry. New York, Knopf, 1923.
The Little Girl, and Other Stories, edited by John Middleton Murry. New York, Knopf, 1924; as *Something Childish, and Other Stories,* London, Constable, 1924.

Poetry

Poems, edited by John Middleton Murry. London, Constable, 1923; New York, Knopf, 1924.
To Stanislaw Wyspianski. Favil Press, 1938.

Letters

The Letters of Katherine Mansfield (two volumes), edited by John Middleton Murry. New York, Knopf, 1928.
Katherine Mansfield's Letters to John Middleton Murry: 1913–1922, edited by John Middleton Murry. New York, Knopf, 1951.

Literary Criticism

Novels and Novelists, edited by John Middleton Murry. Originally in *Athenaeum* (London); New York, Knopf, 1930.
The Critical Writings of Katherine Mansfield, edited with an introduction by Clare Hanson. New York, St. Martin's Press, 1987.

Journals

The Journal of Katherine Mansfield, introduction and notes by John Middleton Murry. New York, Knopf, 1927; definitive edition, London, Constable, 1954.
The Urewera Notebook, edited with an introduction by Ian A. Gordon. London, Oxford University Press, 1978.

Collected Works

The Short Stories of Katherine Mansfield, introduction by John Middleton Murry. New York, Knopf, 1937.
The Scrapbook of Katherine Mansfield, edited by John Middleton Murry. New York, Knopf, 1939.
Collected Stories of Katherine Mansfield. London, Constable, 1945; revised as *The Complete Short Stories of Katherine Mansfield,* Auckland, New Zealand, Golden Press/Whitcombe & Tombs, 1974; edited by Antony Alpers, Auckland, Oxford University Press, 1984.
The Letters and Journals of Katherine Mansfield: A Selection, edited by C. K. Stead. London, Allen Lane, 1977.
The Collected Letters of Katherine Mansfield, edited by Vincent O'Sullivan and Margaret Scott. Oxford, England, Clarendon Press, Volume 1: *1903–1917,* 1984; Volume 2: *1918–1919,* 1987.

Other

Undiscovered Country: The New Zealand of Katherine Mansfield, edited by Ian Gordon. London, Longmans Group, 1974.
Translator, with S. S. Koteliansky, *Reminiscences of Leonid Andreyev* by Maxim Gorki.
Maata (unfinished novel).

*

Adaptations: "The Garden Party" was adapted for television.

Biography: *The Life of Katherine Mansfield* by Ruth Elvish Mantz, London, Constable, 1933; *The Life of Katherine Mansfield* by Antony Alpers, New York, Viking, 1980; *Katherine Mansfield* by Kate Fullbrook, Brighton, England, Harvester Press, 1986; *Katherine Mansfield: A Secret Life* by Clare Tomalin, New York, St. Martin's Press, 1987; *Katherine Mansfield: The Woman and the Writer* by Gillian Boddy, New York, Penguin, 1988.

Bibliography: *The Critical Bibliography of Katherine Mansfield,* edited by Ruth Elvish Mantz, London, Constable, 1931.

Critical Sources: *Katherine Mansfield: A Critical Study* by Sylvia Berkman, New Haven, Connecticut, Yale University Press, 1951; *The Fiction of Katherine Mansfield* by Marvin Magalaner, Carbondale, Southern Illinois University Press, 1971; *Katherine Mansfield and Her Confessional Stories* by Cherry A. Hankin, London, Macmillan, 1983; "Years of Darkness: The Terror of Sexuality in Katherine Mansfield's Fiction" by Kimberley Latta, in *Omnibus*, 6:1, 1983, 38–47; *The English Short Story: A Critical History* by Joanne Trautmann Banks, London, Twayne Publishers, 1985; *Katherine Mansfield: A Study of the Short Fiction* by J. F. Kobler, London, Twayne Publishers, 1990.

* * *

As is frequently noted in critical studies, Katherine Mansfield's writing was an influential development in twentieth-century literature, with her work incorporating many of the breakthroughs that helped define literary modernism in the early part of the century. Mansfield's biographers have also noted her lesbian relationships and bisexuality, with these aspects of her sexual identity first becoming evident while she was enrolled at Queen's College in London from 1903 to 1906. Reconciling these two facets of the author has been a more difficult challenge, however, due in large part to Mansfield's avoidance of homosexuality as a topic in her fiction. The task has been made more problematic due to her husband's treatment of her journals and letters following her death in 1923. Though many volumes of this material were published, the journals and letters were often severely edited and sometimes misconstrued. Later scholarly editions have provided a more reliable picture of Mansfield's life.

Born and raised in New Zealand, Mansfield returned to her native land after attending college in England, but she did not remain there long. Her discontent with the shallow society of colonial Wellington brought her back to London in 1908. She never returned to New Zealand, though her childhood experiences there later furnished her with the subject matter of her most successful stories. In London Mansfield continued her sexually-open lifestyle; she engaged in affairs with both men and women and became pregnant shortly before her marriage to musician George Bowden in 1909. As a result of this behavior, Mansfield's mother took her to a spa in Germany, then left her alone while she endured a miscarriage. Although this has generally been supposed as an effort to conceal the pregnancy, it is more likely, as both Antony Alpers and Gillian Boddy have stated in their biographies, that her mother was seeking the then fashionable water cure for Mansfield's lesbian tendencies. Of the author's lesbian relationships, a certain amount of mystery remains. Mansfield had been linked in a possible affair with Maata Mahapuhu, a Maori princess and fellow student at Queen's College. The unfinished novel *Maata*, however, appears rather to record Mansfield's relationship with friend and lover Ida Baker. Close relationships of this kind recurred in Mansfield's early life, and she repeatedly sought female companionship.

Returning to London, Mansfield quickly joined the literary community, becoming acquainted with writers such as D. H. Lawrence.

She also became romantically involved with editor and literary critic John Middleton Murry, and she married Murry in 1918 when the divorce from her first husband was finalized. Mansfield's first collection of stories was published in 1911, and although the author later said she was unhappy with the book, the stories serve as an introduction to her principal themes.

In these early works, as with most of Mansfield's writing, there is little that deals directly with lesbianism. There is, however, a deep concern with the status of women in society. In her journal for May 1908 she wrote, "It is the hopelessly insipid doctrine that love is the only thing in the world, taught, hammered into women, from generation to generation, which hampers us so cruelly." She gained most of her support and nurturing from women, and her letters to women are warmly affectionate with an underlying sense of complicity, as if women must conspire with one another to resist the male-dominated world. Cherry A. Hankin, in *Katherine Mansfield and Her Confessional Stories,* cites the story "Frau Brechenmacher Attends a Wedding" as an undisguised attack on the sexually-dominant male. In the book *Katherine Mansfield: The Woman and the Writer,* Gillian Boddy calls Mansfield's stories "brave early examples of feminist literature."

The death of Mansfield's beloved brother Lesley in World War I seems to have unblocked her New Zealand experiences. This led to a succession of stories that explored childhood and adolescence and allowed Mansfield to more thoroughly address the dominant themes in her writing. Linda Burnell (the mother in several stories and a figure largely based upon Mansfield's own mother) is clearly worn out by childbearing and seeks only a kind of asexual peace. Aunt Beryl, condemned to spinsterhood, seeks in "At the Bay" to find a relationship but rejects the overdominant advances of both Harry Kember and Mrs. Harry Kember. In "Bliss," through the character of Bertha, Mansfield explores the nature of feminine friendship and female sexuality. Most of the characters in her stories are women and, of the men, almost none show any understanding of the equality between loving individuals that is so important to the women.

The only extant writing with a clearly lesbian theme is the vignette "Leves Amores," now published as an appendix to Clair Tomalin's *Katherine Mansfield: A Secret Life.* Tomalin further suggests that Mansfield's personal experiences of lesbian love appear in the late Ursula episodes in D. H. Lawrence's *The Rainbow,* which do parallel closely Mansfield's early attraction to Edith Bendall. An essay by Kimberley Latta, "Years of Darkness: The Terror of Sexuality in Katherine Mansfield's Fiction," published in *Omnibus,* explores with great insight the sexual nature of the friendships depicted in the stories, and it is clear that female friendships were for Mansfield a way of escaping from the overwhelming male.

Although not an explicitly lesbian writer, Mansfield employs what might be called a feminist approach to life and literature. Scornful of men, whose need is to dominate, she reveals with cruel clarity how their dominance has destroyed any individuality women might have. The latter's economic dependence on men is an ironic result of a world structure that denies women an independent role. Often in her stories, women either reject or are unable to take advantage of independence. This leaves only minor ways of fighting back, and the resistance is often marked by vindictiveness and spite—traits that frequently characterized Mansfield's own relationships. Revealing is the scene in "At the Bay," where the women collectively relax after the trauma of getting Stanley Burnell off to work. This passage illustrates Mansfield's regret about the subordination of women, but also exemplifies the value of female companionship. As other critics have noted, Mansfield was highly critical of women's assigned role, but could not find a satisfactory alternative, only the suggestion that loving relationships with children and other women might make bearable their dependence on men.

—*Murray S. Martin*

———

MARS–JONES, Adam. British short story writer and editor. Born in London, 26 October 1954. Educated at Westminster School; Cambridge University, B.A. 1976, M.A. 1978. Film critic and reviewer, *Independent,* London, 1986—. **Recipient:** Somerset Maugham Award for *Lantern Lecture,* 1982; University of Virginia Benjamin C. Moomaw Prize for oratory. Agent: Peters, Fraser and Dunlop, 503–504 The Chambers, Chelsea Harbour, Lots Road, London SW10 0XF, England, U.K. Address: 42B Calabria Road, Highbury N5 1HU, England, U.K.

WRITINGS

Fiction

"Lantern Lecture," "Hoosh–Mi," and "Bathpool Park," in *Lantern Lecture.* London, Faber, and, without "Lantern Lecture," as *Fabrications,* New York, Knopf, 1981.
"Slim," "An Executor," "A Small Spade," "The Brave," and "Remission," in *The Darker Proof: Stories from a Crisis,* by Mars–Jones and Edmund White. London, Faber, 1987.
"Summer Lightning," in *Best Short Stories 1989,* edited by Giles Gordon and David Hughes. London, Heinemann, and, as *The Best English Short Stories 1989,* New York, Norton, 1989.
"The Changes of Those Terrible Years," in *The Faber Book of Gay Short Fiction,* edited by Edmund White. London and New York, Faber & Faber, 1991.
Monopolies of Loss: Stories (includes "Slim," "An Executor," "A Small Spade," "Summer Lightning," "The Brave," and "Remission"). New York, Knopf, 1993.
The Waters of Thirst. London, Faber, 1993; New York, Knopf, 1994.

Other

Editor, *Mae West Is Dead: Recent Lesbian and Gay Fiction.* London, Faber, 1983.
Venus Envy. London, Chatto & Windus, 1990.

*

Critical Sources: "Britain's New Literary Luminaries" by Craig Brown, in *Harper's Bazaar,* February 1988, 154; review of *The* *Darker Proof* by Joe Arena, in *Washington Monthly,* July–August 1988, 58; review of *Monopolies of Loss* by Richard Canning, in *New Statesman and Society,* 25 September 1992, 57.

*   *   *

Adam Mars–Jones is considered by many to be one of the best short fiction writers on the subject of AIDS in the English language. His stories, which have increasingly focused almost exclusively on the lives of never–too–wealthy, gay, white British men infected and affected by the HIV virus, fit easily into the British belletristic tradition. Unlike many contemporary artists and cultural critics of the AIDS crisis who deal with the syndrome in more *avant–garde* forms, Mars–Jones retains a focus on his characters' nurturing interpersonal relationships in the face of the epidemic. His works are narrated with a strong mixture of wit, camp, and irony by gay characters with AIDS, their care–givers and/or their lovers, reflecting the many facets of London's gay male community.

Two notable transitions have occurred in Mars–Jones' career as an author of short fiction. First, the early acerbic social satire of his award winning *Lantern Lecture* has given way to more somber storytelling, a reflection of the author's obsession with AIDS. In "Hoosh–Mi," one of the author's early works written in 1981, Mars–Jones gives the Queen of England a dose of rabies when she visits Australia. In contrast, his later works tend toward a different type of humor: in 1988's "Remission," a sarcastic tone permeates the story of a man with AIDS trying to mentally reconstruct the few moments of health he experienced while he was taking AZT for all it was worth. Second, Mars–Jones has shifted away from the decision, taken early on in his career, not to mention the acronym AIDS in his stories. Originally this decision was motivated by his desire to reach a wider audience who might turn off at the most clear sight or sound of the disease. Strategically, the story "Slim" (Slim being an African name for AIDS, foreign to British ears), written in 1986, begins: "I don't use that word. I've heard it enough .... I say Slim instead.... I have got Slim." In fact, the word AIDS does not appear in any of the works included in *The Darker Proof,* a short story collection that Mars–Jones authored with American gay litterateur Edmund White. This response to societal AIDS–phobia has given way to a perhaps general realization that we are going to have to live with this epidemic.

Many of Mars–Jones' AIDS stories have appeared in the well–respected British journal *Granta;* several have gone on to publication in *Darker Proof* and, finally, inclusion in 1993's *Monopolies of Loss.* The title of the last collection is a self–reflexive gesture on the part of the author, referring not only to his own type of storytelling monopoly on AIDS but also to the degree in which AIDS now monopolizes his imagination: he says that he can't give up telling the stories of a disease that has so many stories to tell. The gay men in Mars–Jones' short fiction collectively tell the story of a community learning to cope, not only with AIDS or any single character's HIV antibody status, but with the relationship and proper etiquette that develops between the nurturer and the one being nurtured. Typically, the narrator of "Slim" complains about the directness with which his home–care–giver was trained by the Trust program: "He said 'lesions' just the once, but I told him it wasn't a very vivid use of language." This demand for sophisticated style and verbal playfulness from Mars–Jones' characters is fully reflected in the author's unique prose style.

Like many individuals within the gay male community, Mars–Jones' characters are confronted by the transition from the sense of full autonomy that existed during the pre–AIDS years to semi–autonomous interdependency. While AIDS is the agent which produced this change in the community, and while death and bodily dysfunction constantly erupt into the materiality of Mars–Jones' fictional world, the prose has full recourse to a wonderfully bitchy stiff–upper–lip–ness, an adamant and forceful drive to create a witty and meaningful existence in the face of adversity. When the main character from "Remission" determines that AZT is derived from salmon sperm, he declares: "All I say is milt loves me and I love milt! I don't even need to fellate the fish to get at it, though God knows I'd do it if I had to." This comedic coping mechanism also applies to the day–to–day inconvenience of being incapacitated and dependent on others for the most basic of things.

The fullest collection of Adam Mars–Jones' AIDS stories, *Monopolies of Loss,* ends on a rather haunting note for the gay male community in England. "The Changes of Those Terrible Years" tells the story of how finally worn down voluntary AIDS workers can become while simultaneously presenting the most invective criticism that any of the characters with full–blown AIDS has to give to his care–giver. When the narrator tries to comfort Anthony on his death bed, telling him it's okay to stop fighting, Anthony, the narrator's favorite, with difficulty replies: "It's not up to you. *Old* man. Where do you get off telling people when they can die?" After Anthony's death, the narrator puts the house, which he had turned into an AIDS hospice, on the market. Here, as in all his writing, Mars–Jones—who himself worked for a voluntary agency caring for people with AIDS—conscientiously avoids the larger–than–life categories of Hero, Victim, and Savior in favor of the plurality of smaller voices which populate his fictional world.

—Tim Oliver

———

MARTIN, Del (Dorothy L. Martin). American gay activist and writer of nonfiction. Born in San Francisco, California, 5 May 1921. Educated at University of California, Berkeley, 1938–39; San Francisco State College (now University), 1939–41. Married James Martin (divorced); one daughter and two grandchildren; domestic partner of educator and writer Phyllis Lyon, beginning 14 February 1953. Reporter, *Pacific Builder,* San Francisco, 1948–49; editor, *Daily Construction Reports,* Seattle, Washington, 1949–51; free-lance writer, 1951—. Cofounder, Daughters of Bilitis, 1955, founding president of San Francisco chapter, 1955–56, and national president, 1957–60; cofounder, Council on Religion and the Homosexual, 1964; cofounder, Citizens Alert, 1965 (chair, 1971–72); member, Bishop Pike's Diocesan Commission on Homosexuality, 1965–66; treasurer, Intersection, 1967–73; cofounder, San Francisco Women's Centers, 1970; cofounder, Lesbian Mothers Union, 1971; member, Task Force on Homosexuality, San Francisco Mental Health Association, 1971–72; cofounder, Alice B. Toklas Memorial Democratic Club, 1972; member, Bishop Myer's Diocesan Commission on Human Sexuality, 1972–73; cofounder, Community Advisory Board of the Center for Special Problems, 1973; member of national board of directors, National Organization for Women (NOW), 1973–74;

cofounder, Bay Area Women's Coalition, 1974; cofounder, Coalition for Justice for Battered Women, 1975; cochair, NOW's National Task Force on Battered Women and Household Violence, 1975–77; cofounder, La Casa de las Madres, 1976; chair, San Francisco Commission on the Status of Women, 1976–77; cofounder, California Coalition Against Domestic Violence, 1977; cofounder, Lesbian Lobby, 1978; cofounder, San Francisco Feminist Democrats, 1978; member of advisory board, Senior Action in a Gay Environment, 1980–83, and Gay/Lesbian Outreach to Elders, 1984. Member of numerous organizations and committees, including Victims of Crimes Committee, 1975; Police Liaison Committee, San Francisco Human Rights Commission, 1975; Women's Advisory Council, San Francisco Police Department, 1976–77; California State Commission on Crime Control and Violence Prevention, 1980–83; Women's Institute for Freedom of the Press (associate member); National Gay Task Force (charter member); National Lesbian Feminist Organization; Lesbian Caucus; Religious Coalition for Abortion Rights; Mobilization Against AIDS; Lesbian Agenda for Action; ONE, Inc. (honorary member); Southern California Women for Understanding (honorary member); Bay Area Career Women (honorary member). Editor, *Ladder,* 1960–62. Contributor to periodicals, including *Challenge: A Theological Arts Journal, Motive, Open Hands, Osteopathic Physician,* and *On Our Backs.* **Recipient:** American Library Association Gay Book Award for *Lesbian/Woman,* 1972; Prosperos Award of Merit, 1972; Humanist Community of San Jose certificate of recognition, 1973; San Antonio Gay Community Lavender Alcade Service Award, 1978; San Francisco Board of Supervisors certificate of merit and achievement, 1978, commendation, 1980; named honorary citizen of Austin, Texas, 1978; Southern California Women for Understanding First Lesbian Rights Award, 1979; Family Violence Project Gold Star Award, 1981; California State Assembly commendation, 1983; David Award, 1983; City and County of San Francisco Award of Merit, 1985; National Organization for Women Certificate of Appreciation, 1986; honorary doctor of arts from Institute for Advanced Study of Human Sexuality, San Francisco, 1987; Cable Car Award of Merit, 1988; Franklin E. Cook Memorial Award, 1989; American Civil Liberties Union Earl Warren Civil Liberties Award, 1990; George Washington High School Alumni Hall of Merit, 1990. Address: 651 Duncan Street, San Francisco, California 94131, U.S.A.

WRITINGS

Nonfiction

With Phyllis Lyon, *Lesbian/Woman.* San Francisco, Glide Publications, 1972; revised, New York, Bantam, 1973; updated, San Francisco, Volcano Press, 1991.
With Phyllis Lyon, *Lesbian Love and Liberation.* San Francisco, Multi Media Resource Center, 1973.
Battered Wives. Glide Publications, 1976; revised, San Francisco, Volcano Press, 1981.

Contributor

"If That's All There Is," in *Vector,* November 1970.
Lesbians Speak Out. Free Women's Press, 1970.

With Sally Gearhart, "Afterthought: Lesbians as Gays and as Women," in *We'll Do It Ourselves: Combating Sexism in Education,* edited by David Rosen, Steve Werner, and Barbara Yates. Lincoln, University of Nebraska Press, 1974.

The Victimization of Women, edited by Jane Chapman and Margaret Gates. Beverly Hills, California, Sage Publications, 1978.

With Phyllis Lyon, "Reminiscences of Two Female Homophiles," in *Our Right to Love,* edited by Ginny Vida. Englewood Cliffs, New Jersey, Prentice–Hall, 1978.

With Phyllis Lyon, "The Older Lesbian," in *Positively Gay,* edited by Betty Berzon and Robert Leighton. Millbrae, California, Celestial Arts, 1979; updated and edited by Betty Berzon, 1992.

With Phyllis Lyon, "Anniversary," in *The Lesbian Path,* edited by Margaret Cruikshank. Monterey, California, Angel Press, 1980; revised and enlarged, San Francisco, Grey Fox Press, 1985.

Women's Sexual Experience: Explorations of the Dark Continent, edited by Martha Kirkpatrick. Plenum, 1981.

With Phyllis Lyon, "Lesbian Women and Mental Health Policy," in *Women and Mental Health Policy,* edited by Lenore E. Walker. Beverly Hills, California, Sage Publications, 1984.

With Daniel Jay Sonkin and Lenore E. A. Walker, *The Male Batterer: A Treatment Approach.* New York, Springer Publishing, 1985.

Domestic Violence on Trial, edited by Daniel Jay Sonkin. Springer Publishing, 1987.

*

Critical Sources: "A History of the Lesbian Periodical—The Ladder" (masters thesis) by Sarah Elizabeth Boslaugh, University of Chicago, 1984; *Christian Century,* 23 December 1964, 1581; *Ladder* (New York), 1:3, 1975; *American Women Writers: A Critical Reference Guide from Colonial Times to the Present,* edited by Lina Mainiero, New York, Ungar, 1981, 128–129.

Del Martin comments: "The Daughters of Bilitis (DOB) was founded in the oppressive climate of the 1950s when you could be arrested, incarcerated, dishonorably discharged from the military, fired from your job, disowned by your family, and/or confined in an insane asylum just for a state of *being* homosexual.

"Historians tend to forget that such a climate breeds fear, guilt, and isolation. The early years of DOB were spent in peer counseling and discussion to allay the fears and build self esteem. DOB was a beginning, a safe coming–out place. Without self–acceptance and a sense of community and support, there could be no movement as we know it today. Nor could we have dreamed of the social changes that would actually occur in our lifetime.

"Phyllis Lyon and I are proud to have played a part in the evolution from the homophile movement of the 1950s and 1960s to the gay and women's liberation and political–cultural movements of the 1970s, to the emergence of lesbian visibility and passage of gay rights laws of the 1980s, to the political clout of lesbians and gays in the 1990s.

"One word of concern. Lesbians and gays are a reflection of the wide spectrum and diversity of the larger society. We acknowledge our diversity but sometimes do not respect diversity of opinion or strategy of our peoples. There is no one way to promote or create social change. As a lesbian/gay/bisexual movement, we need to honor and validate varying approaches and contributions that may differ because of gender, age, race, ethnicity, religion, or class background. We need to learn from each other, allow individuals to grow in consciousness and come out at their own pace, and understand that different organizations serve diverse populations within our community. The 1993 March on Washington is a vivid example of unity in diversity."

* * *

Del Martin has been an advocate for women since the mid–1950s. She lays claim to many "firsts" as a political activist, organizer, and lesbian feminist. She met her life–long partner Phyllis Lyon in 1949 and, in 1955, they helped to organize the Daughters of Bilitis (DOB), the first national organization in the United States dedicated to lesbian "emancipation." Martin served as president of the original chapter of the DOB in San Francisco, and as the first president of the national organization. The DOB's vehicle, the periodical *Ladder,* which began publication in 1956, was virtually the only forum for lesbian concerns until the 1960s. The *Ladder* promoted a policy of accommodation and appeasement to the heterosexual world rather than direct confrontation; Martin edited this journal during the early 1960s. In the belief that education and research were the means to better understand the "sex variant," the Daughters of Bilitis also fought for changes in existing laws.

Martin and Lyon are especially well known for two pioneering works on lesbian life: *Lesbian/Woman* and *Lesbian Love and Liberation.* These books represent two of the earliest works about lesbians written by lesbians. *Lesbian/Woman* represents the first comprehensive work on what it means to be a lesbian in this society; *Lesbian Love and Liberation* defends a woman's right of sexual choice and individual freedom. *Lesbian/Woman* focuses on the realities of lesbian life and dispels many of the myths and misconceptions about lesbians. A later edition of the volume, revised in 1991, augments the text of the original work with a 20–year update in which Martin and Lyon review both the progress and setbacks experienced by lesbians since 1972. With increased visibility during the 1970s and 1980s, lesbians began to redefine what it means to be lesbian, especially in a homophobic society, and to explore the role of the lesbian in the women's movement. Lesbians experimented with new forms of sexual expression and gained a new self–awareness. A positive self–image appeared in the new literature and the literature itself became increasingly accessible with new bibliographies and periodical and book indexes. New fears also emerged. With the AIDS epidemic, lesbians became increasingly concerned about health issues and attitudes of health professionals. Issues regarding employment, adoption, marriage, gays in the military, concerns of the clergy and of young gays, and ageism also surfaced during this period.

As an activist, Martin has served in various capacities in the National Organization for Women (NOW) since the 1960s, and she has been especially vigorous in the fight against domestic violence. Her influential book *Battered Wives* is helping to raise the consciousness of a nation concerning what has become a national issue. In *The Male Batterer: A Treatment Approach,* she helps define women–battering as a crime and suggests ways to combat it. She was also a founding mother of La Casa de las Madres, a shelter for battered women in San Francisco, and has served on the Coalition for Justice for Battered Women and on the California Commission on Crime Control and Violence Prevention.

—*Jane Jurgens*

MARTINAC, Paula. American novelist and author of short stories. Born in Pittsburgh, Pennsylvania, 30 July 1954. Educated at Chatham College, Pittsburgh, B.A. 1976; College of William and Mary, Williamsburg, Virginia, M.A. 1979. Editor of *Conditions* magazine, 1988–90. Cochair, Board of Directors, New York City Lesbian and Gay Community Services Center; member of International Women's Writing Guild. **Recipient:** Lambda Literary Award for lesbian fiction, 1990; Puffin Foundation grant for teaching of lesbian writing, 1990. Address: c/o Seal Press, 3131 Western Avenue, Suite 410, Seattle, Washington 98121, U.S.A.

WRITINGS

Novels

Out of Time. Seattle, Seal Press, 1990.
Home Movies. Seattle, Seal Press, 1993.

Short Stories

"The Good Daughter," in *Focus: A Journal for Lesbians,* May/June 1983.
"Like Mother, Like...," in *We Are Everywhere: Writings by and about Lesbian Parents.* Freedom, California, Crossing Press, 1988.
"The Tenants," in *Conditions* (Brooklyn, New York), Number 15, 1988.
"Little Flower: A Love Story," in *Binnewater Tides,* summer 1989.
"Mineola, Mineola," in *Sinister Wisdom* (Berkeley, California), summer/fall 1989.
Editor and contributor, *The One You Call Sister: New Women's Fiction.* San Francisco, Cleis Press, 1989.
With Carla Tomaso, *Voyages Out 1: Lesbian Short Fiction.* Seattle, Seal Press, 1989.
"Heroines," in *Conditions* (Brooklyn, New York), Number 17, 1990.
"Pitching Woo," in *Queer City,* 1991.
"Unusual People, Extraordinary Times," in *Art & Understanding,* January–February 1993.

*

Critical Sources: Review by Penny Kaganoff of *Voyages Out 1: Lesbian Short Fiction,* in *Publishers Weekly,* 25 August 1989, 58; review by Ray Olson of *Voyages Out 1: Lesbian Short Fiction,* in *Booklist,* 1 October 1989, 262; review by Kevin M. Roddy of *Voyages Out 1: Lesbian Short Fiction,* in *Library Journal,* December 1989, 172; "Sister's Keepers" by Sally S. Eckhoff, in *Village Voice,* 27 March 1990, 77; "Losing and Finding and Losing Again" by Lynne M. Constantine, in *Belles Lettres* (Gaithersburg, Maryland), spring 1990, 6; review by Penny Kaganoff of *Out of Time,* in *Publishers Weekly,* 13 July 1990, 51; review of *Out of Time,* in *Kirkus Reviews,* 15 August 1990, 1122; review by Rose Fennell of *Out of Time,* in *Lambda Book Report* (Washington, D.C.), October 1990, 44; review by Marie J. Kuda of *Out of Time,* in *Booklist,* 1 October 1990, 255; "Ghost Writing" by Donna Minkowitz, in *Village Voice,* 30 October 1990, 74; "Paula Martinac Fills In the Pages of Lesbian History" by Liz Galst, in *Advocate,* 4 December 1990, 77; "Lesbian Fiction Reinventing Itself" by Lynne M. Constantine, in *Belles Lettres* (Gaithersburg, Maryland), spring 1991, 44; essay by Penny Perkins, in *Contemporary Lesbian Writers of the United States: A Bio–Bibliographical Critical Sourcebook,* edited by Sandra Pollack and Denise D. Knight, Westport, Connecticut, Greenwood Press, 1993.

Paula Martinac comments: "My longer fiction has mostly to do with history and time. I am interested in continuity over time—how different periods in history relate to the present and what lesbians and gay men in particular can learn from them. I am intrigued by photographs and movies and often blend descriptions of them into my narrative; it is their ability to catch specific lost moments in time that fascinates me. Much of my short fiction has been concerned with either family issues or the everyday lives of gay people. Whenever possible, I reach for humor in my fiction, which is almost always set in New York City."

*   *   *

In both her novels and short fiction, Paula Martinac is largely concerned with highlighting the experiences of women. Though the characters she chooses to feature are often homosexual, the focus on lesbians is by no means a given, and she is often able to target the many common denominators between women of differing sexual orientations. Her stories in *Voyages Out 1: Lesbian Short Fiction,* a collection that features Martinac's stories along with those of Carla Tomaso, tend to focus on lesbian issues. These include transitions in relationships and the challenge of "coming out." Ray Olson, writing in *Booklist,* also noted that these stories feature "the subtler, emotional politics between family members, friends, and lovers." The topic in *The One You Call Sister: New Women's Fiction,* of which Martinac is both editor and contributor, is the special relationship between sisters, some lesbians and some not. "Nonsisters may find a new world in the casual clutter of these images of family life," Sally S. Eckhoff remarked in *Village Voice.* "Sisters trying to solve the mysteries of their attachments will also gain some insight," Eckhoff continued, "but may feel in the end that they're looking at an unfinished picture." *Belles Lettres* reviewer Lynne M. Constantine predicted that readers will need to stop to digest each story, because they "so powerfully evoke memory, sensation, regret, longing, and hope that each one will stall any reader who lets it in to the place where fiction touches us most intimately."

Martinac's first novel, *Out of Time,* draws readers into the mystery of an old photo album and the woman who finds it. Susan uncharacteristically steals the book from an antiques shop, and finds herself wondering about the four women in its pictures. Her curiosity turns to obsession when the women begin to talk to Susan, eventually seducing her and luring her into their 1920s world.

Through her exploration of the women's lives, Susan learns about her own history as a lesbian. "Martinac's talent for mood, mystery, and literary seduction shine in this unusually impressive debut," a *Kirkus Reviews* contributor commented.

—*Deborah A. Stanley*

———————

MAUGHAM, Robin. British novelist, playwright, and author of nonfiction, screenplays, and autobiographies. Born Robert Cecil Romer Maugham in London, 17 May 1916; nephew of W. Somerset Maugham. Educated at Eton, and at Trinity Hall, Cambridge. Joined British Army, 1939; served in North Africa, 1942; served with Middle East Intelligence Centre; discharged with honorary rank of captain, 1945. Barrister, London, England, until 1939; writer, 1945–81. Became second Viscount Maugham of Hartfield, 1958; took seat in House of Lords, 1960. Lecturer on Middle East to Royal Institute of International Affairs. *Died in Brighton, England, following a long illness, 13 March 1981.*

WRITINGS

Nonfiction

The 1946 MS. London, War Facts Press, 1943.
Editor, *The Convoy File: Stories, Articles, Poems from the Forces, Factories, Mines, and Fields.* London, Collins, 1945.
Approach to Palestine. London, Falcon Press, 1947.
Nomad, 1947.
North African Notebook. London, Chapman & Hall, 1948; San Diego, California, Harcourt, 1949.
Journey to Siwa, photographs by Dimitri Papadimou. London, Chapman & Hall, 1950; San Diego, California, Harcourt, 1951.
The Slaves of Timbuktu. New York, Harper, 1961.
Search for Nirvana. London, W. H. Allen, 1975.

Novels

The Servant. London, Falcon Press, 1948; San Diego, California, Harcourt, 1949.
Line on Ginger. London, Chapman & Hall, 1949; San Diego, California, Harcourt, 1950; as *The Intruder,* London, New English Library, 1968.
The Rough and the Smooth. San Diego, California, Harcourt, 1951.
Behind the Mirror. San Diego, California, Harcourt, 1955.
The Man with Two Shadows. New York, Harper, 1959.
November Reef: A Novel of the South Seas. London, Longmans, Green, 1962.
The "Joyita" Mystery. Parrish, 1962.
The Green Shade. New York, New American Library, 1966.
The Second Window. London, Heinemann, 1968; New York, McGraw, 1969.
The Link: A Victorian Mystery. London, Heinemann, and New York, McGraw, 1969.

The Wrong People. London, Heinemann, 1970; New York, McGraw, 1971.
The Last Encounter. London, W. H. Allen, 1972; New York, McGraw, 1973.
The Barrier (contains five sonnets by John Betjeman). London, W. H. Allen, and New York, McGraw, 1973.
The Sign. London, W. H. Allen, and New York, McGraw, 1974.
The Corridor. London, W. Kimber, 1980.
The Deserters. London, W. Kimber, 1981; as *Enemy,* San Francisco, Gay Sunshine Press, 1983.

Plays

The Rising Heifer (produced Dallas, Texas, 1952; in England, 1955).
The Leopard, 1956.
Mister Lear (three–act comedy; produced, 1956; later retitled *Just in Time*). London, English Theatre Guild, 1963.
Rise above It (television play), British Broadcasting Corporation (BBC), 1957.
With Philip King, *The Lonesome Road* (three–act; produced, 1957). New York, Samuel French, 1959.
Odd Man In (adaptation of *Monsieur Masure* by Claude Magnier). London, Samuel French, 1958.
The Servant (adaptation of his own book; produced Worthing, England, 1958). London, Davis–Poynter, 1972.
With Philip King, *The Hermit* (produced Harrogate, England, 1959).
Adaptor, *It's in the Bag* (adaptation of *Oscar* by Claude Magnier; produced Brighton, England, 1959).
Adaptor with Willis Hall, *Azauk* (adaptation of the play by Alexandre Rivemale; produced Newcastle–upon–Tyne, England, 1962).
The Claimant (produced Worthing, England, 1962).
The Last Hero (broadcast, BBC–Radio, 1962; televised, 1966).
Winter in Ischia (produced Worthing, England, 1964).
Enemy (two–act; produced London, 1969).

Screenplays

With John Hunter, *The Intruder* (adaptation of his novel *Line on Ginger*), British Lion, 1953.
With Bryan Forbes, *The Black Tent* (adaptation of his serial *Desert Bond* originally appeared in *Chamber's Journal*), Rank Organization, 1956.

Autobiography

Come to Dust (personal account of Libyan Campaign, 1941–42). London, Chapman & Hall, 1947; New York, Viking, 1948.
Escape from the Shadows. London, Hodder & Stoughton, 1972; New York, McGraw, 1973.

Biography

Somerset and All the Maughams. New York, New American Library, 1966.
Conversations with Willie: Recollections of W. Somerset Maugham. New York, Simon & Schuster, and London, W. H. Allen, 1978.

Short Stories

Testament: Cairo 1898. London, Michael de Hartington, 1972.

The Black Tent, and Other Stories, introduction by Peter Burton. London, W. H. Allen, 1973.
The Boy from Beirut, and Other Stories, edited by Peter Burton. San Francisco, Gay Sunshine Press, 1982.

Other

Knock on Teak. London, W. H. Allen, 1976.
Lovers in Exile (collection). London, W. H. Allen, 1977.
The Dividing Line. London, W. H. Allen, 1979.

*

Bibliography: "Select Bibliography of Robin Maugham's Work" by Peter Burton, in *Escape from the Shadows* by Robin Maugham, London, Hodder & Stoughton, 1972.

*   *   *

In world literature, Robin Maugham falls far short of his famous uncle W. Somerset Maugham (with whom he is inevitably compared). For many reviewers, the younger Maugham was more dilettante than artist; others viewed the author as an insightful chronicler of the English upper classes. According to Geoff Puterbaugh, writing in the *Encyclopedia of Homosexuality,* Maugham's literary reputation suffered, in part, because his "real energies were devoted to the bottle and social climbing." Whatever the vagaries of his personal life, Maugham managed to produce several well–received works that explore homosexuality and class structure with what a *Times Literary Supplement* contributor called "a gift for vivid description [and a] knack of hitting off ... a character in a few lines of dialogue." Perhaps foremost among these publications is *The Servant,* a scathing look at the parasitic relationship between an upper–class young man and his manipulative servant. Other Maugham works of note include his play *Enemy,* which tells of a tentative love affair between a British soldier and a German stranded in the desert, and *The Wrong People,* a hard–edged thriller about a homosexual teacher who is offered a gift that comes with a very high price tag. Poet John Betjeman once summed up Maugham's ability to blend complex themes with class consciousness by noting that "here is a real writer ... who has something to say and knows how to say it—a rare combination."

—*Jim Kepner*

————

MAUPIN, Armistead. American novelist, journalist, and public speaker. Born in Washington, D.C., 13 May 1944; grew up in Raleigh, North Carolina. Educated at University of North Carolina at Chapel Hill, B.A. 1966. Served with the U.S. Navy in Vietnam, 1967–70; Lieutenant. Companion of Terry Anderson. Reporter, Charleston *News and Courier,* Charleston, South Carolina, 1970–71; reporter, Associated Press, San Francisco, California, 1971–72; account executive, Lowry, Russom, & Leeper Public Relations, San Francisco, 1973; columnist, *Pacific Sun,* San Francisco, 1974; publicist, San Francisco Opera, 1975; author of serial column "Tales of the City," for *San Francisco Chronicle,* 1976–77, 1981, and 1983; commentator, KRON–TV, San Francisco, 1979. Author of serial column for San Francisco *Examiner,* 1986. Author of dialogue, *La Perichole,* by Jacques Offenbach, produced by the San Francisco Opera Company. Public speaker on gay issues. **Recipient:** Freedoms Foundation Freedom Leadership Award, 1972; Los Angeles Metropolitan Elections Commission Communications Award, 1989; American Library Association's Gay/Lesbian Book Award, 1990, for exceptional achievement. Agent: Amanda Urbin, International Creative Management, 40 West 57th Street, New York, New York 10019, U S A

WRITINGS

"Tales of the City" Series

Tales of the City (originally serialized in *San Francisco Chronicle*). New York, Harper, 1978; in *28 Barbury Lane: A Tale of the City,* 1990.
More Tales of the City (originally serialized in *San Francisco Chronicle*). New York, Harper, 1980; in *28 Barbury Lane: A Tale of the City,* 1990.
Further Tales of the City (originally serialized in *San Francisco Chronicle*). New York, Harper, 1982; in *28 Barbury Lane: A Tale of the City,* 1990.
Babycakes (originally serialized in *San Francisco Chronicle*). New York, Harper, 1984.
Significant Others (originally serialized in San Francisco *Examiner*). New York, Harper, 1987.
Sure of You. New York, Harper, 1989.
28 Barbary Lane: A Tale of the City (contains *Tales of the City, More Tales of the City,* and *Further Tales of the City*). New York, Harper, 1990.
The Complete Tales of the City. New York, Harper, 1991.
Back to Barbary Lane: The Final Tales of the City. New York, Harper, 1991.

Other

Author of introduction, *Mrs. Miniver* by Jan Struther. New York, Harper, 1985.
Author of introduction, *Drawings of the Male Nude,* illustrations by Don Bachardy. Pasadena, California, Twelvetrees Press, 1985.
With others, *Heart's Wheel* (musical), music by Glen Roven, 1990.
Maybe the Moon (novel). New York, HarperCollins, 1992.
Beach Blanket Babylon (dialogue for a stage show).
"Suddenly Home," in *The Faber Book of Gay Short Fiction,* edited by Edmund White. London and New York, Faber & Faber, 1991.

*

Adaptations: A television screenplay adaptation by Richard Kramer of *Tales of the City* is scheduled as a limited series on Channel Four, England, in 1993.

Biography: "Travails of the City" by Steve Warren, in *San Francisco Bay Guardian,* 11 October 1989, 24; "Teller of Tales" by Adam Block, in *Outweek,* 29 October 1989, 42–45; "Armistead Maupin" by Chuck Allen, in *Frontiers 3,* November 1989, 18–21; "For Fifteen Years, He's Told Tales of San Francisco" by Richard Dyer, in *Boston Globe,* 20 November 1989, 32; "Mainstreaming a Cult Classic" by Tony Clifton, in *Newsweek,* 30 November 1989, 77; "A Gay Novelist Writes of Love and AIDS in his *Tales of the City*" by Kim Hubbard and Vicki Sheff, in *People,* 5 March 1990, 51; "Out of the Fog" by Micheline Hagan, in *San Francisco Review of Books,* fall 1992, 5–6.

Interviews: "A Talk with Armistead Maupin," in *Publishers Weekly,* 20 March 1987, 53–54; *Contemporary Authors,* Volume 130, Detroit, Gale, 1990.

Critical Sources: Review by James P. Degnan of *Tales of the City,* in *Hudson Review,* spring 1980, 146–148; review by David Feinberg of *Sure of You,* in *New York Times Book Review,* 22 October 1989, 25–26; *The Gay Novel in America,* by James Levin, New York, Garland, 1991, 288–289; "Armistead Maupin" by Barbara Kaplan Bass, in *Contemporary Gay American Novelists,* edited by Emmanuel S. Nelson, Westport, Connecticut, Greenwood Press, 1993, 255–289.

*   *   *

Armistead Maupin's popular "Tales of the City" novels have appealed to a wide audience, overcoming the gays–only stigma attached to many openly homosexual authors who feature homosexual characters in their work. Although Maupin's work presents issues important to the gay community to a wide audience (a role that he has relished, especially since the epidemic of AIDS), there are elements, which are largely responsible for his popularity, that threaten to undermine the literary viability of his work. The episodic, soap opera–style format of the novels, nearly all of which were first published serially in San Francisco papers, has been criticized as contrived melodrama. Maupin's burlesque of contemporary society has also been read in different ways by different readers, with the line between satire and cliche sometimes becoming difficult to distinguish.

Despite such criticisms, the long history of the continuing series—six novels over an 11–year span—provides a poignant social history of the gay community, contrasting the hedonistic late 1970s with the tragedy that has pervaded the AIDS era. The books follow a recurring cast of characters, who originally shared a San Francisco boarding house, and each installment is rife with historical artifacts, including everything from cocaine and bath houses to AZT and the Persian Gulf War. Maupin's books are more than documents of popular culture, however, and it is his mix of literature and politics that has invited comparisons to earlier socially–conscious authors. Several critics have placed Maupin in the same tradition as nineteenth–century British novelist Charles Dickens, citing Maupin's dramatization of social issues and his affection for the serial format. While the comparison is somewhat apt, Maupin illustrates his contemporary allegiances by replacing Dickens' sentimentality with satire. This combination has obvious popular appeal, and it has allowed Maupin to outline his position on several gay–related issues.

Maupin's homosexual characters are diverse, as capable of both good and bad as their heterosexual counterparts. Maupin also portrays these two groups, gay and straight, as being involved in the same behavior en route to the same conclusions. Gay characters, such as Michael "Mouse" Tolliver, become involved in numerous sexual relationships in the earlier installments of the series; heterosexuals like Mary Ann Singleton go through a similar stage of experimentation. In Maupin's later novels, these escapades yield to longer–term relationships that demand greater commitment and offer greater satisfaction. In this manner, Maupin indicates that sexual orientation has no discernible effect on other aspects of an individual's behavior and that, in many respects, the two groups share similar ideals. This point is carried further by the relationships that develop between homosexuals and heterosexuals in Maupin's work. In daring to put gays and straights together, Maupin breaks down the sexual identity segregation that exists in many works of gay literature. This process emphasizes similarities as much as differences, and demonstrates that strong bonds can develop between homosexuals and heterosexuals.

Coexistent with this intermingling of people with different sexual orientations is an honesty about sexual identity. Maupin's gay characters are generally open about their sexuality, and the heterosexuals are aware and accepting of same–sex relationships. This arrangement provides an implicit message that became more explicit in the course of the "Tales" series: that gays should openly admit their sexual orientation. Maupin's most strident advocacy of coming out occurs in *Sure of You,* the final novel in the series, when Tolliver castigates a fashion designer who hides his homosexuality behind a conventional marriage. Maupin has further promoted a message of sexual openness in his frequent public appearances, and he sees a direct correlation between his roles as activist and writer. "It was no accident that my literary drive emerged as soon as I stopped hiding my sexuality," he related in a *Contemporary Authors* interview. "There was this irresistible urge to tell everything I knew, to explain myself, to demystify a subject that had scared me silly for years."

Since closing the "Tales" series, Maupin has explored new literary interests. His 1992 novel, *Maybe the Moon,* is narrated by a 31–inch tall Hollywood actress who struggles to revive her failing career. By concentrating on such a unique character, Maupin is able to cultivate his penchant for social outcasts while at the same time broadening his literary repertoire. After spending an extended period with the cast of the "Tales" novels, it may take several other variations like *Maybe the Moon* before he earns a critical response that is equal to his popular success. Regardless of Maupin's fate in this regard, he has done much to familiarize the general public with homosexual lifestyles and issues and has rendered compelling, comforting, and entertaining portraits of his gay and lesbian characters.

—*Jeff Hill*

McALMON, Robert. American publisher, poet, novelist, and author of short stories. Born in Clifton, Kansas, 9 March 1896 (some sources indicate January or March 1895). Educated at University of Minnesota, 1916; University of Southern California, 1917–20. Married English poet and novelist Annie Winifred Ellerman

(Bryher), 14 February 1921 (divorced 1927). Edited *Ace* (a magazine about flying), 1918–19; established *Contact* (a magazine that published poetry and criticism) with William Carlos Williams in the early 1920s; moved to Paris in 1921. *Died in Hot Springs, California, 2 February 1956.*

WRITINGS

Poetry

Explorations. London, Egoist Press, 1921.
The Portrait of a Generation, Including the Revolving Mirror. Paris, Contact Editions, 1926.
North America, Continent of Conjecture. Paris, Contact Editions, 1929; reissued, San Diego, Dark Child Press, 1983.
Not Alone Lost. Norfolk, Connecticut, New Directions, 1937.

Short Stories

A Hasty Bunch, afterword by Kay Boyle. Paris, Contact Editions, 1922; Carbondale, Southern Illinois University Press, 1977.
A Companion Volume. Paris, Contact Editions, 1923.
Distinguished Air (Grim Fairy Tales). Paris, Three Mountains Press, 1925; enlarged as *There Was a Rustle of Black Silk Stockings,* New York, Belmont, 1963.
Indefinite Huntress and Other Stories. Paris, Crosby Continental Editions, 1932.
McAlmon and the Lost Generation (includes stories "The Indefinite Huntress," "Blithe Insecurities," "Three Generations of the Same," "The Jack Rabbit Drive," "Wisdom Garnered by Day," "Potato Picking," "In–Between Ladies," "Evening on the Riviera, the Playground of the World," "The Highly Prized Pajamas," "A Romance at Sea," "Mexican Interval," and "Green Grow the Grasses"), edited by Robert E. Knoll. Lincoln, University of Nebraska Press, 1962.
Miss Knight and Others (contains the three stories of *Distinguished Air,* "Miss Knight," and "The Indefinite Huntress"), edited by Edward N. S. Lorusso. Albuquerque, University of New Mexico, 1992.

Other

Post–Adolescence (novel). Paris, Contact Editions, 1923; published with a selection of short stories as *Post–Adolescence: A Selection of Short Fiction,* edited by Edward N. S. Lorusso, Albuquerque, University of New Mexico Press, 1991.
Village: As It Happened through a Fifteen Year Period. Paris, Contact Editions, 1924; reissued and edited by Edward N. S. Lorusso, Albuquerque, University of New Mexico Press, 1990.
Editor, *Contact Collection of Contemporary Writers.* Paris, Contact Editions, 1925.
"New England Victorian Episodes: Pennythinker," in *Pagany,* winter 1930.
"It's All Very Complicated," in *Contact,* February 1932.
Being Geniuses Together: An Autobiography. London, Secker & Warburg, 1938; revised by Kay Boyle as *Being Geniuses Together, 1920–1930,* Garden City, New York, Doubleday, 1968; London, Joseph, 1970; Lincoln, University of Nebraska Press, 1976.

Manuscript Collections: Southern Illinois University, Carbondale; Beinecke Library, Yale University.

Biography: *The Autobiography* by William Carlos Williams, New York, Random House, 1951; *The Heart to Artemis: A Writer's Memoirs* by Bryher, New York, Harcourt, 1962; *That Summer in Paris* by Morley Callaghan, New York, Coward–McCann, 1963; *Alms for Oblivion* by Edward Dahlberg, Minneapolis, University of Minnesota Press, 1964; "Scenes with a Hero" by Kathleen Connell, in *Connecticut Review,* 2:1, 1968, 5–12, reprinted in *Hemingway and the Sun Set* by Bertram D. Sarason, Washington, D.C., NCR/Microcard, 1972, 145–150; *Memoirs of Montparnasse* by John Glassco, Toronto, Oxford University Press, 1970; *Adrift among Geniuses: Robert McAlmon Writer and Publisher of the Twenties* by Sanford J. Smoller, University Park and London, Pennsylvania State University Press, 1975; *Herself Defined: The Poet H. D. and Her World* by Barbara Guest, Garden City, New York, Doubleday, 1984; *John Glassco's Richer World: "Memoirs of Montparnasse"* by Philip Kokotailo, Toronto, ECW Press, 1988; "Foreword" by Gore Vidal, in *Miss Knight and Others,* edited by Edward N. S. Lorusso, Albuquerque, University of New Mexico Press, 1992, ix–xiv.

Critical Sources: *Robert McAlmon: Expatriate Publisher and Writer* by Robert E. Knoll, Lincoln, University of Nebraska Studies (New Series, Number 18), 1957; "Brighter Than Most" by Kay Boyle, in *Prairie Schooner,* spring 1960, 1–4; *Published in Paris: American and British Writers, Printers, and Publishers in Paris, 1920–1939,* New York, Macmillan, 1975; *McAlmon's Chinese Opera* by Stephen Scobie, Montreal, Quadrant Editions, 1980.

*   *   *

Robert McAlmon has been almost completely neglected in the field of gay studies, but the republication of the stories "Miss Knight" and "Distinguished Air" by the University of New Mexico in 1992 should increase interest in his work. Generally known as the most important American expatriate publisher in Paris, his venture, Contact Publishing, an outlet for many of his own works, turned out almost two dozen books by authors such as Bryher, Marsden Hartley, Gertrude Stein, H. D., and Djuna Barnes. His memoir *Being Geniuses Together* is an acerbic, gossipy account of his meetings from 1921 to 1934 with a dazzling array of the major authors and writers of the day. Ironically, McAlmon had enormous difficulty getting his own works published in the United States, and his achievements as a writer have generally been forgotten.

Although primarily a novelist and short story writer, McAlmon wrote poetry throughout his career, producing the volumes *Explorations; The Portrait of a Generation; North America, Continent of Conjecture;* and *Not Alone Lost.* Themes of sexuality appear in various instances in McAlmon's work. In *The Portrait of a Generation* there is a brief character sketch of a massive Italian laborer who is also a transvestite. In "New England Victorian Episodes: Pennythinker," a contribution to *Pagany,* an effete middle–aged man meditates on his frustrated attraction to gazelle–bodied boys.

As a writer of fiction, McAlmon subscribed to beliefs that many have believed stifled his writing. He showed little interest in strong plots, had an aversion for in–depth psychological studies, and claimed that revision spoiled the immediacy of his writing. He wanted to represent psychological types, often specifically American ones. However, such tenets restricted the field in which he could work, and he never reached the achievement of Dos Passos, for example. Praised by Ezra Pound, Kay Boyle, William Carlos Williams, and Katherine Anne Porter, writers with whom he was on good terms at least part of the time, he was often brutally critical of other figures conceded to be his artistic superiors.

Despite his long stays in Paris, McAlmon did not investigate French literature or seriously explore the achievement of gay French contemporaries such as Jean Cocteau, André Gide, and René Crevel. Basically a liberal, he did not take part in explicit political causes. He did denounce fascism in some of his poems, and unlike his longtime gay friend Marsden Hartley, he did not have sympathy for the rise of Adolf Hitler in the early 1930s.

It is hard to chart the course of McAlmon's achievement as a writer of fiction because of the loss of so many later manuscripts. The early short story volumes *A Hasty Bunch* and *A Companion Volume* along with the novella *Post–Adolescence* are artistically his weakest. The autobiographical novella has some interest for its portrait of Marsden Hartley and various famous non–gay characters such as William Carlos Williams. It tells of McAlmon's career as an artists' model at Cooper Union, touching lightly on some of the male artists' desire for his beautiful body.

McAlmon's best work is represented in the novel *Village,* and the three stories in *Distinguished Air.* The novel paints a bleak picture of repressive life in a village on the Great Plains in the years before World War I. In an undeveloped subplot one character, Peter Reynolds, is in love with another young man, Eugene Collins. In 1992, writer Gore Vidal claimed that Peter is a stand–in for McAlmon and that Eugene L. Vidal, Gore's father, is the model for Eugene.

The three stories in *Distinguished Air* take place in Berlin in the early 1920s and center on a world of gay bars, cocaine addiction, alcohol abuse, prostitution, inflation, and expatriate confusion. Again Marsden Hartley serves as the model for a character. The flamboyant gay hero of "Miss Knight" is based on Dan Mahoney, also the model for Djuna Barnes' Matthew O'Connor in *Nightwood,* where he is treated with much greater solemnity. The strength of the story lies not only in its vivid and non–condescending view of a campy queen but in its striking use of phrases such as "rough trade," "real men," "cruising," "pick–ups," "drag," "bitches," and "sisterhood." "Distinguished Air" shines more for its depiction of the gay bar scene with types raunchier than in Christopher Isherwood's later Berlin stories. "The Lodging House" depicts a lesbian milieu.

McAlmon included both new and previously collected stories in his last volume, named eponymously after the best of them, "The Indefinite Huntress." Departing from his usual unpretentious realism, here McAlmon uses motifs from Greek myths as he tells the story of a heterosexual couple both attracted to a beautiful boy. McAlmon published in small magazines about two dozen works of fiction, and a dozen of them are included in Robert E. Knoll's *McAlmon and the Lost Generation.* At least two of them, "Blithe Insecurities" and "Three Generations of the Same," have gay male subtexts. The 1991 edition of *Post–Adolescence* also includes 15 stories (some are also in Knoll's book) including "The Highly–Prized Pajamas" which deals indirectly with lesbianism. An unreprinted story, "It's All Very Complicated" also uses lesbianism in its plot.

Although many of McAlmon's stories have autobiographical roots, one does not see much homosexuality, and the memoir *Being Geniuses Together* is set up to avoid raising questions about McAlmon's intimate life. Since his death, various memoirs have offered accounts of his attraction to men, but they should be approached cautiously. Morley Callaghan in *That Summer in Paris* recounts a 1929 incident when a drunken McAlmon declared his bisexuality and criticized Ernest Hemingway for his vulgar treatment of homosexuals in *The Sun Also Rises.* Kathleen Connell, in a *Connecticut Review* article, wrote that McAlmon said his escape from occupied France was aided by gays in the German army. The discussion of McAlmon in John Glassco's fictionalized *Memoirs of Montparnasse* includes an incident in which a drunken McAlmon got into the bed that the teenage Glassco was sharing with his companion Graeme Taylor. In 1988 Philip Kokotailo's manuscript research revealed that in the early unpublished version of the book Glassco wrote that McAlmon was deeply in love with him and had hoped to separate him from Taylor. Here we have an incident (perhaps the only one on record) that challenges the view of McAlmon as incapable of love. In his poem sequence *McAlmon's Chinese Opera,* Stephen Scobie has McAlmon meditate on whether he might have done better by Marsden Hartley had he become his lover. Edward Dahlberg in *Alms for Oblivion* declared simplistically that McAlmon's homosexuality was rooted in his sham marriage to Bryher, companion of H. D.

In the field of gay studies McAlmon will mostly be remembered for *Distinguished Air.* It raises the question of what attitude one should take toward the confused and wasted lives of some gays, who nevertheless generate admiration through their courage, openness, survival, and sense of humor. Attention to these stories will increase McAlmon's reputation beyond his publishing career.

—*Peter G. Christensen*

McANDREWS, John. *See* **STEWARD, Samuel M(orris).**

McCRAY, Mike. *See* **PRESTON, John.**

McCULLERS, Carson. American novelist, playwright, and author of children's literature. Born Lula Carson Smith in Columbus, Georgia, 19 February 1917. Educated at Columbia University and New York University, 1935–36. Married Reeves McCullers in 1937 (divorced 1940); remarried McCullers in 1945 (committed suicide 1953). Writer. Elected American Academy of Arts and Letters fellow. **Recipient:** Houghton Mifflin fiction fellowship, 1939; Guggenheim fellowships, 1942 and 1946; National Institute of Arts and Letters grant in literature, 1943; New York Drama Critics Circle Award, 1950; Donaldson Award, 1950; Theatre Club, Inc. gold medal, 1950; *Die Welt* younger generation prize, 1965. *Died in Nyack, New York, of complications resulting from a stroke, 29 September 1967.*

WRITINGS

Novels

The Heart Is a Lonely Hunter. Boston, Houghton, 1940; London, Cresset, 1943.
Reflections in a Golden Eye. Boston, Houghton, 1941; London, Cresset, 1942.
The Member of the Wedding. Boston, Houghton, 1946; London, Cresset, 1947.
Clock without Hands. Boston, Houghton, 1961; London, Cresset, 1961.

Plays

The Member of the Wedding: A Play (based on the novel by McCullers; produced New York, 1950). New York, New Directions, 1951.
The Square Root of Wonderful (produced New York, 1957). Boston, Houghton, 1958; London, Cresset, 1958.
Author of narration, *The Ballad of the Sad Cafe* (adaptation by Edward Albee of the novel by McCullers; produced New York, 1963). New York, Atheneum, 1963.

Television Plays

The Invisible Wall, "Omnibus," CBS–TV, 1953.
The Sojourner, NBC–TV, 1964.

Children's Literature

Sweet as a Pickle and Clean as a Pig, illustrations by Rolf Gerard. Boston, Houghton, 1964; London, J. Cape, 1965.
Sucker, illustrations by James Hyes. Mankato, Minnesota, Creative Education, 1986.

Collected Works

The Ballad of the Sad Cafe: The Novels and Stories of Carson McCullers (includes *The Ballad of the Sad Cafe* [originally serialized in *Harper's Bazaar,* 1943], *The Heart Is a Lonely Hunter, Reflections in a Golden Eye,* and *The Member of the Wedding*). Boston, Houghton, 1951; London, Cresset, 1952; as *The Ballad of the Sad Cafe and Other Stories,* New York, Bantam, 1967; as *The Shorter Novels and Stories of Carson McCullers,* London, Barrie & Jenkins, 1972.
Collected Short Stories and the Novel, The Ballad of the Sad Cafe. Boston, Houghton, 1955.
The Mortgaged Heart: The Previously Uncollected Writings of Carson McCullers, edited by Margarita G. Smith. Boston, Houghton, 1971; London, Barrie & Jenkins, 1972.
Collected Stories. Boston, Houghton, 1987.

Other

Author of libretto, *The Twisted Trinity.* Philadelphia, 1946.

Recordings: *Carson McCullers Reads from "The Member of the Wedding" and Other Works,* Metro–Goldwyn–Mayer, 1958.

*

Manuscript Collections: Humanities Research Center, University of Texas; Robert Flowers Collections, Perkins Library, Duke University.

Biography: *The Lonely Hunter: A Biography of Carson McCullers* by Virginia Spencer Carr, Garden City, New York, Doubleday, 1976; "Carson McCullers" by Robert F. Kiernan, in *Concise Dictionary of American Literary Biography: The New Consciousness, 1941–1968,* Detroit, Gale, 1987, 347–357.

Bibliography: *Katherine Anne Porter and Carson McCullers: A Reference Guide* by Robert F. Kiernan, Boston, G. K. Hall, 1976; *Carson McCullers: A Descriptive Listing and Annotated Bibliography of Criticism* by Adrian M. Shapiro, Jackson R. Bryer, and Kathleen Field, New York, Garland, 1980; "Carson McCullers" by Virginia Spencer Carr, in *Contemporary Authors Bibliographical Series,* Volume 1: *American Novelists,* Detroit, Gale, 1986, 293–345; "Carson McCullers" by Margaret B. McDowell, in *Contemporary Authors Bibliographical Series,* Volume 3: *American Dramatists,* Detroit, Gale, 1989.

Critical Sources: *The Ballad of Carson McCullers* by Oliver Evans, New York, Coward–McCann, 1966; *Carson McCullers* by Dale Edmonds, Austin, Steck–Vaughn, 1969; *Carson McCullers* by Lawrence Graver, St. Paul, University of Minnesota Press, 1969; *Carson McCullers* by Richard M. Cook, New York, Ungar, 1975; *The Member of the Wedding: Aspects of Structure and Style* by Eleanor Wikborg, Atlantic Highlands, New Jersey, Humanities Press, 1975; *Carson McCullers* by Margaret B. McDowell, Boston, Twayne Publishers, 1980.

*   *   *

Carson McCullers' importance to American literature was established with the publication of her first novel, *The Heart Is a Lonely Hunter,* in 1940. Her subsequent works, especially *Reflections in a Golden Eye,* in 1941, *The Member of the Wedding,* in 1946, and *Clock without Hands,* in 1961, assured her place in the American literary pantheon. McCullers' genius lies in her ability to simultaneously evoke the comforting ambience of America's past in her depictions of life in a small Southern town, and the discomforting awareness that America's future will challenge and ultimately destroy some of the fundamental assumptions of our culture (i.e., that racial inequality is natural and inevitable and that homosexuality is unnatural and intolerable).

In general, McCullers' works explore the variety and the complexity of human isolation and expose the destructive repercussions of that alienation, especially when the separation of the indi-

258   McCULLERS

GAY & LESBIAN LITERATURE

vidual from society is occasioned by racial and gender bigotry. The pathos of *The Heart Is a Lonely Hunter* probably enabled its first readers to tolerate McCullers' overt message of racial equality, found most obviously in the characterization and exhortations of the black doctor, Benedict Copeland, as well as the covert message of the emotional and psychological authenticity of homosexual love suggested in the feelings of the deaf–mute, John Singer, for Spiros Antonapoulos.

McCullers uses the self–perceptions of her characters to reflect society's prejudices and moral judgements, whereas her authorial observations of the characters reveal no such bias or moral squint. Dr. Copeland, for example, perceives himself as a failure because he has not redeemed his race from the residual bondage of the slave mentality. "He had known the reason for his working and was sure in his heart because he knew each day what lay ahead of him. He would go with his bag from house to house, and on all things he would talk to them and patiently explain. And then in the night he would be happy in the knowledge that the day had been a day of purpose.... There were thousands of such times of satisfaction. But what had been their meaning? Out of all the years he could think of no work of lasting value."

However, McCullers draws the character of Dr. Copeland with dignity, intellect and integrity that foreshadow the charismatic personae of Dr. Martin Luther King, Jr., and Malcolm X. Dr. Copeland's public and private ruminations on "the strong, true purpose" of his mission compel the reader to examine the pattern of racial prejudice that is so prominent in the fabric of American culture.

McCullers approaches the subject of homosexuality with compassionate subtlety. The tenderness of such scenes as John Singer's loving preparation of gifts to take to his hospitalized friend and his return to the house he has shared with Antonapoulos serve to disarm the reader's homophobia. "Singer looked down at the dark front door. He thought of them going out together in the morning and coming home at night. There was the broken place in the pavement where Antonapoulos had stumbled once and hurt his elbow. There was the mailbox where their bill from the light company came each month. He could feel the warm touch of his friend's arm against his fingers."

Ironically, though Singer's love for Antonapoulos is his only joy and his reason for living, homosexuality is one of the few characteristics not attributed to him by the novel's other characters. The poor believe him to be poor and downtrodden; the rich believe he is a wealthy eccentric; the Jews believe he is a Jew; the textile unionists believe he is an organizer for the C.I.O. Dr. Copeland remembers him as a "righteous white man of understanding." As a result, Singer's suicide, which McCullers so unequivocally ties to Antonapoulos' death, is incomprehensible to the other characters.

However, those same readers who shared Singer's pain at the death of Antonapoulos, if their reactions can be gauged by those of the critics, had a difficult time with the blatantly homosexual theme of *Reflections in a Golden Eye*. In retrospect, it is amazing that McCullers' popularity survived the publication of *Reflections in a Golden Eye*, which offered readers no sympathetic characters or relationships to ameliorate the shock value of its focus on Captain Penderton's sexual obsession with Private Williams. The critics were dismayed that McCullers chose to focus on homosexuality, asking, according to Tennessee Williams (in his introduction to the New Classics Series edition of *Reflections in a Golden Eye*), "Why [does she] write about such *dreadful* things?" This work does not celebrate homosexuality. In a scene reminiscent of D. H. Lawrence's writings, McCullers exposes the reader to the paradoxical experi-

ence of unwanted homosexual attraction. Captain Penderton, riding in a deep wood on the military reservation, has been thrown by his wife's horse, Firebird, and is discovered by a nude Private Williams who has been sunbathing in a nearby clearing: "It had happened so quickly that the Captain had not found a chance to sit up or to utter a word. At first he could feel only astonishment. He dwelt on the pure–cut lines of the young man's body. He called out something inarticulate and received no reply. A rage came in him. He felt a rush of hatred for the soldier that was as exorbitant as the joy he had experienced on runaway Firebird. All the humiliations, the envies and the fears of his life found vent in this great anger."

Reflections in a Golden Eye also challenges American society's insistence on the inviolable sanctity of heterosexual marriage by revealing the dysfunctional underside of that institution, an examination replicated 20 years later in Edward Albee's 1962 classic, *Who's Afraid of Virginia Woolf.*

With her next major work, *The Member of the Wedding*, McCullers returns to the gentler approach of *The Heart Is a Lonely Hunter*. The focus is again on the alienation of the individual, with race and gender identification continuing to be the primary examples of how our society isolates its members. The character of Frankie Addams, whose prototype was Mick Kelly in *The Heart Is a Lonely Hunter*, has reached the pivotal age of 12. She is portrayed in the throes of puberty, caught between the freedom of her accustomed androgyny and the hormonal pull of her impending womanhood. Her rapid growth causes her to worry that she may be a freak, like those that so fascinate and repel her at the sideshow: "Frankie had wandered around the tent and looked at every booth. She was afraid of all the Freaks, for it seemed to her that they looked at her in a secret way and tried to connect their eyes with hers, as though to say: we know you. She was afraid of their long Freak eyes."

No longer content to be a child, but unable to shoulder the emotional responsibility of being an adult, Frankie lives in the twilight world of adolescent fantasy where she is free to travel, mingling with the rich and famous, and to enjoy the security of a committed relationship between herself and her brother and his bride. Her sexuality is as changeable as the southern summer weather: at one moment she imagines herself as a marine decorated for bravery, and, in the next moment, she fancies herself as a member of the Women's Army Corps. In her ideal world, "all human beings would be light brown color with blue eyes and black hair. There would be no colored people and no white people to make the colored people feel cheap and sorry all through their lives," and "people could instantly change back and forth from boys to girls, whichever way they felt like and wanted." Her constant companion, six–year–old John Henry, frequently illustrates this ability to "change back and forth" by suddenly showing up in Frankie's cast off dresses and playing with dolls.

Finally, Frankie's ideals are defeated by the demands of acculturation and maturation. She eschews androgyny, calling herself first F. Jasmine and then Frances as her sexuality develops. She makes a new friend, Mary Littlejohn, who introduces her to the privileges of white society, and she even comes to relish the superiority she feels it bestows upon her. The reader feels the regret of losing Frankie as keenly as the death of John Henry.

With *Clock without Hands*, McCullers again brings the reader face to face with the issues of racial bigotry and homophobia. The story of an aging bigot who believes he will singlehandedly raise both the South and a grandson who is in love with a young man of mixed blood, *Clock without Hands* searches for a new definition of passion that transcends the grinding forces of heritage and death.

The old definition (exemplified by ex–congressman Judge Clane, whom the press once described as "one of the fixed stars in that glorious firmament of Southern statesmen") encompasses the fever of racial hatred, the fire of holy homophobia, and the heat of Confederate patriotism. To Judge Clane has fallen the responsibility of raising his orphaned grandson, Jester, whom he plans to send to West Point; but Jester's interests include flying, music, and the young mulatto man, Sherman Pew, who serves as his grandfather's secretary.

Jester does not, at the outset, think of himself as homosexual, however. Having studied the famous *Kinsey Report* regarding the sexual behavior of American men, Jester has decided that "if it turned out he was homosexual like men in the *Kinsey Report*, ... he would kill himself." Yet, in confronting and defying the racial hatred that is the hallmark of his southern heritage, he finds the courage to acknowledge the depth and nature of his feelings for Sherman. Sherman's death at the hands of the town's rednecks releases Jester to take a new look at his world. As he flies above the landscape he marvels at the symmetry and mathematical precision of his environment: "From this height you do not see man and the details of his humiliation. The earth from a great distance is perfect and whole. But this is an order foreign to the heart, and to love the earth you must come closer.... From the air men are shrunken and they have an automatic look, like wound–up dolls. They seem to move mechanically among haphazard miseries. You do not see their eyes. And finally this is intolerable. The whole earth from a great distance means less than one long look into a pair of human eyes. Even the eyes of the enemy."

McCullers offers no magic formula for the defeat of bigotry. There are no easy answers or "happy ever after" endings in her works. Her characters do not save the world, and, in some cases (e.g., John Singer, Sherman Pew, Private Williams and Dr. Copeland), they are unable even to save themselves.

The epiphany revealed to Jester in his flight with Sherman's murderer contains the essence of Carson McCullers' work: that the variety and complexity of humanity are what make life worthwhile. That, ultimately, love and life are richer if, instead of being blind to differences like color and gender, differences are accepted as enhancements of our species.

—Pamela Bigelow

———

McNALLY, Terrence. American playwright and author of screenplays. Born in St. Petersburg, Florida, 3 November 1939. Educated at schools in Corpus Christi, Texas; Columbia University (Henry Adams traveling fellow, 1960), B.A. 1960 (Phi Beta Kappa). Stage manager at Actor's Studio, New York, 1961; tutor to John Steinbeck's children, 1961–62; film critic for *The Seventh Art*, 1963–65; assistant editor for *Columbia College Today*, New York City, 1965–66. Member of American Academy of Arts and Letters, Dramatists Guild (vice–president since 1981). **Recipient:** Stanley Award, 1962; runner–up for Drama Desk Award, 1969; Obie Award, 1974; Dramatists Guild Hull Warriner Award for *Bad Habits*, 1974, for *Frankie and Johnny in the Clair de Lune*, 1987, and *The Lisbon*

Traviata, 1989; Emmy Award for best writing in a miniseries of special for *Andre's Mother*, 1990; Tony Award for Best Book of a Musical for *Kiss of the Spiderwoman*, 1993; Achievements in Playwrighting citations from American Academy of Arts and Letters and National Institute of Arts and Letters; two Guggenheim fellowships, a Rockefeller grant, and a Lucille Lortel Award. Agent: Gilbert Parker, William Morris Agency, 1350 Avenue of the Americas, New York, New York 10019, U.S.A.

WRITINGS

Plays

The Roller Coaster, in *Columbia Review* (New York), spring 1960.
And Things That Go Bump in the Night (produced as *There Is Something Out There*, New York, 1962; revised and produced Minneapolis, Minnesota, 1964; New York, 1965; London, 1977). New York, Dramatists Play Service, 1966; in *Playwrights for Tomorrow I*, edited by Arthur H. Ballet, Minneapolis, University of Minnesota Press, 1966; in *The Ritz, and Other Plays*, 1976.
The Lady of the Camellias (adaptation of book by Alexandre Dumas of play by Giles Cooper; produced New York, 1963).
Tour (produced as part of *The Scene*, Los Angeles, 1967; as part of *Collision Course*, New York, 1968; London, 1971). Published as *Collision Course*, New York, Random House, 1968; in *Apple Pie: Three One–Act Plays*, 1968.
Next (produced Stockbridge, Massachusetts, 1967; New York, 1969; London, 1971). Published in *Apple Pie: Three One–Act Plays*, 1968; in *Sweet Eros, Next, and Other Plays*, 1969.
Botticelli (televised, 1968; produced Los Angeles, 1971; London, 1972). Published in *Apple Pie: Three One–Act Plays*, 1968; in *Sweet Eros, Next, and Other Plays*, 1969; in *Off–Broadway Plays 2*, London, Penguin, 1972.
Apple Pie: Three One–Act Plays (contains *Tour*, *Next*, and *Botticelli*). New York, Dramatists Play Service, 1968.
Sweet Eros (produced New York, 1968; London, 1971). Published as *Sweet Eros, Next, and Other Plays*, 1969; in *Off–Broadway Plays 2*, London, Penguin, 1972.
Witness (produced New York, 1968; London, 1972). Published in *Sweet Eros, Next, and Other Plays*, 1969.
Noon (produced as part of *Chiaroscuro*, Spoleto, Italy, 1968; as part of *Morning, Noon, and Night*, New York, 1968). Published in *Morning, Noon, and Night*, 1969.
¡Cuba Si! (produced New York, 1968). Published in *Sweet Eros, Next, and Other Plays*, 1969; in *Three Plays: ¡Cuba Si!, Bringing It All Back Home, Last Gasps*, 1970.
Here's Where I Belong (produced New York, 1968).
Last Gasps (televised, 1969). Published in *Three Plays: ¡Cuba Si!, Bringing It All Back Home, Last Gasps*, 1970.
Sweet Eros, Next, and Other Plays (contains *Sweet Eros, Botticelli, Next*, and *Witness*). New York, Random House, 1969.
With Israel Horovitz and Leonard Melfi, *Morning, Noon, and Night*. New York, Random House, 1969.
Bringing It All Back Home (produced New York, 1969). Published in *Three Plays: ¡Cuba Si!, Bringing It All Back Home, Last Gasps*, 1970; in *The Ritz, and Other Plays*, 1976.
Three Plays: ¡Cuba Si!, Bringing It All Back Home, Last Gasps. New York, Dramatists Play Service, 1970.

Bad Habits: Ravenswood and Dunelawn (produced New York, 1971). New York, Dramatists Play Service, 1974; in *The Ritz, and Other Plays*, 1976.

Where Has Tommy Flowers Gone? (produced New York, 1971). New York, Dramatists Play Service, 1972; in *The Ritz, and Other Plays*, 1976.

Let It Bleed (produced as part of *City Stops*, New York, 1972).

Whiskey (produced New York, 1973). New York, Dramatists Play Service, 1973; in *The Ritz, and Other Plays*, 1976.

The Ritz (produced as *The Tubs*, New Haven, Connecticut, 1974; revised and produced as *The Ritz*, New York, 1975). Published in *The Ritz, and Other Plays*, 1976.

The Golden Age (produced New York, 1975).

The Ritz, and Other Plays (contains *The Ritz; And Things That Go Bump in the Night; Bringing It All Back Home; Bad Habits: Ravenswood and Dunelawn; Where Has Tommy Flowers Gone?;* and *Whiskey*). New York, Dodd, Mead, 1976.

Broadway, Broadway (produced East Hampton, New York, 1979).

The Lisbon Traviata (broadcast, 1979; produced New York, 1985). New York, Dramatists Play Service, 1986.

It's Only a Play: A Comedy (produced New York, 1982). New York, Dramatists Play Service, 1986.

The Rink: A New Musical, music by John Kander (produced New York, 1984; Manchester, 1987). London and New York, S. French, 1985.

Three Plays by Terrence McNally. New York, Dutton, 1990.

Frankie and Johnny in the Clair de Lune (produced New York, 1987; and in London West End). New York, Dutton, 1991.

Lips Together, Teeth Apart (produced Off–Broadway, 1992). New York, Dutton, 1992.

A Perfect Ganesh (produced New York, 1993).

Screenplays

The Ritz (based on his play of the same title), Warner Bros., 1977.

Frankie and Johnny (based on his play *Frankie and Johnny in the Clair de Lune*), Paramount, 1991.

Television Plays

Botticelli, 1968.
Last Gasps, 1969.
The 5:48 (adaptation of story by John Cheever), PBS, 1979.
"Mama Malone" series, 1983.
Andre's Mother, "American Playhouse" Series, PBS, 1990.

Other

Author of book, *Kiss of the Spider Woman* (based on novel by Manuel Puig; produced in London West End, 1992).
Author of book, *The Rink*.

*

Interviews: "'Ritz' Writer Terrence McNally Is Not an Instinctive Loner" by E. Donnell Stoneman, in *Advocate*, 26 January 1977, 31; "Some Enchanted Arachnid: Playwright Terrence McNally Looks Ahead To a Musical *Kiss of the Spider Woman*" by Steve Warren, in *Advocate*, 24 October 1988, 64–65.

Critical Sources: "Terrence McNally" by Gaynor F. Bradish, in *Contemporary Dramatists*, fourth edition, St. James Press, 1988; "Lanford Wilson and Terrence McNally: On Love, Responsibility, and Sexual Obsession" by L. Bennetts, in *Vogue*, February 1988.

*   *   *

Terrence McNally's creative spirit has produced a large number of works—chiefly plays and screenplays—which span four decades, touching upon many aspects of the "human animal" with a clear eye and deep sensitivity for wry realities. Almost from the outset, McNally's plays have been well–received by both audiences and critics (if occasionally with uncertainty about the author's choice of subject matter). Homosexuality first appears as a theme in *And Things That Go Bump in the Night,* a drama peopled by a family hiding from reality. Into this milieu comes Clarence, an ill–fated character lured to the dysfunctional home by the son (a closeted gay man full of self hatred). As the play progresses, a deliberately confusing series of events ensues and Clarence is driven to suicide. A feeling of grand opera permeates the work, even to the extent of having characters sing portions of various arias and refer to the female lead using the gay slang term "opera queen."

By the time McNally produced *Bringing It All Back Home* five years later, the new frankness of discussion spawned, in part, by the anger of the Stonewall Riots was apparent, with the terms "homosexual" and "lesbian" clearly spelled out and used by the two children whose brother had been killed in Viet Nam. This depiction of homosexual themes continues in *Ravenswood,* where the residents of a resort dedicated to the saving of troubled marriages include Hiram and Francis, a male couple of many years' standing who add to the action with their incessant squabbling. The couple eventually admit to themselves and the audience that "the only reason we stay together is because no one else in the world would put up with us."

McNally's use of homosexual themes and characters eventually resulted in what is considered by many critics the consummate gay farce, *The Ritz.* Carrying on the comedic tradition of such masters of the art as Georges Feydeau, McNally uses virtually every stereotype of New York gay life available to depict the adventures of a straight man hiding out in the famous bathhouse from a brother–in–law who wants to do him out of the family garbage business. In the course of the play, everything from the Broadway establishment to the Mafia and the Andrews Sisters is lampooned without mercy. Despite objections from some liberationists about McNally's characters, *The Ritz* played for 50 weeks on Broadway.

As with *And Things That Go Bump in the Night,* obsession with grand opera performance is at the heart of *The Lisbon Traviata.* Principally revolving around an unheard recording of the opera by Maria Callas desperately sought by one of the main characters, the play takes as its theme the problems of communication between gay men. According to this work, life is merely an opera script to be played out in full, even to the extent of inflicting serious physical injury on one's lover (with medical assistance deferred so that the stanza being heard will not be interrupted).

McNally joined the ranks of playwrights attempting to transfer the complex trauma of AIDS to the stage with his 1990 work for television, *Andre's Mother;* the playwright later wrote the book for the popular musical adaptation of Manuel Puig's *Kiss of the Spider Woman.* Gaynor F. Bradish, in an essay for *Contemporary Drama-*

tists, concludes: "In a theater—in a world, for that matter—always in need of wit and intelligence, Terrence McNally is a very special asset indeed."

—*Robert B. Marks Ridinger*

———

MERRILL, James Ingram. American poet, novelist, playwright, and author of short fiction. Born in New York City, 3 March 1926. Educated at Amherst College, Amherst, Massachusetts, B.A. 1947. Companion of author David Jackson. Contributor to periodicals, including *Hudson Review* and *Poetry.* Member, National Institute of Arts and Letters. **Recipient:** Oscar Blumenthal Prize, 1947; *Poetry* magazine's Levinson Prize, 1949; *Poetry* magazine's Harriet Monroe Memorial Prize, 1951; Morton Dauwen Zabel Memorial Prize for "From the Cupola," 1965; National Book Award in poetry for *Nights and Days,* 1967; Pulitzer Prize for *Divine Comedies,* 1976; Bollingen Prize in Poetry for *Braving the Elements,* 1978; National Book Award in poetry for *Mirabell: Books of Number,* 1979; National Arts Club's Medal of Honor for literature, 1989; Rebekah Johnson Bobbitt National Prize for Poetry, 1990. D.Litt, Amherst College; 1968. Address: 107 Water Street, Stonington, Connecticut 06378, U.S.A.

WRITINGS

Poetry

Jim's Book: A Collection of Poems and Short Stories. New York, privately printed, 1942.
The Black Swan, and Other Poems. Athens, Greece, Icarus, 1946.
First Poems. New York, Knopf, 1951.
Short Stories. Pawlet, Vermont, Banyan Press, 1954.
A Birthday Cake for David. Pawlet, Vermont, Banyan Press, 1955.
The Country of a Thousand Years of Peace. New York, Knopf, 1959; revised, New York, Atheneum, 1970.
Selected Poems. London, Chatto & Windus/Hogarth Press, 1961.
Water Street. New York, Atheneum, 1962.
Violent Pastoral. Privately printed, 1965.
Nights and Days. New York, Atheneum, and London, Chatto & Windus/Hogarth Press, 1966.
The Fire Screen. New York, Atheneum, 1969; London, Chatto & Windus, 1970.
Braving the Elements. New York, Atheneum, 1972; London, Chatto & Windus/Hogarth Press, 1973.
Two Poems: From the Cupola and the Summer People. London, Chatto & Windus, 1972.
Yannina. New York, Phoenix Book Shop, 1973.
The Yellow Pages: 59 Poems. Cambridge, Massachusetts, Temple Bar Bookshop, 1974.
Divine Comedies. New York, Atheneum, 1976; London, Oxford Press, 1977.
Metamorphosis of 741. Pawlet, Vermont, Banyan Press, 1977.
Mirabell: Books of Number. New York, Atheneum, 1978; as "Mirabell's Books of Number" in *The Changing Light at Sandover,* 1982.
Ideas, etc. Jordan Davies, 1980.
Scripts for the Pageant. New York, Atheneum, 1980; in *The Changing Light at Sandover,* 1982.
Santorini: Stopping the Leak. Worcester, Massachusetts, Metacom Press, 1982.
Marbled Paper. Salem, Oregon, Seluzicki Press, 1982.
From the First Nine: Poems 1946–1976. New York, Atheneum, 1982
The Changing Light at Sandover. New York, Atheneum, 1982.
Souvenirs. Nadja, 1984.
Bronze. Nadja, 1984.
Late Settings. New York, Atheneum, 1985.
The Inner Room. New York, Knopf, 1988.
Selected Poems. 1946–1985. New York, Knopf, 1992.

Novels

The Seraglio. New York, Knopf, 1957; London, Chatto & Windus, 1958.
The (Diblos) Notebook. New York, Atheneum, and London, Chatto & Windus, 1965.

Plays

The Birthday: A Play in Verse (produced Massachusetts, 1947).
Tithonus: A Play in Three Acts, 1954.
The Immortal Husband (produced New York, 1955). Published in *Playbook: Plays for a New Theater,* New York, New Directions, 1956.
The Bait (produced New York, 1953). Published in *Artists' Theatre: Four Plays,* edited by Herbert Machiz, New York, Grove Press, 1960.

Other

Recitative: Prose (essays and interviews). San Francisco, North Point Press, 1986.
James Merrill: A Different Person (memoir). New York, Knopf, 1993.

*

Adaptations: *The Changing Light at Sandover* was adapted for the stage as *Voices from Sandover,* produced at Harvard University, Cambridge, Massachusetts, and the Guggenheim Museum, New York.

Manuscript Collections: Washington University Libraries, St. Louis, Missouri.

Interviews: With Ashley Brown, in *Shenandoah,* summer 1968, 3–15; with Donald Sheehan, in *Contemporary Literature,* winter 1968, 1–14; "The Poet: Private" by David Kalstone, in *Saturday Review,* 2 December 1972, 43–45.

Bibliography: "James Merrill: A Bibliographical Checklist" by Jack

W. C. Hagstrom and George Bixby, in *American Book Collector,* November/December 1983, 34–47.

Critical Sources: *Babel to Byzantium* by James Dickey, New York, Farrar, Strauss, 1968; *Alone with America: Essays on the Art of Poetry in the United States since 1950* by Richard Howard, New York, Atheneum, 1971, 327–48; *Five Temperaments: Elizabeth Bishop, Robert Lowell, James Merrill, Adrienne Rich, John Ashbery,* edited by David Kalstone, New York, Oxford University Press, 1977; *The Homosexual Tradition in American Poetry* by Robert K. Martin, Austin, University of Texas Press, 1979; review by Charles Molesworth, in *New Republic,* 26 July 1980; "James Merrill" by Willard Spiegelman, in *Dictionary of Literary Biography,* Volume 5: *American Poets since World War II,* Detroit, Gale, 1980, 53–65; *James Merrill* by Ross Labrie, Boston, Twayne Publishers, 1982; *The Occasions of Poetry: Essays in Criticism and Autobiography,* edited by Tom Gunn, London, Faber, 1982; *James Merrill: An Introduction to the Poetry* by Judith Moffett, New York, Columbia University Press, 1984; *The Consuming Myth: The Work of James Merrill* by Stephen Yenser, Cambridge, Harvard University Press, 1987.

*   *   *

Commenting on poet James Merrill's early career, Richard Howard wrote in *Alone with America* that "the jealous voice of a man capable of no more than objets d'art addressing a man capable of an art transcending objects might easily be the voice of the early James Merrill apostrophizing the writer he was to become: one who managed to make what was merely his poetry into what was necessarily his life." It is a telling observation, for Merrill's career has opened out into life. From the perfect technical intricacy of his early poems, his mastery of language and meter has been joined by a less self–conscious voice—the open, more personally revealing autobiography he uses in such later works as *The Changing Light at Sandover.*

Merrill was born into a wealthy New York family; his father, a stockbroker, was a founder of Merrill, Lynch, Pierce, Fenner & Smith. The material advantages Merrill enjoyed as a child allowed him to attend private schools that placed a high value on the study of verse. In addition, he was greatly influenced by a governess who was fluent in both German and French from whom he gained an early love of language. Despite such early influences, some critics have felt that such affluence resulted in the late maturation of Merrill's natural poetic voice. In *Babel to Byzantium,* James Dickey describes the experience of reading the poet's early works as "[entering] a realm of connoisseurish aesthetic contemplation, where there are no things more serious than gardens (usually formal), dolls, swans, statues, works of art, operas, delightful places in Europe, the ancient gods in tasteful and thought–provoking array, more statues, many birds and public parks, and, always, the 'lovers,' wandering through it all as if they surely lived."

It may be more important to acknowledge that Merrill's position of affluence gave him an unusual breadth of reference that, in the early poems, seems merely rarified, but which, over time, has provided, as David Kalstone points out in the introduction to *Five Temperaments,* "figures who have become resonant in his memory." The objects and places Merrill's reader meets in his early poems appear again throughout the poet's later work, but the figures gain a depth of significance and allusiveness through iteration and the reader's growing familiarity with them. The fine, the exotic, and the mythic are regularly brought together with the commonplace. Private loves and losses have meaning; like the spirits of the dead in *The Changing Light at Sandover,* they surround the living.

Merrill has been criticized for a perceived sensuality and an overrefined sense of detachment in his lyric poems, but the criticism is frequently merely veiled homophobia. Certainly, the sensual is central to Merrill's work. The senses, however, are not untutored—rather, art is their medium, drawing out the merely brutal in an engagement of thought and spirit. "In arguing that the sensual and the spiritual are indivisible," Helen Vendler has written, reviewing *Mirabell: Books of Number,* "Merrill places trust in the affections as a middle term. Faithlessness and infidelities are acts not of the flesh but of the spirit, and they occur when affection doubts or betrays its own powers."

An epic work of 560 pages, *The Changing Light at Sandover* is perhaps Merrill's most well–known work. A trilogy composed of the previously–published "The Book of Ephraim," *Mirabell: Book of Numbers,* and *Scripts for the Pageant,* and concluded by a new coda, the work records years of ouija board sessions that Merrill and his companion David Jackson conducted with spirits from the netherworld. For Merrill, art carries back into life the power to shape, extending the metaphor of the ouija board into an argument on the nature of artistic creation. The spirits with whom Merrill and his lover communicate require human hosts—their "hand" (Jackson) and their "scribe" (Merrill)—if they are to translate themselves from pure timeless abstraction into language and action. "WE ARE THE INSTRUMENTS OF REPLY," a spirit tells them, "ALL THESE OUR CONVERSATIONS COME FROM MEMORY & WORD BANKS / TAPPED IN U."

The "sacred books" of James Merrill have been regarded among this century's major poetic works. Critic Charles Molesworth once noted of the poet in the *New Republic,* "His work asks comparison with that of Yeats and Blake, if not Milton and Dante. But the clearest analogue may be that of Byron, who, desiring a scale both intimate and grand, yet wanting a hero, decided to fill the role himself." Merrill has written of the poet Eugenio Montale, as others have written of Merrill himself: "Any word can lead you from the kitchen–garden into really inhuman depths.... The two natures were always one, but it takes an extraordinary poet to make us feel that, feel it in our spines."

—*Kevin Ray*

———

MEW, Charlotte (Mary). British poet, essayist, and short story writer. Also wrote as Charles Catty. Born in London, 15 November 1870 (some sources say 1869). Attended Gower Street School for Girls in London, briefly boarded with headmistress Lucy Harrison, a famous suffragist; attended lectures at University College, London. Contributor to London periodicals, including *The Yellow Book, Temple Bar, The Englishwoman,* and the *Nation.* **Recipient:** A Civil List pension from the British government, at the recommendation of Walter de la Mare, Thomas Hardy, and John Masefield, 1923. *Died in London, by drinking disinfectant, 24 March 1928.*

WRITINGS

Poetry

The Farmer's Bride (includes "The Forest Road"). London, Poetry
 Bookshop, 1916; enlarged, London, Poetry Bookshop, 1921; as
 Saturday Market, New York, Macmillan, 1921.
The Rambling Sailor, edited by Alida Monro. London, Poetry
 Bookshop, 1929.

Collected Works

Collected Poems, edited by Alida Monro (this edition omits the
 last 54 lines of the poem "In Nunhead Cemetery"). London,
 Duckworth, 1953; New York, Macmillan, 1954.
Collected Poems and Prose, edited by Val Warner. Manchester,
 Carcanet Press, 1981; London, Virago Press, 1982.

Uncollected Poetry

"Song of Sorrow" (as Charles Catty), in *The Yellow Book* (London),
 April 1986.
"The Wind and the Tree" (as Charles Catty), in *The Yellow Book*
 (London), October 1986.

Other

"The Farmer's Bride" and "The Quiet House," in *The Norton Anthology of Literature by Women: The Tradition in English,* edited
 by Sandra M. Gilbert and Susan Gubar. New York, Norton, 1985.
"On the Road to the Sea," in *The Penguin Book of Homosexual
 Verse,* edited by Stephen Coote. New York, Viking Penguin, 1986.
"The Farmer's Bride," "In Nunhead Cemetery," and "On the Road
 to the Sea," in *The Faber Book of 20th Century Women's Poetry,*
 edited by Fleur Adcock. London, Faber and Faber, 1987.
"The Farmer's Bride," "Beside the Bed," and "My Heart Is Lame,"
 in *British Women Writers: An Anthology,* edited by Dale Spender
 and Janet Todd. New York, Peter Bedrick Books, 1989.
"Absence" and "The Cenotaph," in *The Gender of Modernism: A
 Critical Anthology,* edited by Bonnie Kime Scott, with an introduction to Mew by Celeste Schenck. Bloomington and Indianapolis, Indiana University Press, 1990.

*

Manuscript Collections: British Library, London; the Poetry Col-
lection, the Lockwood Memorial Library, State University of New
York at Buffalo; and the Berg Collection, New York Public Library,
New York.

Biography: "The Mystery of Charlotte Mew and May Sinclair:
An Inquiry" by Theophilus E. M. Boll, in *Bulletin of the New York
Public Library,* September 1970, 445–453; "The Charlotte Mew–
May Sinclair Relationship: A Reply" by Mary. C. Davidow, in
Bulletin of the New York Public Library, March 1971, 295–300;
Charlotte Mew and Her Friends by Penelope Fitzgerald, London,
Collins, 1984; with introduction by Brad Leithauser and selected
poems, Reading, Massachusetts, Addison–Wesley, 1988.

Critical Sources: "Charlotte Mew: Biography and Criticism" (dissertation) by Mary C. Davidow, Brown University, 1960; *Modern
British Poetry* by Louis Untermeyer, New York, Harcourt Brace
and World, 1962; "Mary Magdalene and the Bride: the Work of
Charlotte Mew" by Val Warner, in *Poetry Nation Review* (Manchester), Number 4, 1975, 92–106; *A Reader's Guide to Fifty Modern
British Poets* by Michael Schmidt, London, Heinemann, 1979; introduction by Val Warner, in *Collected Poems and Prose,* edited by
Warner, London, Virago Press, 1981, ix–xxii; "Charlotte Mew and
the Unrepentant Magdalene: A Myth in Transition" by Linda
Mizejewski, in *Texas Studies in Language and Literature* (Austin),
fall 1984, 282–302; "Feminism and Deconstruction: Re–Construct-
ing the Elegy" by Celeste Schenck, in *Tulsa Studies in Women's
Literature,* spring 1986, 13–27; *Sexchanges,* Volume 2 of *No Man's
Land: The Place of the Woman Writer in the Twentieth Century,* by
Sandra M. Gilbert and Susan Gubar, New Haven, Connecticut, Yale
University Press, 1989; "Exiled by Genre: Modernism, Canonic-
ity, and the Politics of Exclusion" by Celeste Schenck, in *Women's
Writing in Exile: Alien and Critical,* edited by Mary Lynn Broe and
Angela Ingram, Chapel Hill, University of North Carolina Press,
1989, 225–250; *Victorian Women Poets: Writing Against the Heart*
by Angela Leighton, London, Harvester Wheatsheaf, 1992.

*   *   *

Charlotte Mew might be characterized as a study in contradiction: a self–professed passionate nature, yet noted for her reserve;
a social conformist in her attitudes toward family and society, yet
noted for her mannish clothing and probable lesbianism. Praised by
both the late Victorian Thomas Hardy and the feminist modernist
Virginia Woolf, and championed by Harold and Alida Monro of the
Poetry Bookshop, Mew's poetry was frequently rejected as too
formally irregular for the anthologies of her day and too formally
traditional to be considered modernist. The work of Mew has largely
escaped contemporary critical attention as well. However, her appearance in recent anthologies of women's literature and gay/les-
bian literature indicates a critical reexamination—primarily by feminists—of her work, and the recovery of her literary status as an
important though neglected turn–of–the–century writer.

In 1920, Virginia Woolf said of Mew that she was "unlike anyone
else." Indeed, it is Charlotte Mew's singularity that has troubled
the critical recovery of her work, particularly any attempt to place
her in a historical/literary period. Like many women writers of her
day, Mew wrote in predominantly traditional forms, primarily the
dramatic monologue, which made her poems reminiscent of Victorian poetics, rather than the formal experimentalism of other early
twentieth century writers. Yet contemporary critics have noted
that her traditional forms feature irregular rhythms which reflect
the inner turmoil of her speakers. In this sense Mew's work is
similar to modernist experiments with language and stream of consciousness. Her work then seems to fall within the transition between Victorianism and modernism, and defies easy categorization
by period. Celeste Schenck has argued in "Exiled by Genre: Modernism, Canonicity, and the Politics of Exclusion" that Mew should
be considered a radical modernist, not for her poetics but for her
politics, specifically her emphasis on female sexuality, including
the autoerotic and lesbian. However, Angela Leighton argues in
Victorian Women Poets: Writing Against the Heart for an understanding of Mew as a late Victorian whose works encompass the

themes of Victorian poetry, including that of the fallen woman or prostitute.

Despite the problems of periodization, most critics agree that Mew's emphasis on female experience and female sexuality is central to a historical understanding of her work. A further problem then arises in how to determine the sexuality of Mew, who never admitted to, or, as far as biographers can determine, fulfilled lesbian desire. Val Warner notes, in his introduction to Mew's *Collected Poems and Prose,* that her love of women strongly figures in the themes of "desire and negation, passion and renunciation" that appear throughout her work. Warner adds, "There is no sign in her work that Charlotte Mew accepted her sexuality, and given her concern for appearances, it can hardly be expected of her." Mew was probably a lesbian, yet her sexuality was marked by repression and fear. Penelope Fitzgerald, in *Charlotte Mew and Her Friends,* repeatedly notes Mew's concern for social respectability. Fitzgerald quite persuasively establishes Mew's repressed lesbianism, basing her claims on Mew's strong emotional attachments to women throughout her life, Mew's erotic poetry, and the work of Theophilus Boll. Boll, in an article in the *Bulletin of the New York Public Library,* traces rumors about Mew's attachment to the novelist May Sinclair, and he pursues a close reading of letters and poems exchanged between Mew and Sinclair. Fitzgerald traces Mew's romantic and sexual attractions not only to Sinclair, whose work Mew admired, but also to Ella D'Arcy, with whom Mew worked at *The Yellow Book.* While both women admired Mew's work and Sinclair solicited support for Mew, both women rejected Mew romantically.

A final difficulty is how one then reads Mew's sexuality into her verse. Celeste Schenck locates the strength of Mew's poetry in her lesbianism, claiming in "Exiled by Genre" that Mew has embedded "in what we have learned to call conventional poetry the secret exile of sexual preference." Reading such poems as "On the Road to the Sea" and "The Forest Road" as spoken by women to women, Schenck finds a startling lesbian eroticism in Mew's quiet verse. In "On the Road to the Sea," for example, the speaker states, "We passed each other, turned and stopped for half an hour, then went our way, / I who make other women smile did not make you." Schenck reads the conclusion of "The Forest Road"—which seems to equate desire with sickness, mutual entanglement, and death—as both a double suicide and a mutual female climax. Many other poems explore desire and romantic obsession, often denied or unfulfilled in some way. For example, in "The Farmer's Bride," Mew's most anthologized poem, a farmer addresses his mad bride, who is locked in the attic, and in "In Nunhead Cemetery," a man addresses his dead and buried fiancée. That love may further defy religious disapprobation is evident in "Absence," in which the speaker says, "But call, call, and though Christ stands / Still with scarred hands / Over my mouth, I must answer. So / I will come—He shall let me go!"

The gender of Mew's poetic speakers often seems ambiguous, and perhaps that is critical to her veiling of desire. Mew takes on numerous unstable voices—frustrated lovers, the clinically or romantically insane, fairy children, ambiguously gendered or textually confusing narrators. The speaker of "On the Road to the Sea," for example, has no clearly specified gender. Schenck reads the poem as lesbian, and the poem has been canonized as lesbian in *The Penguin Book of Homosexual Verse.* Yet letters between Mew and Florence Hardy (wife of Thomas Hardy) indicate that Mew intended a male speaker. Hardy had argued with E. M. Forster about the sex of the speaker, Forster insisting on reading the speaker as

female. Reading same–sex desire into the poems remains a tenuous project. Although modern reappraisals may cite not only Mew's biography, but also the precedent of such early critical responses as Forster's, the confusion of sexuality is at stake in any reading.

The themes of madness and death in Mew's work reflect the poet's unhappy life. Mew lost three brothers in youth, and a brother and a sister were committed to mental institutions. Mew and her sister Anne both swore never to be married, for fear of passing on a hereditary insanity. After the death of her mother in 1923, the death of Anne in 1927, and the death of her friend Thomas Hardy in 1928, Mew grew despondent. She entered a nursing home in February of 1928 to seek treatment for neurasthenia, and committed suicide soon afterward by drinking half a bottle of disinfectant.

—Ed Madden

————

MILLAY, E. Vincent. *See* **MILLAY, Edna St. Vincent.**

————

MILLAY, Edna St. Vincent. American poet and dramatist. Also wrote as E. Vincent Millay and Nancy Boyd. Born in Rockland, Maine, 22 February 1892. Attended Barnard College, 1913; Vassar College, A.B., 1917. Married Eugen Jan Boissevain in 1923. Actor with Provincetown Players, 1917–19; free–lance writer for periodicals, 1919–20; traveled in Europe, 1921–23, and the Orient, 1924; gave reading tours, beginning in 1925, and national radio broadcasts, 1932–33; president and presenter of Prix Femina Committee, early 1930s; produced propaganda verse for Writers' War Board during early 1940s. **Recipient:** *Poetry* magazine prize, 1920; Pulitzer Prize for Poetry, 1923; Helen Haire Levinson Prize, for poetry, 1931; laureate of General Federation of Women's Clubs, 1933; Gold Medal of the Poetry Society of America, 1943. Litt.D.: Tufts College, 1925, University of Wisconsin, 1933, Russell Sage College, 1933, Colby College, 1937; L.H.D.: New York University, 1937. *Died at Steepletop, Austerlitz, New York, of a heart attack, 19 October 1950.*

WRITINGS

Poetry

Renascence, and Other Poems (title poem first published under name E. Vincent Millay, in *The Lyric Year,* 1912). New York, Kennerley, 1917.

A Few Figs from Thistles: Poems and Four Sonnets. New York, Shay, 1920; enlarged as *A Few Figs from Thistles: Poems and Sonnets,* New York, Shay, 1921.

Second April. New York, Kennerley, 1921.
The Ballad of the Harp–Weaver. New York, Shay, 1922.
The Harp–Weaver, and Other Poems. New York and London, Harper, 1923.
Poems. London, Secker, 1923.
The Buck in the Snow, and Other Poems. New York and London, Harper, 1928.
Edna St. Vincent Millay's Poems Selected for Young People. New York and London, Harper, 1929.
Fatal Interview, Sonnets. New York and London, Harper, 1931.
Wine from These Grapes. New York and London, Harper, 1934.
Conversation at Midnight. New York and London, Harper, 1937.
Huntsman, What Quarry? New York and London, Harper, 1939.
Make Bright the Arrows: 1940 Notebook. New York and London, Harper, 1940.
Collected Sonnets. New York and London, Harper, 1941.
The Murder of Lidice. New York and London, Harper, 1942.
Collected Lyrics. New York and London, Harper, 1943.
Second April [and] *The Buck in the Snow,* introduction by William Ross Benet. New York, Harper, 1950.
Mine the Harvest, edited by Norma Millay. New York, Harper, and London, Hamilton, 1954.
Collected Poems, edited by Norma Millay. New York, Harper, 1956.
Memorial to D.C.

Drama

And director, *Aria da capo* (produced New York, 1919). New York, Kennerley, 1921; in *Three Plays,* 1926.
The Lamp and the Bell (produced, 1921). New York, Shay, 1921; in *Three Plays,* 1926.
Two Slatterns and a King: A Moral Interlude. Cincinnati, Ohio, Kidd, 1921; in *Three Plays,* 1926.
The King's Henchman (libretto). New York and Birmingham, Fischer, 1926; as *The King's Henchman: A Play in Three Acts,* (produced New York, 1927), New York and London, Harper, 1927.
Three Plays (contains *Two Slatterns and a King, Aria da capo,* and *The Lamp and the Bell*). New York and London, Harper, 1926.
The Princess Marries the Page: A Play in One Act. New York and London, Harper, 1932.

Other

Distressing Dialogues (essays; as Nancy Boyd). New York and London, Harper, 1924.
Edna St. Vincent Millay, edited by Hughes Mearns. New York, Simon & Schuster, 1927.
Fear. New York, Sacco–Vanzetti National League, 1927.
Translator, with George Dillon, and author of introduction, *Flowers of Evil* by Charles Baudelaire. New York and London, Harper, 1936.
Vacation Song. Hanover, New Hampshire, Baker Library Press, 1936.
"There Are No Islands, Any More": Lines Written in Passion and in Deep Concern for England, France, and My Own Country. New York and London, Harper, 1940.
Letters of Edna St. Vincent Millay, edited by Allan Ross Macdougall. New York and London, Harper, 1952.
Take up the Song. New York, Harper, 1986.

Biography: *The Indigo Bunting: A Memoir of Edna St. Vincent Millay* by Vincent Sheehan, New York, Harper, 1951; *Restless Spirit: The Life of Edna St. Vincent Millay* by Miriam Gurko, New York, Crowell, 1962; *The Poet and Her Book: A Biography of Edna St. Vincent Millay* by Jean Gould, New York, Dodd, Mead, 1969; *A Life of One's Own* by Joan Dash, New York, Harper & Row, 1973.

Bibliography: *A Bibliography of the Works of Edna St. Vincent Millay* by Karl Yost, New York, Harper, 1937.

Critical Sources: *Sex Variant Women in Literature; A Historical and Quantitative Survey* by Jeannette Howard Foster, New York, Vantage, 1956; *The Shores of Light* by Edmund Wilson, New York, Vintage Books/Random House, 1961, 744–793; *Edna St. Vincent Millay* by Norman A. Brittin, Boston, Twayne Publishers, 1967, revised, Boston, G. K. Hall, 1982; *A Poet's Alphabet* by Louise Bogan, edited by Robert Phelps and Ruth Limmer, New York, McGraw, 1970, 298–299; *Millay in Greenwich Village* by Anne Cheney, University of Alabama Press, 1975; *Edna St. Vincent Millay: A Reference Guide* by Judith Nierman, Boston, G. K. Hall, 1977; *The First Wave. Women Poets in America, 1915–1945* by William Drake, New York, Macmillan, 1987; *Masks Outrageous and Austere: Culture, Psyche, and Persona in Modern Woman Poets* by Cheryl Walker, Bloomington, Indiana University Press, 1991.

*   *   *

In her review of Edna St. Vincent Millay's *Huntsman, What Quarry?,* poet Louise Bogan called the book "a strange mixture of maturity and unresolved youth." This observation might be as aptly applied to Millay's life as a whole, as she presents herself to the world as a figure whose true identity wavers between two antitheses. Millay has been described as being both "flaming youth" and schoolmarm; she referred to herself as being both harlot and nun. She was a poet who expressed in her verse a love of freedom and risk, yet whose finest thoughts were conveyed within the strictures of the sonnet form. She was both adventurer and claustrophobe, free spirit and homesick child, public figure and elusive recluse.

Some have extended this dichotomy to include Millay's sexual identity. Unfortunately, speculation is difficult to avoid when dealing with Millay. For all the apparent openness of her poetry and letters, they actually reveal little about her private life. Her determination to protect herself from public scrutiny is demonstrated by an incident that occurred in 1948. Harper and Brothers suggested to Millay that a volume of her love poetry be published with a foreword by herself revealing "when, where, and under what impulsion" the poems were written. Millay flatly refused to participate in such a project, stating in her reply, "Of course, you have no possible way of knowing how very reticent a person I am, since I am far too reticent ever to have told you."

In her biographical study of Millay's years in Greenwich Village and her various love affairs, Anne Cheney explores the poet's lesbianism, citing "two reliable sources who prefer to remain anonymous" as her informants as to Millay's enjoyment of lesbian lovemaking. Cheney stresses the importance of the poet's Vassar years to the development of her lesbian tendencies, while Joan Dash, in *A Life of One's Own,* speculates that the roots of Millay's sexual ambiguity can be found in her childhood. Millay's youth was unorthodox for the times. Her mother, Cora Buzzell Millay, chose to divorce Henry Tolman Millay rather than continue to endure his gambling and their mutual incompatibility. This dissolution of the family unit could not have been easy on Millay or her two younger sisters, although her parents' parting was amicable and her father maintained an interest in his children. The girls spent days at a time alone, with Millay, at age 11 or 12, left in charge, while their mother worked as a district nurse to support the family.

Cora Millay was a strong–willed, unconventional woman who was herself a talented writer and musician. Her goals for her daughters were that they should develop their creative abilities and excel. She concentrated her efforts on seeing that Millay and her sisters, Norma and Kathleen, had piano and singing lessons, books, magazines, and exposure to cultural events. However, she also provided them with an example of what could happen to a highly creative woman who had traded her muse for the yoke of family responsibilities: for Cora Millay, love and marriage had resulted in a life of self–sacrifice and frustration. Millay was very conscious of the role her mother played in her own success as a poet. In a letter to her mother written as an adult, Millay wrote: "The reason I am a poet is entirely because / you wanted me to be and intended I should be, even / from the very first."

Cora Millay had intended something else for her oldest child as well—that she be a boy. To family members, Millay was always "Vincent," or "Sefe," which was short for Josephus. She seemed to have slipped into the role of "man of the house" left empty by her absent father, and did her best to create a kind of masculine persona without the benefit of a role model on which it could be based. Cora Millay's ambitions for her eldest daughter, that she be independent, self–fulfilled, and creative, were ones that even a man might have been hard–pressed to fulfill. Millay had seen the results of her father's failure to live up to her mother's expectations. As she wrote to a friend shortly after her own wedding: "I remember a swamp of [cranberries] that made a short– / cut to the railroad station when I was seven. It was / down across that swamp my father went, when my mother / told him to go & not come back. / (Or maybe she said he might come back if he would do / better—but who ever does better?)."

Millay's Vassar years provided her with relationships that were not unlike those she had experienced at home with her younger sisters. Entering college at the age of 21, already a published poet of some fame due to her much–admired poem *Renascence,* Millay became the center of an intimate group whose deep affection for each other long survived their college years. Cheney compares Millay's relationship with these young women to Sappho's with her *hetaerae.*

Memorial to D.C. was written in memory of Dorothy Coleman, a young classmate who died during the influenza epidemic in 1918. In this collection of five poems Millay mourns the loss of the physical reality of her friend, her "big eyes," "thin fingers," and "soft, indefinite–coloured hair." Yet it is the spirit, the beautiful voice, "the music of your talk," that Millay mourns the most.

The importance to Millay of physical contact and the sound of a loved one's voice is revealed in a letter to another old school chum, Anne Gardner Lynch, written in 1921 when Millay was in Europe and feeling lonely: "Oh, if I could just get my arms about you!— And stay / with you like that for hours, telling you so many / things, & listening to all that you must have to say.— / I love you very much, dear Anne, & I always shall."

While in Europe, Millay completed the play *The Lamp and the Bell,* a verse drama in five acts commissioned by the Vassar College Alumnae Association. The play, a costume drama written in the Elizabethan style, centers around the love between two royal step–sisters: Beatrice, the competent princess who runs like a boy, whistles like a boy and rides her horse astride; and Bianca, who is more delicate and sensitive. The unusual closeness of the two is mentioned several times in the play, with Bianca's mother, the queen, twice remarking on the inadvisability of leaving two girls alone together so much. Both princesses fall in love with the same man, but the ensuing complications are resolved in the end, and at the moment of Bianca's death the sisters are reconciled. The play can be seen simply as a celebration of female friendship and loyalty. But as Cheney points out, the relationship between Beatrice and Bianca parallels that between Millay and a member of her Vassar coterie, Charlotte Babcock.

Millay's Greenwich Village years, 1917 to 1920, saw a succession of male lovers, beginning with Floyd Dell and including Edmund Wilson, John Peale Bishop, and Arthur Davison Ficke. Wilson comments on the "spell" Millay "exercised on many ... of all ages and both sexes. Though wooed by many, Millay never let these relationships develop to the point that they could prove to be a threat to her freedom. Her poetry of this time reflects her determination to play at the game of love using men's rules, defiantly claiming a woman's right to be sexually free. In such poems as "Thursday," "To the Not Impossible Him," and the sonnet "I Shall Forget You Presently, My Dear," Millay personifies the flippant, fickle, hedonist who became a symbol of "flaming youth." Floyd Dell's suggestion that Millay undergo Freudian therapy in order to overcome her "sapphic tendencies" was not a welcomed one. Individuality and independence were of too high a value to Millay for her to allow anyone to pry into her inner mind. In the sonnet "Bluebeard" the poet rebukes a lover who has opened "this door you might not open" and revealed that which the poet "kept / Unto myself, lest any know me quite."

As she approached 30, Millay appears to have been torn between a desire for marriage and the fear that marriage would be the end of her as a poet. In Sonnet xxiii she asks her lover, "Cherish you then the hope I shall forget / At length, my lord, Pieria?," likening love to a "bitter crust" thrust down her throat in Sonnet xxv. In *The Concert,* the poet denies her lover's request to accompany her to a concert, saying "You are too much my lover. / You would put yourself / Between me and song."

Yet there is a wistful note to Millay's letter written from Rome on the occasion of her sister Norma's marriage: "Well, both my little sisters are young married women, and me, I am just about three months from being an old maid." The solution to Millay's quandary arrived, shortly after her return from her European sojourn, in the form of Eugen Boissevain. At age 31 Millay married a man 12 years her senior who seemed remarkably suited to her needs. Boissevain's first wife had been the suffragette Inez Milholland, with whom he had shared a brief, unpossessive "open" marriage until her death at 28. Boissevain had played the role of supportive, behind–the–scenes husband to his famous wife, and filled the same role in his marriage to Millay. Although Boissevain was successful in business, Edmund Wilson described him as having "no particular bent or talent of his own," and therefore being led "to the special vocation of assisting the careers of gifted women." Millay had the good fortune of finding a husband who was not afraid to grant her whatever freedom she wished; who was willing to take over the household tasks that Millay so feared would prove a trap; and who filled her mother's role of encouraging her to excel. The most passionate poems written during these years, the sonnet sequence entitled *Fatal Interview,* were inspired not by her marriage, but by her affair with George Dillon with whom she collaborated on a translation of Baudelaire's *Les Fleurs du Mal*. Her marriage did however provide the security, the "love inflexible," and the "militant forgiveness" which Millay had craved from childhood, perhaps from the day she stood and watched her father disappear across the cranberry swamp.

Millay's reputation as a poet was at its height during the 1920s. In 1923 she won the Pulitzer Prize for Poetry, and came to be in great demand for her poetry readings. Her popularity began to wane during the 1930s, and her propaganda writings during World War II enhanced her standing neither with the critics nor the public. The "New Critics" and advocates of "Modern" poetry did not admire Millay's romantic, traditional approach to poetry. Today's rebirth of an interest in feminism and women's studies has raised Millay from the relative obscurity into which she had fallen.

—*Jean Edmunds*

———————

MILLER, Isabel. *See* **ROUTSONG, Alma.**

———————

MILLER, Neil. American journalist and author of nonfiction. Born in Kingston, New York, 1945. Educated at Brown University, B.A.; New York University, M.A. Editor, *Gay Community News*, Boston, Massachusetts, 1975–78; staff writer, *Boston Phoenix*, 1982–86. **Recipient:** American Library Association award for lesbian and gay nonfiction, 1990; Lambda literary award for gay male nonfiction, 1990. Address: 5 Oakland Avenue, Somerville, Massachusetts 01245, U.S.A.

WRITINGS

Nonfiction

In Search of Gay America: Women and Men in a Time of Change. New York, Atlantic Monthly Press, 1989.
Out in the World: Gay and Lesbian Life from Buenos Aires to Bangkok. New York, Random House, 1992.

*

Critical Sources: Review of *In Search of Gay America: Women and Men in a Time of Change*, in *Publishers Weekly*, 24 February 1989, 217; review by Cornelia Jessey of *In Search of Gay America: Women and Men in a Time of Change*, in *Christian Century*, 17 May 1989, 536–538; review by Ben Davis of *In Search of Gay America:*

Women and Men in a Time of Change, in *Wilson Library Bulletin*, June 1989, 119; "Birth of a Queer Nation" by Matthew Parris, in *National Review*, 31 August 1992, 65–67; review by John Weir of *Out in the World: Gay and Lesbian Life from Buenos Aires to Bangkok*, in *Los Angeles Times Book Review*, 29 November 1992.

Neil Miller comments: "I am a journalist by background, and both my books are works of travel–writing and reportage. I have attempted to give a picture of lesbian and gay life outside the centers of gay male culture. In researching *In Search of Gay America: Women and Men in a Time of Change*, for example, I spent time in small towns in the south and midwest, with Latina lesbians in San Antonio, and at a black gay church in Washington, D.C. In working on *Out in the World: Gay and Lesbian Life from Buenos Aires to Bangkok*, I again spent much of my time on the periphery, eschewing the gay 'capitals' of Western Europe for Hong Kong and Johannesburg; an oasis in Egypt; and little towns on the northwest coast of Tasmania. This approach gave me an opportunity to view homosexual identity and community in their earliest stages, to observe the role that culture plays in forming ideas about sex and sexual identity. For me, both books represented a personal journey as well; they afforded me the opportunity, as a white urban gay man, to see what I had in common with gays and lesbians in far–flung parts of the United States and other societies. My travels gave me a sense of the breadth and complexity of the gay and lesbian experience—and how difficult it is to put a stamp on it, to see gay culture as monolithic, to speak about a single 'gay lifestyle'."

*   *   *

Former *Gay Community News* editor Neil Miller traveled throughout the United States to research his first book, *In Search of Gay America: Women and Men in a Time of Change,* and extended his study of homosexuality to 12 countries in *Out in the World: Gay and Lesbian Life from Buenos Aires to Bangkok.* "A book with much to say to a general audience," according to a *Publishers Weekly* reviewer, *In Search of Gay America* is a compilation of glimpses into the day–to–day lives of gays in various communities, from big cities to rural small towns. While many reviewers noted Miller's discovery that gays are often accepted in small communities, Ben Davis pointed out in *Wilson Library Bulletin* that, while "Miller does not find uniform homophobia in the small towns he visited," still "he also does not find that communities ... that have accepted individual gays have significantly changed their attitudes towards homosexuality." Noting Miller's emphasis on the desire for families expressed by many of the gay couples introduced in the book, Cornelia Jessey remarked in *Christian Century* that "Miller's point is that all people ... yearn for the family–oriented, community values so often heralded as the heart of our democracy." Detecting a new "climate of openness and communication," Jessey believes that while Miller "did not see all the changes he had hoped to find, he did discover the sense that there is no going back."

Miller's findings in *Out in the World* spotlight the vast cultural differences that impinge upon the concept of homosexuality. He locates social attitudes in the United States on a spectrum that ranges from Argentinean repression of gay gatherings to Danish government–approved gay marriages. Countries such as Egypt, Japan, and Thailand might acknowledge homosexual experiences as commonplace but reject or cannot comprehend homosexuality as a way of life. In an article for *National Review,* Matthew Parris praised the skepticism, humor, and salience that Miller brings to his "entertaining and readable prose," and found significance in the author's conclusion that "'the homosexual'—as a concept, a type, and an identity—is far from self–evident to most non–Christian and non–Jewish peoples."

—*Deborah A. Stanley*

———

MILLETT, Kate. American feminist, sculptor, photographer, painter, educator, and nonfiction writer. Born Katherine Murray Millett, St. Paul, Minnesota, 14 September 1934. Educated at University of Minnesota, Minneapolis, B.A. 1956 (Phi Beta Kappa); St. Hilda's College, Oxford University, Oxford, England M.A. 1958; Columbia University, New York, Ph.D. 1970. Married Fumio Yoshimura in 1965 (divorced in 1985). Work has appeared in numerous exhibits, including Minami Gallery, Tokyo, Japan, 1963; Judson Gallery, Greenwich Village, New York, 1967; Los Angeles Woman's Building, Los Angeles, California, 1977. Professor of English at University of North Carolina at Greensboro, 1958; kindergarten teacher in Harlem, New York, 1960–61; English teacher at Waseda University, Tokyo, 1961–62; professor of English and philosophy at Barnard College, New York, 1964–69; professor of sociology, Bryn Mawr College, Bryn Mawr, Pennsylvania, 1971; distinguished visiting professor at State College of Sacramento, California, 1971—. Contributor of numerous essays to newspapers and periodicals including *Ms., Semiotext(e), New York Times,* and *Nation.* Member of National Organization of Women; Congress of Racial Equality. Agent: Georges Borchardt, 136 East 57th Street, New York, New York, U.S.A.

WRITINGS

Nonfiction

Sexual Politics. Garden City, New York, Doubleday, 1970.
Prostitution Papers. New York, Banc Books, 1971.
Flying. New York, Knopf, 1974.
Sita. New York, Farrar, Straus, 1977.
The Basement. New York, Simon & Schuster, 1980.
Going to Iran. New York, Coward, McCann, 1981.
The Loony–Bin Trip. New York, Simon & Schuster, 1990.
The Politics of Cruelty. New York, Norton, 1994.

Screenplays

And director, *Three Lives,* Impact Films, New York.

*

Interviews: "The Last Interview in this Issue" by Jeff Goldberg, in *Unmuzzled Ox,* 4:3, 1977, 132–133; "Kate Millett" by Mark

Blasius, in *Semiotext(e), Intervention Series 2: Loving Children* (New York), summer 1980.

Critical Sources: Review by Jonathan Yardley of *Sexual Politics,* in *New Republic,* 1 August 1970, 26, 30–32; review of *Sexual Politics,* in *New York Times Book Review,* 6 September, 1970, 8, 10, 12; review by Germaine Greer of *Sexual Politics,* in *Listener* (London), 25 March 1971, 355–356; review by Jane Wilson of *Flying,* in *New York Times Book Review,* 23 June 1974, 2–3; *Psychoanalysis and Feminism* by Juliet Mitchell, New York, Pantheon Books, 1974; "The Lady's Not For Spurning" by Annette Kolodny, in *Contemporary Literature,* autumn, 1976, 541–562; *Lesbiana: Book Reviews From the Ladder* by Barbara Grier, Tallahassee, Naiad Press, 1976; review by Sara Sandborn of *Sita,* in *New York Times Book Review,* 29 May 1977, 13, 20; review by Anne Taylor of *The Basement,* in *New Republic,* 7–14 July 1979, 35–36; review by Joyce Carol Oates of *The Basement,* in *New York Times Book Review,* 9 September 1979, 14, 24, 26; "Beyond Ideology: Kate Millett and the Case for Henry Miller," in *Perspectives on Pornography,* edited by Gary Day and Clive Bloom, London, MacMillian, 1988; review by Florence King of *The Loony–Bin Trip,* in *Chronicles: A Magazine of American Culture,* June 1990, 43–4; review of *The Loony–Bin Trip,* in *New York Times Book Review,* 3 June 1990, 12; *The Safe Sea of Women: Lesbian Fiction, 1969–1989* by Bonnie Zimmerman, Boston, Beacon Press, 1990.

*   *   *

Since the publication of *Sexual Politics* in 1970, Kate Millett has been in the public eye. This has not always been to her benefit, as she is quick to point out in her several autobiographical memoirs. But it is this conflict between the public and the private—juxtaposed with her deeply held belief that the personal is the political—that is at the basis for all of Millett's thinking and writing. In all of her work Kate Millett has attempted to pose and explore difficult social, political and philosophical questions. She has often drawn upon her own life and experiences to elucidate and exemplify these questions and just as often has been attacked not only for her inquiry but for personalizing her investigation.

Kate Millett was born to a middle–class, but impoverished, family in St. Paul, Minnesota, in 1934. She was an excellent student and graduated with highest honors and a B.A. from the University of Minneapolis in 1956, and an M.A. from Oxford University in 1958. She started a career as a sculptor, painter and photographer in 1959 and moved to Tokyo where she taught English, studied sculpting, and married Fumio Yoshimura, a noted Japanese sculptor. After moving back to the United States in 1963 she taught at Barnard College for several years and entered into a Ph.D. program at Columbia University from which she received her degree in 1970. Her doctoral thesis, titled *Sexual Politics,* which combined literary analysis, sociology and anthropology, was published that year and became an instant best–seller with over 80,000 copies sold the first year.

Sexual Politics was perhaps the first major theoretical work of the second wave of feminism and as such it defined the ideas, strategies and goals of the woman's movement. It also catapulted Millett into the limelight as a major spokeswoman for the movement. In the midst of this media blitz Millett came out as a lesbian—she was asked at a lecture about her sexual identity and answered, as she always did, honestly—a disclosure that was quickly reported in the mainstream press and caused great discussion within the women's movement itself.

While most of the reviews of *Sexual Politics* praised its intelligence, erudition and political acumen, it was also met with some resistance. The woman's movement was still regarded as a threat and it was not uncommon to find critical pieces which referred to "woman's libbers" and "screeching feminists." Even some favorable reviews took exception to Millett's using the blatantly homosexual works of Jean Genet as a blueprint for reviewing gender and sexual roles. Millett's public lesbianism made her an easy target for those who wanted to dismiss her work, her life and the women's movement itself.

As the pressure of the public life increased and Millett was forced into a celebrity status she never sought, her own life began to spin out of control. This period is documented in *Flying*, in 1974, an autobiographical work that details the emotional and psychological dislocations she experienced after the publication of *Sexual Politics*. Not only did she receive public censure for her opinions and her open lesbianism, but her family, particularly her mother, was very upset with her. Millett, however, was determined to be as honest as possible and *Flying*—which she dedicated to her mother—was an attempt to explore exactly what feminists meant when they claimed that the personal was the political.

The revelations of *Flying* were mild compared to those of *Sita*, in 1977. Based on entries from her 1975 journal *Sita*, described and analyzed a destructive sexual and emotional relationship she had with an older woman while living in Berkeley, California, after the publication of *Flying*. While many in the women's movement and the gay and lesbian liberation movement wanted to believe that a relationship between two women would avoid the power struggles and emotional inequities they associated with heterosexuality and heterosexism, Millett's brilliant dissection of human sexual and emotional obsession and destruction within a lesbian relationship was a political breakthrough. The possibility that women might act destructively and hurtfully to one another was an unpopular political and emotional truth that those within the movement did not want to hear. Because Millett used her own life to illustrate her ideas of the complexities of women's experience of sexuality, desire and power, many wrote off *Flying* and *Sita* as overly self–absorbed and egotistical.

Millett followed *Sita* with *The Basement: Meditations on a Human Sacrifice*, in 1980. Based on a true incident in which a young woman was systematically abused, tortured and finally murdered by a group of teenaged boys and girls led by an older woman in whose care she had been placed, *The Basement* is one of Millett's bravest works, for in it she poses the question of why and how women are capable of the same destructive behaviors usually associated with men. Millett was not interested in the simplistic, easy analysis of male power and privilege and was attempting to explore the intricacies of human, and female, behavior. As usual, Millett was a character in *The Basement*—this time serving as reporter and interrogator as well as subject—and included herself and her own life in her investigation of how powerlessness, as well as power, can corrupt.

Going to Iran, published in 1982, documents Millett's trip to Iran after the fall of the Shah and before the rise of the Ayatollah Khomeini. After the collapse of the Shah's regime, a strong feminist movement was fermenting in Iran as part of a broader movement for freedom and social justice. Millett and photographer Sophie Keir documented this movement, as well as its opposition by the state.

In the end Millett and Keir were arrested and expelled by the new government and *Going to Iran* is not only the story of a specific time and place but an examination of how revolutions fail and how political oppression functions on an everyday, personal level.

The publication of *The Loony–Bin Trip* in 1990 brought Millett back into the public eye. In 1973—during the time described in *Flying*—Millett had been briefly committed to a mental hospital by her family. After this she was medicated on lithium to control her mood swings. In 1980, after deciding that the drug was destructive to her creativity as well as her daily life, she made the decision to stop taking it. As her behavior changed, her family and friends reacted and Millett was forced to endure several institutionalizations. In *The Loony–Bin Trip*, Millett argues that "insanity" and "mental illness" are socially constructed labels used against anyone who deviates from the accepted norm. Once again Millett has used her own private life to explore public issues. *The Loony–Bin Trip* was a popular and critical success and engendered heated discussion over a variety of issues from the uses of psychotropic drugs to the role of the artist in society. The power of the book comes from Millett's willingness to break through—as she always has—the artificially constructed categories of "private" and "public" and to make those vital connections between the personal and the political.

—*Michael Bronski*

MISHIMA, Yukio. Pseudonym for Kimitake Hiraoka. Japanese novelist, essayist, playwright, author of short stories, lecturer, and director. Born in Tokyo, 14 January 1925. Educated at Tokyo University, degree in jurisprudence 1947. Civil servant, Japanese Finance Ministry, 1948; writer, beginning 1948. Founder of Tate No Kai (Shield Society). Director of plays and motion pictures, including *Yukoku*, 1965, and *Enjo*. **Recipient:** Shinchosha Publishing Shincho Prize, 1954; Shinchosha Publishing Kishida Prize for Drama, 1955; Yomiuri Newspaper Co. Yomiuri Prize for best novel, 1957, and for best drama, 1961. *Died in Tokyo, by ritual suicide, 25 November 1970.*

WRITINGS

Short Stories

Hanazakari no mori. [Japan], 1944.
Misaki nite no monogatari. [Japan], 1947.
Toadai. [Japan], 1950.
Kaibutsu. [Japan], 1950.
Seijo. [Japan], 1951.
Kamen no kohuhaku sona ta. [Japan], 1951.
Mishima Yukio tampen shu. [Japan], 1951.
Tonorikai. [Japan], 1951.
Mishima Yukio shu. [Japan], 1952.
Hyakuman–en sembei. [Japan], 1960; translated by Edward Seidensticker as "Three Million Yen," in *Death in Midsummer, and Other Stories*, 1966.

Yukoku. [Japan], 1960; translated by Geoffrey Sargent as "Patrio-tism," in *Death in Midsummer, and Other Stories,* 1966.

Mahobin. [Japan], 1961; translated by Edward Seidensticker as "Thermos Bottles," in *Death in Midsummer, and Other Stories,* 1966.

Mishima Yukio tampen senshu. [Japan], 1964; published in six vol-umes, 1971.

Death in Midsummer, and Other Stories (contains "Death in Mid-summer," "Three Million Yen," "Thermos Bottles," "The Priest of Shiga Temple and His Love," "The Seven Bridges," "Patrio-tism," "Dojoji," "Onnagata," "The Pearl," and "Swaddling Clothes"). New York, New Directions, 1966.

Koya yori. [Japan], 1967.

Shishi. [Japan], 1971.

Mishima Yukio judai sakuhin shu. [Japan], 1971.

Acts of Worship: Seven Stories, translation and introduction by John Bester. New York, Kodansha, 1989.

Essays

Kari to emono. [Japan], 1951.

Hagakure nyumon. [Japan], c. 1967; translated by Kathryn N. Sparling as *The Way of Samurai: Yukio Mishima on Hagakure in Modern Life,* New York, Basic Books, 1977.

Fudotoku kyoiku koza. [Japan], 1969.

Wakaki samurai no tame ni. [Japan], 1969.

Mishima Yukio bungaku ronshu. [Japan], 1970.

Ranryo O. [Japan], 1971.

Yukio Mishima on "Hagakure": The Samurai Ethic and Modern Japan, Souvenir Press, 1978.

Plays

Yoru no himawari. [Japan], 1953; translated by Shigeho Shinozaki and Virgil A. Warren as *Twilight Sunflower,* Tokyo, Hokuseido Press, 1958.

Wakodo yo yomigaere. [Japan], 1954.

Hanjo. [Japan], 1955; published in *Kindai nogaku shu,* 1956.

Rokumeikan. [Japan], 1956.

Kindai nogaku shu. [Japan], 1956; translated by Donald Keene as *Five Modern No Plays* (contains "The Damask Drum," "Hanjo," "Kantan," "The Lady Aoi," and "Sotoba komachi"). New York, Knopf, 1957.

Nettaiju. [Japan], 1959; translated as "Tropical Tree," in *Japan Quarterly,* Number 11, 1964.

Mishima Yukio gikyoku zenshu. [Japan], 1962.

Sado koshaku fujin. [Japan], 1965; translated by Donald Keene as *Madame de Sade* (produced New York, 1988), P. Owen, 1968.

Gikyoku kurotokage. [Japan], 1969.

Screenplays

Yukoku (screenplay; based on his own short story). [Japan], 1965.

Novels

Tozoku ["Thieves"], 1948.

Kamen no kokuhaku. [Japan], 1949; translated by Meredith Weatherby as *Confessions of a Mask,* New York, New Direc-tions, 1958.

Ai no kawaki. [Japan], 1950; translated by Alfred H. Marks with introduction by Donald Keene as *Thirst for Love,* New York, Knopf, 1969.

Kinjiki (fiction; two volumes). [Japan], 1954; translated by Alfred H. Marks as *Forbidden Colors,* London, Secker & Warburg, 1968, New York, Berkley Publishing, 1974.

Shiosai. [Japan], 1954; translated by Meredith Weatherby as *The Sound of Waves,* New York, Knopf, 1956.

Kinkakuji. [Japan], 1956; translated by Ivan Morris as *Temple of the Golden Pavilion,* New York, Knopf, 1959.

Utage no ato. [Japan], 1960; translated by Donald Keene as *After the Banquet,* New York, Knopf, 1963.

Gogo no eiko. [Japan], 1963; translated by John Nathan as *The Sailor Who Fell from Grace with the Sea,* New York, Knopf, 1965.

Taido. [Japan], 1967; translated with introduction by Meredith Weatherby and Paul T. Konya as *Young Samurai,* New York, Grove, 1967.

Collected Works

Mishima Yukio sakuhin shu (six volumes). [Japan], 1953–54.

Mishima Yukio senshu (19 volumes). [Japan], 1957–59.

Hojo no umi (novels; four volumes). [Japan], 1969–71; translated as *The Sea of Fertility: A Cycle of Four Novels,* New York, Knopf: Volume 1: *Haru no yuki,* translated by Michael Gallagher as *Spring Snow,* 1972; Volume 2: *Homba,* translated by Michael Gallagher as *Runaway Horses,* 1973; Volume 3: *Akatsuki no tera,* translated by E. Dale Saunders and Cecilia S. Seigle as *The Temple of Dawn,* 1973; Volume 4: *Tennin gosui,* translated by Edward Seidensticker as *The Decay of the Angel,* 1974.

Mishima Yukio (volume of "nihon bungaku kenkyu shiryo sosho" series). [Japan], 1971.

Mishima Yukio. [Japan], 1972.

Mishima Yukio, edited by Ken'ichi Adachi. [Japan], 1973.

Mishima Yukio zenshu (36 volumes), edited by Shoichi Saeki and Jun Ishikawa. [Japan], 1973–76.

Mishima Yukio goroku ["Invitation to Mishimalogy"], edited by Ken Akitsu. [Japan], 1975.

Other

Ma gun no tsuka. [Japan], 1949.

Aporo no sakazuki. [Japan], 1952.

Koi no miyako. [Japan], 1954.

Shi o Kaku shonen ["The Boy Who Wrote Poetry"], 1954.

Shosetsuka no kyuka. [Japan], 1955.

Megami. [Japan], 1955.

Seishun O do ikiru ka. [Japan], 1955.

Shiroari no su. [Japan], 1956.

Kofuku go shuppan. [Japan], 1956.

Gendai shosetsu wa koten tari–uru ka. [Japan], 1957.

Rara to kaizoku. [Japan], 1958.

Hashizukushi. [Japan], 1958.

Bunsho tokuhon. [Japan], 1959; new edition, 1969.

Natsukonoboken. [Japan], 1960.

Ojosan. [Japan], 1960.
Nagasugita haru. [Japan], 1961.
Toka no kiku. [Japan], 1961.
Shisumoru taki. [Japan], 1963.
Ai no shisso. [Japan], 1963.
Nikutai no gakko. [Japan], 1964.
Ongaku. [Japan], 1965.
Hanteijo daigaku. [Japan], 1966.
Mishima Yukio hyoron zenshu. [Japan], 1966.
Eirei no Koe, 1966.
Yakaitfuku. [Japan], 1967.
Mishima Yukio chohen zenshu. [Japan], 1967.
Inochi urimasu. [Japan], 1968.
With Mitsuo Nakamura, *Taidan, ningen to bungaku.* [Japan], 1968.
Waga tomo Hittora. [Japan], 1968.
Mishima Yukio reta kyoshitsu. [Japan], 1968.
Taiyo to tetsu (autobiography). [Japan], 1968; translated by John
    Bester as *Sun and Steel,* New York, Grove, 1970.
Toron Mishima Yukio vs. Todai Zenkyoto. [Japan], 1969.
Raio no Terasu. [Japan], 1969.
Chinsetsu yumiharizuki. [Japan], 1969.
Bunka boei ron. [Japan], 1969.
Mishima Yukio kenkyu. [Japan], 1970.
Sakkaron. [Japan], 1970.
Gensen no kanjo. [Japan], 1970.
Mishima Yukio ten. [Japan], 1970.
Kodogaku nyumon. [Japan], 1970.
Shobu no kororo. [Japan], 1970.
Santao Yuchifu tuan p'ien chieh tso hsuan. [Japan], 1971.
Mishima Yukio no ningenzo. [Japan], 1971.
Mishima Yukio no ski a do miru ka. [Japan], 1971.
Kemono no tawamure. [Japan], 1971.
Ao no jidai. [Japan], 1971.
Shosetsu to wa nani ka. [Japan], 1972.
Nihon bungaku shoshi. [Japan], 1972.
Editor, with Geoffrey Bownas, *New Writing in Japan.* New York,
    Penguin Books, 1972.
Mishima Yukio shonen shi, edited by Kazusuke Ogawa. [Japan],
    1973.
Waga shishunki. [Japan], 1973.
Daiichi no sei. [Japan], 1973.
With Teiji Ito and Takeji Iwamiya, *Sento Gosho.* [Japan], 1977.
Editor, *BA. RA. Kei.: Ordeal by Roses,* photographs by Eikoh Hosoe.
    New York, Aperture Foundation, 1985.

*

Adaptations: *Yukoku* (film adaptation; directed by and starring
Yukio Mishima), 1965; *The Sailor Who Fell from Grace with the
Sea* (film adaptation), 1976; *Temple of the Golden Pavilion* (film
adaptation), Japan.

Biography: *Mishima: A Biography* by John Nathan, Boston, Little,
Brown, 1974; *Life and Death of Yukio Mishima* by Henry Scott
Stokes, New York, Farrar, Straus, 1974.

Critical Sources: *Accomplices of Silence: The Modern Japanese
Novel* by Masao Miyoshi, Berkeley, University of California Press,
1974.

Yukio Mishima's 1949 work, *Kamen no kokuhaku* (*Confessions
of a Mask*), was one of the first important books to deal with the
topic of homosexuality in Japan since Ibara Saikaku's 1687 piece
Nanshoku okagaim (*The Great Mirror of Male Love*). Mishima
based his own life on the first part of Saikaku's work, which celebrated the homosexual love of the ancient samurai. He was also
heavily influenced by themes from the second half which celebrated
the lives of the geisha boys in seventeenth–century Kyoto, Osaka,
and Tokyo. Mishima (born Kimitake Hiraoka) descended from peasant ancestry on his father's side (although both his father and grandfather were high government officials) and from the samurai class
on his mother's side. He was consequently discriminated against as
a young man in Peers' School where students usually claimed noble
ancestry; moreover, he was ostracized because of his early literary
interests. Mishima's *Shi o Kaku shonen* ("The Boy Who Wrote
Poetry") details the agony of a child who thinks in metaphors and
fantasies. While still in school, one of his stories was published in
October, 1944, under "Mishima Yukio," a pen name provided by a
teacher. Subsequently he wrote 40 novels, 18 plays, and numerous
volumes of short stories and essays.

Mishima came of age in postwar Japan; he had not served in the
army but shared in the great changes brought by the events of
Hiroshima and Nagasaki. He published several short stories, studied law for a time, and worked in the Ministry of Finance; but after
his first novel *Tozoku* ("Thieves") appeared in 1948, he pursued
his writing full–time. After publication of *Confessions of a Mask* in
1949, Mishima was quickly recognized as one of Japan's major
authors. The relationship between Japan and the West permeates
both his life and writings. He celebrated ancient Japanese traditions
upholding the responsibilities of the samurai, in classical *waka*
poetry, and in the "No" plays. His own plays use themes from the
West and have influenced Western avant garde theater. *Kindai nogaku
shu* (*Five Modern No Plays*) has reached a wide audience He also
used Western sources and themes. *Sado koshaku fujin* (*Madame de
Sade*) in an unusual twist studies the wife of the Marquis de
Sade, who stood faithfully by her husband until he became an author.

Mishima led a life common to the international set of homosexuals. He enjoyed collecting British antiques, Greek statues, and other
consumer items. He frequented gay bars around the world. In addition to de Sade, he read Oscar Wilde, Marcel Proust, and Haymond
Padiguet, the young, handsome novelist so beloved by Jean Cocteau
who had died in 1923. Unlike many contemporary Western homosexuals, however, he married and fathered two children. His
politics included a dutiful obligation keep his family name alive.

Kinjiki (*Forbidden Colors*) presents numerous scenes from contemporary Japanese homosexual life: parties, bars, lovers, hustlers—all illuminated by the beauty of young men's bodies "waiting for the signal to spring." Mishima's scenes are often sensual and
graphic; for instance, the hero slips "his hand inside the other boy's
tunic.... The heartbeat he felt was violent. The two separated, turned
from each other and hastily tore off their clothing."

The beauty of men's bodies fascinated Mishima. In *Confessions
of a Mask,* he celebrates the exciting smell of soldiers' sweat. He
himself exercised diligently and maintained tight muscles. The male
body in its splendor offered an entry into deeper meanings. In *Taiyo
to tetsu* (*Sun and Steel*) Mishima writes, "Admittedly, I could see
my own muscles in the mirror. Yet seeing alone was not enough to
bring me into contact with the basic roots of my sense of existence." The forbidden fascinated Mishima; he often linked it with
death. Thus in *Ai no kawaki* (*Thirst for Love*) the widow Etsuko,
the mistress of her late husband's father, falls madly in love with a

young, handsome farmer; when the youth responds, she kills him with her father–in–law's scythe. (Mishima told friends that the widow was in fact based on a man.) And in *Gogo no eiko* (*The Sailor Who Fell from Grace with the Sea*) two juveniles kill their idol, a merchant marine officer, when he leaves the service for marriage.

Another great theme in his work is the intertwining of love and death and sadism and masochism. In many of his works Mishima explores questions of meaning and meaninglessness through the use of images such as bodies being pulled apart. The young hero in *Forbidden Colors* parks with a gentle American; suddenly the man rips the boy's shirt off: "Avidly, giant canine teeth, accustomed to meat, sank voraciously into the glowing flesh of the shoulder. Yuichi yelled. Blood ran across the young man's breast." In an article in *Boston Gay Community News,* John Hitzel wrote, "Mishima had learned that the way to make pain pleasing was to eroticize it. 'I tried,' he wrote, 'to hide the pleasure which I took in my pain.' This is the essential underpinning of the sado–masochistic personality. The next step which Mishima took was to eroticize the fear of death so that hara–kiri became the next and last thrill."

Mishima combined continuously speculative ruminations with his remarkable sensuousness. His lifelong speculations on life, destiny, beauty, and nihilism reached a splendid apogee in his final four–volume cycle. The series entitled *Hojo no umi* (*The Sea of Fertility*) included: *Haru no yuki* (*Spring Snow*), *Homba* (*Runaway Horses*), *Akatsuki no tera* (*The Temple of Dawn*), and *Tennin gosui* (*The Decay of the Angel*). The work has baffled critics with its mixture of reincarnation, remarkable descriptions of Benares, transvestism, and nihilism.

Politically, Mishima opposed many modern tendencies and firmly supported the divinity of the emperor. In 1968 he formed a private army of one hundred men, the Tate No Kai (Shield Society), who intended to support their emperor against the radicals of 1968. In *Eirei no Koe* (title means "The Voices of the Heroic Dead"), the spirits of kamikaze pilots denounce the present emperor for having denied his divinity. In 1970, after he had sent the last installment of his *Sea of Fertility* to be published, Mishima led his band against the headquarters of the Japanese Self–Defense Force. Some of the assembled force jeered him, but they fell into silence as he performed (with a beloved comrade) the ancient rite of seppuku. He carefully disemboweled himself with a small sword, and his partner beheaded him and then took his own life. Mishima's death stunned both the Japanese and the international public, but interpreting his seppuku presents as many difficulties as interpreting his writings. Critics might argue whether his act was only a publicity stunt or they might hold that it explained and was the culmination of everything he had ever written. Whatever they might argue, his seppuku was in no way off–handed or desperate. The event went as he had planned. The sequel, however, has remained beyond his control.

Although a traditionalist, Mishima gravitated toward film. In the *Black Lizard* and other films he worked as an actor or director. His fiction has been turned into film. And Paul Schrader's 1985 film *Mishima,* with a score by Philip Glass and a performance by Yasujiro Ozu in the lead role has been banned in Japan because of its portrayal of Mishima's homosexuality.

—*Charles Shively*

MONETTE, Paul. American poet, novelist, and memoirist. Born in Lawrence, Massachusetts, in 1945. Educated at Phillips Academy, Andover, Massachusetts; Yale University, New Haven, Connecticut, B.A. 1967. Companion of Roger Horwitz (died, 1986); companion of Stephen Kolzak (died, 1990); companion of Winston Wilde since 1990. Taught at Milton Academy and Pine Manor College. Active supporter of ACT UP (AIDS Coalition to Unleash Power) and advocate for gay and lesbian rights. **Recipient:** National Book Critics Circle Award nomination, 1988; National Book Award for *Becoming a Man: Half a Life Story,* 1992; honorary degrees from State University of New York College at Oswego, 1992, and Wesleyan University, 1993.

WRITINGS

Poetry

The Carpenter at the Asylum. Boston, Little, Brown, 1975.
No Witnesses, drawings by David Schorr. New York, Avon, 1981.
Love Alone: Eighteen Elegies for Rog. New York, St. Martin's Press, 1988.

Novels

Taking Care of Mrs. Carroll. Boston, Little, Brown, 1978.
The Gold Diggers. New York, Avon, 1979.
The Long Shot. New York, Avon, 1981.
Lightfall. New York, Avon, 1982.
Afterlife. New York, Crown, 1990.
Halfway Home. New York, Crown, 1991.

Memoirs

Borrowed Time: An AIDS Memoir. New York, Harcourt, 1988.
Becoming a Man: Half a Life Story. New York, Harcourt, 1992.

Other

Nosferatu: The Vampire (adaptation of screenplay by Werner Herzog). New York, Avon, 1979.
Scarface (adaptation of screenplay by Oliver Stone). New York, Berkley, 1983.
Predator. New York, Berkeley, 1986.
Havana. Ivy Books, 1991.
Midnight Run. New York, Berkeley, 1990.
(Author of foreword) *A Rock and a Hard Place* by Anthony Godby Johnson. New York, Crown, 1993.

*

Manuscript Collections: University of California, Los Angeles Library special collections.

Biography: "Leaving a Legacy for the Gay Community" by Kay Longcope, in *Boston Globe,* 5 March 1990, 30.

Interviews: "A Story of Life in a Time of AIDS" by Bob Sipchen, in *Los Angeles Times,* 13 June 1988, Section 5, 1; "Paul Monette" by Lisa See, in *Publishers Weekly,* 29 June 1992, 42–43.

Critical Sources: "Dispatches from Aphrodite's War" by William M. Hoffman, in *New York Times,* 11 September 1988, 3; "Fire and Ice" by Richard Labonte, in *Advocate,* 13 September 1988, 65–66; "'The Time before the War': AIDS, Memory, and Desire" by John M. Clum, in *American Literature,* 62:2, 1990, 648–667; review of *Afterlife* by Christopher Davis, in *Lambda Book Report,* 2:3, 1990, 20–21; "Paul Monette: A Gay Novelist in Pursuit of the Human Heart" (review of *Afterlife*) by Susan Brownmiller, in *Chicago Tribune,* 11 February 1990, 3; "An American Romantic" by Eden Ross Lipson, in *New York Times Book Review,* 4 March 1990, 7; review by David B. Feinberg of *Afterlife,* in *Outweek,* 4 April 1990, 59; "Gay Life in the Ruins" (review of *Afterlife*) by John Weir, in *Washington Post,* 26 April 1990, 3; review by Judith Viorst of *Afterlife,* in *New York Times Book Review,* 29 April 1990, 7; review by Walta Borawski of *Halfway Home,* in *Gay Community News,* 21 April–4 May 1991, 7; review by Janice C. Simpson of *Halfway Home,* in *Time,* 6 May 1991, 72; "No Half Measures" by Maria Maggenti, in *Outweek,* 8 May 1991, 56–58; review by K. Orton Williams of *Halfway Home,* in *San Francisco Sentinel,* 9 May 1991, 21; review by Marv Shaw of *Halfway Home,* in *Bay Area Reporter,* 23 May 1991; "All in the Family" by David Kaufman, in *Nation,* 1 July 1991, 21–25, 30; *The Gay Novel in America* by James Levin, New York, Garland, 1991; "Paul Monette" by Michael Lassell, in *Advocate,* 2 June 1992, 34–35; "A Closet of One's Own" (review of *Becoming a Man*) by Robert Dawidoff, in *Los Angeles Times,* 28 June 1992, 10; "A Heart Laid Bare" (review of *Becoming a Man*) by Lawrence Biemiller, in *Washington Post,* 21 June 1992, 1; "Outward Bound" by Maurice Berger, in *Voice,* 30 June 1992, 68; "Paul Monette" by David Román. in *Contemporary Gay American Novelists,* edited by Emmanuel S. Nelson, Westport, Connecticut, Greenwood Press, 1993.

Paul Monette comments: "I'd rather be remembered for loving well than for writing well, and for being a witness to the calamity that has engulfed my people."

*   *   *

Upon receiving the 1992 National Book Award for *Becoming a Man: Half a Life Story,* Paul Monette was catapulted into global recognition as one of the most famous gay writers in the world. At the same time, he was living with AIDS and, in a race against time with the perils of the disease, attempting to complete a book of essays entitled *Last Watch of the Night.*

On a balmy April afternoon in 1993 I chatted with Monette in his warm, cozy, art–filled home in the Hollywood hills above Los Angeles' fabled Sunset Strip. Although he had just returned from a radiation treatment for AIDS, he was alert and energized as ever. I asked him to describe his greatest strength and primary weakness as a writer. "My chief weakness was the closet," he said. "It made virtually everything I wrote until I came out a kind of ventriloquism. Now it turns out I find my greatest strength in exploring myself and my own psyche, testing myself against a rigorous standard of honesty."

Monette explained that he has been influenced as a writer by the essays of Joan Didion and the fiction of Flannery O'Connor. "There's a kind of willingness there to probe a harrowed world. They taught me honesty about writing. But I think the larger influence on the course of my work was the gay generation after the liberation of Stonewall. What I had written earlier was about nothing. When I finally found I could write about being gay, I knew everything was possible. Now I do not write or think in isolation from my tribe. I go with its vicissitudes and triumphs and its constant changing. The hatred of my enemies has spurred me forward."

He finds enormous significance in the emergence of gay and lesbian writing as a powerful force in literature. "It's immensely affirming and exciting that we have produced this documentation of our lives. We are a literature and a psychology that has bloomed with astonishing rapidity. In my lifetime the most powerful literature has come from communities in crisis. Most American writing, however, has become pallid, self–conscious university stuff with precious little to say. In fact, I left poetry behind (with the exception of *Love Alone: Eighteen Elegies for Rog*) because too much of it was writing about nothing, written to a small group of colleagues to get their approval and grants."

I asked Monette to offer an overview of the gay/lesbian content of his past work. He said that his novel *Taking Care of Mrs. Carroll* afforded him a breakthrough moment: "I was proud to have that Dietrich figure at the center, a lesbian from another generation. And all the camp and romanticism of the gay scene in the '60s and early '70s found expression." He discussed his two novels *The Gold Diggers* and *The Long Shot* as a single entity: "I was trying to explore the relationship between gay men and straight women. I did not feel ready to talk about lesbians. Both novels are about friendship and making a family that is not a blood family, but a chosen one. These are gay people and how they live their lives."

Monette feels that his novel *Lightfall* was an anomaly in his work because he was under pressure from his publishers when he wrote it to stop dealing with gay themes. "It is prophetic in that it's about a crazed fundamentalist. It wasn't an easy time for me because I really doubted myself." His next novel, *Afterlife,* provides a broad spectrum of a number of people confronting AIDS. "Everything changed for me after Roger [Horwitz, Monette's lover] was diagnosed with AIDS in 1985. This book records some of the rage of people I admire like Larry Kramer and organizations like ACT UP."

His novel *Halfway Home* is, for Monette, his "lucky star." He said: "I really did get to write the gay love story I always wanted to do. It feels like my best book. I was not afraid to have lesbian characters. I exulted in them. The chosen family wins hands–down. I was able to generate a story that, even in the midst of death, could make the connection of intimacy." *Borrowed Time: An AIDS Memoir* is about his lover Roger's diagnosis and dying. "It struck chords deeper than itself," Monette told me. "I wish I was as wise as the narrator. It lifted me out of myself and enabled me to speak of matters that touched all my people."

His autobiographical work *Becoming a Man: Half a Life Story* brought Monette the maximum of fame and literary acceptance. "I never expected to write nonfiction prose at all. I never thought of myself as a journalist or an essayist. It was totally unknown territory. Although I had all of my education and discipline to help me, it was new. Yet art is inevitably political if one grows up in calamitous times." How, I wondered, does Monette place himself within a larger literary or historical sphere. "This is what is causing so much trouble for the white straight men who wield the power and teach the courses. I am part of the turmoil in which we're trying to add new voices and give a feel of a multicultural world. But I don't feel separatist. One person's truth if told well does not leave anybody out."

Referring to AIDS which has consumed so much of his health and energy, Monette explains that he has continued to write as a way of continuing to breathe. "I've been pleasantly surprised by how [much] I am giving back to my community. There's so much alienation from ourselves as gays and lesbians—the conquest of our own self–hatred—I'm glad to be a figure that gives hope." His life's focus has shifted because of the battleground of his illness. "My life has narrowed to my house and my life with Winston and my two dogs. I'm trying to go over the pieces of my life and see what I cherish and what I believe. This is what I am doing in *Last Watch of the Night.* Simplify—simplify—simplify. I'm not sure what my final words will be."

Paul Monette has confronted being gay in America and AIDS in his work in a deeply involving, confrontational way. Hans Castorp, in Thomas Mann's classic novel *The Magic Mountain,* regretted that he did not live in demanding times. A writer like Monette living today is challenged by a plethora of human and moral crises. The "imprisoned writer" and the "censored artist" are commonplace in our world. A writer provokes controversy, and often wrath, when he or she refuses to bow to conventional demands to remove art's sting and trivialize on demand creative work.

Monette is a symbol of freedom of expression at a moment when serious attempts are being made to suppress such expression, reduce it to a low common denominator, or harness it to serve merely utilitarian purposes. Yet a creative writer cannot thrive in deadening isolation, cut off from the demanding issues and personalities of his or her time. Brutality, prejudice, discrimination, and all forms of dehumanization demand a response as a part of a writer's pact with conscience. A writer cannot remain detached from the shadowy figures—evocative of sculptor Alberto Giacometti's art—who inhabit our city streets in the guise of homeless people; or racism, sexism, and homophobia; or the pandemic of AIDS. Paul Monette's best work in *Borrowed Time* and *Becoming a Man* penetrates the dark night of our collective soul. At precisely this point, he melds his work with his life.

—*Malcolm Boyd*

MORAGA, Cherríe. American educator, editor, publisher, playwright, and poet. Born in Whittier, California, 25 September 1952. Educated at private school in Hollywood, California, B.A. 1974; San Francisco State University, M.A. 1980. High school English teacher, Los Angeles, California, during the mid–1970s; cofounder and administrator, Kitchen Table: Women of Color Press, New York, 1981—; playwright in residence, INTAR (Hispanic–American arts center), 1984; part–time writing instructor, University of California, Berkeley, 1986—. **Recipient:** Before Columbus Foundation American Book Award for *This Bridge Called My Back: Writings by Radical Women of Color,* 1986. Address: c/o Chicano Studies Department, University of California, 3404 Dwinelle Hall, Berkeley, California 94720, U.S.A.

WRITINGS

Editor

With Alma Gómez and Mariana Romo–Carmona, and contributor, *Cuentos: Stories by Latinos.* New York, Kitchen Table: Women of Color Press, 1983.

With Gloria Anzaldúa, and contributor, *This Bridge Called My Back: Writings by Radical Women of Color,* foreword by Toni Cade Bambara. Watertown, Massachusetts, Persephone Press, 1981; revised bilingual edition published as *Esta puente, mi espalda: Voces de mujeres tercermundistas en los Estados Unidos,* edited with Ana Castillo, with Spanish translation by Ana Castillo and Norma Alarcón, San Francisco, Ism Press, 1988.

With Norma Alarcón, *Third Woman,* Volume 4: *The Sexuality of Latinas.* Berkeley, California, Third Woman Press, 1989.

With Ana Castillo and Norma Alarcón, *The Sexuality of Latinas.* Berkeley, California, Third Woman Press, 1992.

Plays

Giving Up the Ghost: Teatro in Two Acts (produced as stage reading, Minneapolis, Minnesota, 1984; produced Seattle, 1987; revised version produced San Francisco, 1987). Minneapolis, Minnesota, West End Press, 1986.

La extranjera, 1985.

Shadow of a Man, 1988.

Heroes and Saints (produced Los Angeles, 1989).

Other

Loving in the War Years: Lo que nunca pasó por sus labios [subtitle means "What Never Passed Her Lips"], (poetry and essays). Boston, South End Press, 1983.

The Last Generation (prose and poetry). Boston, South End Press, 1993.

*

Biography: *Essence,* January 1982, 17; *Ms.,* March 1992, 39.

Interviews: With Mirtha N. Quintanales, in *Off Our Backs,* January 1985, 12–13; with Norma Alarcón, in *Third Woman,* 3:1–2, 1986, 127–134; with Luz María Umpierre, in *Americas Review,* Number 14, 1986, 54–67.

Critical Sources: *New England Review,* summer 1983, 586–87; "All of Our Art for Our Sake" by SDiane Bogus, in *Sinister Wisdom,* fall 1984, 92–106; "Cherríe Moraga's Giving Up the Ghost: The Representation of Female Desire" by Yvonne Yarbro–Bejarano, in *Third Woman,* 3:1–2, 1986, 113–120; *Rocky Mountain Review of Language and Literature,* 41:1–2, 1987, 125–128; "Cherríe Moraga" by Yvonne Yarbro–Bejarano, in *Dictionary of Literary Biography,* Volume 82: *Chicano Writers,* Detroit, Gale, 1989; *Mother Jones,* January–February 1991, 15; *Notable Hispanic American Women,* Detroit, Gale, 1993.

When Cherríe Moraga revealed her homosexuality in the mid–1970s, she began to feel the alienation that she had avoided as a woman of color able to "pass" for a white woman. Moraga wrote of the revelation she experienced in "La Güera," an essay she included in *This Bridge Called My Back: Writings by Radical Women of Color:* "When I finally lifted the lid to my lesbianism, a profound connection with my mother reawakened in me. It wasn't until I acknowledged and confronted my own lesbianism in the flesh, that my heartfelt identification with and empathy for my mother's oppression—due to being poor, uneducated, and Chicana—was realized.... In this country, lesbianism is a poverty—as is being brown, as is being a woman, as is being just plain poor." Moraga's master's degree thesis, *This Bridge Called My Back,* edited with Gloria Anzaldúa, would emerged as a path–making work and win the 1986 Before Columbus Foundation American Book Award. Moraga's later works, which explore her feelings as a lesbian of color, have included essays, poetry, short stories, and plays, all of which continue to challenge American culture and literature.

Born in 1952, in Whittier, California, to a mixed–race couple, Moraga's childhood was bounded by two cultures. Her mother and her mother's family surrounded her with the Spanish language and Mexican American traditions, while her father (of British Canadian descent) and her schools provided her with the Anglo American experience. In 1974, when she earned a bachelor's degree in art from a private college in Hollywood, Moraga became one of the few college–educated people in her family.

After her graduation from college, Moraga taught English at a private Los Angeles high school for two years, and it was during this period that she gradually realized that she wanted to write. Capitalizing on an opportunity presented by a writing class at the Los Angeles Women's Building, she began to write intimately about her lesbianism. "I had known for years that I was a lesbian, had felt it in my bones, had ached with the knowledge, gone crazed with the knowledge, wallowed in the silence of it," she wrote in "La Güera." Moraga ended the silence with this writing and shared her love poems with her writing group. The positive responses she received provided Moraga with the determination to commit herself to write, unabashedly, as a lesbian and about homosexuality.

Moraga began a serious attempt at writing in 1977. Promising herself that she would return to teaching if she made no progress, she moved to San Francisco. There, she worked odd jobs, read works of lesbian literature ranging from Radclyffe Hall's *The Well of Loneliness* to the works of Djuna Barnes, wrote continuously, and discussed her thoughts in cafés with artists, feminists, and other lesbians. When she read a selection of her poems along with Los Angeles poet Eloise Klein Healy in front of an eager coffee-house audience, Moraga decided that her year in San Francisco had been successful and that she would continue to write.

Influenced by Judy Grahn, who wrote specifically about being a lesbian of color, Moraga began to write more and more about her own experience as a Chicana lesbian. A master's thesis for San Francisco State University became a major project—along with Gloria Anzaldúa, Moraga collected essays, letters, and poems from other women of color to create *This Bridge Called My Back: Writings by Radical Women of Color.* Published in 1981 in English and translated into Spanish seven years later as *Esta puente, mi espalda: Voces de mujeres tercermundistas en los Estados Unidos,* this book voiced the concerns of marginalized women who had been heretofore silenced. According to Barbara Smith in the *New England Review,* it was a "groundbreaking collection of Third World Feminist Theory."

Moraga's contributions to *This Bridge Called My Back* and the essays and poems she included in the collection established her as important figure in Chicana and lesbian literature, as well as an inspirational leader in the movement women like her were creating. It was not long before she cofounded the Kitchen Table/Women of Color Press on the East coast and edited *Cuentos: Stories by Chicanas* with Alma Gómez and Mariana Romo Carmona for the group. Containing two stories written by Moraga ("Sin luz" and Pesadilla"), this anthology was the first collection of feminist Chicana writings to be published.

Moraga went on to publish *Loving in the War Years: (Lo que nunca pasó por sus labios),* a collection of poetry—and the first published book of writing by a self–identified Chicana lesbian. This collection includes a number of evocative poems and passionate essays that seek the sources of Moraga's lesbianism, ruminate about the trials it brings her, and celebrate its glories. Throughout the pieces, which are often written in both English and Spanish, Moraga never lets her readers forget her Chicana identity: "I am a Chicana lesbian. My own particular relationship to being a sexual person, and a radical, stands in direct contradiction to, and violation of, the woman I was raised to be."

Moraga wrote her first play, *Giving Up the Ghost,* which she presented at a feminist theater in Minneapolis in mid–1984. At INTAR, the Hispanic–American Arts Center in New York City, with the support of artistic director María Irene Fornes, she was given the opportunity to develop her playwriting skills—the plays *La extranjera, Shadow of a Man,* and *Heroes and Saints,* followed. Among these, *Giving Up the Ghost* is Moraga's most notable play. As Raymund A. Paredes wrote in the *Rocky Mountain Review,* this play "represents the most radical element of contemporary Chicana writing. Moraga portrays heterosexual love as inherently abusive, an act of violent penetration which in the context of the excessively masculine culture of Mexican Americans becomes more brutal still."

With the 1993 publication of *The Last Generation,* a collection of prose and poetry, Moraga re–asserted her identification with the oppressed of the Latin American continent, lamented the assimilation of Latin Americans into the United States, and challenged her readers to fight for radical cultural transformation. Marginalized in the United States by her race, her sexual orientation, and her politics, she felt alienated from even her "pueblo," or her community. She expressed these feelings in "Ni for El Salvador": "I am a woman nearing forty without children. / I am an artist nearing forty without community. / I am a lesbian nearing forty without partner. / I am a Chicana nearing forty without country. / And if it were safe, I'd spread open my thighs / and let the whole world in / and birth and birth and birth life. / The dissolution of self, the dissolution of borders."

Not surprisingly, Moraga's love for women, the very aspect of her identity which has caused her so much pain and brought her infinite inspiration now seems to give her solace. She decides in the poem, "If": "If in the long run / we weep together / hold each other / wipe the other's mouth / dry from the kiss pressed there / to seal the touch / of spirits separated / by something as necessary / as time / we will have done enough."

Moraga's contributions to the literary canon of the feminist, lesbian, Chicana, and women of color movements may be immeasurable. In addition to contributing her own works and voice, she has encouraged other women to write and speak and has even facilitated the publication of their works.

—Ronie–Richele Garcia–Johnson

MORDDEN, Ethan (Christopher). American music critic and historian, novelist, and author of short stories and nonfiction. Born in Heavensville, Pennsylvania, 27 January 1947. Educated at University of Pennsylvania, B.A. 1969. Editor of Romance Division, D.C. Comics, New York City, 1970–71; assistant editor, *Opera News,* New York City, 1974–76. Regular contributor to *Encyclopedia Americana* and *World Book Encyclopedia.* Agent: Dorothy Pittman, John Cushman Associates, Inc., 25 West 43rd Street, New York, New York 10036, U.S.A.

WRITINGS

Fiction

I've a Feeling We're Not in Kansas Anymore (short stories). New York, St. Martin's Press, 1985.
Buddies (short stories). New York, St. Martin's Press, 1986.
One Last Waltz (novel). New York, St. Martin's Press, 1986.
Everybody Loves You: Further Adventures in Gay Manhattan (short stories). New York, St. Martin's Press, 1988.

Nonfiction

Better Foot Forward: The History of American Musical Theatre. New York, Grossman, 1976.
That Jazz!: An Idiosyncratic Social History of the American Twenties. New York, Putnam, 1978.
Opera in the Twentieth Century: Scared, Profane, Godot. New York, Oxford University Press, 1978.
The Splendid Art of Opera: A Concise History. New York, Methuen, 1980.
A Guide to Orchestral Music: The Handbook for Non–Musicians. New York, Oxford University Press, 1980.
The American Theatre. New York, Oxford University Press, 1981.
The Hollywood Musical. New York, St. Martin's Press, 1981; London, David & Charles, 1982.
Movie Star: A Look at the Women Who Made Hollywood. New York, St. Martin's Press, 1983.
Broadway Babies: The People Who Made the American Musical. New York, Oxford University Press, 1983.
Smarts. The Cultural I.Q. Test. New York, McGraw, 1984.
Demented: A Provocative Look at Opera's Greatest Divas. New York, F. Watts, 1984.
Pooh's Workout Book. New York, Dutton, 1984.
Opera Anecdotes. New York, Oxford University Press, 1985.
A Guide to Opera Recordings. New York, Oxford University Press, 1987.
The Hollywood Studios: House Style in the Garden Age of Movies. New York, Knopf, 1988.
The Fireside Companion to the Theatre. New York, Simon & Schuster, 1988.
Medium Cool: The Movies of the 1960s. New York, Knopf, 1990.
Rodgers & Hammerstein. New York, Abrams, 1992.

*

Biography: "Ethan Mordden" by Michael Schwartz, in *Contemporary Gay American Novelists,* edited by Emmanuel S. Nelson, Westport, Connecticut, Greenwood Press, 1993.

Interviews: With Genevieve Stuttaford, in *Publishers Weekly,* 20 June 1980, 10–11.

Critical Sources: "Buddy Stories Your Buddy Never Told You" by Michael Bronski, in *Gay Community News,* 21 December 1986; "Zeitgeist or Poltergeist? Why Gay Books Are So Bad" by T. R. Witomski, in *Gay Community News,* 2 February 1987.

*   *   *

While Ethan Mordden has written well over a dozen books of nonfiction about music, theater, opera, Hollywood, and Broadway—topics of enduring interest to many lesbian and gay readers—his primary contribution to gay literature per se is his fiction. He began telling his tales of gay Manhattan in the monthly gay journal *Christopher Street* in the early 1980s, in a regular column called "Is There a Book in This?" With the 1985 publication of *I've a Feeling We're Not in Kansas Anymore,* it became clear that there was indeed a book, and not just one, but three. Mordden followed *I've a Feeling We're Not in Kansas Anymore* with two more collections of gay stories, *Buddies,* published in 1986, and *Everybody Loves You* which appeared two years later. The three collections are unified into a trilogy by the ubiquitous presence of the autobiographical and eponymous narrator, Bud Mordden, along with Bud's chosen "family": his best friend and arch denizen of gay nightlife Dennis Savage, Dennis' dusty–behind–the–ears young lover, Little Kiwi, and Little Kiwi's disreputable dog, Bauhaus.

Most of the stories in Mordden's trilogy take place in that now–mythical era of gay self–discovery, self–expression, and self–abandon between the Stonewall revolt of June 1969 and the dawn of the AIDS epidemic. As the narrator explains, they encompass tales "of affairs, encounters, discoveries, weekends, parties, secrets, fears, self–promotions—of fantasies that we make real in the telling." While we learn much less about Bud than we do about his expansive circle of comrades, his intrusive, inquisitive presence lends a distinctive feel and a pervasive mood to the stories. "Many jests are made in them," the narrator says of his tales, "though the overall feeling may be sad."

This characteristic melange of humor and pathos derives from the realities of gay life itself and the often traumatic personal histories of the gay men who populate Mordden's stories. These men have generally come to New York as pilgrims from America's vast heartland, where many of them were ridiculed for their perceived inadequacies and abused because of their often painfully obvious inability to conform to the standards of traditional masculine culture. They are wounded and hungry, starved for love, friendship, or simple acceptance. "I am concerned at how often people cry in these pages," says the narrator in *I've a Feeling We're Not in Kansas Anymore.* Faced with this pervasive background of sadness in their lives, the men in Mordden's gay New York have learned to sparkle with wit and to laugh with a vengeance, at themselves, at one another, and at the straight world that once menaced them in their isolation, and that they now valiantly fend off with arms linked. What results is a characteristic gay narrative genre that Mordden himself refers to in *Buddies* as "the New York camp–surreal romance," the archetypal example of which is probably Andrew Holleran's 1979 novel *Dancer from the Dance.* It is a genre whose landmarks exist in a setting historically specific to the 1970s: New York gay bars, discos, and bath houses; leather and drag; opera and show tunes; weekdays at the gym, and weekends at the Pines on Fire Island. Its narration and dialogue are marked by humor, satire, parody, blistering sarcasm, and amused irony.

In some ways, all three installments in Mordden's trilogy are of a piece. As the narrator confides to the reader in *Everybody Loves You*, "I've been trying to tell you that a man–to–man system that doesn't fear sex creates the ultimate in man–to–man friendships." But despite the singleness of purpose, there is a progression. If *I've a Feeling We're Not in Kansas Anymore* is about, as Mordden puts it, "how gay life behaves," and *Buddies* is about "how it feels," then perhaps *Everybody Loves You* can be said to be about how gay life feels about itself, as the introspection so characteristic of the narrator begins to overtake those around him as well. The most concise emblem of this increasing self–awareness is Little Kiwi's sudden insistence on being called by his real name, which turns out to be Virgil. And the context for this shift in perspective is, of course, the AIDS epidemic, most poignantly evoked in "The Dinner Party," in which Bud's friend Cliff reveals his illness, wondering who will be left to know that the Stonewall generation ever lived at all if they all die of AIDS, and whether he himself will be remembered only as the fetching figure he once cut at a cruisey New York leather bar.

Mordden's inventory of fictional writings also includes a novel, *One Last Waltz*. Conceived as a medieval folk saga drawn into modern times, the novel recounts the fortunes of one Dublin Johnny Keogh, who settles in one of New York's old Irish working–class neighborhoods, marries Nora, and sires three sons. Johnny, the eldest son, pursues a criminal career and meets a violent end. Mike becomes an ironworker, and as a compassionate and loving family man, is the antithesis of his womanizing, alcoholic, abusive father. Dennis, who is gay, achieves commercial success as a popular song writer, but struggles to gain Mike's acceptance. *One Last Waltz* shares a similar theme to Mordden's other fictional work. "It occurs to me that all gay life is stories," asserts Mordden in the preface of *I've a Feeling We're Not in Kansas Anymore,* "that all these stories are about love somehow or other."

—*Michael Broder*

————

MORGAN, Claire. *See* **HIGHSMITH, (Mary) Patricia.**

N

NESTLE, Joan. American educator, historian, editor, and author of nonfiction. Born in New York City, 12 May 1940. Educated at Queens College, City University of New York, B.A. 1983; New York University, M.A. 1965. Writing instructor, Queens College, City University of New York, 1966—; cofounder of Lesbian Herstory Archives/Lesbian Herstory Educational Foundation, New York City, 1972—. Member of Poets and Writers, Inc. Contributor to *American Voices, Bad Attitude, Body Politic, Conditions, Gay Community News,* and *Womanews.* **Recipient:** American Library Association Gay Book Award for best gay book, 1988; Lambda Literary Award, 1990. Address: c/o LHEF, Inc., P.O. Box 1258, New York, New York 10116, U.S.A.

WRITINGS

A Restricted Country. Ithaca, New York, Firebrand, 1987.

Editor

With Naomi Holoch, *Women on Women: An Anthology of American Lesbian Short Fiction.* New York, Plume, 1990, Volume 2, 1993.
The Persistent Desire: A Femme–Butch Reader. Boston, Alyson Publications, 1992.

Other

"I Didn't Go Back There Anymore: Mabel Hampton Talks About the South" (interview), in *Feminary,* Number 10, 1977.
"The Lesbian Herstory Archives," in *Focus,* February–March 1979.
"Surviving More and More: Interview with Mabel Hampton," in *Sinister Wisdom* (Rockland, Maine), winter 1979.
"Butch/Fem and Sexual Courage," in *Body Politic,* September 1981.
Author of preface with Deborah Edel, *The Lesbian Periodicals Index.* Tallahassee, Naiad Press, 1986.

*

Biography: "Lesbian Writer Fights Feminist Censors" by Holly Metz, in *Progressive,* August 1989, 16.

Interviews: With Holly Metz, in *American Voice,* winter 1990, 72–84.

Critical Sources: Review by Mary Drake McFeely of *The Lesbian Periodicals Index,* in *Library Journal,* 15 April 1986, 71; review by Penny Kaganoff of *Women on Women: An Anthology of American Lesbian Short Fiction,* in *Publishers Weekly,* 6 April 1990, 111; "Joan Nestle: The Politics of *The Persistent Desire*" by Victoria A. Brownworth, in *Advocate,* 2 June 1992, 39; review by Lisa Nussbaum of *The Persistent Desire: A Femme–Butch Reader,* in *Library Journal,* 15 June 1992, 78; review by Marie J. Kuda of *The Persistent Desire: A Femme–Butch Reader,* in *Booklist,* July 1992, 1913.

Joan Nestle comments: "For most of my adult life, I have been absorbed with the challenge of changing the definition of history. In my teaching in the SEEK program at Queens College, my work with the Lesbian Herstory Archives, my communal readings and performances, I have explored how the human soul resists social and cultural tyrannies. I have learned that when we narrow any definition of who deserves to be free that we endanger the vitality of our own dream of liberation. Femme and butch lesbians stood against sexual bigotry when all they had to protect themselves was their need, their desire, their communal stance. My writing life began in the smoky backroom bars of the 1950s where as a young femme I witnessed both the glory of individual courage and the terror of institutionalized oppression. Now I am in my 50s, and I am still on the track of how the body speaks and what this language means."

*   *   *

Described by *Advocate* contributor Victoria A. Brownworth as "one of the preeminent historians of lesbian life in the United States," Joan Nestle cofounded the Lesbian Herstory Archives and Educational Foundation in New York in 1972. *Progressive* contributor Holly Metz described the archives as "a depository for the diaries, newsletters, photographs, and paintings of working–class lesbians—women the burgeoning women's movement had abandoned, [Nestle] says."

Nestle's studies focus on prejudice, not only from heterosexuals but from within the lesbian community as well. Although Brownworth notes that Nestle takes pride in being thought of as the "quintessential femme woman," the author's adolescence in the Bronx and the Greenwich Village section of Manhattan was marked by the discomfort of being "femme" in a lesbian world that rejected "butch–femme" relationships as unfaithful to the cause. Femme women are considered "the Uncle Toms of the lesbian–feminist movement," Nestle remarked to Brownworth. "So when I began work on *The Persistent Desire,* it was because I wanted people—especially lesbians—to see that butch–femme isn't just some negative heterosexual aping" but a legitimate lifestyle that adds to the diversity of the movement. *The Persistent Desire,* a collection of essays, poetry, fiction, and photographs, contains no pseudonyms.

One of Nestle's requirements for inclusion, she told Brownworth, was that the authors have the courage to identify themselves in print. The book is part of Nestle's ongoing attempt to create a written record of lesbianism less vulnerable to loss than the mostly oral history that has existed so far. *Booklist* reviewer Marie J. Kuda predicted that many of the "thought–provoking essays" included in *The Persistent Desire* are "certain to become keystones for future feminist and gender analyses."

Nestle's work is often opposed by heterosexual women who object to the explicit sexual content of her writing, and by lesbians who oppose not only the graphic sexuality but also Nestle's butch–femme themes, which they see as "putting forth in a positive light an exploitative heterosexual way of relating," Metz reported. In the early 1980s, representatives of the group Women Against Pornography regularly demonstrated at Nestle's speaking engagements. "The antipornography movement is helping to create a new McCarthy period in the lesbian community," Nestle wrote in 1987 in *A Restricted Country.* Although already ostracized by the larger society, lesbians who do not conform to the roles expected of them are further rejected, "distanced and told we are not feminists," Nestle continued, "even though many of us have spent years building the movement." In the years following the Stonewall rebellion, when other gays were slowly gaining ground, butch–femme lesbians were still viewed with contempt, often fired from their jobs or even arrested. Nestle told Metz that she remembers their struggle in her writing: "The work I do is in memory of their courage."

—*Deborah A. Stanley*

NEWMAN, Lesléa. American educator, poet, novelist, and author of short stories and children's fiction. Born in Brooklyn, New York, 5 November 1955. Educated at University of Vermont, B.S. 1977; Naropa Institute, certificate in poetics 1980. Manuscript reader, *Mademoiselle* and *Redbook,* New York City, 1982; book reviewer and writer, *Valley Advocate,* Hatfield, Massachusetts, 1983–87; teacher, University of Massachusetts continuing education, Amherst, 1983–85; director and teacher of creative writing summer program for high school women, Mount Holyoke College, South Hadley, Massachusetts, 1986–88; founder and director, Write from the Heart: Writing Workshops for Women, Northampton, Massachusetts, 1987—. Lecturer and conductor of writing workshops at educational institutions, including Yale University and Amherst, Smith, Swarthmore, and Trinity colleges. Regular contributor to *Conditions, Heresies, Common Lives, Sinister Wisdom,* and *Sojourner.* Member of Society of Children's Book Writers, Authors League of America, Poets and Writers, Feminist Writers Guild, Publishing Triangle, and Academy of American Poets. **Recipient:** Massachusetts Artists Foundation fellowship in poetry, 1989; Lambda Literary Award for *Gloria Goes to Gay Pride,* 1992; *Highlights for Children* fiction writing award for "Remember That," 1992. Agent: Charlotte Raymond, 32 Bradlee Road, Marblehead, Massachusetts 01945, U.S.A. Address: Write from the Heart, P.O. Box 815, Northampton, Massachusetts 01061, U.S.A.

WRITINGS

Novels

Good Enough to Eat. Ithaca, New York, Firebrand Books, and London, Sheba Feminist, 1986.
In Every Laugh a Tear. Norwich, Vermont, New Victoria, 1992.

Short Stories

A Letter to Harvey Milk. Ithaca, New York, Firebrand Books, 1988.
Secrets. Norwich, Vermont, New Victoria, 1990.

Young Adult Fiction

Fat Chance! London, Women's Press, 1993.

Children's Fiction

Heather Has Two Mommies, illustrations by Diana Souza. In Other Words/Inland, 1989.
Gloria Goes to Gay Pride, illustrations by Russell Crockfer. Boston, Alyson Publications, 1991.
Belinda's Bouquet, illustrations by Michael Willhoite. Boston, Alyson Publications, 1991.
Saturday Is Pattyday. Norwich, Vermont, New Victoria, 1993.
Remember That. New York, Clarion Books, forthcoming.
Too Far Away to Touch, Close Enough to See. New York, Clarion Books, forthcoming.

Poetry

Just Looking for My Shoes. Seattle, Back Door Press, 1980.
Love Me Like You Mean It. Santa Cruz, California, HerBooks, 1987.
Sweet Dark Places. Santa Cruz, California, HerBooks, 1991.

Plays

After All We've Been Through (produced Durham, North Carolina, 1989).
Rage (produced New York, 1991).

Nonfiction

"Writing as Self–Discovery," in *Writer,* January 1988.
Somebody to Love: A Guide to Loving the Body You Have. Chicago, Third Side Press, 1991.
Writing from the Heart: Inspiration and Exercises for Women Who Want to Write. Freedom, California, Crossing Press, 1993.

Other

Editor and author of introduction, *Bubbe Meisehs by Shayneh Maidelehs: Poetry by Jewish Granddaughters about Our Grandmothers.* Santa Cruz, California, HerBooks, 1989.
Editor, *Eating Our Hearts Out: Personal Accounts of Women's Relationship to Food.* Freedom, California, Crossing Press, 1993.
Editor, *Bearing the Unbearable: Stories of Losing Loved Ones to AIDS.* Freedom, California, Crossing Press, forthcoming.

Adaptations: *A Letter to Harvey Milk* was produced by Yariv Kohn, York University, Canada, 1990.

Interviews: "Hamp Woman Writes of Lesbian Family" by Natalia Munoz, in *Sunday Republican* (Springfield, Massachusetts), 14 January 1990, E2; "The Jewish Madonna" by Victoria A. Brownworth, in *Lambda Book Report*, November/December 1992, 22.

Critical Sources: "One Step at a Time" (review of *Good Enough to Eat*) by Susanna J. Sturgis, in *Women's Review of Books*, May 1987, 13; review by Joanne Jimason of *Heather Has Two Mommies*, in *Belles Lettres*, winter 1991, 59; "Gay and Lesbian Books for Children," in *Lambda Book Report*, March 1991, 25; *Booklist*, 1992; "Gay Bibliography Rejected by the New York City Schools," in *Publishers Weekly*, 27 April 1992, 18.

Lesléa Newman comments: "Ever since I was a child I have written poems and stories in order to try and understand the world around me, the world inside me and the relationship between the two. Issues of identity and belonging have always been important to me; the position of being an outsider gives one a unique perspective. I write about being a woman, being a Jew and being a lesbian, living in a difficult world in difficult times. Humor runs rampant throughout my work; I use it to remind myself that even in the most trying of times, there is much to be joyful about."

*   *   *

Under the assumption that humans cannot live without nourishment—spiritual, emotional, and actual—and under the assumption that writers and readers meet best on planes that offer these essentials among sensual details, one finds in Lesléa Newman's writing food for the goddess, food for thought, food for a large populace.

Her work, whether directed to children or an adult readership, continually explores issues of lesbian identity and Jewish identity, as well as the political relationships between women and food. Saturated in Yiddish, these predicaments of struggle, discovery and acceptance are so steeped in unique details that they rise above the formulaic, illustrating that Newman heeds her own advice. In "Writing As Self–Discovery" she encourages beginning writers to fill the pages with "sensory detail," noting that "the more specific images you have, the more alive your writing will be." From detailing a grey hospital setting in "Sunday Afternoon" to etching holy domesticity in "One Shabbos Evening," Newman abides by this literary philosophy.

To such vivid settings, she adds solid characterization. In *A Letter To Harvey Milk*, a 1988 collection of short stories, Newman compacts a virtual universe of characters. Rachel, in "The Gift," grows from five years old to adulthood in video–like glimpses, rejecting, accepting and finally celebrating her Judaic background. Like a *tallis,* her faith and beliefs finally rest easily on her shoulders. Other characters confront contemporary issues such as AIDS, relationship struggles, incest—less than desirable situations—but somehow comfortably universal, as they do in another sound collection, *Secrets.*

Her work also highlights eating disorders. *Good Enough To Eat* chronicles the daily struggles of a young woman suffering from bulimia. Throughout most of the novel, the reader finds her possessed and obsessed with food. Sharing an apartment with a whimsical gay man and a vague straight woman, the character continually checks her designated refrigerator shelf, weighing its contents and her self–worth simultaneously. After dipping into her roommate's cache, she chastises herself: "Here you are popping out of your clothes and still you go on eating and eating like there's nothing wrong with you." Later she adds, "It was only a bit of cottage cheese."

These food dilemmas show up elsewhere in Newman's writing. From her poetry, where in "Hunger" she notes that her "thighs grow fat and get in each other's way," to *Somebody To Love: A Guide To Loving The Body You Have*, where she offers candid advice and writing suggestions designed to empower women through their body images, Newman burns the torch for self–acceptance.

She offers the same, realistic exposure for children in *Belinda's Bouquet*, the story of a young girl who arrives at self acceptance. Belinda moves from being a tormented child, teased on the bus for being fat, to a reflective individual after hearing a tale about a gardener who attempts to put all of her marigolds on a diet to make them "thin like the irises," at which point they naturally whither and droop.

Newman manages to step clear of the didactic and continues instead the same Aesopian insight she offered in the groundbreaking book *Heather Has Two Mommies*. In this book, Heather, raised by two lesbians, is confronted in school with a concept of a father, and the child is reduced to tears because she doesn't have the "typical" nuclear family. She learns that many children, not just those with lesbian parents, often have no such family structure. One classmate has a single mother; another has two fathers; still another is part of an adoptive family. Newman continues her pioneering work in *Gloria Goes To Gay Pride*, in which she offers a variety of characters who pivot around Gloria as she participates in the parade. Gays, lesbians, straights, all colorfully portrayed, call for understanding. However, because of content deemed sensitive by several libraries across the nation, Newman's books for children have caused considerable controversy over the issue of lesbian/gay censorship.

Newman's three collections of poetry, *Love Me Like You Mean It, Just Looking For My Shoes,* and *Sweet Dark Places,* reflect yet another outlet for her creativity. Again the human predicament is scoped, illuminated, and celebrated. Her lines reflect real–life situations—sometimes painful, sometimes playful, always candid—as she continues to explore her lesbianism and Jewish identity.

This quest cumulates and unfolds in her 1992 novel *In Every Laugh a Tear* where Newman writes about a mid–life Jewish lesbian caught in the midst of outrage over her grandmother's induction into a nursing home. As Shayna immerses herself into Bubbe's life, sharing the frustrations and fears of aging, Newman consistently stays the great observer, pulls back from any *schmaltz,* offering instead a grandmother who opens a dresser drawer to offer "two American cheese sandwiches." Yet, the old woman's wisdom is not lost. Watching the multitudes pass through the home, she notes: "*Nu,* welcome to God's waiting room." And when the matriarch finally passes, a much stronger Shayna exchanges keepsakes with her mother and promises of commitment with her lover.

In all genres Newman's literary style offers a succession of surprises as she swings from first to third person effortlessly.From hard cadence to a lazy stream of consciousness, the works reveal a woman unafraid of risks. Newman, in an interview for the *Springfield Sunday Republican,* stated that writing is "like being an explorer—when you get scared, you should keep going."

Newman's work, certainly a tribute to her culture and sexual orientation, manages to offer a bridge for those who cannot claim such background elements, offering education, enlightenment and entertainment. One comes away decidedly hungry for more as she assumes her rightful place in the literary canon.

—*Carmen Embry*

———

NIVEN, Vern. *See* **GRIER, Barbara G(ene Damon).**

O

O'HARA, Frank (Francis Russell O'Hara). American poet and dramatist. Born in Baltimore, Maryland, 27 March 1926. Educated at Harvard University, Cambridge, Massachusetts, A.B. 1950; University of Michigan, Ann Arbor (Hopwood award, 1951), M.A. 1951. Served in the U.S. Navy, 1944–46. Museum of Modern Art, New York City, staff member, 1952–53, organizer of circulating exhibitions, 1955–60, assistant curator in department of painting and sculpture exhibitions, 1960–66. Editorial associate, *Art News,* New York City, 1953–55. Poet and playwright in residence, Poet's Theatre, Cambridge, 1956. **Recipient:** Ford Foundation fellowship, 1956; National Book Award, 1972. *Died in Mastic Beach, Long Island, New York, after being struck by a dune–buggy taxicab on Fire Island, 25 July 1965.*

WRITINGS

Poetry

A City Winter, and Other Poems, drawings by Larry Rivers. New York, Tibor de Nagy Gallery Editions, 1952.
Meditations in an Emergency. Palma de Mallorca, Spain, M. Alcover, 1956.
Jackson Pollock (monograph). New York, Braziller, 1959.
Second Avenue. New York, Totem Press, 1960.
Odes, serigraphs by Michael Goldberg. Tiber Press, 1960.
Lunch Poems. San Francisco, City Lights Books, 1964.
Featuring Frank O'Hara. Buffalo, New York, 1964.
Love Poems. New York, Tibor de Nagy Gallery Editions, 1965.
Five Poems. Pratt Adlib Press, 1967.
In Memory of My Feelings: A Selection of Poems, edited by Bill Berkson. New York, Museum of Modern Art, 1967.
Two Pieces. London, Long Hair Books, 1969.
Oranges. New York, Angel Hair Books, 1970.
The Collected Poems of Frank O'Hara, edited by Donald M. Allen. New York, Knopf, 1971.
The Selected Poems of Frank O'Hara, edited by Donald M. Allen. New York, Knopf, 1974.
With Bill Berkson, *Hymns of St. Bridget.* New York, Adventures in Poetry, 1974.
The End of the Far West: 11 Poems, 1974.
Early Writing: 1946–1950, edited by Donald M. Allen. Bolinas, California, Grey Fox Press, 1977.
Poems Retrieved: 1950–1966, edited by Donald M. Allen. Bolinas, California, Grey Fox Press, 1977.

Plays

Try! Try! (produced Cambridge, Massachusetts, 1951).

Change Your Bedding (produced Cambridge, Massachusetts, 1952).
The Houses at Fallen Hanging (produced Living Theatre, 1956).
Awake in Spain (produced Living Theatre, 1960). New York, American Theatre for Poets, 1960.
Love's Labor (produced Living Theatre, 1960). New York, American Theatre for Poets, 1964.
The General's Return from One Place to Another (produced New York, 1964). New York, 1962.
Selected Plays. New York, Full Court Press, 1978.
With V. R. Lang, *A Day in the Life of the Czar; or, I Too Have Lived in Arcadia* (produced New York, 1980).

Exhibition Catalogs

New Spanish Painting and Sculpture: Rafael Canogar and Others. Garden City, New York, Doubleday, 1960.
An Exhibition of Oil Paintings by Frankenthaler. New York, Jewish Museum of the Jewish Theological Seminary of America, 1960.
Franz Kline. Turin, Italy, 1963.
Arshile Gorky. Bonn, Germany, Hermes, 1964.
Robert Motherwell: With Selections from the Artist's Writings. Garden City, New York, Doubleday, 1965.
David Smith, 1907–1965, at the Tate Gallery. London, 1966.
Nakian. Garden City, New York, Doubleday, 1966.

Other

Hartigan and Rivers with O'Hara (an exhibition of pictures, with poems by O'Hara). New York, Tibor de Nagy Gallery Editions, 1959.
Belgrade, November 19, 1963 (letter). Adventures in Poetry, c. 1972.
Art Chronicles 1954–66. New York, Braziller, 1975.
Standing Still and Walking in New York (includes essays, criticism, and an interview with O'Hara), edited by Donald M. Allen. Bolinas, California, Grey Fox Press, 1975.
Homage to Frank O'Hara, edited by Bill Berkson and Joe LeSueur. Berkeley, California, Creative Arts, 1980.

*

Biography: *Frank O'Hara: Poet among Painters* by Marjorie Perloff, New York, Braziller, 1977; *Frank O'Hara* by Alan Feldman, Boston, Twayne, 1979; *City Poet: The Life and Times of Frank O'Hara* by Brad Gooch, New York, Knopf, 1993.

Bibliography: *Frank O'Hara: A Comprehensive Bibliography* by Alexander Smith, Jr., New York, Garland, 1979.

* * *

A poet who celebrated the uncertainties of his time and ridiculed the fraud of traditional poetry, families and values, Frank O'Hara might have enjoyed the shame of his parents, revealed long after his death: that they had fled the town in Massachusetts where he was conceived for Baltimore to await his birth and had falsified his birth record because his mother was pregnant when she married his father. Every record—except his actual birth certificate—records his birth date as 27 June; in fact, O'Hara was born three months earlier, on 27 March. During his formative years, O'Hara attended Catholic schools and was encouraged to enter the priesthood.

To escape the small Massachusetts town of Grafton, O'Hara involved himself in music and movies. He became an excellent pianist and studied to become a composer. On trips to Worcester or Boston for music lessons or to see a movie, he began to pick up sexual partners. In Brad Gooch's *City Poet: The Life and Times of Frank O'Hara,* Larry Rivers, a painter and lover, recalled: "Frank told me that his first homosexual experience was with a stable guy, a guy who took care of the horses, when he was sixteen." In the 1960 work *Second Avenue,* he imagined his father saying, "Do what you want but don't get hurt, / I'm warning you. Leave the men alone, they'll only tease you." As soon as he graduated from high school, he was drafted, entered the navy, and was able to pursue his interests while stationed in Key West and San Francisco. He was trained as a sonar operator and served in the Pacific aboard the USS *Nicholas.*

With the G.I. bill, O'Hara entered Harvard in the fall of 1946 and graduated in the class of 1950. Although he initially intended to study composition, he soon turned to poetry, theater, and the avant garde groups in Cambridge. Here he met Kenneth Koch, John Ashbery, Bunny Lang, and published in the Harvard student magazine. He finished a master's degree at the University of Michigan in 1951 and returned to Cambridge briefly as a resident playwright for the Poet's Theater, but college towns bored him.

O'Hara loved New York City, from which he seldom strayed after 1952, except to spent summers on Long Island, Fire Island, in Provincetown, Maine, or Vermont. Gooch, in his biography, writes that O'Hara "composed a fragmented epic" of New York City, "focusing particularly on the humor and chaos of the growing metropolis and using his experiences as a trail through an ever–changing urban labyrinth."

O'Hara found music, ballet, theater, poetry, love, casual sex, painters, and museums in the city, but he also enjoyed its radical tradition. He had admired F. O. Matthiessen's queerness and socialism at Harvard; in the navy he posed for a photograph with a copy of Dwight Macdonald's anarchist paper, *politics,* where Robert Duncan's essay "The Homosexual in Society" had appeared in August of 1944. He may have been joking when he said the *Communist Manifesto* was his favorite book, but he admired the Russian revolutionary authors and the influence of Vladimir Mayakovsky on his own poetry and theater was profound. While he never clicked with Paul Goodman, he admired his anarchism, his homosexuality, his poetry, and his ideas about literature. He celebrated Nikita

Khruschev and Fidel Castro's kissing at the United Nations. And O'Hara's last poem, "Little Elegy for Antonio Machado," remembered a poet who had died in 1939 while fighting Francisco Franco: "where our futures lie increasingly in fire / twisted ropes of sound encrusting our brains / ... insist on our joining you."

To O'Hara, prejudice was intolerable. He admired African American poets, worked closely with Leroi Jones (Amiri Baaraka), and—in "Ode Salute to the French Negro Poets"— concludes that "the only truth is face to face, the poem whose words become your mouth / and dying in black and white we fight for what we love, not are." His love for black men extended beyond poetry. In "The Movies," O'Hara ("the white heron of your darkness") celebrates his love for a partner sitting beside him.

O'Hara utilized many of the devices of camp in his poetry. A form of covert but pointed speaking, camp could be found throughout the work of Ronald Firbank, one of O'Hara's favorite novelists. One of its earliest definitions came in Christopher Isherwood's *The World in the Evening,* in 1952, and O'Hara, in a poem of that year, "Easter," spoke of "a self–coral serpent wrapped around an arm with no jujubes / without swish / without camp." O'Hara loved swishiness, silliness, giddiness, playful avoidance, wisecracks and the anti–monumental. Allen Ginsberg praised his "common ear / for our deep gossip." O'Hara's "Personism: A Manifesto," which appeared in one version in Leroi Jones' *Jugen* magazine, certainly pokes fun at moral seriousness, but his "Manifesto," because it is funny and irresponsible, is not necessarily false (except in the sense that wigs or a drag queen's breasts are false). Instead, it struggles not to be studied.

A comparison of O'Hara's poetry with the Beats (Jack Kerouac, Allen Ginsberg, Gregory Corso, etc.) helps define his poetry. He shared with them an intense distaste for academics. Appearing on Staten Island with Brahmin Robert Lowell, O'Hara read a poem he had written while coming over on the ferry: "I have been to lots of parties / and acted perfectly disgraceful / but I never actually collapsed / oh Lana Turner we love you get up." Lowell sneered at such frivolity, but even O'Hara's friend John Ashbery, who shared O'Hara's coyness, embraced the Beats. Perhaps music was the difference. Both Ashbery and O'Hara loved classical music; but O'Hara explored jazz and the blues, as did the Beats, although he never ventured into folk music. Ginsberg tried valiantly to reconcile the poets, but his straight friends could be obstreperous.

While never without camp, O'Hara wrote extraordinary series of poems for his many lovers. Virgil Thomson claimed that "after his death a dozen of his lovers turned up looking for the glory of being the chief widow." And Larry Rivers, perhaps Frank's deepest love, said in his eulogy, according to the Gooch biography, that "Frank O'Hara was my best friend. There are at least sixty people in New York who thought Frank O'Hara was their best friend." In a sense, all were his lovers and friends because his poetry encompasses an extraordinary range of the city, life, people."

Not unlike Whitman, O'Hara used the sense of sight intensely. Marjorie Perloff, in her 1977 *Frank O'Hara: Poet Among Painters,* carefully traces the interconnections between him and the painters. Eventually a curator at the Museum of Modern Art and the author of two books and numerous reviews of artists, O'Hara explored everything new. Further study on O'Hara and film, a medium that combines both sound and light, gives substance to his suggestion that "only Whitman and Crane and Williams, of the American poets, are better than the movies."

O'Hara wrote his last poem on (what he did not know was his 40th birthday) 27 March 1966. Nearly a month later, on 25 July

1966, he was struck by a dune–buggy taxicab and killed. Since his death, his reputation has continued to grow. *The Collected Poems of Frank O'Hara,* edited by Donald Allen, appeared in 1971, and new material has continued to surface and be published. His collected letters have yet to appear. Gay liberationists have embraced his work and have further increased his popularity, and biography's such as Gooch's utilize a medium O'Hara loved so much: gossip to open up new illuminations, new inspirations.

—*Charles Shively*

————

ORTON, Joe (John Kingsley Orton). British playwright and actor. Born in Leicester, in 1933. Educated at Royal Academy of Dramatic Art. **Recipient:** London Critics Variety Award, 1964; *Evening Standard* citation for best play of 1966. *Bludgeoned to death in a murder–suicide by his long–time companion, Kenneth Halliwell, 9 August 1967.*

WRITINGS

Plays

Crimes of Passion: The Ruffian on the Stair [and] *The Erpingham Camp* (*The Ruffian on the Stair* broadcast by BBC–Radio, 1964; *The Erpingham Camp* televised by Rediffusion Television, 1966; both plays produced London, 1967; New York, 1969). London, Methuen, 1967.
Entertaining Mr. Sloane (produced London, 1964; on Broadway, 1965). London, Hamilton, 1964; New York, Grove, 1965; with introduction by John Lahr, London, Eyre–Methuen, 1973.
Loot (produced Cambridge, England, 1965; London, 1966; New York, 1968). New York, Grove, 1967.
Funeral Games [and] *The Good and Faithful Servant* (*The Good and Faithful Servant* produced London, 1967; *Funeral Games* produced New York, 1979). London, Methuen, 1970.
What the Butler Saw (produced London, 1969; New York, 1970). London, Methuen, 1969; New York, Grove, 1970.
Orton: The Complete Plays, London, Methuen, and New York, Grove, 1976.

Other

"Until She Screams" (dramatic sketch), in *Oh! Calcutta!,* edited by Kenneth Tynan. New York, Grove, 1969.
Head to Toe (novel), illustrations by Patrick Procktor and Interphot. London, Blond, and New York, St. Martin's Press, 1971.
Up Against It: A Screenplay for the Beatles (unproduced screenplay; produced as musical New York, 1989). London, Methuen, 1979.
The Orton Diaries, edited by John Lahr. New York, Harper, 1986.

Biography: *Prick Up Your Ears: The Biography of Joe Orton* by John Lahr, London, Allen Lane, 1978; *Joe Orton* by Maurice Charney, London, Macmillan, 1984.

Bibliography: *Twenty Modern British Playwrights: A Bibliography, 1956 to 1976,* New York and London, Garland, 1977, 77–83.

Critical Sources: *The Second Wave: New British Drama for the Seventies,* by John Russell Taylor, New York, Hill & Wang, 1971; "Comedy or Farce?" by Frank Marcus, in *London* Magazine, February 1967; "Joe Orton: His Brief Career" by Keath Fraser, in *Modern Drama,* Number 14, 1971; "Comic, Tragic, or Absurd? On Some Parallels between the Farces of Joe Orton and Seventeenth–Century Tragedy," in *English Studies,* Number 59, 1978; "Tragic Farce: Orton and Euripides" by Niall W. Slater, in *Classical and Modern Literature: A Quarterly,* winter 1987; "Joe Orton and the Redefinition of Farce" by Joan F. Dean, in *Theatre Journal,* December 1982; "'The Love of Money Is the Root of All Evil': Joe Orton's *Loot*" by Bert Cardullo, in *Notes on Contemporary Literature,* November 1983; "Joe Orton and the Heterogeneity of the Book" by Michael Beehler, *Sub–stance,* 1982; "Orton's *Loot* as 'Quotidian Farce': The Intersection of Black Comedy and Daily Life" by Maurice Charney, in *Modern Drama,* December 1981; "What Did the Butler See in Orton's *What the Butler Saw?*" by Maurice Charney, in *Modern Drama,* December 1982; "Joe Orton" by John Bull and Frances Gray, in *Essays on Contemporary British Drama,* edited by Hedwig Bock and Albert Wertheim, Munich, Hueber, 1981; "Joe Orton: The Comedy of Ill Manners" by Martin Esslin, in *Contemporary English Drama,* edited by C. W. E. Bigsby and Malcolm Bradbury, New York, Holmes & Meier, 1981; *Because We're Queers: The Life and Crimes of Kenneth Halliwell and Joe Orton* by Simon Shepherd, London, GMP Publishers, 1989.

*   *   *

"I want nothing to do with the civilisation they made. Fuck them!" Such are the words of "Angry Young Man" and internationally famous gay playwright Joe Orton regarding heterosexual society. England's heterosexist supremacy in the 1960s provided ample outrage to spur Orton's literary warfare. His arsenal consisted of madcap farce and macabre comedy. His strategy was simple: rather than promote homosexual characters, he mercilessly satirized heterosexual ones, utilizing brilliant dialogue and strong plots that attacked the pretense of authority figures, religion and hollow respectability.

Enjoying eminence only briefly, playwright Orton became even more famous due to his sensationalistic death at age 34 at the hands of his lover and companion of 14 years. Kenneth Halliwell bludgeoned Orton nine times with a hammer, then immediately committed suicide by taking 22 Nembutals. The exact reason for the murder and suicide is unknown, though speculation abounds, with some claiming it the culmination of jealousy. But Simon Shepherd suggests in *Because We're Queers,* "It was the new society [upper class English theatre elite] with its attitudes and pressures, not [Orton's] promiscuity, which tore them apart." Despite Halliwell's infamy, his contribution to Orton's oeuvre was profound, including immeasurable suggestions, support, encouragement and editing advice.

Orton was born on 1 January 1933, in Leicester, England. "I'm from the gutter," he once said. "And don't you ever forget it because I won't." John Lahr comments in *Prick Up Your Ears* that the "bleak adequacy of the Saffron Lane Estates [in Leicester] had a deceptive violence," and comic violence would become a staple of Orton's plays.

In 1949 Orton acted in a small role in *Richard III* with the Leicester Dramatic Society, then joined the Bats Players and the Vaughan Players. In 1951 he began studies at the Royal Academy of Dramatic Arts where he met and moved in with Kenneth Halliwell. Cohabitating until their deaths, they shared interests in acting at first, then began to write novels and finally plays.

In 1962 the two men were arraigned for stealing and defacing library books. Their mischievous additions of comic imagery and/or text to the covers resulted in six months in jail. Lahr offers, "Prison was more of a turning point in their life than either Orton or Halliwell at first admitted. Orton found a focus for his anger and a new detachment in his writing." Clearly, authority figures became recurring targets in his ensuing work.

Homophobia reigned in Orton's England. As Shepherd points out, "In the '60s ... homosexuality was an 'issue' discussed by those who wanted to reform the law that made it illegal in all circumstances.... Illegality, isolation and pity all had their effects on the way individual homosexuals regarded themselves." On 27 July 1967, less than a month before Orton's death, the Homosexual Bill became law, legalizing private sex between consenting adults.

Orton did *not* write gay plays wallowing in guilt and homosexual angst, however. Rather, he explored relatively uncharted territory in the theatrical portrayal of gays by creating unrepentant, masculine (sometimes threatening) males with versatile sexual natures. Shepard offers that, "In his plays Orton continually infiltrated the action with images of sexy boys.... The young men are characterised with a knowingness which, combined with a casualness about sexual pleasure, constitute a deliberate rejection by Orton of the traditional portrayal of homosexual desire." He continues, "Orton's youths make themselves available to other people's desires. They have not internalised any notion of the forbidden or the special. They show no acceptance of homosexual weirdness or otherness. There is no break between desire and everyday life."

His characters are capable of any extreme when pursuing their immediate goals: blackmail, theft, incest, assault and battery, corpse dismemberment, murder, and more. Lahr states, "Each character has his kingdom—whether holiday camp [*The Erpingham Camp*], psychiatric ward [*What the Butler Saw*] or police squad [*Loot*]. Each is a freak of power and propriety." Interestingly, these comic criminals never indulge in the "crimes" in which Orton partook: mild drug abuse (hashish) and homosexuality. Anonymous sex reinforced his constantly expressed beliefs. "You must do whatever you like," Orton said, "as long as you enjoy it and don't hurt anybody else, that's all that matters." Complete sexual license performed another task in Orton's opinion: "It's the only way to smash the wretched civilisation."

Orton's stylistic use of language appropriately accompanies his scandalous subject matter. Shepard notes the "use of journalese in Orton's plays." The journalese is the type found mostly in the terse sensationalism of tabloid publications. Lahr posits, "The elegance of Orton's comic syntax aspires to perfection while the characters who speak it are unashamedly imperfect. They speak a language of reason but live a life of chaos." Orton simply stated,

"My writing is a deliberate satire on bad theatre."

The Ruffian on the Stair, Orton's first play, (originally titled *The Boy Hairdresser*), contains gay, albeit usually oblique, innuendo. Shepard notes that "homosexual jokes ... creep in at the edges of the conversation." The opening interchange includes Mike's ambiguous announcement, "I'm meeting a man in the toilet." Orton skillfully uses comedy to elicit laughter rather than shock from an admission of mutually consenting homosexual incest, such as when Wilson declares, "[My brother] wore white shorts better than any man I've ever come in contact with."

Loot became Orton's great breakthrough, receiving the *Evening Standard* award and making him internationally famous. Lahr notes, "*Loot* brought Orton's craft to its maturity." Audiences and critics were outraged by the frenzied farce involving an on-stage coffin with an ever-mobile female corpse, a self-righteous Catholic, a murderous nurse, an intrusive policeman, and a pair of bisexual boys. *Loot*'s macabre comic devices put homosexuality into perspective as a minor offense, if an offense at all. As Fay accurately yet impassively states to one of the boys, "Even the sex you were born into isn't safe from your marauding."

In *What the Butler Saw*, Orton's final and most complex farce, madness reigns amongst the "sane" staff of an asylum. Sexual humor abounds. One character advises her husband, "Try a boy for a change. You're a rich man. You can afford the luxuries of life." A policeman seeks a missing cigar (a penis in an earlier draft) from the remains of a Sir Winston Churchill statue. Shepard speculates that "Orton's joking with the penis and the phallus shows him opposing authority but remaining basically committed to masculine sexuality.... The mystique of the penis in British society is preserved by the way it is concealed." Deception on all levels reigns from spoken lies to rampant transvestism.

Aside from his stage plays, Orton had several other works to his credit. A "pornographic sketch" titled "Until She Screams" is one of many scenes in the long-running play *Oh Calcutta!* (which Orton speculated would never be produced). His novel *Head to Toe* was published posthumously. In that work, protagonist Gombold travels aimlessly from head to toe on the body of the giant Atlas, where he encounters strange allegorical characters; the novel is filled with images from Greek mythology. Even in this early work, Orton makes evident his respect for words and their power as weapons in political and social revolution. Orton's only screenplay, *Up Against It*, was written as a vehicle for the Beatles but was rejected for production.

Orton, via his plays, not only successfully vented his rage against a heterosexist society, but he made his enemies (audiences) love the attack. After a decade of preparation, his career began to escalate. For four years he and Halliwell witnessed the phenomenally growing public acceptance of his plays, style and subject matter. Gay and gay-related material progressed from spoken innuendo to an elaborately visual pansexual saturnalia. On 25 May (two and one-half months before their deaths) while relaxing in Tangier, Orton prophetically if not ironically wrote in his diaries, "[Halliwell and I] sat talking of how happy we both felt and of how it couldn't, surely, last. We'd have to pay for it. Or we'd be struck down from afar by disaster because we were, perhaps, too happy."

—*Tom W. Kelly*

OWEN, Wilfred (Edward Salter). British poet. Born in Oswestry, Shropshire, 18 March 1893. Educated at Birkenhead Institute 1900–07; Shrewsbury Technical School, 1907–11. Served in the British Army, 1915–18; became lieutenant; awarded the Military Cross, 1918. Held several positions during his lifetime, including lay assistant, Vicar of Dunsden, Oxfordshire, 1911–13; English tutor, Berlitz School of Languages, Bordeaux, France, 1913–15. *Died in combat, Sambre Canal, France, 4 November 1918.*

WRITINGS

Selected Books: Poems, edited by Siegfried Sassoon. London, Chatto & Windus, 1920; New York, Huebsch, 1921.
The Poems of Wilfred Owen, edited by Edmund Blunden. London, Chatto & Windus, and New York, Viking, 1931.
Thirteen Poems. Northampton, Massachusetts, Gehenna Press, 1956.
The Collected Poems of Wilfred Owen, edited by C. Day Lewis. London, Chatto & Windus, 1963; New York, New Directions, 1964.
Collected Letters, 1967.
Wilfred Owen: War Poems and Others, edited by Dominic Hibberd. London, Chatto & Windus, 1973.
Ten War Poems. Oxford, Taurus Press, 1974.
The Complete Poems and Fragments, edited by Jon Stallworthy. London, Chatto & Windus, 1983.
The Poems of Wilfred Owen, edited by Jon Stallworthy. New York, Norton, 1986.

*

Manuscript Collections: The major repository for manuscripts of Owen's poems is the British Museum, London; Owen's letters are housed at the University of Texas, Austin.

Biography: *Journey from Obscurity: Wilfred Owen 1893–1918* by Harold Owen, London and New York, Oxford University Press, 1963–1965; *Requiem for War: The Life of Wilfred Owen* by Arthur Ormont, New York, Four Winds Press, 1972; *Wilfred Owen* by Jon Stallworthy, London, Oxford University Press, 1974; *Wilfred Owen* by Dominic Hibberd, London, Longman Group, 1975; "Wilfred Owen" by Margaret B. McDowell, in *Dictionary of Literary Biography,* Volume 20: *British Poets 1914–1945,* Detroit, Gale, 1983, 258–269; *Owen the Poet* by Dominic Hibberd, Athens, University of Georgia Press, 1986; *Wilfred Owen: Anthem for a Doomed Youth* by Kenneth Simcox, London, Woburn Press, 1987; "Wilfred Owen" by Margaret B. McDowell, in *Concise Dictionary of British Literary Biography,* Volume 6: *Modern Writers, 1914–1945,* Detroit, Gale, 1992, 304–315.

Bibliography: *Wilfred Owen (1893–1918): A Bibliography* by William White, Kent, Kent State University Press, 1967.

Critical Sources: "The Real War" by Edmund Blunden, in *Athenaeum* (London), 10 December 1920, 807; "Review of Poems by Wilfred Owen," in *London Mercury,* January 1921, 334–336; "En-glish Poets of Today," in *New York Times Book Review,* 15 May 1921, 13, 27; "Edited" by Geoffrey Grigson, in *Saturday Review,* 18 July 1931, 95; "A Dead Poetic Movement" by Gregory Horace, in *Nation,* 25 November 1931, 577–578; "The Poems of Wilfred Owen," in *Hound and Horn,* July–September 1932, 679–681; "Poetry" by Edwin Muir, in *The Present Age from 1914,* edited by Edwin Muir, London, Cresset Press, 1939, 43–128; "Two Prophetic Poems" by D. S. Savage, in *Western Review* (Iowa City), winter 1949, 67–78; "Half Rhyme in Wilfred Owen: Its Derivation and Use" by D. S. R. Welland, in *Review of English Studies,* July 1950, 226–241; "Trench Poets" by Vivian de Sola Pinto, in *Crisis in English Poetry, 1880–1940,* edited by Vivian de Sola Pinto, London, Hutchison's University Library, 1951, 137–157; "Owen's 'The Show'" by Joseph Cohen, in *Explicator,* November 1957; "Wilfred Owen in America" by Joseph Cohen, in *Prairie Schooner* (Lincoln, Nebraska), winter 1957, 339–345; "In Memory of W. B. Yeats and Wilfred Owen" by Joseph Cohen, in *Journal of English and Germanic Philology* (Urbana, Illinois), October 1959, 637–649; "Out of Ugliness" by Louis McNeice, in *New Statesman,* London, 20 October 1960, 623–624; "The Literature of the First World War" by D. J. Enright, in *The Pelican Guide to English Literature,* Volume 7: *The Modern Age,* edited by Boris Ford, Harmondsworth, Middlesex, Penguin Books, 1961, 154–169; "Toward Hysteria" by Hoxie Neale Fairchild, in *Religious Trends in English Poetry,* Volume 5: *1880–1920, Gods of a Changing Poetry,* edited by Hoxie Neale Fairchild, New York, Columbia University Press, 1962, 578–627; "The Truth Told" by D. J. Enright, in *New Statesman,* London, 27 September 1963, 408, 410; "Two War Poets" by G. S. Fraser, in *New York Review of Books,* 19 March 1964, 6–7; *Tribute to Wilfred Owen* by T. J. Walsh, Liverpool, Birkenhead Institute, 1964; "Wilfred Owen, Edward Thomas and D. H. Lawrence" by Anthony Thwaite, in *Contemporary English Poetry: An Introduction,* edited by Anthony Thwaite, London, Heinemann, 1964, 42–53; "The Embattled Truth: Wilfred Owen and Isaac Rosenberg" by Frederick Grubb, in *A Vision of Reality: A Study of Liberalism in Twentieth Century Verse,* edited by Frederick Grubb, New York, Barnes and Noble, 1965, 73–96; "Critics Key: Poem or Personality?" by Gertrude M. White, in *English Literature in Transition, 1880–1920* (Tempe, Arizona), 2:3, 1968, 174–179; "W. B. Yeats and Wilfred Owen" by Jon Stallworthy, in *Critical Quarterly* (Hull, England), autumn 1969, 199–214; *Wilfred Owen* by Gertrude M. White, New York, Twayne, 1969; "Edward Thomas; Wilfred Owen, Isaac Rosenberg; Harold Monro" by C. H. Sisson, in *English Poetry, 1900–1950: An Assessment,* New York, St. Martin's Press, 1971, 71–95; *Wilfred Owen: Chatterton Lecture on an English Poet* by Jon Stallworthy, London, Oxford University Press, 1971; *An Adequate Response: The War Poetry of Wilfred Owen & Siegfried Sassoon* by Arthur E. Lane, Detroit, Wayne State University Press, 1972; "Wilfred Owen's Personality as Revealed by His Letters" by Michele Kaltemback, in *Caliban* (Toulouse, France), Number 10, 1973, 43–54; *Wilfred Owen's Poetry: A Study Guide* by James F. McIlroy, London, Heinemann Educational, 1974; "The Real Wilfred Owen's Life and Legends" by Philip Larkin, in *Encounter* (London), March 1975, 73–81; "Wilfred Owen: A Reassessment" by A. Banerjee, in *Literary Half Yearly* (Mysore, India), July 1977, 85–100; *Wilfred Owen's Strange Meeting: A Critical Study* by Sasi Bhusan Das, Calcutta, Firma KLM, 1977; "Introduction" by Jon Silkin, in *The Book of First World War Poetry,* edited by Jon Silkin, London, Allen Lane, 1978, 11–73; *Wilfred Owen: A Critical Study* by Dennis Welland, London, Chatto & Windus, 1978; "Wilfred Owen and the Georgians" by Dominic Hibberd, in *Review of En-*

glish Studies (Oxford), February 1979, 28–40; "The Analysis of Poetic Texts: Owen's 'Futility' and Davie's 'The Garden Party'" by F. W. Bateson, in Essays in Criticism (Oxford), April 1979, 156–164; Aspects of Wilfred Owen's Poetry by Sasi Bhusan Das, Calcutta, Roy & Roy, 1979; A Concordance to the Poems and Fragments of Wilfred Owen by Donald A. Heneghan, Boston, G. K. Hall, 1979; Tradition Transformed: Studies in the Poetry of Wilfred Owen by Sven Backman, Lund, Sweden, C. W. K. Gleerup, 1979; "Wilfred Owen's 'Mental Cases'" by Mark Sinfield, in Notes and Queries, August 1982, 339–341; Wilfred Owen's Influence on Three Generations of Poets by Sasi Bhusan Das, Calcutta, Roy & Roy, 1982; "Owen's 'Dulce et Decorum Est'" by George V. Griffith, in Explicator, spring 1983, 37–39; The Truth of War: Owen, Blunden, Rosenberg by Desmond Graham, Manchester, Carcanet Press, 1984; "Wilfred Owen's Poetic Development" by James Hepburn, Critic into Anti–Critic, edited by James Hepburn, Columbia, South Carolina, Camden House, 1984, 167–178; "The Critic as Anti–Hero: War Poetry" by Herbert Lomas, in Hudson Review, autumn 1985, 376–389; "Shell Shock and Poetry: Wilfred Owen at Craiglockhart Hospital" by Paul Norgate, in English, spring 1987, 1–35.

*   *   *

Wilfred Owen was born in the village of Oswestry in Shropshire, England, in 1893. He began composing works of poetry at the age of ten, and continued writing to become recognized as one of the world's most eloquent war poets. Only five of Owen's poems were published during his lifetime. Three were published in the Nation magazine and two appeared anonymously in Hydra: Journal of the Craiglockhart War Hospital. Owen's work was featured in the latter publication as he recuperated from injuries suffered in combat during World War I. It was at Craiglockhart Hospital that he met and befriended Siegfried Sassoon, who drew out Owen's poetic instinct.

Owen composed most of his poetry in slightly more than one year. This verse was written from the summer of 1917 to his death in the fall of 1918. Much of his work was published posthumously. Owen described his verse as depicting the pity, shame, and horror of World War I and battle in general, rather than the glory, honor, and majesty which is typically displayed. His poems were written without a nationalistic bias.

Owen's private life still remains an enigma and is open to much speculation. To a large extent his life and poetry were influenced by his domineering mother. Following the poet's death, his family continually guarded and restricted access to his personal life and denied inferences of Owen's latent homosexuality. But through a close scrutiny of themes, leitmotifs, and imagery in Owen's poetics, some readers have observed homosexual tendencies. Some critics point out themes such as patriarchal blood lust, narcissism, injustice collecting, hostility and distaste of women, troop love, antagonism toward God, and masculine imagery. Others cite an underlying current of latent homosexual symbolism in many of Owen's poems. However, in volume three of his Journey from Obscurity: Wilfred Owen, Harold Owen discusses the issue of the poet's alleged latent homosexuality and disinterest in women, stating that Owen's drive and work as poet forced him to remain celibate.

While there is no definitive evidence Owen was an active homosexual, there is high degree of homoeroticism in his juvenile and later poetry. Homoerotic elements can be found in three non–war poems and several unpublished verses, most notably "To Eros," "To the Bitter Sweetheart, A Dream," "To—," and "Maundy Thursday." "To Eros" describes the boy he worships, and in the second poem Eros seduces the speaker in a dream, while taking him to his girlfriend. Later, the lover dismisses the girl. In "To—" two boys become sexually aware of one another while running.

Homoerotic elements are also found in Owen's only definitive love poem "To a Friend (with an Identity Disc)" which implicitly avoids the use of masculine or feminine terms in addressing the friend. In this poem and in some of his other work, Owen includes eroticism that is idealized, romantic, and platonic. His homoerotic tendencies are further detailed in a sonnet dated 10 May 1916, recalling Owen's parting with the de la Touche boys. He writes to his mother that he parts with three of them regretfully, two of them sorrowfully, and one of them most painfully. In various poems, Owen also describes eloquently the beauty of the male physique. Some of the most intimate passages are found in "The Ballad of a Morose Afternoon," which indicates an adolescent infatuation for another young boy. No suggestion is given of its recognition or reciprocation by the other.

Although Owen's private life remains a mystery, a careful analysis of his imagery, themes, and technical style reveals much about his persona. A poet who has left a mark for many generations to come, he is primarily remembered for his revealing depictions of the human suffering of war. He was killed in combat at age 25, just one week before the end of World War I.

—Michael A. Lutes

P

PAGET, Violet. *See* LEE, Vernon.

———

PARKER, Pat (Cook). American poet. Born in Houston, Texas, 20 January 1944. Educated at Los Angeles City College and San Francisco State College (now University). Married 1) Ed Bullins in 1962 (divorced 1966); 2) Robert F. Parker in 1966 (divorced); two children. Has worked as a proofreader, N.C.R. proof operator, waitress, maid, clerk, and creative writing instructor. Director, Feminist Women's Health Center, Oakland, California, 1978—; founder, Black Women's Revolutionary Council, Oakland, 1980. Contributor to *Plexus, Amazon Poetry, I Never Told Anyone,* and *Home Girls.* **Recipient:** WIM Publications Memorial Poetry Award established in her name. *Died of breast cancer, 4 June 1989.*

WRITINGS

Poetry

Child of Myself. Oakland, California, Women's Press Collective, 1972.
Pit Stop: Words. Oakland, California, Women's Press Collective, c. 1974.
WomanSlaughter. Oakland, California, Diana Press, 1978.
Movement in Black: The Collected Poetry of Pat Parker, 1961–1978 (includes work from *Child of Myself* and *Pit Stop*), foreword by Audre Lorde, introduction by Judy Grahn. Oakland, California, Diana Press, 1978.
"Revolution: It's Not Neat or Pretty or Quick," in *This Bridge Called My Back: Writings by Radical Women of Color,* edited by Cherríe Moraga and Gloria Anzaldúa. Watertown, Massachusetts, Persephone Press, 1981.
Jonestown, and Other Madness. New York, Firebrand Books, 1985.

Recordings: *Where Would I Be Without You: The Poetry of Pat Parker and Judy Grahn,* Los Angeles, California, Olivia Records, c. 1976.

*

Interviews: "Pat Parker: Let Me Come to You Strong" by Diane Vozoff, in *Lesbian Tide,* March/April 1977, 13; "Pat Parker Talks about Her Life and Her Work" by Libby Woodwoman, in *Margins,* Number 23, 1987, 60–61.

Critical Sources: Review of *Movement in Black* by Cheryl Clarke in *Conditions: Six,* 1980, 217–225; *This Bridge Called My Back: Writings By Radical Women of Color,* edited by Cherríe Moraga and Gloria Anzaldúa, Watertown, Massachusetts, Persephone Press, 1981; "A Poetry of Survival: Unnaming and Renaming in the Poetry of Audre Lorde, Pat Parker, Sylvia Plath, and Adrienne Rich" by Pamela Annas, in *Colby Library Quarterly* (Waterville, Maine), March 1982, 9–25; *Naming the Waves: Contemporary Lesbian Poetry,* edited by Christian McEwen, London, Virago, 1988; "Pat Parker: A Tribute" by Lyndie Brimstone, in *Feminist Review,* spring 1990, 4–7.

*   *   *

The place of poetry in the world of modern literature has historically been one of diversity. Poetry has been seen at various times as a harmony of voices expressing the personal side of commonly experienced events (as in the battlefield poetry from the First World War), as the matrix of radical opinions and thoughts shaping an entire generation (in "Beat" poet Allen Ginsberg's "Howl"), and as a channel for the definition and discussion of social issues and identities within an evolving or emerging subculture. The myriad challenges posed to mainstream American culture by the civil rights, women's, and gay liberation movements have all required—and found or created—forms of literature to carry their messages to the mainstream public. Where a writer belonged to more than one community, the cast of their creations was marked by a blending of perspectives and emotions. This is particularly true for the gay and lesbian poetry of African Americans, which has only recently begun to be studied as a unique phenomenon in its own right. Of the several women who helped create and shape contemporary lesbian writings, poet Pat Parker was distinctive for her willingness to engage problematic topics such as alcoholism and freedom of speech within her verse.

Born and raised on the outskirts of Houston, the fourth daughter of a Southern Baptist family, Parker left Texas and moved to California following completion of her secondary education. Her lengthy poem "Goat Child," the closest she ever came to writing an autobiography, summarizes some of her childhood and college experiences, as well as her emergence as a writer. She was, as she states in the poem, in search of "new pastures ... golden streets & big money."

Once on the West Coast, Parker attended Los Angeles City College and San Francisco State College. Her arrival in the mid–1960s coincided with the blossoming of the hippie subculture in Haight–Ashbury and the birth of the new gay liberation movement. Incessant debates among lesbian feminists raged over the question of adequate representation for important women's issues, fueled by lesbians who perceived themselves as being relegated to the sidelines. By the time of the Stonewall Riots in 1969, Parker had made a place for herself among the women who would later form the Lesbian Tide Collective and produce the paper of the same name. Recalling meeting her for the first time during this period, the established lesbian poet Audre Lorde would later describe Parker in the preface to *Movement in Black*, the second major collection of Parker's work, as "a young Black poet with fire in her eyes, a beer in her hand and a smile/scowl on her face searching for ... not answers, but inexpressible questions."

In addition to Lorde, it was at this time that Parker was first introduced to Judy Grahn, a fellow refugee from the Southwest whose poetry would interact with her own over the next 20 years. Grahn later admitted that the form of her own work "A Woman Is Talking to Death" had been based upon a familiarity with Parker's "Goat Child."

Parker was to joke that she began to write poetry to silence the criticism her first husband leveled at her prose efforts. Her first collection of poems, *Child of Myself*, appeared in 1972, followed the following year by *Pit Stop*. The title poem of the second collection confronts the issue of alcoholism among women and is one of the few extant modern poems to do so without apology. In November of 1976, during a period of ten months when she had decided to forego giving public readings, and which would end with her performance at the 1977 UCLA Gay Week celebrations, she and Grahn released a joint album of poetry from feminist-owned Olivia Records. The work was entitled *Where Would I Be Without You*, both as a recognition of their friendship and collaboration as artists and as an expression of solidarity and sisterhood.

The murder of Parker's older sister Shirley by her brother-in-law, and the ordeal of his subsequent trial, formed the stuff of the searing lines of *WomanSlaughter*, which Parker took to the International Tribunal on Crimes Against Women held in Brussels in 1976, and later used as the title of her fourth poetry collection. By this time, demand for her work had increased to the point that Diana Press issued the first edition of what has come to be seen as her signature collection, *Movement in Black*.

Parker's final collection of poems, *Jonestown, and Other Madness*, appeared in 1985. It was born because, as she stated in the preface, "We have become too quiet ... turn our minds away from the madness that surrounds us, it is frightening to me that we live with the madness ... to move through our lives ... we are a nation in great trouble." Seeking to express her perceptions of this trouble, Parker drew on the traditions established by a highly varied assortment of African American poets, ranging from Langston Hughes' calls for the rights of black people to the modern voices of Gwendolyn Brooks, Lucille Clifton, Nikki Giovanni, Audre Lorde, Lorraine Hansberry, Zora Neale Hurston, Sonia Sanchez, and Don L. Lee. Always and incessantly, she presents sex between women in her poems, frankly and honestly.

As a contributor to *Plexus, Amazon Poetry*, and the anthologies *I Never Told Anyone, Home Girls*, and *This Bridge Called My Back: Writings By Radical Women of Color*, Parker became widely known among feminist writers of all sexual orientations. In addition to her work as director of the Feminist Women's Health Center in Oakland, California, she also founded that city's Black Women's Revolutionary Council in 1980. Parker died on 14 June 1989, after a struggle with breast cancer.

—*Robert B. Marks Ridinger*

PARNOK, Sophia (Yakovlevna). Russian poet, translator, librettist, playwright, and critic. Also wrote as Andrey Polyanin. Born in Taganrog, Russia, 1885. Educated in Geneva, Switzerland; studied history, philosophy, and law in St. Petersburg. Married (briefly) in 1907; companion of physicist Nina Vedneyeva, 1931–33. Wrote and published a literary journal, 1906; cofounder of Uzel (collectively–operated small press), 1926. *Died in Kirinsky, of heart problems, August 1932.*

WRITINGS

Poetry

Poems. [Russia], 1916.
Roses of Pieria. [Russia], 1922.
The Vine. [Russia], 1923.
Music. [Russia], 1926.
In a Hushed Voice. [Russia], 1928.
Collected Works (includes "Girlfriend" by Marina Tsvetayeva), edited and introduced by Sophia Polyakova, translation by Sonja Franeta. Ann Arbor, Michigan, Ardis, 1979.

Opera

Libretticist, *Almast* (produced, 1930).

*

Biography: "Introduction" by Sophia Polyakova, in *Sophia Parnok: Collected Works,* Ann Arbor, Michigan, Ardis Press, 1979; *The Sunset Days of Yore: Tsvetayeva and Parnok* by Sophia Polyakova, Ann Arbor, Michigan, Ardis Press, 1983.

Critical Sources: "Remembering Sophia Parnok (1885–1933)" by Rima Shore, in *Conditions* (Brooklyn, New York), Number 6, 1980, 177–193; "Russia's Gay Literature and Culture: The Impact of the October Revolution" by Simon Karlinsky, in *Hidden From History: Reclaiming the Gay and Lesbian Past,* edited by Martin Bauml Duberman, Martha Vicunis, and George Chauncy, Jr., New York, New American Library, 1989; "Russia's Gay Literature and History from the Eleventh to the Twentieth Centuries" by Simon Karlinsky, in *Gay Roots,* edited by Winston Leyland, San Francisco, Gay Sunshine Press, 1991.

*　*　*

"Eyes wide open and mouth pressed tight. / I only want to cry out rudely: / "Oh, silly! It's just the opposite— / Close, close your eyes, open your lips for me!" Poet Sophia Parnok made no secret of her sexual orientation in her life or in her work; she wrote these lines for Nina Vedneyeva, the last great love of her life, in Soviet Russia in 1932.

Parnok wrote at a time of severe repression in both Russian literature and culture, for Stalin had imposed his "struggle against lyric poetry." This attempt to bring literature and art in line with the Revolution—and in support of his personality cult—denounced lyric poetry as too personal and bourgeois. Consequently, Parnok's last two published books of poetry were given a very small press run; her final volume of verse, *In a Hushed Voice,* was altered by the censors before its publication in 1928.

Parnok was born in Taganrog, Russia, to Jewish parents—her mother was a doctor and her father a pharmacist. When she was ten her mother died giving birth to twins; the children were raised by a governess whom her father eventually married. Parnok began writing poetry as a young girl, but did not seriously pursue writing until years later. In 1905 she went to Geneva to study music but never finished her studies; instead she returned to Russia to study history, philosophy, and eventually law in St. Petersburg. It was at this point that she began to write seriously, and her first work was published in a literary journal in 1906. Parnok also published several literary reviews, using the male pseudonym Andrey Polyanin in order to be taken more seriously as a critic. Her first book of poetry, *Poems,* was published in 1916 under her own name.

The boldness of her subject matter and language was a sharp contrast to the stifling atmosphere of Soviet Russia. Determined to write despite hard times, Parnok wrote in 1926: "Now I look at poetry as just a means of communication with people. I am happy that there is an eternal language, beyond time, in which I can explain myself to people, and in which I can sometimes find words that everyone can understand." Although her work became more finely crafted, her audience dwindled to her immediate friends. During this period, Parnok had several serious relationships with women and a brief marriage in 1907. *Poems* was followed by more poetry, as well as works of prose, plays, and translations. Unfortunately, much of Parnok's unpublished work has been lost.

After the Russian Revolution, Parnok moved to the Crimea, to Sudak, where she continued to write poetry and the libretto for an opera. She returned to Moscow in 1922 and published four books of poetry in the following years. In 1926 she helped found a collective that operated a small press called "Uzel" (knot or group). They published work that was not officially approved and were soon closed down. After it was completed in 1930, the staging of her libretto, *Almast,* would be Parnok's last link with the public during her lifetime.

Simon Karlinsky, in his pioneering article "Russia's Gay Literature and History from the Eleventh to the Twentieth Centuries," notes that "Parnok's *In a Hushed Voice,* which is clearly a major work by a major poet, went unnoticed in the Soviet press." Fortunately, interest in her work underwent a revival in the 1970s. In 1979 Sophia Polyakova, a professor of Byzantine and classical literature at Leningrad University, published the first collection of poetry by Parnok, not in the Soviet Union but in the United States. Almost a third of the poems had never been published.

Polyakova prefaced her book with a detailed biographical essay on Parnok in which she discussed the poet's relationships with women. Parnok's love affairs greatly influenced her work—particularly a relationship with the famous poet Marina Tsvetayeva, whose poem to Parnok, "Girlfriend," appears in the appendix of Polyakova's book. The moment they met, in October of 1914 at the home of an acquaintance, the two young poets fell in love. Parnok's predilection for women was well–known and the two women carried out an open love affair, despite the fact that Tsvetayeva was married and had a child. A friend of Tsvetayeva's wrote to a mutual acquaintance in the summer of 1915: "Sonya and Marina are an item in Moscow—they are inseparable." This was an exciting period in Russian literary and artistic life—a time of experimentation,

of revolution on every level—and same–sex relationships were even a bit faddish in artistic and intellectual circles. Parnok had already been involved in a five–year relationship with another woman and, although she had married briefly (apparently in order to get her share of the family inheritance), she explained to a male friend who once mistook her friendliness for love: "I never was in love with a man."

Her relationship with Tsvetayeva lasted only two years but it was quite intense, and the two women were an inspiration to each other. They wrote poetry to one other and shared much in common. They travelled to the beautiful Crimea, often to Koktebel, the home of Maximilian Voloshin, where other artistic people gathered. When they parted in 1916 Tsvetayeva called it "the first great catastrophe of my life," and Parnok kept a picture of Tsvetayeva by her bedside until she died.

Following Tsvetayeva were other great loves: actress Lyudmilla Erarskaya, mathematics professor Olga Tsuberbiller, singer Marina Maksakova. Parnok dedicated poems to each of these women, including very personal details in her verse. To Maksakova she wrote: "And I like the sensitivity of these shoulders, / the impetuousness of your buoyant gait, / your frivolous and spare way of speaking, / your taut thighs like those of a mermaid."

A lifelong inspiration for Parnok was the ancient Greek poet Sappho, whom she considered a lesbian literary ancestor. Rima Shore, in her article on Parnok, says: "She envisions herself as the keeper of the flame, singing on Sappho's unfinished songs; she sings of 'Penthesilea,' of strong, fearless Amazons." Parnok, in the person of Aphrodite, wrote in "Dreams of Sappho": "There's talk, Sappho: / They want to know to whom you write your eternal love songs, / Nectar of the gods! To young men or to maids?"

Poet and friend Vladislav Khodasevich painted a vivid portrait of Parnok: "Average in height, on the short side, with fair hair, parted on the side and tied back in a bun, a pale face, which seemed like it had never been young, Sophia Yakovlevna was not very good–looking. But there was something charming and unexpectedly noble about her grey, protruding, attentive eyes, about her intense Lermontov–like look, about the turn of her head, slightly supercilious, about her soft, quite deep voice. Her opinions were independent, her speech direct."

Parnok's death in 1933 was barely mentioned in the Moscow press. Her poor health had grown worse and she died of heart problems in August in the village of Kirinsky, outside Moscow, her lover Nina Vedneyeva at her side. Parnok's friends did not forget her—they met on a regular basis to share their recollections of her after her death, at the home of Olga Tsuberbiller, a former lover. Commenting on Parnok's final years, Polyakova writes, "The relationship with Vedeneyeva was both the most tragic and the most brilliant time of her life: already on the threshold of death, she found the fullness of love and creativity, the greatest blessings on earth."

—*Sonja Franeta*

PASOLINI, Pier Paolo. Italian teacher, artist, actor, writer, film critic, theorist, and director of motion pictures. Born in Bologna, 5

March 1922. Educated at secondary school Reggio Emilia et Galvani, Bologna, graduated 1937; University of Bologna, Ph.D. 1943. Served with Italian Army, 1943. Founder of Academiuta di lenga Furlana (Academy of Friulan Language); secretary of Communist Party cell at Casarsa; cofounder and editor of *Officina*. Director of motion pictures, including *Il Decamerone, Edipo re, Medea,* and *I racconti di Canterbury*. **Recipient:** Special jury prize from Venice Film Festival, 1964; Silver Bear Award, 1971; Golden Bear Award, 1972; special jury prize from Cannes Film Festival, 1974; Karlovy Vary Festival award; Viareggio Prize. *Bludgeoned to death in Ostia, Italy, 2 November 1975.*

WRITINGS

Novels

Ragazzi di vita. Milan, Garzanti, 1955; translated by Emile Capouya as *The Ragazzi,* New York, Grove Press, 1968.
Una vita violenta. Milan, Garzanti, 1959; translated by William Weaver as *A Violent Life,* London, J. Cape, 1968.
Il sogno di una cosa. Milan, Garzanti, 1962.
Teorema. Milan, Garzanti, 1968.

Poetry

Poesie a Casarsa. [Bologna], 1942.
Suite furlan, c. 1947.
Le ceneri di Gramsci ["The Ashes of Gramsci"], Milan, Garzanti, 1954.
L'usignolo della Chiesa Cattolica. Milan, Loganesi, 1958.
Passione e ideologia (1948–1958). Milan, Garzanti, 1960.
La religione del mio tempo. Milan, Garzanti, 1961.
Poesia in forma di rosa. Milan, Garzanti, 1964.
Poesie dimenticate. Societa Filologica Friulana, 1965.
With Laura Betti, *Potentissima signora.* Milan, Loganesi, 1965.
Poesie. Milan, Garzanti, 1970.
Trasumanar e organizzar. Milan, Garzanti, 1971.
Tal cour di un frut: Nel cuore di un fanciullo. Udine, Doretti, 1974.
La nuova giovento: Poesie friulane, 1941–1974. Turin, Einaudi, 1975.
Le poesie. Milan, Garzanti, 1975.
Poems, translation by Norman McAfee and Luciano Martinengo, foreword by Enzo Siciliano. New York, Random House, 1982.
Roman Poems: Bilingual Edition, translation by Lawrence Ferlinghetti and Francesca Valente, preface by Alberto Moravia. San Francisco, City Lights Books, 1986.

Screenplays

With Mario Soldati, *La donna del fiume,* 1955.
With Luis Trenker, *Il prigioniero della montagna,* 1955.
With Federico Fellini, *Le notti de Cabiria,* 1956.
Marisa la civetta, 1957.
Giovanni Mariti, 1958.
With Mauro Bolognini, *La notte brava,* 1959.
La canta delle marane, 1960.
Morte di un amico, 1960.
La giornata balorda, 1960.
With Bolognini, *Il bell'Antonio,* 1960.

La lunga notte del '43, 1960.
With Gianni Puccini, *Il carro armato dell'8 settembre,* 1960.
Accattone ["Beggar"], (adaptation of his own novel, *Una vita violenta;* released by Cino del Duca/Arco, 1961). Capo di Ponte, Edizioni FM, 1961.
With Luciano Emmer, *La ragazza in vetrina,* 1961.
La commare secca, Zibetti, 1962.
Mamma Roma (released by Arco/Cineriz, 1962). Milan, Rizzoli, 1962.
Rogopag ("La ricotta" episode), Arco/Cineriz/Lyre, 1963.
La rabbia (first episode; unreleased). Opus, 1963.
Il vangelo secondo Matteo (released by Arco/Lux, 1964; released in the U.S. as *The Gospel According to St. Matthew*). Milan, Garzanti, 1964.
Comizi d'amore (documentary), Arco, 1964.
Sopralluoghi in Palestina (documentary), 1964.
La terra vista della luna (episode of *Le Streghe* ["The Witches"]), Dino de Laurentis/United Artists, 1965.
Uccellacci e uccellini ["The Hawks and the Sparrows"], (released by Arco, 1966). Milan, Garzanti, 1966.
Edipo re (adaptation of the tragedy by Sophocles; released by Arco, 1967; released in U.S. as *Oedipus Rex*). Milan, Garzanti, 1967.
Che cosa sono le nuvole? (episode of *Cappriccio all'italiana*), Dino de Laurentis, 1967.
Le sequenza del fiore de corta, 1967.
Teorema (adaptation of his own novel). Aetus, 1968.
La sequenza del fiore di carta (episode of *Amore e rabbia*), 1968.
Porcile ["Pigsty"], 1969.
Appunti per un Orestiade africana ["Notes for an African Orestia"], 1970.
Medea (adaptation of the tragedy by Euripides; released by San Marco/Rosima Anstaldt/New Line Cinema, 1970; released in the U.S. as *Medea*). Milan, Garzanti, 1970.
With Sergio Citti, *Ostia.* Milan, Garzanti, 1970.
Il Decamerone (adaptation of the work by Giovanni Boccaccio; released by Produzione Europee Associate/United Artists, 1971; released in the U.S. as *The Decameron*). Published in *Trilogia della vita,* 1975.
I racconti di Canterbury (adaptation of the work by Geoffrey Chaucer; released by United Artists; released in the U.S. as *The Canterbury Tales*). Published in *Trilogia della vita,* 1975.
Il fiore delle Mille e una notte. Published in *Trilogia della vita,* 1975.
Trilogia della vita (includes *Il Decamerone, I racconti di Canterbury,* and *Il fiore delle Mille e una notte*), edited by Giorgio Gattei. Bologna, Cappelli, 1975.
Salo o le Centoventi Giornate di Sodoma ["Salo; or, the 120 Days of Sodom"], 1975.

Plays

Orgia, 1969.
Affabulazione: Pilade (produced Taormina, Italy, 1969). Milan, Garzanti, 1977.
Calderon. Milan, Garzanti, 1973.

Other

Dov ë la mia patria. [Casarsa], 1949.
I parlanti. [Rome], 1951.
Tal cour di un frut. [Tricesimo], 1953.

Dal "diario" (1945–1947). [Caltanissetta], 1954.
La meglio gioventù. [Florence], 1954.
Il canto popolare. [Milan], 1954.
Ragazzi di vita. [Milan], 1955.
Roma 1950, diario. [Milan], 1960.
Sonetto primaverile (1953). [Milan], 1960.
Translator, *Orestiade* by Aeschylus. Turin, Einaudi, 1960.
Contributor, *Donne di Roma* by Sam Waagenaar. Milan, Saggiatore, 1960.
Contributor, *Scrittori della realta dell'VIII al XIX secolo,* edited by Enzo Siciliano. Milan, Garzanti, 1961.
L'odore dell'India. Milan, Loganesi, 1962.
Il sogno di una cosa. [Milan], 1962.
La violenza, drawings by Attardi and others. [Rome], 1962.
Translator, *Il vantone [di] Plauto* by Titus Maccius Plautus. Milan, Garzanti, 1963.
Uccellacce uccellini. [Milan], 1965.
Ali degli occhi azzurri. Milan, Garzanti, 1965; selections translated by John Shepley as *Roman Nights, and Other Stories,* Marlboro, Vermont, Marlboro Press, 1986.
Contributor, *Attalo* by Gioacchino Colizzi. Lara, 1968.
Compiler, *Canzoniere italiano* (anthology; two volumes). Milan, Garzanti, 1972.
Empirismo eretico. Milan, Garzanti, 1972, translated by Ben Lawton and Louise K. Barnett as *Heretical Empiricism,* edited by Barnett, Indiana University Press, 1988.
Il padre selvaggio. Turin, Einaudi, 1975.
La divina mimesis. Turin, Einaudi, 1975.
Scritti corsari. Milan, Garzanti, 1975.
La nuova gioventù. [Turin], 1975.
Lettere agli amici (1941–1945), edited by Luciano Serra. Milan, Guanda, 1976.
Lettere luterane. Turin, Einaudi, 1976; translated by Stuart Hood as *Lutheran Letters,* Atlantic Highlands, New Jersey, Humanities, 1983.
Pasolini in Friuli, 1943–1949. Arti grafiche friulane, 1976.
L'Experience heretique: langue et cinéma. [Paris], 1976.
Le belle bandiere: dialoghi 1960–1965. [Rome], 1977.
Con Pier Paolo Pasolini (interview), edited by Enrico Magretti. Rome, Bulzoni, 1977.
Affabulazione, Pilade. [Milan], 1977.
San Paolo. Turin, Einaudi, 1977.
Le belle bandiere: Dialoghi 1960–1965, edited by Gian Carlo Ferretti. Rome, Editori riuniti, 1977.
Pier Paolo Pasolini e Il Setaccio 1942–43, edited by Mario Kicci. Cappelli, 1977.
I disegni 1941–1975, edited by Giuseppe Zigaina. Milan, Edizioni di Vanni Scheiwiller, 1978.
Theoreme. [Paris], 1978.
Dal diario/Pier Paolo Pasolini, introduction by Leonardo Sciascia, illustrations by Giuseppe Mazzullo. Caltanissetta, Sciascia, 1979.
Descrizioni di descrizioni: Pier Paolo Pasolini a cura di Graziella Chiarcossi. Turin, Einaudi, 1979.
Lettere 1955–1975. Turin, Einaudi, 1988.

*

Biography: *Pier Paolo Pasolini* by Stephen Snyder, Boston, Twayne Publishers, 1980; *Pier Paolo Pasolini* by Pia Friedrich, Boston, G.

K. Hall, 1982; *Pasolini* by Enzo Siciliano, translation by John Shepley, New York, Random House, 1982.

Interviews: *Pasolini on Pasolini* by Oswald Stack, Bloomington, Indiana University Press, 1970; *Entretiens avec Pier Paolo Pasolini* by Jean Duflor, [Paris], 1970; *Con Pier Paolo Pasolini,* edited by Enrico Magretti, Rome, Bulzoni, 1977.

Bibliography: *World Film Directors,* Volume 2: *1945–1985,* edited by John Wakeman, New York, Wilson, 1988, 743–750.

Critical Sources: "Pasolini's Road to Calvary" by John Lane, in *Films and Filming,* March 1963; "Pier Paolo Pasolini and the Art of Directing" by Gordon Hitchens, in *Film Comment,* fall 1965; "Pier Paolo Pasolini Contestatore" by Marc Gervais, in *Sight and Sound,* winter 1968–69; "Pier Paolo Pasolini: Poetry as a Compensation" by John Bragin, in *Film Society Review,* January–March 1969; "Pasolini: Rebellion, Art and a New Society" by Susan Macdonald, in *Screen,* May–June 1969; *Pier Paolo Pasolini* by Marc Gervais, [Paris], 1973; "Pasolini in Persia: The Shooting of 1001 Nights" by Gideon Bachmann, in *Film Quarterly,* winter 1973–74; *Directors and Directions* by John Taylor, [New York], 1975; *Pier Paolo Pasolini* by Stephen Snyder, [Boston], 1980; *Pier Paolo Pasolini: The Poetics of Heresy* by Beverly Allen, Saratoga, California, Anma Libri, 1982; *Pier Paolo Pasolini and the Theatre of the Word* by William Van Watson, Ann Arbor, Michigan, UMI Research Press, 1989; *Pier Paolo Pasolini: Cinema as Heresy* by Naomi Green, Princeton, New Jersey, Princeton University Press, 1990; *Pasolini Requiem* by Barth David Schwartz, New York, Pantheon, 1992.

*   *   *

"To define Pasolini creates embarrassment: poet, director, writer, dramatist.... In reality only one definition can render with precision the area of cultural diligence attended to by Pasolini: intellectual." Stefano Casi's lines in *Desiderio di Pasolini: Omosessualità, arte e impegno intellettuale* aptly describe the breadth of Pasolini's creativity and imply the complexities his ingenuity permeates. Pasolini was first a thinker, and then an artist. Through a variety of artistic media—poetry, film, essay, theater and novel—he investigated and exposed contemporary philosophical constructs, often enraging the academic, political, and artistic status quo by initiating inquiry from a point of view of diversity (a term often used by critics to describe his artistry). Pasolini's work teems with the unconventional and nontraditional. Without a doubt, the author's homosexuality, or as the Italians call it, *inversion,* contributed to Pasolini's predilection to view his subject matter from nonconforming, contrary, yet innovative, perspectives.

Pasolini's earliest work centers around his life in the Friulan provinces. *Poesia a Casarsa* and *Suite furlana* reject the aulic, static Italian language, and seek to create a Friulan koiné, to speak and mythicize in the absolute language of the province, a language that had never been written before. These early short poems create an atmosphere of primitive innocence in the Friulan countryside, playing with light, darkness, butterflies, and fireflies; they are also obsessed with death, mother, and beautiful boys: Narcís, Giovinetto, Dilio, and David. Male eroticism is everywhere, but its presentation is simple and sweet, and content in uncorrupted ignorance.

In October of 1949, Pasolini was arrested and accused of "the corruption of minors and committing obscene acts in a public place." While the charges were eventually dropped, the effects of this incident proved devastating and served as a turning point in his life. Pasolini was stripped of his position as a public school teacher and was expelled from the Italian Communist Party (PCI). Totally humiliated, Pasolini and his mother eventually "fled" the Friulan countryside and resettled in the urban anonymity of Rome.

During the next decade, Pasolini wrote his two most famous novels, *Ragazzi di Vita* (*The Ragazzi*) and *Una vita violenta* (*A Violent Life*). In these works, the author turns his attention away from the innocence of peasant culture and focuses on the plight of the new urban poor, those secluded from the bourgeois benefits of postwar Italy in the slums of the Roman periphery. The novels are actually collections of loosely related vignettes, a structure that reinforces the developmental void experienced by these characters, as if they lived outside the march of history. Pasolini's protagonists are all adolescent males; women, in fact, play only very minor roles in these two works. These are hard–core picaresque novels, where boys run in dangerous packs, searching for the joys of childhood amid filthy fields and the trash laden pools of the Tiber. Young ruffians graduate to thievery and only the strong survive. The less cunning are systematically thinned from the ranks, ending up in brutal Roman prisons, the wounded dying in the open wards of public hospitals. Death is viewed with forced indifference, as the survivors continue on their quest for the only means of subsistence, the almighty lira, which, more often than not, they forfeit to a more cunning or powerful comrade.

The traditional middle–class family unit is totally decimated in these books. Forced into vicious poverty, living in dilapidated buildings, family groups often live one to a room, separated by a scant curtain. Fathers are diminished by drunken disoccupation and mothers—the pillars of Italian society—are reduced to shrilling shrews or penny–pandering painted whores.

To emphasize the harshness of this life, Pasolini replaces his earlier, classical Friulan lexicon, at least in dialogue, with a harsh, often crude and obscene, minimized Roman street vocabulary. What he creates is the *Inferno* of a consumer–oriented society, where lost souls exist in stasis without hope.

Except for a few quick sketches of gay bashing and hustling, homosexuality plays virtually no role in these works. Yet they can be considered love songs of a sort, since the rough, urban poor boys depicted were the constant objects of Pasolini's erotic desires. In his essay in *Desiderio di Pasolini,* Pasolini's cousin, Nico Naldini, reveals significant aspects of the author's sexual proclivities, "In reality, that which attracted him was the rustic world, then the strange world of the Roman sub–proletariat." As for middle class romance, Naldini adds that Pasolini "always refused relationships with bourgeois boys, that is, he never searched them out, never loved them because he found them stripped of all the attractive things that common boys have."

Pasolini was best known for his accomplishments in cinema. As a director, screenwriter, and actor, his visual representations engaged and outraged both his critics and audience. *Accattone* brought to life the unpolished, rough reality of the urban poor. *Il Decameron* cinematically rewrote the medieval rise of the bourgeoisie in sub–proletariat garb, and *Il vangelo secondo Matteo* (*The Gospel According to Saint Matthew*) gave us a Christ of, from, and for the people. *Salò o le Centoventi Giornate di Sodoma* (*Salò; or, the 120 Days of Sodom*), Pasolini's most controversial film, used violence and sado–masochism as a metaphor for the horrors of Fascism.

Pasolini's career came to an abrupt end when, on the night of 1 November 1975, he picked up a young hustler near the Roman railroad station; the next day he was found dead. Pasolini's body had been bashed by a board, mercilessly kicked in the testicles, and run over twice, until his heart burst, with his own car. The next day the hustler, Giuseppe Pelosi, was charged, and eventually convicted, of the crime. One of *The Ragazzi* had concluded *Una vita violenta,* hideously illustrating art as the imitator of life.

—*Joseph P. Consoli*

PATRICK, Robert. American playwright, actor, director, and songwriter. Born in Kilgore, Texas, 27 September 1937. Educated at Eastern New Mexico University. Has held a variety of jobs including dishwasher, autopsy typist, accounts–receivable correspondent, astrologer, and reporter. Waiter, doorman, and stage manager, Caffe Cino, New York City, 1961–63; playwright–in–residence, Old Reliable Theatre Tavern, New York City, 1967–71. Member of the New York Theater Strategy, Playwrights Cooperative, and Actors Studio. **Recipient:** *Show Business* award for best Off–Off Broadway playwright, 1968–69; *Village Voice* Obie award nominee, 1973; Glasgow Citizens' Theatre International play contest first prize, 1973; Rockefeller Foundation playwright–in–residence grant, 1973; Creative Artists Public Service grant, 1976; International Thespian Society Founders Award, 1979.

WRITINGS

Plays

The Haunted Host (produced New York, 1964). Published in *Robert Patrick's Cheep Theatricks!,* 1972.
Mirage (produced New York, 1965). Published in *One Man, One Woman,* 1975.
The Sleeping Bag (produced New York, 1966).
Indecent Exposure (produced New York, 1966).
Halloween Hermit (produced New York, 1966).
Cheesecake (produced New York, 1966). Published in *One Man, One Woman,* 1975.
Lights, Camera, Action (produced New York, 1966). Published in *Robert Patrick's Cheep Theatricks!,* 1972.
Sketches (produced New York, 1966).
The Warhol Machine (produced New York, 1967).
Still–Love (produced New York, 1967). Published in *Robert Patrick's Cheep Theatricks!,* 1972.
Cornered (produced New York, 1968). Published in *Robert Patrick's Cheep Theatricks!,* 1972.
Un Bel Di (produced New York, 1968).
Help, I Am (produced New York, 1968). Published in *Robert Patrick's Cheep Theatricks!,* 1972.
See Other Side (produced New York, 1968).
Camera Obscura (produced New York, 1968).
Absolute Power over Movie Stars (produced New York, 1968).

Preggin and Liss (produced New York, 1968). Published in *Robert Patrick's Cheep Theatricks!*, 1972.

The Overseers (produced New York, 1968).

Angels in Agony (produced New York, 1968).

Salvation Army (produced New York, 1968).

Dynel (produced New York, 1968).

Fog (produced New York, 1969). Published in *Untold Decades: Seven Comedies of Gay Romance*, New York, St. Martin's Press, 1988.

I Came to New York to Write (produced New York, 1969). Published in *Robert Patrick's Cheep Theatricks!*, 1972.

The Arnold Bliss Show (produced New York, 1969). Published in *Robert Patrick's Cheep Theatricks!*, 1972.

Joyce Dynel (produced New York, 1969). Published in *Robert Patrick's Cheep Theatricks!*, 1972.

The Young Aquarius (produced New York, 1969).

Ooooooooops! (produced New York, 1969).

Lily of the Valley of the Dolls (produced New York, 1969).

One Person (produced New York, 1969). Published in *Robert Patrick's Cheep Theatricks!*, 1972.

Silver Skies (produced New York, 1969).

Tarquin Truthbeauty (produced New York, 1969).

The Actor and the Invader (produced New York, 1969).

A Bad Place to Get Your Head (produced New York, 1970).

Bread–Tangle (produced New York, 1970).

Angel, Honey, Baby, Darling, Dear (produced New York, 1970).

The Golden Animal (produced New York, 1970).

Picture Wire (produced New York, 1970).

I Am Trying to Tell You Something (produced New York, 1970).

Shelter (produced New York, 1970).

The Richest Girl in the World Finds Happiness (produced New York, 1970). Published in *Robert Patrick's Cheep Theatricks!*, 1972.

Hymen and Carbuncle (produced New York, 1970). Published in *Mercy Drop, and Other Plays*, 1979.

La Repetition (produced New York, 1970).

Sketches and Songs (produced New York, 1970).

A Christmas Carol (produced New York, 1971).

Youth Rebellion (produced New York, 1972).

Play–by–Play (produced New York, 1972). Published as *Play–by–Play: A Spectacle of Ourselves*, New York, Samuel French, 1975.

Songs (produced New York, 1972).

Something Else (produced New York, 1973). Published in *One Man, One Woman*, 1975.

Ludwig and Wagner (produced New York, 1973). Published in *Mercy Drop, and Other Plays*, 1979.

Mercy Drop (produced New York, 1973). Published as *Mercy Drop, and Other Plays*, 1979.

Simultaneous Transmissions (produced New York, 1973).

The Track of the Narwhal (produced New York, 1973).

Kennedy's Children (produced New York, 1973; London West End, 1975; on Broadway, 1975). Published as *Kennedy's Children: A Play in Two Acts*, London, S. French, 1975; New York, Random House, 1976.

Cleaning House (produced New York, 1973). Published in *One Man, One Woman*, 1975.

Hippy as a Lark (produced New York, 1973).

Blue Is for Boys (produced Hollywood, 1973).

The Golden Circle (produced New York, 1973).

Imp–Prisonment (produced New York, 1973).

The Twisted Root (produced New York, 1973).

Love Lace (produced New York, 1974). Published in *One Man, One Woman*, 1975.

How I Came to Be Here Tonight (produced Hollywood, 1974).

Orpheus and America (produced Los Angeles, 1974).

Fred and Harold, and One Person (produced London, 1976).

My Dear, It Doesn't Mean a Thing (produced London, 1976).

My Cup Runneth Over (produced Brooklyn, 1977). Published as *My Cup Runneth Over: A Play in One Act*, New York, Dramatists Play Service, 1979.

Judas (produced Santa Monica, 1978).

T–Shirts (produced Minneapolis, 1978).

Mutual Benefit Life (produced New York, 1978). New York, Dramatists Play Service, 1979.

Bank Street Breakfast (produced New York, 1979). Published in *One Man, One Woman*, 1975.

Communication Gap (produced Greensboro, 1979).

The Family Bar (produced Hollywood, 1979). Published in *Mercy Drop, and Other Plays*, 1979.

Mercy Drop, and Other Plays (includes *Diaghilev and Nijinsksy*). New York, Calamus, 1979.

All in the Mind (produced New York, 1979).

The Sane Scientist (produced New York, 1979).

Twenty–four Inches (produced New York, 1979).

The Spinning Tree (produced New York, 1979).

Report to the Mayor (produced New York, 1979).

Bread Alone (produced New York, 1979).

50s, 60s, 70s, 80s (produced New York, 1983). Published in *Untold Decades: Seven Comedies of Gay Romance*, 1988.

Big Sweet (produced Richmond, 1984).

No Trojan Women (produced Wallingford, 1985).

Explanation of a Xmas Wedding (produced New York, 1987).

Pouf Positive (produced New York, 1987). Published in *Untold Decades: Seven Comedies of Gay Romance*, 1988.

Untold Decades (produced New York, 1988). New York, St. Martin's Press, 1988; in *Untold Decades: Seven Comedies of Gay Romance*, 1988.

Untold Decades: Seven Comedies of Gay Romance. New York, St. Martin's Press, 1988.

Hello, Bob (produced New York, 1990).

Collected Plays

Robert Patrick's Cheep Theatricks! (includes *The Haunted Host; Lights, Camera, Action; Still–Love; Cornered; Help, I Am; Preggin and Liss; I Came to New York to Write; The Arnold Bliss Show; Joyce Dynel; One Person;* and *The Richest Girl in the World Finds Happiness*). New York, Winter House, 1972.

One Man, One Woman (includes *Mirage; Cheesecake; Something Else; Cleaning House; Love Lace;* and *Bank Street Breakfast*). New York, Samuel French, 1975.

Mercy Drop, and Other Plays (includes *Diaghilev and Nijinsksy; Hymen and Carbuncle; Ludwig and Wagner; Mercy Drop;* and *The Family Bar*). New York, Calamus, 1979.

Untold Decades: Seven Comedies of Gay Romance (includes *Fog; 50s, 60s, 70s, 80s; Pouf Positive;* and *Untold Decades*). New York, St. Martin's Press, 1988.

Other

"Gay Theater's Relationship with Its Audience" (essay), in *Christopher Street* (New York), 23 December 1991.

Biography: "Can a Kid from the Caffe Cino Be Really Big, Baby?" by Michael Feingold, in *Village Voice,* 17 November 1975, 116; "No More Heroes" by Jerry Tallmer, in the *New York Post,* 1 November 1975, 15.

*   *   *

The ground–breaking gay plays of Robert Patrick came into being in a geographical and conceptual space called "Off–Off–Broadway," or "the downtown theater scene," because of its concentration in lofts and other nontraditional spaces. Though theater listings in New York periodicals are still broken down into the categories "Broadway," "Off–Broadway," and "Off–Off–Broadway," that demarcation has become one chiefly of ticket price. In terms of the actual theatrical experiences available in each of the three realms, they are today for the most part indistinguishable. But in the complex and varied theatrical culture of the early 1960s, Off–Off–Broadway was the home of a lively and exciting experimental theater scene, including a flowering of gay theater featuring the works of such playwrights as Doric Wilson, Lanford Wilson, William Hoffman, Robert Heide, George Birmisa, Jean–Claude Van Itallie, and Robert Patrick.

Much of this gay theater germinated and took root at the Caffe Cino, a now–legendary coffee house at 37 Cornelia Street in New York's Greenwich Village that has been called the first Off–Off–Broadway theater. Patrick reports having wandered into the Cino on the heels of a Salvation Army band parade in 1961, when he came to New York to visit a friend from college. Actors were rehearsing a program of excerpts from Oscar Wilde plays. "They were doing it over and over," Robert Patrick told *The Village Voice* in 1975, "and I just went in and sat down, and everybody thought I was with somebody else. And I thought it was a great new idea in theatre to do the same bit over and over—they were so good, I didn't realize they were just rehearsing. And I stayed there, and for three years I had office jobs in the daytime and came there every night. As far as I'm concerned, I still live in the Cino." The Caffe Cino closed its doors in 1968, a few months after owner Joe Cino committed suicide. But by that time, under Cino's nurturing patronage, a new crop of gay playwrights, led by Lanford Wilson, Hoffman, and Patrick, had produced scores of new plays about gay characters and gay life, a realm that had rarely, if ever, been explored in popular theater in any but the most negative and disparaging terms.

Patrick's first play, *The Haunted Host,* which was produced at the Cino in 1964, concerns a gay man who refuses to conform to a straight man's idea of him. Writing of his works since that time, as Patrick noted in *Christopher Street* magazine: "Over half of my more than 100 produced plays have been about gay men. I am proud to have provided more images of gay male possibilities than any other author." One of Patrick's collections, *Untold Decades: Seven Comedies of Gay Romance,* consists entirely of one–act plays, each in a different setting with different characters, that offer a social history of gay male love in America from the 1920s to the 1980s. "My theme here is the effect of repression on the noble spirit," Patrick noted in the preface to *Untold Decades.* Serious themes treated in comic terms characterize much of Patrick's work, as well as a marked propensity for fast pacing, apt puns, and witty one–liners.

Patrick came to international renown with his play, *Kennedy's Children,* which had simultaneous productions on the West End and Broadway in 1975, receiving great critical acclaim and generating widespread popular interest. The play, about how the broken dreams of the 1960s led to the national malaise of the 1970s, takes the form of interlocking monologues by five characters sitting at a bar on the Lower East Side of New York on Valentine's Day in 1974. Each of the five characters is mourning an irreparable loss of a 1960s hero or ideal: for Wanda, it is the assassination of President John Fitzgerald Kennedy; for Mark, it is his own sanity and the dead he left behind in the jungles in which the Vietnam War was fought; for Rona, it is the passing of the radical activism that characterized the 1960s; for Carla, it is the glamour and beauty that died with movie star Marilyn Monroe; and for Sparger, it is the vibrant experimental theater scene that closed its doors when Buffo, the proprietor of the coffeehouse–theater Opera Buffo, committed suicide. It is clear that Buffo and his coffeehouse are modeled on Joe Cino and his legendary cafe. But while Sparger, a gay actor, resembles Robert Patrick in some ways, he is more an amalgam of the many valiant and desperate young theater junkies with whom the playwright came into contact. "I know lots of Spargers," Patrick told the *Village Voice.* "I don't happen to be one of them. I'm a lot older than they are, and a lot more optimistic. And I was a lot less dependent on the ideals of the whole society, so I wasn't as destroyed."

—*Michael Broder*

———

PENNA, Sandro. Italian poet. Born in Perugia, 12 January 1906. Educated at Instituto Tecnico di Perugia, diploma in accounting, 1925. Held a variety of odd jobs, including book store clerk, proofreader, substitute teacher, and salesman. **Recipient:** Viareggio Prize, 1957; Fiuggi Prize, 1970; Bagutta Prize, 1977. *Died in Rome of heart failure, 21 January 1977.*

WRITINGS

Poetry

Poesie. Florence, Parenti, 1938; enlarged, Milan, Garzanti, 1957; enlarged and published as *Tutte le poesie,* Milan, Garzanti, 1970.
Appunti ["Notes"]. Milan, Meridiana, 1950.
Una strana gioia di vivere ["A Strange Joy of Living"]. Milan, All'Insegna del Pesce d'Oro/Scheiwiller, 1956.
Poesie. Milan, Garzanti, 1957.
Croce e delizia ["Suffering and Delight"]. Milan, Longanesi, 1958.
L'Ombra e la luce ["The Shadow and the Light"]. Milan, Scheiwiller, 1975.
Stranezze ["Oddities"]. Milan, Garzanti, 1976.
Il viaggiatore insonne ["The Sleepless Traveler"]. Genoa, San Marco dei Giustiniani, 1977.
Il rombo immenso ["The Loud Buzzing of Bees"]. Milan, Scheiwiller, 1978.

Confuso sogno, edited by Elio Pecora. Milan, Garzanti, 1980; translated in part by George Scrivani as *Confused Dream,* New York, Hanuman, 1988.
This Strange Joy: Selected Poems of Sandro Penna, translation by W. S. Di Piero. Columbus, Ohio State University Press, 1982.
Peccato di gola ["The Sin of Gluttony"]. Milan, Scheiwiller, 1989.

Other

Un pò di febbre ["A Slight Fever"], (essays and articles). Milan, Garzanti, 1973.

*

Biography: *Sandro Penna: La luce e il silenzio* by Giulio Di Fonzo, Rome, Dell'Ateneo, 1981; *Sandro Penna* by Gualtiero De Santi, Florence, Nuova Italia, 1982.

Interviews: With Vittorio Maselli and Gian Antonio Cibotto, in *Antologia popolare di poeti italiani del Novecento,* Florence, Valecchi, 1967.

Critical Sources: "The Undisciplined Eros of Sandro Penna" by Robert S. Dombroski, in *Books Abroad* (Norman, Oklahoma), spring 1973, 304–306.

*   *   *

Sandro Penna's short epigrammatic and platonically dialectical poems display emotions that range from exhilaration to melancholy as they reflect upon his love for boys. Characteristically, he savors an intensely experienced moment, isolates it, and exploits its lyric potential. Seldom suggestive of sexual consummation, his vignettes focus on the gestures or the attributes of a particular boy, such as the confident lighting of a cigarette, the voice of a young worker singing in an empty room, or a young boy urinating against a spindly tree. Sometimes, in the manner of the medieval troubadours, Penna states that he even prefers to watch in safe and silent awe rather than to break forever the magic of the moment.

Yet in other instances the poet urges himself to make a connection ("If you don't speak up he'll never be the one," he notes in *This Strange Joy*). For many years, he and Pier Paolo Pasolini, who was one of Penna's early admirers, are said to have had a running competition to see which of the two could meet more boys. Penna described himself as saturated by a strange joy of living that made him immune to the dangers of the chase. Even when Penna calls himself a "crazed wolf" sniffing the hot shadows in search of companions, his immoderate behavior does not make him feel guilt for his excesses. Sin ceases to exist, he tells us, once sexual attraction has been kindled.

His boys, who are typically upon the threshold of adolescence, are often compared to young animals for their ingenuous grace and sometimes appear adorned by kittens, cats, or puppies, or in an otherwise lush natural setting. One boy harvesting grain wears an apron heavy with fruit. The concept of "light" itself appears in a majority of his poems; and his boys often bask in tints of azure, gold, and white as if their mission were to enlighten the poet's drab existence.

Critics committed to labels are baffled by the straightforward classicism of Penna's lapidary vignettes. He is often classified as a "hermetic" poet on the basis of chronology, but his message, repeated in endless variations, is anything but hermetic. The subject matter of his poetry is boys ("Always boys in my poems," he announces in mock self–accusation in *This Strange Joy*), and his total oeuvre is remarkable for its lack of an evolving philosophy. The difficulty in tracing a philosophical development in Penna's work is further complicated by the fact that his poems were published in nonchronological batches.

Although Penna was never interested in discussing literary theory, cared nothing for literary society, and did not cultivate literary friendships, in his old age he liked to give interviews, which provided him with an opportunity to generate some sorely needed income. Once in an interview, Penna emphasized that he was a pederast instead of a homosexual, a notion that was seized upon and defended by several of his critics. Significantly Penna's favorite word in Italian for the object of his desire is *fanciullo,* ultimately derived from the Latin word *infans* (infant).

Through the efforts of a psychologist he was consulting in 1932, Penna was able to meet Umberto Saba (1883–1957), whose posthumous novel of boy love, *Ernesto,* would be published only after his own death. The older poet encouraged Penna's fledgling efforts to write and publish poetry. Referring to his caressing and seemingly unlascivious vignettes of young boys, Saba later characterized Penna as a singer of frustrated motherhood.

Penna's first volume of poetry was enthusiastically received by Italian critics despite its appearance during the height of the Mussolini regime. It was not until five years after World War II that Penna published his second slender volume of poetry, *Appunti,* but again the critics gave him complimentary reviews.

In 1956, Pasolini gave Penna's literary reputation a boost by reviewing the volume entitled *Una strana gioia di vivere.* The following year, Penna's collected poetry, *Poesie,* was issued. It was this volume that won the coveted Viareggio Prize, which he shared with Pasolini, who had written *Le ceneri di Gramsci* ("The Ashes of Gramsci"), a volume of politically inspired poetry. The victory of two homosexuals in such a highly regarded competition unleashed a spate of homophobia in Italy, and the judges who supported Penna for the prize—Giuseppe De Robertis, Giorgio Caproni, and Leone Piccioni—were singled out for special reproach.

A stranger at life's feast, Penna cultivated the rare ability to enshrine the most vivid moments of his life in a series of picture–perfect lyrics, which, although homoerotic in their majority, have the transcendent power to soar on their own merit and to affect readers far beyond the confines of sexual persuasion.

—*Jack Shreve*

———

PERDURABO, Frater. *See* **CROWLEY, Aleister.**

PETROVSKY, Boris. *See* **MANSFIELD, Katherine.**

———

PICANO, Felice. American novelist, short fiction writer, poet, and publisher. Born in New York City, 22 February 1944. Educated at Queens College of the City University of New York, B.A. 1964. Social worker, New York City Department of Welfare, New York City, 1964–66; assistant editor, *Art Direction,* New York City, 1966–68; assistant manager, Doubleday Bookstore, New York City, 1969–70; free–lance writer, 1970–72; Rizzoli's Bookstore, New York City, assistant manager and buyer, 1972–74; free–lance writer, 1974—; book editor, *New York Native,* 1980–83. Founder and publisher of SeaHorse Press Ltd., 1977—; cofounder and copublisher of the Gay Presses of New York, 1980—. Instructor of fiction writing classes, YMCA West Side Y Writers Voice Workshop, 1982–84. Ernest Hemingway Award finalist, c. 1975. Agents: Jane Berkey (for works published prior to 1992), Jane Rotrosen Agency, 226 East 32nd Street, New York, New York 10016, U.S.A; Malaga Baldi, P.O. Box 591, Radio City Station, New York, New York 10101, U.S.A.

WRITINGS

Novels

Smart as the Devil. New York, Arbor House, 1975.
Eyes. New York, Arbor House, 1976.
The Mesmerist. New York, Delacorte, 1977.
The Lure. New York, Delacorte, 1979.
An Asian Minor: The True Story of Ganymede (novella), illustrations by David Martin. New York, SeaHorse Press, 1980.
Late in the Season. New York, Delacorte, 1981.
House of Cards. New York, Delacorte, 1984.
Ambidextrous: The Secret Lives of Children, Volume 1. Gay Presses of New York, 1985.
To the Seventh Power. New York, Morrow, 1989.
Men Who Loved Me: A Memoir in the Form of a Novel. New York, NAL/Dutton, 1989.

Poetry

The Deformity Lover, and Other Poems. New York, SeaHorse Press, 1978.
Window Elegies. Close Grip Press, 1986.

Contributor

Orgasms of Light, edited by Winston Leland. San Francisco, Gay Sunshine Press, 1979.
Aphrodisiac: Fiction from Christopher Street, edited by Michael Denneny. New York, Coward, 1980.
New Terrors Two, edited by Ramsey Campbell. London, Pan Books, 1980.

Modern Masters of Horror, edited by Frank Coffey. New York, Coward, 1981.
On the Line, edited by Ian Young. Trumansburg, New York, Crossing Press, 1982.
Getting from Here to There: Writing and Reading Poetry, edited by Florence Grossman. Upper Montclair, New Jersey, Boynton/Cook, 1982.
The Christopher Street Reader, edited by Charles Ortleb and Michael Denneny. New York, Coward, 1983.
The Penguin Book of Homosexual Verse, edited by Stephen Coote. New York, Penguin, 1983.
The Male Muse, Number Two, edited by Ian Young. Trumansburg, New York, Crossing Press, 1983.
Not Love Alone, edited by Martin Humphries. London, Gay Mens Press, 1985.
Men on Men, edited by George Stambolian. New York, New American Library, 1986.
Scare Care, edited by Graham Masterson. New York, Tor Books, 1989.
Men on Men, Volume 3, edited by George Stambolian. New York, New American Library, 1990.
The Gay Nineties, edited by Phil Wilkie and Greg Baysans. Freedom, California, Crossing Press, 1991.

Other

Editor, *A True Likeness: An Anthology of Lesbian and Gay Writing Today.* New York, SeaHorse Press, 1980.
Slashed to Ribbons in Defense of Love, and Other Stories. Gay Presses of New York, 1983.
One O'Clock Jump (one–act play; produced Off–Off Broadway, 1986).
With Charles Silverstein, *New Joy of Gay Sex.* New York, HarperCollins, 1992.

*

Adaptations: *Immortal!* (play with music; based on *An Asian Minor: The True Story of Ganymede;* produced Off–Off Broadway, 1986), *Eyes* (screenplay; based on novel of same title), 1986.

Manuscript Collections: Beinecke Rare Books and Manuscript Library–American Collection at Yale University.

Biography: *Contemporary Authors Autobiography Series,* Volume 13, Detroit, Gale, 1991.

Interviews: *Lesenlust* (Berlin), September 1992; *New York Native,* November 1992; *Frontiers,* November 1992; *Edge,* August 1993; *Playboy* (Japan), September 1993; *Esquire* (Japan), October 1993.

Critical Sources: *The Gay Novel in America* by James Levin, New York, Garland, 1991; "Felice Picano" by Will Meyerhofer, in *Contemporary Gay American Novelists: A Bio–bibliographical Critical Sourcebook,* edited by Emmanuel S. Nelson, Westport, Connecticut, Greenwood Press, 1992.

Felice Picano comments: "Gay and lesbian culture has grown so quickly, flourished so, and become so pervasive (and sometimes so important) in our lives that it is very difficult for younger people to realize that it wasn't always there. It wasn't. For those of us who helped to build it, brick by brick, those early, merciless attacks against us and our work in the media (often by closeted gays), the lifelong enmities created, and the continuing closed doors against us in the highest artistic circles are constant reminders of the price we paid for being pioneers. Even worse, are those younger lesbians and gays now in power who ignore and overlook us and our work—which is often at its most mature—and who only present their generation. Those who ignore history are doomed to repeat its mistakes."

*   *   *

Felice Picano is a leader in the modern gay literary movement. Among his works are many novels—both gay and straight, several books of poetry, plays, short stories, a guide to gay sex, and service as a contributor and editor of numerous books. His active involvement in the development of gay presses and a gay literary movement is widely acknowledged. Throughout his life Picano has shaken the status quo. He states in his fictionalized memoirs *Ambidextrous: The Secret Lives of Children:* "I'd already been a fornicator and petty criminal at eleven years old, a drug addict and homosexual at twelve, a seducer, a sexual exhibitionist and successful purveyor of pornography at 13." It was only logical he would help create the gay literary genre.

Following two years of service as a social worker in East Harlem, New York, Picano left for Europe "to break all ties and become a homosexual," he perfunctorily states in *Men Who Loved Me.* After his return from Europe he filled managerial positions in several New York bookstores and performed free–lance writing on the side. While working at Rizzoli's Bookstore, he signed on with literary agent Jane Rotrosen. Through her efforts, Picano's first novel, *Smart as the Devil,* was published in 1975. *Smart as the Devil,* an Ernest Hemingway Award finalist, was followed by two other "straight" novels, *Eyes* in 1976, and *The Mesmerist* in 1977. All three were commercial successes. It was not until 1979, however, that Picano "came out" in his first openly gay thriller, *The Lure.* From that point onward, his literary work was dedicated to the advancement of gay literature.

In 1977 Picano founded the first gay publishing house in New York City, SeaHorse Press. He designed the business as a complete gay endeavor. It would publish solely gay literature and would employ only gay bookbinders, typesetters, artists, and distributors. Some of the most prominent gay literary works of the last two decades can be attributed to SeaHorse. Works by Martin Duberman, Dennis Cooper, Gavin Dillard, Brad Gooch, Doric Wilson, and others fill their catalogues. Several years later Picano collaborated with two other small gay presses to form the Gay Presses of New York (GPNY). By the mid 1980s the alliance held over 70 gay and lesbian titles in print. One of its most notable books was Harvey Fierstein's *Torch Song Trilogy.* GPNY also published Picano's *Slashed to Ribbons in Defense of Love, and Other Stories* and *Ambidextrous.*

Through his work with SeaHorse and GPNY, Picano was influential in gay literary circles. He met frequently with Edmund White, Robert Ferro, Andrew Holleran, George Whitmore, Michael

Grumley, and Christopher Cox. This literary circle became known as the Violet or Lavender Quill Club, the first openly gay author group. The group publicized their books and toured the country promoting them, and its members soon became some of the prominent gay literary figures of the 1980s. From the Violet Quill Club sprang such works as Picano's *Late in the Season* and *An Asian Minor: The True Story of Ganymede,* Ferro's *Family of Max Desir* and *The Blue Star Conspiracy,* Holleran's *Nights in Aruba,* Whitmore's *Confessions of Danny Slocum,* and White's *Boy's Own Story*—as well as numerous others.

The Lure, Picano's quintessential "coming out" novel, succinctly connected his first three straight books, written with a more commercial approach, and his openly gay style that emerged through his affiliation with the Violet Quill Club and SeaHorse. *The Lure* is a fine example of a gay thriller set in Manhattan. The protagonist of the book, Noel Cummings, agrees to act as bait to trap the perpetrator of a series of gay murders. Along the way Cummings discovers his own gay identity. The controversial gay lifestyle of late 1970's New York is openly and unapologetically presented in *The Lure.* As James Levin states in *The Gay Novel in America,* "The theme of coming out was done many times before, but seldom so well as here.... Picano has integrated the homosexual subculture into the traditional thriller." Will Meyerhofer, writing in *Contemporary Gay American Novelists,* finds it to be "the finest example of the gay thriller, a classic."

Picano followed in 1980 with his second gay book, *An Asian Minor.* This was a lighthearted, campy takeoff on a Greek myth. The short novella, with erotic drawings by David Martin, expands the tale from Ovid adding a gay liberation slant. Meyerhofer points out in *Contemporary Gay American Novelists* that this was the first time a Greek myth had been updated with gay sensibility and a high degree of homoeroticism.

Two of the books that Picano is most proud of are his fictionalized memoirs *Ambidextrous: The Secret Lives of Children* in 1985, and *Men Who Loved Me* in 1989. *Ambidextrous* covers his school years from ages 10 to 14, while *Men Who Loved Me* is the author's viewpoint from his early 20s. The books are structured in the style of musical sonatas, complete with variations and fugues. Picano commented in *Contemporary Authors Autobiography Series* that "the books contain all I've learned so far of style, form, and technique in rendering the funny, tragic, sad, frustrating, incomprehensible and ambiguous quotidian of our lives."

Picano's books of poetry, *The Deformity Lover, and Other Poems* and *Window Elegies,* along with other select pieces, express a sense of coming to terms with human nature or contemporary urban living. Many contain autobiographical snippets, often experimental in form, including self interviews, imaginary dialogues, and letters to unknown individuals.

Felice Picano's contribution to contemporary gay literature has been immense. His founding of one of the first gay publishing firms, SeaHorse Press and his involvement in establishing GPNY, has fostered a profound growth in the gay literary genre. Over the course of the last several decades Picano, along with members of the Violet Quill, has been responsible for some of the most heralded gay literature of the 1980s and 1990s. Picano claimed in *Contemporary Gay American Novelists* that perhaps "the reason I lived through these times, knew these people, suffered these losses, became a writer, is so I might bear witness to that era (of AIDS), these people, and these great losses, and make it literature."

—*Michael A. Lutes*

PLANGMAN, Mary Patricia. *See* **HIGHSMITH, (Mary) Patricia.**

POLYANIN, Andrey. *See* **PARNOK, Sophia (Yakovlevna).**

PRATT, Minnie Bruce. American poet, essayist, educator, and activist. Born in Selma, Alabama, 1946. Educated at University of Alabama at Tuscaloosa, B.A. with honors in English 1968; University of North Carolina at Chapel Hill, Ph.D. in English literature 1979. Instructor, Fayetteville State University, Fayetteville, North Carolina, 1975–80; assistant professor, Shaw University, Raleigh, North Carolina, 1980–82; member of graduate faculty, Women's Studies Program, George Washington University, Washington, D.C., 1984–88; adjunct assistant professor, adult degree program, Vermont College at Norwich, 1985–86; faculty member of women's studies program, University of Maryland, College Park, 1984–91; writer in residence, Community Writer's Project, Syracuse, New York, 1988; member of graduate faculty, Union Institute, Cincinnati, Ohio, 1990. Founder, WomanWrites: A Southeastern Lesbian Writers Conference, 1977; member, editorial collective, *Feminary: A Feminist Journal for the South, Emphasizing Lesbian Visions,* 1978–83; founding member, LIPS, lesbian–feminist action group, 1987. **Recipient:** Academy of American Poets Lamont Poetry Selection, 1989; National Endowment for the Arts creative writing fellowship, 1990; Lillian Hellman–Dashiell Hammett Award (with Chrystos and Audre Lorde), Fund for Free Expression, 1991; American Library Association Gay and Lesbian Book Award, 1991; Gustavus Myers Center for the Study of Human Rights in the United States Outstanding Book Award, 1992; District of Columbia Commission on the Arts literature grant, 1992, Lambda Literary Award finalist in nonfiction, 1992. Address: 147 Chestnut Avenue, 4R, Jersey City, New Jersey 07306, U.S.A.

WRITINGS

Essays

"Dear Chrysalis," in *Top Ranking: A Collection of Articles on Racism and Classism in the Lesbian Community,* compiled by Joan Gibbs and Sara Bennett. Brooklyn, New York, February 3rd Press, 1980.
"White Women and White Terror," in *WIN: Twenty Years Later— King's Vision,* August 1983.
With Elly Bulkin and Barbara Smith, *Yours in Struggle: Three Feminist Perspectives on Anti–Semitism and Racism* (includes "Identity: Skin Blood Heart"). Long Haul Press, 1984; Ithaca, New York, Firebrand Books, 1988.

Rebellion: Essays 1980–1991. Ithaca, New York, Firebrand Books, 1991.

Poetry

Sound of One Fork. Durham, North Carolina, Night Heron Press, 1981.
We Say We Love Each Other. Spinsters/Aunt Lute, 1985; Ithaca, New York, Firebrand Books, 1992.
Crime Against Nature. Ithaca, New York, Firebrand Books, 1990.

Other

Lesbian Tongues: Lesbians Talk about Life, Love and Sex (90–minute videotape) by Lil Pitcaithly and Joyce Compton, Washington, D.C., 1989.

*

Interviews: "Southern Women Fight Racism" by Ann Holder, in *Gay Community News,* 2 April 1983, 6, 10; "Toward the Oracle of Ourselves" by Jim Marks, in *Lambda Book Report,* February–March 1990, 6–8, 30; "Explaining in a Way that People Can Hear" by Jennie McKnight, in *Gay Community News,* May 1990; "What She Did for Love" by John–Manuel Andriote, in *Advocate,* 5 June 1990, 64–65; "Close–Up" by Christine Martin, in *1993 Poet's Market,* Cincinnati, Writer's Digest Books, 1992, 129–130; "Interview" by Elaine Auerbach, in *Belles Lettres,* fall 1992, 32–36.

Bibliography: "Sliding Stone from the Cave's Mouth" by Adrienne Rich, in *American Poetry Review,* September/October 1990, 11–16.

Critical Sources: *Au Courant,* March 1987; "National Endowment for the Arts Helps Fund Porn Star's Stage Show" by Valerie Richardson, in *Washington Times,* 5 February 1990, A1; "Crimes of Nature" by Penny Kaganoff, in *Publisher's Weekly,* 2 March 1990, 78; "Gay Literati Celebrate New Era of Acceptance" by Victor F. Zonana, in *Los Angeles Times,* 7 March 1990, E1; "Democracy and Women's Autobiographies" by Anne Koenen in *Amerikastudien/American Studies* (West Germany), 35:3, 1990, 321–336; "The National Endowment for the Arts: Misusing Taxpayers' Money," in *Heritage Foundation Reports,* 18 January 1991; "Sons, Lovers, Immigrant Souls" by Carol Muske, in *New York Times Book Review,* 27 January 1991, 20; "Fund for Free Expression Honors 23 Writers," in *Los Angeles Times,* 22 May 1991, E3; "Rebellion: Essays 1980–1991," in *Publisher's Weekly,* 1 November 1991, 75; "Rebellion: Essays 1980–1991," by Patricia A. Sarles, in *Library Journal,* December 1991, 178, 180; "Check It Out," in *Lambda Book Report,* January/February 1992, 40–1; "Poets Live the Questions: Jewelle Gomez and Minnie Bruce Pratt Discuss Politics and Imagination," in *Out/Look,* spring 1992, 63–71.

*   *   *

Winner of the 1989 Lamont Poetry Selection of the Academy of American Poets, a creative writing fellowship from the National Endowment for the Arts in 1990, and numerous other national awards, Minnie Bruce Pratt is recognized as an eminent poet in the United States. In addition to receiving acclaim for her verse, Pratt is acknowledged as an essayist, activist, lesbian–feminist, and educator. By chronicling her existence in poetry and prose, Pratt has explored themes reflecting the particularities of her life. She has surveyed her European–American, Southern, middle–class upbringing, the early clues of her love of women and the relationships that occurred during her adult years, her ten–year marriage and strained divorce, her battle to retain relationships with her sons, and her subsequent life as a lesbian–poet.

Pratt began writing in earnest after the demise of her marriage in 1975 and her "coming out." In doing so, she rediscovered an affinity for the craft: Drawing on a long tradition of Southern storytelling, Pratt unraveled her past and created her future with words as her guide. Her break into the future created a furor when she fell in love with a woman and lost much of her privilege, including the custody of her two small sons. A self–confessed "good girl," Pratt's rebellion against being forced to choose between her love of women and her children led to her recognition that she had never explored her past, been actively aware of her present, or plotted her future. Nor had Pratt listened to the many voices of her own identity. In her 1990 work, *Crime Against Nature,* Pratt discussed her multiple identities as lesbian poet, ex–wife, daughter, mother, naturalist, feminist, Southerner, "good girl," educator, activist, and marginalized being.

The process of self–identification freed Pratt to bond with minority communities as she detected her place within and outside of these groups. Anne Koenen has said that in Pratt's 1984 essay, "Identity: Skin Blood Heart," she "adopt[ed] the minority approach of linking the individual to the community. Speaking as a white woman, she [wrote] to acknowledge difference and multiplicity, concepts that have been central to feminism over the last years. Pratt demonstrate[d] that the personal is political, [and] confront[ed] her own personal history within the context of racism, sexism, anti–semitism, and homophobia." In her work, Pratt provided a model of personal discovery for lesbians seeking ways to resist and exist with dignity in an often hostile society and to traverse difference without denouncing individuality.

Her earliest publication, a chapbook of poetry published in 1981 entitled *Sound of One Fork,* discussed themes recurrent in her writing—love and racism. One year later, her essay in *Yours in Struggle: Three Feminist Perspectives on Anti–Semitism and Racism* produced an innovative approach to analysis in lesbian–feminist scholarship: a naming of personal racial myths she accumulated in childhood and of her own making. Devoid of guilt and hyperbole, Pratt intermixed historical analysis, theory, and personal accounts to relay the process of understanding herself as an individual.

We Say We Love Each Other, published in 1985, enhanced Pratt's reputation as a lesbian–poet: in *Au Courant,* she was compared to the renowned poets Adrienne Rich, Judy Grahn, and Audre Lorde. *We Say We Love Each Other* consists of three long poems that Pratt entitled "maps." These maps trace the evolution of her identities: feminist, lesbian lover, mother, daughter, social outlaw. In 1990, *Crime Against Nature,* her award–winning volume of poetry, received praise for recording the dissolution of her marriage, her life after the divorce, and her successful relationships with her sons despite society's condemnation of her sexual orientation. *Rebellion: Essays 1980–1991* compiled essays published previously about racism, anti–semitism, violence, money, activism, censorship, and rebellion. These essays are deceptively approachable: upon closer inspection, they offer profundity cloaked in comfortable prose.

While many recurrent themes are found in Pratt's writings (nature, the South, urbanism, art, love, racism, identity, family, sex), her stress on communication pervades. As quoted in *Out/Look,* Pratt noted in an address during the 1991 Creating Change: Lesbian and Gay Leadership conference: "To me my writing is sometimes: A shout to someone to do something; A reminder to myself of what I need to remember, words to center me in a hostile and chaotic universe; A prayer, a justification of need; A repetition to keep my sanity, a stubborn clinging to what I need in order to go on with my life on the edge, on the margin of power." By talking, writing, and sharing, Pratt acknowledged prevalent themes in feminism, democracy, and identity: multiplicity and individualism. Pratt's example invited her audience to record the "maps" of their own lives as she did in *We Say We Love Each Other.* In sum, she incited self–discovery through communication.

While authors of lesbian fiction have produced some uneven works during the last quarter of the twentieth century, lesbian–poets have excelled in communicating many major themes of gay struggle. Pratt's work has continued this tradition and served the two–fold purpose of existing as valuable art in its own right and as representation of lesbian resistance. Upon accepting her award from the Academy of American Poets in 1989, Pratt used the opportunity to give an acceptance speech with political content and to read some of her poems, which referred to her life as a lesbian. An attempt was made by members of the Academy to interrupt her presentation. While shock was not the intention of her speech, Pratt did want to include an acknowledgment of her communities and their support. On another occasion, her poetry was used for political purposes during a National Endowment for the Arts Council meeting when, in protest of Senator Jesse Helm's campaign during the early 1990s to purge the NEA of subversive art, one of Pratt's students read aloud her poem "Peach." The reading of this verse, without the physical presence of Pratt, continued her work of "serving her communities" by paying homage to recalcitrant poets and loving lesbians.

Whether writing a poem, creating an essay, or organizing a protest, Minnie Bruce Pratt has cultivated the concepts of community and personal exchange. As Pratt stated in an 1992 interview with Elaine Auerbach, "I am interested in how we develop power with others. I think it's important that my having access to my own power in my writing doesn't mean draining it away from the community or using it in opposition to others but rather using my power collectively with others to build a transformative future."

—*Cynthia D. Nieb*

———

PRESCOTT, Jack. *See* **PRESTON, John.**

———

PRESTON, John. American novelist, editor, author of nonfiction, and activist. Has also written as Jack Hild, Mike McCray, Preston MacAdam, and Jack Prescott. Born in Framingham, Massachusetts, 11 December 1945. Educated at Lake Forest College, Lake Forest, Illinois, B.A. 1968; University of Minnesota at Minneapolis St. Paul, certified sexual health consultant, 1973. Founder and codirector, Gay House, Inc., Minneapolis, Minnesota, 1970–72; founder and codirector, Gay Community Services, Minneapolis, 1972–74; editor of a newsletter for the Sex Education Council of the United States, New York, New York, beginning 1973; editor, *Advocate,* San Francisco, 1975–76; free–lance writer and editor, 1976–. Regular contributor to *Lambda Book Report;* contributor to *Christopher Street, Front Page, Harper's, Interview, Maine in Print, Philadelphia Gay News, Solares Hill, Steam,* and *Taos Review.* Member of National Writers Union, National Book Critics Circle, PEN, Authors Guild, Maine Writers and Publishers Alliance. **Recipient:** *Front Page* Gay Novel of the Year, 1984; Meridian Theatre's Jane Chambers Playwriters Award, 1984; *Weekly News* (Miami) writer of the year, 1985; Maine State Arts Commission grant, 1989–90; Lambda Literary Award for best anthology, 1993. Agent: Peter Ginsberg, Curtis Brown Associates, 1750 Montgomery Street, San Francisco, California 94111, U.S.A. Address: P.O. Box 5314, Portland, Maine 04101, U.S.A.

WRITINGS

Fiction

Mr. Benson (novel). San Francisco, Alternate Publishing, 1983.
Franny, the Queen of Provincetown (novel). Boston, Alyson Publications, 1983.
I Once Had a Master, and Other Tales of Erotic Love. Boston, Alyson Publications, 1984.
The Mission of Alex Kane (six volumes). Boston, Alyson Publications, Volume 1: *Sweet Dreams,* 1984, revised, New York, Bad Boy, 1993; Volume 2: *Golden Years,* 1984, revised, New York, Bad Boy, 1993; Volume 3: *Deadly Liars,* 1985, revised, New York, Bad Boy, 1993; Volume 4: *Stolen Moments,* 1986, revised, New York, Bad Boy, 1993; Volume 5: *Secret Dangers,* 1986, revised, New York, Bad Boy, 1993; Volume 6: *Lethal Secrets,* 1987, revised, New York, Bad Boy, 1993.
Entertainment for a Master. Boston, Alyson Publications, 1986.
Love of a Master. Boston, Alyson Publications, 1987.
The Heir (novel). Austin, Texas, Liberty Books, 1988.
In Search of a Master. Secaucus, New Jersey, Lyle Stuart, 1989.
Tales from the Dark Lord (short stories). New York, Bad Boy, 1992.
The King (novel; published with a reprint of *The Heir*). New York, Bad Boy, 1993.
The Arena (novel). New York, Bad Boy, 1993.

Editor

Hot Living: Erotic Stories about Safer Sex. Boston, Alyson Publications, 1985.
And contributor, *Personal Dispatches: Writers Confront AIDS.* New York, St. Martin's Press, 1989.
The Big Gay Book: A Man's Survival Guide for the Nineties. New York, Plume, 1991.
And contributor of "Medfield, Massachusetts," and "Portland, Maine," and author of introduction, *Hometowns: Gay Men Write about Where They Belong.* New York, Dutton, 1991.

And author of introduction, *A Member of the Family: Gay Men Write about Their Closest Relations.* New York, Dutton, 1992.
And author of introduction, *Flesh and the Word: An Anthology of Erotic Writing.* New York, Dutton, 1992.
And contributor and author of introduction, *Flesh and the Word 2: An Anthology of Erotic Writing.* New York, Plume, 1993.

Nonfiction

Author of introduction, *$tud* by Phil Andros. Boston, Alyson Publications, 1982.
With Frederick Brandt, *Classified Affairs: A Gay Man's Guide to the Personals.* Boston, Alyson Publications, 1984.
With Glenn Swann, *Safe Sex: The Ultimate Erotic Guide,* photographs by Fred Bissones. New York, Plume, 1987.
Author of introduction, *How to Write and Sell Gay Erotica* by Lars Eighner. Austin, Texas, Liberty Books, 1987.
Author of introduction, *Kvetch* by T. R. Witomski. Berkeley, California, Celestial Arts, 1989.
My Life as a Pornographer, and Other Indecent Acts (essays and articles). New York, Richard Kasak Books, 1993.

Contributor

The Alternative Press Annual, edited by Patricia Case. Philadelphia, Temple University Press, 1984.
Gay Life, edited by Eric Rofes. Garden City, New York, Doubleday, 1986.
The Source Book on Lesbian/Gay Health Care, edited by Michael Shernoff and William Scott. National Lesbian and Gay Health Foundation, 1988.
Leatherfolk. Boston, Alyson Publications, 1991.
Gender and Performance, edited by Laurence Senelick. Hanover, New Hampshire, University Press of New England, 1992.
High Risk, edited by Amy Scholder and Ira Silverberg. New York, Dutton, 1991.
The Erotic Impulse, edited by David Steinberg. Los Angeles, J. P. Tarcher, 1992.
You Can Do Something about AIDS. Boston, Alyson Publications, 1993.

*

Adaptations: *Franny, the Queen of Provincetown* (stage play), produced 1984.

Biography: "John Preston" by Jane L. Troxell, in *Contemporary Gay American Novelists,* edited by Emmanuel S. Nelson, Westport, Connecticut, Greenwood Press, 1993, 320–327.

Interviews: "Between the Covers with John Preston" by Marcia Pally, in *Advocate,* 1 March 1988, 42–47.

Critical Sources: *The Gay Novel in America* by James Levin, New York, Garland, 1991, 337–342.

John Preston comments: "I consider my writing to be an intimate, ongoing conversation with the gay men who have always been my readers. I am very conscious that this is the audience to whom I write, for whom I want to be a voice that was denied all of us, including myself, when I was younger. I hope that the craft of my writing and the integrity of my material is great enough that other people will listen and hear this conversation."

*   *   *

In the highly individualistic world of gay and lesbian writing, it is often the case that each author will choose to specialize in a particular genre. John Preston is an exception to this rule for many reasons. His prolific literary output has ranged from 13 novels through personal essays and articles to pornography, safe sex manuals, self-help books and the editing of several significant anthologies such as *Hometowns: Gay Men Write about Where They Belong.* This constantly expanding body of work may be usefully compared to that of activist priest Malcolm Boyd, except that where Boyd's writings are often highly subjective and take the form of prayers, essays, and biographical testaments to gay and lesbian spirituality, Preston's are frank in their treatment of gay and lesbian self-esteem, sexuality, AIDS, and homophobia, examining and affirming the day-to-day realities experienced by many homosexuals.

Raised in Medfield, Massachusetts, Preston demonstrated an early commitment to social causes, beginning his work in the areas of civil rights and minority education while still in high school. He also worked on a Navajo reservation in New Mexico during this time, then attended Lake Forest College, obtaining his undergraduate degree in 1968. He next relocated to Minneapolis to continue the process of coming out. Drawing on his experience, in 1970 he established the first gay community center in the United States and served as its director for two years while enrolled in the sexual health consulting program at the University of Minnesota. In 1973 he accepted an appointment as editor of the newsletter of the Sex Education Council of the United States and relocated to New York City. His formal involvement with gay and lesbian writing began soon after, with one year's work in San Francisco as editor of the *Advocate* from 1975 to 1976. When he returned to New York in 1978, Preston began working on a lengthy story which would eventually become his classic novel of sadomasochism, power dynamics and gay sex, *Mr. Benson.* The novel was first serialized by Drummer in 1978 and not issued in book form until 1983, but the success of *Mr. Benson* inaugurated Preston's explosively productive career and eventually led the author to return to New England. It is from this reestablished base in Portland, Maine—which he details in *Personal Dispatches: Writers Confront AIDS*—that the ensuing 15 years of creation has been carried out.

An examination of the variety of works produced by Preston quickly reveals six distinct thematic groups: pornographic and erotic writing, often with sadomasochistic overtones, a genre begun with *Mr. Benson* and continued until 1989 by four successive novels; the unique novel-cum-stage-play *Franny, the Queen of Provincetown,* celebrating the courage and humor of being a drag queen (a sharp contrast to other stage depictions of members of the gay world such as Lanford Wilson's 1964 play *The Madness of Lady Bright*); a series of popular adventure novels featuring the gay superhero Alex Kane; several edited anthologies such as *Flesh and the Word*; non-

fiction works on homosexuality for a general audience, an example being *The Big Gay Book: A Man's Survival Guide for the Nineties;* and, subsequent to his own diagnosis as HIV-positive in 1987, several books on safe sexual techniques in the age of AIDS, an outgrowth of his Minnesota training.

Preston's own views on his writing are as diverse as the genres in which he creates. The series of novels and other writings which began with *Mr. Benson* illustrates his constant exploration of the interrelation between sexual fantasy and the "real world," while being in a sense autobiographical. Preston also told the *Advocate*'s Marcia Pally that he considers these books to be "a historical document ... about a time we can't experience anymore." *Franny, the Queen of Provincetown* is an exploration of an ethical way to be gay and middle-aged and was written when Preston himself was in his late 30s. It deals with a drag queen who must reclaim a sense of purpose in life following his lover's death, which he does through the energy of his rage and grief. It received the *Front Page* Gay Novel of the Year Award in 1984. The sexual imagery of the fantasies in *I Once Had a Master* and the other successors to *Mr. Benson* reappears in practical form in instructional books such as *Safe Sex: The Ultimate Erotic Guide,* with Preston adapting the information so that it could be safely utilized in the AIDS era. The compilation *Personal Dispatches: Writers Confront AIDS,* which Preston edited, was a different consideration of the crisis, and the book became a finalist for the Gay and Lesbian Book Award of the American Library Association in 1990. The author has also written extensively for the mainstream press under several pseudonyms, although these books contain no homoerotic content.

—*Robert B. Marks Ridinger*

———

PROSPERO & CALIBAN. *See* **ROLFE, Frederick (William Serafino Austin Lewis Mary).**

———

PROUST, (Valentin-Louis-George-Eugene-) Marcel. French novelist, translator, and essayist. Born 10 July 1871. Educated at Ecole Libre des Sciences Politiques, 1890; Sorbonne, University of Paris, licence es lettres 1895. Served in French Army infantry, 1889–90. Cofounder, *Le Banquet,* 1892; librarian, Mazarine Library, Institut of France, Paris, 1895–1900. Contributor, sometimes under pseudonyms Marc Antoine, Dominique, Echo, and Horatio, to periodicals including *Le Banquet* and *Figaro.* **Recipient:** Prix Goncourt, 1919; named to French Legion of Honor, 1920. *Died in Paris, France, of pulmonary infection, 18 November 1922; buried at Pere-Lachaise Cemetery.*

WRITINGS

A la recherche du temps perdu (*In Search of Lost Time*) Series

Volume 1: *Du Côté de chez Swann* (two volumes). Paris, Grasset, 1913; Paris, Gallimard, 1919; translated by C. K. Scott–Moncrieff as *Swann's Way*, New York, Holt, 1922; chapter entitled "Un amour de Swann" translated by C. K. Scott–Moncrieff as *Un amour de Swann*, New York, Macmillan, 1965; translated by Terence Kilmartin as *Swann in Love*, New York, Random House, 1984.

Volume 2: *A l'ombre des jeunes filles en fleurs* (three volumes). Paris, Nouvelle Revue Francais, 1919; translated by C. K. Scott–Moncrieff as *Within a Budding Grove*, London, Chatto & Windus, and New York, T. Seltzer, 1924.

Volume 3: *Le Côté de Guermantes I*. Paris, Nouvelle Revue Francais, 1920; translated by C. K. Scott–Moncrieff as *Le Côté de Guermantes II*, in *Sodome et Gomorrhe I*, 1921; as *The Guermantes Way*, New York, T. Seltzer, 1925.

Volume 4: *Sodome et Gomorrhe I* (includes *Le Côté de Guermantes II*). Paris, Nouvelle Revue Francais, 1921; as *Sodome et Gomorrhe II* (three volumes), Paris, Gallimard, 1922; translated by C. K. Scott–Moncrieff as *Cities of the Plain*, New York, A. & C. Boni, 1927.

Volume 5: *Sodome et Gomorrhe III: La Prisonnière* (two volumes). Paris, Gallimard, 1923; translated by C. K. Scott–Moncrieff as *The Captive*, London, Knopf, and New York, A. & C. Boni, 1929.

Volume 6: *Albertine disparue* (two volumes). Paris, Gallimard, 1925; translated by C. K. Scott–Moncrieff as *The Sweet Cheat Gone*, London, Knopf, and New York, A. & C. Boni, 1930; translated by Terence Kilmartin as *The Fugitive*.

Volume 7: *Le Temps retrouvé* (two volumes). Paris, Nouvelle Revue Francais, 1927; translated by Frederick A. Blossom as *The Past Recaptured*, New York, Random House, 1934; translated by Andreas Mayer as *Time Regained*, London, Chatto & Windus, 1970.

A la recherche du temps perdu (four volumes). Paris, Gallimard, 1987–89; translated by C. K. Scott–Moncrieff and Terence Kilmartin as *In Search of Lost Time* (six volumes), London, Chatto & Windus, 1992.

Novels

Jean Santeuil, preface by Andre Maurois. Paris, Gallimard, 1952; translated by Gerard Hopkins (three volumes), London, Weidenfeld & Nicolson, 1955; New York, Simon & Schuster, 1956; revised as *Jean Santeuil, précédé de Les Plaisirs et les jours*, Paris, Gallimard, 1971.

Letters

Comment debut a Marcel Proust: Lettres inedites. Paris, Nouvelle Revue Francais, 1925.

Lettres inedites, Paris, Bagneres–de–Bigorre, 1926.

Forty–seven Unpublished Letters from Marcel Proust to Walter Berry, edited and translated by Caresse and Harry Crosby. Paris, Black Sun Press, 1930.

Correspondance generale de Marcel Proust (six volumes). Paris, Plon, 1930–36.

Lettres a la N.R.F. Paris, Gallimard, 1932.

Lettres a un ami, recueil de quarante–et–une lettres inedites adresses a Marie Nordlinger, 1889–1908. Paris, Editions du Calame, 1942.

Lettres a Madame C. Paris, J. B. Janin, 1946.

A un ami: Correspondance inedite, 1903–1922. Paris, Amiot–Dumont, 1948; as *Letters to a Friend*, translation by Alexander and Elizabeth Henderson, Falcon Press, 1949.

Letters of Marcel Proust, translated and edited by Mina Curiss, introduction by Harry Levin. New York, Random House, 1948.

Lettres à André Gide, avec trois lettres et deux textes d'André Gide. Neufchâtel et Paris, Ides et Calendes, 1949.

Lettres de Marcel Proust a Bibesco. France, Guilde du Livre, 1949.

Marcel Proust: Correspondance avec sa mere, edited by Philip Kolb. Paris, Plon, 1953; as *Marcel Proust: Letters to His Mother*, translated and introduced by George D. Painter, London, Rider, 1956; Secaucus, New Jersey, Citadel Press, 1958.

Marcel Proust et Jacques Riviere: Correspondance, 1914–1922, edited by Philip Kolb. Paris, Plon, 1954.

Lettres a Reynaldo Hahn, edited by Philip Kolb. Paris, Gallimard, 1956.

Choix de lettres, edited by Philip Kolb. Paris, Plon, 1965.

Lettres retrouvees. edited by Philip Kolb. Paris, Plon, 1966.

Comment debut a Marcel Proust. Paris, Gallimard, 1969.

Correspondance de Marcel Proust, edited by Philip Kolb. Paris, Plon, 1970.

Correspondance Proust–Copeau. edited by Michael Raimond. Ottawa, Ontario, University of Ottawa, 1976.

Correspondance Marcel Proust–Jacques Riviere (1914–1922), edited by Philip Kolb. Paris, Gallimard, 1976.

Selected Letters (two volumes), edited by Philip Kolb: Volume 1: *1880–1903*, translation by Ralph Mannheim, Garden City, New York, Doubleday, 1983; Volume 2: *1904–1909*, translation by Terence Kilmartin, Oxford, Oxford University Press, 1989.

Mon cher petit: Lettres à Lucien Daudet 1895–1897, 1904, 1908, edited by Michel Bonduelle. Paris, Gallimard, 1991.

Translator

La Bible d'Amiens (*The Bible of Amiens*) by John Ruskin. Paris, Mercure de France, 1904.

And author of introduction, *Sesame et les lys* (*Sesame and Lilies*) by John Ruskin). Paris, Mercure de France, 1906; introduction translated by William Burford in *On Reading*, New York, Macmillan, 1971, reprinted in *On Reading Ruskin: Prefaces to "La Bible d'Amiens" and "Sesame et les Lys" With Selections from Notes to the Translated Texts*, New Haven, Connecticut, Yale University Press, 1987.

Collected Works

Oeuvres completes de Marcel Proust (ten volumes). Paris, Nouvelle Revue Francais, 1929–36.

A la recherche du temps perdu (13 volumes). Translated as *Remembrance of Things Past*, 1922–31; translated by C. K. Scott–Moncrieff and Frederick A. Blossom (two volumes), New York, Random House, 1960; translated by C. K. Scott–Moncrieff and Andreas Mayer; revised by Terrence Kilmartin (three volumes), New York, Random House, 1981.

Marcel Proust: A Selection from His Miscellaneous Writings (contains selections from *Pastiches et mélanges* and *Chroniques*), edited and translated by Gerard Hopkins. A. Wingate, 1948.

The Maxims of Marcel Proust (contains material from *A la recherche du temps perdu*), edited and translated by Justin O'Brien. New York, Columbia University Press, 1948; as *Aphorisms and Epigrams from "Remembrance of Things Past,"* New York, McGraw, 1964.

Other

Portraits de peintre (poetry), 1896.

Les Plaisirs et les jours (prose and poetry), preface by Anatole France. Paris, Calmann–Levy, 1896; translated by Louise Varese as *Pleasures and Regrets,* New York, Crown, 1948; translated by Louise Varese, Gerard Hopkins, and Barbara Dupee as *Pleasures and Days, and Other Writings,* Garden City, New York, Doubleday, 1957.

Pastiches et mélanges (articles). Paris, Gallimard, 1919; selections in *Marcel Proust: A Selection from His Miscellaneous Writings,* 1948.

Chroniques (articles). Paris, Nouvelle Revue Francais, 1927; selections in *Marcel Proust: A Selection from His Miscellaneous Writings,* 1948.

Contre Sainte–Beuve, siuvi de Nouveaux Mélanges (critical essays), edited by Bernard de Fallois. Paris, Gallimard, 1954; translated by Sylvia Townsend Warner as *On Art and Literature, 1896–1919,* New York, Meridian Books, 1958; as *By Way of Sainte–Beuve,* London, Chatto & Windus, 1958; revised edition as *Contre Sainte–Beuve, précédé de Pastiches et Mélanges et suivi de Essais et articles,* Paris, Gallimard, 1971; translated by John Sturrock as *Against Sainte–Beuve, and Other Essays,* New York, Penguin, 1988.

*

Adaptations: *Swann in Love* (film), 1984.

Biography: *Proust* by Clive Bell, London, Hogarth Press, 1928; *Marcel Proust* by Richard H. Barker, Torrance, California, Criterion Press, 1958; *Marcel Proust* (two volumes) by George D. Painter, London, Chatto & Windus, 1959, New York, Random House, 1978; *Marcel Proust* by Patrick Brady, Boston, Twayne Publishers, 1977.

Critical Sources: *Marcel Proust, sa vie, son oeuvre* by Léon Pierre–Quint, Paris, Aux Editions du Sagittaire, Simon Kra, 1925, translated as *Marcel Proust: His Life and Work,* New York, Knopf, 1927; *Comment Marcel Proust a composé son roman* by Albert Feuillerat, New Haven, Yale University Press, 1934; "Genèse de Swann" by Robert Vigneron, in *Revue d'Histoire de la Philosophie et d'Histoire Générale de la Civilisation,* Number 5, 1937, 67–115, reprinted in *Etudes sur Stendhal et sur Proust, recueillies par ses élèves en témoignage de leur reconnaissance* by Robert Vigneron, Paris, A.–G. Nizet, 1978; "Marcel Proust's Duel" by Douglas W. Alden, in *Modern Language Notes,* February 1938, 9104–9106; *Journal 1889–1939* by André Gide, Paris, Gallimard, 1939; *Marcel Proust and His French Critics* by Douglas W. Alden, Los Angeles, Lymanhouse, 1940, second edition, New York, Russell & Russell, 1973; *Introduction to Proust: His Life, His Circle, His Work* by

Derrick Leon, Boston, Kegan Paul, 1940; *Le Sabbat: souvenirs d'une jeunesse orageuse* by Maurice Sachs, Paris, Editions Corréa, 1946, translated by Richard Howard as *Witches' Sabbath,* New York, Stein and Day, 1964; *A la recherche de Marcel Proust* by André Maurois, Paris, Hachette, 1949, translated as *Proust: Portrait of a Genius,* New York, Harper, 1950; *Nostalgia: A Psychoanalytic Study of Marcel Proust* by Milton Miller, Boston, Houghton, 1956; *Proust: The Early Years* by George D. Painter, Boston, Little, Brown, 1959; *Proust: The Later Years* by George D. Painter, Boston, Little, Brown, 1965; *Avec Marcel Proust: causeries–souvenirs sur Cabourg et le Boulevard Haussmann* by Marcel Plantevignes, Paris, A.–G. Nizet, 1966; *Mon Ami Marcel Proust: souvenirs intimes* by Maurice Duplay, Paris, Gallimard, 1971; "Albertine the Ambiguous" by Justin O'Brien, in *Contemporary French Literature* New Brunswick, Rutgers University Press, 1971, 85–114; *Mon Ami Marcel Proust* by Maurice Duplay, 1972; *Monsieur Proust* by Céleste Albaret, Paris, Editions Robert Laffont, 1973; *La Place de la madeleine: écriture et fantasme chez Proust* by Serge Doubrovsky, Paris, Mercure de France, 1974, translated by Carol Mastrangelo Bové and Paul Bové as *Writing and Fantasy in Proust,* Lincoln, University of Nebraska Press, 1986; *Marcel Proust's Grasset Proofs: Commentary and Variants* by Douglas W. Alden, Chapel Hill, North Carolina Studies in the Romance Languages and Literatures, 1978; *Proust and the Art of Love: The Aesthetics of Sexuality in the Life, Times and Art of Marcel Proust* by J(ulius) E(dwin) Rivers, New York, Columbia University Press, 1980; *Maladies of Marcel Proust: Doctors and Disease in His Life and Work* by Bernard Straus, New York, Holmes & Meier, 1980; "Proust, Gide and the Sexes" by Harry Levin and Justin O'Brien, in *PMLA,* Number 65, 1982, 648–653; *Les Amours et la sexualité de Marcel Proust* by Henri Bonnet, Librairie A.–G. Nizet, 1985; "Le plus ancien état du texte proustien après les épreuves Grasset" by Douglas W. Alden, in *Etudes proustiennes VI,* Paris, Gallimard, 1987, 89–114; "Marcel Proust" by Douglas W. Alden, in *Dictionary of Literary Biography,* Volume 65: *French Novelists, 1900–1930,* Detroit, Gale, 1988.

*   *   *

Marcel Proust is recognized as the greatest French author of the twentieth century. His seven–volume masterwork, *A la recherche du temps perdu* (now called by its correct title in the English translation, *In Search of Lost Time*), "comes closer than that of any other French writer of this century to being a summa, a literary monument," as I wrote in the *Dictionary of Literary Biography.* The *Recherche,* which explores one man's search for meaning in his past, secured Proust's reputation in the literary world as a vastly skilled writer capable of great insights. Alden added, "By his style alone Proust stands among the masters. His great work reveals the mind of a *moraliste* or commentator on mores, a great social novelist, a master psychologist, a comic writer, a highly original aesthetician, and a poet."

The question of how much the *Recherche* reflects Proust's own life has been debated among scholars for decades; criticism often focuses on the work's psychological content. George D. Painter, in his biography *Marcel Proust,* believed the *Recherche* was written by Proust as "the symbolic story of his life," adding that it "occupies a place unique among great novels in that it is not, properly speaking, a fiction, but a creative autobiography." Of particular interest to some of Proust's biographers is the role of homosexuality in both the author's life and his work. Unlike his contemporary André Gide, who eventually went public concerning his homosexuality, Proust always feared exposure. Although Proust assigned a prominent role to homosexuals in his great novel, his main character—the one who says "I" and who borrowed so many characteristics from his creator—is always presented as heterosexual. Thus, both the details of Proust's private life and the ultimate interpretation of his work remain a subject of controversy.

During Proust's lifetime, and for more than a decade after his death, critics never suggested that he was homosexual. His first biographer, Léon Pierre–Quint (himself a homosexual according to Henri Bonnet), in 1925 devoted an entire chapter to "Sodome et Gomorrhe," borrowing his title from the volume of the *Recherche* in which Proust goes so thoroughly into homosexuality, but he does not relate the subject in any way to Proust's personal life. Against critics who object to any mention of homosexuality, Pierre–Quint rises in defense of Proust, praises him for his objectivity, and endorses his entire treatment of the subject for its accuracy.

As the Second World War approached and French writers turned their attention toward Moscow, Proust's work went into a momentary eclipse. For this reason two "revelations" went unnoticed; to some scholars, the revelations lend credence to the theory that Proust was a homosexual. The first in 1937 was Robert Vigneron's remarkable discovery (it is unclear how he came upon these facts) that the death of Albertine, the great love of the narrator of the *Recherche*, was inspired by the death of a certain Agostinelli whose airplane fell into the Mediterranean. Proust's affection for his one–time chauffeur and later secretary was the genesis of the Albertine episodes which, according to Albert Feuillerat in his *Comment Marcel Proust a composé son roman* in 1934, Proust added to the volume, *A l'ombre des jeunes filles en fleurs,* before expanding the subject in the posthumously published parts of his long novel. The second revelation, equally unnoticed because of the impending war, was Gide's account in his *Journal* of 1939 of a conversation with Proust in May, 1921. Said Gide: "Far from denying his homosexuality, he flaunts it, and, I could almost say, brags about it. He says that he never loved women spiritually and has never known love except with men." Gide was wrong about the bragging, unless it was to Gide himself, because Proust's correspondence proves that he made every effort to stop the slightest suggestion that he was homosexual.

In 1946 there came another revelation in *Le Sabbat* by Maurice Sachs, a member of the Cocteau coterie and a homosexual by his own admission. In 1928 Sachs was a customer in Le Cuziat's male brothel. He points out for the first time that Le Cuziat resembled in every particular (his knowledge of aristocratic protocol and his cultivated manner) Proust's character Jupien, who opened a male brothel to which the narrator contributed some excess family furniture. Sachs noted that Proust's real furniture was still at Le Cuziat's brothel and also reported his conversations with Le Cuziat, who claimed to have taken Proust to witness a butchering in an abattoir and to have arranged to have a male prostitute defile pictures of Proust's high society lady friends.

In 1949, with Proust's literary reputation again in the ascendance, André Maurois published the first "scientifically" prepared biography of Proust, *A la recherche de Marcel Proust.* Maurois was the first person allowed to consult the store of original documents in the possession of Madame Gérard Mante, Proust's niece. Vigneron's article on Agostinelli had been published in an obscure and now defunct scholarly publication, and Maurois overlooked it, but he

quoted Sachs at length on Le Cuziat's character, however without mentioning any repugnant details. He must have shocked the Proust heirs by asserting that Proust was indeed homosexual as Gide said, and he maintains that Proust used women as a smokescreen to hide his homosexuality. After recounting in detail Proust's emotional attachments to men, a subject which could by this time be constructed from the correspondence, he claimed that in later life Proust kept a series of men as prisoners in his apartment, just as the narrator kept Albertine under surveillance.

In 1959, Maurois' biography had become obsolete because of his failure to discover *Jean Santeuil* and *Contre Sainte–Beuve* among Proust's papers. Painter published the first volume of his monumental biography, *Proust: The Early Years,* in which he startled the "Proustian world" by claiming that Proust had fallen in love as a young man and that he even had sexual relations with the actress Louisa de Mornand. When Painter's second volume, *Proust: The Later Years,* came out in 1965, he startled the entire literary world with his account of some rats that were "pierced with hatpins and beaten with sticks while Proust looked on." By the final years of his life, according to Painter, Proust had become a homosexual pervert.

In 1966 Marcel Plantevignes published a book—filled with misprints and even errors in French—which related his daily visits to Proust in the latter's hotel room at Cabourg, the coastal city on which Balbec was modeled. Proust's relations with this young man were unquestionably platonic, but suddenly Proust challenged Plantevignes' father to a duel for reasons unknown both to Plantevignes senior and junior. When they pierced the mystery and thus avoided the duel, they discovered that Proust had been incensed by a young woman, with whom he had been walking, who taunted him for spending so much time with a young man. Proust thought that the Plantevignes had been spreading "false" rumors about him. The few readers of Plantevignes' book must have recalled another of Proust's duels which was part of Proustian lore ever since Pierre–Quint's biography. In 1896 Jean Lorrain, a homosexual writing under the pseudonym of "Raitif de la Bretonne," attacked Comte Robert de Montesquiou (eventually the model for Proust's epic homosexual character, the Baron de Charlus) for his *Hortensias bleus* and saved some of his abuse for Proust, who had just published a volume of short stories, *Les Plaisirs et les jours.* For years it was assumed that Proust was simply annoyed by the criticism, and that was Maurois' opinion. Painter corrected that view by pointing out what Lorrain also said: that, since Proust had obtained a preface from Anatole France, Lorrain would get for his next volume a preface "from Alphonse Daudet himself, who won't be able to refuse this service to Mme Lemaire or to his son Lucien." Painter goes on to say that Lorrain was accusing Proust of a homosexual relation with Lucien Daudet.

Additional evidence of Proust's homosexuality was uncovered by Henri Bonnet. When Bonnet was writing his book on Darlu, the philosophy professor whom Proust so admired, a French cabinet minister gave him a copy of two Proust letters which Proust's niece refused to let him publish. Bonnet passed the photocopies on to Philip Kolb who did publish them in 1970 in the first volume of his monumental *Correspondance de Marcel Proust.* Written during class at the Lycée Condorcet, the letters are addressed to fellow pupils, Jacques Bizet and Daniel Halévy, to whom Proust (who had been reading Socrates' *Symnosium*) proposed a sexual encounter, a proposal which was rebuffed. In his 1985 *Les Amours et la sexualité de Marcel Proust,* Bonnet discovered an unpublished notebook of Marcel Jouhandeau in which the latter relates his encounter with a male prostitute who told him in detail how he "performed" for Proust.

However, in her 1973 *Monsieur Proust* Céleste Albaret, Proust's former housekeeper for whom he had a tremendous affection, denies that there were any prisoners in the apartment and maintains that, whereas Proust told her what he observed in Le Cuziat's bawdy house, he went there only for the documentation needed to finish the *Recherche*. She also emphasizes her employer's heterosexuality, quoting him as saying that he was "crazy about" Marie Benardaky, the model for Gilberte Swann, and that he even thought of marrying an unnamed person, but his mother opposed him. This much seems probable: that, at the end of his life, despite what Albaret says, Proust's homosexuality turned into a perversion. What it was before is more conjectural. There is no firsthand evidence that, as a handsome young social butterfly, he was an active homosexual, although biographers have supposed that his relations with the young musician Reynaldo Hahn (whom he portrays as the perfect companion, Henri de Réveillon, in *Jean Santeuil*) and then with Lucien Daudet were of that nature. What is more certain is that Proust was an emotional person who sought affection. In his complex psyche, affection could easily turn into jealousy, which explains the motivation of his characters and the theories of love which the narrator of the *Recherche* expounds.

When Proust rose in society and frequented a group of young nobles openly flaunting their heterosexuality, he not only had to pretend to be like them but also "fell in love" with one of them, Bertrand de Fénelon, with whom he went through the full gamut of emotions because Fénelon did not reciprocate. Fénelon became the model for Saint–Loup, a longtime friend of the narrator. Much later Proust discovered that Fénelon was really homosexual, and he made Saint Loup into one near the end of the *Recherche*, even adding a sadistic scene to reinforce the point. Like Fénelon, Saint–Loup was an officer who died at the front, but only after losing his croix de guerre on the way to Jupien's brothel. And then there was Agostinelli, who had a common–law wife to whom he was frequently unfaithful with other women. Proust's passion for him must have paralleled the narrator's anxiety regarding Albertine, whom he suspected of being a lesbian. There are echoes of this passion in Proust's correspondence of the period and then a record of its subsiding. However, there is no proof that Agostinelli reciprocated, either emotionally or physically.

J. E. Rivers, in his 1980 *Proust and the Art of Love: The Aesthetics of Sexuality in the Life, Times, and Art of Marcel Proust*, a scholarly treatise, has also tried to settle once and for all the question of Proust's homosexuality. Frequently citing the *Kinsey Report*, which offered statistical measures of the homosexual population, Rivers maintains that all biographers of Proust have erred in accepting as scientifically correct Proust's own view of homosexuality. In keeping with the naturalist tradition in literature, to which he owed some of his most fundamental attitudes, Proust read Krafft–Ebing and Havelock Ellis and absorbed all of the erroneous science of his times. Homosexuality, says Rivers, is not an illness that necessarily produces a perversion; it is not hereditary either, nor do homosexuals constitute a race unto themselves, the effeminate members of which recognize each other by mysterious signs.

Rivers also rejects the Freudian view that homosexuality is due to an Oedipus complex. Thus he differs with other biographers of Proust, particularly psychiatrist Milton L. Miller, author of *Nostalgia: A Psychoanalytic Study of Marcel Proust*, and Bernard Straus, author of *Maladies of Marcel Proust; Doctors and Disease in His Life and Work*. Nevertheless, Proust himself, who did not know

Freud because he was unknown in France in Proust's day, supplied all of the elements of a Freudian interpretation of his novel by including an important early scene where the narrator, having been dismissed by his father, still manages to obtain his mother's goodnight kiss. Biographers have continued to wonder whether his mother knew that he was a homosexual. Maurice Duplay, a friend of the family, claims in his 1972 *Mon Ami Marcel Proust* that Proust's mother did know and that she recommended to him, "When you go out with Marcel and go to a restaurant or to the theatre, try to take some pretty women with you." Reading the 1953 volume of *Correspondance avec sa mère*, an early publication of Philip Kolb, one has the impression that the relationship between Proust and his mother was strange indeed, for she still treated him as a child when he was a grown man.

As Rivers says, Proust had stereotyped ideas about homosexuality that he codified in his novel in a long essay, which was both a defense of homosexuality and a condemnation of it. At this point the reader hears another voice, to use the terminology of Marcel Muller in *Les Voix narratives dans "La Recherche du temps perdu,"* which is no longer that of the narrator but of the author himself. In the underlying manuscript of this section, this essay, beginning with the homosexual encounter between Charlus and Jupien, was well integrated into the surrounding narrative. Either as bravado or because he was impatient to get to this fundamental subject as soon as possible, Proust completely detached this section and published it with the title *Sodome et Gomorrhe I* as a coda to *Le Côté de Guermantes*. In the original manuscript the narrator, as he waited for the return of the Duchesse de Guermantes, described at great length a bumblebee pollinating an orchid. In the final version bumblebee and orchid become a far–fetched metaphor which presides over the sexual encounter. Through a convenient peephole the narrator sees and hears the opening conversation when the two homosexuals, driven by instinct, meet for the first time. The narrator calls the scene both comical and strange but he also speaks of the "beauty of the glances of M. de Charlus and Jupien" which he compares to "those interrogative phrases of Beethoven." When the omniscient voice of the author intervenes, it tells two sad stories of the young homosexual in bed with his wife and of the lone homosexual landowner pining away in the country. Yet, while defending homosexuality and commiserating with misunderstood homosexuals, Proust lapses into all of the stereotyped terminology of his generation; homosexuals belong to an "accursed race," their sexual tendency is a "vice," their "illness" is incurable. "M. de Charlus looked like a woman; he was one," says a voice. When Gide read the pre–publication pages of *Sodome* in the *Nouvelle Revue Française*, he confided his indignation to his journal.

Shall we say, with Gide, that the *Recherche* was a "camouflage" and that it really belongs to gay and lesbian literature? In the early days of Proust criticism Vigneron maintained that the Eulenburg scandal (Eulenburg was a friend of the Kaiser) and the Oscar Wilde trial and sentencing (Proust knew Wilde slightly and, it is thought, went to see him in his hiding place in Paris), which were the talk of the town, were what inspired Proust to write his great novel. That theory is untenable because the essential ingredients of the *Recherche* were already in the much earlier manuscripts. It now seems clear from the correspondence that when Proust mentioned his intention to write on homosexuality, he was thinking only of an article which ultimately he did not write.

The radical change that Proust made in going from his aborted *Jean Santeuil* to the *Recherche*—the change that some critics believe is further evidence of his homosexuality—was to shift from the third person technique to the first person. It is a curious fact that in his correspondence, Proust says that "I" will do this and "I" will do that when explaining what will happen later in his novel, as though it were autobiographical. To say that Proust merely amputated his Jewishness (his mother was a Jew) and his homosexuality to make his character "I" is not sufficient, for that denies him the rank of a great novelist and overlooks the function of imagination in his work. From the time of *Jean Santeuil,* Proust aspired to universality; in the *Recherche,* "laws," as Proust called his generalizations, were so abundant that Justin O'Brien collected them in a small 1948 volume entitled *The Maxims of Marcel Proust.* Because his aesthetic and technique were based on the subconscious, he thought he could draw his universality from within himself and that he, as an individual, was representative of all humanity.

Similarities do exist between Proust and his narrator, however. Despite the profundity of his observations, which professional psychologists have taken seriously, this narrator who loved his mother (and grandmother as a substitute for the mother) but seemed to feel only jealousy for Albertine, this narrator who always stayed in bed and suffered from a psychosomatic illness analogous to Proust's asthma, seems to have a limited view of life. This limitation might well be blamed on Proust's homosexuality, but this does not make "I" a homosexual precisely because Proust, as a novelist, did not construct him that way. Bowing to the modern vogue for semiology, Rivers tries to find signals that Proust wants his readers to interpret the narrator as a homosexual, but the demonstration is not convincing.

If "I" was not homosexual, his life was crisscrossed with homosexuals. It is thought that Charlus, perhaps the most thoroughly constructed homosexual character in literary history, was to have taken over the novel in the unwritten portion after the Grasset proofs and to have provided a homosexual version of *Un Amour de Swann,* the third person novelette which intrudes in *Du côté de chez Swann.* Although Albertine replaced Charlus as the dominant force in the rest of the novel, the great homosexual lover still remained on center stage as his tragic drama was played out. Critics have said that Proust put his Jewishness into a less prominent character, Bloch, and his sexuality into Charlus. In that case, they overlook the fact that Charlus is an observed character and is modeled on Montesquiou, the haughty noble whose favor Proust courted, not because he was homosexual but because he was the arbiter of aristocratic society as well as a writer with literary connections. Behind Montesquiou's back Proust imitated him, to the amusement of his irreverent friends.

Charlus is conceived entirely in terms of all of the stereotypes which Rivers defined. In spite of his attempts to appear masculine (as a young man he and his friends beat up a homosexual), he appears more and more feminine as he grows older. In the local gossip of Combray, he was thought to be the lover of the Duchesse de Guermantes. When the narrator finally meets him at Balbec, Charlus "behaves" like a homosexual trying to seduce a young man, but the narrator does not recognize him for what he is, nor does he understand when, much later on, Charlus invites him to his house and offers to take him under his protection, an offer which the narrator finally refuses by stamping on Charlus' tall hat. It takes the encounter between Charlus and Jupien to enlighten the narrator on what he calls "inversion." As Charlus grows older he becomes less guarded in his remarks and passes for an oracle on homosexuality, while still pretending not to be homosexual himself, although everyone is now convinced that he is. In one of the most dramatic scenes of this seemingly undramatic novel, Madame Verdurin fi-

nally crushes him and separates him from his lover, Morel, just as she once expelled Swann and tried to separate him from Odette in "Un Amour de Swann." In a kind of Götterdämmerung with German zeppelins cruising overhead, the narrator takes refuge in Jupien's brothel where, through a peephole, he observes Charlus' masochistic and sadistic acts.

If the narrator feels sorry for Charlus, whom he never ceases to admire for his intelligence and erudition, that is not the case for Morel, whom Charlus picks up at a railway junction while the narrator conveniently looks on from a train window. Morel embodies stereotyped characteristics of the homosexual partner. He is sadistic in his announced but unrealized intention to seduce Jupien's niece and then in his persecution of the Verdurin coachman; he prostitutes himself to anyone, once to the Prince de Guermantes while Charlus is looking through another peephole. The latter scene is intentionally comical, as is another in which Charlus pretends to be about to have a duel in order to inspire Morel's sympathy. The narrator cannot stand Morel, although he is a fine musician, because of his pretensions and deceitfulness. In part the model for Morel is Léon Delafosse, the musician whom Proust introduced to Montesquiou.

If male homosexuals come within the purview of the narrator, they do not interfere with his life. Not so the lesbians. In an early short story which Proust published in *Le Banquet* but omitted from *Les Plaisirs et les jours,* "Avant la nuit," a lesbian confesses her guilt as she lies dying, having committed suicide. "Confession d'une jeune fille," which Proust retained in his volume of short stories, was a similar story ending in suicide although the episode is heterosexual. Since the protagonist, who is engaged, kills herself after her mother has seen her having sex with another man, commentators have interpreted this as an expression of Proust's own guilt at a much earlier period in his life. Suicide because of guilt is one of the homosexual stereotypes singled out by Rivers. In a fragment of *Jean Santeuil,* Jean forces his mistress to admit that she is a lesbian; this is clearly a harbinger of Swann's tormenting Odette (usually it is jealousy about her male lovers but he even suspects lesbianism) and of the narrator's persecution of Albertine. In *Du Côté de chez Swann,* to the great annoyance of the poet Francis Jammes and the critic Paul Souday, there is the entirely gratuitous episode of Mademoiselle Vinteuil and her companion defiling the portrait of the composer Vinteuil under the eyes of the boy narrator who has happened to look through the window.

Lesbian characters do not surface again in the *Recherche* until Albertine appears, yet when she is introduced, she does not seem to be lesbian; she is merely the young girl "in blossom," among many others, with whom the narrator becomes infatuated. At the end of the Balbec summer season, Albertine lets the narrator come to her hotel room when she is in bed, but she repels his advances. Time elapses and she visits the now—cynical narrator in his family apartment where, with little hesitation, she becomes his mistress. This relationship, punctuated with periods of pleasant companionship and even thoughts of marriage, followed by periods of indifference on the part of she narrator, fills the summer at Balbec until Albertine dances with her friend Andrée in a sensual manner, and then the narrator learns that she may be a friend of Mademoiselle Vinteuil. This news arouses strong emotions in the narrator, analogous to Swann's jealousy of Odette but yet very different, and he whisks Albertine off to his family's apartment in Paris.

Once there, Albertine becomes the captive referred to in the title of the volume *La Prisonnière.* The narrator spies on her, has her followed, analyzes her language, but never has proof that she is a lesbian. When he is in one of his periods of indifference and has decided that they must separate, she escapes. His emotions become violent and he does all he can by letters and a messenger, Saint–Loup, to persuade her to come back. Her last letter indicates a willingness to come back but she is already dead, having been killed in an equestrian accident. Overcome with grief but still wanting to know the truth, the narrator sends the maitre d'hôtel on a sleuthing expedition and, although he returns with lurid accounts of Albertine's lesbianism, the narrator can never be sure that he was not lying. Interrogating Andrée also begets similar information, but she finally states that she was making everything up to please the narrator, which also might not be true. Thus the narrator is never sure whether Albertine was a lesbian and yet, later on in the *Recherche*, he seems to have convinced himself that she was.

"Albertine the ambiguous," Justin O'Brien once called her in an article in *PMLA*. For innumerable reasons, including Albertine's connection with Agostinelli, boy–like mannerisms, and cohabitation with the narrator in a bourgeois apartment (an unusual action for that time in French society), O'Brien contended that Albertine was not a female but a male transposed, especially because Proust himself said in the *Recherche* that homosexuals, if deeply involved in a novel, transpose the sex of the characters. In a public debate on the subject at the Modern Language Association, Harry Levin replied to O'Brien by arguing that biography should be ignored in judging a work of literature, that all that counts is the text which must be taken at its face value. Rivers has advanced a stronger argument; even though Albertine's behavior might be exceptional in terms of the social behavior of the period, it is still plausible and that is all that counts for the reader. Serge Doubrovsky, in his 1974 *La Place de la madeleine,* has complicated the matter even further by insisting that the heterosexual relations between the narrator and Albertine, described in detail but with some essential elements missing, are ambiguous and perhaps unnatural.

Many a reader and also critics have objected that Proust's conception and theories of love are too pessimistic and therefore unnatural (the argument can also be extended to include the contention that his view of love is fully determined by his homosexual experience). Proust, thought, of course, that his theory of love was applicable to everyone. Again it can be said that none of this matters, that unrequited love does exist and that the story of "I" and Albertine, or of Swann and Odette, is entirely plausible. There is also a different argument for the implausibility of Albertine; that she is so fluid a character that she really does not exist. Anyone who argues that way has missed the whole point of Proust. As the example of Saint–Loup and Rachel demonstrates, the lover creates the loved one who is never as others see her. Rachel is repulsive for the narrator, beautiful for Saint–Loup. Swann wakes up to the fact that Odette was not his type. The narrator defined Albertine as "un être de fuite," a being of flight. In the last analysis, it may be better if nothing were known about Proust's biography in order to achieve the fullest enjoyment of his magnificent text.

—*Douglas W. Alden*

———

PUIG, Manuel. Argentinean novelist and playwright. Born in General Villegas, 28 December 1932. Educated at University of Buenos Aires beginning 1950; Centro Sperimentale di Cinematografia beginning 1955; studied language and literature at private institutions. Served as a translator, Argentina Air Force, 1953. Translator and instructor in Spanish and Italian, London and Rome, Italy, 1956–57; assistant film–director, Rome and Paris, France, 1957–58; worked as a dishwasher, Stockholm, Sweden, 1958–59; assistant film director, Buenos Aires, 1960; film subtitle translator, Rome, 1961–62; clerk, Air France, New York City, 1963–67. Contributor to *Omni*. **Recipient:** *Le Monde* best foreign novel designation, 1968; San Sebastian Festival best script award, 1974, and jury prize, 1978; American Library Association Notable Book award, 1979; *Plays & Players* award, for most promising playwright, 1985. *Died in Cuernavaca, Mexico, 22 July 1990*

WRITINGS

Novels

La traición de Rita Hayworth. Buenos Aires, Sudamericana, 1968; translated by Suzanne Jill Levine as *Betrayed by Rita Hayworth,* New York, Dutton, 1971.
Boquitas pintadas: Folletin. Buenos Aires, Sudamericana, 1969; translated by Suzanne Jill Levine as *Heartbreak Tango: A Serial,* New York, Dutton, 1973.
The Buenos Aires Affair: Novela policial. Buenos Aires, Sudamericana, 1973; translated by Suzanne Jill Levine as *The Buenos Aires Affair: A Detective Novel,* New York, Dutton, 1976.
El beso de la mujer araña. Barcelona, Spain, Seix–Barral, 1976; translated by Thomas Colchie as *The Kiss of the Spider Woman,* New York, Knopf, 1979; translated by Allan Baker, Oxford, Amber Lane, 1987.
Publis angelical. Barcelona, Spain, Seix–Barral, 1979; translated by Elena Brunet, Vintage, 1986.
Eternal Curse on the Reader of These Pages, translated by Puig from English into Spanish as *Maldicion eterna a quien lea estas páginas.* Barcelona, Spain, Seix–Barral, 1980; New York, Random House, 1982.
Sangre de amor correspondido. Barcelona, Spain, Siex–Barral, 1982; translated by Jan L. Grayson as *Blood of Requited Love,* New York, Vintage, 1984.
La cara del villano; Recuerdo de Tijuana. Barcelona, Spain, Seix–Barral, 1985.
Cae la noche tropical. Barcelona, Spain, Seix–Barral, 1988; translated by Suzanne Jill Levine as *Tropical Night Falling,* New York, Simon & Schuster, 1991.

Plays

El beso de la mujer araña (produced Spain, 1981; translated by Allan Baker as *Kiss of the Spider Woman* (produced London, 1985; Los Angeles, 1987). Published with *Bajo un manto de estrellas: Pieza en dos actos,* Barcelona, Spain, Seix–Barral, 1983.
Bajo un manto de estrellas: Pieza en dos actos (produced Spain). Published with *El beso de la mujer araña: Adaptación escénica realizada por el autor.* Barcelona, Spain, Seix–Barral, 1983; translated by Ronald Christ as *Under a Mantle of Stars: A Play in Two Acts,* Lumen Books, 1985.

Misterio del ramo de rosas (produced Spain; as *Mystery of the Rose Bouquet,* London, 1987; Los Angeles, 1989), translation by Allan Baker. London, Faber, 1988.

Screenplays

Boquitas Pintadas, 1974.
El lugar sin límites (adaptation of a novel by Jose Donoso), 1978.
Pubis angelical.

Other

"Growing Up at the Movies: A Chronology" (autobiography), in *Review,* Numbers 4–5, 1971–72.
Contributor, *Le texte familial; textes hispaniques* (colloquium), edited by Georges Martin and N. Castellaro. Toulouse, France, Universite de Toulouse–Le Mirail, 1984.
Contributor, *Drama Contemporary: Latin America,* edited by Marion P. Holt and G. W. Woodward. P.A.J., 1986.

*

Adaptations: *The Kiss of the Spider Woman* (motion picture), Island Alive, 1985; *The Kiss of the Spider Woman* (screenplay) by Leonard Schrader with an introduction by David Weisman, Boston, Faber, 1987; *The Kiss of the Spider Woman* (musical), produced London West End, 1992; on Broadway, 1993.

Interviews: "Author and Translator: A Discussion of *Heartbreak Tango*" by Suzanne Jill Levine, in *Translation,* 2:1–2, 1974, 32–41; with Ronald Christ, in *Partisan Review,* Number 44, 1977, 52–61; "Manuel Puig at the University of Missouri–Columbia" by Katherine Bouman, in *American Hispanist,* 2:7, 1977, 11–12; with Ronald Christ, in *Christopher Street,* April 1979, 25–31; "Betraying a Latin Dream" by Don McPherson, in *Sunday Times* (color supplement), 8 April 1984, 51–52; "From the Pampas to Hollywood: An Interview with Manuel Puig" (1984) by Reina Roffé, translation by Pamela Carmell, in *Bloomsbury Review,* March–April 1988, 14–15; "The Art of Fiction CXIV" by Kathleen Wheaton, in *Paris Review,* winter 1989, 128–147; "Brief Encounter: An Interview with Manuel Puig" (1979) by Jorgelina Corbatta, translated and adapted by Ilan Stavans, in *Review of Contemporary Fiction,* 11:3, 1991, 165–176; "A Last Interview with Manuel Puig" by Ronald Christ, in *World Literature Today,* 65:4, 1991, 571–578.

Bibliography: "Manuel Puig: Selected Bibliography" by David Draper Clark, in *World Literature Today,* 65:4, 1991, 655–662.

Critical Sources: *Suspended Fictions: Reading Novels by Manuel Puig* by Lucille Kerr, Urbana, University of Illinois Press, 1987;

The Necessary Dream: A Study of the Novels of Manuel Puig by Pamela Bacarisse, Cardiff, University of Wales Press, 1988; *Review of Contemporary Fiction,* 11:3, 1991 (William Gass and Manuel Puig issue); *World Literature Today,* 65:4, 1991 (Manuel Puig issue); *Manuel Puig* by Jonathan Tittler, Boston, Twayne Publishers, 1993.

Manuel Puig's work was acclaimed in Latin America from the time his first novel *La traición de Rita Hayworth* (*Betrayed by Rita Hayworth*) was published in Argentina. At the time of his sudden death in 1990, he was arguably one of the best known Latin American authors of the last several decades. Puig is situated among the renowned group of writers, including Julio Cortázar, José Donoso, Carlos Fuentes, Gabriel García Márquez, and Mario Vargas Llosa, whose works began to draw attention to Latin American literature during the 1960s, the period of the so–called "Boom." Puig's work is unique among this literary group in that he combines an interest in popular culture with techniques of experimental fiction, while also turning a critical eye and ear on modern society and culture.

When Puig died, his work had reached many different audiences of readers around the world. Theater–goers and movie fans also became familiar with his name through the successful 1985 film based on his novel *El beso de la mujer araña* (*Kiss of the Spider Woman*), which he adapted for the stage as well. This novel, which is his fourth (he wrote eight in all), seems to have had the greatest impact on the general public, partly because it deals explicitly, and rather inventively, with the question of homosexuality. This question becomes a topic of discussion and debate for the novel's two protagonists, a homosexual and heterosexual. These two characters are thrown together for several months in 1975 as cellmates in an Argentine prison. Valentín, the heterosexual, has been convicted of revolutionary activities, and his is the voice of political activism, of leftist—Marxist, to be precise—theory and practice; Molina, the homosexual, has been convicted of the "corruption of minors," and his is the voice of sentimental and romantic stories, of film fantasies and popular culture. In the juxtaposition of these characters, the novel stages an encounter between incompatible political values and views of homosexuality. What appears at the beginning as a difficult encounter of opposing characters and questions, however, becomes at the end an embrace that resolves apparently irreconcilable differences of political ideology and sexual preference.

Readers familiar with other Puig novels may see in Molina something familiar to an adult version of the protagonist of *Betrayed by Rita Hayworth,* whose name is Toto. *Betrayed by Rita Hayworth* virtually tells the story of Toto's formation, and that formation, it is suggested, is both as an artist (perhaps a writer—Puig states in a number of interviews that the novel was autobiographical) and as a homosexual. However, in that first novel the protagonist's possible sexual orientation is not a matter to which direct and sustained attention is paid, although the question of his sexual identification and preference does get raised here and there in a number of observations made by other characters. The novel seems to hint at but not state what otherwise remains as a constant, if not also critical, subtext to the story being told about its protagonist. It is a text that suggests but does not declare what the outcome will be for Toto, whose obsession with Hollywood movies and devotion to his mother are implicitly bound to one another. It could be argued, then, that this novel of formation is precisely that, a story about how sexual identity and artistic potential are simultaneously shaped through familial attachments and cultural interests.

With *Betrayed by Rita Hayworth* Puig provides a kind of case study not only of an individual but also of a family and a town in

Argentina in the 1930s and 1940s. This novel is the first chapter, so to speak, in the overall story that is told in Puig's works. The story begins in that place and time with *Betrayed by Rita Hayworth*'s tale about childhood and ends in Brazil (where Puig lived for some years in the 1980s) with *Cae la noche tropical* (*Tropical Night Falling*) and its sketch of old age. In between, Puig fashions his own brand of serial and detective fiction, in *Boquitas pintadas: Folletin* (*Heartbreak Tango: A Serial*) and *The Buenos Aires Affair: Novela policial* (*The Buenos Aires Affair: A Detective Novel*); an adventurous combination of Hollywood romance and science fiction in *Pubis angelical;* a story of political exile and personal entanglement in *Maldicion eterna a quien lea estas páginas* (*Eternal Curse on the Reader of These Pages*); and a confusing confessional soap–opera story of young passion in *Sangre de amor correspondido* (*Blood of Requited Love*).

The path to *Kiss of the Spider Woman* and its explicit engagement with theories of homosexuality as well as its overt presentation of a homosexual character is not a thematically direct one. Indeed, in both his second and third novels, published between *Betrayed by Rita Hayworth* and *Kiss of the Spider Woman,* Puig focuses on the sentimental and sexual affairs of heterosexual characters. He also continues to rework, if not also revive, forms of popular or "low" art and culture, as the subtitles of *Heartbreak Tango* and *The Buenos Aires Affair* ("A Serial" and "A Detective Novel") clearly suggest. In the novels that follow *Kiss of the Spider Woman,* popular culture remains a thematic concern and popular narrative models inform both the stories Puig tells and the methods he deploys to tell them.

In *Kiss of the Spider Woman,* Molina, the homosexual character, tells the plots of Hollywood movies to his cellmate Valentín as a kind of nighttime entertainment. Molina is presented as a homosexual whose interests and identity are also bound up with popular culture. Molina's interest in sentimental and romantic forms of popular culture would seem to fit the "feminine" role he desires to play as a homosexual. The novel also focuses directly on the question of homosexuality in a series of footnotes that summarize scientific discourse and sociological studies about the origins and nature of homosexuality. In addition, the two characters talk about homosexual and heterosexual relations; and, based on their own rather different ideas and experiences, they even debate what the differences and similarities between those apparently disparate types of relationships ought to be.

The importance of Puig's writing with regard to the topic of homosexuality may, however, resides less in such explicit discussions about sexual orientation or in the direct representation of a homosexual character than in the way his works erode the hierarchies supporting traditional social orders and cultural codes. Furthermore, his work is significant for gay and gender studies not so much because one or two novels present homosexual themes or figures, but rather because such works both reconsider cultural forms and redefine social values. Puig's writing overall, as well as the novels that take up the question of homosexuality, upsets the privilege of traditionally authorized figures, such as being male and heterosexual, and forms of culture, such as "high" art and "canonical" literature. In his work, female and homosexual figures acquire new value, just as previously undervalued or "low" forms of culture are resituated in positions of importance and interest. Thus, if *Kiss of the Spider Woman* remains as Puig's best known work, it should be seen as representing not a narrow focus on one issue but a radical interrogation of contemporary culture and society.

—*Lucille Kerr*

PURDY, James (Amos). American novelist, short story writer, poet, and playwright. Born in Ohio, 17 July 1923. Educated at University of Chicago, University of Madrid, and University of Puebla, Mexico. Faculty member, Lawrence College (now University), Appleton, Wisconsin, 1949–53; interpreter in Latin America, France, and Spain; editor in Spain; U.S. Information Agency lecturer in Europe, 1982; taught fiction writing at New York University in 1980s. **Recipient:** National Institute of Arts and Letters grant in literature, 1958; Guggenheim fellowship, 1958 and 1962; Ford Foundation grant, 1961; PEN–Faulkner Award nomination, 1985; Rockefeller Foundation grant. Address: 236 Henry Street, Brooklyn, New York 11201, U.S.A.

WRITINGS

Fiction

Don't Call Me By My Right Name, and Other Stories. New York, William–Frederick, 1956; included in *63: Dream Palace: A Novella and Nine Stories,* 1957.

63: Dream Palace. New York, William–Frederick, 1956; as *63: Dream Palace: A Novella and Nine Stories* (contains *63: Dream Palace* and *Don't Call Me By My Right Name, and Other Stories*), London, Gollancz, 1957; uncensored edition with preface by Edith Sitwell, London, Secker & Warburg, 1961.

Color of Darkness (contains "Color of Darkness," "You May Safely Gaze," "Don't Call Me By My Right Name," "Eventide," "Why Can't They Tell You Why?, "Man and Wife," "You Reach for Your Hat," "A Good Woman," "Plan Now to Attend," "Sound of Talking," "Cutting Edge," and "63: Dream Palace"). Privately printed, 1956; as *Color of Darkness: Eleven Stories and a Novella* (contains *63: Dream Palace, Don't Call Me By My Right Name, and Other Stories,* and two stories), New York, New Directions, 1957; London, Secker & Warburg, 1961; with *Malcolm* and introduction by Tony Tanner as *Color of Darkness* [and] *Malcolm,* Garden City, New York, Doubleday, 1974; original edition reissued, with foreword by Edward Albee, as *63: Dream Palace and Other Stories,* Harmondsworth, Penguin, 1981.

Malcolm. New York, Farrar, Straus, 1959; London, Secker & Warburg, 1960; with foreword by Edward Albee, Harmondsworth, England, Penguin, 1980.

The Nephew. New York, Farrar, Straus, 1960; London, Secker & Warburg, 1961; with foreword by Edward Albee, New York, Penguin, 1980.

Children Is All (stories and plays). New York, New Directions, 1962; London, Secker & Warburg, 1963.

Cabot Wright Begins. New York, Farrar, Straus, 1964; London, Secker & Warburg, 1965.

Eustace Chisholm and the Works. New York, Farrar, Straus, 1967; London, J. Cape, 1968.

An Oyster Is a Wealthy Beast (story and poems). Los Angeles, Black Sparrow Press, 1967.

Mr. Evening: A Story and Nine Poems. Los Angeles, Black Sparrow Press, 1968.

On the Rebound: A Story and Nine Poems. Los Angeles, Black Sparrow Press, 1970.

I Am Elijah Thrush. Garden City, New York, Doubleday, and London, J. Cape, 1972; with introduction by Paul Binding, InBook, 1986.

In a Shallow Grave, introduction by Jerome Charyn. New York, Arbor House, 1976; London, W. H. Allen, 1978.

A Day after the Fair: A Collection of Plays and Short Stories. New York, Note of Hand, 1977.

Narrow Rooms. New York, Arbor House, 1978; Godalming, Surrey, England, Black Sheep, 1980.

Lessons and Complaints. New York, Nadja, 1978.

Sleep Tight. New York, Nadja, 1979.

Dream Palaces: Three Novels (contains *Malcolm, The Nephew,* and *63: Dream Palace*). New York, Viking, 1980.

Mourners Below. New York, Viking, 1981; London, Peter Owen, 1984.

On Glory's Course. New York, Viking, 1984.

The Candles of Your Eyes, illustrations by Ed Colker. New York, Nadja, 1985; as *The Candles of Your Eyes and Thirteen Other Stories,* New York, Weidenfeld & Nicolson, 1987.

In the Hollow of His Hand. New York, Weidenfeld & Nicholson, 1986.

The Candles of Your Eyes and Thirteen Other Stories. London, Weidenfeld & Nicholson, 1987.

Garments the Living Wear. San Francisco, City Lights Books, 1989.

63: Dream Palace; Selected Stories, 1956–1987. Santa Rosa, California, Black Sparrow Press, 1991.

Out with the Stars. London, Peter Owen, 1993.

"Sleepers in Moon–Crowned Valleys" Series

Jeremy's Version. Garden City, New York, Doubleday, 1970; London, J. Cape, 1971.

The House of the Solitary Maggot. Garden City, New York, Doubleday, 1974.

Poetry

The Running Sun. New York, Paul Waner Press, 1971.

Sunshine Is an Only Child. New York, Aloe Editions, 1973.

I Will Arrest the Bird That Has No Light, 1978.

Lessons and Complaints. Nadja, 1978.

Don't Let the Snow Fall: a Poem; Dawn: a Story. Utrecht, Holland, Sub Signo Libelli, 1984.

The Brooklyn Branding Parlors, edited by Josh Gosciak and Maurice Kenny, illustrations by Vassilis Vogils. New York, Contact II, 1986.

Are You in the Winter Tree?, 1987.

Collected Poems. Amsterdam, Holland, Athenaeum–Polak & Van Gennep, 1990.

Plays

Mr Cough and the Phantom Sex, 1960.

Cracks (produced New York, 1963).

Wedding Finger. Published in *Antaeus,* Number 10, 1973; New York, New Directions, 1974.

Two Plays (contains *A Day at the Fair* and *True*). Dallas, Texas, New London Press, 1979.

Proud Flesh: Four Short Plays. Northridge, California, Lord John Press, 1981.

Scrap of Paper [and] *The Berrypicker.* Los Angeles, Sylvester & Orphanos, 1981.

Other

Contributor, *New Directions in Prose and Poetry 21.* New York, New Directions, 1969.

Recordings: *Eventide, and Other Stories,* Spoken Arts, 1968; *63: Dream Palace,* Spoken Arts, 1969.

*

Adaptations: *Malcolm* was adapted as a play by Edward Albee, New York, Dramatists Play Service, 1966; *The Running Sun* has been set to music by Robert Helps as *The Running Sun: Soprano and Piano,* New York, C. F. Peters, 1976; other poems by Purdy have been set to music by Richard Hundley; *Sleep Tight* was filmed by Inquiring Systems, Inc.; *In a Shallow Grave* was filmed by Kenneth Bowser and released by Skouras Pictures, 1988.

Biography: *James Purdy* by Henry Chupack, Boston, Twayne Publishers, 1975; *James Purdy* by Stephen D. Adams, New York, Barnes & Noble, 1976; *Dictionary of Literary Biography,* Volume 2: *American Novelists since World War II,* Detroit, Gale, 1978; *Contemporary Authors Autobiography Series,* Volume 1, Detroit, Gale, 1984.

Interviews: With Patricia Lear, in *Story Quarterly,* Number 26, 1989; 55–76.

Bibliography: "James Purdy" by George E. Bush, in *Bulletin of Bibliography,* January–March 1971, 5–6.

Critical Sources: "The Small, Sad World of James Purdy" by Paul Herr, in *Chicago Review,* autumn–winter 1960, 19–25; "The Quaking World of James Purdy" by Warren French, in *Essays in Modern American Literature,* edited by Richard E. Langford, Deland, Florida, Stetson University Press, 1963; *Standards* by Stanley Edgar Hyman, New York, Horizon, 1966; *"The Not–Right House": Essays on James Purdy* by Bettina Schwarzchild, Columbia, University of Missouri Press, 1968; review by Geoffrey Wolfe of *Jeremy's Version,* in *Newsweek,* 12 October 1970, 122; *City of Words* by Tony Tanner, New York, Harper, 1971; "The Paradoxes of Patronage in Purdy" by Frank Baldanza, in *American Literature,* November 1974, 347–356; *The Post–Modern Aura* by Charles Newman, Evanston, Illinois, Northwestern University Press, 1985; *The Gay Novel in America* by James Levin, New York, Garland, 1991; "James Purdy" by James Morrison, in *Contemporary Gay American Novelists,* edited by Emmanuel S. Nelson, Westport, Connecticut, Greenwood Press, 1992.

*   *   *

Throughout his career, critical reception of James Purdy's work has been radically polarized. Purdy's first two major works—*63: Dream Palace* and *Color of Darkness*—were rejected by the major American publishing houses but were privately printed abroad. According to Purdy, some publishers reviewing his early work diagnosed him as insane, but Dame Edith Sitwell, after reading

Color of Darkness, praised his literary merit, calling Purdy "one of the greatest living writers of fiction in our language." Although the publication of *Malcolm* gained him widespread notoriety, critics still questioned his credibility as an artist; in fact, critics became even more vitriolic in their assessment of Purdy's later work. The more extreme critical hostility directed toward Purdy's work, however, has been grounded in a heterosexism which depicts the homosexuality of his characters as the cause of their ruin. Such analyses, so dismissive of Purdy's gay characters, are all too reminiscent of more contemporary portrayals of gay sexuality where gay desire is synonymous with disease and death.

The publication of *Eustace Chisholm and the Works* marked a turning point in Purdy's career. Here, the gay sexuality of his characters is brought to the fore, whereas in his earlier fiction, it could only be construed subtextually. Despite Purdy's more open attitude, his gay characters remained wretched about their own sexuality. They are always trying to escape from it, but such denial has disastrous results. *Eustace Chisholm and the Works* relates the story of Daniel Haws' inability to admit his love for the young and handsome Amos Ratcliffe. Daniel attempts to escape his desire by re-enlisting in the army—what Eustace, as the narrator/historian, refers to as Daniel's "dark bridegroom." Yet this metaphorical marriage only leads Daniel to his eventual murderer, the sadistic Captain Stadger, the most extreme example, within Purdy's oeuvre, of a character's internalized homophobia. In the relationship between Daniel and Amos, Purdy more openly depicts the desire possible between two men that is not limited strictly to a physical or sexual realm; and with Daniel and Stadger, Purdy depicts the figurative and literal death that is inevitable, within Purdy's fictionalized world, when gay desire remains hidden and silent. The triangle these three men form develops a salient motif that would shape much of Purdy's later fiction: the inevitable destruction that occurs when a man cannot accept his desire for another man, with disastrous consequences not only for the object of desire but also, and even more importantly, for himself.

Although Purdy has been innovative in his literary style and narrative method of presentation, his thematic concerns have remained fairly consistent since his early work. One primary narrative interest in Purdy's fiction is a paternal absence and the subsequent attempt to replace him. In Malcolm, for example, the title character has been abandoned by a father we never see, and then upon the advice of the astrologer Mr. Cox to "give yourself up to things," Malcolm encounters a series of father–figures who not only are incapable of providing him with the stability for which he searches but rather, exploit him for their own purposes. Here, as in later works, we follow an exiled protagonist who wanders through the narrative landscape—a nomad in search of home which, presumably, the father–figure will provide. Having failed to find a paternal haven, Malcolm is forced into a heterosexual marriage that provides neither stability nor comfort. Instead, this union ironically signals his eventual demise.

Within Purdy's surreal vision, home seems less a tangible reality than the tenuous creation of the characters' imaginations, especially when his gay characters rely upon a heterosexual paradigm. This unfulfilled search with its continually deferred resolution creates an ominous and pervading sense of alienation within Purdy's narrative world. The protagonists' discomfiture stems from their having been set adrift in a world that is not of their making and one where they are unable to reconcile their sense of self with those definitions disseminated by the culture around them. This incongruity not only forms their relationship to a larger community (whether represented by the family unit, the neighborhood, or the small town) but also extends to their relationships with individual characters. In *Garments the Living Wear,* Purdy turns his attention to AIDS, euphemistically referred to in the narrative as "the pest." Here, one might expect that the desperation felt by the host of characters would produce a bond or even a community—that is, a common emigré status among these characters as they chart their way through the plague–ridden city of the novel. However, in customary Purdy fashion, the dominant thematic tone paints them as self–enclosed exiles—nomads without a tribe or a nation. Divine grace and its attendant promise of both individual and communal salvation, here represented by Jonas Hakluyt, the "new messiah," are shown to be illusory. Even at the end of the novel, when Jared owns the two theatres he has dreamed of, the narrator concludes that this "gift of the theatres without the presence of the giver seemed somehow hollow." Earlier in his career, Purdy described his body of work as the exploration of the American soul; perhaps "hollow" best sums up Purdy's vision of its essence.

—David Norton

R

RAMIEN, Th. *See* HIRSCHFELD, Magnus.

———

RAPHAEL, Lev. American educator and writer of short stories and nonfiction. Born in New York City, 19 May 1954. Educated at Fordham University at Lincoln Center, B.A. 1975; University of Massachusetts at Amherst, M.F.A. 1978; Michigan State University, Ph.D. in American studies 1986. Instructor in education, Michigan State University, East Lansing, 1983–85, assistant professor of American thought and language, 1986–88; writer and scholar, 1988—. Adjunct professor, Fordham University at Lincoln Center, 1976–80, and John Jay College of Criminal Justice of the City University of New York, 1979. Intern with Teacher Development and Organizational Change Project, Institute for Research on Teaching, 1984–86; associate editor, College of Education, 1985–86; educational consultant to numerous municipal and state offices in Michigan. Contributor of short stories and articles to *Redbook, Christopher Street, Frontiers, Hadassah, Commentary, American Imago,* and *Journal of Popular Literature.* **Recipient:** University of Massachusetts at Amherst Harvey Swados Fiction Prize, 1977; *Amelia* Reed Smith Prize, 1988; Lambda Literary Award for gay men's debut, 1990. Address: 4695 Chippewa Drive, Okemos, Michigan 48864, U.S.A.

WRITINGS

With Gershen Kaufman, *The Dynamics of Power: Building a Competent Self.* Cambridge, Massachusetts, Schenkman, 1983; revised as *The Dynamics of Power: Fighting Shame and Building Self–Esteem,* Rochester, Vermont, Schenkman Books, 1991.
Dancing on Tisha B'Av (short stories). New York, St. Martin's Press, 1990.
With Gershen Kaufman, *Stick Up for Yourself!: Every Kid's Guide to Personal Power and Positive Self–Esteem* (young adult), edited by Pamela Espelund. Minneapolis, Minnesota, Free Spirit Press, 1990.
With Gerry Johnson and Gershen Kaufman, *A Teacher's Guide to Stick Up for Yourself: A 10–Part Course in Self–Esteem and Assertiveness for Kids.* Minneapolis, Minnesota, Free Spirit Press, 1991.
Edith Wharton's Prisoners of Shame: A New Perspective on Her Neglected Fiction. New York, St. Martin's Press, 1991.
Winter Eyes. New York, St. Martin's Press, 1992.

Contributor

Men on Men 2, edited by George Stambolian. New York, New American Library, 1988.
"Another Life," in *The Faber Book of Gay Short Fiction,* edited by Edmund White. London and New York, Faber & Faber, 1991.
Certain Voices, edited by Darryl Pilcher. Boston, Alyson Publications, 1991.
"Okemos, Michigan," in *Hometowns: Gay Men Write about Where They Belong,* edited by John Preston. New York, Dutton, 1991.
"Another Life," in *The Faber Book of Gay Short Fiction,* edited by Edmund White. London and Boston, Faber & Faber, 1991.
More Like Minds, edited by Ben Goldstein. London, GMP, 1991.

*

Interviews: *Detroit Jewish News,* 4 January 1991; *Detroit Jewish Bulletin,* 31 July 1992; *Detroit Free Press,* 13 November 1992; *Lansing State Journal,* 14 December 1992; *Outlines* (Chicago), February 1993.

Lev Raphael comments: "From my first published short story, my writing has always been 'about Silence ... the things people don't say,' as Virginia Woolf puts it in *The Voyage Out.*"

* * *

Lev Raphael is one of the most prolific and pioneering of a group of contemporary gay and lesbian writers who explore the place of sexual orientation within the larger context of an ethnic culture and religious tradition. Born and raised in New York City as the son of two Holocaust survivors, he completed much of his training in the fields of English and creative writing at Fordham University and the University of Massachusetts. After completing his doctorate in American studies at Michigan State University, Raphael was appointed assistant professor of American thought and language. His career in education has included serving as consultant to municipal and state offices throughout Michigan. His literary output has ranged from works such as *Stick Up For Yourself!* (for children and young adults, on building self–esteem), to literary analysis (*Edith Wharton's Prisoners of Shame: A New Perspective on Her Neglected Fiction*), to his own independent creations. These latter have chiefly taken the form of dozens of short stories and articles in periodicals and anthologies.

Much of Raphael's short fiction deals with gay and/or Jewish subject matter, often focusing on children of Holocaust survivors.

The stories with gay themes tend to be familiar in form yet unique in setting, dealing with the question of whether it is possible to be gay or lesbian within the restrictive context of observant Judaism. Raphael's debut collection of stories, *Dancing on Tisha B'Av*, explores conflicts of identity, including the cost of being true to one's nature, whether defined by religious belief or sexual orientation; the energy needed to achieve and maintain open and healthy communication; and the price paid by openly gay and lesbian members of the Jewish community. Much of the richness of Lev Raphael's writing stems from his consideration of gay and lesbian subjects through the lens of Jewish folklore, liturgy and ritual, and historical tradition. Examples of this include several stories in which openly gay Jews are barred from reading the Torah [sacred scripture], a gay man assists a woman in discovering more about Judaism and what it may mean for her, and spiritual values are emphasized to a group of gay and straight Jewish students by a stranger who may or may not be the prophet Elijah.

Nowhere is the conundrum of reconciliation of gay and Jewish identities more obviously expressed than in the title of *Dancing on Tisha B'Av*. Tisha B'Av is a day of mourning, memorializing the destruction of the Temple in Jerusalem. The image in the title juxtaposes a profane, celebratory act with a somber and holy occasion, mirroring the way Jewish gays and lesbians have traditionally been viewed by their communities—as distasteful, inappropriate, and out of place. In a broader sense, the title symbolizes the problems of becoming an individual in a world which offers no immutable reference points and where the only seemingly stable things are intangibles such as love (homosexual or heterosexual), humor, and faith. Raphael's novel, *Winter Eyes,* expands upon some of the themes introduced in *Dancing on Tisha B'Av*. Through the story of a boy growing into both an awareness of his heritage as a Jew (including the muted horrors of the Holocaust) and his own emerging manhood, it in some ways parallels Chaim Potok's novel, *My Name Is Asher Lev*. In *Winter Eyes* (whose title is derived from a piece of music), a major theme is the power of unspoken things, ranging from memories of the Holocaust to an awakening sexual drive. While *Winter Eyes* explores these issues, it does not resolve them, with the main character even at the end unsure of his sexual identity.

—*Robert B. Marks Ridinger*

RATTIGAN, Terence Mervyn. British playwright and screenwriter. Born in London, 10 June 1911. Educated at Trinity College, Oxford, 1930–33. Served in the Royal Air Force Coastal Command, 1940–45; flight lieutenant. **Recipient:** Helen Terry Award, 1947 and 1948; New York Drama Critics' Circle Award, 1948; Commander of the Order of the British Empire, 1958; knighted, 1971. *Died in Hamilton, Bermuda, 30 November 1977.*

WRITINGS

Plays

With Philip Heimann, *First Episode* (produced London, 1933; New York, 1934).

French without Tears (produced London, 1936; New York, 1937; revised as *Joie de Vivre,* music by Robert Stolz; produced London, 1960). London, Hamish Hamilton, 1937; New York, Farrar & Rinehart, 1938.

After the Dance (produced London, 1939). London, Hamish Hamilton, 1939.

Follow My Leader (produced London, 1940).

Grey Farm (produced New York, 1940).

Flare Path (produced London and New York, 1942). London, Hamish Hamilton, 1942.

While the Sun Shines (produced London, 1943; New York, 1946). London, Hamish Hamilton, 1944; New York, S. French, 1945.

Love in Idleness (produced London, 1944; New York, 1946). London, S. French, 1945.

The Winslow Boy (produced London, 1946; New York, 1947). London, Hamish Hamilton, and New York, Dramatists Play Service, 1946.

Playbill: The Browning Version and Harlequinade (produced London, 1948; New York, 1949). London, Hamish Hamilton, 1949; New York, S. French, 1950.

Adventure Story (produced London, 1949). London, S. French, 1950.

Who Is Sylvia? (produced London, 1950). London, Evans, 1951.

With John Gielgud, *A Tale of Two Cities* (adaptation of novel by Charles Dickens; produced 1950).

The Deep Blue Sea (produced London and New York, 1952). London, Hamish Hamilton, and New York, Random House, 1952.

The Sleeping Prince (produced London, 1953; New York, 1956). London, Hamish Hamilton, and New York, Random House, 1954.

Separate Tables: Table by the Window and Table Number Seven (produced London, 1954; New York, 1956). London, Hamish Hamilton, and New York, Random House, 1955.

Variation on a Theme (produced London, 1958). London, Hamish Hamilton, 1958.

Ross (produced London, 1960; New York, 1961). London, Hamish Hamilton, 1960; New York, Random House, 1962.

Man and Boy (produced London and New York, 1963). New York, S. French, 1963; London, Hamish Hamilton, 1964.

All on Her Own (produced London, 1974); as *Duologue* (produced London, 1976).

A Bequest to the Nation (produced London, 1970). London, Hamish Hamilton, 1970; Chicago, Dramatic Publishing Company, 1971.

In Praise of Love: Before Dawn and After Lydia (includes *Before Dawn* and *In Praise of Lydia;* produced London, 1973; only *After Lydia* produced New York, 1974). London, Hamish Hamilton, 1973; New York, S. French, 1975.

Cause Celebre (produced London, 1977). London, Hamish Hamilton, 1978.

Collected Plays

Volume 1: *French without Tears, Flare Path, While the Sun Shines, Love in Idleness, The Winslow Boy.* London, Hamish Hamilton, 1953.

Volume 2: *The Browning Version, Harlequinade, Adventure Story, Who Is Sylvia?, The Deep Blue Sea.* London, Hamish Hamilton, 1953.

Volume 3: *The Sleeping Prince, Separate Tables, Variation on a Theme, Ross, Heart to Heart.* London, Hamish Hamilton, 1964.

Volume 4: *Man and Boy, A Bequest to the Nation, In Praise of Love, Before Dawn, After Lydia, Cause Celebre.* London, Hamish Hamilton, 1978.

Screenplays

With Anatole de Grunwald and Anthony Asquith, *French without Tears,* Paramount, 1939.
With Anatole de Grunwald and Patrick Kerwin, *The Day Will Dawn,* Paul Soskin Productions, 1940; as *The Avengers,* 1942.
With Anatole de Grunwald, *Quiet Wedding,* Universal, 1941.
With Wolfgang Wilhelm and Rodney Ackland, *Uncensored,* Twentieth Century–Fox, 1943.
With Anatole de Grunwald, *English Without Tears,* 1944; released in the United States as *Her Man Gilby,* Universal, 1949.
The Way to the Stars, 1946; released in the United States as *Johnny in the Clouds,* United Artists, 1946.
With Graham Greene, *Brighton Rock,* Associated British Picture Corporation, 1947.
With Anatole de Grunwald and Rodney Ackland, *Bond Street,* 1948.
With Anatole de Grunwald, *While the Sun Shines,* Stratford, 1950.
With Anatole de Grunwald, *The Winslow Boy,* Eagle Lion, 1950.
The Browning Version, Universal, 1952.
With David Lean, *The Sound Barrier,* 1952; released in the United States as *Breaking the Sound Barrier.*
The Final Test, Rank, 1954.
The Man Who Loved Redheads, United Artists, 1955.
The Deep Blue Sea, Twentieth Century–Fox, 1955.
The Prince and the Showgirl, Warner Brothers, 1957.
With John Gay, *Separate Tables,* United Artists, 1958.
The VIPs, Metro–Goldwyn–Mayer, 1965.
The Yellow Rolls Royce, Metro–Goldwyn–Mayer, 1965.
Goodbye, Mr. Chips (adaptation of the novel by James Hilton), Metro–Goldwyn–Mayer, 1969.
A Bequest to the Nation, Hal Wallis, 1973.

Television Plays

The Final Test, BBC, 1951.
Heart to Heart, BBC, 1962.
Ninety Years On, BBC, 1964.
Nelson—A Portrait in Miniature, ATV, 1966.
All on Her Own, BBC–2, 1968.
High Summer, Thames Television, 1972.

Radio Plays

A Tale of Two Cities, 1950.
Cause Celebre, BBC Radio 4, 1975.

*

Adaptations: *The Browning Version* (sound recording), Caedmon, 1983.

Biography: *Terence Rattigan: The Man and His Work* by Michael Darlow and Gillian Hodson, London, Quartet Books, 1979; *Terence Rattigan* by Susan Rusinko, Boston, Twayne Publishers, 1983; *The Rattigan Version: Sir Terence Rattigan and the Theater of Character* by B. A. Young, London, Hamish Hamilton, 1983.

Terrence Rattigan's name almost never appears in listings of modern gay playwrights. This is partly due to the fact that Rattigan (who was considered one of Britain's leading playwrights for several decades) never publicly came out during his lifetime. But it is also because his type of writing—the well–made, genteel domestic drama—fell out of favor in the late 1950s when it was eclipsed by the more political, ostensibly more socially responsive drama of such writers as John Osborn, Harold Pinter, Arnold Wesker and Edward Bond. When the openly gay Joe Orton entered the British theater scene in 1964 with *Entertaining Mr. Sloane,* his transgressive, socially disruptive plays defined a new gay sensibility in theater, one that would render the works of Terrence Rattigan, as well as Noel Coward, hopelessly old–fashioned.

Rattigan was born to an upper–class family in London in 1911. He began attending Oxford in 1930 and had his first play *First Episode* (which he coauthored with Philip Heimann) professionally produced in 1933. His first solo play *French Without Tears*—about a group of English schoolboys on vacation on the Riviera—was a huge success and established him as a major voice in the British Theater. He was also employed as a screenwriter for Warner Brothers during this period. Rattigan joined the Royal Air Force in 1940 and wrote several plays about the war. It was *The Winslow Boy*—based on a famous trial in which a schoolboy is accused of stealing five pounds—that brought him serious critical notices and also established him as a playwright whose interests were youth, social hypocrisy and middle class sexual and emotional repression. *The Browning Version*—a bitter domestic drama about a failed classics professor that is a cross between *Goodbye Mr. Chips* and *Who's Afraid of Virginia Woolf*—was considered his best work to date.

As Britain's theater changed during the 1950s Rattigan, tired of being considered simply an entertaining—albeit hugely successful—writer, engaged in a somewhat acrimonious debate in the press with other writers such as Christopher Fry, Peter Ustinov and George Bernard Shaw. This was to be a precursor to harsher theater fights that would occur later in the British Theater with the advent of the "Angry Young Man" school of writers. Rattigan was writing screenplays (originals as well as those from his own stage work) for Hollywood at the time and the critical and popular success of his next three plays—*The Deep Blue Sea, The Sleeping Prince,* and *Separate Tables,* secured Rattigan's reputation as perhaps the major British playwright of the time. They also began to expose, more openly, the gay sensibility in his work.

The Deep Blue Sea is a study of a sexually frustrated middle–class woman that is reminiscent of Tennessee Williams' *The Roman Spring of Mrs. Stone* and *A Streetcar Named Desire,* both of which can be read as studies of the author's own disenfranchised sexuality. *The Sleeping Prince* is a gay romantic fantasy about a life–loving showgirl who has an affair with a stuffy royal; the impulse behind the play was that male sexuality needed to be freer and less socially restricted. *Separate Tables* was a study of British types at a resort hotel and Rattigan had originally intended the character of Major Pollock to be a homosexual who was arrested for unsolicited attentions in a movie theater, but the censorship of the time prohibited such material, and Pollock became a masher instead. This however was something of a breakthrough for Rattigan and his next work *Variation on a Theme*—an updated version of *Camille,* a gay male sensibility staple from Verdi to Charles Ludlam—featured a major homosexual character who gives up a gay relationship to marry a much older woman. Besides the gay character, the play's premise of cross–generational, cross–class love also reflected Rattigan's own life and concerns.

More open homosexual themes were present in *Ross* and *Man and Boy*. *Ross* is a sympathetic portrait of T. E. Lawrence that was open about his homosexuality as well as his sado–masochism. The play was based on a filmscript that Rattigan had been commissioned to write, but it was never produced. *Man and Boy* was an exploration of modern business ethics in which a heterosexual corporate magnate attempts to use his heterosexual son to seduce a business rival. Both plays met with some critical success and it is a sign of cultural change that their homosexual content was generally not remarked upon.

During this time, Rattigan also worked on lucrative Hollywood projects: *The VIPs* capitalized on the public scandal of its stars Elizabeth Taylor and Richard Burton as well as featuring plum, rather campy, roles for Maggie Smith and Margaret Rutherford; *The Yellow Rolls Royce* was a multi–episode romantic comedy–drama that harkened back to the Rattigan of the 1940s; and *Goodbye Mr. Chips* returned to the school–boy themes of Rattigan's early work, although this musical version had none of the playwright's bite or sexualized subtext.

The newer playwrights such as Pinter, Bond and Osborn had become firmly established by now and some established writers of the older school, such as Coward, spoke out forcefully against these new works, labeling them morally corrupt and artistically poor. Rattigan, however, kept an open mind and when he did like a work—as in the case of Orton's *Entertaining Mr. Sloane*, which he respected for its sturdy character development—he invested in the play.

Although Terence Rattigan's work fell out of favor for a period of time several of his plays have been revived in the recent years. This is no surprise since Rattigan's psychological insights, abiding interest in exposing social and sexual hypocrisy, and his unending sympathy for characters whose emotional lives have been hurt by a repressive culture are still as pertinent today as they were 60 years ago.

—*Michael Bronski*

RECHY, John (Francisco). American. Born in El Paso, Texas, 10 March 1934. Educated at Texas Western College, B.A.; New School for Social Research. Served in the U.S. Army in Germany. Teacher in graduate school, University of Southern California. Conductor of writing seminars at Occidental College and University of California. Member of Authors Guild, PEN, and Texas Institute of Letters. **Recipient:** Longview Foundation fiction prize for short story, 1961; International Prix Formentor nominee, for *City of Night;* National Endowment for the Arts grant, 1976; *Los Angeles Times* Book Award nomination for body of work, 1984. Agent: Georges Borchardt Inc., 136 East 57th Street, New York, New York 10022, U.S.A.

WRITINGS

Novels

City of Night. New York, Grove, 1963; London, MacGibbon and Kee, 1964.

Numbers. New York, Grove, 1967.
This Day's Death. New York, Grove, 1969; London, MacGibbon and Kee, 1970.
The Vampires. New York, Grove, 1971.
The Fourth Angel. New York, Viking, and London, W. H. Allen, 1972.
Rushes. New York, Grove, 1979.
Bodies and Souls. New York, Carroll and Graf, 1983; London, W. H. Allen, 1984.
Marilyn's Daughter. New York, Carroll & Graf, 1988.
The Miraculous Day of Amalia Gómez. Boston, Little Brown, 1991.

Plays

Momma as She Became—Not as She Was (produced New York, 1968).
Rushes (produced, 1978).
Tigers Wild (based on his novel *The Fourth Angel;* produced New York, 1986).

Uncollected Short Stories

"Mardi Gras," in *Evergreen Review,* Number 5, 1958.
"The Fabulous Wedding of Miss Destiny," in *Big Table,* Number 3, 1959.
"A Quarter Ahead," in *Evergreen Review,* Number 19, 1961.
"It Begins in the Wind," in *Evergreen Review,* Number 24, 1962.
"Three Kinds of Angels," in *Evergreen Review,* Number 26, 1962.
"Pershing Square," in *London Magazine,* 1:10, 1962.
"Rope Heaven by the Neck," in *Nugget Magazine,* February 1963.
"Times Square, Broadway," in *London Magazine,* 2:11, 1963.
"The Childhood of a Vampire," in *Voices,* edited by Robert Ruben. London, Michael Joseph, 1965.
"By the Motel Pool," in *Evergreen Review,* 1967.
"Return to Los Angeles," in *London Magazine,* 8:3, 1968.
"A Very Hungry Child," in *Notes from Underground,* edited by John Bryan. San Francisco, Notes from Underground Press, 1970.
"Love in the Back Rooms," in *Forum,* May 1978.
"Sun and Moon," "The Snake and the Agouti," and "Black Shadows," in *Bachy: A Journal of the Arts,* Number 17, 1980.
"Dream Report," in *Dreamworks: An Interdisciplinary Quarterly,* edited by Marsha Kinder, 2.2, 1981.
"The Lower Depths," in *Oui Magazine,* February 1983.
"Marilyn at Payne Whitney," in *Southern California Anthology,* Number 5, 1987.
"Marilyn, John F., and Professor Dambert," in *Southern California Anthology,* Number 6, 1988.

Uncollected Nonfiction

"A Case for Cruising," in *Village Voice,* 6 August, 1979.
"Hollywood and Homosexuality," in *Forum,* September, 1980.
"AIDS: Mysteries and Hidden Dangers," in *Advocate,* 22 December 1983.
"On Being a Grove Press Author," in *Review of Contemporary Fiction,* fall 1990.

Contributor

The Moderns, edited by LeRoi Jones. Corinth, 1963.
Voices, edited by Robert Rubens. London, M. Joseph, 1963.

Black Humor, edited by Bruce Jay Friedman. New York, Bantam, 1965.

New American Story, edited by Donald M. Allen and Robert Creeley. New York, Grove, 1965.

Collision Course. New York, Random House, 1968.

Scripts, edited by Floren Harper. Boston, Houghton, 1973.

Passing Through, edited by W. Burns Taylor, Richard Santelli, and Kathleen McGary. Santay Publishers, 1974.

Urban Reader, edited by Susan Cahill and Michele F. Couper. Englewood Cliffs, New Jersey, Prentice–Hall, 1979.

Rediscoveries II, edited by David Madden and Peggy Bach. London, Carroll & Graf, 1988.

Other

The Sexual Outlaw: A Documentary: A Non–fiction Account, with Commentaries, of Three Days and Nights in the Sexual Underground. New York, Grove, 1977; London, W. H. Allen, 1978.

*

Manuscript Collections: Boston University.

Biography: "John Rechy," in *Contemporary Authors Autobiography Series,* Volume 4, Detroit, Gale, 1986, 253–266; "On Being a 'Grove Press Author'" by John Rechy, in *Review of Contemporary Fiction* (Elmwood Park, Illinois).

Interviews: By James R. Giles and Wanda Giles, in *Chicago Review,* Number 25, 1973, 19–31; in *Poets and Writers* (New York), May–June 1992, 25–37.

Critical Sources: *The Confusion of Realms* by Richard Gilman, New York, Random House, 1963; "The Cities of Night: John Rechy's *City of Night* and the American Literature of Homosexuality" by Stanton Hoffman, in *Chicago Review,* 17:2–3, 1964, 195–206; "Larry McMurtry's *Leaving Cheyenne* and the Novels of John Rechy: From Trips along the 'Mythical Pecos'" by James R. Giles, in *Houston Forum,* 10:2, 1972, 34–40; "Religious Alienation and 'Homosexual Consciousness' in *City of Night* and *Go Tell It on the Mountain*" by James R. Giles, in *College English* (Tuscaloosa, Alabama), Number 36, 1974, 369–380; "In Search of the Honest Outlaw: John Rechy" by Juan Bruce–Novoa, in *Minority Voices,* Number 3, 1979, 37–45; "The Sexual Underworlds of John Rechy" by Charles M. Tatum, in *Minority Voices,* Number 3, 1979, 47–52; "Odysseus in John Rechy's *City of Night,*" in *Minority Voices,* Number 3, 1979, 53–62; "John Rechy's Tormented World" by Ben Satterfield, in *Southwest Review* (Dallas), winter 1982, 78–85; "John Rechy" by David G. Byrd, in *Dictionary of Literary Biography Yearbook: 1982,* Detroit, Gale, 1983; *Chicano Literature: A Reference Guide,* edited by Julio A. Martínez and Francisco A. Lomelí, New York, Greenwood Press, 1985; "Contemporary Homosexual Fiction and the Gay Rights Movement" by Trudy Steuernagel, in *Journal of Popular Culture* (Bowling Green, Ohio), winter 1986, 125–134; "Homosexuality and the Chicano Novel" by Juan Bruce–Novoa, in *Confluencia,* fall 1986, 69–77; "John Rechy" by Gregory W. Bredbeck, in *Contemporary Gay American Novelists,* edited by Emmanual S. Nelson, Westport, Connecticut, Greenwood Press, 1993, 340–351.

John Rechy comments: "What I most resent about how my work is often viewed—after thirty years and nine more novels—is that purported evaluations of my writing still focus almost exclusively on the ostensible subject of my first novel, *City of Night;* and that such focus merely reinforces, does not re–examine, the misconceptions that greeted that novel when it appeared in 1963. True, *City of Night* remains my best–known work; yes, it is told in the first person by a male–hustler (a Chicano, half–Mexican, half–Scottish); and yes, it is based on my own experiences; but it is not, as it is often perceived, only some kind of confessional by a male–hustler. It is a literary novel that interprets the raw experiences—with much sadness, yes, and also much humor, the humor of survivors. It has a wide cast of varied characters, and it is written in a deliberate style, very consciously attentive to structure.

"The misconceptions about my first novel began with a venomous review in the *New York Review of Books,* which was followed by a similar review, in terms of the tone of hysteria, by the *New Republic.* Both journals questioned whether or not I truly existed (I had refused to promote the book and left the country to avoid losing the privacy I still cherish), which was a clear attempt to wish away a subject, and a presence, that threatened them powerfully. And so they tried to dismiss me as a serious writer. *City of Night* is frequently referred to as a 'modern classic' and taught in literature courses in major universities. Even so, years later, in 'critical evaluations' of my writing, I still detect the echo of those two strident voices, focusing on *City of Night* as confessional, entrenching the initial misperceptions and ignoring most of what I have written since.

"Structure and style are integral to understanding my work. I have never written a novel that has not gone through at least six complete drafts, some chapters and passages through as many as twenty. The prose in *City of Night* is meant to evoke the moody sounds of the blues, the dark sexual rhythms of the best of rock 'n' roll. Unconventional capitalization and punctuation assert those rhythms. In my second novel, *Numbers,* as the protagonist Johnny Rio drives to Los Angeles, I used a mesmerized prose, surreal imagery, to augur his journey of discovery. When he is back in the familiar sexual arena of Los Angeles, the prose becomes much more direct. As he descends into the literal and symbolic depths of the park where he eventually goes to hunt and number sexual encounters, the imagery darkens. In the end, the book's real theme—death—is revealed. I conceived of *Numbers* as a sexual horror story.

"The only novel of mine I dislike—*This Day's Death*—uses two parallel narratives to construct the psychological trap that snaps together at the end. In *The Vampires,* I chose a cinematic technique, literary equivalents of 'panning shots,' 'close–ups.' I wrote the novel in 'technicolor,' garish splashes of colors to match the extravagant characters gathered on a Caribbean Island, which may be hell. My novel *The Fourth Angel* and my Off–Broadway play *Tigers Wild* (based on the novel), are about four wounded teenagers, veering toward cruelty in order to stop feeling. They are also rebellious angels exiled by their parents to seek a false paradise in drugs. Their L.S.D. experiences are conveyed in a fragmentary, hallucinated prose that alters as their perceptions change, first tempting, then menacing.

"*The Sexual Outlaw* is narrated in a spare prose, to suggest a film 'documentary' as well as the 'purity' and directness of the protagonist's three–day sex–hunt, a ritualized journey. I chose various styles, to match content, in the interwoven essays about the oppression of homosexuals. The book ends with the imagery of a battle fought—lost or won? *Rushes* is an exploration of one night in a leather bar and orgy room, and it is structured after the Catholic Mass. At once dingy and bleak, the bar is constructed like a church. Pornographic drawings on the wall correspond to the stations of the cross. Each 'realistic' passage has an antecedent in the Mass. To suggest the language of the Mass, I employed many words with Latin roots. The novel ends with two 'crucifixions'—one symbolic, mimed, the other literal, violent.

"In *Bodies and Souls,* I explored the series of random events by which destiny manifests itself, only in retrospect. Characters include a pornographic actress, a reactionary judge, a black maid, two teenage male hustlers, an unscrupulous television anchor–woman, a gay male stripper for women, and others, who finally come together in one single act of 'meaningless'—but, here, 'inevitable'—violence. The book opens with the 'ending,' thus underscoring my meaning. In *Marilyn's Daughter,* while telling the story of Normalyn Morgan, a young woman who may or may not be the daughter of Marilyn Monroe and Robert Kennedy, I wove a narrative that explores the power of legend over truth. The novel constantly questions its own reality: Rumor is asserted, then contradicted, denied, reasserted. Marilyn Monroe is seen as a metaphor of artifice refined into art, the star a masterpiece of self–creation. The book contains two of my best portraits of gay men, who also had to reinvent themselves to survive.

"*The Miraculous Day of Amalia Gómez* documents one day in the life of a Mexican American woman whose existence in Los Angeles has turned so unbearable that she believes only a miracle from the Holy Mother can save her. Hers is a day of shattering discoveries that include the fact that her teenage son is hustling the streets. In the earlier passages of the book, I established a 'realistic' tone and style, gradually altering it as the book moves toward the 'magical'—the 'miracle' that Amalia perceives in a gaudy shopping mall.

"After having written ten novels in thirty years (three best–sellers; many highly praised); after having taught and/or lectured on writing, literature, and film; after having published countless essays (ranging from the tragedy of AIDS and the ghettoization of gay art, to the literary styles of Jonathan Swift and Emily Brontë, to the poverty among Mexican Americans in the Southwest); after constantly extending the experimenting with literary forms, I am still too often perceived as a hustler who managed to write a confessional tract about his experiences, instead of a writer who wrote, in part, about hustling—and about many, many other subjects. Whether or not I have succeeded in my artistic goals, I believe that the literary aspects of my writing deserve serious attention when my body of work is evaluated."

*   *   *

John Rechy's 1963 novel of male prostitution *City of Night* was a landmark depiction of homosexual life, albeit an unpleasant side of homosexual life. A best–seller in several countries when it first appeared, *City of Night* was nonetheless denigrated by critics who objected to the book's subject matter. Based in part on Rechy's

own experiences as a gay hustler in New York, San Francisco, Los Angeles, Chicago and New Orleans, *City of Night* features an emotionally–cold male prostitute who insists he is not really gay. After a cross–country trip of sexual adventures, however, he realizes that he has been lying to himself. Rechy's depiction of male prostitutes as desperate for love and acceptance has drawn criticism from some gay critics for perpetuating the idea that homosexuals are emotionally unhealthy. But the book's acknowledged position as an important novel in the history of gay literature has earned it a continuing place in college literature courses.

Rechy was born in El Paso, Texas, and raised in a poor section of that city. He left Texas to attend the New School for Social Research in New York City and serve a tour of duty with the United States Army in Germany. Moving to New York to attend Columbia University, Rechy drifted into making quick money by working in Times Square, the gathering place for the city's male prostitutes. He remembers his first customer in his *Contemporary Authors Autobiography Series* article: "A middle–aged man approaches me and says, 'I'll give you ten dollars and I don't give a damn for you.' Two needs of my time then: to be desired powerfully, and not to be expected to care."

Soon Rechy was hustling in other cities across the country. A letter he wrote to a friend about the chaos of Mardi Gras time in New Orleans, a time filled with drugs and sex for Rechy, became his first published story, "Mardi Gras," which appeared in the *Evergreen Review* and, later, as a chapter in *City of Night.* Much of this novel is a fictionalized retelling of his own experiences, a shaping of the chaos, as Rechy has explained it. *City of Night* follows a circular structure, beginning with the death of the narrator's dog and ending with the question "Why can't dogs go to Heaven?" It also introduces a structure Rechy uses in several later novels, alternating between narrative chapters and chapters of biographical sketches of the characters involved. In addition, Rechy's prose is meant to capture the rhythm and flavor of the blues and rock–and–roll.

Telling the story of a gay hustler who keeps his emotional distance from other people and who refuses to believe that he is gay—he in fact sleeps with women to prove to himself that he is not gay—*City of Night* provides an inside look at the dangerous and joyless profession of male prostitution. The loneliness of the book's central character, and his refusal to express emotion for fear that by doing so he will reveal his true sexual identity, give the story an overwhelming sense of despair. An immediate sensation upon publication, *City of Night* brought Rechy unwanted attention from many quarters. Strangers appeared at his door, while impostors claiming to be him were written up in the newspapers. Because of this trouble, he refused to promote the book with personal appearances. He lived quietly for a time, first with a companion in suburban New York, then in the Caribbean.

After a return visit to his native El Paso, Rechy visited Los Angeles where he was soon frequenting Griffith Park, a haven for gay hustlers. This park is the setting for *Numbers,* Rechy's second novel, which details the sexual exploits of Johnny Rio, who challenges himself to pick up 30 sex partners as quickly as possible. He is interested in the "numbers" in an almost magical effort to ward off aging and death through sex. "Numbers" is also a reference to a book of the Bible that describes a clouded place lit at night by fire, a place that sounded to Rechy much like modern–day Los Angeles. In contrast to the prostitute character in *City of Night,* Rio does not sell sex. He indulges himself in openly gay sexual acts because he enjoys them. Although the story is filled with sexual encounters, the novel ultimately concerns itself with death. Rechy notes in an interview in *Poets and Writers* that "*Numbers* came out of experiences I had in Los Angeles when I was trying to outdo my own sexual record. But it's really a book about dying."

This Day's Death returns to Griffith Park but tells this time of an essentially heterosexual man wrongly accused of a gay sexual crime in the park. His trial drives him to hate the existing sex laws and how they are enforced. At the heart of the novel, however, is his relationship with his mother, a woman he loves deeply but by whom he is manipulated. The mother–son relationship is based in part on Rechy's own relationship with his mother. Written in a cinematic prose of close–ups and technicolor splashes, *This Day's Death* forms the last book in a loose trilogy of novels dealing with the gay experience. In the course of the trilogy the reader encounters a character who denies his gayness, one who accepts and enjoys it, and finally one who makes a strong plea for its acceptance.

In later works Rechy has continued to draw on his own life for inspiration, intentionally blurring the line between fact and fiction. The novel *Rushes,* for example, tells of a sadomasochistic leather bar and orgy room whose activities Rechy equates to a Catholic Mass. Chapter titles are taken from the liturgy of the Mass, while words with Latinate roots are specifically used in the narrative. The Rechy persona spends the evening at the bar drinking and talking with his friends. Their conversations delineate the sadomasochistic desires they share to dominate or be dominated by other men. They also characterize specific tendencies within the gay community of the early 1970s.

In *The Sexual Outlaw,* a nonfiction account of the male prostitute's life, Rechy sought to present the literary equivalent of the film documentary. The book follows a prostitute for three days as he roams Los Angeles engaging in anonymous sex. Interwoven with this account are brief essays about homosexuality, texts of speeches, and direct pleas for tolerance of gays. Speaking in *The Sexual Outlaw* of the relationship between his life and work, Rechy states: "My life is so intertwined with my writing that I almost live it as if it were a novel."

City of Night is Rechy's most popular work and perhaps the one most clearly expressing his vision of gay life. It is undoubtedly the book with which his name is most often associated. Aside from its historical value as one of the first novels to depict the life of the gay hustler, *City of Night* possesses a gritty realism that makes it a powerful work despite occasionally extravagant prose. Rechy sees the novel as having been unfairly categorized by the critical establishment as "homosexual literature" rather than as literature dealing with homosexuality. Many critics, he has said, miss the novel's carefully–wrought structure. This categorization, he believes, has made it easy for critics to dismiss or minimize the importance of the novel by segregating it into a subgenre.

—*Thomas Wiloch*

REES, David (Bartlett). British novelist and children's writer. Born in London, 18 May 1936. Educated at Queens' College, Cambridge, B.A. 1958. Schoolmaster at Wilson's Grammar School, London, 1960–65, and Vyners School, Ickenham, 1965–68; lecturer in English at St. Luke's College, Exeter, 1968–78, and University of Exeter, 1978–84. **Recipient:** Guardian Award commen-

dation, 1976, for *Storm Surge;* Library Association Carnegie Medal, 1978, for *The Exeter Blitz;* Children's Rights Workshop Other Award, 1980, for *The Green Bough of Liberty. Died in London, of AIDS–related complications, 22 May 1993.*

WRITINGS

Fiction for Adults

The Milkman's on His Way. London, GMP, 1982.
The Estuary. London, GMP, 1983.
Islands: A Collection of Short Stories. Stamford, Connecticut, Knights Press, 1984.
Out of the Winter Gardens. London, Olive Press, 1984.
The Hunger. London, GMP, 1986.
Watershed. Stamford, Connecticut, Knights Press, 1986.
Twos and Threes. Exeter, Third House, 1987.
The Wrong Apple. Stamford, Connecticut, Knights Press, 1987.
Flux. Exeter, Third House, 1988.
Quince. Exeter, Third House, 1988.
The Colour of His Hair. Exeter, Third House, 1989.

Nonfiction

The Marble in the Water: Essays on Contemporary Writers of Fiction for Children and Young People. Boston, Horn Book, 1980.
Painted Desert, Green Shade: Essays on Contemporary Writers of Fiction for Children and Young Adults. Boston, Horn Book, 1984.
A Better Class of Blond: A California Diary. London, Oliver Press, 1985.
What Do Draculas Do?: Essays on Contemporary Writers of Fiction for Children and Young Adults. Metuchen, New Jersey, Scarecrow Press, 1990.
Dog Days, White Nights (essays). Exeter, Third House, 1991.
Words and Music (essays on gay literature and music). Brighton, Millivres Books, 1993.

For Young Adults

Storm Surge, illustrations by Trevor Stubley. Lutterworth, 1975.
Quintin's Man. Dobson, 1976.
The Missing German. Dobson, 1976.
The Ferryman, illustrated with old maps and prints. Dobson, 1977.
The Spectrum. Dobson, 1977.
Risks. Heinemann, 1977; Thomas Nelson, 1978.
In the Tent. Dobson, 1979; Boston, Alyson Publications, 1985.
Silence. Dobson, 1979.
The Green Bough of Liberty, illustrated with old maps and prints. Dobson, 1980.
The Lighthouse. Dobson, 1980.
Miss Duffy Is Still with Us. Dobson, 1980.
Waves. Longman, 1983.

For Children

Landslip, illustrations by Gavin Rowe. Hamish Hamilton, 1977.
The Exeter Blitz. Hamish Hamilton, 1978.

Holly, Mud, and Whisky, illustrations by David Grosvenor. Dobson, 1981.

The Flying Island. Exeter, Third House, 1988.

For Young Children

The House That Moved, illustrations by Lazlo Acs. Hamish Hamilton, 1978.

The Night before Christmas Eve, illustrations by Peter Kesteven. Leeds, Wheaton, 1980; Pergamon, 1982.

A Beacon for the Romans, illustrations by Peter Kesteven. Leeds, Wheaton, 1981.

The Mysterious Rattle, illustrations by Maureen Bradley. Hamish Hamilton, 1982.

The Burglar, illustrations by Ursula Sieger. Leeds, Arnold/Wheaton, 1986.

Friends and Neighbours, illustrations by Clare Herroneau. Leeds, Arnold/Wheaton, 1986.

Contributor

Remember Last Summer?, edited by John Foster. Heinemann, 1980.

Cracks in the Image. London, GMP, 1981.

School's O.K., edited by Josie Karavasil. Evans, 1982.

Messer Rondo, and Other Stories. London, GMP, 1983.

Knockout Short Stories. Longman, 1988.

The Freezer Counter (short stories), edited by Rees and Peter Robins. Exeter, Third House, 1989.

Fabulous Tricks (short stories), edited by Rees, Peter Robins, and Dave Royle. Exeter, Third House, 1992.

Other

Editor, with Peter Robins, *Oranges and Lemons: Stories by Gay Men.* Exeter, Third House, 1987.

Contributor, *Something about the Author Autobiography Series,* Volume 5 (autobiographical essay). Detroit, Gale, 1988.

Letters to Dorothy (essays and short stories). Exeter, Third House, 1990.

Not for Your Hands: An Autobiography. Exeter, Third House, 1992.

Packing It In (travel guide). Brighton, Millivres Books, 1992.

*

Manuscript Collections: University of Exeter.

Biography: *Something about the Author Autobiography Series,* Volume 5, Detroit, Gale, 1988.

Interviews: "David Rees" by Peter Burton, in his *Talking to ... Peter Burton in Conversation with Writers Writing on Gay Themes,* Exeter, Third House, 1991, reprinted from *Gay Times* (London), 1991.

Critical Sources: Review of *In the Tent* by Allan A. Cuseo, in *VOYA,* April 1986, 34; review of *The Hunger* by Bill Greenwell, *New Statesman,* 30 May 1986, 106; "Finding a New Niche" by Peter Burton, in *Gay Times* (London), March 1991.

David Rees' literary career conveniently falls into three distinctive "periods": books for children and young adults (*Storm Surge* in 1975, to *Holly, Mud and Whisky* in 1981); novels for adults about homosexuality (*The Milkman's on His Way* in 1982, to *The Colour of His Hair* in 1989); and volumes of essays on, primarily, aspects of gay life (*Letters to Dorothy* in 1990, to *Words and Music* in 1993). For unity of argument, *Not for Your Hands: An Autobiography* in 1992, must be included with work from this last period.

However, social issues, in general, and homosexuality, in particular, are covertly evident from the first book, *Storm Surge,* in which young male attraction to young male is a sub–text. For the first time Rees used the symbolic name Aaron for a sexually potent youth, setting up a prototype who would appear in at least two more books: *In the Tent* in 1979, and *The Estuary* in 1983. It was clear to see, particularly retrospectively, in which direction his writing would go.

There is very little overlapping among the three periods of writing (the 1988 children's book *The Flying Island* had been written at least six years earlier and two of the three volumes of essays on fiction for children coincide appropriately with the first period). It is also worth noting that the stages of Rees' writing career correspond with his own personal development while also representing the three predominant stages in the development of any gay man: coming to terms and self–acceptance; coming out and enjoyment; and establishment and mature reflection. Rees admitted that—as he had not fully come to terms with his homosexuality until relatively late in life (after marriage and fatherhood)—that his writing paralleled his personal progress. In *Talking with David Rees,* he revealed: "I undoubtedly started to write successfully and properly as I came to terms with being gay and came out. I came out when I was thirty–seven and had my first novel accepted for publication that year. That was *Storm Surge.* The two things are inextricably bound up together, there's no doubt about it."

It has also to be accepted that Rees drew deeply upon his own life for inspiration (in each of the three periods of his writing). And once his life had become devoid of dramatic 'incident,' he firstly stopped writing fiction and then stopped writing altogether. In *Talking with David Rees,* he acknowledged that he had said everything he had to say: "The fact that I now feel I haven't any more fiction to write is partly because I think my real active gay life has also come to an end. It's difficult to give good, convincing reasons as to why it should be so, but I think my gay life has been my perpetual source of copy and it really doesn't exist anymore."

"These stories, essays, and poems are probably the last I shall write," Rees declared in a brief statement at the beginning of *Letters to Dorothy.* In *Talking with David Rees* I note that it seemed almost "unbelievable that a writer like Rees, to whom getting words down on paper sometimes appeared a compulsion, should wittingly call to a close his career." The appearance of four more books after that time proved that he still had much to say. There also exists a collection of short pieces, *Odes, Sods and a Few Last Things,* though plans for publication are uncertain.

Before the explicitly homosexual novels which begin the second period with *The Milkman's on His Way,* degrees of homoerotic male bonding can be discerned from *Storm Surge* through *The Missing German, Quintin's Man, Risks* (Rees' own uncertainty about his sexual nature is reflected in this story of the dangers unwittingly faced by two teenage boys hitchhiking from Exeter to

London), *In the Tent* and *The Lighthouse*. (The allusion to Virginia Woolf is deliberate; Rees' work abounds with literary and musical references.)

The Milkman's on His Way can be read as either the last book of the first period or the first book of the second. The story of a wind–surfing teenaged boy coming to terms with his homosexuality and making the transition from Exeter childhood to adult maturity in London with an enduring gay relationship, *The Milkman's on His Way* was at the center of controversy in Britain during the progress into law in 1987 of Clause (now Section) 28, a local government bill which outlaws the promotion of gay literature (i.e., books such as this in school libraries) in schools or local government establishments. With sales in excess of 25,000, *The Milkman* is probably the most successful British gay novel to have appeared from a small, specialist press—though Rees notes, in a biographical note to *Packing It In,* that "it is not one of his more memorable novels."

With 42 titles published in less than 20 years (1975 to 1993), it is hardly surprising that the quality of writing should be variable. It is particularly noticeable that during the second period, when he wrote fiction about gay life which drew directly and deeply from his own life, Rees sometimes appeared to be throwing down onto the pages steaming, bleeding heaps of entrails and then trying but not always succeeding to make sense of the very stuff of his own being.

The final period of Rees' creativity, which could be said to coincide with the decline in his health because of his IIIV–positive status, allowed the writer to indulge a lifelong obsession with literature, travel, and music. These incisive essays "often seem ... interior monologues made manifest and the public expression of sometimes intensely private concerns," as I noted in an article for *Gay Times*.

David Rees' writing is satisfyingly all of a piece, progressing from exploration in the early work to understanding and reflection as the circle is completed. Perhaps a writer created by desire and iron discipline, Rees proved himself adventurous when writing for children and young adults, tackling themes many would consider unsuitable or downright contentious. He was also a writer with an intense desire to communicate and share the experience which at mid–term turned his life completely around, and one who, at the end of his career, helped revive *belles lettres,* a literary form until then thought near extinct.

—*Peter Burton*

RENAULT, Mary. Pseudonym for Mary Challans. British–born South African novelist, historian, and children's writer. Born in London, 4 September 1905; immigrated to South Africa in 1948. Educated at Clifton High School, Bristol; St. Hugh's College, Oxford, M.A.; Radcliffe Infirmary, Oxford, R.S.N. 1936. Worked as a nurse in England. Traveled extensively in Europe and the Mediterranean (especially the Greek islands). President, Pen Club of South Africa; fellow, Royal Society of Literature. **Recipient:** MGM award, 1946; National Association of Independent Schools award, 1963; Silver Pen award, 1971. *Died in Cape Town, South Africa, of bronchial pneumonia, 12 December 1983.*

WRITINGS

Novels

Promise of Love. New York, Morrow, 1939; as *Purposes of Love,* London, Longmans, 1939.
Kind Are Her Answers. New York, Morrow, 1940.
The Friendly Young Ladies. London, Longmans, 1944; as *The Middle Mist,* New York, Morrow, 1945.
Return to Night. New York, Morrow, 1947.
North Face. New York, Morrow, 1948.
The Charioteer. London, Longmans, 1953; London, Allen Lane, 1973.
The Last of the Summer Wine. New York, Pantheon, and London, Longmans, 1956.
The King Must Die. New York, Pantheon, 1958.
The Bull from the Sea. New York, Pantheon, and London, Longmans, 1962; London, Penguin, 1973.
The Mask of Apollo. New York, Pantheon, 1966.
Fire from Heaven. New York, Pantheon, 1969; London, Penguin, 1972.
The Persian Boy. New York, Pantheon, and London, Longmans, 1972.
The Praise Singer. New York, Pantheon, 1978; London, Murray, 1979.
Funeral Games. London, Murray, 1981.

Other

The Lion at the Gateway: Heroic Battles of the Greeks and Persians at Marathon, Salamis, and Thermopylae (for children). New York, Harper's, 1964; London, Longmans, 1965.
The Nature of Alexander (history). New York, Pantheon, and London, Allen Lane, 1975.

*

Critical Sources: *Gay Fictions, Wilde to Stonewall: Studies in a Male Homosexual Literary Tradition* by Claude J. Summers, New York, Continuum, 1990, 156–171.

*   *   *

Mary Renault is one of only a handful of authors published by mainstream publishers to have openly homosexual characters in her works. More remarkable still is that she published these works in the 1950s through the 1970s, when homosexual characters typically ended up either dead or profoundly unhappy. Many of her historical novels are centered in ancient Greece (e.g., *The Last of the Summer Wine* in 1956, *The King Must Die* in 1958, *The Bull from the Sea* in 1962, *The Mask of Apollo* in 1966, *Fire from Heaven* in 1969, *The Persian Boy* in 1972, *The Praise Singer* in 1978, and *Funeral Games* in 1981), with which she had fallen in love during her extensive travels to that region. Yet another unusual facet of Renault's writing was that she was barely fictionalizing history in the historical novels for which she is most well known. She has been lauded for the depth and accuracy of her research.

While all her novels of Greece were critically acclaimed and explored the relationships between Greek men matter–of–factly, the book that may have had the greatest impact for the homosexual community was *The Persian Boy*. In this novel, Renault follows Alexander the Great from the time he begins his campaign against the Persians to his death nearly seven years later. The story is told not through Alexander's eyes or even one of his general's eyes; rather, the narrator is a slave, Bogoas, the Persian boy of the title, who was given to Alexander as a prize of war and with whom Alexander falls in love. They remain lovers until Alexander's death. Bogoas is with Alexander during his greatest triumphs, including Alexander's conquest of India. Alexander, though married twice, kept Bogoas at his side, and was, upon occasion, openly affectionate with him to the cheers of the troops that he led.

For many people, *The Persian Boy* provided their first inkling that homosexuality was tolerated and even encouraged in ancient times. While historians have either only obliquely hinted at or totally ignored the Greek tradition of Athenian teenagers taking men as their first lovers (and often not giving up that relationship even after marriage to a woman), Renault wrote of it as if it were the most common of practices—which it was. By writing of it matter–of–factly, Renault was defying her own society's taboos about homosexuality.

—*Pamela Bigelow*

———

REYNOLDS, Joe. *See* **STEWARD, Samuel M(orris).**

———

RICH, Adrienne (Cecile). American poet, translator, and author of nonfiction. Born in Baltimore, Maryland, 16 May 1929. Educated at Radcliffe College, A.B. (cum laude) 1951. Married Alfred Haskell Conrad in 1953 (died, 1970); three children. Conductor of workshops, YM–YWHA Poetry Center, New York City, 1966–67; visiting lecturer, Swarthmore College, Swarthmore, Pennsylvania, 1967–69; adjunct professor in writing division of Graduate School of the Arts, Columbia University, New York City, 1967–69; lecturer in SEEK English program, 1968–70, instructor in creative writing program, 1970–71, then assistant professor of English, 1971–72 and 1974–75, City College of the City University of New York; Fannie Hurst visiting professor of creative literature, Brandeis University, Waltham, Massachusetts, 1972–73; Lucy Martin Donelly fellow, Bryn Mawr College, Bryn Mawr, Pennsylvania, 1975; professor of English, Douglass College, Rutgers University, New Brunswick, New Jersey, 1976–78; A. D. White Professor–at–Large, Cornell University, 1981–86; Clark Lecturer and distinguished visiting professor, Scripps College, Claremont, California, 1983; Burgess Lecturer, Pacific Oaks College, Pasadena, California, 1986; professor of English and feminist studies, Stanford University, Stanford, California, beginning 1986. Member of advisory boards, Boston Woman's Fund, New Jewish Agenda, and Sisterhood in Support of Sisters in South Africa. Member of Modern Language Association (honorary fellow, 1985—). **Recipient:** Yale Series of Younger Poets prize, 1951; Guggenheim fellowships, 1952 and 1961; Poetry Society of America's Ridgely

Torrence Memorial Award, 1955; Friends of Literature (Chicago) Thayer Bradley Award, 1956; Phi Beta Kappa Poet, College of William and Mary, 1960, Swarthmore College, 1965, and Harvard University, 1966; National Institute of Arts and Letters award for poetry, 1961; Amy Lowell travelling fellowship, 1962; Bollingen Foundation translation grant, 1962; *Poetry* magazine's Bess Hokin Prize, 1963; Bautibak Translation Center grant, 1968; *Poetry* magazine's Eunice Tietjens Memorial Prize, 1968; National Endowment for the Arts grant, 1970; Poetry Society of America's Shelley Memorial Award, 1971; Ingram Merrill Foundation grant, 1973–74; National Book Award, 1974; National Gay Task Force Fund for Human Dignity Award, 1981; Modern Poetry Association/American Council for the Arts Ruth Lilly Poetry Prize, 1986; Brandeis University Creative Arts medal for poetry, 1987; National Poetry Association award, 1987; New York University's Holmes Bobst award for arts and letters, 1989; Lamda Literary Award for lesbian poetry, 1992; Publishing Triangle's Bill Whitehead award for lifetime achievement in lesbian and gay literature, 1992. Litt.D., Wheaton College, 1967, Smith College, 1979, Brandeis University, 1987, and College of Wooster, 1988. Address: c/o W. W. Norton Co., 500 Fifth Avenue, New York, New York 10110, U.S.A.

WRITINGS

Poetry

A Change of World, foreword by W. H. Auden. New Haven, Yale University Press, 1951.
Poems. Fantasy Press/Oxford University Poetry Society, 1951.
The Diamond Cutters, and Other Poems. New York, Harper, 1955.
The Knight, after Rilke. Privately printed, 1957.
Snapshots of a Daughter–in–Law: Poems, 1954–1962. New York, Harper, 1963, revised, New York, Norton, 1967.
Necessities of Life. New York, Norton, 1966.
Focus. [Cambridge, Massachusetts], 1967.
Selected Poems. London, Chatto & Windus, 1967.
Leaflets: Poems, 1965–1968. New York, Norton, 1969.
The Will to Change: Poems, 1968–1970. New York, Norton, 1971.
Diving into the Wreck: Poems, 1971–1972. New York, Norton, 1973.
Poems: Selected and New, 1950–1974. New York, Norton, 1974.
Adrienne Rich's Poetry: Texts of the Poems, The Poet on Her Work, Reviews and Criticism, edited by Barbara Charlesworth Gelpi and Albert Gelpi. New York, Norton, 1975.
Pieces (previously published in *The Will to Change: Poems, 1968–1970*). San Francisco, Poythress Press, 1977.
Twenty–one Love Poems. Emeryville, California, Effie's Press, 1977.
The Dream of a Common Language: Poems, 1974–1977. New York, Norton, 1978.
A Wild Patience Has Taken Me This Far: Poems, 1978–1981. New York, Norton, 1981.
Sources. Woodside, California, Heyeck Press, 1983.
The Fact of a Doorframe: Poems Selected and New, 1950–1984. New York, Norton, 1984.
Your Native Land, Your Life. New York, Norton, 1986.
Time's Power: Poems, 1985–1988. New York, Norton, 1989.
An Atlas of the Difficult World: Poems, 1988–1991. New York, Norton, 1991.
Collected Early Poems, 1950–1970. New York, Norton, 1992.

Nonfiction

Of Woman Born: Motherhood as Experience and Institution. New York, Norton, 1976.

Women and Honor: Some Notes on Lying (monograph). Motheroot Publishing/Pittsburgh Women Writers, 1977.

On Lies, Secrets and Silence: Selected Prose, 1966–1978 (includes "Conditions for Work: The Common World of Women" and "'It Is the Lesbian in Us ...'"). New York, Norton, 1979.

Compulsory Heterosexuality and Lesbian Existence (monograph). Onlywomen Press, 1981.

Blood, Bread and Poetry: Selected Prose, 1979–1986 (includes "Compulsory Heterosexuality and Lesbian Existence" and "Split at the Root: An Essay on Jewish Identity"). New York, Norton, 1986.

Translations

With Aijaz Ahmad and William Stafford, *Poems by Ghalib,* edited by Aijaz Ahmad. New York, Hudson Review, 1969.

Reflections by Mark Insingel. New York, Red Dust, 1973.

De amor oscoro/Of Dark Love by Francisco Alarcon. Santa Cruz, Moving Parts, 1991.

Contributor

The Poet as Critic, edited by Anthony Ostroff. Boston, Little, Brown, 1965.

Author of foreword, *The Works of Anne Bradstreet,* edited by Janine Hensley. Cambridge, Harvard University Press, 1967.

Randall Jarrell, 1914–1965, edited by Robert Lowell, Peter Taylor, and Robert Penn Warren. New York, Farrar, Straus, 1967.

Author of introduction, *The Other Voice,* edited by Joanna Bankier. New York, Norton, 1976.

Author of afterword, *Take Back the Night: Women on Pornography,* edited by Laura Lederer. New York, Morrow, 1980.

Author of epilogue, *The Letters and Journals of Paula Modersohn-Becker.* Metuchen, New Jersey, Scarecrow Press, 1980.

Author of introduction, *My Mama's Dead Squirrel: Lesbian Essays on Southern Culture* by Mab Segrest. Firebrand Books, 1985.

The Tribute of His Peers: Elegies for Robinson Jeffers. New York, Tor House Press, 1989.

Author of introduction, *A Few Words in the Mother Tongue: Poems, Selected and New* by Irena Klepfisz. Eighth Mountain Press, 1990.

Author of foreword, *Rosa Luxemburg, Women's Liberation, and Marx's Philosophy of Revolution* by Raya Dunayevskaya. Champaign, University of Illinois Press, 1991.

Recordings: *Adrienne Rich Reading at Stanford.* Stanford, 1973; with others, *A Sign I Was Not Alone.* Out and Out, 1978.

*

Biography: "Adrienne Rich" by Anne Newman, in *Dictionary of Literary Biography,* Volume 5: *American Poets since World War II,* Detroit, Gale, 1980; "Adrienne Rich" by Elizabeth Meese, in *Dictionary of Literary Biography,* Volume 67: *Modern American Critics since 1955,* Detroit, Gale, 1988.

Interviews: With David Montenegro, in *Points of Departure: International Writers on Writing and Politics,* Ann Arbor, University of Michigan Press, 1991, 5–25; "Adrienne Rich Charts a Difficult World" by David Trinidad, *Advocate,* 31 December 1991, 82–84.

Critical Sources: "Ghostlier Demarcations, Keener Sounds" by Helen Vendler, *Parnassus,* fall/winter 1973; "On Adrienne Rich: Intelligence and Will" by Robert Boyers, in *Salmagundi,* spring/summer 1973; "Adrienne Rich: The Poetics of Change" by Albert Gelpi, in *American Poetry Since 1960* edited by Robert B. Shaw, Cheadle, Cheshire, Carcanet Press, 1973; *Adrienne Rich's Poetry: A Norton Critical Edition* edited by Barbara Charlesworth Gelpi and Albert Gelpi, New York, Norton, 1975; *Five Temperaments* by David Kalstone, New York, Oxford University Press, 1977; "Adrienne Rich and an Organic Feminist Criticism" by Marilyn R. Farwell, in *College English,* October 1977; *Reconstituting the World: The Poetry and Vision of Adrienne Rich* by Judith McDaniel, Argyle, New York, Spinsters Ink, 1979; "Levertov and Rich: The Later Poems" by Linda W. Wagner, in her *American Modern: Essays in Fiction and Poetry,* Port Washington, New York, Kennikat, 1980; "All Too Real" by Helen Vendler, in *New York Review of Books,* 17 December 1981; "The 'I' in Adrienne Rich: Individuation and the Androgyne Archetype" by Betty S. Flowers, in *Theory and Practice of Feminist Literary Criticism* edited by Gabriela Mora and Karen S. Van Hooft, Ypsilanti, Michigan, Bilingual Press, 1982; "A Poetry of Survival: Unnaming and Renaming in the Poetry of Audre Lorde, Pat Parker, Sylvia Plath, and Adrienne Rich" by Pamela Annas, in *Colby Library Quarterly,* March 1982, 9–25; "Adrienne Rich: Poet, Mother, Lesbian Feminist, Visionary" by Katherine Arnup, in *Atlantis,* fall/autumn 1982, 97–110; "Her Cargo: Adrienne Rich and the Common Language" by Alicia Ostriker, in her *Writing Like a Woman,* Ann Arbor, University of Michigan Press, 1983; "The Re–Vision of the Muse: Adrienne Rich, Audre Lorde, Judy Grahn, Olga Broumas" by Mary J. Carruthers, in *Hudson Review,* summer 1983, 293–322; *An American Triptych: Anne Bradstreet, Emily Dickinson, Adrienne Rich* by Wendy Martin, Chapel Hill, University of North Carolina Press, 1984; *Reading Adrienne Rich: Reviews and Re–Visions, 1951–1981,* edited by Jane Roberta Cooper, Ann Arbor, University of Michigan Press, 1984; *The Transforming Power of Language: The Poetry of Adrienne Rich* by Myriam Diaz–Diocaretz, Utrecht, Hes Publishers, 1984; *Translating Poetic Discourse: Questions on Feminist Strategies in Adrienne Rich* by Myriam Diaz–Diocaretz, Amsterdam, John Benjamins, 1985; "Lingua Materna: The Speech of Female History" by Carol Muske, in *New York Times Book Review,* 20 January 1985; *The Aesthetics of Power: The Poetry of Adrienne Rich* by Claire Keyes, Athens and London, University of Georgia Press, 1986; "Adrienne Rich and Lesbian/Feminist Poetry" by Catharine Stimpson, in *Parnassus,* spring 1986, 249–268; "'Love for the World and We Are In It': Adrienne Rich's Work of Repair" by Minnie Bruce Pratt, *Lambda Book Report,* November/December 1991.

*   *   *

During the more than 40 years of her literary career, Adrienne Rich has evolved from a dutiful poet following the masculine poetic tradition of Robert Frost, W. H. Auden, and William Butler Yeats to a radical, lesbian feminist with a commitment to a global perspective. She began this evolution in 1951 with her first volume of poetry, published in the same year that she graduated from Radcliffe. This volume entitled *A Change of World* won the Yale Younger Poets Prize and contains a foreword by Auden, in which he suggested that the new generation of poets, in which he included Rich, would follow the tradition established by the "modern" generation of poets (T. S. Eliot, Frost, Yeats) because there had been no societal revolutions that would enable a poetic revolution. Auden, writing in 1951, had no way of foreseeing the impact of the anti–war, civil rights, and feminist movements on poetry in the coming decades. Those movements, as well as the writings of James Baldwin and Simone de Beauvoir, created dramatic changes in Rich's world view and resulted in revolutions in her poetry. Particularly, Rich's developing feminist consciousness, which can be seen as early as 1963 in such poems as "Planetarium," led to an increased awareness of her lesbianism. These alterations in Rich's world and self view created the contradictions of her life that appear in her art. She demands that she be accountable for every part of her identity. In "Split at the Root," a 1982 essay published in *Blood, Bread and Poetry* which begins to examine the contradictions of her life, Rich lists her various identities: "The middle–class white girl taught to trade obedience for privilege. The Jewish lesbian raised to be a heterosexual gentile. The woman who first heard oppression named and analyzed in the Black Civil Rights struggle. The woman with three sons, the feminist who hates male violence.... The poet who knows that beautiful language can lie, that the oppressor's language sometimes sounds beautiful." Rich claims that each of these selves must be investigated in her work and in her life. Rich's unrelenting self–analysis in her prose and in her poetry has not always been well received by critics. However, Rich demands an honesty of self and a continual critical examination of self.

Part of Rich's continual evolution as a writer includes her struggle to critique and define women's voices, particularly lesbian voices, in her writing as well as in that of others. She has worked to create a poetry and prose that investigates the hidden, the silence, that surrounds what we say about ourselves as lesbians, as women, and as women of color. More particularly, Rich questions what lesbians and women in general purposely do not say or reveal about themselves and why. Although she understands the real problems of unemployment and economic survival, she questions the lesbian who creates art in an environment of self–imposed censorship. In "Conditions for Work: The Common World of Women," an essay originally written as the foreword to the anthology, *Working It Out: 23 Women Artists, Scholars and Scientists Talk about Their Lives and Work*, Rich points out that the "whole question of what it means or might mean to work as a lesbian might have occupied an entire essay in this book." Subtly, Rich indicates that the failing of the lesbian artists in this volume occurs on the level of awareness of self and commitment to self–exposure. These women artists, scholars, and scientists might have written an essay on what it means to work as a lesbian, but no such essay appears. Awareness of self and of the history of one's community (whether that community is lesbian, gay, women's, African American, Hispanic, etc.) is critical for Rich. For the lesbian to find her history she must interpret "the silence and denial that has enveloped lesbianism" and "the social taboos [women in the past] lived among."

As part of a larger awareness of self and in an effort to create community among women, Rich has been working at least since 1976 to persuade all women to see the "lesbian in us." This figure of woman, the lesbian, causes much tension in the women's com-

munity. It is precisely for this reason that Rich critiqued the tension produced by heterosexism that inhibits women's communion with one another in "It is the Lesbian in Us ..." and in her landmark essay, "Compulsory Heterosexuality and Lesbian Existence." In these essays, Rich proposes that women, both lesbian and heterosexual, critically examine heterosexism as an institution that oppresses all women. This critique can range from redefining the words that have been used to oppress lesbians ("dyke," "butch," "bulldagger") to coining the phrases "lesbian continuum" and "lesbian existence" as ways of re–visioning women's relationships with each other outside of the heterosexist framework. The terms "lesbian continuum" and "lesbian existence" have been misunderstood and misapplied by many Rich readers. Rich is concerned that the phrase "lesbian continuum" has been used "by women who have not yet begun to examine the privileges and solipsisms of heterosexuality, as a safe way to describe their felt connections with women, without having to share in the risks and threats of lesbian existence.... *Lesbian continuum*—the phrase—came from a desire to allow for the greatest possible variation of female–identified experience, while paying a different kind of respect to *lesbian existence*—the traces and knowledge of women who have made their primary erotic and emotional choices for women."

Rich has been working to create connections and to foster community among women in her poetry as well as in her prose. *Twenty–one Love Poems* is a series of sonnets concerning the problematics of lesbian love in a society that insists on the invisibility of lesbians. Rather than dwell on the problem of lesbian invisibility, Rich finds strong images of women in the landscapes that surround her. These images of power involve figurative and literal representations of women's bodies. In poem XI, "Every peak is a crater. This is the law of volcanoes, / making them eternally and visibly female. / No height without depth, without a burning core, / though our straw soles shred on the hardened lava." Rich creates a powerful image of a woman's body and sexuality in a landscape which has been raped and wasted because it has been depicted as female in a patriarchal society. This creation of new images of the female body and sexuality stems from Rich's stated desire in "Diving into the Wreck." She desires "the wreck and not the story of the wreck / the thing itself and not the myth."

Because Rich finds that language cannot express the whole of experience and its shifts, she dates her poems; she believes that each poem expresses the feelings and thoughts of the poet at that moment. She does not pretend to write universal, transcendent truths. Rather, her poems are a way of understanding experience. In such volumes as *Your Native Land, Your Life, Time's Power,* and *An Atlas of the Difficult World*, Rich explores the responsibility of a poet to her words and images. In these volumes, lesbianism becomes less a subject in itself than a fact of the poet's world, intrinsic to her experience. Lesbianism does not disappear, but becomes a part of a matrix of issues that Rich brings to her poetry, including an awareness of political movements and global feminisms. This matrix attests to Rich's commitment to making minority voices heard, to making the invisible visible. Rich insists on the complexity of our lives and carefully, with a keen sense of language, records that complexity in her poetry and prose.

In a letter written in November of 1990 to David Montenegro and published in *Points of Departure*, Rich discusses forms of censorship and the costs of artistically trivializing minority voices—including lesbian, gay, working–class, and African American—through stereotype and caricature, in a society that cares little for those voices. According to Rich, capitalism conspires against those minority voices by making certain books and experiences unavailable to those uninitiated in that experience—making minority voices invisible to the greater public. In order to combat the erasure of these experiences, Rich suggests that we "insist in our art on the depth and complexity of our lives, to keep on creating the account of our lives, in poems and stories and scripts and essays and memoirs that are as rich and strange as we ourselves. Never to bend toward or consent to be rewarded for trivializing ourselves, our people, or each other."

What Rich envisioned as a strategy in 1990 has characterized her literary production for some time. By continually investigating the contradictions of her life, Rich presents to the world not a cardboard stereotype of a lesbian, not an easily categorized vision of the world that surrounds us, but the complex vision of the world written by a Jewish–lesbian–feminist–mother who is "rich and strange" and wonderfully so.

—*Andrea R. Cumpston*

RIVERS, Elfrida. *See* **BRADLEY, Marion Zimmer.**

ROLFE, Fr. *See* **ROLFE, Frederick (William Serafino Austin Lewis Mary).**

ROLFE, Frederick (William Serafino Austin Lewis Mary). British novelist, short story writer, essayist, and painter. Also wrote as Baron Corvo; Frederick Baron Corvo; Fr. Rolfe; and Prospero & Caliban, a joint pseudonym with Harry Pirie–Gordon. Born in London, 22 July 1860. Educated at North London Collegiate School, Camden Town, and at Oxford University; studied for the priesthood at Oscott Seminary and Scots College, Rome, 1887–1890; rejected for priesthood, c. 1890. Worked as a school teacher, 1874–1886. *Died of heart disease in Venice, Italy, 23 October 1913.*

WRITINGS

Short Stories

Stories Toto Told Me (originally published in *Yellow Book;* republished in *Bodley Booklets*). London and New York, Lane, 1898; with additional "Toto" stories as *In His Own Image,* London and New York, Lane, 1901; 26 stories culled from both editions as *Stories Toto Told Me,* London, Collins, 1969, New York, St. Martin's Press, 1971.
Three Tales of Venice (originally published in *Blackwood's*). London, Corvine Press, 1950.
The Cardinal Prefect of Propaganda, and Other Stories, introduction by Cecil Woolf. Vene, 1957.

The Armed Hands, and Other Stories and Pieces, edited by Cecil Woolf. London, Cecil and Amelia Woolf, 1972.

Novels

Hadrian the Seventh. London, Chatto & Windus, 1904; New York, Knopf, 1925.
Don Tarquinio: A Kataleptic Phantasmatic Romance. London, Chatto & Windus, 1905.
Don Renato, an Ideal Content: A Historical Romance. London, Francis Griffiths, 1909; with introduction by Cecil Woolf, London, Chatto & Windus, 1963.
With Harry Pirie–Gordon, *The Weird of the Wanderer* (as Prospero & Caliban). London, Rider, 1912.
The Desire and Pursuit of the Whole: A Romance of Modern Venice. London, Cassell, 1934; New York, New Directions, 1953.
With Harry Pirie–Gordon, *Hubert's Arthur* (as Prospero & Caliban). London, Cassell, 1935.
Nicholas Crabbe; or, The One and the Many. London, Chatto & Windus, and New York, New Directions, 1958.
Amico di Sandro (fragment). London, privately printed, 1951.

Essays

Chronicles of the House of Borgia (monographs). London, Richards, and New York, Dutton, 1901; as *A History of the Borgias,* New York, Carleton House, 1931.
The Bull Against the Enemy of the Anglican Race. London, privately printed, 1929.

Poetry

Tarcissus: The Boy Martyr of Rome in the Diocletian Persecution, 1880.
Collected Poems [of] *Fr. Rolfe, Baron Corvo,* edited by Cecil Woolf. London, Cecil and Amelia Woolf, 1972.
Ballade of Boys Bathing. London, Officina Mauritana, 1972.

Letters

Letters to Grant Richards. Peacocks Press, 1952.
Letters to C. H. C. Pirie–Gordon, 1959.
Letters to Leonard Moore, 1960.
Letters of Baron Corvo to Kenneth Grahame, 1962.
Letters to R. M. Dawkins, edited by Cecil Woolf. Vane, 1962.
Without Prejudice: One Hundred Letters from Frederick Rolfe, Baron Corvo, to John Lane, 1963.
The Venice Letters, edited by Cecil Woolf. London, Cecil and Amelia Woolf, 1966.
Letters to James Walsh, introduction by Donald Weeks. London, Bertram Rota, 1972.
The Reverse Side of the Coin: Some Further Correspondence between William Frederick Rolfe and Grant Richards. Edinburgh, Tragara Press, 1974.
Aberdeen Interval: Some Letters from William Rolfe to Wilfred Maynell. Edinburgh, Tragara Press, 1975.
Letters to Harry Bainbridge, edited by Miriam Benkovitz. London, Enitharmon Press, 1977.

Frederick Rolfe and "The Times," 4–12 February 1901. Edinburgh, Tragara Press, 1977.

Other

Translator, *The Rubaiyat of Umar Khaiyam.* London and New York, Lane, 1903.
Ghostwriter, *Agricultural and Pastoral Prospects of South Africa* by Owen Thomas. London, Constable, 1904.
Translator, *The Songs of Meleager.* London, First Edition Club, 1937; New York, Garland, 1972.
With Robert Hugh Benson, *Saint Thomas,* edited by Donald Weeks. Edinburgh, Tragara Press, 1979.

*

Adaptations: *Hadrian VII* (stage play) adapted by Peter Luke, Harmondsworth, Penguin, 1969.

Biography: *The Quest for Corvo* by A. J. A. Symons, New York, Macmillan, 1934; *A Biography of Frederick Rolfe, Baron Corvo* by Cecil Woolf, London, Rupert Hart–Davis, 1957; "The Fascination of the Paranoid Personality" by Pamela Hansford Johnson, in *New Quests for Corvo* edited by Cecil Woolf and Brocard Sewell, London, Icon Books, 1965; *Corvo* by Donald Weeks, London, Josseph, 1971; *Frederick Rolfe: Baron Corvo* by Miriam J.Benkovitz, New York, Putnam, 1977.

Critical Sources: "The Fiction of Frederick Rolfe, Baron Corvo" by Sergio Perosa, in *MOSAIC: A Journal for the Comparative Study of Literature and Ideas* (Manitoba), fall 1971, 111–123; "Frederick Rolfe and His Age: A Study in Literary Eccentricity" by John Tytell, in *Studies in the Twentieth Century,* fall 1972, 69–89; "Frederick Rolfe's Papel Dream" by G. P. Jones, in *MOSAIC: A Journal for the Comparative Study of Literature and Ideas* (Manitoba), winter 1974, 109–122.

*   *   *

Frederick Rolfe, painter, photographer, poet, fiction writer, and would–be Catholic priest, was a romantic genius with a massive persecution complex whose life spanned the late Victorian and Edwardian eras. His fiction is primarily autobiographical and imbued with, if not driven by, recurring homosexual themes.

As a young school master, Rolfe published his first work, *Tarcissus,* an extended poem which romanticized the Roman boy–martyr. Here were established the driving themes of most of Rolfe's later work: fascination with and romanticization of the male adolescent, Roman Catholicism, and Italian culture. *Tarcissus* was a favorite among poetic–minded homosexuals of the time, though its veils of romantic, poetic, and classical imagery made it generally acceptable to the mores of the era. At this time Rolfe also composed various love poems addressed to his young pupil–friends, which contained such religious and romantic cloudiness that they were considered quite acceptable for a schoolmaster with a literary bent.

In a later poem, "The Ballade of Boys Bathing," he recounts an afternoon spent observing "The boys who bathe in St. Andrews Bay," at the instigation of homosexual lawyer and literary editor

Charles Kains Jackson. Rolfe also executed a painting of the subject described. Nude boys cavorting in the water were to appear again and again in Rolfe's later works.

Though born and raised an Anglican, Rolfe was fascinated by the Roman Catholic church from an early age, and he not only converted but aspired to the Catholic priesthood. Attracted to the mysticism and profound rituals of the church rather than the institution itself, Rolfe was expelled from seminaries in Scotland and Rome. After leaving the seminary in Rome, Rolfe became a long–term guest of the English–born widow of a Roman aristocrat. His experiences with the servant boys at her country estate in Genzano resulted in his first major published piece, *Stories Toto Told Me.* Here Rolfe expressed his adulation of the tan, athletic, sinewy adolescent male to the fullest degree. Toto and his friends' every look and movement is described with glowing, sensuous adoration. "Near him, paced to and fro my pure greek," Rolfe wrote in the book, "the strong, magnificent violet–shadowed Vittorio, model fit for Andrea Mantegna, arm in arm with the huge and ruddy Goth, Otone, ablaze with health. The little tender Guido of chrusoberol eyes, and his slight glaukos friend, Ilario, delicately dangled slim frail limbs in the sea from pier steps, cooing each to other like white doves."

Rolfe's most significant and well–known work is *Hadrian the Seventh,* the story of an Englishman, George Rose, who after being shunned by the Catholic priesthood is elected Pope to the shock of the church and the world. The troops of teenaged boys that dominate Rolfe's other works are absent here, but the book does contain a certain homosexual ambiance. In his critical introduction to *Hadrian the Seventh,* Herbert Weinstock warns: "Some readers who might be responsive to this burning tapestry may be alienated momentarily by its pervasive, though covert sexual ambivalence."

Hadrian the Seventh's plot obviously stemmed from Rolfe's frustrated ecclesiastical career, and his bitterness and resentment at being rejected by the Roman Catholic church is manifested here with a vengeance, though there is hardly a work where it is lacking. Rolfe was suited neither by personality, temperament, nor habit for the institutional religious life, but he saw the priesthood as a camaraderie of celibate men in antique garb, a protected society in which his own misogyny and eccentricities would make him acceptable.

The writer's last years were spent in Venice where he penned *The Desire and Pursuit of the Whole: A Romance of Modern Venice* Once again the semi–naked young men, this time in the form of gondolieri, create the continuum as they flex their bronzed muscles and preen themselves by the water. The protagonist, Nicholas Crabbe, keeps a manservant, Zildo, who is actually a girl with boyish features that serves him in the guise of a boy. In a rather bizarre and unbelievable ending, Zildo saves Crabbe's life, and he realizes that he has desired her all along. They decide to get married and live happily ever after.

The Desire and Pursuit of the Whole, like much of Rolfe's work, exhibits his penchant for elaborate fantasies that seem to result directly from the facts of his life. Just as *Hadrian the Seventh* presented a fantasy that placated the failed priest, *The Desire and Pursuit of the Whole* presents a similar fantasy in terms of sexual identity. Rolfe's preoccupation with male figures is present in nearly all of his writings and speculation about his attraction to members of the same sex has been widespread; poet W. H. Auden, for one, branded Rolfe a "homosexual paranoid." Crabbe seems in many ways to be Rolfe's fictional alter–ego and the facts and characters in *The Desire and Pursuit of the Whole* mirror many of the details of Rolfe's years in Venice. What is striking is that Rolfe, who was able to imagine a story in which a failed priest becomes Pope, is unable to write openly of a man's attraction to a man—a situation that is not surprising given the time that he was writing. Instead, Rolfe cloaked homosexual desire in heterosexuality; while Crabbe realizes that he was attracted to the appearance of Zildo when he thought she was a man, it is only when she is safely transformed into a woman that the story reaches its rosy conclusion.

—*Richard Alexei*

————

ROREM, Ned. American composer, essayist, and diarist. Born in Richmond, Indiana, 23 October 1923. Attended University of Chicago Lab School, Northwestern University, Curtis Institute (Philadelphia), Juilliard School of Music. Companion of musician James Holmes. Composer in residence, University of Utah, Salt Lake City, 1965–67; professor of composition, Curtis Institute, Philadelphia, Pennsylvania, 1980—. Musical copyist to Virgil Thomson, New York City, in the 1940s. Member of the American Society of Composers and Performers (ASCAP), PEN, and the American Academy of Arts and Letters. **Recipient:** Music Library Association award for best published song of the year, 1948; George Gershwin Memorial Award, 1949; Lili Boulanger Award, 1950; Fulbright fellowship for study in Paris, 1951–52; Prix de Biarritz, 1951; Eurydice Choral Award, 1954; Guggenheim fellowship, 1957, 1979; National Institute of Arts and Letters award, 1968; ASCAP Deems Taylor Award, 1971 and 1975; Pulitzer Prize in music, 1976; D.F.A., Northwestern University, 1977; Grammy Award, 1989; grants from the Ford Foundation, Lincoln Center Foundation, and Koussevitzky Foundation. Agent: Boosey & Hawkes Inc., 24 East 21st Street, New York, New York 10010–7200, U.S.A.

WRITINGS

Diaries and Essays

The Paris Diary of Ned Rorem. New York, George Braziller, 1966.
Music from Inside Out. New York, George Braziller, 1967.
The New York Diary of Ned Rorem. New York, George Braziller, 1967.
Music and People. New York, George Braziller, 1968.
Contributor, *The Artistic Legacy of Walt Whitman: A Tribute to Gay Wilson Allen.* New York, New York University Press, 1969.
Critical Affairs: A Composer's Journal. New York, George Braziller, 1970.
The Final Diary: 1961–1972. New York, Holt, 1974; as *The Later Diaries of Ned Rorem, 1961–1972.* San Francisco, North Point Press, 1983.
Pure Contraption: A Composer's Essays. New York, Holt, 1974.
An Absolute Gift: A New Diary. New York, Simon & Schuster, 1974.
The Paris and New York Diaries of Ned Rorem: 1951–1961. San Francisco, North Point Press, 1983.

Setting the Tone: Essays and A Diary. New York, Coward, 1983.
Paul's Blues. New York, Red Ozier Press, 1984.
The Nantucket Diary of Ned Rorem, 1973–1985. San Francisco, North Point Press, 1987.
Settling the Score: Essays on Music (anthology of previously published pieces). San Diego, Harcourt, 1988.

Plays

Composer and librettist, *The Robbers.* New York, Boosey & Hawkes, 1956.
The Pastry Shop (one–act; produced New York, 1970).
The Young Among Themselves (one–act; produced New York, 1970).

Other

(Author of foreword) *Jean Cocteau and His World: An Illustrated Biography* by Arthur K. Peters. London, Thames & Hudson, 1987.

*

Biography: "Imagination Snared," by Patrick O'Connor, in *Opera News*, October 1988, 24.

Interviews: "In Prose, in Music—A Master of Composition" with Stephen Greco, in *Advocate*, 4 October 1979, 35–37; "The Priorities of Composer/Writer Ned Rorem" with George Heymont, in *Advocate*, 31 March 1983, 39–42; "Songs for These Times" with George Stambolian, in *Advocate*, 8 December 1987, 58–59, 124–127; "Pose and Compose: It's Hard to Tell the Difference," by David R. Slavitt, in *Philadelphia* magazine, May 1988, 89.

*   *   *

In a media interview done in 1982, Ned Rorem summarized the dual creative tracks of his life by characterizing himself as "a composer who happens to write, not an author who happens to compose ... my prose and music fill opposing needs." This apt description is mirrored in his prolific outpouring of musical forms, ranging from several hundred art songs (of which he is considered the contemporary master) through symphonies and operas to large choral works such as the *Whitman Cantata.* Equally significant to modern musical and cultural history, as well as to the genre of gay and lesbian literature, are his collection of essays on music and the several volumes of his personal diaries published over a period of 21 years.

Reared in a childhood environment that emphasized exposure to the fine arts available in Chicago, Rorem's talent for composition surfaced by the age of nine. Following a varied education in both classical and contemporary music (with an introduction to French culture that would have a significant effect on his later literary creations), the winning of the Gershwin Memorial Award in 1949 provided funding for a long–planned three–month trip to Paris. His actual stay in the cultural world of Paris was to last nine years.

It was during this period that he began to record his life, thoughts, and observations in what would eventually appear in 1966 as *The Paris Diary of Ned Rorem.*

Upon its publication, *The Paris Diary* presented an unparalleled and candid account of the mores and people inhabiting postwar Paris (along with some very private information about prominent cultural figures). In addition, the diary highlighted the processes of growth and development through which Ned Rorem the composer passed. The relevance of the diary to gay and lesbian literature lies in its frank descriptions of Rorem's homosexual love affairs at a time when such subjects were considered unmentionable. Although Rorem would later disavow any intent of being an early gay liberation writer—saying simply that he was too lazy to bother lying about his homosexuality—through the diary's pages readers are offered a deeply drawn portrait of an individual who accepted his desires as merely one part of an integrated, stable personality. It was to be two years before a comparable account would appear in the form of Quentin Crisp's humorously acerbic account *The Naked Civil Servant.* While Rorem had maintained an intermittent diary from childhood, the collective texts of this and the later volumes of his private chronicles, including *An Absolute Gift* and *The Nantucket Diary,* fit into an established continental literary tradition where the diary is considered a separate genre.

Rorem's music has also served as a vehicle for the dissemination of works of numerous poets to a large public audience. The scope of his interest in literature is evident in the diversity of sources upon whom he has drawn for texts and inspiration, which ranges from lines from Homer's *The Iliad* to Catullus and the Psalms through Chaucer and John Dryden to more contemporary writers such as e.e. cummings and W. B. Yeats. The creations of gay and lesbian poets were also given place in Rorem's works. While this is particularly true of the writings of Walt Whitman (whose series of poems dedicated to his younger male lovers, *Calamus,* was adapted as a song cycle), texts from Gertrude Stein, Adrienne Rich, John Ashbery, Sylvia Plath, Frank O'Hara, Paul Monette, and Thom Gunn appear as well. In 1988, Rorem received a commission for a choral work from the Gay Men's Chorus of New York, which resulted in the *Whitman Cantata.* An oratorio entitled *Goodbye Fancy* is also based on Whitman's homoerotic verse. Just as he chronicled his personal life in diaries, so too did Rorem keep written stock of music, writing on the subject in volumes such as *Music from Inside Out, Music and People,* and *Pure Contraption: A Composer's Essays.* In addition to maintaining his diaries, Rorem contributed a regular column to *Christopher Street* during the early 1980s. On 13 May 1984, he received a plaque from the Fund for Human Dignity (then affiliated with the National Gay and Lesbian Task Force) in recognition of his work to educate the public about the lives of lesbians and gay men.

—*Robert B. Marks Ridinger*

ROUTSONG, Alma. American novelist and author of nonfiction. Has also written as Isabel Miller. Born in Traverse City, Michigan, 26 November 1924. Educated at Western Michigan University, 1942–44; Michigan State University, B.A. 1949. Married Bruce Brodie in 1947 (divorced); four daughters. Served as a hospital apprentice, U.S. Navy, 1945–46. Editor, Columbia University, New York City, 1968–71; active in Gay Liberation move-

ment, beginning 1970. **Recipient:** Friends of American Writers award for first book, 1954; Breadloaf fellow, 1958; first annual Gay Book Award of the Gay Liberation Task Force of the Social Responsibilities Round Table of the American Library Association for *A Place for Us,* 1971.

WRITINGS

A Gradual Joy. Boston, Houghton, 1953.
Round Shape. Boston, Houghton, 1959.
A Place for Us (as Isabel Miller). New York, Bleeker Street, 1969; as *Patience and Sarah* (Literary Guild selection), New York, McGraw, 1972.
The Love of Good Women. Tallahassee, Naiad Press, 1986.
Side by Side. Tallahassee, Naiad Press, 1990.
A Dooryard Full of Flowers. Tallahassee, Naiad Press, 1993.

*

Interviews: "1962–1972: Alma Routsong, Writing and Publishing *Patience and Sarah,* 'I Felt I Had Found My People'," in *Gay American History: Lesbians and Gay Men in the U.S.A.; A Documentary,* edited by Jonathan Katz, New York, Crowell, 1976, 433–443.

Critical Sources: Review by M. B. Snyder of *Gradual Joy,* in *Chicago Sunday Tribune,* 16 August 1953, 7; review by Caroline Tunstall of *Gradual Joy,* in *New York Herald Tribune Book Review,* 23 August 1953; review by J. D. Paulus of *Gradual Joy,* in *New York Times,* 23 August 1953, 18; review by Charles Lee of *Gradual Joy,* in *Saturday Review,* 26 September 1953; review of *Patience and Sarah,* in *New York Times Book Review,* 23 April 1972, 40; review of *Patience and Sarah,* in *New Statesman,* 25 August 1972, 26; "Frontierswomen in Love" (review of *Patience and Sarah*) by Bell Gale Chevigny, in *Village Voice,* 20 April 1972, 25; review of *Patience and Sarah,* in *Washington Post Book World,* 4 March 1973, 14; review of *The Love of Good Women,* in *Nation,* 27 December 1986, 742–743; review of *The Love of Good Women,* in *New Pages,* spring 1987, 12; review of *The Love of Good Women,* in *New Directions for Women,* September 1987, 18; review of *The Love of Good Women,* in *New Statesman,* 19 February 1988, 34; review by Patricia Craig of *The Love of Good Women,* in *Times Literary Supplement,* 26 February 1988; *The Safe Sea of Women: Lesbian Fiction, 1969–1989* by Bonnie Zimmerman, Boston, Beacon Press, 1990; review of *Side by Side,* in *Lambda Book Report,* January 1991, 24; review of *Side by Side,* in *New Directions for Women,* November 1991, 20.

*   *   *

In the process of living, each individual seeks in the world about them reflections and responses to the growth and change of his or her private self. Such responses can range from ecstatic affirmation to consistent and harsh condemnation—images and actions rooted in accepted cultural norms and set in place and maintained through a variety of mechanisms, including literature. The power of fiction—to explore taboo subjects and illustrate desired social redefinitions—has historically been one of the first to be wielded by minority groups for its damning and redemptive qualities, qualities necessary to the process of community solidarity. In perhaps no other contemporary case has this molding of self–image been as vital as in the gay and lesbian community in the early 1960s. There the inception of the political and social liberation movements summoned forth a parallel revolt among writers: a revolt against the then–current depiction of the consequences of acknowledging one's homosexuality. To women writing in their new–found lesbian voices, the work of writer Alma Routsong offered an indication of possibilities.

Born in 1924 in Traverse City, Michigan, Routsong received her education at Western Michigan University and Michigan State University, completing her bachelor's degree in 1949 after two years of service as a hospital apprentice in the United States Navy. This military experience would surface in the character of the dedicated WAVE physician in her first novel, *A Gradual Joy,* published in 1953. Although the plot follows the course of a fairly standard postwar romance, indications of Routsong's treatment of women characters as strong and independent was already apparent in this early work of fiction, a viewpoint she was to consistently express in her later writings as an open lesbian. Following her divorce from her husband of 15 years in 1962, Routsong entered a relationship with another woman and began work on a new manuscript, destined to appear in 1969 as *A Place for Us.* The work is more popularly known by the title given it upon its republication in 1972: *Patience and Sarah.*

Sparked by the chance discovery of information in a folk art museum at Cooperstown, New York, on Mary Ann Wilson, who lived with her female companion, Miss Brundidge, in Greene County, New York, in the 1820s, *Patience and Sarah* stands as one of the first contemporary lesbian historical novels. Other works included in this genre are Catherine Ennis' Civil War novel *South of the Line,* the westerns of Penny Hayes, and Peter Greene's 1993 account of Sappho of Lesbos, *The Laughter of Aphrodite.* Set in Connecticut's Housatonic Valley in the year 1816, Routsong's novel tells the interwoven stories of Sarah Dowling and Patience White. Although Sarah was raised to take on tasks traditionally associated exclusively with men, even to the extent of dressing in masculine garb, Patience is, as she herself admits, "the old maid aunt" who is skilled at farm management and possessing an artistic gift as well. The characters of the two women reflect the polarization between the butch and femme stereotypes dominant in the lesbian community at the time of the novel's publication.

The risk of censure in publishing such a work (even privately) under one's own name in the late 1960s led Routsong to adopt the pen name Isabel Miller, a combination of her mother's surname with a rearrangement of the letters of "Lesbia." Following initial rejections from several mainstream publishers and reluctance from her own agent, *Patience and Sarah*'s first run of a thousand copies was produced entirely with private funds. The lesbian community's awareness of Routsong's work came through the efforts of the New York chapter of the Daughters of Bilitis, who invited her to speak, and through Gene Damon, editor of the organization's national lesbian magazine, the *Ladder.* By the time the final copy of the first printing of *Patience and Sarah* was sold, requests for copies were coming from university–sponsored women's studies courses. While critical reaction from the gay press did not prompt the later reissue, reviews in the *New York Times* and the *Village Voice* were highly supportive. The 1971 designation of *Patience and Sarah* as

the recipient of the first Gay Book Award given by the American Library Association's Gay Liberation Task Force marked its formal acceptance and recognition by the community for whom it had originally been created.

Patience and Sarah was followed by two other novels, *The Love of Good Women* in 1986, and the 1990 romance, *Side by Side. The Love of Good Women* begins in America shortly before the end of World War II and follows the emotional transformation of its heroine Gertrude from a docile and accepting wife tolerant of her husband's failings to a free and assertive female capable of initiating major changes in her own life. The cause of much of Gertrude's consciousness–raising comes as the result of interactions with her nightshift coworkers in a factory making engine valves. Combining recognition of the essential contribution made by women to the war effort (as exemplified by the mythical Rosie the Riveter) with sharp consideration of the ways in which postwar society acted to limit their options, *Good Women* also examines lesbian relationships as an alternative in the person of Gertrude's sister–in-law and her housekeeper.

The expansion of the descriptive limits of language permitted in a work of literature dealing with lesbians can be illustrated through a comparison of the text of Routsong's *Patience and Sarah, Side by Side,* and in the 1993 sequel *A Dooryard Full of Flowers.* Researchers seeking to place her work in the context of other pioneering lesbian authors such as Ann Bannon should consult the essays in Bonnie Zimmerman's *The Safe Sea of Women: Lesbian Fiction 1969–1989.*

—*Robert B. Marks Ridinger*

———

RULE, Jane (Vance). American–born Canadian novelist and author of short fiction. Born in Plainfield, New Jersey, 28 March 1931; immigrated to Canada, 1956; became Canadian citizen. Educated at Mills College, B.A. 1952. Has held a variety of jobs including typist, teacher of handicapped children, and store clerk. Teacher of English, Concord Academy, Concord, Massachusetts, 1954–56; assistant director, International House, 1958–59, lecturer in English, 1959–70, then visiting lecturer in creative writing, 1973–74, University of British Columbia, Vancouver. Author of column "So's Your Grandmother" in *Body Politic;* contributor of reviews and articles to periodicals and journals, including *Canadian Literature, Chatelaine, Globe and Mail, Housewife, Queen's Quarterly, Redbook,* and *San Francisco Review.* **Recipient:** Canadian Authors' Association best novel award and best short story award, both 1978; Gay Academic Union Literature Award, 1978; Fund for Human Dignity award of merit, 1983; Canadian Institute for the Blind's Talking Book of the Year Award, 1991. Agent: Georges Borchardt, Inc., 136 East 57th Street, New York, New York 10022, U.S.A.

WRITINGS

Novels

Desert of the Heart. Toronto, Macmillan, and London, Secker & Warburg, 1964; Cleveland, Ohio, World Publishing, 1965; Tallahassee, Naiad Press, 1983.

This Is Not for You. New York, McCall, 1970; Tallahassee, Naiad
Press, 1982; London, Pandora Press, 1987.
Against the Season. New York, McCall, 1971; London, Davies,
1972; Tallahassee, Naiad Press, 1984.
The Young in One Another's Arms. Garden City, New York,
Doubleday, 1977; Tallahassee, Naiad Press, 1984.
Contract with the World. New York, Harcourt, 1980; Tallahassee,
Naiad Press, 1982; London, Pandora Press, 1990.
Memory Board. Tallahassee, Naiad Press, London, Pandora Press,
and Toronto, Macmillan, 1987.
After the Fire. Tallahassee, Naiad Press, London, Pandora Press,
and Toronto, Macmillan, 1989.

Short Stories

Theme for Diverse Instruments. Toronto, Talonbooks, 1975; Tal-
lahassee, Naiad Press, 1990.
Inland Passage, and Other Stories. Tallahassee, Naiad Press, and
Toronto, Lester & Orpen Dennys, 1985.

Other

Lesbian Images (literary criticism). Garden City, New York,
Doubleday, 1975; London, Davies, 1976; London, Pluto Press,
1989.
Outlander: Stories and Essays. Tallahassee, Naiad Press, 1981.
A Hot–Eyed Moderate (essays). Tallahassee, Naiad Press, and
Toronto, Lester & Orpen Dennys, 1985.
"Lesbian Literature Need Readers," in *Index on Censorship: In-
ternational Magazine for Free Expression* (London), October
1990.
"Lesbians and Writers," in *InVersions: Writings by Dykes, Queers,
and Lesbians.* Vancouver, British Columbia, Press Gang Pub-
lishers, 1991.

*

Adaptations: *Desert of the Heart* was filmed by Donna Deitch in
1985 and released as *Desert Hearts.*

Critical Sources: "Jane Rule and the Reviewers" by Judith Niemi,
in *Margins,* August 1975, 34–37; "Strategies for Survival: The
Subtle Subversion of Jane Rule" by Marilyn R. Schuster in *Feminist Studies,* fall 1981, 431–450.; "Jane Rule's *Desert* Blooms
Anew" by Marie J. Kuda, in *GayLife* (Chicago), 21 November 1985;
"Focus Changes for Golden Rule" by Chris Newport, in *Lambda
Book Report,* October/November 1989; "Cruising the Libraries"
by Lee Lynch, in *Lesbian Texts and Contexts,* New York, New
York University Press, 1990; *Safe Sea of Women: Lesbian Fic-
tion, 1969–1989* by Bonnie Zimmerman, Boston, Beacon Press,
1990.

*   *   *

"The silence has finally been broken." With these words, Jane
Rule ended the introductory chapters to her 1975 book *Lesbian
Images* and opened the floodgates of lesbian scholarship. *Lesbian*

Images offered biographical sketches, analysis, and criticism of a
number of mainstream writers and provided an overview of lesbian–identified writing from the 1930s onward. With the exception of Jeannette Howard Foster's pioneer work, *Sex Variant
Women in Literature,* self–published in 1956, a few bibliographies,
and an occasional magazine article, Rule's book was the first to
offer an awareness of the depth and breadth of contemporary lesbian literature. Written just after the American Psychiatric Association had lifted the stigma of mental illness from homosexuality,
but before the advent of women's studies or lesbian studies on
campus, Rule's was a trailbreaking study.

Rule's fiction was somewhat troubling to lesbian readers of the
1970s, many of whom had narrowed the scope of their reading to
make up for lost time, and although lesbians and gays peopled her
books, she did not slide easily into a category for lesbian authors.
This Is Not for You and *Against the Season,* published before *Lesbian Images,* as well as *Contract with the World,* published afterward, while challenging and genre–defying to the more astute
reader, were disappointing to those seeking a quick romantic "fix."
Rule's fiction was based on her desire to "speak the truth as I saw
it ... to portray people as they really are." Her aim was never to be
politically correct or to propagandize; there were homosexuals, heterosexuals, the handicapped, etc., in her work because there were
such people in her life. Critic Bonnie Zimmerman notes of Rule:
"In a literary sense she is one of the most mainstream of writers ...
the least connected to the lesbian feminist or lesbian separatist movement ... universalist in her views." Criticism of her work has since
come full circle: a lesbian review of her final novel *After the Fire*
pronounced her later work less lyrical and more closely allied with
the widely–available "pulp lesbian fiction." The independence of
vision and striking adherence to Rule's own reality of lesbian/writer,
regardless of criticism or censure from virtually all sides, has, with
time, enhanced Rule's contribution to the dissemination of gay and
lesbian culture.

Rule's first novel, *Desert of the Heart,* was published in 1964,
while she and her lover Helen Sonthoff were living in Vancouver
and teaching English at a local university. The women were unpre-
pared for the consequences of publishing a book about a lesbian
love affair and Rule soon found herself a figurehead in the Canadian lesbian movement. The novel would draw Rule into media
prominence again in 1985, after the release of *Desert Hearts,* a
film adaptation by Donna Deitch. The film, which won the Jury
Prize at the 1986 United States Film Festival, was an underground
success and boosted Naiad Press' sales by making *Desert* their
version of a best–seller. Naiad Press responded to the popularity
of the novel by issuing a second reprint featuring stills from the
film on the cover and frontispiece. The renewed media focus on
her work introduced Rule to a new generation of lesbian readers.
Author and reviewer Lee Lynch found that her goals as a writer
changed when she encountered *Desert of the Heart:* "Rule had the
magical ability to treat her gay characters as if they could function
normally in a world large enough to hold them ... it pushed back
even further the walls which squeezed us, sometimes to death. The
young dyke writers growing up will be stronger for [Radclyffe]
Hall and for Rule, and will create a literature ever freer of doom
because of our foremothers."

Considering herself primarily a writer of fiction, Rule was reluctant to accept a commission from Doubleday to write as a les-

bian about lesbians. She spent some time weighing the consequences for herself, her partner, and her family before accepting the task of writing *Lesbian Images*. In the book's introduction, she notes that it was her father who helped her decide that the work was indeed necessary in overcoming the perception by readers that lesbianism was not accepted as "one of the faces of love." When the book was released in 1975, nascent lesbian presses like Diana, Daughters, and Naiad Press were still struggling to get off the ground; feminist and lesbian bookstores were just beginning to reach a viable market. So, to the hundreds of women from the United States and Canada gathered at the second annual Lesbian Writers Conference in Chicago that year, Rule's book and the reissue of Foster's *Sex Variant Women in Literature* burst like twin bombshells. Many shared Rule's insight that being lesbian and a writer were inseparable and, in essence, defined one's politics, most applauded her courage in broaching the mainstream, some criticized her for not being more overt or setting forth their sense of what was "politically correct" in her own fiction. But all hailed *Lesbian Images* as a primer to a "great books" course in lesbian literature.

Rule's selections for *Lesbian Images* are worth noting: included are such notable women writers as Radclyffe Hall, Gertrude Stein, Willa Cather, Vita Sackville–West, Ivy Compton–Burnett, Elizabeth Bowen, Colette, Violette Leduc, Margaret Anderson, Dorothy Baker, and Maureen Duffy. In "Four Decades of Fiction," she covers Alma Routsong, Gale Wilhelm, Djuna Barnes, Elizabeth Cragin, Claire Morgan, Bertha Harris, and Rita Mae Brown. Her nonfiction discussion includes Kate Millett, Jill Johnston, Sidney Abbott, and Barbara Love, as well as Martin and Lyon. Subsequent scholarship would develop the ideas of coding in the work of Cather and Stein, the brutal side of some of Sackville–West's fiction, and other ideas introduced by Rule.

In addition to writing *Lesbian Images* and seven novels, Rule has authored three collections of essays and short fiction. She has also contributed short pieces to the lesbian and gay small press— her short stories have been collected in *Theme for Diverse Instruments* and *Inland Passage;* her essays in *A Hot–Eyed Moderate,* and *Outlander* include works of both genres. In her contribution to the *Index on Censorship,* Rule wrote that her work is still at the mercy of homophobic reviewers, publishing practices, and customs agents in three countries: "No Canadian writer can make a living without reaching the wider audiences for French or English, our two official languages." She has chosen to be published in the United States by Naiad Press and by Pandora Press in England because "Feminist and gay presses are willing to keep books in print long enough to sell by word of mouth.... Only in Canada do I still publish with a mainstream press."

Although Rule's long term reputation and critical acclaim may well be based on her stylistically original fiction, her nonfiction, teaching, and advocacy for lesbian writers have had equal impact on lesbian studies and the creation of a lesbian culture. She has said it best herself: "As a lesbian, I believe it is important to stand up and be counted, to insist on the dignity and joy loving another woman is for me. If that gets in the way of people's reading my books, I have finally to see that it is their problem and not mine.... I regret the distorting prejudices that surround me ... they will not defeat me, either as a lesbian or a writer."

—*Marie J. Kuda*

RUSS, Joanna. American novelist, essayist, critic, and author of short stories and nonfiction. Born in New York City, 22 February 1937. Educated at Cornell University, Ithaca, New York, B.A. (high honors) in English 1957; Yale University, New Haven, Connecticut, M.F.A. in playwriting and dramatic literature 1960. Lecturer in speech, Queensborough Community College, Bayside, New York, 1966–67; instructor, 1967–70, then assistant professor of English, 1970–72, Cornell University, Ithaca, New York; assistant professor of English, State University of New York at Binghamton, 1972–75, and University of Colorado, Boulder, 1975–77; associate professor, 1977–84, then professor of English, University of Washington, Seattle. Contributor of numerous essays to *Chrysalis, Extrapolation, Feminist Review/New Woman Times, Journal of Popular Culture, Ms., Red Clay Reader, Science–Fiction Studies, Signs,* and *Sojourner.* Contributor of short fiction to *Arlington Quarterly, Cimarron Review, Confrontation, Epoch, Galaxy, Little Magazine, Magazine of Fantasy and Science Fiction, Monmouth Review, Northwest Review, Orbit, Red Clay Reader, Sinister Wisdom,* and *William and Mary Review.* Contributor of book reviews to *Magazine of Fantasy and Science Fiction, Sinister Wisdom, Washington Post,* and *Women's Review of Books.* Member of Modern Language Association of America and Science Fiction Writers of America. **Recipient:** Science Fiction Writers of America Nebula Award, for best short story, 1972, and for novella, 1983; National Endowment for the Humanities fellowship, 1974–75; World Science Fiction Convention Hugo Award for best novella, 1983. Address: Department of English, GN–30, University of Washington, Seattle, Washington 98195, U.S.A.

WRITINGS

Novels

Picnic on Paradise. New York, Ace Books, 1968.
And Chaos Died. New York, Ace Books, 1970.
The Female Man. New York, Bantam, 1975.
We Who Are About to.... New York, Dell, 1977.
Kittatinny: A Tale of Magic (for children). New York, Daughters, Inc., 1978.
The Two of Them. New York, Berkeley, 1978.
On Strike against God. Brooklyn, New York, Out & Out, 1979.
Extra(Ordinary) People. New York, St. Martin's Press, 1984.

Short Stories

"The Man Who Could Not See Devils," in *Alchemy and Academe,* edited by Anne McCaffrey. Garden City, New York, Doubleday, 1970.
"Useful Phrases for the Tourist," in *Universe Two,* edited by Terry Carr. New York, Ace Books, 1972.
"When It Changed," in *Again, Dangerous Visions,* edited by Harlan Ellison. Garden City, New York, Doubleday, 1972.
"Corruption," in *Aurora: Beyond Equality,* edited by Vonda McIntyre and Susan Janice Anderson. New York, Fawcett, 1976.
"Little Tales from Nature," in *WomanSpace: Future and Fantasy Stories and Art by Women.* Lebanon, New Hampshire, New Victoria, 1981.

Short Story Collections

The Zanzibar Cat (short stories). Sauk City, Wisconsin, Arkham House, 1983.
The Adventures of Alyx. New York, Pocket Books, 1983.
The Hidden Side of the Moon: Stories. New York, St. Martin's Press, 1987.

Essays

"What Can a Heroine Do? Or Why Women Can't Write," in *Images of Women,* edited by Susan K. Cornillon. Bowling Green, Ohio, Bowling Green University Popular Press, 1972.
"Not For Years But for Decades," in *The Coming Out Stories,* edited by Julia Penelope and Susan J. Wolfe. Watertown, Massachusetts, Persephone Press, 1980.
"Recent Feminist Utopias," in *Future Females: A Critical Anthology,* edited by Marleen Barr. Bowling Green, Kentucky, Bowling Green Popular Press, 1981.
"Sword Blades and Poppy Seed with Homage to (Who Else?) Amy Lowell," in *Heroic Vision,* edited by Jessica Salmonson. New York, Ace Books, 1983.
How to Suppress Women's Writing. Austin, University of Texas, 1983.
Magic Mommas, Trembling Sisters, Puritans and Perverts: Feminist Essays by Joanna Russ. Trumansburg, New York, Crossing Press, 1985.
"To Write 'Like a Woman': Transformations of Identity in the Work of Willa Cather," in *Historical, Literary and Erotic Aspects of Lesbianism,* edited by Monica Kehoe. New York, Haworth Press, 1986.

Other

Author of introduction, *Tales and Stories* by Mary Shelley. Boston, G. K. Hall, 1975.
"Window Dressing" (play), in *The New Women's Theatre,* edited by Honor Moore. New York, Vintage, 1977.
Contributor, *The Norton Anthology of Literature by Women: The Tradition in English,* edited by Sandra Gilbert and Susan Gubar. New York, Norton, 1985.
Houston, Houston, Do You Read? [and] *Souls.* New York, Tor Books, 1989.

*

Manuscript Collections: University of Oregon, Portland, Oregon.

Interviews: "Joanna Russ" by Paul Walker, in *Speaking of Science Fiction: The Paul Walker Interviews,* Oradell, New Jersey, Luna, 1978; "Joanna Russ' Feminist Science Fiction" by Diana Goldfarb, in *Sojourner,* July 1979; "Future Sex: Science Fiction Writer Joanna Russ" by Camilla Decarnin, in *Advocate,* 10 December 1981; "Profile: Joanna Russ," in *Isaac Asimov's Science Fiction Magazine,* February 1983;

Critical Sources: "Speculations: The Subjunctivity of Science Fiction," in *Extrapolation,* Number 15, 1973, 51–59; "Towards an Aesthetic of Science Fiction," in *Science–Fiction Studies,* Number 2, 1975, 112–119; "Of Things to Come" by Gerald Jonas, in *New York Times Book Review,* 4 May 1975, 50; review of *The Female Man* by Alexei and Cory Panshin, in *Magazine of Fantasy and Science Fiction,* August 1975, 50–52; "My Boat," in *Magazine of Fantasy and Science Fiction,* January 1976; "Outta Space: Women Write Science Fiction," in *Ms.,* January 1976, 109–111; "One Giant Step for Science Fiction" by Michael Goodwin, in *Mother Jones,* August 1976, 62–63; "From Where I Work" by Marge Piercy, in *American Poetry Review,* 6:3, 1977, 37–39; "The Work of Joanna Russ" by Marilyn Hacker, in *Chrysalis,* Number 4, 1977; "Fiction: *We Who Are About To...,*" in *New York Times Book Review,* 25 September 1977, 38; "SF and Technology as Mystification," in *Science–Fiction Studies,* Number 5, 1978, 250–260; "Joanna Russ" by Barbara Garland, in *Dictionary of Literary Biography,* Volume 8: *Twentieth Century American Science Fiction Writers,* Detroit, Gale, 1980; *In the Chinks of the World Machine: Feminism and Science Fiction* by Sarah LeFanu, London, Women's Press, 1988; *Feminist Utopias* by Frances Bartkowski, Lincoln, Nebraska, University of Nebraska, 1989.

Joanna Russ comments: "Men give jobs to men. It's typical that my work—which is feminist, radical and often even separatist—should be validated and explained by a male writer, precisely the sort of situation I have worked for twenty–five years to change. I blame [the publisher], not Bronski [author of the essay that follows], whose work is good. Draw your own conclusions!"

*   *   *

The genre of science fiction writing has been seen, historically, as a male venue. While women writers have been granted social permission to write within the field of "gothic" literature, a genre, as Joanna Russ points out in *How to Suppress Woman's Writing,* that has always been dismissed as frivolous, they have been discouraged from writing about the more masculine concerns of space travel, alternative realities, or intergalactic life. This, in spite of the fact that one of the original science fiction novels, *Frankenstein: Or The New Prometheus,* was written by Mary Shelley in 1818. Joanna Russ' writing—fiction, children's literature, and critical essays—are a response the cultural limitations that have been placed upon women's writing and imagination.

The bulk of Russ' fiction writing takes place in a woman–centered context. Her earliest work, *Picnic on Paradise,* and a series of short stories (since collected in *The Adventures of Alyx*) center on the character of Alyx, a sixteenth–century B.C. Mediterranean woman who undertakes a series of adventures that eventually entail time travel. In her 1972 essay "What Can a Heroine Do? Or Why Women Can't Write," Russ states that much Western literature is predicated on the self–actualization of its male characters and on the supporting actions of the female characters who aid the men, many times at the expense of their own lives or development. By placing Alyx as a primary cause of plot and action, Russ reorients the genre of sword and sorcery and science fiction to a feminist perspective. This cross between science fiction and sword and sorcery, or fantasy—what some critics have labeled "speculative fiction"—runs through all of Russ' work. In this manner, she often introduces humanist and feminist themes to a genre that frequently relies heavily upon simple technology and abstract theory.

In *And Chaos Died,* Russ creates a witty combination of the "brave new world" novel juxtaposed with a utopia/dystopia theme.

By pitting a culture that relies solely upon technology against a race of people who are psychic, Russ is able to critique the genre of science fiction from the inside. The critique is furthered by her making Jai, one of the story's protagonists, a gay man, thus subverting the essentially heterosexual paradigm of the form. That same year Russ published "When it Changed," a story that postulated the existence of an all–woman utopian society and what might occur when faced with the arrival of men. The story was reminiscent of Charlotte Perkins Gilman's 1915 novel *Herland,* although Russ' work was more sophisticated and less pedological than its predecessor.

In 1975 Russ received critical and popular acclaim for her novel *The Female Man,* a book that hypothesized five female heroes, all of whom come from different planets and who perhaps may be various components of the same character. *The Female Man* is a structurally, linguistically, and metaphorically complex book. It was one of the first blatantly feminist science fiction works and as such paved the way for much women's writing that was to follow in the genre. It was not just that Russ predicated a female–centered narrative, but that she was willing to ask questions about gender inequality, sexual violence, and the possible innate differences between women and men.

The idea that women and men might be profoundly different is also addressed in *We Who Are About To...,* in which eight space travellers are marooned on a deserted, seemingly inhospitable, planet. While most of the travellers attempt to make a desperate effort to survive, a sole woman explorer decides that death with dignity and self–respect is a wiser, more logical choice. *We Who Are About To...* uses the science fiction genre as a meditation on existentialism and the value of living life. Much science fiction is about a journey outward—to space, to the ocean—but *We Who Are About To...* is a journey into the inner self, a psychological exploration of what it means to be human.

This journey towards self knowledge is the basis for *The Two of Them,* and much of Russ' newer work. In *The Two of Them,* Irene, a teenage time traveler, has to negotiate a hostile male–dominated world that has a profound effect upon her psyche. The idea of a young female hero—present in Russ' writing from the Alyx stories on—is also evident in her next book *Kittatinny: A Tale of Magic* in 1978, and two collections of short stories *The Zanzibar Cat* in 1983, and *Extra(Ordinary) People* in 1984. This commitment to the young female hero is intrinsic to Russ' politic of female self–empowerment. The young women in these stories—*Kittatinny* was written and marketed specifically as a children's book—have powerful desires, imaginations, and wills that allow them to overcome any problem with which a male hero might be faced. In Russ' world the imagination is as potent and willful as any physical force—often the imagination is as *real* as any material act or object—and her female heros rely on their quick wits to help them maneuver their way through the world.

Russ' fictional ideas are mirrored in her two works of non–fiction: *How to Suppress Women's Writing* in 1983, and *Magic Mamas, Trembling Sisters, Puritans and Perverts: Feminist Essays* in 1985. In both books Russ argues passionately for a world and a culture in which women's ideas and opinions are able to be heard and implemented. She suggests that it is only by listening to what women really have to say—and ending the suppression and distortion of their ideas and words—that social change will finally occur.

—*Michael Bronski*

RUSSO, Vito. American activist and author of nonfiction. Born in New York City, 11 July 1946. Educated at Fairleigh Dickinson University, B.A. 1968; New York University, M.A. in cinema, 1974. Film distributor, Museum of Modern Art, New York City, 1971–73, and Cinema 5 Ltd., New York City, 1973–75. Companion of Jeffrey Sevick (died). Cohost of *Our Times,* WNYC, New York City, 1983; AIDS activist. Founding member of the Gay and Lesbian Alliance against Defamation. **Recipient:** American Library Association Gay Book of the Year Award, 1982; Social Responsibilities Roundtable Award, 1982; Stonewall Foundation Award; Emery S. Hetrick Award; Arthur Bell Award. *Died in New York City, of AIDS–related complications, 7 November 1990.*

WRITINGS

Nonfiction

The Celluloid Closet: Homosexuality in the Movies. New York, Harper, 1981, revised, 1987.
Contributor, *Funk and Wagnalls Encyclopedia.* New York, Funk & Wagnalls, 1984.

*

Biography: "Vito Russo, 44; A Historian of Film and a Gay Advocate" by Stephen Holden, in *New York Times,* 9 November 1990.

Interviews: "Vito Russo: The Reel–Life Images of Gays in the Movies" by Scott Anderson, in *Advocate,* 15 October 1981, 36–38; "The Age of AIDS" by Lenny Giteck, in *Advocate,* 22 July 1986, 28–33.

Critical Sources: "The Celluloid Closet: Gays through a Hollywood Lens Darkly" by Boyd McDonald, in *Advocate,* 8 December 1987, 60–61, 70; "A Remembrance of Vito Russo" by Arnie Kantrowitz, in *Advocate,* 18 December 1990, 72–75.

*   *   *

The career of the late activist, critic, writer and film historian Vito Russo centered upon an exploration and evaluation of the types and ranges of imagery through which homosexuals and the idea of homosexuality were presented to the general public via the medium of cinematography. Born in New York City in 1946, he attended Fairleigh Dickinson University and New York University, where he completed his graduate training in cinema in the early 1970s. While working as a film distributor at the Museum of Modern Art, he began contributing book reviews, film reviews, and essays on contemporary theater to a wide variety of publications. These periodicals and books ranged from the mainstream *Esquire, Rolling Stone,* and the *Village Voice,* to the nationally circulated gay news media (in particular the *Advocate* and the *New York Native*). He also served as the national publicity director for the 1983 Academy Award–winning documentary *The Times of Harvey Milk,* which chronicled the work and murder of gay rights activist Milk.

Russo's history and analysis of the presentation of gay images in American film, *The Celluloid Closet: Homosexuality in the Movies,* was one of the first serious studies to appear in the re–evaluation of the relationship of gay persons to the fine arts, preceded only by *Screening the Sexes: Homosexuality in the Movies* by Parker Tyler in 1972 and the 1977 and 1980 editions of the British Film Institute's collection of essays edited by Richard Dyer, *Gays and Film.* Russo's project served as a precursor of such works as *We Can Always Call Them Bulgarians: The Emergence of Lesbians and Gay Men on the American Stage* in 1987, *Acting Gay: Male Homosexuality in Modern Drama* in 1992, and Nicholas de Jongh's *Not in Front of the Audience: Homosexuality on Stage* in 1992, which served a similar purpose for the theater.

During the early 1970s, Russo became involved with New York City's Gay Activists Alliance, organizing film festivals at the group's Firehouse headquarters. It was during those evenings, watching audience reactions to the depiction of the few gay and lesbian characters then admitted to contemporary film scripts, that the idea of researching homosexuals in the cinema crystallized. *The Celluloid Closet* first took form as a film and lecture that Russo eventually presented at more than two hundred film festivals, colleges, and museums in Europe, Australia, and the United States. Unlike its predecessors, Russo's book takes a clear, chronological approach to the norms utilized to determine the form homosexuality would be allowed to take on screen, beginning with the silent film comedies of Fatty Arbuckle, John Bunny, and Wallace Beery, and reaching to the varied depictions of characters with more blatantly homosexual overtones and subtexts in such films as *La Cage aux Folles* and *Cruising.* Based on numerous interviews with actors, screenwriters and directors, its historical emphasis is placed almost entirely on the American film industry, with information on foreign gay filmmakers such as Germany's Rainer Werner Fassbinder included only briefly. Of particular interest is the discussion of the ways in which gay and lesbian characters were portrayed on commercial television programs and in made–for–television films such as the breakthrough 1973 release *That Certain Summer.*

The first edition of *The Celluloid Closet* received the Gay Book of the Year Award from the American Library Association in 1982. In a preface to the expanded 1987 edition, Russo stated a guiding principle of challenge of the Gay and Lesbian Alliance Against Defamation, which he had helped to found in 1986. Summarizing the thesis of his work, he writes: "America was a dream that had no room for the existence of homosexuals. Laws were made against depicting such things onscreen. And when the fact of our existence became unavoidable, we were reflected, onscreen and off, as dirty secrets. We have cooperated for a very long time in the maintenance of our own invisibility. And now the party is over."

Russo's diagnosis with AIDS in 1985 served only to augment and redirect his challenge for social change. In addition to recognition from the American Library Association, he also received numerous awards from gay and lesbian organizations for his tireless efforts promoting increased self–respect for homosexuals. Among these were the Stonewall Foundation award for writing, the Emery S. Hetrick award as an outstanding role model for gay and lesbian youth from the Hetrick–Martin Institute, and the Arthur Bell award from the Human Rights Campaign Fund, the national gay political action committee. Even in the painful weeks prior to his death on 7 November 1990, he remained aware and concerned.

—*Robert B. Marks Ridinger*

S

SACKVILLE–WEST, V(ictoria Mary). British poet, novelist, biographer, garden designer, and author of short stories. Also known as Vita Sackville–West. Born at Knole Castle, Sevenoaks, Kent, 9 March 1892; daughter of Lord Lionel and Lady Victoria Sackville–West. Educated privately and at Miss Woolf's School, London. Married journalist and diplomat Harold Nicolson in 1912; two children. Companion of Rosamund Grosvenor and of authors Violet Keppel Trefusis and Virginia Woolf. Contributor of critical essays to Royal Society of Literature, c. 1927–45; author of gardening column for *London Observer*, 1946–61. Associate of the Bloomsbury literary group; fellow, Royal Society. **Recipient:** Hawthornden Prize for poetry, 1927; Heinemann Prize for poetry, 1946; Companion of Honor, 1948. *Died at Sissinghurst Castle, Cranbrook, Kent, of cancer, 2 June 1962.*

WRITINGS

Poetry

Chatterton. Privately printed, 1909.
Constantinople. Privately printed, 1915.
Poems of West and East. New York and London, John Lane, 1917.
Orchard and Vineyard. New York and London, John Lane, 1921.
The Land. London, Heinemann, 1926; Garden City, New York, Doubleday, Doran & Coy, 1927.
King's Daughter. London, Hogarth Press, 1929; Garden City, New York, Doubleday, Doran, 1930.
Invitation to Cast Out Care, illustrations by Graham Sutherland. London, Faber, 1931.
Sissinghurst. London, Hogarth Press, 1931.
Collected Poems: Volume 1. London, Hogarth Press, and Garden City, New York, Doubleday, Doran, 1933.
Some Flowers. London, Cobden–Sanderson, 1937.
Solitude: A Poem. London, Hogarth Press, 1938; Garden City, New York, Doubleday, Doran, 1939.
Selected Poems. London, Hogarth Press, 1941.
The Garden. London, Joseph, and Garden City, New York, Doubleday, Doran, 1946.

Novels

Heritage. New York, Doran, and London, Collins, 1919.
The Dragon in Shallow Waters. London, Collins, 1921; New York, Putnam, 1922.
Challenge. New York, Doran, 1923.
Grey Wethers: A Romantic Novel. New York, Doran, and London, Heinemann, 1923.

The Edwardians. London, Hogarth Press, and Garden City, New York, Doubleday, Doran, 1930.
All Passion Spent. London, Hogarth Press, and Garden City, New York, Doubleday, Doran, 1931.
Family History. London, Hogarth Press, and Garden City, New York, Doubleday, Doran, 1932.
The Dark Island. London, Hogarth Press, and Garden City, New York, Doubleday, Doran, 1934.
Grand Canyon: A Novel. London, Joseph, and Garden City, New York, Doubleday, Doran, 1942.
The Devil at Westease: The Story as Related by Roger Liddiard. Garden City, New York, Doubleday, 1947.
The Easter Party. London, Joseph, and Garden City, New York, Doubleday, Doran, 1953.
No Sign–Posts in the Sea. London, Joseph, and Garden City, New York, Doubleday, 1961.

Short Stories

The Heir: A Love Story. London, privately printed, 1922; with "The Christmas Party," "Patience," "Her Son," and "The Parrot," New York, Doran, and London, Heinemann, 1922.
Seducers in Ecuador. London, Hogarth Press, 1924; New York, Doran, 1925.
Thirty Clocks Strike the Hour, and Other Stories. Garden City, New York, Doubleday, Doran, 1932.
Death of Noble Gadavary and Gottfried Kuenstler. London, Benn, 1932.

Biographies

Author of introduction and notes, *The Diary of Lady Anne Clifford.* London, Heinemann, 1923.
Aphra Behn: The Incomparable Astrea. London, Howe, 1927; New York, Viking, 1928.
Andrew Marvell. London, Faber, 1929.
Saint Joan of Arc. London, Cobden–Sanderson, and Garden City, New York, Doubleday, Doran, 1936; revised, London, Joseph, 1948.
Joan of Arc. London, Hogarth Press, 1937; New York, Stackpole, 1938.
Pepita. London, Hogarth Press, and Garden City, New York, Doubleday, Doran, 1937.
The Eagle and the Dove: A Study in Contrasts, St. Teresa of Avila and St. Therese of Lisieux. London, Joseph, 1943; Garden City, New York, Doubleday, Doran, 1944.
Daughter of France: The Life of Anne Marie Louise d'Orleans, Duchesse de Montpensier, 1627–1693, La Grande Mademoiselle. London, Joseph, and Garden City, New York, Doubleday, 1959.

Gardening Books

Country Notes. London, M. Joseph, 1939; New York, Harper, 1940.
Country Notes in Wartime. London, Hogarth Press, 1940; Garden City, New York, Doubleday, Doran, 1941.
In Your Garden. London, M. Joseph, 1951; as *V. Sackville–West's Garden Book,* edited by Philippa Nicolson, New York, Atheneum, 1968; as *V. Sackville–West's Garden Book: A Collection Taken from In Your Garden,* London, M. Joseph, 1968.
In Your Garden Again. London, M. Joseph, 1953.
More for Your Garden. London, M. Joseph, 1955.
A Joy of Gardening: A Selection for Americans, edited by Hermine I. Popper. New York, Harper, 1958.
Even More for Your Garden. London, M. Joseph, 1958.
The Illustrated Garden Book: A New Anthology, edited by Robin Lane Fox. New York, Atheneum, 1986.

Other

Knole and the Sackvilles. New York, Doran, and London, Heinemann, 1922; revised, London, Benn, 1958.
Passengers to Teheran. London, Hogarth Press, 1926; New York, Doran, 1927.
Twelve Days: An Account of a Journey across the Bakhtiari Mountains in Southwestern Persia. London, Hogarth Press, and Garden City, New York, Doubleday, Doran, 1928.
Translator, *Duineser Elegian: Elegies from the Castle of Duino by Rainer Marie Rilke.* London, Hogarth Press, 1931.
English Country Houses. London, Collins, 1941.
The Women's Land Army. London, M. Joseph, 1944.
Nursery Rhymes (history). London, Dropmore, 1947.
Faces: Profiles of Dogs. London, Harvill, 1961.
With Harold Nicolson, *Another World than This* (anthology). London, M. Joseph, 1945.
Author of introduction, *Prose and Poetry* by Alice Christiana Meynell. London, J. Cape, 1947.
Berkeley Castle: The Historic Glouchestershire Seat of the Berkeley Family since the Eleventh Century. Derby, English Life Publications, 1972.
Dearest Andrew: Letters from V. Sackville–West to Andrew Reiber, 1951–1952, edited by Nancy MacKnight. New York, Scribner, 1979.
The Letters of Vita Sackville–West to Virginia Woolf. New York, Morrow, 1985.

*

Adaptations: *All Passion Spent* was adapted for British television in early 1990s.

Manuscript Collections: Lilly Library, University of Indiana, Bloomington.

Biography: *V. Sackville–West: A Critical Biography* by Sarah Ruth Watson, Boston, Twayne Publishers, 1972; *Portrait of a Marriage* by Nigel Nicolson, New York, Atheneum, 1973; *The Jessamy Brides: The Friendship of Virginia Woolf and Vita Sackville–West* by Joan Trautmann, University Park, Pennsylvania State Studies, 1973; *V. Sackville–West: A Critical Biography* by Michael Stevens, New York, Scribner, 1974; *Vita: The Life of Vita Sackville–West* by Victoria Glendinning, New York, Knopf, 1983.

Critical Sources: *Sex Variant Women in Literature; A Historical and Quantitative Survey* by Jeannette Howard Foster, New York, Vantage, 1956; *V. Sackville–West* by Sara Ruth Watson, New York, Twayne Publishers, 1972; *Toward a Recognition of Androgyny* by Carolyn Heilbrun, New York, Harper, 1974; *Lesbian Images* by Jane Rule, Garden City, New York, Doubleday, 1975; *Virginia Woolf and Her World* by John Lehmann, New York, Harcourt, 1977; *Virginia Woolf: A Critical Memoir* by Winifred Holtby, Chicago, Academy, 1978; *The Androgyne: Fusion of the Sexes* by Elemire Zolla, London, Thames & Hudson, 1981; "Lighting the Cave: The Relationship between Vita Sackville–West and Virginia Woolf" by Louis DeSalvo, in *Signs,* winter 1982, 195–214; *Echo: A Novel* by Violet Trefusis, translation from the French by Stan Miles, introduction by John Phillips, New York, Viking, 1988; *Violet to Vita: The Letters of Violet Trefusis to Vita Sackville–West, 1910–1921,* edited by Mitchell A. Leaska and John Phillips, New York, Viking, 1989.

*   *   *

Vita Sackville–West passionately wanted two things: to be heir to Knole Castle, the ancestral home of the Sackvilles since the days of Elizabeth I, and to be a writer. Being born a woman in late–Victorian England impinged on both those dreams. Knole, her beloved home, with its seven courtyards (one for each day of the week), 52 staircases (one for each week of the year), and 365 rooms (one for each day of the year), passed through the male line to her cousin. The 50 books published during her lifetime received mixed reviews and she was consigned by the critical establishment to the category of minor English female writer.

Sackville–West was also passionate about women and was known in her day as a Sapphist. She had two intense relationships with other women writers that significantly impacted both her work and theirs. With the renewed interest in all things Bloomsbury during the 1970s, her romantic attachment to Bloomsbury lion Virginia Woolf became common knowledge. Though initial attention centered around the possibility of a sexual relationship between the two women (both were married, and both had a history of prior attachments to other women), interest eventually came to focus on Sackville–West's life and work. This reexamination resulted in a number of biographies in the 1970s and 1980s. In the early 1990s, British television produced both her novel *All Passion Spent* and her son's *Portrait of a Marriage,* the latter concerned the scandal surrounding Sackville–West's elopement with novelist Violet Keppel Trefusis.

Soon after the birth of her second son, Sackville–West learned that her husband, diplomat and biographer Harold Nicolson, was a homosexual still actively involved in sexual relationships with men—information he shared with her after a VD scare. The relationship recounted in *Portrait of a Marriage,* published in 1973, was a reaction to her husband's deceit. Sackville–West and Trefusis had been childhood friends, and on renewing their acquaintance, they fell passionately in love. Sackville–West's side of the relationship was told from the autobiographical notes and diaries of the period discovered by her son Nigel Nicolson after her death in 1962. *Violet to Vita,* the first published collection of her letters, paints Sackville–

West less as a martyr than as a petulant, indecisive woman of her time and social standing. The weight of economic dependence and threat of social ostracism were soon brought to bear, forcing Trefusis into a marriage in name only to assuage her mother. Their affair continued and was punctuated with escapes abroad—sometimes with husbands in hot pursuit—and doomed plans to live together in gypsy abandon.

Challenge, Sackville–West's story of love, jealousy, and betrayal, was written during their affair: Eve was modeled after Trefusis and Julian after Sackville–West. Trefusis read the manuscript as it progressed, occasionally even contributing to it. *Challenge* is a reflection of the concern of both women with the presence of both male and female principals in both the individual and the creative artist, a concern shared by fellow author Woolf. Because of the intervention of both women's families, the book was not widely distributed until its republication in 1974.

The patrician Sackville–West met socialist author Woolf in 1922. Their relationship blossomed into an intense and passionate one, which would taper off into a lifelong friendship. The byproduct of their love was both creatively and commercially successful: Woolf's fascination with Sackville–West, and her knowledge of the Sackville family history and Knole Castle, resulted in the fantasy/biography *Orlando,* published by Woolf's Hogarth Press in 1928. This was the first of Woolf's books to be both popular and financially successful; and the publication of Sackville–West's social satire *The Edwardians* in 1930 put the small press well into the black. When Sackville–West and her husband moved into Sissinghurst Castle, Woolf would make her friend a gift of the original Hogarth press in tribute to her contribution.

In 1928, both Sackville–West and Woolf, along with other Bloomsbury homosexuals, were prepared to testify on behalf of Radclyffe Hall's *The Well of Loneliness,* a pioneering novel whose overt lesbian theme had resulted in its confiscation and an obscenity trial. Woolf's *Orlando* was not subjected to the same censure due to her device of having Orlando, who lived from the seventeenth century through the twentieth century, change sex at intervals throughout the book. The novel has been variously described by critics as a Bloomsbury in–joke or a literary love letter, but all have viewed it as a light exception to Woolf's usual output.

Feminist critics observe that both Woolf and Sackville–West were at the peak of their creativity and productivity during the most intense part of their relationship. They also note the cross influence of each on the other's work, particularly Woolf's *A Room of One's Own, Mrs. Dalloway,* and *To the Lighthouse,* and Sackville–West's *Seducers in Ecuador* and *The Dark Island.* In the latter, the characters of Venn and Shirin are again thought to represent dual aspects of the same individual. Woolf responded to what she saw as the male principal in Sackville–West—a practical extension of Coleridge's theory on the androgynous mind of the creative artist. Indeed, Bloomsbury was preoccupied with the duality of the sexes—Carolyn Heilbrun sees the group as the first example of people practicing androgyny as a way of life.

Although she wrote over a dozen novels and three biographies of strong women—Aphra Behn, Joan of Arc, and Therese of Avila—in her early years Sackville–West was known principally for her poetry. In her later life, her name began to be closely attached to her gardens at Sissinghurst. The complete ouvre of Sackville–West includes a variety of books on gardening, 14 volumes of poetry—including several on local and family history—travel writing, a mystery, and even a book on dogs. Her poem *The Land* won the prestigious Hawthornden Prize in 1927, and *The Garden* was awarded

the Heinemann Prize for poetry in 1947. Jeannette Howard Foster finds evidence of lesbian passion in Sackville's verse. In the end, though, it is her insistence upon living her life as a lesbian and a wife, on her own terms, that has earned her a place as a figurehead in the assimilationist les–bi–gay (lesbian/bisexual/gay) movement of the early 1990s.

—*Marie J. Kuda*

———

SAGARIN, Edward. American educator, sociologist, editor, and author of nonfiction. Also wrote as Donald Webster Cory. Born in Schenectady, New York, 18 September 1913. Educated at Brooklyn College of the City University of New York, B.A. (magna cum laude) 1961; New York University, Ph.D. 1966. Married Esther Gertrude Liphshitz in 1936; one son. Worked in perfume and cosmetic industries, 1939–61; lecturer in sociology, Brooklyn College of the City University of New York, 1962–63, and Pratt Institute, 1963–64; professor of sociology, City College of the City University of New York, 1970–82. *Died in 1986.*

WRITINGS

Nonfiction

The Science and Art of Perfumery. New York, McGraw, 1945, second edition, New York, Greenberg, 1955.

With Robert H. Kinzer, *The Negro in American Business.* New York, Greenberg, 1950.

The Homosexual in America: A Subjective Approach (as Donald Webster Cory). New York, Greenberg, 1951; with new introduction, New York, Arno, 1975.

With Elmer G. Leterman, *The Sale Begins When the Customer Says No!* New York, Greenberg, 1953.

The Anatomy of Dirty Words. Kent, Lyle Stuart, 1962.

With Albert Ellis, *Nymphomania: A Study of the Oversexed Woman.* Gilbert Press, 1964.

Structure and Ideology in an Association of Deviants. New York, Arno, 1966.

With Brandt Aymar, *A Pictorial History of the World's Great Trials: From Socrates to Eichmann.* New York, Crown, 1967; enlarged, New York, Bonanza Books, 1985.

Odd Man In: Societies of Deviants in America. Chicago, Quadrangle, 1969.

With Brandt Aymar, *Laws and Trials that Created History: A Pictorial History.* New York, Crown, 1974.

Deviants and Deviance: An Introduction to the Study of Disvalued People and Behavior. New York, Praeger, 1975.

With Arnold Birenbaum, *Norms and Human Behavior.* New York, Praeger, 1976.

Sociology: The Basic Concepts. New York, Holt, 1978.

With Donal E. J. MacNamara, *Sex, Crime, and the Law.* New York, Free Press, 1978.

Raskolnikov and Others: Literary Images of Crime, Punishment, Redemption, and Atonement, foreword by Marvin E. Wolfgang. New York, St. Martin's Press, 1981.

Novels

Flakes of Snow. New York, Crown, 1974.

Translator

Natural Perfume Materials by Y. R. Naves and G. Mazuver. Reinhold, 1947.
Incest by Emile Durkheim. Kent, Lyle Stuart, 1963.

Editor

With M. S. Balsam, and contributor, *Cosmetics: Science and Technology.* New York, Interscience, 1957, second edition, New York, Wiley–Interscience, Volume 1, 1972, Volume 2, 1972, Volume 3, 1974.
Get Well. Radnor, Pennsylvania, Chilton, 1962.
With Brandt Aymar, *The Personality of the Horse.* New York, Crown, 1963.
Editor, with Albert Teichner, *The Cry for Justice* by Upton Sinclair. Kent, Lyle Stuart, 1964.
With Brandt Aymar, *The Personality of the Dog.* New York, Crown, 1964.
Sex and the Contemporary American Scene. Philadelphia, American Academy of Political and Social Science, 1968.
With Donal E. J. MacNamara, *Problems of Sex Behavior.* New York, Crowell, 1968.
With James M. Henslin, *Studies in the Sociology of Sex.* Appleton, 1971, revised as *The Sociology of Sex: An Introductory Reader,* New York, Schocken, 1978.
With Donal E. J. MacNamara, *Perspectives on Correction: Selected Studies in Social Problems.* New York, Crowell, 1971.
With Arnold Birenbaum, *Social Problems: Private Troubles and Public Issues.* New York, Scribner, 1972.
With Arnold Birenbaum, *People in Places: The Sociology of the Familiar.* New York, Praeger, 1973.
With Terrence P. Thornberry, *Images of Crime: Offenders and Victims.* New York, Praeger, 1974.
Humanistic Psychotherapy: The Rational–Emotive Approach. New York, Crown, 1974.
Deviance and Social Change. Beverly Hills, California, Sage Publications, 1977.
With Fred Montanino, *Deviants: Voluntary Actors in a Hostile World.* Morristown, New Jersey, General Learning Press, 1977.
And author of introduction, *Folkways and Mores* by William G. Sumner. New York, Schocken, 1979.
And contributor, *Criminology: New Concerns; Essays in Honor of Hans W. Mattick.* Beverly Hills, California, Sage Publications, 1979.
Taboos in Criminology. Beverly Hills, California, Sage Publications, 1980.

Other

Compiler, *The Other Minorities: Nonethnic Collectivities Conceptualized as Minority Groups.* Waltham, Massachusetts, Ginn, 1971.
Contributor, *Encyclopedia of Sexual Behavior.* Hawthorn, 1961.

With Robert J. Kelly, "Polylingualism in the United States of America: A Multitude of Tongues amid a Monolingual Majority," in *Language Policy and National Unity,* edited by William R. Beer and James E. Jacob. Totowa, New Jersey, Rowman & Allanheld, 1985.

*

Biography: "Edward Sagarin: 1913–1986" by Donal E. J. MacNamara, in *Crime & Delinquency,* October 1986, 515–517.

Critical Sources: *Lesbiana: Book Reviews from the "Ladder"* by Barbara Grier, Tallahassee, Naiad Press, 1976, 185–186.

*   *   *

Edward Sagarin was a pioneering thinker of the American homophile movement. An expert in the chemistry of perfumes, he took an early interest in the civil rights movement. In 1951, around the time when the American homophile movement was forming in the Los Angeles area, he wrote wrote *The Homosexual in America: A Subjective Approach* under the pseudonym Donald Webster Cory (from *Cory–don,* the title of André Gide's celebrated tract, and Daniel Webster, the great American orator.

This work, epoch–making in its time, remains in many respects unsurpassed. It was not just a confession or an autobiography, but summarized in an excellent, concise, preeminently readable style all that was known on the subject in the middle of the century. To the uninitiated, both heterosexual and homosexual, it described the hypocrisy and pretense imposed on lovers of their own sex by Christian intolerance and revealed the words and ways of the clandestine subculture that had long existed in American cities. It analyzed the semiotics of an erotic encounter and the risks to which the unwary could expose themselves. It surveyed both the psychiatric writings on sexual inversion and works of fiction—novels, short stories, plays—in several languages with veiled or explicit homoerotic themes. It furnished anyone approaching the subject with all the tools needed for further study and investigation. The book argued that homosexual acts harmed no one either physically or mentally and were the private concern of those who engaged in them, therefore the state had no reason to ferret them out and punish them. Most importantly, Sagarin defined homosexuals as a *minority* seeking an end to the discrimination and exclusion inflicted by the heterosexual majority, exactly as racial and ethnic minorities were then beginning to demand abolition of the second–class citizenship imposed on them by the Anglo–Saxon majority. Noting that after 1935 the sexual reform movement had come to a halt, he rebuked the psychiatric profession for failing to enlighten the public on the truth about homosexuality and voiced a cadenced plea for understanding and toleration of those who were still invisible and rightless criminals and pariahs in a country that boasted of its freedom. Last of all, he acknowledged that although invisibility made the burden of hatred and contempt less unendurable, it also perpetuated ignorance and hostility; homosexuals had to become visible as what they were and for what they were, if public opinion was to be altered in a positive direction.

The Homosexual in America was far and away the most influential book on homosexuality of the decade, since the leaders of the movement on the West Coast wrote little more than leaflets and magazine articles. Although Sagarin's plea for support was rejected by psychiatrists, his book became the vade–mecum of every politically conscious member of the gay community in the United States of the 1950s, and it inspired such activists as Frank Kameny to risk a new strategy in the struggle for gay rights by openly challenging the prevailing homophobic beliefs. Sagarin wrote several other books on the subject, but none that equalled in importance this first publication.

Changing professions in mid–life, he took a doctorate in sociology at New York University, writing his dissertation on *Structure and Ideology in an Association of Deviants* in 1966, which analyzed the internal politics of the Mattachine Society, the pioneering homophile organization. About this time a psychological trauma occurred that profoundly altered his outlook. In the midst of a homosexual encounter he suffered a seizure and lost consciousness. When he awoke in the hospital, he was overwhelmed with religious guilt, and renounced the movement entirely. Earlier, claiming that he had been under the spell of the vulgar psychoanalytic notion that sexual orientation was acquired primarily through childhood experiences, his advice to parents in *The Homosexual in America* admonished them that *they* were responsible for their child's homosexuality. In the aftermath of this conversion he echoed the neo–Thomistic argument voiced by the homophobic wing of the psychiatric guild that "homosexuality is always a disease."

Totally alienated from the post–Stonewall gay liberation movement after 1969, he refused to participate in the creation of the Gay Academic Union in 1973. As Professor of Sociology at the City College of New York, he published articles on deviant behavior, criminology, and sexology that even with their biases merit attention because of their critical standpoint. He never ceased to maintain that the legal prosecution and social ostracism of homosexuals was a cruel injustice. Though barely known at his death to the younger generation of gay activists, he was remembered by their elders, whose lives he had changed for the better. More than any other figure of the early American movement, in the darkness of the pre–Stonewall era he had brought them enlightenment and hope.

—*Warren Johansson*

———

SANFORD, Abigail. *See* **FOSTER, Jeannette Howard.**

———

SARTON, (Eleanor) May. Belgium–born American poet, novelist, and writer of nonfiction and children's literature. Born in Wondelgem, 3 May 1912; brought to the United States in 1916; became a naturalized U.S. citizen in 1924. Educated at Shady Hill School, Cambridge, Massachusetts, and Institute Belge de Culture Francaise, Brussels, Belgium; graduated from Cambridge High and Latin School, 1929. Apprentice, Eva Le Gallienne's Civic Repertory Theatre, New York City, 1929–34; founder and director, Associated Actors Theatre, New York City, 1934–37; scriptwriter,

Overseas Film Unit, New York City, 1941–52; Briggs–Copeland Instructor in English Composition, Harvard University, Cambridge, Massachusetts, 1949–52; lecturer, Bread Loaf Writer's Conference, Middlebury, Vermont, 1951–53; lecturer, Boulder Writers' Conference, Boulder, Colorado, 1954; lecturer in creative writing, Wellesley College, Wellesley, Massachusetts, 1960–64; poet–in–residence, Lindenwood College, St. Charles, Missouri, 1965. Phi Beta Kappa visiting scholar, 1960; visiting lecturer, Agnes Scott College, 1972. Fellow, American Academy of Arts and Sciences. **Recipient:** New England Poetry Society Golden Rose Award, 1945; *Poetry* magazine Edward Bland Memorial Prize, 1945; Poetry Society of America Reynolds Lyric Award, 1952; Lucy Martin Donelly fellowship, Bryn Mawr College, 1953–54; Guggenheim fellow in poetry, 1954–55; Johns Hopkins University Poetry Festival Award, 1961; Emily Clark Balch Prize, 1966; National Endowment for the Arts grant, 1966; Sarah Josepha Hale Award, 1972; College of St. Catherine Alexandrine medal, 1975; Deborah Morton Award, Westbrook, 1981; Unitarian Universalist Women's Federation Ministry to Women Award, 1982; Avon/COCOA Pioneer Woman Award, 1983; Human Rights Award, 1985; Fund for Human Dignity Award, 1985; Before Columbus Foundation American Book Award, 1985; University of Maine Maryann Hartman Award, 1986; New England Booksellers Association New England Author Award, 1990. Honorary doctorates from Russell Sage College, 1958, New England College, 1971, Clark University, 1975, Bates College, 1976, Colby College, 1976, University of New Hampshire, 1976, Thomas Starr King School of Religious Leadership, 1976, Nasson College, 1980, University of Maine, 1981, Bowdoin College, 1983, and Goucher College, 1985. Address: P.O. Box 99, York, Maine 03809, U.S.A.

WRITINGS

Poetry

Encounter in April. Boston, Houghton, 1937.
Inner Landscape. Boston, Houghton, 1938.
The Lion and the Rose. New York, Rinehart, 1948.
The Land of Silence. New York, Rinehart, 1953.
In Time Like Air. New York, Rinehart, 1958.
Cloud, Stone, Suit, Vine. New York, Norton, 1961.
A Private Mythology. New York, Norton, 1966.
As Does New Hampshire. Peterborough, New Hampshire, Smith, 1967.
A Grain of Mustard Seed. New York, Norton, 1971.
A Durable Fire. New York, Norton, 1972.
Collected Poems: 1930–1973. New York, Norton, 1974.
Selected Poems. New York, Norton, 1978.
Halfway to Silence. New York, Norton, 1980.
Letters from Maine: New Poems. New York, Norton, 1984.
The Silence Now: New and Uncollected Earlier Poems. New York, Norton, 1988.

Fiction

The Single Hound. Boston, Houghton, 1938.
The Bridge of Years. Garden City, New York, Doubleday, 1946.
Shadow of a Man. New York, Rinehart, 1950.
A Shower of Summer Days. New York, Rinehart, 1952.

Faithful Are the Wounds. New York, Rinehart, 1955.
The Fur Person. New York, Norton, 1956.
The Birth of a Grandfather. New York, Rinehart, 1957.
The Small Room. New York, Norton, 1961.
Joanna and Ulysses. New York, Norton, 1963.
Mrs. Stevens Hears the Mermaids Singing, introduction by Carolyn Heilbrun. New York, Norton, 1965, revised, 1974.
Mrs. Pickthorn and Mr. Hare (fable). New York, Norton, 1966.
The Poet and the Donkey. New York, Norton, 1969.
Kinds of Love. New York, Norton, 1970.
As We Are Now. New York, Norton, 1973.
Punch's Secret (juvenile). New York, Harper, 1974.
Crucial Conversations. New York, Norton, 1975.
A Walk through the Woods (juvenile). New York, Harper, 1976.
A Reckoning. New York, Norton, 1978.
Anger. New York, Norton, 1978.
The Magnificent Spinster. New York, Norton, 1985.
The Education of Harriet Hatfield. New York, Norton, 1989.

Nonfiction

I Knew a Phoenix: Sketches for an Autobiography. New York, Rinehart, 1959.
Contributor, *The Movement of Poetry.* Baltimore, Johns Hopkins University Press, 1962.
Plant Dreaming Deep (autobiography). New York, Norton, 1968.
Journal of Solitude. New York, Norton, 1973.
A World of Light: Portraits and Celebrations. New York, Norton, 1976.
The House by the Sea. New York, Norton, 1977.
Writings on Writing. Orono, Maine, Puckerbrush Press, 1980.
Recovering: A Journal. New York, Norton, 1980.
At Seventy: A Journal. New York, Norton, 1984.
May Sarton: A Self-Portrait, edited by Marita Simpson and Martha Wheelock. New York, Norton, 1986.
Encore: A Journal of the Eightieth Year. New York, Norton, 1993.

Other

Toscanini: The Hymn of Nations (screenplay), 1944.
Valley of the Tennessee (screenplay), 1944.
Underground River (play), Play Club, 1947.

*

Manuscript Collections: Henry W. and Albert A. Berg Collection at the New York Public Library.

Biography: *May Sarton: A Biography* by Lenora Blouin, Metuchin, New Jersey, Scarecrow Press, 1978.

Bibliography: *May Sarton: A Bibliography* by Lenora Blouin, Metuchen, New Jersey, Scarecrow Press, 1978; "A Revised Bibliography" by Lenora Blouin, in *May Sarton: Woman and Poet,* edited by Constance Hunting, Orono, Maine, National Poetry Foundation, 1982, 282–319.

Critical Sources: *The Modern American Political Novel: 1900–1960* by Joseph Blotner, Austin, University of Texas Press, 1966;

May Sarton, by Agnes Silbey, Twayne Publishers, 1972; "May Sarton's Women," in *Images of Women in Fiction,* edited by Susan K. Cornillon, Bowling Green, Ohio, Bowling Green University Popular Press, 1972; *Lesbian Images* by Jane Rule, Garden City, New York, Doubleday, 1975; "'Kinds of Love': Love and Friendship in the Novels of May Sarton" by Jane S. Bakerman, in *Critique,* Number 20, 1979; *Dictionary of Literary Biography Yearbook: 1981,* Detroit, Gale, 1982; *May Sarton: Woman and Poet,* edited by Constance Hunting, Orono, Maine, National Poetry Foundation, 1982; "A Note on May Sarton" by Margaret Cruikshank, in *Journal of Homosexuality,* May 1986, 153; "May Sarton" by Constance Hunting, in *Dictionary of Literary Biography,* Volume 48: *American Poets 1880–1945, Second Series,* Detroit, Gale, 1986; *The Gay Novel in America* by James Levin, New York, Garland, 1991.

*   *   *

In her introduction to the 1974 edition of May Sarton's *Mrs. Stevens Hears the Mermaids Singing,* Carolyn Heilbrun noted that "Sarton's life is a mirror image of the usual American success story. In those wildly famous lives where, Scott Fitzgerald has told us, there are no second acts, the glories and the riches soon betray the writer to madness, impotence, alcohol, literary vendettas.... [F]or Sarton, perhaps uniquely so, considering the accomplishments, there has been little organized acclaim, no academic attention, indifference on the part of the critical establishment.... [S]he has written twenty-seven books and, widely read, is only now beginning to get the critical attention properly due her."

Although Sarton published only one novel and a book of poetry in the 1940s, her output since 1950 has been prodigious. It was during the 1950s that Sarton's readership started to grow and she became a presence in the literary world (this was especially true of her autobiographical work). By the 1980s—due in part to Heilbrun's efforts and and an increased interest in feminist literary issues—Sarton's work began to receive the academic and critical attention that had earlier eluded it.

In essence, Sarton's writings explore the inner workings of human nature. The author's journals and poems are all detailed examinations of her life, emotions and fears. At times, Sarton is reticent with regard to the material details of her life—the name of a lover, the exact nature of a fight with a friend—but she is forthcoming about her perceptions and passions. Many of Sarton's novels, such as *Mrs. Stevens Hears the Mermaids Singing* and *The Education of Harriet Hatfield,* feature investigations into personal interior worlds, worlds often similar to the author's own. When *Mrs. Stevens Hears the Mermaids Singing* was published, it was one of the first mainstream novels to deal with an openly lesbian character without any apology or psychoanalytic explanation. Sarton's portrait of Hilary Stevens is complex; although she leads a bisexual life, Stevens states that it is women who have always been her muse, her inspiration. Taken in this light, Sarton's autobiographical character offers a view of lesbianism that is not simply sexual, but the source of artistic creation as well.

By contemporary standards, *Mrs. Stevens Hears the Mermaids Singing* seems mild, but the novel's publication eventually cost Sarton her teaching job (largely because she was too closely identified with her character). Although she has spoken frequently about her lesbianism, Sarton has not made the fact overtly central to her work. Despite this reticence, the tensions between the private and the political are very much present in Sarton's work and thought. As the author once indicated in *Paris Review:* "The militant lesbians want me to be militant and I'm just not."

In the *Journal of Homosexuality,* Margaret Cruikshank wrote of Sarton: "Obviously, a writer's persona should not be confused with her real life identity. Nevertheless, the experience of talking to May Sarton helped me understand that excluding her work from my article was a political rather than a literary choice, one that revealed my inability to place her *inside* the lesbian feminist movement. This unstated criterion required that the writer have a particular temperament and emotional history, that she be a certain kind of lesbian. If the critic insists on seeing citizenship papers before admitting writers to Lesbian Nation, she may miss not only women of Sarton's generation, but also others whose independence keeps them from political alignments." The world of solitude that Sarton inhabits is not one of rarified sensibility and platitudes. The emotions in her journals and novels are strongly felt and articulated. Anger comes through especially forcefully and knowingly in fictional accounts such as *As We Are Now,* about the social disregard of the elderly, or *Anger,* about emotional repression in relationships. Anger also surfaces in Sarton's journals, particularly when she feels that her privacy has been invaded by uninvited outsiders. The solitude of May Sarton's work is a reflection of the privatization of her own life; it also serves as a source of solace. As Cruikshank remarked: "Solitude and independence have not only been natural choices for Sarton; they seem pre–conditions for her art."

—*Michael Bronski*

———

SCHULMAN, Sarah (Miriam). American novelist, journalist, playwright, and essayist. Born in New York City, 28 July 1958. Educated at Hunter College of the City University of New York. Has held a variety of jobs, including waitress, stagehand, secretary, and teacher. Full–time writer, beginning 1988. Book reviewer, *Advocate* and *New York Times Book Review*. Active in movements for social change: reproductive rights movement, gay and lesbian liberation movement, movement for tenants' rights. Member of ACT–UP, 1987—; founder with Jim Hubbard of the New York Lesbian and Gay Experimental Film Festival, 1986; cofounder of the Lesbian Avengers, 1992. **Recipient:** Kitchen Media Bureau video grant, 1982; Fulbright fellow, 1984; American Library Association Gay Book Award, 1988.

WRITINGS

Novels

The Sophie Horowitz Story. Tallahassee, Naiad Press, 1984.
Girls, Vision, and Everything. Seattle, Seal Press, 1986.
After Delores. New York, Dutton, 1988.
People in Trouble. New York, Dutton, 1990.
Empathy. New York, Dutton, 1992.
Rat Bohemia. New York, Dutton, forthcoming.

Short Stories

"The Penis Story," in *Women on Women,* edited by Joan Nestle and Naomi Holoch. New York, Dutton, 1990.

Nonfiction

My American History: Lesbian and Gay Life during the Reagan/ Bush Years. New York, Routledge, 1994.

Contributor

The Tribe of Diana: Writings by Jewish Women, edited by Melanie Kaye Kantrowitz and Irena Klepfisz. Berkeley, California, Sinister Wisdom Press, 1985.
Things that Divide Us, edited by Faith Conlon, Rachel Da Silva, and Barbara Wilson. Seattle, Seal Press, 1985.
"AIDS and Homelessness: Thousands May Die in the Streets," in *Nation,* 10 April 1989.
"Why I Fear the Future," in *Critical Fictions,* edited by Philomena Mariani. Seattle, Bay Press, 1991.
"The Surprise of the New: Five Women Writers Who Are Making a Difference," in *Advocate,* 21 May 1991.
"What Ideals Guide Our Actions? Artists, Censorship, and Building Community," in *Out–Look,* winter 1991.
Author of introduction, *Love Bites,* by Della Grace. InBook, 1991.
"Is The NEA Good for Gay Art," in *Culture Wars: Documents from the Recent Controversies in the Arts,* edited by Richard Bolton. New York, New Press, 1992.
"Special Food," in *Mother Jones,* January–February 1992.
"Getting Normal," in *Mother Jones,* March–April 1992.

Plays

With Robin Epstein, *Art Failures* (produced New York, 1983).
With Robin Epstein, *Whining and Dining* (produced New York, 1984).
And coproducer, *When We Were Very Young: Radical Jewish Women on the Lower East Side* (produced New York, 1984).
And coproducer, *The Swashbuckler* (adaptation of story by Lee Lynch; produced New York, 1985).
With Robin Epstein, *Epstein on the Beach* (three–act; produced New York, 1985).
Hootenanny Night (produced New York, 1986).
Salome/Psychology (produced New York, 1992).
Empathy (produced New York, 1993).
The Group, Guilty with an Explanation, and *1984* (produced New York, 1993).

*

Manuscript Collections: Lesbian Herstory Archives Special Collection.

Interviews: "Sarah Schulman: 'On the Road' to..." by Denise Kulp, in *Off Our Backs,* December 1986, 20; "Troubled Times" by Andrea Freud Lowenstein, in *Women's Review of Books,* July 1990, 22–23; "La Chanze," in *Interview,* November 1990, 70; "It Could Be Verse" by Eileen Myles, in *Interview,* December 1990, 48.

Critical Sources: *The Safe Sea of Women: Lesbian Fiction, 1969–1989* by Bonnie Zimmerman, Boston, Beacon Press, 1990.

Sarah Schulman comments: "The great challenge facing openly lesbian writers whose work is overtly from a lesbian perspective is to end the marginalization of our voice and see our work accepted as American literature and not a special interest novelty act."

*   *   *

Since the publication of her first novel, *The Sophie Horowitz Story,* in 1984, Sarah Schulman's fiction and essays have provided a constant reminder to writers and readers of the possibilities and responsibilities of lesbian and gay fiction. Throughout all of her writing, Schulman explores the interaction between the nature of art and the reality of politics, examining not only the inherent tensions present there but the inescapable interdependency as well. In Schulman's writing and vision, good, truthful art and politics are inextricably bound together.

Schulman was born in New York City in 1958 into a Jewish, middle–class professional family. From an early age she has been involved in progressive politics and grass roots movements for social change: the women's movement, reproductive rights, lesbian and gay liberation, tenants rights, and most recently she has devoted herself to AIDS work and to promoting lesbian empowerment. She is a founding member of both ACT–UP and the Lesbian Avengers.

After working for years as a waitress and writing essays, reviews, and news for the lesbian and gay press, she published her first novel, *The Sophie Horowitz Story,* about a lesbian reporter attempting to track down two radical feminist bank robbers who have recently resurfaced after ten years underground. Although Schulman relied upon the detective story genre to move her plot along, the novel is also a meditation on the state of lesbian politics and sexuality, as well as the potential of writing as a tool for social change. In her 1986 novel, *Girls, Visions and Everything* (the title comes from a passage in *On the Road* by Jack Kerouac), Schulman sets the action in a lesbian community on New York's lower East Side. Schulman examines the idea of pursuing personal freedom in a city, and a country, that is becoming increasingly hostile and dysfunctional. The novel begins, "Lila Futuransky always knew she wanted to be an outlaw, but she could never figure out which one. [S]he wanted to be free but couldn't decide what that meant."

All of Schulman's novels take place in Manhattan, and in them the city becomes a microcosm of social ills as well as a metaphor for the political and moral corruptions of the broader culture. Schulman insists on exploring the individual's responsibility to her community as well as to the world. In an interview in *Women's Review of Books* she states: "I write about New York City. New York is a very stratified city and your layer of protection determines your sense of responsibility ... because that is the disease of how Americans live, people don't care about something unless it affects them personally. So marginal people know how they live and how the dominant culture lives. Dominant culture people know only how they live. The people who have the most power have the least information and the smallest sense of responsibility."

This view is manifest in Schulman's next three novels. *After Delores* is a lesbian detective *noir* in which an unnamed narrator, obsessed with her ex–lover Delores, stumbles onto a murder. Set in Manhattan's East Village, the plot gives Schulman a chance to satirize various artistic types while considering what it means to be working–poor or homeless in New York. Written in the style of James M. Cain and Dashiell Hammett, *After Delores* examines the role of the isolated individual living in an emotionally and physically dangerous environment.

In *People in Trouble,* Schulman looks at the individual's responsibility to her art as well as collective social problems. *People in Trouble* begins with a quote from Karl Marx: "It is not the consciousness of men that determine their being, but their social being that determine their consciousness." This positions Schulman's idea that political and moral action are inextricably bound up with a clear understanding of material reality. Although *People in Trouble* turns on the romantic triangle of a lesbian, a cross–dressing married woman, and her husband, and is set against the background of urban real estate development, the AIDS crisis, and ACT–UP (called "Justice" here), one of the main themes in the novel is the responsibility of the artist. In her *Women's Review of Books* interview, Schulman states that when she became involved with the art world, "what I found was really appalling to me. I found this group of people who really felt that they were better than other people, more important than other people, and who looked down on other people and didn't feel any responsibility. In fact they felt that the world had a responsibility to them."

In *People in Trouble* Schulman specifically questions the idea that an artist is fulfilling her social responsibility by simply creating art and not partaking in a more active politic. The idea of belonging to—and feeling responsibility for—a group or a community permeates the book. This is a question that Schulman also discusses in the *Women's Review of Books:* "When a straight man says to me 'I don't believe in groups, I'm not a group person,' well, he belongs to the one group that's not called a group. He's unaware of the structure that he's living in. He doesn't feel the responsibility because he feels normal." The idea of the responsibility of the artist in a political world is also addressed in her essay "Why I Fear the Future," in which she quotes W. H. Auden's line, "Not one of my poems ever saved one Jew." She writes at the end of that essay, "Knowing that no large social gains can be won in this period, I still remain politically active. I do this because small victories are meaningful in individual lives. I do this because I don't want to be complicit in a future in which people will die and everyone else will be condemned to vicious banality."

This idea forms the basis for Schulman's novel *Empathy,* in which the main character, Anna O., attempts to make sense of a modern world in which the three mainstays of contemporary thinking—psychoanalysis, communism, and capitalism—are all proven failures. *Empathy* deals with some of the themes of the earlier novels—social responsibility, minoritization, urban decay—but investigates them further through formal invention in an attempt to completely link the personal (and the psychological) with the political. While *People in Trouble* pays tribute to Marx in its epitaph (as well as its analysis), *Empathy* does so to Freud, with Schulman naming two of her characters, Anna O. and Dora, after two of Freud's most famous cases. Schulman also views the work as a challenge to the false linearity of the "coming–out novel," attempting to address the creation of lesbian identity formally as well as in the content of the novel.

Schulman's fiction addresses the very pertinent question of how we might be able to live responsibly and fruitfully in a politically corrupt world. Her political work with ACT–UP and the Lesbian Avengers, as well as other social action groups, has been a major influence on her writing. Her role as an artist has been guided by her political actions and ideals, and she steadfastly refuses to view "art" and "artists" as separate from or above political concerns.

—*Michael Bronski*

SCOPPETTONE, Sandra. American novelist and playwright. Has also written as Jack Early. Born in Morristown, New Jersey, 1 June 1936. Companion of writer Linda Crawford. Full–time professional writer. **Recipient:** Eugene O'Neill Memorial Theatre Award, 1972; Ludwig Vogelstein Foundation grant, 1974; New Jersey Institute of Technology New Jersey Authors Award, 1976; California Reading Association California Young Readers Medal (high school), 1979; (as Jack Early) Private Eye Writers of America Shamus Award, 1985; (as Jack Early) Mystery Writers of America Edgar Allan Poe Award nomination, 1985; Mystery Writers of America Edgar Allan Poe Award nomination for *Playing Murder*, 1986. Agent: Charlotte Sheedy, Sheedy Agency, 611 Broadway, New York, New York 10012, U.S.A.

WRITINGS

Novels

Some Unknown Person. New York, Putnam, 1977.
Such Nice People. New York, Putnam, 1980.
Innocent Bystanders. New York, New American Library, 1983.

"Lauren Laurano" Mystery Series

Everything You Have Is Mine. Boston, Little, Brown, 1991.
I'll Be Leaving You Always. Boston, Little, Brown, 1993.

Novels as Jack Early

A Creative Kind of Killer. New York, F. Watts, 1984.
Razzamatazz. New York, F. Watts, 1985.
Donato and Daughter. New York, Dutton, 1988.

Young Adult Fiction

Trying Hard to Hear You. New York, Harper, 1974.
The Late Great Me. New York, Putnam, 1976.
Happy Endings Are All Alike. New York, Harper, 1978.
Long Time between Kisses. New York, Harper, 1982.
Playing Murder. New York, Harper, 1985.

Children's Fiction

Suzuki Beane, illustrations by Louise Fitzhugh. Garden City, New York, Doubleday, 1961.
Bang Bang You're Dead, illustrations by Louise Fitzhugh. New York, Harper, 1968.

Plays

Home Again, Home Again Jiggity Jig (produced New York, 1969).

Something for Kitty Genovese (produced, 1971).
Stuck (produced Waterford, Connecticut, 1972; New York, 1976).

Screenplays

Scarecrow in a Garden of Cucumbers, Maron–New Line, 1972.
The Inspector of Stairs, Independent, 1975.

Television Plays

Love of Life, CBS–TV, 1972.
A Little Bit Like Murder, ABC–TV, 1973.

*

Adaptations: *The Late Great Me* was filmed by Daniel Wilson Productions, 1982; a teleplay based on *Donato and Daughter* was produced by CBS, 1993.

Manuscript Collections: Kerlan Collection, University of Missouri.

Interviews: With Susan M. Reicha, in *Authors and Artists for Young Adults,* Volume 11, Detroit, Gale, 1993.

Critical Sources: *Speaking for Ourselves,* compiled and edited by Donald R. Gallo, Urbana, Illinois, National Council of Teachers of English, 1990, 186–187; "Murder, She Writes" by Michael Lassell, in *Advocate,* 2 July 1991, 93.

* * *

Much of Sandra Scoppettone's young adult and adult fiction originates in her personal experience as an alcoholic, victim of incest, and lesbian. Scoppettone fills her novels with well–drawn characters in emotionally charged situations. These characters, such as the gay teenage boys in *Trying Hard to Hear You,* the young lesbian lovers in *Happy Endings Are All Alike,* and the lesbian private eye in *Everything You Have Is Mine,* challenge society's conventional assumptions about life and the necessary components for happiness. "I think my childhood traumas had a lot to do with shaping me as a writer," revealed Scoppettone in an interview for *Authors and Artists for Young Adults (AAYA).*

Immediately following graduation from high school, Scoppettone left her overprotective parents in South Orange, New Jersey, and moved to New York City to pursue a writing career. She entered the world of young adult fiction after the publication of two collaborative picture books with Louise Fitzhugh. Scoppettone's first effort in this genre, *Trying Hard to Hear You,* grew out of an experience she had while directing a play for a "Youth on Stage" program in Long Island. The novel presents two sensitive teenage boys, Phil and Jeff, who are discovered to be homosexual and are subsequently ostracized by their group of friends. Told from the viewpoint of 16–year–old Camilla Crawford, Jeff's best friend, the story intensifies when Phil breaks under the pressure and decides to "prove" his sexuality with a girl; the two get drunk and are killed in a car crash. Banned by many libraries because of its subject matter, *Try-*

ing Hard to Hear You presents compassionate characters and realistically portrays typical teenage reactions to homosexuality. Scoppettone also introduces a correlation between the racism encountered by a young interracial couple and the homophobia Phil and Jeff experience. As Camilla accepts Jeff's sexual orientation, she learns that love may find expression in a myriad of ways and Scoppettone makes it clear that the homosexual expression of love is as acceptable and valid as any other.

Happy Endings Are All Alike, a powerful story of lesbianism and rape, was also banned. "That's the one that got the least attention when I wrote it, the least reviews, the least anything. It sold the least because it's about girls," Scoppettone noted. Published in 1978, *Happy Endings Are All Alike* focuses on the lesbian relationship between two teenage girls in a small American town. Jaret and Peggy are spending a loving summer together when Peggy decides to test her sexual orientation by dating a young man. In the meantime, a jealous youth who has been spying on the two girls savagely beats and rapes Jaret, threatening to reveal her lesbianism if she tells anyone. Scoppettone includes the whole spectrum of reactions to lesbianism in *Happy Endings Are All Alike.* Jaret's family accepts her sexual identity and supports her decision to bring charges against her assailant. Others in the community, however, display varying degrees of prejudice. In addition to realistically portraying homosexuality in the novel, Scoppettone also includes a brutal portrayal of rape, leaving no illusions about the violence inherent in the crime. *Happy Endings Are All Alike* concludes as an affirmation of individuality.

Scoppettone's recent adult works are even more personally based than her young adult ones. Having previously written detective/mystery novels under the pseudonym Jack Early, in 1991 Scoppettone created private eye Lauren Laurano for the first mainstream lesbian detective book to be published, *Everything You Have Is Mine.* Laurano is a short, Italian lesbian who loves chocolate, gets queasy at the sight of blood, and has lived with the same partner for a number of years—similarly, Scoppettone is half–Italian and a chocoholic, and has lived with writer Linda Crawford for over twenty years. A wise–cracking feminist, Laurano spends her first adventure trying to solve a rape case that quickly turns into a murder investigation. Although the mystery in *Everything You Have Is Mine* becomes somewhat convoluted, Scoppettone accurately captures the essence of the Greenwich Village and presents a spirited, articulate character in Laurano. The next book featuring Laurano, *I'll Be Leaving You Always,* has the sleuth dealing with the death of a close friend and solving the murder at the same time. Scoppettone commented that she hopes the books featuring Laurano will help women "feel prouder and have more self–esteem as lesbians. I think it's already happening."

—Susan M. Reicha

SHAW, T. E. *See* **LAWRENCE, T(homas) E(dward).**

SHERMAN, Martin. American dramatist. Born in Philadelphia, Pennsylvania, in 1938. Educated at Boston University, B.A. in theater and M.F.A. Playwright–in–residence at Mills College in Oakland, California, and at Playwrights Horizons in New York City, 1976–77; affiliated with Ensemble Studio Theatre in New York City. **Recipient:** Wurlitzer Foundation of New Mexico residency grant, 1973; Dramatist Guild's Elizabeth Hull–Kate Warriner Award, 1979, and League of New York Theaters and Producers' Antoinette Perry Award nomination, 1980, both for stage play; National Endowment for the Arts fellowship, 1980. Agents: Johnnie Planko, William Morris Agency, 1350 Avenue of the Americas, New York, New York 10019, U.S.A.; Margaret Ramsay Ltd., 14A Goodwins Court, London WC2N 4LL, England.

WRITINGS

Plays

Fat Tuesday (produced New York).
Next Year in Jerusalem (produced New York, 1968).
The Night Before Paris (produced Edinburgh and New York). Published in *The Best Short Plays of 1970,* Radnor, Chilton, 1970.
Things Went Badly in Westphalia (produced Storrs, Connecticut). Published in *The Best Short Plays of 1970,* Radnor, Chilton, 1970.
Passing By (produced Australia; New York, 1974; London, 1975). Published in *Gay Plays,* New York, Methuen, 1984.
Cracks (produced Waterford, England, 1975; New York, 1976). Published in *Gay Plays: Volume Two,* New York, Methuen, 1985.
Soaps (produced New York, 1975).
New York! New York! (omnibus; produced New York, 1975).
Rio Grande (produced New York, 1976).
Bent (produced Waterford, England, 1978; London and New York, 1979). London, Amber Lane Press, 1979; New York, Avon, 1980.
Messiah (produced London, 1982; New York, 1984). London, Amber Lane Press, 1982.
A Madhouse in Goa (produced London, 1989).
When She Danced (produced New York, 1990).
A Solitary Thing (produced Oakland, California).
Change (musical), lyrics by Ed Kresley, music by Drey Shepperd. With Drey Shepperd, *Delta Lady.*

Television Plays

Movements, BBC.
Don't Call Me Mama Anymore, CBS–TV.

*

Interviews: "Behind the Scenes At Broadway's Big Shocker *Bent*—Playwright Martin Sherman" by Terry Helbing, in *Advocate,* 10 January 1980, 29, 33; "Martin Sherman on *Bent,* The Problems and Pride of a Gay Play Heard around the World" by David Galligan, in *Advocate,* 9 June 1987, 64–65, 124.

Critical Sources: "'Bent,' Starring Richard Gere" by Walter Kerr, in *New York Times,* 3 December 1979; "Surviving" by Brendan Gill, in *New Yorker,* 17 December 1979, 100–102; review of *A Madhouse in Goa* by William A. Henry III, in *Time,* 3 July 1989, 73; review of

When She Danced in *New Yorker,* 26 February 1990, 98; review of
When She Danced, in *New York,* 5 March 1990, 57.

*   *   *

The career of playwright Martin Sherman has been marked by
the production of works that directly address deeply human issues
as experienced by recognizable people under the restraint of varied
social norms. Born in Philadelphia, Sherman attended Boston University for both undergraduate and graduate training in the fine arts
and made his writing debut with the one–act play *Next Year in
Jerusalem* in 1968. While much of his work was first produced in
the Off–Off–Broadway theaters of New York and by small companies in Australia and Great Britain, he has gone on to make a significant contribution to gay and lesbian literature. Sherman's contribution is best seen in *Passing By,* in 1974, *Cracks,* produced the
following year, and *Bent* in 1979, a powerful dramatic depiction of
the fate of gay people in Nazi Germany.

Passing By is the story of the development, flowering, and abandonment of a relationship between two men in the gay world of
New York in the mid–1970s. It would also prove to be the precursor of later plays by Sherman that would chronicle the horror and
courage of the AIDS pandemic. In *Passing By,* the relationship
between the main characters is tested—not by an unknown virus
such as AIDS but by hepatitis, at the time equally frightening and
uncontrollable, if not fatal. Sherman's dramatic protagonists represent two accepted conventional images of gay career stereotypes:
one is a painter given to hysterics (with some parallels to the title
character of Lanford Wilson's 1964 *The Madness of Lady Bright*)
while the other is an Olympic diver who coolly takes great pride in
his physical prowess and mirrors the standard clone image of the
day. The relationship between the two men eventually falters—not
because of lack of emotional commitment but due to their focus on
career goals rather than personal ones. *Cracks,* the next of Sherman's
work to include homosexuals in the plot, is set in the Los Angeles
home of a recently murdered rock star. The range of characters in
Cracks consists of guests at a party, each suspected of having
committed the crime. Among the characters is a gay man who desires to become a monk and who vows never again to engage in sex
outside the convent walls. The assemblage of stereotyped characters is clearly a satire on the wild Hollywood parties of the 1970's,
a satire heightened by the gradual elimination of the cast by a sharp-
shooter.

While both *Cracks* and *Passing By* are clearly included within
the body of writing comprising "gay theater," the scope of power,
passion, and humanity possible in that genre is best exemplified by
Bent. This play, produced in 1978, is significant in that it was the
first play to publicly depict the treatment of gay people under the
Nazi regime and their incarceration in concentration camps during
World War II. Their camp uniforms carried a pink triangle identifying them as homosexuals—this symbol would later be resurrected
as a mark of pride by the American gay community following the
Stonewall Riots of 1969. The idea for *Bent* originated in 1977, when
Sherman was asked to assist England's gay theater group, Gay
Sweatshop, with its production of Drew Griffiths' and Noel Greig's
cabaret play *As Time Goes By.* It is organized as a three–part historical drama about the gay and lesbian community in England: it
moves from 1896, shortly after the trial of Oscar Wilde, through
Weimar Germany from the stock market disaster until 1934 and the

coming of Nazism, through to the United States and the patrons of
the Stonewall Inn.

In the second section of the play, references to the "pink tri-
angles" appear. The appearance, earlier in 1974, in an issue of *Christopher Street,* of an article by historian Richard Plant on the fate of
homosexuals under Nazism, sparked Sherman's interest in further
exploring the subject. The results of that exploration, *Bent* opens in
Berlin in 1934 during the "Night of the Long Knives," a purge of
homosexuals from the ranks of the Nazi Party membership by
Adolf Hitler that resulted in the death of Ernst Rohm, chief of the
Brown Shirts, as well as dozens of other German officers. It tells
the story of two gay men, Max and Rudy, who had the misfortune
to bring home one of the men marked out for death. As witnesses to
their guest's murder, they flee into hiding, only to be eventually
caught and packed aboard a prison train where Rudy is beaten to
death. In the concentration camp, Max avoids identification as a
homosexual by claiming to be a Jew, thus witnessing the abuse
heaped on the homosexual inmates by guards, who considered gays
to be the lowest form of life. Prior to his own death, Max reclaims
his gay identity through a relationship with another prisoner. The
initial performances of *Bent* during its London premiere season
were met with acclaim mixed with anger at having memories of the
war years revived.

The most recent work by Sherman involving elements of the gay
and lesbian world is the 1989 drama *A Madhouse in Goa.* In structure it is actually two one–act plays, each set amid the romantic
isles of Greece, reminiscent of Lanford Wilson's *Hot l Baltimore* in
that the action occurs among residents of a guesthouse. One of the
main characters is a young American trying to recover from a failed
homosexual love affair. In the second act, set in the early 1990s, it
emerges that the first act of the play was not, in fact, reality but
rather a creation of one of the main characters based on an incident
from his past. The fate of the other guests is spelled out, with one
diagnosed as infected with AIDS. The complete destruction of the
island itself via a volcanic eruption mirrors both the archaeologi-
cally documented end of the island of Thera—a possible source of the
myth of Atlantis—and the parallel erasure of the gay world as it
existed before the casual horrors of the 1980s.

—*Robert B. Marks Ridinger*

———

SHILTS, Randy. American journalist, biographer, and author of
nonfiction. Born in Davenport, Iowa, 8 August 1951. Attended
University of Oregon, B.S. 1975. KQED–TV, San Francisco, correspondent for *Newsroom* and City Hall correspondent for *Ten
O'Clock News,* 1977–80; KTVU–TV, Oakland, California, reporter,
1979–80; *San Francisco Chronicle,* staff reporter, 1981–87, national correspondent, 1988—. Contributor of hundreds of articles
to *San Francisco Chronicle.* Frequent lecturer at universities, professional association gatherings, and national health organization
conferences. **Recipient:** American Society of Journalists and Authors' Outstanding Author Award, 1988; Association for Education in Journalism and Mass Communication's Professional Excellence Award, 1988; Bay Area Book Reviewers' Association Award
for Nonfiction, 1988; American Medical Writers Association's John

P. McGovern Award Lectureship in Medical Writing, 1989; appointed to a Mather Lectureship; named University of Oregon Outstanding Young Alumnus, 1993; Parents and Friends of Lesbians and Gays' Oscar Wilde Award, 1993; California Public Health Association's Outstanding Print Media Award, 1993. Address: c/o *San Francisco Chronicle,* 901 Mission Street, San Francisco, California 94103, U.S.A.

WRITINGS

Biography

The Mayor of Castro Street: The Life and Times of Harvey Milk. New York, St. Martin's Press, 1982.

Nonfiction

And The Band Played On: Politics, People and the AIDS Epidemic. New York, St. Martin's Press, 1987.
Conduct Unbecoming: Lesbians and Gays in the U.S. Military; Vietnam to the Persian Gulf. New York, St. Martin's Press, 1993.

Uncollected Nonfiction

"Talking AIDS to Death?," in *Esquire,* March 1989.
"Is Outing Gays Ethical?," in *New York Times,* 12 April 1990.
"Naming Names," in *Gentleman's Quarterly,* August 1990.
"The Year of the Queer: The Queering of America," in *Advocate,* 1 January 1991.
"Claim Your Gay, Avoid the Draft," in *New York Times,* 7 January 1991.
"The Nasty Business of Outing," in *Los Angeles Times,* 7 August 1991.
"Speak for All, Magic," in *Sports Illustrated,* 18 November 1991.
"Good AIDS, Bad AIDS," in *New York Times,* 10 December 1991.
"What's Fair in Love and War," in *Newsweek,* 1 February 1993.

*

Adaptations: *The Mayor of Castro Street: The Life and Times of Harvey Milk* (film) directed by Oliver Stone, Warner Brothers, c. 1994; *And The Band Played On: Politics, People and the AIDS Epidemic* (television production), Home Box Office, 1993; *Conduct Unbecoming: Lesbians and Gays in the U.S. Military; Vietnam to the Persian Gulf* (television movie), Home Box Office, c. 1994.

Manuscript Collections: Gay and Lesbian Archives, San Francisco Public Library.

Interviews: With P. Holt, in *Publishers Weekly,* 19 March 1982, 6–7; *Contemporary Authors,* Volume 127, Gale, 1989; *Publishers Weekly,* 5 January 1990, 22–23; with Laurie Udesky, in *Progressive,* May 1991, 30; "AIDS and the Media" by John Katz, in *Rolling Stone,* May 1993, 31–32; "The Life and Times of Randy Shilts" by Jeff Yarborough, in *Advocate,* 15 June 1993, 32–39; "The Plutarch of Castro Street" by Mike Weiss, in *West,* 4 July 1993, 8–15.

Critical Sources: "The Making of an Epidemic" by Jim Miller and Pamela Abramson, in *Newsweek,* 19 October 1987, 91; "Unhealthy Resistance" by Daniel S. Greenberg, in *Nation,* 7 November 1987, 526; "Plenty of Blame to Go Around" by H. Jack Geiger, in *New York Times Book Review,* 8 November 1987, 9; "Cries and Whispers of an Epidemic" by Ron Bluestein, in *Advocate,* 24 November 1987, 52–53, 63–67; "A Brief but Deadly History" by Henry Klingeman, in *National Review,* 4 December 1987, 50–52; review by John Stark of *And the Band Played On,* in *People,* 18 January 1988, 16; "An End to the Silence" by Duncan Campbell, in *New Statesman,* 4 March 1988, 22; review by John S. Sullivan of *And the Band Played On,* in *America,* 4 June 1988, 588; "AIDS without End" by Diane Johnson and John F. Murray, in *New York Review of Books,* 18 August 1988, 57–63; review of *And the Band Played On,* in *Progressive,* December 1988, 45; review by Joe Wakelee–Lynch of *And the Band Played On,* in *Utne Reader,* January–February 1991, 136; "A Disease of Society" by Jeffrey Weeks, in *New Statesman,* 26 April 1991, 32; "Well–Known Author on AIDS Reveals He Has the Disease" by Leah Garchik, in *Detroit Free Press,* 17 February 1993, 3C.

* * *

In some ways, Randy Shilts has set the standard by which other works of gay journalism are to be judged. Beginning with his work as an openly gay journalist during college, he moved quickly into the gay press, coming to San Francisco in 1975 as part of the staff of the *Advocate.* His research for a series of articles on gay public health problems, which appeared until 1978, provided a framework of reference for later assessments of the impact of AIDS. His unique position as a reporter in the mainstream press whose beat was specifically designated as the gay community began in 1977 at KQED–TV. An outgrowth of his free–lance reporting prior to his staff position at the *San Francisco Chronicle,* his writing has ranged from book reviews and analytical pieces on movement organizations for major gay and lesbian periodicals through news reports on the complex politics of the Bay Area gay and lesbian community culminating in three major works of contemporary gay social commentary and historiography, *The Mayor of Castro Street: The Life and Times of Harvey Milk, And the Band Played On: Politics, People and the AIDS Epidemic,* and *Conduct Unbecoming: Lesbians and Gays in the U.S. Military.*

The Mayor of Castro Street marks the beginning of modern gay and lesbian political biography. Based upon numerous personal interviews and public records, it is the story of the career and assassination of San Francisco Supervisor Harvey Milk, the first openly gay elected public official in the United States. Through the events in Milk's life, Shilts also details the coalescence of gays as a force in San Francisco and California state political life, in particular the campaign against Proposition Six, a legislative initiative aimed at removing homosexual teachers from all California schools. With the exception of *The Crusaders,* a 1972 compilation by Kay Tobin and Randy Wicker of the biographies of prominent activists, *The Mayor of Castro Street* stands as one of the few full–length biographies available on gay and lesbian leaders. It would be joined subsequently by such works as Troy Perry's *Don't Be Afraid Anymore* and Mike Hippler's *Matlovich: The Good Soldier,* illustrating the breadth of the developing genre.

With the appearance of the AIDS epidemic in late 1981, the face of the American gay and lesbian community was altered forever. As the only reporter working for a major city newspaper exclusively assigned to covering the gay and lesbian community in a city that was being devastated by the disease, Shilts was in a unique position to gather information on both the slow progress of medical research on the virus and the federal government's lack of response to the crisis. In his second book, *And the Band Played On*, Shilts initially presents the human faces of the epidemic at the research laboratories of the National Institute of Health, spotlights local clinics in many cities, and discusses the ever–increasing number of confused, frightened, and angry victims. The final section covers the massive demonstration in Washington, D.C., in 1987, by which time more than 20,000 Americans had died of the disease. *And the Band Played On* created the framework of analysis which later works such as James Kinsella's *Covering the Plague: AIDS and the American Media* would utilize.

One of the most controversial issues for advocates of equal rights for homosexuals has been the historic position taken by the United States armed services that such persons were unsuitable for military life and were to be summarily discharged if discovered. While several internal studies by various branches and numerous articles in the gay and lesbian press repeatedly called for change, little was done to formally research and document the origins and impact of these policies. The first major works on the subject were Allan Bérubé's *Coming Out under Fire: The History of Gay Men and Women in World War Two* and *Gays in Uniform: The Pentagon's Secret Reports,* both published in 1990. The latter reprinted the full texts of two reports and several memoranda from the Defense Personnel Security Research and Education Center done in 1988 and 1989 on the issue of the suitability of gays and lesbians for military service. Both reports found no substantive grounds for the historic prohibition. Shilts' third book, *Conduct Unbecoming,* picks up the subject where Bérubé's earlier analysis ceased and follows the changing conditions of life for the military's gay cadre from the Vietnam War to Operation Desert Storm. Personal accounts of both enlisted personnel and career officers of both genders form the bulk of the text and illumine established policy. The situationally flexible ethics of application of the formal ban on homosexuals in the armed forces during periods of exigency such as Vietnam and the Korean War, both in recruitment and training and under field conditions is a constant theme.

—*Robert B. Marks Ridinger*

SHOCKLEY, Ann Allen. American novelist and author of short stories. Born in Louisville, Kentucky, 21 June 1927. Educated at Fisk University, Nashville, Tennessee, B.A. 1948; Western Reserve University (now Case Western University), Cleveland, Ohio, M.S.L.S. 1959. Divorced; one son and one daughter. Assistant librarian, Delaware State College, Dover, 1959–60; assistant librarian, 1960–66, associate librarian, 1966–69, and curator of Negro collection, Maryland State College (now University of Maryland Eastern Shore), Princess Anne; associate librarian and head of special collections, 1969–75, associate librarian for public services, beginning 1975, now associate librarian for special collections, university archivist, and associate professor of library science, Fisk University. Lecturer at University of Maryland, 1968, Jackson

State College, 1973, and Vanderbilt University. **Recipient:** American Association of University Women short story award, 1962; Fisk University faculty research grant, 1970; University of Maryland Library Administrators Development Institute fellowship, 1974; American Library Association Black Caucus award, 1975; American Library Association Task Force Book Award nomination, 1980; Hatshepsut Award for literature, 1981; Martin Luther King, Jr., Black Author Award, 1982; Susan Koppelman Award, 1988; Outlook Award for outstanding pioneering contribution to lesbian and gay writing, 1990; American Library Association Black Caucus Award for professional achievement, 1992. Agent: Carole Abel, 160 West 87th Street, 7D, New York, New York 10024, U.S.A. Address: Fisk University, 17th Avenue North, Nashville, Tennessee 37203, U.S.A.

WRITINGS

Novels

Loving Her. Indianapolis, Indiana, Bobbs–Merrill, 1974.
Say Jesus and Come to Me. New York, Avon, 1982.

Short Stories

"Abraham and the Spirit," in *Negro Digest,* July 1950.
"The Picture Prize," in *Negro Digest,* October 1962.
"A Far Off Sound," in *Umbra,* December 1963.
"The Funeral," in *Phylon* (Atlanta), spring 1967.
"The President," in *Freedomways,* fourth quarter 1970.
"Crying for Her Man," in *Liberator,* January–February 1971.
"Is She Relevant?," in *Black World,* January 1971.
"Her Own Thing," in *Black America,* August 1972.
"Ah: The Young Black Poet," in *New Letters* (Kansas City, Missouri), winter 1974.
"The More Things Change," in *Essence* (New York), October 1977.
"A Case of Telemania," in *Azalea,* fall 1978.
"The Black Lesbian in American Literature: An Overview," in *Conditions: Five,* autumn 1979.
The Black and White of It (includes "Play It, but Don't Say It," "Holly Craft Isn't Gay," "Home to Meet the Folks," "A Birthday Remembered," and "A Meeting of the Sapphic Daughters"). Tallahassee, Naiad Press, 1980.
"Women in a Southern Time," in *Feminary,* 1982.

Nonfiction

A History of Public Library Services to Negroes in the South, 1900–1955 (monograph). Dover, Delaware State College, 1960.
"Does the Negro College Library Need a Special Negro Collection?," in *Library Journal,* June 1961.
"The Negro Woman in Retrospect: Blueprint for the Future," in *Negro History Bulletin* (Washington, D.C.), December 1965.
"Tell It Like It Is: A New Criteria for Children's Books in Black and White," in *Southeastern Libraries,* spring 1970.
A Handbook for the Administration of Special Negro Collections. Nashville, Tennessee, Fisk University Library, 1970; as *The Administration of Special Black Collections,* 1974.
A Manual for the Black Oral History Program. Nashville, Tennessee, Fisk University Library, 1971.

"Pauline Elizabeth Hopkins: A Biographical Excursion into Obscurity," in *Phylon* (Atlanta), spring 1972.

With Sue P. Chandler, *Living Black American Authors: A Biographical Directory.* New York, Bowker, 1973.

"American Anti–Slavery Literature: An Overview—1693–1859," in *Negro History Bulletin* (Washington, D.C.), April–May 1974.

With Veronica E. Tucker, "Black Women Discuss Today's Problems: Men, Families, Societies," in *Southern Voices,* August–September 1974.

"The New Black Feminists," in *Northwest Journal of African and Black American Studies,* winter 1974.

"Black Publishers and Black Librarians: A Necessary Union," in *Black World,* March 1975.

"Joseph S. Cotter, Sr.: Biographical Sketch of a Black Louisville Bard," in *College Language Association Journal,* March 1975.

"Oral History: A Research Tool for Black History," in *Negro History Bulletin* (Washington, D.C.), January–February 1978.

"The Black Lesbian in American Literature," in *Conditions: Five,* autumn 1979.

"Black Lesbian Biography: Lifting the Veil," in *Other Black Woman,* 1982.

Editor

With E. J. Josey, and contributor, *Handbook of Black Librarianship.* Littleton, Colorado, Libraries Unlimited, 1977.

Afro–American Women Writers, 1746–1933: An Anthology and Critical Guide. Boston, G. K. Hall, 1988.

Other

Contributor, *Impressions in Asphalt* (anthology), edited by Ruthe T. Sheffey and Eugnia Collier. New York, Scribner, 1969.

Contributor, *Black Librarian in America,* edited by E. J. Josey. Metuchen, New Jersey, Scarecrow Press, 1970.

Contributor, *Library Lit. 5,* edited by Bill Katz and Robert Burgess. Metuchen, New Jersey, Scarecrow Press, 1975.

Contributor, *Out of Our Lives: A Selection of Contemporary Black Fiction,* edited by Quandra Prettyman Stadler. Washington, D.C., Howard University Press, 1975.

Contributor, *True to Life Adventure Stories,* edited by Judy Graham. Oakland, California, Diana Press, 1978.

*

Biography: *Dictionary of Literary Biography,* Volume 33: *Afro–American Fiction Writers after 1955,* Detroit, Gale, 1984, 232–236.

Bibliography: *Ann Allen Shockley: An Annotated Primary and Secondary Bibliography* by Rita B. Dandridge, New York, Greenwood Press, 1987.

Critical Sources: "Comprehensive Oppression: Lesbians and Race in the Work of Ann Allen Shockley" by Evelyn C. White, in *Backbone 3,* 1979, 38–40; "Deny, Deny, Deny" (review of *The Black and White of It*) by Karla Jay, in *New Women's Times Feminist Review,* April/May 1981, 17–18; review by Rebecca Sue Taylor of

Say Jesus and Come to Me, in *Library Journal,* 1 May 1982; unpublished letter to Rita Dandridge, 29 January 1984; "Theme and Portraiture in the Fiction of Ann Allen Shockley" (dissertation) by SDiane Bogus, Miami University, 1988.

*   *   *

Ann Allen Shockley put the black lesbian character into twentieth–century American literature. Though not without precedent in such early novels as *Young Man with a Horn* and *Home to Harlem,* but without the currency of the socio–political epithet "Black lesbian," the black woman–loving–woman was never a main character in a novel nor even validated as a human being until Shockley wrote her in. Afterwards came others, notably, the title character in Toni Morrison's *Sula* and Celie in Alice Walker's *The Color Purple.* As a unit, Shockley's three principle fictions which feature black lesbians, *Loving Her, The Black and White of It,* and *Say Jesus and Come to Me,* all explore what Rebecca Sue Taylor in *Library Journal* calls "the triple hardship of being female, Black and lesbian," but in the work of Shockley—not to minimize the import—always there is more at issue than gender, sexual expression, and race. Shockley's fictions demonstrate what I called "the paradigm of the considered whole" in "Theme and Portraiture in the Fictions of Ann Allen Shockley." That is, Shockley provides a reader with an all–inclusive view of the single life of a given twentieth–century character by exaggerating the forces that play upon that life.

In *Loving Her,* the major character Renay Johnson is a young black mother, an emerging lesbian, a working class woman with the aspirations of a classic pianist. If this is not a formula for conflict, add the advent of a first–time sexual and interracial experience with an upper–middle–class white woman, the physical abuse of an alcoholic and ne'er–do–well husband, alienation from her mother and friends, and the death of her preteen daughter, and one gets the classic Shockley composition.

In *The Black and White of It,* a testy and much maligned collection of short stories that show black lesbian women in various walks of life from professor to student, slave to singer, senator to mother, and heterosexual to bisexual, Shockley stratifies the conditions of black lesbian lives but does not relieve the reader of the impression of the aggravated circumstances of such lives. *The Black and White of It* demonstrates that black lesbian lives, collected over time and played out day–to–day, are constrained by all the frustration, resentment, joylessness, desperation and oppression that homophobia and racism leave as byproducts, but the collection declares that to some degree, the moral or ethic code of the Black lesbian character also contributes to her pain and unrelieved unhappiness. Within the stories, Shockley demonstrates the contradictions in the lesbian characters' lives by magnifying the moral flaws in the character against the larger and more oppressive social constructs.

One of the short stories in *The Black and White of It,* entitled "Play It but Don't Say It," depicts a cold, grasping black lesbian senator and compulsive eater named Mattie Brown who denies her lesbianism for fear of exposure and for want of power. Like Holly Craft, a singer who marries to hide her homosexuality in "Holly Craft Is Not Gay," and Lynn, the confused femme in "The Play," who, though lesbian, seeks out men (in the presence of her lover) to validate her femininity, Mattie suffers from a lack of pride or self–esteem, from misplaced values, and from the lack of conviction regarding her choices. When Brown is asked by a room of reporters if she "planned to support legislation in favor of homosexuals that would be especially beneficial to the triple jeopardy associated with black lesbians," she responds, "This is not my concern. You see, there are no such black women." Back in the privacy of their room, Mattie's lover and political secretary, who was present at the interview, asks, "For God's sake, what do you think we are?" For this question, she is slapped. Before the story ends, Mattie has gotten rid of her. The story closes with Mattie going "automatically to the kitchen," an ancillary notation about the relationship between pain and food and how women stuff themselves to stuff the pain—a seemingly irrelevant and anticlimactic ending to a typical Shockley composition.

Critics are almost unanimous in their recognition of the defeatism that characterizes the lives of women in *The Black and White of It.* Evelyn White, in a *Backbone* essay, remarked: "These stories ... have certain debilitating effects. They also inspire very crucial questions about lesbian integrity and respect." Further, Karla Jay, writing in *New Women's Times Feminist Review,* stated, "If we can criticize Shockley, it is for the profusion of denial, the profusion of alcohol. We can secretly hope that she presents things out of proportion, but more likely she honestly portrays the oppressive existence of some closeted, self–destructive lesbians whom we have not reached with our movement." But Shockley is not as bleak as all of that. The "paradigm of the considered whole" dictates a balanced view of the lives of lesbians, and although the overall impression of *The Black and White of It* may be bleak, the work contains stories that validate lesbian relationships in the face of oppression, such as "The Mistress and the Slave Girl," a woman–loving–woman story of a plantation owner and her black house servant during slavery. Quite purposely and purposefully, "Birthday Remembered," "A Special Evening," and "Women in a Southern Time" in this collection serve as counterpoints to the "bleak" portraiture of the lonely spinster professor who takes a student as lover, or the wife who sneaks away to be with her weekend female lover, or the woman in "Love Motion" who fakes orgasm with her husband as she fantasizes about women. Speaking of her work in a letter to Rita Dandridge, her foremost critic and bibliographer, Shockley said, "I consider myself a social[ly] conscious writer." Indeed, her social consciousness is best noted in *Say Jesus and Come to Me.*

In *Say Jesus and Come to Me,* Shockley's intention, she told Dandridge, was to "expose the conservatism and snobbishness of the Black Middle class and academicians.... The Black male oppression of women; the superior attitudes and opportunism of some white women towards Black women in the liberation movement, and even to touch the local (Nashville, Tennessee) music scene." Instead of focusing squarely on "obliterating women's oppression," the ideal espoused by one of the white female feminist characters of the book, Shockley asserts, through main character and lesbian minister Myrtle Black: "I am going to insist on moralistic and humanitarian objectives.... All too frequently they are what get lost in movements." Shockley's work in this satirical book about moral conversion and feminist conviction in the very heterosexual South seems to advocate all her familiar and time–tested themes—the religious and spiritual nature of people and its influence upon their lives, interracial relations, black male and female relations, the psyches of men, and the lives of women, lesbian or otherwise. I believe in *Say Jesus,* as in all of Shockley's work, her narratives are proof of her own moral idealism. However satiric, cynical, or ridiculing her work may appear, however ambiguous and sketchily developed, there is always a reasonable hope for unity, solidarity, brotherhood, honor, nobility, and honesty among people. Possessor of a forensic

rather than a belletristic literary style, Shockley's work provides no great symbols or metaphor, no elements of the beloved black folk tale, but it represents a realistic, though Spartan whole, a view of lives today which compound the problems and possibilities of being human in twentieth–century America.

—SDiane A. Bogus

SILVER, Carol. *See* **GRAHN, Judy.**

SMITH, Barbara. American editor and essayist. Born in Cleveland, Ohio, 16 November 1946. Educated at Mount Holyoke College, South Hadley, Massachusetts, B.A. 1969; University of Pittsburgh, Pennsylvania, M.A. 1971. Instructor, University of Massachusetts, 1976–81, Barnard College, 1983, New York University, 1985; visiting professor, University of Minnesota, 1986, Hobart William Smith College, 1987. Director of Kitchen Table—Women of Color Press. Member and founder of Combahee River Collective, 1974–80; artist in residence, Hambidge Center for the Arts and Sciences, 1983, Millay Colony for the Arts, 1983, Yaddo, 1984, Blue Mountain Center, 1985; member of board of directors, National Coalition of Black Lesbians and Gays, 1985—; member of National Association for the Advancement of Colored Persons. **Recipient:** Outstanding Woman of Color Award, 1982; Women Educator's Curriculum Award, 1983. Address: c/o Kitchen Table—Women of Color, P.O. Box 908, Latham, New York 12110, U.S.A.

WRITINGS

Nonfiction

Toward a Black Feminist Criticism. Brooklyn, New York, Out & Out Books, 1980.
With Elly Bulkin and Minnie Bruce Pratt, *Yours in Struggle: Three Feminist Perspectives on Anti–Semitism and Racism.* New York, Long Haul Press, 1984; with new introduction, Ithaca, New York, Firebrand, 1988.

Editor

With Lorraine Bethel, *Conditions: Five* (black women's issue), 1979.
With Gloria T. Hull and Patricia Bell Scott, *All the Women Are White, All the Blacks Are Men, But Some of Us Are Brave: Black Women's Studies.* New York, Feminist Press at the City University of New York, 1981.
Home Girls: A Black Feminist Anthology. New York, Kitchen Table Press, 1983.

Other

"Towards a Black Feminist Criticism," in *Conditions: Two,* 1977.

With Beverly Smith, "I Am Not Meant to be Alone and Without You Who Understand: Letters from Black Feminists," in *Conditions: Four,* 1979.

"Racism and Women's Studies," in *Frontiers,* spring 1980.

With Tia Cross, Freada Klein, and Beverly Smith, "Face–to–Face, Day to Day, Racism CR," in *Women's Studies Newsletter,* winter 1980, 27–28.

"The Other Black Women" (keynote address at first Eastern Black Lesbian conference, New York, January 1981), in *Gay Community Newes,* February 1981.

Author of foreword, *The Combahee River Collective Statement: Black Feminist Organizing in the Seventies and Eighties.* New York, Kitchen Table—Women of Color Press, 1986.

*

Critical Sources: "In Their Own Words" (review of *Home Girls*) by Thulani Davis, in *Nation,* 25 February 1984, 234–235; "Coming Home" (review of *Home Girls*) by Gabrielle Daniels, in *Women's Review of Books,* March 1984, 6–7.

* * *

American feminist editor and essayist Barbara Smith is known both for editing volumes that concern homosexual black feminism and for being the first writer to characterize as lesbian the relationships between black women in classic black novels. In the late 1970s, Smith presented a paper to the National Conference of Afro–American Writers that identified these relationships in novels written since the 1940s. Her paper, which shocked many of the conference's attendees, was the first to publicly address the subject of black lesbianism. Thulani Davis, writing in the *Nation,* stated that the lesbianism Smith says she uncovers in those novels and discusses in her paper is "basically the closeness and mutual support one often finds among women who are brutalized by life, but the word itself [lesbian] brought alarm. How could something lesbian, however amorphous, step out of black culture's shadows and into the acknowledged landmarks of our genius?"

In *Home Girls: A Black Feminist Anthology,* Smith collected essays and stories from 34 black lesbians living in the United States and the Caribbean. The collection celebrates the contributors' individuality, presenting each woman's opinion of what makes her, as a black lesbian, so different from other black women. Smith believes that these differences and the expression and public acknowledgement of them are what add creativity and life to an interdependent culture, and argues that the suppression of these differences would destroy the vitality of that culture. She calls for inclusion, rather than exclusion, of people who are different, particularly black lesbians. In reviewing *Home Girls, Women's Review of Books* contributor Gabrielle Daniels stated: "Black women who are feminists, who are lesbians, are considered to have 'left' the community. Moreover, since the larger feminist movement is composed of mostly white women, it is cause for more distrust and vitriol leveled against Black feminists." Daniels explained that the "refusal to follow the straight and narrow line as to the role of women in the Black community has generated most of the negative response to Black feminism."

In the anthologies *All the Women Are White, All the Blacks Are Men, But Some of Us Are Brave: Black Women's Studies* and *Yours in Struggle: Three Feminists Perspectives on Anti–Semitism and Racism,* Smith and her fellow editors expand their examination of black lesbianism to include discussions of the sexual, religious, and racial stereotyping to which women of color, and black women in particular, are subjected.

————

SPARROW, Philip. *See* **STEWARD, Samuel M(orris).**

————

SPENDER, Stephen (Harold). British poet, critic, dramatist, translator, and educator. Born in London, 28 February 1909. Educated at University College School; University College, Oxford, 1928–30. Served in the National Fire Service, 1941–44. Married Agnes Marie Pearn in 1936 (divorced); married pianist Natasha Litvin in 1941; one son and one daughter. Counsellor, Section of Letters, United Nations Economic, Scientific, and Cultural Organization (UNESCO), 1947; Elliston Chair of Poetry, University of Cincinnati, Ohio, 1953; Beckman Professor, University of California, Los Angeles, 1959; consultant in poetry in English, Library of Congress, Washington, D.C., 1965–66; from 1970 professor, then professor emeritus of English literature beginning 1977, University College, London. Editor, with Cyril Conolly, *Horizon,* London, 1939–41; from 1953 editor with Melvin J. Lasky, then corresponding editor, 1966–67, *Encounter* magazine, London; cofounder of *Index on Censorship;* president, English Centre, PEN, 1975—; visiting lecturer: Northwestern University, Chicago, 1963; Clark lectures, Cambridge University, 1966; Mellon lectures, Washington, D.C., 1968; Northcliffe lectures, London University, 1969; visiting professor, University of Connecticut, 1969; Vanderbilt University, 1979. **Recipient:** Commander of the British Empire, 1962; Queen's Gold Medal for Poetry, 1971; named Companion of Literature, 1977; knighted by Queen Elizabeth II, 1983; *Los Angeles Times* Book Award nomination, 1986; vice–president of Royal Society of Literature (fellow), 1987—; honorary fellow, University College, Oxford, 1973; fellow, Institute of Advanced Studies, Wesleyan University, 1967. D.Litt.: University of Montpelier, Cornell University, Loyola University, Macerata University. Address: 15 Loudon Road, London NW8, England, U.K.

WRITINGS

Poetry

Nine Experiments: Being Poems Written at the Age of Eighteen. London, privately printed, 1928.

Twenty Poems. London, Basil Blackwell, 1930.

Poems. London, Faber, 1933; New York, Random House, 1934.

Perhaps. London, privately printed, 1933.

Poem. London, privately printed, 1934.

Vienna. London, Faber, 1934; New York, Random House, 1935.

At Night. London, privately printed, 1935.

The Still Centre. London, Faber, 1939.
Selected Poems. New York, Random House, 1940.
I Sit by the Window. New York, Linden Press, c. 1940.
Ruins and Visions: Poems, 1934–1942. New York, Random House, 1942.
Poems of Dedication. New York, Random House, 1947.
Returning to Vienna, 1947: Nine Sketches. Chicago, Banyan Press, 1947.
The Edge of Being. New York, Random House, 1949.
Sirmione Peninsula. London, Faber, 1954.
Collected Poems, 1928–1953. New York, Random House, 1955; revised as *Collected Poems, 1928–1985,* London, Faber, 1985.
Inscriptions. London, Poetry Book Society, 1958.
Selected Poems. New York, Random House, 1964.
The Generous Days: Ten Poems. London, D. Godine, 1969; revised as *The Generous Days,* London, Faber, 1971.
Descartes. London, Steam Press, 1970.
Art Student. London, Poem–of–the–Month Club, 1970.
Recent Poems. London, Anvil Press Poetry, 1978.

Essays

The Destructive Element: A Study of Modern Writers and Beliefs. London, J. Cape, 1935; Boston, Houghton, 1936.
Forward from Liberalism. New York, Random House, 1937.
The New Realism: A Discussion. London, Hogarth Press, 1939; Folcroft, Pennsylvania, Folcroft Press, 1977.
Life and the Poet. London, Secker & Warburg, 1942; Folcroft, Pennsylvania, Folcroft Press, 1974.
European Witness. London, Hamish Hamilton, 1946.
Contributor, *The God that Failed: Six Studies in Communism,* edited by Richard H. Crossman. New York, Harper, 1950.
Learning Laughter. London, Weidenfeld & Nicolson, 1952; New York, Harcourt, 1953.
The Creative Element: A Study of Vision, Despair, and Orthodoxy among Some Modern Writers. London, Hamish Hamilton, 1953; Folcroft, Pennsylvania, Folcroft, 1973.
The Making of a Poem. London, Hamish Hamilton, 1955; New York, Norton, 1962.
The Imagination in the Modern World: Three Lectures. Washington, D.C., Library of Congress, 1962.
The Struggle of the Modern. Berkeley, University of California Press, 1963.
Chaos and Control in Poetry. Washington, D.C., Library of Congress, 1966.
The Year of the Young Rebels. New York, Random House, 1969.
Love–Hate Relationships: A Study of Anglo–American Sensibilities. New York, Random House, 1974.
Eliot. London, Fontana, 1975; as *T. S. Eliot,* New York, Viking, 1976.
Henry Moore: Sculptures in Landscape. London, Studio Vista, 1978; New York, C. N. Potter, 1979.
The Thirties and After: Poetry, Politics, People, 1933–1970. London, Macmillan, and New York, Random House, 1978.
Contributor, *America Observed.* New York, C. N. Potter, 1979.
China Diary, illustrations by David Hockney. London, Thames & Hudson, 1982.
In Irina's Garden with Henry Moore's Sculpture. London, Thames & Hudson, 1986.

Plays

Trial of a Judge: A Tragedy in Five Acts (produced London, 1938). New York, Random House, 1938.
To the Island (produced Oxford, 1951).
Adapter and translator, with Goronwy Rees, *Danton's Death* (adaptation of play by Georg Buechner; produced London, 1939). London, Faber, 1939.
Adapter, *Lulu* (adaptation of plays by Frank Wedekind; produced New York, 1958).
Adapter and translator, *Mary Stuart* (adaptation of play by Johann Christoph Friedrich von Schiller; produced in West End, 1961; on Broadway, 1971). London, Faber, 1959.
With Nicholas Nabokov, *Rasputin's End* (opera). Milan, Ricori, 1963.
Adapter and translator, *The Oedipus Trilogy—King Oedipus, Oedipus at Colonos, Antigone: A Version by Stephen Spender* (three-act; revision produced Oxford, 1983). London, Faber, 1985.

Editor

Poems by W. H. Auden. London, privately printed, 1928.
With Louis Mac Neice, *Oxford Poetry 1929.* London, Basil Blackwell, 1929.
With Bernard Spencer, *Oxford Poetry 1930.* London, Basil Blackwell, 1930.
With John Lehmann and Christopher Isherwood, *New Writing, New Series I.* London, Hogarth Press, 1938.
With John Lehmann and Christopher Isherwood, *New Writing, New Series II.* London, Hogarth Press, 1939.
With John Lehmann, and author of introduction, *Poems for Spain.* London, Hogarth Press, 1939.
Spiritual Exercises: To Cecil Day Lewis. London, privately printed, 1943.
And author of introduction, *A Choice of English Romantic Poetry.* New York, Dial, 1947.
And author of introduction, *Selected Poems,* by Walt Whitman. London, Grey Walls Press, 1950.
Europe in Photographs, by Martin Huerlimann. London, Thames & Hudson, 1951.
With Elizabeth Jennings and Dannie Abbse, *New Poems 1956: An Anthology.* London, M. Joseph, 1956.
And author of introduction, *Great Writings of Goethe.* New York, New American Library, 1958.
And author of introduction, *Great German Short Stories.* New York, Dell, 1960.
And author of introduction, *The Writer's Dilemma.* Oxford, Oxford University Press, 1961.
With Irving Kristol and Melvin J. Lasky, *Encounters: An Anthology from the First Ten Years of "Encounter" Magazine.* London, Basic Books, 1963.
With Donald Hall, *The Concise Encyclopedia of English and American Poets and Poetry.* New York, Hawthorne, 1963; revised, London, Hutchinson, 1970.
And author of introduction, *A Choice of Shelley's Verse.* London, Faber, 1971.
And author of introduction, *Selected Poems of Abba Kovne* [and] *Selected Poems of Nelly Sachs.* London, Penguin, 1971.
The Poems of Percy Bysshe Shelley. Cambridge, England, Limited Editions Club, 1971.

D. H. Lawrence: Novelist, Poet, Prophet. London, Weidenfeld & Nicholson, and New York, Harper, 1973.
W. H. Auden: A Tribute. New York, Macmillan, 1975.

Translator

And author of introduction and commentary, with J. B. Leishman, *Duino Elegies* by Rainer Maria Rilke. New York, Norton, 1939; revised, London, Hogarth Press, 1963.
With Hugh Hunt, *Pastor Hall* (three–act play), by Ernst Toller. John Lane, 1939; bound with *Blind Man's Bluff* by Ernst Toller and Denis Johnson, New York, Random House, 1939.
With J. L. Gili, *Poems* by Federico García Lorca. New York, Oxford University Press, 1939.
With J. L. Gili, *Selected Poems of Federico García Lorca.* London, Hogarth Press, 1943.
With Frances Cornford, *Le Dur desir de Durer* by Paul Eluard. London, Grey Falcon Press, 1950.
And author of introduction, *The Life of the Virgin Mary (Das Marien–Leben)* by Rainer Maria Rilke. New York, Philosophical Library, 1951.
With Frances Fawcett, *Five Tragedies of Sex* by Frank Wedekind. New York, Theatre Arts, 1952.
With Nikos Stangos, *Fourteen Poems* by C. P. Cavafy. Editions Electo, 1977.
Lulu Plays, and Other Sex Tragedies by Frank Wedekind. New York, Riverrun, 1979.

Fiction

The Burning Cactus (short stories). New York, Random House, 1936; Freeport, New York, Books for Libraries Press, 1971.
The Backward Son (novel). London, Hogarth Press, 1940.
Engaged in Writing [and] *The Fool and the Princess* (short stories). New York, Farrar, Straus, 1958.
Reteller, *The Magic Flute: Retold* (juvenile; based on the opera by Wolfgang Amadeus Mozart). New York, Putnam, 1966.
The Temple (novel). New York, Grove, 1988.

Other

With William Sansom and James Gordon, *Jim Braidy: The Story of Britain's Firemen.* Linsay Drummond, 1943.
Author of introduction and notes, *Botticelli.* London, Faber, 1945; New York, Pitman Publishing, 1948.
Author of introduction, *The Dedicated Life in Poetry* [and] *The Correspondence of Laurent de Cayeux* by Patrice de la Tour du Pin. London, Harvill Press, 1948.
World within World: The Autobiography of Stephen Spender. New York, Harcourt, 1951; London, Faber & Faber, 1977.
Contributor, *Ghika: Paintings, Drawings, Sculpture.* London, Lund Humphries, 1964; Boston, Boston Book and Art Shop, 1965.
Author of introduction, *Venice.* New York, Vendome, 1979.
Letters to Christopher Isherwood: Stephen Spender's Letters to Christopher Isherwood, 1929–1939, with "The Line of the Branch"—Two Thirties Journals. Santa Barbara, California, Black Sparrow Press, 1980.
Author of introduction, *Herbert List: Photographs, 1930–1970.* London, Thames & Hudson, 1981.

Contributor, *Hockney Paints the Stage* by Martin Friedman. New York, Abbeville Press, 1983.
The Journals of Stephen Spender, 1939–1983. New York, Random House, 1986.

*

Manuscript Collections: Northwestern University, Evanston, Illinois; Bancroft Library, University of California at Berkeley.

Interviews: "Actively Creative at 70: Poet Stephen Spender" by W. I. Scobie, in *Advocate,* June 1977, 24–25.

Critical Sources: *Poets of the Thirties* by D. E. S. Maxwell, New York, Barnes & Noble, 1969; *The Angry Young Men of the Thirties* by Elton Edmund Smith, Carbondale, Illinois, Southern Illinois University Press, 1975; *Concise Dictionary of British Literary Biography,* Volume 7: *Writers after World War II, 1945–1960,* Detroit, Gale, 1991.

*   *   *

The birth of literature in the twentieth century has been marked and delineated by encompassing political and social events and forces, resulting in a quilted corpus of prose, theatrical works and poetry bearing the distinctive colorations of their decades. While each generation of authors has sought to claim a unit for itself, perhaps none has been as challenged to respond with creative energy to an almost total inversion of the established order of the day as that which came of age between the two world wars. Among the writers who attempted to chronicle and record these years of transition, Stephen Spender is notable. Born into a family headed by the liberal political journalist Harold Spender, young Spender was raised in an atmosphere replete with references to how things had been "before the War." Spender's father made a point of stressing the necessity of work and duty to his children, an attitude only exacerbated upon the death of Spender's mother when he was an adolescent. It was not until his 16th year that the realization came to him that his family was Jewish, his relatives having suppressed this aspect of their history.

Shortly after gaining this knowledge, Spender entered university at Oxford, where he became friends with the young poet W. H. Auden and, through Auden, Christopher Isherwood. Finding life at college somewhat dissatisfying, by the summer of 1929 Spender had concluded that "my own work is to write poetry and novels ... I must live and mature in my writing"; he soon left for a holiday in Germany. In 1930, he returned to Germany with Isherwood and witnessed the culture of the last years of the Weimar Republic. With Spender's private publication in 1928 of the first edition of *Nine Experiments,* the creation of an assemblage of poems that would mark the author as a mature poet had begun. Following World War II, this work was succeeded by a shift in emphasis to intellectual and social history, political and travel commentaries, translations, literary criticism and reviews.

The problem of placing Spender within the field of gay writing lies in the omnipresent aspect of his emotional responses to other men and the fact that he may more properly be described as bisexual rather than homosexual. From Spender's earliest lines of poetry, relationships with other males appear as elements of the text, stated and explored without undue fanfare. This creates a situation where the author's experiences with his own gender are more to be inferred than examined (it should also be noted that the broad, impersonal nature of the subjects addressed in the bulk of Spender's postwar work has not lent them to serve as vehicles for personal insight). Two major exceptions to this are his autobiography and *The Temple,* a novel manuscript originally written in 1929 which was reworked and published in 1988.

Although twice married and a father of two, Spender's frank acknowledgement of his attraction to other men in *World within World* is a forerunner of such later personal accounts as the diaries of composer Ned Rorem and Quentin Crisp's *The Naked Civil Servant. World within World*'s pages offer a thoughtful picture of the gradual evolution of the author's social awareness and concern, a quality noted by many critics as one of the most outstanding aspects of his work. Among the descriptions of Spender's travels are also isolated pieces of commentary on the homosexual lifestyle as it was being lived in the 1930s. One of the first of these is contained in his account of the 1929 holiday in Germany, where "bars for homosexuals" are noted as one of the hallmarks of the advanced Modernist attitudes then in vogue. Spender notes that the prohibition of writing about sexuality in England was one of the motivating factors that stimulated both an urge among young writers to challenge the system by deliberately choosing to discuss or depict the forbidden and the desire to emigrate to a less repressive environment.

World within World also provides a clear explication of the author's opinions about same–gender relations and the validity of various explanations for it. In a carefully considered response to the descriptions of homosexuality then offered by psychologists, the author challenges the idea that a relationship between two people of the same sex automatically excludes any possibility of either party entering into a fulfilling heterosexual relationship. The power of the label "homosexual" is viewed as objectionable, impelling those who accept this identification to "make a choice which, in past times, was not made ... men labeled themselves less and adjusted more."

Reflecting his literary interests, Spender cites William Shakespeare as an example of a writer who, while expressing deep emotional attachments for a young man in his sonnets, also advises the youth to marry and set up a family. Spender's exposure in Berlin to the idea—originally espoused by leaders of the first civil rights movement for homosexuals—that such persons constituted a "third sex" is also evident (although Spender rejects such a notion). To Spender, in order to fulfil one's gifts, a writer must remain in contact with the flow of life, not withdraw to an isolation populated by other persons who feel similarly, unable to participate in what the author terms "the generally held concept of the normal."

An indication of Spender's views on the literary depiction of homosexuality may be gained through an examination of his 1972 review of the E. M. Forster novel *Maurice* in the *Partisan Review.* After noting that he had originally seen the manuscript version in 1935 and summarizing the various plot lines, Spender addresses the nature of the relationship Maurice forms with a gamekeeper. According to Spender, two models of coping with homosexuality are offered in the work: either to give in to the demands of a predominantly heterosexual world or to create one's own. Maurice's choice to remain an "unchanged dedicated" homosexual fits with his rebellion against the smothering limits of custom and convention (much

as Spender's frequent extended residences abroad served him). The validity of homosexual acts as an expression of revolt is sustained, as the lovers do not recognize that there is a subculture of other kin to which they may belong. The relationship remains "a special and separate department of ... life, still more of the world, and it does not have room for more than two people." Given Spender's complex series of emotional involvements with other men throughout his life, these lines apply equally well to the author's own times and writings.

—*Robert B. Marks Ridinger*

SPICER, Jack (John Lester Spicer). American poet. Born in Los Angeles, California, 30 January 1925. Educated at Hollywood High School, 1939–43; University of Redlands, California, 1943–45; University of California at Berkeley, 1945–50, B.A. 1947, M.A. 1950. Held a variety of jobs including private detective, 1945–46; teaching assistant at University of California at Berkeley, 1947–50, 1952–53, and at University of Minnesota 1950–52; lecturer in English at California School of Fine Arts (now San Francisco Art Institute), 1953–55; staff of Rare Book Room at Boston Public Library, 1955–56; researcher, Linguistics Department, University of California at Berkeley, 1957–64; editor of *J* (literary magazine), San Francisco, 1959. *Died in San Francisco, 17 August 1965.*

WRITINGS

After Lorca. San Francisco, White Rabbit Press, 1957.
Admonitions, 1958.
Fifteen False Propositions against God, 1958.
Homage to Creeley. Annapolis, Harold and Dora Dull, 1959.
Billy the Kid. Stinson Beach, Enkidu Surrogate, 1959.
The Heads of the Town Up to the Aether. San Francisco, Auerhahn Society, 1959.
A Red Wheelbarrow and Apollo, 1959.
Sends Seven Nursury Rhymes to Jim Alexander, 1959.
Contributor, *The New American Poetry 1945–1960,* edited by Donald Allen. New York, Grove Press, 1960.
Lament for the Makers. San Francisco, White Rabbit Press, 1962.
The Holy Grail. San Francisco, White Rabbit Press, 1964.
Language. San Francisco, White Rabbit Press, 1965.
Book of Magazine Verse. San Francisco, White Rabbit Press, 1966.
A Book of Music. San Francisco, White Rabbit Press, 1969.
The Collected Books of Jack Spicer (contains all of the above), edited by Robin Blaser. Santa Barbara, California, Black Sparrow Press, 1975.
One Night Stand, and Other Poems, edited by Donald Allen, introduction by Robert Duncan. San Francisco, Grey Fox Press, 1980.
The Tower of Babel, edited by Lewis Ellingham and Kevin Killian. Tenerife, Canary Islands, Zasterle Books, 1993.
Detective Novel, edited by Lewis Ellingham and Kevin Killian. Hoboken, New Jersey, Talisman Books, 1993.

Manuscript Collections: Bancroft Library, University of California, Berkeley; Simon Fraser University Library, Burnaby, British Columbia; Lilly Library, University of Indiana, Bloomington; Archive for New Poetry, University of California, San Diego; Kent State University Library, Kent, Ohio; Olin Library, Washington University, St. Louis, Missouri; The Poetry/Rare Books Collection, State University of New York, Buffalo; Homer Babbidge Library, University of Connecticut, Storrs.

Biography: *Poet, Be Like God: The Life of Jack Spicer* (unpublished manuscript) by Lewis Ellingham and Kevin Killian.

Interviews: "Impressions from an 'Estranged' Poet" by Tove Neville, in the *San Francisco Chronicle,* 29 August 1965.

Bibliography: "A Checklist of the Published Writings of Jack Spicer" by Sanford Dorbin, in *California Librarian* (Sacramento), October 1970, 251–261; "Jack Spicer" by Gary M. Lepper, in *A Bibliographical Introduction to Seventy-five American Authors,* Berkeley, California, Serendipity Books, 1976, 379–382.

Critical Sources: *Caterpillar* (New York), Number 12, 1970 (special Jack Spicer issue); "The Practice of Outside" by Robin Blaser, in *The Collected Books of Jack Spicer,* Santa Barbara, California, Black Sparrow Press, 1975, 269–329; *Manroot* (San Francisco), Number 10, 1975 (special Jack Spicer issue); *Boundary* (Binghamton, New York), Number 26, 1977 (special Jack Spicer issue); "Jack Spicer," by Gilbert Sorrentino, in *Something Said,* Berkeley, California, North Point Press, 1984, 49–67; *Ironwood* (Tucson, Arizona), Number 28, 1986 (special Jack Spicer issue); *ACTS* (San Francisco), Number 6, 1987 (special Jack Spicer issue); "'The City Redefined': Community and Dialogue in Jack Spicer" by Michael Davidson, in *The San Francisco Renaissance: Poetics and Community at Mid-Century,* Cambridge, England, and New York, Cambridge University Press, 1989, 150–171; *Jack Spicer* by Edward Halsey Foster, Boise, Idaho, Boise State University Western Writers Series, 1991.

*   *   *

In the last nine years of his short life, Jack Spicer completed a dozen books of poetry and established a poetic tradition on the West Coast that ran parallel, yet counter, to the contemporaneous Beat movement. As a young Berkeley student in the late 1940s, Spicer quickly met other gay male poets, including Robin Blaser and Robert Duncan. They began a lifelong association which Spicer half-seriously called the "Berkeley Renaissance." His poetry of this period is elegiac, lyrical, magic—without the formal innovations developed later in the 1950s—and heavily homoerotic.

Spicer's finest early poems are the "Imaginary Elegies," which became his contribution to Donald Allen's influential anthology *The New American Poetry 1945–1960.* "When I praise the sun or any bronze god derived from it," he wrote in the first elegy, "Don't think I wouldn't rather praise the very tall blond boy / Who ate all of my potato–chips at the Red Lizard. / It's just that I won't see him when I open my eyes / And I will see the sun." Politically an anarchist, Spicer found his academic career stalled after he refused to sign the Loyalty Oath, an anti–Communist provision required of all state employees in California. Just as problematic in terms of

career was his open and avowed homosexuality.

In 1957, Spicer returned to the Bay Area, after a prolonged absence in New York and Boston. A burst of activity ensued, and a new writing practice began, first with the imitations and translations of *After Lorca,* which, he claimed, had been "dictated" to him, if not by García Lorca, then by a mysterious unknown force he sometimes said might be "Martians." In this conceit he was greatly influenced by the French poet Jean Cocteau, whose 1950 surreal film *Orphee* explores the notion of a poetry given from beyond the grave, and by his poetic hero Yeats, whose experiments in automatic writing fascinated Spicer. These poems never came singly: with Robert Duncan, Spicer conceived and developed the "serial poem," a book–length progression of short poems which combine and reorder themselves into a whole in the same way that individual words and lines alter one another in a single poem.

In San Francisco Spicer began teaching, and young poets flocked to him. He wanted to develop a magic school of writing, a *kreis* modeled on the *Georgekreis,* the mystic cult of poetry and love organized by the modernist German poet Stefan George to preserve the memory of a dead boyfriend. Unlike many of his poetic contemporaries, Spicer insisted that poets should *avoid* writing from their own experience, since the poet's subjectivity "got in the way of" the poem itself. His anarchist convictions led him to refuse copyright on his poetry since he believed that he was in no sense its owner, hardly even its creator. Spicer's own students came to include many of the finest poets, both gay and straight, working in San Francisco. He founded his own magazine, *J,* in 1959, to publish their writing, alongside his own, and in 1964 oversaw another influential monthly journal, *Open Space.*

Trained as a linguist, Spicer worked part–time at Berkeley while maintaining an active, bohemian life in the bars, beaches and streets of San Francisco. He developed important friendships—then quarreled—with most of the "New American" poets of his day, including Charles Olson, Denise Levertov, Robert Creeley, and their gay counterparts Frank O'Hara, John Wieners, and Allen Ginsberg. Spicer was always in love, usually without result, with one or another young man on the scene, and out of the romantic tumult came some of the most moving love poetry of the century. In "Several Years' Love," the poem that begins his book *The Heads of the Town Up to the Aether* we find these enigmatic lines: "Two loves I had. One rang a bell / Connected on both sides with hell / The other'd written me a letter / In which he said I've written better / They pushed their cocks in many places / And I'm not certain of their faces / Or which I kissed or which I didn't / Or which of both of them I hadn't."

Always vivid and original, Spicer's poetry grew increasingly elliptical and disjunctive. By the time of his final work, *Language and Book of Magazine Verse,* his poetry had become an inquiry into the nature, purpose and materiality of language itself, anticipating by a generation recent trends in poetic thought. Following the dictation of the Martians meant that Spicer allowed himself no revision, not even the correction of a misspelled word. Each poem in one of his "books" is in the shape, roughly, of a square: the size of a leaf from a student's notebook, and at its last line the Martian transmissions would fade: the poem would end.

In 1965, despite triumphant appearances at the Vancouver Poetry Festival and the Berkeley Poetry Conference, Spicer was visibly weary and weak. His heavy alcohol habit was destroying his liver, and a paranoia about world and local affairs was continually rising in his soul. At age 40, he collapsed in the elevator of his apartment house, in a squalid section of San Francisco, and was brought to the poverty ward of San Francisco General, where he remained for three weeks, in a coma, until death released him. Ten years later, his executor, the poet Robin Blaser, collected his mature work and published it as *The Collected Books of Jack Spicer*, and this volume remains in print today.

—*Kevin Killian*

————

ST. E. A. of M. and S. *See* **CROWLEY, Aleister.**

————

STAMES, Ward. *See* **STEWARD, Samuel M(orris).**

————

STEIN, Gertrude. American poet, playwright, short story writer, novelist, and literary experimentalist. Born in Allegheny, Pennsylvania, 3 February 1874. Educated at Radcliffe College, Cambridge, Massachusetts; Harvard University, Cambridge, Massachusetts, B.A. 1897; Johns Hopkins Medical School, Baltimore, Maryland, 1897–1901. Lived in Paris. Companion of Alice B. Toklas, 1907–46. Contributor to numerous periodicals, including *Psychological Review*, 1896–98, *Transition*, 1927–29, and *Compass*, 1945. **Recipient:** Medaille de la Reconnaissance Francaise, 1922. *Died in Neuilly–sur–Seine, France, of cancer, 27 July 1946.*

WRITINGS

Novels

Three Lives: The Story of The Good Anna, Melanctha and The Gentle Lena. New York, Grafton Press, 1909; London, John Lane, 1915.
Portrait of Mabel Dodge at the Villa Curonia. Florence, Italy, privately printed, 1912.
The Making of Americans, Being a History of a Family's Progress. Paris, Contact Editions, 1925; New York, A. and C. Boni, 1926.
A Book Concluding With As a Wife Has a Cow, A Love Story. Paris, Editions de la Galerie Simon, 1926.
Ida, a Novel. New York, Random House, 1941.
Things As They Are: A Novel in Three Parts by Gertrude Stein, Written in 1903, Now Published for the First Time. Pawlet, Vermont, Banyan Press, 1950.

Poetry

Tender Buttons: Objects, Food, Rooms. New York, Claire Marie, 1914.
Petits poèmes pour un livre de lecture, translation by Madame la Baronne d'Aiguy. Charlot, France, Collection Fontaine, 1944; as *The First Reader and Three Plays,* Dublin/London, Maurice Fridberg, 1946; Boston, Houghton, 1948.
Two (Hitherto Unpublished) Poems. New York, Gotham Book Mart, 1948.
Lifting Belly, edited by Rebecca Mark. Tallahassee, Naiad Press, 1989.

Plays

Geography and Plays. Boston, Four Seas, 1922.
A Village Are You Ready Yet Not Yet A Play In Four Acts. Paris, Editions de la Galerie Simon, 1928.
Operas and Plays. Paris, Plain Editions, 1932.
In Savoy; or, This Is for a Very Young Man (A Play of the Resistance in France). London, Pushkin, 1946.
Last Operas and Plays, edited by Carl Van Vechten. New York, Rinehart, 1949.
Lucretia Borgia: A Play. New York, Albocondoni Press, 1968.
Selected Operas and Plays, edited by John Malcolm Brinnin. Pittsburgh, University of Pittsburgh Press, 1970.

Collections

Matisse, Picasso, and Gertrude Stein with Two Shorter Stories. Paris, Plain Editions, 1933.
Selected Writings, edited by Carl Van Vechten. New York, Random House, 1949.
Gertrude Stein's America, edited by Gilbert A. Harrison. Washington, D.C., Robert B. Luce, 1965.
A Primer for the Understanding of Gertrude Stein, edited by Robert Bartlett Haas. Los Angeles, Black Sparrow Press, 1971.
Fernhurst, Q.E.D., and Other Early Writings. New York, Liveright, and London, P. Owen, 1971.
The Previously Uncollected Writings of Gertrude Stein, edited by Robert Bartlett Haas. Los Angeles, Black Sparrow Press, Volume 1: *Reflections on the Atomic Bomb,* 1973; Volume 2: *How Writing is Written,* 1974.
The Yale Gertrude Stein: Selections. New Haven, Connecticut, Yale University Press, 1980.

The Yale Edition of the Unpublished Works of Gertrude Stein

Volume 1: *Two: Gertrude Stein and Her Brother, and Other Early Portraits, 1906–1912,* edited by Carl Van Vechten. New Haven, Connecticut, Yale University Press, and London, Oxford University Press, 1951.
Volume 2: *Mrs. Reynolds and Five Earlier Novelettes,* edited by Carl Van Vechten. New Haven, Connecticut, Yale University Press, and London, Oxford University Press, 1952.
Volume 3: *Bee Time, and Other Pieces 1913–1927,* edited by Carl Van Vechten. New Haven, Connecticut, Yale University Press, and London, Oxford University Press, 1953.
Volume 4: *As Fine as Melanctha 1914–1930,* edited by Carl Van Vechten. New Haven, Connecticut, Yale University Press, and London, Oxford University Press, 1954.

Volume 5: *Painted Lace, and Other Pieces 1914–1937,* edited by Carl Van Vechten. New Haven, Connecticut, and London, Oxford University Press, 1955.

Volume 6: *Stanzas in Meditation, and Other Poems,* edited by Carl Van Vechten. New Haven, Connecticut, Yale University Press, and London, Oxford Press, 1956.

Volume 7: *Alphabets and Birthdays,* edited by Carl Van Vechten. New Haven, Connecticut, Yale University Press, and London, Oxford University Press, 1957.

Volume 8: *A Novel of Thank You,* edited by Carl Van Vechten. New Haven, Connecticut, Yale University Press, and London, Oxford University Press, 1959.

Librettos

Four Saints in Three Acts: An Opera to be Sung, music by Virgil Thomson (produced Hartford, Connecticut, 1934). New York, Random House, 1934.

A Wedding Bouquet: Ballet Music by Lord Berners. London, J. & W. Chester, 1938.

Capitals, Capitals: Four Men and a Piano, music by Virgil Thomson (produced New York, 1947).

The Mother of Us All, music by Virgil Thomson (produced New York, 1947). Music Press, 1947.

Preciosilla: For Voice and Piano. G. Schirmer, 1948.

In a Garden: An Opera in One Act, music by Meyer Kupferman. New York, Mercury Music, 1951.

Lectures

Lectures in America. New York, Random House, 1935.

Narration: Four Lectures. Chicago, University of Chicago Press, 1935.

Writings and Lectures 1911–1945, edited by Patricia Meyerowitz. London, P. Owen, 1967; as *Look At Me Now and Here I Am: Writings and Lectures,* Baltimore, Penguin, 1971.

Letters

Sherwood Anderson/Gertrude Stein Correspondence and Personal Essays, edited by Ray Lewis White. Chapel Hill, University of North Carolina Press, 1972.

Dear Sammy: Letters from Gertrude Stein and Alice B. Toklas, edited by Samuel M. Steward. Boston, Houghton, 1977.

The Letters of Gertrude Stein and Carl Van Vechten 1913–1946. New York, Columbia University Press, 1986.

Other

Have They Attacked Mary, He Giggled. West Chester, Pennsylvania, 1917.

Descriptions of Literature. Englewood Cliffs, New Jersey, George Platt Lynes and Adlai Harbeck, 1926.

Composition as Explanation. London, Hogarth Press, 1926.

The Elucidation, 1927.

Useful Knowledge. New York, Payson & Clarke, 1928; London, John Lane/Bodley Head, 1929.

An Acquaintance with Description. London, Seizen Press, 1929.

Lucy Church Amiably. Paris, Plain Editions, 1930; New York, Something Else Press, 1969.

Dix Portraits, English with French translations by Georges Hugnet and Virgil Thomson. Paris, Librarie Gallimard, 1930.

Before the Flowers of Friendship Faded Friendship Faded, Written on a Poem by Georges Hugnet. Paris, Plain Editions, 1931.

How to Write. Paris, Plain Editions, 1931.

The Autobiography of Alice B. Toklas. New York, Harcourt, and London, John Lane/Bodley Head, 1933.

Portraits and Prayers. New York, Random House, 1934.

The Geographical History of America or the Relation of Human Nature to the Human Mind. New York, Random House, 1936.

Is Dead, 1937.

Everybody's Autobiography. New York, Random House, 1937; London, Heinemann, 1938.

Picasso. Paris, Librarie Floury, 1939; translated into English by Alice B. Toklas, London, Batsford, 1938; New York, Scribner, 1939.

The World Is Round. New York, William R. Scott, and London, Batsford, 1939.

Paris France. London, Batsford, and New York, Scribner, 1940.

What Are Masterpieces. Conference Press, 1940; enlarged, New York and London, Pitman, 1970.

Wars I Have Seen. New York, Random House, 1945.

Brewsie and Willie. New York, Random House, 1945.

Four in America. New Haven, Connecticut, Yale University Press, 1947.

Blood on the Dressing Room Floor. Pawley, Vermont, Banyan Press, 1948.

With Leon M. Solomons, *Motor Automatism.* New York, Phoenix Book Shop, 1969.

Gertrude Stein on Picasso, edited by Edward Burns. New York, Liverwright, 1970.

I Am Rose. New York, Mini–Books, 1971.

Money. Los Angeles, Black Sparrow Press, 1973.

*

Manuscript Collections: Beinecke Library, Yale University, New Haven, Connecticut; Bancroft Library, University of California, Berkeley; University of Texas, Austin.

Biography: *Gertrude Stein: Her Life and Work* by Elizabeth Sprigge, New York, Harper, 1957; *The Third Rose: Gertrude Stein and Her World* by John Malcolm Brinnin, Boston, Little, Brown 1959; *Everybody Who Was Anybody: A Biography of Gertrude Stein* by Janet Hobhouse, New York, Putnam, 1975.

Interviews: With Robert Bartlett Haas, in *Unclan Review,* summer 1962, 3–11, spring 1963, 40–48, and winter 1964, 44–48.

Bibliography: *Gertrude Stein: A Bibliography* by Robert A. Wilson, New York, Phoenix Bookshop, 1974.

Critical Sources: *Gertrude Stein in Pieces* by Richard Bridgeman, New York, Oxford University Press, 1970; *A Primer for the Gradual Understanding of Gertrude Stein,* edited by Robert Bartlett Haas, Los Angeles, Black Sparrow Press, 1971; "The Mind, The Body, and Gertrude Stein" by Catherine R. Stimpson, in *Critical Inquiry,* spring 1977; "Is Flesh Advisable?: The Interior Theater of Gertrude Stein" by Elizabeth Fifer, in *Signs,* spring 1979; *A Different Language: Gertrude Stein's Experimental Writing* by Marianne

DeKoven, Madison, University of Wisconsin, 1983; *Critical Essays on Gertrude Stein,* edited by Michael J. Hoffman, Boston, G. K. Hall, 1986; "Beyond the Reaches of Feminist Criticism: A Letter from Paris" by Shari Benstock, in *Feminist Issues in Literary Scholarship,* edited by Shari Benstock, Bloomington, Indiana University Press, 1987, 7–29; *Testimony Against Gertrude Stein* (special issue of *Transition,* February 1935), edited by Eugene Jolas, Servire Press, The Hague.

*   *   *

In *Dear Sammy: Letters from Gertrude Stein and Alice B. Toklas,* author Samuel M. Steward describes a conversation he had with Gertrude Stein in 1939 where she suddenly grabs his knee and asks, "Sammy, do you think that Alice and I are lesbians?" Stein tells Steward that, even though most of their friends know "all about everything" regarding her relationship with Toklas and that homosexuals "do all the good things in all the arts," she wants him not to write about her being a lesbian until "say twenty years after I die, unless it's found out sooner or times change."

Much of Stein's writing, as well as her life, exhibits the same interplay of sudden revelation and cryptic secrecy that can be seen in this episode of Steward's memoirs. Stein wrote some of the most unapologetic and often frankly erotic accounts of lesbian lives in the early part of this century, yet she withheld her work from publication and masked its lesbian content through a variety of innovative stylistic disguises. While she was lionized in her lifetime largely on the strengths of her public persona and her most accessible book, *The Autobiography of Alice B. Toklas,* scholarship on Stein has enjoyed a huge growth in the second half of the century, in part because so much of her work and her life has remained unexplored. In addition, the languages and concepts offered by lesbian, feminist, and postmodernist criticism have created new apertures through which to approach and discuss her work. Stein spoke of herself as ahead of her times, and the burgeoning of scholarship about her work and life seems to indicate she was right.

Times were slow to change in Stein's lifetime, however, and Steward more than kept his promise to her, delaying publication of his memoir and collection of letters until 1977. These personal silences between friends were also reflected in the publishing and criticism of Stein's work, and it was not until the growth of lesbian and feminist scholarship, which began during the same time period, that Stein's writing and life began to be examined more on its own merits and in light of the perspectives her lesbianism might have brought to her writing. Shari Benstock, for example, writing in *Feminist Issues in Literary Scholarship,* argues that Stein's sexuality was central to the innovations in her writing: "Stein's perverse style has intimate connections to her lesbianism, which is the motivating force for this private language, at odds with any accepted forms of meaning, a language exploring seemingly arbitrary and coincidental links between signifier and signified. Stein's style served as a mask for her lesbian subject matter."

Michael J. Hoffman, in his introduction to *Critical Essays on Gertrude Stein,* describes one of the contributions of Stein's feminist critics as being "to relate Stein's sexual preference to the buried life it led in her writings." Scholars such as Catherine Stimpson, Cynthia Secor, Elizabeth Fifer, and Shari Benstock have engaged themselves in unearthing and explicating the ways Stein's sexuality has been encoded in her work, and demonstrate how understanding

the coded sexuality can render Stein's seemingly cryptic style both readable and enjoyable. Among other strategies, these scholars have identified Stein's punning, her plays on gender roles and heterosexual terminology, and parts of her lexicon for lovemaking.

Prior to these relatively recent examinations of the relationship between Stein's life and work, biographical accounts and literary criticism often discussed Stein only in relation to other literary movements or authors; her relationship to cubism and modernism, her influence on such (usually male) authors as Ernest Hemingway and Sherwood Anderson, or stylistic comparisons to James Joyce were more common than examinations of Stein's writing on its own merits. In contrast, Benstock sees Stein as having written from outside the communities of male modernist writers and cubist painters, alienated by virtue of her position not only as a woman, but a lesbian woman writer. According to Benstock, Stein worked her alienation to her advantage. "By maintaining her separatism," states Benstock, "She created the myth that she was at the center of a literary period whose borders were, in reality, sealed against her."

This myth which Stein created by writing *The Autobiography of Alice B. Toklas* precipitated a storm of both popularity and controversy for her career. The editors of *Transition* hurried to put out the *Testimony against Gertrude Stein* issue in order to "straighten out those points with which we are familiar before the book has had time to assume the character of historic authenticity." Editor Eugene Jolas charged that Stein was in no way "concerned with the shaping of the epoch she attempts to describe." He added that there was "a unanimity of opinion that she had no understanding of what really was happening around her," and quoted Henri Matisse as saying she had presented the epoch "without taste and without relation to reality." On the other hand, the surface accessibility of the narrative, the public's curiosity about the famous persons such as Pablo Picasso and Matisse discussed within its pages, and the cleverness of the ending where Stein reveals herself, rather than Toklas, as the author of the "autobiography" brought an increased celebrity to Stein. Stein used the narrative voice of "Alice" to portray herself as a founder of twentieth–century literature and "first class genius" in the company of Picasso and Alfred Whitehead (*Selected Writings*). More subtly, she used the autobiography as a means of expressing her relationship as the "husband" of its narrator. "Before I decided to write this book my twenty–five years with Gertrude Stein," writes the Alice–narrator, "I had often said that I would write, The wives of geniuses I have sat with." By placing Stein in one room among the genius–husbands and Alice in another with the wives, Stein wittily establishes both her artistic importance and her important primary relationship.

Ironically, even though Stein's relationship with Toklas has arguably become the most famous lesbian romance in history, their relationship was often erased or portrayed in nonsexual terms during their lifetimes. Toklas was most often referred to as Stein's "secretary," with even friends colluding in the public masquerade. In his introduction and notes to *Bee Time Vine,* Virgil Thomson uses the term to refer to Toklas, also calling her his "chief informant" on matters regarding Stein. During Stein's lifetime, the only more overt allusions to her sexuality came from people trying to use homophobia as a means to denigrate Stein, such as the authors and artists who contributed to *Transition*'s special issue, *Testimony against Gertrude Stein,* which made references to them as spinsters in "boy scout uniforms" occupying "the family circle [of] two maiden ladies greedy for fame and publicity."

Certainly Stein and Toklas were central to the consistently mixed revelation and disguise of themselves as a couple. Stein and Toklas constantly presented themselves together in public, yet kept their relationship ambiguous. *The Autobiography of Alice B. Toklas* makes it clear that Stein and Toklas live, travel and plan their lives together, yet their relationship is made the center, rather than the overt content of the book.

More important than the secrecy about Stein's "private life" itself, was the fact that a tremendous amount of her writing which could be construed as lesbian was withheld from publication for several decades. Stein's first novel, *Q.E.D.*, the semi–autobiographical story of a lesbian lovers' triangle, was unpublished for almost half a century, because Stein was aware the public was not ready to receive it. In the same conversation with Steward mentioned at the beginning of this essay, Stein explained why she had chosen not to publish *Q.E.D.*, which she had written 35 years earlier. "Well for one thing," she told him, "it was too early to write about such things in our civilization, it was early in the century and everything was puritanical and so it was too soon, maybe not if we were Greek but Greek we weren't."

Q.E.D., which Stein described as "too outspoken for the times even though it was restrained," was finally published in a very limited edition in 1950 under the title *Things As They Are*. To make the story more palatable, or publishable, Stein had much earlier transformed the narrative into heterosexual terms, creating *Three Lives*. Although that book still contained depictions of fierce female attachments, the central relationship was between Melanctha and Jeff Campbell, a male doctor, and the social stigma of their relationship was played out by Melanctha's color and social position, rather than as a lesbian relationship, Stimpson declares in *Critical Inquiry*.

Works like *Q.E.D.*, which described lesbian relationships, and Stein's more explicitly sexual and loving works, such as "Lifting Belly" and "A Sonatina Followed by Another," were among the last to be made available. Stein has "Alice" say in the *Autobiography* that Stein "forgot" about her first novel, but Stimpson notes that even after it was "discovered" Stein chose not to include it in the 1941 Yale catalog of her published and unpublished works, which she helped compile. Toklas, Stein's lifelong companion, lived for many years after Stein's death. Understandably reluctant to have her privacy infringed upon, she finally did publish *Q.E.D.* in a very limited edition. *Q.E.D.* was particularly problematic for Toklas because it chronicled Stein's earlier relationship with May Bookstaver, and Toklas, who spent so much of her last years making sure the archives and publishing of Stein's work was complete, is said to have destroyed Bookstaver's letters to Stein in 1932, according to Stimpson.

Although *Q.E.D.* was the most clearly autobiographical and clearly lesbian in content of Stein's writings, it is the playful erotic dialogues like *Lifting Belly* which often engage the attention of contemporary lesbians. Although the piece attracted little attention when it was first published embedded in *Bee Time Vine*, Naiad Press, a lesbian publishing house, reissued the piece on its own in 1989. The different approaches by the editors of the two volumes indicate how critical time and context are to the understanding of Stein. In the 1953 Yale series, Virgil Thomson introduced the piece by saying "I do not know the meaning of the title." Euphemistically, he tells his readers that poems such as *Lifting Belly* "reveal their content to persons acquainted with the regions they describe or with their author's domestic life." In contrast, Rebecca Mark is able to state in her 1989 Naiad Press introduction, "When I read *Lifting Belly* in *The Yale Gertrude Stein*, I was so excited I told everyone I knew about this erotic, lesbian poem." In *Really Reading*

Gertrude Stein, lesbian poet and gay cultural historian Judy Grahn predicts that "in future time ... all of her stories will come clear to us as we modern people stand more nearly in the center of who we are." While Grahn's scenario may seem optimistic, it does seem that as more lesbian scholars and readers emerge "more nearly in the center of who we are," much of Stein's private, cryptic writing has become more accessible. While Stein studies was once confined strictly to the academy, activists like Grahn and Mark have been working to bring her into the lesbian community at large.

Considering the times in which she was writing, part of Stein's greatness as a writer is that she could create language to describe lesbian life and lovemaking. Reading as a contemporary lesbian, Rebecca Mark wonders "how words which rarely mention a body part can make me feel so aroused." "Lifting belly. Are you. Lifting. / Oh dear I said I was tender, fierce and tender. / Do it. What a splendid example of carelessness. / It gives me a great deal of pleasure to say yes. / Why do I always smile. / I don't know. / You are easily pleased. / I am very pleased."

At the end of the twentieth century, the audience Stein predicted may have finally caught up with her. More comfortable with both nonlinear narratives and lesbian existence, contemporary readers and scholars "acquainted with the regions" Stein describes are finding many of Stein's writings to be newly negotiable and exceedingly pleasing terrain.

—*Jayne Relaford Brown*

———

STEPTOE, Lydia. *See* **BARNES, Djuna.**

———

STEWARD, Samuel M(orris). American educator, poet, novelist, and author of short stories and erotica. Has also written as Phil Andros, Donald Bishop, Thomas Cave, Ted Kramer, John McAndrews, Joe Reynolds, Philip Sparrow, Ward Stames, and Philip Young. Born in Woodsfield, Ohio, 23 July 1909. Educated at Ohio State University, B.A. (cum laude) 1931, M.A. 1932, Ph.D. 1934. Professor of English, Carroll College, Helena, Montana, 1934–35; assistant professor of English, State College of Washington (now Washington State University), Pullman, 1935–36; associate professor of English, Loyola University, Chicago, 1935–46; editor, *World Book Encyclopedia,* 1946–48; associate professor of English, DePaul University, Chicago, 1948–54; tattoo artist, under name Phil Sparrow, in Chicago and Oakland, California, 1952–70; full–time writer, beginning 1970. Contributor of short stories to European magazines, sometimes under pseudonyms Donald Bishop, Thomas Cave, Ted Kramer, John McAndrews, Joe Reynolds, Ward Stames, and Philip Young; contributor to *Illinois Dental Journal* under pseudonym Philip Sparrow. Agent: Jed Mattes, 200 West 72nd Street, New York, New York 10023, U.S.A.

WRITINGS

Novels

Angels on the Bough. Idaho, Caxton, 1936.
Parisian Lives. New York, St. Martin's Press, 1984.
Murder Is Murder Is Murder. Boston, Alyson Publications, 1984.
The Caravaggio Shawl. Boston, Alyson Publications, 1989.

Short Stories

Pan and the Firebird. Harrison, 1930.

Poetry

Love Poems: Homage to Housman. Manroot, 1984.

Erotica as Phil Andros

$tud. Washington, D.C., Guild Press, 1966; revised with an introduction by John Preston, Boston, Alyson Publications, 1982.
The Joy Spot (originally written as private illustrations for artist Neel Bate's *In the Barn* drawings). Parisian Press, 1969; as *Ring Around the Rosy,* [Copenhagen], 1969.
My Brother the Hustler. Parisian Press, 1970; revised as *My Brother, My Self,* San Francisco, Perineum Press, 1983.
Renegade Hustler. San Diego, Greenleaf Classics, 1970; revised as *Shuttlecock,* San Francisco, Perineum Press, 1984.
When in Rome, Do.... Parisian Press, 1971; revised as *Roman Conquests,* San Francisco, Grey Fox Press, 1983.
San Francisco Hustler. Parisian Press, 1971; revised as *The Boys in Blue,* San Francisco, Perineum Press, 1984.
The Greek Way. San Diego, Greenleaf Classics, 1971; revised as *Greek Ways,* San Francisco, Perineum Press, 1984.
Below the Belt, and Other Stories. San Francisco, Perineum Press, 1982.
Different Strokes. San Francisco, Perineum Press, 1984.

Nonfiction

Dear Sammy: Letters from Gertrude Stein and Alice B. Toklas, with a Memoir. Boston, Houghton, 1977.
Chapters from an Autobiography. San Francisco, Grey Fox Press, 1981.
Author of introduction, *Quatrefoil* by James Barr. Boston, Alyson Publications, 1982.
Author of introduction, *The Gay Book of Days* by Martin Greif. Carol Publishing, 1985.
Bad Boys and Tough Tattoos: A Social History of the Tattoo with Gangs, Sailors, and Street-Corner Punks, introduction by Wardell B. Pomeroy. New York, Haworth Press, 1990.
Understanding the Male Hustler, introduction by John DeCecco. New York, Haworth Press, 1991.

*

Manuscript Collections: Mugar Library, Boston University.

Biography: *Advocate,* 24 August 1977; *Christopher Street,* July, 1981; *Advocate,* 11 December 1984.

Critical Sources: *Little Caesar,* Number 12, 1981; *Contemporary Authors,* Volume 112, Detroit, Gale, 1985, 465–466.

Samuel M. Steward comments: "It is almost universally acknowledged that the creative impulse functions best in periods of freedom of expression, when the forces of restriction and censorship and puritanical/religious pressure are the least powerful. As a person who has been alive in each decade of the twentieth century, I can attest to a number of observations on the truth of such an assertion.

"In the 1920s the so-called 'Jazz Age' had to contend with long standing forces of puritanism in order to break free, and to struggle against such movements as Comstock's society for the 'suppression of vice' which endeavored to control the outputs in all fields of the arts—pictorial, dramatic, and literary; the strength of the liberating forces eventually won out. (In the same period, the prohibition of alcoholic drinks was another manifestation of the power of the puritan element.) And most notably, at the mid-century point, McCarthyism threatened another repression, this time however with only a single point of pressure—against the threat of communism.

"But in the last decade of the twentieth century there appeared the most subtle and insidiously pervasive form of censorship yet to be found, one in keeping with the advanced sophistication and experience gained from former battles. This was the invidious barrier termed 'political correctness' which by its very nature invaded all forms of artistic and ordinary communication, suffocating the creative impulses or, at the very least, constricting them within the iron bands of limitations created by incompetent individuals. The worst thing about this form was that it was capable of being established by *anyone,* whether or not he had any qualifications.

"When I created the male hustler Phil Andros in the 1960s, I used him as a literary device because as a hustler he was able to enter all levels of society. He was at that time a quasi-romantic figure, a compound of a vague sort of mystery and fascination. But with the advent of 'political correctness' he became suspect, a disapproved figure whose activities went against the grain of the Noble Ideal of Homosexuality.

"What happened to Phil Andros is merely one example of the sort of constricting censorship that prevails in the last decade of the twentieth century. Unless this iron band can be broken and there can be established a return to a more matriarchal and permissive attitude, the arts in the next century would seem to be in for a rather bad quarter of an hour."

*　　*　　*

Samuel M. Steward is the author of novels, poetry, nonfiction, and erotica, most of the latter authored under the pseudonym Phil Andros. Donning other noms de plume—including Donald Bishop, Thomas Cave, Ted Kramer, John McAndrews, Joe Reynolds, Phil Sparrow, Philip Sparrow, Ward Stames, and Philip Young—Steward is known for his provocative writings about hustling, gay life, and tattooing. In all, Steward is said to have written under 25 pseudonyms, and he has contributed numerous short stories to European journals. Called "the father of us all," by George Whitmore in *Christopher Street*, Steward, through his work, has had a significant influence on later gay male erotic writers.

Born 23 July 1909, in Woodsfield, Ohio, Steward began experimenting with writing at a young age. Moving later to Richmond, Virginia, where his mother died, he was bullied and called a "damn Yankee." He saw acts of Ku Klux Klan violence and cross burnings in Richmond and again later in Woodsfield, which he described as the most culturally deprived corner of America. Upon finding a copy of Havelock Ellis' *Sexual Inversion,* he secretly studied it. When Steward was 14 or 15, his father grew concerned about his son's sexual orientation after finding a compromising note that the youth had written to a salesman. Steward had a hard time convincing his father that nothing had really happened. He believes that he ultimately succeeded, since few people could believe that someone they knew did such things. However, his father advised him to see a female prostitute—a typical remedy then recommended for deviant desires.

Steward attended Ohio State University, obtaining a B.A. cum laude in 1931, an M.A. in 1932, and a Ph.D. in 1934. During his college days, he created a stir by writing a frank qualifying essay on Walt Whitman's *Calamus*. He fell in with a crowd of gays and lesbians and a bohemian clique living in a large house. He studied with the popular Clarence Andrews, who was quite open about gay currents in literature—a subject that other academics almost never mentioned. His doctoral thesis on John Henry Newman's Oxford Movement upset many by discussing his subject's homosexuality.

Steward had temporarily converted to Catholicism, inspired oddly by *The Picture of Dorian Gray* and *Against the Grain,* together with other writings by J. K. Huysmans. From 1934 to 1935 he served as professor of English at Carroll College in Helena, Montana. He left that post after writing an article for a national Catholic magazine that upset many priests. He then worked stints as an assistant professor of English at the State College of Washington, now Washington State University, as an associate professor at Chicago's Loyola University, as editor of *World Book Encyclopedia,* and as associate professor of English at Chicago's DePaul University.

It was in 1937 that he made the first of several intimate visits to American writer Gertrude Stein and Alice B. Toklas. Previously, he had been in correspondence with the pair. He made other calls on notable authors such as Thomas Mann, André Gide, Alfred Douglas, and Thornton Wilder. Eventually his friendship with Stein and Toklas filtered into his writings, including the nonfiction *Dear Sammy: Letters from Gertrude Stein and Alice B. Toklas, with a Memoir,* an entertaining and informative account of their long friendship, and the novels *The Caravaggio Shawl* and *Murder Is Murder Is Murder,* featuring Stein and Toklas as amateur detectives.

Steward came to loathe teaching and opted for a new career as a tattoo artist in Chicago and Oakland, California, under the name Phil Sparrow. He was confidant and father confessor to scores of hustlers, tattooing many of the Hells Angels. A keen observer of others, Steward also kept a detailed account of his sexual encounters. After a long battle with alcoholism, he began writing in earnest, pulling from his varied background and experiences.

Among his works is *$tud,* a 1966 collection of intelligent, humane, and proud erotic stories of hustling in Chicago published under the name Phil Andros. First appearing in the *Der Kreis/Le Cercle,* a Swiss gay magazine, and Kim Kent's more daring Danish magazine *Eos, $tud* was conceived in answer to John Rechy's less positive outlook called *City of Night.* Subsequently, he has issued several additional novels as Andros. Some of these gritty stories were darkly filmed in the mid–1970s. In 1977 Grey Fox Press released Steward's heavily condensed *Chapters from an Autobiography.* Some readers, thrilled by the variety of his experience and the pleasure of his style, longed for the missing parts.

Later story collections include *Below the Belt* and *Different Strokes.* Of his novels, including *Shuttlecock* and *The Joy Spot, Parisian Lives* stands out, as do his Stein and Toklas mysteries. Steward told *Contemporary Authors:* "*Parisian Lives* presents, without excuses or fanfare, a way of life known to thousands: the position of the artist in modern society, the forces which fashion him, his resistance to the major paths which most people follow, and his right to create and enjoy life according to his deepest desires. Stein and Toklas best represented this right of the artist. They lived quietly but independently, didn't give a damn for world opinion. The protagonist of *Parisian Lives,* though imperfect, borrowed much of their absolute courage."

More recently, Steward has returned to writing nonfiction. *Bad Boys and Tough Tattoos: A Social History of the Tattoo with Gangs, Sailors and Street–Corner Punks* and *Understanding the Male Hustler* have established Steward as a natural in the growing field of gay sociology.

Describing the changes in sexual trends during the years and how they have been expressed in his literature, Steward told *Advocate* readers that the sexual practices of the 1920s and 1930s were fairly tame, with sadomasochism becoming more prevalent beginning in the mid–1950s. In a 1977 interview with Karl Maves in *Advocate,* Steward explained: "You have to tread such a fucking narrow line to be a queer these days, that I kind of pine for the old days when you were just an ordinary homosexual getting along and making it and having fun all the way. You didn't have to believe in liberation as the only path to heaven—your attention was far more, like, centered at the crotch, and you could enjoy it without making speeches about it."

Of his erotic literature, Steward told *Contemporary Authors:* "I consider erotica to be the purest form of entertainment, making the most direct connection between reader and writer and material. It is a panacea for lonely old men in hotel rooms at night. I wrote it all for my own amusement, hardly for the financial rewards. The novels lay fallow for a decade, then were revived in the 1980s with fair success. Like Stein, I have written mostly for myself and strangers."

—Jim Kepner

———

STRANG, Lennox. *See* **GRIER, Barbara G(ene Damon).**

———

STRONG, Lennox. *See* **GRIER, Barbara G(ene Damon).**

SVAREFF, Count Vladimir. *See* **CROWLEY, Aleister.**

———

SWINBURNE, A(lgernon) C(harles). British poet, literary critic, and novelist. Born in London, 5 April 1837; spent boyhood at family houses on the Isle of Wight and Northumberland. Educated at Eton College, 1849–56, and Balliol College, Oxford, 1856–60. *Died in London, of double pneumonia, 10 April 1909.*

WRITINGS

Poetry

Poems and Ballads. London, Moxon, 1866; as *Laus Veneris, and Other Poems and Ballads,* New York, Carleton, 1866.
An Appeal to England against the Executions of the Condemned Fenians. Manchester, 1867.
A Song of Italy. London, Hotten, and Boston, Ticknor & Fields, 1867.
Ode on the Proclamation of the French Republic. London, F. S. Ellis, 1870.
An Imitation of A. C. Swinburne's Ode on the Proclamation of the French Republic. London, Provost, 1871.
Songs before Sunrise. London, Ellis, and Boston, Roberts Brothers, 1871.
Songs of Two Nations. London, Chatto & Windus, 1875.
Poems and Ballads, Second Series. London, Chatto & Windus, 1878; New York, Crowell, c. 1885.
Songs of the Springtides. London, Chatto & Windus, 1880; New York, Worthington, c. 1882.
Studies in Song. London, Chatto & Windus, and New York, Worthington, 1880.
Specimens of Modern Poets: The Heptalogia; or, The Seven against Sense. London, Chatto & Windus, 1880.
Tristram of Lyonesse, and Other Poems. London, Chatto & Windus, 1882; Portland, Maine, Mosher, 1904.
A Century of Roundels. London, Chatto & Windus, and New York, Worthington, 1883.
A Midsummer Holiday, and Other Poems. London, Chatto & Windus, 1884.
Selections from the Poetical Works of A. C. Swinburne. London, Chatto & Windus, 1887.
Poems and Ballads, Third Series. London, Chatto & Windus, 1889.
Siena. London, J. C. Hotten, c. 1890.
A Sequence of Sonnets on the Death of Browning. London, privately printed, 1890.
Astrophel, and Other Poems. London, Chatto & Windus, and New York, Scribner, 1894.
Robert Burns: A Poem. Edinburgh, printed for the members of the Burns Centenary Club, 1896.

The Tale of Balen. London, Chatto & Windus, and New York, Scribner, 1896.
A Channel Passage, 1855. London, Heinemann, 1899.
Poems and Ballads, Second and Third Series. Portland, Maine, Mosher, 1902.
A Channel Passage, and Other Poems. London, Chatto & Windus, 1904.
Ode to Mazzini. London, privately printed, 1909.
The Ballade of Truthful Charles, and Other Poems. London, privately printed, 1910.
Border Ballads, edited by Thomas James Wise. Boston, Bibliophile Society, 1912.
Lady Maisie's Bairn, and Other Poems. London, privately printed, 1915.
Poems From "Villon," and Other Fragments. London, privately printed, 1916.
Poetical Fragments. London, privately printed, 1916.
Posthumous Poems, edited by Edmund Gosse and Thomas James Wise. London, Heinemann, 1917.
Rondeaux Parisiens. London, privately printed, 1917.
The Italian Mother, and Other Poems. London, privately printed, 1918.
The Ride from Milan, and Other Poems. London, privately printed, 1918.
A Lay of Lilies, and Other Poems. London, privately printed, 1918.
Queen Yseult; A Poem in Six Cantos. London, privately printed, 1918.
Lancelot, The Death of Rudel, and Other Poems. London, privately printed, 1918.
The Two Knights, and Other Poems. London, privately printed, 1918.
Undergraduate Sonnets. London, privately printed, 1918.
The Springtide of Life: Poems of Childhood, edited and with a preface by Edmund Gosse. London, Heinemann, 1918.
The Queen's Tragedy. London, privately printed, 1919.
French Lyrics. London, privately printed, 1919.
Cleopatra. Leeds, Swan Press, 1924.
Ballads of the English Border, edited by William A. MacInnes. London, Heinemann, 1925.
Pasiphaë, edited by Randolph Hughes. London, Golden Cockerel Press, 1950.
A Choice of Swinburne's Verse, edited by Robert Nye. London, Faber, 1973.
Swinburne: Selected Poems, edited by L. M. Findlay. Manchester, Fyfield Books, 1982.

Plays

The Queen–Mother. Rosamond. Two Plays. London, Pickering, 1860; Boston, Ticknor & Fields, 1866.
Atalanta in Calydon. London, Moxon, 1865; Boston, Ticknor & Fields, 1866.
Chastelard. London, Moxon, 1865; New York, Hurd and Houghton, 1866.
Bothwell. London, Chatto & Windus, 1874.
Erechtheus: A Tragedy. London, Chatto & Windus, 1876.
Mary Stuart. London, Chatto & Windus, and New York, Worthington, 1881.
Marino Faliero. London, Chatto & Windus, 1885.

Locrine: A Tragedy (produced, 1899). London, Chatto & Windus, and New York, Alden, 1887.

The Sisters. London, Chatto & Windus, and New York, United States Book Company, 1892.

Rosamund, Queen of the Lombards: A Tragedy. London, Chatto & Windus, and New York, Dodd, Mead, 1899.

The Duke of Gandia. London, Chatto & Windus, and New York, Harper, 1908.

Fiction

Love's Cross–Currents: A Year's Letters. Portland, Maine, Mosher, 1901; London, Chatto & Windus, 1905; unexpurgated version, edited by Francis Jacques Sypher, London, J. Owen, 1976.

The Chronicle of Queen Fredegond. London, privately printed, 1909.

Lucretia Borgia, edited by Randolph Hughes. London, Golden Cockerel Press, 1942.

Lesbia Brandon, edited by Randolph Hughes. London, Falcon Press, 1952.

The Novels of A. C. Swinburne. New York, Farrar, Straus & Cudahy, 1962.

Criticism

Notes on Poems and Reviews. London, J. C. Hotten, 1866.

William Blake: A Critical Essay. London, Hotten, 1868; New York, Dutton, 1906.

George Chapman: A Critical Essay. London, Chatto & Windus, 1875.

A Note on Charlotte Brontë. London, Chatto & Windus, 1877.

A Study of Shakespeare. London, Chatto & Windus, and New York, Worthington, 1880.

A Study of Victor Hugo. London, Chatto & Windus, 1886.

A Study of Ben Jonson. London, Chatto & Windus, and New York, Worthington, 1889.

Studies in Prose and Poetry. London, Chatto & Windus, and New York, Scribner, 1894.

Percy Dysshe Shelley. Philadelphia, Lippincott, 1903.

The Age of Shakespeare. New York and London, Harper, 1908.

Shakespeare. London and New York, Henry Frowde, 1909.

Three Plays of Shakespeare. New York, Harper, 1909.

Les Fleurs du Mal, and Other Studies. London, privately printed, 1913.

Charles Dickens. London, Chatto & Windus, 1913.

A Study of Victor Hugo's "Les Misérables," edited by Edmund Gosse. London, privately printed, 1914.

Pericles, and Other Studies. London, privately printed, 1914.

Thomas Nabbes: A Critical Monograph. London, privately printed, 1914.

Christopher Marlowe in Relation to Greene, Peele and Lodge. London, privately printed, 1914.

The Character and Opinions of Dr. Johnson. London, privately printed, 1918.

Contemporaries of Shakespeare, edited by Edmund Gosse and Thomas James Wise. London, Heinemann, 1919.

Swinburne as Critic, edited by Clyde K. Hyder. London, Routledge and Kegan Paul, 1972.

Collections

The Poems of Algernon Charles Swinburne (six volumes). London, Chatto & Windus, and New York, Harper, 1904.

The Tragedies of Algernon Charles Swinburne (six volumes). London, Chatto & Windus, and New York, Harper, 1905.

The Complete Works of Algernon Charles Swinburne (20 volumes), edited by Edmund Gosse and Thomas J. Wise. London, Heinemann, and New York, Wells, 1925–27.

A Swinburne Anthology: Verse, Drama, Prose, Criticism, edited by Kenelm Foss. 1955.

The Swinburne Letters (six volumes), edited by Cecil Y. Lang. New Haven, Connecticut, Yale University Press, 1959–62.

Other

Editor, *A Selection from the Works of Lord Byron.* London, Ward, Locke and Co., 1866.

With William Michael Rossetti, *Notes on the Royal Academy Exhibition, 1868.* London, Hotten, 1868.

Editor, *Cristabel, and the Lyrical and Imaginative Poems of S. T. Coleridge.* London, Sampson, Low, 1869.

Under the Microscope. London, White, 1872; Portland, Maine, Mosher, 1899.

Essays and Studies. London, Chatto & Windus, 1875.

Note of an English Republican on the Muscovite Crusade. London, Chatto & Windus, 1876.

Miscellanies. London, Chatto & Windus, 1886; New York, Worthington, 1886.

Dead Love, and Other Unedited Pieces. Portland, Maine, Mosher, 1901.

The Marriage of Monna Lisa. London, privately printed, 1909.

In the Twilight. London, privately printed, 1909.

The Portrait. London, privately printed, 1909.

Of Liberty and Loyalty. London, privately printed, 1909.

Translator, *The Ballade of Villon and Fat Madge* by François Villon. London, privately printed, 1910.

A Criminal Case. London, privately printed, 1910.

The Cannibal Catechism. London, privately printed, 1913.

Félicien Cossu: A Burlesque, edited by Edmund Gosse. London, privately printed, 1915.

Théophile. London, privately printed, 1915.

Ernest Clouët: A Burlesque, edited by Edmund Gosse. London, privately printed, 1916.

A Vision of Bags. London, privately printed, 1916.

The Death of Sir John Franklin. London, privately printed, 1916.

New Writings by Swinburne, edited by Cecil Y. Lang. Syracuse, New York, Syracuse University Press, 1964.

Swinburne Replies, edited by Clyde K. Hyder. 1966.

*

Manuscript Collections: British Library, London; Beinecke Library, Yale University; Rutgers University Library; National Library of Wales; Brotherton Library, Leeds University; Harry Ransom Humanities Research Center, University of Texas, Austin; New York Public Library; Mayfield Library, Syracuse University; Huntington Library, San Marino, California; Public Library of New

South Wales; Pierpont Morgan Library, New York; Free Library of Philadelphia; Trinity College, Cambridge University; Library of Congress; Harvard University Library; Princeton University Library; University of Michigan Library.

Biography: *The Life of Algernon Charles Swinburne* by Edmund Gosse, New York, Macmillan, 1917; *La Jeunesse de Swinburne, 1837–1867* by Georges Lafourcade (two volumes), London, Oxford University Press, 1928; *Swinburne: A Literary Biography* by Georges Lafourcade, London, Bell, 1932; "Swinburne's Lost Love" by Cecil Y. Lang, in *PMLA,* Number 74, 1959, 123–130; *Swinburne: A Critical Biography* by Jean Overton Fuller, London, Chatto & Windus, 1968; *Swinburne: Portrait of a Poet* by Philip Henderson, New York, Macmillan, 1974; *Swinburne: The Poet in His World* by Donald Thomas, New York, Oxford University Press, 1979.

Bibliography: *A Bibliography of the Writings of Swinburne* by Thomas James Wise (two volumes), London, privately printed, 1919 and 1920, published as *A Bibliography of the Writings in Prose and Verse of Algernon Charles Swinburne,* Volume 20 of *The Complete Works of Algernon Charles Swinburne,* London, Heinemann, and New York, Wells, 1927; *Algernon Charles Swinburne: A Bibliography of Secondary Works, 1861–1980* by Kirk H. Beetz, Metuchen, New Jersey, Scarecrow Press, 1982.

Critical Sources: *Swinburne's Literary Career and Fame* by Clyde K. Hyder, Durham, North Carolina, Duke University Press, 1933; *Swinburne's Theory of Poetry* by T. E. Connolly, Albany, State University of New York Press, 1964; *The Crowns of Apollo: Swinburne's Principles of Literature and Art* by Robert L. Peters, Detroit, Wayne State University Press, 1965; "Swinburne's Dearest Cousin: The Character of Mary Gordon" by F. A. C. Wilson, in *Literature and Psychology,* 19:2, 1969, 89–99; *Swinburne: The Critical Heritage,* edited by Clyde K. Hyder, London, Routledge, Kegan Paul, 1970; *The Romantic Agony* by Mario Praz, second edition, New York, Oxford University Press, 1970; "Swinburne, Sade, and Blake: The Pleasure–Pain Paradox" by Julian Baird, in *Victorian Poetry,* spring–summer 1971, 49–75; "*La Soeur de la Reine* and Related 'Victorian Romances' by Swinburne" by Gillian Workman, in *Harvard Library Bulletin,* Number 21, 1973, 356–364; "The Aesthetics of Androgyny in Swinburne's Early Poetry" by Anthony H. Harrison, in *Tennessee Studies in Literature,* Number 23, 1978, 87–99; "Swinburne's Masochism" by William B. Ober, in *Boswell's Clap, and Other Essays,* Carbondale, Southern Illinois University Press, 1979, 43–48; *Swinburne: An Experiment in Criticism* by Jerome McGann, Chicago, University of Chicago Press, 1981; "Sapphistries" by Susan Gubar, in *Signs,* Number 10, 1984, 43–62; "Closer than a Brother: Swinburne and Watts–Dunton" by John O. Jordan, in *Mothering the Mind: Twelve Studies of Writers and Their Silent Partners,* edited by Ruth Perry and Martine Watson Brownley, New York, Holmes and Meier, 1984, 204–216; "Swinburne's Dramatic Monologues: Sex and Ideology" by Thais E. Morgan, in *Victorian Poetry,* summer 1984, 175–195; "Poetry and Obscenity: Baudelaire and Swinburne" by Richard Sieburth, in *Comparative Literature,* fall 1984, 343–353; "A. C. Swinburne" by David G. Riede, in *Dictionary of Literary Biography,* Volume 35: *Victorian Poets after 1850,* Detroit, Gale, 1985; "Nature, Sex, and Decadence" by Camille A. Paglia, in *Pre–Raphaelite Poets,* edited by Harold Bloom, New York, Chelsea, 1986; "A. C. Swinburne" by

Donald Gray, in *Dictionary of Literary Biography,* Volume 57: *Victorian Prose Writers after 1867,* Detroit, Gale, 1987; "H. D. and A. C. Swinburne: Decadence and Sapphic Modernism" by Cassandra Laity, in *Feminist Studies,* Number 15, 1989, 461–84, reprinted in *Lesbian Texts and Contexts,* edited by Karla Jay, Joanne Glasgow, and Catherine Stimson, New York, New York University Press, 1990, 217–240; *Masculine Desire: The Sexual Politics of Victorian Aestheticism* by Richard Dellamora, Chapel Hill, University of North Carolina Press, 1990; "Swinburne's Sappho: The Muse as Sister–Goddess" by Joyce Zonana, in *Victorian Poetry,* Number 28, 1990, 39–50; "'Erotion', 'Anactoria', and the Sapphic Passion" by Robert A. Greenberg, in *Victorian Poetry,* Number 29, 1991, 79–87.

*   *   *

In examining the sexual content and themes of Algernon Charles Swinburne's writing, a variation in Swinburne's outlook and effect becomes evident. In his writing in the 1860s and 1870s, Swinburne made himself a provocative public presence by deliberately transgressing the conventions by which sexuality was represented in respectable mid–Victorian literature. In addition to violating the moral taboos of the period, Swinburne's early work stressed the interplay of sexuality—including homosexuality—and art, and the manner in which both elements impact on human existence. In other writings, however, Swinburne was less effective in this area. At times his sexually–charged work could degenerate into self–indulgent sketches that were closer to pornography than a sophisticated exploration of human actions. He also, in his later works, distanced himself from the provocative and compelling explorations of his early career, moving toward a more acceptable but ultimately less insightful position regarding alternative sexuality and its ramifications.

After leaving Oxford without taking a degree in 1860, Swinburne came up to London to make a life in literature, supported by an allowance from his father. He announced what was coming in a review in which he helped to introduce the poetry of Charles Baudelaire to English readers: "It has the languid, lurid beauty of close and threatening weather," he wrote of Baudelaire's verse, "a heavy, heated temperature, with dangerous hot–house scents in it." That metaphor also describes Swinburne's own *Poems and Ballads* in 1866, the book that gave him his reputation. Reviewers of the time called the poems obscene, bestial, and blasphemous. John Morley in the important weekly *Saturday Review* wrote that the book was a "revolt against the current notions of decency and dignity." Robert Buchanan, in a caricature that reveals how and why some readers thought that Swinburne had deviated from the conventions of morality, imagined the author as "long–ringletted, flippant–lipped, down–cheeked, amorous–lidded."

These responses resulted from the figures in Swinburne's poems that indulge in practices that his contemporaries considered unnatural. In "Dolores," for example, the Lady of Pain receives as well as renders pain, "The white wealth of thy body made whiter, / By the blushes of amorous blows." Similarly, the dark, decadent pleasures that excite the ferociously amorous empress in "Faustine" include "Stray breaths of Sapphic song" that "Shook the fierce quivering blood in you / By night." Ironically, the dominant theme of *Poems and Ballads* is the ultimate exhaustion and joylessness of sensual desire, the failure of flesh finally to satisfy. Swinburne was right to say in his reply to his critics, *Notes on Poems and Reviews,* that if his poems had to meet a moral test, "the upshot seems to me moral rather than immoral." But the reviewers who protested the indecorousness of his poems were responding to some of the figures and allusions in the work, rather than the poet's more elusive intentions. In two poems about hermaphroditism, Swinburne confounds conventional categories of gender even as he uses the hermaphrodite to epitomize the painful frustrations of desire. "Lift up thy lips, turn round, look back for love," he writes in "Hermaphroditus," a poem that portrays a "Blind love" that "casts out rest" because nothing "Shall make thee man and ease a woman's sighs, / Or make thee woman for a man's delight." Similarly, in "Fragoletta," the "sweet low bosom, thy close hair, / Thy strait soft flanks and slenderer feet" of the boy–woman make her finally sterile, inert, "still as Love that dies / For love of thee."

Sappho, the Greek lyric poet of Lesbos who was by legend bisexual, was a central figure in Swinburne's work. His invocation of Sappho, however, was more than a means of shocking Victorian mores, and the presence of the Greek poet indicates a deeper intention in Swinburne's focus on sexuality. This intention is revealed when Sappho speaks the dramatic monologue "Anactoria" from *Poems and Ballads.* Here she curses the female lover who has left her, but Sappho's cruelty—she wishes "That I could drink thy veins as wine, and eat / Thy breasts like honey"—is not only a metaphor for the self–annihilating pleasures of love; her parody of the eucharist mocks the violent providence of God, "Who hath made all things to break them one by one."

Sappho's further response to God's actions is the poetry that results in part from her sexuality and frustration; the songs she makes from her pain, she insists, will triumph over God's wasteful power. A decade after *Poems and Ballads* Swinburne chose a line from Sappho—"Nightingale of Lovely Song"—as the epigraph of his long meditative poem "On the Cliffs." In the poem he identifies the "strange manlike maiden" with the nightingale and also invokes the legend of Philomela, whom the gods transformed into a nightingale to protect her, and who in turn transformed the pain and terror of her rape into song. Sappho and the bird, "The small dark body's Lesbian loveliness / That held the fire eternal," pit their song against time, a force that "wastes all songs as roseleaves kissed and frayed." As in "Anactoria," Sappho triumphs: in her lyrics pain and loss are not transcended, but engaged and resolved in a harmony like that of eternity, "Where pain makes peace with pleasure" and "where love and song make strife, / Fire everlasting of eternal life."

In these poems Sappho's lesbianism and bisexuality serve not as signs of sterility but as figures that contain Swinburne's idea of the romantic poet as extraordinary. It is precisely because the poet is extraordinary that she and he are open to various realms of fleshly experience and to intimations of order beyond the pain of individual histories. Swinburne also played with this theme in *Lesbia Brandon,* an unfinished novel that was written in the 1860s and 1870s but not published until 1952. Two of the central characters in the novel, Lesbia Brandon, "poetess and pagan," and Herbert Seyton are sometimes described as androgynous. Herbert looks so like his sister that in one scene he dresses as a girl and is taken for her twin. Lesbia, whose father thinks "she is half–male as it is," turns out Sapphics that are as good as those of any boy at Eton and writes love poems in which "she always takes the man's part." As a boy Herbert is in love with his sister, Lady Wariston, and professes his passion in the usual Swinburnian way: "Oh, I should like you to tread me to death! darling!" His tutor, Denham, is also in love with

Lady Wariston, and he eases the pain of his repressed desire by beating Herbert in generously described floggings: "Hating her with all his heart as he loved her with all his senses, he could punish her through her brother, hurt her through her skin."

In *Lesbia Brandon* Swinburne presents a litany of controversial sexual situations, including adultery, potential incest, homoeroticism expressed or displaced in sadism and masochism, the confusion of genders in androgyny, cross–dressing, and the narcissism of loving oneself in a brother or sister. He plays these elements against a ground populated by stuffy or cynical upper–class men and women for whom sexual desire is a memory or a prurient topic of scandal. But for all this ammunition, his fragmentary novel does not as effectively explore the deeper issues that are present in his early poetry. Lesbia Brandon, whose sexual ambiguity and talent as a poet promise to make her a powerful antagonist to her society, appears only fitfully in the novel. Herbert's passion for his sister and his relationship with Denham become occasions for self–indulgent set–pieces describing flogging and states of yearning in which the pain of unconsummation is itself the pleasure. *Lesbia Brandon* often reads like Swinburne's sketches on flogging published anonymously in a pornographic journal and *The Whippingham Papers* in the 1880s, or like the gleeful references in his letters of the 1860s and 1870s to sodomy, lesbianism, bestiality, and the writings of Sade. All these attentions seem private, particular, and obsessive. Not only are they disconnected from the public discourse on sexuality and its representation in which *Poems and Ballads* and Swinburne's reviews participated, they also seem unconnected to the large themes and purposes of his own writing in which his depiction of uncommon sexual identities and pleasures also said something about the painful limits of fleshly experience and the special character of poets who make their songs on its boundaries.

In the second half of his career Swinburne withdrew from, and sometimes repudiated, the provocations of his earlier writing. He continued to amuse himself by writing poems and sketches about flogging, some of which he exchanged with a cousin, Mary Gordon Leith, to whom years before he had probably proposed marriage. In his published poetry, however, he no longer addressed explicitly erotic subjects or advanced unorthodox ideas about politics and the pain and possibilities of human experience. He showed his new decorousness as early as the second series of *Poems and Ballads* in 1878, in a poem on the death of Theophile Gautier, the author of *Mademoiselle de Maupin,* one of the "golden books" of Swinburne's young manhood in which lesbianism plays an important part. In the poem Swinburne refers discreetly only to "Veiled loves that shifted shapes" and "Flowers double–blossomed, ... / Sweet as the bride–bed, stranger than the grave." By failing to display the forthright approach to homosexuality that had marked his earlier work, Swinburne indicated the course that his writings would follow for the remainder of his career.

Further proof of the poet's changed outlook is evident in his varying attitudes toward the work of American poet Walt Whitman. After lavishly praising Whitman's work, Swinburne later withdrew his appreciation of Whitman citing the American's "unhealthily demonstrative and obtrusive animalism." Swinburne also cut himself off from previous companions of the 1860s and 1870s who he considered disreputable, and in letters and conversation professed an abhorrence of sodomy. He lived through the generation of Walter Pater, Oscar Wilde, and Aubrey Beardsley as an isolated eminence apparently uninterested in the sometimes profoundly unsettling representations and reconceptions of sexuality current in the 1890s.

Despite this change in outlook, Swinburne's energetic self–promotion in the 1860s and 1870s made him a pivotal figure regarding the presentation and consideration of sexuality that lay outside the mainstream. He was a rebel against literary, social, and moral orthodoxies, and he presented engaging images of fluid sexual identities and erotic practices that extended and complicated the meaning of sexual desire. These actions give him and his writing a central place in the literature of sexuality and in the history of ideas about its nature and appropriate expression.

—*Donald Gray*

————

SYMMES, Robert Edward. *See* **DUNCAN, Robert.**

T

TARN, Pauline Mary. *See* VIVIEN, Renée.

TEASDALE, Sara. American poet. Born in St. Louis, Missouri, 8 August 1884. Educated privately. Married Ernst B. Filsinger in 1914 (divorced 1929). **Recipient:** Poetry Society Award, 1917; Columbia Poetry Prize (later named Pulitzer Prize), 1918. *Died in New York City, of an overdose of sleeping pills, 29 January 1933.*

WRITINGS

Poetry

Sonnets to Duse, and Other Poems. Boston, Poet Lore, 1907.
Helen of Troy, and Other Poems. New York and London, Putnam, 1911; revised, New York, Macmillan, 1922.
Rivers to the Sea. New York, Macmillan, 1915.
Love Songs. New York, Macmillan, 1917.
Vignettes of Italy: A Cycle of Nine Songs for High Voice, 1919.
Flame and Shadow. New York, Macmillan, 1920; revised, 1924.
Dark of the Moon. New York, Macmillan, 1926.
Stars To–Night: Verses New and Old for Boys and Girls, illustrations by Dorothy P. Lathrop. New York, Macmillan, 1930.
A Country House, drawings by Herbert F. Roese. New York, Knopf, 1932.
Strange Victory. New York, Macmillan, 1933.

Other

Editor, *The Answering Voice: One Hundred Love Lyrics by Women.* Boston, Houghton, 1917; enlarged edition, New York, Macmillan, 1928.
The Collected Poems of Sara Teasdale, 1937.

*

Biography: *Sara Teasdale: A Biography* by Margaret Haley Carpenter, Norfolk, Pentelic Press, 1977; *Sara Teasdale* by Carol B. Schoen, Boston, Twayne Publishers, 1986; *Sara Teasdale: Woman and Poet* by William Drake, Knoxville, University of Tennessee Press, 1989.

Critical Sources: *Sara Teasdale* by Carol B. Schoen, Boston, Twayne Publishers, 1986.

*   *   *

Although Sara Teasdale was not a prolific poet, her poetry has a timelessness that transcends the fads of the genre. Teasdale wrote primarily from the heart about things of the heart. While she was alive, Teasdale received some critical acclaim, but the sense of that acclaim seemed to be for a poet who wrote "women's" poetry, not an unusual concept for the early years of the twentieth century.

Teasdale will not be remembered as a writer of poems about politics or pithy intellectual issues. She will not be remembered for her poems about the social issues of her day. In her early poems, when Teasdale was not writing about love and all the nuances associated with love—unrequited, gone bad, regained, or lost forever—she wrote about things that struck her fancy as she traveled on the Continent. As she grew older, her poems became darker in nature, and often turned to death and dying.

Teasdale's first collection, *Sonnets to Duse, and Other Poems,* published in 1907, deals with womanhood in two contradictory ways. On the one hand, the poems celebrate female beauty and power, while on the other, they portray women as fragile and weak. In *Helen of Troy, and Other Poems* in 1911, Teasdale explores tragic love through six monologues written from the point of view of well–known female characters from literature. The collection also includes "Union Square," written after the poet's visit to New York City. In this poem, which reviewers denounced as scandalous, Teasdale longs to reveal her love for someone, and she envies the prostitutes' assertiveness in sexual matters. Teasdale published the prize–winning volume, *Love Songs,* in 1917. A combination of new love poems and poetry from previous collections, the book also includes the series, "Interlude: Songs out of Sorrow," reflecting the first of many periods of depression that would lead to the poet's suicide in 1933.

Teasdale's love poems are genderless for the most part. The reader cannot tell to or about whom the poems were written. Her biographers, however, are sure that they were written to one of two men with whom, they insist, she was madly in love. The poems could just as easily have been written to two women with whom Teasdale had intense friendships. And, it must be noted, the "Duse" in the title of her first published book of poems was a woman, an actress whom Teasdale never met and never saw act, but whom Teasdale admired nevertheless. Teasdale was 23 at the time that she wrote *Duse.*

In letters exchanged with Marion Cummings Stanley during an intense two–year friendship, one finds passages filled with "romantic effusions." Why, if her personal correspondence with women was full of romantic effusions, is it not possible that some of the poems from these periods of intense friendships were written about/to these friends?

Two of her books were dedicated to people whose initials were used rather than their names. For instance, *Flame and Shadow* in 1920, was dedicated to "E." with the dedication being in French and ending with "*De tous mes jours*" (all my days). In 1917, Teasdale dedicated *Love Songs* to "E." and the dedication starts off with, "I have remembered beauty in the night." Teasdale's early biographers, who were men, insist that "E." is Ernst Filsinger, whom Teasdale married in 1914, but from whom she was estranged by the time these two books were published. "E." could have been Eunice Tietjens, a woman Teasdale met in 1913 and with whom she had an intense friendship for a few years, and who remained her friend until her death. It is commonly assumed that the poems written to "M." or entitled "For M." were written to a woman. Teasdale's biographers agree that "M." is Margaret Conklin, a young college student whom Teasdale befriended, and with whom, in 1927, she traveled to Europe. It is nearly impossible to determine whether Teasdale's relationships with her women friends went beyond platonic friendship, but many of her poems were genderless, while her private correspondence to her friends was effusively romantic. Those poems suggest that perhaps they, too, were directed toward women.

—*Pamela Bigelow*

THERION, Master. *See* **CROWLEY, Aleister.**

THOMAS, Paul. *See* **MANN, (Paul) Thomas.**

TOKLAS, Alice B(abette). American journalist, publisher, and author of cookbooks. Born in San Francisco, California, 30 April 1877. Educated at the University of Washington, 1893–95; studied music privately. Companion of author Gertrude Stein (died 1946). Lived in Paris. Owner and publisher of Plain Edition, a press devoted to publishing Stein's works. *Died in Paris, 7 March 1967.*

WRITINGS

Cookbooks

The Alice B. Toklas Cook Book. New York, Harper, and London, Joseph, 1954.
Aromas and Flavors of Past and Present, introduction and notes by Poppy Cannon. New York, Harper, and London, Joseph, 1958.
Author of introduction, *The Artists' and Writers' Cookbook* by Beryl Barr and Barbara Turner Sachs. Contact Editions, 1961.

Articles

"They Who Came to Paris to Write," in *New York Times Book Review,* 6 August 1950.
"Between Classics," in *New York Times Book Review,* 4 March 1951.
"Some Memories of Henri Matisse: 1907–1922," in *Yale Literary Magazine* (New Haven, Connecticut), fall 1955.
"Fifty Years of French Fashions," in *Atlantic Monthly* (Boston), June 1958.
"The Rue Dauphine Refuses the Revolution," in *New Republic* (Washington, D.C.), 18 August 1958.
"Sylvia and Her Friends," in *New Republic* (Washington, D.C.), 19 October 1959.

Other

Translator, *The Blue Dog, and Other Fables for the French* by Anne Bodart. Boston, Houghton, 1956.
What Is Remembered (memoirs). New York, Holt, and London, Joseph, 1963.
Staying on Alone: Letters of Alice B. Toklas, edited by Edward Burns. New York, Liveright, 1973.

*

Manuscript Collections: Beinecke Library, Yale University, New Haven, Connecticut; Bancroft Library, University of California, Berkeley.

Biography: *The Autobiography of Alice B. Toklas* by Gertrude Stein, New York, Random House, 1933; *Gertrude Stein in Pieces* by Richard Bridgeman, New York, Oxford University Press, 1970; *The Biography of Alice B. Toklas* by Linda Simon, Garden City, New York, Doubleday, 1977.

*   *   *

The first thing that must be said about Alice B. Toklas, as if the whole world did not already know, is that she did not write *The Autobiography of Alice B. Toklas.* That book, which was a popular success on two continents, was written by Gertrude Stein. The second thing that must be said when you ask about Toklas' contribution to lesbian and gay culture, is that her contribution was the work of Gertrude Stein. Which is not to deny Stein authorship of the works of Gertrude Stein, but rather to say that Stein was the work of Toklas and, as Toklas set about her work for Stein, she enabled the other to work.

Toklas and Stein loved good food. Toklas prepared excellent meals for Stein, as well as for the many guests at their table, and wrote about preparing good food, remarked on good friends, and told generally good stories in her *The Alice B. Toklas Cookbook.* Toklas' name has also become famous in the counter culture for "Alice B. Toklas Brownies" which, in the hippie days, were laced with cannabis, and for the "Alice B. Toklas Democratic Club" which fostered the likes of Harvey Milk in San Francisco. Toklas also gained a degree of notoriety for extolling the sensual pleasures of eating artichokes, which she did frequently, alone or with friends.

Toklas survived Stein by 21 years, but the death of her companion did not put an end to her work. As she had made it her goal to get the writings of Stein published in her lifetime—going to the point of selling a Picasso to create her own imprint, Plain Editions, which would publish Stein's *Lucy Church Amiably*—so she worked on after her friend's death to see that her works were properly published by Yale University Press. Toklas presented her readers a picture of Gertrude Stein at work in her memoir, *What Is Remembered,* published in 1963. And she demonstrated her own love of good gossip in *Staying on Alone: Letters of Alice B. Toklas,* published six years after her death. It is through the gossip of friends of both Toklas and Stein that we learn a good many gay tidbits: "Have you read Mercedes de Acosta's book—*Here Lies the Heart,*" she wrote to Anita Loos, adding, "You can't dispose of Mercedes lightly—she has had the two most important women in the U.S.—Greta Garbo and Marlene Dietrich."

Toklas has turned up in every principal piece of criticism or commentary on Stein. She is also a character in *Murder Is Murder Is Murder: A Gertrude Stein–Alice B. Toklas Mystery* by Samuel Steward, who wrote about gay male studs under the pseudonym Phil Andros, was a tattoo artist to the Hell's Angels, and served as the subject of one of Kinsey's first studies. Toklas and Stein had numerous other literary friends, some of whom did not like one woman but were fond of the other. Author and memoirist Bryher preferred to sit with Toklas while her lover, poet H. D., sat with the geniuses and Stein. And Ernest Hemingway came often to talk or enjoy the bounty of Toklas' kitchen, but made no pretense about his dislike for her.

In truth, in literature and in life, Toklas and Stein were inseparable. They have moved beyond the numerous adaptations of their relationship in fiction, film, and stage into the folklore of two continents. From the time Toklas met Stein in Paris after leaving earthquake–torn San Francisco in 1907, she chose to share her life with Stein as both woman and art. Together they lived an extraordinary life, whether it be rattling off to the front in World War I with a supply of bandages, screaming up and down Chicago's Lake Shore Drive in a police car, testing fate as Jews in Occupied France during two wars, or one writing, and the other typing, radical prose. In her biography of Toklas, Linda Simon finishes what George Bridgeman began in *Gertrude Stein in Pieces,* showing us the sexual puns and fun in the art and lives of these two extraordinary women. After Stein's death, Toklas became keeper of the flame. That Stein remains so much a part of the literary life of the world today is largely to her credit.

—*Marie J. Kuda*

TOURNIER, Michel (Edouard). French novelist and author of short fiction. Born in Paris, 19 December 1924. Educated at Collège Saint–Erembert and Collège Municipal, Saint–Germain–en–Laye; Université de Paris–Sorbonne; University of Tübingen. Producer and director, Radiodiffusion–Télévision Française (RTF), Paris, 1949–54; press attaché and radio announcer, Europe Numero Un, 1955–58; director of literary services, Editions Plon, Paris, 1958–

68; host of television series "La Chambre noire" ("The Black Room"), 1960–65. Founder of Rencontres Internationales de Photographie, an annual festival held in Arles, France. **Recipient:** Académie Française Grand Prize for Novel, 1967; Goncourt Prize, 1970; Chevalier, Légion d'Honneur; Commandeur, Ordre Nationale du Mérite; member, Académie Goncourt, since 1972. Address: Le Presbytère, Choisel, 78460 Chevreuse, France.

WRITINGS

Novels

Vendredi; ou, Les Limbes du Pacifique. Paris, Gallimard, 1967; revised, 1978; translated by Norman Denny as *Friday; or, The Other Island,* London, Collins, and Garden City, New York, Doubleday, 1969.

Le Roi des aulnes. Paris, Gallimard, 1970; translated by Barbara Bray as *The Erl–King,* London, Collins, 1972; as *The Ogre,* Garden City, New York, Doubleday, 1972.

Vendredi; ou, La Vie sauvage (for children). Paris, Flammarion, 1971; translated by Ralph Manheim as *Friday and Robinson: Life on Experanza Island,* New York, Knopf, and London, Aldus, 1972.

Les Météores. Paris, Gallimard, 1975; translated by Anne Carter as *Gemini,* London, Collins, and Garden City, New York, Doubleday, 1981.

Gaspard, Melchior et Balthazar. Paris, Gallimard, 1980; translated by Ralph Manheim as *The Four Wise Men,* London, Collins, and Garden City, New York, Doubleday, 1982; revised as *Les Rois mages,* Paris, Gallimard, 1983.

A Garden at Hammamet (original title, *Un Jardin à Hammamet*), translated by Barbara Wright, illustrations by Leila Menchari. Northridge, California, Lord John Press, 1985.

Gilles et Jeanne. Paris, Gallimard, 1983; translated by Alan Sheridan as *Gilles and Jeanne,* London, Methuen, 1987.

La Goutte d'or. Paris, Gallimard, 1985; translated by Barbara Wright as *The Golden Droplet,* London, Collins, and Garden City, New York, Doubleday, 1987.

Le Médianoche amoureux. Paris, Gallimard, 1989; translated by Barbara Wright as *The Midnight Love Feast,* London, HarperCollins, 1991.

Short Stories

Amandine; ou, Les Deux Jardins ["Amandine; or, The Two Gardens"]. Rouge et Or, 1977.

Le Coq de bruyère (includes "La famille Adam," "La fin de Robinson Crusoé," "La Mère Noël," "Amandine ou les deux jardins," "La fugue du petit Poucet," "Tupik," "Que ma joie demeure," "Le nain rouge," "Tristan Vox," "Les suaires de Véronique," "La jeune fille et la mort," "Le coq de bruyère," L'aire du muguet," and " "Le fétichiste"). Paris, Gallimard, 1978; translated by Barbara Wright as *The Fetishist, and Other Stories,* London, Collins, 1983; Garden City, New York, Doubleday, 1984.

Le Fugue du Petit Poucet ["Tom Thumb Ran Away"] (a Christmas story). Rouge et Or, 1979.

Pierrot; ou, Les Secrets de al nuit. Paris, Gallimard, 1981.

Barbedor. Paris, Gallimard, 1982.

L'Aire de Muquet. Paris, Gallimard, 1982.

Sept Contes. Paris, Gallimard, 1984.

Plays

Le Fétichiste: Un Acte pour un homme seul (based on author's short story; produced Paris, 1974; translated by Barbara Wright produced as *The Fetishist* Off–Broadway, 1984; Edinburgh, 1987).

Other

Le Nain rouge, illustrations by Anne–Marie Soulcié. Montpellier, Fata Morgana, 1975.

Le Vent Paraclet (literary autobiography). Paris, Gallimard, 1977; translated by Arthur Goldhammer as *The Wind Spirit: An Autobiography,* Boston, Beacon Press, 1988; London, Collins, 1989.

La Famille des enfants (photo collection; commentary by the author). Paris, Flammarion, 1977.

Canada: Journal de voyage, photographs by Édouard Boubat. Montréal, La Presse, 1977; as *Journal de voyage au Canada,* Paris, Laffont, 1984.

With Joseph Göbbels, *Derniers carnets.* Paris, Flammarion, 1977.

With Georges Lemoine, *Des Clefs et des serrures* ["Of Keys and Locks"]. Paris, Editions du Chêne/Hachette, 1979.

Le Vol du vampire ["The Flight of the Vampire"]. Paris, Mercure de France, 1981.

Vues de dos, photographs by Édouard Boubat. Paris, Gallimard, 1981.

L'Aire du muguet ["The Lily of the Valley Rest Area"]. Paris, Gallimard, 1982.

With Konrad R. Müller, *François Mitterand.* Paris, Flammarion, 1983.

Le Vagabond immobile, designs by Jean–Max Toubeau. Paris, Gallimard, 1984.

Marseille; ou, Le Présent incertain (photo collection). Paris, PUF, 1985.

Le Tabor et le Sinaï: Éssais sur l'art contemporain. Paris, Belfond, 1988.

Recordings: *Robinson et Tiffauges,* Paris, Desalle, c. 1974.

*

Adaptations: Several stories published in the collection *Le Coq de bruyere* have been adapted for and broadcast on French television.

Interviews: "An Interview with Michel Tournier" by Penny Hueston, in *Meanjin,* May 1978, 401–408; "Michel Tournier: Le Secret d'un livre est la patience" by Jacques Chancel, in *Figaro–Dimanche,* 9 December 1979, 29; "Michel Tournier: 'Je me suis toujours voulu écrivain croyant'" by J. M. de Montrémy, in *Croix,* 10 November 1980, 8; "Michel Tournier: 'J'ai pris la plume et j'ai inventé la vérité'" by Roger d'Ivernois, in *Journal de Genève,* 9 January 1981, 13; "Qu'est–ce que c'est que la littérature? Un Entretien avec Michel Tournier" by Jean–Jacques Brochier, in *Magazine Littéraire,* Number 179, 1982, 80–86.

Critical Sources: *Sud,* spring 1980 (special Tournier issue); *Michel Tournier* by William Cloonan, Boston, Twayne Publishers, 1985; *Michel Tournier* by David Bevans, Amsterdam, Rodopi, 1986; *Sud,* winter 1985–1986 (special Tournier issue); *Michel Tournier: Philosophy and Fiction* by Colin Davis, Oxford, Clarendon Press, 1988;

"Michel Tournier" by William Cloonan in *Dictionary of Literary Biography,* Volume 83: *French Novelists since 1960,* Detroit, Gale, 1989.

*   *   *

Michel Tournier's novels evince an enormous interest in sexuality, but, despite superficial appearances, they do not display an exclusive concern with homosexuality as such. The originality of Tournier's approach to sexuality emerges in his depictions of possible forms of sexual expression that are not focused uniquely on the genitals. Freud claimed that infants were naturally "polymorphous perverse," that they took an erotic pleasure in all parts of their body, as well as in surrounding objects. The development into maturity, according to Freud, involved the gradual abandonment of everything except genitalia as sources of sexual pleasure. Whatever the merits of Freud's thesis, it is consistently, albeit ironically, evoked and challenged in Tournier's writing.

The most politically–aware gay character in Tournier's works is Alexander Surin, The Gemini, a wealthy, self–proclaimed "dandy of sewage," who travels around France in search of physical pleasure that is never without intellectual enlightenment. Alexander carries a cane that conceals a rapier, but his real weapon is his tongue. His life is a continuous denunciation of bourgeois hypocrisy and its attendant cult of sex only in the service of breeding. If his gayness has made him different, this difference is the vantage point from which he views the stupidities which surround him. Alexander may be a warrior in the service of homosexuality, but he is not always a happy one. His life is a constant struggle to expose and deride the straight world whose predictably narrow views are leading the world to hell. When his young lover, Daniel, dies in an accident that was in some small degree Alexander's fault, the older man loses interest in these daily battles, and permits himself to become a murder victim.

Tournier's fiction features a number of other homosexual characters as well. In addition to Alexander Surin's friend, Thomas Koussek, a gay priest who, as a boy, aspired to make love to the crucified Christ, there is a set of twins, Jean and Paul—Alexander's nephews—who are lovers, at least until Jean attempts to break away and experience the heterosexual world. The preceding list of characters can easily give the impression that Tournier's novels are a celebration of the bittersweet joys of gayness. Nothing, however, could be more misleading.

Gayness produces some striking characters and dramatic situations in Tournier's works, but there is little in his presentation about the societal problems confronting gays that would distinguish his treatment from those of other authors. In his novels the liberty of sexual expression is in principle simply taken for granted, even though it is apparent that his gay characters have a more difficult time than the straights. Some, like Alexander Surin, respond to this pressure with brilliance and verve; others, like Achille Mage in *Golden Droplet,* do little besides employ the trappings of artistic creativity as a ploy for seducing unsuspecting boys.

In other works Tournier examines the limits of human sexuality, dealing not only with gay sexual desires but other, less common forms of erotic expression. In *Friday; or, The Other Island,* Tournier rewrites the classic Robinson Crusoe story. In his version, Crusoe arrives on the island as a rather typical married Englishman. During his years as a castaway, he progresses through stages where he literally makes love to the island because its form resembles that of a woman's body; where he allows his understanding of eroticism to be transformed by Friday, even though they never have sex, into an intensely amorous relationship with his natural habitat; and finally where he describes himself as transformed into a woman engaged in love–making with the sun.

In *The Ogre*, Abel Tiffauges derives erotic satisfaction from *la phorie*, which is the act of carrying little boys on one's shoulders. *La phorie* may be taken quite literally, and its significance limited to a satisfaction that attends carrying a child, or it can be given a broader interpretation which would permit it to symbolize any form of non–genitally stimulated erotic pleasure.

While *la phorie* is Tournier's most striking representation of the possibility of a non–genital sexuality, his treatment of it, as his treatment of all sexual matters, is suffused with irony and ambiguity. Abel is a chronic self–deceiver convinced that he has some vast, vaguely–articulated destiny; this leads him into collaboration with the Nazis. Robinson Crusoe in *Friday* has a propensity for cosmic statements and associations that make it equally dangerous to take all his pronouncements at face value. The origin of both characters' incapacity to view themselves without a significant dose of hyperbole may well lie in their refusal to confront in a direct manner the reality of their sexual distinctiveness.

Certainly, the failure to accept one's sexuality, whatever its nature, has disastrous consequences in Tournier's fiction. In *Gilles and Jeanne*, Gilles de Rais, the friend and admirer of Joan of Arc, begins his career as a hero in the French struggle against the English and then ends his life as a criminal convicted of raping and murdering thousands of children, mostly boys. Gilles' transformation from aspiring saint to certain sinner was surely influenced by his intense personal disillusionment that followed the rigged trial and execution of Joan of Arc. Yet throughout his life, as a soldier preparing for his next battle, or as a wealthy noble discovering ways to lure children to his chateau, Gilles forever avoided confronting himself as a sexual being. This refusal contributed to Gilles' death, as well as the deaths of many others.

The consequences of denying one's sexuality are indeed grim in Tournier, but the pleasures of knowing one's identity, or even the possibilities inherent in moving beyond traditional gender categorizations, are great. A story which appears in *The Fetishist, and Other Stories* may well be emblematic of the joyful potential inherent in a sense of self which eschews sexual stereotyping of any sort. In "Mother Christmas" ("La Mere Noel") a village teacher must play the role of Santa Claus at a Christmas celebration. During this ceremony, the teacher's infant child is attending midnight mass across the street. When the baby begins to cry, the teacher is quickly summoned. Santa Claus strides into the church, pushes back the famous white beard, opens the mandatory red coat, and offers her breast to her hungry son.

—*William Cloonan*

TREMBLAY, Michel. French Canadian dramatist, novelist, and author of short fiction. Born in Montréal, Québec, 25 June 1942. Educated at the Institut des Arts Graphiques. Linotypist, 1963–66. Since 1964 writer. **Recipient:** Radio Canada prize, 1964; Méritas

Trophy, 1970, 1972; Canada Council award, 1971; Chalmers award, 1972, 1973, 1974, 1975, 1978, 1986, and 1989; Victor Morin prize, 1974; Canadian Film Festival award, 1975; Ontario Lieutenant–Governor's Medal, 1976 (twice); Québec Ministry of International Relations France–Québec prize, 1981 and 1985; Festival du Théâtre des Ameriques award, 1985; City of Montréal grand prize, 1989; Prix du Public, 1990; Grand Prix du Public, 1990; Jacques–Cartier Lyon prize, 1991. Chevalier, 1984, and Officier, 1991, de l'Ordre des Arts et des Lettres (France). Honorary doctorate: Concordia University, 1990; McGill University, 1991. Agent: Agence Goodwin, 839 est, rue Sherbrooke, Suite 2, Montréal, Québec H2L 1K6, Canada.

WRITINGS

Plays

Le Train (broadcast on radio, 1964; produced Montréal, 1965). Montréal, Leméac, 1990.

Messe noir (adaptations of selected stories from his *Contes pour buveurs attardés* (produced Montréal, 1965).

Cinq (includes *Berthe; Johnny Mangano and His Astonishing Dogs; Gloria Star;* first produced Montréal, 1966). Revised as *En Pièces détachées* (produced Montréal, 1969), with *La Duchesse de Langeais*, Montréal, Leméac, 1970; translated by Allan Van Meer as *Like Death Warmed Over* (produced Winnipeg, Manitoba, 1973), Toronto, Playwrights Co–op, 1973; as *Montréal Smoked Meat* (produced Toronto, 1974), Vancouver, Talon, 1975; as *Broken Pieces* (produced Vancouver, 1974); as *Trois Petit Tours* (television adaptation; broadcast, 1969), Montréal, Leméac, 1971; in *La Duchesse de Langeais, and Other Plays*, 1976.

Les Belles–Soeurs (produced Montréal, 1968). Montréal, Holt, 1968; translated by John Van Burek and Bill Glassco as *Les Belles–Soeeurs*, Vancouver, Talon, 1974; as *The Guid Sisters* (produced Toronto and Glasgow, 1987), Toronto, Exile, 1988; London, Hern, 1991.

With André Brassard, *Lysistrata* (adaptation of the play by Aristophanes; produced Ottawa, 1969). Montréal, Leméac, 1969.

Les Paons (produced Ottawa, 1971). Montréal, CEAD, 1969.

L'Effet des rayons gamma sur les vieux–garçons (adaptation of *The Effect of Gamma Rays on Man–in–the–Moon Marigolds* by Paul Zindel; produced Montréal, 1970). Montréal, Leméac, 1970.

La Duchesse de Langeais (produced Montréal, 1970). With *En Pièces détachées*, Montréal, Leméac, 1970; in *La Duchesse de Langeais, and Other Plays*, 1976.

"...Et Mademoiselle Roberge boit un peu..." (adaptation of *And Miss Reardon Drinks a Little* by Paul Zindel; produced Montréal, 1972). Montréal, Leméac, 1971.

Les Paons (fantasy; produced, 1971).

Le Pays du dragon (adaptation of four one–act plays by Tennessee Williams; produced Montréal, 1971).

À Toi, pour toujours, ta Marie–Lou (produced Montréal, 1971). Montréal, Leméac, 1971; translated by John Van Burek and Bill Glassco as *Forever Yours, Marie–Lou* (produced Toronto, 1974), Vancouver, Talon, 1975.

Demain matin Montréal m'attend (produced Montréal, 1972). Montréal, Leméac, 1972.

Hosanna (produced Montréal, 1973; Toronto, 1974; New York; Birmingham and London, 1981). With *La Duchesse de Langeais,*

Montréal, Leméac, 1973; translated by John Van Burek and Bill Glassco, Vancouver, Talon, 1974.

Mistero buffo (translation and adaptation of the play by Dario Fo; produced Montréal, 1973).

Bonjour, là, bonjour (produced Ottawa, 1974). Montréal, Leméac, 1974; (translation by John Van Burek and Bill Glassco produced, 1975), Vancouver, Talon, 1975.

Mademoiselle Marguerite (adaptation of *Aparaceu a Margarida* by Roberto Athayde; produced Ottawa, 1976). Montréal, Leméac, 1975.

Les Héros de mon enfance (musical comedy; produced Eastman, Québec, 1975). Montréal, Leméac, 1976.

Surprise! Surprise! (produced Montréal, 1975). With *Damnée, Manon, sacrée Sandra*, Montréal, Leméac, 1977; in English, in *La Duchesse de Langeais, and Other Plays*, 1976.

Sainte–Carmen de la Main (produced Montréal, 1976). Montréal, Leméac, 1976; translated by John Van Burek as *Saint Carmen of the Main* (broadcast BBC Radio, 1987), Vancouver, Talon, 1981.

La Duchesse de Langeais, and Other Plays (includes *La Duchesse de Langeais; Berthe; Johnny Mangano and His Astonishing Dogs; Gloria Star; Surprise*). Vancouver, Talon, 1976.

Damnée Manon, sacrée Sandra (produced Montréal, 1977). With *Surprise! Surprise!*, Montréal, Leméac, 1977; (translation by John Van Bureck produced in U.S., 1981), Vancouver, Talon, 1981; as *Sandra/Manon* (produced Edinburgh and London, 1984).

L'Impromptu d'Outremont (produced Montréal, 1980). Montréal, Leméac, 1980; translated by John Van Burek as *The Impromptu of Outremont* (produced, 1981), Vancouver, Talon, 1981.

Les Grandes Vacances (produced Montréal, 1981).

Les Anciennes Odeurs (produced Montréal, 1981). Montréal, Leméac, 1981; translated by John Stowe as *Remember Me*, Vancouver, Talon, 1984.

With Kim Yaroshevskaya, *Oncle Vania* (adaptation of the play by Anton Chekhov). Montréal, Leméac, 1983.

Albertine en cinq temps (produced Ottawa, 1984). Montréal, Leméac, 1984; translated by John Van Burek and Bill Glassco as *Albertine in Five Times* (produced Toronto, Edinburgh, and London, 1986), Vancouver, Talon, 1987; London, Hern, 1991.

Le Gars de Québec (adaptation of *Le Revizov* by Nikolai Gogol; produced Montréal, 1985). Montréal, Leméac, 1985.

Six Heures au plus tard, adaptation of the play by Marc Perrier. Montréal, Leméac, 1986.

Le Vrai Monde? (produced concurrently in Ottawa and Montréal, 1987). Montréal, Leméac, 1987; translated as *The Real World* (produced London, 1990), Vancouver, Talon, 1988.

Nelligan (opera libretto; produced Montréal, 1990). Montréal, Leméac, 1990.

La Maison suspendue (produced Montréal, 1990). Montréal, Leméac, 1990; in English, Vancouver, Talon, 1991.

Théâtre I. Arles, Actes Sud, 1991.

Radio Plays

Le Train, 1964.
Saint Carmen of the Main, 1987.

Television Plays

Trois Petits Tours, from his plays, 1969.

Fiction

Contes pour buveurs attardés (short stories). Montréal, Editions du Jour, 1966; translated by Michael Bullock as *Stories for Late Night Drinkers*, Vancouver, Intermedia Press, 1977.

La Cité dans l'oeuf (fantasy novel). Montréal, Editions du Jour, 1969.

C't'à ton tour, Laura Cadieux. Montréal, Editions du Jour, 1973.

Le Cœur découvert: Roman d'amours. Montréal, Leméac, 1986; translated by Sheila Fischman as *The Heart Laid Bare*, Toronto, McClelland and Stewart, 1989; as *Making Room*, London, Serpent's Tail, 1990.

Le Premier Quartier de la lune. Montréal, Leméac, 1989.

Les Vues animées. Montréal, Leméac, 1990.

"Chroniques du plateau Mont–Royal" Series

La Grosse Femme d'à côté est enceinte (first novel in tetralogy). Montréal, Leméac, 1978; translated by Sheila Fischman as *The Fat Woman Next Door Is Pregnant*, Vancouver, Talon, 1981; London, Serpent's Tail, 1991.

Thérèse et Pierrette à l'école des Saints–Anges (second novel in tetralogy). Montréal, Leméac, 1980; translated by Sheila Fischman as *Therese and Pierrette and the Little Hanging Angel*, Toronto, McClelland and Stewart, 1984.

La Duchesse et le roturier (third novel in tetralogy). Montréal, Leméac, 1982.

Des Nouvelles d'Édouard (fourth novel in tetralogy). Montréal, Leméac, 1984.

Films

Screenplay and dialogue, with André Brassard, *Françoise Durocher, Waitress*, 1972.

Screenplay and dialogue, with André Brassard, *Il était une fois dans l'est*, 1973.

Scenario and dialogue, *Parlez–Vous d'amour*, Films 16, 1976.

Scenario and dialogue, *Le Soleil se lève en retard*, Films 16, 1977.

Le Cœur découvert, 1986.

Le Grand Jour, 1988.

Six Heures plus tard, 1988.

Le Vrai Monde?, 1991.

Other

Québec, trois siècles d'architecture, with Claude Paulette and Luc Noppen. Montréal, Libre Expression, 1979.

*

Adaptations: *Saint Carmen of the Main: Opera in Two Acts*, music by Sydney Hodkinson, libretto by Lee Devin, Associated Music Publishers, 1986.

Manuscript Collections: Bibliothèque Nationale du Canada, Ottawa.

Interviews: "Interview with Tremblay" by Michel Beaulieu, in *Perspectives*, 17 February 1973, 6–9; "Interview with Tremblay" by Geraldine Anthony, in her *Stage Voices: Twelve Canadian Playwrights Talk About Their Lives and Work*, Toronto and Garden City, New York, Doubleday, 1978, 275–291; "Where to Begin the Accusation," by Renate Usmiani, in *Canadian Theatre Review* (Toronto), Number 24, 1979.

Bibliography: By P. Lavoie, in *Voix et Images* (Montréal), winter 1982.

Critical Sources: "Michel Tremblay's Seduction of the 'Other Solitude'" by Catherine McQuaid, in *Canadian Drama* (Guelph, Ontario), Number 2, 1976; *Stage Voices: Twelve Canadian Playwrights Talk About Their Lives and Work*, edited by Geraldine Anthony, Garden City, New York, Doubleday, 1978; "Five Short Plays by Tremblay" by Bruce Serafin, in *Essays on Canadian Writing* (Toronto), Number 11, 1978; "The Tremblay Opus: Unity in Diversity" by Renate Usmiani in *Canadian Theatre Review* (Toronto), Number 24, 1979; *Michel Tremblay: A Critical Study* by Renate Usmiani, Vancouver, Douglas and McIntyre, 1982; "From Alienation to Transcendence: The Quest for Selfhood in Michel Tremblay's Plays" by John Ripley, in *Canadian Literature* (Vancouver), Number 85, 1980; "Michel Tremblay and the Fantastic of Violence" by Ruth B. Antosh, in *Aspects of Fantasy*, edited by William Coyle, Westport, Greenwood, 1986; "Structures of Impasse in Michel Tremblay's *Albertine en cinq temps*" by Elaine Hopkins Garrett, in *Québec Studies* (Montréal), Number 4, 1986; "Michel Tremblay" by Renate Usmiani, in *Dictionary of Literary Biography*, Volume 60: *Canadian Writers Since 1960*, Gale, 1987; "An Eye for an Ear: *Fifth Business* and *La Grosse Femme d'à côté est enceinte*" by Gregory J. Reid, in *Studies in Canadian Literature*, 14:2, 1989; "Canadian Author and Dramatist" by B. A. Came in *Macleans*, 30 December 1991, 36–37.

*   *   *

Unlike most writers, whose early work reflects the experience of their childhood and early youth, Michel Tremblay creates for the reader a world in which the autobiographical element unfolds progressively and by degrees as his universe expands; this is particularly true for the revelation of his sexual orientation. Although the homosexual element is present throughout his work, it first appears in a largely objective manner with the political symbolism of the transvestite figures of his early plays. The central transvestite character reappears in the autobiographical epic of *Les Chroniques du Plateau Mont Royal*. Finally, in the third phase of the author's work, Tremblay himself takes center stage, first thinly disguised as Jean–Marc, the professor of French, and at last openly in the stories of *Les Vues animée* ("The Movies"), which tell how the boy Michel first discovers and faces his "abnormal" proclivities. And so the cycle closes.

When Tremblay's first play, *Les Belles–soeurs*, exploded on the theatre scene of Québec in 1968, his bombshell was entirely linguistic. His bold introduction of *joual*, the Montréal working class dialect, as a dramatic idiom was immediately seen as a political statement and Tremblay marked as a political writer. Thus, when his transvestite characters appeared, especially *La Duchesse de Langeais*, 1970, and *Hosanna*, 1973, they, too, took on political significance. Tremblay himself encouraged this view, calling *Hosanna* an "allegory about Québec" and declaring Québeckers "a

people who have been in disguise for 200 years." His transvestites' multiple disguises reflect the alienation, isolation and postcolonial identity crisis of Québec. However, these characters carry a human pathos far beyond political symbolism: Sandra, in the 1977 *Damnée Manon, Sacrée Sandra*, awaiting her lover in a grotesque imitation of the Virgin Mary; Claude/Hosanna, tragically disappointed in her efforts to impress as Elizabeth Taylor and Cleopatra; and especially the grande dame of them all, the Duchesse de Langeais, alias Edouard, humble shoe salesman, who has picked this romantic character from Balzac for his new self, superimposing upon it countless imitations of famous actresses in their star roles, including Galina Ulanovna's Dying Swan. Besides these central characters, Tremblay has created a host of minor fringe figures to fill in the background of life on the "Main", the seedy street in East Montréal which is their particular world—most important among these fringe figures are the double chorus of "whores" and "transvestites" in *Sainte Carmen de la Main*.

With the victory of the Parti Québécois in 1976, Tremblay's political ardor cooled. At the same time, he turned from drama to fiction, beginning an ambitious project to recreate the world of his childhood with the novel series *Les Chroniques du Plateau Mont Royal*. It was a truly epic undertaking, creating, in minute detail, a background for the characters of the plays, tracing their origin and development on and around rue Fabre, the street where he was born. "Je me suis fait le chantre de la rue Fabre" ("I have made myself the bard of rue Fabre"), he said of this undertaking.

Tremblay himself appears marginally in the novel series, always under the impersonal designation of "l'enfant de la grosse femme" ("the fat woman's child"). However, two entire volumes of the series are devoted to the Duchesse: *La Duchesse et le roturier* and *Des Vouvelles d'Édouard*. The first volume follows the evolution of "l'oncle Édouard," from his first timid attempts at a double life ("roturier" commoner, during the day; "duchesse" at night) through his increasing involvement with the demi–monde of show business to his eventual decision to cross over: "J'ai décidé de casser le moule ... Définitivement. De pus avoir honte. De pus me cacher ... Défier le monde, c'est tout c'qui nous reste pour qu'ils nous endurent" ("I've decided to break the mold ... Definitely. Not to feel ashamed any more. Not to hide myself any more ... To defy them ... that's all we have left so they put up with us.") The book ends on a triumphant note, as the "duchesse" makes her first public appearance. "Édouard avait entr'ouvert la porte qui menait peut–être à la liberation" ("Édouard had opened the door which would perhaps lead to liberation.").

Most of the following volume deals with the intensely disappointing experiences of Édouard's one and only trip to Paris, which convinces him for good of the advantage of illusion over reality. The book also brings to a close the life of the Duchesse, ignominiously murdered on a parking lot by the notorious Toothpick, henchman of Maurice, "king of the Main," to whom the aging drag queen has become an embarrassment.

While working on the early volumes of the *Chroniques du Plateau Mont Royal*, Tremblay also returned to playwriting. This time, his plot is clearly autobiographical. In *Les anciennes odeurs* ("Remember me"), he explores the relationship between a homosexual couple who have broken up, but whose tenderness and complicity persist. Jean–Marc, a professor of French and a novelist, unable to tolerate the unceasing infidelities of Luc, an actor, now lives with another man; when Luc comes to visit, all their pain, frustration and hostility comes to the surface—along with their enduring love.

Jean–Marc reappears as the central character of Tremblay's 1986 novel, *Le Coeur découvert* ("The Heart Laid Bare"). The book explores in detail the tentative, gradual evolution of a deep and eventually fully committed love relationship. At 39, Jean–Marc falls in love with 24–year–old Mathieu, who has only recently discovered his sexual orientation. Mathieu, previously married, has a four–year–old son whom he adores. Thus, both men bring into the relationship a mass of emotional encumbrances: Jean–Marc, his "family" of lesbian friends; Mathieu, his son, his ex–wife, the ex–wife's new husband, and his mother. With great delicacy, tenderness and humor, Tremblay traces the path of the relationship, masterfully recreating moments of joy and wonderment, as well as the occasional panic, especially when the confirmed bachelor faces his first confrontation with the cherubic Sebastien, Mathieu's son. The most successful character of this unusually warm and endearing novel emerges in this irresistible four–year–old, who adjusts to his own unorthodox position in life—three daddies and an unidentified number of mummies—with a panache the adults can only envy.

With *Les Vues animées* ("The Movies"), in 1990, Tremblay completes his journey into the past. He now lets us discover the films and early television of his childhood that shaped his life and work. His first experience of horror movies at the age of five leads to a continuing fascination with the supposed "monsters," toward whom he feels compassion, as the films "were always on the side of the so–called normality." Walt Disney cartoons arouse his first vague but troubling sexual disquiet. However, it is a musical, *La Parade des soldats de bois,* which brings him to self–discovery. He watches Tom–Tom approach the crying Bo–Peep and prepare to comfort her with a kiss: "Alors cette chose tout–a–fait inattendue et qui allait changer ma vie se produisit" ("Then this totally unexpected thing happened, which would change my life"): the realization that he would wish to be in Bo–Peep's place, not in the boy's. Almost immediately, he admits to himself that this is something he has known all along, but tried to deny. "Mais voila, ça y était, et il fallait y faire face!" ("But there it was, it had to be faced!") As he faces the shame and condemnation that he knows await him, a terrible sadness descends upon him; back in his room, he wants to die. Eventually, writing proves his salvation: "Plus tard, je commencerais à écrire pour me soulager, me confesser, me purger d'un secret trop grand pour moi" ("Eventually, I would start writing, for relief, to confess, to purge myself of a secret too great for me.")

Suitably, this volume of recollections concludes with a previously unpublished novelette, written at the age of 16, which describes the agonies of a young boy, Jocelyn, attempting to come to terms with his homosexuality. This Jocelyn obviously is but one of the characters that Jean–Marc, in *The Heart Laid Bare,* calls "those others, so many of them, for whom sexual choice was a Calvary, sometimes long and painful. And often disastrous."

—Renate Usmiani

––––––––––

TRISTRAM. *See* **HOUSMAN, A(lfred) E(dward).**

––––––––––

TRYPHÉ. *See* **BARNEY, Natalie (Clifford).**

TYLER, Parker. American poet and nonfiction writer. Born in New Orleans, Louisiana, 6 March 1907. Educated at Chicago Latin School. From 1954–59, editorial associate of *Art News,* then reviewer and managing editor of *Art News Annual,* 1959, Art Foundation Press, Inc., New York City; lecturer on film, School of Visual Arts, New York City, spring 1962; lecturer, Midwest Film Festival, University of Chicago, 1963; critic. Associate editor, *Blues* (magazine of verse), 1929–30; associate editor, *View,* 1940–47; film correspondent, *Kenyon Review,* 1947–50; sponsor and consultant, Cinema 16, beginning 1950; film reviewer, *Theatre Arts,* 1953; member of board, Creative Film Foundation, 1958–60. **Recipient:** *New Republic* citation for best new Off–Broadway production, 1952; Longview Award for poetry, 1958; Chapelbrook Foundation grant, 1959–61; Ingram–Merrill Foundation grant, 1960; Ford Foundation grant, 1963; Guggenheim fellowship, 1965. *Died in New York City, 24 July 1974.*

WRITINGS

Poetry

Three Examples of Love Poetry. Oakland, California, Parnassus, 1936.
The Metaphor in the Jungle. Grand Junction, Colorado, James A. Decker, 1940.
The Granite Butterfly: A Poem in Nine Cantos. Belfast, Maine, Bern Porter, 1945.
The Will of Eros: Selected Poems, 1930–1970. Santa Barbara, California, Black Sparrow Press, 1972.

Nonfiction

With Charles Henri Ford, *The Young and Evil.* Paris, Obelisk Press, 1933.
The Hollywood Hallucination. Creative Age Press, 1944; with introduction by Richard Schickel, New York, Simon & Schuster, 1970.
The Magic and Myth of the Movies. New York, Holt, 1947; with introduction by R. Schickel, New York, Simon & Schuster, 1970.
Chaplin. New York, Vanguard, 1948; as *Chaplin: Last of the Clowns,* New York, Horizon, 1972.
How to Solve the Mystery of "Rashomon." New York, Cinema 16, 1952.
Conrad Marca–Relli (monograph). Georges Fall, 1960.
The Three Faces of the Film: The Art, the Dream, the Cult. London, Yoseloff, 1960; revised, San Diego, California, A. S. Barnes, 1967.
Classics of the Foreign Film: A Pictorial Treasury. New York, Citadel, 1962.
Florine Stettheimer: A Life in Art. New York, Farrar, Straus, 1963.
Every Artist His Own Scandal: A Study of Real and Fictive Heroes. New York, Horizon, 1964.
The Divine Comedy of Pavel Tchelitchew. New York, Fleet, 1966.
Sex, Psyche, Etcetera in the Film. New York, Horizon, 1969.
Renoir. Garden City, New York, Doubleday, 1969.
Van Gogh. Garden City, New York, Doubleday, 1969.
Degas/Lautrec. Garden City, New York, Doubleday, 1969.
Cezanne/Gaugin. Garden City, New York, Doubleday, 1969.
Screening the Sexes: Homosexuality in the Movies. New York, Holt, 1972.

The Shadow of an Airplane Climbs the Empire State Building: A World Theory of Film. Garden City, New York, Doubleday, 1972.
Carl Pickhardt. New York, Horizon, 1972.
A Pictorial History of Sex in Films. Secaucus, New Jersey, Citadel, 1974.
Early Classics of the Foreign Film (part of Citadel Film series). Carol Publishing Group, 1989.

Other

Editor, *Modern Things.* Salem, New Hampshire, Galleon, 1934.
With Pavel Tchelitchew, *Yesterday's Children.* New York, Harper, 1944.
The Screen (play; produced New York, 1952).
Author of introduction, *Films of Greta Garbo* by Michael Conway. Carol Publishing Group, 1968.
Underground Film: A Critical History. New York, Grove, 1969.
Author of introduction, *The Films of Mae West* by Jon Tuska. Carol Publishing Group, 1973; revised as *The Complete Films of Mae West,* 1992.

*

Critical Sources: *Commonweal,* 6 March 1970, 623; *Choice,* January 1971, 1523–1524; *Times Literary Supplement,* 18 June 1971, 705; *New York Times Book Review,* 17 December 1972, 2; *Washington Post Book World,* 19 August 1973, 13.

*   *   *

Parker Tyler was born 6 March 1907 in New Orleans. He attended Chicago Latin School and later became involved in New York's avant garde literary world. This involvement led to his writing, with Charles Henri Ford, *The Young and Evil* in 1933. Ford was living in Mississippi at the time and Tyler had moved from Chicago to Greenwich Village, where be came involved with a bohemian set. Tyler's letters so engaged Ford that they decided to write a book based upon Tyler's experiences. *The Young and Evil* was published by the Obelisk Press in Paris and for some time the book was detained at customs for obscenity. Once it made it into the United States it was widely, and to some degree favorably, reviewed. Gertrude Stein, Djuna Barnes and Louis Kronenberger all praised it and even with limited circulation *The Young and Evil* gained a solid reputation.

The book itself was a series of sketches and scenes in which Ford and Tyler's characters camped, compared sex lives and beauty hints, and minimally involved themselves with art and politics. While most other gay–themed novels of the time presented characters who were unhappy, psychologically maimed products of unhappy homes, *The Young and Evil* had little interest in etiology and even less in dwelling on its characters' discontents. The book's elliptical, resonant style was elusive and imagistic rather than descriptive and it was no surprise that both Ford and Parker turned to poetry and then cinema in their later careers.

Parker Tyler's volumes of poetry include *Three Examples of Love Poetry* in 1936, and *The Granite Butterfly: A Poem in Nine Cantos* in 1945, both published after *The Young and Evil.* He took up book reviewing, art criticism and film reviewing and it was *The Hollywood Hallucination* in 1944 that started him on his career as a film critic and analyst. With the publication of *The Magic and Myth of the Movies* in 1947, *Chaplin* in 1948, *Sex, Psyche, Etcetera in the Film* in 1969, *Screening the Sexes: Homosexuality in the Movies* in 1972, *The Shadow of an Airplane Climbs the Empire State Building: A World Theory of Film* in 1972, and *A Pictorial History of Sex in Films* in 1974, he established himself over more than two decades as one of the most innovative, perceptive film critics and theorists.

Most writing on film during these years was either in the form of newspaper or magazine reviewing (much of which—with a few exceptions, like James Agee—was haphazard newspaper hack work) or analytic theoretical criticism such as Siegfried Kracauer's *From Calagri to Hitler.* Tyler's contribution to film criticism, however, was to locate the energy and the drive of the film in its ability to depict eroticism. This was not simply the eroticism of the occasional nude or the sexual situation but what might be called now the erotics of representation. The lure of the movies—as Tyler titled his 1947 book—was "the magic and myth" of the experience. Movies were literally a huge projection of fantasy onto a large screen. He postulated that when we respond to movies in a primal way—what critic Pauline Kael calls "Kiss, Kiss, Bang, Bang"—that is primarily a sexual, or at very least, an erotic response.

British novelist Brigid Brophy, in a critical biography on Ronald Firbank, *Prancing Novelist,* postulates that all fiction is a form of masturbatory fantasy. This, on its frankest level, is a cornerstone of Tyler's film theory and the genius of his work. He understood that the erotic response was the primary connection that we have to films and he attempted to explicate this in detail. We respond to movies intellectually (of course) but more profoundly on the level of instinctual pleasure. Being alone in the theater, in the dark, seeing a fantasy on the screen is a sexual experience.

Much of Tyler's criticism also entails how sexuality and sexual mores have changed over the decades. In "The Awful Fate of the Sex Goddesses," Tyler examines the role of great screen sex symbols and notes how a Clara Bow or a Gloria Swanson can no longer exist in film today. Tyler was interested in charting the cultural changes in sexuality—for he understood that film, life and sex were, on some level, interconnected—but he was more interested in exploring what these large sexual images on the silver screen meant for the common audience.

With the advent of the second wave of feminism and gay liberation, Parker Tyler's criticism seemed out of date. While newer political writers such as Molly Haskell and Vito Russo wrote critiques of issues of representation—issues which were concerned with "positive" on "negative" images of homosexuals or women—Tyler was still attempting to elucidate an analysis that dealt with the power of onscreen sexual archetypes upon audiences' lives and sexual fantasies and emotions. In much the same way that Tyler and Ford had no intention of portraying the "positive homosexual" in *The Young and Evil,* but were more interested in presenting the resonant extreme, Tyler's film criticism took the same approach.

As a result much of Tyler's theories had limited, cultist appeal, and though he had some prominence as a writer, his readership was small. The difficulty of reading Parker Tyler in this cultural context was helped by the publication of Vito Russo's *The Celluloid Closet* in 1981. Russo's work gave us the context and ideology to see how culture and politics work in conjunction with one another to create certain specific types of representation. This freed us to begin to understand how Tyler's work refocuses the issue on the relationship between the film image and the inner life of the viewer.

The meaning and sense of much post–modern film criticism—the variety and diversity of readings and personal evaluation of material—is similar to what Parker Tyler was advocating in the late 1940s, 1950s, and 1960s in his film criticism. In many ways, film criticism and gay liberation have "grown up" to be able to understand what Parker Tyler was writing more than four decades ago.

—*Michael Bronski*

V

VEREY, Rev. C. *See* CROWLEY, Aleister.

———

VIDAL, (Eugene Luther) Gore. American novelist, short story writer, playwright, screenwriter, and essayist. Has also written as Edgar Box. Born at U.S. Military Academy, West Point, New York, 3 October 1925. Editor, E. P. Dutton, New York, 1946; lived in Antigua, Guatemala, 1947–49; Democratic Party candidate for Congress in the 29th District of New York, 1960; member of President's Advisory Committee on the Arts, 1961–63; host of television program *Hot Line,* 1964; lived in Italy, 1967–76; cofounder of New Party, 1968–71; cochair of People's Party, 1970–72; ran for nomination as Democratic Party senatorial candidate in California, 1982. Writer and lecturer; appears frequently on television and radio talk shows. **Recipient:** Mystery Writers of America Edgar Allan Poe award for television drama, 1955; Screen Writers Annual award nomination and Cannes Critics Prize for screenplay for *The Best Man,* 1964; National Book Critics Circle award for criticism for *The Second American Revolution, and Other Essays,* 1982; named honorary citizen of Ravello, Italy, 1983; Prix Deauville for *Creation,* 1983. Agent: Owen Laster, William Morris Agency, 1350 Avenue of the Americas, New York, New York 10019, U.S.A.

WRITINGS

Novels

Williwaw. New York, Dutton, 1946; reprinted, New York, New American Library, 1968.
In a Yellow Wood. New York, Dutton, 1947; London, New English Library, 1967.
The City and the Pillar. New York, Dutton, 1949; London, John Lehmann, 1949; revised, London, Heinemann, 1965.
The Season of Comfort. New York, Dutton, 1949.
A Search for the King: A Twelfth–Century Legend. New York, Dutton, 1950.
Dark Green, Bright Red. New York, Dutton, 1950; reprinted, New York, New American Library, 1968.
The Judgment of Paris. New York, Dutton, 1953; London, Heinemann, 1953; revised, Boston, Little, Brown, 1965.
Messiah. New York, Dutton, 1954; revised, Boston, Little, Brown, 1965; London, Heinemann, 1968; with introduction by Eliza-
beth A. Lynn, Boston, Gregg Press, 1979.
Three: Williwaw; A Thirsty Evil: Seven Short Stories; Julian, the Apostate. New York, New American Library, 1962.
Julian. London, Heinemann, and Boston, Little, Brown, 1964; with illustrations by David Whitfield, Geneva, Switzerland, Edito–Service S.A., 1974.
Washington, D.C. London, Heinemann, and Boston, Little, Brown, 1967.
Myra Breckinridge. Boston, Little, Brown, 1968; excised edition, London, Blond, 1968.
Two Sisters: A Novel in the Form of a Memoir. Boston, Little, Brown, 1970.
Burr. New York, Random House, 1973; limited edition, Franklin Center, Pennsylvania, Franklin Library, 1979.
Myron. New York, Random House, 1974, London, Heinemann, 1975.
1876. New York, Random House, and London, Heinemann, 1976.
Kalki. New York, Random House, and London, Heinemann, 1978; limited edition with illustrations by George H. Jones, Franklin Center, Pennsylvania, Franklin Library, 1978.
Creation. New York, Random House, 1981.
Duluth. New York, Random House, and London, Heinemann, 1983.
Lincoln. New York, Random House, and London, Heinemann, 1984; limited edition with illustrations by Thomas B. Allen, Franklin Center, Pennsylvania, Franklin Library, 1984.
Myra Breckenridge [and] *Myron.* New York, Random House, 1986.
Empire. New York, Random House, 1987; limited edition, Franklin Center, Pennsylvania, Franklin Library, 1987.
Hollywood: A Novel of America in the 1920s. New York, Random House, 1990.
Live from Golgotha. New York, Random House, 1992.

Short Stories

A Thirsty Evil: Seven Short Stories (contains "Three Stratagems," "The Robin," "A Moment of Green Laurel," "The Zenner Trophy," "Erlinda and Mr. Coffin," "Pages from an Abandoned Journal," and "The Ladies in the Library"). New York, Zero Press, 1956; limited edition, San Francisco, Gay Sunshine Press, 1981.
"Pages from an Abandoned Journal," in *The Faber Book of Gay Short Fiction,* edited by Edmund White. London and New York, Faber & Faber, 1991.

Essays

Rocking the Boat. Boston, Little, Brown, 1962.
Sex, Death, and Money. New York, Bantam, 1968.
Reflections upon a Sinking Ship. Boston, Little, Brown, and London, Heinemann, 1969.

Homage to Daniel Shays: Collected Essays, 1952–1972. New York, Random House, 1972; as *Collected Essays, 1952–1972,* London, Heinemann, 1974; as *On Our Own Now,* Panther, 1976.
Matters of Fact and of Fiction: Essays, 1973–1976. New York, Random House, 1977.
With others, *Great American Families.* New York, Norton, and London, Times Books, 1977.
With Robert J. Stanton, *Views from a Window: Conversations with Gore Vidal,* edited by Robert J. Stanton and Gore Vidal. Secaucus, New Jersey, Lyle Stuart, 1980.
The Second American Revolution, and Other Essays. New York, Random House, 1982.
Armageddon?; Essays, 1983–1987. London, A. Deutsch, 1987.
At Home; Essays, 1982–1988. New York, Random House, 1988.
Screening History. Cambridge, Harvard University Press, 1992.
United States; Essays, 1951–1991. New York, Random House, 1992.

Plays

Visit to a Small Planet: A Comedy Akin to a Vaudeville (produced on Broadway, 1957). Boston, Little Brown, 1957; revised, New York, Dramatists Play Service, 1959.
The Best Man: A Play of Politics (produced on Broadway, 1960). Boston, Little, Brown, 1960; revised, New York, Dramatists Play Service, 1977.
On the March to the Sea: A Southron Comedy (adaptation of television play *Honor;* produced Bonn, Germany, 1961).
Three Plays (contains *Visit to a Small Planet: A Comedy Akin to a Vaudeville; The Best Man: A Play of Politics;* and *On the March to the Sea: A Southron Comedy*). London, Heinemann, 1962.
Romulus: A New Comedy (adaptation of work by Freidrich Duerrenmatt; produced on Broadway, 1962). New York, Dramatists Play Service, 1962.
Weekend: A Comedy in Two Acts (produced New Haven, Connecticut, and on Broadway, 1968). New York, Dramatists Play Service, 1968.
With others, *An Evening with Richard Nixon* (produced New York, 1972). New York, Random House, 1972.

Screenplays

The Catered Affair, Metro–Goldwyn–Mayer, 1956.
I Accuse, Metro–Goldwyn–Mayer, 1958.
With Robert Hamer, *The Scapegoat,* Metro–Goldwyn–Mayer, 1959.
With Tennessee Williams, *Suddenly Last Summer,* Columbia, 1959.
The Best Man (based on play of same title; United Artists, 1964). Published as *The Best Man: A Screen Adaptation of the Original Play,* Irvington Publishers, 1989.
With Francis Ford Coppola, *Is Paris Burning?,* Paramount, 1966.
The Last of the Mobile Hotshots, Warner Brothers, 1970.

Television Plays

Barn Burning, 1954.
Dark Possession, 1954.
Smoke, 1954.
Visit to a Small Planet, 1955.
The Death of Billy the Kid, 1955.
Dr. Jekyll and Mr. Hyde, 1955.

A Sense of Justice, 1955.
Summer Pavilion, 1955.
The Turn of the Screw, 1955.
Stage Door, 1955.
Visit to a Small Planet, and Other Television Plays (contains *Visit to a Small Planet; Barn Burning; Dark Possession; The Death of Billy the Kid; A Sense of Justice; Smoke; Summer Pavilion;* and *The Turn of the Screw*). Boston, Little, Brown, 1956.
Honor, 1956.
Portrait of a Ballerina, 1956.
The Indestructible Mr. Gore, 1959.
Dear Arthur, 1960.
Dress Gray (adaption of novel by Lucian Truscott), NBC–TV, 1986.
Gore Vidal's "Billy the Kid," TNT, 1989.

Mystery Novels (as Edgar Box)

Death in the Fifth Position. New York, Dutton, 1952; limited edition, Armchair Detective Library, 1991.
Death before Bedtime. New York, Dutton, 1953; limited edition, Armchair Detective Library, 1991.
Death Likes It Hot. New York, Dutton, 1954; limited edition, Armchair Detective Library, 1991.
Three by Box: The Complete Mysteries of Edgar Box (contains *Death in the Fifth Position; Death Before Bedtime;* and *Death Likes It Hot*). New York, Random House, 1978.

Other

Editor, *Best Television Plays.* Ballantine, 1965.
A Conversation with Myself. New York, Bantam, 1974.
Author of introduction, *The Edith Wharton Omnibus.* Garden City, New York, Doubleday, 1978.
Author of introduction, *The Collected Stories of Paul Bowles.* Santa Rosa, California, Black Sparrow Press, 1983.
Author of introduction, *All Trivia* by Logan Pearsall Smith. New York, Ticknor & Fields, 1984.
Vidal in Venice, edited by George Armstrong, photographs by Tore Gill. New York, Summit Books in association with Antelope, and London, Weidenfeld and Nicholson in association with Channel Four Television and Antelope, 1985.
Author of introduction, *The Collected Stories* by Tennessee Williams. New York, New Directions, 1985.
Author of introduction, *Finistere* by Fritz Peters. Seeker Press, 1985.
Author of introduction, *The Golden Bowl* by Henry James. Viking Penguin, 1985.
Author of forward, *Dawn Powell.* QPB, 1989.
Author of foreword, *Head of a Sad Angel: Stories 1953–1966* by Alfred Chester, edited by Edward Field. Santa Rosa, California, Black Sparrow Press, 1990.
Author of foreword, *Impossible H. L. Mencken: A Selection of His Best Newspaper Stories,* edited by Marion E. Rodgers. Garden City, New York, Doubleday, 1991.
Author of introduction, *Where Joy Resides: A Christopher Isherwood Reader,* edited by Don Bachardy and James P. White. Farrar, Straus, 1991.
Who Owns the U.S.? Odonian Press, 1992.

Recordings: *An Evening with Richard,* Ode Records, 1973.

Manuscript Collections: Wisconsin Historical Society, Madison.

Interviews: *Fag Rag,* winter 1974; *Gay Sunshine,* winter, 1975; *Views from a Window: Conversations with Gore Vidal,* edited by Robert J. Stanton and Gore Vidal, Secaucus, New Jersey, Lyle Stuart, 1980; "Gore Vidal: The Writer as Citizen" by Claudia Dreifus, in *Progressive,* September 1986, 36; "Gore Vidal" by Mark Matousek, in *Interview,* June 1987, 92; "Grandson of a 'Populist Demagogue'" by Herbert Mitgang, in *New York Times Book Review,* 14 June 1987, 42; "The Rise and Fall of the American Empire" by Alvin P. Sanoff, in *U.S. News and World Report,* 13 July 1987, 62; "Gore Vidal" by David Sheff, in *Playboy,* December 1987, 51; "The Chore of Being Gore" by Andrew Kopkind, in *Interview,* June 1988, 62; "Tug of War" by Colin Wright, in *New Statesman and Society,* 3 November 1989, 43; "Through the Looking Glass" by Howard Means, in *Washingtonian,* February 1990, 78; "Mailer and Vidal: The Big Schmooze" by Carole Mallory, in *Esquire,* May 1991, 105; "'J.F.K.' Is Not What He Had in Mind" by Michael Anderson, in *New York Times Book Review,* 30 August 1992, 27.

Bibliography: *Gore Vidal: A Primary and Secondary Bibliography* by Robert J. Stanton, Boston, G. K. Hall, 1978.

Critical Sources: "Gore Vidal: The Search for a King" by John W. Aldridge, in his *After the Lost Generation: A Critical Study of the Writers of Two Wars,* New York, McGraw–Hill, 1951, 170–183; *Gore Vidal* by Ray Lewis White, Boston, Twayne Publishers, 1968; *The Apostate Angel: A Critical Study of Gore Vidal* by Bernard F. Dick, New York, Random House, 1974; "Gore Vidal" by Robert Graalman, in *Dictionary of Literary Biography,* Volume 6: *American Novelists since World War II,* Detroit, Gale, 1980; "The Mysteries of Edgar Box (aka Gore Vidal)" by Earl F. Bargainnier, in *Clues* (Bowling Green, Ohio), spring–summer 1981, 45–42; "Narrative Patterns in the Novels of Gore Vidal" by David Barton, in *Notes on Contemporary Literature* (Carrollton, Georgia), September 1981, 3–5; *Gore Vidal* by Robert F. Kiernan, New York, Ungar, 1982; "Political Change in America: Perspectives from the Popular Historical Novels of Michener and Vidal" by Samuel M. Hines, Jr., in *Political Mythology and Popular Fiction,* edited by Ernest J. Yanarella and Lee Sigelman, Westport, Connecticut, Greenwood Press, 1988, 81–99; "Collecting Mystery Fiction: Edgar Box (Gore Vidal)" by Otto Penzler, in *Armchair Detective* (New York), winter 1989, 38; *Gay Fictions, Wilde to Stonewall: Studies in a Male Homosexual Literary Tradition* by Claude J. Summers, New York, Continuum, 1990; "Gore Vidal: A Grandfather's Legacy" by Marvin J. LaHood, in *World Literature Today* (Norman, Oklahoma), summer 1990, 413–417; *The Gay Novel in America* by James Levin, New York, Garland, 1991; "My O My O Myra" by Catherine R. Stimpson, in *New England Review* (Middlebury, Vermont), fall 1991, 102–115; *Gore Vidal: Writer against the Grain* edited by Jay Parini, New York, Columbia University Press, 1992; "Gore's Lore" by Arthur Lubow, in *Vanity Fair,* September 1992, 126; "A Gadfly in Glorious, Angry Exile" by Martha Duffy, in *Time,* 28 September 1992, 64–66; "Gore Vidal" by Joel Shatzky, in *Contemporary Gay American Novelists,* edited by Emmanuel S. Nelson, Westport, Connecticut, Greenwood Press, 1993.

Gore Vidal is considered by many critics to be one of the most influential American writers of the post–World War II period. Although his work encompasses a wide variety of subjects and ideas, Vidal has gained a certain level of renown for his depiction of homosexual characters and themes. The author's career began with the publication of his first novel, *Williwaw,* in 1946. Written while Vidal was recuperating from a bout of rheumatoid arthritis, *Williwaw* takes place on an Army transport ship against the backdrop of an Artic squall (or "williwaw"). This debut novel—often characterized as "atypical" of Vidal's best work—was hailed by reviewers as being both compelling and finely honed.

It was in his second novel, *In a Yellow Wood,* that Vidal first focused on homosexuality as a thematic device. The story unfolds as a day in the life of Robert Holton, a conventional man who has just returned from the war to a perfunctory job in New York City. During the evening, Holton meets an old friend married to an internationally famous gay artist; eventually, the young clerk accompanies these companions to a gay bar where Holton encounters a number of snobbish, somewhat feminine patrons. While the bar trip is a relatively minor incident in the novel, it serves to illustrate Holton's struggle to reconcile the lure of his ordered life with his desire to embrace the unconventional.

In 1948, Vidal created a stir with his full–length study of a gay man in *The City and the Pillar.* The novel's protagonist, Jim Willard, is a handsome, athletic tennis instructor who projects a very "boy next door" image. Willard's depiction disturbed a number of critics, many of whom felt that the impact of the author's interesting characterization was lost amid thematic generalities and haphazard editing. Still, other voices hailed Vidal's willingness to take a new look at some long–standing stereotypes by presenting a "hero" who was as incapable of love and committment as many of his fictional heterosexual peers.

Vidal's next five novels were critical and commercial failures. Much of the critics' hostile stance was due to factors such as the author's stylistic experimentation and presentation of complex—and sometimes confusing—themes. Even though these works did little to advance Vidal's literary reputation, they nevertheless offered some interesting homosexual plot lines and characters. In *A Season of Comfort,* for example, heterosexual character Bill Giraud is presented as superficially happy and successful. He is haunted, however, by the memory of a sexual dalliance with Jimmy, the high school athletic hero. Later in life, Giraud—who feels that he could never have sex with a man again—decides that this earlier affair was an important, constructive part of his personal development.

In 1954, Vidal decided to seek financial stability by moving to Hollywood where he wrote film scripts and television dramas. While some critics have found homosexual subtexts in the author's script for *Ben Hur* and his adaption of Tennessee Williams' *Suddenly Last Summer,* this stage in Vidal's career appeared to be more concerned with money–making than making waves. In light of his previous work, Vidal seemed to be burying his "homosexual enfant terrible" image, an effort that was rewarded by favorable critical reaction to works like *Visit to a Small Planet.*

Having established the financial independence he craved, Vidal returned to fiction in 1964 with a formula that led to both critical and popular success, a formula epitomized by the book *Julian.* The story is told as the journal of eccentric fourth–century Roman emperor Julian (with added margin notes and letters by two of the ruler's aging contemporaries). While the main thrust of *Julian* concerns with the emperor's observations about his life and times, the novel also serves up a great deal of insouciant and ribald gossip

(gossip that often centers around homosexual activities).

In the midst of penning his historical tomes, Vidal created one of his most campy and controversial works. *Myra Breckinridge* offers a colorful central character in the figure of a homosexual male turned female via a sex change operation. As a protagonist, Myra is both fascinating and repellent; she holds forth on a variety of subjects (most notably the connection between sex and power) and engages in all manner of sexual escapades. Through Myra's thoughts and actions, Vidal turned popular and psychoanalytic ideas about gender identity inside out. Many critics found Vidal's open approach to sexuality in modern society refreshing and humorous, while others considered the book's blatant sexuality borderline pornography. In many respects, a large part Vidal's success with *Myra Breckinridge* was the result of his refusal to merely lecture or leave difficult issues unresolved.

In his more recent books, such as the controversial mock–history *Live from Golgotha,* Vidal treats all manner of subjects, including homosexuality, in much the same irreverent manner. When looking at these later works—where the depiction of homosexuals and homosexuality seems a natural part of the author's narrative—Vidal's early presentations of homosexuality emerge both prescient and quaint. Perhaps the emphasis on homosexuality as a theme and character device does some disservice to the author, whose body of work is diverse with regard to both theme and characterization. Nevertheless, readers should not overlook the Vidal's ground–breaking willingness to take chances with a complex subject at a time when doing so could have meant professional disaster.

—*James Levin*

VIVIEN, Renée. British and French poet and short fiction writer. Also wrote as R. Vivien and René Vivien. Born Pauline Mary Tarn in London, England, 8 June 1877. Family moved to Paris one year after her birth, and returned to London in 1886 after her father's death. Educated by English governess. Companion of Natalie Clifford Barney and Baroness Hélène van Zuylen de Nyevelt. Financially independent as result of inheritance. Writer in Paris from 1898 until 1909. *Died in Paris, of anorexia and alcoholism, 18 November 1909.*

WRITINGS

Poetry

Cendres et poussières. Paris, Lemerre, 1902.
Du vert au violet. Paris, Lemerre, 1903.
Evocations. Paris, Lemerre, 1903.
La Vénus des aveugles. Paris, Lemerre, 1904.
Etudes et préludes. Paris, Lemerre, 1904.
A l'heures des mains jointes. Paris, Lemerre, 1906; translated by Sandia Belgrade as *At the Sweet Hour of Hand in Hand,* Tallahassee, Naiad Press, 1979.
Chansons pour mon ombre. Paris, Lemerre, 1907.

Flambeaux éteints. Paris, Sansot, 1908.
Silages. Paris, Sansot, 1908.
Poèmes en prose. Paris, Sansot, 1909.
Le vent des vaisseaux. Paris, Sansot, 1910.
Dans un coin de violettes. Paris, Sansot, 1910; translated by Margaret Porter and Catherine Kroger as *The Muse of Violets,* Tallahassee, Naiad Press, 1977.
Hallions. Paris, Sansot, 1910.
Poésies complètes, I. Paris, Lemerre, 1934.
Poésies complètes, II. Paris, Lemerre, 1934.

Novellas

La Dame à la louve. Paris, Lemerre, 1904; translated by Karla Jay and Yvonne M. Klein as *The Woman of the Wolf, and Other Stories,* New York, Gay Presses of New York, 1983.
Une Femme m'apparut. Paris, Lemerre, 1905; translated by Jeannette Howard Foster as *A Woman Appeared to Me,* Tallahassee, Naiad Press, 1979.
Anne Boleyn: Reproduction en fac–similé des épreuves uniques de l'edition jamais tiré de Lemerre (1909). Muizon, France, L'Ecart, 1982.

Short Stories

Brumes de fjords. Paris, Lemerre, 1902.

Translator

L'Etre double by Paule Riversdale. Paris, Lemerre, 1904.
Sapho. Paris, Lemerre, 1909.

*

Manuscript Collections: Fonds lettéraire Jacques Doucet, Paris.

Biography: "Forgotten Lesbian Poet: Renée Vivien" by Gene Damon and Lee Stuart in *Lesbian Lives,* edited by Barbara Grier and Coletta Reid, Oakland, California, Diana Press, 1976.

Critical Sources: *The Pure and the Impure* by Colette, New York, Farrar, Straus and Giroux, 1967; "Rhetoric and Images of Feminism in the Poetry of Renée Vivien" (dissertation) by Jeanne Louise Manning, 1981; "Return to Mytilène: Renée Vivien and the City of Women" by Elyse Blankley in *Women Writers and the City: Essays in Feminist Literary Criticism,* edited by Susan Merrill Squier, Knoxville, University of Tennessee Press, 1984, 45–67; "The Disciples of the Tenth Muse: Natalie Clifford Barney and Renée Vivien" (dissertation) by Karla Jay, 1984; "Sapphistries" by Susan Gubar, in *Signs: Journal of Women in Culture and Society* (Durham, North Carolina), autumn 1984, 43–62; "Daughters' Exile: Renée Vivien, Gertrude Stein, and Djuna Barnes in Paris" (dissertation) by Elyse Blankley, 1985; "Renée Vivien in the Night Garden of the Spirit" by Alice Parker, in *Aspects of Fantasy: Selected Essays from the Second International Conference on the Fantastic in Literature and Film,* edited by William Coyle, Westport, Connecticut, Greenwood Press, 1986, 7–15; "'Drunk with Chastity': The Poetry of Renée Vivien" by Pamela J. Annas, in *Women's Studies: An Interdisciplinary Journal* (Flushing, New York), Number 13, 1986, 1–2, 11–22;

"The Problematics of French 'Poesie Feminine': Early Twentieth Century Parisian Women Poets" (dissertation) by Tama Lea Engelking, 1987; *The Amazon and the Page* by Karla Jay, Bloomington, Indiana University Press, 1988; "Sapho 1900: Imaginary Renée Vivien and the Rear of the Belle Époque" by Elaine Marks, in *Yale French Studies* (New Haven, Connecticut), Number 75, 1988, 175–189; "The Erotic and the Sacred: Art and Ritual in the Lives of Natalie Barney and Her Circle" (dissertation) by Vicki L. Kirsch, 1991; "Fleurs du Mal or Second–Hand Roses?: Natalie Barney, Romaine Brooks, and the Originality of the Avant–Garde" by Bridgett Elliott and Jo–Ann Wallace in *Feminist Review,* spring 1992, 6–30.

*   *   *

In *The Pure and the Impure,* Colette depicts Renée Vivien as beautiful, childlike, and charming, but also as obscene and self–destructive, living in stifling and dimly–lit rooms and gargling toilet water to mask her alcohol consumption. Colette's reminiscences of Vivien and her relationship with the wealthy and domineering Baroness Hélène Van Zuylen de Nyevelt, who wielded a frightening influence over Vivien, provide a disturbing picture of the dissipated atmosphere of the talented poet's life. The oppressive image that emerges could easily have been drawn from Symbolist literature and is even more tragic for being real.

Little is known of the early life of the poet Vivien. She was the daughter of an English father and an American mother. In 1898 she gained financial independence through an inheritance from her paternal grandfather and arrived in Paris, rebelling against her oppressive family and the restrictions of Victorian England. The following year she met Natalie Barney, with whom she began a tempestuous relationship. Her novella *Une Femme m'apparut* is based on their affair.

In 1904, Vivien and Barney traveled to Lesbos with the intent of founding an artistic community of lesbian poets and intellectuals. While this project was not a success, it may have provided much of the inspiration for the Academy of Women founded by Barney in Paris years later. During this time Vivien purchased a villa there, and even after the failure of the colony, spent a portion of each year in solitude at this retreat. She filled her garden with exotic plants and birds, and hung over her garden gate a sign with "Paradise" carved in Greek.

In spite of her alcoholism and anorexia, Vivien was prolific in her work, producing numerous volumes of poetry, two novellas, and a book of short stories over the course of ten years. She often wrote in Sapphic meter, and her work has been praised for its purity of form. Vivien's accomplishments are even more extraordinary as she wrote primarily in her second language. Her first volumes of poetry were published under the name R. Vivien. Critics who praised the passionate romantic verses to women were later embarrassed when Vivien's gender became public knowledge.

Vivien's work is marked by diverse influences, including Classical Greek philosophy, French Symbolism, and American feminism. She frequently drew from decadent and symbolist traditions, giving them a unique lesbian interpretation. She found models in history, in Greek and Christian mythologies, and in the medieval tradition of courtly love. Religion, mysticism, and death were frequent themes. In her hands, clichés of the period were used to promote a world centered around women. She wrote about lesbian love for a female audience—not for male titillation—lending lesbianism a legitimate voice.

Vivien and her circle have frequently been trivialized by critics who dismiss them as curiosities or concentrate solely on their lifestyles, rather than their work. They have been viewed primarily as imitations of earlier movements. More recently, scholars such as Bridgett Elliot and Jo–Ann Wallace have interpreted Vivien's use of familiar literary and artistic forms as a strategy to depict the visible lesbian of the early twentieth century. In the 1970s, interest in Vivien's work was revived by French and English–speaking feminists and lesbians. Her valuable contributions as an early openly lesbian author make her an integral part of gay and lesbian literary history, just as they made her a central figure in the lesbian expatriate community flourishing in Paris in the early twentieth century.

—*Melissa J. Delbridge*

W

WARNER, Sylvia Townsend. British poet, novelist, and short story writer. Born in Harrow, Middlesex, 6 December 1893. Privately educated. Lived with poet Valentine Ackland (died 1969). Member of editorial committee of *Tudor Church Music,* London, 1923–29; supporter of the British Communist Party until the 1940s; regular contributor to *New Yorker,* 1936–78. Fellow of the Royal Society of Literature; honorary member of the American Academy of Arts and Letters; sponsor of the Rachel Carson Trust. **Recipient:** Prix Menton, 1968. *Died in Maiden Newton, Dorsetshire, 1 May 1978.*

WRITINGS

Poetry

The Espalier. London, Chatto & Windus, and New York, Dial, 1925.
Time Importuned. London, Chatto & Windus, and New York, Viking, 1928.
Opus 7: A Poem. London, Chatto & Windus, and New York, Viking, 1931.
Rainbow. New York, Knopf, 1932.
With Valentine Ackland, *Whether a Dove, or Seagull.* New York, Viking, 1933; London, Chatto & Windus, 1934.
Two Poems. Derby, Hopkins, 1945.
With Reynolds Stone, *Boxwood.* Privately printed, 1957; Monotype Corp., 1958; enlarged, London, Chatto & Windus, 1960.
King Duffus, and Other Poems. Wells, Clare, 1968.
Azrael, and Other Poems. Newbury, Libanus, 1978; as *Twelve Poems,* London, Chatto & Windus, 1980.
Collected Poems, edited by Claire Harman. Manchester, Carcanet, and New York, Viking, 1983.

Novels

Lolly Willowes; or, The Loving Huntsman. London, Chatto & Windus, and New York, Viking, 1926; with introduction by Anita Miller, Academy Chicago Limited, 1979.
Mr. Fortune's Maggot. London, Chatto & Windus, and New York, Viking, 1927.
The True Heart. London, Chatto & Windus, and New York, Viking, 1929.
Summer Will Show. London, Chatto & Windus, and New York, Viking, 1936.
After the Death of Don Juan. London, Chatto & Windus, 1938, and New York, Viking, 1939.

The Corner that Held Them. New York, Viking, 1948.
The Flint Anchor. New York, Viking, 1954.
Lolly Willowes, and Mr. Fortune's Maggot. New York, Viking, 1966.

Short Stories

"Some World Far from Ours" and "Stay, Corydon, Thou Swain." London, Mathews and Marrot, 1929.
Elinor Barley. London, Cresset, 1930.
A Moral Ending, and Other Stories. London, Jackson, 1931; enlarged as *The Salutation,* London, Chatto & Windus, and New York, Viking, 1932.
More Joy in Heaven, and Other Stories. London, Cresset, 1935.
With Graham Greene and James Laver, *Twenty–four Short Stories.* London, Cresset, 1939.
The Cat's–Cradle Book. New York, Viking, 1940; London, Chatto & Windus, 1960.
A Garland of Straw: Twenty–eight Stories. New York, Viking, 1943; as *A Garland of Straw, and Other Stories,* London, Chatto & Windus, 1943; as *A Garland of Straw; Twenty–eight Stories,* New York, Viking, 1943.
The Museum of Cheats: Stories. London, Chatto & Windus, and New York, Viking, 1947.
Winter in the Air, and Other Stories. London, Chatto & Windus, 1955; New York, Viking, 1956.
A Spirit Rises: Short Stories. New York, Viking, 1962.
Swans on an Autumn River: Stories. New York, Viking, 1966; as *A Stranger with a Bag, and Other Stories,* London, Chatto & Windus, 1966.
The Innocent and the Guilty. New York, Viking, 1971.
Kingdoms of Elfin. New York, Viking, 1977.
One Thing Leading to Another, and Other Stories, edited by Susanna Pinney. New York, Viking, 1984.
Selected Stories of Sylvia Townsend Warner. New York, Viking, 1988.

Nonfiction

The Portrait of a Tortoise: Extracted from the Journals of Gilbert White. London, Chatto & Windus, and Toronto, Oxford University Press, 1946.
Somerset. London, Elek, 1949.
Jane Austen: 1775–1817. London and New York, Longmans, Green, 1951; revised, 1957.
Sketches from Nature. London, Clare, 1963.
T. H. White: A Biography. London, J. Cape, 1967; New York, Viking, 1968.
Scenes of Childhood. New York, Viking, 1982.

Other

Editor, with others, *Tudor Church Music* (ten volumes). Oxford
   University Press, c. 1925–30.
Author of score, *Alleluia, Anthem for Five Voices*. London, Oxford,
   1925.
The Maze: A Story to Be Read Aloud. London, Fleuron, 1928.
"Notation; the Growth of a System," in *The Oxford History of
   Music*. London, Oxford, 1929.
This Our Brother. London, Cambridge, 1930.
Editor and author of introduction, *The Weekend Dickens*. London,
   Machelose, and New York, Lorring & Mussey, 1932.
The People Have No Generals. London, Newport, 1941.
Translator, *By Way of Saint–Beuve* by Marcel Proust. London,
   Chatto & Windus, 1958; as *On Art and Literature: 1896–1917*,
   New York, Dell, 1964; as *Marcel Proust on Art and Literature,
   1896–1919*, New York, Carroll & Graf, 1984.
Translator, *A Place of Shipwreck* by Jean René Huguenin. London,
   Chatto & Windus, 1963.
Author of prologue, *The Book of Merlyn* by T. H. White. Austin,
   University of Texas Press, 1977.
Letters, edited by William Maxwell. New York, Viking, 1983.

*

Biography: *For Sylvia: An Honest Account* by Valentine Ackland,
New York, Norton, 1985; *This Narrow Place: Sylvia Townsend
Warner and Valentine Ackland: Life, Letters, and Politics, 1930–
1951* by Wendy Mulford, London, Pandora Press, 1988.

Critical Sources: "The Mastery of Miss Warner" by John Updike,
in *New Republic*, 5 March 1966, 23–25; *Who Was Who Among
English and European Authors 1931–1949*, Detroit, Gale, 1978;
"Sylvia Townsend Warner 1893–1978: A Celebration," edited by
Claire Harmon, in *PN Review 23*, 8:3, 1981–82, 30–61; "Sylvia
Townsend Warner" in *Modern British Literature*, compiled and ed-
ited by Denis Lane and Rita Stein, New York, Ungar, 1985, 564–
566; "Sylvia Townsend Warner" by Barbara Brothers, in *Dictio-
nary of Literary Biography*, Volume 34: *British Novelists, 1890–
1929: Traditionalists*, Detroit, Gale, 1985, 277–281; *This Narrow
Place: Sylvia Townsend Warner and Valentine Ackland: Life, Letter,
and Politics, 1930–1951* by Wendy Mulford, London, Pandora
Press, 1988; "Summer Will Show" by Julie Abraham in *Nation*, 19
March 1988; "This Narrow Place" by Sara Maitland, in *New Statesman & Society*, 10 June 1988; *British Women Writers: A Critical
Reference Guide*, edited by Janet Todd, New York, Continuum,
1989, 692–695; "A Dangerous Relevance" (review of *Sylvia
Townsend Warner: A Biography* by Claire Harman, and *For Sylvia:
An Honest Account* by Valentine Ackland) by P. N. Furbank, in
Times Literary Supplement, 28 July–3 August 1989, 815–16; "Ex-
iled to Home: The Poetry of Sylvia Townsend Warner and Valen-
tine Ackland" by Gillian Spraggs, in *Lesbian and Gay Writing: An
Anthology of Critical Essays*, edited by Mark Lilly, Philadelphia,
Temple University Press, 1990, 109–125; "Sylvia Townsend
Warner" by Evelyn Gettone, in *Encyclopedia of Homosexuality*,
edited by Wayne R. Dynes, New York, Garland, 1990, 1383–1384;
The Feminist Companion to Literature in English by Virginia Blain,
Patricia Clements, and Isobel Grundy, New Haven, Yale University

Press, 1990; "Sylvia Townsend Warner and the Counterplot of
Lesbian Fiction" by Terry Castle, in *Sexual Sameness: Textual Dif-
ferences in Lesbian and Gay Writing*, edited by Joseph Bristow,
London, Routledge, 1992, 128–147; *The Bloomsbury Guide to
Women's Literature*, edited by Claire Buck, Englewood Cliffs, New
Jersey, Prentice Hall, 1992, 1123–1124.

*   *   *

Sylvia Townsend Warner's way of life is a celebration of paradox. She enjoyed the tranquil retirement of a country gentlewoman,
as well as political and social unorthodoxy. She struggled with the
constraints on individual expression imposed by social class and
grappled with various means of personal liberation. She acknowledged both repressive formal codes of behavior and the disruptive
influence of some external force or power. She was drawn to both
the eccentricities of human behavior while being a great friend of
nature. This celebration is nowhere more evident than in her diverse
oeuvre.

One of the most neglected twentieth–century British writers of
stature, Warner was the product of an upper–middle–class
Edwardian family upbringing. After being privately educated she
intended to study musical composition in Vienna with Arnold
Schoenberg, but the outbreak of World War I made this impossible.
For a time she worked as a relief munitions worker. Following her
father's death in 1916, she relocated to London, pursuing a career as
a musicologist and serving on the editorial committee for the Ox-
ford/Carnegie edition of the ten–volume *Tudor Church Music*.

By the mid–1920s, with a large collection of friends in and out of
London's Bloomsbury district, the sociable Warner was a figure on
the city's scene. Since "coming out" in 1911 or 1912, she moved in
diverse circles, initially socializing with friends of her parent's generation, then in the 1920s with the Powys Circle in the vicinity of
the village of Chaldon in Dorset. It was here, through her friendship
with novelist Theodore Powys, that she met, and in 1930 fell in
love with, a young female would–be writer named Valentine Ackland.
Their passionate affair lasted, through various vicissitudes, for 40
years. Warner's letters record very movingly that their relationship
was the central fact in both women's lives.

Warner and Ackland's conversion to and acceptance of lesbianism were somewhat different. After Warner "came out," she skillfully avoided both suitors and marriage, although several long–term
affairs were sustained, including those with musicologist Percy
Buck and sculptor Stephen Tomlin. Ackland, who was 24 years old
when she met Warner, had been involved in a number of lesbian and
heterosexual affairs. However, Warner never suffered from repressive conventionality as Ackland did. Some critics note that Warner's
two fantastic novels, *Lolly Willowes* and *Mr. Fortune's Maggot*,
were pointing toward her conversion to lesbianism. P. N. Furbank
writes: "At all events the mere fact of homosexuality seems not to
have worried her at all; and having abundant social confidence, and
a sure sense of values, she did not have to bother greatly over
neighborly gossip or public opinion." Ackland, on the other hand,
struggled with the paradox of lesbian existence in a patriarchal society. The partnership of the two is the subject of a study by Wendy
Mulford called *This Narrow Place: Sylvia Townsend Warner and
Valentine Ackland: Life, Letters and Politics, 1930–1951*, which
gives more space to Warner's work and pays greater attention to the
novels than the poems. Mulford's study is shaped by her experi-

ence of living in the house which was Warner and Ackland's home for 32 years.

Warner and Ackland neither hid nor emphasized their lesbianism or their relationship. The 1930s and 1940s were decades characterized by political turmoil and imminent violence, by political seriousness and optimism, by cultural upheaval. The times were fertile and supportive of a partnership like Warner and Ackland's, which ultimately transcended its rural and domestic roots to become a unity both literary and political. Nonetheless, it is important to note that the two lived in a culture in which the desire of one woman for another was stigmatized as unnatural, inordinate, taboo, and a dangerous personal and social commitment.

Sharing a joint commitment to the resistance of European fascism, the two joined the Communist Party of Great Britain in 1935, and political activities dominated their lives for several years. Their passionate commitment, as writers and as individuals, to the left, took them to Spain to support the government and to work for the Red Cross during the Spanish Civil War. Warner remained a self–proclaimed anarchist until her death.

In 1936, one of Warner's stories was accepted by *New Yorker*. During the next 40 years she contributed some 150 stories and nine poems to the magazine. Noted by many—including John Updike and her friend and editor at *New Yorker* for roughly 40 years, William Maxwell—her success in these pages brought her a solid reputation and considerable income, but had its impact on Ackland. Serious illness marked her later days. Ackland left the Party, drifting toward the political center, and joined the Catholic Church. She eventually became a Quaker. She died of cancer in 1968.

Warner won distinction in many spheres—as a musicologist, a novelist, a poet, a writer of short stories, and a biographer. Her reputation both in her lifetime and since has been founded more securely in her prose. A British traditionalist, she wrote fiction characterized by her strong narrative skills, imaginative energy, originality of plot and setting, and oscillation between realistic and fabulous modes. She made her writing debut in 1925 as a poet with a collection entitled *The Espalier*. This was followed by the novel *Lolly Willowes; or, The Loving Huntsman*, published in 1926, the year she met Ackland. Warner's reputation was both fixed and made by this novel. The book is both a pastoral romance and a feminist parable in which the masculine, sterile and conventional values of the town are challenged by the feminine, fecund, and subversive countryside. *Lolly Willowes* went through several impressions and was a primary selection of the Book–of–the–Month–Club.

Similarly lending itself to whimsical interpretation, *Mr. Fortune's Maggot*, an early selection of the Literary Guild and Warner's second novel, includes a male homosexual who is implicit and central to the story. This pastoral idyll explores the theme of self–liberation. In it, a missionary "sodomite" falls in love with a convert, a young boy named Lueli. Warner followed *Mr. Fortune's Maggot* with *The True Heart*, her third and most mellow novel. Here she retells the story of Cupid and Psyche in a nineteenth–century East Anglican setting. The fable is an affirmation of love as a power that overcomes all odds.

The theme of liberation from ideological constraints and awareness of alternative realities is central to *Summer Will Show* and *After the Death of Don Juan*. *Summer Will Show* was begun in 1932, less than five years after Radclyffe Hall's explicitly lesbian novel *The Well of Loneliness* had been banned from publication as a result of a famous obscenity trial. *Summer Will Show* has been called a *Well of Loneliness* with antiracist, anticapitalist politics, a lesbian ver-

sion of *Sammy and Rosie Get Laid* set in the revolutionary Paris of 1848. A novel of social protest—feminist and economic, it is a fictional account of collisions among the classes, genders and sexualities. It is the story of Sophia Willoughby, an upper–class Englishwoman of country background and estranged wife of an English gentleman, and Minna Lemuel, an East European Jewish artiste and the discarded mistress. Like Warner and Ackland, these characters have an affinity that transcends class and cultural barriers. Skillfully interweaving sexual and historical stories, politics, and form, Warner succeeds in telling her story and in cataloging devices for preliberation lesbian narratives. The sexual element in the relationship between Sophia and Minna is not an issue, however. As Gillian Spraggs in an essay for *Lesbian and Gay Writing* notes, "although unstressed, it is certainly not unspoken; it pervades the second half of the book."

Warner's sixth and most ambitious novel, *The Corner that Held Them*, while less praised than *Lolly Willowes*, is respected as a witty, amusing, and memorable novel of medieval convent life as viewed through twentieth–century eyes. It continues to be recognized as one of the most sustained works of historical imagination of our time. *The Flint Anchor*, her last novel, traces the decline and fall of a domestic tyrant in an east–coast English fishing port in the first part of the last century. Male homosexuality is an incidental motif in this chronicle.

Warner's short stories were published in book form beginning in 1929. Recurrent themes are the struggle of an overlooked person for recognition, the painful effects of mutual incomprehension, and moments of sharp insight into obscure lives. Her feeling for the marginalized and emotionally derelict is expressed in many of her stories. In 1971's *The Innocent and the Guilty*, the author presents the predicaments of modern man, his isolation, alienation, loneliness and sexual confusion. Her experience of living as a lesbian informs some of her best writing.

Likened as a poet to a "'feminine Thomas Hardy' (although with more range and less plangency)" in *The Feminist Companion to Literature in English*, Warner exhibits a graceful and inconsequent fancy in her verse and in several novels. The first two volumes of essentially lyric poetry contain subject matter that is romantically marginal or otherworldly. Ghosts, witches, faery lovers, gypsies, village idiots, distraught widows, eerie old women and men vie for the reader's attention. Settings include abandoned gardens, ruins, and countryside in bleak or rainy weather. Warner's poetry is put to the critical fore by Clare Harmon in a *PN Review 23* essay which includes poems, an interview, photos, letters, and personal recollections.

Warner's nonfiction includes a biography of T. H. White, the author of the novels that became the basis for the musical *Camelot*, and a study of Jane Austin, as well as a travel guide and sketches on nature. *Whether a Dove, or Seagull*, a joint collection containing poems by Warner and Ackland, stands as a poetic achievement and as a record of a loving and creative partnership between two women. Most of the poems are interesting and impressive love poems written by either poet to the other. None of the poems are signed and few are titled, an arrangement which seems to have suggested itself as a result of their developing political commitment. The volume is evidence of the presence and force of the lesbian theme in Warner's work as a whole. Her work in this volume conforms to precedents in earlier volumes (landscape) and markedly departs from them (seasons, weather, characters, theme of reciprocated passion and shared delight, image of the house and house fires). Spraggs writes in *Lesbian and Gay Writing* that awareness of the kind of relationship enjoyed by the lovers is "even more pertinent to a fruitful reading [of some of the poems.]" Eroticism and sexual explicitness are evident in some of the work.

Although Warner has been appreciated by both her literary peers and others, critical studies of her work are few. John Updike and Glen Cavaliero have, for years, led the critical pack. *Sexual Sameness: Textual Differences in Lesbian and Gay Writing* includes a chapter by Terry Castle entitled "Sylvia Townsend Warner and the Counterplot of Lesbian Fiction." Castle nominates *Summer Will Show* an exemplary "lesbian" fiction and adds: "What makes this novel paradigmatically 'lesbian,' in my view, is not simply that it depicts a sexual relationship between two women, but that it so clearly, indeed almost schematically, figures this relationship as a breakup of the supposedly 'canonical' male–female–male erotic triangle." Castle demonstrates that this kind of subverted triangulation, or "erotic 'counterplotting'" is characteristic of lesbian novels in general. She notes that Warner's "plotting ... illustrates ... what we might take to be the underlying principle of lesbian narratives itself: namely, that for female bonding to 'take,' as it were, to metamorphose into explicit sexual desire, male bonding [male homosexual bonding] must be suppressed."

As lesbian and gay writing is increasingly celebrated, Warner's generally under–read, even unknown, texts, and certainly, under–appreciated ones, may at last emerge from neglect and the critical assessment her fiction deserves may at last appear.

—*Sarah Barbara Watstein*

———

WARREN, Patricia Nell. American novelist, editor, and artist. Has also written as Patricia Kilina. Born in Helena, Montana, 15 June 1936. Educated at Stephens College, A.A. 1955; Manhattanville College of the Sacred Heart (now Manhattanville College), B.A. 1957. Married George O. Tarnawsky in 1957 (divorced 1973). Copyeditor, 1959–63, and associate book editor, beginning 1959, *Reader's Digest,* Pleasantville, New York; staff writer, *Runner's World,* Mountain View, California, beginning 1971. Publicity and women's director, National Road Runners, 1972. Regular contributor to *Cats, All Cats,* and *Cat World;* contributor to *Modern Maturity* and *American West.* **Recipient:** *Atlantic* College Fiction Contest first prize for a short story, 1954; Walt Whitman Award for Excellence in Gay Literature, 1978. Agent: Paul R. Reynolds, Inc., 12 East 41st Street, New York, New York 10017, U.S.A

WRITINGS

Novels

The Last Centennial. New York, Dial, 1971.
The Front Runner. New York, Morrow, 1974.
The Fancy Dancer. New York, Morrow, 1976.
The Beauty Queen. New York, Morrow, 1978.
One Is the Sun. New York, Ballantine, 1991.

Other

Translator, with George O. Tarnawsky, *Ukrainian dumy* (poetry). Toronto, Canadian Institute of Ukrainian Studies, and Cambridge, Massachusetts, Ukrainian Research Institute, 1979.

*

Interviews: "Still a Front–Runner" by Stuart Timmons, in *Advocate,* 7 June 1988, 66–67.

Critical Sources: "Contemporary Homosexual Fiction and the Gay Rights Movement" by Trudy Steuernagel, in *Journal of Popular Culture,* winter 1986, 125–133; *The Gay Novel in America* by James Levin, New York, Garland, 1991, 265–268.

*   *   *

Beginning with the publication of her first prize–winning story in the *Atlantic's* college fiction contest in 1954, Patricia Nell Warren has worked in several genres of literature. Her output has ranged from translations of Ukrainian poetry to numerous articles for popular periodicals such as *Cat World, Modern Maturity,* and *American West* (this last reflecting her pride in her home state of Montana) as well as five novels. She has also been deeply involved in publishing, serving as copyeditor and associate book editor for *Reader's Digest* and a staff writer for *Runner's World* since 1971. Her importance to the development of gay and lesbian literature was established with three novels which appeared in the 1970s, *The Front Runner, The Fancy Dancer,* and *The Beauty Queen.*

In all her writing, Warren draws upon her own experiences to provide detail and create a solid, believable world with well–drawn characters. Her first gay–themed novel, *The Front Runner,* appeared in 1974 and was an outgrowth of her own questions regarding her identity as a woman and her awareness of people's sexual needs. It is the story of a love affair between an athlete, distance runner Billy Sive, and his coach, Harlan Brown, and is filled with intricate information on the world of contemporary intercollegiate, international, and Olympic track competition. Related themes such as the problems of intergenerational relationships, gays and lesbians as parents, the state of the contemporary gay rights movement, and the institutionalized homophobia in professional sports are all explored. Warren's own feminism is reflected in the strong and capable character of Betsy, a lesbian athlete who chooses to be artificially inseminated with the semen of Sive after he is assassinated at the Olympic Games. The opening dedication is offered "to all the athletes who have fought for human rights in sports and to the young gay runner I met at a party, who gave me the idea for this book." *The Front Runner* was one of the first openly gay novels to make the *New York Times* best–seller list, with the mass–market edition proclaiming it to be "the first honest popular novel about homosexual love." While the death of Sive echoes the fatalism of an older generation of gay and lesbian characters whose lives regularly came to some unfortunate end, the assassination also comes at his moment of Sive's supreme triumph as a man and an athlete.

Warren continued her examination of environmental homophobia in *The Fancy Dancer*, published in 1976. Like *The Front Runner*, this work again questions the role of sexuality and the social limitations placed on it through the story of Tom Meeker, a young priest in rural Montana. Through his efforts to achieve a sexual self against the boundaries set by both rural society and the Roman Catholic Church, Warren shifts her focus from organized sport to organized religion as her subject of analysis. The sense of estrangement and alienation felt by Meeker is challenged by his feelings for Vidal Stump, a local outcast who becomes his first lover. In some ways, this is perhaps the quietest of Warren's three gay novels, involving an introspective pilgrimage and eventual connection with the world through Meeker's acceptance of himself as a gay man with a valid vocation. The range of opinion on the issue of homosexuality within the Church is reflected in the persons of Father Doric (another homosexual priest), Father Vance (Meeker's parish superior), and Father Matt (who earlier discouraged his friendship with Doric in the seminary).

In 1978, Warren again added to the genre of gay and lesbian literature with *The Beauty Queen*. Full of parallels to the contemporary "Save Our Children" campaign headed by fundamentalist Christian entertainer Anita Bryant, it tells the story of Jeannie Coulter, a former public figure who determines to gain political power (in this case, the governorship of New York) through a religiously–flavored campaign against what she terms "homosexualism." In the course of the novel, she is forced to confront her own unresolved feelings over her mother's death and her father's homosexuality. Such topics as employment discrimination, violence against gays and lesbians, and sadomasochism are also explicitly raised in the subplots concerning two homosexual New York City police officers and their lovers.

—*Robert B. Marks Ridinger*

———

WATMOUGH, David (Arthur). British–born Canadian novelist and short story writer. Born in London, 17 August 1926; raised on a farm in St. Kew near Bodmin, Cornwall. Educated at King's College, London, 1945–49. Served in the British Royal Navy, 1944–45. Immigrated to Vancouver, British Columbia, 1962; became Canadian citizen in 1969. Companion of Floyd St. Clair since 1951. Began his writing career during his teen years with Cornish newspapers; tutor in English in Paris and Lyons, 1949–52; writer and editor, Holy Cross Press, New York City, 1953–54; talks producer, Third Programme, British Broadcasting Corp., London, 1955; editor, Ace Books, 1957; feature writer and reviewer, *San Francisco Examiner*, 1958–60; drama and art critic, *Vancouver Sun*, Vancouver, British Columbia, 1965–69; regular columnist, *Vancouver Step* (a bi–monthly arts magazine), 1991–93. Broadcaster for British Broadcasting Corp., Canadian Broadcasting Corp., and KPFA–Radio, Berkeley, California. Editor of *Homosexuality and the Theatre*, special issue of *Canadian Theatre Review*, fall 1976. **Recipient:** Canada Council bursary awards, 1968 and 1970; Canada Council senior arts grant, 1976 and 1986. Address: 3358 West First Avenue, Vancouver, British Columbia V6R 1G4, Canada.

WRITINGS

Novels

No More into the Garden. Toronto and Garden City, New York, Doubleday, 1978.
The Year of Fears. Oakville, Ontario, Mosaic Press, 1988.
Thy Mother's Glass. Toronto, HarperCollins, 1992.
The Time of the Kingfishers. Toronto, HarperCollins, in press.
Deadheads and Yellow Broom (sequel to *Thy Mother's Glass*), in progress.

Short Stories

Ashes for Easter, and Other Monodramas (includes "In the Mood" and "Wickanninish Memory"). Vancouver, Talonbooks, 1972.
Love and the Waiting Game: Eleven Stories (contains "All Kinds of Harvesting," "Flies, Lizards, and Bonar Law," "Love and the Waiting Game," "The Time of the Wind," "Rosemary," "Seduction," "Return of the Native," "Bell Bottoms on Plymouth Hoe," "Giulietta," "Cousin Petherick and the Will," and "Fathers and Sons"). Ottawa, Oberon Press, 1975.
From a Cornish Landscape. Padstow, England, Lodenek Press, 1975.
The Connecticut Countess: Chronicles of Davey Bryant (includes "Cousin Petherick and the Will," "False Start," and "Inside Out"). Trumansburg, New York, Crossing Press, 1984.
Fury (includes "Fury," "One for All" and "Nelly Moriarty and the Jewish Question"). Ottawa, Oberon Press, 1984.
Vibrations in Time (includes "I Hate Queers" and "The Savage Gardener"). Toronto, Mosaic Press, 1986.

Contributor

"The Audience as Critic," in *Canadian Theatre Review,* fall 1975.
"Ashes for Easter," in *Cornish Short Stories.* Harmondsworth, Penguin, 1976.
"Confessionalism and the First Person; or, The Future of Fiction," in *Canadian Fiction Magazine,* Numbers 32/33, 1979/1980.
"Black Memory," in *On the Line: New Gay Fiction,* edited by Ian Young. Trumansburg, New York, Crossing Press, 1981.
"On Coming to British Columbia: Some Personal and Literary Reflections," in *Canadian Literature,* spring 1984.
"Fury," in *Best Canadian Stories of 1983.* Ottawa, Oberon Press, 1984.
"The Wounded Christmas Choir Boy," in *Canadian Christmas Stories.* Kingston, Ontario, Quarry Press, 1990.
"Eurydice, May I Kiss the Cop?," in *Certain Voices.* Boston, Alyson Publications, 1991.
"Thank You Siegfried Sassoon," in *Indivisible.* New York, New American Library/Plume, 1991.
"The Horses," in *Dalhousie Review* (Halifax), 1991.

Other

A Church Renascent: A Study in Modern French Catholicism. London, S.P.C.K., 1951.

Names for the Numbered Years: Three Plays (contains "Friedhof," "My Mother's House Has Too Many Rooms," and "Do You Remember One September Afternoon?"), illustrations by Claude Breeze. Vancouver, Bau–Xi Press, 1967.

Editor and author of introduction, *Vancouver Fiction*. Winlaw, British Columbia, Polestar Press, 1985.

The Unlikely Pioneer: Opera from the Pacific to the Prairies. Oakville, Ontario, Mosaic Press, 1986.

Recordings: *Pictures from a Dying Landscape* (contains "Trading in Innocence," "Ashes for Easter," and "First Job"), Toronto, Kenata Records, 1972; *Vibrations* (compact disc; contains "A First Death," "The Reluctant Club," and "Thank You Siegfried Sassoon"), Vancouver, The Writer's Voice, 1991.

*

Interviews: "Interview with David Watmough" by Geoff Hancock, in *Canadian Fiction Magazine*, winter 1976, 65–83.

Critical Sources: "Performer of Many Parts" by Paul Grescoe, in *Canadian Magazine*, 18 November 1972, 36–38; "The Novel that Never Ends: David Watmough's Reminiscent Fictions" by George Woodcock, in his *The World of Canadian Writing: Critiques and Recollections*, Vancouver, Douglas and McIntyre, 1980, 211–221; *Lizard in the Grass* by John Mills, ECW Press, 1980; "David Watmough" by Jerry Wasserman, in *Dictionary of Literary Biography*, Volume 53: *Canadian Writers since 1960, First Series*, Detroit, Gale, 1986; Keynote Address given by David Watmough at the "Words without Borders" event at Celebration 90, August 1990; "Family Man" by Marvin Shaw, in *Advocate*, 25 February 1992, 81.

David Watmough comments: "I see my novels and stories as essentially family–oriented. Not surprisingly, perhaps, for one who has lived with his partner for over forty years. My fiction is invariably written from a first–person standpoint as I seek to pervade it with the authoritative flavor of personal twentieth–century experience. But woe betide the reader who confuses my protagonist, Davey Bryant, with his creator, David Watmough. Down that path lies a morass of factual error which could lead to madness!"

*   *   *

Canadian author David Watmough makes the center of his short stories and novels Davey Bryant, his fictional alter ego, a projection of Watmough himself who is different from his creator but similar enough to be a candid picture of the author. Throughout the course of Watmough's novels, Davey epitomizes the life of the gay male in the twentieth century as he travels throughout England, the United States, and Canada in search of adventure.

In *Ashes for Easter, and Other Monodramas*, the truthful side of Davey emerges: In "In the Mood," he yields to a gay passion and seduces a black American G.I. outside a dance in his Cornish home town when he is barely into his teens. But there is also the evasive Davey, who coolly lies to some detectives getting information on the murder of a gay young German in "Wlckanninish Memory." These stories powerfully illustrate the gay man's drive to be truthful about himself and his dreadful need to shield who he is from potentially harmful authority. Juxtaposed stories like these are a prime characteristic of Watmough's art; time and again he uses Davey's differing experiences and the conflicting emotions they raise to further illuminate the complexities of his fictional character.

In the short story collection *Fury*, two stories show the gay youth caught in the anti–Semitic dilemma endemic to our times. In "One for All," Davey knows the fright and fear of violent bigotry when he and friend Charlie Lazarus are trapped in a confrontation between Communists and British Fascists in London's East End. But in a subsequent story, "Nelly Moriarty and the Jewish Question," loyalty and resentment fight within him again.

The cost of deception is a recurrent theme in Watmough's fiction. In "Cousin Petherick and the Will," a Cornwall story in *The Connecticut Countess: Chronicles of Davey Bryant*, members of Davey's family learn that they will not share in the legacy of their sometimes–despised relative because he has willed a large part of it to a strapping young man he had admired for years. The story "Inside Out" has Davey himself being deceived: the paroled criminal Davey believes he is helping tricks him in the helpless fashion of one who can't do otherwise.

In *Vibrations in Time*, two more stories dramatically demonstrate both the omnipresent threat of homophobia and Davey's growing tendency to challenge it. In "The Savage Gardener," he is brutally confronted by a youth who extorts money from him, a turn of events poignantly contrasted with a memory of a sweet Cuban boy he had once encountered at the same lakeside spot. While Davey backs down in this situation—partly because more bashers are just off the scene—in the succeeding story, "I Hate Queers," he asserts himself against a famous photographer whose homophobia is grounded in professional jealousy.

But not all of Davey Bryant's adventures are serious. A vital part of his character is picaresque, and comic episodes abound throughout Watmough's books. In the author's first novel, *No More into the Garden*, a spurious archimandrite lures Davey into a dinner with "the Alabama giantess," who feasts Davey wildly as a prelude to bed. In "False Start," a story collected in *The Connecticut Countess*, Davey becomes Brother Dominic in a brief fervor of religious zeal and chaperons a group of younger boys and girls through a visit to a related Dutch church. The devout expedition goes completely awry when the kids desert pious intentions for sexual shenanigans.

The novel *Thy Mother's Glass* demonstrates a significant development in Watmough's fiction. Although the importance of family in the life of the "gay everyman" has been a vital part of much of the author's ouvre, this work concentrates on that value in a new way: the book alternates from Davey's point of view to his mother Isabella's. By the "glass" in the title, Watmough means a mirror, and the psychological resemblance of mother and son is artfully nurtured. By no means hewing to the older analysis of gay sons as products of a dominant mother and a weak father, the novel traces the relationship as one that is loving and mutually influential. Also, it enables Watmough to start several years prior to Davey's birth and to depict Isabella as an intelligent and independent young woman clearly capable of developing similar qualities in her son. While not forecasting the desertion by his creator of Davey as protagonist and narrator, this shift should be understood as yet another forward step in Watmough's juxtaposition of related but contrasting dualities.

A unique high point in Watmough's career occurred in August, 1990, when he and author Jane Rule served as honorary co–hosts at "Words Without Borders," part of an arts event called Celebration 90. In his keynote address at the opening session, Watmough recounted significant portions of his own life and career and projected his ideas on the state of gay writing today and how it could best develop. "Thorny relations which flare up between gay men and gay women, bisexual dilemmas, gay pedophilia and the promiscuous patterns of many of us are all surely viable territories for further development," he noted, and went on to add: "As an author gazing down the barrel of our century's final decade, I see the upcoming role of the gay writer as one continually changing and evolving."

—Marvin Shaw

———

WAUGH, Evelyn (Arthur St. John). British novelist, short story writer, and essayist. Born 28 October 1903, in Hampstead, London. Educated at Hertford College, Oxford, 1921–24, and Heatherley's Art School, 1924. Served with Royal Marines, 1939–40, Commandos, 1940–43, and the Royal Horse Guards, 1943–45, in Crete, North Africa, and Yugoslavia; became major. Married 1) Evelyn Gardner, 1928 (divorced, 1930; marriage annulled, 1936); 2) Laura Herbert, 1937; children include the writer Auberon, Margaret, Teresa, Harriet, James, and Septimus. Worked as a school teacher, a journalist for the London *Daily Express,* and a war correspondent in Abyssinia (now Ethiopia). **Recipient:** Hawthornden Prize, 1936; Black Memorial Prize, 1953; named Royal Society of Literature fellow and companion of literature, 1963; honorary degree from Loyola College; refused to accept Commander of the British Empire award. *Died in Combe Florey, Somerset, 10 April 1966.*

WRITINGS

Novels

Decline and Fall. London, Chapman & Hall, 1928; Garden City, New York, Doubleday, Doran, 1929.
Vile Bodies. London, Chapman & Hall, and New York, Cape & Smith, 1930.
Black Mischief. London, Chapman & Hall, and New York, Farrar & Rinehart, 1932.
A Handful of Dust. London, Chapman & Hall, and New York, Farrar & Rinehart, 1934.
Scoop. London, Chapman & Hall, and Boston, Little, Brown, 1938.
Put Out More Flags. London, Chapman & Hall, and Boston, Little, Brown, 1942.
Brideshead Revisited: The Sacred and Profane Memories of Captain Charles Ryder. London, Chapman & Hall, and Boston, Little, Brown, 1945; revised, Chapman & Hall, 1960.
Scott–King's Modern Europe. London, Chapman & Hall, 1947; Boston, Little, Brown, 1949.

The Loved One: An Anglo–American Tragedy. London, Chapman & Hall, and Boston, Little, Brown, 1948.
Helena. London, Chapman & Hall, and Boston, Little, Brown, 1950.
Men at Arms. London, Chapman & Hall, and Boston, Little, Brown, 1952.
Love among the Ruins: A Romance of the Near Future. London, Chapman & Hall, 1953.
Officers and Gentlemen. London, Chapman & Hall, and Boston, Little, Brown, 1955.
The Ordeal of Gilbert Pinfold: A Conversation Piece. London, Chapman & Hall, and Boston, Little, Brown, 1957.
Unconditional Surrender. London, Chapman & Hall, 1961; as *The End of the Battle,* Boston, Little, Brown, 1962.
Basil Seal Rides Again; or, The Rake's Regress. London, Chapman & Hall, and Boston, Little, Brown, 1963.
Sword of Honour (contains *Men at Arms, Officers and Gentlemen,* and *Unconditional Surrender*). London, Chapman & Hall, 1965; Boston, Little, Brown, 1966.

Short Stories

Mr. Loveday's Little Outing, and Other Sad Stories. London, Chapman & Hall, and Boston, Little, Brown, 1936; expanded as *Charles Ryder's Schooldays, and Other Stories,* 1982.
Work Suspended: Two Chapters of an Unfinished Novel. London, Chapman & Hall, 1942; expanded as *Work Suspended, and Other Stories Written before the Second World War,* 1949.
Tactical Exercise. Boston, Little, Brown, 1954.

Travel

Labels: A Mediterranean Journal. London, Duckworth, 1930; as *A Bachelor Abroad,* New York, Cape & Smith, 1930.
Ninety–two Days: The Account of a Tropical Journey through British Guinea and Part of Brazil. New York, Farrar & Rinehart, 1934; as *Ninety–two Days: A Journey in Guinea and Brazil,* London, Duckworth, 1986.
Waugh in Abyssinia. London and New York, Longmans, Green, 1936.
Tourist in Africa. London, Chapman & Hall, and Boston, Little, Brown, 1960.

Criticism

P.R.B.: An Essay on the Pre–Raphaelite Brotherhood, 1847–1854. London, Graham, 1926.
Rosetti: His Life and Works. London, Duckworth, and New York, Dodd, Mead, 1928.

Other

The World to Come (poems). Westminster Press, 1916.
Remote People. London, Duckworth, 1931; as *They Were Still Dancing,* New York, Farrar & Rinehart, 1932.
An Open Letter to His Eminence, the Cardinal Archbishop of Westminster. London, Whitefriars, 1933.
Edmund Campion: Scholar, Priest, Hero, and Martyr. London, Longmans, Green, and New York, Sheed & Ward, 1935.

Robbery Under Law: The Mexican Object Lesson. London, Chapman & Hall, 1939; as *Mexico: An Object Lesson,* Boston, Little, Brown, 1939.

When the Going Was Good. London, Duckworth, and Boston, Little, Brown, 1946.

Wine in Peace and War. London, Saccone & Speed, 1947.

The Holy Places (essays). London, Queen Anne, 1952; New York, Queen Anne & British Book Centre, 1953.

The World of Evelyn Waugh, edited by Charles J. Rolo. Boston, Little, Brown, 1958.

The Life of the Right Reverend Ronald Knox, Fellow of Trinity College, Oxford, and Protonotary Apostolic to His Holiness Pope Pius XII. London, Chapman & Hall, 1959; as *Monsignor Ronald Knox, Fellow of Trinity College, Oxford, and Protonotary Apostolic to His Holiness Pope Pius XII,* Boston, Little, Brown, 1959.

A Little Learning: The First Volume of an Autobiography. London, Chapman & Hall, 1964; as *A Little Learning: An Autobiography, the Early Years,* Boston, Little, Brown, 1964.

The Diaries and Letters of Evelyn Waugh, edited by Michael Davie. London, Weidenfeld & Nicolson, 1976; Boston, Little, Brown, 1977.

A Little Order: A Selection from the Journalism of Evelyn Waugh, edited by Donat Gallagher. London, Eyre Methuen, 1977; Boston, Little, Brown, 1981.

The Letters of Evelyn Waugh, edited by Mark Amory. New York, Ticknor & Fields, 1980.

The Essays, Articles and Reviews of Evelyn Waugh, edited by Donat Gallagher. Boston, Little, Brown, 1984.

Evelyn Waugh, Apprentice: The Early Writings, 1910–1927, edited and with an introduction by Robert Murray Davis. Norman, Oklahoma, Pilgrim Books, 1985.

*

Adaptations: *The Loved One* was filmed by Metro–Goldwyn–Mayer in 1965; *Decline and Fall* was filmed as *Decline and Fall of a Bird Watcher* by Twentieth Century–Fox in 1969; *Brideshead Revisited* was filmed for television by Granada Television in 1981; *A Handful of Dust* was adapted into a 1988 film by screenwriters Tim Sullivan and Derek Granger and director Charles Sturridge.

Biography: *Evelyn Waugh: Portrait of an Artist* by Frederick J. Stopp, Boston, Little, Brown, 1958; *Evelyn Waugh: Portrait of a Country Neighbor* by Frances Donaldson, London, Weidenfeld & Nicolson, 1967, Chilton, 1968; *My Brother Evelyn, and Other Profiles* by Alec Waugh, Farrar, Straus, 1967; *Evelyn Waugh: A Biography* by Christopher Sykes, Boston, Little, Brown, 1975; *Evelyn Waugh: The Early Years, 1903–1939* by Martin Stannard, Norton, 1987; *Evelyn Waugh: The Later Years, 1939–1966* by Martin Stannard, Norton, 1992.

Bibliography: *Evelyn Waugh: A Checklist of Primary and Secondary Materials,* edited by Robert Murray Davis and others, Whitston, 1972; *A Catalogue of the Evelyn Waugh Collection at the Humanities Research Center* by Robert Murray Davis, University of Texas at Austin/Whitston, 1981; *A Bibliography of Evelyn Waugh,* edited by Paul A. Doyle and others, Whitston, 1986.

Critical Sources: *Evelyn Waugh* by Christopher Hollis, London, Longmans, Green, 1954; *Roman Holiday: The Catholic Novels of Evelyn Waugh* by A. A. DeVitis, Bookman Associates, 1956; *Evelyn Waugh Newsletter and Studies* Garden City, New York, Nassau College, 1962—; *Evelyn Waugh* by Malcolm Bradbury, Oliver & Boyd, 1964; *The Satiric Art of Evelyn Waugh* by James F. Carens, University of Washington Press, 1966; *Evelyn Waugh* by Paul A. Doyle, Eerdmans, 1969; *Evelyn Waugh* by David Lodge, New York, Columbia University Press, 1971; *Evelyn Waugh and His World,* edited by David Pryce–Jones, Boston, Little, Brown, 1973; *Evelyn Waugh's Officers, Gentlemen and Rogues: The Fact Behind His Fiction* by Gene D. Phillips, Nelson–Hall, 1975; *Evelyn Waugh, Writer* by Robert Murray Davis, Norman, Oklahoma, Pilgrim Books, 1981; *The Picturesque Prison: Evelyn Waugh and His Writing* by Jeffrey Heath, McGill–Queens University Press, 1982; *The Writings of Evelyn Waugh* by Ian Littlewood, London, Basil Blackwell, 1983; *Evelyn Waugh: A Reference Guide* by Margaret Morriss and D. J. Dooley, London, G. K. Hall, 1984; *Evelyn Waugh: The Critical Heritage,* edited by Martin Stannard, Routledge & Kegan Paul, 1984; *A Reader's Companion to the Novels and Short Stories of Evelyn Waugh* by Paul A. Doyle, Pilgrim Books, 1988; *Evelyn Waugh* by Kathryn W. Crabbe, Continuum, 1988; *The Ironic World of Evelyn Waugh* by Frederick L. Beaty, Northern Illinois University Press, 1992.

*   *   *

When Evelyn Waugh attempted to have *Decline and Fall,* his first novel, accepted for printing in 1928, the publisher rejected it on the grounds of "indelicacy." A second publisher agreed to issue the book if some of the improprieties were toned down. In order to get the novel published, Waugh made the requested changes. The principal problem centered around the explicit portrayal of a homosexual schoolmaster named Captain Edgar Grimes. According to the novel, Grimes had held teaching posts at several prep schools, but his homosexual activities with the boys always led to the termination of his employment. Since he had connections in the education system, he always managed to find another teaching position. In fact in World War I he was saved from a court martial in the British army because of the "Old Boys' Network."

The character of Grimes, based on Richard Young, a fellow teacher of Waugh's at Arnold House early in Waugh's career, is an entertaining companion, a well–travelled adventurer, and a lively spirit. When he presumably dies during an attempted prison escape, Waugh observes that he "was of the immortals ... a life force.... Surely he had followed in the Bacchic train of distant Arcady, and played on the reeds of myth by forgotten streams, and taught the childish satyrs the art of love?" Grimes is not censured by the novelist for his homosexual behavior. In order to have the novel published, though, Waugh decreased the number of explicit homosexual references and implications in the story.

Waugh's next full scale portrait of a homosexual occurs in *Put Out More Flags,* published in 1942. Ambrose Silk is a sensitive and intelligent aesthete. He has had several male lovers and becomes very distressed over an abortive affair with a young German.

Ambrose works for the Ministry of Information, writing articles which are designed to support the British war effort. He is innocently naive and trusting so he falls victim to the schemes of an unprincipled character named Basil Seal, who manages to get Ambrose fired and causes him to flee to Ireland while confiscating his living quarters and possessions. Waugh once admitted that Silk was modelled on Brian Howard, a well–known Oxford aesthete and homosexual who ultimately died from a drug overdose.

Two left–wing poets, Parsnip and Pimpernel, are referred to in the novel. Both quickly leave England when World War II commences in order to take up residence in the United States. Parsnip is based on W. H. Auden, while Pimpernel represents Christopher Isherwood. At the time of the war, several Englishmen of draft age departed the country to avoid participating in the struggle against Adolf Hitler and the Nazis. Many members of the British public were outraged at this occurrence because of what was regarded as cowardly and unpatriotic behavior. Waugh makes his disdain for Parsnip and Pimpernel very vivid, and their homosexuality adds to the negative presentation. Although he was over age at the beginning of the conflict, Waugh immediately volunteered for military service, and his satire of the two writers is based more on their perceived cowardice than on their homosexuality.

Waugh's most famous novel, *Brideshead Revisited,* presents an intimate relationship between Sebastian Flyte and Charles Ryder. It has been argued by scholars whether the two young men have an actual sexual relationship or simply a very intense platonic intimacy. In the novel their is no hint of physical sexuality. The very successful PBS television adaptation of the book, however, suggests that the two men, who had met at Oxford, were sexually involved.

One of the reasons Waugh omits notions of homosexuality between Sebastian and Charles is to contrast their characters with another of Waugh's personalities, Anthony Blanche. Blanche, who is based both on Harold Acton and Brian Howard, is the epitome of the Oxford aesthete and one of the most memorable characters in twentieth–century fiction. Blanche is intellectually brilliant and immensely cultured. He moves from one homosexual relationship to another, and yet is such a superlative conversationalist that he at times almost takes over the novel. In fact, in preliminary draft versions of the book, Waugh had to tone down Blanche's role, giving him less conversation and emphasizing such negative qualities as jealousy, dishonesty, and scandal–mongering. *Brideshead Revisited* thus presents a detailed view of a cosmopolitan homosexual who has engaged in numerous homosexual relationships as well as a relationship, which may or may not have involved physical intimacy, between Sebastian and Charles.

Much of the latter material is unquestionably based on two homosexual romances Waugh himself experienced at Oxford—one with Richard Pares, the other with Alastair Graham. Homosexual relationships at Oxford were at that time not uncommon because women were rarely involved in university life. Waugh's close relationship with Pares appears not to have culminated in physical expression, while his measure of intimacy with Graham has been debated. Regardless, the idyllic Arcadian early association between Sebastian and Charles certainly reflects upon time that Waugh spent with Pares and Graham. Charles Ryder observes that for a time he achieved something he had not know: "A happy childhood, and though its toys were silk shirts and liqueurs and cigars and its naughtiness high in the catalogue of grave sins, there was something of nursery freshness about us that fell little short of the joy of innocence."

The most significant homosexual characters in Waugh's last novels are Sir Ralph Brompton and Corporal–Major Ludovic. Brompton is an influential figure in *The End of the Battle,* while Ludovic appears in *Officers and Gentlemen* as well as in *The End of the Battle.* Brompton, a retired ambassador, is a tall, handsome dandy, smooth and slick, who becomes a diplomatic advisor to British Hazardous Operation Headquarters in World War II. He is an avowed Communist attempting to spread his political views both in England and abroad. Ludovic, who once had a homosexual liaison with Brompton, is a more complex and reclusive figure. In the chaos that surrounds the British military evacuation from Crete, he is portrayed as both brave and unscrupulous. After the war, he purchases an estate in Italy and engages in a homosexual relationship with an American officer he had met earlier in London. He is successful in a new writing career.

In his *Letters* and *Diaries,* Waugh frequently makes disparaging references to homosexuals. In all fairness, however, it must be noted that in his various satiric moods or in his manic–depressive phases, no group—not even churchmen or nannies—is spared the sting of his vitriolic pen. In the novels, the matter is not so clear–cut. Grimes is admired, and both Sebastian and Charles are portrayed favorably. Even Anthony Blanche, who is totally involved in homosexuality, is presented with an ambivalence that overall is not unfavorable. On the other hand, homosexuals like Parsnip and Pimpernell are satirized for their alleged cowardice, and Sir Ralph Brompton is despised for his Communism. Such reactions are understandable given Waugh's strong feelings about fighting the Nazis and his consistent hatred of Communism, which, as he frequently emphasized, would take away basic human liberties. In the world of Waugh's fiction, then, the author's treatment of homosexuality fluctuates depending on the characters' motives and on the circumstances in which they are involved.

—*Paul A. Doyle*

———

WEEKS, Jeffrey.   British social scientist and nonfiction writer. Born in Rhondda, Wales, 1 November, 1945. Educated at University of London, B.A. (honours) 1967, M.Phil. 1973; University of Kent, Ph.D. 1983. History teacher, Sidcup Grammar School, London, 1969–70; research officer, London School of Economics and Political Science, London, 1970–77; fellow in sociology, University of Essex, Colchester, 1978–79; lecturer in sociology, University of Kent at Canterbury, 1980–83; research fellow, University of Southampton, Southampton, 1983–85; assistant registrar, Council for National Academic Awards, London, 1986–90; professor of social relations, University of the West of England (formerly Bristol Polytechnic), Bristol, 1990—. Contributor to numerous anthologies. Member of British Sociological Association, Writers Guild of Great Britain. **Recipient:** Socialist Review Book Award, 1986; University of Manchester Simon Senior fellowship, 1989–90. Address: 26 Dresden Road, London N19 3BD, England, U.K.; Faculty of Economics and Social Service, University of the West of England, Frenchay Campus, Bristol B516 1QY, England, U.K.

WRITINGS

With Sheila Rowbotham, *Socialism and the New Life: The Personal and Sexual Politics of Edward Carpenter and Havelock Ellis.* London, Pluto Press, 1977.
Coming Out: Homosexual Politics in Britain from the Nineteenth Century to the Present. London, Quartet, 1977; second edition, 1990.
Sex, Politics, and Society: The Regulation of Sexuality since 1800. London, Longman, 1981; second edition, 1989.
Sexuality and Its Discontents: Meaning, Myths and Modern Sexualities. London, Routledge, 1985.
Sexuality. Chichester, Ellis Horwood, 1986.
Against Nature: Essays on History, Sexuality and Identity. London, Rivers Oram, 1991.

Editor

With Chris Cook and others, *Sources in British Political History, 1900–1951* (five volumes). London, Macmillan, 1974–78.
Family Directory: Information Resources on the Family. London, British, Library, 1986.
Family Studies—Information Needs and Resources: The Report of the Review Panel on Family Studies. London, British Library, 1986.
With Kevin Porter, *Between the Acts: Lives of Homosexual Men, 1885–1967.* London, Routledge, 1990.

Other

"Inverts, Perverts, and Mary–Annes: Male Prostitution and the Regulation of Homosexuality in England in the Nineteenth and Early Twentieth Centuries," in *Hidden from History: Reclaiming the Gay and Lesbian Past,* edited by Martin Bauml Duberman, Martha Vicinus, and George Chauncey, Jr. New York, New American Library, 1989.

*

Critical Sources: "Loyal Oppositions: The Goal of Gay and Lesbian Politics" by David Bergman, in *Lambda Book Report,* November/December 1991.

Jeffrey Weeks comments: "Looking back over my writings over the past twenty years I see three overwhelming preoccupations: with sexual identities, both personal and social, and with the complex forces that shape them; with the changing patterns of social regulation that attempt to control and at the same time construct sexuality, and give rise to the patterns of discourse which attempt to define what is right or wrong, legitimate or illegitimate at any particular time, and present as truth what is often in fact historical and contingent. Underlying all these apparently disparate themes is a more consistent interest: with value systems, and with their attendant cultural and political implications. This theme has now become the explicit thread linking my most recent researches and writings, from the question of values in an age of uncertainty to the implications for social policy of community based responses to HIV and AIDS."

At a time when theoretical approaches to gay, lesbian, and bisexual studies are entering a new phase of sophistication, Jeffrey Weeks has emerged as a central theoretician of a constructionist approach to the study of human sexuality. In the book that he co–authored with Sheila Rowbotham, *Socialism and the New Life,* Weeks describes the sex researcher Havelock Ellis as not so much a new thinker as a synthesizer of the work of others. Ellis' *Sexual Inversion* brings together for an English–language readership the sex research of various continental and English scholars. In his work Weeks shows that he also has a penchant for summarizing and recombining the sex research done by others. Many of his major publications—such as *Sexuality and Its Discontent* and *Against Nature*—contain lucid accounts of the theoretical positions of Edward Carpenter, Magnus Hirschfeld, Karl Heinrich Ulrichs, Alfred Kinsey, Michel Foucault, and others. The history he provides of these researchers' projects is not a simply descriptive one. Coming as he has out of a British left tradition, Weeks has actively recast these pioneers' conclusions and linked their work with those aspects of contemporary theories about sexuality that he finds most viable.

Weeks has always approached sexuality as a highly political field of study that has social and cultural as well as individual importance. From his first publications in the 1970s, he has been at his most eloquent when discussing the potential connections between socialism—conceived in a Western European libertarian sense—and sexuality. His various writings in this area form the most important aspects of his own theoretical work. Weeks' training both as a historian and sociologist has similarly given him a perspective on the history of sexuality that is often missing from other major accounts, which tend to be historical but undertheorized. By positioning himself in his writings somewhat outside the usual channels of the academy, Weeks—like Simon Watney in Britain and Cindy Patton in the United States—has also developed an awareness of people dealing with grass roots political organization and support groups. This sensitivity to actual experience has made the political edges of his writing particularly acute.

Although Weeks has mainly been interested in the broad field known as sexuality or sex research, he often focuses on homosexuality in his work. And although much of his writing deals with sexuality in toto, his own recounting of the work of others often involves exploring the changing definitions and understandings of the concept of homosexuality since the Victorian period to the present. His most significant intervention into gay studies might in fact be his argument for an anti–natural definition of homosexual identity. That is, he is adamantly against using biological nature–based or sociobiological genetic–based theories to explain why there are people willing to call themselves gay. This definitional praxis occurs throughout his work and dovetails with his concentration on the political and social critiques of sexuality. Foucault's three–volume analysis of sexuality, *Histoire de la sexualite,* is often Weeks' touchstone between his own social constructionist theories of homosexuality and those in other fields—such as literary studies, psychology, and classical studies. Indeed he is adept at putting together various fields that have been kept apart by twentieth–century categories and specializations. This willingness to learn from many disciplines in order to stay at the forefront of theories about sexuality is balanced by a pragmatic interest in the idea of community and the problems that individual identity and choice can create. The current challenge in a multicultural society—to balance individual freedoms with the needs of a community as a whole—is not a new problem for Weeks, but one that has recurred in his work. Weeks' current goal is to formulate for these questions a real and practical, and not just a theoretical, answer.

—Shelton Waldrep

WELCH, (Maurice) Denton. British novelist, diarist, visual artist, poet, and author of short fiction. Born in Shanghai, China, 29 March 1915. Attended St. Michael's School, Uckfield, Sussex, 1926–29; Repton School, beginning 1929; Goldsmith School of Art, New Cross, London, 1933. *Died in Kent, 30 December 1948.*

WRITINGS

Novels

Maiden Voyage. London, Routledge, 1943; New York, Penguin, 1983.
In Youth is Pleasure (self–illustrated). London, Routledge, 1945; New York, Oxford University Press, 1982; with foreword by William Burroughs, New York, Dutton Obelisk, 1985.
A Voice Through a Cloud. London, John Lehmann, 1950; New York, Penguin, 1983.

Short Stories

Brave and Cruel, and Other Stories. London, Hamish Hamilton, 1949.
A Last Sheaf. London, John Lehmann, 1951.
I Left My Grandfather's House. London, Lion & Unicorn Press, 1958.
Dumb Instrument, edited by Jean–Louis Chevalier. London, Enitharmon Press, 1976.
"When I Was Thirteen," in *The Faber Book of Gay Short Fiction,* edited by Edmund White. London and New York, Faber & Faber, 1991.

Journals

The Denton Welch Journals, edited by Jocelyn Brooke. London, Hamish Hamilton, 1952.
The Journals of Denton Welch (unexpurgated edition), edited by Michael De–La–Noy. London, Allison & Busby, 1984.

Collected Works

Denton Welch: A Selection from His Published Works (self–illustrated), edited with an introduction by Jocelyn Brooke. London, Chapman Hall, 1963.
The Stories of Denton Welch, edited by Robert Phillips. New York, Dutton, 1986.

Biography: *Denton Welch: The Making of a Writer* by Michael De–La–Noy, London, Viking/Penguin, 1984.

*   *   *

"When asked what writer has most directly influenced my own work I can answer without hesitation: Denton Welch." Thus begins the foreword by William Burroughs to a 1985 edition of Welch's novel, *In Youth Is Pleasure.* It is a factor that Burroughs, author of *The Naked Lunch,* shares with many other first–person narrators, for Welch was a pioneer of sexually frank autobiographical fiction with a confessional bias.

Author of several novels and short stories that closely parallel the author's life, as well as journals and poetry, Welch's seeming self–absorption was a result of personal misfortune. A major influence on Welch's early life was his American mother whose tragic death from kidney disease at age 41 would haunt much of his writing. Their relationship had been unusually close; in early childhood the two had traveled between China and England—as well as visit Korea and Canada—where they would stay in expensive hotels and rented houses. Several years later, in 1935, Welch's life was again visited by tragedy when he was run over by a car during a bicycle outing. The injuries that he sustained from this accident left physical scars as lasting as the emotional scars left by the loss of his mother.

It might be said that Welch's theme *was* himself and that he recognized this as not only a reality but a potential limitation. In June 1943, on the publication of *Maiden Voyage,* his first novel, Welch wrote in a letter to an old school friend: "I think I shall always be writing about myself—so I am warning you! Perhaps my next book may be broader, fuller, but it also may *not* be." In fact, Welch never strayed far from the path of vigorously scrutinizing the self. But so objective and candid was his approach to self–portraiture that he neither suffered the restrictions of a blinkered solipsism nor invited the reader's boredom because of an overly–constricted focus.

The triple strengths of Welch's writing express themselves most naturally in the short story and short novel genres: relentless honesty, a vigorously pared autobiographical theme, and a flair for detail springing from the author's prior vocation as an artist. Welch not only painted some singular surrealistic canvases but furnished some fanciful still–life designs to illustrate the text of such books as *In Youth Is Pleasure* and, even more plentifully, *Denton Welch: A Selection From His Published Works,* which also features 13 of Welch's poems.

Some of the author's finest evocations of minuscule detail, deliberately assembled to create a telling mosaic, are found in *The Journals* (especially the unexpurgated version). Here, as elsewhere, Welch never allows his detailed eroticism to degenerate into a crude pornography because his mastery of a truly honed prose never permits him to abandon his goal of absolute verbal precision. His style is consistent throughout the body of his work—an indelible literary signature found on virtually every page. Characteristic of Welch's style is a passage from his first novel, *Maiden Voyage:* "It was raining and I was alone. My aunt and my brother were out. I sat on the settle in the dining room and watched the rain soaking into the lawn.... I went to the sideboard and opened one of the cupboards. A breath of salt, pepper, mustard, green baize, jeweller's rouge, wine and spirits escaped. The whisky decanter glistened from the bottom shelf, as prickly as a prison wall. The prisms and roses seemed too sharp to touch and the glittering stopper was like a diadem. I pulled it up with the soft crunch and squeak of glass on glass, and smelt the whisky."

It is hardly surprising that this meticulous miniaturist has largely remained the choice of the connoisseur and lover of truly self–conscious writing. His gay affirmation, as well as his refusal to stray far from domestic concerns, has also played a part in keeping him from both the center of gay literary awareness and mainstream acceptance of his artistic worth. In a sampling of major literary reference volumes, there is no specific mention of the sexual hetero-doxy that is such an informing element in Welch's writing and which he invoked without embarrassment or guilt.

While Welch's skill at summoning small details and patterning them to make probing assertions is apparent, he is not afraid to tread more vigorous waters when the occasion warrants. The use of pain in his last and possibly finest novel, *A Voice Through a Cloud,* is a brilliant tour de force, exceeded in sheer poignancy only by his short story "At Sea" which in brief, diamond–hard strokes evokes the grieving love between a dying mother and her jealousy–plagued small son. It is this kind of skillfully controlled narrative, lit with a heart–wrenching candor, that gives the work of Welch its literary significance. In honor of his work, during the last years of his life Welch was saluted by such prominent luminaries of the British literary establishment as Edith Sitwell, E. M. Forster, Cyril Connoly, and Vita Sackville–West; he delighted in such recognition, though often from his sickbed.

Few twentieth–century authors of elevated style and finished prose are more deserving of renewed attention than Denton Welch, and certainly no gay writer more demands literary resurrection. In the highly competitive field of gay writing that focuses on child-hood and adolescence, it can be reasonably argued that in Welch we have the ultimate genius of the genre and the finest exponent of the century.

—David Watmough

———

WHITE, Edmund (Valentine III). American novelist, biographer, editor, and educator. Born in Cincinnati, Ohio, 13 January 1940. Educated at University of Michigan, B.A. 1962. Senior editor, Time, Inc., Book Division, New York City, 1972–73. Assistant professor of writing seminars, Johns Hopkins University, Baltimore, Mary-land, 1977–79. Adjunct professor of creative writing, Columbia University School of the Arts, New York City, 1981–83; profes-sor, Brown University, 1990—. Instructor in creative writing at Yale University, New York University, Johns Hopkins University, and George Mason University, Fairfax, Virginia. Executive director of New York Institute for the Humanities, 1981–82. Editor, *Satur-day Review* and *Horizon;* contributing editor, *Vogue* and *House and Garden.* **Recipient:** University of Michigan Hopwood Awards for fiction and drama, 1961 and 1962; Ingram Merrill grants, 1973 and 1978; Guggenheim fellowship, 1983; American Academy and Insti-tute of Arts and Letters award for fiction, 1983; named Chevalier de l'Ordre des Artes et Lettres, 1993. Agent: Maxine Groffsky, Maxine Groffsky Literary Agency, 2 Fifth Avenue, New York, New York 10011, U.S.A.

WRITINGS

Nonfiction

With Charles Silverstein, *The Joy of Gay Sex: An Intimate Guide for Gay Men to the Pleasures of a Gay Lifestyle.* New York, Crown, 1977.
States of Desire: Travels in Gay America. New York, Dutton, 1980.
Genet: A Biography. New York, Knopf, 1993.

Novels

Forgetting Elena. New York, Random House, 1973.
Nocturnes for the King of Naples. New York, St. Martin's Press, 1978.
A Boy's Own Story. New York, Dutton, 1982.
Caracole. New York, Dutton, 1985.
The Beautiful Room Is Empty. New York, Knopf, 1988.

Other

Blue Boy in Black (play; produced New York, 1963).
Contributor, *Aphrodisiac* (short stories). London, Chatto & Windus, 1984.
With Adam Mars–Jones, *The Darker Proof: Stories from a Crisis.* New York, New American Library/Plume, 1988.
"Back to Mackinac" in *House and Garden* (New York), June 1990.
"Out of the Closet, Onto the Bookshelf: A Prominent Gay Writer Chronicles the Emergence of a New Literature," in *New York Times Magazine,* 16 June 1991.
"Editor, and contributor of Skinned Alive," in *The Faber Book of Gay Short Fiction.* London and New York, Faber & Faber, 1991.

*

Interviews: *Library Journal,* 15 February 1973, *Alive and Writ-ing: Interviews* by Larry McCaffery, University Press of Illinois, 1987, 257–274; "The Importance of Being: Armistad Maupin and Edmund White" by Walter Kendrick, in *Village Voice,* 28 June 1988, 22; *Paris Review* (New York), fall 1988, 47–80; "An Interview with Edmund White," in *Missouri Review* (Columbia, Missouri), 13:2, 1990, 89–110; "From Paris to Providence: An Interview with Edmund White" by Alfred Corn, in *Christopher Street* (New York), October 1991, 13.

Critical Sources: "Edmund White" by William Goldstein, in *Pub-lishers Weekly,* 24 September 1982, 6–8; "Imagining Other Lives" by Leonard Schulman, in *Time,* 30 July 1990; *The Gay Novel in America* by James Levin, New York, Garland, 1991; "Edmund White" by David Bergman, in *Contemporary Gay American Novel-ists,* edited by Emmanuel S. Nelson, Westport, Connecticut, Green-wood, 1993, 386–394.

Edmund White comments: "My two direct influences have been contradictory ones—Vladimir Nabokov and Christopher Isherwood.

From Nabokov, I acquired a delight in applying a dandy's fastidious standards to everyday American life. Through Isherwood, whose hold on my imagination came to supplant Nabokov's, I learned to admire a sober style and a searching sincerity. I find myself oscillating even now between these two writers, both admirable."

*   *   *

Edmund White has often said that what interests him as a writer and as a critic is not to see with a "psychological eye", but with a "sociological eye," and yet, as he acknowledged in an interview with Kay Bonetti in the *Missouri Review,* "the philosophical novelist, like Thomas Mann, is someone I tend to loathe and the very concrete novelist who has very few ideas, like Colette, is someone I tend to admire." It is a constant, an abiding base for his work, a taste for the particular, the concrete, which reveals, through its place within a society, the meaning (and range of meanings) of that place. Indeed, if nothing else, it sets his work apart from the two primary forms the American novel has taken in the second half of the twentieth century: the metafictional novel, turning in upon its own technique and concerned with questions of knowability, of uncertainty; and the more conventional and more popular novel of psychological sentiment. White's first novel, *Forgetting Elena,* which has been variously described as dreamlike—a baroque fantasy—was praised on its publication by such literary luminaries as Vladimir Nabokov, Gore Vidal, and John Ashbery. The intricacy and elaborate quality of its surface style pricks out the equally intricate, nearly hermetic facets of the Fire Island society he describes: feverish, intensely competitive, elegant nearly to the exclusion of any other concern. White explained its attraction to Bonetti: "The idea of writing about a culture that had a surface democracy, but an actual hierarchy, and where morality has been replaced by esthetics ... fascinated me. It seemed to be true of how a certain group of highly privileged gay men were living in the seventies."

With his second novel, *Nocturnes for the King of Naples,* White moderated the oblique, apparent fantasy of *Forgetting Elena* and produced a book whose boundaries match those of the visible world, yet whose impulses remain indirect, artistically more concerned with the latent and the suggestive than with the obvious. In *Nocturnes,* in fact, one can witness the modulations between White's two styles, between the elaborate fantasy of *Forgetting Elena* and *Caracole* and the direct, almost plain style of *A Boy's Own Story* and *The Beautiful Room Is Empty.* In his elaborate early style, White's sociological, or rather structuralist, underpinning comes clearest, with character and identity dissolving into a meeting and conflicting series of social and linguistic codes. The self is a thing constructed out of bits of the world. "My appearance," his narrator observes in *Nocturnes,* "was composed of allusions to things or people I admired—the slacks from an old gangster movie, the shoes and socks from the athletes I'd watched at school circling the track, the jacket from a veteran whom I'd studied once during a two-hour layover in a bus terminal, the gauzy shirt from a circus barker whose masculinity had become all the more pungent through dandyism." This interplay of elaborate and plain styles is reflected in White's observation of old and new gay styles, which he outlined for *Christopher Street* in 1991. "Whereas," he wrote,"such earlier gay esthetic sensibilities as dandyism or camp had proceeded through indirection

and puzzling, deliberately intimidating, reorderings of traditional values, the new esthetic, which I dubbed the Pleasure Machine, was frank, hedonistic, devoid of irony."

All commentators trying to capture what is, at any time, essential about a new culture stumbling into being, strive to see their subject as Alexis de Tocqueville saw the new American democracy, as a unique eruption, a severance of past from future. In 1840, concluding *La Democratie en Amerique,* he wrote that "although the revolution that is taking place in the social condition, the laws, the opinions, and the feelings of men is still very far from being terminated, yet its results already admit of no comparison with anything that the world has ever before witnessed.... As the past has ceased to throw its light upon the future, the mind of man wanders in obscurity."

At a time when international gay life has undergone a revolution of its own, accomplishing a profound and startling break with the past, and when the past has "ceased to throw light upon the future," has ceased to be a firm territory from which one may predict what will come, White has attempted to articulate the blind experiment as gay men in particular, and society more generally, have sought out new relationships to one another, to social institutions, and to conceptions of gender and humanity. *States of Desire: Travels in Gay America,* completed as the decade of radical liberation was ending, and with AIDS not yet on the horizon, provides as close to a poetics as White has given. Reaching out from New York to the west coast, then drawing back across a continent to where he began, White offers a geography of life rewritten by desire, rewritten as desire. What began as journalism, a travelogue, is appropriated for another purpose and the particular here becomes not simply representative of a place and a mode of life but a link in a chain of understanding. Here, more clearly than he had done before, White draws on work of French theorists—Barthes, Hocquenghem, Foucault—to insist that the modes of living and desiring he describes reveal people engaged in a social critique. At such time, his work is a light thrown onto "the mind of man wander[ing] in obscurity."

Although he had been a prominent and popular gay writer before the publication of *A Boy's Own Story,* and had been admired for the confident craftsmanship of his novels, White was still perhaps best-known, at least in gay circles, as the coauthor of *The Joy of Gay Sex.* But his third novel consolidated his reputation as a writer of fiction, and pushed him immediately to the forefront of that post–Stonewall generation of openly gay writers who in a short time were self-consciously transforming gay writing and publishing. These writers, many of them members of the Violet Quill, a writers' club founded in New York in 1979, broke with earlier generations by electing to identify themselves, explicitly, as gay writers and to take as their subject the rapidly evolving urban gay subcultures that in 1970s America was altering gay and straight life alike. Writing for *Christopher Street* in the early 1990s, looking back on that time, White noted that in those years "the old polarities that had functioned in an earlier period of gay life (butch/femme, older/younger, richer/poorer) and that had been patterned after borrowed social forms (husband/wife, teacher/student, gentleman/worker) had been rejected in favor of a new tribalism. To be sure, this equality was only apparent ... but on a sweaty disco floor at dawn, surrounded by a congeries of half–nude bodies, the interchangeability of human beings did seem real enough."

The change that AIDS brought to gay life coincided with the emergence of White's more direct mature style, and the elegant sensitivity of *A Boy's Own Story* brought a startling clarity of observation to the three stories he contributed to *The Darker Proof,* a short story collection that also features four pieces by Adam Mars–Jones. Where the earlier fiction drew energy from the sense of being at the center of things, now, without choosing it, that center had grown white hot. Personal history was overtaken by an impersonal history and became an extension of a broad public discourse. In a *Christopher Street* interview with Alfred Corn, White explained that "I was diagnosed early, around '85. The first year–and–a–half I was quite depressed, really ... I stayed at home, and in a way, I was out of touch with friends of mine in America who were ill— which some people thought was just cowardice, as it partly was, but I didn't get much gratification out of that form of cowardice— in other words, facing it and going through it with people is somehow enriching, perhaps, or at least realistic."

It has sometimes been claimed that White flirts with the role of satirist, more in the earlier novels than the later ones, but one must admit in the end that he is no satirist, though a casual humor suffuses his work. Satire requires distance, requires that the purveyor remain both removed from his subject and passionately involved with it, an antagonist, for the satirist is at heart a reformer, outraged by what he sees. White, though briefly touching satire in *Forgetting Elena* and *Nocturnes for the King of Naples,* and glancingly in *States of Desire,* works best from within, as a part of the world he describes. In White one does not find a satirist's rage, nor does one find him standing back from cosmopolitan gay society, surveying, wary. Rather his humor is mild, pervasive, not pointed. In his mature style, irony is diffused by a larger humanity. Beginning with *A Boy's Own Story* and deepening with the stories in *The Darker Proof* and *The Beautiful Room is Empty,* White has returned to the model of Colette, a writer not of ideas, but of concrete lives. His subject is, as it has been from the start, the world, but it is a world apprehended through the observation of his own life. "It's as though I peeled away the fantasy layer, in a style that was extremely ornate and appropriate to that particular vision" he told Bonetti in the *Missouri Review.* "Then I was ready to deal with the painful reality of my youth in a more direct way. If my goal now was to tell the truth, I wasn't going to disguise it with a style that was very rhetorical."

—*Kevin Ray*

WHITE, Patrick (Victor Martindale). British–born Australian novelist and playwright. Born in London, 28 May 1912. Educated at King's College, Cambridge, B.A. 1935. Served with the Royal Air Force, 1940–45; intelligence officer. **Recipient:** Australian Literature Society Herbert Crouch Medal, 1956; Miles Franklin Award, 1958 and 1962; W. H. Smith & Son literary award, 1959; brotherhood award from National Conference of Christians and Jews, 1962; Nobel Prize for literature, 1973. *Died in Sydney, Australia, 30 September 1990.*

WRITINGS

Novels

Happy Valley. London, Harrap, 1939; New York, Vantage, 1940.

The Living and the Dead. New York, Viking, 1941.
The Aunt's Story. New York, Viking, 1948.
The Tree of Man. New York, Viking, 1955.
Voss. New York, Viking, 1957.
Riders in the Chariot. New York, Viking, 1961.
The Solid Mandala. New York, Viking, 1966.
The Vivisector. New York, Viking, 1970.
The Eye of the Storm. London, J. Cape, 1973; New York, Viking, 1974.
A Fringe of Leaves. London, J. Cape, 1976; New York, Viking, 1977.
The Twyborn Affair. New York, Viking, 1979.
Memoirs of Many in One, by Alex Xenophon Demirjian Gray. New York, Viking, 1986.

Short Stories

The Burnt Ones. New York, Viking, 1964.
The Cockatoos: Shorter Novels and Stories. London, J. Cape, 1974; New York, Viking, 1975.
Three Uneasy Pieces. London, J. Cape, 1988; New York, Random House, 1989.

Poetry

The Ploughman, and Other Poems. Boston, Beacon Press, 1935.
Poems. Soft Press, 1974.

Plays

Return to Abyssinia (produced London, 1947).
The Ham Funeral (produced Adelaide, 1961). Published in *Four Plays,* 1965.
The Season at Sarsaparilla (produced Adelaide, 1962). Published in *Four Plays,* 1965.
A Cheery Soul (produced Melbourne, 1963). Published in *Four Plays,* 1965.
Night on Bald Mountain (produced Adelaide, 1964). Published in *Four Plays,* 1965.
Four Plays (contains *The Ham Funeral; The Season at Sarsaparilla; A Cheery Soul;* and *Night on Bald Mountain*). London, Eyre & Spottiswoode, 1965; New York, Viking, 1966.
Big Toys, 1977.
Signal Driver, 1981.
Netherwood, 1983.

Other

Flaws in the Grass: A Self–Portrait (autobiography). New York, Viking, 1981.
The Night of the Prowler (screenplay adaptation by White of his short story of the same name), Chariot/International Harmony, 1979.

*

Biography: *Patrick White: A Life* by David Marr, New York, Knopf, 1991.

Bibliography: *A Bibliography of Patrick White* by Janette Finch, Libraries Board of South Australia, 1966.

Critical Sources: *Beyond All This Fiddle: Essays 1955–1967* by A. Alvarez, New York, Random House, 1969; *The Mystery of Unity: Theme and Technique in the Novels of Patrick White* by Patricia A. Morley, Montréal, McGill–Queen's University Press, 1972; *Patrick White as Playwright* by J. R. Dyce, Queensland, University of Queensland Press, 1974; *The Eye in the Mandala* by Peter Beatson, London, Elek, 1976; *Patrick White* by Ingmar Bjorksten, Queensland, University of Queensland Press, 1976; *Patrick White's Fiction: The Paradox of Fortunate Failure* by Carolyn Bliss, New York, St. Martin's Press, 1986; "Patrick White's Style–Again" by Rodney S Edgecombe in *Antipodes*, 1:2, 1987, 83–87; *Patrick White: Fiction and the Unconscious* by David J. Tacey, Melbourne, Oxford University Press, 1988; *Critical Essays on Patrick White,* edited by Peter Wolfe, Boston, G. K. Hall, 1990; "Patrick White—The International Legacy" (a symposium), in *Antipodes*, 6:1, 1992, 5–58; "On the Limits of Archetypal Criticism" by Rick Wallach, in *Antipodes*, 6:2, 1992, 133–138.

*   *   *

Patrick White received the Nobel Prize for Literature in 1973, the only Australian to be so honored. He was, in fact, born in London, but his parents took him back to Australia four months later. He always claimed to be a Londoner and to despise Australians. His family were major landholders in New South Wales and Queensland, corresponding to the landed gentry of England. He himself disputed this claim to belong to Australia's aristocracy and referred to his family as nouveaux riches. Even so he enjoyed many things about this easy life, including the racehorses in which many of his family specialized, and by which they prospered. Contradictions of this sort are frequent in his writing and his life: A homosexual who never felt the need to "come out"; a great writer always uncertain of his reputation. These factors are explored fully in David Marr's *Patrick White: A Life,* and White's own self–portrait. Both are essential reading and provide keys to his often enigmatic novels, since they help place his writing in the context of his life.

White later returned to England to study at King's College, Cambridge, where he also met his first lover. His life after that was somewhat nomadic. In 1939 he travelled to America, where his first novel *Happy Valley* was published to rave reviews. Its publication coincided with the fall of France in 1940, and White felt he should go on to England and offer his services in the war. He joined the Royal Air Force and was posted, first to the Sudan and then to Alexandria. This period marked the turning point in his life. Not only did White receive the Herbert Crouch Medal for *Happy Valley,* he published *The Living and the Dead* and met Manoly Lascaris, who became his lover for the rest of his life. Lascaris was a descendant of former Byzantine emperors. Meeting him introduced White to perhaps the most bizarre of expatriate communities: the Greeks who had been expelled from Smyrna by the Turks and who formed an inbred society in cosmopolitan Alexandria. Many years later this experience would blend with his own boyhood experience as a jackeroo (the Australian equivalent of a ranch hand) on the family farms to become *The Twyborne Affair* and *Memoirs of Many in One.* These novels, which followed his receipt of the Nobel Prize, baffled many of the critics, who could not understand how these contradic-

tory traditions could be combined in one work, and White was felt to be scoring off Australia. The same bafflement greeted his self–portrait and, indeed, *Flaws in the Glass* is by no means easy reading. It is sprawling and disconnected, and great bluntness (on political affairs) is accompanied by great reticence (on personal affairs).

White saw no need to write the "great Australian homosexual novel" though he was urged to do so. He despised those who surrounded themselves with fellow homosexuals, yet he made no bones about his own homosexual nature, which he thought to be the source of his creativity. For him homosexuality meant a blending of masculine and feminine, and he credited his feminine side with the insight that enabled him to depict so accurately the spiritual and psychological inner beings of his characters. Although there are few overtly homosexual figures in his novels, and they are often singled out for criticism for shallowness, there are frequent deep, almost mystical friendships, such as that between Voss and Harry Robarts. His "heroes" are mystics, driven to pursue the mandala that he saw as the image of life, seeking always for meaning below the surface.

Although Marr makes a close connection between White's homosexuality and his success as a writer, others have questioned the connection. The most extreme is David Tacey, who, in applying Jungian analysis to White's writings, concludes that he "literalizes his desire for his father in a way which obscures symbolic meaning," leading to the disorderly chaos of his last novels. This interpretation has been rebutted by Rick Wallach, though even he feels that White's creativity is somewhat strained. In part this attitude results from Wallach's uneasiness with the gay content.

White's primary concern as a novelist is the exploration of the inner lives of his characters. Diverse as these are, they may be divided into those with spiritual insight and those who are earth–bound. For the latter White frequently shows great contempt, an attitude he also held towards the place–seekers and money–grubbers in Australian society. Increasingly he sought to explore the multiple personality layers that can be found in anyone, and to show that only awareness of these hidden depths can bring wholeness. Often his most admired characters have to come through turbulent moments to achieve personal calm. Examples are Elizabeth Hunter in *The Eye of the Storm* and Ellen Roxburgh in *A Fringe of Leaves.* Perhaps the most well–known is the explorer Voss, in the novel of the same name, who achieves peace only in death, becoming part of the land. The element of mysticism so prominent in the novels of his middle period reflects his own view that life has great depths and great possibilities that are too often denied, to the impoverishment of the spirit.

Toward the end of his writing career he found more and more need to explore the dual sexual capabilities of the human personality. This is prefigured by the experiences of the women referred to earlier, who emerge from harrowing experiences strengthened but also with a strong sense of the ambiguities inherent in living. *The Twyborne Affair* expands this sense of ambiguity by offering a triple view of one person, as Eudoxia, Eddie, and Eadith. Throughout certitude about sexual identity remains elusive, though the homosexual rape of Eddie (a jackeroo like White himself) suggests a sexual ambivalence on the part of Australians toward homosexuals, something akin to the hidden sexual history of the American West. Similarly the novel intertwines White's own experiences in London, the Greek diaspora, and Australia. Even more complex, *Memoirs of Many in One* is an elaborate literary construct. White, in the role of editor of the memoirs of Alex Gray, is able to take elements of his own life and recreate from them an elusive reality, which recalls to some extent White's exotic creations. Between these two novels came *Flaws in the Glass,* intended to suggest the impossibility of ever fully understanding any other person or even one's self, because all is refracted through mirrors, which may distort and conceal as much as they reveal.

White was a private man who poured his life into his writings. He felt no need to explain or to excuse his personality. That was for others to accept. His novels record a long love–hate relationship with Australia, but an even deeper feeling that he gained spiritual strength from the conflict, as he did from trying to reconcile the masculine and feminine sides of his own personality. For him life was fragile and uncertain (he was a life–long asthmatic), but nevertheless to be faced with spirit and courage.

—*Murray S. Martin*

———

WILDE, Oscar (Fingal O'Flahertie Wills). Irish–born British poet, playwright, novelist, and short story writer. Also wrote as C.3.3. and Sebastian Melmoth. Born 16 October (some sources say 15 October) 1854 (some sources say 1856) in Dublin. Educated at Trinity College, Dublin, 1871–73; Magdalen College, Oxford, B.A. (first class honors) 1878. Married Constance Mary Lloyd, 29 May 1884 (died 7 April 1898); one son. Toured United States and Canada as lecturer, 1882; toured the British Isles as lecturer, 1883–84. Journalist and book reviewer in London, 1884–87; member of editorial staff, *Woman's World* (periodical), London, 1887–89. Prisoner at institutions including Old Baily, Wandsworth Prison, Reading Jail, and Pentonville Prison, 1895–97. Traveler in Switzerland, Italy, and France, under pseudonym Sebastian Melmoth, 1897–1900. Author of such lectures as "Art and the Handicraftsman" and "Lecture to Art Students." Contributor of articles, essays, reviews, and criticism such as "Woman's Dress," "More Radical Ideas Upon Dress Reform," "Sermon in Stones at Bloomsbury," "Mrs. Langtry as Hester Grazebrook," "London Models," "Some Cruelties of Prison Life," "Oscar Wilde on Poets and Poetry," "Slaves of Fashion," " Costume," and "The American Invasion" to periodicals, including *Pall Mall Gazette, Dramatic Review, Woman's World, New York World, Court and Society Review, English Illustrated Magazine,* London *Daily Chronicle, Blackwood's Edinburgh Magazine,* and *Chameleon.* Contributor of poems to periodicals, including *Dublin University Magazine, Irish Monthly, Kottabos, Our Continent, In a Good Cause, Court and Society Review, Art and Letters, Centennial Magazine, Lady's Pictorial,* and *Burlington.* Translator into English, sometimes under pseudonym Sebastian Melmoth. **Recipient:** Oxford Univeristy's Newdigate Prize for Poetry, 1878. *Died in Paris, after a short illness, 30 November 1900; buried in Bagneux Cemetery, Paris; reinterred in 1909 in Pere–Lachaise Cemetery (French national cemetery), Paris.*

WRITINGS

Poetry

Newdigate Prize Poem: Ravenna, Recited in the Theatre, Oxford, 26 June 1878. Oxford, T. Shrimpton & Son, 1878.

Poems (includes "Helas," "E Tenebris," "Panthea," "Impressions"). London, David Bogue, and Boston, Roberts Brothers, 1881; with illustrations by Charles Ricketss, London, Elkin Mathews & John Lane, 1892.

The Sphinx, illustrations by Charles Ricketts. London, Elkin Mathews & John Lane, and Boston, Copeland & Day, 1894; with illustrations by Melvin Leipzig, Three Kings Press, 1969.

The Ballad of Reading Gaol (as C.3.3., Wilde's prison number). London, L. Smithers, 1896; with illustrations by Frans Masereel, London, Journeyman Press, 1978.

The Harlot's House (first published in *The Dramatic Review,* 11 April 1885), illustrations by Althea Gyles. London, Mathurin Press/L. Smithers, 1904; with illustrations by Daphne Lord, Surrey, Keepsake Press, 1967.

Poems in Prose (first published in *Fortnightly Review,* July 1894; contains "The Artist," "The Doer of Good," "The Disciple," "The Master," "The House of Judgment," "The Teacher of Wisdom"). London, privately printed, 1905; revised as *Prose Poems* (contains "The Master," "The Disciple," "The House of Judgment," "The Doer of Good," "The Artist"), illustrations by Margaret McCord, Downpatrick, Crannog Press, 1973.

Pan, a Double Villanelle, and Desespoir, a Sonnet. Boston, J. W. Luce, 1909.

Remorse: A Study in Saffron, notes by Majl Ewing. Los Angeles, William Andrews Clark Memorial Library, 1961.

Serenade, illustrations by Rigby Graham. Privately printed, 1962.

Some Early Poems and Fragments. Privately printed, 1974.

Collected Poetry

The Poems of Oscar Wilde. New York, F. M. Buckles, 1906.

The Poems of Oscar Wilde. London, Methuen, 1908.

The Poetical Works of Oscar Wilde, Including Poems in Prose. Portland, Maine, T. B. Mosher, 1908.

The Poetical Works of Oscar Wilde, introduction by Nathan Haskell Dole. New York, Crowell, 1913.

Panthea, and Other Poems, edited by George Sylvester Viereck. Girard, Kansas, Haldeman–Julius, 1925.

The Poems of Oscar Wilde, illustrations by Jean de Bosschere. New York, Boni & Liveright, 1927.

The Harlot's House, and Other Poems, illustrations by John Vasos. New York, Dutton, 1929.

Poems, selected and introduced by Denys Thompson. London, Chatto & Windus, 1972.

Mervyn Peake, Oscar Wilde: Extracts from the Poems of Oscar Wilde, foreword by Maeve Gilmore, illustrations by Mervyn Peake. London, Sidgwick & Jackson, 1980.

Plays

Vera; or, The Nihilists: A Drama in Four Acts (produced New York, 1883). London, privately printed, 1880; as *Vera; or, The Nihilists: A Drama in a Prologue and Four Acts,* privately printed, 1902; London, L. Smithers, 1904.

The Duchess of Padua: A Tragedy of the XVI Century, Written in Paris in the XIX Century (produced as *Guido Ferranti: A Tragedy of the XVI Century* on Broadway, 1891; London, 1907). New York, privately printed, 1883; as *The Duchess of Padua* bound with *Salome,* New York, F. M. Buckles, 1906.

Salomé: Drame en un acte (produced Paris, 1896; London, 1905; New York, 1906). Paris, Librarie de L'Art Independant, and London, Elkin Mathews & John Lane, 1893; with illustrations by Andre Derain, New York, Limited Editions Club, 1938; translated by Alfred Bruce Douglas as *Salomé: A Tragedy in One Act*, illustrations by Aubrey Beardsley, London, Elkin Mathews & John Lane, and Boston, Copeland & Day, 1894; with introduction by Holbrook Jackson, illustrations by Aubrey Beardsley, New York, Limited Editions Club, 1938; with introduction by Holbrook Jackson, illustrations by Valenti Angelo, Baltimore, Heritage Press, 1945; with additions, illustrations by Aubrey Beardsley, New York, Dover, 1967; as *Salome* bound with *The Importance of Being Earnest* and *Lady Windermere's Fan*, introduction by Edgar Saltus, New York, Boni & Liveright, 1919; bound with *The Importance of Being Earnest*, introduction by Louis Kronenberger, New York, Collier, 1962; translated by R. A. Walker as *Salome*, illustrations by Aubrey Beardsley, London, Heinemann, 1957; translated by Vyvyan Holland as *Salome*, illustrations by Frank Martin, London, Folio Society, 1957.

Lady Windermere's Fan (produced London, 1892; New York, 1893). London, Elkin Mathews & John Lane, 1893; as *Lady Windermere's Fan: A Play about a Good Woman*, London, L. Smithers, 1903; bound with *Salome* and *The Importance of Being Earnest*, introduction by Edgar Saltus, New York, Boni & Liveright, 1919; bound with *The Importance of Being Earnest*, introduction by John Gielgud, illustrations by Tony Walton, New York, Limited Editions Club/J. Roberts Press, 1973; with commentary and notes by Patricia Hern, London, Methuen, 1985.

A Woman of No Importance (produced in West End, 1893). London, John Lane, 1894; bound with *An Ideal Husband*, New York, Boni & Liveright, 1919.

The Importance of Being Earnest: A Trivial Comedy for Serious People (produced London, 1895). London, L. Smithers, 1899; bound with *Salome* and *Lady Windermere's Fan*, introduction by Edgar Saltus, New York, Boni & Liveright, 1919; as *The Importance of Being Earnest: A Trivial Comedy for Serious People, in Four Acts as Originally Written*, New York Public Library, 1956; as *The Original Four-Act Version of The Importance of Being Earnest: A Trivial Comedy for Serious People*, foreword by Vyvyan Holland, London, Methuen, 1957; with illustrations by Cecil Beaton, London, Folio Society, 1960; bound with *Lady Windermere's Fan*, introduction by Louis Kronenberger, New York, Collier, 1962; as *The Importance of Being Earnest: A Trivial Play for Serious People*, introduction by Adeline Hartcup, London, Methuen, 1966; bound with *Lady Windermere's Fan*, introduction by John Gielgud, illustrations by Tony Walton, New York, Limited Editions Club/J. Roberts Press, 1973; New York, Samuel French, 1977.

An Ideal Husband (produced in West End and on Broadway, 1895). London, L. Smithers, 1899; bound with *A Woman of No Importance*. New York, Boni & Liveright, 1919.

A Florentine Tragedy (produced London, 1906), opening scene by Sturge Moore. Boston, J. W. Luce, 1908.

For Love of the King: A Burmese Masque. London, Methuen, 1922.

La Sainte Courtisane: Or, The Woman Covered with Jewels.

Collected Plays

The Plays of Oscar Wilde, Volume 1: *Lady Windermere's Fan; A Woman of No Importance;* Volume 2: *The Importance of Being Earnest; An Ideal Husband;* Volume 3: *The Duchess of Padua; Vera: Or, The Nihilists; Salome;* Volume 4: *A Florentine Tragedy; La Sainte Courtisane: Or, The Woman Covered With Jewels; Salome*. Boston, J. W. Luce, 1905–20.

The Plays of Oscar Wilde (contains *Lady Windermere's Fan; A Woman of No Importance; The Importance of Being Earnest; An Ideal Husband; Vera: or, The Nihilists; The Duchess of Padua;* and *Salome*), illustrations by Frederic W. Goudy. New York, H. S. Nichols, 1914.

Plays (contains *Lady Windermere's Fan; A Woman of No Importance; An Ideal Husband;* and *The Importance of Being Earnest*), illustrations by Donia Nachshen. London, Collins, 1931.

Comedies (contains *The Importance of Being Earnest; Lady Windermere's Fan; An Ideal Husband;* and *A Woman of No Importance*). New York, Grosset & Dunlap, 1931.

Five Famous Plays (contains *Lady Windermere's Fan; A Woman of No Importance; An Ideal Husband; The Importance of Being Earnest;* and *Salome*), introduction by Alan Harris. London, Duckworth, and New York, Scribner, 1952.

Selected Plays (includes *The Importance of Being Earnest; An Ideal Husband; Lady Windermere's Fan; A Woman of No Importance;* and *Salome*). London, Penguin, 1954.

Plays, introduction by Tyrone Guthrie. London, Collins, 1961.

Five Plays (contains *Lady Windermere's Fan; A Woman of No Importance; An Ideal Husband; The Importance of Being Earnest;* and *Salome*), introduction by Hesketh Pearson. New York, Bantam 1964.

Plays. London, Penguin, 1964.

Five Major Plays. New York, Airmont, 1970.

Three Plays (contains *Lady Windermere's Fan; An Ideal Husband;* and *The Importance of Being Earnest*), introduction by H. Montgomery Hyde. London, Methuen, 1981.

Wilde: Comedies: A Casebook (contains *Lady Windermere's Fan; A Woman of No Importance; An Ideal Husband;* and *The Importance of Being Earnest*), edited by William Tydeman. New York, Macmillan, 1982.

Two Society Comedies (contains *A Woman of No Importance*, edited by Ian Small; and *An Ideal Husband*, edited by Russell Jackson). New York, Norton, 1983.

The Importance of Being Earnest, and Other Plays. New York, New American Library, 1985.

Fiction

The Picture of Dorian Gray (novel; originally appeared in *Lippincott's Monthly Magazine*, July 1890). As *The Picture of Dorian Gray: Original Text—1890*, Adler's Foreign Books, 1964; revised and enlarged, London and New York, Ward, Lock, 1891; with introduction by Peter Faulkner, Dutton, 1976.

Lord Arthur Savile's Crime: A Study of Duty. London, privately printed, 1904; as *Lord Arthur Savile's Crime: A Study in Duty*, illustrations by Dorothea Braby, Story Classics, 1954.

The Birthday of the Infanta. Portland, Maine, T. B. Mosher, 1905; with illustrations by Leonard Lubin, Viking, 1979.

The Fisherman and His Soul. Portland, Maine, T. B. Mosher, 1907; with illustrations by Mallette Dean, Grabhorn Press, 1939.

The Young King [and] *The Star-Child*. Portland, Maine, T. B. Mosher, 1909.

The Selfish Giant. Herrin, Illinois, V. and H. W. Trovillion, 1932; with illustrations by Lisbeth Zwerger, Saxonville, Massachusetts, Picture Book Studio, 1984; bound with *The Happy Prince,* foreword by Hal W. Trovillion, Herrin, Illinois, Trovillion Private Press, 1945.

The Happy Prince, foreword by Hal W. Trovillion, illustrations by William J. Goodacre. Herrin, Illinois, Trovillion Private Press, 1940; bound with *The Selfish Giant,* foreword by Hal W. Trovillion, Herrin, Illinois, Trovillion Private Press, 1945.

(Presumed author) *Teleny: Or, The Reverse of the Medal* (novel). Olympia Press, 1958; as *Teleny: A Novel Attributed to Oscar Wilde,* edited by Winston Leyland, Gay Sunshine Press, 1984.

The Canterville Ghost, illustrations by Wallace Goldsmith. Boston, International Pocket Library, 1965.

Little Hans, the Devoted Friend, illustrations by Robert Quackenbush. New York, Bobbs–Merrill, 1969.

The Remarkable Rocket, illustrations by Henry E. Coleman. Graham–Johnston, 1974.

The Star Child, abridged by Jennifer Westwood, illustrations by Fiona French. Bristol, Florida, Four Winds Press, 1979.

The Nightingale and the Rose, illustrations by Freire Wright and Michael Foreman. Oxford, Oxford University Press, 1981.

Collected Fiction

The Happy Prince, and Other Tales (contains "The Happy Prince," "The Nightingale and the Rose," "The Selfish Giant," "The Devoted Friend," and "The Remarkable Rocket"), illustrations by Walter Crane and Jacomb Hood. London, D. Nutt, and Boston, Roberts Brothers, 1888; with illustrations by Rudolph Ruzicks, Stanford, Connecticut, Overbrook Press, 1936; bound with *A House of Pomegranates,* preface by John Espey, London, Garland, 1977.

Lord Arthur Savile's Crime, and Other Stories (contains "Lord Arthur Savile's Crime," "The Sphinx Without a Secret," "The Canterville Ghost," and "The Model Millionaire"). London, Osgood, McIlvaine, and New York, Dodd, Mead, 1891.

A House of Pomegranates (contains "The Young King," "The Birthday of the Infanta," "The Fisherman and His Soul," and "The Star–Child"), illustrations by C. H. Shannon. London, Osgood, McIlvaine, 1891; New York, Dodd, Mead, 1892; with illustrations by Jessie M. King, London, Methuen, 1915; bound with *The Happy Prince, and Other Tales,* preface by John Espey, London, Garland, 1977.

The Happy Prince, and Other Fairy Tales (contains "The Happy Prince," "The Nightingale and the Rose," "The Selfish Giant," "The Young King," "The Star–Child," "The Fisherman and His Soul," and "The Birthday of the Infanta"). New York, Brentano's, 1909; bound with *A House of Pomegranates,* preface by John Espey, London, Garland, 1977.

Fairy Tales (contains "The Happy Price," "The Young King," "The Star–Child," "The Selfish Giant," "The Nightingale and the Rose," "The Devoted Friend," "The Remarkable Rocket," "The Birthday of the Infanta," and "The Fisherman and His Soul"). New York, Putnam, 1913.

The Happy Prince, and Other Stories (contains "The Happy Prince," "The Nightingale and the Rose," "The Selfish Giant," "The Young King," "The Star–Child," "The Fisherman and His Soul," and "The Birthday of the Infanta"), illustrations by Spencer Baird Nichols. New York, Frederick A. Stokes Co., 1931.

Ben Kutcher's Illustrated Edition of A House of Pomegranates, and the Story of the Nightingale and the Rose (contains "The Happy Prince," "The Nightingale and the Rose," "The Selfish Giant," "The Young King," "The Star–Child," "The Fisherman and His Soul," and "The Birthday of the Infanta"), introduction by H. L. Mencken, illustrations by Ben Kutcher. New York, Moffat, Yard, 1918.

The Fisherman and His Soul, and Other Fairy Tales, illustrations by Theodore Nadejen. New York, Farrar & Rinehart, 1929.

Stories (contains *The Picture of Dorian Gray; Lord Arthur Savile's Crime, and Other Stories; A House of Pomegranates;* and *The Happy Prince, and Other Tales*), illustrations by Donia Nachshen. London, Collins, 1931; with introduction by John Guest, 1952.

The Happy Prince, and Other Tales (contains "The Happy Prince," "The Fisherman and His Soul," "The Birthday of the Infanta," "The Young King," "The Star–Child," "The Nightingale and the Rose," and "The Selfish Giant"), illustrations by Everett Shinn. Philadelphia, Chicago, John C. Winston, 1940.

The Happy Prince: The Complete Fairy Stories of Oscar Wilde (contains *The Happy Prince, and Other Tales* and *A House of Pomegranates*), illustrations by Philippe Jullian. London, Duckworth, 1952; New York, Macmillan, 1953; with critical notes by Vyvyan Holland, 1965; as *The Complete Fairy Stories of Oscar Wilde,* 1970; as *The Fairy Stories of Oscar Wilde,* illustrations by Harold Jones, introduction by Naomi Lewis, London, Gollancz, 1976.

Fairy Tales, illustrations by Charles Mozley. London, Bodley Head, 1960; as *Complete Fairy Tales,* New York, F. Watts, 1961.

The Happy Prince, and Other Stories, introduction by Micheal Mac Liammoir, illustrations by Lars Bo. London, Penguin, 1962.

The Picture of Dorian Gray and Selected Stories, foreword by Gerald Weales. New York, New American Library, 1962.

The Young King, and Other Fairy Tales, introduction by John Updike, illustrations by Sandro Nardini and Enrico Bagnoli. New York, Macmillan, 1962.

The Happy Prince, and Other Stories, illustrations by Peggy Fortnum. New York, Dutton, 1968.

The Short Stories of Oscar Wilde (contains "The Portrait of Mr. W. H."; *Lord Arthur Savile's Crime, and Other Stories; A House of Pomegranates;* and *The Happy Prince, and Other Tales*), introduction by Robert Gorham Davis, illustrations by James Hill. New York, Limited Editions Club, 1968.

Lord Arthur Savile's Crime, and Other Stories (contains "Lord Arthur Savile's Crime," "The Canterville Ghost," "The Model Millionaire," "The Young King," "The Fisherman and His Soul," "The Happy Prince," "The Devoted Friend," and "The Portrait of Mr. W. H."). London and New York, Penguin, 1973.

Complete Shorter Fiction, edited and introduced by Isobel Murray. Oxford, Oxford University Press, 1980.

The Birthday of the Infanta, and Other Tales (contains "The Birthday of the Infanta," "The Selfish Giant," "The Nightingale and the Rose," "The Young King," and "The Happy Prince"), illustrations by Beni Montresor. New York, Atheneum, 1982.

Oscar Wilde Stories and Fairy Tales, illustrations by Zevi Blum. Franklin Center, Pennsylvania, Franklin Library, 1983.

Nonfiction

The Soul of Man Under Socialism (originally appeared in *Fortnightly Review,* February 1891). Published in *The Soul of Man Under Socialism* [by Wilde, and] *The Socialist Ideal—Art* [and] *The Coming Solidarity* [by William Morris and W. C. Owen]),

New York, Humboldt, 1892; as *The Soul of Man*, London, privately printed, 1895; with preface by Robert Ross, London, Arthur L. Humphreys, 1912.

The Portrait of Mr. W. H. (essay; originally appeared in *Blackwood's Edinburgh Magazine*, July 1889). Portland, Maine, T. B. Mosher, 1901, revised as *The Portrait of Mr. W. H. as Written by Oscar Wilde Sometime after the Publication of His Essay, of the Same Title, and Now First Printed from the Original Enlarged Manuscript Which for Twenty–six Years Has Been Lost to the World*, New York, M. Kennerley, 1921; revised again as *The Portrait of Mr. W. H.: The Greatly Enlarged Version Prepared by the Author after the Appearance of the Story in 1889 but Not Published*, edited and introduced by Vyvyan Holland, London, Methuen, 1958.

Phrases and Philosophies for the Use of the Young (originally appeared in Chameleon, December 1894). Privately printed, 1902.

The Rise of Historical Criticism. Privately printed, Sherwood Press, 1905; reprinted, Philadelphia, Pennsylvania, R. West, 1978.

De Profundis (originally appeared in full in *Letters*, edited by Rupert Hart–Davis, New York, Harcourt, 1962; published in England as *The Letters of Oscar Wilde*, R. Hart–Davis, 1962). Published with preface by Robert Ross, New York, Putnam, 1905; enlarged, 1909; with introduction by Frank Harris, New York, Modern Library, 1926; revised as *De Profundis: Being the First Complete and Accurate Version of "Epistola: In Carcere et Vinculis," the Last Prose Work in English of Oscar Wilde*, introduction by Vyvyan Holland. New York, Philosophical Library, 1950; London, Methuen, 1950; unexpurgated edition published as *De Profundis: Unexpurgated*, introduction by Jacques Barzun, Vintage Books, 1964.

Impressions of America (includes lecture text), edited and introduced by Stuart Mason. Sunderland, Keystone Press, 1906.

Decorative Art in America (includes "House Decoration," lecture text, letters, reviews, and interviews), edited and introduced by Richard Butler Glaenzer. New York, Brentano's, 1906.

The Suppressed Portion of "De Profundis," by Oscar Wilde, Now for the First Time Published by His Literary Executor. New York, Robert Ross, P. R. Reynolds, 1913.

A Critic in Pall Mall: Being Extracts from Reviews and Miscellanies. London, Methuen, 1919.

The Critic as Artist: A Dialogue. De Roos, 1957.

Collected Nonfiction

Intentions (essays; contains "The Decay of Lying," "Pen, Pencil, and Poison," "The Critic as Artist," and "The Truth of Masks"). London, Osgood, McIlvaine, and New York, Dodd, Mead, 1891.

Oscariana: Epigrams (excerpts), compiled by Constance Mary Lloyd Wilde. Privately printed, 1895; revised and enlarged, London, Arthur L. Humphreys, 1912.

Essays, Criticisms, and Reviews (collection of editorials first published in *Woman's World*, November 1887 to June 1889; contains "A Fascinating Book," "A Note on Some Modern Poets," "Some Literary Notes," and "Literary and Other Notes"). Privately printed, 1901.

Sebastian Melmoth (excerpts; includes epigrams and aphorisms, and *The Soul of Man Under Socialism*). London, Arthur L. Humphreys, 1904.

Epigrams and Aphorisms (excerpts), introduction by George Henry Sargent. Boston, J. W. Luce, 1905.

The Wisdom of Oscar Wilde, selected and introduced by Temple Scott. New York, Brentano's, 1906.

Great Thoughts from Oscar Wilde, selected by Stuart Mason. New York, Dodge Publishing, 1912.

Aphorisms of Oscar Wilde (contains "On Men and Women," "On Civilisation," "On Art," "On Vices, Virtues, and Emotions," and "On Everything"), selected and arranged by G. N. Sutton. London, Methuen, c. 1914.

The Essays of Oscar Wilde. New York, A. & C. Boni, 1935.

Essays, edited and introduced by Hesketh Pearson. London, Methuen, 1950; as *The Soul of Man Under Socialism, and Other Essays*, introduction by Philip Rieff. New York, Harper, 1970.

Epigrams: An Anthology, compiled by Alvin Redman, introduction by Vyvyan Hollad. A. Redman, 1952; New York, Day, 1954; as *The Wit and Humor of Oscar Wilde*, New York, Dover, 1959.

Wit and Wisdom, compiled by Cecil Hewetson. London, Duckworth, 1960; as *Wit and Wisdom of Oscar Wilde*, New York, Philosophical Library, 1967.

Literary Criticism of Oscar Wilde, edited by Stanley Weintraub. Lincoln, University of Nebraska Press, 1968.

The Artist as Critic: Critical Writings of Oscar Wilde, edited by Richard Ellmann. New York, Random House, 1969.

The Wit of Oscar Wilde, compiled by Sean McCann. Frewin, 1969.

Witticisms of Oscar Wilde, compiled by Derek Stanford. London, John Baker, 1971.

Wilde Things: The Delicious and Malicious Epigrams of Oscar Wilde, illustrations by Aubrey Beardsley. Sussex, Attic Press, 1972.

Letters

With James Abbott McNeill Whistler, *Wilde v. Whistler: Being an Acrimonious Correspondence on Art between Oscar Wilde and James A. McNeill Whistler* (first published in *The Gentle Art of Making Enemies* by Whistler, Heinemann, 1890). Privately printed, 1906.

Letters After Reading. New York, P. R. Reynolds, 1921; as *After Reading: Letters of Oscar Wilde to Robert Ross*, Beaumont, 1921.

After Berneval: Letters of Oscar Wilde to Robert Ross, illustrations by Randolph Schwabe. Beaumont, 1922.

Oscar Wilde's Letters to Sarah Bernhardt, edited by Sylvestre Dorian. Girard, Kansas, Haldeman–Julius, 1924.

Some Letters from Oscar Wilde to Alfred Douglas, 1892–1897, preface by William Andrews Clark, Jr., notes by Arthur C. Dennison, Jr., and Harrison Post, additional material by A. S. W. Rosenbach. London, W. A. Clark/J. H. Nash, 1924.

Sixteen Letters from Oscar Wilde, edited and notes by John Rothenstein. London, Faber & Faber, and New York, Coward–McCann, 1930.

Letters (includes first publication of full text of *De Profundis*), edited by Rupert Hart–Davis. New York, Harcourt, 1962; as *The Letters of Oscar Wilde*, London, Rupert Hart–Davis Ltd., 1962.

Selected Letters of Oscar Wilde, edited by Rupert Hart–Davis. Oxford, Oxford University Press, 1979.

Berneval: An Unpublished Letter, notes and introduction by Jeremy Mason. Tragara Press, 1981.

Oscar Wilde—Graham Hill: A Brief Friendship (letters), notes and introduction by Jeremy Mason. Tragara Press, 1982.

More Letters of Oscar Wilde, edited by Rupert Hart–Davis. London, J. Murray, and New York, Vanguard Press, 1985.

General Omnibus Volumes

Poems by Oscar Wilde, Together with His Lecture on the English Renaissance (includes lecture first published in *New York Tribune*, 10 January 1882). Privately printed, 1903.

The Best of Oscar Wilde: Being a Collection of the Best Poems and Prose Extracts of the Writer, collected by Oscar Herrmann, edited by W. W. Massee, illustrations by Frederick Ehrlich. Avon Press, 1905.

Fairy Tales and Poems in Prose. New York, Boni & Liveright, 1918.

Art and Decoration: Being Extracts from Reviews and Miscellanies by Oscar Wilde (includes *Phrases; Philosophies for the Use of the Young; La Sainte Courtisane: or, The Woman Covered With Jewels;* and *The Rise of Historical Criticism;* "House Decoration," "Art and the Handicraftsman," "Lecture to Art Students," "Mrs. Langtry as Hester Grazebrook," "Slaves of Fashion," "Woman's Dress," "More Radical Ideas Upon Dress Reform," "Costume," "The American Invasion," "Sermons in Stones at Bloomsbury," "London Models," and "L'Envoi"). London, Methuen, 1920.

The Picture of Dorian Gray, The Importance of Being Earnest, The Ballad of Reading Gaol, and Other Works of Oscar Wilde (includes *The Critic as Artist; The Soul of Man Under Socialism; Lady Windermere's Fan;* and "Letter to Robert Ross, 31 May 1897"), introduction by Hesketh Pearson. New York, Dutton, 1930; as *Plays, Prose Writings, and Poems*, 1955; revised, introduction by Isobel Murray, 1975.

The Writings of Oscar Wilde: Poems, Short Stories, Plays, Novels, Fairy Tales, Letters, Dialogues, and Philosophy. Union City, New Jersey, William Wise, 1931.

Poems and Essays, illustrations by Donia Nachshen. London, Collins, 1931.

The Best Known Works of Oscar Wilde, Including the Poems, Novels, Plays, Essays, Fairy Tales and Dialogues (includes *Poems; The Picture of Dorian Gray; Lady Windermere's Fan; Salome; A Woman of No Importance; An Ideal Husband; The Importance of Being Earnest; The Critic as Artist;* and *The Decay of Lying;* essays and fairy tales). New York, Blue Ribbon Books, 1931.

The Works of Oscar Wilde, illustrations by Donia Nachshen, London, Collins, 1932.

The Poems and Fairy Tales of Oscar Wilde. New York, B. A. Cerf/ D. S. Klopfer, 1932.

The Poems of Oscar Wilde (includes essay "Oscar Wilde on Poets and Poetry"). New York, A. & C. Boni, 1935.

The Best Known Works of Oscar Wilde, Including the Poems, Novels, Plays, Essays and Fairy Tales. Kansas City, Missouri, Halcyon House, 1940.

The Portable Oscar Wilde, selected and edited by Richard Aldington. New York, Viking, 1946; revised edition selected and edited by Richard Aldington and Stanley Weintraub, 1981.

Selected Works, with Twelve Unpublished Letters (includes *The Decay of Lying; The Critic as Artist; The Picture of Dorian Gray; Salome; The Importance of Being Earnest; De Profundis; Poems; Poems in Prose;* and reviews, anecdotes, and letters). London, Heinemann, 1946.

Works, edited and introduced by G. F. Maine. London, Collins, 1948; New York, Dutton, 1954; new edition, London, Collins, 1963.

Selected Essays and Poems (includes *The Soul of Man Under Socialism; The Decay of Lying; De Profundis; Poems;* and *The Ballad of Reading Gaol*), introduction by Hesketh Pearson. London and New York, Penguin, 1954; as *De Profundis, and Other Writings*, 1973.

Poems and Essays, introduction by Kingsley Amis. London, Collins, 1956.

Oscar Wilde: Selections From the Works of Oscar Wilde, edited and introduced by Graham Hough. New York, Dell, 1960.

Selected Writings, introduction by Richard Ellmann. Oxford, Oxford University Press, 1961.

Intentions, and Other Writings. Garden City, New York, Doubleday, 1961.

Works, introduction by John Gilhert. London, Spring Books, 1963; as *The Works of Oscar Wilde*, 1977.

De Profundis (includes *The Ballad of Reading Gaol*), notes by Rupert Hart–Davis, additional material by W. H. Auden. Avon Books, 1964.

Selected Writings of Oscar Wilde, edited and introduced by Russell Fraser. New York, Houghton, 1969.

Poems in Prose and the Preface to The Picture of Dorian Gray. Mason Hill Press, 1974.

The Illustrated Oscar Wilde (includes "Preface" to *The Picture of Dorian Gray;* "The Uses of Criticism" from *The Critic as Artist;* "On Christ" from *De Profundis; The Soul of Man Under Socialism; The Ballad of Reading Gaol; The Importance of Being Earnest; The Portrait of Mr. W. H.; Phrases and Philosophies for the Use of the Young;* and "The Happy Prince," "The Young King," "The Devoted Friend," "The Selfish Giant," "Lord Arthur Savile's Crime," and "The Canterville Ghost"), edited and introduced by Roy Gasson. Jupiter, 1977.

The Annotated Oscar Wilde: Poems, Fictions, Plays, Lectures, Essays, and Letters, edited, with introduction and notes, by H. Montgomery Hyde. New York, C. N. Potter, 1982; as *The Annotated Oscar Wilde*, London, Orbis, 1982.

The Picture of Dorian Gray, and Other Writings (includes *Lady Windermere's Fan; Salome; An Ideal Husband; The Importance of Being Earnest;* and *The Ballad of Reading Gaol*), edited and introduced by Richard Ellmann. New York, Bantam, 1982.

Complete Works

The Writings of Oscar Wilde, Volume 1. *A House of Pomegranates, The Happy Prince, and Other Tales;* Volume 2: *Lady Windermere's Fan; The Importance of Being Earnest;* Volume 3: *Lord Arthur Savile's Crime; The Portrait of Mr. W. H., and Other Stories;* Volume 4: *Poems Including Ravenna; The Ballad of Reading Gaol; The Sphinx*, introduction by Richard Le Gallienne; Volume 5: *The Picture of Dorian Gray;* Volume 6: *Intentions;* Volume 7: *A Woman of No Importance; An Ideal Husband;* Volume 8: *Essays, Criticisms, and Reviews;* Volume 9: *What Never Dies, A Romance by Barbey d'Aurevilly, Translated into English by Sebastian Melmoth (Oscar Wilde);* Volume 10: *Epigrams; Phrases and Philosophies for the Use of the Young;* Volume 11: *Salome; The Duchess of Padua; Vera;* Volume 12: *Poems in Prose;* Volume 13: *De Profundis, from the Original, Unexpurgated German Edition translated by Henry Zick;* Volume 14: *Essays and Stories, by Lady Wilde (Speranza);* Volume 15: *His Life, With a Critical Estimate of His Writings.* London, New York, A. R. Keller, 1907.

Works (15 volumes), edited by Robert Ross, Volume 1 (Volume 10 of U.S. edition): *The Duchess of Padua;* Volume 2 (Volume 6 of U.S. edition): *Salome; A Florentine Tragedy; Vera;* Volume 3 (part of Volume 7 of U.S. edition): *Lady Windermere's Fan;* Volume 4 (Volume 8 of U.S. edition): *A Woman of No Importance,* Volume 5 (Volume 9 of U.S. edition): *An Ideal Husband;* Volume 6 (part of Volume 7 of U.S. edition): *The Importance of Being Earnest;* Volume 7 (Volume 5 of U.S. edition): *Lord Arthur Savile's Crime, and Other Prose Pieces* (contains *Lord Arthur Savile's Crime, and Other Stories; The Portrait of Mr. W. H.; Poems in Prose;* and *The Rise of Historical Criticism*); Volume 8 (Volume 3 of U.S. edition): *Intentions and The Soul of Man;* Volume 9 (Volume 1 of U.S. edition, which adds *Pan, a Double Villanelle* and *Desespoir, A Sonnet*): *Poems* (contains *Poems; The Harlot's House; The Sphinx; The Ballad of Reading Gaol;* and uncollected poems, translations); Volume 10 (Volume 2 of U.S. edition): *A House of Pomegranates; The Happy Prince, and Other Tales;* Volume 11 (Volume 11 of U.S. edition): *De Profundis* (includes four letters written from Reading prison); Volume 12 (Volume 4 of U.S. edition): *The Picture of Dorian Gray;* Volume 13 (Volumes 12 and 13 of U.S. edition): *Reviews;* Volume 14 (Volume 15 of U.S. edition): *Miscellanies* (contains *Phrases and Philosophies for the Use of the Young; The Rise of Historical Criticism; La Sainte Courtisane: or, The Woman Covered With Jewels;* essays, criticism, letters, and lectures); Volume 15 (not included in U.S. edition): *For the Love of the King: A Burmese Masque,* 1922. London, Methuen, 1908 (unless otherwise indicated); Boston, J. W. Luce, 1910; U.S. edition published as *The First Collected Edition of the Works of Oscar Wilde, 1908–1922* (15 volumes), New York, Barnes & Noble, 1969.

Second Collected Edition of the Works of Oscar Wilde (14 volumes), edited by Robert Ross, Volume 1: *Lord Arthur Savile's Crime; The Portrait of Mr. W. H., and Other Stories;* Volume 2: *The Duchess of Padua;* Volume 3: *Poems, with The Ballad of Reading Gaol* (includes *The Sphinx; Ravenna; Pan; Desespoir*); Volume 4: *Lady Windermere's Fan;* Volume 5: *A Woman of No Importance;* Volume 6: *An Ideal Husband;* Volume 7: *The Importance of Being Earnest;* Volume 8: *A House of Pomegranates;* Volume 9: *Intentions;* Volume 10: *De Profundis;* Volume 11: *Essays and Lectures;* Volume 12: *Salome; La Sainte Courtisane; A Florentine Tragedy;* Volume 13: *The Picture of Dorian Gray,* Paris, Charles Carrington, 1910; Volume 14: *Salome, A Tragedy in One Act,* illustrations by Aubrey Beardsley, London, John Lane, 1912. London, Methuen, 1909 (except as noted).

The Works of Oscar Wilde, introduction by Richard Le Gallienne, Volume 1: *Poems;* Volume 2: *Dorian Gray;* Volume 3: *A House of Pomegranates; The Happy Prince, and Other Tales;* Volume 4: *Lord Arthur Savile's Crime, and Other Stories; The Portrait of Mr. W. H.; A Florentine Tragedy;* Volume 5: *Lady Windermere's Fan; The Importance of Being Earnest;* Volume 6: *A Woman of No Importance; An Ideal Husband;* Volume 7: *Salome; The Duchess of Padua; Vera; Or, The Nihilists;* Volume 8: *De Profundis* (includes supplementary letters); *The Soul of Man Under Socialism; Of Him Who Died at No. 13. by L. C. van Noppen;* Volume 9: *Poems in Prose; The Priest and the Acolyte; L'Envoi; Some Cruelties of Prison Life; Lecture on the English Renaissance; Wilde v. Whistler; The Rise of Historical Criticism; The Truth of Masks;* Volume 10: *Intentions; The Decay of Lying; Pen, Pencil, and Poison; The Critic as Artist;* Volume 11: *Epigrams; Oscariana; Sebastian Melmoth; Phrases and Philosophies; Oscar Wilde's Literary Art; Correspondence; Impressions of America; Oscar Wilde in America;* Volume 12: *Essays, Criticisms, and Reviews;* Volume 13: *What Never Dies: A Romance by Barbey D'Aurevilly, Translated into English by Sebastian Melmoth*

(Oscar Wilde); Volume 14: *Essays and Stories by Lady Wilde (Speranza);* Volume 15: *His Life, With a Critical Estimate of His Writings*). New York, Lamb, 1909; reprinted in 15 volumes as *The Sunflower Edition of the Works of Oscar Wilde,* New York, AMS Press, 1972; as *The Works of Oscar Wilde,* new introduction by Stanley Weintraub, New York, AMS Press, 1980.

Complete Works of Oscar Wilde, edited by Robert Ross, Volume 1: *Poems;* Volume 2: *The Picture of Dorian Gray; A House of Pomegranates;* Volume 3: *The Happy Prince, and Other Tales; Lord Arthur Savile's Crime, and Other Stories; The Portrait of Mr. W. H.; Poems in Prose; The Rise of Historical Criticism;* Volume 4: *Intentions; The Soul of Man Under Socialism;* Volume 5: *Salome; A Florentine Tragedy; Vera: Or, The Nihilists;* Volume 6: *Lady Windermere's Fan; The Importance of Being Earnest;* Volume 7: *A Woman of No Importance; An Ideal Husband;* Volume 8: *The Duchess of Padua; De Profundis;* Volume 9: *Reviews;* Volume 10: *Miscellanies, Essays and Criticism, Letters, Unpublished Manuscripts, Lectures, Bibliography.* New York, Bigelow, Brown, 1921.

The Complete Works of Oscar Wilde, Volume 1: *Poems,* introduction by Richard Le Gallienne; Volume 2: *Vera, and Other Early Plays* (includes *The Duchess of Padua*), introduction by J. Forbes Robertson; Volume 3: *The Happy Prince, and Other Fairy Tales,* introduction by William Butler Yeats; Volume 4: *The Picture of Dorian Gray,* introduction by C. Kernshan, review by Walter Pater; Volume 5: *Intentions,* introduction by Edgar Saltus; Volume 6: *Lord Arthur Savile's Crime, The Portrait of Mr. W. H., and Other Stories,* introductions by R. B. Glaenzer and C. Smyth; Volume 7: *Lady Windermere's Fan; A Woman of No Importance,* introduction by A. B. Walkley; Volume 8: *The Importance of Being Earnest; An Ideal Husband,* introduction by J. Drinkwater; Volume 9: *Salome, and Other Plays,* introduction by Arthur Symons; Volume 10: *The Soul of Man Under Socialism, and Other Essays,* introduction by John Comer Powys; Volume 11: *De Profundis, Lectures and Essays,* introductions by M. Monahan and W. F. Morse; Volume 12: *Criticisms and Reviews,* introduction by P. Colum. Garden City, New York, Doubleday, 1923.

Complete Works of Oscar Wilde, introduction by Vyvyan Holland. London, Collins, 1948; new edition, 1966.

Other

Author of introduction (later collected separately as "L'envoi"), *Rose Leaf and Apple Leaf,* by Rennell Rodd. J. M. Stoddard, 1882.

Author of scenario, *Mr. and Mrs. Daventry: A Play in Four Acts* by Frank Harris (produced, 1900), introduction by H. Montgomery Hyde. Richards Press, 1956.

Defendant, *The Trial of Oscar Wilde From the Shorthand Reports* (court transcripts), preface by Charles Grolleau. Paris, Charles Carrington, 1906.

Defendant, *Oscar Wilde: Three Times Tried* (court transcripts). London, Ferrestone Press, 1912.

Defendant, *The Trials of Oscar Wilde: Regina (Wilde) v. Queensberry* [and] *Regina v. Wilde and Taylor* (court transcripts), edited and introduced by H. Montgomery Hyde, foreword by Travers Humphreys. W. Hodge, 1948; as *The Three Trials of Oscar Wilde,* University Books, 1956, enlarged as *Famous Trials, Seventh Series: Oscar Wilde,* Penguin, 1963; augmented edition as *The Trials of Oscar Wilde,* New York, Dover, 1973.

Adaptations: *Lady Windermere's Fan* was adapted for motion pictures, including *Lady Windermere's Fan,* Ideal Film, 1917, Warner Brothers, 1925, and *The Fan,* Twentieth–Century Fox, 1949; *Salome* was adapted for motion pictures, including *A Modern Salome,* Hope Hampton Productions, 1920, and *Salome,* Nazimova Productions, 1922, Raymond Rohauer, 1951, rereleased, 1967, Columbia Pictures, 1953; *A Woman of No Importance* was adapted as a film released by Select Pictures, 1922; *Lord Arthur Savile's Crime, and Other Stories* was adapted as *Flesh and Fantasy,* Universal Pictures, 1943; "The Canterville Ghost" was adapted as a film released by Loew's, 1944; *The Picture of Dorian Gray* was adapted as a film released by Loew's, 1945; *An Ideal Husband* was adapted as a film released by British Lion Film Corp., 1948; "The Birthday of the Infanta" was adapted as a film released by Realm Television Productions, 1949; *The Importance of Being Earnest* was adapted as a film released by Universal International Films, 1953; *The Ballad of Reading Gaol* was adapted as *Man of Rope,* British Film Institute, 1961, Films Incorporated, 1971; "The Selfish Giant" was adapted as a film released by Weston Woods Studios, 1971, Pyramid Films, 1972; "The Happy Prince" was adapted as a film released by Potterton Productions, 1973; "The Remarkable Rocket" was adapted as a film released by Pyramid Films, 1975.

Picture of Dorian Gray was adapted for the stage by Grace Constant Lounsbery as a three–act play, published by Simpkin, Marshall, 1913, by Constance Cox as a two–act play published by Fortune Press, 1948, and by John Osborne as *The Picture of Dorian Gray: A Moral Entertainment,* Faber, 1973; "The Canterville Ghost" was adapted for the stage as *The Saturday Evening Ghost,* Samuel French, 1936, by Darwin R. Payne as *The Canterville Ghost,* Coach House Press, 1963, and for television by Bell System Family Theatre, broadcast by NBC–TV, 1975; Wilde's scenario was developed by Frank Harris into the four–act stage play *Mr. and Mrs. Daventry,* published by Richards Press, 1956; "The Nightingale and the Rose" was adapted for the stage by Ralph Moreno, published by Hartmes Handpress, 1958; "Lord Arthur Savile's Crime" was adapted by Constance Cox as a three–act play published by Samuel French, 1963.

Salome was adapted for an opera by Richard Strauss, produced in Dresden, Germany, 1905; "The Nightingale and the Rose" was adapted for a symphonic poem for large orchestra by Alexander Stinert, 1950; *Lady Windermere's Fan* was adapted by librettist Don Allan Clayton for the Off–Broadway musical comedy *A Delightful Season,* 1960.

Manuscript Collections: William Andrews Clark Memorial Library, University of California, Los Angeles; New York Public Library; Beinecke Library, Yale University; University of Edinburgh Library; and Magdalen College, Oxford Univerty.

Biography: *The Unrecorded Life of Oscar Wilde* by Rupert Croft–Cooke, New York, McKay, 1972; *Oscar Wilde* by Sheridan Morley, New York, Holt, Rinehart & Winston, 1976; *Oscar Wilde* by Richard Ellmann, London, Hamish Hamilton, 1987, New York, Knopf, 1988.

Bibliography: *Bibliography of Oscar Wilde* by Stuart Mason, London, Laurie, 1914; *Oscar Wilde: An Annotated Bibliography of Criticism* by E. H. Hickhail, London, Macmillan, 1978.

Critical Sources: *Oscar Wilde Discovers America* by Lloyd Lewis and Henry Justin Smith, 1882, New York, Harcourt, 1936; *The Letters of Oscar Wilde,* edited by Rupert Hart–Davis, New York, Harcourt, 1962; *Complete Works of Oscar Wilde,* edited by J. B. Foreman, with introduction by Vyvyan Holland, New York, Harper, 1966; *Oscar Wilde: The Critical Heritage,* edited by Karl Beckson, London, Routledge and Kegan Paul, 1970; *Oscar Wilde* by Richard Ellmann, New York, Knopf, 1988; *Gay Fictions, Wilde to Stonewall: Studies in a Male Homosexual Literary Tradition* by Claude J. Summers, New York, Continuum, 1990.

*   *   *

Universally acknowledged as the wittiest poet, literary critic, novelist, short story writer, and playwright of the late nineteenth century, Oscar Wilde achieved fame early in life—chiefly the result of his American lecture tour in 1882—but later, at the height of his powers, he suffered subsequent disgrace when he was convicted and imprisoned for homosexual offenses in the most sensational trials of the century. The tragic conclusion of his career was foreshadowed, however, in such a work as *The Picture of Dorian Gray,* which, Wilde said in a letter to Lord Alfred Douglas, secretly contained "the note of Doom that like a purple thread runs through the gold cloth" of his homoerotic novel. In a letter to another friend, Wilde willingly accepted his symbolic "martyrdom," which he believed essential if homosexuals were ever to be accepted by society.

Oscar Fingall O'Flahertie Wills Wilde was born in Dublin on 16 October 1854, the second son of parents prominent in Ireland's cultural and professional life. His father, Dr. William Ralph Wills Wilde, was an internationally well–known ear and eye surgeon, the founder of a hospital in 1853, and the author of some 20 books on such subjects as Irish archaeology and antiquarian subjects as well as the 1853 *Aural Surgery,* the standard textbook on the subject. In 1864, Queen Victoria knighted him for his work in directing the medical census in Ireland. Wilde's mother, Lady Wilde (born Jane Francesca Elgee), was prominent in political and literary circles as "Speranza," a pseudonym meaning "hope," designed to inspire Irish nationalists as well as feminists. During her long life, she published many volumes of poems, essays, stories, and collections of folklore.

Wilde received his primary school education at the Portora Royal School in Enniskillen, Ulster, and in October of 1871, he entered Trinity College, Dublin, where he won awards in classical studies. While at Trinity, Wilde was absorbed by Hellenism, which he interpreted as the union of body and soul, as opposed to Christianity, which traditionally denigrated the body in favor of the soul. Hellenism appealed to his homoerotic interests, reenforced by his study of Plato's dialogues, such as the *Symposium,* which discusses homosexual love between men and between men and boys. In June of 1874, after completing three years at Trinity College, he was awarded a scholarship to attend Magdalen College, Oxford University.

During his years at Oxford, he not only distinguished himself by his extensive learning but also achieved renown for his brilliant talk. In his fourth year, he won the Newdigate Prize for his 1878 poem *Ravenna,* which was published and recited publicly at the Sheldonian Theatre. While at Oxford, he attended the lectures of Walter Pater and John Ruskin, both of whom stressed the experience of art as the key to a full life: Pater urging immersion in intense aesthetic sensations; Ruskin urging the study of great art, which could reveal a world divinely ordered. By surrounding himself with artistic objects, such as blue china and peacock feathers, Wilde assumed the role of an Aesthete. In 1881, he published *Poems,* which revealed his devotion to such poets as Keats, Swinburne, and Rossetti (a devotion, some critics contended, bordering on plagiarism).

By 1881, Punch's cartoons contained a figure resembling Wilde as the arch–Aesthete; as a result, Gilbert and Sullivan's operetta, *Patience,* implied that Wilde was the principal object of this satire of Aestheticism, though Swinburne and Rossetti were also suspected as models for the "fleshly" and "idyllic" poets. The producer of *Patience,* Richard D'Oyly Carte, engaged Wilde to give a series of lectures in America to publicize the production there. For most of 1882, Wilde lectured in the United States and Canada on such topics as the aesthetic movement, house decoration, and nineteenth–century Irish poets. In the early weeks, he appeared on stage in aesthetic costume in imitation of the characters in *Patience:* in knee breeches, velvet jacket, and a sunflower or lily in his buttonhole—dress that provoked charges of "unmanliness." On his return to London, he began reviewing of books in various periodicals and newspapers; arranging for the production of his Romantic tragedy *Vera; or the Nihilists* in 1883, which failed in New York; and editing *Woman's World* between 1887 and 1889. In 1884, he married Constance Lloyd, later an author. Two children were born: Cyril in 1885, killed in action in 1915; and Vyvyan in 1886.

In 1888, Wilde published his first volume of fairy tales, *The Happy Prince, and Other Tales,* which reveals prominent homoerotic themes and fantasies of martyrdom. In "The Happy Prince," a male Swallow fulfills various requests from the statue of the Happy Prince, such as helping the poor by stripping the gold leaf and precious gems from the statue, but when winter comes, the bird refuses to leave the Prince for Egypt. When the Prince kisses the Swallow on the lips, the bird falls dead at his feet. But the power of love—here clearly homoerotic—results in God's elevation of the dead bird and the self–mutilated statue into Paradise.

In the July 1889 issue of *Blackwood's Edinburgh Magazine,* Wilde expressed the theme of homosexual martyrdom in more obvious form in his story "The Portrait of Mr. W. H." Here the quest for the identity of Mr. W. H. (called, in the dedication of Shakespeare's sonnets, as the work's "onlie begetter") involves the effeminate Cyril Graham, who, in school, had always performed female leads in Shakespeare's plays. In order to affirm the truth that the object of Shakespeare's love was Mr. W. H.—Willie Hughes, "some wonderful boy–actor of great beauty"—Cyril kills himself, "the youngest and the most splendid of all the martyrs of literature," as a "sacrifice to the secret of the Sonnets." Such a martyr's death eventually appeals to Cyril's friend, who, when he accepts the theory concerning W. H., threatens suicide but ironically dies not as a martyr but a victim of tuberculosis—a chararacteristic compromise by Wilde on the implicit homoeroticism of the story to avoid critical attacks. In his *Oscar Wilde,* Richard Ellmann remarks that Wilde told the story of Willie Hughes to the statesmen Arthur Balfour and Herbert Asquith, both of whom "advised him not to print it, lest it corrupt English homes."

A portrait—like that in "The Portrait of Mr. W. H."—is also the central symbol of Wilde's most daring work, *The Picture of Dorian Gray,* which appeared in one issue of *Lippincott's Monthly Magazine* in July of 1890. When it appeared in book form in 1891, it contained six additional chapters and a preface delineating the idea of "art for art's sake," the idea that art should be concerned with its own perfection rather than with moral, political, or religious issues.

The homoerotic myth of Narcissus (a small bronze statuette of whom Wilde had on his mantelpiece in his Tite Street home) pervades both character and plot in the novel, which depicts Dorian's narcissistic adoration of his own image in his portrait. Lord Henry Wotton, his mentor, has collected some 17 photographs of the beautiful Dorian, whom he refers to as "a Narcissus," and later, after rejecting the actress Sibyl Vane, who subsequently kills herself, Dorian, "in boyish mockery of Narcissus," kisses or pretends to kiss "those painted lips [of his portrait] that now smiled so cruelly at him."

The painter of the portrait, Basil Hallward, refuses to exhibit it because, as he says, he has put too much of himself into it. Hallward's erotic attraction to Dorian is further dramatized by his own account of their first meeting at a party: "When our eyes met, I felt that I was growing pale. A curious sensation of terror came over me. I knew that I had come face to face with some one whose mere personality was so fascinating that, if I allowed it to do so, it would absorb my whole nature, my whole soul, my very art itself." Later, Hallward confesses to his homoeroticism by remarking that he had never cared for women (a remark that Wilde removed in the second version in an attempt to pacify his critics). Late in the novel, Hallward asks Dorian, who has acquired an unsavory reputation: "Why is your friendship so fatal to young men?" Dorian eventually plunges a knife into the disfigured painting in order to kill this embodiment of conscience, an act that ironically restores it to its original beauty, whereas Dorian is found dead, his hideous body symbolizing his moral decline.

The critical reactions to Wilde's novel, particularly the first version, indicated that many reviewers had grasped its homosexual subtext. The *Daily Chronicle* of 30 June 1890, for example, called it "a tale spawned from the leprous literature of the French *De'cadents—a* poisonous book ... [of] effeminate frivolity ... [and] unbridled indulgence in every form of secret and unspeakable vice." In the *Athenaeum* of 27 June 1891, the reviewer of the second version charged that the novel was "unmanly, sickening, vicious" (such terms as "unspeakable vice" and "unmanly" were usually Victorian code words for homosexuality).

In his second volume of tales, the 1891 *A House of Pomegranates,* Wilde later regarded one of the stories, "The Young King," as another foreshadowing of his own tragic destiny. The 16–year–old lad shows "signs of that strange passion for beauty that was destined to have so great an influence over his life." Indeed, the tapestries in his palace depict the "Triumph of Beauty" (for Wilde, beauty—whether in art or in young men and boys—is frequently associated with homoerotic impulses). When the Young King's dreams reveal the suffering of his people who prepare for his coronation, he rejects luxurious raiment, dons peasant clothes, and wears a crown of thorns, associated with Christ's crucifixion, accompanied by transformation and elevation. At the end of the story, no one dares look upon the Young King's face, "for it was like the face of an angel."

Wilde's most notable literary successes occurred in the theater with his four society comedies, beginning with *Lady Windermere's Fan* in 1892. His witty dandies reveal Wilde's own narcissistic impulses, as in *An Ideal Husband* in 1895, in which Lord Goring remarks: "To love oneself is the beginning of a lifelong romance." In his greatest play, *The Importance of Being Earnest* in 1895, Wilde focuses on the comic implications of the double life, as in Jack Worthing's adoption of the name "Ernest" when in town to indulge in pleasure, and in Algernon Moncrieff 's invention of a sick friend named "Bunbury," who provides Algernon with an excuse to avoid social obligations. Indeed, Wilde was leading a more daring double life in his homosexual affairs with "renters" (male prostitutes), casual pick–ups, and his own circle of friends, including the young Lord Alfred Douglas, whose father, the Marquess of Queensberry, provoked Wilde into charging him with libel for accusing him of "posing as somdomite" (misspelling the offensive word).

The evidence at the Queensberry trial turned against Wilde, who was himself arrested and convicted in criminal trials held in April and May of 1895 under the notorious Criminal Law Amendment Act of 1885, which stipulated that any homosexual acts committed either in private or in public were punishable by two years at hard labor. Wilde served the specified term principally at Reading Prison, the setting of his most famous poem *The Ballad of Readinq Gaol* in 1898, which expresses the mystery of his own self–destructiveness in the famous refrain that "all men kill the thing they love." While in prison, Wilde had written a long autobiographical letter to Douglas (later published as *De Profundis*), which explores his pain and suffering provoked by his relationship with Douglas and with homophobic society at large. Ironically, while defending his own homosexuality, Wilde regards Queensberry as a degenerate Philistine and rejects the view of the Italian criminologist Cesare Lombroso, who regarded homosexuality as a congenital pathology. In the process, as Claude J. Summers writes in *Gay Fictions*, Wilde emerges as "Saint Oscar, a kind of Harlequin Christ–figure who transforms his victimization into a martyrdom."

When released in May of 1897, he immediately left England for France, assuming the name of "Sebastian Melmoth," derived from the Christian martyr St. Sebastian and the title of the Gothic 1820 novel *Melmoth the Wanderer* by Wilde's great–uncle, Charles Maturin. Shortly before his death on 30 November 1900, Wilde wrote to his friend George Ives, a poet and criminologist who had organized a secret order of homosexuals to advance the "Cause": "Yes: I have no doubt we shall win, but the road is long, and red with monstrous martyrdoms. Nothing but the repeal of the Criminal Law Amendment Act would do any good." A step in that direction occurred on the 100th anniversary of Wilde's birth when the London County Council authorized a commemorative blue plaque to be placed on his former home on Tite Street. Three years later, the Criminal Law Amendment Act was repealed.

—Karl Beckson

WILLIAMS, Tennessee. American playwright, poet, novelist, and short fiction writer. Also wrote under original name, Thomas Lanier Williams. Born in Columbus, Mississippi, 26 March 1911. Educated at University of Missouri, 1931–33; Washington University, St. Louis, Missouri, 1936–37; University of Iowa, A.B. 1938. Contributor of stories to *Esquire*. **Recipient:** Group Theatre Award for *American Blues*, 1939; Rockefeller Foundation Grant, 1940; American Academy of Arts and Letters Award, 1944; New York Drama Critics Circle Award, Sidney Howard Memorial Award, Donaldson Award, and *Sign* Annual Award, all for *The Glass Menagerie*, 1945; New York Drama Critics Circle Award, Donaldson Award, and Pulitzer Prize, all for *A Streetcar Named Desire*, 1948;

elected to National Institute of Arts and Letters, 1952; New York Drama Critics Circle Award and Pulitzer Prize for *Cat on a Hot Tin Roof*, 1955; *London Evening Standard* Drama Award for *Cat on a Hot Tin Roof*, 1958; New York Drama Critics Circle Award for *The Night of the Iguana*, 1962; first place in London Critics' Poll for Best New Foreign Play for *The Night of the Iguana*, 1964–65; Brandeis University Creative Arts Medal, 1964–65; National Institute of Arts and Letters Gold Medal, 1969; first centennial medal of the Cathedral of St. John the Divine, 1973; elected to Theatre Hall of Fame, 1979; Kennedy Center Honors award, 1979; Medal of Freedom, 1980. L.H.D. and H.L.D. *Died in New York City, 25 February 1983.*

WRITINGS

Plays

Cairo! Shanghai! Bombay! (as Thomas Lanier Williams; prologue and epilogue by Bernice Dorothy Shapiro; produced Memphis, 1935).

The Magic Tower (as Thomas Lanier Williams; produced Webster Groves, Missouri, 1936).

Headlines (as Thomas Lanier Williams; produced St. Louis, 1936).

Candles to the Sun (as Thomas Lanier Williams; produced St. Louis, 1937).

Fugitive Kind (as Thomas Lanier Williams; produced St. Louis, 1937.)

Spring Song (as Thomas Lanier Williams; produced Iowa City, Iowa, 1938).

Not about Nightingales (as Thomas Lanier Williams), 1939.

American Blues (as Thomas Lanier Williams; includes *Candles to the Sun, Fugitive Kind, Spring Storm, Not about Nightingales;* produced, 1939).

The Long Goodbye (produced New York, 1940). Published in *27 Wagons Full of Cotton, and Other One–Act Plays*, 1946.

Battle of Angels (produced Boston, 1940; revised as *Orpheus Descending,* produced on Broadway, 1957; London, 1959). Revision originally published in *Pharos* (Murray, Utah), with a note by Margaret Webster and an account of the first production in Boston by Williams, spring 1945; as *Battle of Angels,* New York, New Directions, 1945; as *Orpheus Descending, with Battle of Angels: Two Plays,* New York, New Directions, 1958; as *Orpheus Descending,* London, Secker & Warburg, 1958; as *The Fugitive Kind, with Battle of Angels: Two Plays,* preface by Williams, New York, New Directions, 1959; as *The Fugitive Kind,* New York, New American Library, 1960; bound with *Something Unspoken* and *Suddenly Last Summer,* Harmondsworth, Penguin in association with Secker & Warburg, 1961; revised, New York, Dramatists Play Service, 1975; bound with *The Night of the Iguana,* Harmondsworth, Penguin, 1968; bound with *The Glass Menagerie* and *A Streetcar Named Desire,* New York, New Directions, 1971; bound with *Cat on a Hot Tin Roof* and *Suddenly Last Summer,* New York, New Directions, 1971; bound with *The Rose Tattoo* and *Camino Real,* Harmondsworth, Penguin, 1976.

This Property Is Condemned (produced New York, 1942; London, 1953; included in *Three Short Plays,* produced Dallas, 1948; included in *Three Premieres,* produced Off–Broadway, 1956). Published in *27 Wagons Full of Cotton, and Other One–Act Plays*, 1946.

With Donald Windham, *You Touched Me!* (suggested by the short story of the same title by D. H. Lawrence; produced Cleveland, 1943; on Broadway, 1945). New York, French, 1947.

The Purification (produced Pasadena, 1944; Cambridge, England, 1955; Off–Broadway, 1959). Published in *27 Wagons Full of Cotton, and Other One–Act Plays,* 1946.

The Glass Menagerie (based on story "Portrait of a Girl in Glass" by Williams; produced Chicago, 1944; on Broadway, 1945; London, 1958). New York, Random House, 1945; London, Lehmann, 1948; bound with *A Streetcar Named Desire,* edited by E. Martin Browne, Harmondsworth, Penguin in association with Secker & Warburg, 1959; bound with *Sweet Bird of Youth* and *A Streetcar Named Desire,* Harmondsworth, Penguin in association with Secker & Warburg, 1962; revised, with introduction by E. R. Wood, London, Heinemann Educational, 1968; bound with *Battle of Angels* and *A Streetcar Named Desire.* New York, New Directions, 1971.

Stairs to the Roof (produced Pasadena, 1945).

Moony's Kid Don't Cry (included in *Two One–Act Plays,* produced Nantucket, 1946; New York, 1947; London, 1971). Published in *The Best One–Act Plays of 1940,* edited by Margaret Mayorga, Dodd, 1940; included in *American Blues: Five Short Plays,* 1948.

The Last of My Solid Gold Watches (produced Los Angeles, 1947). Published in *27 Wagons Full of Cotton, and Other One–Act Plays,* 1946.

Portrait of a Madonna (produced Los Angeles, 1947; New York, 1959). Published in *27 Wagons Full of Cotton, and Other One–Act Plays,* 1946.

Lord Byron's Love Letter (produced, New York, 1947). Published in *27 Wagons Full of Cotton, and Other One–Act Plays,* 1946.

Auto–da–Fe (produced New York, 1947; Bromley, Kent, 1961). Published in *27 Wagons Full of Cotton, and Other One–Act Plays,* 1946.

The Lady of Larkspur Lotion (produced New York, 1947; London, 1968). Published in *27 Wagons Full of Cotton, and Other One–Act Plays,* 1946.

Summer and Smoke (based on story "The Yellow Bird" by Williams; produced Dallas, 1947; on Broadway, 1948; revised as *Eccentricities of a Nightingale* and produced Nyack, New York, 1964; Guildford, Surrey, 1967; on Broadway, 1976). Published as *Summer and Smoke,* New York, New Directions, 1948; London, Lehmann, 1952; as *The Eccentricities of a Nightingale* [and] *Summer and Smoke,* New York, New Directions, 1964; bound with *The Rose Tattoo,* and *Camino Real,* New York, New Directions, 1971.

A Streetcar Named Desire (produced on Broadway, 1947; London, 1949). New York, New Directions, 1947; London, Lehmann, 1949; revised acting edition, New York, Dramatists Play Service, 1953; bound with *The Glass Menagerie,* edited by E. Martin Browne, Harmondsworth, Penguin in association with Secker & Warburg, 1959; bound with *Sweet Bird of Youth* and *The Glass Menagerie,* Harmondsworth, Penguin in association with Secker & Warburg, 1962; with introduction by Williams, New York, New American Library, 1963; bound with *Battle of Angels* and *The Glass Menagerie,* New York, New Directions, 1971.

Ten Blocks on the Camino Real (revised as *Camino Real,* produced on Broadway, 1953; London, 1957). Originally published in *American Blues: Five Short Plays,* 1948; as *Camino Real,* Norfolk, Connecticut, New Directions, 1953; London, Secker & Warburg, 1958; bound with *The Rose Tattoo,* edited and introduced by E. Martin Browne, Harmondsworth, Middlesex, Penguin in association with Secker & Warburg, 1958; bound with *The Eccentricities of a Nightingale, Summer and Smoke,* and *The Rose Tattoo,* New York, New Directions, 1971; bound with *The Rose Tattoo* and *Orpheus Descending,* Harmondsworth, Penguin, 1976.

The Rose Tattoo (produced Chicago, 1950; on Broadway, 1951; London, 1959). New York, New Directions, 1951; London, Secker & Warburg, 1954; bound with *Camino Real,* edited and introduced by E. Martin Browne, Harmondsworth, Middlesex, Penguin in association with Secker & Warburg, 1958; bound with *The Eccentricities of a Nightingale, Summer and Smoke,* and *Camino Real,* New York, New Directions, 1971; bound with *Camino Real* and *Orpheus Descending,* Harmondsworth, Penguin, 1976.

I Rise in Flame, Cried the Phoenix: A Play about D. H. Lawrence (produced Off–Broadway, 1953; London, 1971), with a note by Frieda Lawrence. Norfolk, Connecticut, New Directions, 1951.

27 Wagons Full of Cotton (produced New Orleans, and as part of a triple bill entitled *All in One* on Broadway, 1955). Published in *27 Wagons Full of Cotton, and Other One–Act Plays,* 1946.

Cat on a Hot Tin Roof (produced on Broadway, 1955; London, 1958). New York, New Directions, 1955; London, Secker & Warburg, 1956; bound with *The Milk Train Doesn't Stop Here Anymore,* Harmondsworth, Penguin, 1969; bound with *Orpheus Descending* and *Suddenly Last Summer,* New York, New Directions, 1971; revised, New York, New Directions, 1975; bound with *The Milk Train Doesn't Stop Here Anymore,* and *The Night of the Iguana,* Harmondsworth, Penguin in association with Secker & Warburg, 1976.

Something Unspoken (produced Lake Hopatcong, New Jersey, 1955; with *Suddenly Last Summer* as *Garden District,* Off–Broadway and London, 1958). Published in *27 Wagons Full of Cotton, and Other One–Act Plays,* 1948; as *Garden District; Two Plays: Something Unspoken* [and] *Suddenly Last Summer,* London, Secker & Warburg, 1959; bound with *Orpheus Descending* and *Suddenly Last Summer,* Harmondsworth, Penguin in association with Secker & Warburg, 1961; bound with *Baby Doll: The Script for the Film* and *Suddenly Last Summer,* Harmondsworth, Penguin, 1968.

Three Players of a Summer Game (produced Westport, Connecticut, 1955). London, Secker & Warburg, 1960.

Sweet Bird of Youth (produced Coral Gables, Florida, 1956; on Broadway, 1959; Watford, Hertfordshire, 1968), with foreword by Williams. New York, New Directions, 1959; London, Secker & Warburg, 1961; revised, New York, Dramatists Play Service, 1962; bound with *A Streetcar Named Desire* and *The Glass Menagerie,* Harmondsworth, Penguin in association with Secker & Warburg, 1962.

The Case of the Crushed Petunias (produced Cleveland, 1957; New York, 1958; Glasgow, 1968). Published in *American Blues: Five Short Plays,* 1948.

Suddenly Last Summer (with *Something Unspoken* as *Garden District,* produced Off–Broadway and London, 1958). New York, New Directions, 1958; published as *Garden District; Two Plays: Something Unspoken* [and] *Suddenly Last Summer,* London, Secker & Warburg, 1959; bound with *Orpheus Descending* and *Something Unspoken,* Harmondsworth, Penguin, 1961; bound with *Baby Doll: The Script for the Film* and *Something Unspoken,* Harmondsworth, Penguin in association with Secker & Warburg, 1968; bound with *Cat on a Hot Tin Roof* and *Orpheus Descending,* New York, New Directions, 1971.

Talk to Me Like the Rain and Let Me Listen (produced Westport, Connecticut, 1958; New York, 1962). Published in *27 Wagons Full of Cotton, and Other One–Act Plays,* 1946.

Period of Adjustment (produced Miami, 1958, codirected by Williams; on Broadway, 1960; Bristol, 1961; London, 1962; simultaneously published in *Esquire*). Published as *Period of Adjustment: High Point Over a Cavern; a Serious Comedy,* New York, New Directions, 1960; London, Secker & Warburg, 1961; revised as *Period of Adjustment; or, High Point is Built on a Cavern: A Serious Comedy,* New York, Dramatists Play Service, 1961.

I Rise in Flame, Cried the Phoenix (included in *Two Short Plays,* produced Off–Broadway, 1959).

The Night of the Iguana (based on the short story by Williams; produced Spoleto, Italy, 1959; Miami, 1960; revised version produced on Broadway, 1961; London, 1965). Originally appeared in *Esquire,* February 1962; New York, New Directions, 1962; Harmondsworth, Penguin in association with Secker & Warburg, 1964; revised, New York, Dramatists Play Service, 1963; bound with *Orpheus Descending,* Harmondsworth, Penguin, 1968; bound with *Cat on a Hot Tin Roof,* Harmondsworth, Penguin, 1976; bound with *Cat on a Hot Tin Roof* and *The Milk Train Doesn't Stop Here Anymore,* Harmondsworth, Penguin, 1976.

The Enemy: Time. Published in *Theatre* (New York), March 1959.

Hello from Bertha (produced Bromley, Kent, 1961). Published in *27 Wagons Full of Cotton, and Other One–Act Plays,* 1946.

To Heaven in a Golden Coach (produced Bromley, Kent, 1961).

The Milk Train Doesn't Stop Here Anymore (produced Spoleto, Italy, 1962; revised version produced on Broadway, 1963; London, 1968). Typescript edition, New York, Moon Lake Productions and Two Rivers Enterprises, c. 1962; New York, New Directions, and London, Secker & Warburg, 1964; bound with *Cat on a Hot Tin Roof,* Harmondsworth, Penguin, 1969; bound with *Cat on a Hot Tin Roof* and *The Night of the Iguana,* Harmondsworth and Baltimore, Penguin, 1976.

The Dark Room (produced London, 1966). Published in *American Blues: Five Short Plays,* 1948.

The Mutilated (with *The Gnädiges Fräulein* as *Slapstick Tragedy,* produced on Broadway, 1966). New York, Dramatists Play Service, 1967.

The Gnädiges Fräulein (with *The Mutilated* as *Slapstick Tragedy,* produced on Broadway, 1966; as *The Latter Days of a Celebrated Soubrette,* produced New York, 1974). Originally appeared in *Esquire,* August 1965; typescript edition as *Two Slapstick Tragedies: The Mutilated* [and] *The Gnädiges Fräulein,* New York, Studio Duplicating Services, c. 1966; New York, Dramatists Play Service, 1967.

The Seven Descents of Myrtle (produced on Broadway, 1968; revised as *Kingdom of Earth,* produced Princeton, New Jersey, 1975). Originally appeared as "Kingdom of Earth," in *Esquire,* February 1967; typescript edition as *Kingdom of Earth: A Play in Seven Scenes,* New York, Studio Duplicating Service, 1967; as *The Kingdom of Earth; The Seven Descents of Myrtle,* New York, New Directions, 1968; revised, New York, Dramatists Play Service, 1969.

The Two–Character Play (produced London, 1967; revised as *Out Cry* and produced Chicago, 1971; on Broadway, 1975). New York, New Directions, 1969; as *Out Cry,* New York, New Directions, 1973.

At Liberty (produced New York, 1968). Published in *American Scenes,* edited by William Kozlenko, New York, Day, 1941.

In the Bar of a Tokyo Hotel (produced Off–Broadway, 1969; London, 1971). New York, Dramatists Play Service, 1969.

The Strangest Kind of Romance (a dramatization of short story "The Malediction" by Williams; produced London, 1969). Published in *27 Wagons Full of Cotton, and Other One–Act Plays,* 1946.

I Can't Imagine Tomorrow (produced PBS–TV, 1970). Originally published in *Esquire,* March 1966; included in *Dragon Country: A Book of Plays,* 1970.

A Perfect Analysis Given by a Parrot (with *The Frosted Glass Coffin,* produced Key West, Florida, 1970). New York, Dramatists Play Service, 1958; both plays published in *Dragon Country: A Book of Plays,* 1969.

The Parade. New York, A. Meyerson, c. 1970.

The Long Stay Cut Short; or, The Unsatisfactory Supper (produced London, 1971). Published in *American Blues: Five Short Plays,* 1948.

Confessional (produced Bar Harbor, Maine, 1970; revised as *Small Craft Warnings,* produced Off–Broadway, 1972; London, 1973). Typescript edition as *Confessional: A Play in Two Scenes,* New York, Studio Duplicating Service, c. 1970; published as *Small Craft Warnings,* New York, New Directions, 1972; London, Secker & Warburg, 1973.

Old Folks Not at Home; or, The Frosted Glass Coffin (produced Key West, Florida, 1970 as *The Frosted Glass Coffin*). Typescript edition, New York, A. Wood, MCA Artists, 1970.

The Red Devil Battery Sign (produced Boston, 1975; revised and produced Vienna, 1976). New York, New Directions, 1988.

Demolition Downtown: Count Ten in Arabic (produced London, 1976).

This Is (An Entertainment) (produced San Francisco, 1976).

Vieux Carré (produced on Broadway, 1977). New York, New Directions, 1979.

Tiger Tail (produced Atlanta, 1978).

Creve Coeur (produced Charleston, South Carolina, 1978; as *A Lovely Sunday for Creve Coeur,* produced Off–Broadway, 1979). Published as *A Lovely Sunday for Creve Coeur,* New York, New Directions, 1980.

Kirche, Kutchen und Kinder (produced Off–Off Broadway, 1979).

Clothes for a Summer Hotel: A Ghost Play (produced on Broadway, 1980). New York, New Directions, 1983.

Some Problems for the Moose Lodge (included in *Tennessee Laughs,* produced Chicago, 1980; expanded as *A House Not Meant to Stand,* produced Chicago, 1981; revised version produced Chicago, 1982).

Steps Must Be Gentle: A Dramatic Reading for Two Performers. New York, Targ Editions, 1980.

The Travelling Companion, in *Christopher Street,* November 1981.

Something Cloudy, Something Clear (produced Off–Off–Broadway, 1982). New York, Dramatists Play Service, 1981.

Will Mr. Merriwether Return from Memphis? (produced Key West, Florida, 1980).

The Remarkable Rooming–house of Mme. Le Monde. New York, Albondocani Press, 1984.

Beauty Is the Word; Hot Milk at Three in the Morning, in *Missouri Review,* Volume 7, Number 3, 1984.

Ten by Tennessee (one–act plays; produced New York, 1986).

Me, Vashya.

Life Boat Drill.

Of Masks Outrageous and Austere.

Collected Plays

27 Wagons Full of Cotton, and Other One–Act Plays (contains *27 Wagons Full of Cotton: A Mississippi Delta Comedy; The Purification; The Lady of Larkspur Lotion; The Last of My Solid Gold Watches; Portrait of a Madonna; Auto–Da–Fee: A Tragedy in One–Act; Lord Byron's Last Love Letter; The Strangest Kind of Romance: A Lyric Play in Four Scenes; The Long Goodbye; Hello from Bertha;* and *This Property Is Condemned*). Norfolk, Connecticut, New Directions, 1945; London, Grey Walls Press, 1947; enlarged (adding *Something Wild; Talk to Me Like the Rain and Let Me Listen;* and *Something Unspoken*), New York, New Directions, 1953.

American Blues: Five Short Plays (contains *Moony's Kid Don't Cry; The Dark Room; The Case of the Crushed Petunias; The Long Stay Cut Short, or The Unsatisfactory Supper;* and *Ten Blocks on the Camino Real*). New York, Dramatists Play Service, 1948.

Four Plays (contains *The Glass Menagerie; A Streetcar Named Desire; Summer and Smoke;* and *Camino Real*). London, Secker & Warburg, 1956.

Five Plays (contains *Cat on a Hot Tin Roof; The Rose Tattoo; Something Unspoken; Suddenly Last Summer;* and *Orpheus Descending*). London, Secker & Warburg, 1962.

Three Plays (contains *The Rose Tattoo; Camino Real;* and *Sweet Bird of Youth*). New York, New Directions, 1964.

Dragon Country: A Book of Plays (contains *In the Bar of a Tokyo Hotel; I Rise in Flame, Cried the Phoenix; The Mutilated; I Can't Imagine Tomorrow; Confessional; The Frosted Glass Coffin; The Gnädiges Fräulein;* and *A Perfect Analysis Given by a Parrot*). New York, New Directions, 1969.

Three by Tennessee Williams (contains *Sweet Bird of Youth; The Rose Tattoo;* and *Night of the Iguana*). New York, New American Library/Dutton, 1976.

Tennessee Williams: Four Plays (contains *Summer and Smoke; Orpheus Descending; Suddenly Last Summer;* and *Period of Adjustment*). New York, New American Library/Dutton, 1976.

Selected Plays (limited edition), illustrations by Herbert Tauss. Franklin Center, Pennsylvania, Franklin Library, 1977.

Tennessee Williams: Eight Plays, introduction by Harold Clurman. Garden City, New York, Doubleday, 1979.

Selected Plays, illustrations by Jerry Pinkney. Franklin Center, Pennsylvania, Franklin Library, 1980.

The Theatre of Tennessee Williams Series

Volume 1: *Battle of Angels; The Glass Menagerie;* [and] *A Streetcar Named Desire.* New York, New Directions, 1972.

Volume 2: *The Eccentricities of a Nightingale; Summer and Smoke; The Rose Tattoo;* [and] *Camino Real.* New York, New Directions, 1972.

Volume 3: *Cat on a Hot Tin Roof; Orpheus Descending;* [and] *Suddenly Last Summer.* New York, New Directions, 1972.

Volume 4: *Sweet Bird of Youth; Period of Adjustment;* [and] *The Night of the Iguana.* New York, New Directions, 1972.

Volume 5: *The Milk Train Doesn't Stop Here Anymore; Kingdom of Earth (The Seven Descents of Myrtle); Small Craft Warnings;* [and] *The Two–Character Play.* New York, New Directions, 1976.

Volume 6: *27 Wagons Full of Cotton, and Other Short Plays.* New York, New Directions, 1981.

Volume 7: *In the Bar of a Tokyo Hotel, and Other Plays.* New York, New Directions, 1981.

Screenplays

With Gore Vidal and Luchino Visconti, *Senso,* c. 1949; with Paul Bowles, as *The Wanton Countess,* Domenico Forges Davanzati, 1954.

The Glass Menagerie, with Peter Berneise, Warner Brothers, 1950.

A Streetcar Named Desire, with Oscar Saul, Warner Brothers, 1951. Published as *A Streetcar Named Desire: A Screen Adaptation Directed by Elia Kazan,* Irvington, 1989.

With Hal Kanter, *The Rose Tattoo,* Paramount, 1955.

Baby Doll, Warner Brothers, 1956. Published as *Baby Doll: The Script for the Film, Incorporating the Two One–Act Plays Which Suggested It: 27 Wagons Full of Cotton* [and] *The Long Stay Cut Short, or The Unsatisfactory Supper,* New York, New Directions, 1956; as *Baby Doll: The Script for the Film,* New York, London, Secker & Warburg, 1957; bound with *Something Unspoken* and *Suddenly Last Summer,* Harmondsworth, Penguin, 1968.

With Gore Vidal, *Suddenly Last Summer,* Columbia, 1959.

With Meade Roberts, *The Fugitive Kind* (based on *Orpheus Descending* by Williams), United Artists, 1959. Published as *The Fugitive Kind,* New York, New Directions, 1958; London, Secker & Warburg, 1959.

Boom (based on *The Milkman Doesn't Stop Here Anymore*), Universal, 1968.

With Lanford Wilson, *The Migrants* (teleplay), "Playhouse 90," CBS–TV, 1974.

Stopped Rocking, and Other Screenplays (includes *Stopped Rocking; All Gaul Is Divided; The Loss of a Teardrop Diamond;* and *One Arm*), introduction by Richard Gilman. New York, New Directions, 1984.

Novels

The Roman Spring of Mrs. Stone. New York New Directions, and London, Lehmann, 1950.

Moise and the World of Reason. New York, Simon and Schuster, 1975; London, W. H. Allen, 1976.

Short Stories

One Arm, and Other Stories (contains "One Arm," "The Malediction," "The Poet," "Chronicle of a Demise," "Desire and the Black Masseur," "Portrait of a Girl in Glass," "The Field of Blue Children" [first published in *Story,* summer 1939], "The Important Thing," "The Angel in the Alcove," "The Night of the Iguana," and "The Yellow Bird"). New York, New Directions, 1948.

Hard Candy: A Book of Stories (contains "Three Players of a Summer Game," "Two on a Party," "The Resemblance between a Violin Case and a Coffin," "Hard Candy," "Rubio y Morena," "The Mattress by the Tomato Patch," "The Coming of Something to the Widow Holly," "The Vine," and "The Mysteries of the Joy Rio"). New York, New Directions, 1954.

Three Players of a Summer Game, and Other Stories (contains "Three Players of a Summer Game," "The Important Thing," "One Arm," "Portrait of a Girl in Glass," "The Coming of Something to the Widow Holly," "Two on a Part," "The Yellow Bird,"

"The Field of Blue Children," The Resemblance between a Violin Case and a Coffin," and "The Night of the Iguana"). London, Secker & Warburg, 1960.

The Knightly Quest: A Novella and Four Short Stories (contains "The Knightly Quest," "Mama's Old Stucco House" [originally appeared in *Esquire,* January 1965], "Man Bring This Up Road" [originally appeared in *Mademoiselle* (New York), July 1959, and as "Man Brings This Up Road" in *International* (London), spring 1965], "The Kingdom of Earth," and *Grand*). New York, New Directions, 1967; revised and enlarged as *The Knightly Quest: A Novella and Twelve Short Stories,* London, Secker & Warburg, 1968.

Eight Mortal Ladies Possessed: A Book of Stories (contains "Happy August the Tenth," "The Inventory at Fontana Bella," "Miss Coynte of Greene," "Sabbaths and Solitude," "Completed," and "Oriflamme"). New York, New Directions, 1974; London, Secker & Warburg, 1975.

It Happened the Day the Sun Rose. Los Angeles, Sylvester and Orphanos, 1981.

Collected Stories (contains "The Vengeance of Nitocris" [originally appeared in *Weird Tales,* June 1928], "A Lady's Beaded Bag," "Something by Tolstoi," "Big Black: A Mississippi Idyll," "The Accent of a Coming Foot," "27 Wagons Full of Cotton," "Sand," "Ten Minute Stop," "Gift of an Apple," "The Field of Blue Children," "In Memory of an Aristocrat," "The Dark Room," "The Mysteries of the Joy Rio," "Portrait of a Girl in Glass," "The Angel in the Alcove," "Oriflamme," "The Vine," "The Malediction," "The Important Thing," "One Arm," "The Interval," "Tent Worms," "Desire and the Black Masseur," "Something about Him," "The Yellow Bird," "The Night of the Iguana," "The Poet," "Chronicle of a Demise," "Rubio y Morena," "The Resemblance between a Violin Case and a Coffin," "Two on a Party," "Three Players of a Summer Game," "The Coming of Something to the Widow Holly," "Hard Candy," "Man Bring This Up Road," "The Mattress by the Tomato Patch," "The Kingdom of Earth," "Grand," "Mama's Old Stucco House," "The Knightly Quest," "A Recluse and His Guest," "Happy August the Tenth," "The Inventory at Fontana Bella," "Miss Coynte of Greene," "Sabbatha and Solitude," "Completed," "Das Wasser Ist Kalt," "Mother Yaws," and "The Killer Chicken and the Closet Queen'), introduction by Gore Vidal. New York, New Directions, 1985.

"Two on a Party," in *The Faber Book of Gay Short Fiction,* edited by Edmund White. London and New York, Faber & Faber, 1991.

Poetry

"The Summer Belvedere," in *Five Young American Poets,* edited by James Laughlin. New York, New Directions, 1944.

In the Winter of Cities: Poems. Norfolk, Connecticut, New Directions, 1956; enlarged, Norfolk, Connecticut, New Directions, 1964.

Androgyne, Mon Amour: Poems. New York, New Directions, 1977.

Memoirs

Grand (limited edition). New York, House of Books, 1964; originally appeared in *Esquire,* November 1966; published in *The Knightly Quest: A Novella and Four Short Stories,* New York, New Directions, 1967.

Memoirs. Garden City, New York, Doubleday, 1975; London, W. H. Allen, 1976.

Letters

Tennessee Williams' Letters to Donald Windham, 1940–65, edited with commentary by Donald Windham. New York, Sandy Campbell, 1976.

Five O'Clock Angel: Letters of Tennessee Williams to Maria St. Just, 1948–1982. New York, Knopf, 1990.

Other

"Questions without Answers," in *New York Times,* 3 October 1948.

Lord Byron's Love Letter: Opera in One Act (libretto by Williams based on his play; music by Raffaello de Banfield; produced London, 1964). New York, G. Ricordi, 1955.

"Tennessee Williams Presents His POV," in *New York Times Magazine,* 12 June 1960.

Author of introduction, *Reflections in a Golden Eye* by Carson McCullers. Bantam, 1961.

With David Newman, "The Agent as Catalyst," in *Esquire,* December 1962.

Contributor, *Oh! Calcutta!* (produced Off–Broadway, 1969).

"Survival Notes: A Journal," in *Esquire,* September 1972.

"Let Me Hang It All Out," in *New York Times,* 4 March 1973.

Focus on Tennessee Williams: A Giant of Stage Realism Discusses His Foremost Plays (sound recording), Center for Cassette Studies, 1975.

"The Blessings and Mixed Blessings of Workshop Productions," in *Dramatists Guild Quarterly,* autumn 1976.

"I Have Written a Play for Artistic Purity," in *New York Times,* 21 November 1976.

Author of introduction, *Feminine Wiles* by Jane Bowles. Santa Barbara, California, Black Sparrow Press, 1976.

Where I Live: Selected Essays, edited by Christine R. Day and Bob Woods. New York, New Directions, 1978.

*

Adaptations: *The Roman Spring of Mrs. Stone* was filmed by Warner Brothers in 1961; *Sweet Bird of Youth* was filmed in 1962; *Period of Adjustment* was filmed in 1962; *The Night of the Iguana* was filmed by Metro–Goldwyn–Mayer in 1964; *This Property Is Condemned* was filmed by Paramount in 1966; *I Can't Imagine Tomorrow* and *Talk to Me Like the Rain and Let Me Listen* were televised together under the title *Dragon Country,* 3 December 1970, by New York Television Theatre; an adaptation of *The Seven Descents of Myrtle* was filmed by Warner Brothers in 1970 under the title *The Last of the Mobile Hot–Shots; Summer and Smoke: Opera in Two Acts,* New York, Belwin–Mills, 1972, was adapted from play by Williams with music by Lee Holby and libretto by Lanford Wilson; an audio recording of Rosemary Harris and James Farentino in the Lincoln Center Repertory Theater production of *A Streetcar Named Desire* was produced by Caedmon in 1973; *The Glass Menagerie* was filmed by Burt Harris for Cineplex Odeon in 1987; *A Streetcar Named Desire* was filmed for television in 1984 and broadcast on

ABC–TV; *Cat on a Hot Tin Roof* was filmed for television in 1984 by International TV Group; *Summer and Smoke* was filmed for television in 1989 and broadcast on NBC–TV; *Confessions of a Nightingale* (a one–man–show impersonation of Williams) by Charlotte Chandler and Ray Strickland was performed by Strickland.

Manuscript Collections: Humanities Research Center, University of Texas at Austin.

Biography: *Tennessee Williams: Rebellious Puritan* by Nancy M. Tischler, New York, Citadel Press, 1961; *Remember Me to Tom* by Edwina Dakin Williams (as told to Lucy Freeman), New York, Putnam, 1963; *Tennessee Williams and Friends* by Gilbert Maxwell, 1965; *Tennessee Williams: A Biography* by Catharine R. Hughes, Englewood Cliffs, New Jersey, Prentice–Hall, 1978; *Tennessee Williams: An Intimate Biography* by Dakin Williams and Shepherd Mead, New York, Arbor House, 1983; *As If: A Personal View of Tennessee Williams,* New York, Sandy Campbell, 1985; *The Kindness of Strangers, the Life of Tennessee Williams* by Donald Spoto, Ballantine, 1986; *Lost Friendships: A Memoir of Truman Capote, Tennessee Williams, and Others,* New York, Paragon House, 1989; *Costly Performances, Tennessee Williams: The Last Stage, a Personal Memoir* by Bruce Smith, Paragon House, 1990.

Interviews: "A Man Named Tennessee" by Robert Rice, in *New York Post,* 21 April–4 May 1958; "Williams and Kazan and the Big Walkout" by Arthur Gelb, in *New York Times,* 1 May 1960, 1; "Williams on Williams" by Lewis Funke and John E. Booth, in *Theatre Arts,* January 1962, 16–19, 72–73; *A Look at Tennessee Williams,* 1969; "Tennessee Williams Survives" by Tom Buckley, in *Atlantic Monthly,* November 1970, 98; "Tennessee Williams—A Candid Conversation," in *Playboy,* April 1973, 69–84; "Tennessee Williams on Art and Sex" by Mel Gussow, in *New York Times,* 3 November 1975, 49; *Conversations with Tennessee Williams,* edited by Albert J. Devlin, University Press of Mississippi, 1986.

Bibliography: "Tennessee Williams: Twenty–five Years of Criticism" by Delma E. Presley, in *Bulletin of Bibliography,* March 1973, 21–29; "*A Streetcar Named Desire:* Twenty–five Years of Criticism" by S. Alan Chesler, in *Notes on Mississippi Writers,* fall 1974, 44–53; *Tennessee Williams: A Bibliography* by Drewey Wayne Gunn, Metuchen, New Jersey, Scarecrow Press, 1980.

Critical Sources: *New York Times,* 3 October 1948; "The Plays of Tennessee Williams" by Henry Popkin, in *Tulane Drama Review,* March 1960, 45–67; *The Dramatic World of Tennessee Williams* by Francis Donahue, New York, Ungar, 1964; *Village Voice,* 24 February 1972; *Tennessee Williams' Letters to Donald Windham, 1940–1965,* edited by Donald Windham, New York, Sandy Campbell, 1976; *Tennessee Williams, a Tribute,* edited by Jac Thorpe, 1977; *The World of Tennessee Williams* by Richard F. Leavitt, London, W. H. Allen, 1978; *Los Angeles Times,* 28 February 1983; *Los Angeles Times,* 6 March 1983; "Tennessee Williams' Legacy" by Andrea Dworkin, in *Ms.,* June 1983, 106; *Dictionary of Literary Biography Documentary Series,* Detroit, Gale, Volume 4: *Tennessee Williams,* edited by Margaret A. Van Antwerp and Sally Johns, 1984; "Intro-

duction" by Gore Vidal to *Collected Stories* by Tennessee Williams, New York, New Directions, 1985; *Tennessee Williams,* New York, St. Martin's Press, 1987; "Tennessee Williams: Someone to Laugh at the Squares With" by Gore Vidal, in his *At Home: Essays 1982–1988,* New York, Random House, 1988; *The Gay Novel in America* by James Levin, New York, Garland, 1991; *Communists, Cowboys, and Queers: The Politics of Masculinity in the Work of Arthur Miller and Tennessee Williams* by David Savran, University of Minnesota Press, 1992.

*   *   *

Dubbed "Tennessee" by his University of Iowa fraternity brothers because of his drawl, Thomas Lanier Williams is considered a genius of the American theatre, changing its style and content and becoming its psychological and poetic master for 40 years. During the 1940s, his award–winning *The Glass Menagerie, A Streetcar Named Desire,* and *Summer and Smoke,* which have since become universal classics, earned him critical acclaim as the nation's greatest new playwright. Although Williams is generally considered a major innovator in the theatre, he was faulted by some critics for his oblique, albeit sensitive, treatment of homosexuality. Whereas many gays complained that he touched on gay themes too indirectly, Williams' dramatic treatment of homosexuality was actually bold for the time; and most critics believe that the tension Williams created made for better theatre. Williams, many critics believe, reached his creative peak in the 1940s. Thereafter, critics began to attack Williams for traversing familiar ground in his later plays, which Williams constantly reworked. Gore Vidal, a friend of Williams from the late 1940s to the early 1960s, noted that it was not at all unusual for Williams to frequently revise his own work. "I once found him revising a short story that had just been published. 'Why,' I asked, 'rewrite what's already in print?' He looked at me, vaguely; then he said, 'Well, obviously it's not finished.' And went back to his typing." However, by the late 1970s, this joyously poetic, master psychologist of the American stage had come to seem almost pathetic and sadly dated. "As Tennessee Williams's powers failed (drink/drugs/age), he turned himself into a circus," commented Vidal. "If people would not go to his new plays, he would see to it that they would be able to look at him on television and read about him in the press." But according to Andrea Dworkin in a *Ms.* commentary on Williams' literary legacy, "No great artist, which he was, writes without an almost merciless objectivity. Williams' own romanticism and others' trivializing perceptions of his homosexuality obscure the tremendous objectivity of his work: his insides are there (not in any simple way) and so are our own. He was destroyed mostly by his own lucidity, not the drugs or drink that made that lucidity endurable. He thought of writing as an escape from reality, but in an artist of his magnitude it never is. Writing distills reality, so the burden of it is heavier and on the artist alone. 'Sometimes,' he wrote, still about writing, 'the heart dies deliberately, to avoid further pain.'"

In 1975, he published his *Memoirs,* which detailed the homosexual side of his life (though several friends complained that he had left them out). Some critics suggested that by condensing Williams' manuscript, editors had unduly emphasized his sex life; others found the *Memoirs* a pathetic self–portrait (Williams considered doing another autobiographical work that would include more of his experiences in the theatre). In 1976, partly in response to Williams having slighted their 25–year relationship in the *Memoirs,* Donald Windham released *Tennessee Williams' Letters to Donald Windham, 1940–1965,* which offered a more upbeat portrayal of the playwright. The frankness of *Memoirs* ended any possible charge of Williams being closeted—though he had accepted his homosexuality early and *Time* magazine had specifically outed him decades before; but he became more political near the end of his life, campaigning for gay rights with a 1982 fund letter for the Human Rights Campaign Fund to help elect congressmen who would oppose what many considered a homophobic Family Protection Act. He died in early 1983 at New York's midtown Hotel Elysee, having choked on a bottle cap; it was later revealed that he had taken barbiturates. In his memory, 30 Broadway theatres dimmed their lights.

Born in Columbus, Mississippi, Williams was raised in St. Louis. His early childhood was filled with pleasant memories centered around his grandparents; his maternal grandmother was especially influential in his life and provided funds for him to attend the University of Missouri in Columbia. However, because he enjoyed reading and writing over more athletic pursuits, Williams elicited the epithet "Miss Nancy" from his father; and when Williams failed R.O.T.C., he was forced to withdraw from the university and enter the tedium of a shoe company. Recalling the celebration of Williams' 37th birthday, Gore Vidal indicates that Williams insisted it was his 34th. When later confronted with the discrepancy in birth dates, Williams told him, "I do not choose to count as part of my life the three years that I spent working for a shoe company." Vidal points out that although Williams had only spent ten months in the position, the reason he had changed his birth date was to enter a play contest open only to those no older than 25.

He was 24 when his first play, *Cairo! Shanghai! Bombay!* about sailors and prostitutes, was produced. Like many artists, Williams was amazed at what "straight" critics and academics made out of his works. Expecting the story of a play to have a beginning, middle, turning point, crisis and end, these critics also expected a theme. In 1948, he wrote in the *New York Times:* "I have never been able to say what was the theme of my play and I don't think I've ever been conscious of writing with a theme in mind. I am always surprised, when, after a play has opened, I read in the papers what the play was about.... Usually, when asked about a theme, I look vague and say 'It's a play about life.'" His gay vision had leaped beyond linear structuring. He would not write plays about homosexuality—desiring not, he said, to limit his audience to gays.

Those gays who wanted everything spelled out found his work elusive, and some gay drama critics excluded him entirely. Others, who had learned to read between the lines, found him an exemplar of what is meant by gay consciousness. It was not necessarily about having sex on stage, or even about mentioning the word; it was a special, sometimes wounded, often humorous way of looking at the world—as an outsider inside the nest. In his later years, Williams dealt more openly with homosexuality, as in the novel *Moise and the World of Reason,* and his very frank *Memoirs,* as he had much earlier in his short story collections, *One Arm, and Other Stories* in 1948, and *Hard Candy, and Other Stories* in 1954. Almost scandalously homoerotic when they appeared, for a long time, these stories led an underground existence.

As they had done with Christopher Isherwood, Paul Goodman, and as others did much later with Edward Albee, a few brash Los Angeles gay liberationists, full of self–righteous omniscience, confronted Williams at one of his public appearances to raise his consciousness. Hurt by the attack, he defended the writer's right to his own vision, free from slogans and dogmas of the moment. Williams

told New York journalist Arthur Bell in the *Village Voice,* "I've nothing to hide. Homosexuality isn't the theme of my plays. They're about all human relationships." Moreover, Williams was annoyed by critics who repeatedly said that he hated women, that his wonderful women characters did not conform to the idealized heterosexual stereotypes of glamour gal, wife or mother, or that Blanche Du Bois and others were really drag queens in disguise. In a *Gay Sunshine* interview, he expressed anger at this charge, adding that he never understood transvestites or transsexuals, and that homosexuals were not trying to imitate women: "We are simply trying to be comfortably assimilated by our society." In one television interview with Dick Cavett, he turned away in annoyance when asked about those great women characters. "I'm tired of talking about that. I came here to discuss my homosexuality, and if we're not going to talk about that, I might as well leave."

Famed for his powerfully motivated, frustrated and poetic women characters, Williams also portrayed many sexually magnetic, predatory and self–defeating males, and others sadly broken down by demands of the macho role. *A Streetcar Named Desire* was a Broadway smash in 1947, winning the Pulitzer prize. Williams, however, was denounced as decadent by some critics who had previously admired him, and bitterly criticized by later gays who wanted a more explicit rendering of the subject than Williams' tentative introduction of an off–stage sympathetic gay theme. Yet, for its time, the play was almost revolutionary and it remains a major stage and film classic. *The Rose Tattoo* hit Broadway in 1950; Daniel Mann's powerful 1955 film vehicle for Anna Magnani and Burt Lancaster was another strong example of gay vision without necessary mention of homosexuality. Like Carson McCullers and William Inge, both close friends, Williams brought the mystique of the sexy superstud to the American stage. *Camino Real,* 1953, a dreamplay, included as characters Lord Byron, World War II's "Kilroy," Casanova and Camille, and had much of interest for perceptive gay theatre goers. *Suddenly Last Summer,* staged in 1958 and filmed in 1959 with a screenplay by Williams, explores a mother's and a wife's tug–of–war over an off–screen homosexual artist murdered by boys at the beach. His 1959 novel, *The Roman Spring of Mrs. Stone,* was filmed in 1961 and shockingly portrayed an American school teacher's unsettling encounter with a young Italian hustler. Here, more than in the plays, critics said that Mrs. Stone really personified an aging male homosexual. *Moise and the World of Reason,* published in 1975 and largely forgotten, was a specifically gay novel—a wonderfully wacky story of three lost souls in Greenwich Village. Few critics knew what to make of it; however, calling it a "symbolic novel," James Levin pointed out in *The Gay Novel in America* that in "homosexuality is not presented realistically."

In a 1983 article answering critics who accused Williams of writing "homosexual fantasies in heterosexual drag," *Los Angeles Times* critic Dan Sullivan reported: "Williams once told a reporter that homosexuality was a comfortable life style for him—a life style he pursued fairly publicly in his later years—but he was interested in drawing the larger world. He did this with the accuracy of an artist who has a great deal of firsthand emotional information about other men and women, and who knows that their longings aren't any different in kind than his, only differently directed." In the *Los Angeles Times,* Vidal once called Williams "the sort of writer who does not develop; he simply continues," complaining that Williams never seemed to read other writers, or learn from them or from experience. Williams consistently ducked questions of why he did not deal directly with gay love and gay culture in his plays; and in that sense, as Vidal has said, Williams did not evolve. He wrote about troubled individuals, but apparently could not find dramatic fodder in gay life beyond that.

Sullivan continued: "There is, in his best plays, an area of ambiguity that disturbs some people today, particularly those who think Williams should have been more out front as a gay artist in the 1950s. He's been blamed, for example, for leaving up in the air the question of whether Brick in *Cat on a Hot Tin Roof* was or wasn't homosexual. For me, this ambiguity is one of the strengths of his plays. It reflects a fruitful tension between Williams the searcher after the whammo theatrical effect, and Williams the poet, who knows the power of something unspoken. The tension is particularly true to the mood of the 1950s, which wasn't yet ready to call absolutely every spade a spade. But it has more to do with artistic tact than social repression.... Williams' decline as an artist has something to do with his loss of tact.... Illusion, tact, the veil over the bulb, leads to truth in the best of his plays, the truth that there's mystery at everybody's heart, that people aren't be solved." Williams' "deepest reality was that of an artist—a most serious one. Gore Vidal suggests that he was a bit of an ignoramus about literature. Perhaps, but he wrote some fine poetry." And his poetry, *In the Winter of Cities* and *Androgyne, Mon Amour,* should satisfy those who want things spelled out.

"Sex is an energy that pervades all of our imagination and most of our acts and that manifests itself in every human relationship," relates Louis Auchincloss in the afterword to *Dictionary of Literary Biography Documentary Series.* "It took the genius of Tennessee Williams to dramatize this universality. His heroes and heroines are sexual impulses, his plots a kind of sexual intercourse. The presence of lust or love in every episode and piece of dialogue in his plays is what gives the warmth and glow even to his brutes and villains." Yet, even if much of his work was not specifically or overtly about gays, all of Williams' vision was unmistakably and brilliantly gay. He wrote five or six of the best plays in modern American drama, and many of his so-called lesser plays continue to be performed. He was one of the finest and most humanely insightful American writers, attuned to the poetry of wounded souls. But his lingering difficulty in accepting his own gayness kept him, I think, from understanding the potential drama in its non-sexual components.

—*Jim Kepner*

WILLIAMS, Thomas Lanier. *See* **WILLIAMS, Tennessee.**

WILLY. *See* **COLETTE, (Sidonie–Gabrielle).**

WILLY, Colette. *See* **COLETTE, (Sidonie–Gabrielle).**

WILSON, Barbara (Ellen). American novelist and short story writer. Born in Long Beach, California, 17 October 1950. Publisher, Seal Press, Seattle, Washington. **Recipient:** Columbia Translation Prize. Address: c/o Seal Press, 3131 Western Avenue, Suite 410, Seattle, Washington 98121, U.S.A.

WRITINGS

Novels

Ambitious Women. Seattle, Spinsters, 1982, second edition, 1986; London, Women's Press, 1983.
Cows and Horses. Portland, Oregon, Eighth Mountain Press, 1988; London, Virago Press, 1989.

"Pam Nilsen" Crime Series

Murder in the Collective. Seattle, Seal Press, and London, Women's Press, 1984.
Sisters of the Road. Seattle, Seal Press, 1986; London, Women's Press, 1987.
The Dog Collar Murders. Seattle, Seal Press, and London, Virago Press, 1989.

"Cassandra Reilly" Mystery Series

Gaudi Afternoon. Seattle, Seal Press, 1990; London, Virago Press, 1991.
Trouble in Transylvania. Seattle, Seal Press, and London, Virago Press, 1993.

Short Stories

Talk and Contact (contains "Package Tour," "Postcard Views of the World," "Resemblances," "Travellucinations," "Turtles Do It," "Furniture," "Occupational Therapy," "Frankenstein," "The Growth Spurt," and "Talk and Contact"). Seattle, Seal Press, 1978.
Thin Ice (contains "Thin Ice," "Drive–away," "S.A.S.E.," "In the Archives," "Looking for the Golden Gate," "Earthquake Baroque," "Pity," "Emily's Arrows," "Disasters," "The Investment," "Sense and Sensitivity," "Stalingrad," and "Phantom Limb Pain"). Seattle, Seal Press, 1981.
Walking on the Moon: Six Stories and a Novella (contains "Il Circo delle donne," "Take Louise Nevelson," "How to Fix a Roof," "Hearings," "The Hulk," "Miss Venezuela," and "Walking on the Moon"). Seattle, Seal Press, 1983; London, Women's Press, 1986.
Miss Venezuela (includes stories from *Thin Ice, Walking on the Moon* plus "Starfish," "Crater Lake," and "The Back Door of America"). Seattle, Seal Press, 1988.

Uncollected Short Stories

"Murder at the International Feminist Book Fair," in *Reader I Murdered Him,* edited by Jen Green. London, Women's Press, 1989; New York, St. Martin's Press, 1990.
"We Didn't See It," in *Lesbian Love Stories,* edited by Irene Zahava. Watsonville, California, Crossing Press, 1989.

"The Theft of the Poet," in *A Woman's Eye,* edited by Sara Paretsky and Martin H. Greenberg. New York, Delacorte, 1990.
"Is This Enough for You?," in *Lesbian Love Stories,* Volume 2, edited by Irene Zahava. Watsonville, California, Crossing Press, 1991.
"The Death of a Much–Travelled Woman," in *The Fourth Woman Sleuth Anthology,* edited by Irene Zahava. Watsonville, California, Crossing Press, 1991.

Other

The Geography Lesson (for children), illustrations by Gregory MacDonald. Seattle, Seal Press, 1977.
Editor, with Faith Conlon and Rachel de Silva, *The Things That Divide Us* (short stories). Seattle, Seal Press, 1985; London, Sheba, 1986.
Translator, *Cora Sandel: Collected Short Stories.* Seattle, Seal Press, 1985.
Translator, *Nothing Happened* by Ebba Haslund. Seattle, Seal Press, 1987.
"The Erotic Life of Fictional Characters," in *An Intimate Wilderness: Lesbian Writers on Sexuality,* edited by Judith Barrington. Portland, Oregon, Eighth Mountain Press, 1991.
"My Work," in *Inversions: Writing by Dykes, Queers, and Lesbians,* edited by Betsy Warland. Vancouver, British Columbia, Press Gang Publishers, 1991.

*

Interviews: With Barbara Findlen, in *Ms.,* November/December 1991, 78.

Critical Sources: Sketch by Lyn Pykett, in *Twentieth–Century Crime and Mystery Writers,* New York, St. Martin's Press, 1985; review of *The Dog Collar Murders,* in *Publishers Weekly,* 17 March 1989, 90; review by Marilyn Stasio of *Gaudi Afternoon,* in *New York Times Book Review,* 25 November 1990, 22; "The Feminist Counter–Tradition in Crime: Cross, Grafton, Paretsky, and Wilson" by Maureen T. Reddy, in *The Cunning Craft: Original Essays on Detective Fiction and Contemporary Literary Theory,* edited by Ronald G. Walker, Macomb, Western Illinois University, 1990, 174–187.

Barbara Wilson comments: "Much of my work, whether serious or humorous, subversive or traditional, springs from an attempt to come to terms with death and loss. Crime writing has given me permission to be playful while tackling social issues, however, I do not consider myself a mystery writer. The fluid nature of emerging lesbian literature has encouraged experimentation. I am still very much in the process of learning how to say what I need to say."

* * *

Barbara Wilson's writings provide insight into the political, social, and emotional ramifications of the struggle to redefine our culture's view of women by liberating it from male expectations. Wilson's female characters reflect the variety of women in real life:

they are of all ages and all physical types, represent a variety of skills and professions, and their racial and family backgrounds are diverse. Some are straight, some are bisexual, some are lifelong lesbians and some are just discovering their women–centered sexuality. And as Marilyn Stasio remarks in the *New York Times Book Review,* Wilson draws her characters "with affection and humor."

In her earlier stories and novels, Wilson described the process of women learning to rely upon the strengths of their gender in a male–dominated world and to define themselves without reference to men, an act fraught with political and social consequence. In these works, such as *Ambitious Women* and the first two Pam Nilsen mysteries, Wilson's characters confront such issues as violence against women, racism and homophobia. The sexuality of the characters in these works, while treated as essential, is sometimes of secondary importance to their social and political consciousness. Moreover, according to Lyn Pykett in *Twentieth–Century Crime and Mystery Writers,* Wilson is one of several lesbian/feminists who have been instrumental in transforming the essentially conservative genre of detective fiction to reflect "a leftist politics and a radical sexual politics." In her study of the feminist counter–tradition in detective fiction, Maureen T. Reddy explains that "feminism is the source of each detective's authority and therefore of her power, while each murderer's corrupt definition and destructive use of power is rooted in patriarchal, capitalist ideology, which is seen finally to lack legitimate authority."

In later works, beginning with *Cows and Horses* and *The Dog Collar Murders,* to the stylized mysteries, *Gaudi Afternoon* and *Trouble in Transylvania,* Wilson writes from a more strongly defined lesbian perspective. In *Cows and Horses,* a novel about the end of a long relationship, lesbian desire is one of the main focuses. The struggle to define sexuality is also the driving element of *The Dog Collar Murders,* a mystery about the "porn wars" of the 1980s in North America. Calling the novel "clever and illuminating," a *Publishers Weekly* reviewer notes that it manipulates the mystery genre to examine "issues at the heart of feminist debate over sexuality, pornography and violence against women." In the two Cassandra Reilly novels, *Gaudi Afternoon* and *Trouble in Transylvania,* Wilson takes a more playful approach to lesbian desire, as she explores gender definition and confusion.

Most of the characters in Wilson's short stories are female, and Wilson focuses on their relationships, especially family relationships. Several of her most memorable characters are girls at various stages of physical and emotional development, portrayed in the often painful, sometimes comic process of learning to love and forgive their all–too–human siblings and parents. For example, Wilson creates a character named Kate through a series of several stories. Each story presents a vignette from Kate's life as she evolves from a young girl to a middle–aged woman, and demonstrates how that evolution changes her relationships with her father and brother. The title story of *Miss Venezuela* highlights the dreamy, self–conscious fantasies of a pre–teen girl watching the Miss Universe contest with her family. Calling this collection "provocative and perceptive," a *Publishers Weekly* contributor notes that the stories portray "women struggling with the love of men, women, family and self."

Many of Wilson's stories and novels take place in Seattle or the West Coast, and critics praise her keen rendering of the sights and sounds of that region, but increasingly she has used foreign settings to tell the stories, not only of North American women, but of women in England, Spain, and Eastern Europe. Her view of politics and sense of place have expanded to become more international.

Her vision of the infinite variety of women is empowering and her work enriches our understanding of what it means to be female in the late twentieth century. Wilson combines politics, humor, and lyricism in work that has steadily progressed in complexity to treat issues of desire, language and gender.

—Pamela Bigelow

————

WILSON, Doric. American playwright and author of screenplays. Has also written as Howard Aldon. Born in Los Angeles, California, 24 February 1939. Apprenticed to Richland Players, Washington, 1952–58; studied with Lorraine Larson, Tri–Cities, Washington, 1955–58; attended University of Washington, 1958–59. Founding member and playwright–in–residence, Barr/Wilder/Albee Playwrights Unit, New York City, 1963–65; artistic director, Ensemble Project, New York City, 1965–68; founding member and playwright–in–residence, Circle Repertory Company, New York City, 1969–71; founding artistic director, TOSOS Theatre Company, New York City, 1969–71; playwright–in–residence, The Glines, New York City, 1978–82, and Jerry West's Funtastic Shows, Portland, Oregon, 1983–84; director, New City Theatre Playwright's Workshop, Seattle, 1985; director and playwright–in–residence, Pioneer Square Theatre, Seattle, beginning 1986. Director of plays, including *The Madness of Lady Bright*, 1974; *The Hostage*, 1975; and *What the Butler Saw*, 1975. Contributor of articles and reviews to magazines and newspapers, including *Villager* and *Other Stages*. Member, Board of Advisers, Hibbs Gallery and Visual Arts Center, New York City, beginning 1981. **Recipient:** San Francisco Cable Car Award for *Forever After*, 1981; Citation for Service to the Gay Community from New York Gay and Lesbian Independent Democrats, 1982; Jane Chambers Award for Significant Contribution to the Development of Gay Theatre, 1982; National Gay Theatre Award for best play of 1982 for *Street Theatre; Villager* award, 1983; *Newsmaker* award, 1984. Address: c/o JH Press, P.O. Box 294, Village Station, New York, New York 10014, U.S.A.

WRITINGS

Plays

And He Made a Her (produced New York, 1961).
Babel, Babel, Little Tower (produced New York, 1961).
Now She Dances!: A Short Play in Direct Reference and in Direct Reply to "Salome" by Oscar Wilde (produced New York, 1961; revised version produced New York, 1975).
Pretty People (produced New York, 1961).
In Absence (produced New York, 1968).
It Was a Very Good Year (produced New York, 1970).
Body Count (produced New York, 1971).
The West Street Gang (and director; produced New York, 1977). Included in *Two Plays*, 1979.
Ad Hoc Committee (produced New York, 1978).
Surprise (produced New York, 1978).

Turnabout (as Howard Aldon; produced Richland, Washington, 1979).
A Perfect Relationship: A Domestic Comedy in Two Acts (produced New York, 1979). Included in *Two Plays*, 1979; New York, Sea Horse Press, 1983.
Two Plays (contains *The West Street Gang* and *A Perfect Relationship*). New York, Sea Horse Press, 1979.
Forever After: A Vivisection of Gaymale Love, without Intermission (and director; produced New York, 1980). New York, JH Press, 1980.
Street Theatre: The Twenty–seventh of June (produced New York, 1981). New York, JH Press, 1981.
Saints on a Secret Mission (produced Seattle, 1986).

Other

"Caffe Cino" in *Other Stages* (New York), March 1981.

*

Manuscript Collections: Lincoln Center Library of the Performing Arts, New York City.

Interviews: "A Perfect Relationship with Gay Theater: Playwright Doric Wilson" by Robert Chesley, *Advocate*, 5 April 1979, 33–34; "Doric Wilson: A Lively Look at Gay Revolt As 'Street Theater,'" in *Advocate*, 1 April 1982, 37–39.

Critical Sources: *Lavender Culture* by Karla Jay and Allen Young, New York, Jove, 1979; "Images of the Gay Male in Contemporary Drama" by James W. Carlsen, in *Gayspeak: Gay Male and Lesbian Communication*, edited by James W. Chesebro, New York, Pilgrim, 1981, 165–174; "Gay Plays, Gay Theatre, Gay Performance" by Terry Helbing, in *Drama Review* (New York), March 1981; review by Michael Feingold of *Forever After*, in *Voice Literary Supplement*, December 1981, 6.

*   *   *

The decade immediately following the Stonewall Riots of 1969 witnessed a uniquely diverse explosion of creativity in virtually all fields of literature and the fine arts as lesbian and gay writers, painters, and poets claimed a new freedom to both express themselves and create institutions which would foster and preserve the growth of a gay sensibility. Nowhere was this phenomenon more visible than in theatre, where local companies (many of them with only very brief spans of performance) were founded to provide venues for works exploring the meanings of homosexuality. Through the career of playwright and director Doric Wilson, it is possible to follow this process almost from its very beginning.

His involvement with the theatre began with a six–year apprenticeship with a company in the Richland, Washington, area, followed by a short period at the University of Washington in Seattle. With two completed (if unperformed) plays in hand, he decided to relocate to New York City for training as a set designer in the early 1960s. Formal entrance to that city's theatrical world was provided when the Caffe Cino, a coffeehouse in Greenwich Village which was the home of the emerging Off–Off Broadway movement, chose one of his works for performance in 1961. In 1963, Wilson was invited by Edward Albee, Richard Barr and Clinton Wilder to join the Playwright's Unit, another prominent Off–Off Broadway venture, an association which lasted until the group decided to produce Mart Crowley's *The Boys in the Band* in 1965. Three years as artistic director for the Ensemble Project followed, and Wilson was involved with the Circle Repertory Company as both a founding member and playwright–in–residence at the time of the Christopher Street riots.

The brave new environment of the gay liberation movement offered Wilson an opportunity to utilize his experience in theatre administration to create the first professional openly gay theatre company in 1969. Known as TOSOS (The Other Side of Silence), it began as a cooperative venture to give gay artists in whatever medium a safe place to present their work. Supported chiefly by Wilson's wages as a bartender, TOSOS lasted for five years, ending its existence with the premiere of Wilson's first play dealing explicitly with gay life, *The West Street Gang*, in 1977. The satire is set in a Lower West Side bar and addresses the issue of harassment and violence against gay men (one of the earliest such appearances of the topic as a plot line) through a confrontation of the patrons with the leader of a local gang. While the setting and structure of the work recall Lanford Wilson's *Balm in Gilead,* the mood of the piece is emphatically different, mirroring the anti–gay political campaign of conservative Anita Bryant, the publicity seeking of many gay organizations, and popular (if inaccurate) coverage of the gay community in mainstream media. With *A Perfect Relationship,* the 1979 offering which marks Wilson's next examination of gay reality, the emphasis shifts from group reaction to the internal dynamics of emotional bonds between two men and issues of honesty and commitment. Placing the common situation of two roommates who become lovers—without consciously realizing it—on stage puts the urban world of gay America in the 1970s and its ethos regarding factors important in building and sustaining healthy partnerships into high relief, some of it comic. This theme persists in the successive work, *Forever After,* which received the San Francisco Cable Car Award in 1981. Here, the scene is once more an apartment in New York City, where an anniversary celebration of an "equal but independent cohabitation" turns into a wry commentary by the muses of comedy and tragedy on not only same–sex pairings but also on the function of gay theatre itself. Paralleling this growth and diversification in performance and craft was Wilson's increasing involvement with the off–stage aspects of management and composition as playwright–in–residence and director with The Glines company of New York and the New City Theatre Playwright's Workshop and Pioneer Square Theatre of Seattle.

It is with the 1982 production of *Street Theater* that the writer comes full circle, using the stage as a venue to present the experience of gay history to a more general public, continuing the tradition begun by Jonathan Katz in his 1972 play *Coming Out!* Drawing heavily on his own first–hand knowledge of Greenwich Village, the play in some ways complements its predecessor by portraying the situation of gay people on the eve of the Stonewall Riots through a series of characters ranging from a drag queen, a tough but caring lesbian, and a leatherman with a keen political sense to a naive flower child, a corrupt vice squad officer, and a gay man in analysis to overcome his homosexuality. The idea of illustrating the Stonewall events on stage had long attracted Wilson, but it was a random encounter with two blatant queens on the street which finally sparked the form of the piece. Challenging the accepted rhetoric of the time which placed anger over oppression as the driving force behind the liberation movement, Wilson views the need to establish a distinctive gay cultural identity as the primary motivation fueling the early efforts for change. *Street Theater* was the recipient of the *Villager* Best Play Award in 1983 and the Jane Chambers Award for 1982/1983. While Wilson's career was to develop further—with involvement in more than one hundred Off and Off–Off Broadway plays as director, writer, or producer and the writing of *Saints on A Secret Mission* and *An Object of Affection*—his true significance for gay literature lies in his role as one of the founders and definers of gay theatre and some of its most challenging works.

—*Robert B. Marks Ridinger*

WILSON, Lanford (Eugene). American dramatist. Born in Lebanon, Missouri, 13 April 1937. Educated at Ozark High School, Missouri; Southwest Missouri State College, Springfield, 1955–56; San Diego State College (now University), 1956–57; University of Chicago, 1957–58; University of Missouri, Ph.D. 1985. Worked at various jobs, and in advertising, Chicago, 1957–62; director, actor, and designer for Caffe Cino and Cafe La Mama theatres, New York City, beginning 1962. Founding member and resident playwright and director, Circle Repertory Company, New York City, 1969—. Member of Dramatists Guild Council. **Recipient:** Vernon Rice–Drama Desk Award for *The Rimers of Eldritch,* 1966–67; Rockefeller Foundation grant, 1967, 1974; ABC–Yale University fellowship, 1969; Guggenheim grant, 1970; Obie award, 1972 for *The Hot l Baltimore,* 1975 for *The Mound Builders,* and 1984; Emmy Award nomination for *The Migrants,* 1972; Outer Critics Circle award, 1973 for *The Hot l Baltimore;* Drama Critics Circle award, 1973 for *The Hot l Baltimore,* and 1980; American Institute of Arts and Letters award, 1974; Academy Award, 1974; Pulitzer Prize for *Talley's Folly,* 1980; Brandeis award, 1981. Agent: Bridget Aschenberg, International Creative Management, 40 West 57th Street, New York, New York 10019, U.S.A. Address: c/o Circle Repertory Company, 186 West Fourth Street, New York, New York 10014, U.S.A.; Box 891 Sag Harbor, New York 11963, U.S.A.

WRITINGS

Plays

So Long at the Fair (produced New York, 1963).
No Trespassing (produced New York, 1964).
Home Free! (also director; produced New York, 1964; London, 1968). Included in *Balm in Gilead, and Other Plays,* 1965; with *The Madness of Lady Bright,* London, Methuen, 1968.
The Madness of Lady Bright (also director; produced New York, 1964; London, 1968). Included in *Eight Plays from Off–Off Broad-*

way, edited by Nick Orzel and Michael Smith, New York, Bobbs–Merrill, 1966; in *The Rimers of Eldritch, and Other Plays,* 1967; in *Gay Plays: The First Collection,* New York, Avon Books, 1979; with *Home Free!,* London, Methuen, 1968.

Balm in Gilead (produced New York, 1965; Edinburgh, 1986). Included in *Balm in Gilead, and Other Plays,* 1965.

Ludlow Fair (produced New York, 1965; Edinburgh, 1967; London, 1977). Included in *Balm in Gilead, and Other Plays,* 1965.

Balm in Gilead, and Other Plays (comprises *Balm in Gilead; Ludlow Fair; Home Free!*). New York, Hill & Wang, 1965.

Sex Is Between Two People (produced New York, 1965).

The Rimers of Eldritch (also director; produced New York, 1965). Included in *The Rimers of Eldritch, and Other Plays,* 1967.

This Is the Rill Speaking (also director; produced New York, 1965). Included in *The Rimers of Eldritch, and Other Plays,* 1967.

Days Ahead (produced New York, 1965). Included in *The Rimers of Eldritch, and Other Plays,* 1967.

The Sand Castle (produced New York, 1965). Included in *The Sand Castle and Three Other Plays,* 1970; in *Best Short Plays 1975,* New York, Dodd, Mead, 1976.

Miss Williams: A Turn (produced New York, 1965).

Wandering: A Turn (produced New York, 1966). Included in *The Rimers of Eldritch, and Other Plays,* 1967; in *The Sand Castle, and Three Other Plays,* in *Collision Course,* New York, Dramatists Play Service, 1970.

The Rimers of Eldritch, and Other Plays (comprises *The Rimers of Eldritch; Days Ahead; This Is the Rill Speaking; Wandering: A Turn*). New York, Hill & Wang, 1967.

Untitled Play, music by Al Carmines (produced New York, 1968).

The Gingham Dog (produced Washington, D.C., 1968; New York, 1969; Manchester, 1970). New York, Hill & Wang, 1970.

Lemon Sky (produced Buffalo and New York, 1970). New York, Hill & Wang, 1970.

Serenading Louie (produced Washington, D.C., 1970; New York, 1976). New York, Dramatists Play Service, 1976; in *Best Plays of 1975–1976,* New York, Dodd, Mead, 1976; revised version (produced New York, 1984), New York, Hill & Wang, 1985.

The Sand Castle, and Three Other Plays (comprises *The Sand Castle, Sextet [Yes]; Stoop; Wandering for Voices*). New York, Dramatists Play Service, 1970.

The Great Nebula in Orion (produced Manchester, 1971; New York, 1972; London, 1981). Included in *The Great Nebula in Orion and Three Other Plays,* 1973; in *Best Short Plays 1972,* New York, Dodd, Mead, 1973.

Sextet (Yes): A Play for Voices (produced New York, 1971). Included in *The Sand Castle and Three Other Plays,* 1970.

Ikke, Ikke, Nye, Nye, Nye (produced New Haven, Connecticut, and New York, 1972; London, 1981). Included in *The Great Nebula in Orion and Three Other Plays,* 1973.

The Family Continues (produced New York, 1972). Included in *The Great Nebula in Orion and Three Other Plays,* 1973.

The Great Nebula in Orion and Three Other Plays (comprises *The Great Nebula in Orion; The Family Continues; Victory on Mrs. Dandywine's Island; Ikke, Ikke, Nye, Nye, Nye*). New York, Dramatists Play Service, 1973.

The Hot l Baltimore (produced New York, 1973; London, 1976). New York, Hill & Wang, 1973; in *Best Plays of 1972–1973,* New York, Dodd, Mead, 1973; in *The Obie Winners: The Best of Off-Broadway,* Garden City, New York, Doubleday, 1980.

The Mound Builders (produced New York, 1975). New York, Hill & Wang, 1976.

Brontosaurus (produced New York, 1977; London, 1982). New York, Dramatists Play Service, 1978.

5th of July (produced New York, 1978; revised as *Fifth of July,* produced New York, 1980; Bristol, 1987). Included in *Best Plays of 1977–1978,* New York, Dodd, Mead, 1978; New York, Hill & Wang, 1979.

Talley's Folly (produced New York, 1979; London, 1982). New York, Hill & Wang, 1980; in *Best Plays of 1979–1980,* New York, Dodd, Mead, 1980.

Bar Play, in *Holidays* (produced Louisville, 1979).

A Tale Told (produced New York, 1981; revised version as *Talley and Son,* produced New York, 1985). New York, Hill & Wang, 1986.

Thymus Vulgaris (produced New York, 1981). New York, Dramatists Play Service, 1982; in *Best Short Plays 1982,* New York, Dodd, Mead, 1983.

Angels Fall (produced Miami, 1982). New York, Hill & Wang, 1983; in *Best Plays of 1982–1983,* New York, Dodd, Mead, 1983.

Say deKooning (produced Southhampton, New York, 1985).

Sa–Hurt? (produced New York, 1986).

A Betrothal (produced London, 1986). New York, Dramatists Play Service, 1986; in *Best Short Plays 1987,* New York, Dodd, Mead, 1988.

Burn This (produced Los Angeles and New York, 1987). New York, Hill & Wang, 1988.

Abstinence: A Turn. New York, Hill & Wang, 1989; in *Best American Short Plays 1990,* New York, Applause Theatre Book Publishers, 1991.

The Moonshot Tape. Included in *The Moonshot Tape, and A Poster of the Cosmos,* New York, Dramatists Plays Service, 1990.

A Poster of the Cosmos. Included in *The Moonshot Tape, and A Poster of the Cosmos,* New York, Dramatists Play Service, 1990; in *Best Short Plays 1989,* New York, Applause Theatre Company, 1990.

Redwood Curtain (produced Seattle, 1992; New York, 1993). New York, Hill & Wang, 1992.

Teleplays

Stoop, "New York Television Theatre," WNET (New York), 1969.

With Tennessee Williams, *The Migrants,* "Playhouse 90," CBS, 1974.

Taxi, "Hallmark Hall of Fame," NBC, 1978.

Other

One Arm (screenplay; adaptation of story by Tennessee Williams), 1970.

Author of libretto, *Summer and Smoke: An Opera in Two Acts,* music by Lee Hoiby (adaptation of play by Tennessee Williams; produced St. Paul, 1971; New York, 1972). New York, Belwin Mills, 1972.

"Observations of a Resident Playwright" (essay), in *New York Times,* 23 April 1978.

"Meet Tom Eyen, Tom Eyen," in *Horizon,* July 1979.

Translator, *The Three Sisters* by Anton Chekhov (produced Hartford, Connecticut, 1985; New York, 1986). New York, Dramatists Play Service, 1984.

Interviews: "Lanford is One 'L' of a Playwright" by Guy Flately, in *New York Times,* 22 April 1973, Section 2: 1, 21; "Lanford Wilson—Can He Score on Broadway?" by Robert Berkvist, in *New York Times,* 17 February 1980, Section 2: 1, 3; "Portrait: Lanford Wilson" by Jennifer Allen, in *Life,* June 1980, 29–30; "The Most Populist Playwright" by Ross Wetzsteon, in *New York,* 8 November 1982, 40–45; "Recreating the Magic: An Interview with Lanford Wilson" by Gene A. Barrett, in *Ball State University Forum,* spring 1984, 57–74; "I Write the World As I See It Around Me" by Michiko Kakutani, in *New York Times,* 8 July 1984, Section 2: 4, 6; "Lanford Wilson Comes Home" by Samuel Freedman, in *New York Times Magazine,* 30 August 1987, 28, 63–64; "Talking to ... Lanford Wilson and Terrence McNally: On Love, Responsibility, and Sexual Obsession" by Leslie Bennetts, in *Vogue,* February 1988, 216, 220.

Bibliography: *Contemporary Authors Bibliographical Series,* Volume 1: *American Dramatists,* Detroit, Gale, 1989.

Critical Sources: "Lanford Wilson" by Arthur Sainer, in *Contemporary Dramatists,* New York, St. Martin's Press, 1973; "Plainsongs and Fancies" by Trish Dace, in *Soho Weekly News,* 5 November 1980, 20; "Lanford Wilson" by Gautam Dasgupta, in *American Playwrights: A Critical Survey,* Volume 1, edited by Gautam Dasgupta and Bonnie Marranca, New York, Drama Book Specialists, 1981, 27–39; "Lanford Wilson" by Ann Crawford Dreher, in *Dictionary of Literary Biography,* Volume 7: *Twentieth–Century American Dramatists,* Detroit, Gale, 1981; "Images of the Past in the Plays of Lanford Wilson" by Henry Schvey, in *Contemporary American Drama,* Munich, Huebler, 1981, 225–240; "Broadway Bound: Simon, Kopit, McNally, Wilson" by Ruby Cohn, in her *New American Dramatists 1960–1980,* New York, Grove, 1982; "Images of America; Wilson, Weller, and Horovitz" by Barry Witham, in *Theatre Journal,* May 1982, 223–232; *A Critical Introduction to Twentieth–Century American Drama,* Volume 3: *Beyond Broadway,* Cambridge University Press, 1985, 26–28, 219, 417; "Lanford Wilson" by Harold Branam, in *Critical Survey of Drama,* Volume 5, edited by Frank N. Magill, Englewood Cliffs, New Jersey, Salem, 1985, 2095–2103; *Lanford Wilson* by Gene A. Barnett, Boston, G. K. Hall, 1987; *Lanford Wilson* by Mark Busby, Boise, Idaho, Boise State University Press, 1987; "Down and Out in Lebanon and New York: Lanford Wilson" by William Herman, in his *Understanding Contemporary American Drama,* Columbia, University of South Carolina Press, 1987, 196–271; "The Comic Vision of Lanford Wilson" by Martin J. Jacobi, in *Studies in the Literary Imagination,* fall 1988, 199–134; "Some Kind of Future: The War for Inheritance in the World of Three American Playwrights of the 1970s" by James F. Schlatter, in *South Central Review,* spring 1990, 59–74.

*   *   *

The steady stream of works produced by playwright Lanford Wilson since his debut has explored a wide range of human emotions and situations through an often bewildering variety of characters. A basic feature of virtually all Wilson's work is an examination of society and its flaws through dialogue by people who are either on its margins or completely outside accepted frames of reference.

From the very beginning, homosexuals have been part of the world Wilson created for his audiences. His first play to be staged at Caffe Cino in New York, the 1965 work *Balm in Gilead,* is set in a seedy all–night coffee shop on Upper Broadway on Halloween night. Among the 29 characters inhabiting this shadowy world are gay and lesbian hustlers. The portrayal of such individuals as human beings with recognizable needs is itself notable for this period of American theater; setting the play on Halloween, a night traditionally associated with superficial masks hiding underlying reality, reinforces the atmosphere of alienation sought by the author.

The most prominent of his early one–act plays which portrays an openly gay character is *The Madness of Lady Bright,* first performed in 1964. It is the story of Leslie Bright, an aging homosexual gradually falling to pieces in his apartment on Manhattan on a stifling summer afternoon. The work is principally a monologue by the title character addressed to his mirror, in the course of which he reveals his life history, his emotional problems, and finally renounces his efforts to retain a hold on reality and to connect with a world which has no interest in him. Wilson depicts this latter quality graphically by having the only responses Bright receives to his spate of desperate phone calls be American Airlines and Dial–a–Prayer. Two ancillary characters, distinguished only by gender, provide illustration for and commentary on his deterioration. Produced before the beginning of the contemporary gay liberation movement at the Stonewall Riots of 1969, it is in some ways offered as a specimen of social attitudes towards gays in general (and transvestites in particular, which Leslie Bright is) as they existed in American society in the middle years of the 1960s.

By the time of *The Great Nebula in Orion* in 1971, the world has clearly undergone significant changes from the condemnatory atmosphere of hatred and denigration of homosexuals shown in Wilson's previous work. The play tells of the chance meeting of two old school friends and their discussion over drinks of their lives. In the course of these reminiscences, it emerges that one of the women is a lesbian, a fact that is treated without the psychiatric condescension of *The Madness of Lady Bright.* The playwright has moved away from presenting his audience with an expected stereotype and instead offers an individual accepting of herself and able to reach out to her friend.

The gradual progression of gay people from stage caricatures to recognizably familiar people culminates in Wilson's 1978 work *5th of July.* The gay relationship between two of the main characters is taken as an established fact, with more attention placed on the service of one of them in the Vietnam War and the loss of his legs. An earlier failed relationship with one of a couple interested in purchasing his family home is also explored. From the portrayal of gays as the ultimate outsiders with whom members of the audience would have trouble identifying (as in the case of Leslie Bright or the men and women of *Balm in Gilead*), the image of a gay man as the consummate insider, a disabled war veteran injured defending his country, indicates the considerable shift in social attitudes over the intervening 14 years of change.

—*Robert B. Marks Ridinger*

————

WINSLOE, Christa. German sculptress, novelist, playwright, and scriptwriter. Born in Darmstadt, 23 December 1888. Educated at girls' schools in East Germany and Switzerland. Married the

Hungarian sugar cane baron Ludwig Hatvany in 1913 (separated); companion of American journalist Dorothy Thompson, 1932–33; lived with Swiss author Simone Gentet. Active in France's anti–fascist movement. *Murdered, with Simone Gentet, in Cluny, France, c. 6 June 1944.*

WRITINGS

Novels

Das schwarze Schaf ["The Black Sheep"], c. 1913.
Das Mädchen Manuela. Translated by Agnes Neill Scott as *The Child Manuela: The Novel of Mädchen in Uniform,* New York, Farrar & Rinehart, 1933.
Life Begins, translation by Agnes Neill Scott. London, Chapman & Hall, 1935; as *Girl Alone,* New York, Farrar & Rinehart, 1936.
Passeggiera ["Passengers"], 1938.
Männer kehren heim ["Men Return Home"].

Plays

Ritter Nérestan ["Knight Nérestan"] (produced Leipzig, 1930). As *Gestern und heute* ["Yesterday and Today"], Berlin, 1930; adapted by Barbara Burnham as *Children in Uniform: A Play in Three Acts,* London, Gollancz, 1932; New York, S. French, 1933; as *Girls in Uniform,* in *The Best Plays of 1932–1933,* edited by Burns Mantle, New York, Dodd, Mead, 1933.
Der Schritt hinüber, 1940.

Film Scripts

With F. Dardam, *Mädchen in Uniform* (based upon Winsloe's play *Ritter Nérestan*), [Germany], 1931; released in France as *Jeunes Filles en Uniforme* (adaptation of French text by Colette).
Jeunes filles en détresse, 1940.
Schicksal nach Wunsch, 1941.
Aiono, 1943.

*

Adaptations: *Mädchen in Uniform* (film adaptation of *Ritter Nérestan*), 1931.

Manuscript Collections: A few unpublished essays are included in the papers of Dorothy Thompson at Syracuse University Library.

Critical Sources: *Sex Variant Women in Literature; A Historical and Quantitative Survey* by Jeannette Howard Foster, New York, Vantage, 1956, 236–238; *Dorothy and Red* by Vincent Sheean, Boston, Houghton, 1963, 207–249; *Dorothy Thompson: A Legend in Her Time* by Marion K. Sanders, New York, Avon, 1974, 179–181, 188–193, 195, 200; *Gay American History: Lesbians and Gay Men in the U.S.A.* by Jonathan Katz, New York, Crowell, 1976, 556–562, 663; *The Celluloid Closet* by Vito Russo, New York, Harper, 1981, 56–58; *"I Thought People Like That Killed Themselves": Lesbians, Gay Men and Suicide* by Eric E. Rofes, San Francisco, Grey Fox Press, 1983, 11, 140–141; *Gay/Lesbian Almanac* by Jonathan Katz, New York, 1983, 470–472, 479; "From Repressive Tolerance to Erotic Liberation: 'Mädchen in Uniform'" by B. Ruby Rich, in *Re–Vision: Essays in Feminist Film Criticism,* edited by Mary Anne Doane, Patricia Mellencamp, and Linda Williams, Los Angeles, American Film Institute, 1984, 100–130; "Lesbians and Film: Some Thoughts" by Caroline Sheldon, in *Gays and Film,* revised edition edited by Richard Dyer, New York, Zoetrope, 1984, 5–26; *We Can Always Call Them Bulgarians: The Emergence of Lesbians and Gay Men on the American Stage* by Kaier Curtin, Boston, Alyson Publications, 1987, 161–168; "Distance and Desire: English Boarding School Friendships" by Martha Vicinus, in *Hidden from History: Reclaiming the Gay and Lesbian Past,* edited by Martin Bauml Duberman, Martha Vicinus, and George Chauncey, Jr., New York, Meridian, 1990, 212–229, 524; *The Gay and Lesbian Liberation Movement* by Margaret Cruikshank, New York, Routledge, 1992; "Redressing the 'Natural': The Temporary Transvestite Film" by Chris Straayer, in *Wide Angle,* January 1992, 36–54; *Vampires and Violets: Lesbians in Film* by Andrea Weiss, New York, Penguin, 1993.

*   *   *

Christa Winsloe was the enigmatic author of the novel *The Child Manuela*—the stage adaptation of which was performed both in the United States and Europe under several titles. She also received credit for the screenplay for the 1931 film version entitled *Mädchen in Uniform.* The original novel, which was not published in Germany until after the success of both film and play adaptations, is considered one of the last examples of lesbian fiction to be issued before "Nazi ascendancy wiped out homosexual literature," according to Jeannette H. Foster in her *Sex Variant Women in Literature.* The play, staged variously as *Gestern und Heute* in the original German and *Girls in Uniform* or *Children in Uniform* in English translation, was eclipsed in its U.S. productions by the popularity of the film version released to American audiences in 1932: the stage production opened the day following the announcement that the film *Mädchen in Uniform* was named Best Motion Picture of the Year by the New York film critics. Even so, some critics found it "infinitely superior" to the film, a theatrical experience "no intelligent playgoer can afford to miss."

Most of Winsloe's novel is concerned with the early life of Manuela Meinhabis in the first decades following the turn of the century—but prior to World War I. Both the play and film adaptations depart from the novel in that they begin near the novel's end, the point at which the young woman is enrolled in a boarding school catering to the daughters of the Prussian upper classes. Manuela's spartan school is run by a cold martinet who rules her teachers and pupils with military efficiency, much to the chagrin of the sensitive, passionate teenager. In the novel, Manuela has had previous infatuations with other women and girls; in the play and film, other than the untimely death of her mother little of her early history is known. Manuela is attracted to Fraulein von Bernberg, a teacher who is also the object of affection of many of her fellow pupils. During a school play, Manuela assumes a role in male costume and declares her love before the other students. According to Chris Straayer, this assumption of male privilege defies "society's hegemony," setting off a chain of events that, in both the novel and the stage adaptation, lead to the young woman's suicide.

The conclusion of the film version is at variance with Winsloe's novel, and there has been much discussion about the possible existence of two versions of the film's finale. Sources close to the making of the film recall an ending close to that of both the novel and play in the German version, rather than the more familiar one—where Manuela is saved by fellow students—in the copy distributed in France, England, and the United States. In her definitive article on the film, R. Ruby Rich cites an interview with one of the film's stars, Hertha Thiele, who recalls shooting the suicide, but says that version was scrapped before the release of the film. The significance of the film's ending as a defeat of the headmistress—who represents authoritarianism and militarism—has been especially noted by those who see the film as an indictment of the rising Nazi movement. In fact, one of the acts of Nazi propaganda minister Goebbels was to remove *Mädchen in Uniform* from circulation in Germany. Others find the film's "happy ending" a cop-out and, holding the play in higher esteem as a lesbian work than the overt anti-fascist polemic embodied in the film, see the stage drama as an early example of homosexual self-destruction following rejection—personal and political.

Of all Winsloe's work, the film version of *Mädchen in Uniform* is the most significant in its contribution to lesbian culture, not only for its content, but because of its history in the United States. An early talkie, written and directed by women, with an all women cast and crew, the film boasted a French text adaptation by Colette which, while included in the French edition of *Colette at the Movies,* is reduced to a mention in the introduction to the English translation. Censorship by—and personal agendas of—the establishment are tools which have been used to subvert positive images of lesbians and promote stereotypes in the media. By the time the film arrived in the United States, the Hays Office's censorship had cut from it all evidence of overt lesbianism that would otherwise prevent its release. According to Vito Russo, John Krimsky, who bought the film's United States distribution rights in 1932, refused to allow the film to be shown in any context that suggested it dealt with lesbianism. His estate continued to control distribution in like manner after his death in the late 1970s. The eventual release of *Mädchen in Uniform* on video-cassette made it generally accessible in other than pirated versions or showings in film festivals. Public showings from the 1980s onward finally exhibited it in a sexual-political consort: Program notes from these festivals by scholarly critics have restored the work to a position central to the study of women in the cinema.

The film is seen as a precursor to a number of lesbian boarding-school-genre novels and plays that would be filmed and offered in America as censorship guidelines relaxed with the industry's threat from television. *Olivia* (France, 1950), *Therese and Isabelle* (Germany, 1968), *The Children's Hour* (United States, 1961), *Picnic at Hanging Rock* (Australia, c. 1975), and a 1958 English-dubbed German technicolor remake of *Mädchen in Uniform* itself were all permitted because they allowed interpretation on a schoolgirl crush level and were safe from the lesbian sexual stereotype. Rich makes the strongest case for *Mädchen in Uniforms'* unique value to the culture: "It is the film revival most key to establishing a history of lesbian cinema." She sees its importance as only truly understood when the film is viewed as a lesbian text—a film with lesbian sexuality as its central subject. Interpretation and dialogue continue. A group of leather lesbians viewing the video version at a benefit in the early 1990s hailed it as a lost S/M classic, while an art house was also showing it in the context of an exploration of fascism to feminism in women's films.

Winsloe would create an overt lesbian in the character of Fax in her novel *Girl Alone,* published in England as *Life Begins.* Set in prewar Munich, Fax is passionately in love with a young sculpture student named Eva-Maria who rooms with her. There are other lesbian characters in the book, and each is portrayed matter-of-factly as part of the milieu in which she moves. Eva-Marie, the novel's protagonist, is just about to succumb to her roommate's attentions when Fax abruptly takes another woman lover. Disillusioned, the young sculptress leaves the Bohemian life to seek spiritual answers in Assisi, returning to throw herself into her art and "to begin to live."

Jacket notes on the 1936 publication of *Girl Alone* describe Winsloe as the daughter of a high German officer who married a Hungarian Baron. "Under the name of the Baroness Hatvany, she is well known in European art circles for her sculpture, which has received many prizes in notable exhibitions throughout the Continent." However, a more detailed and most-often quoted source of information about Winsloe is Vincent Sheean's biography of novelist Sinclair Lewis and his wife Dorothy Thompson, *Dorothy and Red.* Thompson, a noted foreign correspondent, was expelled from Germany by Hitler in 1934, and is considered by many to have been one of the best political journalists of the prewar period. In the chapter entitled "A Rather Strange Interlude," Sheean draws heavily from edited portions of Thompson's diaries to document her love affair with Winsloe. In 1933, their romance carried them from Vienna to Portofina where Winsloe had a house in an area that became a gathering point for German intelligentsia in exile from the Nazis. Later, the two women traveled to Munich and then to America where they spent late spring at Thompson's home in Vermont, and returned to Europe in midsummer. Both Winsloe and Thompson would divorce—Thompson and Lewis separated in 1937, and Sheean's biography closes with their divorce in 1942.

Marion Sanders picks up the later connection between Winsloe and the famous journalist in her biography *Dorothy Thompson: A Legend in Her Time,* noting that Winsloe was murdered in the South of France in June 1944. Though Winsloe's killer was discovered, Thompson was unsuccessful in unearthing the full story of the circumstances surrounding Winsloe's death and always assumed her friend was assassinated for her outspoken antifascist stance. After her successes in the 1930s, Winsloe would continued to write, though little else was published, until her death. There are a few unpublished essays of hers among Thompson's papers at Syracuse University Library.

—*Marie J. Kuda*

WINTERSON, Jeanette. British novelist and author of short stories and nonfiction. Born in Lancashire, 27 August 1959. Educated at St. Catherine's College, Oxford, M.A. 1981. Held a variety of jobs including ice-cream van driver, make-up artist in a funeral parlour, and domestic assistant in a mental hospital. **Recipient:** Publishing for People award, Whitbread award for first novel, and Booksellers Association of Great Britain and Ireland award, all 1985; John Llewellyn Rhys Memorial prize for fiction, 1987; American Academy of Arts and Letters' E. M. Forster Award

1989; British Association of Film and Television Arts award, Prix Italia, FIPA d'argent (Cannes), and Ace award for best drama, all 1991. Agent: International Creative Management, 40 West 57th Street, New York, New York 10019, U.S.A.

WRITINGS

Novels

Oranges Are Not the Only Fruit. London, Pandora Press, 1985; New York, Atlantic Monthly Press, 1987.
The Passion. London, Bloomsbury, 1987; New York, Atlantic Monthly Press, 1988.
Sexing the Cherry. London, Bloomsbury, 1989; New York, Knopf, 1991.
Written on the Body. London, J. Cape, 1992; New York, Knopf, 1993.

Uncollected Short Stories

"Orion," in *Winter's Tales 4* (new series), edited by Robin Baird–Smith. London, Constable, and New York, St. Martin's Press, 1988.

Screenplays

Oranges Are Not the Only Fruit (television adaptation of her novel), 1990.
Great Moments in Aviation. London, BBC Enterprises/Miramax, 1993.

Other

Fit for the Future: The Guide for Women Who Want to Live Well. London, Pandora Press, 1980.
Boating for Beginners, illustrations by Paula Youens. London, Methuen, 1985.
Editor, *Passion Fruit: Romantic Fiction with a Twist.* London, Pandora Press, 1986.

*

Critical Sources: "With the Lord in Wigan" by Roz Kaveney, in *Times Literary Supplement,* 22 March 1985, 326; "... and Before" by Emma Fisher, in *Times Literary Supplement,* 1 November 1985, 228; "Between Two Worlds" by Sarah Gold, in *Washington Post Book World,* 1 October 1987; "Rollicking 'Oranges' Uses Its Daring Humor to Get Religion" by Joseph Olshan, in *Chicago Tribune,* 8 November 1987, 8; review by Ursula Hegi of *Oranges Are Not the Only Fruit,* in *New York Times Book Review,* 8 November 1987, 26; "Sating a Passion for High Romance" by Alan Cheuse, in *Chicago Tribune,* 5 July 1988; *The Safe Sea of Women: Lesbian Fiction, 1969–1989* by Bonnie Zimmerman, Boston, Beacon Press, 1990; review by Nancy Wigston of *Sexing the Cherry,* in *Toronto Globe and Mail,* 31 March 1990; "A Journey through Time, Space and Imagination" by Michiko Kakutani, in *New York Times,* 27 April 1990; review by Richard Eder of *Sexing the Cherry,* in *Atlantic

Monthly,* 3 May 1990; "A Cornucopia of Earthy Delights" by Michael Dirda, in *Washington Post Book World,* 13 May 1990, 9; "Fingers in the Fruit Basket: A Feminist Reading of *Oranges Are Not the Only Fruit*" by Rebecca O'Rourke, in *Feminist Criticism: Theory and Practice,* edited by Susan Sellers, University of Toronto Press, 1991, 57–69.

Jeannette Winterson comments: "I am not interested in gay/lesbian literature *for its own sake.* I am interested in literature. I am an experimental writer and a sophisticated one. My personal life is *not* a way into my work and never has been."

*   *   *

Jeannette Winterson entered the English literary scene in 1985 with an exuberant coming of age story, *Oranges Are Not the Only Fruit.* The novel's heroine, Jeannette (no surname is given), brings immediately to mind Molly Bolt of Rita Mae Brown's *Rubyfruit Jungle.* Unlike many protagonists in coming out narratives, Jeannette is relatively untroubled by her same sex romantic and sexual desires; what bothers her is how others interpret these feelings. When challenged in front of her Pentecostal congregation about her adolescent love for Melanie, Jeannette counters, "To the pure all things are pure. It's you not us." Like Molly Bolt, Jeannette is illegitimate and adopted, "tainted" from birth with the mark of illicit sexual desire, signifying her position both as outsider and as independent spirit. Both heroines have strong–minded adoptive mothers and weak–willed fathers, a pattern common to lesbian novels. The daughter's strong will is equal to the mother's and conflicts with the mother's need to dominate and to control the sexuality of the incipient lesbian. Eventually, however, the lesbian daughter learns to appreciate the strength, even the idiosyncrasy of the mother which allows her to function in a patriarchal system.

Oranges Are Not the Only Fruit follows a tradition in lesbian autobiographical novels in which a protagonist, whose life highly mirrors the author's, recounts her coming to a lesbian identity. Jeannette in *Oranges Are Not the Only Fruit* is named after the author and shares many of the same experiences, growing up in the Midlands within a strict religious tradition, working in a funeral parlor, and as an ice cream truck driver. Like Audre Lorde's *Zami,* however, *Oranges Are Not the Only Fruit* invites the reader to see the autobiographical story *as a story,* a myth of the self. Winterson overlays the novel with both biblical and folk tale references; the eight chapters of *Oranges* are named after the first eight books of the Old Testament, while feminist fairy tales interrupt the linear flow of the narrative.

Oranges Are Not the Only Fruit places Winterson within a lesbian literary tradition; but to what extent her first or later novels are "lesbian" has been disputed from the outset. For example, in her article "Fingers in the Fruit Basket: A Feminist Reading of *Oranges Are Not the Only Fruit,*" published in *Feminist Criticism: Theory and Practice,* Rebecca O'Rourke repeats the words of one of her students who "was also quite clear that it wasn't a lesbian book ... that lesbian issues were not at its heart and it was not addressed primarily to a lesbian readership." Though Winterson may not place lesbian identity development in the thematic foreground, she does make Jeannette's same sex–attraction central to other themes which O'Rourke calls primary in the novel: "religion, the nature of mothering, the nature of ambition."

Winterson has become a critical success and is noted for the wealth of classical, mythical, folk, and historical references contained in her short, clever, philosophically challenging novels. While retaining many lesbian signifiers within her body of references, Winterson fragments both the characters and the narrative, becoming one of the leading post–modern—or even "queer"—lesbian writers. The element of fairy or morality tale grows within the narrative, and in later novels, history, briefly explicated in *Oranges Are Not the Only Fruit*, becomes a central theme.

A young French villager, Henri, who becomes cook to Napoleon, and a beautiful, young, red–haired Venetian woman named Villanelle, alternately narrate Winterson's 1987 novel, *The Passion*. Villanelle's grand passion is an unnamed aristocratic woman, while Henri's is first the myth of Napoleon, then Villanelle. Though one of the novel's grand obsessions is of one female character for another, Winterson treats same–sex love casually. When Villanelle, working at the casino dressed as a young man, first meets the female object of her desire she states, "I am pragmatic about love and have taken my pleasure with both men and women but I have never needed a guard for my heart." Both *The Passion* and her later novel, 1992's *Written on the Body*, reveal that Winterson is more interested in describing the process and truths of love, obsession, and passion, than in justifying or explicating same–sex attraction.

Sexing the Cherry concerns even more tangentially questions of gay and lesbian identity. Though the novel is filled with feminist retellings of folk tales and classical myths, some with newly lesbian outcomes, its alternating, time–travelling narrators are the desexualized foundling, Jordan, and his enormous Rabelaisian adoptive mother, Dog–Woman. Winterson depicts sex, especially the hypocrisy of sex, hilariously in her third novel, but same–sex sexuality is not a prevalent theme.

From her discourse on love in *Written on the Body*, Winterson removes some of the familiarity of gendered and sexed roles in lovemaking. All characters save for the narrator are identified by sex, but by refusing to provide the narrator with a gender, Winterson allows the reader of any sexuality to read his or her own longing into the story. Because Winterson is a woman and the primary object of desire in the novel is also a woman, the reader can read the novel as lesbian. However, Winterson's clear invitation to separate questions of gender from love and desire would certainly redefine traditional definitions of lesbian writing. It is debatable whether *Written on the Body* meets even the expanded reading of lesbian literature which Bonnie Zimmerman, writing about *Oranges Are Not the Only Fruit* in her book, *The Safe Sea of Women*, describes as "express[ing] general experiences and desires through the 'slant' given by a lesbian point of view." However, no matter what the number of exclusively lesbian characters Winterson writes into her texts, she likely will continue to be read as a lesbian novelist by many lesbian critics. Her use of same–sex or ungendered eroticism, homophilic references, and feminist or lesbian sensibility, while not focusing solely on questions of lesbian identity and experience, certainly would seem to invite a lesbian reading.

—*Terry L. Allison*

WITTIG, Monique. French novelist. Born in Alsace, 1935 (some sources say 1936); immigrated to the United States in 1976; daughter of poet Henri Dubois. Educated at Sorbonne, University of Paris. Worked for Biblioteque Nationale; proofreader for Editions de Minuit, 1964; lecturer. **Recipient:** Prix Medicis, 1964.

WRITINGS

Novels

L'Opoponax. Paris, Editions de Minuit, 1964; translated by Helen Weaver as *The Opopopnax*, New York, Simon & Schuster, 1966.
Les Guérillères. Paris, Editions de Minuit, 1969; translated by David Le Vay, New York, Viking, 1971.
Le Corps lesbien. Paris, Editions de Minuit, 1973; translated by David Le Vay as *The Lesbian Body*, New York, Morrow, 1975.
Virgile, non. Paris, Editions de Minuit, 1985; translated by David Le Vay and Margaret Crosland as *Across the Acheron*, London, P. Owen, 1987.

Other

With Sande Zeig, *Brouillon pour un dictionnaire des amantes*. Paris, Grasset, 1976; translated as *Lesbian Peoples: Material for a Dictionary*, New York, Avon, 1979.
"Paradigm" (essay), in *Homosexualties and French Literature*, edited by Elaine Marks and George Stambolian. Ithaca, New York, Cornell University Press, 1979.
With Sande Zeig, *Le Voyage sans fin* (play; translation produced as *The Constant Journey*, Plainfield, Vermont, 1984). Paris, Vlasta, 1985.
The Straight Mind, and Other Essays. Boston, Beacon Press, 1992.

*

Critical Sources: "A Cosmogony of O: Wittig's *Les Guérillères*" by Erica Ostrovsky, in *Twentieth Century French Fiction*, edited by George Stambolian, New Brunswick, Rutgers University Press, 1975; *Women of Iron and Velvet* by Margaret Crosland, New York, Taplinger, 1976; "Language and the Vision of a Lesbian–Feminist Utopia in Wittig's *Les Guérillères*," in *Frontiers*, spring/summer 1981; "The Text as Body/Politics: An Appreciation of Monique Wittig's Writings in Context" by Hélène Vivienne Wenzel, in *Feminist Studies* (New York), summer 1981, 264–87; "Amazons and Mothers? Monique Wittig, Hélène Cixous and Theories of Women's Writing" by Diane Griffin Crowder, in *Contemporary Literature*, summer 1983; "Language and Childhood: *L'Opoponax* by Monique Wittig" by Jean H. Duffy, in *Forum for Modern Language Studies*, October 1983; "Women and Language in *Les Guérillères* by Monique Wittig," in *Stanford French Review*, winter 1983; "Monique Wittig" by Jean H. Duffy, in *Beyond the Nouveau Roman: Essays on the Contemporary French Novel*, edited by Michael Tilby, New York, Berg/St. Martin's Press, 1990, 201–228; *Vlasta*, Number 4, 1985 (special Monique Wittig issue); "Guérillères Warfare: Monique Witting, Straight Shooter" by Cindy Patton, in *Village Voice*, 30 June 1992.

French novelist and feminist theorist Monique Wittig has always gone well beyond the feat of explicitly portraying lesbians and lesbianism in her text; she has devised, in fact, a theory of lesbianism as the route to social revolution that has largely shaped the thinking of French and American radical lesbian feminists. Writing at the same time that a number of other French women intellectuals turned to language as a possible source for change in women's lives, Wittig both shared in what has been called French feminism and rebelled against the beliefs of many of her peers; her work has since become central to debates about women's liberation and "queer theory."

The student revolts that shook Paris in 1968 created upheaval across French culture and sparked a feminist movement among French women. Mostly students and intellectuals, many of the women claimed that male dominance, enforced in every aspect of culture, controlled women most powerfully through language. Consequently, they claimed, women could only begin to free themselves by using language in radical ways. Wittig emerged as one of the strongest proponents of this philosophy, expanding the field for rebellion from gender alone to sexuality, as well. Each of her novels and all of her essays, in one way or another, take the radical use of language as their subject. Her first novel, *The Opoponax*, began this project, but subtly enough that many critics overlooked the radical lesbianism in the story of a girl's boarding–school romance. By 1969, however, when *Les Guérillères* first appeared, Wittig's political and theoretical agenda was unavoidably apparent.

Like most of her later texts, *Les Guérillères* borrowed its form from the "masterpieces" of Western literature. In this case, the epic conventions of *The Aeneid*—Virgil's classical poem about the origins of Rome—served as a starting point for Wittig's tale of the overthrow of patriarchy by armies of revolutionaries known only as *guérillères* and *elles*. (The first term, which Wittig created, is a feminized form of the French for *guerillas*.) Wittig wanted to redefine the second (the third–person, plural, feminine pronoun in French) as a universal designation, much as English speakers use *he* to refer to men and women. Wittig sought a revolution in language on two levels at once: first, in the use of a classical text for decidedly non–classical purposes, and second, in the radical disruption of conventions of language. *The Lesbian Body*, issued in France in 1973 as *Le Corps Lesbien*, reinterprets the "Song of Songs"—an ancient love poem associated with the Bible—as a celebration of lesbian desire. *Across the Acheron*, published in French as *Virgil, non*, retells the story of Dante's *Divine Comedy* from the perspective of a lesbian heroine visiting the circles of hell (which are now peopled by heterosexual men and women).

While Wittig developed her theories of radical lesbianism and language, several heterosexual women intellectuals, including Hélène Cixous, developed a theory and a style of writing that became known as *écriture féminine*. The term translates loosely as "writing from the body"—from, specifically, the female body—and insists that a particular style will be produced by the writer with a woman's body. Meant to counter the dominance of styles produced by centuries of male writers, *écriture féminine* celebrated an abstraction called *woman*. Wittig, however, saw the danger of continuing to equate women with their bodies, no matter how positive the intention. In place of this, Wittig developed her notion of "the lesbian" as the most significant revolutionary category. Consequently, each of her major literary works consistently takes a lesbian or an army of lesbians as its protagonist, leaving the story of *woman* aside or presenting it as the opposite of lesbianism.

"[I]t would be incorrect to say that lesbians associate, make love, live with women, for 'woman' has meaning only in heterosexual systems of thought and heterosexual economic systems. Lesbians are not women." With these words from an essay called "The Straight Mind," Wittig challenges the fundamental assumptions of liberal feminism and designates a far more radical purpose for her own work. Her desire to distinguish between *lesbian* and *woman* is based on the belief that liberal feminism cannot do enough to liberate women. Wittig argues, both in her novels and in an extensive collection of essays, that the very word *woman* must be discarded. In her 1985 essay "The Mark of Gender," Wittig declares that "[women] is one of those gender–marked words ... which I never use in French. For me it is the equivalent of *slave*, and, in fact, I have opposed its use whenever possible."

In order to disrupt this system of slavery, a new term—one that is neither *man* nor *woman*—must emerge. Wittig suggests that language is just the place to imagine such a term. "The only thing to do," she says in the preface to *The Straight Mind, and Other Essays*, "is to stand on one's own feet as an escapee, a fugitive slave, a lesbian." *Les Guérillères* and *The Lesbian Body* each imagine a single step in that process, the first describing the revolution itself, the second trying to envision the utopia that will follow that revolution. But, as Wittig explains in "The Mark of Gender," even that image of utopia is a kind of revolution: "'I' has become so powerful in *The Lesbian Body* that it can attack the heroes of love, and lesbianize them, lesbianize the symbols, lesbianize the gods and the goddesses, lesbianize the men and the women." Here, as in all of Wittig's work, her use of the term "lesbian" is the lever that she uses to pry apart a social structure that she perceives to be sexist and heterosexist. In this sense her lesbianism is not only explicit in her work, but is its most significant quality.

—*Ondine E. Le Blanc*

———

WOOLF, (Adeline) Virginia. British publisher, novelist, essayist, diarist, and author of short fiction. Born in London, 25 January 1882; daughter of the writer Sir Leslie Stephen. Self–educated. Married Leonard Woolf in 1912 (died, 1969). Founder, with brother Thoby Stephen, of *Hyde Park Gate News* (a weekly paper), 1891–95; Morley College, London, England, instructor in English, c. 1905–07; founder and operator of Hogarth Press with husband, beginning 1917. Also wrote essays under name Virginia Stephen. **Recipient:** Prix *Feminina* from *Feminina* and *Vie Heureuse* reviews, 1928. *Committed suicide by drowning in the Ouse River, Lewes, Sussex, 28 March 1941.*

WRITINGS

Novels

The Voyage Out. London, Duckworth, 1915; revised, New York, Doran, 1920.
Night and Day. London, Duckworth, 1919; New York, Doran, 1920.
Jacob's Room. Richmond, Hogarth, 1922; New York, Harcourt, 1923.

Mrs. Dalloway. London, Hogarth, and New York, Harcourt, 1925.
To the Lighthouse. London, Hogarth, and New York, Harcourt, 1927.
Orlando: A Biography. London, Hogarth, and New York, Crosby Gaige, 1928.
The Waves. London, Hogarth, and New York, Harcourt, 1931.
The Years. London, Hogarth, and New York, Harcourt, 1937.
Between the Acts. London, Hogarth, and New York, Harcourt, 1941.

Short Stories

Two Stories Written and Printed by Virginia Woolf and L. S. Woolf. Richmond, Hogarth, 1917; story by Virginia Woolf published separately as *The Mark on the Wall,* Richmond, Hogarth, 1919.
Kew Gardens. Richmond, Hogarth, 1919; Folcroft, Pennsylvania, Folcroft Press, 1969.
Monday or Tuesday. London, Duckworth, 1919; New York, Doran, 1920.
A Haunted House, and Other Short Stories. London, Hogarth, 1943; New York, Harcourt, 1944.
The Complete Shorter Fiction of Virginia Woolf, edited by Susan Dick. New York, Harcourt, 1985.

Essays and Criticism

Mr. Bennett and Mrs. Brown. London, Hogarth, 1924; Folcroft, Pennsylvania, Folcroft Press, 1977.
The Common Reader. London, Hogarth, and New York, Harcourt, 1925.
A Room of One's Own. London, Hogarth, and New York, Harcourt, 1929.
The Common Reader, Second Series. London, Hogarth, 1932; as *The Second Common Reader,* New York, Harcourt, 1932.
Three Guineas. London, Hogarth, and New York, Harcourt, 1938.
The Death of the Moth, and Other Essays. New York, Harcourt, 1941; London, Hogarth, 1942.
The Moment, and Other Essays. London, Hogarth, 1947; New York, Harcourt, 1948.
The Captain's Death Bed, and Other Essays. London, Hogarth, and New York, Harcourt, 1950.
Granite and Rainbow. London, Hogarth, and New York, Harcourt, 1958.
Contemporary Writers. London, Hogarth, 1965; New York, Harcourt, 1966.
Collected Essays (four volumes). London, Hogarth, 1966–67; New York, Harcourt, 1967.
The London Scene: Five Essays. New York, F. Hallman, 1975.
Moments of Being (autobiographical essays), edited by Jeanne Schulkind. London, Chatto & Windus, 1976; New York, Harcourt, 1978.
Books and Portraits: Some Further Selections from the Literary and Biographical Writings of Virginia Woolf, edited by Mary Lyon. London, Hogarth, 1977; New York, Harcourt, 1978.
Women and Writing. London, Women's Press, 1979; edited by Michéle Barrett, New York, Harcourt, 1980.
The Essays of Virginia Woolf, edited by Andrew McNeillie. New York, Harcourt, 1986.

The Letters of Virginia Woolf Series

Volume 1: *The Flight of the Mind, 1888–1912,* edited by Nigel Nicolson and Joanne Trautmann. London, Hogarth, 1975; as *The Letters of Virginia Woolf,* Volume 1: *1888–1912,* New York, Harcourt, 1975.
Volume 2: *The Question of Things Happening, 1912–1922,* edited by Nigel Nicolson and Joan Trautmann. London, Hogarth, 1976; as *The Letters of Virginia Woolf,* Volume 2: *1912–1922,* New York, Harcourt, 1976.
Volume 3: *A Change of Perspective, 1923–28,* edited by Nigel Nicolson and Joan Trautmann. London, Hogarth, 1977; as *The Letters of Virginia Woolf,* Volume 3: *1923–1928,* New York, Harcourt, 1978.
Volume 4: *A Reflection of the Other Person, 1929–1931,* edited by Nigel Nicolson and Joan Trautmann. London, Hogarth, 1978; as *The Letters of Virginia Woolf,* Volume 4: *1929–1931,* New York, Harcourt, 1979.
Volume 5: *The Sickle Side of the Moon, 1932–1935,* edited by Nigel Nicolson and Joan Trautmann. London, Hogarth, 1979; as *The Letters of Virginia Woolf,* Volume 5: *1932–1935,* New York, Harcourt, 1979.
Volume 6: *Leave the Letters Till We're Dead, 1936–1941,* edited by Nigel Nicolson and Joan Trautmann. London, Hogarth, 1980; as *The Letters of Virginia Woolf,* Volume 6: *1936–1941,* New York, Harcourt, 1980.

Other Collected Letters

Virginia Woolf and Lytton Strachey: Letters, edited by Leonard Woolf and James Strachey. New York, Harcourt, 1956.
The Hogarth Letters. London, Chatto & Windus, 1985.

Other

Street Haunting. San Francisco, Westgate Press, 1930.
On Being Ill. London, Hogarth, 1930.
Beau Brummell. New York, Rimington & Hooper, 1930.
A Letter to a Young Poet. London, Hogarth, 1932; Folcroft, Pennsylvania, Folcroft Press, 1975.
Flush, A Biography. London, Hogarth, and New York, Harcourt, 1933.
Walter Sickert: A Conversation. London, Hogarth, 1934; Folcroft, Pennsylvania, Folcroft Press, 1970.
Reviewing. London, Hogarth, 1939; Folcroft, Pennsylvania, Folcroft Press, 1969.
Roger Fry: A Biography. London, Hogarth, and New York, Harcourt, 1940.
A Writer's Diary: Being Extracts from the Diary of Virginia Woolf, edited by Leonard Woolf. London, Hogarth, 1953; New York, Harcourt, 1954.
Hours in a Library. New York, Harcourt, 1958.
Nurse Lugton's Golden Thimble. London, Hogarth, 1966.
Mrs. Dalloway's Party: A Short Sequence, edited by Stella McNichol. London, Hogarth, 1973; New York, Harcourt, 1975.
The Waves: The Two Holograph Drafts, transcribed and edited by John W. Graham. Toronto and Buffalo, University of Toronto Press, 1976.
Freshwater: A Comedy, edited by Lucio P. Ruotolo, illustrations by Loretta Trezzo. New York, Harcourt, 1976.

The Diary of Virginia Woolf, edited by Anne Olivier Bell, Volume 1: *1915–1919;* London, Hogarth, 1977; New York, Harcourt, 1979; Volume 2: *1920–1924,* London, Hogarth, and New York, Harcourt, 1978; Volume 3: *1925–1930,* London, Hogarth, and New York, Harcourt, 1980; Volume 4: *1931–1935,* London, Hogarth, and New York, Harcourt, 1982.

The Pargiters: The Novel–Essay Portion of "The Years," edited by Mitchell A. Leaska. New York Public Library, 1977.

Rupert Brooke. Burford, England, Cygnet Press, 1978.

Virginia Woolf's Reading Notebooks, edited by Brenda R. Silver. Princeton, New Jersey, and Guildford, Surrey, Princeton University Press, 1982.

Melymbrosia: An Early Version of "The Voyage Out," edited by Louise A. DeSalvo. New York, New York Public Library, 1982.

The Virginia Woolf Reader. San Diego, Harcourt, 1984.

A Passionate Apprentice. London, Hogarth, and San Diego, Harcourt, 1990.

Nurse Lugton's Curtain. San Diego, Harcourt, 1991.

Paper Darts. London, Collins & Brown, 1991.

*

Manuscript Collections: Henry W. and Albert A. Berg Collection of English and American Literature, New York Public Library; Charleston Papers, King's College, Cambridge; Monk's House Papers, University of Sussex Library; Washington State University's Library at Pullman, Washington; University of Texas at Austin.

Biography: *Beginning Again: An Autobiography of the Years 1911 to 1918* by Leonard Woolf, New York, Harcourt, 1964; *All the Way: An Autobiography of the Years 1919 to 1939* by Leonard Woolf, New York, Harcourt, 1967; *The Journey Not the Arrival Matters: An Autobiography of the Years 1939 to 1969* by Leonard Woolf, New York, Harcourt, 1970; *Virginia Woolf: A Biography* by Quentin Bell, New York, Harcourt, 1972; *The Jessamy Brides: The Friendship of Virginia Woolf and Vita Sackville West* by Joan Trautmann, University Park, Pennsylvania, Pennsylvania State Studies, 1973; *Virginia Woolf and Her World* by John Lehmann, New York, Harcourt, 1975; *A Marriage of the Minds* by George Spater and Ian Parsons, New York, Harcourt, 1977; *Woman of Letters: A Life of Virginia Woolf,* New York, Oxford University Press, 1978; *Virginia Woolf: A Writer's Life* by Lyndall Gordon, Oxford, Oxford University Press, 1984; *Virginia Woolf: Life and London; A Biography of Place* by Jean Moorcroft Wilson, New York, Norton, 1988.

Bibliography: *Virginia Woolf: An Annotated Bibliography of Criticism,* by Robin Majumdar, New York and London, Garland, 1976; *A Bibliography of Virginia Woolf* by B. J. Kirkpatrick, Oxford, Clarendon Press, 1980.

Critical Sources: *The Well of Loneliness* by Radclyffe Hall, New York, Covici–Friede, 1928; *Mimesis: The Representation of Reality in Western Literature* by Erich Auerbach, translation by Willard R. Trask, Princeton, Princeton University Press, 1953; *Modern Fiction Studies,* autumn, 1972 (special Virginia Woolf issue); *Virginia Woolf and the Androgynous Vision* by Nancy Topping Bazin, New Brunswick, New Jersey, Rutgers University Press, 1973; *Toward a Recognition of Androgyny* by Carol G. Heilbrun, New York, Knopf, 1973; *Portrait of a Marriage* by Nigel Nicholson, New York,

Anthenaeum, 1973; *Virginia Woolf: A Critical Reading* by Avrom Fleishman, Baltimore, Johns Hopkins University Press, 1975; *The Bloomsbury Group: A Collection of Memoirs, Commentary, and Criticism* by S. P. Rosenbaum, Toronto, University of Toronto Press, 1975; *Bulletin of the New York Library,* winter, 1977 (special Virginia Woolf issue); *Virginia Woolf: Sources of Madness and Art* by Jean O. Love, Berkeley and London, University of California Press, 1977; *Bloomsbury: A House of Lions* by Leon Edel, Philadelphia and New York, Lippincott, 1979; *Continuing Presences: Virginia Woolf's Use of Literary Allusion* by Beverly Ann Schlack, University Park, Pennsylvania State University Press, 1979; *Virginia Woolf: Revaluation and Continuity,* edited by Ralph Freedman, Berkeley and London, University of California Press, 1980; *The Absent Father: Virginia Woolf and Walter Pater* by Perry Meisel, New Haven and London, Yale University Press, 1980; *Surpassing the Love of Men: Romantic Friendship and Love between Women from the Renaissance to the Present* by Lillian Faderman, New York, Morrow, 1981; *New Feminist Essays on Virginia Woolf,* edited by Jane Marcus, Lincoln, University of Nebraska Press, 1981; *All That Summer She Was Mad* by Stephen Trombley, New York, Continuum, 1982; *Virginia Woolf's Literary Sources and Allusions: A Guide to the Essays* by Elizabeth Steele, New York and London, Garland, 1983; *Virginia Woolf: A Guide to Research* by Thomas Jackson Rice, New York and London, Garland, 1984; "Liberty, Sorority, Misogyny," "Taking the Bull by the Udders: Sexual Difference in Virginia Woolf—A Conspiracy Theory," and "Sapphistry: Narration as Lesbian Seduction in *A Room of One's Own*" by Jane Marcus, in *Virginia Woolf and the Languages of Patriarchy,* Bloomington, Indiana University Press, 1987, 75–95, 136–62, and 163–87; "'If I Saw You Would You Kiss Me?': Sapphism and the Subversiveness of Virginia Woolf's *Orlando*" by Sherron E. Knopp, in *PMLA,* January 1988, 23–34; *Who Killed Virginia Woolf?: A Psychobiography* by Alma Halbert Bond, Human Sciences Press, 1989; *Virginia Woolf: The Impact of Childhood Sexual Abuse on Her Life and Work* by Louise A. DeSalvo, Boston, Beacon Press, 1989; "Sexual Identity and *A Room of One's Own:* 'Secret Economies' in Virginia Woolf's Feminist Discourse" by Ellen Bayuk Rosenman, in *Signs: Journal of Women in Culture and Society,* spring 1989, 634–650.

*   *   *

Virginia Woolf loved women, emotionally and physically. She neither lived nor wrote from a traditional point of view, so to impose a rigid grid of heterosexual interpretation upon her life and her texts is to leave undeveloped their rich homoerotic texture. For many years, Woolf biographers and scholars did just that, even though relationships with women were central to the author's life and texts. In many critical studies, Woolf's lesbian interactions were interpreted as mere friendships, thus denying their erotic implications. Emphasis on her obsession with her mother, her breakdowns, and her avant–garde lifestyle focused much critical attention on her pathologies, her need for care–taking by others, and her eventual suicide.

Certain facts concerning Woolf's sexuality, in keeping with the bohemian picture of a writer, could not be suppressed—her lesbian liaison with Vita Sackville–West, her close relationships with women throughout her lifetime, her presumed platonic marriage to Leonard Woolf, and the absence of any male romantic figures in her writings.

These aspects of her life were employed to depict Woolf as uninterested in a physical relationship, as a child in search of her mother, as a dysfunctional wife, or as an asexual creature. And, because much biographical information about Woolf came from family members or others who had a vested interest in protecting individual reputations, an accurate representation of the author could not emerge.

Woolf's preference for female protectors and confidants is well documented. She declared her love for women openly in a letter written in 1930: "But I am the most passionate about women. Take away my affections and I should be like sea weed out of water; like the shell of a crab, like a husk. All my entrails, light, marrow, juice, pulp would be gone. I should be blown into the first puddle and drown.... It is true that I only want to show off to women. Women alone stir my imagination." Involvements with Madge Vaughan and Violet Dickinson preceded Woolf's best–known relationship, with Vita Sackville–West; a later liaison developed between the author and Dame Ethel Smyth. As Jane Marcus points out in *Virginia Woolf and the Languages of Patriarchy*, in these friendships Woolf was "never seduced, betrayed, or abandoned."

The experiences of Woolf's personal life are reflected in the complex expression of homoeroticism found in her works. Marcus stresses that "female heterosexuality is most often represented in Woolf's fiction as victimization or colonization." Woolf introduced the homoerotic element in *Mrs. Dalloway* through the relationship of Clarissa Dalloway and Sally Seton, in *Between the Acts* through Miss LaTrobe, the lesbian artist, and in *A Room of One's Own* through the mysterious relationship of the scientists, Chloe and Olivia. Other lesbian narratives can be identified in works such as *To the Lighthouse* (most specifically in the relationship between Lily Briscoe and Mrs. Ramsay), *Orlando* (in the gender metamorphosis of the main character), and *The Pargiters*.

Woolf's inclusion of lesbianism in her texts was sometimes buried beneath one or more heterosexual plots and other times exhibited as a main theme. Homoerotic pairings were often juxtaposed with dysfunctional male/female dyads, and can be read as constructions of alternative relationships—relationships which lie outside of heterosexual structures. Aware of the prohibitions against overt homosexuality during the time in which she lived, Woolf often encoded, or disguised, her lesbian narratives. In a letter to Vita Sackville–West, the author made reference to "Moments of Being: 'Slater's Pins Have No Points,'" a short story with a lesbian sub plot. She wrote, "Sixty pounds just received from America for my little Sapphist story of which the Editor has not seen the point, though he's been looking for it in the Adirondacks." Woolf clearly found both irony and delight in the fact that the encoded lesbian narrative remained undiscovered by the American editor.

Woolf was keenly aware of the dangers of being too obviously a sapphist. Citing an early fragment of *A Room of One's Own*, Marcus observes that after the words "Chloe liked Olivia," the author wrote: "The words covered the bottom of the page: the pages had stuck. While fumbling to open them there flashed into my mind the inevitable policeman ... the order to attend the Court; the dreary waiting; the Magistrate coming in with a little bow." These latter references describe Radclyffe Hall's obscenity trial over the novel *The Well of Loneliness*. Banned by English courts, the book significantly affected novelists' freedom to write about lesbianism. At one point, Woolf had planned to testify at the trial; even without this testimony, she was aware of the suit's possible implications.

As Ellen Bayuk Rosenman notes in *Signs: Journal of Women in Culture and Society*, Woolf had no workable cultural definition of lesbianism that bore resemblance to her own same–sex relationships. "No understanding of lesbianism existed that explained her personal relationship with Sackville–West, as private experience and public understandings shared no common ground," Rosenman writes. Neither the depiction of Stephen Cordon in Radclyffe Hall's novel nor the prevailing interpretations of lesbianism by sexologists Havelock Ellis and Richard von Kraft–Ebing seemed appropriate representations of what Woolf experienced. Rosenman concludes that it is not surprising that, under these circumstances, Woolf did not openly—or at times even positively—portray lesbian experience.

In *PMLA*, Sherron Knopp emphasizes Woolf's awareness of the homophobic time in which she lived, as well as the author's disassociation from lesbian definitions of the day. Knopp references a passage from *Orlando* as proof that Woolf understood the penalties for sapphism: "For she was extremely doubtful whether, if the spirit [of the age] had examined the contents of her mind carefully, it would not have found something highly contraband for which she would have had to pay the full fine. She had only escaped by the skin of her teeth." As Knopp alleges, "The examination [that] Orlando passes 'by the skin of her teeth' could not be plainer, and *The Well of Loneliness* provided a timely illustration of the 'full fine' one could expect to pay for *not* passing."

Woolf nonetheless continued to inscribe homoerotic desire as she understood it in her works, bringing "buried things to light and [making] one wonder what need there had been to bury them" as she insists in *A Room of One's Own*. Her value to lesbian and gay history, as well as literary production, lies then in her repeated lesbian plots and subplots, and in her personal struggle to express the experiences of her own life in her texts. That Woolf left us a trail of these experiences in her own words, in her diaries and letters, and in her fiction and nonfiction, is evidence of the importance that lesbian relationships had in her life.

—*Pamela J. Olano*

Y-Z

YOUNG, Philip. *See* STEWARD, Samuel M(orris).

———

YOURCENAR, Marguerite. Belgian–born American and French novelist, poet, essayist, and translator. Born Marguerite de Crayencour in Brussels, 8 June 1903; immigrated to United States, naturalized U.S. citizen, 1947; French citizenship restored, 1980. Educated privately. Professor of comparative literature at Sarah Lawrence College, 1940–50. **Recipient:** Prix Femina–Vacaresco, 1951; Newspaper Guild of New York Page One Award, 1955; Prix Combat, 1963; Prix Femina, 1968; Prix Monaco, 1973; French Ministry of Culture Grand Prix National des Lettres, 1975; Academie Francaise Grand Prix de la Litterature, 1980; National Arts Club Medal of Honor for Literature, 1985; commander of Legion of Honor (France). L.T.D. from Smith College, 1961, from Bowdoin College, 1968, from Colby College, 1972, and from Harvard University, 1981. *Died in Maine, 17 December 1987.*

WRITINGS

Novels

Alexis; ou, Le Traite du vain combat ["Alexis; or, Treatise on Useless Combat"]. [Paris], 1929; revised, Paris, Plon, 1965; translated by Walter Kaiser as *Alexis,* New York, Farrar, Straus, 1984.
La Nouvelle Eurydice ["The New Eurydice"]. Paris, Grasset, 1931.
Dernier du reve ["Coin of Dreams"]. Paris, Grasset, 1934; revised, 1959; as *A Coin in Nine Hands,* translation by Dori Katz, New York, Farrar, Straus, 1982.
Le Coup de grâce. Paris, Gallimard, 1939; translated by Grace Frick as *Coup de Grâce,* New York, Farrar, Straus, 1957.
Memoires d'Hadrien. Paris, Plon, 1951; translated by Grace Frick as *Memoirs of Hadrian,* New York, Farrar, Straus, 1954; as *"Memoirs of Hadrian" and Reflections on the Composition of "Memoirs of Hadrian,"* New York, Farrar, Straus, 1989.
L'Oeuvre au noir ["The Work in Black"]. Paris, Gallimard, 1968; translated by Grace Frick as *The Abyss,* New York, Farrar, Straus, 1976.

Poetry

Le Jardin des chimeres ["The Garden of the Chimeras"]. Paris, Librairie Acadèmique, 1921.

Les Dieux ne sont pas morts ["The Gods Are Not Dead"]. Paris, Editions Sansot, 1922.
Feux. [Paris], 1936; revised, Paris, Gallimard, 1974; translated by Dori Katz as *Fires,* New York, Farrar, Straus, 1981.
Les Charites d'Alcippe. [Brussels], 1956; as *The Alms of Alcippe,* Targ Editions, 1982.

Short Stories

La Mort conduit l'attelage ["Death Drives the Team"]. Paris, Grasset, 1934.
Nouvelles Orientales. Paris, Gallimard, 1938; translated by Alberto Manguel as *Oriental Tales,* New York, Farrar, Straus, 1985.
Comme l'eau qui coule. Paris, Gallimard, 1982; translated by Walter Kaiser as *Two Lives and a Dream,* New York, Farrar, Straus, 1987.

Essays

Les Songes et les sorts ["Dreams and Spells"]. Paris, Grasset, 1938.
Sous benefice d'inventaire ["With Reservations"]. Paris, Gallimard, 1962; revised, 1978; translated by Richard Howard as *The Dark Brain of Piranesi, and Other Essays,* New York, Farrar, Straus, 1984.
Le Temps, ce grand sculpture: Essais. Paris, Gallimard, 1983; translated by Walter Kaiser as *That Mighty Sculptor, Time,* New York, Farrar, Straus, 1989.
En pelerin et en etranger. Paris, Gallimard, 1990.

Plays

Electra; ou, La Chute des masques. Paris, Plon, 1954.
Le Mystere d'Alceste [and] *Qui n'a pas son minotaure?* Paris, Plon, 1963.

Other

Pindare. Paris, Grasset, 1932.
Author of critique, and translator from the Greek, with Constantin Dimaras, *Presentation critique de Constantin Cavafy, 1863–1933* ["Critical Presentation of Constantin Cavafy"]. Paris, Gallimard, 1958.
Translator from the English, *Fleuve profond, sombre riviere: Les Negro spirituals* ["Deep, Dark River"]. Paris, Gallimard, 1964.
Author of critique, and translator from the English, *Presentation critique d'Hortense Flexner.* Paris, Gallimard, 1969.
Théâtrè (two volumes). Paris, Gallimard, 1971; translated by Dori Katz, as *Plays,* New York, Performing Arts Journal Publications, 1985.

Le Labyrinthe du monde, Volume 1: *Souvenirs pieux*, Paris, Gallimard, 1974; Volume 2: *Archives du nord*, Paris, Gallimard, 1977; Volume 3: *Quoi?: L'Eternite*, Paris, Gallimard, 1990.

Translator, *La Couronne et la lyre* ["The Crown and the Lyre"], (classical Greek poems). Paris, Gallimard, 1979.

Anna Sonor, 1979.

Suite d'estampes pour Kou–Kou–Hai. High Loft, 1980.

Les Yeux ouverts: Entretiens avec Matthieu Galey. Paris, Centurion, 1980; translated by Arthur Goldhammer as *With Open Eyes: Conversations with Matthieu Galey*, Boston, Beacon Press, 1986.

Discours de reception de Mme Marguerite Yourcenar a l'Academie Francaise et reponse de M. Jean d'Ormesson. Paris, Gallimard, 1981.

Mishima; ou, La Vision du vide (biography). Paris, Gallimard, 1981; translated by Alberto Manguel as *Mishima: A Vision of the Void*, New York, Farrar, Straus, 1986.

Un Homme obscur, 1982.

Oeuvres romanesques. Paris, Gallimard, 1982.

Blues et gospels. Paris, Gallimard, 1984.

*

Interviews: *Entretiens radiophoniques avec Marguerite Yourcenar* by Patrick de Rosbo, Paris, Mercure de France, 1972, 77.

Critical Sources: *Entretiens radiophoniques avec Marguerite Yourcenar* by Patrick de Rosbo, Paris, Mercure de France, 1972, 77; "A Synopsis of Proust's Remarks Concerning Homosexuality" by William C. Carter, in *Proust Research Association Newsletter*, Number 10, 1973, 22; "Sexuality in Gide's Self–Portrait" by Wallace Fowlie, "Triumphs and Tribulations of Homosexual Discourse" by Jean–Paul Aron and Roger Kempf, and "The Homosexual Paradigm in Balzac, Gide, and Genet" by Gerald H. Storzer, in *Homosexualities and French Literature*, edited by George Stambolian and Elaine Marks, Cornell University Press, 1979, 151, 186, 256; "The Homosexual Paradigm in Balzac, Gide, and Genet" by Gerald H. Storzer, in *Homosexualities and French Literature*, edited by George Stambolian and Elaine Marks, Cornell University Press, 1979, 186; "Les facteurs homosexuels de la création littéraire: le cas d'Albert Camus" by Jean Gassin, in *Australian Journal of French Studies* (Clayton, Australia), May–August 1980, 190; *Marguerite Yourcenar in Counterpoit*, Lanham, Maryland, University Press of America, 1983; "Mirrors and Masks in *Denier du rêve*" by C. Frederick Farrell and Edith R. Farrell, in *Marguerite Yourcenar in Counterpoint*, Lanham, Maryland, University Press of America, 1983; *Marguerite Yourcenar* by Pierre L. Horn, Boston, Twayne Publishers, 1985; "Marguerite Yourcenar" by Peter G. Christensen, in *Encyclopedia of Homosexuality*, edited by Wayne R. Dynes, New York, Garland, 1990; *The Gay Novel in America* by James Levin, New York, Garland, 1991.

*   *   *

Marguerite Yourcenar will always be known for breaking the almost 350–year tradition of an all–male French Academy. It was not the first time that her life and work proved unconventional.

Born Marguerite Antoinette Jeanne Marie Ghislaine Cleenewerck de Crayencour on 8 June 1903, Yourcenar spent her childhood moving about with her father, almost 50 years her senior, as he pursued the life of a wealthy socialite interested in gambling and women. She supplemented her education by tutors with the monuments and cultural offerings of Paris and the Riviera. Her first exile, caused by the outbreak of World War I, was in England where she learned both English and Latin. Back in Paris, she studied Greek, learned Italian on her own, and explored world literature with her father.

Her writing career began in her teens with two privately published books. By her early 20s she had launched two ambitious projects: a life of the emperor Hadrian and a vast saga, "Remous" ["Eddies"], covering much of Europe over many centuries. Three segments of it formed *La Mort conduit l'attelage* ["Death drives the team"] published in 1934. Rewritten, they became the principal works of her maturity: *Memoirs of Hadrian*, *The Abyss*, and *Two Lives and a Dream*.

In 1929, the Wall Street crash swallowed most of her mother's legacy, (mismanaged by her half–brother), and her father died penniless. Yourcenar, however, published her first novel and sealed the rupture with her family by deciding to spend her remaining fortune on ten years of "luxurious freedom"—largely in Greece and Italy—which yielded eight books. In 1939, her money gone and no work available, she accepted the invitation of an American friend, Grace Frick, for a lecture tour in the United States.

The outbreak of World War II prevented Yourcenar's return. She became a United States citizen in 1947 and soon bought a house in Northeast Harbor, Maine, where she lived—with frequent and prolonged travels abroad—until her death in 1987. Her election to the Academy in 1980 came just four months after the death of Grace Frick, her translator, assistant, and companion of 40 years.

Her writings, as well as her lifestyle, were controversial: one of her strongest terms of condemnation is the phrase "right–thinking." Her books often defy classification: is *Fires* poetry or prose?; *Hadrian* a novel or an essay?; *Le Labyrinthe du monde* ["The Labyrinth of the World"] history? autobiography? or a novel form as yet undefined?

Of her themes, none is more multifaceted than love. Its importance varies with the work, depending entirely on the protagonists and their milieu; different kinds of love and of forms to express them reflect its variety. Whether the loves be heterosexual, homosexual, bisexual, lesbian, incestuous, or other–worldly, however, they are judged by the same criteria; the most noteworthy involve the lover's whole being.

Despite a Catholic upbringing, Yourcenar always acknowledges the importance of the flesh but aims at a relationship that expresses a union with the divine, like the Hindu *maithuma*. Both a disease and a vocation, love is based on aesthetic, metaphysical, and moral values, while its historical or mythical sources obviate the need for explanations.

Her first novel, *Alexis*, whose subtitle, "The Treatise of Vain Struggle," reminds us of André Gide, is based on living models and shows society's effects on someone with homosexual leanings. In a personal letter, the protagonist tries to explain to his wife—and perhaps to himself—why he is leaving her and their child (conceived because of a "duty" to continue an ancient family line) in order to gain the freedom he needs for his art. Written in the style of the examination of conscience, he berates himself for what he considers shameful "trangressions"; for he has internalized the values of his Protestant upbringing. The word "homosexual" never appears; he refers to the afternoon on which he "encountered beauty."

For Alexis there is a difference between pleasure and love. The latter is directed toward an idealized concept of women; the former, pursued in secret, often with anonymous partners, is indispensable. The failure of marriage to bring fulfillment is a constant. Clytemnestra, a mythological model in *Fires,* spent her early life preparing to be a good wife, before realizing that Agamemnon doesn't care enough to come home on furlough. In the "Preface" to "Electra" she and Aegisthus are described as an "old couple ... who didn't wait for the grave to start to rot together."

This description would be apt for other married people. If there is love, one is usually trapped; if couples stay together it is often for an undesirable end, like preserving the status quo. Especially in her autobiographical *Le Labyrinthe du monde,* women cope as best they can—sometimes by assuming a domineering role—within their male–dominated society and frequently die in childbirth often after an excessive number of pregnancies. The image of blood is often associated with women, as in *A Coin in Nine Hands*: "killing, giving birth, you're all good at that, you women: at all the operations that involve blood." Clytemnestra says she bled more bearing her children than Agamemnon did when dying. To the "I" in *Fires* who comments, "A child is a hostage. Life has you," infanticides, actual and proposed, respond. Hadrian is satisfied with the Roman system of choosing and adopting a successor. Zeno, as he prepares for death in *The Abyss,* wonders, and perhaps shares the Lady of Froso's hope "which lies deeper than mere bodily desire" to give him a son, even though that would mean that he "would not get out of this labyrinth until the end of time."

Fires, Yourcenar's only book devoted to love, illustrates or underscores most of her themes. It was written in part to get over an unhappy love affair with the nameless "man I loved." Passages from her diary alternate with prose poems whose protagonists are primarily mythical women. "You are God" the "I" writes; Mary Magdalene goes beyond physical love to a love for Christ, while Antigone and Phaedo go beyond the human to devote themselves to an ideal. Antinous is a god for Hadrian, but he also serves as a model of beauty, the subject of innumerable art works.

Sappho closes this collection. She "rises" as an acrobat rather than a poet, and she is saved from her suicide attempt by the safety net of her art. Her lover, Attys, leaves her; and she begins to prefer a young man, who has just enough feminine qualities to be attractive. Then he appears in women's clothing, denying Sappho the opportunity of being the passive partner and showing her that she will always rediscover Attys in new forms. This blend of the sexes is very common in Yourcenar's work—names proper to both are one indication—and may explain Yourcenar's propensity for bisexual characters. Circumstances also dictate the practices of a given time, as Proust points out. There are few lesbians in these works, but Marguerite of Austria, an historical example, makes a cameo appearance in *The Abyss.*

Achilles and Patrocles represent, perhaps most clearly, the exchanging of roles between the sexes. Achilles, according to legend, was hidden, disguised as a girl, in the court of Lycomedes. There he made love to Deidamia and later strangled her—or his feminine side—and was helped to escape by Misandre, a more masculine woman who would have gone with him were she not "a prisoner of her breasts." The sketch ends with his legendary duel with Penthesilea, transposed into a dream–sequence ballet where changing costumes reflect the passing of ages. His falling in love after her death—"the iron rape"—is explained because she was a woman worthy of being a friend, the only one who resembled Patrocles.

This Greek, military ideal of love is the one underlying Yourcenar's next novel *Coup de grace.* Its first person narrator, Erick, a mercenary soldier who despised women insofar as they were "feminine," loved his cousin and comrade–in–arms, Conrad, described in feminine terms as having "the gentleness of a young girl," and was loved by Sophie, Conrad's sister. Erick found Sophie attractive under pseudo–battle conditions—they watched an aerial bombardment from an exposed position—but spurned and assaulted her when she curled her hair and dressed for a ball. The resemblance between brother and sister is underscored: Sophie appears to be "a brother to her brother"; and, when Erick executes her in the end, he has the impression that it is Conrad who is dying a second time. He agrees to be her executioner, perhaps to show his superior detachment, perhaps because he took her request as a definitive proof of her love. When his imagined scenario fails—he turns his head and misses his shot—he blames it on Sophie, deciding that her motive was to bequeath him remorse. He concludes: "One is always trapped, somehow, in dealings with women." Hercules in "Alcestes" echoes him: "With women, you know, one can never be sure."

Women whom Yourcenar favors are steadfast, but they are often seen through men's eyes. Hadrian considers most of them frivolous or shallow, except for his adopted mother, Plotina, who fills for him the role, valued by Yourcenar, of *parèdre* (god's consort). Plotina's virtues are wisdom, loyalty, and self–control, not "feminine" qualities. Zeno, too, values the one woman, the Lady of Froso, who worked beside him and had her own expertise to contribute. Condemnation of the other sex is common. Marcella, the heroine of *Coin* comments: "All men are cowards."

Although *Memoirs of Hadrian,* Yourcenar's most famous novel, was written to illustrate the "good prince," readers have been most fascinated by this second–century emperor's love affair with Antinous, whose sacrificial suicide represented the low point in Hadrian's life. They compare themselves to Achilles and Patrocles and even visit their graves. Another pseudo–battle, a dangerous lion hunt, replaces actual battlefield experience. Yet, enamored as he was, Hadrian does not love wisely. Interested in other love objects—men and women—he allows Antinous to feel neglected, for which he reproaches himself bitterly when it is too late. Self–centered love is always condemned by Yourcenar.

Yourcenar's other great historical novel, *The Abyss,* chronicles the life of a sixteenth–century alchemist/physician, Zeno. It is a quest for enlightenment and self–discovery, so he has little time for love. Like Hadrian and Erick he sees women primarily as wearers of dresses and perfumes; he prefers "a body like [his] own," which can give him pleasure without long–term commitments. His cousin, Henry Maximilian, spells out the heterosexual position. Despite men like Socrates and Anacreon, he likes women because they are different.

This novel is also one of the best representations of several themes that have been identified in the works of other gay and lesbian writers: travel, the mask and the outsider. Aron and Kempf point out that in Gide "a geographical difference ... covers a political difference," while Fowlie adds: "This wandering pattern of life is often the homosexual's." As Hadrian moved about as a soldier and emperor, Zeno traveled to study medicine and alchemy and, as Yourcenar herself, to know the world. Because his work was suspect, his books condemned, and his sexual preferences illegal, he was forced to wear a "mask," which as Storzer says of Gide and Genet, "is to experience a form of death."

Persecuted outsiders have many names in Yourcenar: Protestants, like the one in *Archives* whom Yourcenar "adopts" as a cousin;

witches, gathered in covens to affirm their identity against the world; homosexuals, listed in *Archives* with other groups as examaples of people condemned to death in some societies; and revolutionaries, such as those in *A Coin.* Gassin, discussing Camus, writes "homosexuality/persecution." If condemnation by the church and society is a constant, the consequences vary—from the scorn Alexis feels to death at the stake for Zeno. It is in this larger context of minority experiences that Yourcenar places homosexuality for Rosbo, while still insisting that more of the characters are bisexual. Whatever their differences from the norm, however, any oppressed group acting from worthy needs and motives receives Yourcenar's sympathy and support.

—*C. Frederick Farrell, Jr., and Edith R. Farrell*

ZIMMERMAN, Bonnie. American educator and writer of nonfiction. Born in Chicago, Illinois, 1947. Educated at Indiana University and State University of New York at Buffalo. Educator and writer. Companion of Berlene Rice. Member of Women's Studies department, San Diego State University. **Recipient:** Lambda Literary Award for *The Safe Sea of Women,* 1991.

WRITINGS

Nonfiction

"'Lesbianism 101': Teaching Lesbian Courses," in *Radical Teacher,* November 1980.
"What Has Never Been: An Overview of Lesbian Feminist Literary Criticism," in *Feminist Studies* (College Park, Maryland), fall 1981.
"Exiting from Patriarchy: The Lesbian Novel of Development," in *The Voyage In: Fictions of Female Development,* edited by Elizabeth Abel, Marianne Hirsch, and Elizabeth Langland, Hanover, New Hampshire, University Press of New England for Dartmouth College, 1983.
"The Politics of Transliteration: Lesbian Personal Narratives," in *Signs: Journal of Women in Culture and Society* (University of Chicago), summer 1984.
"Feminist Fiction and the Postmodern Challenge," in *Postmodern Fiction: A Bio–Bibliographical Guide,* edited by Larry McCaffery, New York, Greenwood Press, 1986.
"'The Dark Eye Beaming': Female Friendship in George Eliot's Fictions," in *Lesbian Texts and Contexts: Radical Revisions,* edited by Karla Jay, Joanne Glasgow, and Catharine R. Stimpson, New York University Press, 1990.
The Safe Sea of Women: Lesbian Fiction, 1969–1989. Boston, Beacon Press, 1991; London, Onlywomen Press, 1992.
"Seeing, Reading, Knowing: The Lesbian Appropriation of Literature," in *(En)Gendering Knowledge,* edited by Joan Hartman and Ellen Messer–Davidow, University of Tennessee Press, 1991.

Interviews: Unpublished interview with Jayne Relaford Brown.

Critical Sources: Review by Julie Abraham of *The Safe Sea of Women,* in *Nation,* 3 December 1990, 706; review by Richard Labonte of *The Safe Sea of Women,* in *Advocate,* 24 September 1991, 95; review by Sally Munt of *The Safe Sea of Women,* in *Feminist Review,* spring 1992, 94–99; review by Jewelle Gomez of *The Safe Sea of Women,* in *Multi–Cultural Review,* 1:1, 1992.

Bonnie Zimmerman comments: "I have had the privilege and great good luck to participate in the past two decades of lesbian feminist politics and culture. Unlike too many people in our alienated society, I have been able to pursue a true vocation: a life in which emotional fulfillment, political activism, and remunerative work actually complement each other, rather than warring incessantly. Becoming a lesbian—and proclaiming it out loud—was the best thing I ever did, both personally and professionally. I highly recommend it to every woman."

*   *   *

One of the early openly lesbian professors in academia, Bonnie Zimmerman has been a pioneer in lesbian studies and literary criticism. She has served as a faculty member and frequent chair of the Women's Studies Department at San Diego State University since 1978, where she was active in establishing a Women's Studies major and also developed an interdisciplinary course, "Woman–Identified Women," which studies lesbian literature, history, theory and identity politics. She has written numerous articles on lesbian issues, including ground–breaking essays on lesbian studies ("Lesbianism 101"), the lesbian as reader ("Seeing, Reading, Knowing") and an overview of lesbian feminist criticism ("What Has Never Been"). Zimmerman is best known for her volume *The Safe Sea of Women: Lesbian Fiction, 1969–1989,* an overview and analysis of contemporary lesbian fiction.

The Safe Sea of Women discusses the major symbols and structures of most of the more than two hundred lesbian novels written in the first 20 years of the gay liberation movement. Zimmerman examines the ways in which lesbian literature both mirrors and creates a sense of lesbian identity and community. As she states in her preface, "I view lesbian fiction as the expression of a collective 'myth of origins' with four primary divisions...: the lesbian self, the lesbian couple, the lesbian community, and community and difference." Zimmerman's book explores how each of these categories has been presented in lesbian fiction since the late 1960s. After examining these ongoing themes and the emerging trends of the late eighties, she concludes with a speculation about three possible trajectories for the future of lesbian fiction: a literature in which lesbians are "normalized" and depicted as different only in terms of sexual preference; a literature which emphasizes lesbians as outside of and separate from mainstream society; a combination of the two, where the lesbian hero lives within society, yet possesses a special understanding and knowledge drawn from her lesbian imagination.

In an interview with Jayne Relaford Brown, Zimmerman stated, "My history is very close to the history of the writers who are writing this literature, starting in the early seventies. Part of what I want this book to be is a history, a literary history of the lesbian movement. Even though it's not organized in a strictly historical way, I think someone reading the book would get ... a sense of what the last twenty years, at least on the cultural front, have been like."

Zimmerman went on to discuss the relationship she sees between lesbians and lesbian literature, commenting that there seems to be a "dialectic" between lived experience and literature, particularly for lesbians. "I think we [lesbians] are probably just as much shaped by the fictions we read as the fictions are shaped according to what we think of as our real lives," Zimmerman said. A few generations ago, she stated, lesbians shaped their lives after Stephen Gordon, the central character of Radclyffe Hall's *The Well of Loneliness*, then Beebo Brinker, the heroine of Ann Bannon's novels. In the seventies, she says, "the movement exploded and created all kinds of new images." Lesbians could then choose, says Zimmerman, to model themselves after audacious characters like Rita Mae Brown's Molly Bolt in *Rubyfruit Jungle*. While Zimmerman stipulates that lesbians do not merely imitate fictional characters, she emphasizes their importance to lesbian culture: "Culture and ideology, words, images, language in its broadest sense, does shape our reality. Especially, I think, in that particular culture I identify in this book, symbols are tremendously important. It is an extremely mythic culture that we have created, full of symbols of Amazons and Lesbian Nation and all that, so of course literature is going to be an important part of the way we invent our lives."

With her extensive teaching and writing about lesbian literature, Zimmerman has also contributed to the ways in which lesbians in the late twentieth century "invent our lives." "Any piece of literary criticism," she states in the preface to *The Safe Sea of Women*, "is in its own way the creation of another story." In her interview with Brown, she defined her function as a lesbian literary critic in terms of being "of service" to lesbian culture. "One of the nicest compliments I've had in my entire career," stated Zimmerman, "came from a writer whose works I discuss in my book, and twice she has said to me, 'Thank you for showing me what we're doing.'" While Zimmerman acknowledges that the biases of her own history as a "white, professional academic who 'came out' in the context of the women's liberation movement of the early 1970s" affect the story she creates about lesbian literature, she looks forward to many more diverse perspectives on contemporary lesbian writing. "The 'contradictions' between our accounts," states Zimmerman, "may well provide the space in which future lesbian literature flourishes."

—Jayne Relaford Brown

Advisors and Contributors

Adolphs, Dieter Wolfgang. Associate Professor of German, Department of Humanities, Michigan Technological University, Houghton, Michigan; author of *Literarischer Erfahrungshorizont: Aufbau und Entwicklung der Erzählperspektive im Werk Thomas Manns,* 1985. **Essay:** Thomas Mann.

Alden, Douglas W. Professor Emeritus, University of Virginia, Charlottesville; author of *Marcel Proust and His French Critics; Marcel Proust's Grasset Proofs; Jacques de Lacretelle; First Readings in French Masterpieces; Premier Manuel; Grammaire et Style;* editor of twentieth-century volumes of *A Critical Bibliography of French Literature;* editor, since 1949, of *French XX Bibliography.* **Essay:** Marcel Proust.

Alexei, Richard. Free-lance writer and consultant; culinary writer and chef in San Francisco. **Essay:** Jack Kerouac and Frederick Rolfe.

Allison, Terry L. Associate Collections Librarian, California State University, San Marcos; author of several articles in library science; conducting research on the colonial tradition in gay male writing. **Essay:** Jean Genet, Guy Hocquenghem, Alan Hollinghurst, and Jeanette Winterson.

Anderson, Andrew A. Associate Professor of Spanish, University of Michigan, Ann Arbor; author of *Lorca's Late Poetry: A Critical Study,* 1990; *García Lorca: "La zapatera prodigiosa,"* 1991; editor of Lorca's *Antología poética,* 1986, *Diván del Tamarit, Llanto por Ignacio Sánchez Mejías, Seis poemas galegos, Poemas sueltos,* 1988. **Essay:** Federico García Lorca.

Barclay, Donald A. Reference Librarian, New Mexico State University Library, Las Cruces. **Essay:** Willa Sibert Cather.

Barrie, Cecily M. Free-lance writer and literary researcher; regular reviewer for *Canadian Book Review Annual.* **Essay:** Amy Lowell.

Beckson, Karl. Professor of English, Brooklyn College of the City University of New York; author or editor of ten books on various figures of the 1890s, including *Oscar Wilde: The Critical Heritage,* 1970; *London in the 1890s: A Cultural History,* 1993; and *The Oscar Wilde Encyclopedia,* forthcoming. **Essay:** Oscar Wilde.

Benkov, Edith. Professor of French, San Diego State University, California; specializes in Medieval and Renaissance literature and feminist criticism; has published articles on Crétien de Troyes, Marie de France, Christine de Pizan, Louise Labé, and Medieval theatre; is currently working on a study of cross-dressing and genre in Renaissance theatre. **Essays:** Violette Leduc and Vernon Lee.

Bigelow, Pamela. Free-lance writer. **Essays:** Ann Bannon, Ursula Le Guin, Carson McCullers, Mary Renault, Sara Teasdale, and Barbara Wilson.

Bogus, SDiane A. Professor of Composition and American Literature, DeAnza College, Cupertino, California; author of *Dyke Hands and Sutras Erotic and Lyric, For the Love of Men: Poems for Gay Men,* and *The Chant of the Women of Magdalena;* editor of Woman in the Moon Publications, a lesbian small press. **Essay:** Ann Allen Shockley.

Boney, Bradley. Doctoral candidate and assistant instructor, University of Texas at Austin; author of reviews for *Drama Review;* currently working on dissertation about AIDS and the theatre. **Essays:** Larry Kramer.

Boyd, Malcolm. Please see his own entry. Chaplain of AIDS Ministries, Episcopal Diocese of Los Angeles; author of *Are You Running with Me, Jesus?, As I Live and Breathe, Malcolm Boyd's Book of Days, Gay Priest,* and *Take Off the Masks;* former president of PEN West. **Essay:** Paul Monette.

Broder, Michael. Free-lance writer; contributor to *AIDS Patient Care, Brooklyn Free Press, City Limits, Courier-Life, Columbia College Today, Downtown, New York Post, QW, Spin,* and *Village Voice.* **Essays:** Allan Gurganus, Tony Kushner, and Ethan Mordden, Robert Patrick.

Brodsky, Ira N. Free-lance writer. **Essay:** Paula Gunn Allen.

Bronski, Michael. Free-lance writer; author of *Culture Clash: The Making of Gay Sensibility,* 1984; contributor to numerous periodicals. **Essays:** Edward Albee, Dorothy E. Allison, Neil Bartlett, Blanche McCrary Boyd, Christopher Bram, Rita Mae Brown, Dennis Cooper, Mart Crowley, Melvin Dixon, Maureen Duffy, Christopher Durang, Ranier Werner Fassbinder, David B. Feinberg, Robert Ferro, Jewelle Gomez, Doris Grumbach, Thom Gunn, Patricia Highsmith, Andrew Holleran, Jill Johnston, Kate Millett, Terence Mervyn Rattigan, Joanna Russ, May Sarton, Sarah Schulman, and Parker Tyler.

Brown, Jane Relaford. Lecturer, San Diego State University and Southwestern College; author of *The Face We Choose,* forthcoming. **Essays:** Judy Grahan, Gertrude Stein, and Bonnie Zimmerman.

Burton, Peter. Commissioning Editor, Millivres Books, Brighton, East Sussex, England; features and reviews editor of *Gay Times;* author of *Rod Steward: An Authorised Biography,* 1977; *Parallel Lives: A Memoir,* 1985; and *Talking to ... in Conversation with Writers Writing on Gay Themes,* 1991. **Essay:** David Rees.

Cancalon, Elaine D. Professor of French, Florida State University, Tallahassee; author of *Techniques et personnages dan les récits d'André Gide,* 1970; *Fairy-tale Structures and Motifs in "Le Grand Meaulnes,* 1975; and articles on Gide, Flaubert, Buzzati, Marie-Claire Blais, Verlaine, Borges, and Anne Hébert. **Essay:** André Gide.

Christensen, Paul. Professor of Modern Literature, Texas A&M University, College Station; author of *Charles Olson: Call Him Ishmael,* 1979; *In Love, In Sorrow: The Complete Correspondence of Charles Olson and Edward Dahlberg,* 1990; *Minding the Underworld: Clayton Eshleman and Late Postmodernism,* 1991; poetry includes *The Vectory,* 1977; *Signs of the Whelming,* 1983; and *Weights & Measures,* 1985; poet. **Essays:** Hart Crane and Allen Ginsberg.

Christensen, Peter G. Lecturer in English, Marquette University, Milwaukee, Wisconsin; specialist in twentieth-century comparative literature; frequent contributor to *Film Criticism, Review of Contemporary Fiction, Classical and Modern Literature,* and *Dada/Surrealism.* **Essays:** J. R. Ackerley, Truman Capote, C. P. Cavafy, and Robert McAlmon.

Cloonan, William. Professor of French, Florida State University, Tallahassee. **Essay:** Michel Tournier.

Consoli, Joe. Humanities Bibliographer, Alexander Library, Rutgers University, New Jersey; author of *Giovanni Boccaccio: An Annotated Bibliography;* currently working on new translation of *Il Novellino;* member of board of editors for *Italian Quarterly.* **Essays:** Aldo Busi and Pier Paolo Pasolini.

Cruikshank, Margaret. Department of English, City College of San Francisco; author of *The Gay and Lesbian Liberation Movement.*

Cumpston, Andrea R. Doctoral candidate, University of Alabama, Tuscaloosa; currently working on a study of lesbian desire in nineteenth-century American novels. **Essay:** Adrienne Rich.

Curry, Renee R. Assistant Professor of English, California State University, San Marcos; author of articles on Elizabeth Bishop and May Sarton, and on film directors John Waters and Tim Hunter. **Essay:** Bryher.

Delbridge, Melissa J. Archivist, Duke University, Durham, North Carolina. **Essay:** Romaine Brooks, Janet Flanner, Renée Vivien.

Doyle, Paul A. Professor of English, Nassau Community College, Garden City, New York. **Essay:** Evelyn Waugh.

Dynes, Wayne R. Professor at Hunter College of the City University of New York; cofounder of New York chapter of Gay Academic Union in 1973; compiled and annotated *Homosexuality: A Research Guide;* editor-in-chief of the multiple-award-winning *Encyclopedia of Homosexuality;* coeditor of *Studies in Homosexuality* for Garland Publishing, 1992. **Essay:** William S. Burroughs.

Eddy, Ron. GMP Publishers, London, England; author of articles in *Aquarist & Pondkeeper,* and *Leselust;* regular contributor to *London Scene.*

Edgar, Kathleen J. Free-lance writer. **Essay:** Jane Chambers.

Edmunds, Jean. Free-lance writer. **Essay:** Edna St. Vincent Millay.

Embry, Carmen. Reference Librarian, Coordinator of Bibliographic Instruction, Ekstrom Library, University of Louisville, Kentucky; author of *When Sanibel Becomes You,* 1993; editor of *Kentucky Libraries, 1989-1993.* **Essay:** Lesléa Newman.

Farrell, C. Frederick, Jr. Professor of French and Chair of the Division of the Humanities; University of Minnesota, Morris; co-author, translator, and editor of books and articles concerning Marguerite Yourcenar, Gaston Gachelard, Louise Labé, Eméric Crucé, and François Mauriac. **Essay:** Marguerite Yourcenar.

Farrell, Edith R. Associate Professor of French, University of Minnesota, Morris; co-author, translator, and editor of books and articles concerning Marguerite Yourcenar, Gaston Gachelard, Louise Labé, Eméric Crucé, and François Mauriac. **Essay:** With C. Frederick Farrell, Jr., Marguerite Yourcenar.

Franeta, Sonja. Instructor in Russian literature; free-lance writer. **Essays:** Mikhail Kuzmin and Sophia Parnok.

Garcia-Johnson, Ronnie-Richele. Graduate student, Univeristy of Michigan, Ann Arbor; free-lance writer. **Essay:** Cherríe Moraga.

Gough, Cal. Reference librarian and social science book selector in Central Library of the Atlanta-Fulton Public Library, Atlanta, Georgia; member of American Library Association's Gay and Lesbian Task Force and helped establish Library Information Clearinghouse; co-editor, *Gay and Lesbian Library Service,* 1990, co-author, *The Booklover's Guide to Atlanta,* 1992; executive board member of local gay and lesbian history project in Atlanta.

Gray, Donald. Professor of English, Indiana University, Bloomington. **Essay:** A. C. Swinburne.

Hansen, Roland C. Readers' Services Librarian, John M. Flaxman Library, School of the Art Institute of Chicago; treasurer, and former secretary and co-chair of Social Responsibilities Round Table of the Gay and Lesbian Task Force of the American Library Association; contributor to *Complete Book of Research;* compiler, *AIDS and the Arts: A Bibliography.*

Hill, Jeff. Free-lance writer. **Essay:** Armistead Maupin.

Hollinghurst, Alan. Please see his own entry. Poet and novelist; poetry editor, *Times Literary Supplement,* London.

Holzberger, William G. Professor of English, Bucknell University, Lewisburg, Pennsylvania. **Essay:** A. E. Housman.

Jay, Karla. Please see her own entry. Professor, Pace University; co-editor of *Out of the Closets: Voice of Gay Liberation;* co-author of *The Amazon and the Page: Natalie Clifford Barney and Renée Vivien;* general editor of *The Cutting Edge: Lesbian Life and Literature.* **Essay:** Natalie Barney.

Johansson, Warren. Independent scholar and free-lance researcher and writer; specialities are Slavic, Indo-European and Semitic philology and history of ideas; founding member of Scholarship Committee of Gay Academic Union in New York City, of Gay Alumni of Columbia, of Visibility Action Committee of the Gay and Lesbian Alliance Against Defamation; associate editor of *Encyclopedia of Homosexuality,* 1990; currently at work on *Homosexuality from the Old Testament to the New: The Sources of Christian Intolerance,* and *Homosexuality, Pederasty, Intersexuality.* **Essays:** Colette, Aleister Crowley, Wayne R. Dynes, Havelock Ellis, Magnus Hirschfeld, and Edward Sagarin.

Johnson, Richard A. Lucia, Ruth, and Elizabeth MacGregor Professor of English, Mount Holyoke College, South Hadley, Massachusetts; author of *Man's Place: An Essay on Auden,* 1973; coauthor of *Common Ground,* 1993. **Essay:** W. H. Auden.

Jurgens, Jane. Reference Librarian, Northeastern Illinois University, Chicago; member of Gay and Lesbian Task Force of the American Library Association. **Essays:** Margaret Cruikshank, Katherine Forrest, Michel Foucault, Radclyffe Hall, T. E. Lawrence, Phyllis Ann Lyon and Del Martin.

Kasinec, Denise. Free-lance writer. **Essay:** Lillian Faderman.

Kelly, Tom W. Free-lance writer and playwright; contributor of articles and reviews on books, theatre, art, and assorted community interest stories to the gay presses in San Francisco, Oregon, Seattle, and Los Angeles. **Essays:** Daniel Curzon and Joe Orton.

Kepner, Jim. Gay activist; founder of International Gay and Lesbian Archives; has taught gay studies since 1956; author of more than 2,000 articles for gay press publications; at work on *Gay Spirit Rising, The Loves of a Long-Time Activist,* and *The Posthumous Trial of Roman Novarro.* **Essays:** Elsa Gidlow, Barbara G. Grier, Joseph Hansen, Langston Hughes, Jonathan Katz, Robin Maugham, Samuel M. Steward, and Tennessee Williams.

Kerr, Lucille. Professor of Spanish and Comparative Literature, University of Southern California; author of *Suspended Fictions: Reading Novels of Manuel Puig,* 1987, and *Reclaiming the Author: Figures and Fictions from Spanish America,* 1992; review editor of *Latin American Literary Review.* **Essay:** Manuel Puig.

Killian, Kevin. Poet, playwright, and novelist; author of *Shy,* 1989, and *Bedrooms Have Windows,* 1989; currently cowriting a biography of Jack Spicer. **Essay:** Jack Spicer.

Kuda, Marie J. Independent scholar, historian, archivist, writer and lecturer who has been an activist for over 25 years; author of *Women Loving Women: A Select and Annotated Bibliography of Women Loving Women in Literature,* 1975; free-lance reviewer for several publications, including *Booklist.* **Essays:** June Arnold, Pat Califia, Tee A. Corinne, Jeannette Howard Foster, Karla Jay, Rosamund Lehmann, Jane Rule, Vita Sackville-West, Alice B. Toklas, and Christa Winslow.

Le Blanc, Ondine. Graduate student, University of Michigan, Ann Arbor. **Essays:** Djuna Barnes, Hilda Doolittle, and Monique Wittig.

Levin, James. Professor of History, City College of New York, and attorney in private practice; author of *The Gay Novel in America,* 1983, and *Reflections of the Homosexual Rights Movement,* 1983. **Essays:** Gore Vidal.

Lutes, Michael A. Assistant Librarian, University Libraries, University of Notre Dame, Indiana; regular contributor to *Library Journal* and *Choice.* **Essays:** Wilfred Owen and Felice Picano.

Madden, Ed. Poet, and doctoral candidate, University of Texas at Austin; at work on dissertation on Charlotte Mew, Michael Field, and fin-de-siecle lesbian poetry; contributing editor, *Borderlands: Texas Poetry Review;* reviewer for *Texas Triangle: The Lesbian and Gay News Weekly.* **Essay:** Charlotte Mew.

Malinowsky, H. Robert. Principal Bibliographer and Professor, University of Illinois at Chicago; author of *Science and Engineering Literature,* 1980; *International Directory of Gay and Lesbian Periodicals,* 1987; *AIDS Information Sourcebook,* 1988-91; *Science and Technology Annual Reference Review,* 1989-91; and *Best Science and Technology Reference Books for Young People,* 1993; former president of Mountain Plains Library Association and the Special Libraries Association.

Marie, Jacquelyn. Women's Studies/Reference Librarian, University of California, Santa Cruz; contributor to *Women's Annual* and *Across Cultures.* **Essays:** Gloria Anzaldúa.

Martin, Murray S. Free-lance writer. **Essays:** Dennis Altman, E. M. Forster, D. H. Lawrence, Katherine Mansfield, and Patrick White.

McNab, James. Chairperson and Professor of French, University of North Carolina, Wilmington; author of *Radiquet;* has published articles on Cocteau, Radiquet, Mauriac, and Cubism; currently at work on authors of the post-World War I period. **Essay:** Jean Cocteau.

Nieb, Cynthia D. Department of History, Cornell University, New York. **Essay:** Minnie Bruce Pratt.

Norton, David. Doctoral candidate in English and Critical Theory, University of Washington, Seattle; currently at work on dissertation on "Queer Bodies and National Identity." **Essay:** James Purdy.

Olano, Pamela J. Doctoral candidate, University of Minnesota; contributor to *Virginia Woolf: Themes and Variations,* 1993, and *The Cutting Edge: Lesbian Life and Literature;* currently at work on *The Lavender Menace.* **Essay:** Virginia Woolf.

Oliver, Tim. Doctoral candidate, State University of New York at Stony Brook; currently at work on dissertation on gal male avant-garde films and gay spectatorship in relation to community liberationist discourse. **Essay:** Adam Mars-Jones.

Percy, William A., III. Professor of History, University of Massachusetts, Boston; co-editor of *Encyclopedia of Homosexuality,* 1990; co-author of *Outing: Shattering the Conspiracy of Silence,* 1993. **Essays:** Allan Bérubé, Martin B. Duberman, and Robert Duncan.

Ramsay, Anders. Free-lance writer. **Essay:** Becky Birtha.

Ray, Kevin. Curator of Manuscripts, Washington University, St. Louis, Missouri. **Essays:** David Leavitt, James Merrill, and Edmund White.

Reicha, Susan M. Free-lance writer. **Essay:** Sandra Scoppettone.

Ridinger, Robert B. Marks. Associate Professor, University Libraries, Northern Illinois University; compiler of *An Index to "The Advocate," the National Gay Newsmagazine, 1967-1982,* 1983, and *The Homosexual and Society: An Annotated Bibliography,* 1990; poet. **Essays:** Malcolm Boyd, Robert Chesley, Quentin Crisp, John D'Emilio, Andrea Dworkin, Richard W. Hall, Audre Lorde, Terrence McNally, Pat Parker, John Preston, Lev Raphael, Ned Rorem, Alma Routsong, Vito Russo, Martin Sherman, Randy Shilts, Stephen Spender, Patricia Nell Warren, Doric Wilson, and Lanford Wilson.

Rolls, Allison. Doctoral student, University of Michigan, Ann Arbor; free-lance writer. **Essay:** Elizabeth Bowen and I. Compton-Burnett.

Rosco, Jerry. Associate editor, *Torso, Playguy,* and *Mandate* magazines in New York; co-editor of *Glenway Wescott, 1937-1955,* 1990; currently at work on biography *Glenway Wescott Personally.* **Essay:** Charles Henri Ford.

Schiff, Adam L. Associate Librarian for Technical Services, California Academy of Sciences, San Francisco; member of American Library Association's Gay and Lesbian Task Force; served on its steering committee and the ALA Gay/Lesbian Book Award committee; editor of *Biofeedback;* founding member of Special Libraries Association Natural History Caucus.

Shaw, Marvin S. Retired teacher of English, Skyline College, San Bruno, California; co-author of *A Viewer's Guide to Art,* 1991; frequent contributor to San Francisco *Bay Area Reporter,* and the *Advocate.* **Essay:** David Watmough.

Shelton, Pamela L. Free-lance writer. **Essay:** James Baldwin.

Shively, Charles. Professor of American Studies, University of Massachusetts, Boston; active in gay presses; author of *Neustra Señora de Los Dolores,* 1975; *Calamus Lovers, Walt Whitman's Working Class Camerados,* 1987; *A History of the Conception of Death in America, 1650-1860,* 1988, and *Drum Beats, Walt Whitman's Civil War Boy Lovers,* 1989; active in gay presses. **Essays:** John Ashbery, James Broughton, Edward Carpenter, Luis Cernuda, Yukio Mishima, and Frank O'Hara.

Shreve, Jack. Department of Humanities, Allegany Community College, Cumberland, Maryland. **Essay:** Sandro Penna.

Smith, Jeanette. Associate professor and head of government documents, New Mexico State University Library; contributor to *Extrapolation.* **Essay:** Marion Zimmer Bradley.

Stanley, Debbie A. Free-lance writer. **Essays:** Harlan Greene, Paula Martinac, Neil Miller, and Joan Nestle.

Stetco, Dayna. Free-lance writer. **Essay:** Mary Daly.

Streeter, David. Pomona Public Library, Pomona, California.

Summers, Claude J. William E. Stirton Professor in the Humanities and Professor of English, University of Michigan-Dearborn; author of *Christopher Isherwood,* 1980; *E. M. Forster,* 1983; *Gay Fictions, Wilde to Stonewall,* 1990; and numerous other books and essays on seventeenth- and twentieth-century English and American literature. **Essay:** Christopher Isherwood.

Taraba, Suzy. Member of Gay and Lesbian Task Force of the American Library Association, Durham, North Carolina.

Thompson, Dawn. Doctoral candidate in Canadian Comparative Literature, University of British Columbia, Vancouver. **Essay:** Marie-Claire Blais.

Ulloa, Justo C. Professor of Spanish and Spanish American Literature, Virginia Tech, Blacksburg; author of *Sobre José Lezama Lima y sus lectores: quia v compendio bibliográfico,* 1987; editor-in-chief of Cuban Literary Studies series of the Society of Spanish and Spanish American Literature, Boulder, Colorado. **Essay:** With Leonor A. Ulloa, José Lezama Lima.

Ulloa, Leonor A. Professor of Spanish and Spanish American Literature, Radford University, Radford, Virginia; author of numerous articles on modern Latin American fiction; editor and founder of *MIFLC,* the official organ of the Mountain Interstate Foreign Language Conference. **Essay:** With Justo C. Ulloa, José Lezama Lima.

Usmiani, Renata. Department of English, Mount St. Vincent University, Halifax, Nova Scotia. **Essay:** Michel Tremblay.

Waldrep, Shelton. Doctoral candidate, Duke University, Durham, North Carolina; managing editor of *Lesbian and Gay Studies Newsletter,* a publication of the Gay and Lesbian Caucus for the MLA; author of articles, reviews, and poetry in the United States, United Kingdom, and Canada. **Essay:** Jeffrey Weeks.

Watmough, David. Please see his own entry. Canadian novelist and short story writer; author of *Ashes for Easter,* 1962; *Thy Mother's Glass,* 1992; and *The Time of the Kingfishers,* forthcoming; currently at work on sequel to *Thy Mother's Glass* entitled *Deadheads and Yellow Broom.* **Essay:** Denton Welch.

Watstein, Sarah Barbara. Associate Librarian for Public Services, Jacqueline Grennan Wexler Library, Hunter College of the City University of New York; compiler of bibliographies; co-author of *AIDS and Women, A Sourcebook,* 1990; contributor to *Feminist Bookstore News, Body Positive,* and *Visibilities.* **Essay:** Sylvia Townsend Warner.

Wiloch, Thomas. Free-lance writer and poet; author of *Stigmata Junction,* 1985; *Paper Mask,* 1988; *The Mannikin Cypher,* 1989; *Tales of Lord Shanith,* 1989; *Night Rain,* 1991; *Decoded Factories of the Heart,* 1991; *Narcotic Signature,* 1992; *Lyrical Brandy,* 1993. **Essays:** John Boswell, Jane Bowles, Paul Bowles, Harvey Fierstein, and John Rechy.

General Index

Y-Z

Nationality Index

(Authors are listed alphabetically under
country of origin and/or their country of citizenship.

United States

Gender Index

Male

A

B

C

D

E-F

G

H-I

K

L

M

General Subject and Genre Index

Education

Encoding/Oblique or Masked References

Eroticism

Essays

Expatriate Community

Family/Societal Relationships

Feminism

Fiction (Novels)

Fiction (Short Stories)

Fiction (Genre)

Obscenity

Parents of Gays and Lesbians

Pederasty

Philosophy

Poetry

Politics, Political and Social History

Pornography

Prostitution, Hustling

Psychology

Race Relations, Multiculturalism

Gay and Lesbian Literary Awards

American Library Association
Gay/Lesbian Book Award

1993   Nonfiction
> *Making History: The Struggle for Gay and Lesbian Equal Rights, 1945-1990, An Oral History,*
> Eric Marcus

       Literature
> *Ceremonies: Prose and Poetry,* Essex Hemphill

1992   Nonfiction
> *Odd Girls and Twilight Lovers: A History of Lesbian Life in Twentieth Century America,*
> Lillian Faderman

       Literature
> *Halfway Home,* Paul Monette

1991   Nonfiction
> *Encyclopedia of Homosexuality,* Wayne Dynes, Editor

       Literature
> *Crime Against Nature,* Minnie Bruce Pratt

1990   Nonfiction
> *In Search of Gay America: Women and Men in a Time of Change,* Neil Miller

       Literature
> *Eighty-Sixed,* David B. Feinberg

       Exceptional Achievement
> Armistead Maupin, "Tales of the City" Series

1989   *After Delores,* Sarah Schulman
       The Swimming-Pool Library, Alan Hollinghurst

1988   *And the Band Played On: Politics, People, and the AIDS Epidemic,* Randy Shilts
       A Restricted Country, Joan Nestle

1987   *The Spirit and the Flesh: Sexual Diversity in American Indian Culture,* Walter Williams

1986   *Sex and Germs: The Politics of AIDS,* Cindy Patton

1985   *Another Mother Tongue: Gay Words, Gay Worlds,* Judy Grahn

1984   *Sexual Politics/Sexual Communities: The Making of a Homosexual Minority in the United States, 1940-1970,*
       John D'Emilio

1983	No Award
1982	*Surpassing the Love of Men: Romantic Friendship and Love between Women from the Renaissance to the Present*, Lillian Faderman *Black Lesbians: An Annotated Bibliography*, J. R. Roberts, Compiler *The Celluloid Closet: Homosexuality in the Movies*, Vito Russo
1981	*Christianity, Social Tolerance, and Homosexuality: Gay People in Western Europe from the Beginning of the Christian Era to the Fourteenth Century*, John Boswell
1980	*Now the Volcano: An Anthology of Latin American Gay Literature*, Winston Leyland, Editor
1979	*Now That You Know: What Every Parent Should Know About Homosexuality*, Betty Fairchild and Nancy Howard
1978	*Our Right to Love*, Ginny Vida, Editor
1977	*Familiar Faces, Hidden Lives*, Howard Brown
1976	No Award
1975	*Homosexuality: Lesbians and Gay Men in Society, History, and Literature*, Jonathan Katz, Editor
1974	*Sex Variant Women in Literature: A Historical and Quantitative Survey*, Jeannette Howard Foster
1973	No Award
1972	*The Gay Mystique*, Peter Fisher *Lesbian/Woman*, Del Martin and Phyllis Lyon
1971	*Patience and Sarah*, Isabel Miller

Lambda Literary Awards

1993   Fiction
        Running Fiercely toward a High Thin Sound, Judith Katz
        Let the Dead Bury the Dead, Randall Kenan

      Nonfiction
        Eleanor Roosevelt, Blanche Wiesen Cook
        Becoming a Man, Paul Monette

      Poetry
        Counting Myself Lucky, Edward Field
        Undersong, Audre Lorde

      Humor
        Dykes to Watch Out For (The Sequel), Alison Bechdel

      Mystery
        Crazy for Loving, Jaye Maiman
        Bit Tango, Elizabeth Pincus
        The Hidden Law, Michael Nava

      Science Fiction/Fantasy
        Ammonlite, Nicola Griffith
        China Mountain Zhang, Maureen F. McHugh

      Anthologies
        A Member of the Family, John Preston, Editor
        Persistent Desire, Joan Nestle, Editor

      Young Adult Literature
        When Heroes Die, Penny Raife Durant

      Editor's Choice
        Gay Ideas, Richard Mohr

      Publisher's Service Award
        Craig Fodwell, Founder
        Oscar Wilde Memorial

1992   Fiction
        What the Dead Remember, Harlan Greene
        The Gilda Stories, Jewelle Gomez
        The Revolution of Little Girls, Blanche McCrary Boyd

      Nonfiction
        The Zuni Man-Woman, Will Roscoe
        Cancer in Two Voices, Sandra Butler and Barbara Rosenblum

      Poetry
        The Road Before Us: 100 Black Gay Poets, Assoto Saint, Editor
        Atlas of the Difficult World: Poems 1988-1991, Adrienne Rich

      Humor
        Putting On the Ritz, Joe Keenan

Mystery
> *A Country of Old Men*, Joseph Hansen
> *Murder Tradition*, Katherine V. Forrest

Science Fiction/Fantasy
> *The Dark Beyond the Stars*, Frank M. Robinson
> *The Gilda Stories*, Jewelle Gomez

Anthologies
> *Brother to Brother*, Essex Hemphill, Editor
> *Chicana Lesbians: The Girls Our Mothers Warned Us About*, Carla Trujillo, Editor

Children's/Young Adult Literature
> *The Duke Who Outlawed Jelly Beans*, Johnny Valentine

Editor's Choice
> *Odd Girls and Twilight Lovers: A History of Lesbian Life in Twentieth-Century America*, Lillian Faderman

Lesbian/Gay Small Press Book Award
> *Gay Roots: Twenty Years of Gay Sunshine*, Winston Leyland, Editor

Publisher's Service Award
> Barbara Grier and Donna McBride of Naiad Press

1991   Fiction
> *The Body and Its Dangers*, Allen Barnett
> *Out of Time*, Paula Martinac

Nonfiction
> *Coming Out Under Fire*, Allan Bérubé
> *The Safe Sea of Women*, Bonnie Zimmerman

Poetry
> *Decade Dance*, Michael Lassel
> *Going Back to the River*, Marilyn Hacker

Humor
> *New, Improved Dykes to Watch Out For*, Alison Bechdel

Mystery
> *Gaudi Afternoon*, Barbara Wilson
> *Ninth Life*, Lauren Wright Douglas
> *Howtown*, Michael Nava

Science Fiction/Fantasy
> *Gossamer Axe*, Gael Baudino
> *Magic's Price*, Mercedes Lackey
> *Secret Matter*, To Johnson

Anthologies
> *Men on Men 3*, George Stambolian, Editor
> *Women on Women*, Joan Nestle and Naomi Holoch, Editors

AIDS
> *The Way We Live Now*, Elizabeth Osbourn, Editor

Debut
> *Her,* Cherry Muhanji
> *Dancing on Tisha B'av,* Lev Raphael

Editor's Choice
> *The Encyclopedia of Homosexuality,* Wayne Dynes, Editor

Gay Men's Small Press Book Award
> *Daddy's Roommate,* Michael Wilhoite

Lesbian Small Press Book Award
> *Different Mothers,* Louise Rafkin, Editor
> *Making Face/Making Soul,* Gloria Anzaldúa

Publisher's Service Award
> Phil Wilkie and Greg Baysans
> *The James White Review*

1990   Fiction
> *Eighty-Sixed,* David B. Feinberg
> *The Bar Stories,* Nisa Donnelly

Nonfiction
> *In Search of Gay America,* Neil Miller
> *Really Reading Gertrude Stein,* Judy Grahn, Editor

Poetry
> *Poets for Life,* Michael Klein, Editor

Humor
> *Gay Comics,* Robert Triptow, Editor

Mystery
> *The Beverly Malibu,* Katherine V. Forrest
> *Simple Suburban Murder,* Mark Zubro

Science Fiction/Fantasy
> *What Did Miss Darrington See?,* Jessica Amanda Salmonson, Editor
> *Somewhere in the Night,* Jeffrey N. McMahan

Anthologies
> *Hidden from History: Reclaiming the Gay and Lesbian Past,*
> Martin Bauml Duberman, Martha Vicinus, and George Chauncey, Jr., Editors
> *Intricate Passions,* Tee A. Corinne, Editors
> *Out the Other Side,* Cristian McEwen and Sue O'Sullivan, Editors

Young Adult/Children's
> *Losing Uncle Tim,* MaryKate Jordan

AIDS
> *Reports from the Holocaust,* Larry Kramer

Debut
> *The Names of the Moons of Mars,* Patrica Roth Schwartz
> *The Irreversible Decline of Eddie Socket,* John Weir

Editor's Choice
>   *Lifting Belly* by Gertrude Stein, Rebecca Mark, Editor

Gay and Lesbian Small Press Book Award
>   *My Life As a Mole*, Larry Mitchell

Publisher's Service Award
>   Carol Seajay
>   *Feminist Bookstore News*

1989   Fiction
>   *The Beautiful Room Is Empty*, Edmund White
>   *Trash*, Dorothy Allison

Nonfiction
>   *Borrowed Time*, Paul Monette
>   *Lesbian Ethics*, Sarah Hoagland

Poetry
>   *Gay and Lesbian Poetry in Our Time*, Carl Morse and Joan Larkin, Editors

Mystery/Science Fiction
>   *Skiptrace*, Antoinette Azolakov
>   *Goldenboy*, Michael Nava

AIDS
>   *Borrowed Time*, Paul Monette

Debut
>   *Bird-Eyes*, Madelyn Arnold
>   *The Swimming-Pool Library*, Alan Hollinghurst

Editor's Choice
>   *Why Can't Sharon Kowalski Come Home?*, Karen Thompson and Julie Andrzejewski

Gay Men's Small Press Book Award
>   *Goldenboy*, Michael Nava
>   *The Delight of Hearts*, Almad al-Tifashi

Lesbian Small Press Book Award
>   *Trash*, Dorothy Allison

Publisher's Service Award
>   Sasha Alyson

Publishing Triangle Awards

1993   Bill Whitehead Award for Lifetime Achievement in Gay and Lesbian Literature
            Samuel Delany

         Ferro-Grumley Award for Best Gay Male and Best Lesbian Fiction of the Year
            Bastard Out of Carolina, Dorothy Allison
            Let the Dead Bury the Dead, Randall Kenan

         Gregory Kolovakos Award for AIDS Writing
            The Man with Night Sweats, Thom Gunn

1992   Bill Whitehead Award for Lifetime Achievement in Lesbian and Gay Literature
            Adrienne Rich

         Ferro-Grumley Award for Best Gay Male and Best Lesbian Fiction of the Year
            Vanishing Rooms, Melvin Dixon
            The Revolution of Little Girls, Blanche McCrary Boyd

         Gregory Kolovakos Award for AIDS Writing
            To the Friend Who Did Not Save My Life, Hervé Guibert

Additional Authors of
Gay and Lesbian Literature

Abbott, Sidney
Ackland, Valentine
Acosta, Mercedes de
Adam, Barry D.
Adelman, Marcy
Aldridge, Sarah
Aleixandre, Vincente
Allen, Jeffner M.
Almodovar, Pedro
Alther, Lisa
Altolaguirre, Manuel
Ameen, Mark
Anderson, Jack
Anderson, Margaret C.
Anderson, Shelly
Anderson, Sherwood
Anshaw, Carol
Aragon, Louis
Arenas, Reinaldo
Arnold, C. D.
Arnold, Madelyn
Arthur, Frederick de
Arvin, Newton
Asch, Sholem
Ash, John
Averill, Harold
Azolakov, Antoinette
Babe, Thomas
Babilla, Assurbanipal
Bahr, Hermann
Bailey, Derrick Sherwin
Bailey, Paul
Baker, Dorothy
Baker, Nikki
Bang, Herman
Barnett, Allen
Barr, James
Barrett, Martha B.
Bartel, Paul
Bataille, Georges
Bates, Katherine Lee
Baudino, Gael
Bayer, Sandy
Beach, Sylvia
Beachy, Stephen
Beam, Joseph
Bechdel, Alison
Becker, Carol
Bell, Arthur
Bell, Neal
Belloc, Denis
Benavente, Jacinto
Benedict, Ruth F.
Bennett, Alan

Benson, A. C.
Benson, E. F.
Bentley, Eric
Bergman, David
Bernard, Frits
Berrill, Kevin
Berzon, Betty
Bianchi, Tom
Biren, Joan E. (Jeb)
Birmisa, George
Bishop, Elizabeth
Blaman, Anna
Block, Francesca L.
Blumenfeld, Warren J.
Bogle, Darlene
Boffin, Tessa
Bogus, SDiane A.
Bommer, Lawrence
Boone, Bruce
Borer, Alain
Botto, Antonio
Bourdet, Edouard
Bowne, Alan
Boye, Karin
Brady, Maureen
Bradley, Katherine Edith
Brainard, Joe
Brand, Adolf
Brant, Beth
Brantenberg, Gerd
Brasch, Charles
Brass, Perry
Brecht, Bertolt
Bright, Susie
Broch, Hermann
Bronner, Arnold
Bronski, Michael
Brook, Richard
Brossard, Nicole
Broumas, Olga
Brown, Arch
Brown, Foreman
Brown, Howard
Brown, Pamela
Brown, Richard W.
Browning, Frank
Browning, Oscar
Bruckner, Ferdinand
Bryan, Jed A.
Bulkin, Elly
Bullough, Vern
Bumbalo, Victor
Bunch, Charlotte
Burns, John Horne

Burt, Simon
Busch, Charles
Butler, Sandra
Byrd, Stephanie
Cade, Cathy
Calderon, Sara Levi
Caldwell, Joseph
Callan, Michael
Cameron, Peter
Campbell, Michael
Campbell, Roy
Camus, Renaud
Cant, Bob
Carlquist, Sherwin
Carman, Bliss
Carr, Emily
Casal, Mary
Casement, Roger
Cassady, Marsh
Castleman, Riva
Castro, Rick
Cavin, Susan
Champagne, John
Chatwin, Bruce
Cheever, John
Chesebro, James William
Chester, Alfred
Chubb, Ralph Nicholas
Cixous, Hélène
Clark, Donald Henry
Clark, J. Michael
Clarke, Cheryl
Clarke, Dorothy
Clausen, Jan
Clutha, Janet
Coe, Christopher
Cohen, Daniel
Connolly, Cyril
Cooper, Edith
Copeland, Jeff
Corn, Alfred
Cornwell, Anita
Couperus, Louis
Courage, James Francis
Coutinho, Edilberto
Craigin, Elisabeth
Crevel, Rene
Crimp, Douglas
Cruse, Howard
Cunningham, John
Cunningham, Michael
Curb, Rosemary
Cutler, Stan
Damata, Gasparino

Daney, Serge
D'Annunzio, Gabriele
Dante, Nicholas
Dar, David
Davenport, Doris
Davenport, Guy
Davidson, Michael
Davis, Ben
Davis, Christopher
Day, F. Holland
Dean, Elizabeth
de Haan, Jacob Israel
DeJean, Joan
Delany, Samuel R.
DeLynn, Jane
Deming, Barbara
Denisoff, Dennis
D'Hondt, John
Diaman, N. A.
Dickinson, Anna Elizabeth
Dillard, Gavin
Dilsner, Ludwig
Dodson, Owen
Dollimore, Jonathan
Donnelly, Nisa
Dorcey, Mary
Dorn, Edward
Douglas, Alfred
Douglas, Lauren Wright
Douglas, Norman
Dover, Kenneth
Dowell, Coleman
Dreher, Sarah
Driggs, John H.
Dukokz, Kazimir
Dunne, Gary
Duplechan, Larry
Duvert, Tony
Dyer, Charles
Edelman, Scott
Edwards, George R.
Edwards, Nicky
Egbuton, J. Z.
Eichberg, Rob
Eisenstein, Sergei
Ekelund, Vilhelm
Ellenzweig, Allen
Ellis, Walter M.
Enquist, Per Olof
Esenin, Sergei
Essart, Fiona
Evans, Arthur
Eyen, Tom
Falco, Kristine L.

Fennelly, Tony
Ferenczi, Sandor
Fernandez, Dominique
Fichte, Hubert
Finn, Stephen
Finn, William
Firbank, Ronald
Fisher, Peter
Fitzroy, A. T.
Fletcher, Beryl
Flood, Gregory
Flynn, Michael
Foote, Mary Anna Hallock
Fornes, Maria Irene
Forrester, Alice
Forster, J.
Foster, David William
Fox, John
Fraser, James
Fraser, Jean
Frechette, David
Freedman, Estelle
Friday, Nancy
Friedlaender, Benedict
Friedman, Sanford
Fricke, Aaron
Fries, Kenny
Fritscher, Jack
Fuller, Henry Blake
Gaines, Steven
Gale, Patrick
Galloway, David
Gambone, Philip
Gammon, Carolyn
Garber, Marjorie
Gardiner, James
Gardner, Layce
Garrett, Kristen
Gayle, Marilyn
Gearhart, Sally Miller
Gee, Maurice
Gellert, Roger
George, Stefan
Gervais, Paul
Giantvalley, Scott
Giles, Jane
Gilgun, John F.
Gill, John
Gilligan, Sharon
Giorno, John
Giovani, Leo
Glasgow, Joanne
Glines, John
Gluck, Robert
Gloeden, Baron von
  Wilhelm
Goldman, Emma
Gombrowicz, Witold
Gomez-Arcos, Aghstin

Gonsalves, Roy
Gooch, Brad
Goodman, Bernice
Goodman, Paul
Goodwin, Joseph P.
Gordon, Billi
Gosse, Edmund
Gould, Janice M.
Goytisolo, Juan
Grae, Camarin
Gray, Stephen
Green, Robert
Greenberg, David F.
Greene, Bette
Greenfield, Freddie
Greenspan, Judy
Grief, Martin
Grierson, Francis Durham
Griffin, Caroline
Grimsley, Jim
Grover, Jan Zita
Gruen, John
Grumley, Michael
Guerin, Daniel
Guibert, Hervé
Guyon, Rene Charles Marie
Hacker, Marilyn
Hadleigh, Boze
Hagedorn, Jeff
Hale, Keith
Halliburton, Richard
Hampton, Christopher
Hampton, Susan
Hankel, Frances
Hanscombe, Gillian
Harbeck, Karen
Hardy, J. E.
Harris, Bertha
Hart, Jack
Hartley, L. P.
Hartley, Marsden
Harvey, Stephen
Harvie, Ron
Harwood, Lee
Heide, Robert
Helbing, Terry
Heller, Nancy G.
Hellman, Lillian
Hemmings, Susan
Herbert, John
Herdt, Gilbert
Higgins, Colin
Hinsch, Bret
Hirschberg, Herbert
Hite, Molly
Hoagland, Sarah Lucia
Hoban, Gordon
Hobson, Laura Z.
Hodges, Beth

Hoffman, William M.
Hollerith, J. P.
Holmes, B. L.
Holsclaw, Doug
Home, William Douglas
Home, Stewart
Horowitz, Gene
Howard, Richard
Hsienyung, Pat
Hughes, Holly
Hugo, Giles
Huston, Bo
Hutchins, Loraine
Hwang, David Henry
Ide, Arthur Frederick
Indiana, Gary
Innaurato, Albert
Isensee, Rik
Island, David
Islas, Arturo
Itiel, Joseph
Ivanov, Viacheslav
  Ivanovich
Ives, George Cecil
Iwaszkiewicz, Jaroslaw
Jackson, Graham
Jackson, Isaac
Jacob, Naomi Ellington
Jahnn, Hans Henny
Jahr, Clifford
James, Henry
Jarry, Alfred
Jewett, Sarah Orne
Johnson, Cary Alan
Johnson, Lionel
Johnson, Paul R.
Johnson, Sonia
Johnson, Toby
Jolley, Elizabeth
Jones, James W.
Jordan, MaryKate
Jouhandeau, Marcel Henri
Kallman, Chester
Kampmann, Christian
Kanter, Lynn
Kantrowitz, Arnie
Karásekze Loovic, Jife
Kaye/Kantrowitz, Melanie
Kearnes, Michael S.
Kenna, Peter
Keenan, Joe
Kelly, Dennis
Kelly, George E.
Keneally, Thomas (Michael)
Kennedy, Evelyn
Kennedy, Pagan
Kenny, Maurice
Kikel, Rudy
Killian, Kevin

Kim, Willyce
King, Francis
Kirk, Marshall
Kirkwood, James
Kitzinger, Celia
Klaich, Dolores
Klepfisz, Irena
Kliuev, Nikolai
Koelsch, William Alvin
Kondoleon, Harry
Konecky, Edith
Kotz, Cappy
Kovalev, Mikhail A.
Kovick, Kris
Krohnke, Friedrich
Kupffer, Elisar von
Kwitny, Jonathan
Lacey, Edward
Lackey, Mercedes R.
Lagerloef, Selma
Lane, Ann J.
Lapidus, Jacqueline
Larkin, Joan
Lassell, Michael
Latzky, Eric
Lauren, Jessica
Lauritsen, John
Laws, Jay B.
Lechon, Jan
Lehmann, John
Lemke, Jurgen
Letellier, Patrick
LeVay, Simon
Leventhal, Stan
Levin, James
Levin, Jenifer
Leyland, Winston
Lidstone, Margot Jane
Livia, Anna
Locke, Alain
Lonsdale, Frederick
Louis, Pierre
Loulan, Jo Ann
Love, Barbara J.
Lox, Ginger
Lucas, Craig
Ludlam, Charles
Luhan, Mabel Dodge
Lynch, Lee
Lynch, Michael
Lynes, George Platt
MacDonald, Ingrid
Mackay, John Henry
Mackay, Mary
Mackenzie, Compton
Mackenzie, Ronald
MacLeod, Anne
Macpike, Loralee
Maddy, Yulisa Amadu

Madsen, Hunter
Mains, Geoff
Malouf, David
Manahan, Nancy
Manley, Joey
Mann, Emily
Mann, Klaus
Manning, Rosemary
Manrique, Jaime
Mapplethorpe, Robert
Marchant, Anyda
Marcus, Eric
Marcus, Frank
Marinetti, Filippo Tommaso
Marsh, Edward Howard
Martin, Violet Florence
Martin du Gard, Roger
Mason, Timothy
Matthiessen, F. O.
Mattison, Andrew M.
Mauriac, Francois
Mauries, Patrick
Mazumdar, Maxim
McCauley, Stephen
McClenaghan, Tom
McConnell, Vicki P.
McDonald, Boyd
McDowell, Michael
McGehee, Peter
McKay, Festus Claudius
McMahan, Jeffrey N.
McNaught, Brian Robert
McNeill, John J.
McNeill, Sandra
McNeill, Wayne
McPherson, Scott
McWhirter, David P.
Mead, Margaret
Mead, Taylor
Medker, Richard
Mellow, James
Meredith, William
Merrick, Gordon
Meshchersky, Vladimir
  Petrovich
Meyer, Thomas
Michaels, Grant
Miller, Merle
Miller, Susan
Mingovits, Victor
Mitchell, Larry
Mitzel, John
Mohin, Lilian
Mohr, Richard D.
Money, John W.
Monk, Ray
Monro, Harold
Montherlant, Henry de
Montley, Patricia
Moorhead, Finola

Moorhouse, Frank
Morell, Mary
Morganstein, Linda
Morris, Michael
Morris, Sidney
Moskovitz, Jerome
Mountainwater, Shekhinah
Muhanji, Cherry
Munro, H. H.
Murray, Stephen O.
Mushroom, Merril
Musil, Robert
Myles, Eileen
Nagrodskaya, Yevdokia
  Appolonovna
Namjoshi, Suniti
Natalie, Andrea
Natzler, Caroline
Nava, Michael
Navarre, Yves
Nelson, Alice Ruth Moore
  Dunbar
Nelson, Charles
Nelson, Chris
Nichels, Thom
Nichols, Rosalie
Nicolson, Harold George
Niles, Blair
Nin, Anais
Nkoki, Simon
Norse, Harold
Novello, Ivor
Nugent, Richard Bruce
Nungesser, Lon
Ohio, Denise
Oleson, Amy
Oliver, Mary
Orlovsky, Peter
Ortleb, Charles
Osborne, John
Osborne, Karen Lee
Osirio, Miguel Angel
Oxenberg, Jan
Oxendine-Santana, Bill
Pankhurst, Christabel
Paradis, Yves
Park, Jacquelyn Holt
Parker, Pam
Parmar, Pratibha
Parnell, Peter
Patrick, John
Paul, Rick
Peladan, Josephin
Pelle, Marie-Paule
Penelope, Julia
Penteado, Darcy
Percy, Walker
Perkins, Rachel
Perry, Troy
Pessoa, Fernando

Peters, Robert L.
Peyrefitte, Roger
Pfanner, James
Phelan, Shane
Phillips, Edward O.
Pickett, James Carroll
Pickett, James Carroll
Pierce, Charles
Pintauro, Joe
Plante, David
Plomer, William Charles
  Franklin
Plumpe, Friedrich Wilhelm
Poirier, Jean
Ponse, Barbara
Pope, Penelope
Porter, Dorothy
Potts, Cherry
Pougy, Liane de
Praunheim, Rosa von
Price, Edwards Reynolds
Radiguet, Raymond
Rafkin, Louise
Raitt, Suzanne
Rambova, Natacha
Rand, Jordan
Ransom, Rebecca
Rathbone, Eleanor
Raymond, Diane
Rayn, Jay
Redon, Joel
Reed, John
Reed, Paul
Reid, Forrest
Reid, John
Reidinger, Paul
Reineig, Christa
Reinig, Christa
Reve, Gerard
Rhodes, Dusty
Rice, Anne
Rickel, Boyer
Rilke, Rainer Maria
Rist, Darrell Yates
Ritts, Herb
Rivers, Diana
Robins, Peter
Robson, Ruthann
Rodi, Robert
Rodway, Margaret R.
Roman, Richard
Roof, Judith
Roscoe, Will
Rosenblum, Barbara
Rostand, Maurice
Roussel, Raymond
Rozanov, Vasily Vasilievich
Rubin, Amy Kateman
Rubin, Gayle
Rueda, Enrique T.

Russell, Paul
Rutledge, Leigh W.
Sachs, Maurice
Saint, Assoto
Salinas, Pedro
Salmonson, Jessica Amanda
Sanders, Timothy
Sands, Regine
Sargeson, Frank
Sassoon, Siegfried
Saum, Karen
Saylor, Steven
Schenkar, Joan
Schiller, Greta
Schneebaum, Tobias
Schreiber, Ron
Schulman, Sheila
Schuyler, James Marcus
Schwartz, Patricia Roth
Schwartz, Ruth L.
Scott, Duncan Campbell
Seaton, Maureen
Sedaris, David
Segrest, Mab
Serna, Idella
Shaffer, Peter
Shairp, Mordaunt
Sherwood, Bill
Showalter, Elaine
Silva, Aguinaldo
Silverstein, Charles
Simon, Linda
Smith, Evan
Smith, Rosamond
Smyth, Dame Ethel
Soldatow, Sasha
Soestmeyer, Axel
Somerville, Edith
Soulie de Morant, George
Spain, Nancy
Spanbauer, Tom
Spears, Steve J.
Sperr, Martin
Springer, Nancy
Stadler, Matthew
Stambolian, George
Stanford, Adrian
Steakley, James D.
Stein, Diane
Stevens, David
Stevenson, Edward Iraneus
  Prime
Stewart, Jean
Strachey, Lytton
Strindberg, August
Sudermann, Hermann
Sullivan, Louis
Summers, Claude J.
Surcicle, Pat
Swallow, Jean

Swicegood, Thomas
Swenson, May
Szymanowski, Karol
Tate, Velma
Tavel, Ronald
Taylor, Carole
Taylor Cecil Philip
Taylor, Kyna Janine P.
Taylor, Sheila Ortiz
Tell, Dorothy
Terry, Megan
Tessina, Tina
Thompson, Dorothy
Thompson, Karen
Thompson, Mark
Thorstad, David
Thurman, Wallace
Timmons, Stuart
Tobin, Kay
Toder, Nancy
Tolan, Kathleen
Tolins, Jonathan
Tom of Finland
Tomiko, Yamakawa
Torrès, Tereska
Toussel, Raymond
Townsend, Larry
Townsend, Prescott
Townshend, Peter
Trifonov, Gennady
Trinidad, David
Tsui, Kitty
Tsvetaeva, Marina
Tusquets, Esther
Underwood, Reginald
Valentine, Johnny
Van Danzig, Rudi
Van Druten, John
van Itallie, Jean-Claude
Van Vechten, Carl
Vega
Veidt, Conrad
Viaud, Julien
Vincinus, Martha
Vining, Donald
Virtue, Noel
Visconti, Luchino
Vogel, Bruno
Wahl, Loren
Wakefield, Tom
Walker, Alice
Walpole, Hugh
Warland, Betsy
Watney, Simon
Weathers, Carolyn
Wedekind, Frank
Weinberg, George
Weinberg, Thomas S.
Weir, John

Weirauch, Anna Elisabet
Weiss, Ruth
Welch, Pat
Wells, Jess
Weltner, Peter
Wentworth, Taylor Anne
Wescott, Glenway
Whale, James
Whitmore, George
Whittman, Carl
Wicker, Randolfe Hayden
Wilcox, Michael
Wilhelm, Gale
Willhoite, Michael
Williams, George Emlyn
Williams, Walter
Wilmer, Val
Wilson, Angus
Wilson, Anna
Wilson, Douglas
Winant, Fran
Windham, Donald
Wingrove, Brian L.
Wings, Mary
Wohlbruck, Adolf
Wolfe, Chris Anne
Wolff, Charlotte
Woodberry, George Edward
Woodlawn, Holly
Woods, Gregory
Woollcott, Alexander
Yosano, Akiko
Young, Allen
Young, Ian
Zane, David
Zapata, Luis
Ziegler, Alexander
Zinovieva-Annibal, Lydia
Zubro, Mark Richard

Selected Anthologies and Critical Studies

Fiction

Aphrodisiac: Fiction from Christopher Street, Coward, McCann, & Geoghegan, 1980.
Bushfire: Stories of Lesbian Desire, edited by Karen Barber, Alyson Publications, 1992.
By Word of Mouth: Lesbians Write the Erotic, edited by Lee Fleming, Gynery Books, 1989.
Certain Voices, edited by Darryl Pilcher, Alyson Publications, 1991.
Contemporary Gay American Novelists, edited by Emmanuel S. Nelson, Greenwood Press, 1993.
Contemporary Lesbian Writers of the United States, edited by Sandra Pollock, Greenwood Press, 1993.
Cracks in the Image: Stories by Gay Men, edited by Richard Dipple, Alyson, 1981.
Daughters of Darkness: Lesbian Vampire Stories, edited by Pam Keesey, Cleis Press, 1993.
Different: An Anthology of Homosexual Short Stories, edited by Stephen Wright, Bantam, 1974.
Discontents: An Anthology of New Queer Writers, edited by Dennis Cooper, Amethyst Press, 1991.
Disorderly Conduct, edited by M. Mark, Serpent's Tail, 1991.
Dykescapes, edited by Tina Portillo, Alyson Publications, 1991.
Embracing the Dark, edited by Eric Garber, Alyson Publications, 1992.
Erotica: An Anthology of Women's Writing, edited by Margaret Reynolds, Pandora, 1990.
Erotica: Women's Writings from Sapho to Margaret Atwood, edited by Margaret Reynolds, Fawcett, 1992.
First Love/Last Love: New Fiction from Christopher Street, Putnam, 1985.
Flesh and the Word: An Anthology of Erotic Writing, edited by John Preston, Dutton, 1992.
Flesh and the Word 2: An Anthology of Erotic Writing, edited by John Preston, Plume, 1993.
Heat: Gay Erotic Fiction from the American Southwest, Lavender Press, 1990.
In a Different Light: An Anthology of Lesbian Writers, edited by Carolyn Weathers, Clothespin Fever Press, 1989.
Indivisible: New Short Fiction by West Coast Gay and Lesbian Writers, edited by Terry Wolverton, Plume, 1991.
Intricate Passions, edited by Tee Corinne, Banned Books, 1989.
InVersions: Writing by Dykes, Queers and Lesbians, edited by Betsy Warland, Press Gang, 1992.
Lesbian Bedtime Stories, edited by Terry Woodrow, Tough Dove Books, 1989.
Lesbian Bedtime Stories 2, edited by Terry Woodrow, Tough Dove Books, 1990.
Lesbian Fiction: An Anthology, edited by Elly Bulkin, Persephone, 1981.
Lesbian Love Stories, edited by Irene Zahava, Crossing Press, 1989.
Lesbian Love Stories 2, edited by Irene Zahava, Crossing Press, 1991.
Lesbian Short Fiction, edited by Paula Martinac and Carla Tomaso, Seal Press, 1989.
May West Is Dead: Recent Lesbian and Gay Fiction, edited by Adam Mars-Jones, Faber, 1988.
Men on Men 3: Best New Gay Fiction, edited by George Stambolian, Plume, 1990.
Men on Men 4: Best New Gay Fiction, edited by George Stambolian, Dutton, 1992.
Men to Men: The Best New Gay Fiction, edited by George Stambolian, New American Library, 1986, 1988.
More Like Minds, edited by Ben Goldstein, GMP, 1991.
New Lesbian Writing: An Anthology, edited by Margaret Cruickshank, Grey Fox Press/Subterranean, 1984.
Now the Volcano: An Anthology of Latin American Gay Literature, edited by Winston Leyland, Gay Sunshine, 1979.
On the Line: New Gay Fiction, edited by Ian Young, Crossing, 1981.
Other Countries: Black Gay Voices, Other Countries, 1988.
OutRage: 1993 Australian Gay and Lesbian Short Story Anthology, Designer Publications, 1992.
Piece of My Heart: A Lesbian of Colour Anthology, Sister Vision Press, 1992 (finalist for ALA G/L book award).
Shadows of Love: American Gay Fiction, edited by Charles Jurrist, Alyson, 1988.
Shorts: An Anthology, edited by Octavio Roca and M. Korsmo, Thane, 1987.
Speaking for Ourselves: Short Stories by Jewish Lesbians, edited by Irene Zahava, Crossing Press, 1990.
The Christopher Street Reader, edited by Michael Denneny, Putnam, 1984.
The Erotic Naiad, edited by Barbara Grier, 1992.
The Exploding Frangipani: Lesbian Writing from Australia and New Zealand, Women's Press, 1990.
The Faber Book of Gay Short Fiction, edited by Edmund White, Faber & Faber, 1992.
The Freezer Counter: Stories by Gay Men, edited by David Rees and Peter Robins, Third House, 1989.
The Lesbian Home Journal: Stories from "The Ladder," edited by Barbara Grier and Coletta Reid, Diana Press, 1976.
The Power and the Glory, and Other Lesbian Stories, collected by Miriam Saphira, Papers Inc. (New Zealand), 1992.
Tide Lines: Stories of Change by Lesbians, edited by Lee Fleming, Gynergy Books, 1991.

Travelling on Love in a Time of Uncertainty: Contemporary Australian Gay Fiction, BlackWattle, 1991.
What Did Miss Darrington See?, edited by Jessica Amanda Salmonson, Feminist Press, 1990.
Wild Hearts, Shebe Feminist, 1992.
Women on Women, edited by Joan Nestle and Naomi Holoch, Plume, 1990.
Word of Mouth: Short-Short Stories by 100 Women Writers, Volume 2, edited by Irene Zahava, Crossing Press, 1992.

Nonfiction

Amazing Grace: Stories of Lesbian and Gay Faith, edited by Malcolm Boyd and Nancy Wilson, Crossing Press, 1991.
And Thus Will I Freely Sing: An Anthology of Lesbian and Gay Writing from Scotland, Polygon, 1989.
Blood Whispers: Los Angeles Writers on AIDS, Gay and Lesbian Community Services Center, 1991.
Brother to Brother: New Writings by Black Gay Men, edited by Essex Hemphill, Alyson, 1991.
Chicana Lesbians: The Girls Our Mothers Warned Us About, edited by Carla Trujillo, Third Woman, 1991.
Coming Out: An Anthology of International Gay and Lesbian Writings, edited by Stephen Likosky, Pantheon, 1992.
Flaunting It: Lesbian and Gay Studies, edited by Cheryl Kader and Thomas Piontek, Indiana University Press, 1992.
Gay Culture in America, edited by Gilbert Herdt, Beacon, 1992.
Happy Endings: Lesbian Writers Talk about Their Lives and Work, edited by Kate Brandt, Naiad Press, 1993.
High Risk: An Anthology of Forbidden Writings, edited by Amy Scholder and Ira Silverberg, Dutton, 1991.
Hometowns: Gay Men Write About Where They Belong, edited by John Preston, Plume, 1992.
How Do I Look?: Queer Film and Video, edited by Bad Object-Choices, Bay Press, 1992.
In the Life: A Black Gay Anthology, edited by Joseph Beam, Alyson, 1986.
Indivisible, edited by Terry Wolverton and Robert Drake, Plume, 1991.
An Intimacy of Equals, edited by Lilian Mohin, Onlywomen Press, 1992.
An Intimate Wilderness: Lesbian Writers on Sexuality, edited by Judith Barrington, Eighth Mountain Press, 1991.
Leatherfolk: Radical Sex, People, Politics and Practice, edited by Mark Thompson, Alyson Publications, 1992.
Lesbian Culture: An Anthology, edited by Julia Penelope, Crossing Press, 1993.
A Lotus of Another Color: A South Asian Anthology, Alyson, 1992.
Loving in Fear: Lesbian and Gay Survivors of Childhood Sexual Abuse, Queer Press, 1991.
A Member of the Family: Gay Men Write about Their Families, edited by John Preston, Dutton, 1992.
Our Lives: Lesbian Personal Writings, edited by Frances Rooney, Second Story Press, 1991.
Out the Other Side: Contemporary Lesbian Writing, edited by Christian McEwen, Crossing Press, 1989.
Personal Dispatches: Writers Confront AIDS, edited by John Preston, St. Martin's Pres, 1989.
Pink Ink: An Anthology of Australian Lesbian and Gay Writers, Wicked Women Publications, 1991.
Queer City, Portable Lower East Side, 1991.
Sisters, Sexperts, Queers: Beyond the Lesbian Nation, edited by Arlene Stein, Plume, 1993.
The Persistent Desire: A Femme-Butch Reader, edited by Joan Nestle, Alyson Publications, 1992.
What a Lesbian Looks Like, Routledge, 1992.
What Lesbians Do in Books, edited by Elaine Hobby and Chris White, Women's Press, Ltd., 1992.

Poetry

Amazon Poetry, edited by Elly Bulkin and Joan Larkin, Out, 1975.
Games of Venus: An Anthology of Greek and Roman Erotic Verse from Sappho to Ovid, Routledge, 1992.
Gay and Lesbian Poetry in Our Time: An Anthology, edited by Carl Morse and Joan Larkin, St. Martin's, 1988.
Here to Dare: Ten Gay Black Poets, edited by Assotto Saint, Galiens, 1992.
Lesbian Poetry: An Anthology, Persephone Press, 1981.
The Male Muse: Gay Poetry Anthology, edited by Ian Young, Crossing, 1973.
Naming the Waves: Contemporary Lesbian Poetry, edited by Christian McEwen, Crossing, 1988.
Orgasms of Light, edited by Winston Leyland, Gay Sunshine, 1977.
The Penguin Book of Homosexual Verse, edited by Stephen Coote, Allen Lane, Penguin, 1987.
Poets for Life, edited by Michael Klein, Crown, 1990.
The Road Before Us: 100 Gay Black Poets, edited by Assoto Saint, Galiens Press, 1991.
The Son of the Male Muse: Gay Poetry Anthology, Crossing, 1983.
Twentysomething: Poems, edited by Martin Humphries, GMP, 1991.
Unending Dialogue: Voices from an AIDS Poetry Worshop, Faber & Faber, 1993.
Whatever You Desire: A Book of Lesbian Poetry, edited by Mary Jo Bang, Oscars, 1990.

Drama

The First Anthology of Lesbian Plays, edited by Kate McDermott, Aunt Lute, 1985.
Gay Plays: An International Anthology, Ubu Repertory Theater Publications, 1989.
Gay Plays: The First Collection, edited by William M. Hoffman, Avon, 1979.
Gay Plays: Volume One, edited by Michael Wilcox, Methuen, 1984.
Gay Plays: Volume Two, edited by Michael Wilcox, Methuen, 1985.
Gay Plays: Volume Three, edited by Michael Wilcox, Methuen, 1987.
Gay Plays: Volume Four, edited by Michael Wilcox, Methuen, 1990.
Gay Swestshop: Four Plays and a Company, edited by Michael Osment, Methuen, 1989.
Homosexual Acts: Five Short Plays from the Gay Season at the Almost Free Theatre, Inter-Action Imprint, 1975.
Lesbian Plays: One, edited by Jill Davis, Methuen, 1987.
Lesbian Plays: Two, edited by Jill Davis, Methuen, 1989.
Making Out: Plays by Gay Men, edited by Robert Wallace, Coach House Press, 1992.
Out Front: Contemporary Gay and Lesbian Plays, edited by Don Shewey, Grove Press, 1988.
Places, Please! The First Anthology of Lesbian Plays, edited by Kate McDermott, Spinsters, Company, 1986.
She's Always Liked the Girls Best: Lesbian Plays, edited by Claudia Allen, Third Side Press, 1992.
Strike while the Iron Is Hot: Sexual Politics in Theatre, edited by Michelene Wandor, Journeyman Press, 1980.
Tough Act to Follow: One-Act Plays on the Gay/Lesbian Experience, edited by Noreen C. Barnes, Alamo Square, 1992.
The Way We Live Now: American Plays and the AIDS Crisis, Theater Communications Group, 1990.

Critical Studies

Acting Gay: A History of Homosexuality in Drama, John M. Clum, Columbia University Press, 1992.
American Drama and the Emergence of Social Homophilia, Gene Touchet, University of Florida Press, 1974.
An Analysis of the Treatment of the Homosexual Character in Drama, Donald L. Loeffler, Arno Press, 1975.
Gay and Lesbian Themes in Latin American Writing, David W. Foster, University of Texas Press, 1991.
Gay and Lesbian Plays Today, edited by Terry Helbing, Heinemann, 1993.
Gay Fictions: Wilde to Stonewall, Claude J. Summers, Continuum, 1990.
The Gay Novel in America, James Levin, Garland, 1991.
The Gay Novel: The Male Homosexual Image in America, James Levin, Irvington, 1983.
Gayspeak: Gay Male and Lesbian Communication, edited by James W. Chesebro, Pilgrim, 1981.
The Homosexual as Hero in Contemporary Fiction, Stephen D. Adams, Barnes & Noble, 1980.
The Homosexual Tradition in American Poetry, Robert K. Martin, University of Texas, 1979.
Lesbian and Gay Writing: An Anthology of Critical Essays, edited by Mark Lilly, Temple University Press, 1990.
The Lesbian in Literature, Barbara G. Grier, Naiad Press, 1981.
Lesbian Studies Present and Future, edited by Margaret Cruikshank, Feminist Press, 1982.
Like a Brother, Like a Lover, George M. Sarotte, Anchor Press/Doubleday, 1978.
Literary Visions of Homosexuality, edited by Stuart Kellogg, Haworth, 1993.
New Lesbian Criticism: Literary and Cultural Readings, edited by Sally Munt, Columbia University Press, 1992.
Not in Front of the Audience: Homosexuality on Stage, Nicholas de Jongh, Routledge, Chapman & Hall, 1992.
Playing the Game: The Homosexual Novel in America, Roger, Austen, Bobbs-Merrill, 1977.
Queer Theatre, Stefan Brecht, Suhrkamp, 1978.
The Safe Sea of Women: Lesbian Fiction 1969-1989, Bonnie Zimmerman, Beacon, 1990.
Sex Variant Women in Literature, Jeannette H. Foster, Naiad, 1985.
Sexual Anarchy: Gender and Culture at the Fin de Siecle, Elaine Showalter, Penguin, 1991.
The Sexual Dimension in Literature, edited by Alan Bold, Vision Press, 1983.
Sexuality in Western Art, Edward Lucie-Smith, Thames & Hudson, 1992.
Sweet Dreams: Sexuality, Gender, and Popular Fiction, edited by Susannah Radstone, Lawrence & Wishart, 1988.
The Voyage In: Fictions of Female Development, University Press of New England, 1983.
We Can Always Call Them Bulgarians, Kaier Curtin, Alyson, 1987.

General

Encyclopedia of Homosexuality, edited by Wayne Dynes, Garland, 1990.
Eyes of Desire: A Deaf Gay and Lesbian Reader, edited by Raymond Luczak, Alyson, 1993.

Gay and Lesbian Library Service, edited by Cal Gough and Ellen Greenblat, McFarland, 1990.

Gay Roots: An Anthology of Gay History, Sex, Politics and Culture, edited by Winston Leyland, Gay Sunshine, 1991.

Gay Sunshine Interviews, edited by Winston Leyland, Gay Sunshine Press, 1978, 1982, 1984.

Hidden from History: Reclaiming the Gay and Lesbian Past,
edited by Martin Bauml Duberman, Martha Vicinus, and George Chauncey, Jr., New American Library, 1990.

Inside/Out: Lesbian Theories, Gay Theories, edited by Diana Fuss, Routledge, 1991.

Intricate Passions, edited by Tee A. Corinne, Banned Books, 1990.

Lesbians, Gay Men, and the Law: A Reader, edited by William B. Rubenstein, New Press, 1993.

Out the Other Side, edited by Cristian McEwen and Sue O'Sullivan, Crossing Press, 1990.

Peculiar People: Mormons and Same-Sex Orientation, edited by Wayne Schow, Signature Books, 1991.

Silverleaf's Choice: An Anthology of Lesbian Humor, edited by Ann E. Larson, Silverleaf Press, 1990, 1992.

Voicing Our Visions: Writings by Women Artists, edited by Mara R. Witzling, Universe Publishing, 1992.

Women, Girls and Psychotheraphy: Reframing Resistance, edited by Carol Gilligan, Haworth Press, 1992.

Women of the 14th Moon: Writings on Menopause, edited by Dena Taylor, Crossing Press, 1992.

GAY & LESBIAN LIT

ISBN 1-55862-174-1

90000

9 781558 621749